AF570787

American Sculpture
in the Museum of American Art
of the Pennsylvania Academy
of the Fine Arts

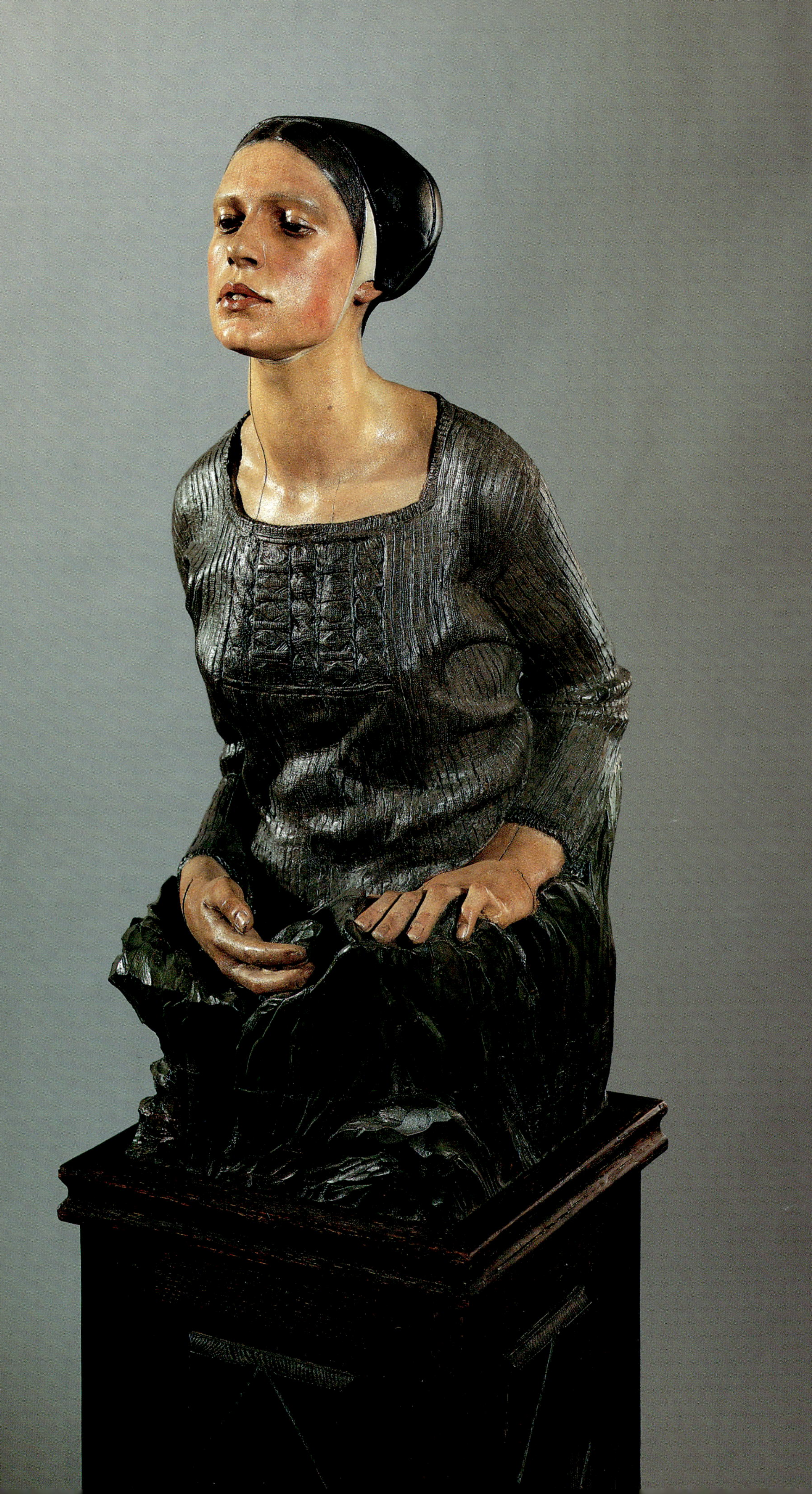

AMERICAN SCULPTURE

in the Museum of American Art of the Pennsylvania Academy of the Fine Arts

By Susan James-Gadzinski
and Mary Mullen Cunningham

Editors: Jacolyn A. Mott, Linda Bantel
Contributors: Theresa Z. Esperdy, Michael W. Panhorst, Judith E. Stein, Sylvia Yount

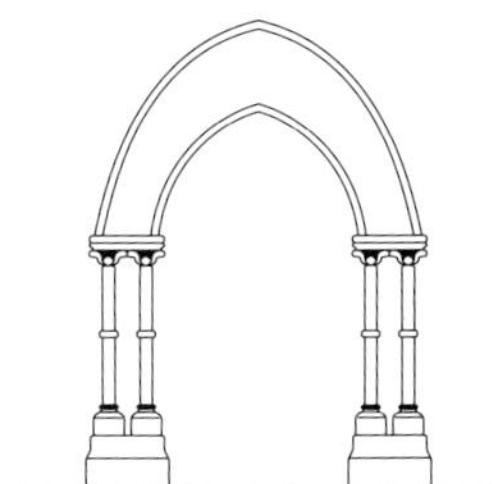

Museum of American Art of the Pennsylvania Academy of the Fine Arts, Philadelphia
in association with the University of Washington Press, Seattle and London

This publication is made possible by grants from
The Pew Charitable Trusts,
The Andrew W. Mellon Foundation, and the
National Endowment for the Arts

Production Editor, Susan James-Gadzinski
Editorial Consultant, Dr. Eric Gadzinski
Photographer, Rick Echelmeyer

Designer, Klaus Gemming, New Haven, Connecticut
Typesetter, dix!, Syracuse, New York
Printer and Binder, Stamperia Valdonega, Arbizzano (Verona), Italy

FRONT COVER: Roberts, *Hypathia*, pp. 88–89
BACK COVER: Ward, *Freedman*, pp. 80–81
FRONTISPIECE: Kendall, *Quest*, pp. 168–70
p. viii: Jennewein, *Memory*, pp. 238–39
p. xii: Grafly, *In Much Wisdom*, pp. 129–30

Distributed by the University of Washington Press,
P.O. Box 50096, Seattle, WA 98145-5096

LIBRARY OF CONGRESS CATALOGUING-IN-PUBLICATION DATA
Pennsylvania Academy of the Fine Arts. Museum of American Art.
American sculpture in the Museum of American Art of the Pennsylvania Academy of the Fine Arts / by Susan James-Gadzinski and Mary Mullen Cunningham ; editors, Jacolyn A. Mott, Linda Bantel ; contributors, Theresa Z. Esperdy . . . [et al.].
p. cm.
Includes bibliographical references and index.
ISBN 0-295-97692-6 (paperback)
1. Sculpture, American—Catalogs. 2. Sculpture—Pennsylvania—Philadelphia—Catalogs. 3. Pennsylvania Academy of the Fine Arts. Museum of American Art—Catalogs. I. James-Gadzinski, Susan, 1955– II. Cunningham, Mary Mullen, 1959– . III. Bantel, Linda.
IV. Mott, Jacolyn A., 1935– . V. Title.
NB205.P46 1997
730'.973'07474811—dc21 97-35152
CIP

PRINTED AND BOUND IN ITALY

Contents

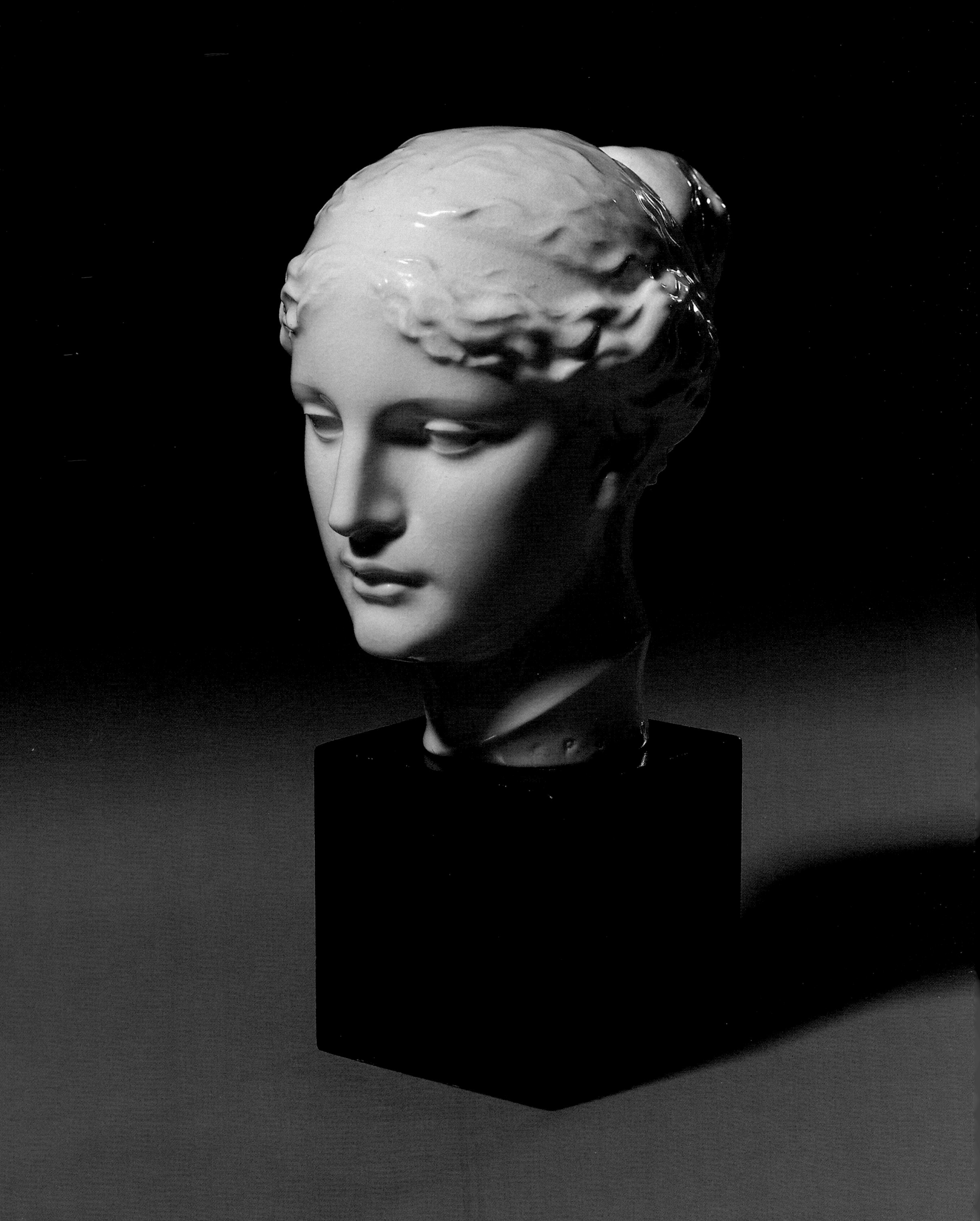

Foreword

The special purposes of this Academy have influenced the nature of its collections as they have grown over nearly two centuries. The Pennsylvania Academy of the Fine Arts was founded in 1805, based upon the model of the Royal Academy in London, "to promote the Cultivation of the Fine Arts" in the United States by educating artists and exhibiting their work. The understanding that the Academy would acquire works of art (or their copies) to fulfill its educational mission was written into its original charter, and has informed the growth of its collections since the first part of the nineteenth century. At the time of its creation, there was no other institution of its kind in this country, and since 1805 its collections have grown in conjunction with the growth of American art.

To read through this catalogue with this in mind is to encounter not just the history of a collection, but of our nation's artistic culture. There are many ways in which to read a catalogue of this kind—for biographical information, for interpretations of the individual works—but one informative exercise, in relation to our institutional history and our place in the history of American art, is to take stock of the accession numbers assigned to the individual works, and the information they provide about the sculptures' dates of acquisition. Many of these works, it may be observed, entered our collections at the time of their creation, their exhibition at the Academy, or shortly thereafter. They were acquired as the paragons of artistic achievement in a nascent artistic culture, and they collectively serve as the embodiment of this culture's growth and maturation.

A catalogue of this ambition requires considerable time and the dedicated efforts of many minds to achieve. Special acknowledgment should be made of the vision and efforts of my predecessors, Frank H. Goodyear, Jr. and Linda Bantel, who are responsible for the conception and nurturing of this publication. Susan James-Gadzinski has worked devotedly to bring this project to completion. Together with co-author Mary Mullen Cunningham, and contributors Theresa Z. Esperdy, Michael W. Panhorst, Judith E. Stein, and Sylvia Yount, she has realized a resource of admirable breadth and intelligence, documenting one of the most important collections of American sculpture in the world. The authors are to be congratulated for realizing a source of information that will sustain the scholarship in American art history for many generations to come. Klaus Gemming, who has designed this handsome publication, is also to be congratulated for the care and intelligence he has brought to every detail of this catalogue's design.

This publication has been realized with the support of The Pew Charitable Trusts, The Andrew W. Mellon Foundation, and the National Endowment for the Arts. Additional support from the NEA, the Institute of Museum Services, The Getty Grant Program, The Rittenhouse Foundation, and The Provincial Foundation has resulted in the conservation of many of the works documented by this catalogue. We are grateful to these funders for enabling us to continue an educational mission begun nearly two centuries ago.

Daniel Rosenfeld

The Edna S. Tuttleman Director of the Museum of American Art

Preface

THIS PROJECT was initiated by then Curator, and later Director and President, Frank H. Goodyear, Jr., and the Board of Directors of the Pennsylvania Academy of the Fine Arts. Curator and later Edna S. Tuttleman Director of the Museum, Linda Bantel, and I began this sculpture catalogue to complement the paintings checklist that was published in 1989.

All of the objects were examined and conserved, when necessary, by sculpture conservator Virginia Naudé, now president of Norton Art Conservation. The collection was painstakingly photographed by Rick Echelmeyer. Funding for this project has been provided by The Pew Charitable Trusts, The Andrew W. Mellon Foundation, and the National Endowment for the Arts. Sculpture conservation has been funded by the NEA, the Institute for Museum Services, The Getty Grant Program, The Rittenhouse Foundation, and The Provincial Foundation.

Cataloguing and researching were performed by Mary Mullen Cunningham, Theresa Z. Esperdy, and myself, with the assistance and advice of Virginia Naudé, Mark Bockrath, the Museum's Chief Conservator, and their assistants, as well as Linda Bantel. Artists' biographies and object entries were divided among various authors with the bulk of the writing falling to Cunningham (mostly 19th century) and myself (mostly 1890s–1950s). Michael W. Panhorst wrote about Samuel Murray and Charles Bregler. Theresa Z. Esperdy, Sylvia Yount, and Judith E. Stein contributed several entries.

Some of this research first came to light in the 1986–87 major chronological and thematic exhibition of about 200 sculptures from the Museum's collection. Work on the catalogue both supported and profited from work on the exhibition. During the course of compiling the catalogue, it was decided to restructure it to concentrate on the Museum's unique historical strengths. Artists whose objects predate 1951 have complete biographical and object entries. Later works are checklisted and illustrated. The medals and cameos collection is featured in an illustrated checklist in the Appendix.

Additional fine work by Judith E. Stein (Red Grooms and Morris Gallery exhibition artists), Theresa Z. Esperdy (medals and cameos), and by Jean Henry (regional and national artists post-1960), is available for study in the artists' research files in the curatorial department of the Museum. Many thanks to the artists who provided information on their career and production.

In the summer of 1994, editor Jacolyn A. Mott completed her work on the manuscript and retired from a distinguished career with the Museum. Linda Bantel's spirit and guidance is evident throughout the book. Her successor, Daniel Rosenfeld, along with President Gresham Riley, provided encouragement and advice in the final completion of the publication. Klaus Gemming has created an elegant design and been supremely patient throughout the entire endeavor, providing guidance and advice gleaned from years of experience with art publications.

I am especially grateful to my co-author, the contributing authors, the Museum staff, the editors, and the conservators. In addition, numerous assistants have contributed to the project over the years, including Serena Orteca, Anne Monahan, William Gremmel, Sheila Raman, Gabrielle Zitani, Audrey Lewis, Barbara Veith, and David Rashkis. Most recently, the assistance of Exhibition Coordinator Sarah L. James; Curator of Collections Sylvia Yount; Archivist Cheryl Leibold; Rights and Reproductions Manager Barbara Katus; and Administrative Assistants Naida Das and Christian Dean, has been invaluable in the completion of this catalogue. I also wish to thank former Pennsylvania Academy Librarian Marietta Boyer for her inexhaustible assistance throughout the years.

Other individuals who have provided assistance include: Dorothy Allen, Carl Alpert, Louise Todd Ambler, Marjorie Pingel Balge, Ruth and Mansfield Bascom, Gladys Edgerly Bates, Arthur Beale, Wolfgang Behl, Elizabeth W. Bendiner, Victoria Rosin Bieber, Carole I. Binswanger, Lawrence Campbell, Ward Childs, Janis C. Conner, Andrew Connors, Susan Danly, David B. Dearinger, Lauretta Dimmick, Adolph Dioda, John Dryfhout, Alice Levi Duncan, Ilene Susan Fort, Kathleen A. Foster, Frederick Fried, Abigail Booth Gerdts, William H. Gerdts, Morris Goldsmith, Kathryn Greenthal, Renee Gross, George Gurney, Mary Jane Hamilton, Walker Hancock, Jonathan Harding, Donna J. Hassler, Daniel Hodgson, Edward Fenno Hoffman III, Liz Jarvis, Evelyn Müller Johnson, Mary Alice Kennedy, Andrew J. Kozar, Paula M. Kozol, Antoinette Kraushaar, Joan S. Martin, Annette Masling, Susan E. Menconi, Dan Miller, John Milley, Mrs. Henry Mitchell, Theodora Morgan, Milo M. Naeve, Paul Nakian, Marina Pacini, April Paul, Bennard B. Perlman, Jan Seidler Ramirez, Joel Rosenkranz, Louise Rossmassler, Walter Rotan, Lorraine and Charles Rudy, Robin Salmon, Marion San-

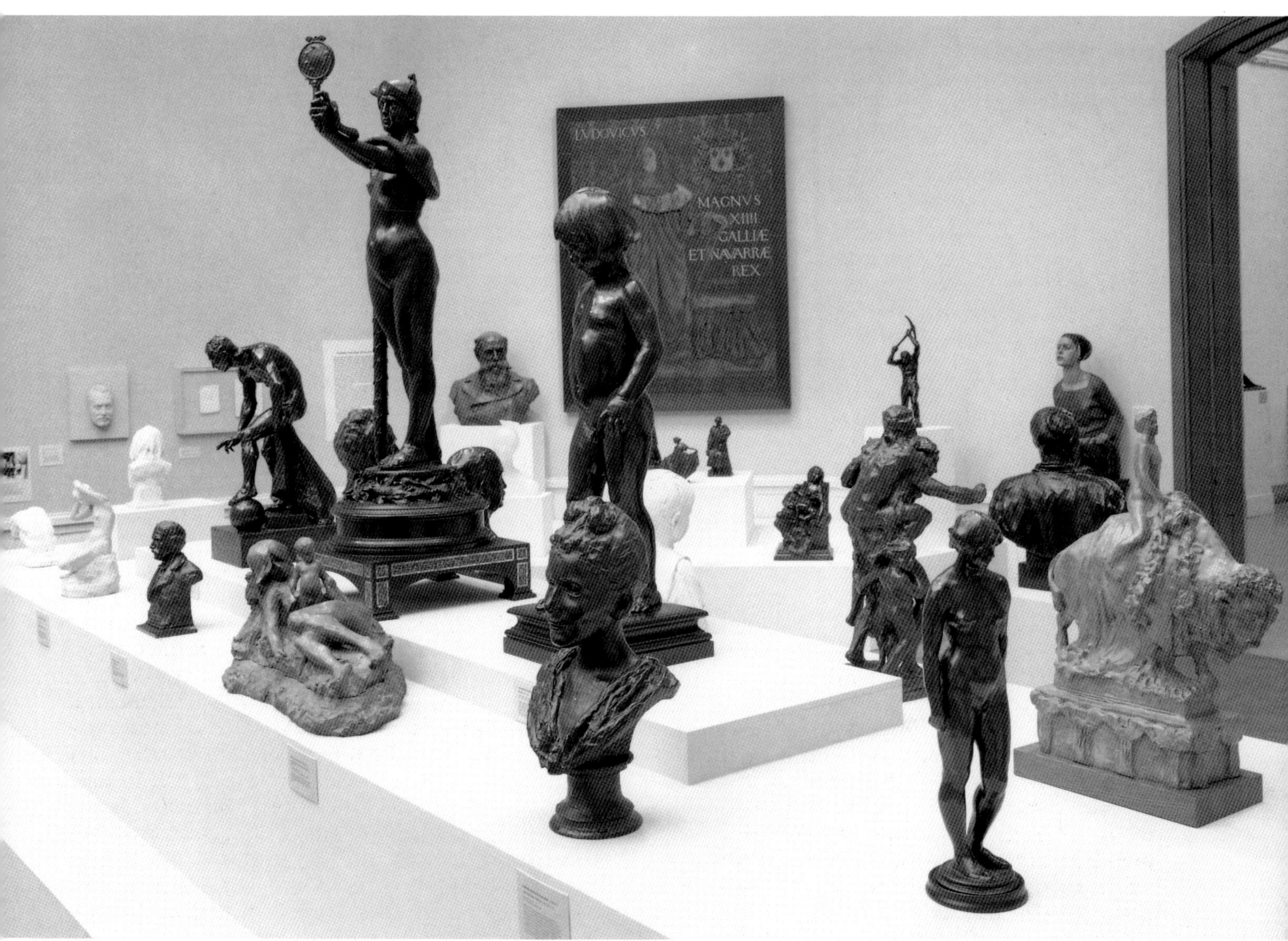

View of Exhibition "Sculpture at the Pennsylvania Academy of the Fine Arts," 1986–87,
The Archives of the Pennsylvania Academy of the Fine Arts

ford, Philip Schiavo, Darrel Sewell, Lewis I. Sharp, Pamela H. Simpson, John Smith, Suzanne Smith, Thomas P. Somma, Davidson Sommers, Regina Soria, Linda Stanley, Catherine Stover, Charles Stuckey, Roberta K. Tarbell, Alexander Tatti, Steve Tatti, Judy Throm, Pam Violanti, Anthony Visco, Cheryl Vogler, Jeanne L. Wasserman, Phoebe Dent Weil, Jody Wilkie, Gretchen Worden, Margaret K. Yarnall, and Kimberly King Zea.

Institutions whose staff were especially helpful and deserve special note include: the National Museum of American Art, the Archives of American Art, and the Index of American Sculpture, all part of the Smithsonian Institution, Washington, D.C.; The Free Library of Philadelphia, and The Historical Society of Pennsylvania, both in Philadelphia; The Metropolitan Museum of Art, the Frick Art Reference Library, the National Sculpture Society, and the New York Public Library, Central Branch, all in New York; and the Museum of Fine Arts, Boston.

To the staff, board, donors, artists, docents, and visitors who have long awaited the publication of this book, many thanks for your patience. Finally, Mary Mullen Cunningham and I would like to express our appreciation to our husbands Anthony Cunningham and Eric Gadzinski, and daughters Flannery and Madeleine, and Alice and Emily for their invaluable love and support.

It is with great pride that this collection can now become widely known and available to all.

Susan James-Gadzinski

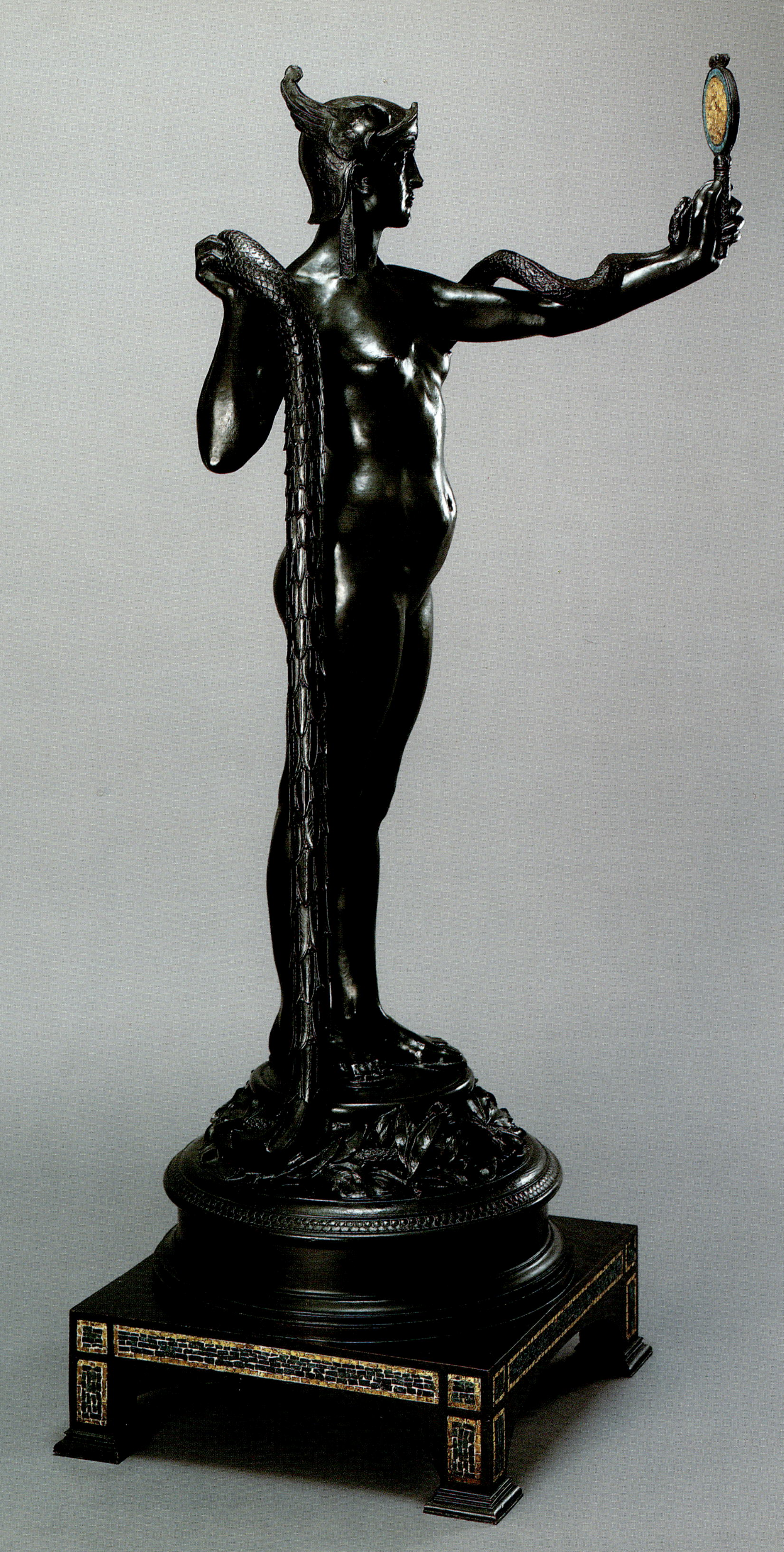

The American Sculpture Collection

THE Pennsylvania Academy of the Fine Arts, founded in 1805, holds the distinction of being the oldest art school and museum in the country. Drawing, painting, and sculpture were (and still are) considered the primary modes of expression in both areas of the institution. Sculpture has always been the stepchild of the other two; although a knowledge of modeling has often been considered helpful for depictions of three-dimensionality in drawing or painting. It is the interrelationship between the institution's Museum and School that yields the richness and significance of the art collection.

The Museum's American sculpture collection of 400 objects was formed over 190 years by the efforts of administrators, collectors, curators, and sculptors. Early acquisitions by the institution consisted of antique casts (now considered part of the School's collection), portrait busts of the Founding Fathers, and European sculptures. Most of the latter have found more appropriate homes as, in the last twenty years, the Museum has focused more on collecting and exhibiting American art.

Sculptor William Rush was one of three artists among seventy-one individuals who were instrumental in forming the Pennsylvania Academy. (Seven of Rush's portrait busts, an eagle, and a fragment of a civic sculpture are in the collection.) Among the first items purchased for the new institution were sculptures, in the form of plaster casts taken from Greek and Roman busts and statues of mythological subjects in French and Italian collections. Despite a fire in 1845 that destroyed most of the antique gallery, some of the original casts still exist. These casts were made available for drawing "to persons of good character," and they continue to be used by beginning Academy students.

During the early years of the Academy, training in clay modeling was sporadic. Joseph Alexis Bailly taught it briefly, from 1876–78, using antique casts as live models were too difficult to obtain. (Several important works by Bailly are in the collection.) Over the next decade, there continued to be a room set aside for modeling and "a ton of the best clay" was purchased for the use of interested students.

In the 1880s, Thomas Eakins gave occasional critiques of sculptural work. He encouraged the creation of small clay models to be used as props (a practice he had learned in Paris) when determining the arrangement of a painting's composition. Eakins also encouraged casting parts of the body in plaster to preserve dissections and for use as a teaching device. Modeling from animals, such as the horse and cow, and casting from their anatomy, was also begun at this time. Examples of this work are in the Museum's collection, as are portrait busts of Eakins and his circle.

A sculpture department was formed in 1892 under the direction of former Eakins student Charles Grafly, who had also trained in Paris. This coincided with a national interest in sculpture after Philadelphia's Centennial Exposition in 1876 and during the World's Columbian Exposition in Chicago of 1892–93. Grafly traveled widely prior to commencing his teaching appointment in order to determine an appropriate curriculum for the new department. His emphasis on complete knowledge of human anatomy continued the Eakins tradition. Students came from all over the country to study with Grafly, an uncompromising teacher. One especially promising student, Daniel Carl Müller, studied for twenty years with Grafly at night while working full-time as a professional carver of carousel animals.

Students were then and are now encouraged to compete for an opportunity to undertake foreign study. The awarding of scholarship money began in 1902 as the William Emlen Cresson Traveling Scholarships, and each year since then several sculpture students have been chosen for this honor. (Other traveling scholarships to Europe and elsewhere are now also offered.) Grafly's tenure saw the endowment of student competition prizes in sculpture, like those offered in Paris: the Edmund Stewardson Prize in 1899 and the Anna Katharine Stimson Prize in 1917. Modeling from animals resumed at the Academy country school in Chester Springs, Pennsylvania in the 1920s under the direction of former Grafly student Albert Laessle.

Walker Hancock, who took over from his teacher Charles Grafly after Grafly's sudden death in 1929, expanded the School's curriculum to include classes in stone carving, plaster casting, and architectural competitions with the University of Pennsylvania. Hancock, Laessle, Harry Rosin, and Charles Rudy carried on many of Grafly's teachings into the late 1960s. (The Museum has a strong collection of works by Grafly and his students, including Emily Clayton Bishop, Beatrice Fenton, Laessle, Hancock, Rudy, and Rosin, that were often purchased directly from the artists.)

Since the 1960s, the sculpture curriculum has

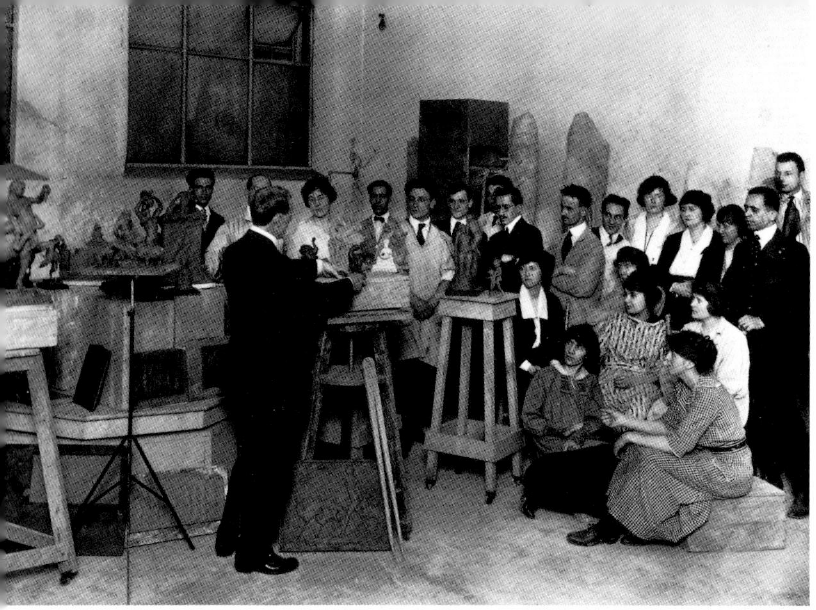

Charles Grafly and His Composition Class at the Pennsylvania Academy of the Fine Arts, about 1921, The Archives of the Pennsylvania Academy of the Fine Arts (unidentified photographer)

been further expanded to include welding, bronze casting, various technologies, and a Master's Degree program.

The Museum's collection grew through the years from purchases made at the annual juried exhibitions of paintings and sculptures that ran from 1811 to 1968. The exhibitions attracted submissions from throughout the United States as well as from expatriate artists in Europe. In 1913, the George D. Widener Memorial Gold Medal was first awarded for the best sculpture displayed in the Museum's annual exhibition. (The medal was designed by Albert Laessle in 1916.) Several of the award-winning sculptures, such as works by José de Creeft, Harry Rosin, and Anna Hyatt Huntington, were then acquired by the Museum. Other works by Widener Award-winning sculptors were also purchased over the years.

Influential art collectors and Academy board members, such as Henry C. Gibson, Joseph Harrison, Jr., Edward H. Coates, Edward Carey, and James L. Claghorn, donated important works to the institution. Large-scale neoclassical sculptures were commissioned specifically for the Museum, including: *Jerusalem* by William Wetmore Story, and *Penelope* by Rinaldo Rinaldi. Special funds for the acquisition of works of art were endowed by Joseph E. Temple, Henry C. Gibson, John Lambert, and Henry D. Gilpin.

The tradition of exhibiting and supporting the work of contemporary artists continued after the 1968 demise of the annual exhibitions in the form of the Morris Gallery exhibition program. Works by such sculptors as Tom Butter, Bill Freeland, Brian Meunier, Charles Fahlen, Robinson Fredenthal, and Judy Moonelis were purchased from Morris Gallery exhibitions. The establishment of the Award of American Art and its coordinated purchase of a work from the honoree has yielded important works by Nancy Graves and Frank Stella. Several recent sculptures by Academy graduates, including James Lloyd and Eiko Fan, were selected by the Museum Director for purchase from annual exhibitions by the Fellowship, the Academy's alumni association. In the last decade, exhibitions by such sculptors as Red Grooms, Duane Hanson, Mary Frank, and Nam June Paik have been featured in the Museum's galleries, resulting in additions to the collection.

Committee purchases of significance include the Louise Nevelson assemblage donated by friends of Bonnie Wintersteen. Other acquisitions have been designed to fill in some of the historical gaps in the collection, such as William Wetmore Story's *Semiramis,* John Rogers's *Checkers up at the Farm,* and Beatrice Fenton's *Bacchanale,* or enrich areas of strength, such as William Rush's head of the *Nymph of the Schuylkill,* and works by the circle of Thomas Eakins.

This collecting activity has yielded a body of work with a strong emphasis on the figure, which has been an emphasis in the teaching of the School. Areas of particular depth include portrait busts, neoclassical marble sculpture, French-inspired bronze figures, and direct carvings in stone and wood. Artists represented include past Academy teachers and students, additional members of the greater Philadelphia artistic community, as well as more prominent modern artists such as Gaston Lachaise, Alexander Calder, Chaim Gross, David Smith, Isamu Noguchi, George Segal, Leonard Baskin, Mary Frank, and Siah Armajani.

This collection's richness lies in the wide variety of materials and techniques represented by the works. Moreover, its significance lies in the overview it affords of the many modes of sculptural production in America from 1780 to 1995.

Susan James-Gadzinski

Reader's Guide to the Catalogue

THE PURPOSE of this catalogue is to provide scholars, students, and the general public with a reference book on the American sculpture collection of the Museum of American Art of the Pennsylvania Academy of the Fine Arts. The book is meant to complement the illustrated checklist of the Museum's American paintings collection, published in 1989. The entire sculpture collection was examined, catalogued, researched, conserved (when necessary), and photographed for this purpose.

Organization
The book consists of biographical and object entries, and is organized chronologically by the birthdate of the sculptor. Where there is more than one object in the collection by an artist, the works are arranged chronologically by execution date.

Biographies
Most of the artists represented in the catalogue are either American by birth or naturalization, or were educated in the United States, or worked here for a period of time. In addition, several foreign sculptors are included, on the basis of their portrayal of American sitters, or because their work was specifically commissioned for the Museum. Within the text, references to other sculptors featured in the catalogue are indicated by small capitals, and further information can be found in their biographies. Life dates are given for sculptors whose works are not represented in the collection, although some may have works listed in the 1951 to 1995 checklist, or in the medals and cameos checklist in the Appendix.

Use of PAFA
The acronym PAFA is used in Notes, References, and Exhibitions sections, when referring to the Pennsylvania Academy of the Fine Arts or more recently to its Museum of American Art.

Dates of Works
The composition date for any sculpture is given beneath its title. If there is a secondary date, such as a cast date or carving date, it appears on the line that describes the sculpture's media.

Bronze Casting
For sculpture that includes a foundry mark, information on the casting method is included in the media line. Otherwise, the casting information appears on the inscription line, along with any information on the foundry.

Measurements
Measurements are given in three dimensions (height x width x depth) in both inches and centimeters. Measurements of auxiliary bases and pedestals are given for those elements designed by the sculptor as part of the work. All dimensions were taken by the sculpture conservator.

Inscriptions
The artist's signature and any inscriptions are located in relation to the object, i.e., on the front or back of the work at its own (or proper) left or right. Inscriptions that are thought to be the work of another hand, are identified where possible. Any foundry mark or foundry information is listed on a separate line after the other inscriptions.

Credit Line and Accession Number
The credit line identifies the source of each work. This is followed by the accession number indicating the year the work came into the collection, and numbers indicating the sequence of that work within the year, and where necessary, within a group of works.

Exhibitions
All the known exhibitions of a work are listed in chronological order. Much of the information comes from artists' questionnaires in the Museum's registrarial files or from inquiries in the curatorial research files.

An asterisk (*) after the exhibition year indicates a work's appearance in an *Annual Exhibition of Paintings and Sculpture* of the Pennsylvania Academy of the Fine Arts.

Ex Collections
Ex Collections refer to all known owners of the object, and their years of ownership. The artist is listed here only if the work remained in his or her collection more than a few years.

Related Works
Other casts or versions of a sculpture are mentioned, where known, in the text of the entry. Citations using (q.v.) or (qq.v.) indicate another object entry or entries to consult for further information.

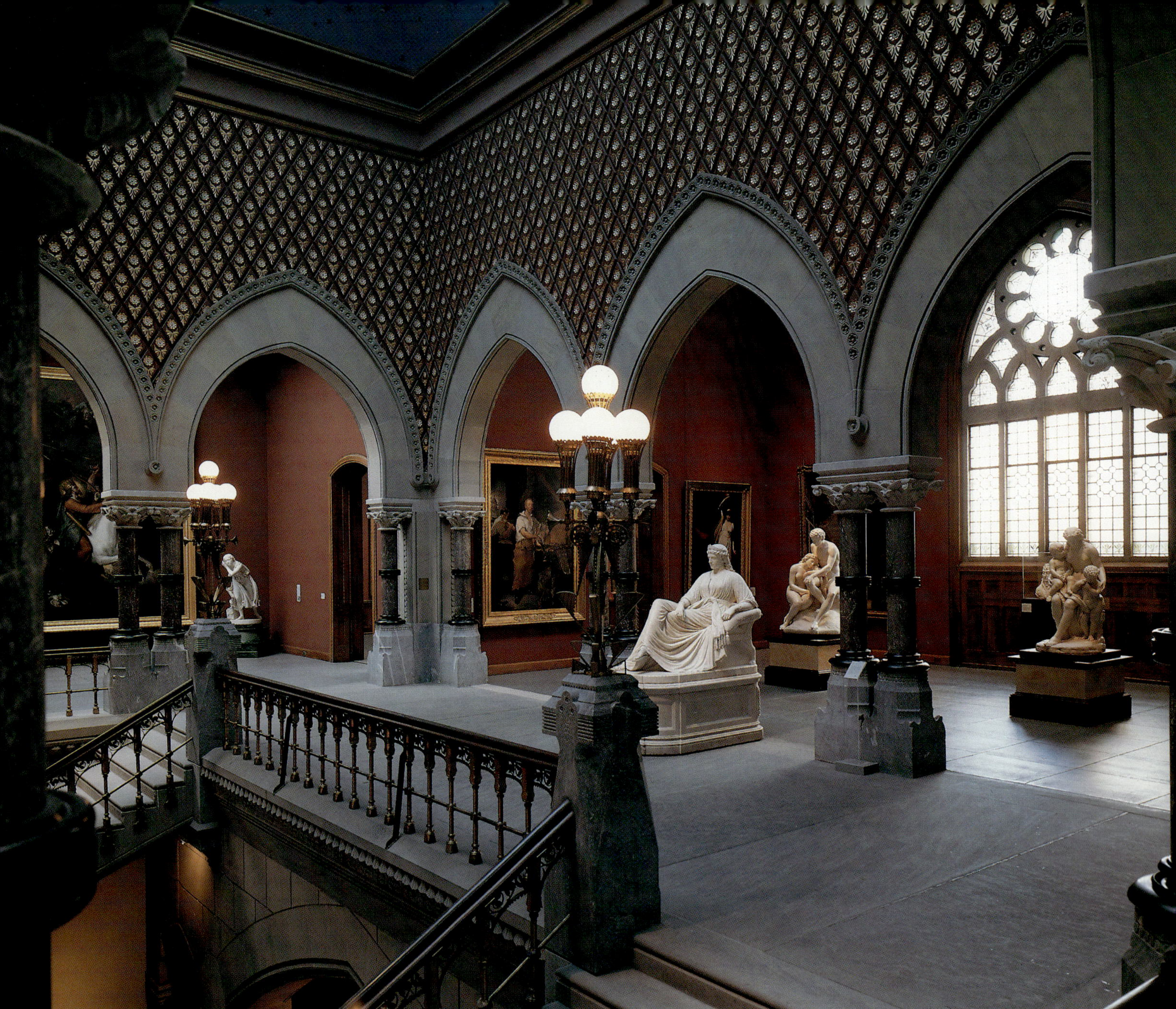

Grand Stairhall. Museum of American Art,
The Archives of the Pennsylvania Academy of the Fine Arts

Checklist 1951 to 1995
Works dating from 1951 to 1995 are checklisted and illustrated. For works by artists represented by biographies and object entries in the catalogue, the checklist contains a cross reference to the catalogue material where an illustration and more information can be found.

Medals and Cameos Checklist
The medals and cameos are checklisted and illustrated in the Appendix. Where there are duplicates in the collection, only one example is illustrated.

Index
The index lists artists, titles of works, and sitters. The numbers refer to pages, not catalogue or checklist numbers.

Authors' Index
Page numbers are listed for each author's entries. Several artists have object entries written by different authors.

Susan James-Gadzinski

Catalogue

Jean Antoine Houdon

1741–1828

Jean Antoine Houdon, the foremost French sculptor of the eighteenth century, was born in Versailles to parents of modest means. He grew up in Paris in an artistic environment, for his father was the concierge at the Ecole des Elèves Protégés. Established for art students who had won the Prix de Rome, the school prepared them for their Roman sojourns. When Houdon was fifteen, he enrolled at the Royal Academy of Painting and Sculpture. His principal master was Michel Ange Slodtz (1705–1764), but he also studied with Jean Baptiste Lemoyne (1704–1778) and Jean Baptiste Pigalle (1714–1785). In 1761 Houdon won first prize in the Prix de Rome competition and was sent to study for three years at the Ecole des Elèves Protégés. He embarked for Rome in 1764.

Houdon received his first important commission while a student at the French Academy in Rome. In 1767 he was hired to make statues of Saint Bruno and Saint John the Baptist for the church of Santa Maria degli Angeli in Rome. While he worked on these statues, Houdon perfected his knowledge of anatomy by dissecting cadavers under the direction of a physician at a Roman hospital. As a preliminary study for the statue of John the Baptist, he modeled a detailed anatomical figure called *L'Ecorché* (The Flayed Man). The figure won him immediate acclaim, and a plaster cast of it was purchased by the French Academy in Rome. Houdon's *L'Ecorché* became a staple for art schools in both Europe and the United States. The Pennsylvania Academy of the Fine Arts acquired a cast in 1805. It was the only modern work in the group of casts selected in Paris for the Pennsylvania Academy by Nicholas Biddle and Houdon.[1]

Houdon had returned to Paris in the autumn of 1768. The following summer, the Royal Academy accepted him as an exhibitor in the Salons, a necessary step for achieving success as an artist in eighteenth-century France. In the Salon of 1769 he showed many of his Roman works, including reductions of the statues of Saint Bruno and Saint John the Baptist. Houdon continued to exhibit regularly in the Salons until 1814.

Portraiture accounted for the majority of Houdon's commissions throughout his career. During the 1770s, his skills as a portraitist were honed in numerous busts of French nobles, wealthy bourgeoisie, and foreign royalty. A staunch realist, Houdon was able to make his busts appear lifelike. Even in marble, he captured the feel of hair and skin, and achieved a sense of the underlying structure of a face. Probably more than any other sculptor, Houdon exploited eyes for emotional and dramatic effect. He often gave his portraits a sidelong gaze and employed a variety of techniques to make the eyes appear real.

Today, Houdon is primarily remembered for his series of great men of the Enlightenment. Probably the best known of these is the powerful seated figure of Voltaire, made in 1780. Houdon also modeled likenesses of Diderot, Rousseau, and Lafayette. His busts of Benjamin Franklin, George Washington,[2] and Thomas Jefferson are among the most enduring images of these American Founding Fathers.

In 1785 Jefferson helped secure a commission for Houdon from the Virginia legislature to create a marble statue of George Washington for the state capitol at Richmond. In preparation, Houdon traveled to the United States and, at Mount Vernon, made a life mask and modeled a bust of Washington. Back in Paris, Houdon created the lifesize statue, which was installed in the rotunda of the Virginia capitol in 1796. As America's first public statue and something of a marvel, it provided an important incentive for further patronage of sculptors in the United States. Although Houdon continued to produce sculpture until about 1814, his reputation declined in the wake of the French Revolution and the increasing popularity of the stark neoclassical style of Antonio Canova, the favored sculptor of Napoleon.

Notes

1. Nicholas Biddle to Joseph Hopkinson, William Meredith, and Charles W. Peale, Nov. 20, 1805, History of PAFA file, PAFA Archives. The third page of this letter refers to Houdon's *L'Ecorché:* "A Full length statue intended for students. This altho' modern is so highly esteemed, & seems so well calculated for the purpose of an Academy that it has been added with a conviction that it would be acceptable."

2. The Pennsylvania Academy purchased a plaster cast of Houdon's bust of George Washington from the 1862 sale of Rembrandt Peale's possessions. By 1932 it had disappeared from the collection.

References

1911 Charles Henry Hart and Edward Biddle, *Memoirs of the Life and Works of Jean Houdon, The Sculptor of Voltaire and of Washington,* Philadelphia: privately printed.
1975 H.H. Arnason, *The Sculptures of Houdon,* New York: Oxford University Press.

John Paul Jones

1780

a.
Plaster, painted to resemble terracotta; cast about 1788
27¾ x 19⅛ x 12″ (70.5 x 48.6 x 30.5 cm)
Signed and dated under right shoulder: *houdon f.* 1780
Source unknown, 1864.3

b.
Bronze with black patina; cast in 1905 from original plaster in PAFA collection
27¾ x 20 x 10″ (70.5 x 50.8 x 25.4 cm)
Signed and dated under right shoulder: *houdon f.* 1780
Sand cast by Bureau Brothers, Philadelphia
Pennsylvania Academy purchase, 1905.5

JOHN PAUL JONES (1747–1792), the popular naval hero of the American Revolution, scored his most notable victory in 1780 while commanding the French-financed *Bonhomme Richard.* He defeated the larger and more powerful British warship *Serapis* during a fierce encounter in which an early demand for his surrender elicited his now-famous reply, "I have not yet begun to fight." Jones's audacity and bravery earned him the adulation of all Paris. In the spring of 1780, the Parisian Masonic Lodge of the Nine Sisters, of which Jones was a member, commissioned Jean Antoine Houdon to execute this likeness. Jones was thirty years old. A fastidious man of slight build, he chose to be depicted in his naval uniform with the ribbon and medal of the French Order of Military Merit suspended from the buttonhole of his left lapel. The pose and expression that Houdon captured in the bust reflect the keen mind and resolute spirit of the young Jones. Houdon exhibited a terracotta-colored plaster cast of the bust at the Paris Salon of 1781. The same year he completed the marble version for the Masonic Lodge (collection of the United States Naval Academy, Annapolis).[1]

Houdon, *John Paul Jones,* plaster

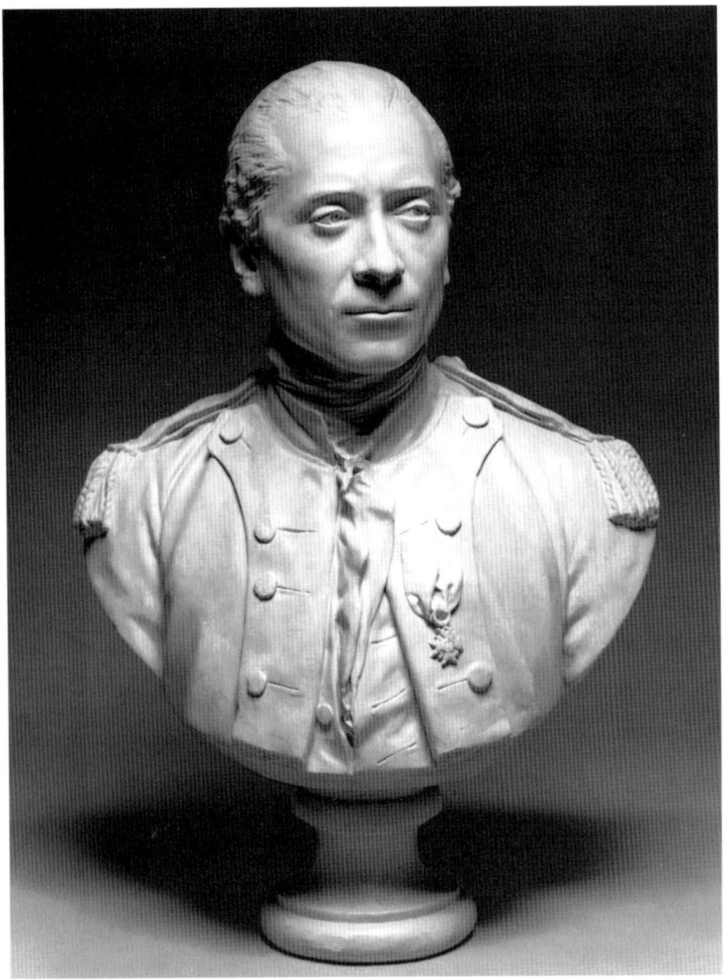

Jones was pleased with Houdon's portrait and, between 1784 and 1791, ordered at least twenty casts for American and French friends.[2] Among the earliest casts were those to be given to William Carmichael, the American minister to Spain; George Washington; and Thomas Jefferson (probably the one now in the Museum of Fine Arts, Boston). In 1788 Jones ordered casts for eight other American friends.[3] The one given to Major General William Irvine, then a Pennsylvania delegate to the Continental Congress in New York, was a plaster cast made in 1788 or 1789 and bears a remnant of the wax seal of Houdon's atelier. It probably arrived at the Pennsylvania Academy of the Fine Arts in 1832. That year a "bronzed" plaster cast of John Paul Jones by an unidentified artist was listed in the catalogue of the Academy's twenty-first annual exhibition. The bust appeared again in the annual exhibition catalogues from 1864 to 1866 and 1868 to 1870; by then it was attributed to WILLIAM RUSH. Although this attribution is curious inasmuch as the bust is signed, such oversights occurred in the early catalogues. Finally, the 1892 catalogue of the permanent collection correctly attributed the bust to Jean Antoine Houdon.

Like the plaster that Houdon exhibited in the Paris Salon of 1781, this bust was originally painted to simulate terracotta. At some point, however, it was painted black to resemble bronze and remained so until 1989, when the original terracotta color was restored. It seems likely that the "bronzing" was applied before 1832, especially because the inscription "Presented by Paul Jones to Maj. Genl Wm. IRVINE" was painted in gold on top of the bronzing on the underside of the chest.

In 1903 at the expense of Dr. Edward Emerson of Concord, Massachusetts, a mold was made from this bust by the Philadelphia plaster casters Tognarelli and Company. Two plasters were made for Emerson, who presented them to the Concord Free Public Library and the Museum of Fine Arts, Boston. Emerson gave the mold to the Pennsylvania Academy, and it remains in the collection today. Two more plasters were cast in 1903: one for CHARLES GRAFLY and another for Dr. Weir Mitchell. Mitchell presented his to the United States Naval Academy. All of these busts are inscribed "copy after the original at the Pennsylvania Academy of the Fine Arts."

Notes

1. H.H. Arnason, *Sculpture by Houdon,* exhib. cat. (Worcester, Mass.: Worcester Art Museum, 1964), p. 70.

2. An excellent source for locations of the many copies of this bust and their histories is "The Bust of John Paul Jones," an unpublished typescript written about 1975 by James W. Cheevers, associate director and senior curator, U.S. Naval Academy, copy in PAFA object file.

3. These eight men—Major General Arthur St. Clair, John Ross, John Jay, Major General William Irvine, Charles Thomas, Colonel Jeremiah Wadsworth, James Madison, and Edward Carrington—are listed in John Paul Jones to William Short, Sept. 15/26, 1788, enclosed in John Paul Jones to Thomas Jefferson, August 29/Sept. 9, 1788, Library of Congress. Typed extract from letter and enclosure, PAFA object file.

References

1911 Charles Henry Hart and Edward Biddle, *Memoirs of the Life and Works of Jean Houdon, The Sculptor of Voltaire and of Washington,* Philadelphia: privately printed, p. 132. **1970** Louis E. Marrits, *Modeled Portrait Sculpture,* South Brunswick, N.J.: A.S. Barnes and Company, p. 185 (ill.).

Exhibited (plaster)

1944–45 PAFA, *Star Presentation,* cat. no. 9 (ill.). **1992–93** PAFA, *Masterworks of American Art, 1750–1950.* **1994–96** PAFA, *Two Centuries of Collecting at the Museum of American Art.*

Exhibited (bronze)

1936 Dallas Museum of Fine Arts, *Texas Centennial Exposition.* **1945** John Wanamaker department store, Philadelphia, *Portraits of Warriors,* sponsored by War Finance Committee, U.S. Treasury Department. **1974–75** Second Bank of the United States, Philadelphia, *Masterworks of American Art, 1740–1840.* **1978** PAFA, Peale House, *The Early Schools of the Pennsylvania Academy of the Fine Arts, 1805–1868.*

Joel Barlow

1803–4

a.
Plaster; cast between 1804 and 1812
23 x 20 x 12½" (58.5 x 50.8 x 31.7 cm)
Signed and dated under right shoulder: *houdon an* XII [Year 12 (the twelfth year of the French Republic, i.e., 1803)]
Inscribed under left shoulder: *J. Barlow 50 ans*
Source unknown, 1879.9

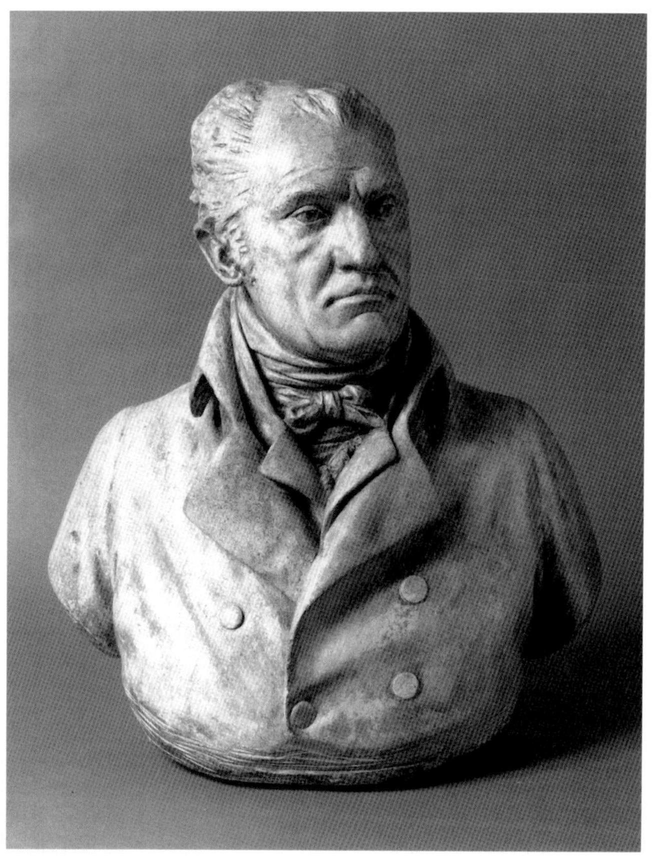

Houdon, *Joel Barlow,* plaster (a)

b.
Plaster; cast in 1912 from a marble version
27½ x 20½ x 11½" (69.8 x 52.1 x 29.2 cm)
Gift of Judge Peter T. Barlow, 1914.6

JOEL BARLOW (1754–1812) was reared on a Connecticut farm and was graduated from Yale College in 1778. Early in his career he tried his hand at law, teaching, and publishing; but his real love was writing. In 1787 he published *The Vision of Columbus,* an epic poem that brought him wide acclaim. The following year, an ill-fated business venture took him to France, where he began his evolution from conservative New Englander to liberal Republican. From 1790 to 1792 he resided in London, where he befriended Thomas Paine and wrote radical political tracts. His treatise "Advice to the Privileged Orders," published in 1792, stirred strong reaction on both sides of the English Channel: he was banned from England and proclaimed an honorary citizen in France. There Barlow amassed a fortune buying and selling French goods. His improved circumstances enabled him to indulge his varied interests, chief among which were politics, literature, art, agriculture, and technology. Appointed United States consul to Algiers in 1795, he effected the release of American prisoners in Africa. Barlow returned home to the United States in 1805. He was frequently sought out for his business knowledge and political acumen, and in 1811 President James Monroe appointed him minister to France. He died the following year in Poland while attempting to meet with Napoleon to negotiate a commerce treaty.

Joel Barlow posed for this likeness in Paris in 1803, but it was probably completed the following year because Houdon inscribed Barlow's age as fifty and he would not have turned fifty until March 23, 1804. The bust is one of the strongest works of Houdon's late period; and it effectively captures the aggressive, dogmatic personality of the sitter. This portrait (probably a plaster version) was exhibited at the Paris Salon of 1804 along with Houdon's bust of the inventor and painter Robert Fulton (Musée du Louvre, Paris), who was Barlow's intimate friend.

The early plaster in the Pennsylvania Academy of the Fine Arts was first recorded in 1812, when it appeared in the supplement to the annual exhibition catalogue. It was listed in the Inventory of Property of the Pennsylvania Academy of about 1813. This suggests that it was officially part of the collection by that time, yet no record of its acquisition survives.[1] The signature, date, and inscription on this plaster appear also on ones in the National Academy of Design in New York, the New-York Historical Society, and the National Portrait Gallery in Washington, D.C. All these plasters have closed backs; according to the Houdon scholar H.H. Arnason, this suggests that they were cast from a marble version or versions.[2] The White House owns a marble that descended from the sitter, although it is neither signed nor inscribed.[3] Charles Henry Hart and Edward Biddle, in their 1911 book, mentioned two additional marbles: one then in the possession of a great-grandnephew of the sitter, H.P. Chambers of Washington, Pennsylvania, and another once owned by James Madison but lost by 1911.[4] Robert Fulton inquired about having a marble carved in 1813,[5] but even if it was made, it would have been too late to have been the prototype for the Pennsylvania Academy's plaster. No matter what its derivation, the long history and fine details of this plaster point to its having originated in Houdon's studio.

Notes

1. Inventory, about 1813, History of PAFA file, PAFA Archives.

2. Arnason 1975, p. 24.

3. Barlow had acquired this by 1808; see Joel Barlow to Houdon, August 25, 1808, Houghton Reading Room, Harvard University, Cambridge. The Pennsylvania Academy's second plaster was made in 1912 from this marble version.

4. Charles Henry Hart and Edward Biddle, *Memoirs of the Life and Works of Jean Houdon, The Sculptor of Voltaire and of Washington* (Philadelphia: privately printed, 1911), p. 263.

5. See Robert Fulton to Ruth Baldwin Barlow, June 12, 1813, Houghton Reading Room, Harvard University, quoted in H.H. Arnason, *Sculpture by Houdon*, exhib. cat. (Worcester, Mass.: Worcester Art Museum, 1964), p. 126.

Reference

1975 H.H. Arnason, *The Sculptures of Houdon*, New York: Oxford University Press, pp. 100, 119.

Exhibited

1812* suppl., cat. no. 131. **1816** PAFA, *Exhibition at the Pennsylvania Academy of the Fine Arts*, p. 7. **1816** PAFA, *Exhibition at the Pennsylvania Academy of the Fine Arts*, cat. no. 142. **1817*** cat. no. 327. **1818*** cat. no. 327. **1819*** cat. no. 306. **1820*** cat. no. 162. **1821*** cat. no. 230. **1822*** cat. no. 283. **1823*** cat. no. 223. **1824*** cat. no. 450. **1825*** cat. no. 486. **1826*** cat. no. 475. **1827*** cat. no. 475. **1828*** cat. no. 453. **1829*** cat. no. 394. **1830*** cat. no. 349. **1838** PAFA, *Exhibition of the Pennsylvania Academy of the Fine Arts*, cat. no. 99. **1944–45** PAFA, *Star Presentation*, cat. no. 10 (ill.). **1951** Detroit Institute of Arts, *The French in America, 1500–1875*. **1964** Worcester Art Museum, Mass., *Sculpture by Houdon*, cat. pp. 120–24 (ill.). **1967** PAFA, *The First Forty Years: Early Acquisitions to the Academy's Permanent Collection*, cat. no. 9. **1976** National Gallery of Art, Washington, D.C., *The Eye of Thomas Jefferson*. **1977–78** Octagon, American Institute of Architects Foundation, Washington, D.C., *Dolley and the Great Little Madison*. **1986–87** PAFA, *Sculpture at the Pennsylvania Academy of the Fine Arts*.

Giuseppe Iardella

Died about 1831

Skilled stone carvers were scarce in America during the late eighteenth and early nineteenth centuries. Most were brought from Italy where the trade had a rich and honored history. One of the Italians, Giuseppe Iardella, came to Philadelphia about 1794 to carve the architectural sculpture for Robert Morris's mansion. It was being erected on Chestnut Street between Seventh and Eighth streets under the direction of the French architect Pierre Charles L'Enfant. Within three years of Iardella's arrival, however, construction of the mansion came to a halt. Morris, a wealthy financier of the American Revolution, had lost his vast fortune through land speculation. The unfinished mansion, which had come to be called Morris's Folly, was demolished about 1800. Much of the decorative carving that Iardella had produced was purchased by James Traquair, the owner of a local marble yard. Traquair incorporated some of Iardella's decorations into his building at Tenth and Market streets and presumably sold the rest.[1]

Four bas-relief panels that Iardella executed for Morris's Folly are extant. Three depict allegories of the arts—*Drama, Music,* and *Painting.* Each contains a pair of putti that float on a cloud and grasp symbols of the relevant art. In the fourth panel, the putti hold a large medallion that was undoubtedly intended to receive an inscription. *Drama* and *Music* were purchased by the architect Benjamin Henry Latrobe, who cut them into lunettes and incorporated them into the facades of the new wings that he built onto the Chestnut Street Theatre between 1801 and 1806.[2] The other two panels survive in the original rectangular format. About 1926 *Painting* was built into the rear entrance to Olney, a privately owned historic home in Joppa, Maryland.[3] The fourth panel is part of the Drayton Tomb at the Magnolia Plantation and Garden in Charleston, South Carolina.

Sometime after work stopped on Morris's Folly, Giuseppe Iardella was hired by James Traquair to carve marble busts of America's founders. These busts were copies after original works by European sculptors, such as Giuseppe Ceracchi (1751–1801) and Jean Jacques Caffieri (1725–1792). Iardella was listed as a sculptor in the Philadelphia City Directory in 1802 and 1803. Later, he opened his own stonecutting business and probably concentrated his efforts on architectural decorations. Until 1817, he and his partner, Christopher Hocker, operated a marble yard on Race Street.[4] Sometime after this, Iardella may have worked for Peter Fritz, the proprietor of the Stone Cutting and Marble Mantle Manufactory, located at 226 Race Street. A book published in 1831 commented that, when passing this establishment, one could not fail to notice "the two dogs carved in stone, by the celebrated Jardella, lately deceased."[5]

Notes

1. Abraham Ritter, *Philadelphia and Her Merchants* (Philadelphia: published by the author, 1861), p. 200.

2. Ironically, in 1798 in a severe criticism of the design of Morris's Folly, Latrobe had written of Iardella's work: "There is a profusion of wretched sculpture. . . . The capitals of the columns are of the worst taste." Benjamin Henry Latrobe, *The Journal of Latrobe* (New York: D. Appleton and Company, 1905), p. 91.

3. The relief had been given to the owner of Potts Quarry near Conshohocken, Pa., to satisfy a claim of $2,500 against Morris's bankrupt estate for stone supplied for Morris's Folly. Mr. Potts built the relief into a wall of the home he was erecting near Conshohocken. Known as Angel House, it was destroyed in 1926; but the sculpture was salvaged by J. Alexis Shriver for Olney. See Shriver, "Permanence or Change?; The History of Old Olney Again Brings Up an Unsettled Question," *Baltimore Sun*, May 27, 1928, pp. 12–13.

4. J. Thomas Scharf and Thompson Westcott, *History of Philadelphia, 1609–1884* (Philadelphia: L.H. Everts and Company, 1884), vol. 2, p. 1067.

5. James Mease and Thomas Porter, *Picture of Philadelphia* (Philadelphia: Robert DeSilver, 1831), vol. 2, p. 118. The sculptor's name was also spelled Jardella.

Alexander Hamilton

About 1804
After Giuseppe Ceracchi (1751–1801), 1794
Marble
23¼ x 12½ x 9¼" (59.1 x 31.8 x 23.5 cm)
Pennsylvania Academy purchase, by subscription (about 1811), 1814.2

Giuseppe Iardella carved this copy of Giuseppe Ceracchi's 1794 life portrait of Alexander Hamilton (1757–1804). The copy was previously attributed to the Irish immigrant sculptor John Dixey (about 1765–1820) because it was thought to be the one that he presented to the Columbian Society of Artists in 1814. Originally called the Society of Artists of the United States, the Columbian Society was founded at Philadelphia in 1810 to promote the arts in

Iardella, *Alexander Hamilton*

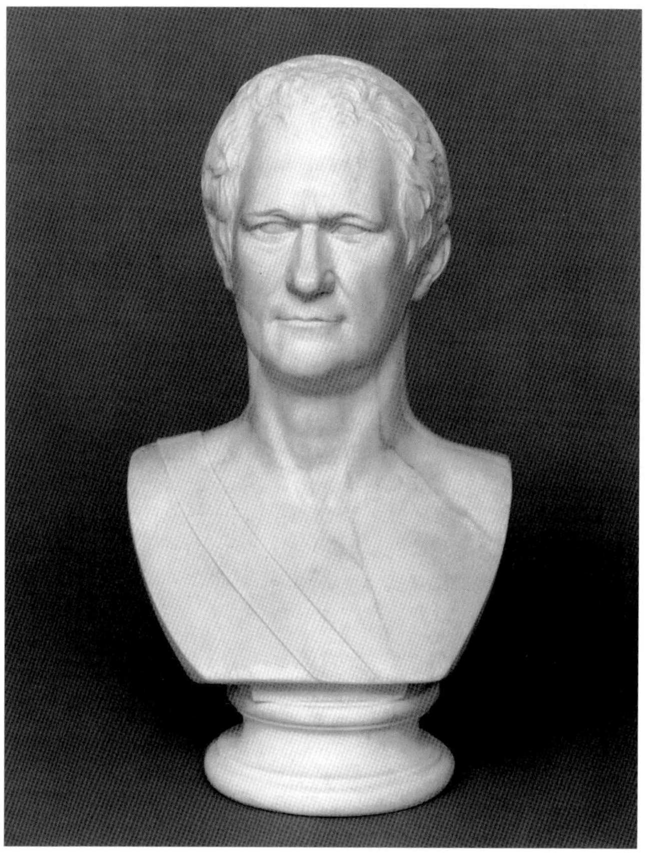

America. It was closely affiliated with the Pennsylvania Academy of the Fine Arts and held its meetings and annual exhibitions at the Academy until 1815. The Ceracchi-type bust of Hamilton that Dixey made was in plaster, however, rather than marble.[1] Dixey's plaster probably entered the Pennsylvania Academy's collection after 1815. It last appeared in 1890 in the catalogue of the permanent collection, and there is no record of its disposal.

In the Academy's catalogues of the permanent collection and the annual exhibitions, the Dixey plaster is often confused with the marble version by Iardella; and both are often misattributed. The correct attribution of the marble bust was established by an 1847 letter addressed to the president and directors of the Pennsylvania Academy by Adam Traquair, a city commissioner and a son of the stonecutter James Traquair. According to Adam Traquair, in the early days of the Academy he placed in the galleries a bust of Alexander Hamilton carved in Italian marble by Giuseppe Iardella. A number of subscribers gave a total of about $110 for its purchase. Traquair claimed that, in exchange for the bust, the Academy had issued him a certificate good for two shares of Academy stock, drawn upon Charles N. Bancker, then treasurer of the Academy, but that the certificate was lost by Bancker's countinghouse.[2]

Iardella undoubtedly carved this bust while he was employed by James Traquair. In 1804 Traquair advertised marble busts of the late General Alexander Hamilton at a price of one hundred dollars and busts of George Washington that were carved by "an artist whom the celebrated Ceracchi employed in executing the busts of Washington, Jefferson, Hamilton and Rittenhouse."[3] During his first trip to Philadelphia in 1791–92, Ceracchi had modeled from life the clay portrait busts of twenty-seven distinguished Americans. He returned to Philadelphia in 1794 with marble versions of his busts of Alexander Hamilton, George Washington, Thomas Jefferson, and David Rittenhouse, as well as marble medallion portraits of James Madison and John Adams. Iardella did not arrive in Philadelphia until the same year; therefore, he could have carved these busts in Italy under Ceracchi's direction and may well be the artist to whom Traquair refers. In any event, this marble copy by Iardella was probably acquired by the Pennsylvania Academy in 1811 and is almost certainly the one that was shown that year in the first annual exhibition of the Society of Artists of the United States. It subsequently appeared in an inventory made about 1813 of the Academy's collection.

Notes

1. Dixey cast a number of plaster copies. On Sept. 20, 1804, an advertisement in the *New York American Citizen* announced "that a mould from this bust [Ceracchi's Hamilton] has just been completed under the direction of Mr. John Dixey . . . and that one cast is finished from it in plaster of Paris."

2. Adam Traquair to PAFA, Sept. 16, 1847, PAFA Archives. He misattributes the original to JEAN ANTOINE HOUDON, rather than Ceracchi.

3. "Marble Bust of General Hamilton," *Poulson's American Daily Advertiser*, Philadelphia, Nov. 16, 1804, p. 4.

Exhibited

1811 PAFA, *First Annual Exhibition of the Society of Artists*, cat. no. 417. **1816** PAFA, *Exhibition of Mr. Allston's Picture of The Dead Man Restored to Life by Touching the Bones of the Prophet Elisha . . . in addition to the stationary pictures of the Academy*, p. 7. **1816** PAFA, *Exhibition of Mr. C.R. Leslie's Picture of the Murder of Rutland and Mr. Allston's Dead Man Restored . . .*, cat. no. 146. **1817*** cat. no. 359. **1818** PAFA, *Exhibition of Paintings, Statues, Prints, etc. at the Pennsylvania Academy of the Fine Arts*, cat. no. 383. **1818*** cat. no. 359. **1819*** cat. no. 360. **1820*** cat. no. 315. **1821** PAFA, *Exhibition of Paintings, Statues, Prints, etc. at the Pennsylvania Academy of the Fine Arts*, cat. no. 202. **1822*** cat. no. 256. **1823*** cat. no. 231. **1824*** cat. no. 458. **1825*** cat. no. 492. **1826*** cat. no. 481. **1827*** cat. no. 481. **1828*** cat. no. 459. **1829*** cat. no. 432. **1830*** cat. no. 386. **1831*** cat. no. 81. **1832*** cat. no. 81. **1834*** cat. no. 95. **1836–38, 1840** PAFA, *Exhibition of the Pennsylvania Academy of the Fine Arts*, cat. no. 95. **1843** PAFA, *Exhibition of Paintings, Statues, and Casts at the Pennsylvania Academy of the Fine Arts*, cat. no. 6. **1845** PAFA, *Exhibition of Paintings, Statues and Casts at the Pennsylvania Academy of the Fine Arts*, p. 16 (shown in front of building). **1847** *Exhibition of Paintings, Statues and Casts at the Pennsylvania Academy of the Fine Arts*, cat. no. 530. **1848** PAFA, *Exhibition of the Paintings and Statuary at the Pennsylvania Academy of the Fine Arts*, cat. no. 441. **1849*** cat. no. 358. **1851*** cat. no. 374. **1852*** cat. no. 373. **1853*** cat. no. 409. **1854*** cat. no. 401. **1855*** cat. no. 528. **1856*** cat. no. 562. **1857*** cat. no. 474. **1858*** cat. no. 545. **1859*** cat. no. 415. **1860*** cat. no. 439. **1861*** cat. no. 380. **1862*** cat. no. 380. **1864*** cat. no. 280. **1865*** cat. no. 168. **1866*** cat. no. 168. **1868*** cat. no. 390. **1869*** cat. no. 300. **1937** Pennsylvania Museum of Art, Philadelphia, *Signers of the Constitution*. **1974–75** Second Bank of the United States, Philadelphia, *Masterpieces of American Art, 1740–1840*. **1978** PAFA, Peale House, *The Early Schools of the Pennsylvania Academy of the Fine Arts, 1805–1868*, checklist no. 9.

ATTRIBUTED TO GIUSEPPE IARDELLA

Benjamin Franklin

About 1804
After Jean Jacques Caffieri (1725–1792), 1777
Marble
23⅝ x 19½ x 13" (60 x 49.5 x 33 cm)
Pennsylvania Academy purchase, 1811.1

In March of 1777, while Benjamin Franklin (1706–1790) served in Paris as American minister to France, he sat for a portrait by the French sculptor Jean Jacques Caffieri. That likeness, in terracotta, is preserved in the Bibliothèque Mazarine, Paris. Caffieri's archrival, JEAN ANTOINE HOUDON, made a bust of Franklin the following year. Franklin preferred the Caffieri portrait and ordered at least six plaster casts for his family and friends. Throughout the nineteenth century, both busts were copied extensively. In the United States, the Caffieri-type was often incorrectly attributed to either Houdon or the Italian sculptor Giuseppe Ceracchi (1751–1801). No marble version has been conclusively assigned to Caffieri, and it seems unlikely that he ever carved one.[1]

This marble replica was at the Pennsylvania Academy of the Fine Arts by June 1811, when WILLIAM RUSH and Rembrandt Peale were appointed by the Academy's directors to secure its purchase from Jean Simon Chaudron, a well-known local clock maker and silversmith.[2] Where and from whom Chaudron acquired the bust are unknown; but he may have supplied Rush and Peale with the mistaken attribution to Giuseppe Ceracchi, whose name was not connected with the work until July 8th, when "Cerraci" was listed as the artist in the Academy's record of the purchase for $120.[3] This attribution has long been questioned. Charles Coleman Sellers hypothesized that, although the bust was not carved by Ceracchi, it was sent to Chaudron from Italy through Ceracchi's agency, thus causing his name to be associated with it.[4] Isotopic analysis has revealed that the marble was quarried in Italy,[5] but Italian marble would have been readily available in the United States. It was being imported during the early nineteenth century by James Traquair of Philadelphia. There seems to have been, however, at least one prototype Caffieri bust in Italy to support the conjecture that this copy was carved there. In 1790 a full-length statue of Franklin was commissioned by William Bingham from Francesco Lazzarini (d. 1808) for the Library Company of Philadelphia, and a bust of Franklin by Caffieri was borrowed from the Pennsylvania Hospital and sent to Italy as a model. A marble copy in the American Philosophical Society in Philadelphia is purported to be of Italian workmanship and may be based on this model.[6] The Philosophical Society's marble has the upright posture and distinctly carved pupils of Caffieri's original terracotta, whereas the one in the Pennsylvania Academy has a forward thrust and blank stare that suggest a model further removed from the original.

Charles Henry Hart in 1911 was the first to recognize the Pennsylvania Academy's marble as a Caffieri type. He believed that this and several other Caffieri-type replicas in American museums were incorrectly attributed to Ceracchi because he had executed busts of several founding fathers during two visits to the United States in the 1790s and was, with the exception of Houdon, the sculptor best known to Americans. Hart suggested that this bust was carved in Philadelphia at James Traquair's marble yard by either Giuseppe Iardella or John Dixey.[7] At present, Hart's hypothesis remains the most convincing. Ulysses Desportes, the leading scholar on Ceracchi, doubts that an artist of his stature would have spent time carving a copy of another sculptor's work.[8] Furthermore, Ceracchi did not typically employ the dead eye that is seen in this bust. Atypical of the early Caffieri copies as well, this treatment indicates a conservative artist with a deep respect for classical models.[9] Giuseppe Iardella's few known sculptures all display the dead eye.

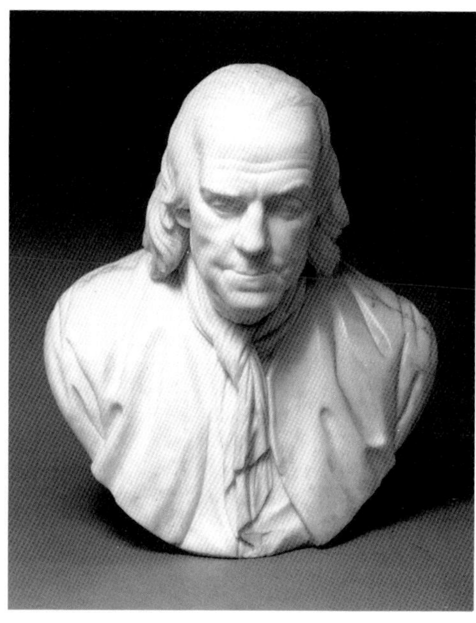

Attributed to Iardella, *Benjamin Franklin*

A stronger case can be made for Iardella as sculptor of this bust than John Dixey. The earliest known advertisement by Traquair offering such busts for sale was in 1804.[10] Iardella was still working for Traquair at that time, but Dixey had been gone for three years. He moved to New York in 1801.

Notes

1. The Detroit Institute of Arts owns an unsigned marble attributed to Caffieri. See Charles Coleman Sellers, *Benjamin Franklin in Portraiture* (New Haven: Yale University Press, 1962), p. 212.

2. Ibid., p. 208. The writer incorrectly cites Charles Willson Peale rather than his son Rembrandt as one of the appointees.

3. PAFA donation book, 1810–52, PAFA Archives.

4. Sellers 1962, p. 209.

5. Norman Herz to Virginia Norton Naudé, Oct. 1, 1986, PAFA object file.

6. *A Catalogue of Portraits and Other Works of Art in the Possession of the American Philosophical Society* (Philadelphia: American Philosophical Society, 1961), p. 33.

7. Charles Henry Hart and Edward Biddle, *Memoirs of the Life and Works of Jean Houdon, The Sculptor of Voltaire and of Washington* (Philadelphia: privately printed, 1911), p. 98.

8. Sellers 1962, p. 209.

9. Ibid.

10. "Marble Bust of General Hamilton," *Poulson's American Daily Advertiser*, Philadelphia, Nov. 16, 1804, p. 4.

Exhibited
1813* cat. no. 2. **1816** PAFA, *Exhibition of Mr. Allston's Picture of The Dead Man Restored to Life by Touching the Bones of the Prophet Elisha . . . in addition to the stationary pictures of the Academy*, p. 7. **1816** PAFA, *Exhibition of Mr. C.R. Leslie's Picture of the Murder of Rutland and Mr. Allston's Dead Man Restored . . .*, cat. no. 131. **1817*** cat. no. 331. **1818*** cat. no. 381. **1818** PAFA, *Exhibition of the Paintings, Statues, Prints, etc. at the Pennsylvania Academy of the Fine Arts*, cat. no. 277. **1819*** cat. no. 267. **1820*** cat. no. 121. **1821*** cat. no. 207. **1821** PAFA, *Exhibition of the Paintings, Statues, Prints, etc. at the Pennsylvania Academy of the Fine Arts*, cat. no. 207. **1822*** cat. no. 261. **1823*** cat. no. 236. **1824*** cat. no. 463. **1853*** cat. no. 443. **1854*** cat. no. 426. **1855*** cat. no. 503. **1856*** cat. no. 557. **1856** PAFA, *Fall Exhibition of the Pennsylvania Academy of the Fine Arts*, cat. no. 298. **1857*** cat. no. 480. **1858*** cat. no. 535. **1859*** cat. no. 411. **1860*** cat. no. 442. **1861*** cat. no. 379. **1862*** cat. no. 379. **1863*** cat. no. 376. **1864*** cat. no. 287. **1865*** cat. no. 171. **1866*** cat. no. 171. **1867*** cat. no. 382. **1868*** cat. no. 413. **1869*** cat. no. 323. **1937** Pennsylvania Museum of Art, Philadelphia, *Signers of the Constitution*. **1944–45** PAFA, *Star Presentation*, cat. no. 4 (ill.). **1952** University of Pennsylvania. **1986–87** PAFA, *Sculpture at the Pennsylvania Academy of the Fine Arts*.

Unidentified Artist

Eagle

About 1805
Pine, painted gold
19½ x 36 x 8" (49.5 x 91.4 x 20.3 cm)
Gift of B.I. de Young, 1947.12

THIS EAGLE was formerly attributed to WILLIAM RUSH; but the carving technique, design, and joinery do not relate to his known eagles. For example, the feathers are flat and undifferentiated unlike those of the Rush eagle (q.v.). There is also no known history that links this eagle to Rush.

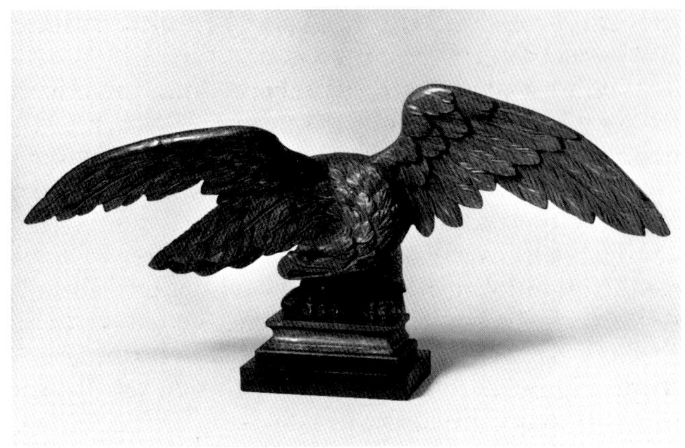

Unidentified Artist, *Eagle*

Reference
1982 Linda Bantel et al., *William Rush, American Sculptor*, exhib. cat., Philadelphia: PAFA, pp. 179–80, fig. 127.

Exhibited
1937 Pennsylvania Museum of Art, Philadelphia, *William Rush 1756–1833: The First American Sculptor*, cat. no. 53. **1959** Westmoreland County Museum of Art, Greensburg, Pa., *250 Years of Art in Pennsylvania*. **1960** Old Westbury Gardens, N.Y., sculpture exhibition. **1988** Katonah Gallery, N.Y., *The American Eagle: Symbol and Spirit, 1782–1882*.

Ex Collection
B.I. de Young, ?–1947 (on loan to PAFA, 1911–47).

William Rush

1756–1833

William Rush was born in Philadelphia to Joseph Rush, a ship carpenter, and Rebecca Lincoln Rush. As a child, William showed a talent for carving and drawing. He was apprenticed in his early teens to Edward Cutbush, a highly skilled carver from London, and within about three years outshone his teacher. Probably by 1774 Rush had his own business carving ornaments for ships. Soon after the outbreak of the Revolution, he joined the American cause and was commissioned an ensign in the Fourth Regiment of Foot of Lieutenant Colonel Wills's Philadelphia Militia. In 1780 Rush married Martha Simpson Wallace; and, two years later, his son John was born, the first of ten children. JOHN RUSH also became a carver and joined his father's business.

William Rush carved figureheads and ornaments for merchant ships, especially those owned by Stephen Girard. Rush usually carved American subjects—Indians and contemporary heroes like George Washington and Benjamin Franklin—but he also carved such historical figures as Sir Walter Raleigh and Captain John Smith; and, for Girard who named some of his ships after French philosophers, Rush carved the likenesses of Voltaire and Rousseau. Rush's figureheads were admired at home and abroad for their masterful carving and poses. By the time of the Grand Federal Procession, July 4, 1788 (celebrating both the anniversary of the Declaration of Independence and the Constitution's ratification by ten of the thirteen states), Rush was a leader among the carvers and gilders. Thus it is not surprising that he designed and executed their elaborate exhibit for the procession. When Congress established the U.S. Navy on March 27, 1794, and ordered six frigates built, Rush was chosen to create symbolic carvings for them.

On December 29, 1794, Rush joined a group of forty artists, including Charles Willson Peale, to organize an art academy, later called the Columbianum, a forerunner of the Pennsylvania Academy of the Fine Arts. Its purpose was to collect old master paintings and casts of antique statuary, establish classes, and hold art exhibitions; but the group was short-lived. In 1801 Rush helped in the reconstruction of a mastodon skeleton for Peale's natural-history museum by carving missing bones. On October 16, 1801, Rush was elected to the Common Council and served on it or the Select Council until 1826. In 1805 he helped found the Pennsylvania Academy of the Fine Arts and served as a director for all but one year until his death in 1833.

The Embargo Act of 1807 ended the shipbuilding industry in Philadelphia, and Rush turned to other interests. In 1808 for the Chestnut Street Theatre, he carved his first architectural statues, *Comedy* and *Tragedy* (Philadelphia Museum of Art). He served on the City Council's Watering Committee, which built a waterworks at Philadelphia's Centre Square; and in 1809 Rush carved *Allegory of the Schuylkill River,* a fountain of a woman and a bittern for the grounds of the waterworks (*Head of the Nymph* [q.v.]).

In 1810 the Society of Artists elected Rush its first president and in 1811 appointed him professor of sculpture. That year he began exhibiting sculpture at the Pennsylvania Academy; and, the following year, he was elected an academician, at the top of a list that included the painters Thomas Sully, Benjamin West, and John Singleton Copley. In 1813 Rush supervised the Academy's first class using live models.

Rush was one of the earliest American sculptors to create busts of soldiers, statesmen, and scientists for the libraries of middle-class gentlemen. His portraits were made from life or from memory. In 1815 he carved his most ambitious portrait, a full-length figure of George Washington (Independence Hall, Philadelphia).[1] All his wooden sculptures were painted white to simulate antique marble sculptures, thereby anticipating the neoclassical style that was soon to prevail in America. Rush executed commissions for crucifixes, angels, and eagles for churches; figures of the Virtues for Masonic Hall; decorations for bridges; and designs for city parks.

In the 1820s he was on the City Council committee that oversaw the expansion of the waterworks at Fairmount on the Schuylkill River; and he and his son carved figures for the millhouse entrances. In 1824 Rush was a founding member of the Franklin Institute. When General Lafayette visited Philadelphia on his grand tour, Rush was on the City Council committee to organize activities. In 1825 he was made an honorary member of New York's American Academy of the Fine Arts. William Rush never went abroad for study or travel and rarely left Philadelphia, but he emerged as an extremely gifted craftsman and self-taught artist whose career flourished in a critical period in American history.

Note

1. PAFA has a bronze cast from the mold CHARLES GRAFLY made in 1916 from the wooden original; the plaster cast he made is in the School's cast collection.

Reference

1982 Linda Bantel, "William Rush, Esq.," in *William Rush, American Sculptor,* exhib. cat., Philadelphia: PAFA, pp. 9–30.

Eagle

About 1810
Painted pine
30⅜ x 32 x 12⅝" (77.2 x 81.3 x 32.1 cm)
Gift of Wilson Mitchell, 1922.12

THE EAGLE, emblem of American resolve and independence, was very popular during the eighteenth century; and Rush carved a number of them. This one was made from six separate pieces of wood. A wire, set deep within the head and visible in the mouth, indicates a provision for something to be held in the bird's beak.

While there is no documentary evidence to link this eagle with William Rush, the carving and joinery are consistent with his technique. The detailed carving of the feathers is similar to that of the eagle he carved in 1811 for Saint John's Lutheran Church and of *Exhortation* and *Praise* in Saint Peter's Church, Philadelphia.

Exhibited
1937 Pennsylvania Museum of Art, Philadelphia, *William Rush, 1756–1833: The First American Sculptor,* cat. no. 54. **1949** Art Institute of Chicago, *From Colony to Nation: An Exhibition of American Painting, Silver and Architecture from 1650 to the War of 1812,* cat. no. 100. **1951** Denver Art Museum, *Life in America.* **1955** PAFA, *The One Hundred and Fiftieth Anniversary Exhibition,* cat. no. 11. **1982** PAFA, *William Rush, American Sculptor,* cat. no. 37 (ill.). **1986–87** PAFA, *Sculpture at the Pennsylvania Academy of the Fine Arts.* **1987** New York Public Library. **1988** Katonah Gallery, N.Y., *The American Eagle: Symbol and Spirit, 1782–1882.* **1989** PAFA, *"The Birds and the Beasts Will Teach Us."*

Head of the Nymph (Fragment from "Allegory of the Schuylkill River")

1809
Pine
10 x 9½ x 10" (25.4 x 24.1 x 25.4 cm)
Henry S. McNeil Fund, 1990.8

THIS PINE HEAD is all that remains of one of William Rush's earliest public works. The full-length statue of the nymph and bittern exists in an 1872 bronze cast on loan to the Philadelphia Museum of Art by the Fairmount Park Commission.

Rush was on the City Council's Watering Committee that built the waterworks in Centre Square (now the site of City Hall). The pumphouse, designed by the architect Benjamin Henry Latrobe, featured a fountain with Rush's figure in front of it, as shown in John Lewis Krimmel's 1812 painting *Fourth of July in Centre Square* (Museum of American Art, Pennsylvania Academy of the Fine Arts).

The figure of the nymph was carved from a live model, Louisa Vanuxem (1782–1874), who was the daughter of James Vanuxem, the chairman of the committee. The eyes feature Rush's typical treatment: carved-out pupils with an incised line around the iris. The intricate deeply carved curls and top knot are also characteristic of his work.

The fountain was moved to the new waterworks on the Schuylkill River at Fairmount in the later 1820s. Deteriorating, it was cast in bronze; and the wood figure was repainted and then reinstalled in a protected location. About 1900, the figure, which had by then nearly disintegrated, was moved inside where it was discovered by a descendant of the model, John S. Wurts, who rescued the head and part

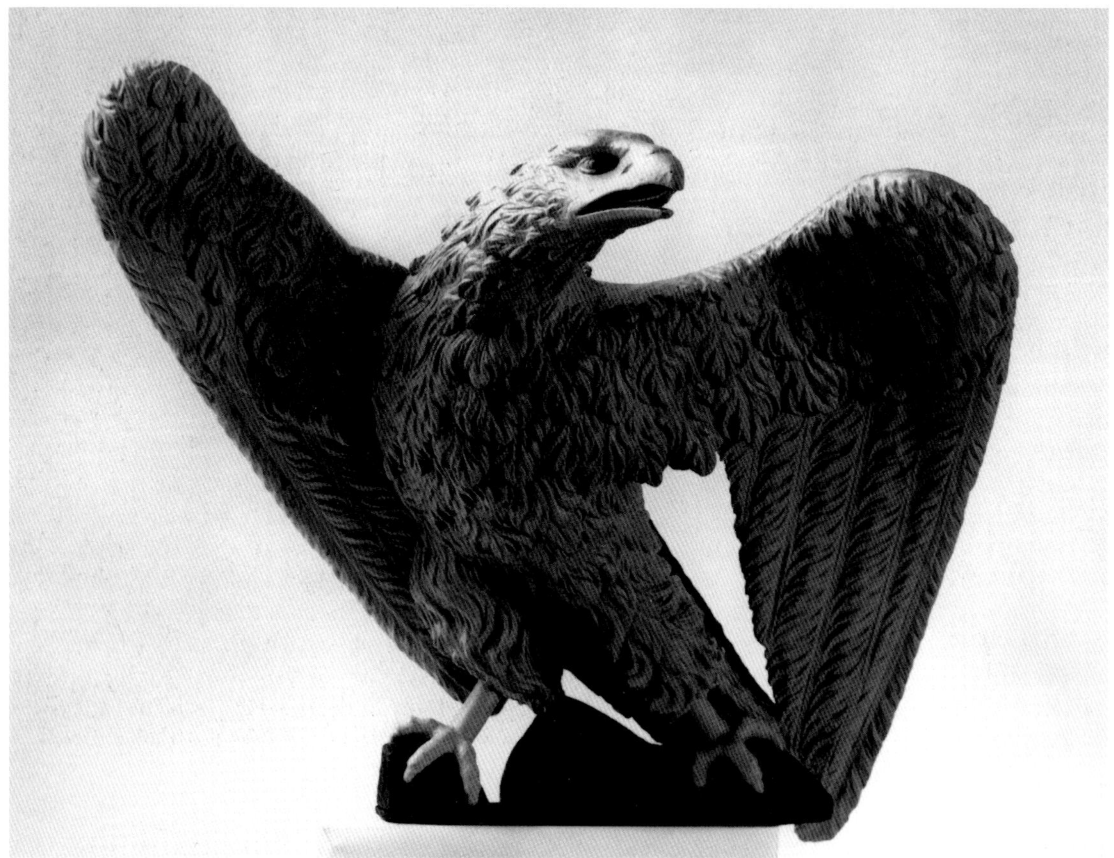

Rush, *Eagle*

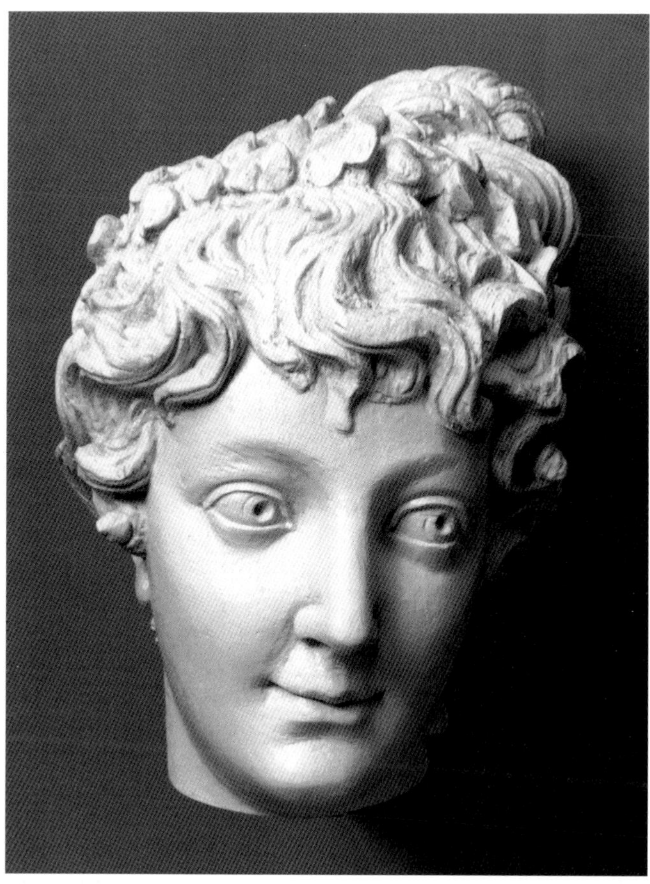

Rush, *Head of the Nymph*

of the bird (present whereabouts unknown). Several casts of the head were then made in bronze (the Museum of American Art has one).

Exhibited
1937 Pennsylvania Museum of Art, Philadelphia, *William Rush, 1756–1833: The First American Sculptor,* cat. no. 5b. **1955** PAFA, *The One Hundred and Fiftieth Anniversary Exhibition,* cat. no. 22. **1975** Philadelphia Museum of Art, *La Première Pose: The Nude in Philadelphia.* **1982** PAFA, *William Rush, American Sculptor,* pp. 35–37, cat. no. 35 (ill.). **1992–93** PAFA, *Masterworks of American Art, 1750–1950.* **1994–96** PAFA, *Two Centuries of Collecting at the Museum of American Art.*

Ex Collections
City of Philadelphia, 1809–about 1900; John S. Wurts, Philadelphia, about 1900–58; private collection, 1958–90.

Joseph Wright

About 1810
Terracotta
19¾ x 16½ x 10″ (50.2 x 41.9 x 25.4 cm)
Source unknown, 1813.1

Born in Bordentown, New Jersey, Joseph Wright (1756–1793) was the only son of Patience Lovell Wright, a noted modeler of wax portraits. After her husband died, she took Joseph to England, where they lived from 1772 to 1782. He learned clay and wax modeling from his mother and painting from Benjamin West. According to the American art historian William Dunlap, Wright taught William Rush to model. (Wright was in Philadelphia from 1783 to 1786.) It is thought that, as an homage to his deceased mentor, Rush modeled this portrait from memory years after Wright's death. It is one of Rush's earliest works in terracotta.

Exhibited
1811* cat. no. 458a. **1818** PAFA, *Exhibition of the Paintings, Statues, Prints, etc. at the Pennsylvania Academy of the Fine Arts,* cat. no. 355. **1819*** cat. no. 333. **1820*** cat. no. 189. **1937** Pennsylvania Museum of Art, Philadelphia, *William Rush, 1756–1833: The First American Sculptor,* cat. no. 10 (ill.). **1944–45** PAFA, *Star Presentation,* cat. no. 35, pl. 18. **1949** Art Institute of Chicago, *From Colony to Nation: An Exhibition of American Painting, Silver and Architecture from 1650 to the War of 1812,* cat. no. 99. **1955** PAFA, *The One Hundred and Fiftieth Anniversary Exhibition,* cat. no. 18. **1973** PAFA, *Held in Trust,* checklist no. 197. **1982** PAFA, *William Rush, American Sculptor,* cat. no. 38 (ill.). **1986–87** PAFA, *Sculpture at the Pennsylvania Academy of the Fine Arts.*

Rush, *Joseph Wright*

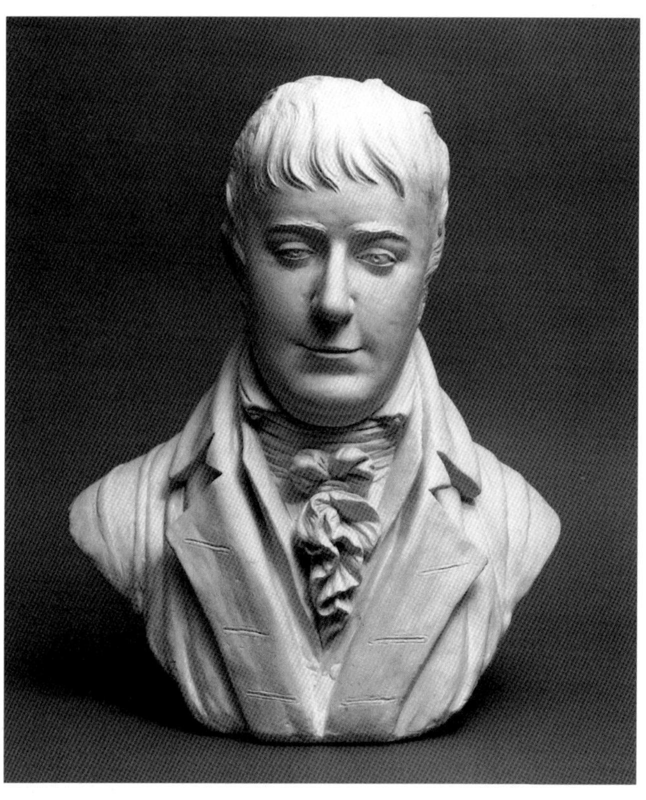

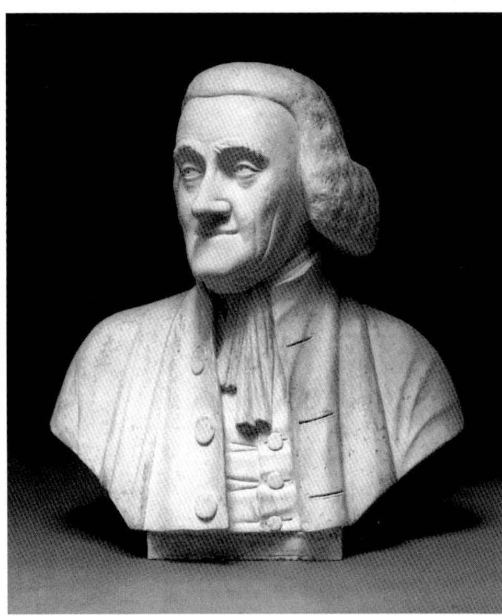

Rush, *Samuel Morris*

Samuel Morris

1812
Plaster; cast in 1905
21½ x 20 x 11½" (54.6 x 50.8 x 29.2 cm)
Signed on back: Wm. Rush/fect.
Gift of The Schuylkill Fishing Company of the State in Schuylkill, 1905.8

THIS IS one of three casts made by P.G. Tognarelli of Philadelphia[1] from the painted pine original owned by the Schuylkill Fishing Company of the State in Schuylkill in Cornwells Heights, Pennsylvania. (The pine bust has been on loan to the Pennsylvania Academy of the Fine Arts since 1980, in exchange for this plaster.) The wooden head is one of only two signed sculptures by Rush, and it retains its original paint.

Samuel Morris (1734–1812) was active in politics and served as governor of the Schuylkill Fishing Company, a society founded in 1732 for the purpose of fishing and feasting. After he died, the pine bust was commissioned by the society and installed in a place of honor in its new building. No portraits had been made during Morris's lifetime so Rush must have worked from memory.

Note

1. One of the other casts is owned by the First Troop Philadelphia City Cavalry; the whereabouts of the other is unknown. Additional casts were made in 1928 and 1943 for Morris descendants.

Reference

1982 Linda Bantel et al., *William Rush, American Sculptor*, exhib. cat., Philadelphia: PAFA, pp. 126, 128.

Benjamin Rush

1812
Terracotta
18¾ x 15½ x 12½" (47.6 x 39.4 x 31.8 cm)
Source unknown, 1864.6

THIS IS a portrait of Dr. Benjamin Rush (1745–1813), the sculptor's second cousin, who was a signer of the Declaration of Independence and an influential Philadelphia physician and author. On March 12, 1815, William Rush wrote to the painter Benjamin West in London and explained how he modeled this likeness using actual head measurements (New-York Historical Society).

Like JEAN ANTOINE HOUDON, Rush made terracotta busts for display so that he could take orders for plaster casts. As of 1982 there were four known plaster replicas of this bust—at the Library Company of Philadelphia, the College of Physicians of Philadelphia, the collection of the late Andrew Oliver in Boston, and Pennsylvania Hospital in Philadelphia. The whereabouts of two other replicas is unknown.

References

1937 Henri Marceau, *William Rush, 1756–1833: The First American Sculptor*, Philadelphia: Pennsylvania Museum of Art, p. 42. **1975** Robert Erwin Jones, M.D., "Portrait Busts of Benjamin Rush, M.D., by his contemporaries," *Antiques* 108 (July), fig. 22, pp. 109, 111–12. **1981** William H. Gerdts, *The Art of Healing: Medicine and Science*

Rush, *Benjamin Rush*

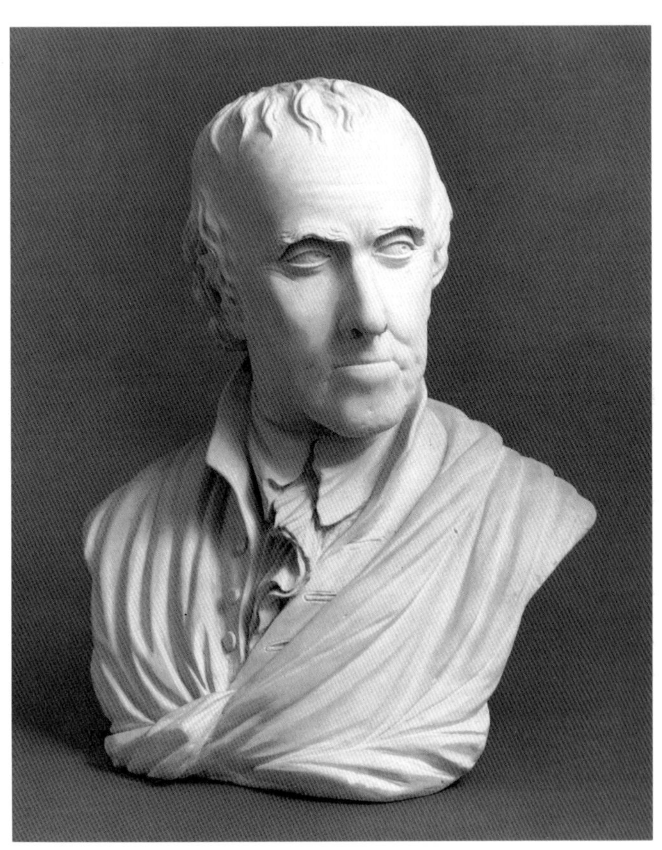

in American Art, exhib. cat., Birmingham, Ala.: Birmingham Museum of Art, p. 12 (ill.).

Exhibited
1814* cat. no. 43. **1815*** cat. no. 6. **1816** PAFA, *Exhibition of Mr. Allston's Picture of the Dead Man Restored to Life by Touching the Bones of the Prophet Elisha . . . in addition to the stationary pictures of the Academy*, p. 8. **1816** PAFA, *Exhibition of Mr. C.R. Leslie's Picture of the Murder of Rutland and Mr. Allston's Dead Man Restored . . .*, cat. no. 150. **1817*** cat. no. 362. **1818*** cat. no. 362. **1818** PAFA, *Exhibition of the Paintings, Statues, Prints, etc. at the Pennsylvania Academy of the Fine Arts*, cat. no. 355. **1819*** cat. no. 272. **1820*** cat. no. 118. **1821*** cat. no. 216. **1822*** cat. no. 269. **1823*** cat. no. 209. **1824*** cat. no. 436. **1825*** cat. no. 472. **1826*** cat. no. 461. **1827*** cat. no. 461. **1828*** cat. no. 439. **1829*** cat. no. 402. **1830*** cat. no. 357. **1831*** cat. no. 87. **1832*** cat. no. 87. **1834*** cat. no. 87. **1836–38, 1840** PAFA, *Exhibition of the Pennsylvania Academy of the Fine Arts*, cat. no. 87. **1843** PAFA, *Exhibition of paintings, statues, and casts at the Pennsylvania Academy of the Fine Arts*, cat. no. 87. **1865*** cat. no. 214. **1866*** cat. no. 214. **1868*** cat. no. 400. **1869*** cat. no. 311. **1926** PAFA, *A Gallery of National Portraiture and Historic Scenes*, checklist no. 440. **1944–45** PAFA, *Star Presentation*, cat. no. 32, pl. 8. **1955** PAFA, *One Hundred and Fiftieth Anniversary Exhibition*, cat. no. 16 (ill.). **1982** PAFA, *William Rush, American Sculptor*, p. 52, cat. no. 49 (ill.), figs. 45, 73, 74.

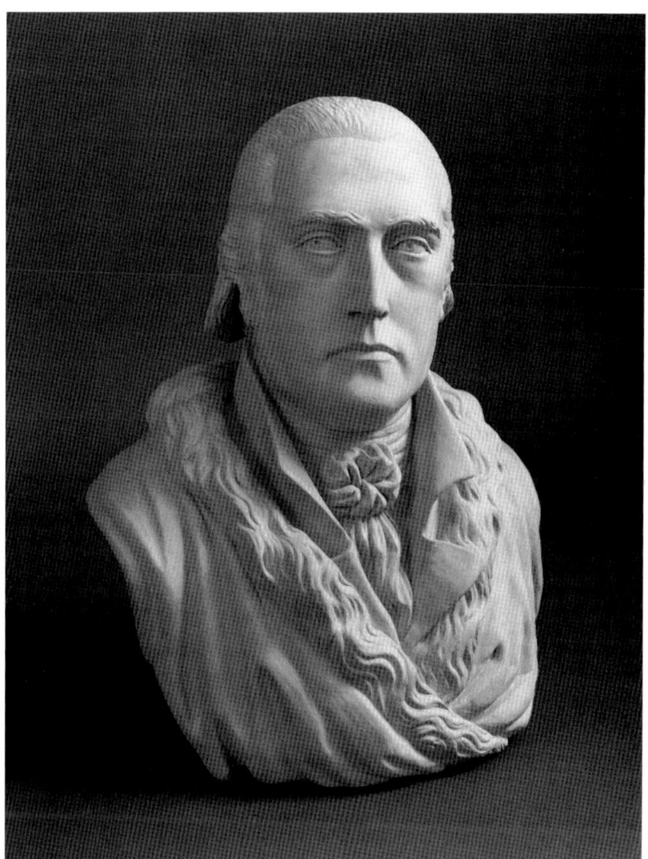
Rush, *Philip Syng Physick*

Philip Syng Physick

1812–13
Terracotta
19 x 14¾ x 11¼" (48.2 x 37.5 x 28.5 cm)
Source unknown, 1944.28

Dr. Philip Syng Physick (1768–1837) was called the father of American surgery. He worked with Dr. Benjamin Rush (portrait bust [q.v.]) during the yellow-fever epidemic in Philadelphia.

This bust may have been owned by the Pennsylvania Academy of the Fine Arts since 1865 inasmuch as an unattributed bust of Physick is listed then in the catalogue of the permanent collection.

Four plaster casts exist in Philadelphia: at the American Philosophical Society, the Library Company of Philadelphia, the College of Physicians, and in the collection of Robert Erwin Jones, M.D. Two others are unlocated.

Exhibited
1813* cat. no. 139. **1814*** cat. no. 42. **1815*** cat. no. 7. **1816** PAFA, *Exhibition of Mr. Allston's Picture of the Dead Man Restored to Life by Touching the Bones of the Prophet Elisha . . . in addition to the stationary pictures of the Academy*, p. 8. **1816** PAFA, *Exhibition of Mr. C.R. Leslie's Picture of the Murder of Rutland and Mr. Allston's Picture of the Dead Man Restored . . .*, cat. no. 151. **1817*** cat. no. **363.** **1818*** cat. no. **363.** **1818** PAFA, *An Exhibition of the Paintings, Statues, Prints, etc. at the Pennsylvania Academy of the Fine Arts*, cat. no. 363. **1819*** cat. no. 341. **1820*** cat. no. 197. **1821*** cat. no. 218. **1821** PAFA, *Exhibition of the Paintings, Statues, Prints, etc. at the Pennsylvania Academy of the Fine Arts*, cat. no. 218. **1822*** cat. no. 271. **1823*** cat. no. 211. **1824*** cat. no. 438. **1825*** cat. no. 474. **1826*** cat. no. 463. **1827*** cat. no. 463. **1828*** cat. no. 441. **1829*** cat. no. 404. **1830*** cat. no. 359. **1834*** cat. no. 110. **1836–38, 1840** PAFA, *Exhibition of the Pennsylvania Academy of the Fine Arts*, cat. no. 110. **1843** PAFA, *Exhibition of Paintings, Statues, and Casts at the Pennsylvania Academy of the Fine Arts*, cat. no. 87. **1866*** cat. no. 477, unattributed. **1868*** cat. no. 477, unattributed. **1926** PAFA, *A Gallery of National Portraiture and Historic Scenes*, checklist no. 434. **1937** Pennsylvania Museum of Art, Philadelphia, *William Rush, 1756–1833: The First American Sculptor*, cat. no. 27 (ill.), pp. 40–42. **1944–45** PAFA, *Star Presentation*, cat. no. 31. **1955** PAFA, *One Hundred and Fiftieth Anniversary Exhibition*, cat. no. 21. **1965** Philadelphia Museum of Art, *The Art of Philadelphia Medicine*, cat. no. 40. **1982** PAFA, *William Rush, American Sculptor*, p. 86, fig. 75, cat. no. 60 (ill.).

Caspar Wistar

1812–13
Terracotta
20 x 17 x 13½" (50.8 x 43.2 x 34.3 cm)
Source unknown, 1864.7

AT THE TIME that William Rush modeled this portrait of Dr. Caspar Wistar (1761–1818), they were working together to make anatomical models for Wistar's anatomy students at the University of Pennsylvania. Wistar, who held medical degrees from the University of Pennsylvania and the University of Edinburgh, had been a distinguished teacher at the College of Physicians in Philadelphia. Then he was appointed a full professor at the University of Pennsylvania, and in 1810 a chair of anatomy was created for him.

Three plaster replicas of this terracotta are in Philadelphia at the American Philosophical Society, the College of Physicians of Philadelphia, and Pennsylvania Hospital. A fourth, originally at Wistar Institute of Anatomy and Biology, is presently unlocated.

Exhibited
1813* cat. no. 140. **1815*** cat. no. 2. **1817*** cat. no. 392. **1818*** cat. no. 392. **1818** PAFA, *Exhibition of the Paintings, Statues, Prints, etc. at the Pennsylvania Academy of the Fine Arts,* cat. no. 272. **1821*** cat. no. 217. **1821** PAFA, *Exhibition of the Paintings, Statues, Prints, etc. at the Pennsylvania Academy of the Fine Arts,* cat. no. 217. **1822*** cat. no. 270. **1823*** cat. no. 210. **1824*** cat. no. 437. **1825*** cat. no. 473. **1826*** cat. no. 462. **1827*** cat. no. 462. **1828*** cat. no. 440. **1829*** cat. no. 403. **1830*** cat. no. 358. **1831*** cat. no. 89. **1832*** cat. no. 89. **1834*** cat. no. 89. **1836–38, 1840** PAFA, *Exhibition of the Pennsylvania Academy of the Fine Arts,* cat. no. 89. **1843** PAFA, *Exhibition of Paintings, Statues, and Casts at the Pennsylvania Academy of the Fine Arts,* cat. no. 89. **1937** Pennsylvania Museum of Art, Philadelphia, *William Rush, 1756–1833: The First American Sculptor,* cat. no. 26 (ill.). **1944–45** PAFA, *Star Presentation,* cat. no. 34. **1949** Art Institute of Chicago, *From Colony to Nation: An Exhibition of American Painting, Silver and Architecture from 1650 to the War of 1812,* cat. no. 98. **1965** Philadelphia Museum of Art, *The Art of Philadelphia Medicine,* cat. no. 32 (ill.). **1973** PAFA, *Pennsylvania Academicians,* checklist no. 56. **1982** PAFA, *William Rush, American Sculptor,* pp. 54, fig. 48, p. 88, fig. 79, cat. no. 59 (ill.). **1986–87** PAFA, *Sculpture at the Pennsylvania Academy of the Fine Arts.*

Rush, *Caspar Wistar*

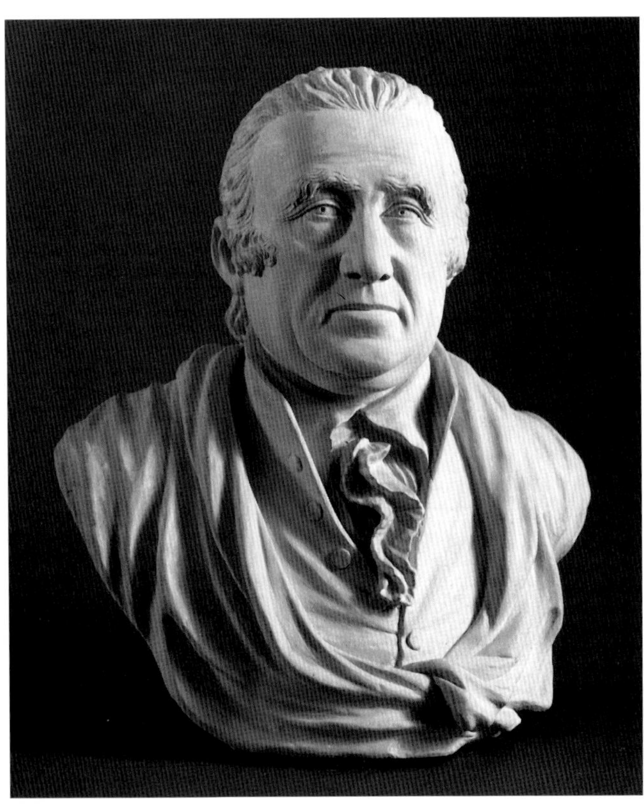

Self-Portrait

About 1822
Terracotta
15½ x 18 x 11" (39.4 x 45.7 x 27.9 cm)
Source unknown, 1849.1

THIS BUST was first exhibited at the Pennsylvania Academy of the Fine Arts in 1822. It had been recorded as part of the permanent collection by 1849. William Rush, who achieved fame as a carver of wood, depicted himself emerging from a pine knot. The illusion that he created by making terracotta look like wood is a stunning display of his technical virtuosity.

There are no known plaster replicas, but several bronzes were cast posthumously, in 1905 (the Museum of American Art of the Pennsylvania Academy has one) and 1970. One bronze is at the National Portrait Gallery in Washington, D.C.

Exhibited
1822* cat. no. 40. **1823*** cat. no. 40. **1824*** cat. no. 40. **1825*** cat. no. 40. **1826*** cat. no. 40. **1827*** cat. no. 40. **1828*** cat. no. 40. **1829*** cat. no. 40. **1830*** cat. no. 40. **1831*** cat. no. 108. **1832*** cat. no. 108. **1834*** cat. no. 108. **1836–38, 1840** PAFA, *Exhibition of the Pennsylvania Academy of the Fine Arts,* cat. no. 108. **1843** PAFA, *Exhibition of Paintings, Statues, and Casts at the Pennsylvania Academy of the Fine Arts,* cat. no. 108. **1849*** cat. no. 412. **1855*** cat. no. 477. **1856** PAFA, *Fall Exhibition of the Pennsylvania Academy of the Fine Arts.* **1858*** cat. no. 520. **1860*** cat. no. 403. **1865*** cat. no. 228. **1866*** cat. no. 228. **1868*** cat. no. 448. **1869*** cat. no. 360. **1926** PAFA, *A Gallery of National Portraiture and Historic Scenes.* **1937** Pennsylvania Museum

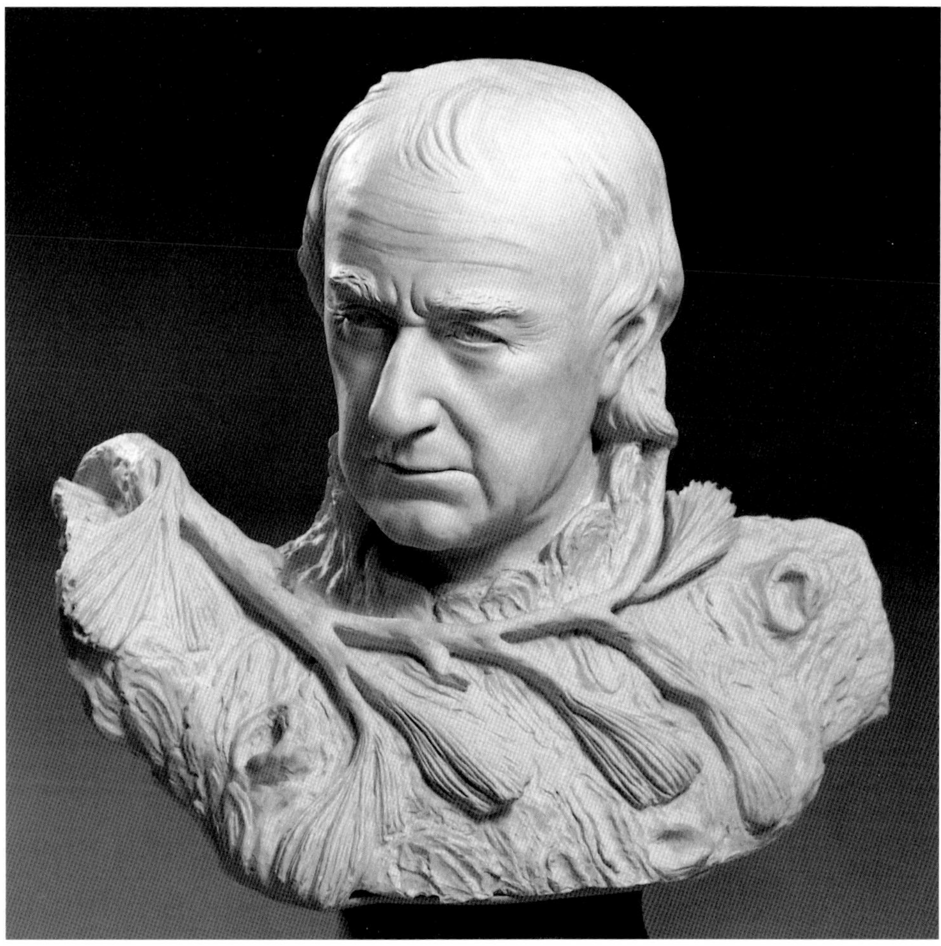

Rush, *Self-Portrait*

of Art, Philadelphia, *William Rush, 1756–1833: The First American Sculptor,* cat. no. 42 (ill.). **1944–45** PAFA, *Star Presentation,* cat. no. 33, pl. 27. **1973** PAFA, *Pennsylvania Academicians,* checklist no. 55. **1976** PAFA, *In This Academy,* cat. no. 34, p. 15 (ill.). **1982** PAFA, *William Rush, American Sculptor,* pp. 86–87, figs. 76–78, cat. no. 90 (ill.), color ills. on cover and pl. 7. **1986–87** PAFA, *Sculpture at the Pennsylvania Academy of the Fine Arts.* **1992–93** PAFA, *Masterworks of American Art, 1750–1950.* **1994–96** PAFA, *Two Centuries of Collecting at the Museum of American Art.*

Marquis de Lafayette

1824
Terracotta
21 x 18¾ x 11¼" (53.3 x 47.6 x 28.6 cm)
Gift of Dr. William Rush Dunton, Jr., 1911.3

DURING his 1824 tour of the United States, the marquis de Lafayette (1757–1834) spent a week in Philadelphia and was elaborately entertained. William Rush's statues *Wisdom* and *Justice* (on loan to the Museum of American Art of the Pennsylvania Academy of the Fine Arts by the Fairmount Park Commission) were featured in a temporary civic arch for the occasion.

It is said that Rush observed Lafayette during an official dinner and then modeled this bust from memory. A few days later, he showed it to Lafayette who called it an excellent likeness.

Rush never exhibited this bust during his lifetime. It remained in his family until his great-grandson presented it to the Pennsylvania Academy in 1911. The first cast was made in plaster in 1912 by the Academy for the Schuylkill Fishing Company of the State in Schuylkill in exchange for a plaster cast of the bust of Samuel Morris (q.v.). Bronzes were cast in 1970; one of them is at the National Portrait Gallery in Washington, D.C.

References
1987 Beatrice Garvan, *Federal Philadelphia,* exhib. cat., Philadelphia: Philadelphia Museum of Art, cat. no. 250, fig. 31. **1989** Queens Museum, Flushing, N.Y., *Lafayette, Hero of Two Worlds,* exhib. cat., fig. 158, p. 169.

Exhibited
1824 Franklin Institute, Philadelphia. **1937** Pennsylvania Museum of Art, Philadelphia, *William Rush, 1756–1833: The First American Sculptor,* cat. no. 43 (ill.). **1944–45** PAFA, *Star Presentation,* cat. no. 30, pl. 26. **1955** PAFA, *One Hundred and Fiftieth Anniversary Exhibition,* cat. no. 13 (ill.). **1973** PAFA, *Held in Trust,* cat. no. 194. **1976** PAFA, *In This Academy,* cat. no. 35. **1982** PAFA, *William Rush, American Sculptor,* cat. no. 94 (ill.), color pl. 8. **1986–87** PAFA, *Sculpture at the Pennsylvania Academy of the Fine Arts.* **1994–96** PAFA, *Two Centuries of Collecting at the Museum of American Art.*

Ex Collections
William Rush, 1824–33; probably his daughter Mary Simpson Dunton, 1833–87; probably her grandson William Rush Dunton, Jr., 1887–1911.

Rush, *Marquis de Lafayette*

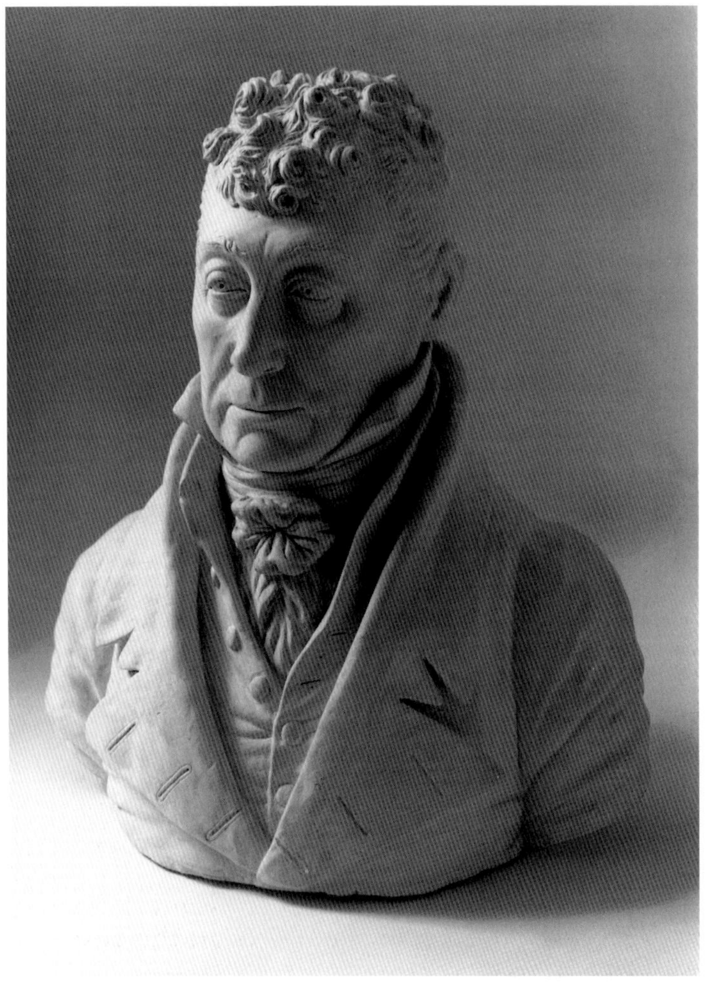

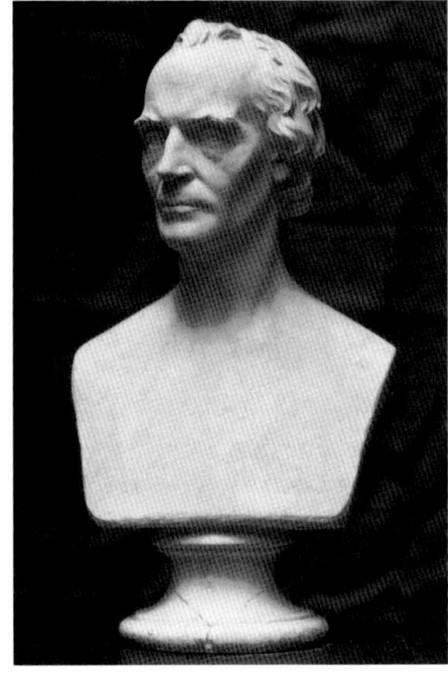

Unidentified Artist, *Unidentified Man*

Unidentified Artist

Unidentified Man

About 1820–30
Plaster, painted white
25 x 13¾ x 10¼″ (63.5 x 34.9 x 26 cm)
Source unknown, 1832.1

THIS BUST was originally thought to be the work of WILLIAM RUSH, but the bare chest and the modeling of the facial details do not relate to any of his known portraits.

John Rush

1782–1853

Little is known about the life and career of John Rush, the eldest child of the sculptor WILLIAM RUSH. According to the Philadelphia city directories, John Rush was employed in 1809 as a shipwright and by 1814 as a carver. According to bills, he was by then helping repair his father's figureheads. By 1819 he was an equal partner in his father's shop William Rush and Son, and they were working on carvings for the ship *Columbus.* In 1820 and 1821 they worked on figures of four of the Masonic virtues for Philadelphia's Masonic Hall. During the 1820s, John Rush carved and repaired ship's carvings for the vessels *Ellen, Potomac, Superb, Helvetius,* and *Rousseau.* He worked with his father on allegorical figures in 1825 and on *Mercury* in 1828 and 1829 for the Fairmount Waterworks. By then William Rush was in his seventies and apparently working less. John's name disappears from the records at about this time, and he may have gone to Cincinnati, as this later clipping implies:

> Our city suffered a loss in the death of the late William Rush not only on account of the moral worth and public spirit of that gentleman, but especially in reference to his pre-eminence as an artist. Mr. Rush had no equal in this country, we believe, as a carver, and ship owners have felt his loss in the ornamental parts of those vessels which are the pride of our port, and which claim admiration in all parts of the world which they visit. The son of Mr. Rush, who inherited his father's taste and received his father's instruction, removed some time since to Cincinnati where his works were greatly admired. But the death of his father has induced the son to return to his native city to continue the business which was for a short time interrupted, and we may now look for more of those beautiful figure-heads and stern decorations which give the finish to a Philadelphia ship.[1]

John Rush may have helped his father secure perhaps his final commission in 1830 from "a gentleman in Covington, opposite Cincinnati" for busts of Thomas Jefferson, James Madison, George Washington, and General Lafayette. The person who commissioned William Rush to model or cast the busts and who motivated the younger Rush to move to Cincinnati was probably Nicholas Longworth. He was the well-known patron of many sculptors of the time, including HIRAM POWERS, SHOBAL VAIL CLEVENGER, and Henry Kirke Brown (1814–1866). Longworth's sponsorship enabled them to study and work in the United States and Italy.

Back in Philadelphia, John Rush is known to have produced an eagle for the Fairmount Waterworks in 1835; carvings in 1836 and 1837 for the vessel *Pennsylvania,* based on his father's 1824 designs; and the *Goddess of Liberty* about 1840 for the top of the courthouse in Reading, Pennsylvania. He carved eight allegorical figures in the 1840s for the George W. Carpenter estate in Germantown, a northern suburb of Philadelphia. About Carpenter, Linda Bantel wrote, "It is curious and perhaps to John Rush's credit that this wealthy patron, who could have afforded to go to Europe for the best in marble statuary, chose instead a local woodcarver."[2] Perhaps John Rush has not been given enough credit, and he deserves to emerge from his father's shadow.

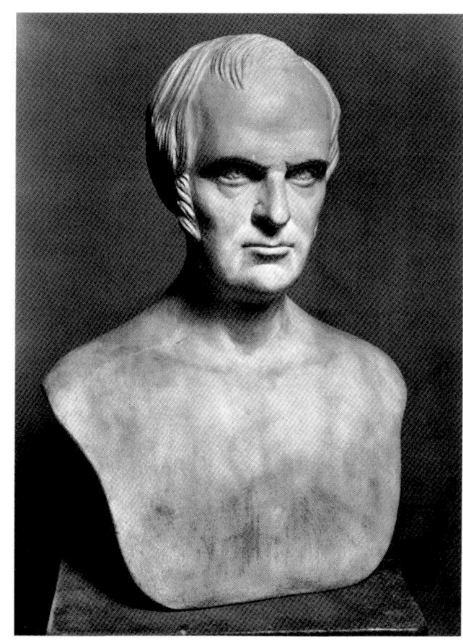

Attributed to Rush, *David Rittenhouse*

Notes

1. *United States Gazette,* Philadelphia, April 15, 1833, p. 2.
2. Linda Bantel, "William Rush Esq." in *William Rush, American Sculptor* (Philadelphia: PAFA, 1982), p. 25.

ATTRIBUTED TO JOHN RUSH

David Rittenhouse

About 1840
Pine, painted white
24 x 17 x 10½" (61 x 43.2 x 26.7 cm)
Gift of John F. Lewis, Jr., 1951.28

DAVID RITTENHOUSE (1732–1796) was an astronomer who taught at the University of Pennsylvania. He was also the first director of the United States Mint and president of the American Philosophical Society from 1791 to 1796.

There are no other known busts by John Rush with which to compare this example. The chest is blank, unlike those his father created, which are all clothed. This feature represents a later innovation of the neoclassical style that was emerging in the late 1820s. The hair is not as intricately carved nor as highly textured as in William Rush's busts. The joinery also differs from his father's technique: nails are used here, whereas William Rush used glue.

John Rush was one of the sculptors who worked for George W. Carpenter from whose estate this bust was sold in 1893.

Exhibited
1937 Pennsylvania Museum of Art, Philadelphia, *William Rush, 1756–1833: The First American Sculptor* (not in cat.). **1982** PAFA, *William Rush, American Sculptor,* pp. 184–85, 187, fig. 135, checklist no. 59.

Ex Collections
George W. Carpenter estate sale, 1893; George Staub, Washington, D.C., by 1937–51; Elizabeth K. Sharpe, Conshohocken, Pa., 1951; George F. Kearney, 1951; John F. Lewis, Jr., Philadelphia, 1951.

John Frazee

1790–1852

John Frazee is believed to be the first American-born sculptor to execute a bust in marble. Despite a lack of European training, he gleaned a vast amount of information about sculpture and its production from the scanty resources available in early nineteenth-century America.[1] The busts that he produced demonstrate his knowledge of neoclassicism and mark his place in the beginning of this international style in America.

The youngest of ten children, Frazee was born in Rahway, New Jersey, shortly before his father abandoned the family. In their struggle against poverty, there was little opportunity for formal education. Aside from a couple of years in school and lessons from his grandmother, John Frazee was self-educated. His passions ran to art and music. Apprenticed at the age of fourteen to a mason named William Lawrence, Frazee became enamoured of stone carving. His first attempt was a plaque commemorating Lawrence's completion of a bridge over the Rahway River. In 1808 Frazee was sent to New Brunswick, New Jersey, to help in the building of a bank. There he persuaded Ward Baldwin, an experienced stone cutter, to instruct him in carving.

For the next several years, Frazee carved gravestones, first in Rahway and then in New Brunswick. During this time, he also developed his singing skills. For a time he augmented his income by running a singing school in Rahway. In 1817 he helped compile *The New-Brunswick Collection of Sacred Music.*

Frazee moved to New York in 1818. He and his brother William established a marble cutting shop, specializing in memorials and mantlepieces. John was responsible for most of the decorative carving and lettering. An example from this period is the memorial for Sarah Haynes, 1821, located in Trinity Church, New York.

Although he had produced only a few sculptures, Frazee achieved sufficient recognition to be elected a member of the American Academy of the Fine Arts in 1824. A bylaw of the academy required new members to present a piece of their work to the institution within a year of their election. In 1824 the marquis de Lafayette visited the United States, and several members of the American Academy persuaded him to sit for a portrait by Frazee. The sculptor completed a plaster likeness and presented it to the American Academy to fulfill the membership requirement. Favorable reaction to the bust helped Frazee secure a commission for a memorial to the eminent New York lawyer John Wells. Completed in 1825, it is located in Saint Paul's Chapel. The portrait of Wells atop this memorial is thought to be the first marble bust executed by an American sculptor. Frazee was the only sculptor among the artists who founded the National Academy of Design the following year.

In 1831, two years after dissolving his partnership with his brother, Frazee entered into business with one of his journeyman carvers, Robert E. Launitz (1806–1870). Born in Latvia, Launitz had studied with the Danish neoclassicist Bertel Thorwaldsen (1770–1844) before coming to the United States in 1828. Launitz's neoclassical training augmented Frazee's inclination towards that style. The heroic quality of Frazee's bust of John Jay and the use of the dead eye demonstrate the sculptor's complete assimilation of neoclassicism. Commissioned by the federal government in 1831, this bust marks Frazee's place as the first American sculptor to secure congressional patronage.

During the early 1830s, the Boston Athenaeum commissioned seven portraits from Frazee. Among them are his busts of Daniel Webster, Nathaniel Bowditch, and Chief Justice John Marshall. The Pennsylvania Academy of the Fine Arts owned a version of the Marshall bust, but it was lost sometime before 1944.

With his health waning and the pressures of a large family mounting, Frazee accepted a salaried position as architect and superintendent of the New York Custom House from 1834 to 1841. He produced little sculpture during his later years. Neither his fondest dream, a congressional commission for a figure of Thomas Jefferson, nor his well-received plan for a colossal monument to George Washington was ever realized.

Note

1. Although a few art academies existed in the United States during the early 1880s, none offered instruction in

sculpture. Frazee's earliest exposure to sculpture included the antique casts at the American Academy of the Fine Arts, New York, and the carvings of foreign sculptors working in the United States, such as Giuseppe Ceracchi (1751–1801) and Enrico Causici (active in the United States, 1822-about 1826).

References

1835 John Frazee, "The Autobiography of Frazee, the Sculptor," *North American Magazine* (April and June), reproduced as a pamphlet for the exhibition *John Frazee, Sculptor* at National Portrait Gallery, Washington, D.C., April 25-August 24, 1986. **1978** Linda Hyman, "From Artisan to Artist: John Frazee and the Politics of Culture in Antebellum America," Ph.D. diss., City University of New York. **1986** Jean Henry and Dennis Montagna, "John Frazee and the Emergence of American Neoclassical Sculpture," unpublished typescript, PAFA research file. **1986** Frederick S. Voss, with essay by Dennis Montagna and Jean Henry, *John Frazee, Sculptor,* Washington, D.C., and Boston: National Portrait Gallery, Smithsonian Institution, and Boston Athenaeum, pp. 17–55.

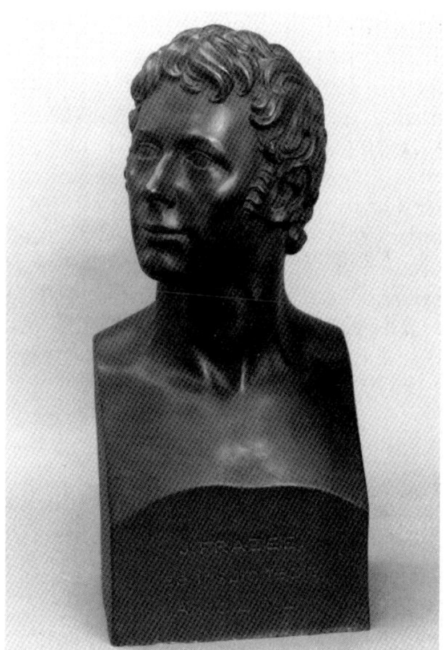

Frazee, *Self-Portrait*

Self-Portrait

1827

Bronze with black patina; sand cast in 1905

22½ x 9¾ x 9½" (57.2 x 24.8 x 24.1 cm)

Signed and dated on front (incised): J. FRAZEE./se ipsum fecit/ Anno L.A.LII [year of American liberty 52 (i.e., 1828)]

Foundry mark stamped on back at lower right: BUREAU BROS/[PHILA]

Cast by the Pennsylvania Academy from original plaster in Academy's collection, 1905.4

THE YEAR that he modeled this self-portrait, 1827, John Frazee exhibited a plaster version at the National Academy of Design in New York. No doubt he dated the work the following year because he anticipated its completion in marble.[1] Unfortunately, the carving was never done.

Frazee was thirty-seven years old when he modeled this portrait, but he depicted himself as a much younger man. The herm design, lacking shoulders and drapery, may have been inspired by the similarly constructed portrait of Alexander the Great attributed to Lysippus, fourth century, B.C. (Musée du Louvre, Paris). Frazee was probably familiar with a plaster cast of the Greek work in the American Academy of the Fine Arts, New York.

This bronze version of Frazee's self-portrait was cast from a plaster owned by the Pennsylvania Academy of the Fine Arts.[2] Now lost, that plaster may have been the one that Frazee showed in the Pennsylvania Academy's 1832 annual exhibition.[3] It is possible that he never removed the plaster after the exhibition. This was not uncommon in the early nineteenth century, because most sculptors viewed plasters only as models. A plaster version, however, does not appear again in the Pennsylvania Academy's records until the 1864 catalogue of the permanent collection. It is also listed in the two dozen subsequent permanent-collection catalogues, published by the Academy between 1864 and 1903 when they were discontinued. The plaster was missing by 1940 when a checklist of the Academy's sculpture collection was compiled.[4] A photograph made about 1902 of the Pennsylvania Academy's plaster shows the last line of the inscription as "Anno L.A.LIII" with the third *I* extending only three-fourths as high as the other two.[5] This clearly differs from the inscriptions on the other two known plasters, at the National Academy of Design (donated by the sculptor from the 1827 National Academy exhibition mentioned earlier) and the National Portrait Gallery, which read "Anno L.A.LII." It appears from the photograph that the inscription on the Pennsylvania Academy's plaster was tampered with and that the final period was extended upward.[6] On the Academy's bronze version, the third *I* is only faintly visible. Possibly the foundry was instructed to correct the erroneous date before making the cast. A plaster version was cast at the same time for the sculptor's youngest daughter, Lydia Frazee Belknap, of Yonkers, New York.[7]

Notes

1. About the dating system and its possible symbolism for Frazee, see Frederick Voss, *John Frazee, Sculptor* (Washington, D.C., and Boston: National Portrait Gallery, Smithsonian Institution, and Boston Athenaeum), p. 74.

2. Frazee never worked in bronze; but, at the turn of the century, bronze casts were considered a preferable, more permanent record of a sculptor's work. When this bronze

was made, the Pennsylvania Academy also had three other sculptures cast into bronze: WILLIAM RUSH's terracotta *Self-Portrait,* JEAN ANTOINE HOUDON's plaster *John Paul Jones,* and SHOBAL VAIL CLEVENGER's plaster *Joseph Hopkinson* (qq.v.).

3. No record exists of a donor for the Academy's plaster, and no mention of its purchase or arrival into the collection can be found. In the catalogue *Carved and Modeled: American Sculpture, 1810–1940* (New York: Hirschl and Adler Galleries, 1982, p. 16), Susan Menconi states that the plaster was deposited at the Pennsylvania Academy about 1865 on long-term loan by the sculptor's family; but there is nothing to confirm this. The 1864 catalogue of the permanent collection lists the Pennsylvania Academy as the owner, and the bust is never placed in the appendix of works on deposit that appears in most of the permanent collection catalogues. Furthermore, if the bust had been lent by the sculptor's family, the artist's daughter Lydia Frazee Belknap would probably have known; but in 1905, she wrote to the Academy, asking permission to have a plaster copy made and inquiring how this could be done (Lydia Belknap to John E.D. Trask, Nov. 2, 1905, PAFA Archives).

4. The last mention is in 1934, when the Pennsylvania Academy informed Stephen Millet, a descendant of the sculptor, that two plaster casts of the plaster in its collection could be made for him (minutes, meeting of the board of directors, Nov. 14, 1934, PAFA Archives). Mr. Millet, however, never ordered the casts (S. Millet to Mary Mullen Cunningham, interview, April 1986).

5. The date of this photograph was assigned on the basis of the catalogue number A617 that appears on the bust and corresponds to the 1902 and 1903 permanent-collection catalogues.

6. The Academy's 1864 catalogue of the permanent collection recorded the inscription on the bust "Anno L.A.LII." Clearly it had not yet been defaced.

7. Minutes, meeting of the board of directors, Nov. 6, 1905, PAFA Archives. This may be the cast purchased in 1982 by the National Portrait Gallery from Hirschl and Adler Galleries, New York. The inscription on the National Portrait Gallery's bust, however, has the final period. If this plaster and the Pennsylvania Academy's bronze were indeed cast from the same model, one would expect their inscriptions to be identical. One possible explanation is that the plaster caster and Bureau Brothers foundry corrected the inscription differently.

Exhibited

1915 Panama-Pacific International Exposition, San Francisco, cat. no. 2806. **1951–52** Detroit Institute of Arts and Toledo Museum of Art, *Travelers in Arcadia,* cat. no. 46 (ill.). **1953** Philadelphia Art Alliance, *Nineteenth Century Philadelphia Architecture.* **1957** Newark Museum, N.J., *Early New Jersey Artists: Eighteenth and Nineteenth Centuries,* cat. no. 30 (ill.). **1962** PAFA, *Forgotten Favorites: Selections from the Permanent Collection.* **1965** New Jersey State Museum, Trenton, *New Jersey and the Artist,* intro. to cat. by Selden Rodman, [p. 13]. **1974–75** Second Bank of the United States, Philadelphia, *Masterworks of American Art, 1740–1840.* **1976** Rutgers University Art Gallery, New Brunswick, N.J., *The City of New Brunswick from the Revolution to the First World War, Its Art, Architecture, Industry and Life.* **1976** Whitney Museum of American Art, New York, *Two Hundred Years of American Sculpture,* p. 23 (ill.).

Rinaldo Rinaldi

1793–1873

The Italian sculptor Rinaldo Rinaldi was born in Padua, the son of a wood carver. He demonstrated a talent for his father's profession at an early age. While a teenager, he carved statues for many churches around Padua, including a group of angels for the church of San Antonio. In 1810 he entered the Academy of Fine Arts in Venice, where he took classes in painting and sculpture and won several prizes. He was the first sculptor to receive the Rome prize, a stipend that enabled him to live in Rome and study with the renowned neoclassicist Antonio Canova (1757–1822). Rinaldi and Canova developed a great affection for one another, and Canova is said to have treated his young protegé like a son. Under Canova's tutelage, Rinaldi executed a bust of the painter Andrea Mantegna for the Pantheon.

Later, Rinaldi studied with Luigi Zandomeneghi (1778–1850); but he remained a devoted disciple of Canova. His many mythological statues, portrait busts, and funerary monuments display the high finish associated with the school of Canova. Rinaldi became a member of the Academy Saint Luke in Rome in 1826 and a member of the congregation of virtuosos of the Pantheon in 1827. Rinaldi was one of the six Italian sculptors selected to execute a memorial to Canova for the church of Santa Maria dei Frari in Venice. Rinaldi's contribution was a lion and a female figure.[1] The memorial's composition and figures were directly inspired by one of Canova's own masterpieces, The Maria Christina monument in Augustiner-Kirche in Vienna.

Note

1. Hugh Honour, "Canova's Studio Practice—II: 1792–1822," *Burlington Magazine* 114 (April 1972), p. 229.

Reference

1964 Gérard Hubert, *La Sculpture dans l'Italie Napoléonienne,* Paris: Editions E. de Boccard, p. 263.

Penelope

1851
Marble
86½ x 29½ x 26½" (141.5 x 74.9 x 66.1 cm)
Signed and dated on base's left side: Rinaldo Rinaldi F./ Roma 1851
Gift of Dr. John Rhea Barton, 1851.2

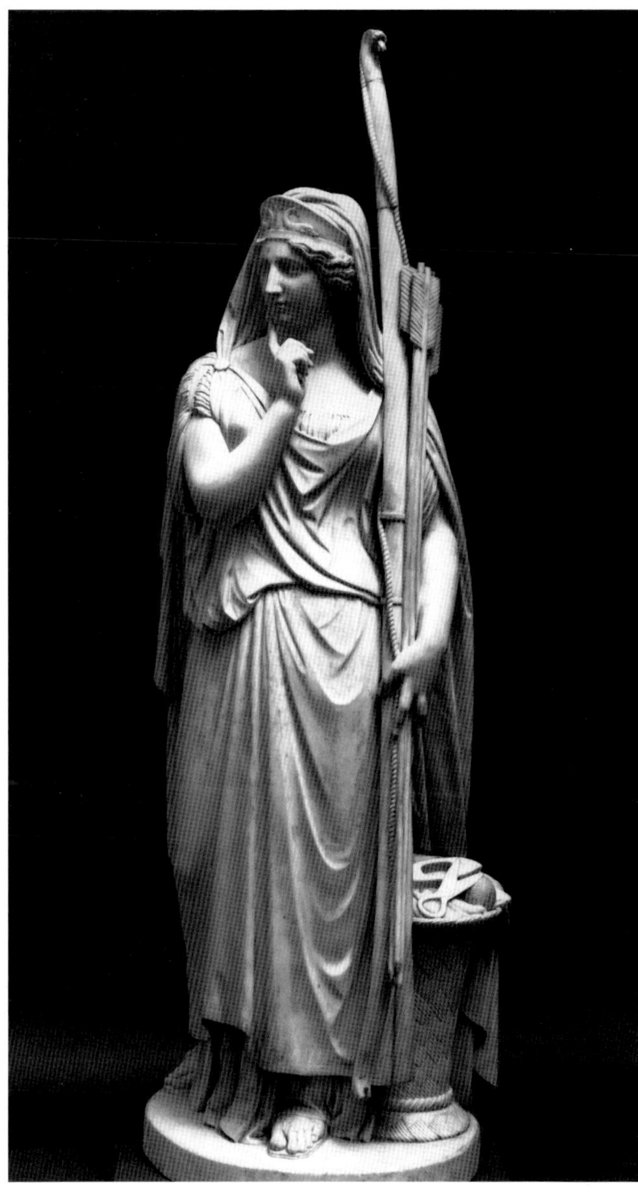

Rinaldi, *Penelope*

In 1851 the Philadelphia surgeon John Rhea Barton visited Rinaldo Rinaldi's studio in Rome and chose this marble statue of Penelope as a gift for the Pennsylvania Academy of the Fine Arts. In a letter informing the Academy of his gift, Barton made much of the fact that the sculpture was "original and unrepeated."[1] Yet, this was probably because the piece had only recently been completed. Like other neoclassical sculptors, Rinaldi would certainly have kept a model of the statue on display in his studio and, if another customer had requested the statue, it would have been carved again.

The subject of the statue comes from Homer's *The Odyssey.* Penelope, the wife of Odysseus, was besieged by suitors during her husband's long absence. For several years, she put them off by promising to choose a new husband when she had finished her weaving, which she secretly undid every night. Her trickery was eventually discovered, but she was saved by the arrival of Odysseus in disguise. Recognizing him as she sat among her suitors, Penelope proposed that they compete for her hand by a trial of strength and skill in archery, which she knew only Odysseus could win. The statue shows Penelope, holding the bow and arrows, about to make this challenge:

> Here is my lord Odysseus' hunting bow.
> Bend and string it if you can. Who sends an arrow
> through iron axe-helve sockets, twelve in line?
> I join my life with his, and leave this place, my home.[2]

In 1981, during conservation of this statue, it was discovered that many small pits on the surface of the marble had been filled with plaster. These pits were most likely produced by the removal of dark iron pyrites.[3] Because of the demand of nineteenth-century art patrons for flawless white marble, it was not uncommon for neoclassical sculptors to touch up their statues in this manner.

Notes

1. J. Rhea Barton to the president and directors of the Pennsylvania Academy of the Fine Arts, June 16, 1851, PAFA object file.
2. Quoted from Book 21, "The Test of the Bow," translated by Robert Fitzgerald (New York: Anchor Books, 1963), p. 393.
3. Virginia Norton Naudé, Conservation Report, March 1, 1981, PAFA object file.

Exhibited

1853* cat. no. 283. **1854*** cat. no. 244. **1855*** cat. no. 277. **1858*** cat. no. 464. **1857*** cat. no. 316. **1858*** cat. no. 347. **1859*** cat. no. 362. **1860*** cat. no. 358. **1861*** cat. no. 418. **1862*** cat. no. 417. **1863*** cat. no. 401. **1864*** cat. no. 259. **1865*** cat. no. 164. **1866*** cat. no. 164. **1867*** cat. no. 322. **1868*** cat. no. 374. **1869*** cat. no. 272. **1972** PAFA, *Acres of Art,* checklist no. 82. **1986–87** PAFA, *Sculpture at the Pennsylvania Academy of the Fine Arts.*

Horatio Greenough

1805–1852

Horatio Greenough was the first American sculptor to study in Italy. His lead set in motion an artistic migration of American sculptors that lasted over twenty-five years. Greenough was born in Boston to socially prominent parents. His father, David

Greenough, was a successful real-estate dealer and an indulgent parent to his eleven children. Several of the children pursued careers in the arts; and the youngest, RICHARD S. GREENOUGH, followed in Horatio's footsteps to become the second sculptor in the family.

After gaining attention through his early drawings and chalk carvings, Horatio Greenough was introduced to William S. Shaw, the librarian of the Boston Athenaeum. Shaw gave Greenough entrée to the Athenaeum's cast collection. Greenough received some early instruction in clay modeling and carving from Solomon Willard (1783–1861), an artisan and architect, and from J.B. Binon (active in Boston, 1818–1820), a French sculptor. Alpheus Carey, a local tombstone cutter, also helped him with his carving technique.

In 1821 Greenough entered Harvard College. There he studied art history and continued to model busts. He was befriended by Joseph Cogswell, the college librarian, who lent him plaster casts and drawings to copy. During his junior year, Greenough met the painter Washington Allston; and they formed a lasting friendship. Allston provided Greenough with a guiding hand and encouraged him to go to Italy. Having accepted this advice and a letter of introduction to the famous neoclassicist Bertel Thorwaldsen (1770–1844), Greenough arrived in Rome in the fall of 1825. Thorwaldsen helped him begin his studies working from the antique. During this time, Greenough modeled his first ideal piece, *The Dead Abel.* Extremely ambitious, he overworked and became seriously ill. He returned home in March of 1827 to recuperate.

Greenough spent the next year modeling portraits, including those of President John Quincy Adams and Chief Justice John Marshall. Eager to return to Italy, he set sail again late in the spring of 1828. Although his destination was Florence, he spent the summer in Carrara, where he supervised the craftsmen translating his busts into marble and perfected his own carving skills. Throughout his career, Greenough employed stone carvers for rough work but did the finishing himself. In December 1828, Greenough reached Florence. For several months, he studied with Lorenzo Bartolini (1777–1850), who encouraged him to work from live models rather than copy antique sculptures.

The American author James Fenimore Cooper arrived in Florence about the same time as Greenough, and the two struck up a friendship. Greenough modeled Cooper's portrait in January of 1829 (Boston Public Library). In turn Cooper, who had been charmed by the singing putti in Raphael's painting *The Madonna del Baldacchino,* 1508–9 (Pitti Palace, Florence), commissioned Greenough to create a sculpture with a similar theme. Greenough finished *The Chanting Cherubs* in 1830 (whereabouts unknown), and Cooper was so pleased that he sent it on tour to several American cities. The American public, however, was shocked by the nudity of the cherubs and disappointed that they did not actually sing.

In 1832, at the urging of Cooper and Allston, the United States Congress commissioned Greenough to create a statue of George Washington for the Capitol. Greenough finished the colossal clay model late in 1835. The seated, half-nude figure was inspired by descriptions of the statue of Zeus by the Greek sculptor Phidias that once stood in the Temple of Elis at Olympia. When it arrived at the Capitol in December 1841, Greenough's statue was ridiculed by critics and public alike and eventually removed from its honorable site. Today, the statue is housed in the National Museum of American History, Smithsonian Institution, Washington, D.C.

In 1837 Greenough received another congressional commission. The work was to be a companion to *The Discovery Group* by Luigi Persico (1791–1860). The pair of sculptures would eventually flank the great stairs leading to the Capitol. Greenough's *The Rescue Group* depicts the conflict between the Anglo-Saxon and aboriginal races. The major project of his later years, it was not installed at the Capitol until 1852, the year he died. By 1958 *The Rescue Group* had seriously deteriorated and was placed in storage.

During his later years, Greenough spent many hours writing about his aesthetic theories. *The Travels, Observations, and Experiences of a Yankee Stonecutter* (New York, 1852) is a compilation of these writings under the pseudonym Horace Bender.

References

1963 Nathalia Wright, *Horatio Greenough: The First American Sculptor,* Philadelphia: University of Pennsylvania Press. **1972** Nathalia Wright, ed., *Letters of Horatio Greenough: American Sculptor,* Madison: University of Wisconsin Press. **1972** Sylvia E. Crane, *White Silence—Greenough, Powers, and Crawford, American Sculptors in Nineteenth-Century Italy,* Coral Gables: University of Miami Press. **1984** Wayne Craven, *Sculpture in America,* Newark: University of Delaware Press, pp. 101–11. **1986** *American Figurative Sculpture in the Museum of Fine Arts, Boston,* Boston: Museum of Fine Arts, pp. 4–26.

Marquis de Lafayette (Marie Joseph Paul Yves Roch Gilbert du Motier de Lafayette)

1831
Marble; carved in 1832–33
25¾ x 23½ x 12¾" (65.3 x 59.7 x 32.3 cm)

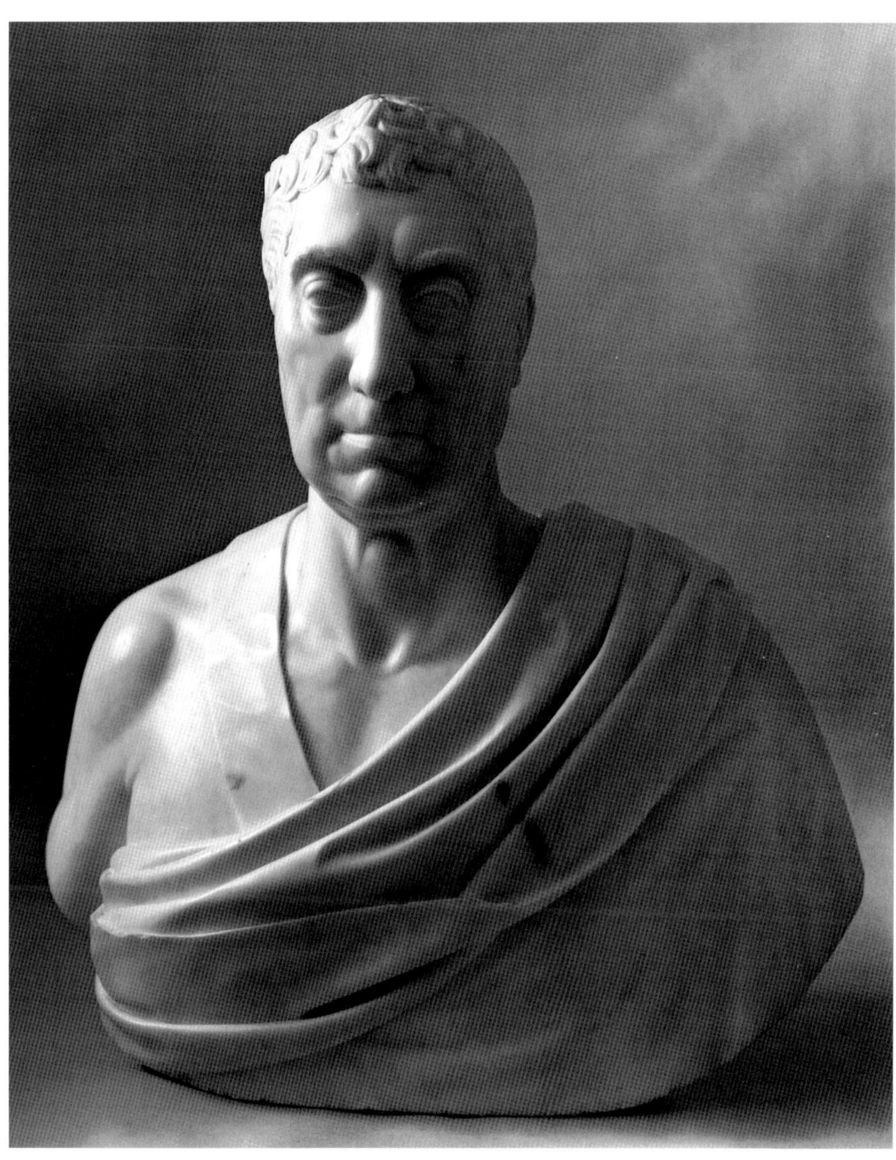

Greenough, *Marquis de Lafayette*

Signed on back [monogram]: HG
Gift of Francis Kinloch, 1834.2

Horatio Greenough conceived the idea of executing a portrait of the marquis de Lafayette (1757–1834) late in 1830. He felt that his budding career would be advanced by a bust of the famous general. Greenough therefore wrote to his friend James Fenimore Cooper, then residing in Paris, to solicit his aid in arranging the sittings. Lafayette initially opposed the idea because he had promised the French sculptor Pierre Jean David d'Angers (1788–1856) that the bust made by d'Angers would be his official portrait. Eventually Lafayette relented and agreed to pose for Greenough, provided that Cooper keep him company at each sitting.[1]

Detained in Florence for several months, Greenough arrived in Paris in August of 1831. Lafayette was deeply involved in political affairs, and Greenough had to wait until the middle of October to begin the bust. Even then, Lafayette could spare but a few minutes at a time. Finally one morning, Cooper captivated Lafayette for two hours with stories and conversation so that Greenough could complete the bust.[2]

Back in Florence early in 1832, Greenough began to translate the bust into marble. When it was finished, he sold it to Francis Kinloch, a South Carolinian who had come to Florence in 1832 to study painting.[3] Greenough had met him earlier in America.[4] Kinloch gave the bust of Lafayette to the Pennsylvania Academy of the Fine Arts in 1834.[5] Unfortunately, his gift seems to have gone unrecorded. The 1847 accession number was probably assigned retroactively on the basis of the *Catalogue of the Paintings and Statuary at the Pennsylvania Academy of the Fine Arts* published that year.

Greenough executed two other versions of the bust of Lafayette. One is lifesize (about 1833, Massachusetts State House, Boston) and varies slightly from the Museum of American Art of the Pennsylvania Academy's. The other is a reduction (about 1833, Museum of Fine Arts, Boston).

Notes

1. Nathalia Wright 1963, p. 90.
2. Horatio Greenough to Rembrandt Peale, Nov. 8, 1831, Historical Society of Pennsylvania, microfilm, roll no. P23, frame no. 541, Archives of American Art, Smithsonian Institution, Washington, D.C.
3. *Philadelphia National Gazette and Literary Review,* July 24, 1834, cited in Nathalia Wright to Joseph Fraser, Jr., director of the PAFA, May 4, 1961, PAFA object file.
4. Nathalia Wright, "Francis Kinloch: A South Carolina Artist," *South Carolina Historical Magazine* 61 (1960), pp. 99–100.
5. *Philadelphia National Gazette and Literary Review,* July 24, 1834, see n. 3.

References

1963 Nathalia Wright, *Horatio Greenough: The First American Sculptor,* Philadelphia: University of Pennsylvania Press, pp. 90–93, [pl. 11]. **1967** Denys Sutton, "The Luminous Point," *Apollo* 85 (March), p. 216, fig. 6. **1972** Sylvia E. Crane, *White Silence—Greenough, Powers, and Crawford, American Sculptors in Nineteenth-Century Italy,* Coral Gables: University of Miami Press, pp. 63 (ill.), 442. **1978** Lynette I. Rhodes, *American Folk Art from the Traditional to the Naive,* Cleveland: Cleveland Museum of Art, p. 29, fig. 7. **1982** Linda Bantel, "Sculpture at the Pennsylvania Academy," *Antiques* 121 (March), p. 708 (ill.). **1986** *American Figurative Sculpture in the Museum of Fine Arts, Boston,* Boston: Museum of Fine Arts, p. 14.

Exhibited

1834* cat. no. 98. **1836*** cat. no. 105. **1837*** cat. no. 105. **1838*** cat. no. 105. **1840*** cat. no. 105. **1847** PAFA, *Exhibition of Paintings, Statues and Casts, at the Pennsylvania Academy of the Fine Arts,* cat. no. 523. **1849*** cat. no. 372. **1850*** cat. no. 379. **1851*** cat. no. 388. **1852*** cat. no. 395. **1853*** cat. no. 444. **1854*** cat. no. 423. **1855*** cat. no. 558. **1856** PAFA, *Fall Exhibition of the Pennsylvania Academy of the Fine Arts,* cat. no. 303. **1857*** cat. no. 481. **1858*** cat. no. 537. **1859*** cat. no. 408. **1860*** cat. no. 438. **1861*** cat. no. 395. **1862*** cat. no. 396. **1863*** cat. no. 381. **1864*** cat. no. 285. **1865*** cat. no. 170. **1866*** cat. no. 170. **1867*** cat. no. 380. **1868*** cat. no. 411. **1869*** cat. no. 321. **1975** Second Bank of the United States, Philadelphia, *Masterworks of American Art, 1740–1840.* **1978–79** PAFA, *350 Masterpieces of American Art.* **1986** National Portrait Gallery, Washington, D.C., *John Frazee, Sculptor* (did not travel to Boston Athenaeum). **1986–87** PAFA, *Sculpture at the Pennsylvania Academy of the Fine Arts.* **1989** Queens Museum, Flushing, N.Y.; Historical Society of Pennsylvania, Philadelphia; and Museum of Our National Heritage, Lexington, Mass., *Lafayette, Hero of Two Worlds: The Art and Pageantry of His Farewell Tour of America, 1824–1825,* fig. 162, pp. 172, 173–75.

HIRAM POWERS

1805–1873

Hiram Powers was born on a farm near Woodstock, Vermont. When he was thirteen, his family moved west and eventually settled in Cincinnati. His father died shortly thereafter, and the young Powers was compelled to find work. After a number of odd jobs, he secured an apprenticeship in Luman Watson's clock-and-organ factory, where he acquired mechanical skills. In 1825 the Prussian sculptor Frederick Eckstein (about 1775–1852) arrived in Cincinnati, and Powers soon became one of his pupils. He learned how to model clay and make plaster casts. Powers's talent for modeling and his mechanical aptitude secured his employment at Joseph Dorfeuille's Western Museum in 1828. At the time, the Western was essentially a wax museum with an admission fee of ten cents. Mrs. Francis Trollope, the English author who traveled throughout the United States collecting information for her book on the domestic manners of Americans, was in Cincinnati then; and, with her advice, Powers designed a waxwork loosely based on Dante's *Inferno* for the museum. It was mechanically operated and became one of the city's major attractions.

In 1834 the Cincinnati real-estate tycoon and art patron Nicholas Longworth sponsored a trip for Powers to Washington, D.C., and provided him with a letter of introduction to President Andrew Jackson. Powers created one of the most realistic and enduring images of Jackson (Metropolitan Museum of Art, New York). Before returning to Cincinnati, Powers also modeled busts of Vice President Martin Van Buren (New-York Historical Society), Chief Justice John Marshall (U.S. Supreme Court), and others. During the winter of 1836–37, Powers went to Boston to model portraits, including those of Daniel Webster (National Museum of American Art, Smithsonian Institution) and John C. Calhoun (North Carolina Museum of Art, Raleigh).

With financial backing from both Longworth and Colonel John Preston of South Carolina, Powers was able to take his wife and two children to Italy in the fall of 1837.[1] HORATIO GREENOUGH helped the newcomers get settled in Florence and even commissioned Powers to model his portrait. Initially, Powers concentrated on filling orders for the busts that he had modeled in the United States. His talent in this area was quickly recognized; and by 1839 Bertel Thorwaldsen (1770–1844), Lorenzo Bartolini (1777–1850), and Horatio Greenough all acknowledged him to be the preeminent portraitist.[2] The Powers family was quickly assimilated into the Anglo-American community in Florence. The sculptor and his wife socialized with such notables as Nathaniel Hawthorne and Robert and Elizabeth Barrett Browning. Powers's studio became a major attraction for American tourists making the Grand Tour.

About 1839 Powers began to create ideal sculpture. That year he completed *Ginevra,* the bust of a young woman in classical attire, and worked on his first full-length statue, *Eve Tempted.* In 1841 he executed the standing *Fisher Boy* and formulated the idea for his most famous statue, *The Greek Slave.* Inspired by the Greek war for independence, it depicts a beautiful Greek girl abducted by Turks and about to be sold into slavery. Powers began work on the clay model for the statue in June 1842. The first marble version (a total of six were made) was completed in 1844 and was purchased by an Englishman who exhibited it at Grave's Pall Mall in London in the summer of 1845. Between 1847 and 1849, two versions of the statue were shown to great acclaim in major American cities.[3]

During the later part of his career, Powers produced a series of ideal female statues, including *America, California, Eve Disconsolate,* and *The Indian Girl.* In July of 1916, the Pennsylvania Academy of the Fine Arts purchased original plasters of *America* and *California* from two of Powers's daughters through his grandson, Charles W. Lemmi.[4] Both plasters fell into disrepair and were probably disposed of between 1940 and 1944.[5] The Pennsylvania Academy deaccessioned three other works by Powers: a bust of John Quincy Adams was sold in 1898, and in 1950 a marble bust *Ginevra* and a second marble replica of *Proserpine* were sold.[6]

Notes

1. Richard P. Wunder, "The Irascible Hiram Powers," *American Art Journal* 4 (Nov. 1972), p. 11.
2. Wayne Craven, *Sculpture in America* (Newark: University of Delaware Press, 1984), p. 114.
3. The second version of the statue, owned by the New Orleans banker James Robb, was exhibited at the Pennsylvania Academy in the summer of 1848. Robb offered to sell *The Greek Slave* to the Academy, and in January 1849 his offer was accepted. Problems arose during the bargaining, however, and the sale was never completed. See Minutes, meeting of the board of directors, Jan. 8, 1849, PAFA Archives.
4. PAFA to Charles W. Lemmi, July 19, 1916, PAFA Archives.
5. Both statues were recorded on the list of sculpture in the permanent collection, compiled Nov. 26, 1940; but in 1944, *America* was recorded as unlocated on the registrar's object card, now in the Powers file, Works no longer in collection, PAFA Archives.
6. Powers file, ibid.

References

About 1969 Clara Louise Dentler, "White Marble: The Life and Letters of Hiram Powers, Sculptor," typescript, microfilm, roll nos. 1102–3, Archives of American Art, Smithsonian Institution, Washington, D.C. **1974** Richard P. Wunder, *Hiram Powers: Vermont Sculptor,* Taftsville, Vermont: Countryman Press. **1975** Donald Martin Reynolds, *Hiram Powers and His Ideal Sculpture,* Ph.D. diss., Columbia University, New York: Garland Series reprint, 1977. **1977** Donald Martin Reynolds, "The 'Unveiled Soul': Hiram Powers's Embodiment of the Ideal," *Art Bulletin* 59 (Sept.), pp. 394–414. **1991** Richard P. Wunder, *Hiram Powers: Vermont Sculptor, 1805–1873,* 2 vols., Newark: University of Delaware Press.

Proserpine

1843
Marble; carved about 1860
25 x 19 x 10" (63.5 x 48.2 x 25.4 cm)
Signed on back at center: H. POWERS.
Gift of John Livezey, 1864.5

ACCORDING to Roman mythology, Proserpine (known in Greek as Persephone), the goddess of spring, was abducted each year by Pluto, the god of

Powers, *Proserpine*

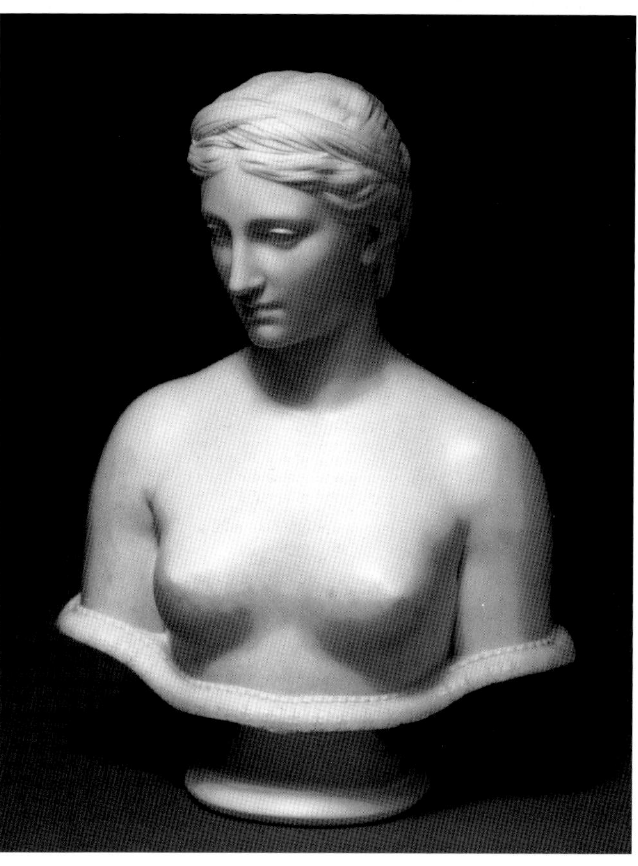

the underworld, and held captive for several months. Her release brought springtime back to earth. Hiram Powers completed his original model for *Proserpine* in 1843.[1] The first marble replica was made for the Philadelphia publisher and art collector Edward L. Carey. In that bust (Philadelphia Museum of Art), Proserpine's breast and shoulders emerge from an elaborate basket of flowers.[2] This design was laborious and expensive to carve, so Powers immediately made a second version with a simpler basket filled with acanthus leaves. In 1849 Powers simplified the termination still more, as a simple band of foliated ornament like that on this bust. Powers also produced some marble replicas that have no termination ornament of any sort. *Proserpine* was Powers's most popular ideal bust; he probably executed close to two hundred marble replicas of it in full and reduced scale.[3]

Carved about 1860, this marble bust was selected from the sculptor's studio in Florence by John Livezey of Philadelphia.[4] After Livezey received the work the following year, he wrote to Powers of his intention to give it to the Pennsylvania Academy of the Fine Arts. He also complained about two veins in the marble and claimed that this was not the sculpture upon which he had placed his private mark when he was in Florence.[5] In a heated reply, Powers accounted for the absence of Livezey's mark by explaining that he always cleaned a sculpture that had been sitting in his studio for any length of time. He asserted that he had sent the correct bust and told Livezey to return it for a complete refund if he doubted Powers's integrity.[6] Livezey responded that he trusted Powers's word and was quite satisfied with the bust.[7] Although no acquisition record survives, Livezey probably gave the bust to the Pennsylvania Academy in 1864. That year it was shown for the first time at the Pennsylvania Academy, in the forty-first annual exhibition, and was listed in the catalogue as the property of the Academy, given by John Livezey.

Notes

1. Wunder 1991, vol. 2, p. 188.
2. The bust owned by Carey was shown in the PAFA's twenty-sixth annual exhibition in 1849.
3. Wunder 1991, vol. 2, p. 189.
4. Powers to Livezey, Feb. 1861, microfilm, roll no. 1141, frame no. 205, Archives of American Art, Smithsonian Institution, Washington, D.C.
5. Livezey to Powers, March 24, 1861, microfilm, roll no. 1141, frame no. 312, ibid.
6. Powers to Livezey, April 12, 1861, microfilm, roll no. 1141, frame no. 341, ibid.
7. Livezey to Powers, May 14, 1861, microfilm, roll no. 1141, frame no. 374, ibid.

Reference

1991 Richard P. Wunder, *Hiram Powers: Vermont Sculptor, 1805–1873,* Newark: University of Delaware Press, vol. 2, p. 195.

Exhibited

1864* cat. no. 327. **1865*** cat. no. 187. **1866*** cat. no. 187. **1867*** cat. no. 400. **1868*** cat. no. 447. **1869*** cat. no. 359. **1876*** cat. no. 654. **1940** Baltimore Museum of Art, *Romanticism in America.* **1962** PAFA, *Forgotten Favorites: Selections from the Permanent Collection.* **1974–75** Second Bank of the United States, Philadelphia, *Masterworks of American Art, 1740–1840.* **1978–79** PAFA, *350 Masterpieces of American Art.* **1986–87** PAFA, *Sculpture at the Pennsylvania Academy of the Fine Arts.* **1988** Glencairn Museum, Bryn Athyn, Pa., *New Light: Ten Artists Inspired by Swedenborg,* cat. no. 4, as *Persephone.*

Robert Ball Hughes

1806–1868

A native Londoner, Robert Ball Hughes entered the Royal Academy of Arts in 1818. About two years into his studies, he was hired as a studio assistant by Edward Hodges Baily (1788–1867), a neoclassical sculptor who had studied under John Flaxman (1755–1826). Hughes showed four works at the Royal Academy in London between 1822 and 1828.[1] The relief *Pandora Brought by Mercury to Epimethus,* exhibited in 1824, won a gold medal.[2]

Hughes immigrated to the United States in 1829 and settled in New York. He was enthusiastically received there and was befriended by the president of the American Academy of the Fine Arts, the painter John Trumbull.[3] Sculpture commissions were scarce in the United States at this time, however, and Hughes soon discovered competition and poor remuneration. Even Trumbull paid him inadequately for the portrait bust made of him about 1834 (Yale University Art Gallery, New Haven).[4] One of Hughes's favorites, the bust depicts Trumbull in a toga to which is pinned the medal of the Order of the Cincinnati.

Hughes received several commissions for monumental sculpture during his early years in the United States; but, as was typical of the times, portraiture proved to be his mainstay. In 1831 he completed the model for a relief memorial to Bishop Henry Hobart. Four years later, the finished marble was installed in Trinity Church, New York. It depicts the dying bishop slumped in a chair, his gaze directed by the allegorical figure of Religion toward the Cross, the symbol of eternal life. In April of 1835, Hughes's standing marble statue of Alexander Hamilton (statuette of Hamilton [q.v.]) was installed at the New York Merchants' Exchange.

About 1838 Hughes moved to Philadelphia. He was drawn there by a commission for an equestrian monument of George Washington, sponsored by the Order of the Cincinnati. Although the commission never materialized, Hughes's model survives at the Society for the Preservation of New England Antiquities in Boston. Hughes submitted five medallion portraits and three plaster busts to the Artists' Fund Society Exhibition of 1840, held at the Pennsylvania Academy of the Fine Arts.

In the hope of finding a more receptive audience for his work, Hughes moved to Boston in 1840. About two years later, he made a statue of Charles Dickens's character Oliver Twist (location unknown). It proved to be very popular and was exhibited at the Crystal Palace in London in 1851. He executed statues of other literary subjects, including Nell Trent, 1858 (Boston Athenaeum), the heroine of another Dickens tale, *The Old Curiosity Shop.*

In 1838 Hughes was commissioned to make an effigy of the eminent Boston mathematician and astronomer Nathaniel Bowditch. Hughes's plaster model (Boston Athenaeum) depicts Bowditch seated with a copy of his book *The Practical Navigator* propped on his right knee and a globe and sextant beside his chair. When Hughes tried to have the piece cast, he ran into great difficulty: nothing so large had yet been cast in the United States, and the advanced casting techniques of the European foundries were still unknown. Finally, in 1847 a bronze was cast by the Boston copper dealer and bell founder Henry N. Hooper and placed on Bowditch's grave in Mount Auburn Cemetery.[5] It was defective, however, and had to be recast in 1887 by the French foundry Gruet Jeune.

Hughes passed his later years in relative obscurity. With few patrons, he was reduced to making cameos and wax medallions. He even took up pyrography, the technique of burning drawings into wood.[6]

Notes

1. Algernon Graves, *The Royal Academy of Arts: A Complete Dictionary of Contributors and Their Work from Its Foundation in 1769 to 1904* (New York: Burt Franklin, 1972), vol. 2, p. 187.
2. Craven 1984, p. 71.
3. It is somewhat ironic that Trumbull received Hughes with open arms, given his negative communication to JOHN FRAZEE, just three years earlier, that nothing in sculpture would be wanted "in this country, for yet a hundred years." Quoted in *Dictionary of American Biography,* s.v. "Frazee, John." On the other hand, it is certainly understandable that Trumbull, having himself undergone rigorous training in England under Benjamin West, would feel a kinship with Hughes (who had a similar English education) and a lack of confidence in the self-taught Frazee.
4. Brumbaugh 1958, p. 423.
5. Michael Edward Shapiro, *Bronze Casting and American Sculpture, 1850–1900* (Newark: University of Delaware Press, 1985), p. 32.
6. Albert TenEyck Gardner, *American Sculpture: A Catalogue of the Collection of The Metropolitan Museum of Art* (New York: Metropolitan Museum of Art, 1965), pp. 6–7.

References

1957 Georgia Stamm Chamberlain, "The Portrait Busts of Robert Ball Hughes," *Art Quarterly* 20 (Winter), pp. 383–86. **1958** Thomas B. Brumbaugh, "A Ball Hughes Correspondence," *Art Quarterly* 21 (Winter), pp. 423–27. **1984** Wayne Craven, *Sculpture in America,* Newark: University of Delaware Press, pp. 70–76.

Alexander Hamilton

About 1829
Marble; carved about 1865 by an unidentified artist
27¼ x 10½ x 8¼" (69.2 x 26.7 x 21 cm)
Inscribed on front of base: HAMILTON
Gift of Mrs. John K. Mitchell, 1917.11

ONE OF Robert Ball Hughes's original plasters was undoubtedly used as the model for this marble statuette of Alexander Hamilton (1757–1804), but there is no evidence that the marble was carved by Hughes or under his direction. The replica was made at the request of Eliza Hamilton Schuyler, Hamilton's granddaughter. Although she died in 1863 before the carving could be done, she asked her husband to see to its completion as a gift for her sister-in-law, Angelica Livingston Hamilton.[1]

Hughes modeled the statuette in preparation for a large marble statue for the New York Merchants' Exchange on Wall Street. He completed the statuette, or at least a version of it, by November 1829.[2] Today plaster casts are owned by the Detroit Institute of Arts; the Schuyler Mansion State Historic Site in Albany; and the Museum of the City of New York.[3] However, these three plasters differ slightly from one another. It may be that they are working versions of the statuette, which was not approved by the Merchants' Exchange until December 1830. The plaster in the Museum of the City of New York, which was presented by Hamilton's descendants, is the closest in appearance to the Pennsylvania Academy's marble and may have been the source for it.

In December of 1830, Hughes's statuette was approved on behalf of the Merchants' Exchange by a committee that included Philip Hone, the former

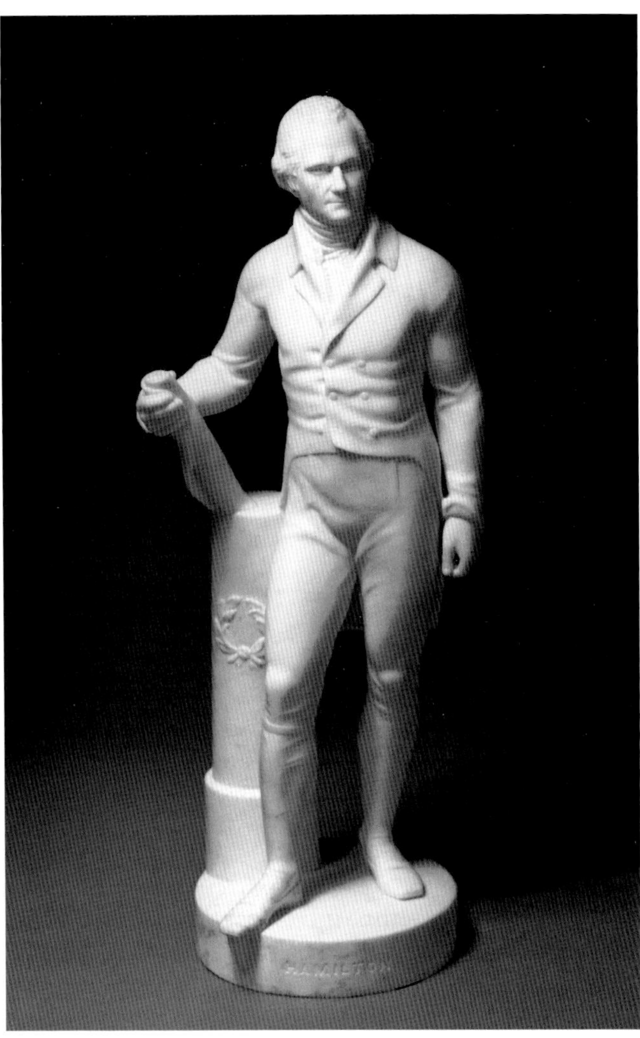

Hughes, *Alexander Hamilton*

mayor of New York, and John Trumbull, the painter.[4] Hughes ordered a large block of Carrara marble for the full-scale statue, and the marble arrived the following October.[5] It was not until January 1834, however, that Hughes wrote to Trumbull, who was president of the American Academy of the Fine Arts, to ask if he could use the institution's statue gallery to execute his full-scale model.[6] He must have begun work shortly thereafter, because the marble statue was finished by March 1835. Hughes had recruited English stonecutters to do the carving[7]; and, soon after they began, an imperfection appeared in the marble. To conceal it, Hughes changed Hamilton's contemporary coat and breeches to a toga. Like the statuette, the full-scale figure held a scroll in the right hand, possibly Hamilton's famous 1804 report on funding the national debt. This was the first full-length statue to be carved in marble in America, and it was widely praised when it was unveiled in the rotunda of the Merchants' Exchange. Sadly, the statue was destroyed just eight months later during a great conflagration that ruined a large section of New York.

Notes

1. George L. Schuyler to Mrs. Alexander Hamilton, Sr., April 22, 1865, typed transcript in PAFA Archives.
2. *Charleston [S.C.] Courier,* Nov. 14, 1829, under "Hughes" in sec. 4(b), Anna Wells Rutledge Papers, microfilm, roll no. 116, Archives of American Art, Smithsonian Institution, Washington, D.C.
3. An undated note in the object file in the Schuyler Mansion State Historic Site says that four plasters were made from the original and presented to the Hamilton family.
4. Georgia Stamm Chamberlain, "The Ball Hughes Statue of Alexander Hamilton," *Studies on American Painters and Sculptors of the Nineteenth Century* (Annandale, Va.: Turnpike Press, 1965), p. 7.
5. *Charleston [S.C.] Courier,* Oct. 19, 1831, under "Hughes" in sec. 4(b), Anna Wells Rutledge Papers, microfilm, roll no. 116, Archives of American Art.
6. Wayne Craven, *Sculpture in America* (Newark: University of Delaware Press, 1984), p. 73.
7. Chamberlain 1965, p. 7.

Exhibited

1937 Philadelphia Museum of Art, *Signers of the Constitution.* **1986** National Portrait Gallery, Washington, D.C., *John Frazee, Sculptor,* p. 43, fig. 21. **1986–87** PAFA, *Sculpture at the Pennsylvania Academy of the Fine Arts.*

Ex Collections

Mrs. Alexander Hamilton, Sr. (Angelica Livingston Hamilton), about 1865; Dr. and Mrs. John K. Mitchell, until 1917.

Washington Irving

1836
Plaster, painted white
27½ x 19¼ x 11" (69.8 x 48.9 x 27.9 cm)
Inscribed on back of base: Published as the/Act Directs by/Ball Hughes, May 1/1836
Gift of Thomas Sully, 1861.2

Washington Irving (1783–1859) spent seventeen years in Europe, during which time he published a number of his most famous works, including *The Sketch Book,* which contains "The Legend of Sleepy Hollow" and "Rip Van Winkle"; *History of the Life and Voyages of Christopher Columbus;* and *The Alhambra.* When he returned to the United States in 1832, it was as an internationally renowned author.

Robert Ball Hughes, who may have met Irving when they both lived in London, modeled this likeness in New York in 1836, four years after the writer's celebrated return home. The bust is idealized and draped with the ubiquitous toga in the neoclassical style that Hughes learned from Edward Hodges

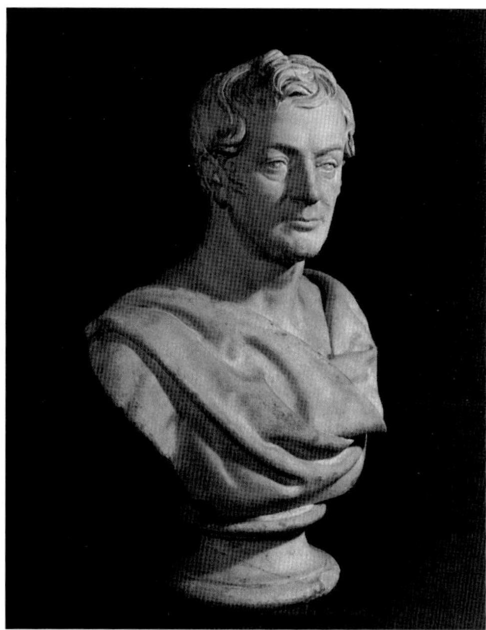

Hughes, *Washington Irving*

Baily in London. Another version, bare-chested, is inscribed, "This is the only bust for which Mr. Washington Irving ever sat."[1]

Hughes made numerous plaster casts of his busts of Irving, which he sold for fifteen dollars each.[2] At the same time HIRAM POWERS was getting ten times that much for a similar work.[3] This bust was given to the Pennsylvania Academy in 1861 by the painter Thomas Sully, who served as a director of the Academy for many years. Sully and Irving became friends during their youth. Before Irving's departure for England in 1815, the two often went on outings together—Sully toting his sketchbook and Irving, his notebook.[4]

Notes

1. Regarding a plaster cast of this version, see A.J. Philpott, "Bust of Washington Irving Owned by O'Connell Family; Work by Robert Ball Hughes Found in Dorchester Shed," *Boston Daily Globe*, Oct. 27, 1941, typescript in PAFA object file.
2. *New York Mirror*, Sept. 10, 1836, p. 83.
3. Wayne Craven, *Sculpture in America* (Newark: University of Delaware Press, 1984), p. 74.
4. Edward Biddle and Mantle Fielding, *The Life and Works of Thomas Sully* (Lancaster, Pa.: Wickersham Press, 1921), p. 25.

Shobal Vail Clevenger

1812–1843

During the second quarter of the nineteenth century, Cincinnati was emerging as an active center for the arts. Shobal Vail Clevenger was one of many sculptors, including HIRAM POWERS and Henry Kirke Brown (1814–1866), to begin his career there under the watchful eye of the art patron Nicholas Longworth.

Born in Middletown, Ohio, Clevenger was the son of a weaver and the third of ten children. His initiation into the field of sculpture, like that of many nineteenth-century sculptors, came through the trades. During his early teens, he moved to Centerville to follow in his brother's footsteps and learn to be a mason. Sickness, possibly the beginnings of tuberculosis, forced him to return home for a period of recuperation after which he apprenticed himself to David Guion, a Cincinnati gravestone cutter. At Guion's, Clevenger perfected his skills and soon proved more adept than his master in carving stone. He stayed with Guion for four years and did most of the shop's ornamental work. Following his apprenticeship, Clevenger married and moved to Xenia, where he tried unsuccessfully to open his own shop. He returned to Cincinnati to work as a journeyman carver for Guion, but before long he and a partner opened a stone-carving establishment of their own. About this time, Clevenger may have studied briefly with Frederick Eckstein (about 1775–1852), a German-born sculptor who was in Cincinnati trying to establish an academy of fine arts.

In 1835 Ebenezer Smith Thomas, the editor of the *Cincinnati Daily Evening Post*, encouraged Clevenger to carve a bust in stone. Clevenger complied and used Thomas as his model. After completing the bust in clay, Clevenger tried in vain to secure a piece of marble in which to carve it. Driven by his desire to precede Hiram Powers in completing the first stone bust west of the Mississippi, he carved it in sandstone.

Clevenger soon caught the eye of Nicholas Longworth, who made it possible for him to attend anatomy classes at the Ohio Medical College during the winter of 1836–37. Continuing his portrait work, he carved in sandstone the future president William Henry Harrison and the anatomy instructor Dr. John Eberle. Though Clevenger longed to go to Italy, Longworth thought him not quite ready and sent him east instead. Clevenger's first stop was Lexington, Kentucky, where he modeled a portrait of the statesman Henry Clay in 1837. Because Clay gave him a certificate stating that the likeness was correct, the bust helped Clevenger's reputation a great deal. (A marble version was shown in the annual exhibitions of the Pennsylvania Academy from 1851 to 1853 and again in 1855.) By January 1838 Clevenger was in Washington, D.C., where he modeled portraits of John Quincy Adams, Daniel Webster, and Martin Van Buren. Clevenger had arrived in Boston by March 1839 and from there took brief trips to New York and Philadelphia during the spring. In Boston he modeled busts of many prominent citizens, including Lemuel Shaw, Harrison Gray Otis, and Washington Allston (q.v.).

Finally in the autumn of 1840, Clevenger left for Italy. He settled in Florence where his clay models were translated into marble. Several of Hiram Powers's assistants helped with the carving. Twenty busts were completed in marble and shipped home. Clevenger modeled six additional portrait busts, including Louis Bonaparte and Hiram Powers. In the spring of 1842, he completed his first ideal head, entitled *The Lady of the Lake* (whereabouts unknown), and was working on an ideal statue called *The Indian.* Unfortunately, he had little time to complete new work; for, within two years of his arrival in Italy, he was deathly ill with tuberculosis. Hoping to see his home once again, Clevenger embarked on a return voyage—only to die at sea in September of 1843. In New York a subscription fund was organized to have *The Indian* carved in marble under the supervision of Hiram Powers. Now lost, the piece is known only through an engraving.[1] Powers also oversaw the completion of some of Clevenger's portrait busts for the benefit of the sculptor's destitute wife and children.

Note

1. "Clevenger," *United States Magazine and Democratic Review* 14 (Feb. 1844), frontispiece.

References

1839 "Shobal Vail Clevenger, The Sculptor," *Southern Literary Messenger* 5 (April), pp. 262–64. **1844** "Clevenger," *United States Magazine and Democratic Review* 14 (Feb.), pp. 202–6. **1966** Thomas B. Brumbaugh, "Shobal Clevenger: An Ohio Stonecutter in Search of Fame," *Art Quarterly* 29, pp. 29–45. **1984** Wayne Craven, *Sculpture in America,* Newark: University of Delaware Press, pp. 180–87.

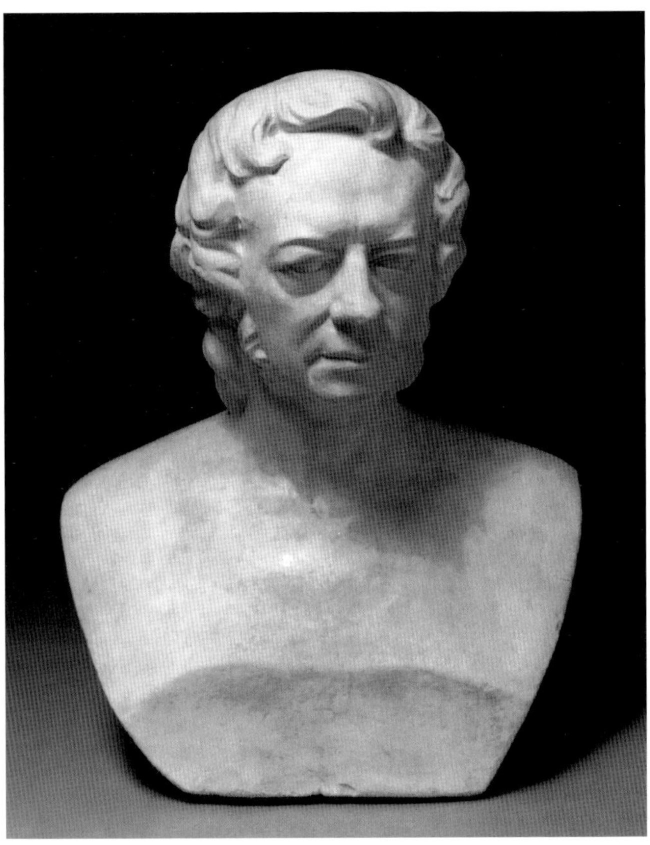

Clevenger, *Washington Allston*

Washington Allston

1839
Plaster
21 x 17 x 9½" (53.3 x 43.2 x 24.2 cm)
Source unknown, 1848.2

SHOBAL VAIL CLEVENGER's bust of Washington Allston (1779–1843) was commissioned in 1839 by the trustees of the Boston Athenaeum to recognize Allston's position as the foremost American romantic painter of his day. Allston, who had been suffering from a severe attack of neuralgia, wrote to William T. Andrews, the secretary of the board of trustees, on August 21, 1839: "I feel deeply sensible to the honour done me; and whenever my state of health shall be such as to allow me of it, I shall be happy to comply with the request."[1] It was probably in the fall that Allston was well enough to sit for the portrait. Clevenger and the painter George Flagg, who was Allston's nephew, worked concurrently on portraits of Allston. Clevenger completed a plaster model in time for the first sculpture exhibition at the Boston Athenaeum, in 1839.[2] Washington Allston was pleased with Clevenger's likeness of him and wrote to his family in North Carolina: "My friends here think it could not be more like me: as well as I know my own face so think I."[3] But the painter's emaciated features were shown too realistically to suit his family; and, after his death in 1843, they commissioned Edward Brackett (1818–1903) to make another bust (Metropolitan Museum of Art, New York).

Clevenger's work in Boston was facilitated by the trustees of the Athenaeum, who provided him with a studio. To show his appreciation, Clevenger gave the Athenaeum eight plaster busts, including one of Allston (no longer in the collection). The trustees in return commissioned a marble version of the Allston portrait. The marble was carved in Italy and remains today at the Boston Athenaeum. Little is known about the provenance of the plaster bust at the Museum of American Art of the Pennsylvania Academy of the Fine Arts. In the Pennsylvania Academy's 1848 collection catalogue, it was listed as belonging to the institution and may have arrived in the collection before that date. The 1848 accession number was most likely assigned during the 1940s and based on the 1848 catalogue. The National Academy of Design in New York also owns a plaster, purchased from Mrs. Clevenger in 1843.

Notes

1. Jonathan Harding, *The Boston Athenaeum Collection: Pre-Twentieth Century American and European Painting and Sculpture* (Boston: Boston Athenaeum, 1984), p. 22.
2. Wayne Craven, *Sculpture in America* (Newark: University of Delaware Press, 1984), p. 184.
3. Brumbaugh 1966, pp. 38–39.

References

1857 E.P. Peabody, "Last Evening with Allston," *Emerson's Magazine and Putnam's Monthly* 5 (Oct.), p. 502. **1903** Lorado Taft, *The History of American Sculpture,* New York: Macmillan Company, p. 100 (ill.). **1966** Thomas B. Brumbaugh, "Shobal Clevenger: An Ohio Stonecutter in Search of Fame," *Art Quarterly* 29, pp. 29–45, figs. 3, 4 (ills.). **1973** William H. Gerdts, *American Neo-Classic Sculpture: The Marble Resurrection,* New York: Viking Press, pp. 106, 107 (ill.).

Exhibited

1849* cat. no. 367. **1850*** cat. no. 405. **1851*** cat. no. 421. **1852*** cat. no. 449. **1853*** cat. no. 416. **1854*** cat. no. 438. **1855*** cat. no. 510. **1856** PAFA, *Fall Exhibition of the Pennsylvania Academy of the Fine Arts,* cat. no. 296. **1858*** cat. no. 522. **1859*** cat. no. 441. **1860*** cat. no. 397. **1865*** cat. no. 208. **1866*** cat. no. 208. **1868*** cat. no. 382½. **1869*** cat. no. 292. **1951** Detroit Institute of Arts and Toledo Museum of Art, *Travelers in Arcadia,* cat. no. 25. **1976** PAFA, *In This Academy,* cat. no. 7. **1986–87** PAFA, *Sculpture at the Pennsylvania Academy of the Fine Arts.*

Isaac P. Davis

About 1839
Plaster
22 x 16 x 8" (55.9 x 40.6 x 20.3 cm)
Source unknown, 1876.7

Isaac P. Davis (1799–1883) was born in Plymouth, Massachusetts. A rope manufacturer by trade, he was active in Boston's social life and on intimate terms with men like Daniel Webster, who in 1841 helped him secure an appointment as naval officer for the port of Boston. Davis was a patron of the arts and served on the board of trustees of the Boston Athenaeum from 1830 to 1845. Among his many artist friends were Gilbert Stuart, Washington Allston, Thomas Sully, Hiram Powers, and Shobal Vail Clevenger.[1] Undoubtedly, Clevenger modeled Davis's bust in Boston in 1839. The same year he carved a marble bust (now in the Boston Athenaeum) of Isaac's brother, Judge John Davis, a former president of the Boston Athenaeum.

The plaster bust of Isaac Davis probably came to the the Pennsylvania Academy of the Fine Arts through the Artists' Fund Society of Philadelphia, of which Davis was an honorary, amateur member. Founded in 1824 by artists dismayed by the fact that the board of directors of the Pennsylvania Academy was made up of businessmen rather than artists, the society was organized to allow artists "control of their own professional affairs."[2] When this bust was first exhibited at the Pennsylvania Academy, in the fall of 1856, it was listed as the property of the Artists' Fund Society. From the 1840s through the 1860s, the

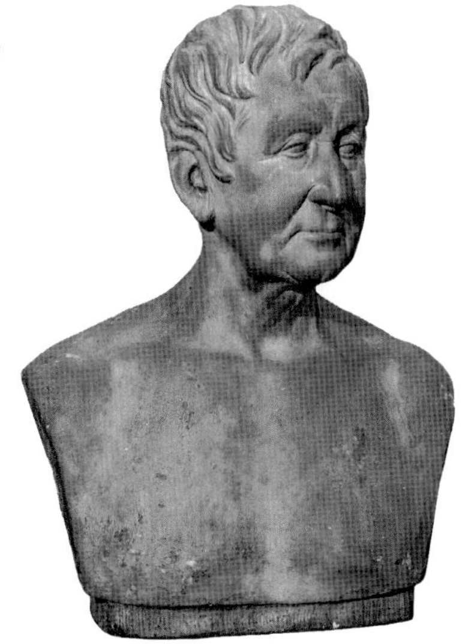

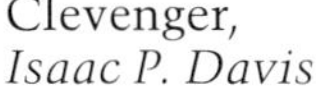

Clevenger,
Isaac P. Davis

activities of the society were intimately bound up with those of the Academy. From 1840 to 1866, the society rented an exhibition hall from the Pennsylvania Academy; and when the society moved to new quarters in 1866, it may have had to dispose of part of its permanent collection—with some works being assimilated into the Academy's collection. The 1876 accession date for the bust was probably assigned during the 1940s, based on the 1876 catalogue *Property and Loan Exhibition of the Pennsylvania Academy of the Fine Arts* in which the piece was listed as belonging to the Academy.

Notes

1. "Biographical Sketch of Isaac P. Davis," *Proceedings of the Massachusetts Historical Society*, 1869–70, pp. 94–99.

2. *Catalogue of the First Exhibition*, Artists' Fund Society of Philadelphia, 1835, p. 3, PAFA Archives.

Reference

1966 Thomas B. Brumbaugh, "Shobal Clevenger: An Ohio Stonecutter in Search of Fame," *Art Quarterly* 29, p. 38, fig. 8 (identified erroneously as *Bust of Joseph Hopkinson* [q.v.]).

Exhibited

1856 PAFA, *The Fall Exhibition of the Pennsylvania Academy of the Fine Arts*, cat. no. 274. **1876** PAFA, *Property and Loan Exhibition of the Pennsylvania Academy of the Fine Arts*, cat. no. 281.

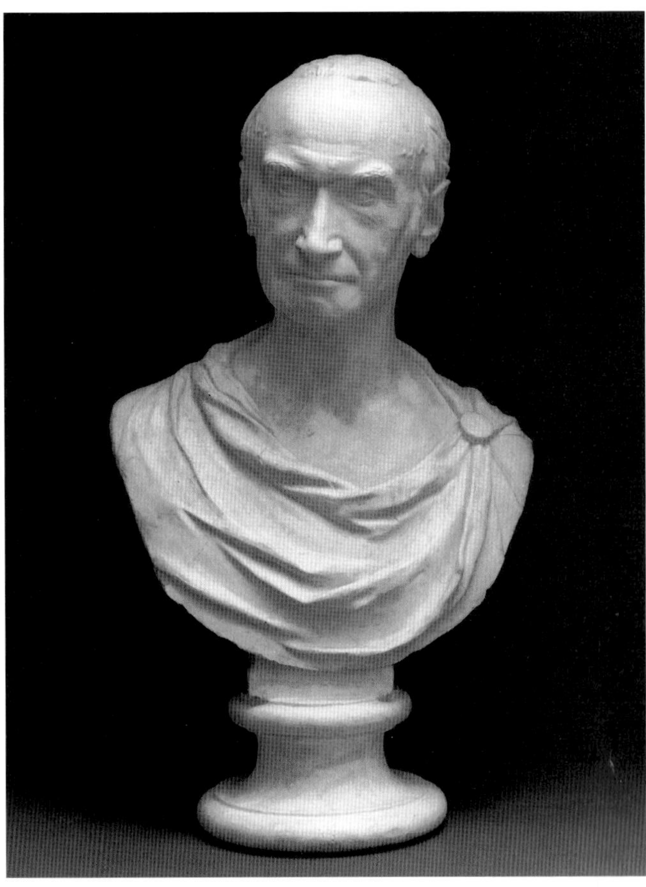

Clevenger, *Joseph Hopkinson*, plaster

Joseph Hopkinson

1839

a.
Plaster
26 x 15 x 11" (66 x 38.1 x 28 cm)
Annotated in pencil on right side of integral base:
Clevenger/Sculp
Source unknown, 1847.4

b.
Bronze with black patina; sand cast in 1905
26 x 15 x 11" (66 x 38.1 x 28 cm)
Foundry mark stamped on top of integral base:
BUREAU BROS./PHILA.
Purchased by the Pennsylvania Academy, 1905.3

THIS PORTRAIT of the congressman and jurist Joseph Hopkinson (1770–1842), a sixty-nine-year-old native Philadelphian, was modeled during Shobal Vail Clevenger's brief visit to Philadelphia in the spring of 1839. Although the face is completely realistic, the shoulders are draped in a Roman toga, a common device for representing statesmen. This combination of neoclassical idealism and American realism is typical of the busts created by early nineteenth-century American sculptors before they ventured to Italy.

Joseph Hopkinson was the son of Francis Hopkinson, a signer of the Declaration of Independence, and the son-in-law of Thomas Mifflin, the first governor of Pennsylvania. Joseph Hopkinson served as a United States congressman from 1814 to 1820 and in 1828 was appointed a judge of the federal district court for eastern Pennsylvania by President John Adams. Hopkinson is most often remembered as the author of "Hail, Columbia," which he set to the tune of the "President's March" in 1798.

Hopkinson was affiliated with many of Philadelphia's cultural institutions. He was one of the seventy-one founders of the Pennsylvania Academy of the Fine Arts and served as its second president, from 1813 until his death in 1842. An able manager, he helped the fledgling Academy attain financial stability and was instrumental in expanding its collection and enlarging its original building.

This portrait may have been commissioned by the Pennsylvania Academy. The fact that the raised lines from the mold were not smoothed away on the plaster model suggests that Clevenger intended it merely as an intermediate step in the process of translating the bust into marble and did not plan to exhibit it. Clevenger probably took the plaster model with him when he went to Italy in 1840. This may explain its being exhibited at the Academy for the first time as late as 1847, inasmuch as the sculptor's meager estate took some time to be settled. The plaster remained almost continuously on view at the Academy from 1847 to 1869. Although Clevenger himself never worked in bronze, the Pennsylvania Academy had the bust cast in bronze in 1905 by the Bureau Brothers Foundry.

Reference (plaster)
1966 Thomas B. Brumbaugh, "Shobal Clevenger: An Ohio Stonecutter in Search of Fame," *Art Quarterly* 29, p. 38, fig. 10 (identified erroneously as *Bust of Isaac P. Davis* [q.v.]).

Reference (bronze)
1930 "Bust of Hopkinson Found in Academy," *Philadelphia Public Ledger*, April 27 (ill.), microfilm, roll no. 57, frame no. 268, PAFA Archives.

Exhibited (plaster)
1847 PAFA, *Exhibition of paintings, statues and casts, at the Pennsylvania Academy of the Fine Arts*, cat. no. 534. **1849*** cat. no. 375. **1850*** cat. no. 381. **1851*** cat. no. 425. **1852*** cat. no. 398. **1853*** cat. no. 449. **1854*** cat. no. 418. **1855*** cat. no. 506. **1856*** cat. no. 556. **1856** PAFA, *Fall Exhibition of the Pennsylvania Academy of the Fine Arts*, cat. no. 306. **1858*** cat. no. 547. **1859*** cat. no. 396. **1860*** cat. no. 463. **1861*** cat. no. 578. **1862*** cat. no. 543. **1865*** cat. no. 207. **1866*** cat. no. 207. **1868*** cat. no. 882. **1869*** cat. no. 291. **1976** PAFA, *In This Academy*, cat. no. 8, pp. 20 (ill.), 274.

Exhibited (bronze)
1975–76 Whitney Museum of American Art, New York, *A Portrait of Young America*.

Joseph Mozier

1812–1870

Joseph Mozier was born in Burlington, Vermont, to parents of French origin.[1] Part of his youth was spent in Mount Vernon, Ohio, but by 1831 he was a partner in the dry-goods firm of Tweed, Mozier and Company in New York. During his years in business, Mozier pursued art as a hobby. Sculpture particularly interested him. In 1844, following the death of SHOBAL VAIL CLEVENGER, Mozier helped New York's Mercantile Library Association raise funds to have Clevenger's statue *The Indian* carved in marble.[2] Mozier also provided space, possibly at his dry-goods establishment on Bond Street, for the exhibition of a small plaster study of the figure.[3] By 1845 Mozier had sufficient capital to retire from business and devote himself to sculpture. He took his family abroad and, after visiting the major cities of Europe, settled in Florence to study.

Between 1847 and 1850, Mozier's work was regularly seen in the annual exhibitions of the National Academy of Design in New York. His address was not listed in the Academy's 1847 or 1848 exhibition catalogues, but in 1849 it was given as 673 Broadway, New York; in the 1850 catalogue, his address was simply listed as Italy; and in 1857, as Rome.[4] It was probably during the early 1850s that Mozier established his permanent residence in Rome.

Although most of Mozier's sculptures shown at the National Academy of Design were marble busts, he turned at an early stage to full-length statues, which he was able to sell in extraordinary numbers. Thus he was not forced, like most of his contemporaries, to model portraits for the revenue they could bring in. To some extent, Mozier's success can be attributed to his business acumen. He catered to the Victorian penchant for the sentimental and anecdotal, and he shied away from nude figures, which were difficult to sell. Mozier often borrowed his subjects from contemporary literature. His *White Lady of Avenel*, by 1867 (private collection, New Haven), was inspired by Sir Walter Scott's *The Monastery*. His 1859 statue *Wept of Wish-ton-Wish* (Yale University Art Gallery, New Haven) depicts the heroine of James Fenimore Cooper's romance of the same name. It concerned a white girl who was captured by Indians and chose to remain with them. The story was very popular at mid-century when people felt nostalgic about life in the wilderness during colonial times. Mozier executed at least two statues of Indians: *Pocahontas*, about 1848 (private collection), and *The Indian Girl's Lament*, about 1857 (location unknown), inspired by a poem by William Cullen Bryant. Mozier also created many statues depicting biblical figures, such as *Rebecca at the Well*, 1857 (New York Public Library, on loan to the New-York Historical Society); *The Prodigal Son* (q.v.); *Queen Esther*, about 1859; *Jephthah's Daughter*, 1865; *Rizpah*, by 1867 (whereabouts of the last three are unknown).

During the 1850s and 1860s, Mozier's Roman studio was a common stop for American tourists in Italy. In 1855 Henry A. Stone purchased a pair of marble statues, *Truth* and *Silence*, from Mozier's studio. Stone gave the statues to the Mercantile Library Association of New York,[5] where they remained un-

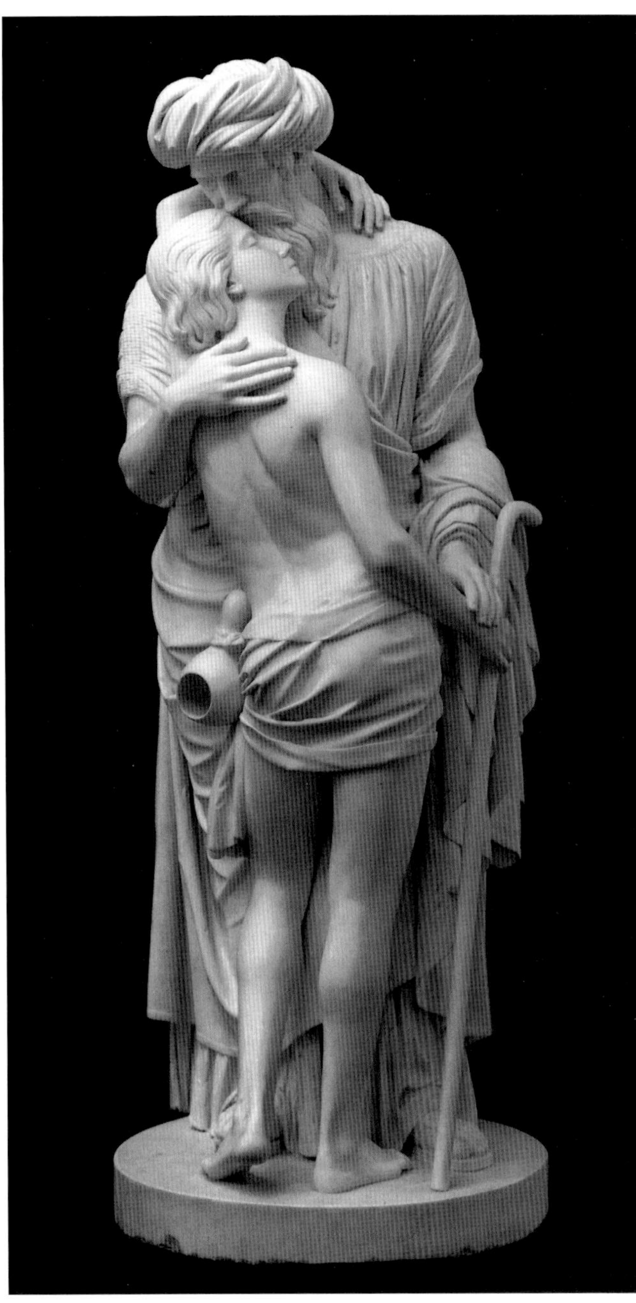

Mozier, *The Prodigal Son*

til 1984 when they were sold to a private collector. In 1858 Nathaniel Hawthorne visited Mozier's studio. He was unimpressed with most of the sculptor's work but commented favorably on two genre pieces, *Girl with Cat and Dog* and *Boy Mending a Pen.*

By 1866 Mozier had completed *Il Penseroso,* a full-length statue of the goddess of melancholy, inspired by John Milton's poem of the same title. During the 1870s and early 1880s, one version of *Il Penseroso* was housed in the United States Capitol. It was eventually purchased for the Capitol from Mozier's widow but was transferred in 1888 to the Smithsonian Institution.[6] It is now in the collection of the National Museum of American Art. Another copy, possibly that owned by James L. Claghorn and shown at the Pennsylvania Academy of the Fine Arts in 1869–70, is now in Memorial Hall, Fairmount Park, Philadelphia. About 1867 Mozier completed a statue of Undine, the water nymph who was the heroine of a romance by Baron de la Motte-Foqué and an opera by Albert Lortzing. Mozier swathed the nymph in revealing wet drapery. William H. Gerdts has called the piece "one of the most notable American examples of the see-through illusionism popular in Italy at mid-century."[7] In 1867 *Undine* took the grand prize at the Rome Art Exhibition.[8] One copy of it is now owned by the University of Dayton in Ohio, and another is in a private collection in New York.

Notes

1. "Obituary: Joseph Mozier," London *Art Journal* 23 (Jan. 1, 1871), p. 6.
2. Richard P. Wunder, "The Irascible Hiram Powers," *American Art Journal* 4 (Nov. 1972), p. 11.
3. *National Academy of Design Exhibition Record, 1826–1860* (New York: printed for New-York Historical Society, 1943), p. 45.
4. Ibid.
5. "Sketchings: Editorial Correspondence," *Crayon* 2 (Fall 1855), p. 216.
6. Charles E. Fairman, *Art and Artists of the Capitol of the United States of America* (Washington, D.C.: Government Printing Office, 1927), p. 317.
7. William H. Gerdts, *American Neo-Classic Sculpture: The Marble Resurrection* (New York: Viking Press, 1973), p. 89.
8. *Dictionary of American Biography,* s.v. "Mozier, Joseph."

References

1870 "Death of an American Sculptor in Switzerland—His Career," *New York Times,* Oct. 30, p. 3. **1876** Rodman J. Sheirr, "Joseph Mozier and His Handiwork," *Potter's American Monthly* 6, no. 49 (Jan.), pp. 24–28. **1878** William J. Clark, Jr., *Great American Sculptures,* Philadelphia: Gebbie and Barrie, pp. 120–21. **1903** Lorado Taft, *The History of American Sculpture,* New York: Macmillan Company, pp. 110–11.

The Prodigal Son

About 1857
Marble; carved in 1858
76 x 30¾ x 31" (193 x 78.1 x 78.8 cm)
Signed on side of plinth near father's right foot:
MOZIER .Sc:/ROME
Gift of J. Gillingham Fell, 1869.2

SCULPTURES with two figures, like *The Prodigal Son,* were relatively common in the mid-nineteenth century. Their popularity was linked to the vogue for narrative art and its demand for characters. In addition, group pieces gave sculptors a chance to display their virtuosity in composition and modeling. This sculpture depicts the Old Testament story of the wastrel son's repentant homecoming and the warm reception by his father. Mozier also called this piece *Prodigal's Return.*[1]

The March 1857 edition of the *Crayon* (p. 92) noted that *The Prodigal Son* could be seen in Mozier's Roman studio. This probably referred to the plaster model, however, because in April 1858 Nathaniel Hawthorne wrote that he had recently seen the plaster and its duplicate "taking shape out of an immense block of marble." Although Hawthorne, who was one of Mozier's harshest critics, acknowledged that the group possessed merit, his enthusiasm was quelled by the rumor that Mozier had stolen or adapted the idea from the work of a student in the French Academy.[2] Another contemporary author had nothing but praise for *The Prodigal Son* and described it as an example of the "naturalistic school of Art [which makes] no attempt to idealize or give a poetical version of the subject . . . but is presented with a feeling of genuine pathos which is most striking."[3] In 1878 the artist and critic William J. Clark, Jr., praised it as Mozier's most important work.[4]

J. Gillingham Fell, a member of the board of directors of the Pennsylvania Academy of the Fine Arts, bought *The Prodigal Son* when he visited Mozier's studio in the spring of 1869. It was shipped direct to the Pennsylvania Academy as a gift. In April, Fell wrote to the Academy's president, Caleb Cope, that "after some anxious deliberation [I] came to the conclusion that this group combined as many of the qualities which will render it acceptable to *our* taste as any I have met."[5]

Two restorations, using polyester resin, have been made to the sculpture: in 1981, the father's missing right thumb was replaced; and in 1985, the curved top of the father's staff, which had been missing for many years, was restored based on 1876 and 1878 engravings of the piece.[6]

Notes

1. Joseph Mozier to James Claghorn, April 28, 1869, PAFA object file.
2. Lorado Taft, *The History of American Sculpture* (New York: Macmillan Company, 1903), p. 111.
3. London *Art Journal* 2 (April 1, 1859), p. 124.
4. William J. Clark, Jr., *Great American Sculptures* (Philadelphia: Gebbie and Barrie, 1878), p. 120.
5. J. Gillingham Fell to Caleb Cope, March 27, 1869, PAFA object file.
6. Conservation reports, March 1, 1981, and Sept. 24, 1985, PAFA object file.

References

1876 Rodman J. Sheirr, "Joseph Mozier and His Handiwork," *Potter's American Monthly* 6 (Jan.), p. 25 (engraved ill.). **1973** William H. Gerdts, *American Neo-Classic Sculpture: The Marble Resurrection,* New York: Viking Press, p. 59, fig. 16. **1982** Regina Soria, *Dictionary of Nineteenth Century American Artists in Italy, 1760–1914,* Rutherford, N.J.: Fairleigh Dickinson University Press, p. 238 (ill.).

Exhibited

1876* cat. no. 628. **1972** PAFA, *Acres of Art,* cat. no. 67. **1978–79** PAFA, *350 Masterpieces of American Art.* **1986–87** PAFA, *Sculpture at the Pennsylvania Academy of the Fine Arts.*

Thomas Crawford

1813?-1857

Thomas Crawford was probably born in New York in 1813 to Irish immigrant parents.[1] As a child, he took lessons at a local drawing school and collected a small group of plaster casts.[2] At the age of fourteen, Crawford apprenticed himself to a wood carver. A few years later, he began to draw at the National Academy of Design and possibly there met JOHN FRAZEE. By 1832 Crawford was working as a stonecutter in the firm of Frazee and Launitz. During the next three years, Crawford not only carved architectural ornaments and funerary monuments but also worked on several marble busts. It is likely that both Frazee and Launitz offered Crawford instruction in clay modeling. Robert Launitz (1806–1870), who had studied in Rome under Bertel Thorwaldsen (1770–1844), encouraged Crawford to do the same and gave him a letter of introduction to Thorwaldsen.

Crawford arrived in Rome in September 1835 and studied with Thorwaldsen for about a year. The influence of his mentor's neoclassical style can be seen in Crawford's early work. To support himself, he modeled portrait busts of Americans on the Grand Tour. One of the most noteworthy is of the young Boston lawyer Charles Sumner. When Sumner visited Rome in the spring of 1839, he and Crawford began a long friendship. The portrait that Crawford modeled was put into marble in 1842 and is now in the Museum of Fine Arts, Boston.

Back in Boston, Sumner started a subscription fund to purchase a marble version of Crawford's first ideal work, *Orpheus and Cerberus,* 1843 (Museum of Fine Arts, Boston). In Crawford's unique portrayal of the myth, Orpheus has already tamed the three-headed dog, Cerberus, and is peering into the Underworld in search of his wife. Through Sumner's efforts, the sculpture arrived in Boston in the fall of 1843. It was the highlight of the first exhibition of Crawford's work, which was held in a specially built structure on the grounds of the Boston Athenaeum in May 1844. *Orpheus and Cerberus* received high praise; and, because the figure wore a fig leaf, there was no criticism of its nudity. Other early works by Crawford include a small dancing child called *Genius of Mirth,* 1843 (Metropolitan Museum of Art, New York), and his most neoclassical work, *Hebe and Ganymede,* modeled in 1842 and completed in marble by 1851 (Museum of Fine Arts, Boston).

During the summer of 1844, Crawford traveled back to the United States to marry Louisa Ward, a New York socialite. He returned again after winning a competition in 1849 for a monument to General George Washington for Richmond, Virginia. The contract entailed the creation of an equestrian statue of Washington, six statues of other famous Virginians, and six eagles at a cost of $53,000. Crawford finished the bronze equestrian figure and statues of Thomas Jefferson and Patrick Henry as well as plaster models for figures of John Marshall and George Mason before his untimely death. The monument was eventually completed by RANDOLPH ROGERS.

During the few remaining years before a cancerous tumor behind his left eye forced him to stop working in 1856, Crawford was widely recognized. The Pennsylvania Academy of the Fine Arts elected him an honorary professional member on April 10, 1854. He was the major contributor of sculpture to the United States Capitol. In 1853 he began work on the pediment sculptures for the Senate wing, which depict past and present civilizations of America. The models were sent to Washington, D.C., where they were carved in marble.[3] The last figure was put into place in 1863. During 1855 and 1856, Crawford was working on the models for the bronze doors to the Senate and the House of Representatives. Both sets of doors portray themes of war and peace and were finished after Crawford's death by WILLIAM HENRY RINEHART. Crawford also modeled the colossal figure of Freedom that surmounts the Capitol dome. It was cast in bronze in the United States by the self-taught sculptor and founder Clark Mills (1810/15–1883). On December 2, 1863, when the head of the figure was hoisted into place, cannon shots rang out in salute.

Notes

1. Gale 1964, p. 5.

2. Thomas Hicks, *Thomas Crawford; His Career, Character, and Works: A Eulogy* (New York: D. Appleton and Company, 1858), p. 9.

3. Captain Montgomery Meigs, chief engineer of the Capitol, to Henry D. Gilpin, president of the PAFA, Sept. 27, 1856, PAFA Archives. Meigs inquired whether the Academy would be interested in having on deposit the plaster models for Crawford's pediment. He added that Mrs. Crawford favored the idea. The Academy's board of directors formed a committee in December 1857 to communicate with Meigs; but the models, which are now lost, were never sent to the Academy.

References

1846 C. Edwards Lester, *The Artists of America,* New York: Baker and Scribner, reprinted New York: Kennedy Galleries, 1970, pp. 235–57. **1875** Samuel Osgood, *Thomas Crawford and Art in America,* New York: John F. Trow and Printers. **1964** Robert Gale, *Thomas Crawford: American Sculptor,* Pittsburgh: University of Pittsburgh Press. **1972** Sylvia E. Crane, *White Silence—Greenough, Powers and Crawford, American Sculptors in Nineteenth Century Italy,* Coral Gables: University of Miami Press.

Peri at the Gates of Paradise

1854–56
Marble; carved in 1856–57
69¾ x 27¾ x 24″ (177.2 x 70.5 x 62 cm)
Signed and dated on side of plinth at back left:
T. CRAWFORD/FECIT.ROMA.1856
Inscribed on front vertical surface of plinth: PERI
Bequest of Clarissa A. Burt, 1917.9

THIS IS a variant of the angelic theme that was popular with American sculptors of the mid-nineteenth century. A *peri* in Persian mythology is a fallen angel. Thomas Crawford's statue was inspired by the opening lines of the Irish poet Thomas Moore's poem "Paradise and the Peri" from his 1817 book *Lalla Rookh:* "One Morn a Peri at the gate of Eden stood disconsolate." In the poem, the peri tries and fails many times to regain entry to Paradise. Finally, she finds the repentant tears of an old man and offers them to God, who, in return, readmits her.

Soon after visiting Crawford's Roman studio in February 1854, the Philadelphian Arthur A. Burt ordered a marble statue and pedestal for which he prepaid half the purchase price, or two hundred pounds. The remainder was due upon completion and included delivery to Philadelphia.[1] In late April, Crawford sent Burt a photograph of his clay study for the *Peri.* The sculptor emphasized that the statue would be superior to the study and added that he was preparing to begin the full-scale model.[2] Crawford was then in the midst of working on his Capitol commissions, however, and had little time to devote to the model. He continued working on it intermittently for about two years.

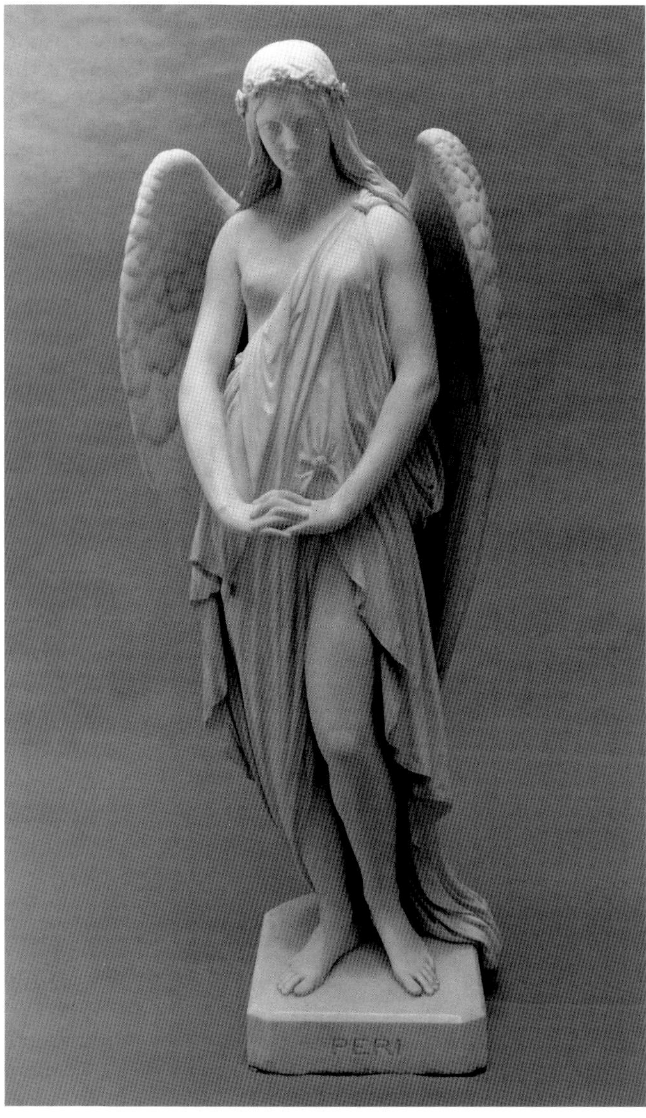

Crawford, *Peri at the Gates of Paradise*

When Crawford became incapacitated by a cancerous tumor, studio assistants carved the *Peri* in marble. The sculptor's wife, Louisa, wrote to Arthur Burt on April 21, 1857, that the statue was ready to be shipped from Rome. She characterized the remuneration as less than adequate and expressed surprise that her husband had agreed to bear the burden of the shipping charges.[3] Burt responded by sending a copy of his agreement with Crawford along with words of admiration for the sculptor's work and his hopes for Crawford's recovery.[4]

Peri at the Gates of Paradise came to the Pennsylvania Academy of the Fine Arts in 1917 through the bequest of Burt's wife, Clarissa. Another carving of the same statue, of unknown date and provenance, is in the Corcoran Gallery of Art, Washington, D.C.

Notes

1. Contract signed by Thomas Crawford, Feb. 28, 1854, PAFA Archives.

2. Thomas Crawford to Arthur A. Burt, April 26, 1854, PAFA Archives. The photograph is in the PAFA "Peri" object file.

3. Louisa Crawford to Arthur Burt, April 21, 1857, PAFA Archives.

4. Arthur Burt to Louisa Crawford, May 8, 1837, PAFA Archives.

Reference

1982 Linda Bantel, "Sculpture at the Pennsylvania Academy," *Antiques* 121 (March), p. 708, fig. 4.

Exhibited

1972 PAFA, *Acres of Art,* cat. no. 26. **1978–79** PAFA, *350 Masterpieces of American Art: 1720–1978.* **1986–87** PAFA, *Sculpture at the Pennsylvania Academy of the Fine Arts.*

Hugh A. Cannon

1812?–1865

Although Hugh A. Cannon's birthplace has been reported as either Ireland or Pennsylvania, a death record in the Philadelphia City Archives reveals that he was born in Philadelphia.[1] Cannon served an apprenticeship under John Struthers, a highly regarded marble mason and the owner of a busy Philadelphia stoneyard. In 1837 Cannon's name first appeared in the Philadelphia directory, where he is listed as a marble mason. According to the *United States Gazette,* however, Cannon was more inclined towards sculpture than the traditional aspects of masonry like hewing stone for buildings. By September 1838, he had completed a marble bust of Nicholas Biddle and was working on one of Henry Clay (qq.v.) at his studio in the lower story of the old Masonic Hall in Filbert Street west of Eighth Street.[2]

Cannon endeavored to educate himself in his chosen profession by studying at the Pennsylvania Academy of the Fine Arts. In November 1839, after having submitted satisfactory recommendations to President Joseph Hopkinson, Cannon was granted free access to the Pennsylvania Academy's statue gallery so that he could draw from the antique casts.[3] In 1840 his bust of Chief Justice John Marshall was shown in the Artist's Fund Society exhibition in Philadelphia. His work was also seen in New York. In 1841 he exhibited marble busts of Henry Clay and Edwin Forrest at the Apollo Association, the forerunner of the American Art-Union.

On September 13, 1847, J. Struthers and Son, Cannon's former employer, signed a contract with the city of Philadelphia to build a memorial honoring Frederick Graff, the engineer of the Fairmount Waterworks.[4] They designed a free-standing architectural niche, containing a marble bust, and hired Cannon to execute the bust. When the monument was finally erected on July 29, 1848, Cannon's bust of Graff was acclaimed for its faithful resemblance and beautiful execution.[5] Today, the bust is very weathered; and Cannon's signature, if it existed, has been thoroughly obliterated.

According to the reminiscences of the sculptor J. Augustus Beck (1831-about 1915), Cannon worked during 1848 in Lancaster, Pennsylvania, for the stone carver Major Charles Howell.[6] Although we have no record of the nature of Cannon's work for Howell, it must have been well regarded because in 1854 Cannon received an important commission for a large wooden statue of the inventor Robert Fulton for the facade of the newly built Fulton Opera Hall in Lancaster.[7] Cannon portrayed Fulton standing and attired in contemporary dress with an unrolled scroll in his left hand. He may have based the head of Fulton on the two best-known likenesses of the inventor, those by JEAN ANTOINE HOUDON (by 1802, Musée du Louvre, Paris) and Benjamin West (1806, New York State Historical Association, Cooperstown, N.Y.). It is estimated that Cannon received between 300 and 375 dollars for the statue.[8] According to Beck, who visited Cannon in his Philadelphia studio about this time, he had several other wooden statues in progress.[9]

In 1851 ISAAC BROOME began to study wood and marble carving with Cannon. At that time, Broome later recalled, Cannon's major patron was George W. Carpenter, the wealthy owner of the leading wholesale drug firm in Philadelphia. Carpenter had an elaborate estate in Germantown, called Phil-Ellena, which was embellished with paintings and sculpture. The exact nature of the sculptural work that Cannon did for the estate remains a mystery. According to Broome, Cannon had difficulty supporting his family during the 1850s, so Carpenter employed him as the manager of his considerable city real estate. Cannon continued in this capacity for a number of years during which he completed no sculpture. Broome recalled Cannon with fondness and described him as a "broad minded intellectual man" whose "associates were the literate actors, artists, and the prominent physicians of that time."[10]

Notes

1. Board of Health Death Register, 1865, p. 170, Philadelphia City Archives.
2. *United States Gazette,* Sept. 4, 1838, p. 2.
3. Permit, Nov. 26, 1839, Applications and Permits to Copy Paintings, 1837–45, Committee on Instruction, PAFA Archives.
4. Philadelphia City Council Watering Committee Papers, 1847, Philadelphia City Archives.
5. *North American and United States Gazette,* Philadelphia, July 31, 1848, p. 2.
6. Beck letter of about 1904 quoted in "Fulton Hall and Its Graven Image," *Papers Read before the Lancaster County Historical Society,* Dec. 6, 1918, vol. 22 (Lancaster, Pa., 1918), p. 147.
7. Today the sculpture, which was conserved in 1984, is housed inside the opera house. A fiberglass cast has been placed in the original niche.
8. In 1825, twenty-three years earlier, William Rush and his son John were paid $450 for their two wooden sculptures *Allegory of the Schuylkill River in Its Improved State* and *Allegory of the Waterworks.*
9. "Fulton Hall and Its Graven Image," 1918, pp. 146–48.
10. Isaac Broome to Harrison Morris, Feb. 25, 1900, PAFA Archives.

Nicholas Biddle

1838
Marble
23½ x 16½ x 8" (59.7 x 42 x 20.3 cm), with base
Source unknown, 1850.1.1

NICHOLAS BIDDLE (1786–1844) was born in Philadelphia into a well-established Quaker family. Educated at the University of Pennsylvania and the College of New Jersey in Princeton, he was graduated from the latter institution at the age of fifteen as valedictorian. A noted author, Biddle contributed articles to the *Port-Folio* and helped to establish it as America's preeminent literary magazine. In 1814 he published his *History of the Expedition of Captains Lewis and Clark.* Today, Biddle is best remembered as a financier. He helped stabilize the Bank of the United States after its reorganization in 1818. As its president from 1823 to 1827, however, he was ultimately blamed for its failure.

An ardent art lover, Biddle sat for portraits by myriad artists. The Italian sculptor E. Luigi Persico (1791–1860) executed one in 1837. Cannon could have seen it the following year when a plaster cast was exhibited at the Pennsylvania Academy of the Fine Arts. That same year Cannon completed this likeness of Biddle, which closely resembles Persico's bust, especially in its use of the dead eye, a neoclassical device not seen in Cannon's other known portraits. Although he overtly copied the work of other sculptors, Cannon probably modeled this bust from life.[1] In 1918 the art critic Edward Biddle, Nicholas's grandson, wrote that he possessed a letter from Hugh

Cannon asking Nicholas Biddle to inspect the just-finished bust.[2] It therefore seems likely that Cannon made this bust for Biddle or at least at his request.

This bust was formerly believed to have been presented to the Pennsylvania Academy in 1850 by Daniel W. Coxe, a director of the Bank of the United States. Although Coxe gave Cannon's self-portrait and his portrait of Henry Clay to the Academy in 1850, there is no record that he gave this piece. It seems more likely that the Academy acquired this bust through Mrs. Hopkinson (probably Mrs. Francis Hopkinson, née Ann Biddle, the sister of Nicholas Biddle), who lent the bust to the Pennsylvania Academy's thirty-third annual exhibition in 1856. Although there is no record of its gift, the bust was recorded as the property of the Pennsylvania Academy in the catalogue of the 1857 annual exhibition.

Notes

1. The Maryland Historical Society owns a bust by Cannon after the Italian sculptor Antonio Capellano (active in the United States, 1815-about 1827), but Cannon's signature makes it clear that it is a copy: Gen. W.H. Winder/by H. Cannon/1843/from a bust by Capellano 1820.

2. "Fulton Hall and Its Graven Image," *Papers Read before the Lancaster County Historical Society,* Dec. 6, 1918, vol. 22 (Lancaster, Pa., 1918), p. 147.

Reference

1975 Nicholas B. Wainwright, "Nicholas Biddle in Portraiture," *Antiques* 108 (Nov.), p. 962 (ill.).

Exhibited

1856* cat. no. 564. **1856** PAFA, *The Fall Exhibition of the Pennsylvania Academy of the Fine Arts,* cat. no. 282. **1857*** cat. no. 482. **1858*** cat. no. 533. **1859*** cat. no. 418. **1860*** cat. no. 441. **1861*** cat. no. 381. **1867*** cat. no. 378. **1868*** cat. no. 405. **1869*** cat. no. 315. **1973** PAFA, *Held in Trust,* cat. no. 30. **1974–75** Second Bank of the United States, Philadelphia, *Masterworks of American Art, 1740–1840.* **1975–76** Whitney Museum of American Art, *A Portrait of Young America.* **1978–79** PAFA, *350 Masterpieces of American Art: 1720–1978.*

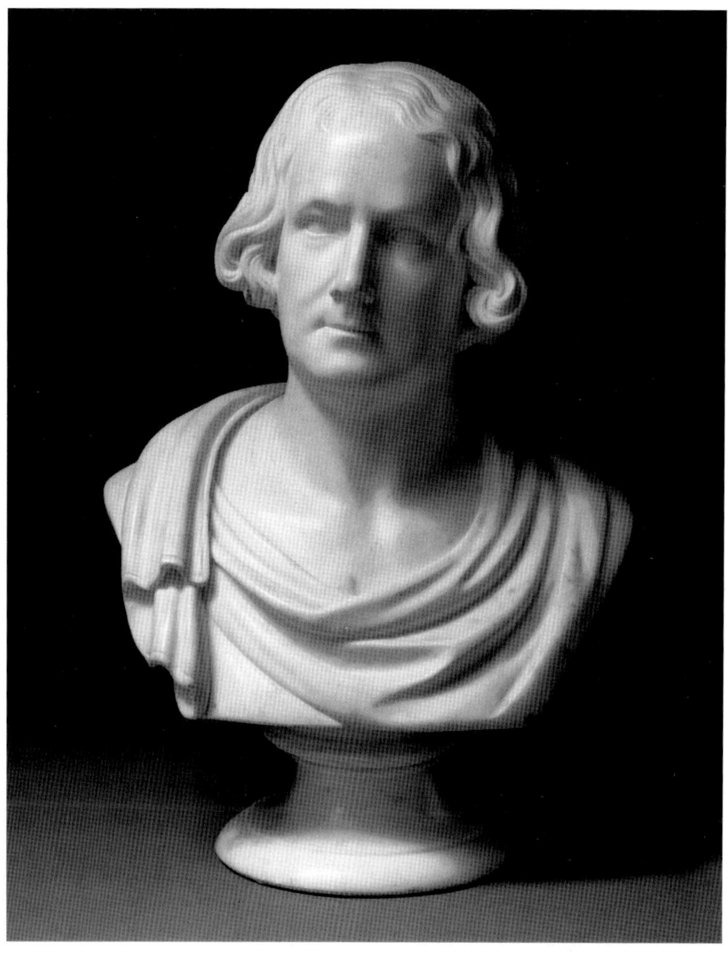

Cannon, *Nicholas Biddle*

Henry Clay

1838
Marble
28 x 17 x 9" (71 x 43.2 x 23 cm), with base
Signed vertically on back: H CANNON/fecit
Gift of D.W. Coxe, 1850.1.3

HENRY CLAY (1777–1852) was born in Hanover County, Virginia. In 1797, at the age of twenty, he established himself as a criminal lawyer in Lexington, Kentucky, where his great skill as an orator was quickly recognized. He was elected to the United States Senate in 1806 and served until 1811. That year he ran for the House of Representatives, in which he served almost continually until 1825. Under President John Quincy Adams, he served as secretary of state from 1825 to 1827 and then returned to the Senate in 1831. His great desire to be president was never realized, although he ran for the office several times. He made his strongest bid for the presidency in 1844 but was defeated by James Knox Polk. Clay was extremely influential and popular in the South, particularly in his home state of Kentucky. In 1849 his urgings of moderation and compromise helped delay the onset of the Civil War.

On September 4, 1838, the *United States Gazette* reported that Cannon had almost finished a portrait bust of Henry Clay. It is not known if Clay sat for the bust, but the *Gazette* reported the likeness to be "truly astonishing—the features and expression of [the] great statesman and orator are perfect." In March of 1841, Cannon offered a marble version for sale at an exhibition at the Apollo Association in New York.[1] It seems likely that this is the one now in the collection of the Museum of American Art of

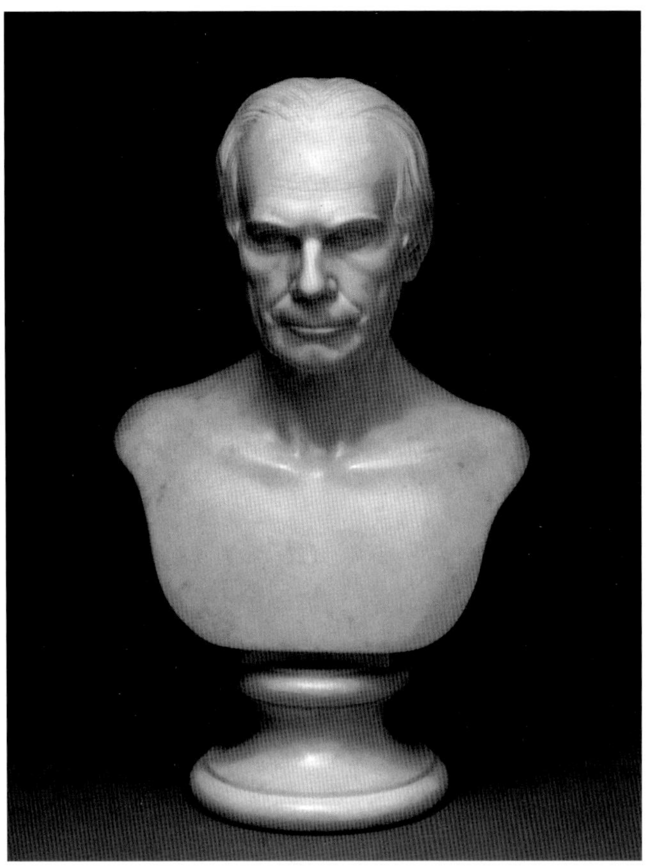

Cannon, *Henry Clay*

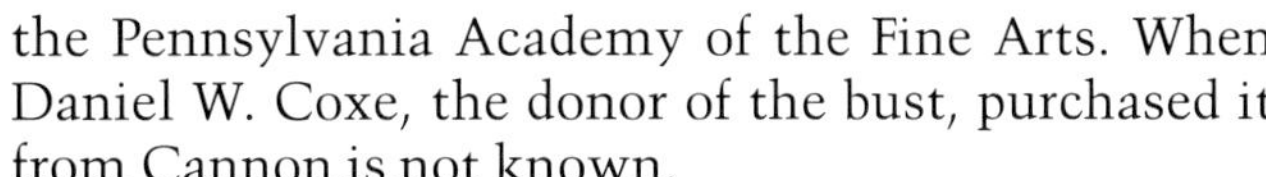

the Pennsylvania Academy of the Fine Arts. When Daniel W. Coxe, the donor of the bust, purchased it from Cannon is not known.

Note

1. Mary Bartlett Cowdrey, *American Academy of the Fine Arts and American Art-Union Exhibition Record, 1816–1852* (New York: New-York Historical Society, 1953), p. 55.

Exhibited

1851* cat. no. 392. **1852*** cat. no. 297½. **1853*** cat. no. 484. **1854*** cat. no. 397. **1855*** cat. no. 533. **1856*** cat. no. 566. **1856** PAFA, *The Fall Exhibition of the Pennsylvania Academy of the Fine Arts,* cat. no. 291. **1857*** cat. no. 476. **1858*** cat. no. 532. **1859*** cat. no. 420. **1860*** cat. no. 440. **1861*** cat. no. 393. **1862*** cat. no. 394. **1863*** cat. no. 383. **1864*** cat. no. 283. **1865*** cat. no. 169. **1866*** cat. no. 169. **1867*** cat. no. 390. **1868*** cat. no. 332. **1978–79** PAFA, *350 Masterpieces of American Art: 1720–1978.*

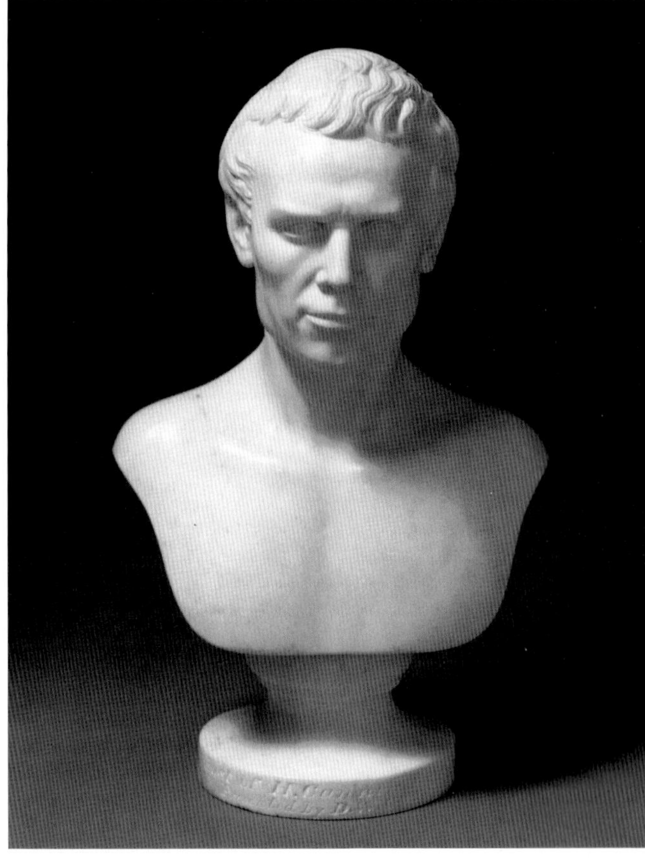

Cannon, *Self-Portrait*

Self-Portrait

About 1845
Marble
26 x 16½ x 9" (66 x 42 x 23 cm), with base
Inscribed on front of base: Bust of H. Cannon, Sculpt./
Presented by D.W. COXE.
Gift of D.W. Coxe, 1850.1.2

ALTHOUGH there are no other known images of Hugh A. Cannon with which to compare this self-portrait, it can be assumed to be a fair likeness. Judging by his busts of Biddle and Clay, Cannon was not given to great idealizations. Rather, his first priority in portraiture, like that of most of his contemporaries, was to capture a good likeness. The lifelike quality of this bust is largely due to the drilled pupils of the eyes, which lend animation and intensity to the face.

Daniel W. Coxe, the son of the wealthy Philadelphia political economist Tench Coxe, seems to have given Cannon considerable patronage. In October 1850, he presented this bust and the one of Henry Clay (q.v.) to the Pennsylvania Academy of the Fine

Arts.[1] At the same time, he deposited with the Academy a bust of himself by Cannon,[2] which, after Coxe's death, was returned to his brother Charles.[3]

Notes

1. *Donations to the Pennsylvania Academy of the Fine Arts,* Oct. 7, 1850, p. 59, PAFA Archives.
2. Although the entry of Oct. 7, 1850, in the PAFA donation book records this as a bust of Mr. Coxe's nephew, it is later consistently recorded as depicting Daniel Coxe himself.
3. Charles Coxe to Caleb Cope, Oct. 17, 1861, and Property Register, Oct. 18, 1861, PAFA Archives.

Exhibited

1851* cat. no. 419. **1852*** cat. no. 444. **1854*** cat. no. 395. **1855*** cat. no. 535. **1856*** cat. no. 567. **1857*** cat. no. 483. **1858*** cat. no. 540. **1859*** cat. no. 403. **1860*** cat. no. 453. **1865*** cat. no. 166. **1866*** cat. no. 166. **1867*** cat. no. 370. **1868*** cat. no. 396. **1869*** cat. no. 307. **1876*** cat. no. 630. **1973** PAFA, *Held In Trust,* cat. no. 31. **1976** Philadelphia Museum of Art, *Philadelphia: Three Centuries of American Art,* cat. no. 280 (ill.).

Guido Butti

Active in the United States, 1852–about 1864

Very little is known about Guido Butti. He may have immigrated to the United States from his native Italy in 1852. He appears in the New York city directory of 1852–53 as "artist, sculptor & modeller of the human figure, & ornamental work of every style." He is not listed, however, in the directories of 1853–54 or 1854–55. Presumably he left New York for Washington, D.C., around 1854.

Butti was probably lured to Washington by the hope of securing ornamental work for the new wing of the United States Capitol. According to Charles E. Fairman:

> The work of Mr. Butti at the Capitol was largely that of a modeler. He had reached that degree of proficiency where he modeled so that others might reproduce his work in marble. Very many of his works doubtless exist about the Capitol, but as the carving was done by different sculptors there is very little in the matter of record to identify his work.[1]

Nonetheless, the date books of the chief engineer, Montgomery C. Meigs, provide a few clues to Butti's work for the Capitol. On January 28, 1856, Meigs recorded that he bargained with Butti about carving the marble for Thomas Crawford's statue of a revolutionary soldier for the Senate pediment and that Butti was executing the models for the ornamental mantel in the Senate antechamber.[2]

Meigs also hired Butti to work on the northern extension of the old General Post Office in Washington. He executed the models for the building's Corinthian capitals, as well as the sculptures over the west entrance gate.[3]

Notes

1. Charles E. Fairman, *Art and Artists of the Capitol of the United States of America* (Washington, D.C.: United States Government Printing Office, 1927), p. 167.
2. Papers of Montgomery C. Meigs, Library of Congress Manuscript Division, microfilm, roll no. 1, frame no. 319.
3. Meigs's notes of payment to Butti are in the Records of the Architect of the Capitol, Washington, D.C.

Railroad and Telegraph or Steam and Electricity

1856
Plaster, painted beige
54 x 120 x 10" (137.2 x 304.8 x 25.4 cm)
Deposited by the United States Government, 1.1856

These allegorical spandrel figures, as well as the keystone mask of Fidelity, were modeled and cast in plaster by Guido Butti between January and June of 1856. They are models for the marbles that adorn the arch of the west entrance to the former General Post Office, located on E Street between Seventh and Eighth streets, in Washington, D.C.[1] Butti executed this ornamental group under the aegis of the Post Office extension program, which, like the similar project at the Capitol, was supervised by Montgomery C. Meigs. Butti agreed to carve the spandrels and mask in marble for two thousand dollars, but it is not certain whether he did the carving or not.[2] While a voucher showing payment to him of one thousand dollars for the modeling and casting of the group survives, none for the carving has come to light.[3]

For many years, these models were erroneously attributed to Thomas Crawford, who produced a great deal of sculpture for the Capitol. In 1856 Crawford and Meigs communicated about architectural sculpture for the keystones of the General Post Office,[4] but Crawford never completed the work because he developed a malignant tumor in 1856 and died the following year.

In 1926 Charles E. Fairman, the curator of the United States Capitol, informed the Pennsylvania Academy of the Fine Arts that the attribution of these models to Crawford was incorrect. He cited several documents in the archives of the Architect of the

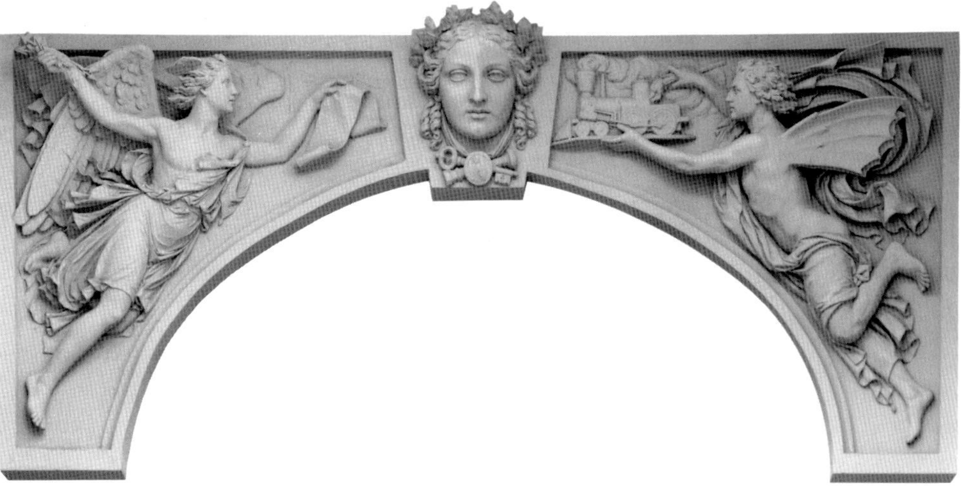

Butti, *Railroad and Telegraph or Steam and Electricity*

Capitol, among them the previously mentioned voucher of payment to Butti and a November 1856 photograph annotated on the back with Butti's name and showing the marbles in situ at the General Post Office.[5] Apparently the erroneous attribution to Crawford, which dates back to 1856, originated in the records of the Pennsylvania Academy. On September 15, 1856, Montgomery C. Meigs offered to deposit these plaster models at the Academy.[6] Soon thereafter, he wrote to Henry D. Gilpin, the president of the Academy, concerning a different matter—the disposition of the plaster models for Thomas Crawford's pediment for the Capitol. In this letter, Meigs wrote that both he and Crawford would like to see the plaster models for the pediment placed at the Pennsylvania Academy, although he added that this would be sometime in the future, as the carving had barely begun. It was the last paragraph of Meigs's letter that confused Gilpin. Meigs wrote: "The plaster models which I propose to send now are those from which certain figures were cast for the west gate of the Gen. Post Office Building. They need some slight repairs which I expect to have completed in a few days & I will then send them."[7] Because Meigs had not mentioned the name of the sculptor of the General Post Office models in either of his letters, Gilpin assumed that they were by Crawford. When the plasters arrived at the Pennsylvania Academy, Gilpin wrote to Meigs informing him of the safe arrival of the "reliefs of Mr. Crawford."[8] Meigs realized the mix-up and hastened to inform Gilpin that the reliefs were the work of Guido Butti. On the bottom of the letter that Gilpin sent to him, Meigs scrawled, "Mistaken not Crawford but Butti's so informed Mr. G. by a letter not recorded. Written at home and sent in a hurry." Although this correction was noted by the Pennsylvania Academy, Crawford's name continued to be associated with the models.[9]

The iconographical relationship of Butti's allegorical figures of the railroad and telegraph to the Post Office is somewhat vague. The theme seems to be a general one of communication and expansion. Although railroad companies had contracts with the Post Office at this time, the telegraph had nothing to do with the postal service in the 1850s.[10] Butti may have included the figure of the telegraph simply as a tribute to the invention and its creator, Samuel F.B. Morse, who in 1845 opened the world's first telegraph office on the site covered by the northeast side of the building.[11] The keystone mask is identified as Fidelity by these attributes—a dog (shown on a medallion), a key, and a sealing-wax stamp. The mask probably has no direct relationship to the spandrel figures but rather was intended to fit into the comprehensive decorative scheme that Montgomery Meigs envisioned for the building, which included fifteen keystone masks representing human passions.

Notes

1. During the early twentieth century, this building housed the Tariff Commission. When the commission changed its name to the International Trade Commission, the building became known as the ITC building. It now belongs to the Government Services Administration.

2. Agreement signed by Guido Butti, June 27, 1856, Records of the Architect of the Capitol.

3. Voucher of payment to Butti, ibid.

4. Robert Gale, *Thomas Crawford: American Sculptor* (Pittsburgh: University of Pittsburgh Press, 1964), p. 164.

5. Charles E. Fairman to John Andrew Myers, May 5, 1926, PAFA object file.

6. Montgomery C. Meigs to Caleb Cope, Sept. 3, 1856, PAFA object file.

7. Montgomery C. Meigs to Henry D. Gilpin, Sept. 27, 1856, ibid.

8. H.D. Gilpin to M.C. Meigs, Oct. 10, 1856, Records of the Architect of the Capitol.

9. See PAFA Fall exhibition catalogue, 1856, cat. no. 231.

10. Richard John to Mary Mullen Cunningham, April 28, 1987, PAFA research file.

11. "Old Land Office in Washington Thought Architectural Treasure," United States Tariff Commission, typescript, about 1928, General Post Office Clipping File, Martin Luther King, Jr., Memorial Library, Washington, D.C.

Exhibited

1856 PAFA, *Fall Exhibition of the Pennsylvania Academy of the Fine Arts,* cat. no. 231. **1857*** cat. no. 312. **1858*** cat. no. 340. **1859*** cat. no. 394. **1860*** cat. no. 359. **1861*** cat. no. 371. **1862*** cat. no. 371. **1863*** cat. no. 404. **1864*** cat. no. 18. **1865*** cat. no. 199. **1866*** cat. no. 199. **1876–present** Permanent display in the main galleries of the Museum.

Erastus Dow Palmer

1817–1904

Erastus Dow Palmer was born in Pompey, New York, where he spent his early childhood on his grandfather's farm. When he was nine, his family moved to Utica, and he began to work with his father as a carpenter. For about ten years after the death of his father in 1834, Palmer made his living in that trade, first in the town of Dunkirk on Lake Erie and later back in Utica. In 1843 he carved a cameo likeness of his wife, which he showed to Thomas R. Walker, a local lawyer and art lover. With Walker's help, Palmer discovered a market for his cameos and gradually gave up carpentry. Walker wrote letters of introduction to artists and collectors for Palmer and encouraged him to make large-scale sculpture.[1]

In 1849 Palmer moved to Albany, where he lived for the rest of his life. His first sculpture in the round, *The Infant Ceres,* 1849–50 (private collection, Santa Barbara), was shown at the National Academy of Design, in New York, in 1851. During the 1850s, Palmer became intimately involved in the art community in Albany. He helped organize exhibitions at the Albany Gallery of Fine Arts and became the chief promoter in Albany for the *Crayon,* a journal of art and aesthetics.

In 1853 he began work on his first full-length figure in the round, called *The Indian Girl* or *The Dawn of Christianity,* 1856 (Metropolitan Museum of Art, New York). Commissioned by the New York merchant Hamilton Fish, it depicts a semi-nude Indian girl finding a crucifix lost by Christian missionaries. The statue proved to be the highlight of *The Palmer Marbles,* his solo exhibition in New York in late 1856. The exhibition received wide acclaim. It was advertised as the first show in America of marble sculpture carved entirely by an American craftsman without the aid of European artisans. Palmer's growing reputation was abetted by friends and patrons. In December 1856, Dr. James H. Armsby of Albany intimated in a letter to the Pennsylvania Academy of the Fine Arts that the Academy might do well to show Palmer's work in its galleries.[2] Accordingly, Palmer was invited to exhibit in February (just a month and a half later); but his schedule did not permit it.[3]

Palmer finished his most famous statue, *The White Captive,* in 1859 (Metropolitan Museum of Art). Also commissioned by Hamilton Fish, it portrays a Christian girl who has been stripped and bound by Indians. Palmer intended *The White Captive* to be a companion to *The Dawn of Christianity,* with the latter representing the effect of the Christian on the savage and the former, the effect of the savage on the Christian. Although *The White Captive* is an entirely nude figure, its religious narrative made it acceptable to a prudish public. In fact, Anson G. Chester, a critic who saw the plaster model of *The White Captive* in the spring of 1858, praised Palmer's daring. Chester applauded the fact that neither of the figure's hands cover her genital area in the attitude of "conscious shame" so often employed by sculptors (seen, for example, in *The Greek Slave* by HIRAM POWERS). "If the world is not extra squeamish," he continued, "this one manly innovation will be the making of [Palmer]."[4] Many critics praised Palmer's ability to present a thoroughly American subject. This choice of subject by a self-taught native artist, together with his consistent use of Christian themes, ingratiated him with the public and critics alike.

During the post-Civil War era, Palmer turned increasingly to bronze as a medium, but he received relatively few commissions during this period. His last major commission was for a bronze statue of the eighteenth-century jurist and diplomat Robert R. Livingston for Statuary Hall of the United States Capitol. The commission was awarded to Palmer by the State of New York just before his first trip to Europe. After traveling through England, Belgium, Italy, and France, Palmer settled in Paris for two months to model the Livingston statue. Two bronzes of it were cast in Paris by the Barbidienne foundry;

the second cast was destined for the state capitol in Albany. One of the bronzes was exhibited in Philadelphia at the Centennial Exposition, where it won a first-class medal.

Notes

1. Webster 1983, p. 19.
2. Minutes, meeting of the board of directors, Dec. 8, 1856, and minutes, meeting of the committee on exhibitions, Dec. 20, 1856, PAFA Archives.
3. Minutes, meeting of the committee on exhibitions, Dec. 23, 1856. Palmer's reply is recorded in minutes, meeting of the board of directors, Feb. 9, 1857, PAFA Archives.
4. "Palmer, the Sculptor," *Syracuse Daily Journal*, April 3, 1858, from the New York Public Library, microfilm, roll no. N50, frame no. 1073, Archives of American Art.

References

1856 Erastus Dow Palmer, "Philosophy of the Ideal, 1856," *Crayon* 3 (Jan.), reprinted in *American Art Review* 2 (May-June 1975), pp. 70–77. **1856** "Masters of Art and Literature; Erastus Dow Palmer," *Cosmopolitan Art Journal* 1 (Nov.), pp. 7–49. **1972** J. Carson Webster, "Erastus D. Palmer: Problems and Possibilities," *American Art Journal* 4 (Nov.), pp. 34–43. **1983** J. Carson Webster, *Erastus D. Palmer: Sculpture—Ideas*, Newark: University of Delaware Press.

Spring

1855
Marble
23⅝ x 15½ x 10½" (60 x 39.4 x 26 cm)
Pennsylvania Academy purchase, 1857.2

Erastus Dow Palmer completed the clay model for this allegorical bust of Spring by the end of May 1855. He idealized the likeness of Annie Walker, the daughter of his friend and first patron, Thomas T. Walker.[1] In the catalogue of Palmer's 1856 exhibition in New York, where *Spring* was seen publicly for the first time, the art historian Henry T. Tuckerman described it as the "sweetest type of maidenhood," embodying the "mysterious and enchanting season" in the childlike bosom, fresh parted lips, and wreath of ripening grass.[2]

At least eight marble versions of *Spring* were carved by Palmer's shop. The one in the Museum of American Art of the Pennsylvania Academy of the Fine Arts was the first. Palmer's account book records that it was carved by Charles Calverly (1833–1914) and finished by Launt Thompson (1833–1894), Palmer's studio assistants.[3] The piece was originally carved for Edward D. Morgan, who was elected governor of New York in 1858 and later served as a United States senator. Because the marble had a slight defect, however, Palmer carved another for Morgan. The first version was purchased by the Cosmopolitan Art

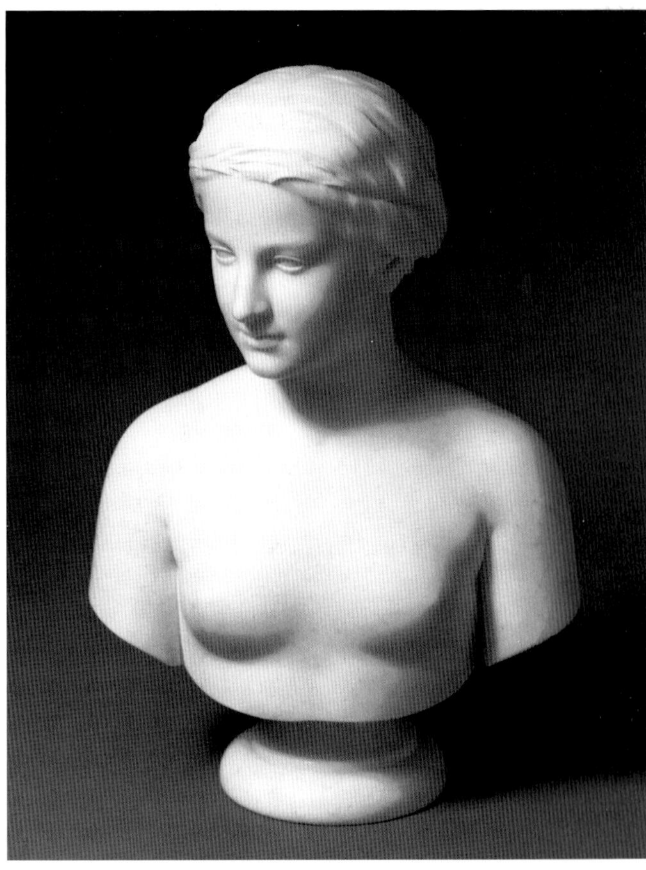

Palmer, *Spring*

Association of New York and awarded to Mrs. E.L. Howland as a distribution prize. She offered the bust for sale in the Pennsylvania Academy's 1857 annual exhibition from which the Academy bought it for $350.[4]

Notes

1. J. Carson Webster, *Erastus D. Palmer: Sculpture—Ideas* (Newark: University of Delaware Press, 1983), pp. 176–77.
2. *Catalogue of the Palmer Marbles at the Hall Belonging to the Church of the Divine Unity, 548 Broadway, New York* (Albany: J. Munsell, 1856), p. 7. Even more sentimental than Tuckerman's prose was the poem about *Spring* written by an unidentified woman and included in the catalogue.
3. Webster 1983, pp. 176–77.
4. Minutes, meeting of the board of directors, Sept. 14, 1857, PAFA Archives.

References

1856 *Cosmopolitan Art Journal* 1 (Nov.), p. 48 (engraved ill.). **1856** *Leslie's* 5 (Nov. 22), p. 372 (engraved ill.).

Exhibited

1856 Church of the Divine Unity, New York, *The Palmer Marbles*, cat. no. 3. **1857*** cat. no. 318. **1858*** cat. no. 355. **1859*** cat. no. 369. **1860*** cat. no. 348. **1861*** cat. no. 385. **1862*** cat. no. 386. **1863*** cat. no. 390.

1864* cat. no. 325. **1867*** cat. no. 402. **1868*** cat. no. 422. **1869*** cat. no. 354. **1963** PAFA, *Forgotten Favorites: Selections from the Permanent Collection.* **1975** Second Bank of the United States, *Masterworks of American Art, 1740–1840.* **1978–79** PAFA, *350 Masterpieces of American Art.* **1986–87** PAFA, *Sculpture at the Pennsylvania Academy of the Fine Arts.*

Ex Collections
Cosmopolitan Art Association, New York, about 1855–56; Mrs. E.L. Howland, 1856–57.

Richard S. Greenough

1819–1904

Born in Jamaica Plains, Massachusetts, a suburb of Boston, Richard Saltonstall Greenough was the eleventh and last child of David and Betsy Bender Greenough. He was educated at Charles W. Greene's school in Jamaica Plains and at the Boston Latin School from which he was graduated at the age of seventeen. It was probably because his father's real-estate business had suffered substantial losses that Richard did not attend Harvard College as four older brothers had done. Instead, he entered the accounting department of the merchant business owned by two of his brothers. They soon became aware of his desire to follow in the footsteps of another brother, the sculptor HORATIO GREENOUGH. Accordingly, they sent him to Italy in 1837; and he joined Horatio in Florence. Unfortunately, Richard became seriously ill and was forced to return to Boston after only six months.

Nonetheless, within two years, Richard Greenough had opened a sculpture studio. As an unknown sculptor, he had difficulty finding patrons; and in 1843 he wrote to his fellow sculptor Henry Kirke Brown (1814–1866) to inquire about the state of patronage in Albany, as he was considering quitting Boston.[1] Nothing came of this, however, and Greenough's situation in Boston improved when his plaster bust of the prominent historian William Hickling Prescott was given to the Boston Athenaeum by the sitter in 1844 and exhibited there. It received a good deal of attention, and the demand for Greenough's work rose accordingly. One of his earliest extant marble pieces (1846, Museum of Fine Arts, Boston) depicts the small child Augustus Edward May.

In 1848 Greenough returned to Italy. For several years, he worked in Rome where most of the second-generation American neoclassicists had their studios. Like most of them, he earned his living by making portrait busts of American travelers. His 1849 marble bust of Cornelia Van Rensselaer (New-York Historical Society) is typical of mid-nineteenth-century neoclassical portraiture in its concern with costume. Greenough also produced a number of ideal sculptures like *Cupid Warming an Icicle,* about 1848 (whereabouts unknown), which catered to the Victorian penchant for sweet and sentimental subjects.

In 1853 Greenough visited Boston and brought with him a recently completed plaster model for an ideal statue entitled *Shepherd Boy with an Eagle.* It was cast in bronze by the Ames Foundry in Chicopee, Massachusetts, and purchased by subscription in 1857 for the Boston Athenaeum, where it remains today. Greenough probably went to Boston at the behest of friends eager for him to secure the commission for a statue of Benjamin Franklin to be erected in front of City Hall. The commissioners of the statue wanted it to be executed by an American; and Greenough, a native Bostonian, was a logical choice. To ensure a correct and realistic representation, he was lent the clothes that Franklin wore to the signing of the treaty of alliance with France, which were preserved at the Massachusetts Historical Society. In 1856 the bronze statue was unveiled amid great fanfare. It was praised by critics and the public alike, and thousands of small lead and chalk copies were sold. The pedestal was designed by one of the sculptor's brothers, the architect Henry Greenough. Upon it appear four bronze bas-reliefs, depicting scenes from Franklin's life. Thomas Ball (1819–1911) executed two of the reliefs: *Declaration of Independence* and *Treaty of Peace and Independence, September 3, 1783.* They are overshadowed, however, by the simpler and more elegant reliefs by Richard Greenough: *Franklin as a Printer* and *Experiment with Lightning.*

While at work on the Franklin statue, Greenough received a commission for a seated figure of John Winthrop, the first governor of Massachusetts, to be placed in the chapel of Cambridge's Mount Auburn Cemetery. In 1856 the marble was carved in Paris, where Greenough had established a studio. It is hardly more than a costume piece and fails to impart a sense of vigor or monumentality to the figure. Although Greenough continued to work in Paris for about twenty years, his work displays little tendency towards the active surfaces characteristic of the French Beaux-Arts style. His *Carthaginian Girl,* 1863 (Boston Athenaeum), is typically neoclassical in its style and narrative content. Based on the *Venus de Milo,* it depicts a semi-nude Carthaginian girl who cuts her long hair so that it can be used to string the bows with which her kinsmen defend their city during the Second Punic War. Less static is Greenough's swooning *Mary Magdalene,* 1866 (Brooklyn Museum).

By the mid-1870s, the sculptor had returned to Rome. During the last decades of his life, he also spent time in Newport, Rhode Island. In 1876 he executed a standing marble figure of Governor John Winthrop for Statuary Hall in the Capitol in Washington, D.C.[2] Greenough's last major work, a lifesize marble dated 1882, depicts Circe offering a cup of enchanted wine to an unseen Ulysses (Metropolitan Museum of Art, New York).

Notes

1. Richard S. Greenough to Henry Kirke Brown, Feb. 22, 1843, Gratz Collection, Historical Society of Pennsylvania, Philadelphia.
2. A bronze version of this statue, originally cast for Boston's Scollay Square, is now on the grounds of the First Church in Boston.

References

1955 Thomas B. Brumbaugh, "Horatio and Richard Greenough: A Critical Study with a Catalogue of Their Sculpture," Ph.D. diss., Ohio State University. **1963** Thomas B. Brumbaugh, "The Art of Richard Greenough," *Old-Time New England* 53 (Jan.-March), pp. 61–78.

Greenough, *Huntington Frothingham Wolcott*

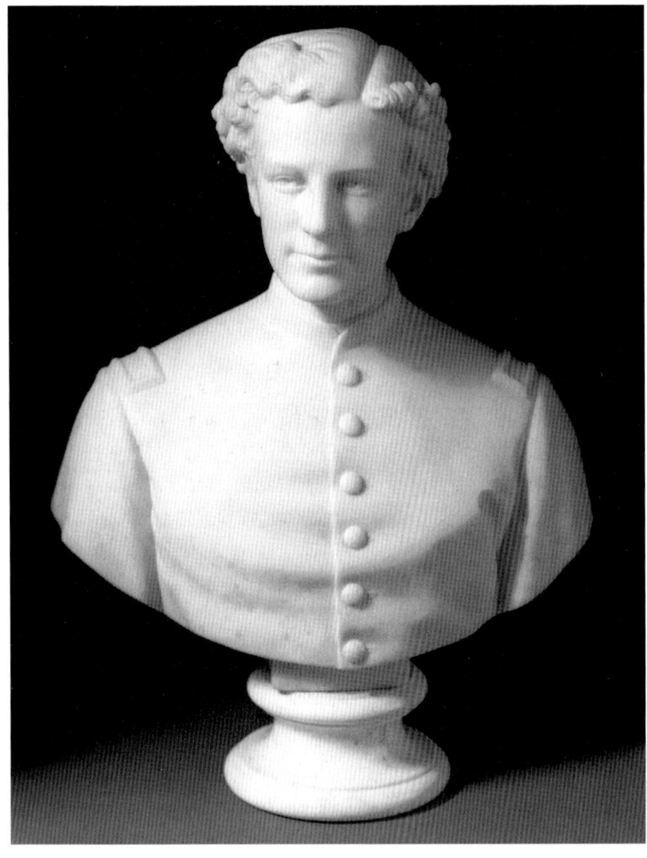

Huntington Frothingham Wolcott

1867
Marble
22 x 19½ x 9½" (56 x 49.5 x 24.2 cm)
Signed and dated on back: R.S.GREENOUGH./SCT.PARIS. 1867.
Pennsylvania Academy purchase, 1970.19

When the Civil War broke out in 1861, fifteen-year-old Huntington Frothingham Wolcott (1846–1865) was a student at Mr. Dixwell's private school in Boston. He became deeply convinced that it was his duty to fight in the Union Army, but his parents refused to let him enlist until he reached the age of nineteen. Early in 1865, the governor of Massachusetts commissioned Wolcott a second lieutenant in the second Massachusetts Cavalry. Under the command of General Philip H. Sheridan, he fought in the decisive battle of Five Forks in Virginia. Wolcott survived the war but was ill with typhoid fever. He died on June 9, 1865, at his home in Boston.[1]

This bust was commissioned by Huntington Wolcott's stepmother, his mother's sister.[2] Richard S. Greenough completed it in Paris in 1867, two years after Wolcott's death. That same year, WILLIAM MORRIS HUNT painted a three-quarter-length portrait of Wolcott (Museum of Fine Arts, Boston). The two portraits are similar and are probably based on the same photograph of the young soldier in uniform. Greenough succeeded in evoking a sense of life in this bust while also paying attention to small details like the buttons of Wolcott's uniform. Each one is emblazoned with an eagle and a shield inscribed with the letter *C* for *Cavalry.*

The original pedestal for this bust survives. It is covered with dark red velvet except for the top and bottom moldings, which are ebonized wood. Incised around the top molding is an extract from a letter that Wolcott sent to his stepmother shortly before his nineteenth birthday.[3] It expresses his desire to join the Union Army: "Dear Mamma you must let me go I feel so about it I think it would be sweet to die for my country." This echoes a line from the Roman poet Horace: "It is sweet and honorable to die for your country" (*Odes* 3.2.3). Wolcott was probably familiar with it, as the poem was part of the traditional academic curriculum. The bust remained in the Wolcott family until it was bought by a Boston art dealer in 1965.

Notes

1. William Lawrence, *Roger Wolcott* (Boston and New York: Houghton, Mifflin and Company, 1902), pp. 17–31.
2. Maury A. Bromsen to William B. Stevens, August 4, 1970, PAFA object file.
3. Lawrence 1902, p. 25.

Exhibited
1972 PAFA, *Acres of Art*, cat. no. 41. **1978–79** PAFA, *350 Masterpieces of American Art.* **1986–87** PAFA, *Sculpture at the Pennsylvania Academy of the Fine Arts.* **1994–96** PAFA, *Two Centuries of Collecting at the Museum of American Art.*

Ex Collections
Wolcott family, about 1867–1965; Maury A. Bromsen, 1965–70.

Atherton Blight

1878
Marble
30 x 22½ x 11½" (76.2 x 57.1 x 29.2 cm)
Signed and dated on back: R.S.GRENOUGH. [*sic*] SC^T./ ROMA, 1878.
Gift of Mr. Atherton Blight, 1893.1

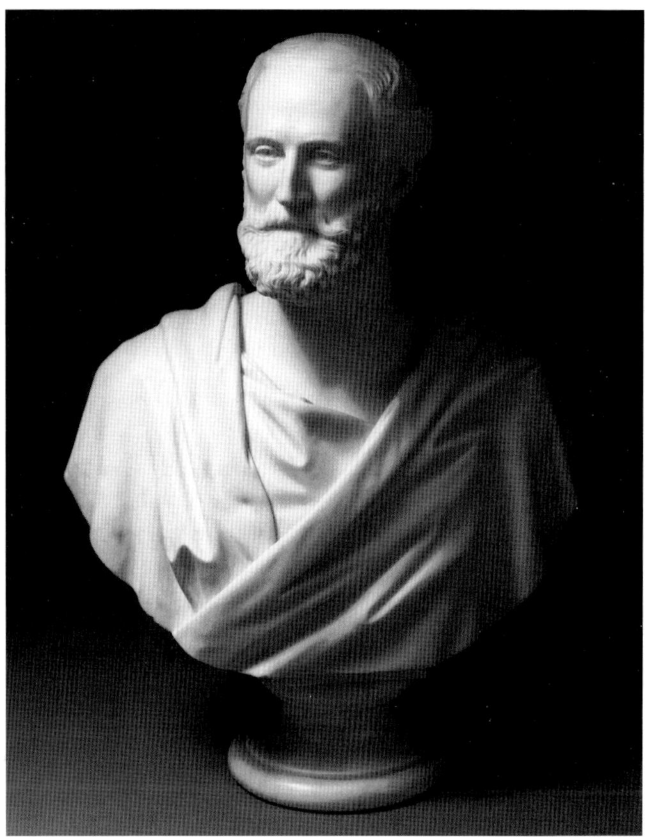

Greenough, *Atherton Blight*

ATHERTON BLIGHT (1833/34–1909), a scholar and master of foreign languages, was Richard Greenough's son-in-law and a long-time resident of Philadelphia.[1] He served on the board of directors of the Pennsylvania Academy of the Fine Arts from 1878 to 1885, the Committee of Finance from 1879 to 1882, and the Committee of Instruction in 1884. Greenough executed this bust in Rome in 1878, when Blight was in his mid-forties. Although it was undoubtedly done from life, there is little sense of personality in the bust. The highly finished marble, the meticulously rendered hair and beard, and the toga are all *retardataire.*

Blight had deposited this bust at the Pennsylvania Academy by 1880 and possibly as early as 1878, the year it was executed and Blight's first year as a director of the Academy. In the 1880 catalogue of the permanent collection, it was listed in the appendix of deposited works. On December 19, 1892, Harrison S. Morris, the managing director of the Pennsylvania Academy, wrote to Blight explaining that changes were being made in the installation of the Academy's permanent collection and that his bust had been removed from the galleries and placed in the directors' room. Morris added that it could remain there until Blight desired "to make other disposal of it."[2] From Cannes, France, Blight responded to Morris that, because his house in Philadelphia was rented and his summer home in Newport, Rhode Island, was closed, he would greatly appreciate it if the bust could remain at the Academy until the spring, when he hoped to return to the United States.[3] Blight never collected the sculpture, however, and his desire to have it remain at the Pennsylvania Academy, where he had "passed many pleasant hours," was probably expressed verbally. Eleven years later, when Blight wrote to the president of the Academy offering as a gift from his daughters a marble statue by Richard Greenough entitled *Nemesis,* he made no mention of the bust.[4]

Notes
1. Obituary, *New York Times,* Nov. 5, 1909, p. 9.
2. Harrison S. Morris to Atherton Blight, Dec. 19, 1892, PAFA Archives.
3. Atherton Blight to Harrison S. Morris, Jan. 2, 1893, PAFA object file.
4. Atherton Blight to the president of the PAFA, Nov. 21, 1904, including a photograph of *Nemesis,* PAFA Archives.

Ex Collection
The sitter (on deposit at the PAFA, about 1878–93).

William Wetmore Story

1819–1895

William Wetmore Story was born in Salem, Massachusetts, and reared in Cambridge. His mother, the former Sarah Waldo Wetmore, came from a prominent Boston family. His father, Joseph Story, was a justice of the United States Supreme Court and a respected Harvard College law professor. Young William enjoyed the advantages of affluence and an intellectually stimulating home life. From his teenage years, he wrote, drew, and modeled clay. Story received his undergraduate and law degrees from Harvard in 1838 and 1840, respectively. Shortly thereafter, he began to practice law in the offices of Charles Sumner and George Hillard. During the 1840s, Story published several important law treatises, as well as some poetry and prose. A prolific writer, he published fiction, poetry, essays, and criticism throughout his career. In 1843 he married Emelyn Eldridge of Boston. They socialized with the Boston literati, including Ralph Waldo Emerson, Nathaniel Hawthorne, and Story's boyhood friend James Russell Lowell.

Ironically, it was the death of his father in 1845 that launched Story's career as a sculptor. Even though he was only an amateur modeler, a group of Boston citizens commissioned him to make a memorial statue of his father for Mount Auburn Cemetery. To prepare, he went to Rome with his family in 1847. Although he returned to Boston and his law practice several times over the course of the next few years, he found it impossible to fend off his growing desire to become a professional sculptor. The acclaim that the marble statue of his father received in Boston in 1855 gave Story the impetus to abandon his legal practice and join the community of expatriate artists in Rome.

In their commodious apartment in the Palazzo Barberini, the Storys played host to many Anglo-American travelers. They regularly entertained an intimate circle of friends that included the American sculptor Harriet Hosmer (1830–1908) and the poets Robert and Elizabeth Barrett Browning. The Storys' elegant soirées often included the staging of a play in their small theater or William's dramatic reading of one of his newest verses. Still, his early years in Italy were not entirely carefree. Although he received a few commissions for portraits, including one of the abolitionist Theodore Parker, 1860 (Boston Public Library) and one of Josiah Quincy, about 1861 (Harvard University, Cambridge), there was little interest in his idealized sculpture. This finally changed in 1862, when Pope Pius IX admired his work and paid to send *Cleopatra,* 1858 (Los Angeles County Museum), and the *Libyan Sibyl,* 1860 (Metropolitan Museum of Art, New York), to the International Exhibition in London. The English critics praised Story's work, and the sculptures became star attractions of the exhibition. *Cleopatra* also brought Story significant attention in the United States after it became widely known that Nathaniel Hawthorne used the statue as the model for his protagonist's masterpiece in his 1860 romance *The Marble Faun.* These early sculptures set the tone for much of Story's subsequent ideal work. He preferred characters caught in emotional or psychological turmoil and drew his subjects from history, literature, mythology, and the Bible. His figures are generally in static neoclassical poses, but their stories unfold through facial expressions and props. Among his most popular such works were *Saul When the Evil Spirit was upon Him,* 1863 (Fine Arts Museums of San Francisco); *Medea Meditating the Death of Her Children,* 1866 (Museum of Fine Arts, Boston); and *Alcestis Returning from the Other World,* 1874 (Wadsworth Athenaeum, Hartford).

Independently wealthy, Story was not compelled to turn out portrait busts to earn a livelihood, as were most of his American colleagues. Among his relatively small production are busts of his friends Robert and Elizabeth Barrett Browning, 1866 (Boston Athenaeum). Story produced several notable portrait monuments, including one of Joseph Henry, 1881 (plaster, National Museum of American Art), the first secretary of the Smithsonian Institution, and one of Chief Justice John Marshall, 1884 (U.S. Supreme Court, Washington, D.C.).

References

1897 Mary E. Phillips, *Reminiscences of William Wetmore Story,* Chicago and New York: Rand, McNally and Company. **1969** Henry James, *William Wetmore Story and His Friends,* New York: Kennedy Galleries and Da Capo Press, reprint of original 1903 two-volume edition. **1972** William H. Gerdts, "William Wetmore Story," *American Art Journal* 4 (Nov.), pp. 16–33. **1985** Jan M. Seidler, "A Critical Reappraisal of the Career of William Wetmore Story (1819–1895), American Sculptor and Man of Letters," Ph.D. diss., Boston University.

Jerusalem in Her Desolation (also called *Jerusalem* and *Jerusalem Lamenting*)

1873
Marble
67 x 42 x 46" (170.2 x 106.7 x 116.8 cm)
Pedestal: 35 x 42 x 46" (88.9 x 106.7 x 116.8 cm)
Signed and dated on right side within a circle: WWS [monogram]/ROMA 1873
Inscribed in raised letters at front: JERUSALEM; and at lower left side of figure, the Latin text of Lamentations 1:1–2.
Gift of Mr. and Mrs. Arthur Klein, 1986.41

IN LATE 1870 or early 1871, William Wetmore Story was commissioned by Nancy McClellan Grigg of Paris to make this statue, *Jerusalem in Her Desolation,* for ten thousand dollars. Mrs. Grigg, who had grown up in Philadelphia as a member of a prominent local family, intended to present the statue to the Pennsylvania Academy of the Fine Arts.[1]

While Mrs. Grigg would certainly have had some say in the selection of the theme for the sculpture, the subject clearly reflects Story's taste. Drawn to tragic literary themes, he was especially fond of depicting brooding females. He went to the Bible for inspiration and found his personification of Jerusalem in the Lamentations of Jeremiah, chapter 1, verses 1 and 2, in which the prophet mourns the destruction of the holy city and the deportation of its citizens by King Nebuchadnezzar of Babylon in 586 B.C.:

1 How doth the city sit solitary,
 that was full of people!
how is she become as a widow!
 she that was great among the nations, and
 princess among the provinces,
how is she become tributary!

2 She weepeth sore in the night,
 and her tears are on her cheeks:
among all her lovers
 she hath none to comfort her:
all her friends have dealt treacherously with her,
 they are become her enemies.

Sitting upon broken walls, Story's personification of Jerusalem is despondent, yet regal. Her expression suggests not only sorrow but also bitterness and a determination to overcome calamity. Victorian audiences liked the narrative quality of Story's sculptures; and they particularly enjoyed his attention to details like the phylactery, a symbol of Jewish piety, that Jerusalem wears upon her forehead. Even the critic James Jackson Jarves, who deplored Story's melodramatic subjects, found it impossible not to admire his "rightly chosen" ornaments.[2]

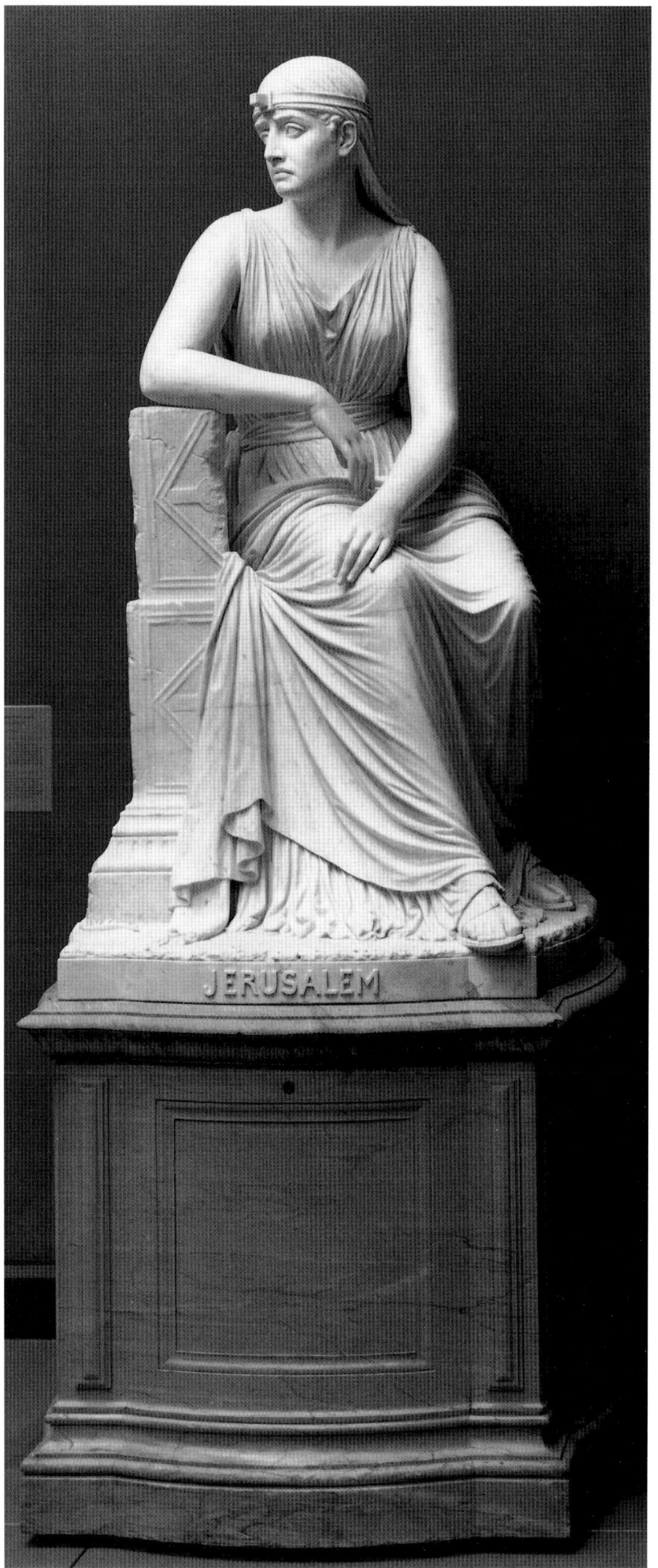

Story, *Jerusalem in Her Desolation*

Before it was shipped to Philadelphia, *Jerusalem in Her Desolation* was exhibited in London at Holloway and Son's Gallery in August 1873; and at the sculptor's request, quotations from the Lamentations were hung on the walls surrounding the statue. The London *Art-Journal* of that month lauded the figure and noted, "The general impression of the design is that of majestic sorrow; and the execution of the work throughout is most careful."[3] The British writer A.W. Kinglake conveyed to Story his admiration for the piece and recounted his fortunate meeting with a female acquaintance who delightfully pointed out the statue's individual "beauties."[4]

Not until April 22, 1876, was *Jerusalem in Her Desolation* finally introduced in Philadelphia. With great pomp and circumstance, the statue was unveiled during the opening ceremony of the Pennsylvania Academy's new building at Broad and Cherry streets.[5] Although the statue was hailed by the Academy as a major new acquisition, the Philadelphia art critic William J. Clark found it unworthy of such distinction. In his book *Great American Sculptures*, published in 1878, Clark denigrated the sculpture: "There is a stiffness and a total lack of grace in the lines of the figure for which there is no reason and no excuse."[6] Twenty-six years later, the American sculptor and author Lorado Taft, adopting an even harsher tone, called Jerusalem "amateurish."[7] Yet, in general, the statue was admired, and it remained in the collection of the Pennsylvania Academy for eighty-five years.

In 1949 the Pennsylvania Academy formed a committee to evaluate its sculpture collection and recommend works for disposal. According to the Academy's president, John F. Lewis, "for reasons of lack of space, and also changed tastes, the Academy is willing and anxious to get rid of [Jerusalem], even though in its day it represented a cherished work of art and still has very considerable impact."[8] In December 1951, *Jerusalem in Her Desolation* was given to the Philadelphia Memorial Park, a cemetery in Frazer, Pennsylvania where it was installed outdoors.

By 1972 the Academy had realized that a major treasure and part of its history had been given away. Negotiations were initiated to retrieve the sculpture. Finally, in 1986 *Jerusalem in Her Desolation* was returned to the Pennsylvania Academy as a gift of Mr. and Mrs. Arthur Klein. Exposure to the elements had been extremely detrimental, and in 1992 the sculpture underwent extensive conservation.

Story made a slightly smaller version of *Jerusalem in Her Desolation* for his great patron, Count Palffy of Paris. It was carved in 1877 but dated 1879 (Ponce Art Museum, Puerto Rico).[9]

Notes

1. Nancy McClellan Grigg (Mrs. John Grigg) to James Claghorn, president of the PAFA, April 7, 1873, and Ward B. Haseltine to James Claghorn, May 22, 1873, PAFA object file.

2. James Jackson Jarves, *Art Thoughts: The Experiences and Observations of an American Amateur in Europe* (New York: Hurd and Houghton, 1869), p. 311.

3. London *Art-Journal* (August 1873), p. 255.

4. Quoted in Henry James, *William Wetmore Story and His Friends* (New York: Kennedy Galleries and Da Capo Press, 1969; reprint of original 1903 two-volume edition), vol. 2, p. 298.

5. London *Art-Journal* 2 (June 1876), p. 192.

6. Clark 1878, p. 93.

7. Taft 1903, p. 155.

8. John F. Lewis to Philip Klein, president of the Philadelphia Memorial Park, June 22, 1949, PAFA object file.

9. Jan Seidler Ramirez to Mary Mullen Cunningham, March 15, 1991, PAFA object file.

References

1878 William J. Clark, Jr., *Great American Sculptures*, Philadelphia: Gebbie and Barrie, p. 93. **1888** *Art Stationer* 1 (August), p. 40, frontispiece. **1897** Mary E. Phillips, *Reminiscences of William Wetmore Story*, Chicago and New York: Rand, McNally and Company, pp. 167–68, 182. **1903** Lorado Taft, *The History of American Sculpture*, New York: Macmillan Company, pp. 150, 155–56. **1976** *In This Academy*, Philadelphia: PAFA, pp. 33, 48, 49 (ill.).

Exhibited

1873 Holloway and Son's Gallery, London. **1876*** cat. no. 595.

Ex Collections

PAFA, 1873–1951; Philadelphia Memorial Park, Frazer, Pa., 1951–86.

Semiramis

1873
Marble
54½ x 34½ x 65½" (138.4 x 87.6 x 166.4 cm)
Pedestal: 27¾ x 34½ x 65½" (70.5 x 87.6 x 166.4 cm)
Signed on back of chair: WWS [monogram]/Roma 1873
Inscribed on front of plinth: SEMIRAMIS; and on side of plinth: STOREY [*sic*] Sc.
Gift of Mr. and Mrs. Jacob M. Kaplan, 1982.12

IN POPULAR CULTURE the historical Semiramis, an Assyrian queen who was Babylonian by birth and lived and reigned about 800 B.C., has been overshadowed by her mythical identity. A number of legends have become attached to her. During the late eighteenth and nineteenth centuries, the most widespread conception was based largely on Voltaire's 1748 play. In his dramatic tragedy *Semiramis*, the beautiful and ambitious queen of Babylon conspires with her lover, Assur, to poison her husband. Before he dies, the king beseeches a trusted friend to spirit away his young son, Ninias. For the next fifteen years, Semiramis rules Babylon with great skill; but, all the while, remorse for her crime and wretchedness at the loss of her son increase. Because she refuses to marry Assur and install him as king, he plots her downfall. To foil Assur, whom she now despises, Semiramis proposes to marry a brave young warrior who is really the son she believes to be dead. Ninias is warned against the incestuous liaison by his father's ghost, who demands that the son avenge him. Led by the ghost, Ninias enters his father's dark tomb and plunges his sword into a shadowy figure that he takes to be Assur but, in fact, is his own mother. Voltaire's play provided the basis for the 1822 opera *Semiramide* by Rossini. For many years, it was regarded as one of the composer's greatest achievements. William Wetmore Story undoubtedly saw a performance, possibly with his favorite diva, the Italian Adelaide Ristori, in the title role.

This legendary Semiramis has exactly the character that William Wetmore Story found compelling, the kind that he repeatedly selected for his idealized sculptures. He liked to portray figures caught in a maelstrom of conflicting emotions. He was especially attracted to females who exploited their sexual powers for personal gain or vengeance—such as Cleopatra, Delilah, Judith, and Medea.

Story's sculpture of Semiramis captures the still-proud queen seated on her throne as if contemplating the evil that she has done and her ultimate destiny. Her languid pose is somewhat awkward, and her legs are disconcertingly elongated. As usual, Story paid close attention to the details of the figure's physiognomy and costume. Semiramis's facial features are of the appropriate Semitic type, with a long nose and

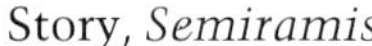
Story, *Semiramis*

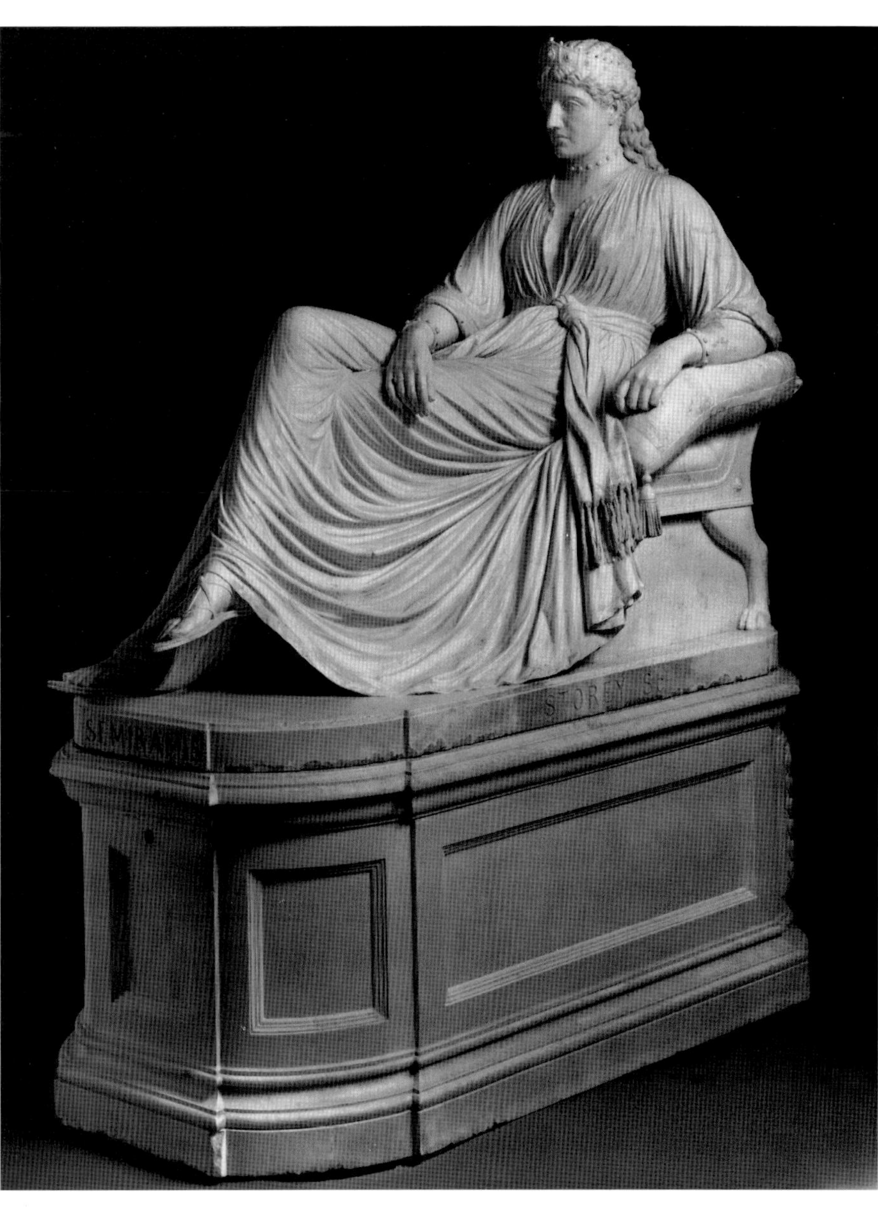

full lips. The Assyrians are known to have worn exquisite jewelry; and Semiramis is bedecked with bracelets, a necklace, and a jeweled diadem.

Story completed his clay model of *Semiramis* sometime in 1872; and, before the year was over, he had received two commissions for it in marble.[1] The statue belonging to the Museum of American Art of the Pennsylvania Academy of the Fine Arts was the first to be carved. It was ordered by Ernst Leopold Benzon, a shrewd German-American who had amassed a fortune in the mercantile trade in London. Benzon was a friend of Story and Robert Browning, both of whom he occasionally entertained at his country house near Pillochry, Scotland. In September 1873, not long after *Semiramis* had been delivered to London, Benzon died. Browning wrote to Story concerning the statue and its fate the following June: "I duly waited on the Semiramis and had every impression you could desire or expect of her grandeur and voluptuousness. I don't know what they intend to do with it. . . . I know . . . nothing at all, about the arrangements under poor Benzon's will."[2] Benzon's widow must have decided to sell the statue because, in July of 1874, it was on display at Holloway and Son's Gallery in London. The London *Art-Journal* reported that Benzon's death made the work "open to a purchaser," but whether one was found at that time is not known.[3] In any event, *Semiramis* remained in England until it was given to the Pennsylvania Academy in 1982.

Critical reaction to *Semiramis* seems to have been mixed. The London *Art-Journal* of 1874 described the statue as "dignified in attitude and regal in expression." According to the reviewer, the only fault with the work was one common to American sculptors—namely a tendency to multiply the number of folds in the drapery until the "grandeur of arrangement" is lost.[4] Unsurprisingly, Lorado Taft, a stickler for correct anatomy and proportion, disliked the statue. He saw the second version, owned by the New York entrepreneur and philanthropist William Blodgett when it was exhibited at the Metropolitan Museum of Art in New York late in the century.[5] Taft wrote that *Semiramis* "shows no trace of sculptural inspiration. It has neither grace nor power—scarcely, indeed, a definite pose."[6]

Because it had been displayed outdoors for years, the statue required conservation and restoration when it came to the Pennsylvania Academy. Numerous losses were replaced, including most of the nose, the front part of the crown, both thumbs, both big toes, and the front part of each sandal. These restorations were made on the basis of photographs of the second version of the sculpture.

Notes

1. Jan Seidler Ramirez to Mary Mullen Cunningham, March 15, 1991, PAFA object file.
2. Robert Browning to William Wetmore Story, June 9, 1874, quoted in Gertrude Reese Hudson, ed., *Browning to His American Friends* (New York: Barnes and Noble, 1965), p. 174.
3. London *Art-Journal* (July 1874), p. 223.
4. Ibid.
5. The second version was commissioned by William Blodgett, who also owned a copy of Story's *Medea.* According to Jan Seidler Ramirez (see n. 1), after the dispersal of Blodgett's collection during the latter part of the nineteenth century, this version of *Semiramis* dropped from sight. In the early 1980s, it was offered for sale by a Los Angeles art gallery and was bought by a private collector.
6. Lorado Taft, *The History of American Sculpture* (New York: Macmillan Company, 1903), p. 156.

Reference

1984 Linda Bantel, "William Wetmore Story's Semiramis," *A Growing American Treasure: Acquisitions since 1978,* Philadelphia: PAFA, p. 22.

Exhibited

1874 Holloway and Son's Gallery, London. **1986–87** PAFA, *Sculpture at the Pennsylvania Academy of the Fine Arts.*

Edward Sheffield Bartholomew

1822–1858

A member of the second generation of American sculptors to settle in Italy, Edward Sheffield Bartholomew became an ardent practitioner of mid-nineteenth-century neoclassicism. Born in Colchester, Connecticut, he was the eldest son of Sarah and Abial Lord Bartholomew. The family moved to Hartford when Edward was in his early teens. A difficult transition to a new home was compounded by his father's disapproval of his predilection for art. He was apprenticed to a dentist, Dr. William S. Crane, with whom he remained for about four years. Though uninclined towards dentistry, the skills he learned from Dr. Crane supported him while he studied art at the National Academy of Design in New York. After about a year in New York, Bartholomew returned to Hartford in 1845 to assume the position of curator of the newly built Wadsworth Athenaeum.

Shortly after his return to Hartford, Bartholomew discovered he was color-blind. He gave up painting and took up sculpture. James G. Batterson, a local marble cutter, supplied him with the necessary tools and taught him to carve marble. One of Bartholomew's earliest works is a marble bas-relief of Mrs. Lydia H. Sigourney, about 1845–48 (Wadsworth Athenaeum). She was a contemporary author whom Bartholomew greatly admired.

In 1848 Bartholomew returned to New York to study anatomy. During this stay, he contracted smallpox, which left him lame and sickly. Undaunted by poor health, he was determined to study in Italy. With financial help from Enoch Pratt, a Baltimore merchant and financier whom he had met some years earlier, Bartholomew sailed for Rome in 1850.[1] There, he studied under the then-renowned sculpture instructor Luigi Ferrari (1810–1894), who urged him to devote himself to bas-relief. Bartholomew accepted his advice; among the earliest pieces that he produced in Rome are marble relief portraits of two Baltimoreans: James Howard McHenry in the guise of the blind Homer and William George Read as Belisarius (1852 and 1853, respectively; both, Maryland Historical Society, Baltimore). The sculptor probably received these commissions through Enoch Pratt, who became an important patron. While visiting Rome in 1855, Pratt bought two ideal statues in marble, *Campaspe* and *Shepherd Boy,* for his new home (both undated, Peabody Institute of the Johns Hopkins University, Baltimore). Bartholomew's bust of Pratt, about 1855, is in the Enoch Pratt Free Library in Baltimore. By 1856 Bartholomew had numerous commissions, many of which were never completed —for he died in Naples in the spring of 1858.

The sculptor's best-known ideal work, *Eve Repentant,* was begun in 1858. A posthumous replica is in the Wadsworth Athenaeum. The original was purchased by Joseph Harrison, Jr., of Philadelphia. He received it in January 1859, after Bartholomew's death. Shortly thereafter, Harrison exhibited the statue at the Pennsylvania Academy of the Fine Arts. An admission fee was charged to view it in order to help Bartholomew's mother, who was in severe financial straits.[2]

Notes

1. Alexandra Lee Levin, "Enoch Pratt as Patron of Edward S. Bartholomew, Sculptor," *Maryland Historical Magazine* 51 (Dec. 1956), pp. 267–72.

2. Minutes, meeting of the board of directors, Jan. 24, 1859, PAFA Archives.

References

1858 "Masters of Art and Literature; Edward S. Bartholomew," *Cosmopolitan Art Journal* 2 (Sept.), pp. 184–85. **1866** Henry T. Tuckerman, "Two of our Sculptors: Akers and Bartholomew," *Hours at Home* 2 (April), pp. 530–32. **1896** Susan Underwood Crane, "Edward Sheffield Bartholomew," *Connecticut Quarterly* 2 (July-Sept.), pp. 202–14. **1956** Alexandra Lee Levin, "Enoch Pratt as Patron of Edward S. Bartholomew, *Maryland Historical Magazine* 51 (Dec.), pp. 267–72. **1962** William G. Wendell, "Edward Sheffield Bartholomew, Sculptor," *Wadsworth Atheneaum Bulletin,* pp. 1–18. **1970** Henry W. French, *Art and Artists in Connnecticut,* New York: Da Capo Press, pp. 112–18.

James L. Claghorn

About 1858
Marble
30 x 22 x 16" (76.2 x 55.9 x 40.6 cm)
Gift of Mrs. James L. Claghorn, 1884.3

DURING the mid-nineteenth century, portraiture was the "bread and butter" of many young sculptors. It provided them with both the means to support themselves and the chance to broaden their reputations so that they might be awarded commissions for idealized works. Because Edward Sheffield Bartholomew's career spanned only about a decade, a large part of his oeuvre consists of busts like this one of the native Philadelphian James Lawrence Claghorn (1817–1884). An important businessman and the president of the National Bank of Philadelphia, Claghorn must have been pleased with this dignified representation.[1] Bartholomew borrowed con-

Bartholomew, *James L. Claghorn*

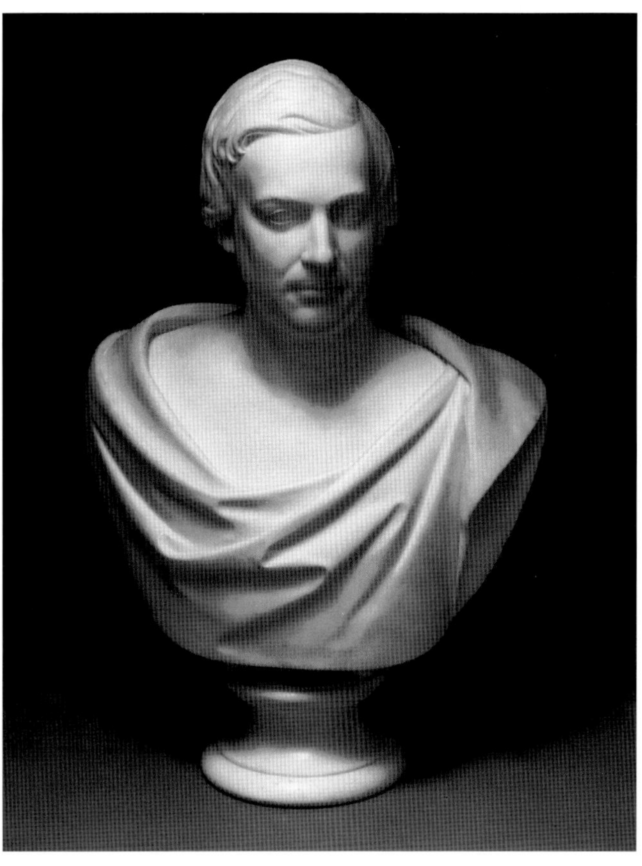

ventions from the neoclassical school, such as the smooth surface and the dead eye, to give the bust a noble and timeless quality. The sitter himself may have requested the toga, a neoclassical affectation still fairly popular at mid-century.

Claghorn was president of the board of directors of the Pennsylvania Academy of the Fine Arts from 1872 until his death. At various times, he also served as president of the Philadelphia School of Design for Women and treasurer of the Fairmount Park Art Association. An avid art collector, Claghorn exhibited his premier print collection at the Pennsylvania Academy during December 1874 and January 1875. The proceeds from the exhibition helped complete the Academy's Victorian building.[2]

Upon presenting her husband's bust to the Academy in 1884, Mrs. Claghorn noted that the portrait had been made about 1858.[3] If this date is correct, the commission was most likely received during Bartholomew's last visit to the United States in late 1857. He may not have had the opportunity to oversee its translation into marble because of his premature death in May of 1858.

Notes

1. James L. Claghorn, obituary, *New York Times*, August 27, 1884, p. 5.
2. *Exhibition of Prints (Claghorn Collection)* (Philadelphia: PAFA, 1875), exhib. cat., p. 38, PAFA Archives.
3. Minutes, meeting of the board of directors, Oct. 13, 1884, PAFA Archives.

Exhibited

1876* cat. no. 662.

Ex Collections

James L. Claghorn, about 1858–84; his wife, Julia, 1884.

William Morris Hunt

1824–1879

William Morris Hunt is remembered primarily as a painter—for portraits and landscapes and for helping to introduce the French Barbizon school of painting to the United States. He was born in Brattleboro, Vermont, to Jane Leavitt Hunt and Jonathan Hunt, a United States congressman. Two of William's siblings also exhibited artistic talent. Jane, the eldest, painted watercolors. A younger brother, Richard, became a renowned architect who designed Beaux-Arts-style mansions for American industrial tycoons.

When Hunt was eight years old, his father died and the family moved to New Haven, Connecticut. There, he took drawing lessons from a Sicilian artist named Spiridione Gambardella. After the family moved to Boston in 1828, Hunt studied modeling with the sculptor John Crookshanks King (1806–1882) and also learned to carve cameos. Cameo portraits of himself and his three brothers were made into a bracelet, now in the Museum of Fine Arts, Boston. In 1840 Hunt entered Harvard College, but his artistic and musical pursuits allowed him little time for traditional studies, and he was dismissed after his junior year.

During the fall of 1843, Hunt traveled through Europe with his family. In 1844 he was in Rome studying with the American sculptor Henry Kirke Brown (1814–1866), and the following year he attended the Düsseldorf Academy in Germany. He found the methods taught at Düsseldorf tedious; and, before a year had passed, he moved to Paris with the hope of studying under the sculptor James Pradier (1790–1852). Pradier's atelier was full, however, and Hunt enrolled in the painting classes of Thomas Couture, whose style and bold use of color he particularly admired. He also studied with Antoine Louis Barye (1796–1875), the well-known animal sculptor. Hunt modeled a medallion portrait of Thomas Couture in 1848 (Brooks Memorial Library, Brattleboro) and a study of horses (q.v.) for an allegorical theme that was finally realized in the painting *The Flight of Night*, 1879 (New York State Capitol, Albany, now obscured by a dropped ceiling). During this time, he decided to concentrate on painting rather than sculpture. Under the influence of François Millet, Hunt's paintings began to exhibit the rather blurred edges characteristic of the Barbizon painters.

Hunt returned to Boston in 1855 and married Louisa Dumaresque Perkins, a granddaughter of Thomas Handasyd Perkins, one of the city's wealthiest merchants. From 1856 to 1862, the couple resided in Newport, Rhode Island. Through his wife, Hunt formed important society connections and began to garner portrait commissions. With the outbreak of the Civil War, the Hunts moved to Boston. There, in the spring of 1868, Hunt began to teach a painting class for women. Helen Knowlton, one of his students, jotted down his remarks to the class. After much coaxing, Hunt edited these notes; and they were published in a volume entitled *Talks on Art*.

In 1878 Hunt was commissioned to paint two large murals in the Assembly Chamber of the New York State Capitol, in Albany. One was *The Flight of Night*; the other portrayed Christopher Columbus. The murals were completed within a year and were hailed as a success by the critics. (Unfortunately,

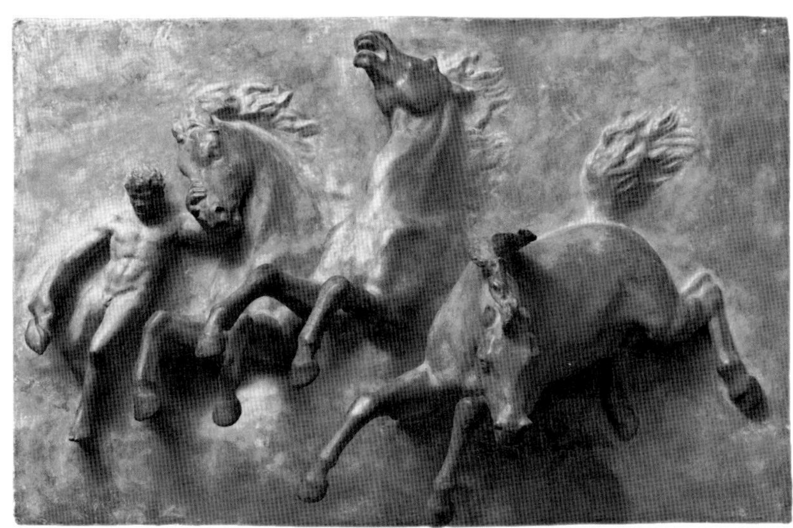
Hunt, *The Flight of Night*

within ten years, they were severely damaged by dampness, resulting from an improperly built vault.) The physical and emotional strain of creating the murals took a huge toll on Hunt. He stopped painting; and in September 1879, while visiting the writer Celia Thaxter at Appledore, Isle of Shoals, off the coast of New Hampshire, he drowned in a pond.

References

1899 Helen M. Knowlton, *Art-Life of William Morris Hunt*, Boston: Little, Brown and Company. **1923** Martha A.S. Shannon, *Boston Days of William Morris Hunt*, Boston: Marshall Jones Company. **1979** *William Morris Hunt: A Memorial Exhibition*, Boston: Museum of Fine Arts.

The Flight of Night (also called *Horses of Anahita*)

About 1848–50
Plaster, painted ochre, pink, and brown; cast about 1898
19½ x 29 x 11" (49.5 x 73.7 x 27.9 cm)
Stamped on bottom edge: COPYRIGHT/MAR 4, 1880/BY ESTATE/WILLIAM M. HUNT/L.D. HUNT. ADM X.
Caster's mark stamped on bottom edge: P.P CAPRONI & [BRO.] BOSTON [around perimeter of circular stamp]; PLASTIC/ARTS [inside circle]
Pennsylvania Academy purchase, 1898.11

In 1846, while William Morris Hunt was studying in Düsseldorf, a younger brother, Leavitt, sent him a translation of the sixth-century Persian poem *Anahita*. It describes the goddess of night, Anahita, and her flight from the coming dawn. The poem fascinated Hunt, and its conceptualization occupied him off and on for more than thirty years. Sadly, the culmination of his work on the theme, his 1879 mural *The Flight of Night* in the New York State Capitol, Albany, deteriorated miserably. Hunt painted the mural directly onto the wall, and excessive moisture from an improperly built vault caused the paint to peel. Today the ruined mural is hidden by a dropped ceiling.

According to Henry Angell, a Boston eye specialist and Hunt's close friend, the artist first put his image of Anahita on paper in 1847. An early sketch (about 1847–50), possibly the earliest surviving record of Hunt's work on the theme, belongs to the Institute of American Architects in Washington, D.C. The drawing depicts Anahita driving her three "night mares," led by an attendant who is just vaguely delineated. To the right of Anahita appear a mother and child, representing the positive aspects of night—sleep and repose. Except for some minor adjustments, Hunt's conception of the theme changed remarkably little over the many years that he worked on it.[1]

Hunt undoubtedly made this high relief to study the exact poses of the horses and their attendant, who, as a symbol of darkness, carries an inverted torch. Henry Adams pointed out that the relief shows considerable familiarity with French romantic sculpture and was probably executed during Hunt's early days in Paris while he studied with Antoine Louis Barye (1796–1875).[2]

Numerous plaster casts of this relief exist. They date from various periods and editions. Although it is not known whether Hunt had his original clay model cast into plaster while in Paris, this seems likely. In any case, an early plaster cast was lent by one of the artist's younger brothers, the architect Richard Morris Hunt, to an 1866 exhibition at the National Academy of Design, in New York.[3] It seems that Richard

Morris Hunt was especially fond of the relief and incorporated it into several of the homes he designed in Newport, Rhode Island.[4] Other plaster casts had probably been made by 1866. Hunt surely would have kept at least one in his possession. According to Hunt's student and biographer, Helen Knowlton, a relief of *The Flight of Night* (presumably a plaster cast but possibly the original clay model) was at a local caster's shop when fire destroyed Hunt's Boston studio in 1872. The relief thus escaped injury. Unfortunately, Knowlton does not mention the caster's name.[5] We do know, however, that after 1880 two Boston casting firms, P. Gariboldi and P.P. Caproni and Brother, made plaster casts of the relief.[6] The cast in the Museum of American Art of the Pennsylvania Academy of the Fine Arts was made by the latter firm and was purchased in 1898, probably to complement the Museum's recent acquisition of an 1878 oil-and-chalk sketch for the Albany mural.

Notes

1. For a chronology of Hunt's work on the theme, see Henry Adams, "The Development of William Morris Hunt's *The Flight of Night,*" *American Art Journal* 15 (Spring 1983), pp. 43–52.

2. Ibid., p. 47. Adams notes that the small scale and the style of Hunt's relief recall Barye's bronzes of horses. Paula M. Kozol, "William Morris Hunt," *American Figurative Sculpture in the Museum of Fine Arts, Boston* (Boston: Museum of Fine Arts, 1986), p. 140, points out that Hunt owned a cast of Barye's *Turkish Horse* at this time. Kozol suggests several other works that Hunt could have seen in Paris and that might have inspired him in his work on this relief. Among them is the stucco relief *Horses of the Sun,* attributed to Robert Le Lorrain (1666–1743), on the facade of the Hôtel de Rohan.

3. Kozol 1986, p. 140, has suggested that this may be the cast now owned by the Metropolitan Museum of Art, New York.

4. At least three homes designed by Richard Morris Hunt in Newport have casts of the relief. One is the Colonel George Waring House, now known as the Hypotenuse House. Cora Lee Gibbs to Mary Mullen Cunningham, March 16, 1989, PAFA research file.

5. Helen M. Knowlton, *Art-Life of William Morris Hunt* (Boston: Little, Brown and Company, 1899), p. 81.

6. A cast by P. Gariboldi is in the Isabella Stewart Gardner Museum, Boston.

Exhibited

1989 PAFA, *"The Birds and the Beasts Will Teach Us."*

Randolph Rogers

1825–1892

Randolph Rogers spent most of his career in Rome among other expatriate sculptors, including THOMAS CRAWFORD, Harriet Hosmer (1830–1908), WILLIAM HENRY RINEHART, and WILLIAM WETMORE STORY. Rogers was financially successful and enjoyed patronage from the wealthy Americans who frequented the artists's studios. His most popular works expressed the romance and pathos that Victorian audiences found so appealing.

Rogers was born in Waterloo, New York, to John and Sara McCarthy Rogers. Between 1829 and 1834, his father moved the family to Ann Arbor, Michigan, where Randolph spent the remainder of his childhood.[1] During his teens, he became particularly interested in woodcuts and wood engraving. Rogers moved to New York about 1847 to seek employment as an engraver. Unsuccessful in this attempt, he was hired as a dry-goods clerk by John Steward and Lycurgis Edgerton. When his employers discovered his talent for sculpture, they provided him with the funds to go to Italy. Rogers arrived in Florence in 1848 and began to study with the renowned neoclassical sculptor Lorenzo Bartolini (1777–1850) at the Academy of Saint Mark. He taught Rogers to model in clay and plaster and instilled in him a fondness for naturalism. After Bartolini's death, Rogers moved to Rome, where he established a studio in 1851.

Success came quickly. An ideal bust entitled *Night* was shown in New York at the National Academy of Design in 1852.[2] His first large-scale work portrayed an Old Testament theme, *Ruth Gleaning* (1853). It was extremely popular, and more than thirty replicas were produced by Rogers's studio.[3] Rogers drew his subjects from contemporary literature, the Bible, and mythology. *Nydia, the Blind Girl of Pompeii* (q.v.), about 1853, based on the heroine of Edward Bulwer-Lytton's novel *The Last Days of Pompeii,* was described in 1878 as "one of the most popular statues that has ever been executed by an American artist."[4] Like *Ruth Gleaning, Nydia* was replicated many times during Rogers's life.[5] Versions of both statues were exhibited in 1876 at the Centennial Exposition in Philadelphia.

In 1855, while on a brief trip to the United States, Rogers sought and received the commission for the great bronze doors at the eastern entrance to the rotunda of the Capitol. He portrayed Columbus's discovery of America in an elaborate design based on Lorenzo Ghiberti's (1381–1455) Gates of Paradise

(1425–52) for the Florence Baptistry. Rogers returned to Rome in late 1855 to continue work on the doors. They were sent to Munich for casting in 1861 and installed in the Capitol in 1862.

In 1857, in the midst of his work on the doors for the Capitol, Rogers was asked by Governor Henry Alexander Wise of Virginia to complete Virginia's Washington Monument, a project of the recently deceased Thomas Crawford. Rogers executed the statues of Thomas Nelson and Meriwether Lewis. He also altered Crawford's design by adding six seated allegorical figures. Throughout his career, Rogers received many public commissions for commemorative and funerary monuments. Among his most notable memorial portraits is the marble statue of John Adams, 1854–59, made for Mount Auburn Cemetery in Cambridge, Massachusetts. Following Abraham Lincoln's death in 1865, Rogers was commissioned by the city of Philadelphia to create a monument. The bronze statue of Lincoln seated, holding a pen in one hand and the Emancipation Proclamation in the other, was placed near Lemon Hill in Fairmount Park in 1871. Two years later, Rogers used a similar design in his bronze commemorative statue of William Henry Seward for New York. Seward had served as governor of New York from 1837 to 1842 and as secretary of state under two presidents, Lincoln and Johnson. Rogers's most important tomb monument was the *Angel of Resurrection*, 1862, for the Samuel Colt Memorial at Cedar Hill Cemetery in Hartford, Connecticut.

Rogers executed several war memorials, including *The Sentinel*, 1863, in Cincinnati; Soldiers National Monument, 1865–69, for Gettysburg National Park; the Michigan Soldiers and Sailors Monument, 1867–72, in Detroit; and the Worcester Civil Monument, 1871–74, in Massachusetts.

In 1874 Rogers created his last work based on a mythological subject—*The Lost Pleiad* (Art Institute of Chicago). He also was commissioned to make a bronze Victory-type figure entitled *The Genius of Connecticut* for the Connecticut State Capitol. It adorned the dome of the building until 1938.

During his lifetime, Rogers was awarded many honors. In 1873 in Rome, he became the first American to be elected an academician of the Academy of Saint Luke, where he was professor of sculpture.[6] He was also knighted in 1884 by King Umberto I in honor of his achievements as an American sculptor in Italy.[7]

Randolph Rogers possessed a keen business sense. Beginning in 1867, he kept a detailed journal in which he recorded his commissions and accounts. The journal is now part of the University of Michigan Historical Collections in Ann Arbor. Rogers donated all his plaster casts to the University of Michigan in 1885.[8] Only three are still in existence.

Notes

1. Researched and written with major contribution by Audrey Lewis, 1988 Museum intern. M.F. Rogers 1971, p. 10.
2. *Dictionary of American Biography,* s.v. "Rogers, Randolph."
3. Wayne Craven, *Sculpture in America* (Newark: University of Delaware Press, 1984), p. 313.
4. William J. Clark, Jr., *Great American Sculptures* (Philadelphia: Gebbie and Barrie, 1878), p. 75.
5. Rogers himself probably never learned to carve in marble. He employed numerous marble carvers.
6. M.F. Rogers 1971, pp. 134–35.
7. Ibid., p. 149.
8. Ibid., p. 155.

References

1910 Elihu Vedder, *The Digressions of V,* New York: Houghton Mifflin Company, pp. 329–30, 375–76. **1927** Charles Fairman, *Art and Artists of the Capitol of the United States of America,* Washington, D.C.: U.S. Government Printing Office, pp. 153–57, 478–79. **1971** Millard F. Rogers, Jr., *Randolph Rogers, American Sculptor in Rome,* Amherst: University of Massachusetts Press. **1973** William H. Gerdts, *American Neo-Classic Sculpture: The Marble Resurrection,* New York: Viking Press, pp. 34–35, 86, 120–21.

Nydia, the Blind Girl of Pompeii

About 1853
Marble
54¼ x 25½ x 35" (138.2 x 64.8 x 88.9 cm)
Signed on side of plinth near capital: Randolph Rogers,/ Rome.
Gift of Mrs. Bloomfield Moore, 1895.5

Nydia, the Blind Girl of Pompeii was inspired by a character in Edward Bulwer-Lytton's popular 1834 novel *The Last Days of Pompeii.* Randolph Rogers chose to portray her as she escapes from the erupting Mount Vesuvius and searches for her lost companions, including the man she loves. Her courage is described by Bulwer-Lytton:

> Guiding her steps, then, by the staff which she always carried, she continued, with incredible dexterity, to avoid the masses of ruin that encumbered the path. . . . Weak, exposed, yet fearless, supported by but one wish, she was a very emblem of Psyche in her wanderings; of Hope, walking through the Valley of the Shadow; of the Soul itself—lone but undaunted amidst the dangers and the snares of life![1]

Rogers's sculpture captured the qualities of purity and bravery that so appealed to the Victorian public.

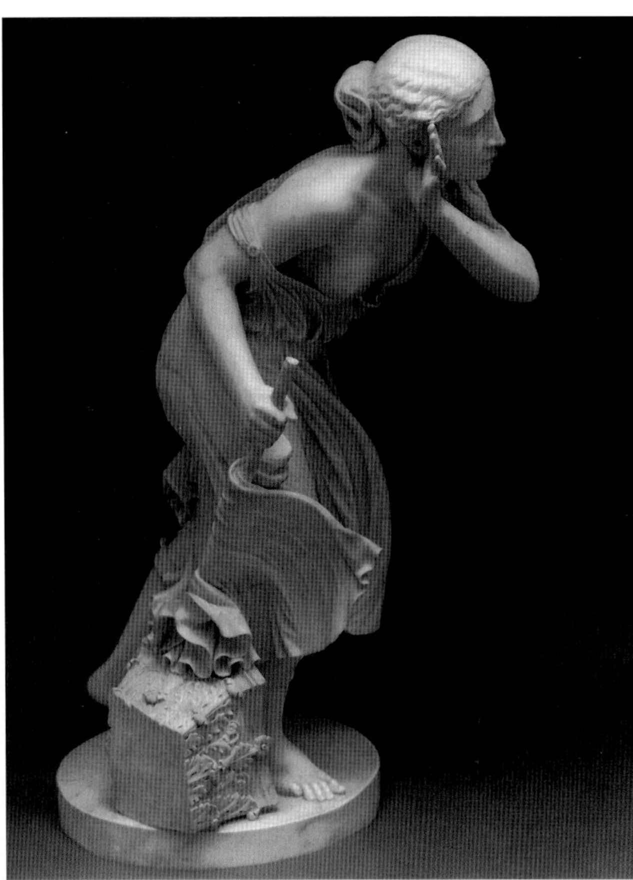

Rogers, *Nydia, the Blind Girl of Pompeii*

The face is sweet and has softly rounded, idealized features. The dramatic vitality of the swirling drapery has invited comparisons with the Hellenistic Greek sculpture *Old Market Woman* (Metropolitan Museum of Art, New York), as well as with the work of the Italian baroque master Gian Lorenzo Bernini (1598–1680). Rogers wrote that *Nydia* was an expensive piece to carve because of the deep undercutting of the drapery.[2]

Rogers's wife stated in an unpublished biography of her husband that *Nydia* was commissioned by J.D. Bates of Boston.[3] No commission has been documented elsewhere, however, including the Bates collection. In any event, Rogers produced numerous versions. A visitor to his Roman studio in 1866 recorded in her diary that the sculptor had put twenty-five Nydias into marble.[4] Rogers's own journal lists fifty-two orders for the statue between 1867 and 1888.[5] This frequent replication was viewed with humor by some of Rogers's contemporaries; an American visitor to his studio recalled seeing "seven Nydias, all in a row, all listening, all groping, and seven Italian marble-cutters at work cutting them out. It was a gruesome sight."[6] Replicas of *Nydia* reside in many museums across the United States, including the Metropolitan Museum of Art, New York; Museum of Fine Arts, Boston; the Detroit Institute of Arts; and the National Museum of American History, Washington, D.C.

This version was owned by Mr. and Mrs. Bloomfield Moore, who lived in a Frank Furness-designed mansion on Broad Street in Philadelphia.[7]

Notes

1. Edward G.E. Bulwer-Lytton, *The Last Days of Pompeii* (New York: Dodd, Mead and Company, reprinted in 1946), p. 348.
2. Randolph Rogers to Henry S. Frieze, April 3, 1859, Michigan Historical Collections at the University of Michigan, Ann Arbor. Quoted in Millard F. Rogers, Jr., *Randolph Rogers, American Sculptor in Rome* (Amherst: University of Massachusetts Press, 1971), p. 39.
3. Rosa Gibson Rogers, *Biography of Randolph Rogers*, unpubl. MS in Michigan Historical Collections at the University of Michigan. Quoted in M.F. Rogers 1971, pp. 37–38.
4. Frances W. Dunn, diary, Jan. 23, 1866, Michigan Historical Collections at the University of Michigan. Quoted in M.F. Rogers 1971, p. 96.
5. M.F. Rogers 1971, pp. 200–4.
6. D.M. Armstrong, *Day Before Yesterday* (New York: Charles Scribner's Sons, 1920), p. 195.
7. The interior of their home with *Nydia* displayed in the entrance hall, is illustrated in *Artistic Houses*, New York: D. Appleton and Co., vol. 1, 1883, p. 153.

Reference

1993 Joyce K. Schiller, "Nydia: A Forgotten Icon of the Nineteenth Century," *Bulletin of the Detroit Institute of Arts*, vol. 67, no. 4, pp. 36–45.

Exhibited

1962 PAFA, *Forgotten Favorites: Selections From the Permanent Collection.* **1976** Whitney Museum of American Art, New York, *200 Years of American Sculpture*, cat. no. 50. **1986–87** PAFA, *Sculpture at the Pennsylvania Academy of the Fine Arts.*

Abraham Lincoln

About 1866
Marble
27 x 21 x 13½" (68.6 x 53.3 x 34.2 cm)
Gift of Richard D. Wood, 1866.1

After Abraham Lincoln (1809–1865) was assassinated, there arose a great national desire to perpetuate the memory of the fallen president. Paintings, monuments, and portrait busts were commissioned by civic groups and private individuals. No formal record exists of the commission for this bust, but it is believed to have been created in 1866 for Richard D. Wood, of Philadelphia. No additional replicas are known to exist. Rogers gave a plaster version, possibly the model for this marble, to the University of Michigan in 1886; but it no longer survives.

Philadelphia was one of the first cities to initiate a subscription campaign for a Lincoln monument and, by 1866, had raised $22,000.[1] A committee on design, headed by Charles Janeway Stille, may have known about this marble bust when, in mid-December 1866, it invited Rogers to compete for the commission. In any case, when Rogers sent several designs to Stille in March of 1867, he suggested that the committee might want to look at the bust belonging to Wood.[2] Rogers was apparently unaware that Wood had donated the bust to the Pennsylvania Academy of the Fine Arts on December 27, 1866.[3] The sculptor seems to have made use of a version of this bust in creating the likeness for the proposed monument. On January 22, 1868, he sent another design to Stille, again asked the committee to look at the bust, and added that "it is said to be very good but I now feel certain I can improve upon it."[4]

Rogers may have used photographs or daguerreotypes in creating the likeness. He may have obtained a cast of the life mask of Lincoln made by LEONARD VOLK in 1860.[5] Other works that Rogers may have known include a bust of Lincoln made in 1861 by Thomas Dow Jones (1811–1891) and painted portraits made in 1864 by William E. Marshall and Francis B. Carpenter.

Rogers, *Abraham Lincoln*

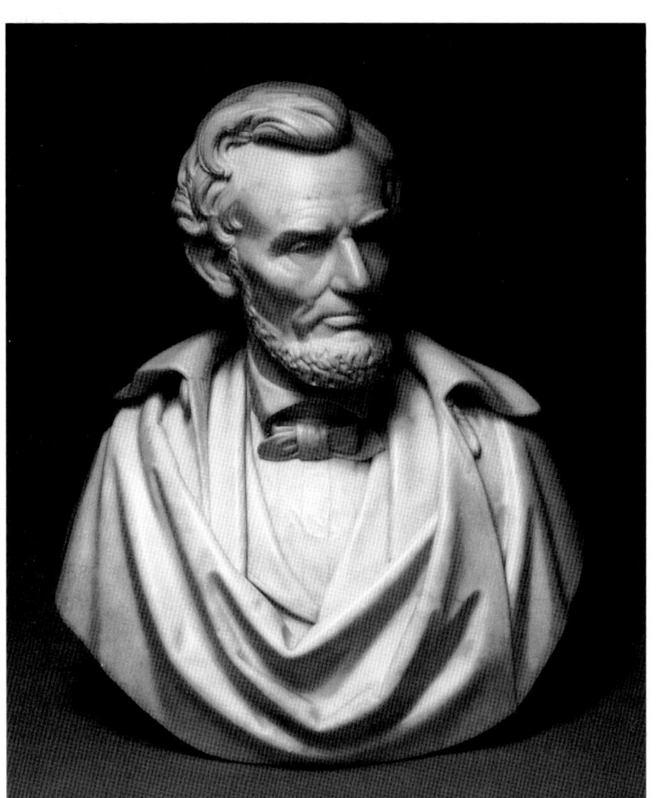

Notes

1. Wayne Craven, "Abraham Lincoln," in Wainwright 1974, p. 46.
2. Randolph Rogers to Charles Janeway Stille, March 25, 1867, Charles Janeway Stille Papers, Historical Society of Pennsylvania, Philadelphia: "I must beg of the Committee not to look upon these hasty sketches as perfect likenesses of Mr. Lincoln. I had only time to give an idea of him. . . . Mr. R.D. Wood of Philadelphia has a bust by me of Mr. Lincoln which is said to be good. I wish you would examine it."
3. Miscellaneous Records, 1864–76, p. 18, PAFA Archives. The formal acceptance of the bust is recorded in Minutes, meeting of the board of directors, Jan. 14, 1867, PAFA Archives.
4. Randolph Rogers to Charles Janeway Stille, Jan. 22, 1868, Charles Janeway Stille Papers, Historical Society of Pennsylvania.
5. Wayne Craven, "Abraham Lincoln," in Wainwright 1974, p. 50.

References

1971 Millard F. Rogers, Jr., *Randolph Rogers: American Sculptor in Rome,* Amherst: University of Massachusetts Press, p. 102 (ill.). **1974** Nicholas B. Wainwright, ed., *Sculpture of a City: Philadelphia Treasures in Bronze and Stone,* New York: Walker Publishing Company, p. 345.

Exhibited

1867* cat. no. 313. **1868*** cat. no. 384. **1869*** cat. no. 295. **1978–79** PAFA, *350 Masterpieces of American Art.* **1986–87** PAFA, *Sculpture at the Pennsylvania Academy of the Fine Arts.* **1994–96** PAFA, *Two Centuries of Collecting at the Museum of American Art.*

Joseph A. Bailly

1825–1883

Born in Paris, Joseph Alexis Bailly was the son of Joseph Philidor Bailly, a furniture manufacturer. The young Bailly studied at the French Institute and worked in his father's factory. During the revolution of 1848, he was sympathetic to the rebels. Conscripted into the French army, he was forced to flee for his life after he shot at the captain of his regiment. Bailly found sanctuary in England and studied briefly with Edward Hodges Baily (1788–1867), a member of the Royal Academy and a participant in the sculptural decoration of the facade of Buckingham Palace.

Joseph Bailly soon came to America, initially to New Orleans. Following sojourns in New York, Philadelphia, and Buenos Aires, he settled in Philadelphia in 1850. He opened a wood-carving shop and quickly gained a local reputation for portraits and decorative items, including wood carvings, wax carvings, and cameos.[1] Bailly then worked briefly in the shop of the German-born cabinetmaker Gottlieb Vollmer before opening a sculpture studio in 1854 with Charles Bushor (originally spelled Buschor, 1823–1885).[2] Between 1855 and 1857, Bushor and Bailly were occupied with two large commissions. For the Grand Lodge of the Freemasons, they carved furniture and eight female figures personifying the Masonic virtues.[3] They also carved the ornament for Philadelphia's new Academy of Music. Bushor and Bailly's shop was located at 47 South Eighth Street, a four-story building elaborately adorned with carvings and statues. A contemporary advertisement for their establishment tells of an attached drawing school.[4]

Between 1851 and 1878, Bailly showed numerous works in wood, wax, plaster, marble, and bronze at the Pennsylvania Academy of the Fine Arts. From 1851 to 1868, he participated in each annual exhibition except the three from 1855 to 1857, when he was occupied with the Masonic and Academy of Music commissions. Bailly exhibited seven works in 1876 when, after a five-year hiatus, the Academy resumed the annual exhibitions in its new building at Broad and Cherry streets. He was represented by three works in the 1878 annual; and in 1884, a year after his death, one of his portraits was included in the fifty-fifth annual exhibition.

Bailly was elected an associate of the Pennsylvania Academy in 1859 and was made an academician the following year. In the early 1860s he began to teach voluntarily in the Academy School. By this time, he was quite successful and had many commissions. During the 1860s and 1870s, he executed a number of funerary monuments, including those of General Francis E. Paterson, about 1868; William E. Cresson, 1869; and William F. Hughes, 1870 (all in Laurel Hill Cemetery, Philadelphia). Bailly's *Aurora,* shown at the Centennial Exposition in Philadelphia, was called "a piece of magic . . . a powerful stimulant of our wonder" by the critic Edward Strahan.[5] Also at the exposition, displayed in the rotunda of Memorial Hall, was his equestrian statue of President Guzman Blanco, part of a large commission that Bailly had received from the Venezuelan government. Strahan's review of the centennial noted that, if one stood at the corner of Sixth and Chestnut streets, it was possible to see three of Bailly's works: the marble *George Washington* in front of Independence Hall, the bronze *Benjamin Franklin* on the corner of the Ledger Building, and the horses supporting the escutcheon on the Ledger Building.[6]

In the fall of 1876, the Pennsylvania Academy offered a class in clay modeling for the first time and engaged Joseph Bailly as instructor.[7] Initially, Bailly's students worked from both live models and antique casts; but, during the 1877–78 term, lack of funds prohibited the hiring of models and enrollment dropped dramatically.[8] For the 1878–79 year, the Academy's directors decided to appropriate funds for models for the class but not for Bailly's salary. The class continued that year without official instruction, although THOMAS EAKINS offered criticism on occasion.[9]

Notes

1. According to Abigail Schade, "Joseph A. Bailly (1825–1883)," in *Philadelphia: Three Centuries of American Art* (Philadelphia: Philadelphia Museum of Art, 1976), p. 383, Bailly won first prize in 1852 for an oak carving in the Franklin Institute's annual exhibition. This may be the same carving that Bailly showed in the PAFA's 1852 annual exhibition: *Bouquet,* cat. no. 427, carved from one piece of American oak.

2. Schade 1976, p. 353.

3. Henry Houston Hawley, *Charles Buschor: Designer and Manufacturer of Furniture and Interior Decorations,* master's thesis, University of Delaware, June 1960, p. 6. (A typescript is in The Masonic Library and Museum of Pennsylvania, Philadelphia.)

4. Carl W. Dreppard, *Victoriana; The Cinderella of Antiques* (Garden City: Doubleday, 1950), p. 207.

5. Edward Strahan, *The Art Gallery of the Exhibition, a Selection from the Paintings and Sculpture* (Philadelphia: Gebbie and Barrie, 1877), p. 58.

6. Ibid., pp. 56, 58. Bailly's marble *George Washington* was moved inside City Hall and a bronze replica erected in its place. See "Plaque is stolen in City Hall from Statue of Washington," *Philadelphia Evening Bulletin,* Nov. 19, 1948.

7. Minutes, meeting of the board of directors, Dec. 13, 1875, PAFA Archives.

8. Average attendance reports, 1876–77, in minutes, meeting of the committee on instruction, 1856–80; minutes, meeting of the board of directors, Oct. 8, 1877, PAFA Archives.

9. Minutes, meeting of the board of directors, June 10, 1878; Fairman Rogers to George Corliss, Oct. 7, 1878, PAFA Archives.

References

1878 William J. Clark, Jr., *Great American Sculptures,* Philadelphia: Gebbie and Barrie, pp. 104–5. **1964** *Dictionary of American Biography,* s.v. "Bailly, Joseph A."

Unidentified Child

1860s
Marble
15 x 11¾ x 6¾" (38.1 x 32.3 x 17.1 cm)
Signed on back of base: JABailly [initials in monogram]
Gift of Mrs. Daniel Stillwell Ewing, 1932.3

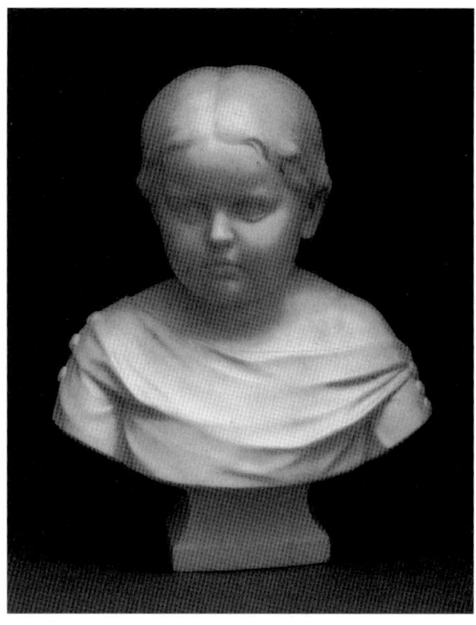

Bailly, *Unidentified Child*

JOSEPH A. BAILLY did a considerable business in portraiture and must have experimented a good deal with various methods of truncating and draping busts. The buttoned tunic slipping off the child's left shoulder gives this charming portrait a spontaneous and playful quality. In its unpretentiousness the bust resembles contemporary genre sculpture.

A facile worker, Bailly was skilled not only in marble but also in wood and bronze. His subject matter ran the gamut from flower bouquets to animal sculpture to idealized allegorical figures.

Exhibited
1986–87 PAFA, *Sculpture at the Pennsylvania Academy of the Fine Arts.*

Paradise Lost

1863–68
Marble
61 x 37½ x 42″ (155 x 94 x 106.8 cm)
Signed on back: *J.ABailly* [initials in monogram]
Bequest of Henry C. Gibson, 1892.6.2

DURING the 1860s and 1870s, Joseph A. Bailly was the most renowned sculptor in Philadelphia. As such, he was compelled to model idealized subjects because they were considered the greatest sculptural challenge of his day. *Paradise Lost,* which takes its title from Milton's epic poem, represents the dejected Adam and Eve after being banished from Paradise. Thus it was also known as *The Expulsion.* Although Bailly's handling of the theme appears overly sentimental to the modern viewer, its obvious religious and moral narrative is precisely what appealed to Victorian Americans. The figures are quite sensuous, but Bailly concealed enough of their nudity to keep them within the range of Victorian acceptability. Instead of the typical fig leaf, a piece of fur is draped across Adam's loins, thus recalling Genesis 3:21 wherein God clothes the couple in "coats of skins" before sending them away from Eden.

In 1863 Bailly showed a small plaster model of *Paradise Lost* in the fortieth annual exhibition of the Pennsylvania Academy of the Fine Arts. The following year, he entered full-size plasters of both *Paradise Lost* and its companion piece, *First Prayer* (q.v.), in the annual exhibition. Probably in hope of finding a patron to commission marbles of the pair, Bailly left the plasters on view at the Pennsylvania Academy throughout 1864. Henry Clay Gibson, a wealthy

Bailly, *Paradise Lost*

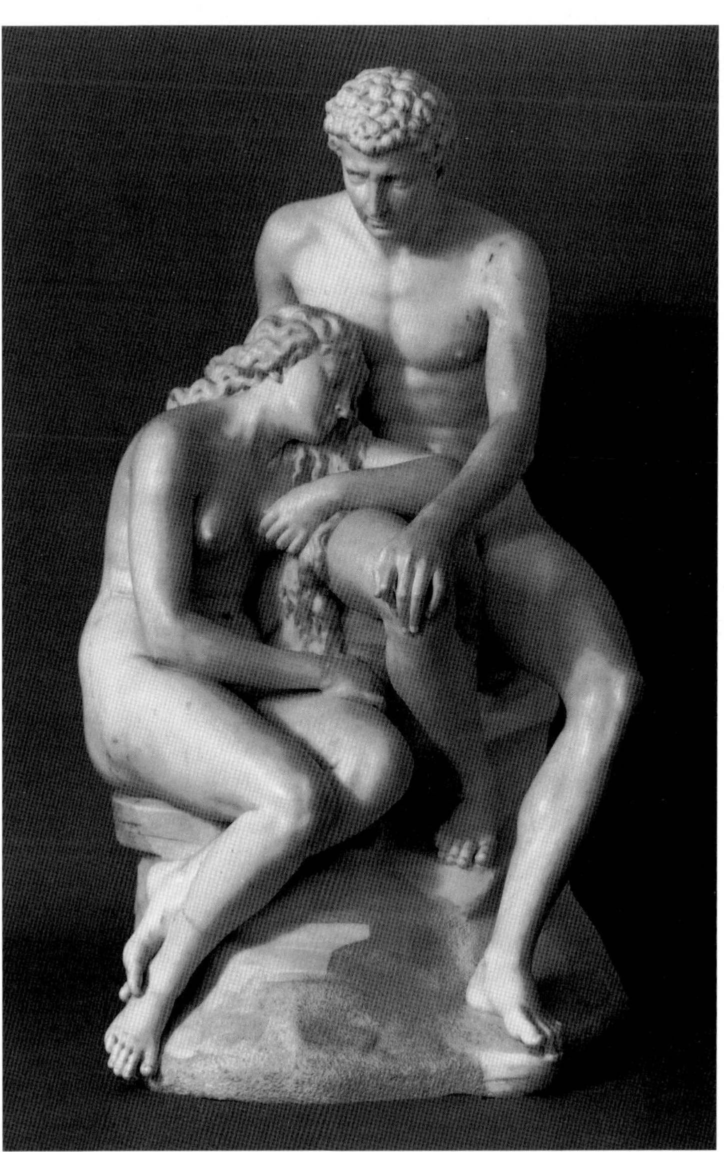

Philadelphia art collector, may have seen them there and decided then to offer Bailly the commission.

In January 1865, the two plaster statues were sent to New York; but the purpose is unclear.[1] They may have been sent for exhibition. On the other hand, Bailly, although an adept carver himself, may have hired a New York craftsman to translate them into marble. In any event, the marbles were completed by 1868, when they went on view at the Pennsylvania Academy, courtesy of their owner, Henry C. Gibson. The statues were moved in 1871 to Gibson's new home, designed and built by Frank Furness and George C. Hewitt at 1612 Walnut Street. Gibson had Bailly's two sculptures installed in the dining room, where they flanked Auguste Friedric Albrecht Schenck's painting *The Last Hour.*[2]

Bailly, *First Prayer*

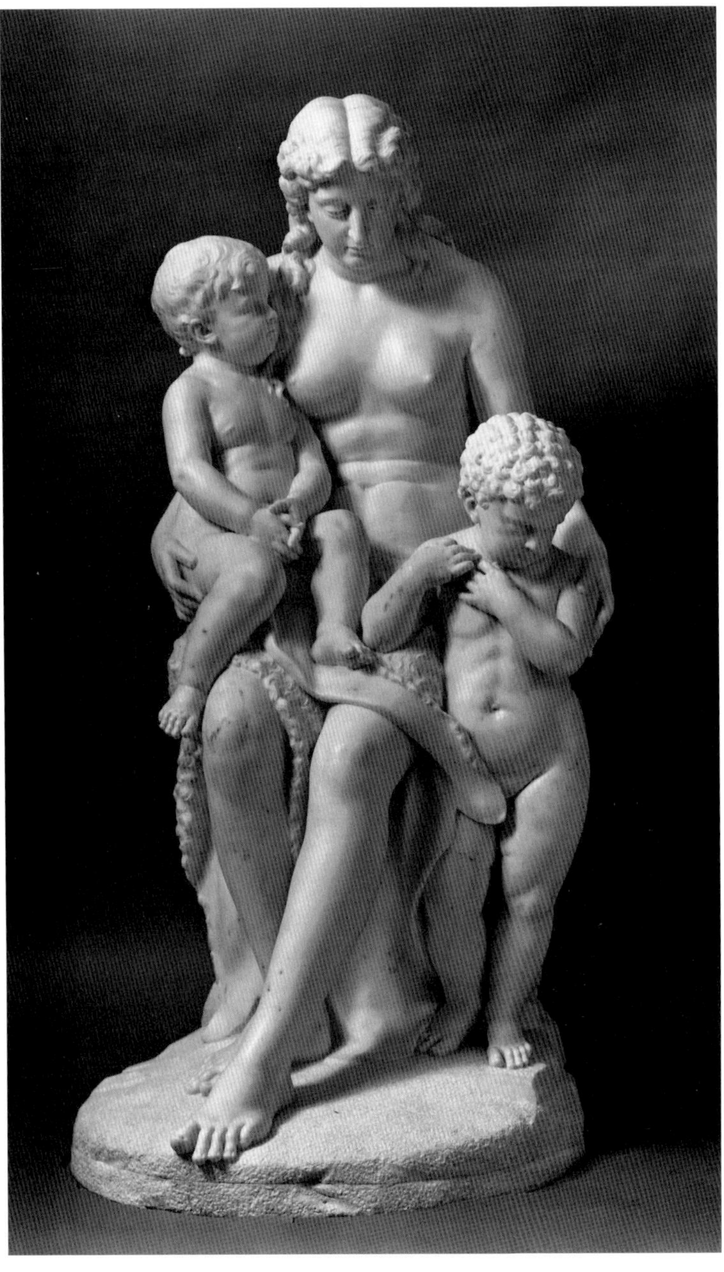

Notes

1. Chronology of Henry Clay Gibson, filed under "Beneficient Connoisseurs Exhibition: Gibson," Curator's file, PAFA Archives.

2. Photograph, PAFA Archives.

References

1973 William H. Gerdts, *American Neo-Classic Sculpture: The Marble Resurrection,* New York: Viking Press, no. 126, pp. 116–17 (ill.). **1975** David Sellin, "The First Pose: Howard Roberts, Thomas Eakins and a Century of Philadelphia Nudes," *Bulletin, Philadelphia Museum of Art* 70 (Spring), p. 11 (ill.). **1976** Wayne Craven, "Images of a Nation in Wood, Marble and Bronze," in *200 Years of American Sculpture,* New York: David R. Godine in association with the Whitney Museum of American Art, pp. 42 (ill.), 44.

Exhibited

1972 PAFA, *Acres of Art,* cat. no. 6. **1973** PAFA, *Held in Trust, One Hundred Sixty-Six Years of Gifts to the Pennsylvania Academy of the Fine Arts,* cat. no. 41. **1974** PAFA, *The Beneficent Connoisseurs (Gibson Collection),* cat. no. 2. **1976** Philadelphia Museum of Art, *Philadelphia: Three Centuries of American Art,* cat. no. 330 (ill.). **1978–79** PAFA, *350 Masterpieces of American Art: 1720–1978.* **1984–85** PAFA, *A Growing American Treasure: Recent Acquisitions and Highlights from the Permanent Collection.* **1986–87** PAFA, *Sculpture at the Pennsylvania Academy of the Fine Arts.*

Ex Collection

Henry C. Gibson, 1868–92.

First Prayer

1864–68
Marble
57½ x 29 x 33" (146 x 73.7 x 83.8 cm)
Signed on back: *J.ABailly.* [initials in monogram]
Bequest of Henry C. Gibson, 1892.6.6

THIS COMPANION to *Paradise Lost* (q.v.) represents Eve with her children Cain and Abel. In both sculptures, the depiction of Eve is based on the same model, who had distinctly classical features. Here she bows her head as if trying to impart her knowledge of the power of God to her small children.

The highly polished marble and the intricate patterns of the hair, fleece, and rock are typical of marble sculpture of the mid-nineteenth century. Following a technique popularized by JEAN ANTOINE HOUDON, the sculptor retained a speck of marble in the eyes of the figures in order to give them a lifelike sparkle.

References

1976 Wayne Craven, "Images of a Nation in Wood, Marble and Bronze," in *200 Years of American Sculpture,* New York: David R. Godine in association with the Whitney Museum of American Art, pp. 42 (ill.), 43. **1982** Linda

Bantel, "Sculpture at the Pennsylvania Academy," *Antiques* 121 (March), p. 709, fig. 6.

Exhibited
1974 PAFA, *The Beneficient Connoisseurs (Gibson Collection)*, cat. no. 3. **1984–85** PAFA, *A Growing American Treasure: Recent Acquisitions and Highlights from the Permanent Collection.* **1986–87** PAFA, *Sculpture at the Pennsylvania Academy of the Fine Arts.*

Ex Collection
Henry C. Gibson, 1868–92.

Abraham Lincoln

1865
Metal alloy
10 x 6½ x 4¾" (25.4 x 16.5 x 12.1 cm)
Signed at center back: JABailly [initials in monogram]
Inscribed at back of left shoulder: Patent; at back of right shoulder: May/1865.; at center back in arc: [W]ARNER MISK[E]Y MERRILL PHILA
Gift of Warner M. Merrill, 1944.14

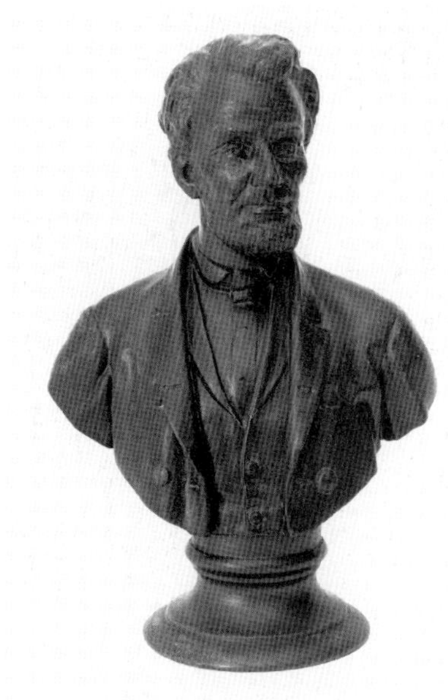

Bailly, *Abraham Lincoln*

A NUMBER of sculptures of Abraham Lincoln (1809–1865) were patented by various artists in 1865. There were at least eight busts, three medallions, one monument, and one statuette.[1] Joseph A. Bailly patented this cabinet-size bust a month after the president's assassination. Patinated like bronze, it is composed of a lightweight metal alloy that is much less expensive than bronze and more durable than plaster. Bailly obviously hoped to sell many of these busts to an American public mourning the death of one of its greatest heroes. A commercial production rather than a serious study of character or sculptural form, this bust is not unusual in Bailly's oeuvre. Lorado Taft observed that he did a "considerable business in portraits and clever specimens of commercial art."[2]

Bailly produced other historical portraits, which, like this one, were cast in editions. At the Great Logan Square Fair, in Philadelphia in 1864, he donated six portrait busts of General Ulysses S. Grant and six busts of General George Gordon Meade to be sold for the benefit of the United States Sanitary Commission, which was in charge of medical services on the battlefield.[3]

In the forty-second annual exhibition of the Pennsylvania Academy of the Fine Arts, in 1865, Bailly offered for sale a statuette of Abraham Lincoln that may have been this image. If so, Bailly most likely began work on the bust before Lincoln's death, which occurred just ten days before the opening of the exhibition.

Notes

1. Albert TenEyck Gardner, *Yankee Stonecutters: The First School of Sculpture, 1800–1850* (New York: Columbia University Press, 1945), p. 53.
2. Lorado Taft, *The History of American Sculpture* (New York: Macmillan Company, 1903), p. 505.
3. *Catalogue of Paintings, Drawings, Statuary, Etc., of the Art Department in the Great Central Fair Held in Logan Square, June, 1864, for the Benefit of the U.S. Sanitary Commission* (Philadelphia: 1864), p. 25.

William Emlen Cresson

1866
Plaster, painted to resemble terracotta
21⅛ x 17½ x 4½" (53.6 x 44.5 x 11.4 cm)
Signed and dated on front at lower left: J.ABailly. 1866. [initials in monogram]
Bequest of Priscilla P. Cresson, 1902.1.1

JOSEPH A. BAILLY'S terracotta-colored plaster relief of William Emlen Cresson (1843–1868) at the age twenty-three hints at the sculptor's experience in carving cameos and furniture. The volute and acanthus ornament that frames the lower portion of the bust recalls carved decorations on Victorian furniture. Bailly produced relief sculptures throughout his career. Between the years 1858 and 1868, he showed six of them in the annual exhibitions of the Pennsylvania Academy of the Fine Arts.

The painter William Emlen Cresson was a child prodigy who, at the age of eleven, had a painting accepted for the Pennsylvania Academy's thirty-first annual exhibition. In 1860 he was a classmate of Mary Cassatt in the Academy's antique class;[1] and

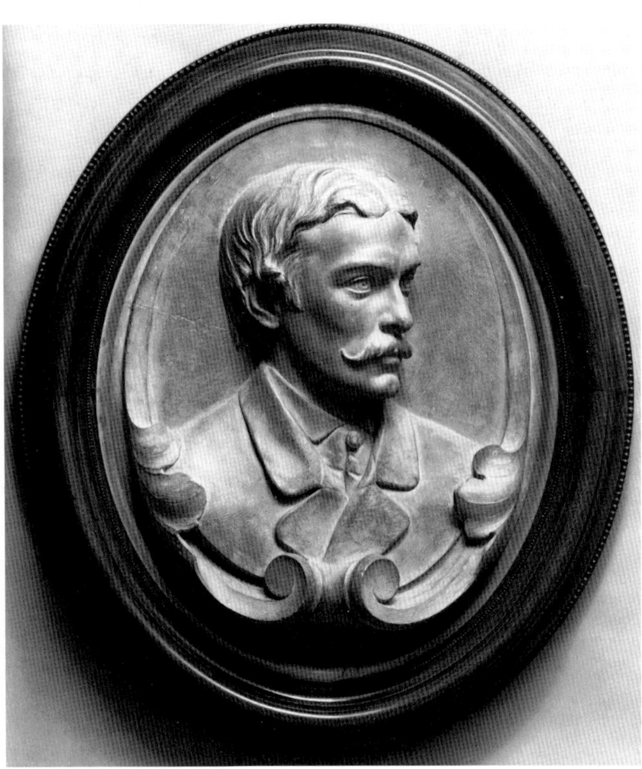

Bailly, *William Emlen Cresson*

he later participated in the annual exhibitions of 1865, 1867, and 1868. Six of his paintings remain in the Academy's collection. Elected an academician in 1867, Cresson died the following year at the age of twenty-five.

Emlen and Priscilla Cresson, William's parents, were prominent Philadelphia Quakers who were very much interested in the arts. After their son's death, they established a trust fund, the income from which was to be used for European travel scholarships for meritorious Pennsylvania Academy students. The first Cresson scholarship was given in 1902; they are still awarded today.

The Cressons commissioned Joseph Bailly to model a seated statue for their son's tomb in Laurel Hill Cemetery. Completed in 1869, the extraordinarily advanced work depicted Cresson with palette and brushes (they are now missing) and was cast by the Robert Wood Foundry of Philadelphia.

Note

1. Listed in Antique Class Register, 1859–69, PAFA Archives, as Wm. Prichett Cresson (*Prichett* was his mother's maiden name).

Reference

1906 "City's Great Art Prizes," *Philadelphia Record*, Jan. 14 (ill.).

Exhibited

1973 PAFA, *Held in Trust*, cat. no. 3. **1975–76** Whitney Museum of American Art, *A Portrait of Young America*. **1976** PAFA, *In This Academy*, cat. no. 3. **1978–79** PAFA, *350 Masterpieces of American Art: 1720–1978*. **1980** PAFA, Peale House, *The Pennsylvania Academy Schools, 1876–1900*. **1986–87** PAFA, *Sculpture at the Pennsylvania Academy of the Fine Arts*.

Ex Collection

Emlen and Priscilla Cresson, 1866–1902.

William Henry Rinehart

1825–1874

William Henry Rinehart was one of the second generation of American neoclassical sculptors. Born near Union Bridge, Maryland, he was the fifth of eight sons of Israel and Mary Snader Rinehart, prosperous farmers of Pennsylvania German heritage. As a boy, William showed little interest in farming or schooling. Tradition has it that he was discovered modeling a clay bust of his mother rather than doing his chores, so his father put him to work at the marble quarry on the family farm. This proved fortunate for young Rinehart. His temperament and skills were well suited to the tasks of polishing and lettering stone. By his early twenties, he had joined the Baltimore marble firm of Baughman and Bevan. He attended evening art classes at the Maryland Institute of Mechanic Arts, where he won a gold medal in 1851 for a stone relief copy of David Teniers's painting *The Smokers*, 1851 (National Museum of American Art, Washington, D.C.). Occasional commissions for portrait busts began to come his way, and in 1853 an exhibition of his sculpture was held at the Maryland Historical Society.

With the financial backing of William T. Walters, the Baltimore railroad tycoon and art patron, Rinehart set sail for Florence in 1855. Among the works from this first Italian sojourn are two reliefs, *Day* and *Night*, 1856 (also called *Morning* and *Evening*, Peabody Institute of Johns Hopkins University, Baltimore). They reveal the influence of Bertel Thorwaldsen (1770–1844), the prominent Danish neoclassicist, who made his home in Florence. During the summer of 1856, Rinehart accompanied the American sculptor Joel T. Hart (1810–1877) to London. Rinehart returned briefly to Baltimore in 1857 before settling permanently in Rome the following year. He came to be regarded as one of the most affable American artists in Rome, and his studio was a popular haunt for American travelers.

Like most neoclassical sculptors, Rinehart supported himself largely through portraiture. Between 1859 and his death in 1874, he executed over eighty portrait busts. Many depict prominent American financiers and industrialists, such as William Wilson Corcoran, a native of Washington, D.C., and the founder of the Corcoran Gallery; William P. Wilstach, a Philadelphia merchant and art collector; and Thomas Alexander Scott, another Philadelphian and president of the Union Pacific Railroad. Rinehart executed several charming full-length portraits of children, including one of Henry Elliott Johnston, Jr., as *Cupid Stringing His Bow,* 1874 (National Museum of American Art, Washington, D.C.).

Rinehart was a prodigious worker, and during his short career he produced a fair number of ideal statues. The sentimental group *Sleeping Children,* executed in 1859 for the cemetery plot of Mr. and Mrs. Hugh Sisson of Baltimore, was tremendously popular; and Rinehart sold at least eighteen marble copies of it (one is at Yale University Art Gallery, New Haven). Most of his ideal works were based on historical or mythological figures. In 1874 William Corcoran purchased a marble version of Rinehart's *Endymion,* the youthful shepherd beloved by the goddess Diana, which is now in the Corcoran Gallery of Art in Washington, D.C. The Metropolitan Museum of Art in New York owns three ideal statues by Rinehart: *Antigone,* 1870; *Latona and Her Children,* 1872; and *Clytie,* 1872. The statue of Clytie, the nymph who fell in love with the sun god, Apollo, and turned into a sunflower, was considered by Rinehart to be his masterpiece.

He also executed several important public works. In 1866 Louisa Crawford, the widow of the sculptor THOMAS CRAWFORD, asked Rinehart to complete her husband's commission for the bronze doors to the Senate and the House of Representatives in the United States Capitol. The state of Maryland commissioned him in 1869 to create a bronze statue of Roger Brooke Taney, Chief Justice of the United States Supreme Court. It was cast at the Ferdinand von Muller Foundry in Munich and installed at Annapolis in 1870. A second bronze cast was given to the city of Baltimore by William T. Walters. Although Rinehart depicted Taney heavily draped in neoclassical fashion, the seated figure displays a greater naturalism than the sculptor's ideal works. Yet, for the most part, Rinehart continued to produce smooth neoclassical marbles and was little affected by the growing trend towards active surfaces and the use of bronze in the late nineteenth century.

Rinehart never married, and his will directed that his estate be used for the advancement of sculpture in America. Under the careful control of the executors, William T. Walters and Benjamin F. Newcomer, a Baltimore railroad executive, Rinehart's estate was allowed to appreciate until 1891. It was then used to establish the Rinehart School of Sculpture at the Maryland Institute and to endow the Rinehart Scholarship to allow young sculptors to study in Paris or Rome.

References
1939 William Sener Rusk, *William Henry Rinehart, Sculptor,* Baltimore: Norman T.R. Munder. **1948** Marvin Chauncey Ross and Anna Wells Rutledge, *A Catalogue of the Work of William Henry Rinehart, Maryland Sculptor, 1825–1874,* Baltimore: Peabody Institute and Walters Art Gallery. **1948/1949** Marvin Chauncey Ross and Anna Wells Rutledge, eds., "William H. Rinehart's Letters to Frank B. Mayer, 1865–1870," *Maryland Historical Magazine* 43 (June), pp. 127–38, and 44 (March), pp. 52–57.

Hero

About 1865–66
Marble, carved in 1869
33¾ x 24 x 11¾" (85.7 x 61 x 29.8 cm)
Signed and dated on back: WM. H. RINEHART SCVLP.^{T}
ROMA 1869
Bequest of Henry C. Gibson, 1892.6.70

ACCORDING to Greek legend, Hero was a priestess of Aphrodite. Every night she was visited at her home in Sestos by her lover, Leander, who swam across the Hellespont from Abydos to see her. One night the wind blew out her lamp, which was Leander's beacon, and he drowned. When his body washed up on the shore, the grief-stricken Hero flung herself into the water to be united for eternity with her lover.

In his *Heroides,* the Roman poet Ovid retold the tale of Hero and Leander in the form of imagined letters penned by the lovers. Lord Byron became infatuated with Ovid's account and was largely responsible for reawakening interest in the story in the nineteenth century. Byron reenacted Leander's nightly feat by swimming across the Hellespont himself in 1810. Prideful of this accomplishment, he often flaunted it in his poems and letters. In 1813 he published *The Bride of Abydos,* inspired not only by Ovid's story but also by his own experiences in the Middle East.

Poorly educated in the classics, William Henry Rinehart discovered many of the themes for his sculpture in the work of contemporary artists rather than in the classical literary tradition. Several other nineteenth-century sculptors were attracted to the story of Hero and Leander, and Rinehart may have

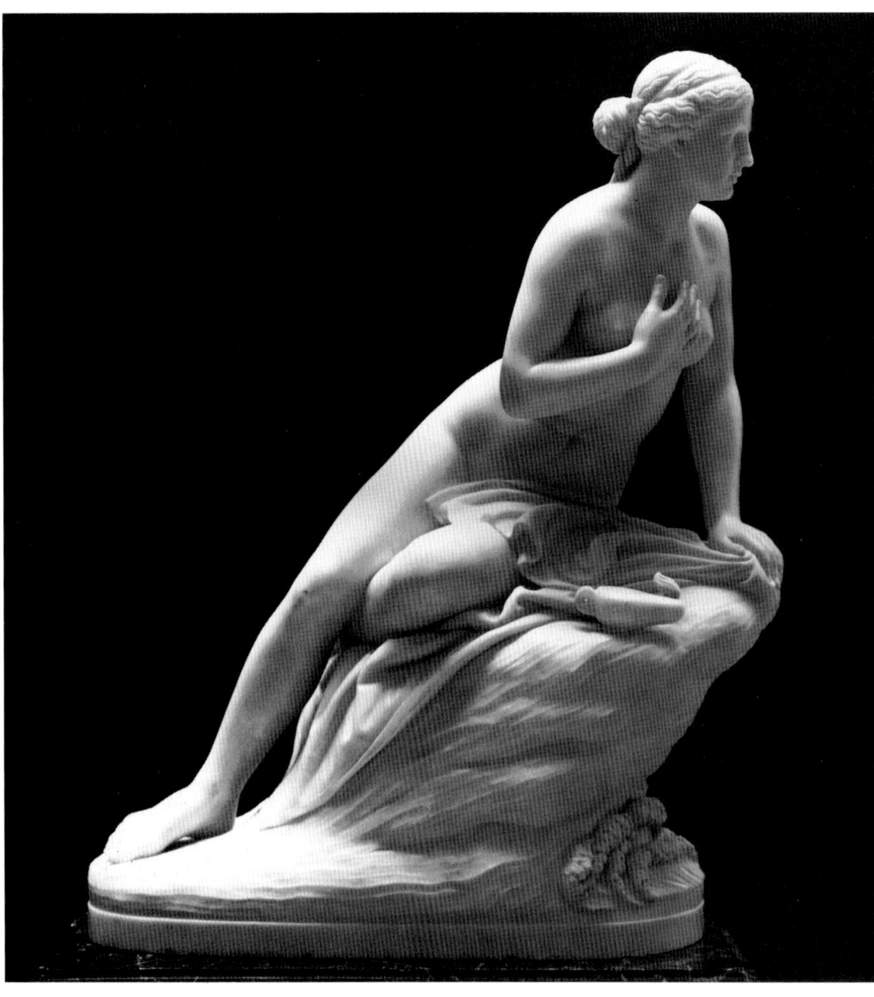

Rinehart, *Hero*

followed their lead when he depicted the pair of lovers. In 1848 Carl Johann Steinhauser (1813–1872), a German sculptor who lived in Rome from 1835 to 1863, executed a group statue of Hero and Leander;[1] and WILLIAM WETMORE STORY, an American resident in Rome, made a statue entitled *Hero Searching for Leander* in 1858. Rinehart probably completed his model for *Leander* in 1859 because his account book records payments to a stone carver for blocking out a statuette of Leander during the late summer and fall of that year.[2] The first mention of *Hero* in Rinehart's account book appears almost six years later, in May 1865, when he recorded payment to a workman for sawing a block for *Hero.*[3] Even though there seems to have been a large interval between the production of the two statues, it is clear that Rinehart conceived them as a pair. Twin waves lap at the bases of both works. While Leander disrobes in preparation for his fateful swim, Hero peers out at the stormy sea in search of him. The flame in her lamp wavers, a portent of the impending tragedy.

Several factors no doubt played a role in Rinehart's decision to place *Hero* and *Leander* on separate bases. Certainly the poignancy of the lovers' separation in the legend itself suggested that they be separated in stone, as well. The Victorian sensibilities of Rinehart's American patrons also probably influenced him. A statue that united the nude lovers in an embrace ran the risk of being deemed too explicit. Furthermore, there were economic considerations. Statues of single figures required less marble and could therefore be priced more affordably. Rinehart obviously expected to sell *Hero* and *Leander* separately. In fact only one pair was ever purchased. Edward Clark of New York bought the first marble of *Leander* (Newark Museum, N.J.) in 1865 and the first marble of *Hero* the following year (Peabody Institute of Johns Hopkins University in Baltimore). Nineteenth-century art patrons generally preferred female nudes, and *Hero* proved to be much more popular than *Leander.* According to Rinehart's records, only two marble statues of *Leander* were carved, while nine were made of *Hero.*[4] (The Chrysler Museum in Norfolk, Va., and the collection of JoAnn and Julian Ganz, Jr., Los Angeles, both have a marble of *Hero.* The National Museum of American Art, Smithsonian Institution, owns a plaster.)

Scholars have noted the similarity of *Hero*'s pose to the classical Roman marble *Nymph with a Shell,* about 150 B.C. (Musée du Louvre, Paris) and to *Ariadne on the Panther,* 1803–14 (Städtische Skulpturensammlung im Liebieghaus, Frankfurt am Main, Germany), by the German neoclassicist Johann Heinrich von Dannecker.[5] Rinehart may have admired *Nymph with a Shell* at the Louvre during visits to Paris in the 1850s. Also, a cast of it was at the French Academy in Rome, and it was widely known through copies and reductions.[6] Dannecker's *Ariadne on the Panther* was highly regarded in the nineteenth century and was also well known through small porcelain replicas reproduced by the Minton factory in England in the 1840s.[7]

The version of *Hero* at the Museum of American Art of the Pennsylvania Academy is displayed on a maroon stone pedestal.

Notes

1. Steinhauser's *Hero and Leander* was purchased by the PAFA in 1848 and remained in the collection until 1950, when it was deemed worthless and destroyed.
2. William Henry Rinehart Account Book, 1858–62, pp. 11–12, William Henry Rinehart Papers, Archives of American Art, microfilm, roll no. 3116, frame nos. 705–6.
3. William Henry Rinehart Account Book, "Libra Maestro," 1862–74, p. 11, ibid., frame no. 765.
4. Marvin Chauncey Ross and Anna Wells Rutledge, *A Catalogue of the Work of William Henry Rinehart, Maryland Sculptor, 1825–1874* (Baltimore: Peabody Institute and Walters Art Gallery, 1948), pp. 25, 28.
5. For comparison with *Nymph with a Shell,* see William L. Vance, *America's Rome* (New Haven: Yale University Press, 1989), vol. 1, pp. 263–64; and with *Ariadne on the Panther,* see Lorado Taft, *The History of American Sculpture* (New York: Macmillan Company, 1903), p. 175, and Gerdts 1974, p. 85.
6. Francis Haskell and Nicholas Penny, *Taste and the Antique: The Lure of Classical Sculpture, 1500–1900* (New Haven: Yale University Press, 1981), p. 281.
7. H.W. Janson, *19th-Century Sculpture* (New York: Harry N. Abrams, 1985), pp. 62–63.

References

1974 William H. Gerdts, *The Great American Nude: A History in Art,* New York: Praeger, pp. 81, 85, 96 (ill.). **1976** Wayne Craven, "Images of a Nation in Wood, Marble and Bronze," in *200 Years of American Sculpture,* New York: Whitney Museum of American Art, pp. 43–44, 58 (ill.).

Exhibited

1972 PAFA, *Acres of Art,* cat. no. 83. **1974** PAFA, *The Beneficient Connoisseurs (Gibson Collection),* cat. no. 70. **1984–85** PAFA, *A Growing American Treasure: Recent Acquisitions and Highlights from the Permanent Collection.* **1986–87** PAFA, *Sculpture at the Pennsylvania Academy of the Fine Arts.* **1994–96** PAFA, *Two Centuries of Collecting at the Museum of American Art.*

Ludwig Drake

1826–1897

Born in Pyrmont, Germany, Ludwig Drake was one of seventeen siblings. An elder brother, Friedrich (1805–1882), also a sculptor, was a disciple of Christian Daniel Rauch (1777–1857), the neoclassicist who was a favorite of the Prussian court. Friedrich had a successful studio in Berlin, and in 1837 he invited Ludwig to study with him and Christian Rauch. Remaining in Berlin after his studies were completed, Ludwig Drake assisted in his brother's studio and worked in a factory that made tile stoves. Soon he was able to set himself up in a private studio and secure his own commissions. In 1856 he showed two busts—the Christ Child and another child at the Berlin Academy. Drake produced many portraits, including a bust of General von Pfuel in 1868 and a statuette of Kaiser Wilhelm I in 1884. In 1871 he executed a group sculpture for the Potsdam railway station. His greatest achievement, however, was the sculptural decoration for the front of the British embassy in Berlin, formerly Strousberg Palace.

Reference

1913 Ulrich Thieme and Felix Becker, *Allgemeines Lexikon der Bildenden Kunstler* (Leipzig: Verlag von E.A. Seemann), vol. 9, p. 539.

Simon Gratz I

About 1840–50
Plaster, painted white
25½ x 17 x 12" (64.8 x 43.2 x 30.5 cm)
Signed behind right shoulder: *L Drake/[feci]t*
Presented by Miss Gratz, 1909.3

Simon Gratz (1773–1839) was born in Philadelphia. His father, Michael, had immigrated to Philadelphia from Upper Silesia, Germany, in 1759 to join his elder brother in business. After a few years as a prosperous merchant, Michael Gratz married Miriam Simon of Lancaster. Simon was the third of their twelve children. Following in his father's footsteps,

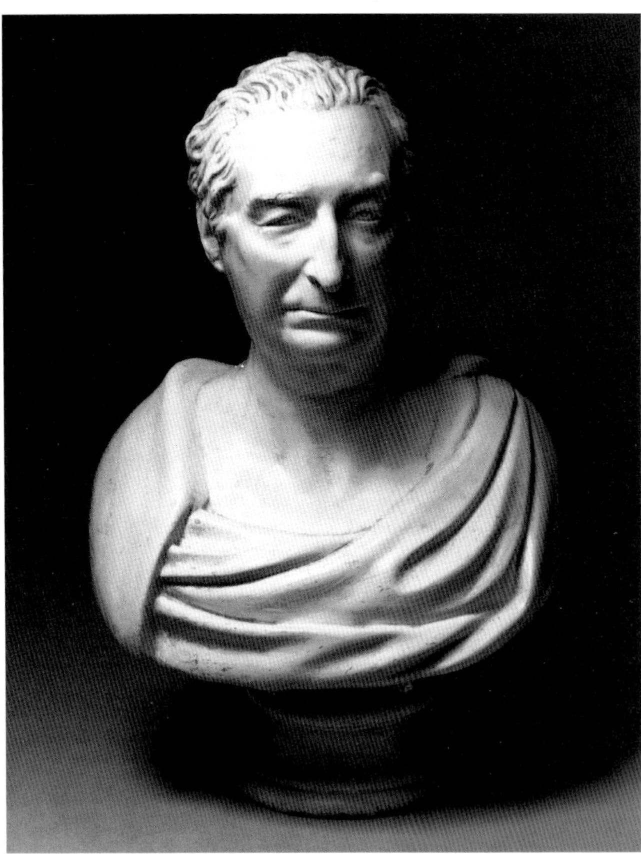

Drake, *Simon Gratz I*

Simon became a merchant and, together with a younger brother, Hyman, established Gratz Brothers at 231 Market Street. The Gratzes were one of Philadelphia's most prominent Jewish families. Among them were a number of philanthropists, notably Simon's sister Rebecca, who is also remembered for her great beauty and deep religious convictions.[1] Simon Gratz was one of the seventy-one founders of the Pennsylvania Academy of the Fine Arts in 1805. His brother Hyman served on the board of the Pennsylvania Academy from 1834 to 1857.[2]

Ludwig Drake probably executed this bust in Germany after Gratz's death, because it does not appear that the sculptor ever visited the United States. A member of the Gratz family may have commissioned the bust to be modeled from a daguerreotype. It was not uncommon for wealthy Americans to commission European artists during the mid-nineteenth century. Although the choice of Ludwig Drake may appear unusual today, it could have been an obvious one for a family with German forebears.

Notes

1. Rebecca Gratz was a friend of the American author Washington Irving. He recounted tales of her to Sir Walter Scott, who patterned Rebecca in *Ivanhoe* after her.
2. Leach 1912, p. 6.

Reference

1912 Frank Willing Leach, "Old Philadelphia Families CXXXIX: Gratz," *Philadelphia North American,* Dec. 1, sec. 6, p. 6 (ill.).

Exhibited

1969 Historical Society of Pennsylvania, Philadelphia, Rebecca Gratz Centenary.

Leonard Volk

1828–1895

Leonard Wells Volk was born in Wellstown (now Wells), New York, but spent much of his youth on a farm in Berkshire County, Massachusetts. His father, Garret Volk, was a marble cutter, who had perfected his trade while working on New York's City Hall. When Leonard was sixteen, he became an apprentice at the marble yard of his father and elder brother in Pittsfield, Massachusetts. After graduating to journeyman carver, he worked in western Massachusetts and then in upstate New York. For a time he was a partner of one of his brothers in Batavia. He was also in Bethany, where he met Emily C. Barlow, a doctor's daughter, who would later become his wife. In the autumn of 1848, Volk took a job in Saint Louis. He rented a studio and in his free time began to draw and to model in clay. One of his earliest busts, modeled from a daguerreotype, portrayed Dr. Barlow. Another early work was a marble copy of a bust of Henry Clay by Joel T. Hart (1810–1877).

In April 1852, Leonard Volk and Emily Barlow were married. They settled in Galena, Illinois.[1] The marriage proved propitious for his career because Emily's cousin, the Illinois senator Stephen A. Douglas, took a particular interest in the young sculptor. Like most mid-nineteenth-century American sculptors, Volk yearned to visit Italy, where the facilities for studying sculpture were the best in the world. With financial assistance from Douglas, he was able to make the trip. He departed from New York in September of 1855, stopped in London to see the Elgin Marbles, and visited Paris for the Exposition Universelle. But he spent most of his year-and-a-half sojourn in Italy. He worked from antique casts at the French Academy in Rome and modeled his first full-length statue, which depicted George Washington cutting down the cherry tree.[2] He was kindly received by the American sculptors in Rome, including RANDOLPH ROGERS, whose likeness he sculpted.[3] Before returning to the United States in June 1857, he spent several months in Florence.

When Volk arrived home, Stephen Douglas helped him set up a studio in Chicago. Unfortunately, 1857 was a difficult year. The country was experiencing a serious depression, and Volk was forced to spend most of his time carving cameos to make ends meet. The turbulent election campaign between Douglas and Abraham Lincoln for the United States Senate took place the following year, and Volk was commissioned to execute a lifesize statue of Douglas (now in the Old State Capitol, Springfield, Illinois). In 1859 the statue of Douglas, along with four other sculptures by Volk, was exhibited in the Chicago Exhibition of the Fine Arts, the first major art show of the Mid-west.[4] The exhibition was curated by Volk and held at Burch's Building at the corner of Wabash Avenue and Lake Street.

During the Lincoln-Douglas debates, Volk had met Lincoln, who promised to sit for the sculptor when time permitted. This occurred two years later, when Lincoln was in Chicago on legal business. To reduce the number of sittings, Volk made his well-known life mask of Lincoln (q.v.). The finished product of these sittings, a herm-type bust, was patented by Volk on June 12, 1860 (a plaster version is in the National Portrait Gallery, Washington, D.C.). After Lincoln's assassination in 1865, Volk received numerous orders for it.[5] His first marble version was probably the one purchased by Chicago's Crosby Art Association in 1866 and shown the following year at the Exposition Universelle in Paris.[6] Through his busts of Lincoln, Volk achieved a lasting fame and a modicum of financial success.

Volk was well respected and very active in Chicago art circles. In 1861 he helped organize the Chicago Art Union. In 1863 and 1865, he organized the art galleries for the Sanitary Fairs that benefited soldiers wounded in the Civil War. After the war, he was one of the founders of the Chicago Academy of Design and served as its president for eight years.

In 1866, five years after the death of Stephen A. Douglas, Volk designed a monument to mark his benefactor's grave. The colossal monument is dominated by a nine-foot-tall statue of Douglas atop a soaring marble shaft. Four female allegorical figures adorn the base. The sarcophagus is surmounted by a bust of the senator made by Volk in 1857–58.[7] His other important works include a statue of Lincoln at the New State Capitol Building in Springfield; the first Civil War soldiers' monument in the country, in Girard, Pennsylvania; and a soldiers' monument in Rock Island, Illinois. Volk also contributed a bronze statue of Lincoln to the soldiers' monument in Rochester, New York. At the World's Columbian Exposition, held in Chicago in 1893, he showed three portrait busts.[8] That same year, he executed a bronze statue of General James Shields as the contribution of Illinois to Statuary Hall in the United States Capitol.

Notes

1. *Dictionary of American Biography*, s.v. "Volk, Leonard."
2. *Biographical Sketches of the Leading Men of Chicago*, 1868, p. 338. Volk visited Italy again in December 1868, and January 1871. In 1872 he ordered the first shipment of Carrara marble to Chicago.
3. Volk undoubtedly executed this bust in Rome. He exhibited a plaster cast of it at the 1859 Chicago Exhibition of the Fine Arts.
4. The other works that Volk exhibited were (1) the cast of a bust of Randolph Rogers, (2) the cast of a statue of George Washington in his youth, (3) a statuette in clay, and (4) a portrait statue of a child (the five-year-old son of S.H. Kerfoot). In a letter to Kerfoot, dated Nov. 7, 1892, and preserved at the Chicago Historical Society, Volk claimed this to be the first statue executed in Chicago. It was destroyed in the Chicago fire of 1871.
5. Volk executed this bust in full and half sizes and with various truncations. A toga-draped version is at the Chicago Historical Society, and a 1914 bronze replica of a version truncated at the neck is at the Metropolitan Museum of Art, New York.
6. *Biographical Sketches of the Leading Men of Chicago*, 1868, p. 340. Later this bust was housed at the Chicago Historical Society. It was destroyed during the great fire of 1871.
7. *History of the Douglas Monument at Chicago* (Chicago: Chicago Legal News Company, 1880).
8. They were *Colonel William Hale Thompson*, *Colonel Hascall*, and *Bust of a Lady*.

References

1868 *Biographical Sketches of the Leading Men of Chicago*, Chicago: Wilson and St. Clair, pp. 335–42. **1951** Donald Charles Durman, *He Belongs to the Ages: The Statues of Abraham Lincoln*, Ann Arbor: Edwards Brothers, pp. 3–5. **1984** Wayne Craven, *Sculpture in America*, Newark: University of Delaware Press, pp. 240–42.

Life Mask of Abraham Lincoln

1860
Bronze; cast about 1952
9¾ x 8⅛ x 6½" (24.8 x 21.6 x 16.5 cm)
Inscribed faintly on back at right below support rod: GEORGE A/SHUSTE[N]/1952/PHILA. PA: and again at left on angle: GEO[R] SHUSTE[N]
Charles Bregler's Thomas Eakins Collection, purchased with the partial support of the Pew Memorial Trust, 1985.68.1.23

IN APRIL 1860, in preparation for modeling a bust, Leonard Volk made a cast of the face of Abraham

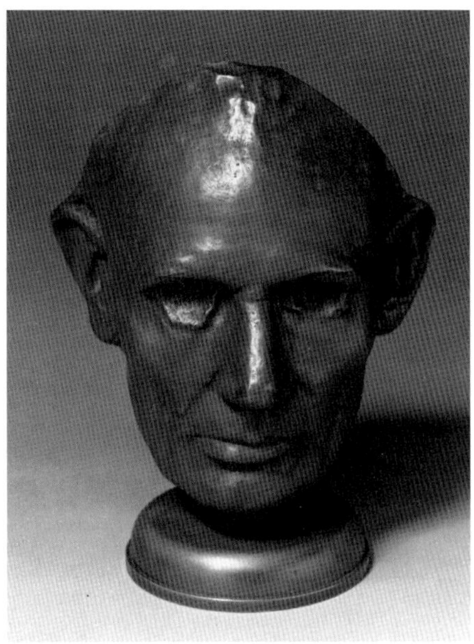

Volk, *Life Mask of Abraham Lincoln*, bronze

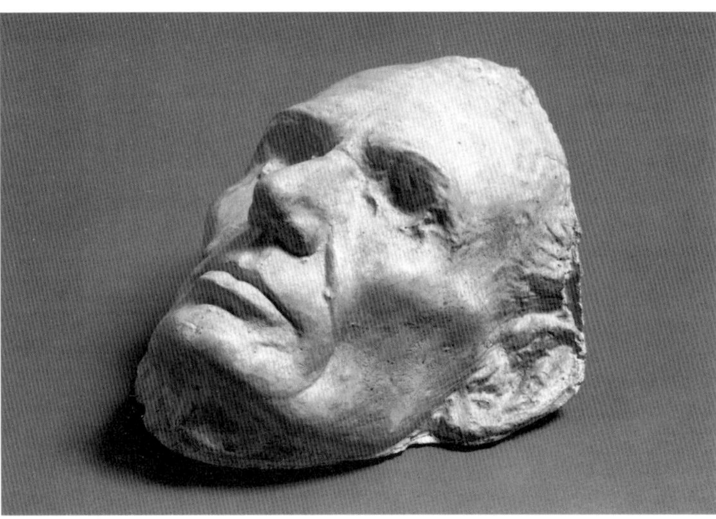

Volk, *Life Mask of Abraham Lincoln*, plaster (a)

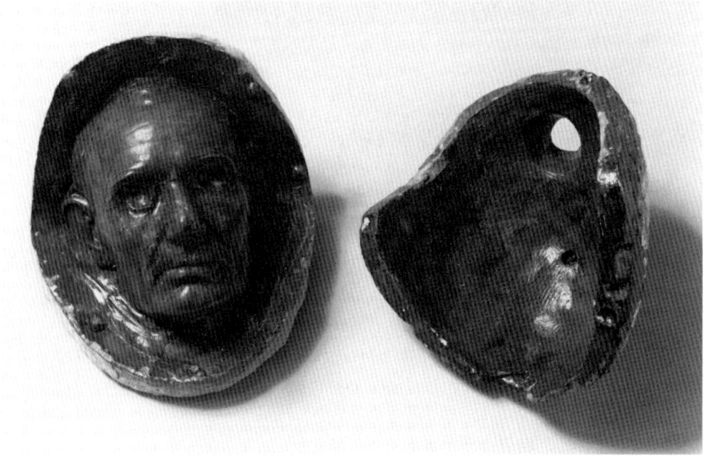

Volk, *Life Mask of Abraham Lincoln*, plaster (b)

Lincoln (1809–1865).[1] Two months later, when Lincoln was nominated for the presidency, Volk visited him at his home in Springfield, Illinois, and made casts of his hands. Volk subsequently used these casts when he executed his statues of Lincoln for the New State Capitol in Springfield and for the soldiers' monument in Rochester, New York. In the late nineteenth and early twentieth centuries, Volk's well-known mask was used as a model by many Lincoln portraitists.

The lack of detail in this replica of Volk's 1860 life mask indicates that it is a *surmoulage*, several generations removed from the original plaster. Its direct model is impossible to determine, but the replica probably dates from the early twentieth century. The faint inscription on the back appears to have been incised after casting and probably refers to an owner. The surface of the bronze is blackened with carbon or soot. There is probably no patina under the blacking.

In 1885 Richard Watson Gilder, the editor of the *Century Magazine*, noticed a replica of the Lincoln mask in the studio of the Canadian-born painter Wyatt Eaton. He had been given the replica by Leonard Volk's son, Douglas, a painter, who owned his father's original Lincoln casts.[2] Recognizing the importance of Volk's casts, Gilder encouraged his close friend the sculptor AUGUSTUS SAINT-GAUDENS and two other men, Thomas B. Clarke and Erwin Davis, to form a committee to purchase the casts for the federal government by soliciting subscriptions for replicas at fifty dollars for a set of the mask and the hands in plaster, seventy-five dollars for a bronze mask and plaster hands, and eighty-five dollars for a set entirely of bronze.[3] Thirty individuals and three institutions subscribed. Augustus Saint-Gaudens inscribed each of the bronze masks with the name of the subscriber, the date of Volk's original, and the date of casting—February 1886. With the subscription funds, the original plaster casts were purchased from Douglas Volk. They and a set of bronze casts were presented to the United States Government to be preserved at the National Museum (now the National Museum of American History, Smithsonian Institution). A condition of the gift precludes the government from making any replicas from the original plasters. Furthermore, the government was allowed to make no casts from the bronzes until January 1, 1896. The thirty-three subscribers were asked not to cast replicas for ten years, and Leonard Volk and his heirs were asked not to sell replicas for less money than was paid by the thirty-three subscribers.[4]

Notes

1. See L.W. Volk, "The Lincoln Life Mask and How It Was Made," *Century Magazine* 23 (1881), pp. 223–27.

2. Homer Saint-Gaudens, ed., *The Reminiscences of Augustus Saint-Gaudens* (New York: Century Company, 1913), vol. 1, p. 355.

3. Kathryn Greenthal, *Augustus Saint-Gaudens: Master Sculptor* (New York: Metropolitan Museum of Art, 1985), p. 126.

4. Augustus Saint-Gaudens, Thomas B. Clarke, and Richard Watson Gilder to the National Museum, Feb. 1, 1886, National Museum of American History, Smithsonian Institution. In 1891 Volk sent a set of casts free of charge to the English artist G.F. Watts. See Leonard Volk to Charles L. Hutchinson, Jan. 7, 1891, Chicago Historical Society.

Life Mask of Abraham Lincoln

1860

a.
Plaster; possibly cast in 1891
10½ x 8½ x 5⅝" (26.7 x 21.6 x 14.3 cm)
Annotated by Charles Bregler in pencil on back behind right ear: Life Mask/by/Volk 1860/Chicag[o]
Charles Bregler's Thomas Eakins Collection, purchased with the partial support of the Pew Memorial Trust, 1985.68.1.24

b.
Plaster, attached to mother mold; possibly cast in 1891
9 x 11 x 12" (22.9 x 27.9 x 30.5 cm)
Charles Bregler's Thomas Eakins Collection, purchased with the partial support of the Pew Memorial Trust, 1985.68.1.22a, b

IT IS BELIEVED that these two plaster versions of Leonard Volk's life mask of Lincoln belonged to THOMAS EAKINS and descended from him to his student, Charles Bregler. Eakins and WILLIAM R. O'DONOVAN used a replica of Volk's life mask in 1891 when they were working together on the equestrian relief portrait of Abraham Lincoln for the Soldiers and Sailors Memorial Arch in Grand Army Plaza, Brooklyn, New York. When these casts were made and by whom are unknown. Perhaps Eakins cast them himself from a replica owned by O'Donovan.[1] It is clear that the two casts are closely related, and the quality of detail in them suggests that they are not many generations removed from the original.

Note

1. At the fifty-second annual exhibition of the PAFA, in 1881, William O'Donovan showed a *Bronze relief from Volk life mask of Lincoln*, so he probably owned a cast of the mask himself.

GEORGE STARKEY

Died 1889/90

Nothing is known about George Starkey's background. Even the location and date of his birth remain mysteries. He may have arrived in Philadelphia in 1870, when he was first listed as a sculptor in the city directory. By that time, Starkey had become an accomplished sculptor. In either 1870 or 1871, he exhibited a lifesize statue, *Ruth*, in the Chestnut Street display window of the Philadelphia jewelry store Bailey and Company, now Bailey, Banks and Biddle.[1] In 1871 he executed a marble portrait bust of Benjamin Franklin Peale (q.v.). Starkey continued to be listed as a sculptor in the Philadelphia directories through 1873.

In 1875 he settled in Scranton, with his wife, Anna, and their sons, George, Jr., and Frank. That year, he was listed in the Scranton city directory as a marble cutter. The following year, however, he was designated a sculptor with a studio at 226 Lackawanna Avenue.[2] In Philadelphia in 1879, a medallion head by Starkey, entitled *The Lily of the Valley*, was exhibited by its owner, J.A. Price, in the fiftieth annual exhibition of the Pennsylvania Academy. Two years later, in 1881, Starkey exhibited a relief, *Head of Christ*, at the Pennsylvania Academy's fifty-second annual exhibition. He offered the head and copies of it for sale at fifty dollars each. Most likely the piece was not sold and Starkey decided to present it to the Pennsylvania Academy; for, only three and a half months after the exhibition closed, he gave the Academy a medallion head of Christ in copper (now lost).

In the Scranton city directories of 1882 through 1885, Starkey was listed simply as artist; but, in 1886, he advertised as a sculptor and painter. The following year, his son George embarked upon a career of his own; and both father and son were listed as artists. In 1888 and 1889, they advertised as ornamental modelers. George Starkey died in Scranton in 1889 or 1890.

Notes

1. Undated clipping, about 1870–71, from the *Philadelphia Bulletin*, Howard Roberts Scrapbook, microfilm, roll no. 3657, frame no. 61, Archives of American Art, Smithsonian Institution, Washington, D.C.

2. Information from Scranton city directories courtesy of Dorothy Allen, executive director, Lackawanna Historical Society, Scranton, Pa.

Benjamin Franklin Peale

1871
Marble
24 x 23 x 13" (61 x 58.4 x 33 cm)
Signed and dated on back: Geo. Starkey Sc./1871.
Gift of Mrs. Benjamin Franklin Peale through Florence I. Gibson, 1876.1

THIS posthumous portrait of Benjamin Franklin Peale (1795–1870) was probably commissioned by his widow. George Starkey would have used a photograph or a painted portrait as his model. The carving, which was almost certainly done by Starkey himself, is very skillful. The sculptor was most likely at mid-career when he created this work. Its naturalistic style, execution in marble, and the use of the dead eye and the toga suggest that he had been steeped in the late neoclassical tradition, which continued well into the second half of the nineteenth century in provincial areas.

Benjamin Franklin Peale was the fourteenth child of Charles Willson Peale. The elder Peale asked the members of the American Philosophical Society to choose the name for his son. The Society's selection honored its chief founder and Philadelphia's illustrious patriot.[1] Appropriately, Benjamin Franklin Peale, always called Franklin, inherited his namesake's inventiveness. He became a skilled mechanic, inventor, and administrator. After an unsuccessful venture in the cotton business, Franklin Peale joined his brother Titian in managing the museum in Philadelphia founded by their father and located in the upper story of the State House (now Independence Hall). To the museum's physical-science exhibits, Franklin Peale contributed several of his own inventions, including a magnet capable of lifting three hundred pounds. Peale resigned from the museum in 1833 to take a position at the United States Mint; and, from 1840 to 1854, he served as chief coiner. He invented a steam coining press that replaced the more laborious hand press. In 1864, ten years after resigning from the mint, he was elected president of the Hazelton Coal and Railroad Company in Philadelphia.[2]

Peale was involved in many of Philadelphia's cultural and educational institutions. Elected a member of the American Philosophical Society in 1831, he served as one of its curators for many years. He was a member of the board of directors of the Pennsylvania Academy of the Fine Arts from 1855 to 1870. At the time of his death, he was also president of the Musical Fund Society, which he had helped found, and president of the Pennsylvania Institution for Instruction of the Blind.

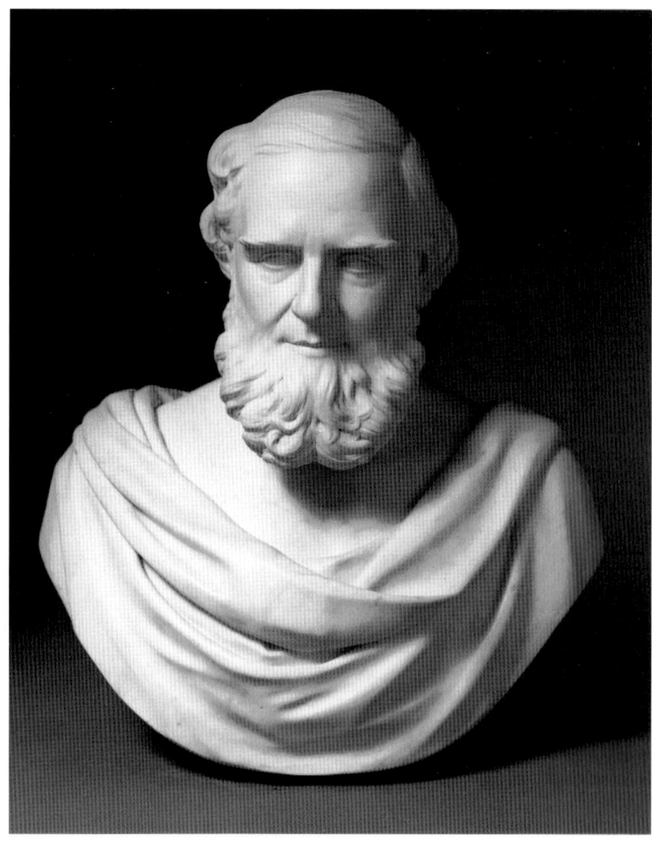

Starkey, *Benjamin Franklin Peale*

Sometime before her death in 1875, Peale's wife, née Caroline E. Girard, deposited this bust at the Pennsylvania Academy. In 1876 Florence I. Gibson, Mrs. Peale's niece and the executor of her estate, wrote that Mrs. Peale had intended the bust to be a gift, although it had never been so recorded. Florence Gibson confirmed the gift, and the Academy accessioned the work.[3]

Notes

1. Robert Patterson, "An Obituary Notice of Franklin Peale," read before the American Philosophical Society, Dec. 16, 1870, *Proceedings of the American Philosophical Society Held at Philadelphia for Promoting Useful Knowledge* 11 (Jan. 1867-Dec. 1870).
2. Charles Coleman Sellers, *Charles Willson Peale: Later Life (1790–1827)* (Lancaster, Pa.: Lancaster Press, 1947), vol. 2, pp. 382–83.
3. Florence I. Gibson to Caleb Cope, Jan. 29, 1876, PAFA object file.

W. Marshall Swayne

1828–1918

William Marshall Swayne was born in Pennsbury Township, Chester County, Pennsylvania. He was the second of five children of William and Mary Ann Marshall Swayne. Marshall was only ten years old when his father died. The child went to live with his grandfather at Acadia, the family homestead, located in nearby East Marlborough Township. The property was the remainder of a huge tract of land purchased by an ancestor, Francis Swayne, in 1711. Marshall Swayne attended both public and private schools in Chester County and, about 1840, was enrolled at the Westtown Friends Boarding School.[1] As a young man, he taught school and worked in a country store.

When his grandfather died in February 1848, Marshall and his older brother, Benjamin, inherited the homestead. Two years later, Marshall bought out his brother's share of the property. While Marshall earned his livelihood by farming and burning limestone at Acadia,[2] his interest in sculpture was developing. He received his first recognition as a sculptor in June 1850, when he was twenty-one years old. At an exhibition of horticulture, mechanical arts, and fine arts held at the Chester County Historical Society, he won an honorable mention for a clay bust (no longer extant) of Dr. Emmor Worth, Jr.[3] Two years later, Swayne showed a plaster bust of Dr. Benjamin Pennock in the twenty-ninth annual exhibition of the Pennsylvania Academy of the Fine Arts. Henry S. Evans, publisher of the *West Chester Village Record,* wrote of the Pennock bust: "I had the pleasure of seeing it side by side with works of distinguished sculptors, ancient and modern, in the late exhibition of the Academy of Fine Arts, in Philadelphia; and pointed to it with just pride as the production of a citizen of my own native county." Evans continued his flattering review by suggesting that, if Swayne would like to take up sculpture as a profession, he should go to Italy and study with HIRAM POWERS or some other master sculptor. Evans further proposed that the citizens of Chester County should sponsor Swayne's trip, if he himself lacked the necessary financial resources. Evans added that he would like to see Swayne execute a bust of William Darlington, the distinguished president of the National Bank of Chester County.[4] Swayne did indeed model Darlington's likeness in 1858. A plaster version dating from that year and a marble version carved in 1864 both survive at the Chester County Historical Society in West Chester. As for Evans's suggestion of study in Italy, Swayne was probably uninterested. He would soon become thoroughly convinced that American artists should remain at home in order to promote the formation of a national school of art.

In 1858 Swayne decided to sell Acadia because of mounting financial pressures, which were in part connected to a growing family. He had four children by this time and would have four more in the coming years. His desire to earn a living from sculpture prompted him to go to Washington, D.C., where he hoped to secure commissions for portrait busts of the country's eminent men. He arrived there late in 1858 armed with a letter of introduction from William Darlington to Thomas U. Walter, the architect of the United States Capitol.[5] Within a month or so, Swayne was busy modeling a bust of the well-known abolitionist Joshua Reed Giddings and an ideal bust of Little Eva from Harriet Beecher Stowe's *Uncle Tom's Cabin.*[6] In 1859 he modeled a bust of Samuel Houston, the senator from Texas. At about the same time, Swayne met the sculptor Henry Kirke Brown (1814–1866), who soon became his mentor. Following the older artist's suggestion, Swayne copied and drew from sculptures housed in the Capitol. Brown advised him not to make a special study of anatomy because "you can get a far more serviceable knowledge of [anatomy] . . . by drawing and modeling than you can by book or the scalpel."[7]

Although Swayne lived primarily in Washington from 1858 to 1867, his family remained in Chester County; and he made frequent trips home. In September 1860, he received an important commission from the citizens of Chester County for a marble bust of General Anthony Wayne to be placed in the county courthouse (now in the Chester County Historical Society).

Financial concerns no doubt prompted Swayne to begin working as a clerk in the United States Treasury Department in June 1863. He continued to sculpt in his free hours. Included among the life busts that he modeled are several members of Lincoln's cabinet: William Henry Seward, secretary of state; Salmon P. Chase, secretary of the treasury; and Edwin M. Stanton, secretary of war.[8] In March 1864, Henry C. Townsend of Philadelphia commissioned Swayne to execute a marble bust of President Lincoln on condition that it be finished in time for the Great Central Fair to be held in Philadelphia that same year for the benefit of wounded Union soldiers. Lincoln sat for Swayne in a makeshift studio in the library of the solicitor of the Treasury Department. Swayne, recalling the sittings, fondly noted that Lincoln told stories, recited poetry, and engaged him in pleasant conversation.[9] Unfortunately, Swayne contracted smallpox and was not able to finish the plaster model for the marble until the fair was nearing its close. Although the plaster was shown at the end of the fair, it appears that the marble was never carved.[10] Today a plaster version, painted to simulate bronze, is in the National Museum of American History, Smithsonian Institution. Swayne also produced a three-foot-high model for a statue of Lincoln delivering his last inaugural address. In 1865 the model was shown in the forty-fifth annual exhibition of the Pennsylvania Academy of the Fine Arts. Swayne executed several other designs for monuments, including two for equestrian statues of General George Gordon Meade and General Anthony Wayne. However, Swayne was never commissioned to produce a major monument.

He modeled a life portrait of President Andrew Johnson in 1865; and, two years later, the president appointed him United States Collector of Internal Revenue for the seventh district of Pennsylvania, Swayne's home region. He continued to sculpt and, in September 1870, wrote to his old friend William Darlington about his desire to open a sculpture studio in West Chester, provided he could secure sufficient commissions to warrant it.[11] Of the numerous portrait busts by Swayne preserved today in the Chester County Historical Society, most date before 1870. It appears that he received few commissions during his later years. Swayne was living in Chester County in the town of Kennett Square when he died in 1918 at the age of ninety.

Notes

1. "Memories written by A. Canova Swayne," contained in Swayne scrapbook, pp. 1–2, Chester County Historical Society.

2. Ibid.

3. Certificate of honorable mention preserved in Swayne scrapbook, ibid.

4. *The West Chester [Pa.] Village Record,* June 29, 1852, preserved ibid.

5. Copy of letter preserved ibid.

6. Swayne also produced two ideal busts, entitled *Autumn* and *Inez.* See his "List of works in sculpture modeled in the order in which they were executed by W. Marshall Swayne," Dec. 1914, Chester County Historical Society.

7. Henry Kirke Brown to W. Marshall Swayne, Dec. 8, 1859, preserved in Swayne scrapbook. This advice notwithstanding, Brown lent Swayne his copy of *Wilson's Anatomy.*

8. Swayne also executed half-size bas-reliefs of these three sitters. They were offered for sale along with his reliefs of George Washington, Abraham Lincoln, and Secretary of the Navy Gideon Wells, at the Christian Commission's fair held in Washington in 1863 for the benefit of hospitalized Union soldiers.

9. See A. [*sic*] Marshall Swayne, "Reminiscences Concerning the Modelling of a Bust of Lincoln," *The Federal Architect,* July 1940, Swayne scrapbook, p. 45, Chester County Historical Society. In his later years, Swayne enjoyed recounting his experience with Lincoln. He gave several public talks about it, and his reminiscences appeared in various publications. Swayne recalled that about nine months after he had modeled Lincoln's portrait, he met the president at a reception. Lincoln greeted him by saying, "you're the man that made the mud head of me" and told him that, although he had sat for several other sculptors afterwards, he liked Swayne's bust the most.

10. At the fair, the bust was displayed with a placard that read, "Model of a Bust of A. Lincoln now being executed in marble by Wm. Marshall Swayne of Washington D.C. To be purchased by subscription for the Union League of Philadelphia as an ornament for their new house. Presented to the Great Central Fair by Henry C. Townsend." Apparently, the subscription fund was not successful, as the bust is not in the league's collection.

11. W. Marshall Swayne to William Darlington, Sept. 2, 1870, Chester County Historical Society.

References

William Marshall Swayne Scrapbook, compiled chiefly by Antonio Canova Swayne, Chester County Historical Society, West Chester. **1936** Albert Cook Myers, "William Marshall Swayne, Chester County's Sculptor of Lincoln: 1828–1918," *Yesterday in Chester County Art,* West Chester: Art Center.

Henry Charles Carey

1878
Plaster
22½ x 19½ x 13" (57.1 x 49.5 x 33 cm)
Signed on back: W.M. Swayne Scp./Kennet [*sic*] Square,/Pa.
Gift of James L. Claghorn, 1878.2.2

MARSHALL SWAYNE'S oeuvre primarily consists of plaster portrait busts like this one of the Philadelphia publisher and economist Henry Charles Carey (1793–1879). It was Swayne's custom to work from life, and Carey sat for this portrait in April and May of 1878.[1] The sculptor may also have employed a photograph for reference, as one that looks remarkably similar to this bust is preserved in the Swayne scrapbook at the Chester County Historical Society. The sculptor has accurately represented the elderly Carey's sagging jowls and heavy brow. It is tempting to compare this bust to Roman portraiture of the Augustan Age (31 B.C.–A.D. 68). Like a Roman marble modeled from a wax death mask, this bust has a harsh realism in its portrayal of the sitter's features and the underlying bone structure. It fails, however, to capture the texture and mobility of the skin. To give the eyes a lifelike appearance, Swayne employed a technique similar to the revolutionary one of JEAN ANTOINE HOUDON: he cut out all but a small fragment of the iris, the fragment denoting the reflection of light in the eye.

Henry Carey was the eldest son of nine children

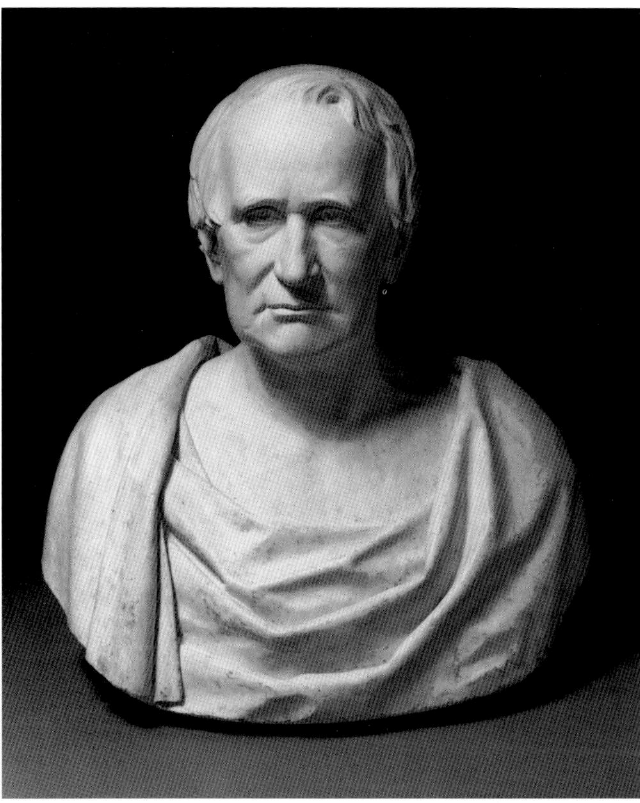

Swayne, *Henry Charles Carey*

born to Mathew and Bridget Flahavan Carey. In 1874 Mathew Carey left Dublin, for the United States and established himself as a publisher in Philadelphia. When Henry Carey was twenty-four years old, he became a partner in his father's firm, Carey, Lea and Carey. During his career, Henry Carey published works by Thomas Carlyle, Washington Irving, and Sir Walter Scott. Carey wrote a book entitled *Essays on the Rate of Wages* when he was forty-two years old; and soon after, he left the publishing business to devote himself to the study of economics. He wrote several other important books that brought him an international reputation in the field.

It was probably the donor, James L. Claghorn, who commissioned Swayne to model Henry Carey's portrait. As president of the Pennsylvania Academy of the Fine Arts, Claghorn surely knew that Henry and his sister Maria intended to bequeath the important art collection of their deceased brother, Edward, to the Pennsylvania Academy.

Note

1. PAFA Art Property Register, 1877–97, May 14, 1878, PAFA Archives.

James L. Claghorn

1878
Plaster
30 x 21 x 14" (76.2 x 53.3 x 35.6 cm)
Signed on back: W.M. Swayne Scp./Kennet [*sic*] Square,/Pa.
Annotated erroneously in pencil above signature (largely effaced): JOSEPH [CLA]GH[OR]N
Gift of James L. Claghorn, 1878.2.3

MARSHALL SWAYNE modeled this bust of the native Philadelphian James L. Claghorn (1817–1884) during the spring of 1878 at the same time that he modeled Henry Carey's portrait (q.v.).[1] Claghorn, who was then president of the Pennsylvania Academy of the Fine Arts, probably commissioned both busts, which he presented to the Academy on May 14, 1878. Although they were made at the same time, the Claghorn bust has a naive or primitive quality not evident in the Carey bust. The eyes contribute greatly to this effect, because they are not sculptural like those of the Carey bust but rather are simply drawn in, with little change in the depth of surface. The regularly repeated lines that define the hair and the cumbersome drapery with its profusion of folds also look

Swayne, *James L. Claghorn*

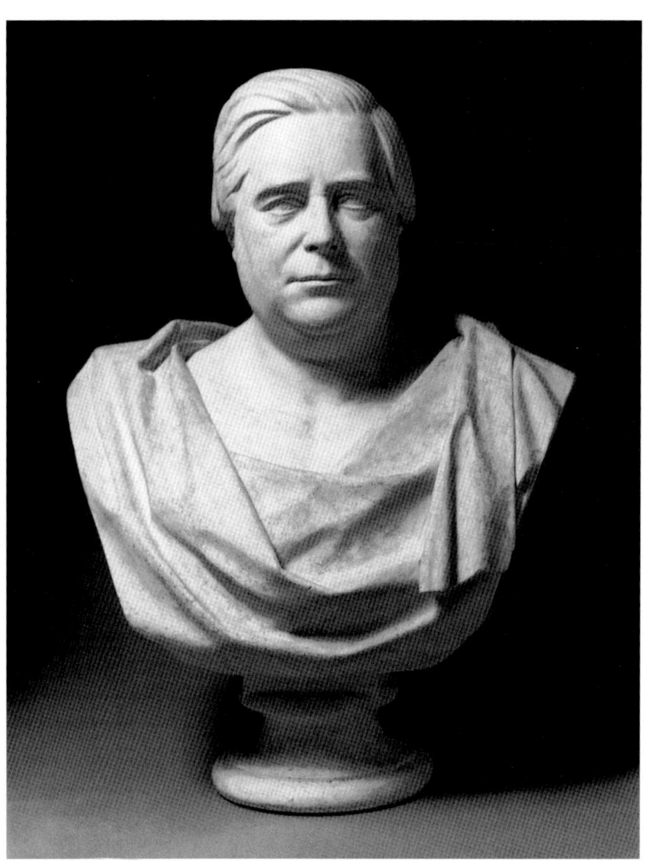

naive. Nonetheless, comparison with two contemporary photographs of Claghorn preserved in the Pennsylvania Academy Archives shows the bust to be an excellent likeness. It also has a stong sense of personality, which is evident when it is compared to the portrait of Claghorn (q.v.) executed twenty years earlier by EDWARD SHEFFIELD BARTHOLOMEW.

Note

1. PAFA Art Property Register, 1877–97, May 14, 1878, PAFA Archives.

John Rogers

1829–1904

Like Currier and Ives, the name John Rogers is synonymous with American popular art of the nineteenth century. Between 1860 and 1893, Americans bought about eighty thousand of Rogers's mass-produced plaster statuettes, appropriately called "Rogers groups."[1] The most popular ones depicted sentimental genre scenes, such as *Weighing the Baby* and *Fetching the Doctor;* but he also executed literary, dramatic, and historical images. At an average price of fourteen dollars, Rogers groups were well within the reach of middle-class Americans, who purchased them as wedding, anniversary, and birthday gifts.

Born in Salem, Massachusetts, John Rogers was the son of prominent parents of modest means. He attended Boston's English High School and later worked as a mechanic at the Amoskeag Mills in Manchester, New Hampshire. At the age of twenty, he took up clay modeling as a hobby. His early predilection for literary and genre subjects may have been reinforced by seeing three sculptures by ROBERT BALL HUGHES at the Boston Athenaeum; they illustrated scenes from Charles Dickens and Laurence Sterne.[2] One, made about 1851, of Nell Trent, the heroine of Dickens's *The Old Curiosity Shop,* may have inspired Rogers to attempt the same subject.

During the financial panic that swept the United States in 1857, Rogers lost his job as manager of a railroad repair shop in Hannibal, Missouri. That loss precipitated his decision to pursue sculpture as a career. With the financial assistance of an aunt and uncle, he went to Paris, where he studied briefly with Antoine Laurent Dantan (1798–1878). Rogers then made his way to Rome and spent a few weeks in the atelier of the British neoclassical sculptor Benjamin Edward Spence (1822–1866), who advised him to keep his work simple and to avoid the use of accessories. Rogers, however, considered these details essential to his storytelling; he had no intention of pursuing sculpture in the grand tradition, which he considered "out of his depth."[3]

Discouraged by the classical theories on sculpture that were prevalent in Europe, Rogers returned home in the spring of 1859. During the following summer in New York, he patented and mass-produced *The Slave Auction.* This piece was well received by critics and abolitionists, such as Henry Ward Beecher, but failed to sell because of its controversial subject matter.[4] Rogers showed it in the 1860 annual exhibition of the National Academy of Design.

The Civil War provided Rogers with subject matter for some of his most popular groups. *The Council of War,* of 1868, which depicts General Ulysses S. Grant, Secretary of War Edwin McMasters Stanton, and President Abraham Lincoln, displays Rogers's talent as a portraitist. He executed a number of portraits that were not replicated en masse, such as the 1892 bust *William Cullen Bryant* (New-York Historical Society). Though primarily remembered for his diminutive groups, Rogers occasionally worked on a large scale. He created two major monuments: an equestrian statue of General John Reynolds for Philadelphia in 1884 and a memorial to Abraham Lincoln for Manchester, New Hampshire, in 1892. The statue of Lincoln earned Rogers a bronze medal at the World's Columbian Exposition in Chicago in 1893, the same year that a crippling illness forced him to retire.

Notes

1. David Bourdon, "An intimate regard for everyday life made a homely art," *Smithsonian* 6 (May 1975), p. 51.
2. David H. Wallace, "The Art of John Rogers: 'So Real and So True,' " *American Art Journal* 4 (Nov. 1972), p. 60.
3. Wayne Craven, *Sculpture in America* (Newark: University of Delaware Press, 1984), p. 360.
4. Ibid., p. 361.

References

1967 David H. Wallace, *John Rogers: The People's Sculptor,* Middletown, Conn.: Wesleyan University Press.
1979 Harold Holzer and Joseph Farber, "The Sculpture of John Rogers," *Antiques* 115 (April), pp. 756–68.

Checkers up at the Farm

1875
Plaster, painted beige; cast in 1877
20 x 17 x 12½" (50.8 x 43.2 x 31.8 cm)
Signed on top of base on front: JOHN ROGERS/NEW YORK; dated at back of base near figure of woman: PATENTED/ DECEMBER 28 187[5]

Inscribed on front of base: CHECKERS/UP AT THE FARM
Gift of Mrs. Alfred Bendiner in memory of Judge and Mrs. William B. Linn, 1974.6

JOHN ROGERS'S *Checkers up at the Farm* is the last and most sophisticated version of four different groups of checker players. He began working on the theme in his early twenties, long before he entertained any thought of pursuing a career in sculpture. His first version, *Checker Players,* about 1850, is his earliest surviving group and exists only in its original clay form (Society for the Preservation of New England Antiquities, Boston). It displays two caricaturelike figures with overly large heads. One sits at a high-backed bench with his head thrown back in glee, for he has cornered his opponent, who leans forward on his stool in disbelief. Rogers based this group on an engraving after a painting by the English artist Sir David Wilkie.[1]

Rogers modeled a second version of the theme while in Chicago in 1859. It earned him his first public notice when it was raffled off to benefit the U.S. Sanitary Commission at the Chicago Cosmopolitan Bazaar. Through the sale of twenty-five-cent tickets, it brought in the considerable sum of seventy-five dollars. Also in clay, this group is now lost, but it probably looked very much like the checker players that Rogers created in plaster the following year.[2] In this version, the poses are similar to the 1850 group; but the two players are elegantly proportioned and seated on a wooden settee. Rogers showed this group in the thirty-fifth annual exhibition of the National Academy of Design, in New York in 1860.

Rogers's work on the checkers theme culminates in his most complex and popular version, *Checkers up at the Farm.* Here, the group is expanded to four figures by the addition of a woman onlooker, holding a young child. Rogers patented this image on December 28, 1875, and exhibited it in the Centennial Exposition in Philadelphia, where it won a bronze medal. Between April 1877, when Rogers began to publish *Checkers up at the Farm* and 1892, when he sold his business, over five thousand copies of the group were sold. It was his second most popular group (*Coming to the Parson* was the first), and over fifty copies are still known to exist.

Notes

1. David H. Wallace, "The Art of John Rogers: 'So Real and So True,' " *American Art Journal* 4 (Nov. 1972), p. 59.
2. Mr. and Mrs. Chetwood Smith, *Rogers Groups: Thought & Wrought by John Rogers* (Boston: Charles E. Goodspeed and Company, 1934), p. 49.

Exhibited

1986–87 PAFA, *Sculpture at the Pennsylvania Academy of the Fine Arts.*

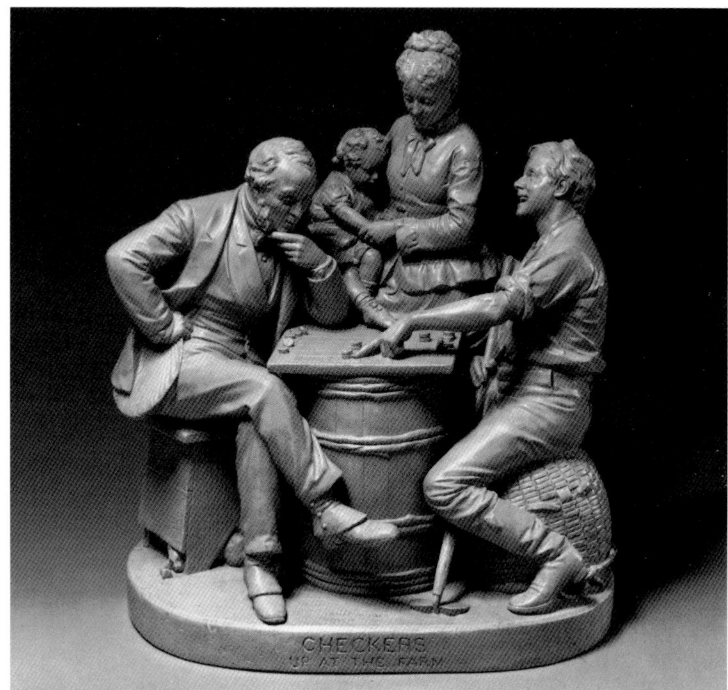

Rogers, *Checkers up at the Farm*

Ex Collections

Mr. and Mrs. T. Steward Wood, Wayne, Pa.; their daughter and her husband, Judge William B. Linn, to about 1952; Mr. and Mrs. Alfred Bendiner, Malvern, Pa., about 1952–74.

JOHN QUINCY ADAMS WARD

1830–1910

John Quincy Adams Ward was a revitalizing force in American sculpture during the third quarter of the nineteenth century. Rejecting the romantic classicism brought home by American sculptors trained in Italy, he followed the naturalistic style espoused by Henry Kirke Brown (1814–1866). Unlike most sculptors of his generation, Ward never went abroad to study. Although he was not opposed to European training, he believed American sculptors should create an indigenous art.

Named after the sixth president of the United States, Ward was the fourth of eight children born to John and Eleanor Macbeth Ward. He grew up on a farm in Urbana, Ohio, and, as a boy, spent many contented hours modeling clay in the workshop of a local potter and dreaming of becoming a sculptor. Seeing his dissatisfaction with farming, his parents enrolled him in an anatomy class in the hope that he would pursue a medical career, but his desire to become a sculptor remained firm.

When he was nineteen and recuperating from ill health, Ward went to Brooklyn, New York, to stay with his sister. She encouraged him to visit the nearby studio of Henry Kirke Brown. Impressed with the work that the young man showed him, Brown accepted him as a student. Within a year, Ward had become Brown's paid assistant; and, for the next seven years, he learned and practiced the profession under the eye of his mentor. He left Brown's employ in 1856. Two years later, he settled in Washington, D.C., where he worked on several busts of political figures, including Hannibal Hamlin, soon to be vice-president under Abraham Lincoln, and Senator John Park Hale. Ward also completed two uncommissioned statuettes, an ideal figure called *The Indian Hunter* and a standing figure of the Ohio pioneer Simon Kenton. Both statuettes were exhibited at the Pennsylvania Academy of the Fine Arts in 1859.

In New York, during the Civil War years, Ward supplemented his income by modeling decorative objects for the Ames Manufacturing Company. He was elected an academician of the National Academy of Design in 1863 after showing his sculpture of a black slave entitled *Freedman* (q.v.) in the annual exhibition. His reputation was firmly secured the following year when he exhibited an enlarged version of *The Indian Hunter* in an art gallery on Broadway. Ward had gone out West to make pencil and wax sketches of native Americans before embarking on the large version. It was praised for its realism and ethnological accuracy, and funds were raised to have the piece cast in bronze and erected in New York's Central Park. Before the bronze was set up in the park, it was shown at the Exposition Universelle in Paris in 1867, where it was hailed as a truly American effort.

In the post-Civil War decades, the fervor to immortalize America's heroes in bronze reached its climax; and Ward, a skilled portraitist, was the sculptor of the hour. In 1865 he received a commission for the Commodore Matthew C. Perry Monument for Newport, Rhode Island. It was the first of Ward's many collaborations with the architect Richard Morris Hunt. First introduced to the Beaux-Arts style by Hunt, Ward was further exposed to it in 1870 in Paris during his first trip to Europe. Eventually, he integrated some of the characteristics into his own naturalistic style. A new and richer texture is apparent in his 1879 equestrian figure of Major General George Henry Thomas, located in Washington, D.C. The Garfield Monument, completed in 1887, also for Washington, shows the sculptor's assimilation of the Beaux-Arts style in the lively poses of the three figures that personify stages in the life of President James A. Garfield.

In the early 1890s, Ward completed two of his best-known monuments, the Henry Ward Beecher Monument in Brooklyn, New York, and a seated statue of Horace Greeley, the founder of the *New York Tribune* (now located in City Hall Park, New York). At the turn of the century, Ward was seventy years old. Despite the two major equestrian figures already underway, he accepted the task of designing the sculptural program for the pediment of the New York Stock Exchange. Finished in 1904 with the help of PAUL WAYLAND BARTLETT, it was Ward's last major work.

References

1910 Obituary, *New York Times,* May 2, p. 9. **1985** Lewis I. Sharp, *John Quincy Adams Ward: Dean of American Sculpture,* Newark: University of Delaware Press, pp. 17–96.

Freedman

1863
Plaster, tinted yellow ochre
20¼ x 15 x 7" (51.4 x 38.1 x 17.8 cm)
Signed on front of base: J.Q.A.Ward Sculptor
Gift of the artist, 1866.2

AFTER BEING SHOWN at the Pennsylvania Academy of the Fine Arts in the spring of 1863, this piece remained there and Ward presented it to the Academy in 1866. In return, the board of directors elected him an honorary member. Concurrently with the Pennsylvania Academy's spring exhibition, another plaster cast of this work was on view at the National Academy of Design in New York. A critic for the *New York Times* noted that it was a welcome respite from the tedious and interchangeable representations of "Hope, Faith [and] Innocence" that littered American sculpture.[1] Ward's ability to transcend the banal and portray a contemporary moral issue realistically was greatly appreciated. In his 1864 book *The Art-Idea,* the critic James Jackson Jarves wrote, "We have seen nothing in our sculpture more soul-lifting or more comprehensively eloquent. It tells in one word the whole sad tale of slavery and the bright story of emancipation."[2]

While historically linked to Abraham Lincoln's Emancipation Proclamation, the *Freedman* was undoubtedly an expression of Ward's own antislavery sentiments. About the piece, he wrote, "I intended it to express—not one set free by any proclamation so much as by his own love of freedom and a conscious *power* to [break] things—the struggle is not over with him. (As it never is in life) yet I have tried to express a degree of hope in this undertaking."[3]

Growing up in Ohio farm country, Ward had been acquainted with several black families, and he paid tribute in a 1908 newspaper essay to a childhood friend called Uncle Caesar.[4] The *Freedman* is not a portrait, however, but rather an idealization, created by selecting features from several models. Although, when first exhibited, the *Freedman* was seen as lacking classical prototypes, Lewis I. Sharp has noted its relationship to the Greek *Belvedere Torso,* mid-first century B.C. (Museo Pio-Clementino, Vatican City); and indeed Ward's appreciation and study of classical sculpture is well documented.[5]

According to the art historian Henry T. Tuckerman, six bronze casts of the *Freedman* were originally made.[6] Lewis Sharp has catalogued three original 1863 casts, as well as three later authentic casts. Bronzes were exhibited at the Exposition Universelle in Paris in 1867, the National Academy of Design in 1868, and the Panama-Pacific International Exposition in San Francisco, in 1915, after the artist's death. A bronze of *Freedman* is in the collection of the National Academy of Design; it was presented by Ward about 1900 to replace a broken portrait bust that had been his diploma presentation in 1863.[7]

In 1981, when the Pennsylvania Academy conserved its example of the *Freedman,* a coat of white paint that was not original was removed from the surface, and the sculpture's yellow-ochre color was revealed. Ward probably deemed the darker color more appropriate to the subject matter; and, because he planned to exhibit the piece, he tinted the plaster before varnishing it. During conservation, several major losses were restored.[8] The most significant losses, the left forearm and the entire right arm, were recast, using one of the existing bronzes as a model. The manacle and broken chain—crucial iconographic details—were modeled anew, cast, and replaced.

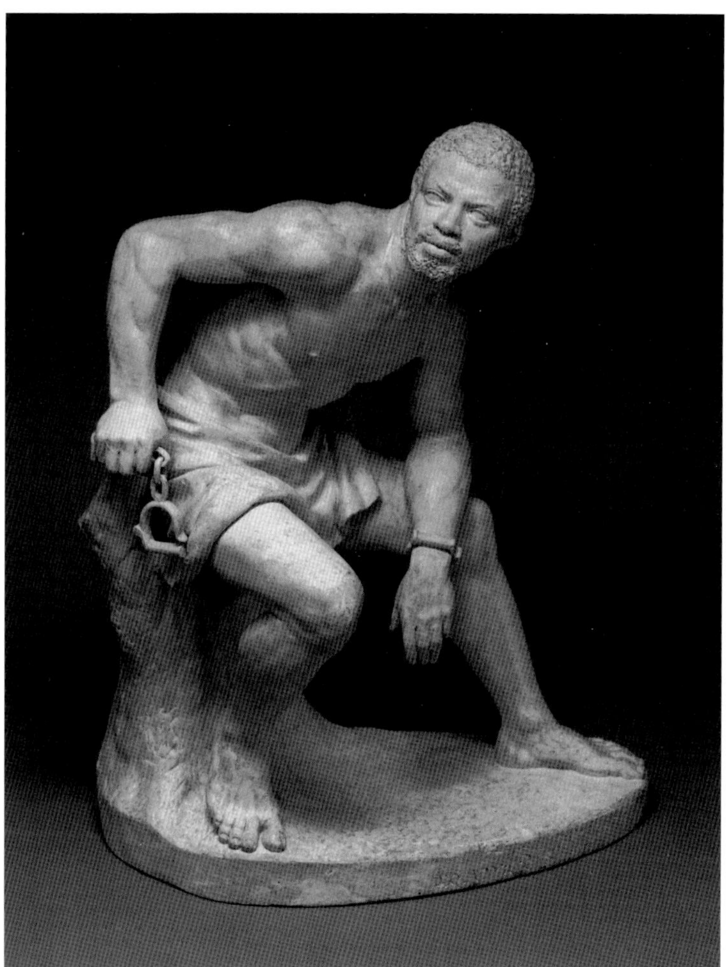

Ward, *Freedman* (see also back cover)

Notes

1. "Mr. Ward's Statue of the Fugitive Negro, at the Academy of Design," *New York Times,* May 3, 1863, p. 5.
2. James Jackson Jarves, *The Art-Idea* (first published in 1864; reprinted Cambridge, Mass.: Belknap Press of Harvard University, 1960), p. 225.
3. John Quincy Adams Ward to J.R. Lambdin, April 2, 1863, Albert Rosenthal Papers, Archives of American Art, Smithsonian Institution.
4. *Dictionary of American Biography,* s.v. "Ward, John Quincy Adams."
5. Lewis I. Sharp, *John Quincy Adams Ward: Dean of American Sculpture* (Newark: University of Delaware Press, 1985), p. 42.
6. Henry T. Tuckerman, *Book of the Artists* (first published in 1867; reprinted New York: James F. Carr, 1967, p. 581.
7. David B. Dearinger, "John Quincy Adams Ward," *An American Collection: Paintings and Sculpture from the National Academy of Design* (New York: National Academy of Design, 1989), exhib. cat., pp. 48–49.
8. The application of white paint and the losses may have occurred about 1883 while the sculpture was being used for teaching purposes as part of the Pennsylvania Academy's cast collection. See *The Olympia Galleries Important Collection of Photographs by Thomas Eakins* (New York: Sotheby Parke Bernet, Nov. 1977), sale no. 4044B, cat. no. 504 (ill. [on shelf in background]).

Exhibited

1863* cat. no. 394. **1864*** cat. no. 288. **1867*** cat. no. 389. **1868*** cat. no. 444. **1869*** cat. no. 356. **1986–87** PAFA, *Sculpture at the Pennsylvania Academy of the Fine Arts.* **1994–96** PAFA, *Two Centuries of Collecting at the Museum of American Art.*

Isaac Broome

1835–1922

Isaac Broome was born in Valcartier in the province of Quebec but was reared in Philadelphia. At the age of sixteen, he began to study wood and stone carving with his neighbor, the sculptor HUGH A. CANNON.[1] Cannon had studied at the Pennsylvania Academy of the Fine Arts, and he exhibited there. It seems likely that he encouraged Broome to do the same. Broome may have attended the Pennsylvania Academy during the early 1850s and was certainly at work there by September of 1856, when he was issued a permit to copy a painting.[2] His name appears in the Academy's life-class register of about 1858 and in the antique-class register of 1859.[3]

Broome first exhibited at the Pennsylvania Academy in 1855: he showed a bust of a gentleman and an ideal piece called *Memory* in the thirty-second annual exhibition. Three years later, in the thirty-fifth annual exhibition, his first bust carved in marble, a portrait of Mrs. Francis Peters, was shown.[4] He also participated in the annual exhibitions from 1859 through 1869 and in 1876, 1878, 1903, and 1906. With the exception of *Memory* and *The Wandering Psyche,* shown in 1906, all the works that Broome exhibited at the Pennsylvania Academy were portraits in the round or in relief.

In several obituaries and in Broome's listing in *Who's Who in America,* it is recorded that between 1855 and 1856 he worked on the statues designed by THOMAS CRAWFORD for the east pediment of the United States Capitol. Although no records confirming Broome's employment as a stone carver could be located in the archives of the Capitol,[5] it is possible that he was an unpaid apprentice and thus his name went unrecorded. If so, he probably did not work very long on the pediment statues inasmuch as he was back in Philadelphia in September of 1856.

Sometime between 1857 and 1858, Broome traveled to Italy, France, and England. While abroad, he visited museums and collected art for American patrons. He maintained a studio in Rome for a time and there translated into marble several busts of Americans.[6] In Italy he studied Greek and Etruscan pottery, which piqued an interest in ceramics that remained throughout his life.[7]

Following his return to the United States, Broome resumed his studies at the Pennsylvania Academy in 1860.[8] That year, he was made an associate of the Academy; the next year, he was elected an academician. About 1865 he moved to Pittsburgh and established himself as a manufacturer of terracotta objects, such as vases, fountains, and architectural ornaments. Pittsburgh proved to be a poor market for his wares, however, and he returned to sculpting and painting. In 1871 he attempted to open a terracotta works in Brooklyn, New York, but was forced to abandon the venture when the board of health ruled his kilns a fire hazard.[9]

In 1875 Broome was hired by Ott and Brewer, owners of the Etruria Pottery in Trenton, New Jersey, to design and model objects in parian. His designs were featured in the Etruria Pottery's display at the Centennial Exhibition in Philadelphia, 1876; and his *Baseball Vase* and *Cleopatra* (both, New Jersey State Museum, Trenton) were awarded medals. The *Baseball Vase* stands thirty-four inches high and is embellished with baseball motifs, including three baseball players modeled in the round and frozen in action. *Cleopatra* is a bust of polychromed parian with an exquisitely detailed costume.

After the Centennial Exhibition, Broome's expertise in ceramics was widely touted; and, in 1878, he was appointed a special commissioner of ceramics to the Exposition Universelle in Paris by joint order of the United States Government and the State of New Jersey. He remained in Europe for about two years collecting information on various potteries and ceramic techniques. Throughout the 1880s and 1890s, he lectured and wrote about ceramics.

In 1883 Broome accepted a position as modeler and designer of tiles at the Trent Tile Company in Trenton. Two years later, he helped establish the Broome Providential Tile Works in that city. He also worked at the Beaver Falls Art Tile Company in Pennsylvania. His tile designs include a head of Sappho and a series representing various aspects of the arts.[10]

Broome had a powerful interest in sociology and, in 1890, published *The Brother,* a scathing indictment of the American industrial-labor system. He was a leader and teacher at the Ruskin Co-Operative, an industrial settlement in Ruskin, Tennessee, and, in 1902, wrote *The Last Days of the Ruskin Co-Operative Association.*

During his later years, Broome held the position of scientific and technical expert for Lenox, Incorporated, in Trenton. He was a personal friend of Walter Scott Lenox; and, at the age of eighty-four, Broome painted four panels representing the seasons for Lenox's home.[11]

Notes

1. Isaac Broome to Harrison S. Morris, managing director of the PAFA, Feb. 25, 1900, PAFA Archives.

2. Permit issued Sept. 24, 1856, Committee on Instruction, File of Applications and Permits to Copy Paintings, 1856–69, PAFA Archives.

3. Life Class Register, about 1858–69, and Antique Class Register, 1859–69, PAFA Archives. At that time, the school year seems to have run from October 1 to March 31.

4. *Descriptive Catalogue of the Permanent Collection of Works of Art* (Philadelphia: PAFA, 1900), p. 105. In 1878 Mrs. Peters's bust and probably that of her husband were deposited in the Pennsylvania Academy by a Mrs. Barstow of South Carolina. They remained in the collection until 1950 when, along with a plaster head of a baby by Broome, they were deaccessioned and sold through Samuel T. Freeman's auction house in Philadelphia.

5. Telephone interview with the Arts and Reference Department of the Architect of the Capitol, by Mary Mullen Cunningham, Jan. 23, 1987, PAFA research file.

6. "His Life Devoted to Art Productions: Isaac Broome, Former Noted Designer for Local Potteries and Tile Work, Is Giving Himself to Classic Sculpture," about 1916, clipping file, Art Department, Trenton Free Library.

7. Edwin Atlee Barber, *Pottery and Porcelain of the United States* (Watkins Glen, originally published 1893; reprinted in New York: Century House Americana, 1971), p. 371.

8. Student Registration Card, 1860, PAFA Archives.

9. Barber 1893, pp. 371–72.

10. Ibid., pp. 362, 367, 370, 374.

11. Harry J. Podmore, "Veteran Trenton Artist Produces Wonderful Work in Clay and Oil: Professor Isaac Broome's Attractive Group Paintings Representing the Four Seasons to Adorn Walls of Proposed New Residence of Walter Scott Lenox," *Trenton Sunday Times Advertiser*, Dec. 26, 1919, vertical file, Trenton Free Library.

References
1922 Obituary, *Trenton Times*, May 5, vertical file, Trenton Free Library. **1922** Obituary, *Trenton State Gazette*, May 17, ibid. **1973** Barbara White Morse, "Tiles Made by Isaac Broome, Sculptor and Genius," *Spinning Wheel* (Jan.–Feb.), pp. 18–22. **1962** *Who Was Who in America*, vol. 1, 1897–1942, Chicago: A.N. Marquis Company, p. 144.

Benjamin Franklin

1857–58
Marble
22 x 21 x 14" (55.9 x 53.3 x 35.6 cm)
Source unknown (1858), 1944.16

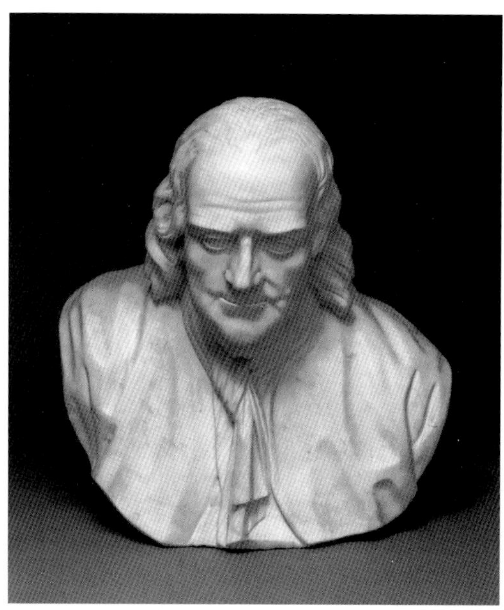

Broome, *Benjamin Franklin*

THIS IMAGE of Benjamin Franklin (1706–1790) is based on the life portrait modeled in 1777 by the French sculptor Jean Jacques Caffieri (1725–1792). The date 1857–58 has been assigned to Broome's portrait because it appeared at the Pennsylvania Academy of the Fine Arts in 1858 [1] and because Broome is believed to have carved his first marble portrait only a year earlier.[2]

Broome's model for the bust of Franklin is unknown. He may have copied the Caffieri-type bust of Franklin attributed to GIUSEPPE IARDELLA, which had been owned by the Pennsylvania Academy since 1811 (q.v.). But there are discrepancies between the two that make it difficult to reconcile them as model and copy. For instance, Broome's lacks the forward thrust of the head found in Iardella's bust. Also, Broome delineated the pupils in the eyes; while, on the earlier bust, the eyes are blank. Because Broome was in Rome during 1857–58, he may have used one of the numerous Italian copies of Caffieri's bust as his model.[3] Possibly he executed this bust for practice before beginning to carve marble versions of the plaster busts that he had brought with him from Philadelphia. In 1858 Broome's bust of Franklin was installed on the portico outside the Pennsylvania Academy's building on Tenth and Chestnut streets.[4] It provided a companion to the colossal head of Napoleon that had stood on the other side of the portico for several years. Later, the Napoleon was replaced by the bust of Franklin attributed to Giuseppe Iardella. Since 1858 these two busts of Franklin had been confused in the Academy's records. In fact, it was not until the 1876 *Catalogue of the Property and Loan Exhibition of the Pennsylvania Academy of the Fine Arts* was published that Broome was correctly recorded as the sculptor of this bust. Although Broome's bust had been listed as the property of the Pennsylvania Academy in the 1858 permanent collection catalogue, it was not formally accessioned until 1944.

Notes

1. *Catalogue of the Thirty-fifth Annual Exhibition of the Pennsylvania Academy of the Fine Arts* (Philadelphia: PAFA, 1858), pp. 28–29. In this catalogue, both Broome's bust and the one now attributed to Iardella are erroneously attributed to the Italian sculptor Giuseppe Ceracchi (1751–1801).

2. *Descriptive Catalogue of the Permanent Collection of Works of Art* (Philadelphia: PAFA, 1900), p. 105, lists bust of Mrs. Francis Peters as his first marble portrait.

3. Charles Coleman Sellers, *Benjamin Franklin in Portraiture* (New Haven: Yale University Press, 1962), p. 203.

4. *Catalogue,* 1858, p. 29.

Exhibited

1935 At dedication of new Philadelphia Post Office, Thirtieth and Chestnut Streets. **1952** Houston Hall, University of Pennsylvania, Philadelphia. **1975** Second Bank of the United States, Philadelphia, *Masterworks of American Art, 1740–1840.* **1978–79** PAFA, *350 Masterpieces of American Art: 1720–1978.*

Pierce Francis Connelly

1841–1932

Pierce Francis Connelly, the fifth child of Pierce and Cornelia Peacock Connelly, was born in the small town of Grand Coteau, Louisiana. His parents were natives of Philadelphia, where his paternal grandfather, Henry Connelly, was a well-known furnituremaker. The maelstrom of his early childhood deeply affected Frank Connelly. Just before his birth, his father, an Episcopal minister, resolved to become a Roman Catholic priest. In 1845 Pierce Connelly took his family to Rome where he and Cornelia were granted an official separation by Pope Gregory XVI. The following year, Pierce was ordained; and Cornelia, after taking a formal vow of chastity, entered the convent of the Sacred Heart at Trinità dei Monti. In 1847 the pope ordered Cornelia to England to establish a new teaching order. The three surviving children were placed in English schools. Frank, at four years of age, was sent to the Hampstead School for boys. In 1847 Pierce Connelly experienced a change of heart and began a long and desperate fight to prevent Cornelia from becoming a nun. He eventually gave up and finally left the Catholic Church. In 1853 he took his daughter, Adeline, and Frank to Florence, where, upon returning to the Episcopal fold, Pierce became a minister of the American Episcopal Church. Frank never understood his mother's deep religious convictions. As a young man, he saw her only a few times; and the meetings were strained and traumatic for both of them.[1]

Frank Connelly was further educated at Marlborough College in Wilshire, England. There, the young man's talent for drawing emerged.[2] On April 1, 1861, he entered the Ecole des Beaux-Arts in Paris. His sponsor was the French painter Charles Gleyre whose atelier was one of the most popular for students interested in traditional academic training and preparation for the Ecole's entrance examinations.[3] Gleyre ran his atelier free of tuition, and that may have attracted Connelly.[4] Described as "rather eccentric," Connelly also may have felt a kinship with the brooding and introspective Gleyre.[5] Nonetheless, Connelly did not remain long in Paris; by 1863 he was studying in Rome.[6] Then, during the late 1850s or early 1860s, he spent some time in Philadelphia, probably visiting his uncle Harry Connelly, a wealthy wine dealer.[7] Frank joined the Philadelphia Sketch Club, where he was known as "Father Connelly" because of his parents' religious affiliations.[8]

Sometime during 1864–65 Connelly returned to Florence and began to work in the sculpture studio of HIRAM POWERS. In 1865 Connelly executed a marble bust of Shakespeare's Cordelia, from *King Lear.* Her meticulously rendered brocade costume reflects the late neoclassical concern with textured surfaces.[9] In this century, *Cordelia* was used as the model for the mannequins of the First Ladies at the National Museum of History and Technology, Smithsonian Institution.[10] By 1868 Connelly had opened a studio on the Piazza Donatello in Florence.

Several high-ranking Englishmen were among his friends, and they undoubtedly paved the way for a number of important commissions. In 1870 Connelly traveled to England where he executed busts of English nobles, including a full-length seated statue of Louisa Drummond, the duchess of Northumberland (collection of the duke of Northumberland, Lyon House).[11] In 1871, at the Royal Academy of Arts, he exhibited busts of Henry George (Earl Percy) and Algernon George (the sixth duke of Northumberland).[12]

When John Forney, of Philadelphia, visited Florence to select art for the American Centennial Exhibition, he was greatly impressed by Connelly's work.[13] At the exhibition, Connelly was represented by eleven works, far more than any of the other sculptors. The sculptor and critic Lorado Taft praised Connelly's half-lifesize bronze group *Honor Arresting the Triumph of Death* as one of the most impressive works in the art department of the centennial.[14] Finished in 1869, it was inspired by the Civil War. After the exhibition, Connelly deposited the work at the Pennsylvania Academy and tried unsuccessfully to sell it to the Academy.[15] The sculpture was removed in 1939, when Connelly's daughter, Maria Cornelia Connelly Borghese, gave it to Rosemont College in Rosemont, Pennsylvania, an institution run by the Sisters of the Holy Child Jesus, the order founded by Frank Connelly's mother.[16]

After visiting Philadelphia for the Centennial Exhibition, Connelly traveled to New Zealand, probably at the invitation of his friend and patron Sir John Logan Campbell, whom he had met in Florence in 1864. Connelly arrived in Auckland, early in 1877 and began to paint and draw the exquisite countryside. He exhibited sketches, drawings, and photographs of his sculpture at the exhibition of the Auckland Society of Artists in 1877. In December 1877, he ascended Mount Tongariro to sketch and paint. This mountain was regarded as taboo by the natives, who seized his horse and sketchbooks. Connelly also visited Sydney, Australia, and, in 1878, won the sculpture competition for a memorial to the community leader Thomas Mort. Connelly spent his later years in Florence, where he resided with his daughter.[17]

Notes

1. Juliana Wadham, *The Case of Cornelia Connelly* (New York: Pantheon Books, 1957), p. 145.
2. Harry Connelly Groome, *The Groome Family and Connections: A Pedigree* (Philadelphia: J.B. Lippincott Company, 1907), p. 77.
3. Barbara Weinberg, "Nineteenth Century American Painters at the Ecole des Beaux Arts," *American Art Journal* 13 (Fall 1981), p. 72.
4. Albert Boime, *The Academy and French Painting in the Nineteenth Century* (New Haven: Yale University Press, 1986), pp. 58, 61.
5. Albert TenEyck Gardner, *American Sculpture: A Catalogue of the Collection of the Metropolitan Museum of Art* (New York: Metropolitan Museum of Art, 1965), p. 38.
6. *Catalogue of the Fortieth Annual Exhibition of the Pennsylvania Academy of the Fine Arts* (Philadelphia: PAFA, 1863), p. 20.
7. Groome 1907, p. 78.
8. David Sellin, "The Centennial," *Sculpture of a City: Philadelphia's Treasures in Bronze and Stone* (New York: Walker Publishing Company, 1974), p. 85. See also handwritten notes about various Philadelphia Sketch Club members, probably by Hugh A. McCann, bound with PAFA annual exhibition catalogue, vol. 1852–66, PAFA Archives.
9. William H. Gerdts, *American Neo-Classic Sculpture: The Marble Resurrection* (New York: Viking Press, 1973), p. 116.
10. *The First Ladies Hall: The National Museum of History and Technology, Smithsonian Institution* (Washington, D.C.: Smithsonian Institution Press, 1980), introduction.
11. Colin Shrimpton to Mary Mullen Cunningham, April 8, 1987, PAFA research file.
12. Algernon Graves, *The Royal Academy of Arts: A Complete Dictionary of Contributors and Their Work from Its Foundation in 1769 to 1904* (New York: Burt Franklin, 1972), vol. 2, p. 122.
13. John W. Forney, *A Centennial Commissioner in Europe, 1874–1876* (Philadelphia: J.B. Lippincott and Company, 1876), p. 10.
14. Lorado Taft, *The History of American Sculpture* (New York: Macmillan Company, 1903), p. 261.
15. See Prince M. Borghese to PAFA, April 5, 1921; Borghese to PAFA, Oct. 20, 1921; Pierce Francis Connelly to John F. Lewis, March 18, 1922, Connelly file, Works no longer in collection, PAFA Archives.
16. Order of Maria Cornelia Borghese with seal of American Consul in Rome, July 11, 1939, ibid.
17. Megan Minoque, "Pierce Francis Connelly," 1984 research paper in archives of Society of the Holy Child Jesus, Rosemont, Pa.

Unidentified Gentleman

1867
Marble
22 x 16 x 7" (56 x 40.8 x 18 cm)
Signed and dated on back of integral base: P.F. CONNELLY Fecit Flor 1867
Pennsylvania Academy purchase (1910), 1944.17

WHEN the Pennsylvania Academy of the Fine Arts purchased this bust in 1910, it was thought to depict the painter William Emlen Cresson (1843–1868).[1] In 1942, however, the Works Progress Administration catalogued the American portraits at the Pennsylvania Academy and identified the sitter as the painter William Henry Lippincott (1849–1920). It may have been at this point that LIPPINCOT (*sic*) and the date 1840 were scrawled in pencil on the back of the bust.[2]

Connelly, *Unidentified Gentleman*

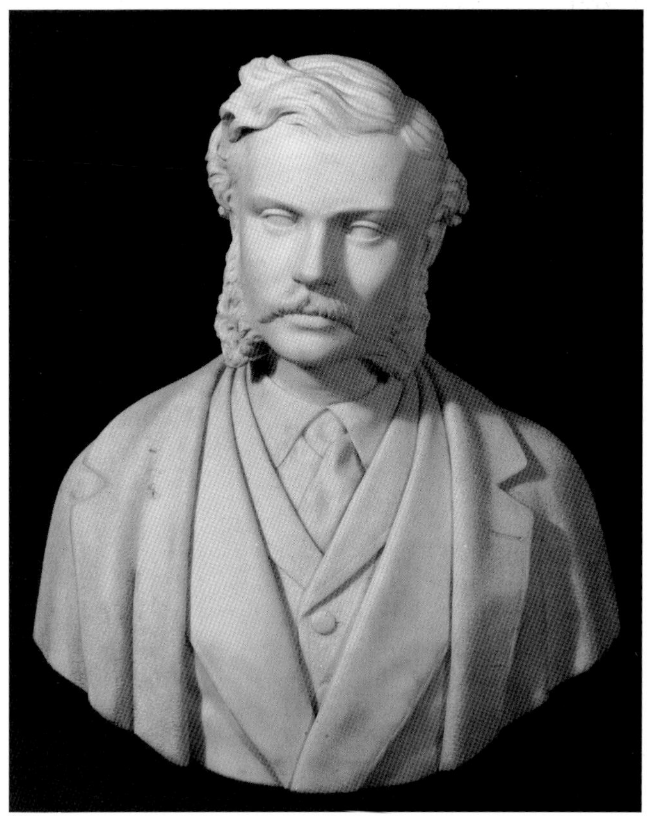

(This annotation was removed during conservation in 1985.) Obviously, the WPA cataloguers believed it to be an entirely different bust from the one acquired in 1910, which was subsequently recorded as no longer in the collection.[3] This explains why the bust was assigned a 1944 accession number.

The sitter's identity is still in question. Frank Connelly may have been acquainted with William Cresson through the Philadelphia Sketch Club. Cresson studied in Paris during 1867, but there is no evidence that he went to Florence. It is important to note, however, that the inscription "Flor" does not necessarily mean that Connelly modeled the bust in Florence. He may have modeled it during a trip to Philadelphia in the early or mid 1860s and simply had it carved in marble upon his return to Florence. Cresson was the only son of well-to-do parents who could have easily afforded a marble bust. Comparison with several surviving images of Cresson, including the relief portrait (q.v.) by JOSEPH A. BAILLY, does not eliminate him as a possible sitter. They reveal, however, that he parted his hair in the middle, unlike the man shown here.

The identification of the sitter in 1942 as William Henry Lippincott seems to have been based on the mention in *Artists of the Nineteenth Century and Their Works* of a bust of Lippincott by Connelly in Philadelphia.[4] William Henry Lippincott would have been only nineteen years old in 1867; and, although this in itself does not rule him out as a possible sitter, a photograph of him as a middle-aged man bears little resemblance to the bust. The bust displays a stronger resemblance to Joshua Lippincott (1814–1880), who was for many years a director of the Commercial National Bank in Philadelphia.[5] He would have been fifty-three years old in 1867, however, and this bust appears to portray a much younger man.

To this profusion of possible sitters must be added Connelly himself. A photograph of the sculptor as a young man matches the bust remarkably well.[6] Connelly, who had taken up sculpture just a few years before executing this bust, often used members of his family as models. It would not have been unusual for him to model a self-portrait, but to spend the money to have it carved in marble would have been remarkable.

During the conservation of this bust in January 1986, traces of plaster were found lodged in the ears and in other pockets. This may indicate that a plaster mold was made from the marble.[7] The whereabouts of replicas, if in existence, are presently unknown.

Notes

1. Minutes, meetings of the board of directors, April 5, 1909, and Feb. 7, 1910, PAFA Archives.
2. The inscription "1840" is odd. The WPA cataloguers erroneously believed it to be Connelly's birth date. See *Inventory of American Portraiture (in Painting and Sculpture) in the Permanent Collection of the Pennsylvania Academy of the Fine Arts*, part of survey of American portraiture in Pennsylvania, 1942, vol. 1, p. 291, unpublished typescript, PAFA Archives.
3. Card file of works no longer in permanent collection, PAFA Archives.
4. Clara Erskine Clement and Laurence Hutton, *Artists of the Nineteenth Century and Their Works* (Boston: Houghton, Osgood and Company, 1879), p. 151.
5. "Old Philadelphia Families CVI; Lippincott," *Philadelphia North American*, April 14, 1912, sec. 6, p. 6.
6. "Family Album," *Pylon* 29 (Special issue, 1968), p. 23.
7. Conservation report, Jan. 8, 1986, PAFA object file.

Exhibited

1962 PAFA, *Forgotten Favorites: Selections from the Permanent Collection.* **1986–87** PAFA, *Sculpture at the Pennsylvania Academy of the Fine Arts.*

Howard Roberts

1843–1900

By choosing to study in Paris in 1866 rather than in Florence or Rome, Howard Roberts placed himself in the vanguard of American sculptors. Although his major works are in marble, not bronze, they display the new naturalism and vigorous modeling that was the hallmark of the Ecole des Beaux-Arts in Paris.

Roberts was born into a well-to-do Philadelphia family. His paternal grandfather, Algernon Roberts, had served as an officer in the Pennsylvania Militia during the Revolution. Howard was educated at the Classical Institute of the Reverend John W. Faires and probably began classes at the Pennsylvania Academy of the Fine Arts in 1860 or 1861. At the Academy, he studied sculpture under JOSEPH A. BAILLY and, in 1863, was registered in the life class.[1] Roberts exhibited a low relief entitled *Cordelia* at the Pennsylvania Academy's annual exhibition in 1863 and, the following year, a statue entitled *Cupid.* In 1864 he was elected an associate member of the Pennsylvania Academy, an honor that gave him free access to the Academy's classes.

In 1861 Roberts was among the sixteen students and alumni of the Pennsylvania Academy who signed the charter of the Philadelphia Sketch Club. Other signers included the painters Earl Shinn, Daniel Ridgway Knight, and Robert Wylie. Roberts served as treasurer for the club in 1865. The first Annual Prize Exhibition of the Sketch Club was held in December of that year at the Pennsylvania Academy. Roberts exhibited and offered for sale three works: *Mephistopheles, Shan't Have It,* and *Evening.*[2]

Following the end of the Civil War, Roberts and his friend Earl Shinn set sail for Paris in April of 1866. They applied for admission to the Ecole des Beaux-Arts but were told that they would have to wait for openings to occur. In the meantime, they went to Pont-Aven in Brittany, where a colony of American artists had formed around their fellow Philadelphian Robert Wylie. By the fall, Roberts had yet to be accepted at the Ecole, so he enrolled at the private atelier of the sculptor Charles Alphonse Gumery (1827–1871). If it had not been for the arrival of THOMAS EAKINS in Paris in September 1866, Roberts might never have entered the Ecole. Eakins was undaunted by the obstacles and succeeded in gaining admission for himself and (quite unintentionally) the other Americans, including Roberts.[3]

At the Ecole des Beaux-Arts, Roberts studied under Augustin Alexandre Dumont (1801–1884) and developed a sound understanding of the human form. He visited Italy with Earl Shinn in 1868 and then returned to Paris before going home in 1869. Back in Philadelphia, Roberts set up his studio at 1731 Chestnut Street. He was soon favored with commissions from Philadelphia's high society. In the spring of 1870, Earl Shinn penned a newspaper account of the works executed by Roberts since his return from Paris. It notes two portrait busts: one of a well-known homeopathic physician and the other of a young lady. During his first years home, Roberts also produced several ideal busts, including one entitled *Lucile,* inspired by the novel of that name by Owen Meredith. It embodied the figure to the waist and included both arms. Roberts's statuette *Hester Prynne and Baby Pearl at the Pillory,* inspired by Nathaniel Hawthorne's *Scarlet Letter,* was exhibited in the window of the Philadelphia jewelry store Bailey and Company (now Bailey, Banks and Biddle) in April 1872.[4]

In 1873 Roberts returned to Paris for eighteen months. There, he completed the model for *La Première Pose,* 1873–76 (Philadelphia Museum of Art), a virtuoso study of a nude female model at her first sitting. The finished marble was shipped to Philadelphia for the Centennial Exhibition, where it was awarded one of the three medals given to American sculpture. Although it received wide acclaim, it was also criticized; many Americans were not yet willing to accept a nude devoid of narrative context. The critic Lorado Taft applauded Roberts's success in creating such a beautiful figure. But Taft was a stickler for realism, and he found the model's pose affected and "too professional" to elicit a true sense of modesty.[5]

Roberts was an energetic presence in the Philadelphia art scene of the 1870s. He served as vice-president of the Philadelphia Sketch Club in 1871 and 1872 and as president from 1873 to 1877. In 1878 he showed *Lot's Wife* (private collection), his most modernistic sculpture, at the first exhibition of the Society of American Artists, in New York. The sculpture captures the moment when the unfortunate woman is being turned to salt. That same year, Roberts won a statewide competition for a statue to be installed in the nation's Statuary Hall, which was established in 1864 in the old chamber of the House of Representatives in the Capitol. Roberts's finished marble statue of the Pennsylvania inventor Robert Fulton was installed there in 1883. Little is known about the sculptor's later years. He died in Paris in 1900.

Notes

1. Life-Class Register, about 1858–69, PAFA Archives.
2. *First Annual Prize Exhibition of the Philadelphia Sketch Club Held at the Pennsylvania Academy of the Fine Arts,* Dec. 1865, PAFA Archives.
3. Thomas Eakins to his father, Benjamin, Oct. 13, 1866, PAFA Archives, relates that Eakins and Roberts, former classmates at the PAFA, felt a mutual dislike.
4. David Sellin, "The First Pose: Howard Roberts, Thomas Eakins and a Century of Philadelphia Nudes," *Bulletin, Philadelphia Museum of Art* 70 (Spring 1975); reprinted with additional material as *The First Pose, 1876: Turning Point in American Art; Howard Roberts, Thomas Eakins and a Century of Philadelphia Nudes* (New York: W.W. Norton and Company, 1976), pp. 22–23.
5. Lorado Taft, *The History of American Sculpture* (New York: Macmillan Company, 1903), p. 257.

References

About 1867–94 Howard Roberts scrapbook, microfilm, roll no. 3657, Archives of American Art, Smithsonian Institution, Washington, D.C. **1878** William J. Clark, Jr., *Great American Sculptures,* Philadelphia: Gebbie and Barrie, pp. 101–4. **1976** Joe Rischl, "Howard Roberts," *Philadelphia: Three Centuries of American Art,* Philadelphia: Philadelphia Museum of Art, pp. 394–95.

Eleänore

1870
Marble
25¼ x 17 x 11" (64.1 x 43.2 x 28 cm)
Signed and dated at right: HRoberts. 1870 [initials in monogram]
Bequest of Henry C. Gibson, 1892.6.11

HOWARD ROBERTS executed this bust in his Philadelphia studio shortly after returning from Paris. While still in progress—and untitled—it was described in detail in a Philadelphia newspaper.[1] Roberts obviously named the piece after it was finished.

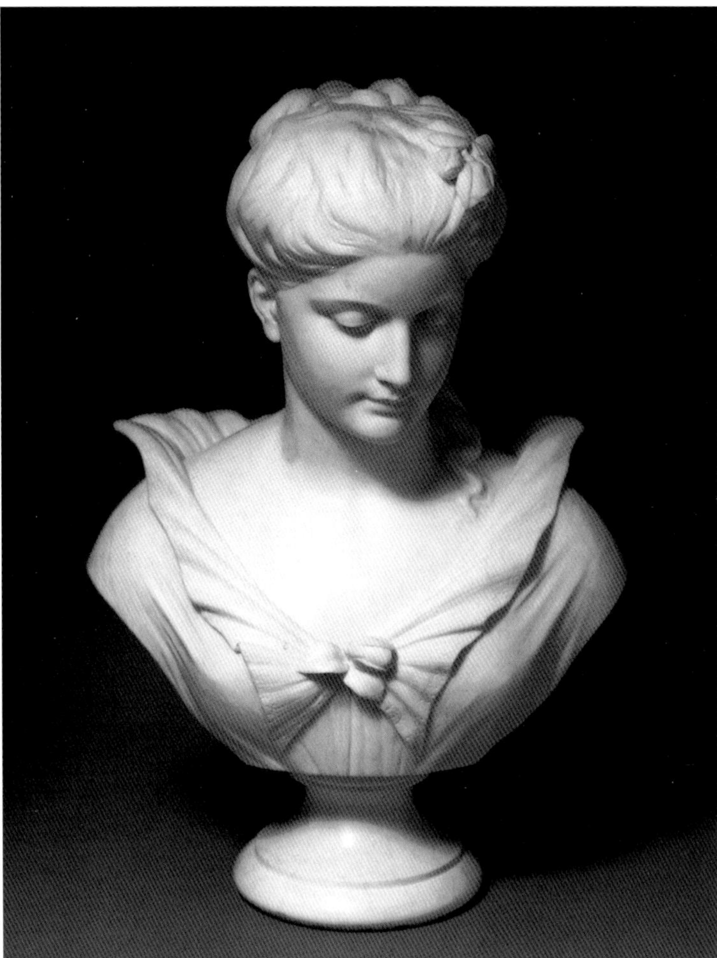

Roberts, *Eleänore*

He took the title from Alfred Lord Tennyson's poem "Eleänore," which begins, "Thy dark eyes open'd not." Roberts undoubtedly employed a model to sit for the bust.[2] Although he idealized her, the sculpture retains a sense of the individual.

In April 1870, Roberts exhibited *Eleänore* and another idealized bust at Bailey and Company, a Philadelphia jewelry store that offered its display windows as exhibition space for artists.[3] *Eleänore* was purchased by the Philadelphia art collector Henry Gibson, who gave it to the Pennsylvania Academy of the Fine Arts.

Notes

1. Unidentified Philadelphia newspaper clipping, 1870, from the Howard Roberts scrapbook, microfilm, roll no. 3657, frame no. 60, Archives of American Art, Smithsonian Institution, Washington, D.C.
2. *Philadelphia Bulletin,* 1870, newspaper clipping, microfilm, roll no. 3657, frame no. 61, ibid.
3. Ibid.

Reference

1975 David Sellin, "The First Pose: Howard Roberts, Thomas Eakins and a Century of Philadelphia Nudes," *Bulletin, Philadelphia Museum of Art* 70 (Spring); reprinted in 1976 with additional material as *The First Pose, 1876: Turning Point in American Art; Howard Roberts, Thomas Eakins and a Century of Philadelphia Nudes,* New York: W.W. Norton and Company, p. 22 (ill.).

Exhibited

1870 Bailey and Company, Philadelphia. **1962** PAFA, *Forgotten Favorites: Selections from the Permanent Collection.* **1974** PAFA, *The Beneficent Connoisseurs (The Henry C. Gibson Collection),* cat. no. 71, as *Eleanor.* **1978–79** PAFA, *350 Masterpieces of American Art.* **1986–87** PAFA, *Sculpture at the Pennsylvania Academy of the Fine Arts.* **1994–96** PAFA, *Two Centuries of Collecting at the Museum of American Art.*

Roberts, *Hypathia* (see also front cover)

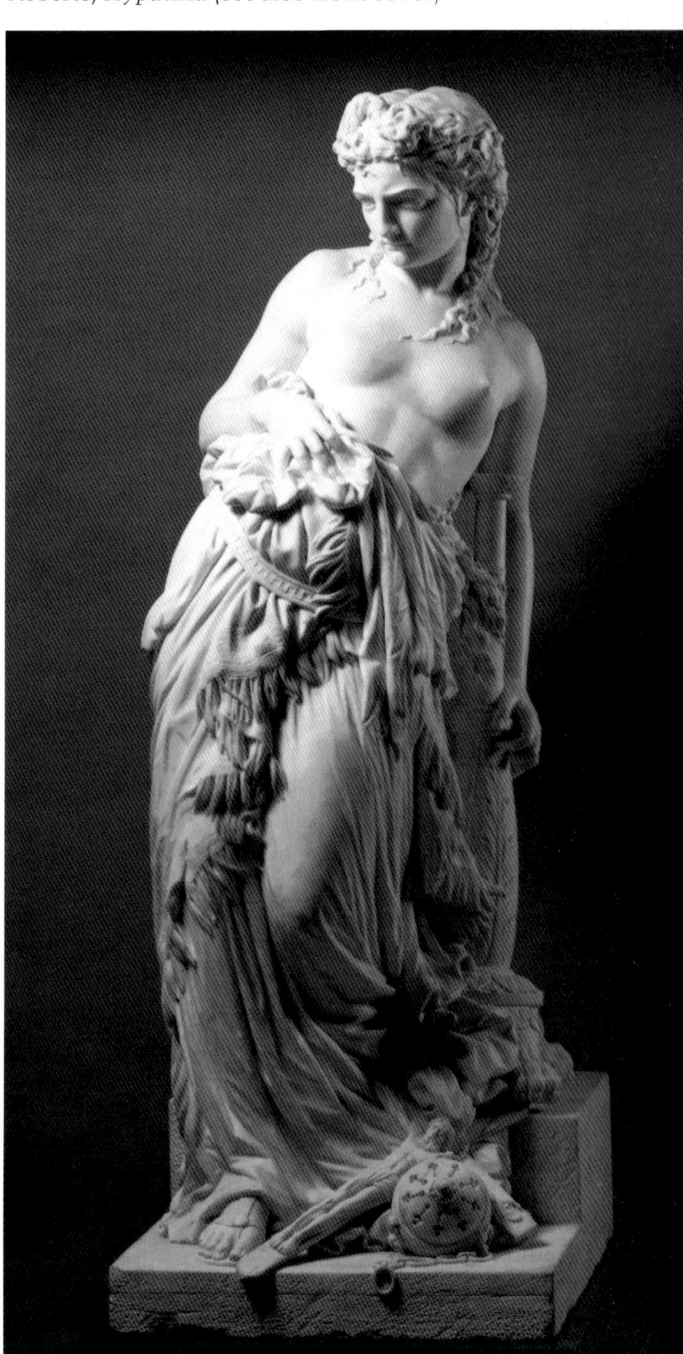

Ex Collection
Henry C. Gibson, 1870–92.

Hypathia

1873
Marble; carved in 1877
67 x 23¾ x 28½" (170.2 x 60.3 x 72.4 cm)
Signed on plinth at front left: HRoberts. [initials in monogram]
Gift of Mrs. Pauline L. Roberts, 1928.1

HYPATHIA was a beautiful neoplatonic philosopher said to have been murdered in Alexandria in A.D. 415 by a band of monks. This sculpture was inspired by Charles Kingsley's 1853 novel, *Hypathia.* The statue depicts the pagan philosopher turning from flight to face the fanatic band that has driven her into a church to slay her. In typical Victorian fashion, accessories—crucifix, censer, and candlestick—are used to convey the story.

Hypathia was Howard Roberts's first attempt to model a lifesize figure. He completed the plaster model in 1873 and probably intended to show the marble at the Centennial Exhibition in Philadelphia. He took the plaster model to Paris where he planned to have it carved in marble; but once in Paris, he became engrossed with a new work, *La Première Pose,* 1873–76 (Philadelphia Museum of Art), an academic nude from life. Roberts decided to complete it rather than *Hypathia* for the Centennial Exhibition. He hoped that it would attract more attention than the literary theme of *Hypathia* and would also generate favorable comparisons with the avant-garde French sculpture that would be shown close to it. Perhaps he was also influenced by the fact that Peter F. Rothermel had independently chosen Hypathia as the subject for a painting that he planned to show at the centennial.[1]

Roberts shipped the plaster model of *Hypathia* back to Philadelphia, where it was cut in marble in 1877. Upon completion, it was exhibited at Earle's Galleries, 816 Chestnut Street. According to Roberts's friend the critic William J. Clark, *Hypathia* did more to increase the sculptor's fame than *La Première Pose* because it "appealed to a wider range of tastes, and a different order of sympathies."[2]

In 1894 Roberts left Philadelphia for an indefinite stay in Europe. Before going, he made arrangements for a long-term loan of *Hypathia* to the Pennsylvania Academy of the Fine Arts.[3] The statue remained at the Academy and, in 1928, was formally donated by the sculptor's wife.

Notes

1. Sellin 1975, pp. 23–24, 28.
2. William J. Clark, Jr., *Great American Sculptures* (Philadelphia: Gebbie and Barrie, 1878), p. 103.
3. Howard Roberts to Harrison S. Morris, managing director of PAFA, Feb. 22, 1894, PAFA object file.

References

1975 David Sellin, "The First Pose: Howard Roberts, Thomas Eakins and a Century of Philadelphia Nudes," *Bulletin, Philadelphia Museum of Art* 70 (Spring); reprinted in 1976 with additional material as *The First Pose, 1876: Turning Point in American Art; Howard Roberts, Thomas Eakins and a Century of Philadelphia Nudes,* New York: W.W. Norton and Company, p. 23 (ill.). **1982** Linda Bantel, "Sculpture at the Pennsylvania Academy," *Antiques* 121 (March), p. 701 (ill.).

Exhibited

1877 Earle's Galleries, Philadelphia. **1905*** cat. no. 1030. **1978–79** PAFA, *350 Masterpieces of American Art.* **1986–87** PAFA, *Sculpture at the Pennsylvania Academy of the Fine Arts.*

DENNIS B. SHEAHAN

Died after 1910

Few biographical facts have come to light about Dennis B. Sheahan, who was active in New York between 1873 and 1910. He executed bronze and marble portraits in a late neoclassical style. His imposing, over-lifesize bronze bust of the Irish poet Thomas Moore, made in 1879, stands on a granite pedestal in New York's Central Park. Sheahan's portraits and genre sculptures were exhibited at the National Academy of Design in 1876, 1877, 1878, and 1881, as well as the National Sculpture Society in 1898.

He catered to the growing vogue for narrative sculpture that arose in the United States during the last quarter of the nineteenth century. The titles of sculpture that he exhibited at the National Academy of Design, like *Hamlet* and *General Custer's Last Charge,* suggest their popular appeal. One of his narrative works, a plaster statuette entitled *Frank Mayo as Davy Crockett,* 1883, is in the New-York Historical Society.

Joseph Harrison, Jr.

1874
Marble
23⅜ x 20⅞ x 13⅛" (59.4 x 53 x 33.3 cm)
Signed and dated on back: D B SHEAHAN Sculp[t] New York 1874
Bequest of Mrs. Joseph Harrison, Jr., 1912.14.5

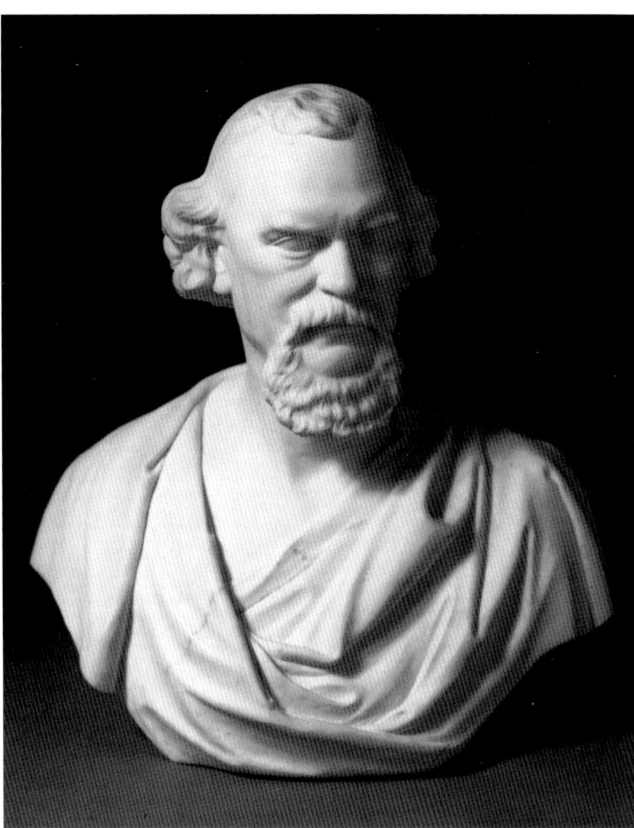

Sheahan, *Joseph Harrison, Jr.*

SARAH HARRISON probably commissioned Dennis B. Sheahan to execute this marble portrait of her husband shortly after his death on March 27, 1874. Although Harrison had been sickly during the last years of his life, the bust represents him as a vital elderly gentleman. Sheahan's neoclassical style seems particularly appropriate for a likeness of Harrison, an art collector who loved grandeur and history in art.

A self-made man, Joseph Harrison, Jr. (1810–1874), amassed his fortune by building locomotives. During the 1840s, he spent several years in Russia overseeing the construction of trains for the rail line from Saint Petersburg to Moscow. While in Europe, he began to indulge his passion for art and collected both European and American works. In London during the early 1850s, he acquired several important American paintings, including the first of Gilbert Stuart's Vaughan-type portraits of George Washington, 1795 (National Gallery of Art, Washington, D.C.), and Benjamin West's *Penn's Treaty with the Indians,* 1771–72 (Museum of American Art, Pennsylvania Academy of the Fine Arts). It was also in England in 1852 that Harrison bought George Catlin's entire Indian gallery for about forty thousand dollars. Catlin's gallery encompassed hundreds of canvases that he had painted to record American Indian life, as well as his extensive collection of Indian artifacts. Unfortunately, because of a bitter dispute between Harrison and Catlin, the entire collection was relegated to storage in several Philadelphia warehouses for over a quarter of a century, until 1879 when Sarah Harrison donated it to the Smithsonian Institution.[1]

When Harrison returned in 1852 from his long European stay, he built a mansion on Rittenhouse Square in Philadelphia to house his growing art collection. At the sale of the Peale Museum's collection in Philadelphia in 1854, Harrison acquired several additional important paintings, including Charles Willson Peale's masterpiece *The Artist in His Museum,* 1822 (Museum of American Art, Pennsylvania Academy of the Fine Arts). Harrison became a leading figure in Philadelphia art circles and in 1854 was elected to the board of directors of the Pennsylvania Academy of the Fine Arts. He patronized several Philadelphia artists, including Christian Schussele and Thomas Buchanan Read.

In 1878, four years after her husband's death, Sarah Harrison gave eleven paintings to the Pennsylvania Academy in his memory. She bequeathed five more paintings and this bust of Harrison to the Academy in 1912. These two gifts included such masterpieces as Benjamin West's *Penn's Treaty with the Indians* and *Christ Rejected,* 1814; Charles Willson Peale's *The Artist in His Museum;* John Vanderlyn's *Ariadne Asleep on the Island of Naxos,* 1809–14; and Rembrandt Peale's large porthole portrait *George Washington, Patriae Pater,* about 1824.

Notes

1. "Joseph Harrison, Jr., a forgotten art collector," *Antiques* 102 (Oct. 1972), pp. 660–68.

Exhibited

1974 PAFA, *The Beneficent Connoisseurs (The Joseph and Sarah Harrison Collection),* cat. no. 6. **1976** PAFA, *In This Academy,* cat. no. 37.

THOMAS EAKINS

1844–1916

Born in Philadelphia, Thomas Eakins was the son of the writing master and professional calligrapher Benjamin Eakins (portrait bust by SAMUEL MURRAY [q.v.]), who unfailingly supported his career as an artist. As a student at Central High School, Thomas showed an aptitude for drawing. Beginning in the fall of 1862, he studied for three years at the Pennsylvania Academy of the Fine Arts, where classes were loosely supervised by Peter Frederick Rothermel and Christian Schussele. Eakins also took anatomy instruction at Jefferson Medical College. In 1866 he went to Paris and studied at the Ecole des Beaux-Arts in the atelier of the academic painter Jean Léon Gérôme, whose belief in studying sculpture to learn form and anatomy led Eakins to seek instruction from the sculptor Augustin Alexandre Dumont (1801–1884).

Eakins returned to Philadelphia in 1870. When the Pennsylvania Academy opened its new building in 1876, he began to assist Schussele, the ailing head of the school, and the new professor of anatomy, Dr. William Williams Keen, a leading Philadelphia surgeon. Eakins succeeded Schussele as professor of drawing and painting in 1879 and was named director in 1881. He reorganized the school's curriculum and based it in part upon that of the Ecole des Beaux-Arts in Paris. He reduced the length of time during which students drew from plaster casts and moved them into a coeducational class sketching a clothed model. They then advanced to segregated life classes in which they painted from the nude figure. Eakins made all students—not just sculptors—model in clay and wax. He believed this helped the painters to understand human movement and achieve a sense of three-dimensionality in their work.

Eakins's views on teaching were so controversial that in 1886 he was asked to resign from the Pennsylvania Academy. Among the students who followed him to the Art Students' League of Philadelphia were Samuel Murray, CHARLES GRAFLY, and CHARLES BREGLER. Eakins was to influence generations of Pennsylvania Academy students through Grafly and A. STIRLING CALDER who went on to teach many of his theories. Eakins shared a studio with Murray and WILLIAM R. O'DONOVAN in the 1890s and collaborated with Murray on the figures for the Witherspoon Building in Philadelphia and with O'Donovan on the horses for the Soldiers and Sailors Memorial Arch in Brooklyn.

Most of Eakins's sculptures were studies for paintings, i.e., William Rush models (q.v.), horse studies for *Fairman Rogers Four-in-Hand,* wax models for *The Swimming Hole,* and studies for *Arcadia* (q.v.). These sculptural studies were among the many tools —such as photographs, pencil drawings, watercolor and oil sketches, and anatomical studies—that he used to create a convincing illusion on canvas of three-dimensional forms.

Reliefs were another of his interests, deriving from his admiration for the Parthenon friezes, which he knew from replicas in the Pennsylvania Academy's cast collection. Eakins lectured and wrote about the subject and executed several commissioned reliefs—*Spinning* and *Knitting* (qq.v.) and, about 1893, the reliefs for the Battle Monument in Trenton—as well as reliefs for his own purposes—the *Arcadia* series.

References
1977 Phyllis D. Rosenzweig, *The Thomas Eakins Collection of the Hirshhorn Museum and Sculpture Garden,* Washington, D.C.: Hirshhorn Museum. **1982** Lloyd Goodrich, *Thomas Eakins,* Cambridge, Mass.: Harvard University Press for the National Gallery of Art, vols. 1 and 2. **1989** Kathleen A. Foster and Cheryl Leibold, *Writing about Eakins: The Manuscripts in Charles Bregler's Thomas Eakins Collection,* Philadelphia: University of Pennsylvania Press. **1997** Kathleen A. Foster, *Thomas Eakins Rediscovered,* New Haven, Conn.: Yale University Press.

Five models for *"William Rush Carving the Allegorical Figure of the Nymph of the Schuylkill"*

1876–77
Plaster, cast in 1931 from original wax models
Charles Bregler's Thomas Eakins Collection, purchased with the partial support of the Pew Memorial Trust, 1985.68.1.1.1–5

Allegory of the Waterworks
4⅝ x 8⅜ x 2¾" (11.8 x 21.3 x 7 cm)
Inscribed by Charles Bregler at back: EAKIN [*sic*]

William Rush
7⅛ x 4¼ x 5" (18.1 x 10.8 x 12.7 cm)
Inscribed by Charles Bregler at back: EAKINS;
underneath: I

Water Nymph and Bittern
(Allegory of the Schuylkill River)
9½ x 4¼ x 2⅝" (24.1 x 10.8 x 6.7 cm)

Head of the Water Nymph
7⅜ x 4½ x 3½" (18.7 x 11.4 x 8.9 cm)
Inscribed by Charles Bregler underneath base: IV/EAKINS

George Washington
8⅛ x 4⅛ x 2⅝" (20.6 x 10.5 x 6.7 cm)
Inscribed by Charles Bregler underneath base: IV

THOMAS EAKINS created several paintings between 1876 and 1908 on the theme of WILLIAM RUSH and his model for the *Allegory of the Schuylkill River,* including the 1876–77 painting at the Philadelphia Museum of Art. Eakins felt a kinship to Rush for they both were Philadelphians who strongly believed in the realistic depiction of the human body and the

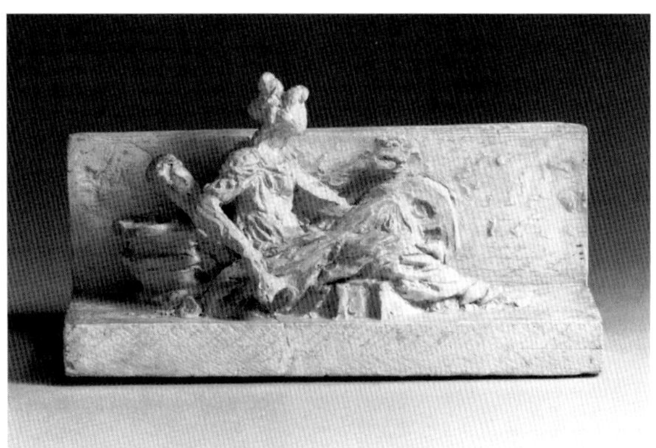

Eakins, *Allegory of the Waterworks*

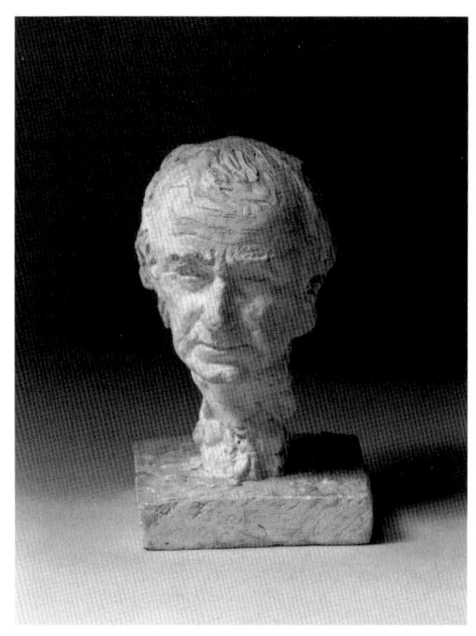

Eakins, *William Rush*

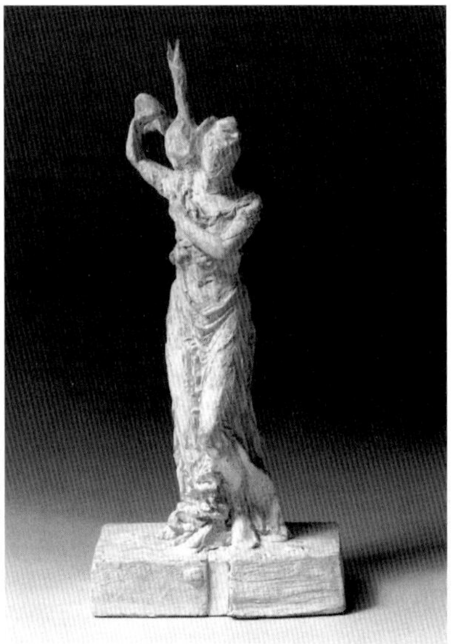

Eakins, *Water Nymph and Bittern*

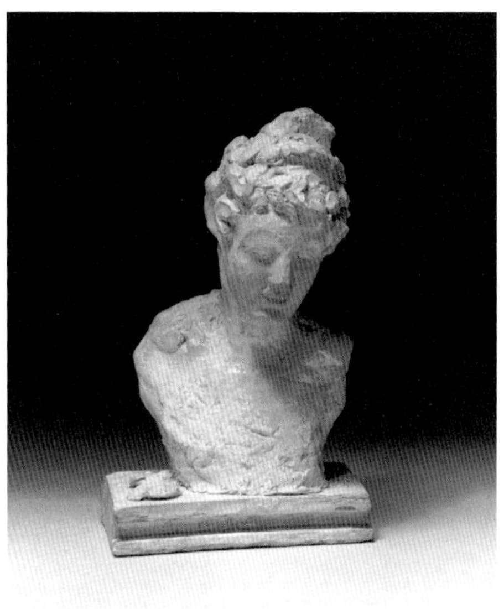

Eakins, *Head of the Water Nymph*

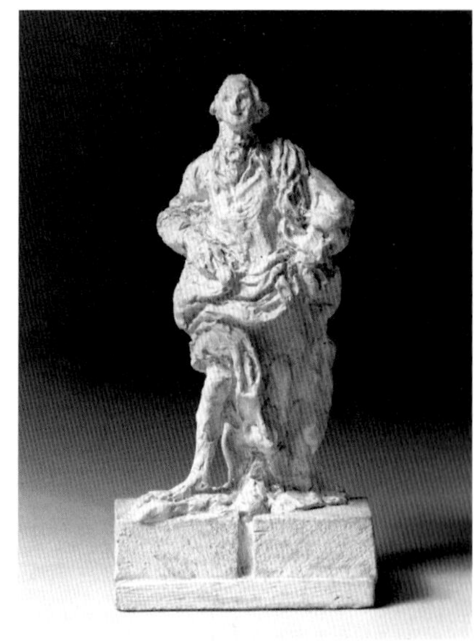

Eakins, *George Washington*

use of nude models. Eakins spent two years on this project, seeking out Rush's notebooks, interviewing his friends, visiting his workshop, and studying his sculpture. Eakins worked from Rush's *Allegory of the Waterworks,* 1825 (Fairmount Park Commission); Rush's terracotta self-portrait (q.v.); the portrait of Rush attributed to Rembrandt Peale, before 1813 (Independence Hall); Rush's *Allegory of the Schuylkill River* (pine head, [q.v.]; bronze cast [from original, complete figure], Philadelphia Museum of Art); and his wooden sculpture of *George Washington,* 1815 (Independence Hall). Images of sculptures that were not executed by Rush until years later appear anachronistically in the background of Eakins's painting.

Eakins made six wax studies for the painting: five are in the Philadelphia Museum of Art; the study for the nude model, which was once owned by Susan Macdowell Eakins, is no longer extant. Samuel Murray and Susan Eakins had five sets of plasters cast from the original waxes between October 14 and 16, 1931. The sets, in the order of casting, are currently owned by the Philadelphia Museum of Art (#1), Newark Museum in New Jersey (#2 or #3), the Museum of American Art of the Pennsylvania Academy of the Fine Arts (#4), and the Hirshhorn Museum and Sculpture Garden in Washington, D.C. (part of #5—*George Washington, Water Nymph and Bittern,* and *Allegory of the Waterworks*). Perhaps *George Washington, Water Nymph and Bittern,* and *William Rush,* formerly owned by Seymour Adelman, now in the Dietrich Collection, are from the other set (either #2 or #3). The original molds for the set of five plasters were sold at the estate sale of Susan Macdowell Eakins, but they are now lost. In about 1965 three sets of bronzes were cast from Seymour Adelman's plasters of *George Washington, Water Nymph and Bittern,* and *William Rush.* Bronze sets are at Bryn Mawr College and the Philadelphia Museum of Art; a *Water Nymph and Bittern* is in a private collection; and the Yale University Art Gallery has a *Water Nymph and Bittern* and a *William Rush.*

Exhibited
1991–92 PAFA, *Thomas Eakins Rediscovered: At Home, At School, At Work.*

Ex Collections
Susan Macdowell Eakins, 1931–about 1932; Charles Bregler, gift, about 1932–58; his wife, Mary Picozzi Bregler, 1958–85.

Twenty Anatomical Casts and a Model 1877–82

a) Five Animal Casts

Ecorché Cat
1877
Painted plaster
14 x 25¾ x 3⅝" (35.6 x 65.4 x 9.2 cm)
Signed and dated under cat's body on background of relief: EAKINS/1877
Pennsylvania Academy purchase, 1991.7.15
Reference
1974 Gordon Hendricks, *The Life and Work of Thomas Eakins,* New York: Grossman Publishers, fig. 110, p. 131.
Exhibited
1991–92 PAFA, *Thomas Eakins Rediscovered: At Home, At School, At Work.*

Front Leg of Cat
1877
Painted plaster
11½ x 4⅜ x 1½" (29.2 x 11.1 x 3.8 cm)
Pennsylvania Academy purchase, 1991.7.16

Hind Leg of Cat
1877
Painted plaster
13¼ x 4½ x 3⅛" (33.7 x 11.4 x 7.9 cm)
Pennsylvania Academy purchase, 1991.7.17

Front Leg of Horse
1877
Plaster
Length: 28¼" (71.8 cm)
Pennsylvania Academy purchase, 1991.7.18

Hind Leg of Horse
1877
Plaster
Length: 33¼" (84.5 cm)
Pennsylvania Academy purchase, 1991.7.19

b) Fifteen Human Casts

Right Foot
1877
Painted plaster
7¼ x 3½ x 9" (18.4 x 8.9 x 22.9 cm)
Signed and dated on sole of foot: EAKINS/1877
Inscribed with anatomical notations
Pennsylvania Academy purchase, 1991.7.7
Exhibited
1965 Philadelphia Museum of Art, *The Art of Philadelphia Medicine,* cat. no. 89 (ill.). **1976** PAFA, *In This Academy.* **1986–87** PAFA, *Sculpture at the Pennsylvania Academy of the Fine Arts.* **1990** PAFA, *The Academic Tradition.*

Left Foot
About 1877
Plaster
6 x 3½ x 10" (15.2 x 8.9 x 25.4 cm)
Charles Bregler's Thomas Eakins Collection, purchased with the partial support of the Pew Memorial Trust, 1985.68.1.3

Front of Neck and Part of Shoulder
1877–80
Painted plaster
8¾ x 15⅝ x 5" (22.2 x 39.7 x 12.7 cm)
Inscribed by Charles Bregler (incised) on cut-off: CAST/b[y]/EAKINS
Signed by Thomas Eakins (painted) beneath right shoulder: T.E./ Eakins
Charles Bregler's Thomas Eakins Collection, purchased with the partial support of the Pew Memorial Trust, 1985.68.1.2
Exhibited
1990 PAFA, *The Academic Tradition.* **1991–92** PAFA, *Thomas Eakins Rediscovered: At Home, At School, At Work.* **1992** PAFA, *Eakins the Teacher.*

Left Arm, Hand, and Part of Shoulder
1877–80
Painted plaster
30½ x 9½ x 4" (77.5 x 24.1 x 10.2 cm)
Inscribed with anatomical notations
Pennsylvania Academy purchasc, 1991.7.3

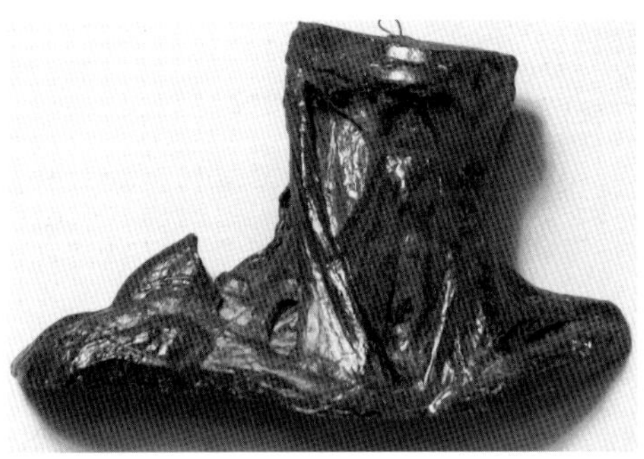

Eakins, *Front of Neck and Part of Shoulder*

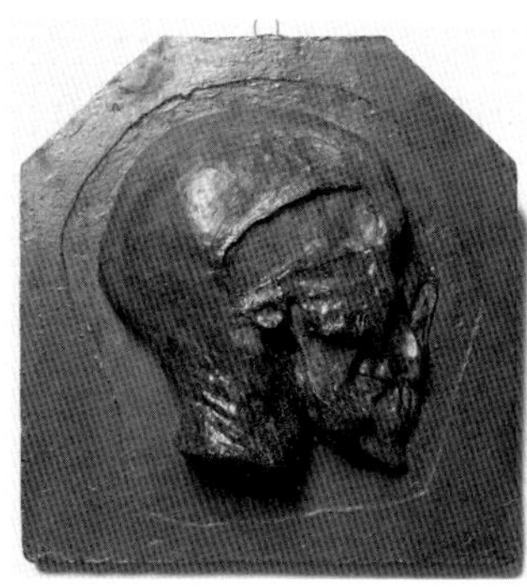

Eakins, *Right Side of Head*

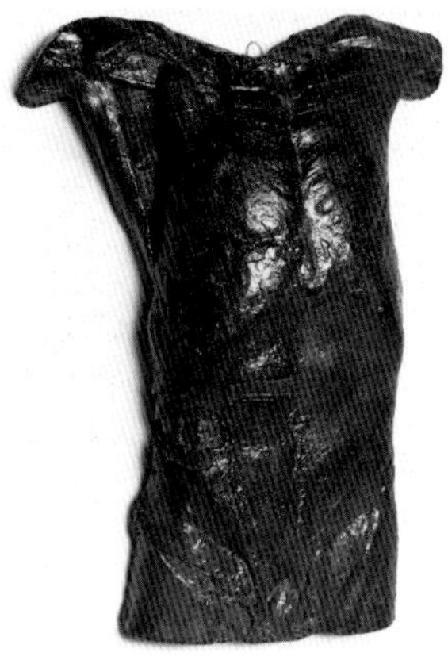

Eakins, *Front of Male Torso*

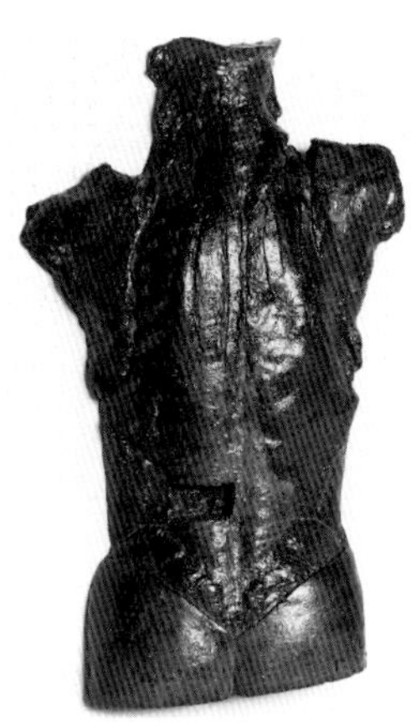

Eakins, *Back of Male Torso*

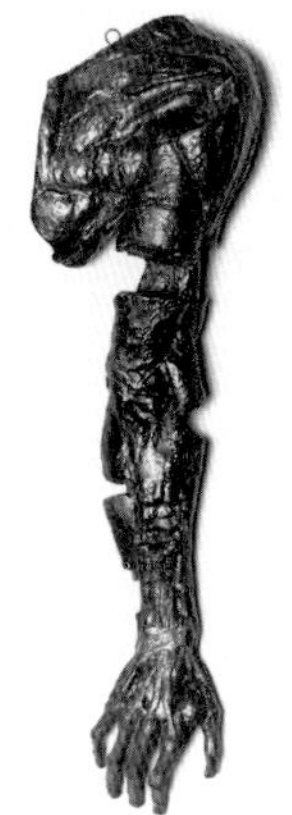

Eakins, *Right Shoulder, Arm, and Hand*

Exhibited
1986–87 PAFA, *Sculpture at the Pennsylvania Academy of the Fine Arts.*

Left Arm, Hand, and Part of Shoulder
1877–80
Painted plaster
30½ x 9 x 4" (77.5 x 22.9 x 10.2 cm)
Pennsylvania Academy purchase, 1991.7.5

Left Side of Neck and Chin
1877–80
Painted plaster
9½ x 9 x 4⅝" (24.1 x 22.9 x 11.8 cm)
Pennsylvania Academy purchase, 1991.7.9

Right Side of Head
1877–80
Painted plaster
12½ x 12 x 4½" (31.8 x 30.5 x 11.4 cm)
Illegible PAFA seal on back
Inscribed with anatomical notations
Pennsylvania Academy purchase, 1991.7.10
Exhibited
1976 PAFA, *In This Academy.* **1986–87** PAFA, *Sculpture at the Pennsylvania Academy of the Fine Arts.* **1991–92** PAFA, *Thomas Eakins Rediscovered: At Home, At School, At Work.*

Left Knee
1877–80
Painted plaster
10¼ x 5⅛ x 3¾" (26 x 13 x 9.5 cm)
Illegible PAFA seal on top cutoff
Signed on cutoff (incised): T.E.
Inscribed with anatomical notations
Pennsylvania Academy purchase, 1991.7.11
Exhibited
1965 Philadelphia Museum of Art, *The Art of Philadelphia Medicine,* cat. no. 89a. **1986–87** PAFA, *Sculpture at the Pennsylvania Academy of the Fine Arts.*

Front of Male Torso
1880
Painted plaster
29 x 20 x 7⅝" (73.7 x 50.8 x 19.4 cm)
Signed and dated (in raised letters) within seal in shape of palette on back: PENNA. ACAD./FINE ARTS./EAKINS/ 1880.
Inscribed with anatomical notations
Pennsylvania Academy purchase, 1991.7.1
Reference
1974 Gordon Hendricks, *The Life and Work of Thomas Eakins,* New York: Grossman Publishers, fig. 110, p. 131.
Exhibited
1965 Philadelphia Museum of Art, *The Art of Philadelphia Medicine,* cat. no. 88 (ill.). **1975–76** Whitney Mu-

seum of American Art, *A Portrait of Young America.* **1976** PAFA, *In This Academy,* cat. no. 63. **1986–87** PAFA, *Sculpture at the Pennsylvania Academy of the Fine Arts.* **1991–92** PAFA, *Thomas Eakins Rediscovered: At Home, At School, At Work.*

Back of Male Torso
1880
Painted plaster
30½ x 19 x 6⅝" (77.5 x 48.3 x 16.8 cm)
Signed and dated on back: EAKINS/80/P.A.F.A.
Inscribed with anatomical notations
Pennsylvania Academy purchase, 1991.7.2
Exhibited
1965 Philadelphia Museum of Art, *The Art of Philadelphia Medicine,* cat. no. 88a. **1975–76** Whitney Museum of American Art, *A Portrait of Young America.* **1986–87** PAFA, *Sculpture at the Pennsylvania Academy of the Fine Arts.* **1991–92** PAFA, *Thomas Eakins Rediscovered: At Home, At School, At Work.*

Right Shoulder, Arm, and Hand
1880
Painted plaster
27½ x 7¼ x 4½" (69.9 x 18.4 x 11.4 cm)
Signed and dated (in raised letters) within seal in shape of palette on back: PENN ACAD/FINE ARTS/EAKINS/1880
Signed below seal in black paint: TE
Incised in the side cutoff: 2
Inscribed with anatomical notations
Pennsylvania Academy purchase, 1991.7.4
Exhibited
1986–87 PAFA, *Sculpture at the Pennsylvania Academy of the Fine Arts.*

Back of Shoulder
1880
Painted plaster
18½ x 13 x 4½" (47 x 33 x 11.4 cm)
Pennsylvania Academy purchase, 1991.7.6

Left Shoulder
1880
Painted plaster
8 x 7½ x 3" (20.3 x 19.1 x 7.6 cm)
Inscribed with anatomical notations
Pennsylvania Academy purchase, 1991.7.13

Left Half of Vertebral Column, Pelvis, and Upper Half of Thigh
About 1880
Painted plaster
7⅛ x 20¾ x 6⅜" (18.1 x 52.4 x 16.2 cm)
Inscribed with anatomical notations
Pennsylvania Academy purchase, 1991.7.8
Exhibited
1986–87 PAFA, *Sculpture at the Pennsylvania Academy of the Fine Arts.*

Left Leg, Thigh, and Pelvis
About 1880
Painted plaster
38¼ x 8⅜ x 7½" (97.2 x 21.3 x 19.1 cm)
Signed (incised) on cutoff: E
Inscribed with anatomical notation
Pennsylvania Academy purchase, 1991.7.12
Exhibited
1986–87 PAFA, *Sculpture at the Pennsylvania Academy of the Fine Arts.* **1991–92** PAFA, *Thomas Eakins Rediscovered: At Home, At School, At Work.* **1992** PAFA, *Eakins the Teacher.*

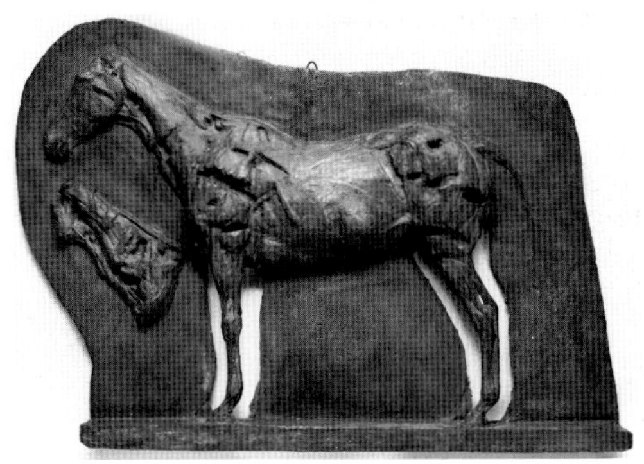

Eakins, *The Mare Josephine*

c) One Model

The Mare Josephine (Ecorché Anatomical Model)
1882
Plaster, painted gray
22¼ x 31 x 3" (56.5 x 78.7 x 7.6 cm)
Signed and dated at lower center: EAKINS/1882
Pennsylvania Academy purchase, 1991.7.14
Exhibited
1975–76 Whitney Museum of American Art, *A Portrait of Young America.* **1976** PAFA, *In This Academy,* cat. no. 62. **1989** PAFA, *"The Birds and the Beasts Will Teach Us."*

IN THE ANATOMY CLASSES during the years that Thomas Eakins taught at the Pennsylvania Academy of the Fine Arts, Dr. William Williams Keen gave thirty lectures: eight on the skeleton, twelve on the muscles, four on the facial features, two on the skin and hair, and four on posture, proportions, and sexual differences. He used live models, skeletons, drawings, and JEAN ANTOINE HOUDON'S *Ecorché,* or figure without skin, which had been in the school for many years and was painted by Eakins to show the information he had gleaned from his dissections. All advanced students were required to dissect human and animal cadavers. Eakins then cast portions of the cadavers in plaster, using gelatin molds, and painted and labeled them for use in the classroom.[1]

Plaster anatomical casts have always been important in teaching students about light, shade, and form. Eakins cast his from actual corpses in order to create a permanent record of the dissections done at the Pennsylvania Academy. They provided information about scale and volume that no anatomical book illustrations could convey. Eakins performed his dissections from an artistic rather than a medical point of view; superficial, or surface-influencing, bones and muscles are exposed to illustrate size, form, origin, and insertion. Cross-sections clearly demonstrate the depth and order of overlying muscles. The muscle fiber, cartilage, bone, and skin are painted in a naturalistic way with red indicating muscles, yellow the tendons, white the bone, and brown the skin. On most of the human casts, the revealed parts are identified by inscriptions of their Latin names in block letters. Many of the casts appear in photographs of the Art Students' League of Philadelphia and of Eakins's studio at 1330 Chestnut Street, where they must have commonly served as reference tools. Copies were apparently used at the Pennsylvania Academy after Eakins's time, but the original set is no longer extant.

The set of eighteen anatomical casts and one model that were purchased by the Pennsylvania Academy in 1991 were once owned by Thomas Eakins, who gave them to his friend and colleague SAMUEL MURRAY. He taught at Moore College of Art and Design to which he apparently presented the casts in 1934. They were on loan to the Pennsylvania Academy from 1960 until the sale in 1991. Although several sets of plaster casts were made in Eakins's lifetime, including one given to the University of Pennsylvania for its assistance in obtaining dissecting material and another given to the Academy of Natural Sciences for its loan of skeletons, the Pennsylvania Academy's is the only set known to be extant. Two of the casts (left foot and front of neck) were purchased by the Academy in 1985 from Charles Bregler's Thomas Eakins Collection. They were apparently given to Bregler in 1938 by Eakins's widow, Susan Macdowell Eakins.

Sixteen of the anatomical casts in bronze are at the Philadelphia Museum of Art, thirteen of them duplicate plasters at the Museum of American Art of the Pennsylvania Academy; the whereabouts of plasters for the other three (right hand, right elbow, and right thigh, leg, and foot) are unknown.[2]

The anatomy of the horse, cat, and dog was of great interest to Eakins. In 1876–77 he made casts of a dissected cat (qq.v.) and a dog (whereabouts unknown). The anatomy classes of Eakins and Dr. Keen focused especially on the horse. A skeleton was borrowed from the Academy of Natural Sciences for use in the classroom, and each winter Eakins took a group of students to M.L. Shoemaker and Company, a bone-boiling factory, where they could study and dissect the cadavers of horses. In January of 1881 Eakins had a ramp built behind the Pennsylvania Academy so that a horse could be brought into the freight elevator and up to the sculpture studio. In the summers, students continued their study of live horses at the farm of Fairman Rogers, the chairman of the Pennsylvania Academy's Committee on Instruction. *The Mare Josephine (Ecorché)* of 1882 is an anatomical model of a horse owned by Fairman Rogers that Eakins had used as a live model in 1878. When Josephine died in 1882, the cadaver was probably donated to the school, where it was dissected by the students. Eakins then modeled this ecorché relief showing the muscular system of the horse with a detail of the neck muscles at the left. A bronze cast of the ecorché relief made in 1930 is in the Philadelphia Museum of Art. In 1891–92 Eakins modeled sculptures of horses for William O'Donovan's figures of Lincoln and Grant on the Soldiers and Sailors Memorial Arch in Brooklyn.

Notes

1. Thirteen of the casts are polychromed with oil paint. Four are painted a uniform, matte red-brown (a human left arm [1991.7.5], the ecorché cat, and the cat legs). Three are unpainted (the horse's legs and the human cast of the left foot).

2. See Theodor Siegl, *The Thomas Eakins Collection* (Philadelphia: Philadelphia Museum of Art, 1978), pp. 82–87.

Reference

1997 Kathleen A. Foster, *Thomas Eakins Rediscovered,* New Haven, Conn.: Yale University Press.

Knitting

1882–83

a.

Plaster, painted brown

20¾ x 17¼ x 4½" (52.7 x 43.8 x 11.4 cm)

Torn paper label on back: Knitting/by Thomas Eakins./ 1330 Chestnut St./Philadelphia.; in another hand: *R[e]turn/as Bros/*[B]*way*

Charles Bregler's Thomas Eakins Collection, purchased with the partial support of the Pew Memorial Trust, 1985.68.1.5

Reference

1992 Mark F. Bockrath, Virginia N. Naudé, and Debbie Hess Norris, "Thomas Eakins: Painter, Sculptor, Photographer," *Journal of the American Institute for Conservation* 31 (Spring), pp. 56–60, figs. 2, 4.

Exhibited
1883* cat. no. 415. **1991–92** PAFA, *Thomas Eakins Rediscovered: At Home, At School, At Work.*

b.
Bronze with brown patina; sand cast in 1886
20 x 16½ x 5" (50.8 x 41.9 x 12.7 cm)
Paper label on back of bronze: [A]rt Club./ E[X]HIBITION./ TO APRIL 4th./[So]ciety American Ar./Name, Thomas Eakins/ Title, Knitting/Price [crossed out] Return to Haseltine
Group of three stacked paper labels originally on back of bronze, now in object file: on bottom, printed: RETURN TO/T. A.WILMURT, /54 EAST 13th STREET,/NEW YORK; in the middle: *E. H. Coates;* on top, form label with lower-case lettering in ink: *[P]roperty of* PENNSYLVANIA ACADEMY OF THE FINE ARTS, 1887./ TITLE *Knitting* /ARTIST *Thomas Eakins*/[1]/20 *Presented by Edward H. Coates*
Foundry mark probably on back at top center, obscured by original label: BUREAU BROS./ PHILA.
Gift of Edward H. Coates, 1887.2.1

References
1933 Lloyd Goodrich, *Thomas Eakins: His Life and Work,* New York: Whitney Museum of American Art, cat. no. 505. **1974** Gordon Hendricks, *The Life and Work of Thomas Eakins,* New York: Grossman Publishers, fig. 151, pp. 164–66. **1976** Wayne Craven, "Images of a Nation in Wood, Marble and Bronze," in *200 Years of American Sculpture,* New York: David R. Godine in association with the Whitney Museum of American Art, cat. no. 115 (ill.).

Exhibited
1887 Society of American Artists, New York. **1970** Whitney Museum of American Art, New York, *Thomas Eakins Retrospective Exhibition.* **1970–71** Worcester Art Museum, Mass., *Thomas Eakins: His Photographic Works.* **1975–76** Whitney Museum of American Art, *A Portrait of Young America.* **1976** PAFA, *In This Academy,* cat. no. 224. **1983** Detroit Institute of Arts, *The Quest for Unity: American Art Between World's Fairs, 1876–1893,* cat. no. 75a (ill.), pp. 152–53. **1986–87** PAFA, *Sculpture at the Pennsylvania Academy of the Fine Arts.* **1992** PAFA, *Eakins the Teacher.* **1994–96** PAFA, *Two Centuries of Collecting at the Museum of American Art.*

Spinning

1882–83

a.
Plaster, painted brown
21 x 17⅜ x 4¼" (53.3 x 44.1 x 10.8 cm)
Torn paper label on back: by Th[omas Eakins]/1330 [Che]st[nut]/Philadelphi[a]; in another hand: *1*[8]*7 Broadway/N.Y.*
Charles Bregler's Thomas Eakins Collection, purchased with the partial support of the Pew Memorial Trust, 1985.68.1.6

Reference
1992 Bockrath et al., pp. 56–60, figs. 1, 3 (ills.).

Exhibited
1883* cat. no. 414. **1991–92** PAFA, *Thomas Eakins Rediscovered: At Home, At School, At Work.*

b.
Bronze with brown patina; sand cast in 1886
20 x 16½ x 3" (50.8 x 42 x 7.5 cm)
Foundry mark on back at top center: BUREAU BROS./ PHILA.
Gift of Edward H. Coates, 1887.2.2

References
1933 Goodrich, cat. no. 504. **1969** Moussa A. Domit, *The Sculpture of Thomas Eakins,* Washington, D.C.: Corcoran Gallery of Art, cat. no. 10 (ill.), pp. 8, 21, 43. **1974** Hendricks, fig. 152, pp. 164–66. **1976** Craven, cat. no. 114 (ill.).

Exhibited
1887 Society of American Artists, New York. **1970** Whitney Museum of American Art, *Thomas Eakins Retrospective Exhibition.* **1970–71** Worcester Art Museum, Mass., *Thomas Eakins: His Photographic Works.* **1975–76** Whitney Museum of American Art, *A Portrait of Young America.* **1976** PAFA, *In This Academy,* cat. no. 225. **1983** Detroit Institute of Arts, *The Quest for Unity: American Art Between World's Fairs, 1876–1893,* cat. no. 75b (ill.), p. 153. **1986–87** PAFA, *Sculpture at the Pennsylvania Academy of the Fine Arts.* **1992** PAFA, *Eakins the Teacher.* **1994–96** PAFA, *Two Centuries of Collecting at the Museum of American Art.*

THOMAS EAKINS was intrigued by relief sculpture and the technical problems it presented.[1] In 1882 he eagerly accepted his first sculpture commission from the architect Theophilus P. Chandler for reliefs to adorn the chimneypiece in a house being built at 2032 Walnut street for the businessman James P. Scott.[2] Eakins's original plan called for three reliefs. *Spinning* and *Knitting* were to flank a central panel of a man chopping wood, as illustrated in Eakins's sketch of about 1882 (Charles Bregler's Thomas Eakins Collection).[3] This active subject was abandoned in favor of one depicting an old man reading, probably because it was in keeping with the calm tone set by *Spinning* and *Knitting.*

The fireplace, which was located in a grand center hall, was massive; and the reliefs were to be placed on the chimneypiece about three feet above eye level. From the landing of the nearby staircase, one could look down and see the fireplace on the opposite wall. Eakins therefore felt compelled to make the reliefs read from different angles. He modeled *Spinning* on a smaller scale than *Knitting* because it would have been closer to the viewer descending the staircase.

Although Eakins worked the models in clay, the final reliefs were to be in stone. Bronze casts were to be the intermediate stage. Eakins wanted the stone carvings to look as close as possible to his clay origi-

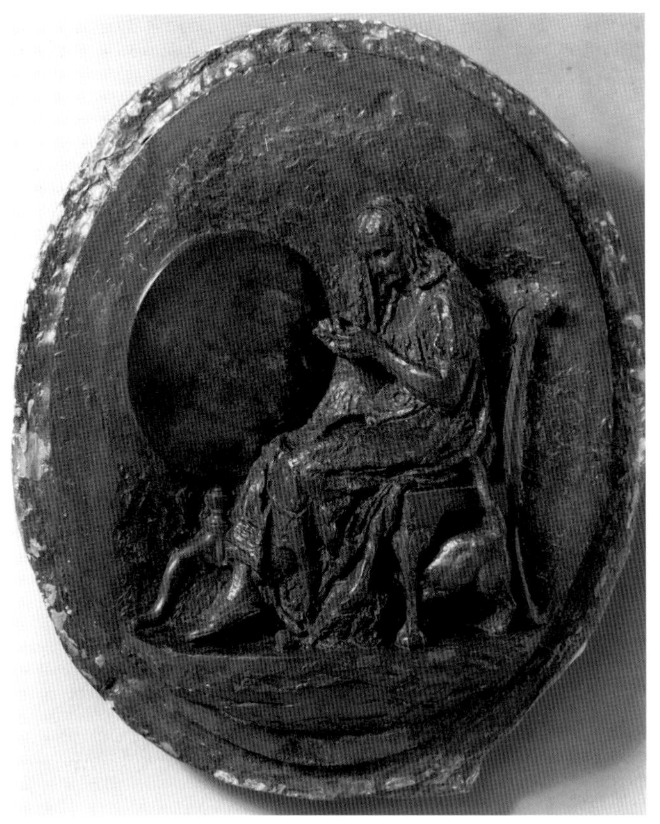

Eakins, *Knitting,* plaster

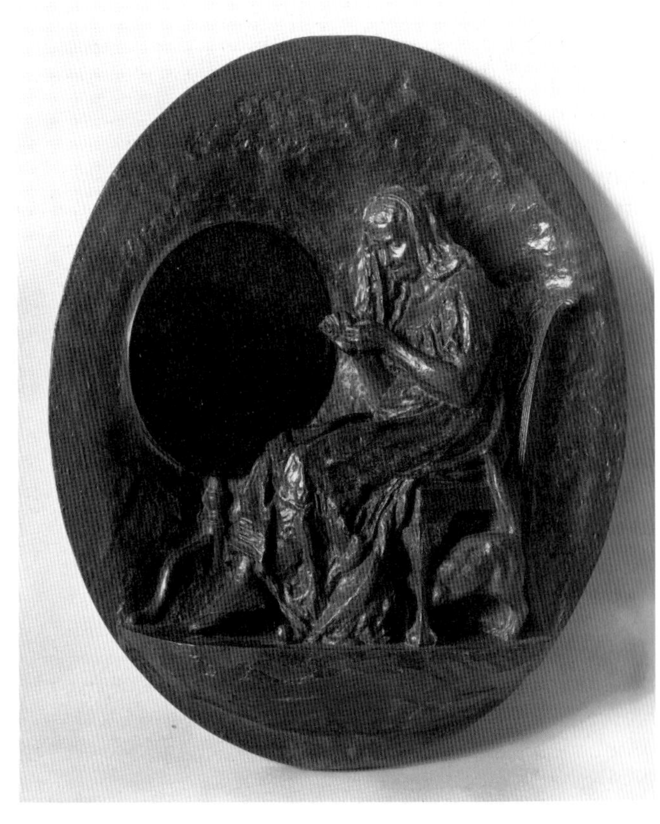

Eakins, *Knitting,* bronze

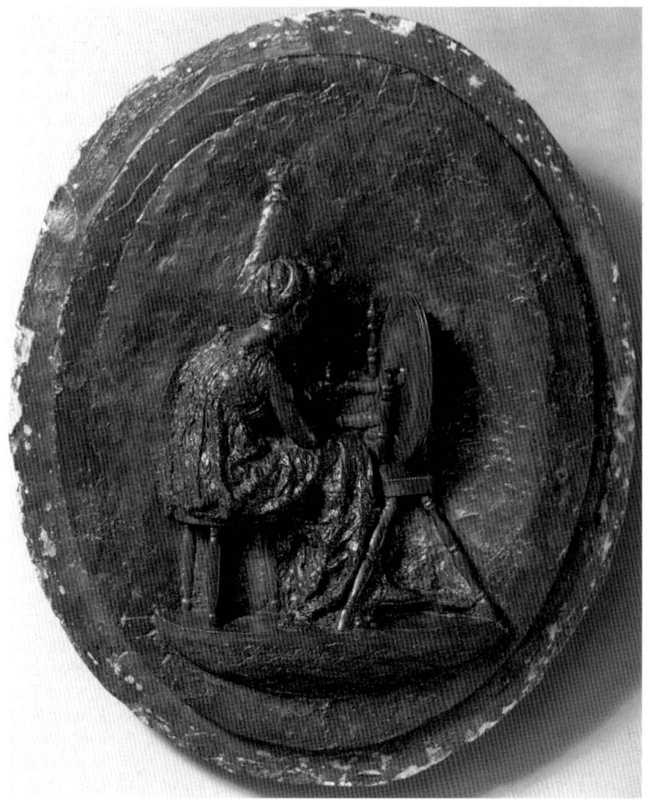

Eakins, *Spinning,* plaster

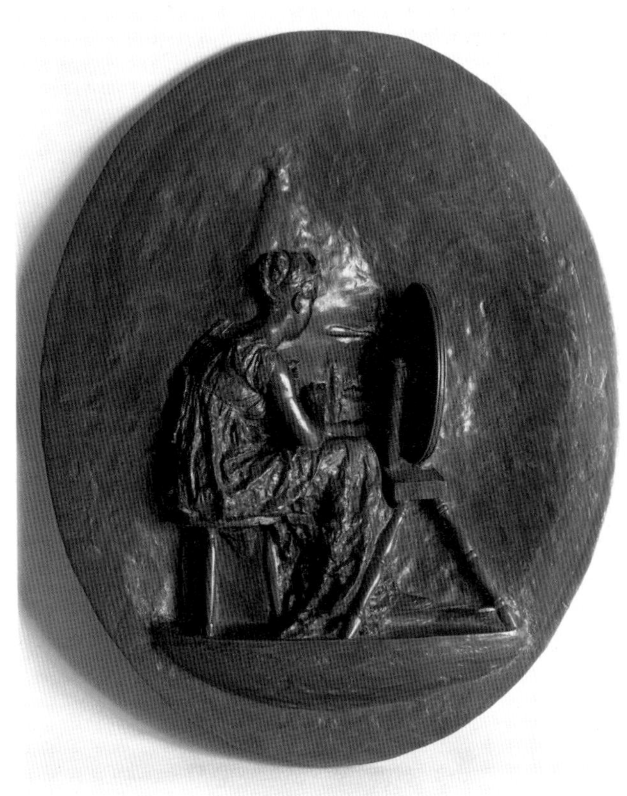

Eakins, *Spinning,* bronze

nals and thus decided to employ a New York stone cutter using a steam copying machine. Eakins intended to finish the stone himself with the women models once again in front of him.

James Scott saw plaster casts of *Spinning* and *Knitting* sometime in the spring of 1883. He was unimpressed and apparently thought Eakins was spending too much time and money on live models, thereby inflating the final cost. Scott did not want the reliefs carved in stone and refused to pay for the work that Eakins had already completed. The dispute was finally settled two years later through the efforts of Edward H. Coates, a director of the Pennsylvania Academy of the Fine Arts. Scott paid Eakins five hundred dollars. Eakins kept the plaster models, which the Museum of American Art of the Pennsylvania Academy now owns; and in 1886 he had the Bureau Brothers foundry cast two sets in bronze. Edward Coates purchased one set for presentation to the Academy. The other is in a private collection.

In 1986 the Pennsylvania Academy's plaster reliefs were X-rayed and discovered by sculpture conservator Virginia Norton Naudé to be assemblages, not casts.[4] Metal armature was discovered in the projecting legs of the spinning wheel and stool in *Spinning* and in the cat in *Knitting.* The tabletop in the latter relief was found to have been applied to the relief surface. Therefore, several elements on each relief were modeled separately and then attached to the relief where they did not require the extra support an armature provides. This led to the conclusion that these examples were the originals from which all the others were cast. Additional rims of plaster were attached to the reliefs to serve as part of a mother mold in the casting process, and both reliefs and rims were coated with shellac indicating a step in the casting process.

In 1930 Susan Macdowell Eakins had two sets lost-wax cast in bronze at Roman Bronze Works in New York. They are now owned by the Philadelphia Museum of Art and the Hirshhorn Museum and Sculpture Garden in Washington, D.C. Other sets of plasters are in private collections and the Art Institute of Chicago. A plaster of *Spinning* is in the Philadelphia Museum of Art; a plaster of *Knitting* is the Corcoran Gallery of Art. A plaster study of the earlier version of *Knitting* before Eakins remodeled the head of the woman is in a private collection. At least twelve casts in bronze were made in recent years by Hirschl and Adler in New York and Alva Museum Replicas.

Notes

1. Thomas Eakins, "Sculpture Relief," original manuscript, Archives of the Philadelphia Museum of Art.
2. See letters in Kathleen A. Foster and Cheryl Leibold, *Writing about Eakins: The Manuscripts in Charles Bregler's Thomas Eakins Collection* (Philadelphia: University of Pennsylvania Press, 1989), p. 155.
3. See Kathleen A. Foster, *Thomas Eakins Rediscovered,* cat. no. 206 (New Haven, Conn.: Yale University Press, 1997).
4. See Virginia Norton Naudé, Conservation Reports, Nov. 6, 1989, PAFA object files with x-radiographic images.

References

1978 Theodor Siegl, *The Thomas Eakins Collection,* Philadelphia: Philadelphia Museum of Art, plasters, pp. 99–101; text adapted in "*Spinning* and *Knitting:* Two Sculptural Reliefs by Thomas Eakins," *Philadelphia Museum of Art Bulletin* 74 (June 1978), pp. 18–22. **1983** Evan Turner, "Thomas Eakins: The Quest for Truth," in *The Art Institute of Chicago Centennial Lectures,* Museum Studies 10, Chicago: Contemporary Books, pp. 164–72.

An Arcadian

1883
Plaster, painted green
8 x 5¼ x ¾" (20.3 x 13.3 x 1.9 cm)
Charles Bregler's Thomas Eakins Collection, purchased with the partial support of the Pew Memorial Trust, 1985.68.1.4

ALTHOUGH Thomas Eakins criticized the academic practice of copying antique casts, he valued Greek

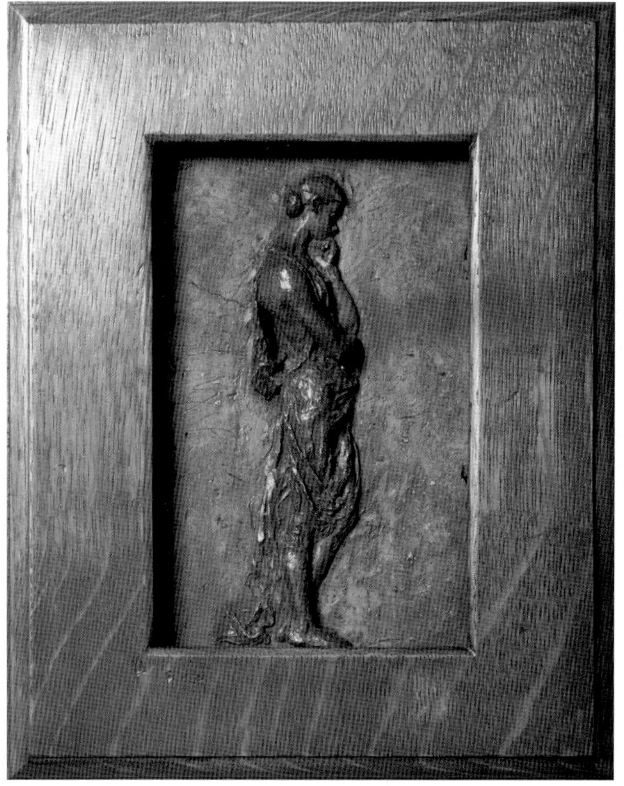

Eakins, *An Arcadian*

art, especially Phidias's Parthenon frieze, and he placed his models for photographs and paintings in poses from antique sculpture. He was fascinated by Arcadian subjects inspired by Roman poetry and depicted them in nearly twenty sculptures, oil paintings, and photographs.[1] Eakins copied this draped female figure standing in profile from his larger 1883 relief *Arcadia* (plaster, Philadelphia Museum of Art). The latter sculpture shows a procession of draped and nude males and females listening to music played on the pipes by a figure who may be the god Pan, seated directly in front of the figure that Eakins reused for the Academy's relief. He also did a separate, larger relief, *A Youth Playing the Pipes,* 1884 (plaster, Philadelphia Museum of Art; bronze, Hirshhorn Museum and Sculpture Garden, Washington, D.C.), that relates closely to his 1883 *Arcadia* painting (Metropolitan Museum of Art, New York). At the time, Eakins was lecturing on relief sculpture and giving special praise to those done in ancient Greece. His interest in reliefs had been reinforced by his recent commission for *Spinning* and *Knitting* (qq.v.).

The Pennsylvania Academy's plaster was probably painted green to simulate a bronze patina. There is a bronze cast of *An Arcadian,* made in 1930, in the Fine Arts Museum of San Francisco. The Arcadian works were never exhibited in Eakins's lifetime but were given as gifts to friends, colleagues, and students.

Note

1. Marc Simpson, "Thomas Eakins and His Arcadian Works," *Smithsonian Studies in American Art* 1 (Fall 1987), p. 83.

Reference

1933 Lloyd Goodrich, *Thomas Eakins: His Life and Work,* New York: Whitney Museum of American Art, cat. no. 507.

Exhibited

1986–87 PAFA, *Sculpture at the Pennsylvania Academy of the Fine Arts.* **1991–92** PAFA, *Thomas Eakins Rediscovered: At Home, At School, At Work.*

ATTRIBUTED TO THOMAS EAKINS

1880s
Plaster

Hand of Child (Margaret Crowell)
2¾ x 4¾ x 8¼" (7 x 12.1 x 21 cm)

Hand of Child (Margaret Crowell)
2⅜ x 3¾ x 6¾" (6 x 9.5 x 17.1 cm)

Hand of Adult Male
3¼ x 6¾ x 10⅝" (8.3 x 17.1 x 27 cm)

Purchased with funds donated by the Pennsylvania Academy Women's Committee, 1988.10.64–66

THESE life casts of hands were purchased along with photographs and other works from the Gordon Hendricks Collection. They are poor in quality and bear little resemblance to the fine quality casts that Thomas Eakins is known to have produced.

WILLIAM R. O'DONOVAN

1844–1920

William Rudolf O'Donovan was born in Preston County, Virginia, to James Hayes O'Donovan and the former Mary Bright. During his early teens, William was apprenticed to a marble cutter at Carmichael's stoneyard in Greene County, Pennsylvania. Apparently his carving skills quickly surpassed those of his master, and he ran away before his apprenticeship was completed.[1] When the Civil War broke out in April 1861, O'Donovan enlisted in Virginia's Staunton Artillery and served until Robert E. Lee surrendered at Appomattox Court House on April 9, 1865. After the war, O'Donovan lived for a time in Virginia and then went to Baltimore. In 1867 his ambition to become a sculptor led him to New York. He later wrote to his sister, Janet O'Donovan Abraham, that, during his first two years in New York, he "endured horrible poverty and humiliation" and despaired of being able to compete with the European-trained sculptors.[2] Aside from his early apprenticeship, O'Donovan is believed to have been entirely self-taught. By 1869 or 1870, he had established a studio on Broadway. During the 1870s, he acquired a reputation as a sculptor of realistic portraits, and he modeled likenesses of many eminent citizens and fellow artists. Beginning in 1874, he often showed his portraits at the National Academy of Design. Later, he exhibited in New York at the Society of American Artists and the Architectural League and in Philadelphia at the Pennsylvania Academy of the Fine Arts. The list of his sitters is formidable. Among them were the poets Walt Whitman and Clarence Edmund Stedman, the painter THOMAS EAKINS (q.v.), and Major General Joseph Wheeler. The bust of the latter is now in the National Museum of American Art, Smithsonian Institution, Washington, D.C.

In the fall of 1877, O'Donovan was among the founding members of the Tile Club, a small group of artists who gathered to decorate tiles but whose tacit purpose was to eat, drink, and fraternize. William Merritt Chase, Winslow Homer, Edwin Austin Abbey, and AUGUSTUS SAINT-GAUDENS were also members. Many of the Tile Club members had studios in the Tenth Street Studio Building at 51 West Tenth Street. O'Donovan rented a studio there from 1878 to 1880.[3] As a member of the Tile Club and a resident of the Tenth Street Studio Building, O'Donovan was surrounded by cognoscenti of American art.

During the early 1870s, O'Donovan became very much interested in spiritualism. He read the *Spiritualistic Journal* and admired the sermons of Henry Ward Beecher.[4] To his sister, O'Donovan wrote that art should reflect nature, the divine revelation of God. Rather than displaying an artist's skill for its own sake, a work of art "must be simple and unpretentious as truth itself."[5] O'Donovan's spiritualism is evident in the art criticism that he wrote for newspapers and magazines.[6]

At the National Academy of Design's annual exhibition in 1878, O'Donovan exhibited busts of fellow Tenth Street residents William Page, Winslow Homer (q.v.), and William H. Beard. The bust of Page was very highly regarded and prompted O'Donovan's election as an associate member of the National Academy. The bust was purchased by a group of Page's friends who presented it to the National Academy, where it remains today. O'Donovan seems to have been particularly inspired by the work of William Page. He called Page's portraits "quiet" and "matter of fact" and lamented that they were passed over for the works of "surface painters."[7] O'Donovan empathized with Page's Swedenborgian beliefs.

O'Donovan was well known for his soldier's monuments. In 1881, for Tarrytown, New York, he executed a statue commemorating the capture of the British spy Major Andre. O'Donovan modeled statues of George Washington for the Peace Monument, 1882, Newburgh, New York; for the Battle of Trenton Memorial, 1893, Trenton, New Jersey; and, one of an unknown date for Caracas, Venezuela. In 1891 he was commissioned to make the lifesize equestrian reliefs of Abraham Lincoln and Ulysses S. Grant for the Soldiers and Sailors Memorial Arch in Grand Army Plaza, at the entrance to Prospect Park, Brooklyn, New York. O'Donovan hired Thomas Eakins, an expert in the anatomy of the horse, to collaborate with him on the project. Like O'Donovan, Eakins was an ardent realist. To create the two horses, O'Donovan and Eakins decided against the typical method of combining the best characteristics from several animals to make an ideal composite; instead, they searched for a particular horse for each rider. Eakins modeled the horses; O'Donovan, the riders. O'Donovan used LEONARD VOLK's life mask of Lincoln (q.v.) and a death mask of Grant, as well as live models. The finished reliefs were installed in the arch in 1895. Their intense realism contrasts markedly with the idealized heroism typical of contemporary monuments. For this reason, the reliefs were criticized severely by the press and the public and were even threatened with removal.[8]

In addition to sculpture, O'Donovan painted landscapes in watercolor, pastel, and tempera. Many of his paintings were made in the vicinity of Rye, New York, where he spent summers. In 1919, the year before his death, O'Donovan had a show of tempera paintings at the Cottier and Company Gallery in New York.[9]

Notes

1. Preface to letters of William Rudolf O'Donovan, Historical Society of Pennsylvania, Philadelphia. Information supplied by O'Donovan's niece, Perle J. Abraham.
2. William O'Donovan to Janet O'Donovan Abraham, March 16, 1871, typed transcript, ibid.
3. Annette Blaugrund, "The Tenth Street Studio Building: A Roster, 1857–1895," *American Art Journal* 14 (Spring 1982), p. 71.
4. W.R. O'Donovan to J.O. Abraham, April 6, 1872, typed transcript, Historical Society of Pennsylvania.
5. W.R. O'Donovan to J.O. Abraham, Feb. 11, 1877, ibid.
6. See for instance, William R. O'Donovan, "A Statue of Shakespeare," *Lippincott's Monthly* 11 (June 1874), pp. 118–23.
7. W.R. O'Donovan to J.O. Abraham, May 8, 1875, typed transcript, Historical Society of Pennsylvania.
8. Lloyd Goodrich, *Thomas Eakins* (Cambridge: Harvard University Press, 1982), vol. 2, p. 112.
9. "American Sculptor's Notes in Color," *New York Sun*, Dec. 27, 1919.

References

1920 Obituary, *New York Times*, April 21, p. 9. **1962** *Dictionary of American Biography*, s.v. "O'Donovan, William Rudolf."

Winslow Homer

1876
Bronze with brown patina; sand cast in 1911
12 x 6 x 4¾" (30.5 x 15.2 x 12.1 cm)
Signed and dated on back: O DONOVAN/1876
Inscribed on front: HOMER.
Foundry mark on back: BUREAU BRO'S/FOUNDERS
Cast in bronze by the Pennsylvania Academy from the original owned by Thomas Eakins, 1911.2

IT WAS PROBABLY during the early 1870s that Winslow Homer (1836–1910) and William R. O'Donovan first met. O'Donovan modeled this diminutive likeness of Homer in 1876. The following year, he showed the bust (most likely a plaster version) at the

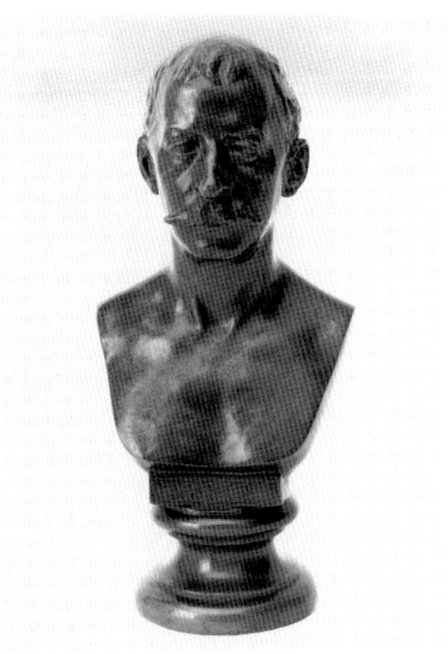

O'Donovan, *Winslow Homer*

National Academy of Design, in New York. In 1879 a plaster was shown in the second exhibition of the Society of American Artists, which was mounted first in New York and then in Philadelphia, at the Pennsylvania Academy of the Fine Arts.

In 1892 O'Donovan gave a plaster version of the bust (whereabouts unknown) to his friend THOMAS EAKINS. The Pennsylvania Academy borrowed Eakins's bust in 1911 to have this bronze made for its permanent collection. Other bronze versions of the bust are in the Metropolitan Museum of Art, New York, and the Corcoran Gallery of Art, Washington, D.C. A plaster that descended through Winslow Homer's family is in the Colby College Museum of Art, Waterville, Maine.

Exhibited
1972 Cosmopolitan Club, Philadelphia, exhibition of works from PAFA. **1991–92** PAFA, *Thomas Eakins Rediscovered: At Home, At School, At Work.*

Alice Gerson

1884
Plaster
7½ x 5⅝ x ½" (19.4 x 14.2 x 1.5 cm)
Inscribed on front at bottom: [To A]lice Gerson/From/ William Rudolf/[O'Donovan]; and dated at upper right: 1884.
Annotated in ink on paper label affixed to back: *Bas Relief/by William. Rudolph. ODonovan/Presented by Mrs. Talcott William[s]/[Mar] 4, 1912.*
Gift of Mrs. Talcott Williams, 1912.7.1

ALICE GERSON (1864–1927) was twenty years old when William R. O'Donovan modeled this portrait. Two years later, she married the painter William Merritt Chase.

O'Donovan was surely familiar with the relief sculptures of AUGUSTUS SAINT-GAUDENS. The two exhibited together in several shows and were fellow members of the Tile Club. O'Donovan's placement of this figure and his use of a bottom border are reminiscent of Saint-Gaudens's relief portraits. In addition, the horizontal scoring that O'Donovan employed to define the border often appears in the background of Saint-Gaudens's reliefs.

Exhibited
1986–87 PAFA, *Sculpture at the Pennsylvania Academy of the Fine Arts.*

Marie Heimlicher

1884
Plaster
10⅜ x 8 x ½" (26.3 x 20.4 x 1.3 cm)
Signed on front at bottom: William Rudolf O'Donovan fecit

O'Donovan, *Alice Gerson*

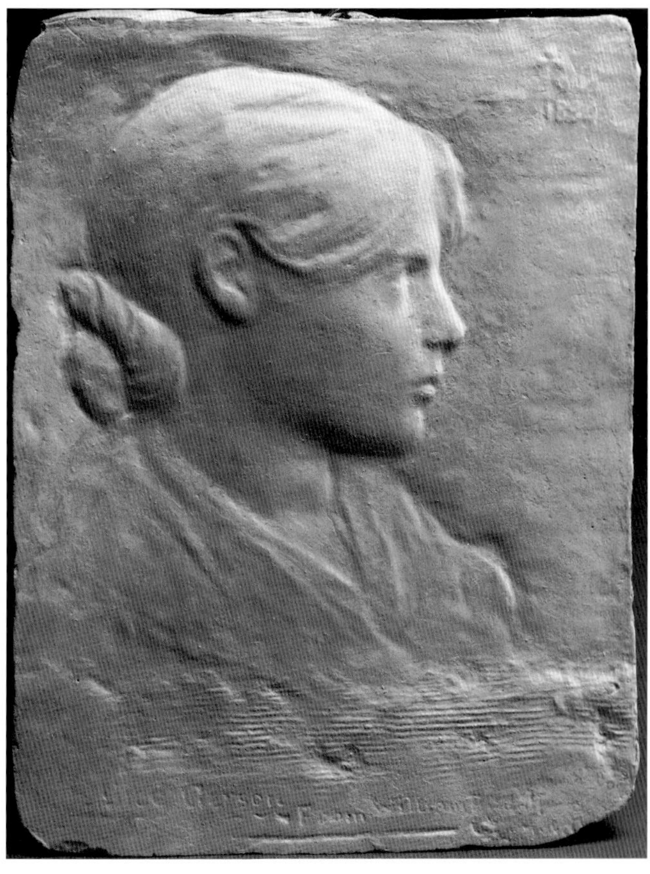

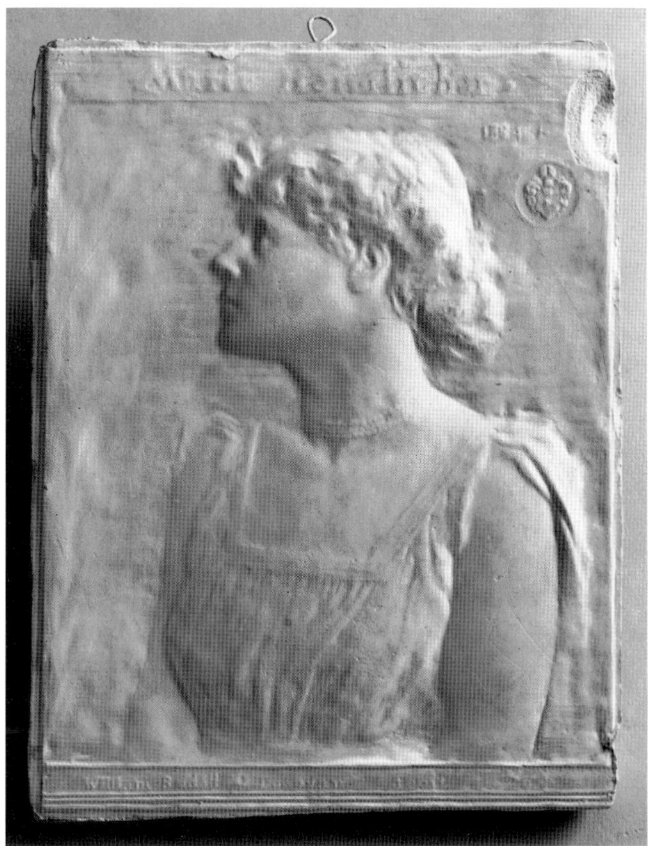

O'Donovan, *Marie Heimlicher*

Inscribed in raised letters on front at top: Marie Heimlicher/1884
Annotated in ink on paper label affixed to back: *Bas Relief/by William Rudolph ODonovan/Presented by/ Mrs Talcott Williams/Mar 4, 1912.*
Gift of Mrs. Talcott Williams, 1912.7.2

NOTHING IS KNOWN about Marie Heimlicher, the sitter in this relief portrait. William R. O'Donovan modeled her likeness in very low relief, using soft amorphous forms and no undercutting. Many of the forms, such as the beads and letters, have a peculiar flattened surface. O'Donovan's use of lettering reveals the influence of AUGUSTUS SAINT-GAUDENS, the most famous exponent of the relief portrait. As Saint-Gaudens so often did, O'Donovan incorporated the sitter's coat of arms into this portrait. A bronze version of this relief is in the Hirshhorn Museum and Sculpture Garden, Washington, D.C.

Exhibited
1986–87 PAFA, *Sculpture at the Pennsylvania Academy of the Fine Arts.*

Thomas Eakins

1892
Plaster, tinted pink
11 x 6⅝ x 4⅜" (27.9 x 16.8 x 11.1 cm)
Annotated by Charles Bregler in pencil on back: Thomas Eakins/modeled/by/O Donavan [*sic*]
Charles Bregler's Thomas Eakins Collection, purchased with the partial support of the Pew Memorial Trust, 1985.68.1.21

WILLIAM R. O'DONOVAN modeled a bust of Thomas Eakins (1844–1916), and Eakins in turn painted a portrait of O'Donovan while the two artists were working together in 1892 on the equestrian relief portraits of Abraham Lincoln and Ulysses S. Grant for the Soldiers and Sailors Memorial Arch, Brooklyn, New York. O'Donovan undoubtedly made this relief portrait in preparation for his bronze bust of Eakins. There are traces of hand modeling, and a mold line runs vertically through the center of the face: these facts suggest that this is not a mask cast from life.

O'Donovan and Eakins exchanged their finished portraits of one another. Both were shown in New

O'Donovan, *Thomas Eakins*

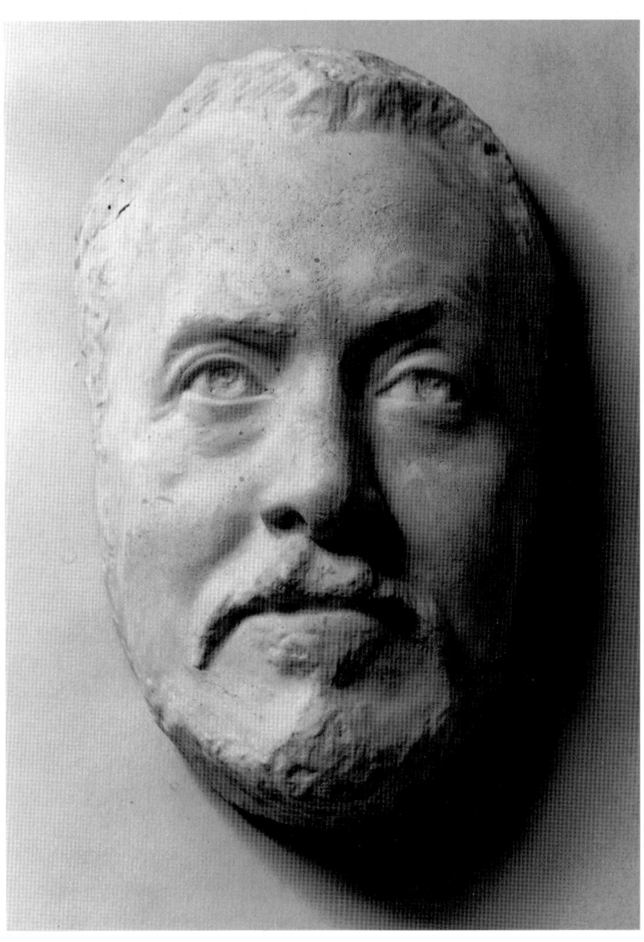

York at the National Academy of Design's 1892 annual exhibition.[1] O'Donovan's bronze bust of Eakins was shown at the World's Columbian Exposition in Chicago, in 1893.[2] The present whereabouts of both portraits are unknown.[3]

Notes

1. Maria Naylor, ed., *The National Academy of Design Exhibition Record, 1861–1900* (New York: Kennedy Galleries, 1973), vol. 1, cat. no. 439; and vol. 2, cat. no. 497.
2. *Official Directory of the World's Columbian Exposition* (Chicago: W.B. Conkey Company, 1893), cat. no. 86.
3. Lloyd Goodrich, *Thomas Eakins* (Cambridge: Harvard University Press, 1982), vol. 1, p. 125, suggests that Mrs. Eakins, who had strong likes and dislikes about images of her husband, destroyed the bust.

Exhibited

1986–87 PAFA, *Sculpture at the Pennsylvania Academy of the Fine* Arts. **1991–92** PAFA, *Thomas Eakins Rediscovered: At Home, At School, At Work.*

Ex Collections

Thomas Eakins, 1892–1916; his wife, Susan Macdowell Eakins, 1916–38; Charles Bregler, 1938–58; his wife, Mary Picozzi Bregler, 1958–85.

Ida Waugh

About 1847–1919

Primarily remembered as a painter and illustrator, Ida Waugh created a fair number of sculptures early in her career. She was the daughter of the landscape and portrait painter Samuel Bell Waugh and his first wife, Mary Z. Mendenhall.[1] His second wife, Mary Eliza Young, a painter of miniatures, was the mother of Frederick Judd Waugh, who became a well-known marine painter. Reared in this artistic milieu, Ida began her art training with her father, who was a recognized force in the artistic community of Philadelphia. He participated regularly in the annual exhibitions of the Pennsylvania Academy of the Fine Arts and was elected an academician in 1860.

With his encouragement, Ida Waugh exhibited at the Pennsylvania Academy for the first time in 1863; she entered a statuette entitled *The Contraband* in the fortieth annual exhibition. She went on to show plaster sculptures in the annual exhibitions from 1865 to 1867 and again in 1876. She is recorded as a student at the Academy in 1867[2] and was elected an associate the following year. Associates were professional members of the institution from whose ranks the academicians were chosen. In October of 1869, her signature, along with those of Emily Sartain and Catherine Drinker, appeared on a petition requesting the continuation of the women's life class, which the Academy had instituted the previous April.[3] The petition was successful, and the class continued under the tutelage of Christian Schussele.

Ida Waugh never married, and she may have turned to commercial art to support herself. During the 1870s, she began producing illustrations for the Boston chromolithographic firm of Louis Prang and Company and became rather well known for sentimental children's book illustrations. Waugh exhibited both sculpture and paintings at the Centennial Exposition in Philadelphia but, by the 1880s, seems to have substituted painting for sculpture as her primary artistic medium.

Following in the footsteps of her half-brother, Frederick, Ida Waugh went to Paris in 1888 and enrolled in the Académie Julian. There she studied under Jùles Joseph Lefebvre. While in Paris, she was also a student of Jean Joseph Benjamin-Constant and Paul Louis Delance. She is recorded as having been at the Académie Delecluse from 1891 to 1892.

Her work was included in the Gallery of Honor in the Women's Building of the World's Columbian Exposition in Chicago in 1893. She was awarded the Norman W. Dodge Prize at the National Academy of Design in New York in 1896 for her portrait of Dr. Paul J. Sartain, the son of the Philadelphia printmaker John Sartain. During her later years, she maintained homes on Bailly Island, Maine, and in New York, where she died on January 25, 1919.

Notes

1. Obituary, *New York Times*, Jan. 27, 1919, p. 13.
2. Student card, PAFA Archives.
3. Minutes, meeting of Committee on Instruction, Oct. 11, 1869, PAFA Archives.

Fancy Head

By 1865
Plaster, painted pink
8⅞ x 7 x 4¼" (22.5 x 17.8 x 10.8 cm)
Gift of James L. Claghorn, 1878.2.4

This intimate, high-relief, plaster medallion of a young girl was modeled from life.[1] It was lent to the 1865 annual exhibition of the Pennsylvania Academy of the Fine Arts by the owner, James L. Claghorn. Ida Waugh entered another plaster medallion, *Saint Agnes,* in the same exhibition. Painted and presented as finished pieces, these decorative medallions may have been inspired by the popular Victorian cameo. The curved truncation of the shoulders in *Fancy*

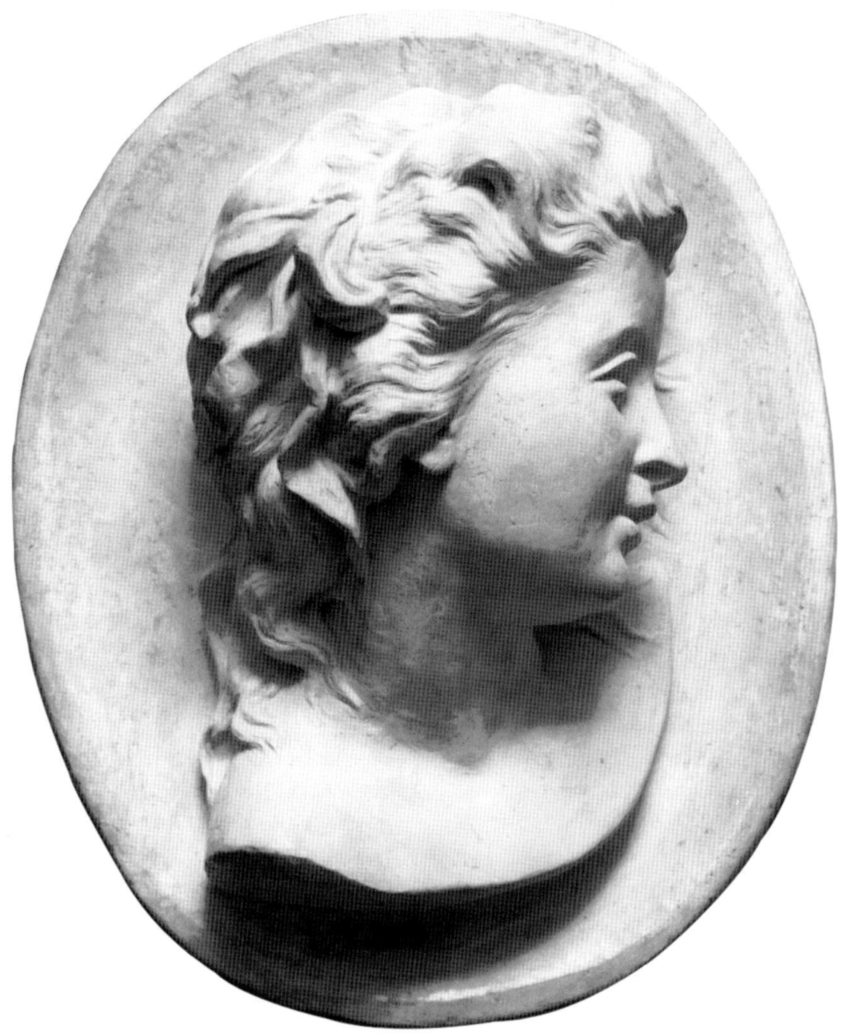

Waugh, *Fancy Head*

Head particularly recalls the treatment of a cameo.

Though certainly not replicated en masse like the plaster genre groups of JOHN ROGERS, Waugh's plaster medallions may have had a similar commercial purpose. As a new middle class emerged in Victorian America, the demand for affordable art to decorate the home encouraged the widespread use of plaster as an inexpensive sculpture medium. In addition to *Fancy Head,* for example, James L. Claghorn owned the Rogers group called *Country Post Office* and displayed it prominently in the study of his Logan Square home.[2] The epitome of the successful Victorian middle-class businessman, Claghorn pursued a number of interests in art. He was an avid print collector and a supporter of the Pennsylvania Academy to which he donated *Fancy Head* in 1878.

Notes

1. PAFA Art Property Register, 1877–97, July 17, 1878, PAFA Archives. When Claghorn gave this medallion portrait to the Pennsylvania Academy, it was framed and glazed.
2. Photograph, PAFA Archives.

Exhibited

1865* cat. no. 806. **1974** PAFA, *The Pennsylvania Academy and Its Women, 1850–1920,* cat. no. 12. **1986–87** PAFA, *Sculpture at the Pennsylvania Academy of the Fine Arts.*

Ex Collection

James L. Claghorn, about 1865–78.

Henry J. Ellicott

1847–1901

Henry Jackson Ellicott was born in 1847 in Anne Arundel County, Maryland. He studied at the National Academy of Design, in New York, where he received instruction from William Henry Powell and Emanuel Leutze. He also studied under Constantino Brumidi. In 1876 Jackson moved to Philadelphia. Two years later, he exhibited for the first time at the Pennsylvania Academy of the Fine Arts, in the forty-ninth annual exhibition. During the next thirteen years, he showed in four more of the Academy's annuals, ending with the sixty-first annual exhibition in 1891, just prior to his move to Washington, D.C.

During the administration of President Benjamin Harrison, Ellicott was appointed Superintendent and Chief Modeler for the U.S. Treasury Department. In 1892 he wrote that most of his time was spent modeling military monuments.[1] One important project was an equestrian statue of George B. McClellan, the Civil War general, for Philadelphia, the city in which he was born. Other examples of Ellicott's work can be found in Boston, New York, Gettysburg, and Pittsburgh. He died in Washington in 1901.

Note

1. Henry Jackson Ellicott to J. Woodward, Feb. 18, 1892, PAFA Archives.

References

1904 "Henry J. Ellicott," *The National Cyclopaedia of American Biography* 12, New York: James T. White and Company, p. 122. **1984** Glenn B. Opitz, ed., *Dictionary of American Sculptors*, Poughkeepsie, N.Y.: Apollo, p. 115.

Ellicott, *John Sartain*

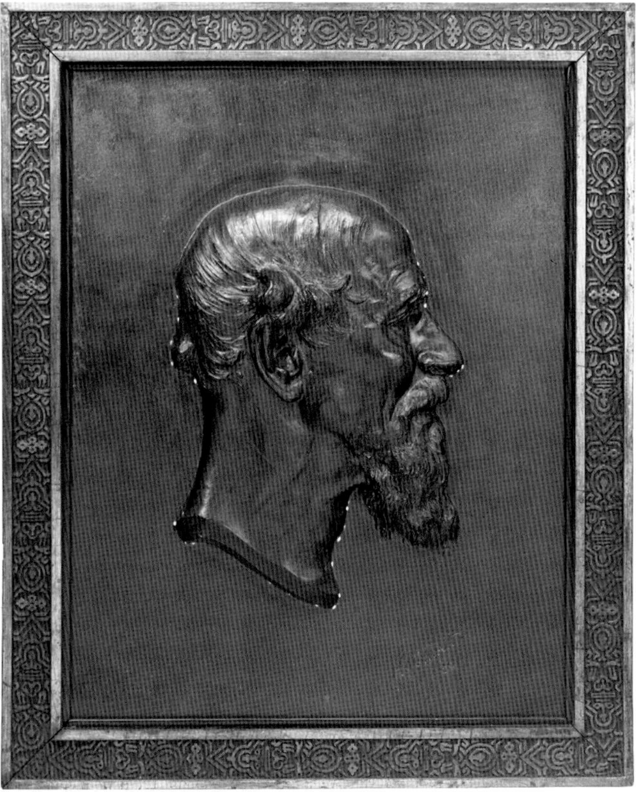

John Sartain

About 1888
Bronze with brown patina; sand cast by 1891
22¼ x 17¼ x 3" (56.5 x 43.8 x 7.6 cm)
Signed on front at lower right: HJ Ellicott/Sc
Inscribed at lower left: John Sartain
Foundry mark on truncation of bust: [B]UREAU BROS./ [PHILA]
Gift of John Sartain, 1891.13

John Sartain (1808–1897), was born in London and immigrated to the United States in 1830. He settled in Philadelphia, where he came under the patronage and influence of Thomas Sully. Sartain is credited with being not only the earliest but also the leading practitioner of the art of mezzotint engraving in America. For twenty-three years, he was associated with the Pennsylvania Academy of the Fine Arts as an academician and a member of the board of directors and was responsible for the arrangement of galleries and rooms there. He enjoyed a long and prolific career as an engraver until his death in 1897.

This bronze portrait, executed in extremely high relief, is a good likeness of Sartain in his later years. It was modeled by Henry J. Ellicott sometime prior to 1891; perhaps around 1888 when he modeled Sartain's likeness for the *Commemorative Medal of the 50th Anniversary of the Monument Cemetery* (see Appendix). The relief was in Sartain's collection by January of 1891, when it was included in the sixty-first annual exhibition of the Pennsylvania Academy.[1] Sartain gave it to the Academy in November of 1891 in exchange for a terracotta bust of himself by Franz Engdahl. In December 1891, the sculptor wrote of his desire to present a "portrait medallion" to the Academy.[2] Probably he was referring to the medal that was an 1891 gift.

Notes

1. John Sartain to Henry Whipple, Jan. 14, 1891, PAFA Archives.
2. Henry J. Ellicott to PAFA, Dec. 18, 1891, PAFA Archives.

Exhibited
1891* cat. no. 488.

Commemorative Medal of the 50th Anniversary of the Monument Cemetery, 1888: See Appendix.

Augustus Saint-Gaudens

1848–1907

Augustus Saint-Gaudens was born to a French father and an Irish mother in Dublin at a time when the potato famine was forcing many people to flee Ireland. Six months after Saint-Gaudens's birth, his family, too, departed for the United States. They settled in New York, where the father crafted fancy boots for ladies and gentlemen. As a teenager, Augustus was apprenticed to a cameo carver. One of his early employers in the trade, Jules Le Brethon, instructed him in clay modeling and encouraged his artistic aspirations. Between 1864 and 1866, Saint-Gaudens took evening drawing classes at both the Cooper Union for the Advancement of Science and Art and the National Academy of Design.

In 1867 he traveled to Paris to see the Exposition Universelle and to continue his art studies. He supported himself by carving cameos while he studied sculpture at the Ecole Gratuité de Dessin, commonly called the Petite Ecole, and then at the Ecole des Beaux-Arts under François Jouffroy (1806–1882).

When the Franco-Prussian War broke out in 1870, Saint-Gaudens went to Rome. There, he began his first full-scale figure, a statue of Hiawatha; but he fell ill with malaria and had to return home to recuperate. Back in New York, he executed a number of portraits, including those of Edwin W. Stoughton, 1872–73 (John and Mabel Ringling Museum of Art, Sarasota) and William M. Evarts, 1872–74 (private collection). Saint-Gaudens also received an important commission for an allegorical statue of Silence for the Masonic Temple then under construction in New York (now at the Masonic Soldiers' and Sailors' Hospital, Utica, N.Y.). He returned to Rome to work on *Silence* and to carve *Hiawatha* in marble (private collection) for Edward D. Morgan, a former governor of New York.

In New York in 1875, Saint-Gaudens secured work on several small decorative projects through Tiffany and Company. The following year, he was hired by John LaFarge to assist on the mural paintings for Henry Hobson Richardson's Trinity Church in Boston. It was the first of a number of projects on which he worked with LaFarge. Others include a reredos for Saint Thomas's Church in New York (destroyed by fire in 1905); the King Family Tomb in Newport, Rhode Island; and the decorations for the home of Cornelius Vanderbilt II on Fifth Avenue in New York.[1]

In 1877 Saint-Gaudens returned to Paris and began work on the bronze relief sculptures that were to bring him wide acclaim. Among them are several portraits of his artist friends, including Jules Bastien-Lepage, 1880 (Museum of Fine Arts, Boston) and William Merritt Chase, 1888 (American Academy of Arts and Letters, New York). One of the best known is *Robert Louis Stevenson,* modeled from life in 1887–88 (three versions in numerous collections).

By the 1880s Saint-Gaudens had become a major force in the New York art world. In 1881 his bronze statue of Admiral David Farragut was unveiled in Madison Square Park. That same year, Saint-Gaudens was elected president of the Society of American Artists, a group that he had helped found in 1877 in reaction to the conservative policies of the National Academy of Design.[2] Saint-Gaudens was also an influential teacher, who, beginning in 1888, spent almost ten years at the Art Students League of New York.

Saint-Gaudens's famous standing figure of Abraham Lincoln was erected in Chicago's Lincoln Park in 1887. His friend and frequent collaborator, the architect Stanford White, designed the pedestal and surrounding exedra. For White's Madison Square Garden in New York, Saint-Gaudens executed a colossal gilded weathervane depicting the goddess Diana.[3] It was hoisted atop the building in 1891. The same year, the sculptor's mortuary statue for the grave of Marian Hooper Adams was erected in Rock Creek Cemetery in Washington, D.C. Another major monument, which had occupied his time intermittently from 1884, was erected in 1897 across from the State House in Boston. It was the Shaw Memorial relief, commemorating a Civil War hero who was fatally wounded while leading his black regiment in battle.

The last major work of Saint-Gaudens's career was an equestrian statue of General William Tecumseh Sherman, 1903 (Grand Army Plaza, Brooklyn, N.Y.). Two years later, at the request of President Theodore Roosevelt, Saint-Gaudens designed the United States ten-dollar and twenty-dollar gold pieces. After 1905, when Saint-Gaudens learned that he had cancer, he spent more and more time at Aspet, his country estate, in Cornish, New Hampshire (today, a National Historical Site).

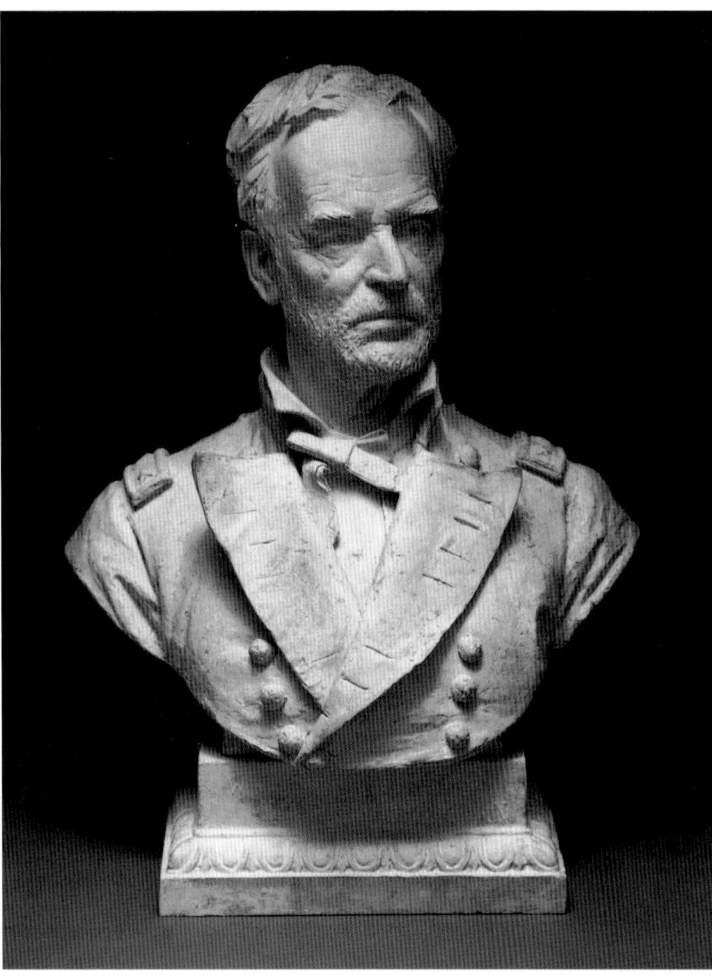

Saint-Gaudens, *William Tecumseh Sherman*

Notes

1. The mansion was torn down in 1925. Two objects survive: Saint-Gaudens's caryatid mantlepiece (Metropolitan Museum of Art, New York) and a panel depicting Ceres (Saint-Gaudens National Historic Site, Cornish, N.H.).

2. The Society of American Artists was short-lived, and in 1890 Saint-Gaudens was elected an academician of the National Academy of Design.

3. The statue, which was made of gilded copper, proved too heavy to turn and was replaced by a smaller version in 1894. The latter was removed in 1925 when the original Madison Square Garden was demolished and is now at the Philadelphia Museum of Art. The first version was destroyed by fire while on display at the Columbian Exposition; a fragment survived although it is now unlocated.

References

1913 Homer Saint-Gaudens, ed., *The Reminiscences of Augustus Saint-Gaudens,* 2 vols., New York: Century Company. **1969** Louise Hall Tharp, *Saint-Gaudens and the Gilded Era,* Boston: Little, Brown and Company. **1982** John H. Dryfhout, *The Work of Augustus Saint-Gaudens,* Hanover, N.H.: University Press of New England. **1985** Kathryn Greenthal, *Augustus Saint-Gaudens, Master Sculptor,* New York: Metropolitan Museum of Art.

William Tecumseh Sherman

1888
Plaster, cast about 1892
29½ x 21¾ x 12¾" (74.9 x 55.2 x 32.3 cm)
Signed and dated on proper right side of figure in raised letters from a circular stamp: COPYRIGHT BY AVGVSTVS ST GAVDENS/M/DCCCX/CII
Inscribed in raised letters on front of base: WILLIAM-TECVMPSEH [*sic*]-/SHERMAN
Deposited by Mrs. Alexander M. Thackara, 1.1897

WILLIAM TECUMSEH SHERMAN (1820–1891) earned his reputation as a brilliant military tactician during the Civil War. In 1864 he led the "March to the Sea" from Chattanooga, Tennessee, to Savannah, Georgia, where his troups succeeded in cutting off the main supplies to the Confederate Army. Upon the inauguration of Ulysses S. Grant as president in 1869, Sherman succeeded him as commander of the United States Army.

It was not without some prodding that the testy sixty-eight-year-old general consented to pose for Augustus Saint-Gaudens during the winter of 1888.[1] Sherman was tired of being pestered by "damned sculptors," but Whitelaw Reid, the editor of the *New York Tribune,* and Rachel Sherman Thorndike, one of the general's daughters, helped convince him to sit for Saint-Gaudens.[2] Sherman proved to be an excellent sitter except when Saint-Gaudens moved too far behind him. Then, Saint-Gaudens later wrote, "his head turned too, very much, someone observed, as if he was watching out for his 'communications from the rear.' " Sherman chatted amiably with the sculptor about the Civil War and the men he knew. It was a memorable experience for Saint-Gaudens, who regretted that he did not record their conversations.[3]

This superb likeness was modeled in about eighteen sittings of two hours each.[4] The sculptor and historian Lorado Taft (1860–1936) called the bust "one of the most vivid things ever made, a head that startles one who unexpectedly encounters it."[5] The deeply creased face, stubbled beard, and piercing eyes give the head a lifelike quality. The skewed tie is fitting as Sherman was known to be careless of his appearance and often unkempt.[6]

Although the bust was not commissioned, several of Sherman's children were extremely pleased with the likeness. Mary Elizabeth "Lizzie" Sherman, the general's second oldest child, wrote to Saint-Gaudens: "To see so fine a likeness of my dear father affords me the utmost satisfaction & happiness."[7] At least two daughters acquired casts of the bust.[8] This plaster cast came to the Museum of American Art of the Pennsylvania Academy of the Fine Arts through Sherman's fifth child, Mrs. Alexander Thackara, née

Eleanor Mary Sherman. She acquired the bust directly from Saint-Gaudens's studio.[9] It is undoubtedly an early cast, possibly dating from 1892, the year of the copyright.[10] It is very similar to the plaster version at the Fogg Art Museum in Cambridge, Massachusetts, and to at least one of the plaster versions at the Saint-Gaudens National Historic Site in Cornish, New Hampshire. The bases of these early plasters are decorated with an egg-and-dart molding, while the later versions have a larger, more elaborate base with a pillow of ribbon-bound laurel.[11] The inscriptions also differ: on the early plaster casts, Sherman's middle name is spelled incorrectly as *Tecumpseh,* and his surname appears on a separate line; in the later, more elegant design, the spelling error has been corrected and the inscription fitted into a single line.[12] Exactly when Saint-Gaudens made these changes is unknown. He probably reworked the base before the bust was first cast in bronze, but this date is also elusive.[13] The sculpture may not have been cast in bronze until 1900, when Saint-Gaudens exhibited a bronze at the twenty-fifth anniversary exhibition of the American Fine Arts Society, in New York.[14] This bust later served as a study for the equestrian monument of Sherman, 1903 (Grand Army Plaza, Brooklyn, N.Y.).[15] In fact, Saint-Gaudens hardly altered the head at all.

Notes

1. See William T. Sherman to Saint-Gaudens, Jan. 24, 1888, and March 3, 1888, Dartmouth College Library, Hanover, N.H.
2. Royal Cortissoz, *The Life of Whitelaw Reid* (New York: Charles Scribner's Sons, 1921), vol. 2, p. 379.
3. Homer Saint-Gaudens, ed., *The Reminiscences of Augustus* Saint-Gaudens (New York: Century Company, 1913), vol. 1, p. 381.
4. Ibid., pp. 378, 381.
5. Lorado Taft, *Modern Tendencies in Sculpture* (Chicago: University of Chicago Press, 1921), p. 112.
6. William T. Sherman, *Memoirs of General William T. Sherman by Himself,* foreword by B.H. Liddell Hart (Bloomington: Indiana University Press, 1957), p. v.
7. Lizzie Sherman to Augustus Saint-Gaudens, undated (1888), Dartmouth College Library.
8. Augusta Saint-Gaudens to Rachel Sherman Thorndike, Jan. 30, 1908, ibid., indicates that Thorndike, the general's sixth child, acquired a bronze version from the sculptor's wife in early Feb. 1908.
9. Edward H. Coates, former president of the PAFA, to John F. Lewis, president of the PAFA, April 18, 1913, PAFA object file.
10. Alexander M. Thackara to Harrison S. Morris, managing director of the PAFA, about April 23, 1897, PAFA object file: "I send you by messenger a plaster reproduction of St. Gaudens' bust of General Sherman, made by St. Gaudens himself, also a pedestal upon which it has generally stood." This seems to imply that the Thackaras had the bust in their collection for some time.
11. Bronze versions that have the base of ribbon-bound laurel are located at the Metropolitan Museum of Art, New York; the Bronx Community College Hall of Fame, N.Y.; the United States Military Academy, West Point, N.Y.; and the Saint-Gaudens National Historic Site, Cornish, N.H.
12. A plaster cast of the Sherman bust reproduced in the *Century Magazine* 5 (June 1897), p. 183, exhibits a base that differs from the early style as seen in the Museum of American Art of the Pennsylvania Academy's piece and from the other known versions, as well. It was probably an intermediary solution for the inscription of the general's name appears to be on one line.
13. The Henry Bonnard Bronze Company to Mrs. Saint-Gaudens, Sept. 9, 1907, Saint-Gaudens Papers, Dartmouth College Library, in response to her request for an estimate to cast this bust in bronze: "We made two copies for Mr. St. Gaudens some years ago."
14. The exhibition history of the various versions of this bust is given in John H. Dryfhout, *The Work of Augustus Saint-Gaudens* (Hanover, N.H.: University Press of New England, 1982), p. 168.
15. H. Saint-Gaudens 1913, vol. 2, p. 124.

Exhibited

1986–87 PAFA, *Sculpture at the Pennsylvania Academy of the Fine Arts.*

Ex Collection

Mrs. Alexander M. Thackara, about 1892–97.

Mr. and Mrs. Wayne Mac Veagh

1902–3
Marble
39¼ x 58 x 1½ to 2⅜" (varies) (99.7 x 147.3 x 3.8 to 6 cm)
Signed and dated in lower right corner: MDCC/A ST G
[in monogram]/CCII
Gift of Captain Stuart Farrar Smith, 1941.16

FROM 1901 to 1904, Augustus Saint-Gaudens spent the late winter and early spring seasons in Washington, D.C.[1] It was probably there at one of the numerous social gatherings that he met Mr. and Mrs. Mac Veagh.

Isaac Wayne Mac Veagh (1833–1917) was born in Chester County, Pennsylvania. He was graduated tenth in his class from Yale University, entered the legal profession, and served as district attorney in Chester County from 1859 to 1864. In 1866, four years after the death of his first wife, Mac Veagh married Virginia Rolette Cameron (d. after 1923). She was the daughter of Simon Cameron, a Republican political boss in Pennsylvania, whom Mac Veagh eventually opposed. In 1876 the Mac Veaghs moved to Philadelphia, and they maintained a home in the area from then on. Mac Veagh was a tireless fighter against political injustice. His legal skills and bipartisan appeal earned him the position of attorney general under President James Garfield. Mac Veagh served as ambassador to Italy from 1893 to 1895. In

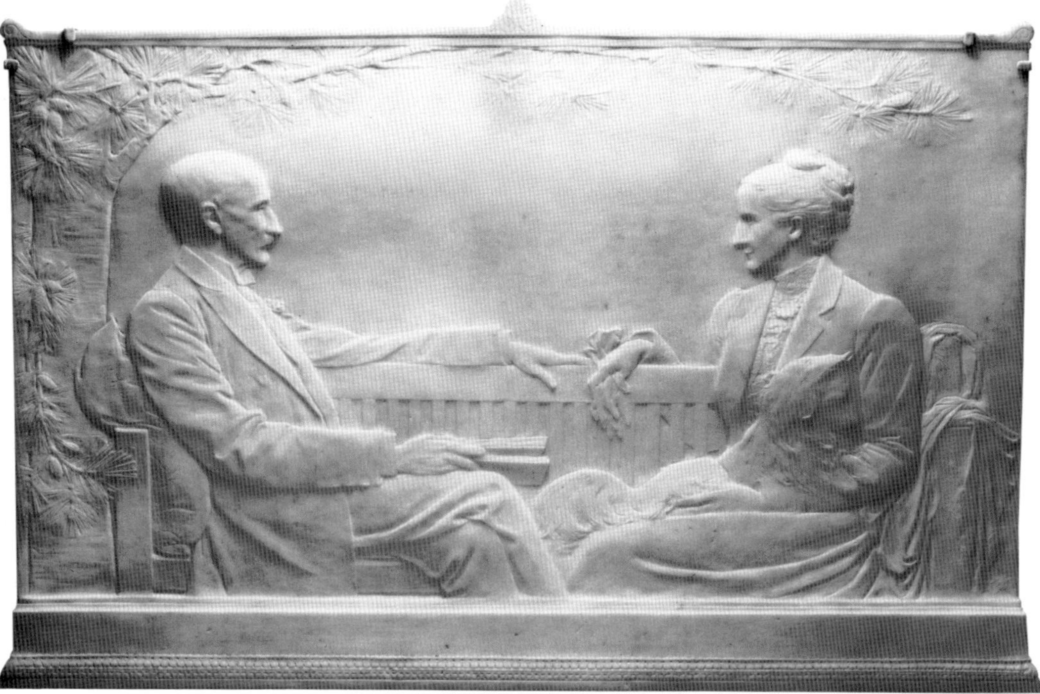

Saint-Gaudens, *Mr. and Mrs. Wayne Mac Veagh*

1897 he returned to the legal profession and established a practice in Washington, D.C.

Mr. and Mrs. Mac Veagh commissioned this portrait in 1902 for twelve thousand dollars.[2] Although Saint-Gaudens began the portrait in Washington, D.C., it was probably completed at his Cornish, New Hampshire, estate in 1903.[3] His studio assistants Frances Grimes (1869–1963) and Henry Hering (1874–1949) helped with the work as Saint-Gaudens's health was failing.[4] It is tempting to attribute some of the shallow modeling that appears in the relief—for example, Mr. Mac Veagh's coat sleeves —to a hand other than the sculptor's.

As he so often did in his relief portraits, Saint-Gaudens set the subjects against a plain background. The pine tree, a significant design element, is confined to the left and upper perimeters and not allowed to interfere with the gaze of the sitters. Saint-Gaudens's working drawings for this portrait indicate that he toyed with the idea of having only one, rather than both, of the Mac Veaghs rest a hand on the back of the bench.[5] The final solution, however, draws the figures together in a touching and elegant manner.

When this marble relief was ready to be installed at the Mac Veaghs' Washington home in December 1904, Saint-Gaudens sent along Frances Grimes to make sure that it was correctly placed upon its easel and well lighted.[6] The easel, which remains with the piece today, was constructed of golden oak by the well-known furniture makers Davenport and Company, according to Saint-Gaudens's instructions.[7]

The Mac Veaghs were delighted with the relief, but Mrs. Mac Veagh thought she would prefer it in bronze, so the couple ordered a cast. In February 1906, when the bronze was completed, they moved this marble version to their home in Bryn Mawr, outside Philadelphia.[8] Today, the bronze cast is in the Corcoran Gallery of Art, Washington, D.C.

In 1922 the Mac Veaghs' daughter, Margaretta Cameron Mac Veagh Farrar Smith, deposited this relief at the Pennsylvania Academy of the Fine Arts. "It was my father's desire that this marble should ultimately be presented to the Academy of Fine Arts," she wrote.[9] The gift was made by her husband in 1941 after her death.

Notes

1. John H. Dryfhout, *Augustus Saint-Gaudens: The Portrait Reliefs* (New York: Grossman Publishers, 1969), cat. no. 50, unpaginated.
2. John H. Dryfhout, *The Work of Augustus Saint-Gaudens* (Hanover, N.H.: University Press of New England, 1982), p. 248.
3. Dryfhout 1969 suggests the relief was completed at Cornish "because the furnishings and suggestion of trees came from the Cornish estate."
4. Dryfhout 1982, p. 248.

5. Homer Saint-Gaudens, ed., *The Reminiscences of Augustus Saint-Gaudens* (New York: Century Company, 1913), vol. 2, p. 129.

6. Augustus Saint-Gaudens to Messrs. Davenport, undated draft of letter, and Saint-Gaudens to Wayne Mac Veagh, August 27, 1904, both Saint-Gaudens Papers, Dartmouth College Library, Hanover, N.H.

7. Wayne Mac Veagh to Augustus Saint-Gaudens, Dec. 19, 1904, ibid.

8. Mac Veagh to Saint-Gaudens, Feb. 26, 1906, ibid.

9. M. Farrar Smith to John Andrew Myers, secretary of PAFA, Oct. 31, 1922, PAFA object file.

References

1976 *In This Academy*, Philadelphia: PAFA, p. 47 (ill.). **1982** Linda Bantel, "Sculpture at the Pennsylvania Academy," *Antiques* 121 (March), p. 713 (ill.).

Exhibited

1972 PAFA, *Acres of Art*, checklist no. 93. **1986–87** PAFA, *Sculpture at the Pennsylvania Academy of the Fine Arts*. **1994–95** PAFA, *Two Centuries of Collecting at the Museum of American Art*.

Ex Collections

Mr. and Mrs. Wayne Mac Veagh, 1904-before 1922; their daughter, Mrs. Margaretta Cameron Mac Veagh Farrar Smith, by 1922, when she deposited it at the Pennsylvania Academy, until 1941; her husband, Captain Stuart Farrar Smith, 1941.

World's Columbian Exposition Commemorative Presentation Medal, 1892–94: See Appendix.

Albert Van den Berghen

1850–1921

Little is known about Albert Louis Van den Berghen, a Belgian sculptor born in Vilvorde and trained at the Ecole de Dessin et de Modelage in Brussels. His obituary in the *Chicago Evening Post* provides the most information. Unfortunately, much of it has not been verifiable. Van den Berghen immigrated to the United States in 1876. It is said that he found work with AUGUSTUS SAINT-GAUDENS in New York.[1] What he did for Saint-Gaudens is unknown. It may have been modeling or plaster casting but appears to have been incidental.

About 1880 Van den Berghen went to Washington, D.C., where he assisted in decorating the War and Navy libraries (in the Old Executive Office Building) and the Library of Congress.[2] From Washington, he moved to Philadelphia. His name appears in Gopsill's Philadelphia Directory from 1886 to 1889. He is listed as a sculptor in each of these years except 1887, when he is designated as an engraver. Other than *Ecce Homo* (q.v.), none of his work from this period has come to light. From Philadelphia, Van den Berghen went to Chicago to assist with the sculptural decorations for the World's Columbian Exposition of 1893. His obituary lists five projects on which he worked: the Brazil, Indiana, Mines and Mining, Government, and Electrical buildings. It also reports that he was "congratulated for his representation of 'Baltimore.' "

Van den Berghen remained in Chicago after the exposition. He apparently made plaster decorations for seasonal displays at Marshall Field's department store. He was an instructor at the Art Institute of Chicago for perhaps four years.[3] In 1900 Van den Berghen had a studio on Madison Street near Wells Street and seems to have earned his living chiefly through architectural sculpture.[4] He executed an overmantle panel depicting mermaids for a home on Lake Michigan and a mantlepiece for a home designed by Spencer and Powers in River Forest.[5] In 1903 he modeled four heads illustrating various states of intoxication for Chicago's Majesty Bar, which was later destroyed.[6] His standing bronze statue of Abraham Lincoln entitled *All Men Are Created Equal* was cast by the American Art and Bronze Company of Chicago and erected in Racine, Wisconsin. A bronze replica of the statue is in Clinton, Illinois.[7]

Van den Berghen seems to have had a wide variety of interests. During his last years, he wrote a book about sociology and religion. At his memorial service, the writers Clarence Darrow and Eleanor Gridley paid him tribute.[8]

Notes

1. Obituary, *Chicago Evening Post*, Dec. 20, 1921, Chicago Historical Society.

2. Ibid. Elsa Santoyo, curator, Old Executive Office Building, Washington, D.C., telephone interview with Mary Mullen Cunningham, March 19, 1989, said that the records of the building and decoration program have no information about Van den Berghen. John Knowlton, archivist, Library of Congress, telephone interview with Mary Mullen Cunningham, March 15, 1989, said that the decoration of the library began about 1886 (by then Van den Berghen was already in Philadelphia) and that artists outside of Washington were commissioned to create works for the library, but nothing about Van den Berghen has yet been found.

3. Mary Jane Hamilton, archivist, Art Institute of Chicago, to Susan James-Gadzinski, March 3, 1992, PAFA research file, states that he was an instructor for at least two years. His obituary says four years.

4. "A.L. Van den Berghen, Sc.," *Chicago History* 2 (Fall 1949), p. 156.

5. William Gray Purcell, "Spencer and Powers, Architects," *Western Architecture* 20 (April 1914), p. 37.

6. "A.L. Van den Berghen, Sc." (Fall 1949), p. 156.

7. F. Lauriston Bullard, *Lincoln in Marble and Bronze*

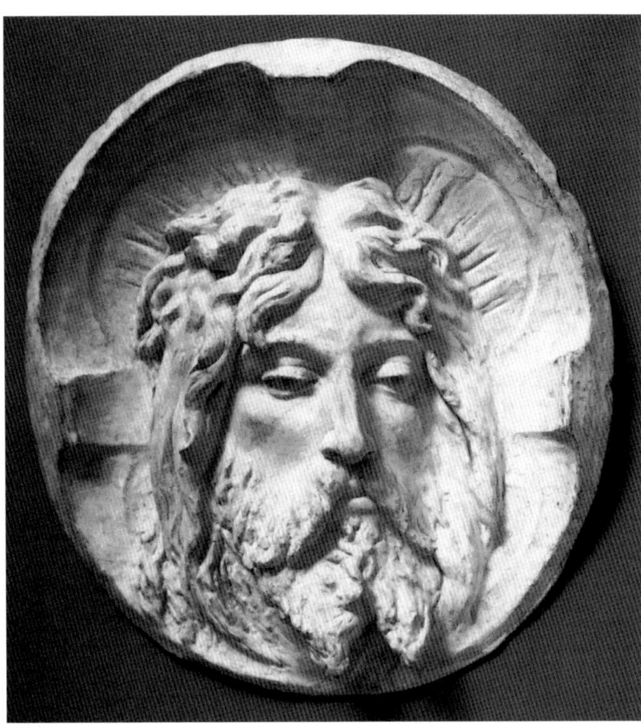

Van den Berghen, *Ecce Homo*

(New Brunswick, N.J.: Rutgers University Press, 1952), p. 255.

8. Obituary, *Chicago Evening Post,* Dec. 20, 1921, Chicago Historical Society.

Ecce Homo

About 1886–89
Papier-mâché
18¾ x 17½ x 4¾" (47.6 x 44.5 x 12.1 cm)
Typed label on back: Title Ecce Hom[o]/By–A.L. Van den [Berghen]
Deposited by Mrs. Sarah B. Wister in 1889 and given to the Pennsylvania Academy, probably after 1892, 1889.4

ALBERT VAN DEN BERGHEN most likely modeled this high-relief medallion of Jesus Christ between 1886 and 1889, when he lived in Philadelphia. The downcast eyes and elongated face give the head an elegant pathos and call to mind many northern European depictions of Christ. Made of papier-mâché reinforced with jute fiber, the medallion is very light. Its curved shape suggests that it was meant to be recessed into a wall rather than framed for hanging. It is therefore assumed to be a model for a stone carving.

Mrs. Sarah B. Wister brought the medallion to the Pennsylvania Academy of the Fine Arts in April 1889 and presented it to the Committee on Exhibitions for consideration. The committee accepted the medallion for exhibition.[1] Whether the sculptor or Mrs. Wister owned the piece is unclear. In the 1892 catalogue of the Pennsylvania Academy's permanent collection, the medallion appears under the heading of loaned sculpture, but the owner is not listed.

Note

1. Minutes, meeting of Committee on Exhibitions, April 8, 1889, p. 80, PAFA Archives.

JOHN JOSEPH BOYLE

1851–1917

The son of Irish immigrants, John Joseph Boyle was born in New York and grew up in Philadelphia. His father, a stone cutter, died when John was six years old. As a young man, he took up his father's trade by entering an apprenticeship at a stoneyard. During the evenings, he attended Central High School and the drawing classes at the Franklin Institute. In 1875 he took an anatomy class with THOMAS EAKINS at the Sketch Club. The following year, he came to the Pennsylvania Academy of the Fine Arts to study under Eakins and the sculptor JOSEPH A. BAILLY. Boyle sailed for Europe in 1877 to begin three years of training with Augustin Alexandre Dumont (1801–1884) and Aimé Millet (1819–1891) at the Ecole des Beaux-Arts in Paris.

Boyle achieved some recognition for his early portraits, but his first major commission came in 1880 from Martin Ryerson, a Chicago lumber tycoon. Ryerson had a particular affection for the Ottawa Indians and wanted to erect a monument to them in Chicago's Lincoln Park. Following the lead of JOHN QUINCY ADAMS WARD, who had traveled West to study native Americans some twenty years earlier, Boyle spent two months on a reservation in North Dakota to prepare for the commission. Back in Philadelphia, he completed the piece, entitled *An Indian Family,* or *The Alarm,* in 1884.[1] It was so highly regarded in Philadelphia that the Fairmount Park Association commissioned him to create a similar sculpture called *Stone Age in America.* This time, Boyle went to Paris to work. He exhibited a plaster version of the piece in the 1886 Paris Salon, where it won an honorable mention. Two years later, the finished bronze was installed in Fairmount Park. Both *An Indian Family* and *Stone Age in America* benefit from Boyle's lively modeling and his ability to convey narrative without excessive detail. He continued to depict native Americans. In 1891 he exhibited *Indian Sculpture: An Illustration in Bas-relief* in the sixty-first annual exhibition of the Pennsylvania Academy.

At the turn of the century, Boyle participated in two major projects. For the World's Columbian Exposition, in Chicago in 1893, he supervised the sculptural decoration of the Transportation Building. In 1901 he returned, for the last time, to an aboriginal theme when he created a pair of plasters entitled *The Savage Age in the East* and *The Savage Age in the West* for the Pan-American Exposition in Buffalo, New York. The pair, along with works by other sculptors representing the Despotic Age, suggested the superiority of the democratic system of government and of the United States in particular.

In his mature years, Boyle modeled a number of noteworthy historical portraits. Among these are the 1893 statues of Plato and Francis Bacon in the upper story of the Rotunda of the Library of Congress, the seated Benjamin Franklin of 1900 that was given to Philadelphia by Justus C. Strawbridge and is now on the campus of the University of Pennsylvania, and the statue of Commodore John Barry unveiled in Washington, D.C., in 1914.

Boyle returned to the Pennsylvania Academy in 1895 to teach for one year while CHARLES GRAFLY took a leave of absence. Boyle had a fruitful relationship with the Academy and was represented in the annual exhibitions of 1883, 1891–92, 1895, 1908–10, 1912, 1915, and 1919. He also served on the jury of selection for sculpture in 1895/96 and 1898.

By 1902 Boyle had moved his permanent residence from Philadelphia to New York, where he served on the Art Commission from 1906 to 1919. He was a charter member of the National Sculpture Society and an associate of the National Academy of Design. He died in New York at the age of sixty-six.

Note

1. *The Corn Dance,* a sculpture that Boyle showed at the Pennsylvania Academy's annual exhibition of 1883, may also have had a native-American theme.

References

1917 "John J. Boyle Dies; A Pioneer Sculptor," *Philadelphia Public Ledger,* Feb. 11, p. 13. **1922** "Autobiography of John J. Boyle," *Fairmount Park Art Association, an Account of Its Origin and Activities from Its Foundation in 1871. Issued on the Occasion of Its Fiftieth Anniversary, 1921,* Philadelphia, p. 193. **1974** *Sculpture of a City: Philadelphia's Treasures in Bronze and Stone,* New York: Walker Publishing Company, pp. 111–17. **1976** Abigail Schade, "John J. Boyle (1851–1917)," in *Philadelphia: Three Centuries of American Art,* Philadelphia: Philadelphia Museum of Art, pp. 431–32.

Tired Out

1887
Bronze with brown patina; lost-wax cast
22 x 14¼ x 14⅝" (56 x 36.2 x 37.2 cm)
Signed and dated on back of chair at top: J.J. Boyle. sculpt Florence 1887
Foundry mark on base at back: THIEBAUT FRES/fondeurs
Gift of Mrs. John J. Boyle, 1919.1

IN THIS UNIQUE CAST of *Tired Out,* an exhausted young mother and her two children are depicted with forthright naturalism.[1] John Joseph Boyle has made no attempt at lofty idealism. The acanthus ornamentation on the chair seems simply to show the influence of the sculptor's eight-month sojourn in Italy and not to be a classical allusion. During the late nineteenth century, secular representations of motherhood were common in Europe, but they were usually presented under the guise of Charity, Joy, or some other personification. In the 1870s, however, the French sculptor Jules Dalou (1838–1902) made intimate genre scenes of young women that were widely produced in bronze and porcelain. They may have provided some inspiration for this sculpture. An American, BESSIE POTTER VONNOH, explored the

Boyle, *Tired Out*

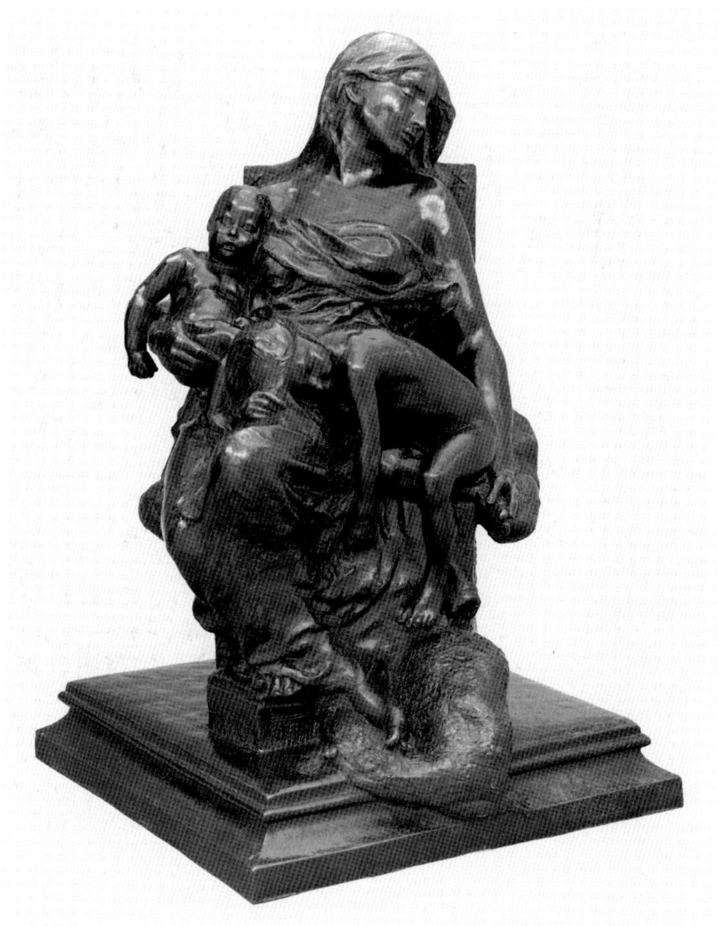

same genre and, in the late 1890s, turned out a series of sculptures on motherhood.

In 1887 Boyle returned to Paris to have *Tired Out* cast by the Thiebaut Frères Foundry, which at the time was busy casting his *Stone Age in America.* When he exhibited *Tired Out* at the World's Columbian Exposition, in Chicago in 1893, it won a medal and was cited in *What to See and Where to Find It—Gems of the Fair, 10,000 Facts.* Because it was shown in many exhibitions, including the Pan-American Exposition, in Buffalo in 1901, and the Panama-Pacific International Exposition, in San Francisco in 1915, the piece became one of Boyle's best-known works.

Note

1. Mrs. John (Elizabeth C.) Boyle to John F. Lewis, Jan. 16, 1919, PAFA object file.

Exhibited

1893 *World's Columbian Exposition,* Chicago, cat. no. 15. **1898** Galleries of the American Fine Arts Society, New York, *Third Exhibition of the National Sculpture Society,* cat. no. 35. **1901** *Pan-American Exposition,* Buffalo, N.Y., cat. no. 1546. **1908** Fifth Regiment Armory, Baltimore, *Exhibition of the National Sculpture Society under the Auspices of the Municipal Art Gallery of Baltimore,* cat. no. 63. **1909** Buffalo Fine Arts Academy, Albright Art Gallery, *A Collection of Small Bronzes; Lent by the National Sculpture Society,* cat. no. 25 (traveled to the Art Institute of Chicago; City Art Museum, Saint Louis; Worcester Art Museum, Mass.). **1915** *Panama-Pacific International Exposition,* San Francisco, cat. no. 533. **1916** Buffalo Fine Arts Academy, Albright Art Gallery, *Exhibition of Contemporary American Sculpture; Held under the auspices of the National Sculpture Society,* cat. no. 112. **1919*** cat. no. 395. **1978–79** PAFA, *350 Masterpieces of American Art: 1720–1978.* **1983** Detroit Institute of Arts, *The Quest for Unity: American Art Between World's Fairs, 1876–1893,* cat. no. 73 (ill.). **1986–87** PAFA, *Sculpture at the Pennsylvania Academy of the Fine Arts.* **1993** National Museum of American Art and National Portrait Gallery, Washington, D.C., *Revisiting the White City: American Art at the 1893 World's Fair,* cat. no. 21, plate 30, pp. 147, 359 (ill.).

Ex Collections

The artist, 1887–1917; his wife, Elizabeth C., 1917–19.

Art Club of Philadelphia Medal, about 1890: See Appendix.
Carol H. Beck Gold Medal, 1909: See Appendix.

J. William Fosdick

1858–1937

James William Fosdick was born in Charlestown, Massachusetts, and educated in the city's public schools. When William was about sixteen, his father bought some burnt-wood pictures by ROBERT BALL HUGHES which inspired the young man to try his hand at this method of picturemaking in which red-hot tools are applied to wood.[1] Fosdick probably continued to produce "fire etchings,"[2] as he later dubbed these works, throughout his approximately four years of study under Otto Grundmann at the school of the Museum of Fine Arts in Boston.

Fosdick went to Paris in 1881 and enrolled at the Académie Julian, where he studied painting under Gustave Rudolph Boulanger, Jules Joseph Lefebvre and Raphael Collin. In the summer of 1884, he cut short a painting excursion to Normandy and returned home to execute his first major burnt-wood commission.[3] Having heard Fosdick's talent praised by Mrs. Robert Ball Hughes,[4] Edward D. Adams of New York commissioned him to create a Renaissance-style border for the dining room of his new home in the "Villard Complex" on Madison Avenue, built by McKim, Mead and White.[5]

At this early stage, Fosdick's tools were primitive and consisted of simple plaster-handled metal rods heated in a charcoal furnace. Soon, however, he discovered a surgical instrument for cauterizing wounds that could be adapted to his purposes. The tool allowed Fosdick to work more quickly and in greater comfort because it eliminated the need for a furnace. A glass or nickel receptacle housed the heat source—a sponge saturated with naphtha or alcohol. Attached to the receptacle were two long rubber tubes, one connected to a bellows to control the flame and the other tipped with a platinum point. Typically, Fosdick worked the entire panel with the red-hot platinum point and then alternated between it and an emery cloth to achieve the effect he desired.[6]

In 1888 Fosdick had an exhibition in Paris of his burnt-wood decorations. He was greatly encouraged by the favorable reactions of his French teachers and resolved to intensify his efforts.[7] Returning home, he set up a studio in New York and soon secured a reputation as the foremost exponent of the art. He also painted murals, wrote letters to the *New York Times* on a variety of subjects, and occasionally reviewed art exhibitions.[8] He was a staunch defender of the crafts movement.[9]

In 1895 a burnt-wood frieze by Fosdick won the gold medal for mural decoration at the Atlanta Exposition.[10] It depicted the meeting of Francis I of France and Henry VIII of England in 1520 at a place near Calais that became known as the "Field of the Cloth of Gold." In the spring of 1896, Fosdick was honored with a one-man exhibition at the Pennsylvania Academy of the Fine Arts. It included forty-eight works, primarily burnt-wood panels but also charcoal studies and paintings on wood. His burnt-wood triptych *The Adoration of Jeanne D'Arc,* 1896 (National Museum of American Art, Smithsonian Institution, Washington, D.C.), provided the focal point. It was installed, as Fosdick had suggested, in a setting made reminiscent of a chapel by blocking off the gallery's skylights, draping the walls, and using concealed gas burners to light the work from above.[11] On April 7th, Fosdick gave a talk in the gallery and demonstrated his fire-etching technique. He also showed the audience his collection of burnt-wood decorations from various nations, ranging from naive works by Fiji Islanders to sophisticated designs by Swiss craftsmen.[12]

Throughout the 1890s, Fosdick exhibited at the New York Architectural League, where his work attracted the attention of prominent architects. Most of his major commissions were for the decoration of churches and private homes and were garnered for him by architects. During these years of the so-called American Renaissance, the country's new millionaires were building lavish homes; and Fosdick produced burnt-wood decorations for several of them. In 1897 he executed decorative panels for the library of Georgian Court, the country home of the railroad executive George J. Gould in Lakewood, New Jersey.[13] Fosdick also produced work for the homes of the New York mayor William F. Havemeyer in Seabright, New Jersey; Adolph Lewisohn in New York; and the art collector William T. Evans in Montclair, New Jersey.

In 1900 Fosdick was given a retrospective exhibition at the Lotos Club in New York. He was a member of numerous art associations, including the Architectural League of New York; the National Society of Mural Painters, for which he served as recording secretary from about 1897 to 1900; the New York Society of Craftsmen; the National Arts Club; the Copley Society; and the North Shore Art Association of Gloucester, Massachusetts. Fosdick also served a term as president of the American Alumni of the Académie Julian.[14]

Notes

1. Biographical information, typescript, Fosdick object file, National Museum of American Art, Smithsonian Institution, Washington, D.C.
2. J. William Fosdick to Harrison S. Morris, managing director of the PAFA, Feb. 21, 1896, PAFA Archives.
3. "The Fire Etcher's Work," *New York Times,* Feb. 14, 1892, p. 17.
4. E. Ball Hughes to Edward D. Adams, about 1880, quoted in Albert TenEyck Gardner, *American Sculpture: A Catalogue of the Collection of The Metropolitan Museum of Art* (New York: Metropolitan Museum of Art, 1965), p. 7.
5. "The Fire Etcher's Work," 1892, p. 17.
6. Ibid.
7. Ibid.
8. See, for example, *New York Times:* "At the 'Trysting Elms,' " June 20, 1926, p. 10x; "Sir George Henschel More 'Boheme' History and Casts," Oct. 19, 1930, p. 10x; "Gari Melchers as a Student," Dec. 9, 1932, p. 20.
9. J. William Fosdick, "American Handicraft: The Fourth Annual Exhibition of the National Society of Craftsmen," *Art and Progress* 2, no. 4 (Feb. 1911), pp. 100–3.
10. J. William Fosdick to Harrison S. Morris, Feb. 28, 1896, PAFA Archives, and *Descriptive Catalogue of the Permanent Collections of Works of Art* (Philadelphia: PAFA, 1897), p. 20.
11. Fosdick to Morris, Feb. 4, 1896, and Morris to Fosdick, Feb. 11, 1896, PAFA Archives.
12. *Philadelphia Inquirer,* April 7, 1896, p. 4.
13. Fosdick to Morris, Sept. 21, 1897, PAFA Archives. Sister M. Christina Geis, telephone interview with Mary Mullen Cunningham, Jan. 8, 1986, confirmed that Georgian Court still exists as part of Georgian Court College, and Fosdick's work is intact.
14. Obituary, *New York Times,* Sept. 15, 1937, p. 23.

Reference
1985 Peter Hastings Falk, ed., *Who Was Who in American Art,* Madison, Conn.: Sound View Press, p. 209.

King Louis XIV

1895
Basswood, fire-etched; gilded letters
84 x 60⅛ x 1¼" (213.4 x 152.7 x 3.2 cm)
Signed and dated at lower right: J.W.FOSDICK·1895·
Inscribed in large gilded letters, at upper left: LVDOVICVS; at center right: MAGNVS/XIIII./GALLIÆ/ET/NAVARRÆ/REX.
Henry D. Gilpin Fund, 1896.3

J. WILLIAM FOSDICK completed this burnt-wood relief panel of the French king Louis XIV (1638–1715) in 1895, and the following year it was included in his exhibition at the Pennsylvania Academy of the Fine Arts. The Academy purchased the panel from the exhibition and installed it in the library.[1] The 1896 exhibition catalogue described the work as a decorative panel adapted from existing images of Louis XIV in the museum at Versailles. Fosdick undoubtedly based his work on the 1839 marble statue of the Sun King by Philippe Henri Lemarie (1798–1880). Although he reversed Lemarie's image, Fosdick borrowed the pose and copied the royal trappings in minute detail.

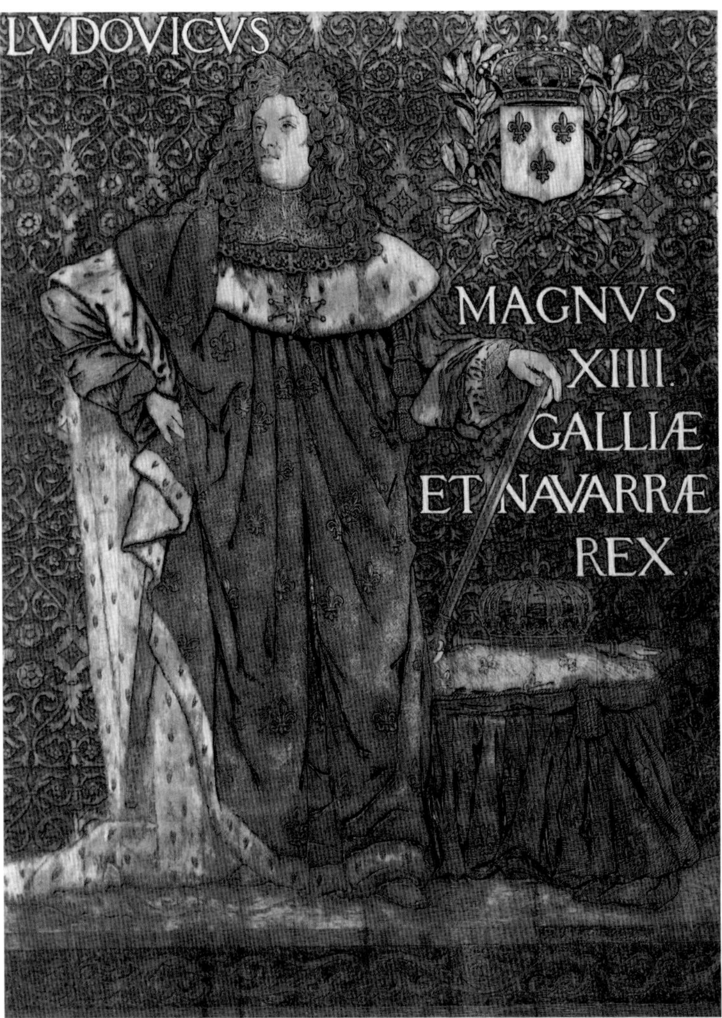

Fosdick, *King Louis XIV*

Fosdick achieved subtle effects of color in his panels through the application of a variety of pigment stains and subsequent buffing.[2] In this panel, areas such as the hands, the feet, and the ermine trim have been buffed to reveal some of the natural color of the basswood. The light color combined with Fosdick's fine, burnt lines give the ermine a remarkably tactile quality.

Notes

1. J. William Fosdick to Harrison S. Morris, managing director of the PAFA, Sept. 21, 1897, PAFA Archives.

2. Solvent tests indicate that Fosdick probably applied a greatly thinned brown oil-pigment stain and buffed it off certain areas before brushing on a wax-resin varnish.

Exhibited

1896 PAFA, *Pictures of the Glasgow School* and *The Adoration of Jeanne D'Arc and other Burnt Wood Decorations by J. William Fosdick,* cat. no. 139. **1900** Lotos Club, New York, retrospective. **1938–86** University of Pennsylvania, Philadelphia, long-term loan. **1986–87** PAFA, *Sculpture at the Pennsylvania Academy of the Fine Arts.* **1988–94** PAFA, front lobby.

William Partridge

1861–1930

William Ordway Partridge was born in Paris to American parents. His father, an amateur painter and avid art collector, was a successful agent for the New York merchant Alexander T. Stewart. William Partridge was educated in the United States, including some early training in the fine arts at Adelphi Academy, a secondary school in Brooklyn, New York (now Adelphi University). Partridge entered Columbia University in the autumn of 1881. There, he continued to study art and developed a keen interest in the theater. Forced to withdraw from Columbia because of ill health, he went abroad and traveled in Germany, Italy, and France. He spent several months in Florence studying with the sculptor Fortunato Galli (d. 1918). By October 1883, Partridge was in Paris, where he attended lectures at the Ecole des Beaux-Arts although he never officially enrolled as a student. He also received limited instruction from the most well-known French sculptor of the day, Marius Jean Antonin Mercié (1845–1916).[1]

Partridge's interest in the theater remained strong; and, when he returned to the United States in the spring of 1884, he enrolled at the American Academy of Dramatic Arts in New York. He participated in several theatrical productions but preferred to give dramatic readings of the works of Keats, Shelley, and Shakespeare. He earned his living in this way during the late 1880s in Boston and counted Isabella Stewart Gardner among his admiring patrons.[2] He continued to sculpt and received encouragement from his cousin John Rogers. In 1887 Partridge modeled *Nearing Home,* a portrait of an old woman, which was later carved in marble (Corcoran Gallery of Art, Washington, D.C.). The favorable critical response that it received undoubtedly whetted Partridge's desire to study sculpture in earnest. His marriage in 1887 to Mrs. Augusta Merriam, a wealthy widow from Milton, Massachusetts, provided him with the financial resources to study abroad. In 1887 he went to Rome to begin two years of training with the Polish sculptor Pio Welonski (1849–1931).

Returning home in 1889, Partridge established a studio in Milton. The following year, he won the competition for a statue of William Shakespeare to be erected in Lincoln Park in Chicago. He took a studio in Paris in order to model the statue and visited London to study death masks that purported to be of Shakespeare. In London, he executed a portrait in low relief of the British actor Sir Henry Irving that was shown in the Royal Academy. Partridge received favorable reviews for his first major showing at the World's Columbian Exposition, in Chicago in 1893. He exhibited ten sculptures, including his model for the Shakespeare statue; busts of Edward Everett Hale, 1891 (bronze, Union League Club of Chicago) and James Russell Lowell, 1892 (bronze, whereabouts unknown; a plaster version is in the Public Library, Muskegon, Michigan); and a model for his statue of Alexander Hamilton, which was to be erected in Brooklyn, New York, by the Hamilton Club in 1896.

Partridge's fast-growing prestige resulted in many commissions for monumental works. In 1895 he executed a statue of General Ulysses S. Grant, which the Union League of Brooklyn presented to the city and erected on Bedford Avenue. In 1899 Partridge was selected to contribute a statue to the large temporary arch erected in New York to celebrate the homecoming of Admiral George Dewey, the hero of the Spanish-American War. No longer extant, Partridge's statue for the arch depicted Dewey's mentor, Admiral David Farragut. Other monumental works by Partridge include the baptismal font, 1904, for the Washington National Cathedral in Washington, D.C.; a statue of Horace Greeley, 1914, for Chappaqua, New York; a statue of Thomas Jefferson, 1914, for Columbia University in New York; and a statue of Pocahontas, 1922, for Jamestown, Virginia.

Partridge was accepted in affluent society. His oeuvre contains numerous portrait busts, many depicting prominent professionals and businessmen. In making a portrait, Partridge emphasized those physiognomic details that he believed captured the individual's personality. Around the turn of the century, his work began to display a greater impressionism. Although he continued to model faces with a high degree of finish, he treated bodies in a free sketchlike manner. This is apparent in several of his busts of men of arts and letters, such as Alfred Tennyson, 1899 (bronze, National Museum of American Art, Smithsonian Institution, Washington, D.C.) and Richard Wagner, 1912 (whereabouts unknown).

Partridge and his wife divorced in 1904; and, in Venice the following year, he married the poet Margaret Ridgely Schott. Partridge was himself an author, who published two books of poetry: *The Song-Life of a Sculptor* in 1894 and *Sonnets and Lyrics* in 1902. He lectured and wrote extensively about art, especially sculpture. His *Technique of Sculpture*, published in 1895, is an important document of nineteenth-century sculptor's methods. In his writing, Partridge encouraged the foundation of an American school of sculpture. Although he had high praise for the work of AUGUSTUS SAINT-GAUDENS, JOHN QUINCY ADAMS WARD, and Daniel Chester French (1850–1931), Partridge was opposed to their domination of the National Sculpture Society, in New York. To counter what he considered the monopoly of the National Sculpture Society, he helped found the Society of American Sculptors in 1904.[3] He supported a democratic membership and the establishment of a permanent exhibition space for the new society, but it lasted less than six years.

Notes

1. Marjorie Pingel Balge, "William Ordway Partridge (1861–1930): American Art Critic and Sculptor," Ph.D. diss., June 1982, University of Delaware, pp. 2–4.
2. Ibid., p. 7.
3. Ibid., p. 23.

References

1900 William Chauncy Langdon, "William Ordway Partridge, Sculptor," *New England Magazine* 22 (June), pp. 382–98. **1914** *The Works in Sculpture of William Ordway Partridge, M.A.*, New York: John Lane Company. **1948** W. Francklyn Paris, "William Ordway Partridge, Sculptor," *The Hall of American Artists*, New York University: Architectural Forum, vol. 4, unpaginated. **1974** *William O. Partridge: American Sculptor*, Plattsburgh, N.Y.: Art Gallery at State University of New York, College of Arts and Sciences, exhib. cat., essay by Marjorie P. Balge.

William Wood

1895
Bronze with green patina; sand cast
27½ x 27 x 15½" (69.9 x 68.6 x 39.4 cm)
Signed and dated on right shoulder: *W.O Partridge/95*
Foundry mark stamped below signature: GORHA[M] MFG. CO./FOUNDERS
Henry D. Gilpin Fund, 1983.25

BORN IN GLASGOW, Scotland, William Wood (1808–1894) immigrated to the United States at the age of nineteen and settled in New York. He became a successful businessman but lost all his assets during the financial panic of 1857. He later worked in banking until 1869, when he retired. That year, he joined Thomas Hunter and others to promote the cause of education and became one of the founders of the Normal College of the City of New York. Established to train more and better-qualified women teachers for the city's elementary schools, the Normal College was renamed Hunter College in 1914 to honor Thomas Hunter, the school's first president.[1]

Shortly after Wood's death in 1894, a committee composed of the faculty and associate alumnae of the Normal College commissioned William Partridge to produce this larger-than-lifesize bust. The committee presented it to the college during a memorial service honoring Wood.[2] Also in 1895 Partridge executed

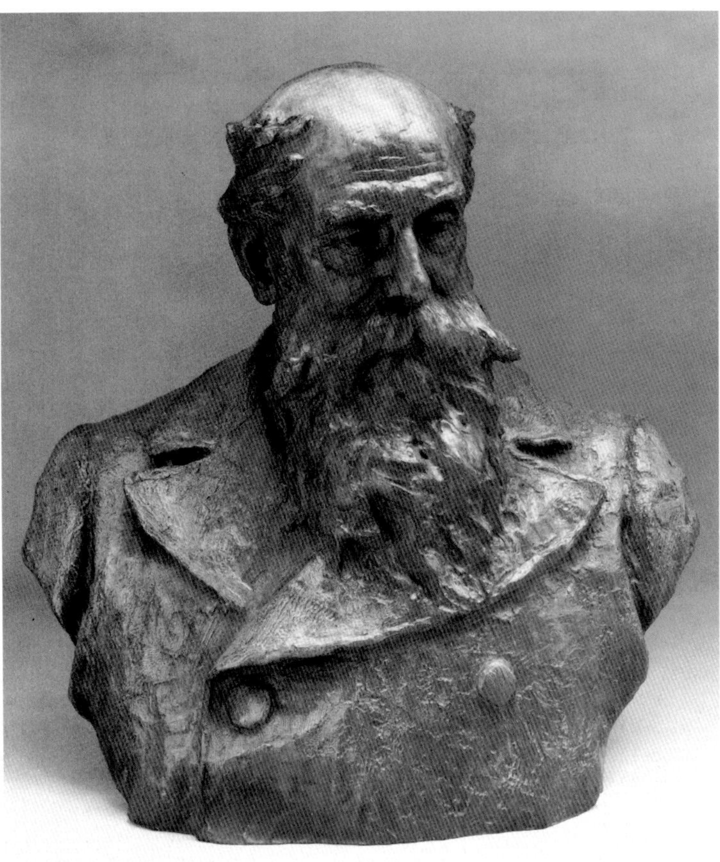

Partridge, *William Wood*

a statuette of William Wood (present whereabouts unknown).[3]

To model the bust, Partridge undoubtedly worked from photographs. He may also have used a portrait of Wood that was presented to the associate alumnae of the Normal College on May 23, 1890 (Hunter College Archives). It had been painted that year by Ruth Merington, a London-born artist. Judging by her painting and photographs of Wood in the Hunter College Archives, Partridge's portrait is a good likeness of the portly Wood. Modeled in the Beaux-Arts style, the sculpture is alive with texture and tool marks. Like many of Partridge's portrait busts, the face demonstrates a greater degree of finish than the chest and shoulders. The original dark green patina has lightened from exposure outdoors.

Notes

1. Samuel White Patterson, *Hunter College: Eighty-Five Years of Service* (New York: Lantern Press, 1955), pp. 3, 15.

2. "In William Wood's Memory," unidentified newspaper clipping from the scrapbook of the artist's daughter, Mrs. William A.M. Burden collection.

3. *The Works in Sculpture of William Ordway Partridge, M.A.* (New York: John Lane Company, 1914), p. lx.

Exhibited

1986–87 PAFA, *Sculpture at the Pennsylvania Academy of the Fine Arts.*

Ex Collections

Normal College (now Hunter College), New York, 1895-after 1914; private collections, after 1914–83.

Charles Grafly

1862–1929

Charles Allan Grafly, Jr., was born in Philadelphia of German, Dutch, and Quaker heritage. He was the youngest of eight children of Charles Grafly, Sr., and Elizabeth Simmons.[1] His father farmed in Bucks County. At various times, he also made shoes and worked in a tobacco shop and at the Philadelphia Gas Works. Charles, Jr., enjoyed working with his hands like his maternal grandfather, Garrett Simmons, who apparently cut silhouettes at the Peale Museum in Philadelphia. As a boy, Grafly produced sketches and mechanical drawings. He is said to have developed an interest in sculpture after seeing the Centennial Exposition, in 1876.[2] Perhaps he was captivated by the colossal arm of the Statue of Liberty by the French sculptor Frédéric Auguste Bartholdi (1834–1904) or by the nude female figure *La Première Pose* by HOWARD ROBERTS, who had been trained at the Pennsylvania Academy of the Fine Arts and in Paris. Despite his father's wish that he take over the family farm, Grafly apprenticed himself at the age of seventeen to the Struthers Stoneyard, then the oldest and largest of its kind in the United States. His major project during most of his four years there was helping to carve ornaments and figures for Philadelphia's City Hall, from the designs of the sculptor Alexander Milne Calder (1846–1923). Because he was having difficulty carving human anatomy convincingly, Grafly enrolled in evening drawing classes at the Spring Garden Institute in 1882 and soon became an instructor of freehand drawing. The next year, he began studying with THOMAS EAKINS at the Pennsylvania Academy, where he took classes in modeling and anatomy and later dissected cadavers. When Eakins left the Academy in 1886, Grafly was one of the students who followed him to the newly created Art Students' League of Philadelphia. A short time later, Grafly returned to the Academy to study with the painter Thomas Anshutz (see portrait by Grafly [q.v.]), another of Eakins's former students.

In the fall of 1888, Grafly fulfilled his dream of

going to Paris for further study. He joined a group from the Academy that included the painter Robert Henri who was later joined by Edward Redfield. After a stopover in London where Grafly was impressed by the Elgin Marbles, the students arrived in Paris and enrolled at the Académie Julian. Grafly studied modeling with the sculptor Henri Michel Chapu (1833–1891), painting with salon painter Adolphe William Bouguereau, and drawing with Tony Robert-Fleury. Chapu asked Grafly and EDMUND STEWARDSON to assist him with an allegorical figure, *Steam Being Confined by Man,* for the Exposition Universelle of 1889. In February 1890 at the Académie Julian, a five-day competition was held in which Grafly won the *prix d'atelier*—a monetary prize and a medal. His figure of a posed female model was cast in plaster and permanently installed on the wall of the school. This honor had never before been given an American.[3] Grafly took the rigorous entrance examination for the more prestigious Ecole des Beaux-Arts but was turned down at least twice (one time because a history paper was late).

Grafly's first public success came when his busts *Daedalus* and *Saint Jean* were accepted for the 1890 Paris Salon. That year, he returned briefly to Philadelphia to work on his first commission, a figure of William Penn for a local insurance company. Grafly went back to Paris in the fall with A. STIRLING CALDER, who had recently introduced him to the woman who would become his wife, Frances Sekeles. In the Paris Salon of 1891, he won an honorable mention for a female figure *Mauvais Présage* (present whereabouts unknown). The death of his father soon after brought Grafly back to Philadelphia, where he began teaching at the Pennsylvania Academy and at Drexel Institute (now Drexel University). He created the Academy's first sculpture department and put the subject on an equal footing with painting for the first time. In June 1895 he married and returned to Paris. He explained to his mother that "I could not stay in America without starving body and soul and losing the little recognition I have." He was going abroad "to gain new ideas, new experiences"[4] and to work on a sculpture group, later called the *Vulture of War* (q.v.), that he envisioned as his masterpiece. He received weekly criticisms from the sculptor Jean Dampt (1853–1946). In Paris in 1896, his daughter, Dorothy, was born; and the family soon returned to the United States.

Grafly set up a studio in Philadelphia and never went back to Europe. He taught at Drexel Institute for several more years and at the Pennsylvania Academy until his death. He sent his sculpture to all the major exhibitions and won medals at many of them, including the World's Columbian Exposition, in 1893 in Chicago; the Exposition Universelle of 1900, in Paris; and the Pan-American Exposition, in 1901 in Buffalo. The Pennsylvania Academy awarded him the Academy Gold Medal in 1899 "for distinguished services in art and to the Academy."

His first portrait commission for a public monument came in 1898 from the Fairmount Park Art Association. It involved modeling busts of John B. Gest and Admiral David Porter, and a figure of Major General John Reynolds for the Smith Memorial, to Pennsylvania's Civil War heroes. Grafly was commissioned to execute a symbolic outdoor sculpture, *Fountain of Man,* for the Pan-American Exposition, in 1901, and figures of *Truth, Electricity,* and *Thomas Jefferson* for the Louisiana Purchase Universal Exposition, in 1904. He was commissioned to produce allegorical figures—*England* in 1903 and *France* in 1904—for the exterior of the New York Customs House. In 1906 they were carved in marble by Piccirilli Brothers of New York. The National Academy of Design, in New York, in 1902 elected Grafly an associate and an academician in 1905.

In 1905 Grafly bought property in Lanesville, Massachusetts, and built a home and studio called "Fool's Paradise." He spent summers there and most of the rest of the year in Philadelphia until 1917, when he began living in Lanesville year round and commuting between teaching jobs at the Pennsylvania Academy and the school of the Museum of Fine Arts in Boston. Grafly served on the Municipal Art Jury of Philadelphia from its inception in 1912 until his death. He was commissioned in 1913 to produce a sculpture group, the *Pioneer Mother Memorial,* for the Panama-Pacific International Exposition in San Francisco.[5] In 1925 he received a public commission for a figure of President James Buchanan for a park in Lancaster, Pennsylvania. Because of Grafly's long involvement with the memorial to General Meade in Washington, D.C. and his work on other commissions, his former student and assistant ALBERT LAESSLE was given the commission for the General Galusha Pennypacker Memorial for Logan Square, Philadelphia. It was completed in 1934, according to Grafly's sketch of about 1921–26.

Charles Grafly died tragically in 1929, a victim of a hit-and-run automobile accident. Among the numerous pallbearers at his funeral were his former students Albert Laessle and ALBIN POLÁŠEK and artists such as Hugh Breckenridge (see portrait by Grafly [q.v.]), Edward Redfield, Robert Henri, and Albert Rosenthal. A memorial exhibition of eighty-eight of Grafly's works was held at the Pennsylvania Academy in 1930 at the time of the 125th annual exhibition. Other memorial exhibitions were held in Washington, D.C., and Boston. Grafly was honored posthumously at the Hall of American Artists at New York University with a bust modeled by Polášek. In 1930 the mayor of Philadelphia Harry A. Mackey, proposed that Grafly's sculpture be gathered in a building under municipal auspices as a memorial tribute; but nothing came of it.[6]

In 1972 more than 200 sculptures, mostly of plaster, were donated to Wichita State University's Edwin A. Ulrich Museum of Art, and the Grafly family papers to the University's Ablah Library Special Collections Archives. In 1996 the Ulrich Museum held an exhibition of Grafly's work with a catalogue by Dr. Pamela H. Simpson, of Washington and Lee University, and Donald E. Knaub, director of the Ulrich Museum, that includes an edited version of Dorothy Grafly Drummond's biography of her father.

Notes

1. Much of this biography is culled from Pamela H. Simpson's 1974 doctoral dissertation.
2. Craven 1984, p. 437.
3. D. Grafly, 1929, p. 79, PAFA Archives. This biography of Charles Grafly was written by his daughter in 1929, according to Dr. Pamela H. Simpson. Several typed versions exist, including the original transcript and a photocopy of the one in the Archives of the Pennsylvania Academy of the Fine Arts. The latter was given by the author at an unknown date (possibly 1941, when she lent her father's sculpture). A somewhat longer version is in the Ablah Library, Wichita State University, and bears the title "Charles Grafly, American." Pages cited in the notes to the Grafly entries in this catalogue are from the version in the Academy archives. The biography, abridged and edited, appears in the 1996 exhibition catalogue *The Sculptor's Clay: Charles Grafly (1862–1929)* published by the Edwin A. Ulrich Museum of Art, Wichita State University.
4. Ibid., p. 91.
5. *Pioneer Mother Memorial* is now in Golden Gate Park.
6. "Grafly Studio Estate Treasures Soon Will Be Westward Bound," *Philadelphia Inquirer,* July 21, 1972, p. 20.

References

1899 Lorado Taft, "Charles Grafly Sculptor," *Brush and Pencil* 3 (March), pp. 343–53. **1901** Vittoria C. Dallin, "Charles Grafly's Work," *New England Magazine* 25 (Oct.), pp. 228–35. **1903** Helen W. Henderson, "Charles Grafly, Sculptor: An Apostle of Symbolism," *Booklovers Magazine* 2 (Nov.), pp. 6, 7, 500–505. **1910** John E.D. Trask, "Charles Grafly, Sculptor: An Appreciative Note," *Art and Progress* 1 (Feb.), pp. 83–89. **1918** Anna Seaton-Schmidt, "Charles Grafly in His Summer Home," *American Magazine of Art* 10 (Dec.), pp. 52–58. **1929** "Charles Grafly, Sculptor, Dead," *New York Times,* May 6, p. 25. **1929** Dorothy Grafly, "Sculptor's Clay," typescript of biography of Charles Grafly. **1972** Moissaye Marans, "Charles Grafly as Teacher," *National Sculpture Review* 21 (Fall), pp. 20, 26. **1972** John Harbeson, "Charles Grafly as Collaborator," *National Sculpture Review* 21 (Fall), pp. 21, 25, 26. **1974** Pamela H. Simpson, "The Sculpture of Charles Grafly," Ph.D. diss., University of Delaware, Newark. **1984** Wayne Craven, *Sculpture in America,* Newark: University of Delaware, pp. 437–42. **1986** Kathryn Greenthal, Paula M. Kozol, Jan Seidler Ramirez, *American Figurative Sculpture in the Museum of Fine Arts, Boston,* Boston: Museum of Fine Arts, pp. 286–92. **1996** Pamela H. Simpson and Donald E. Knaub, *The Sculptor's Clay: Charles Grafly (1862–1929),* Wichita, Kans.: Edwin A. Ulrich Museum of Art, exhib. cat.

Daedalus

1889

a.
Painted plaster
28 x 20 x 14" (71.1 x 50.8 x 35.6 cm)
Signed and dated on base below right shoulder: GRAFLY/PARIS/ 1889.
Inscribed in relief on front of base: DÆDALVS
Henry D. Gilpin Fund, 1891.4

b.
Bronze with brown patina; sand cast about 1892
24¾ x 19 x 15½" (62.9 x 48.3 x 39.4 cm)
Signed, dated, and inscribed as above
Foundry mark beneath left shoulder: BUREAU BROS./ PHILA.
Henry D. Gilpin Fund, 1892.2

THIS BUST was modeled in Paris about one year after Charles Grafly arrived there to study. He had already adopted the lively surface texture then in vogue in Paris. The subject is the mythological figure Daedalus, who made wings so that he and his son, Icarus, could fly from prison.

According to Grafly's diary, he was working on a sculpture of Daedalus and Icarus in January 1890, probably soon after completing this bust. The subject may have been assigned by his teacher Henri Michel Chapu.[1] Mythological subject matter was very popular at the time. Grafly may have been inspired by a figure of Icarus by the British sculptor Alfred Gilbert (1854–1934) that had received notice in the press when it was shown in Paris at the 1889 Exposition Universelle.[2] In 1894 Grafly modeled a bust of *Icarus,* wearing a band around his upper arm for securing the wings.[3]

The plaster version of this bust was shown at the 1890 Paris Salon and the following year at the Pennsylvania Academy, where it was awarded an honorable mention from the Temple Trust Fund and was purchased. After it was accidentally broken and then repaired, Grafly encouraged the Academy to "reproduce the head in a more substantial material" and discussed his preference for bronze rather than marble.[4] The Academy had this bronze made about April 1892 when the president reported that he had authorized the bust to be cast by Bureau Brothers.[5] In 1894

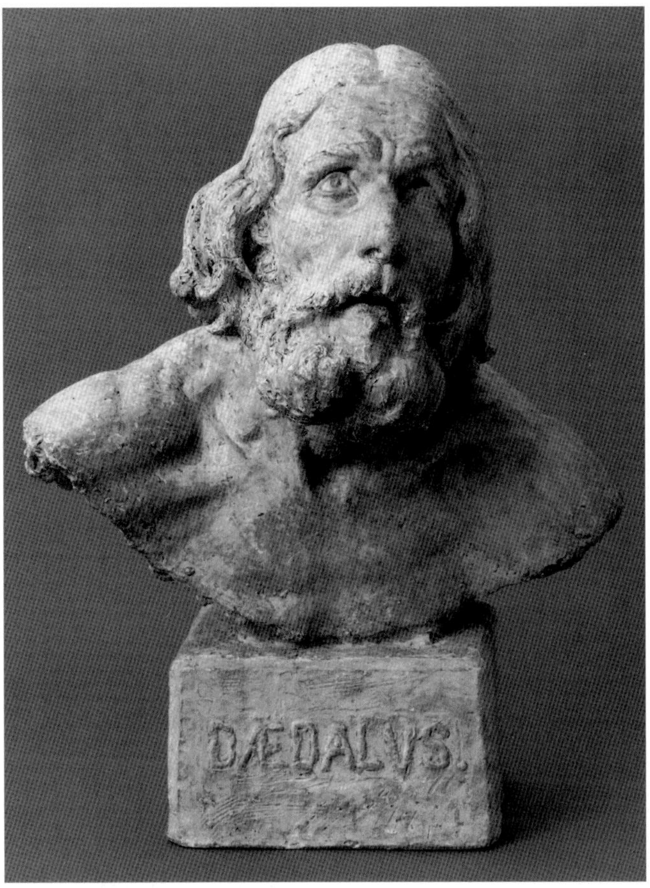

Grafly, *Daedalus*, plaster

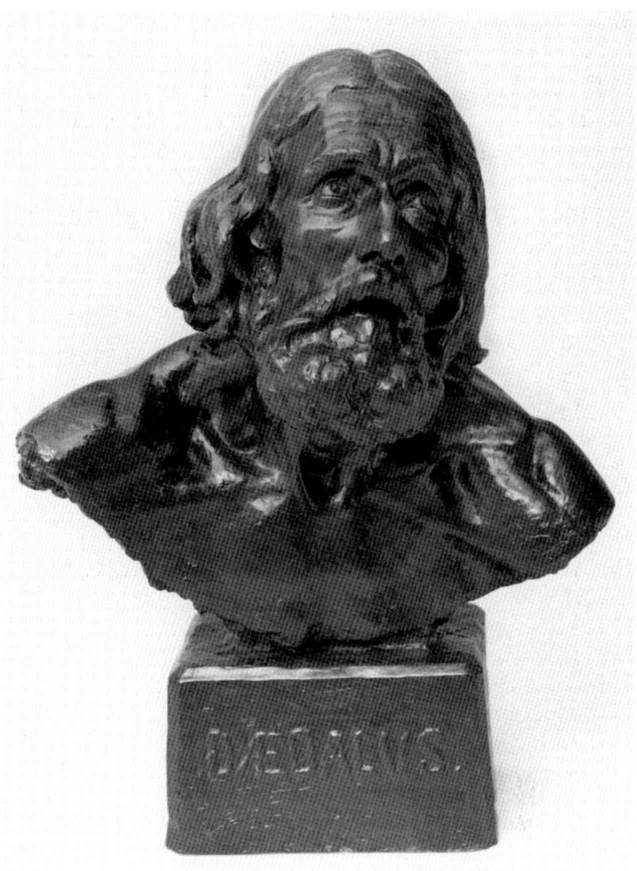

Grafly, *Daedalus*, bronze

the costs of the purchase and the casting were transferred to the Gilpin Fund, hence the credit line.[6]

The Museum of American Art of the Pennsylvania Academy owns the only known versions of this bust. Grafly received a medal when the plaster was exhibited with *Mauvais Présage* at the World's Columbian Exposition, in 1893.

Notes

1. Simpson 1974, pp. 133–34. Grafly's diaries of 1889–90 are in the Ablah Library, Wichita State University.
2. Simpson 1974, p. 134.
3. *Icarus* in plaster and a posthumous bronze cast are owned by the Edwin A. Ulrich Museum of Art, Wichita State University.
4. Minutes, meeting of the committee on exhibitions, March 6, 1891, p. 147, PAFA Archives, and Charles Grafly to Edward H. Coates, president of the PAFA, March 28, 1891, PAFA object file.
5. Minutes, meeting of the board of directors, April 11, 1892, PAFA Archives.
6. Minutes, meeting of the board of directors, Feb. 12, 1894, PAFA Archives.

References (plaster)
1899 Lorado Taft, "Charles Grafly Sculptor," *Brush and Pencil* 3 (March), p. 349 (ill.). **1974** Pamela H. Simpson, "The Sculpture of Charles Grafly," Ph.D. diss., University of Delaware, Newark, cat. no. 10.

References (bronze)
1962 Bennard B. Perlman, *The Immortal Eight: American Painting from Eakins to the Armory Show, 1870–1913,* New York: Exposition Press; published as *Painters of the Ashcan School: The Immortal Eight,* New York: Dover Publications, 1988, p. 39 (ill.). **1974** Pamela H. Simpson, "The Sculpture of Charles Grafly," Ph.D. diss., University of Delaware, Newark, cat. no. 10, pp. 131 (ill.), 132. **1993** *Revisiting the White City: American Art at the 1893 World's Fair,* exhib. cat., Washington, D.C.: National Museum of American Art and National Portrait Gallery, Smithsonian Institution, cat. no. 123, p. 366 (ill.).

Exhibited (plaster)
1890 *Paris Salon,* cat. no. 3948, as *Dédale.* **1891*** cat. no. 489.

Exhibited (bronze)
1893 PAFA, *Works of Art to be Exhibited at the World's Columbian Exposition,* cat. no. 168. **1893** *World's Columbian Exposition,* Chicago, cat. no. 49. **1901** Saint Botolph Club, Boston, *Exhibition of Sculpture by Mr. Chas. Grafly of Philadelphia,* checklist no. 4. **1930** PAFA, *Memorial Exhibition of Work by Charles Grafly,* cat. no. 28. **1930** Brooklyn Museum, *Exhibition of Sculpture: Recent*

Work by Distinguished Sculptors, cat. no. 143. **1931** Museum of Fine Arts, Boston, *Memorial Exhibition of Sculpture by Charles Grafly.* **1955** PAFA, *150th Anniversary Exhibition,* cat. no. 189. **1965** Newman Galleries, Philadelphia, *Daniel Garber Paintings; Charles Grafly Sculpture.* **1983** Detroit Institute of Arts, *The Quest for Unity: American Art Between World's Fairs 1876–1893,* cat. no. 77 (ill.). **1984–85** PAFA, *A Growing American Treasure: Recent Acquisitions and Highlights from the Permanent Collection.* **1986–87** PAFA, *Sculpture at the Pennsylvania Academy of the Fine Arts.* **1996** Edwin A. Ulrich Museum of Art, Wichita State University, Kans., *The Sculptor's Clay: Charles Grafly,* cat. no. 21.

Aeneas and Anchises

1893
Bronze with green and brown patina; lost-wax cast by 1915
27 x 12¼ x 15" (68.6 x 31.1 x 38.1 cm)
Signed and dated on top of base: GRAFLY/1893
Foundry mark on back of base: ROMAN BRONZE WORKS N-Y
Gift of the Fellowship of the Pennsylvania Academy of the Fine Arts, 1928.14

CHARLES GRAFLY first worked on studies for this composition in the winter of 1890–91 while in Paris. The modeling of the piece reflects the vitality and spontaneity that he learned there. It was not completed until 1893 when he was back in Philadelphia. Perhaps the advent of his teaching responsibilities at Drexel Institute (now Drexel University) and the Pennsylvania Academy of the Fine Arts delayed its completion.

Depicted here is the dramatic flight from the burning city of Troy, described in Virgil's *Aeneid.* Aeneas leads his young son and carries his father, Anchises, who holds the household gods.

The plaster version of this group is at the Edwin A. Ulrich Museum of Art at Wichita State University. There are two other bronzes. The earlier, with a brown patina, was made by Bureau Brothers foundry. It was given to Edward Redfield by Grafly and is now in a private collection. The other, made by the Roman Bronze Works, is at the Delaware Art Museum, Wilmington. It was on loan to the Museum of the Pennsylvania Academy from 1941 to 1962.

The Academy's cast is probably the one that was returned to Grafly in April 1927 from the estate of John E.D. Trask.[1] Grafly had sent the group to Trask in 1915 "for private exposition" when Trask was the director of art at the Panama-Pacific Exposition, San Francisco. Grafly had tried to present the group to Trask's lawyer in 1926 "as a remembrance of Mr. Trask as well as myself," for Grafly already had a cast in his collection.[2] One of these casts was shown at the Sesquicentennial International Exposition in Philadelphia in 1926.

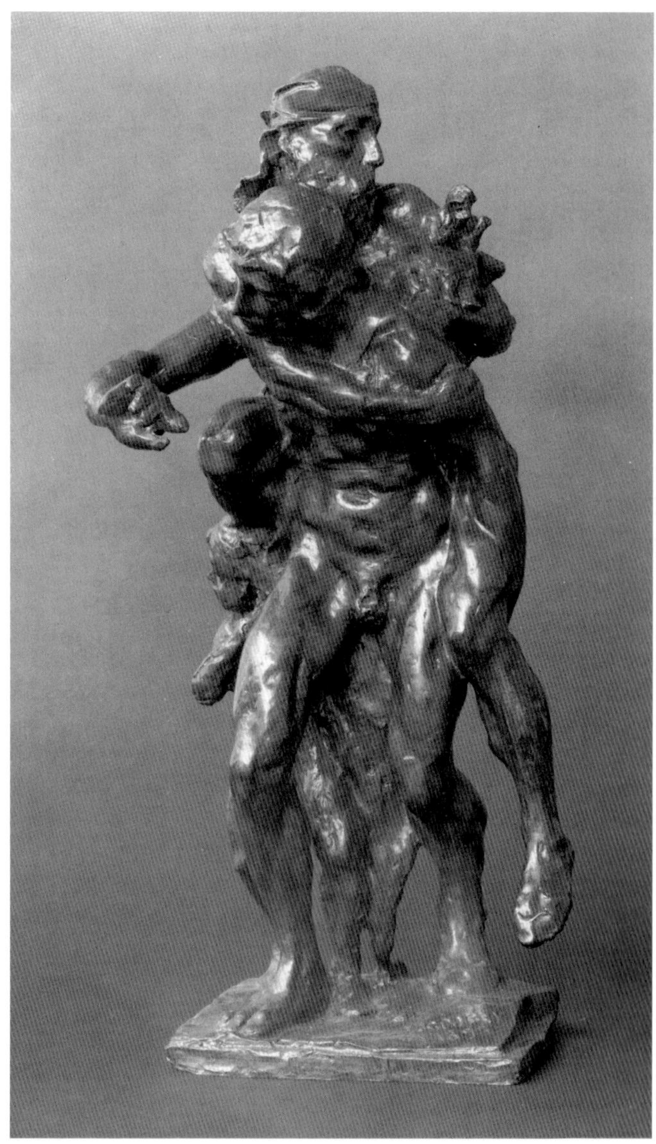

Grafly, *Aeneas and Anchises*

Notes

1. Grafly's handwritten receipt, April 14, 1927, Ablah Library, Wichita State University.

2. Charles Grafly to Joseph M. Dohan, July 12, 1926, ibid.

References

1972 Moissaye Marans, "Charles Grafly as Teacher," *National Sculpture Review* 21 (Fall), p. 20 (ill.). **1974** Pamela H. Simpson, "The Sculpture of Charles Grafly," Ph.D. diss., University of Delaware, Newark, pp. 30, 31 (ill.), 32, cat. no. 30. **1975** Jeremy Cooper, *Nineteenth Century Romantic Bronzes: French, English and American Bronzes, 1830–1915,* London: David & Charles, fig. 123, p.

122. **1984** Wayne Craven, *Sculpture in America*, Newark: University of Delaware, fig. 12.11, p. 461.

Exhibited
1928 PAFA, annual Fellowship exhibition, cat. no. 125. **1955** PAFA, *150th Anniversary Exhibition*, cat. no. 186, pp. 114, 117 (ill.). **1959** Philadelphia National Bank, exhibition for Philadelphia Sketch Club centennial celebration. **1965** Newman Galleries, Philadelphia, *Daniel Garber Paintings; Charles Grafly Sculpture.* **1970** University of Nebraska-Lincoln, Sheldon Memorial Art Gallery, *American Sculpture*, cat. no. 63 (ill.). **1975** William Penn Memorial Museum, Harrisburg, exhibition of works of art from the PAFA. **1976** Philadelphia Museum of Art, *Philadelphia: Three Centuries of American Art*, cat. no. 376 (ill.), p. 440. **1978–79** PAFA, *350 Masterpieces of American Art: 1720–1978.* **1984–85** PAFA, *A Growing American Treasure: Recent Acquisitions and Highlights from the Permanent Collection.* **1986–87** PAFA, *Sculpture at the Pennsylvania Academy of the Fine Arts.* **1996** Edwin A. Ulrich Museum of Art, Wichita State University, Kans., *The Sculptor's Clay: Charles Grafly*, cat. no. 31.

Ex Collections
John E.D. Trask, 1915–26; his estate, 1926–27; the artist, 1927–28.

Vulture of War

1895–99
Bronze with red-brown patina; lost-wax cast between 1906 and 1929
32 x 14 x 16" (81.3 x 35.6 x 40.6 cm)
Foundry mark on back of base: ROMAN BRON[ZE WO]RKS N.Y.
Gift of Dorothy Grafly, 1959.14

CHARLES GRAFLY returned to Paris in July 1895 to create a masterpicce "to further [his] reputation as a sculptor."[1] The statue later came to be called *Vulture of War*. By September he had completed a working sketch composed of two figures.[2] "I find that all the sins of the human race are fostered by idleness," he wrote,

> and from this fact I've taken my subject—idleness and its fruits—cruelty goes hand in hand with idleness, destroys love, springing from the lap of idleness upon ground that is not stable. I've taken two strong male figures powerful yet emaciated, slothful yet full of life, one reclining, the other standing, symbolic of the influence idleness has for the bad.[3]

Vittoria C. Dallin visited Grafly's studio in Paris in 1896, saw the large-scale *Vulture of War*, and was told that the group would consist of four figures: the central figure, War, swings a man as if he were a scythe, his outstretched arm and hand (which holds a flaming torch) forming the blade. Across the "scythe" rests the form of a lifeless woman, representing Death and Destruction. Upon War's back is a vulture ready to reap from the carnage his impious harvest.[4]

Grafly never completed the over-lifesize group that he envisioned, although he did exhibit the large-scale version. Both show a figure hovering over a globe that symbolizes Earth, and dragging a bag containing the spoils of war. Photographs of Grafly modeling the bust of Hugh Henry Breckenridge (q.v.) in Philadelphia in 1898 show in the background the large-scale plaster figure for the *Vulture of War*, but without a head,[5] although the complete figure was exhibited several times. At the close of the Louisiana Purchase Universal Exposition in 1904, Grafly was unable to pay the cost of having the sculpture returned to Philadelphia, and it was stored at the City Art Museum of Saint Louis and later destroyed.[6]

In Philadelphia between 1896 and 1898, Grafly made a plaster reduction of the *Vulture of War*. It was exhibited at the Pennsylvania Academy's sixty-seventh annual exhibition in 1898 and remained

Grafly, *Vulture of War*

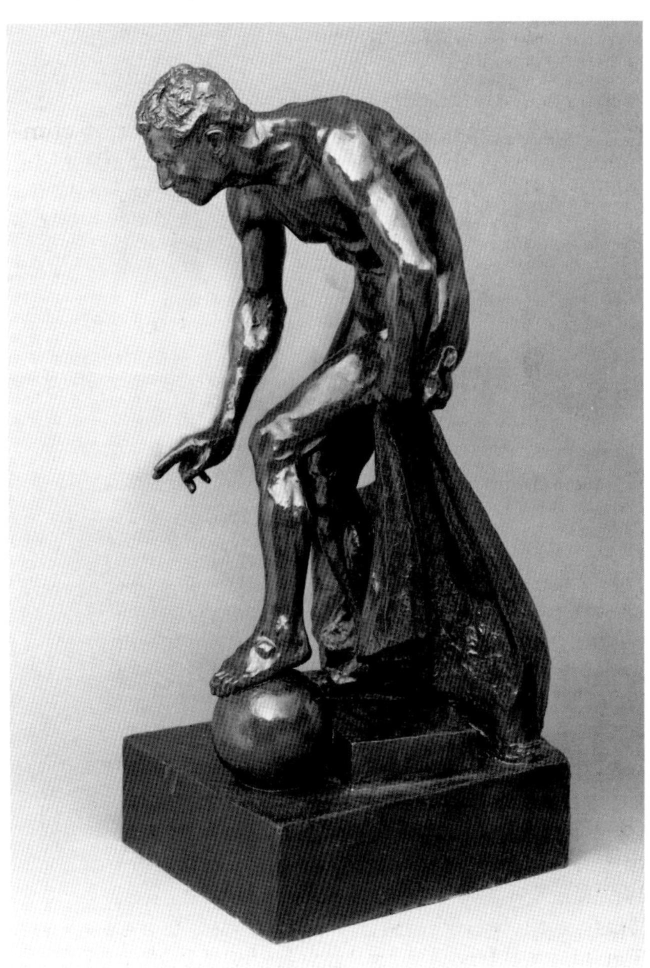

stored at the Academy, from which it was borrowed for exhibition.[7] The bronze that is now in the collection of the Museum of American Art of the Pennsylvania Academy was cast in the artist's lifetime, sometime after 1906 when he began patronizing the Roman Bronze Works. However, the plaster version —rather than the bronze—was shown at the 1930 Pennsylvania Academy memorial exhibition.

A posthumous cast was produced in 1936 by the Gorham Company and given to Brookgreen Gardens in South Carolina the following year. There are at least four bronze heads from the reduction of the *Vulture of War* in private collections and a large-scale, plaster, helmeted head (Edwin A. Ulrich Museum of Art, Wichita State University).

Notes

1. Charles Grafly to father-in-law, Leopold Sekeles, a note included with dated letter from Frances Sekeles Grafly to Sekeles, Sept. 15, 1895, Ablah Library, Wichita State University.

2. Grafly's early sketch exists in plaster at the Edwin A. Ulrich Museum of Art, Wichita State University.

3. C. Grafly to L. Sekeles, Sept. 15, 1895.

4. Vittoria C. Dallin, p. 229, states that the visit took place in the summer of 1895; but, according to Grafly to Sekeles, Sept. 15, 1895, he was only then about to begin work on the figure.

5. Photograph file, Ablah Library.

6. A museum inventory, about 1905, lists *Vulture of War.* A museum inventory of modern casts, about 1907, lists *Vulture of War,* register no. 30, as lent by the artist. A list, dated Jan. 19, 1933, of "Modern Casts to be disposed of" lists *Vulture of War* on page 4 with a symbol signifying "Destroyed Spring of 1933 (Reported Apr 11)." Grafly's plasters *Thomas Jefferson* and *Truth,* also from the Louisiana Purchase Universal Exposition, were destroyed at the same time. The documents are all in the Saint Louis Art Museum Archives.

7. Charles Grafly to Harrison S. Morris, managing director of the PAFA, March 26, 1901, PAFA Archives. The plaster version is now at the Edwin A. Ulrich Museum of Art.

References

1965 D. Grafly, "Newman Holds Exhibition to Celebrate Centennial," *Philadelphia Bulletin,* Jan. 31 (ill.), clipping file, Free Library of Pennsylvania, Philadelphia. **1968** Beatrice Gilman Proske, *Brookgreen Gardens Sculpture,* Brookgreen Gardens, S.C., rev. ed., p. 48. **1974** Pamela H. Simpson, "The Sculpture of Charles Grafly," Ph.D. diss., University of Delaware, Newark, cat. no. 50 (ill.).

Exhibited

1936 Temple University Art Galleries, Philadelphia, *Exhibition of Sculpture by Charles Grafly,* cat. no. 12. **1955** PAFA, *150th Anniversary Exhibition,* cat. no. 195 (ill.). **1962** Woodmere Art Gallery, Philadelphia, *An Invited Exhibition by Pennsylvania Members of the National Academy of Design,* checklist no. 20. **1965** Newman Galleries, Philadelphia, *Daniel Garber Paintings; Charles Grafly Sculpture.* **1984–85** PAFA, *A Growing American Treasure: Recent Acquisitions and Highlights from the Permanent Collection.* **1986–87** PAFA, *Sculpture at the Pennsylvania Academy of the Fine Arts.*

Symbol of Life

1897
Bronze with black patina; cast in 1897–98; ivory ball
37½ x 24¼ x 19¾" (95.3 x 61.6 x 50.2 cm)
Signed and dated on top of base at back, between woman's feet: Chas. Grafly/1897
Sand cast by Bureau Brothers, Philadelphia
Gift of Dorothy Grafly, 1971.1

THIS WORK is one of the symbolic groups that Charles Grafly produced after his return from France. When asked about the significance of *Symbol of Life,* Grafly responded,

> It was my purpose to develop the truth that all life, to achieve the highest and best, must be rooted on a perfect sphere. The woman symbolized nature firmly but kindly directing and encouraging man, holding constantly before him the goal—perfection; producing fruit that he may struggle to realize in himself the highest and best possibilities implanted within him. Ivory, silver and gold have been employed to symbolize strength, purity and truth by fostering which only can the highest and best be reached.[1]

The symbolism baffled the author and fellow sculptor Lorado Taft (1860–1936), who marveled at Grafly's modeling of the figures:

> I have never passed the group without walking around it, and around again, so big and masterly is its workmanship. . . . I glory in the construction of those two figures; the bigness of handling; the gravity of the faces and dignity of carriage; the hanging of the flesh upon the bones; the sinuous flow of the surface, so contrasting in the two; the power and the subtlety of modeling of all things essential, and the noble disregard of impertinent and importunate details. I delight in the very way in which the nails are not done.[2]

The ivory ball originally bore a gold and silver sprig of wheat that rose above the heads of the figures.[3] The modeling of the figures is smoother with more emphasis on anatomy than that of his works done in Paris. Grafly won a gold medal at the Paris Exposition Universelle of 1900 when this work, *From Generation to Generation,* the large-scale *Vulture of War* (qq.v.), and two portrait busts were shown. He also received a gold medal when *Symbol of Life* and *From Generation to Generation* were exhibited in the South Carolina Inter-State and West Indian Exposition in 1901–2. No other versions of this sculpture are extant; the plaster was broken,[4] perhaps in the casting of the bronze, and was probably discarded. It was most likely cast by Bureau Brothers, like *From Generation to Generation.* The plaster *Head of a*

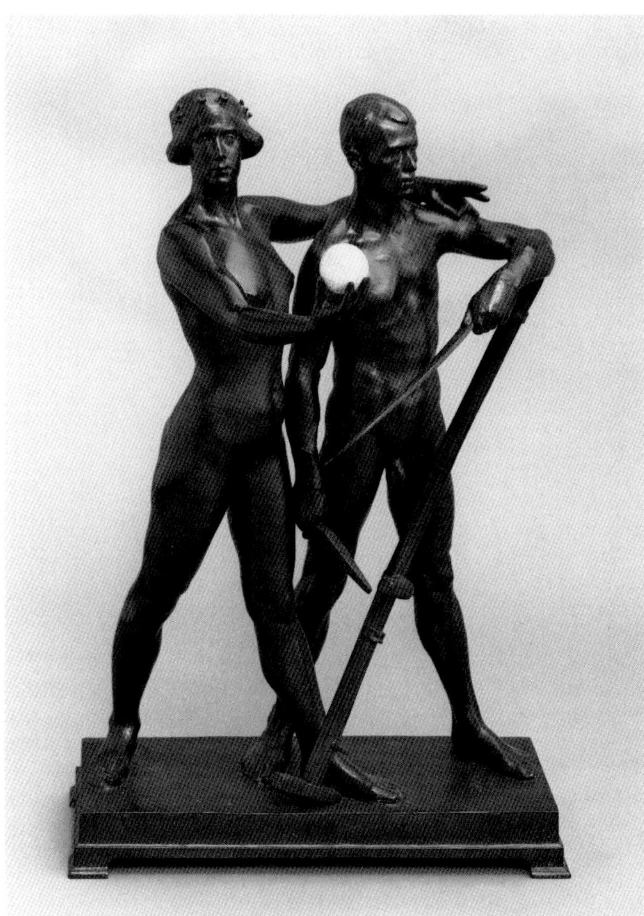

Grafly, *Symbol of Life*

Woman (Edwin A. Ulrich Museum of Art, Wichita State University) has a crown and hairstyle similar to those of *Symbol of Life* and is probably a study for it.

In 1898 *Symbol of Life* was to have been shown at a New York jeweler's; but because "of the prejudice in the mind of the public against viewing anything so 'Manly' in a private Establishment such as ours while [there is not] the least objection to such a display in an art exhibition,"[5] its appearance was cancelled.

Notes

1. Dorothy Grafly, *Sculptor's Clay,* typescript of biography of Charles Grafly, 1929, p. 105.
2. Taft, "Charles Grafly Sculptor," *Brush and Pencil,* p. 348.
3. Undated photograph, Ablah Library, Wichita State University.
4. Charles Grafly to J.T. Coolidge, Sr., Museum of Fine Arts, Boston, Feb. 20, 1908, Ablah Library, Wichita State University.
5. E.H. Wikles (?) to Harrison S. Morris, Feb. 14, 1898, PAFA Archives.

References

1899 Lorado Taft, "Charles Grafly Sculptor," *Brush and Pencil* 3 (March), pp. 344–45 (ills.). 347–48. **1904** Julian Zolnay, *The Art Department Illustrated: Louisiana Purchase Exposition,* Saint Louis, p. 371 (ill.). **1925** Lorado Taft, *The History of American Sculpture,* New York: Macmillan Company, fig. 95, p. 506. **1974** Pamela H. Simpson, "The Sculpture of Charles Grafly," Ph.D. diss., University of Delaware, Newark, pp. 38–41, fig. 5, cat. no. 64 (ill.).

Exhibited

1898* cat. no. 804 (ill.). **1898** American Fine Arts Society, New York, *Third Exhibition of the National Sculpture Society,* cat. no. 83. **1900** Paris, *Exposition Universelle,* cat. no. 21. **1901** Saint Botolph Club, Boston, *Exhibition of Sculpture by Mr. Chas. Grafly of Philadelphia,* checklist no. 2. **1901** Buffalo, *Pan-American Exposition,* cat. no. 1586. **1901–2** Charleston, *South Carolina Inter-State and West Indian Exposition.* **1904** Saint Louis, *Louisiana Purchase Universal Exposition,* cat. no. 2118. **1906** Art Association of Indianapolis, John Herron Art Institute, *Inaugural Exhibition,* cat. no. 303. **1908** Fifth Regiment Armory, Baltimore, *Exhibition of the National Sculpture Society Under the Auspices of the Municipal Art Gallery of Baltimore,* cat. no. 145. **1909** Art Museum, Eden Park (Cincinnati Art Museum), *Sixteenth Annual Exhibition of American Art,* cat. no. 169. **1909–10** Buffalo Fine Arts Academy, Albright Art Gallery, *A Collection of Small Bronzes Lent by the National Sculpture Society,* cat. no. 59 (traveled to the Art Institute of Chicago; the City Art Museum, Saint Louis; and the Worcester Art Museum in Massachusetts). **1911** Saint Botolph Club, Boston, *Sculpture by Charles Grafly; Paintings by Daniel Garber,* checklist no. 21. **1912** Museum of Fine Arts, Boston. **1926** Philadelphia, *Sesquicentennial International Exposition,* cat. no. 1126. **1930** PAFA, *Memorial Exhibition of Work by Charles Grafly,* cat. no. 53. **1936** Temple University Art Galleries, Philadelphia, *Exhibition of Sculpture by Charles Grafly,* cat. no. 1. **1984–85** PAFA, *A Growing American Treasure: Recent Acquisitions and Highlights from the Permanent Collection.* **1986–87** PAFA, *Sculpture at the Pennsylvania Academy of the Fine Arts.* **1996** Edwin A. Ulrich Museum of Art, Wichita State University, Kans., *The Sculptor's Clay: Charles Grafly,* cat. no. 33.

Ex Collections

The artist, about 1898–1929; his family, 1929–71 (lent to the PAFA by Dorothy Grafly, 1941–71).

From Generation to Generation

1897–98
Bronze with black patina; sand cast in 1898–99
49 x 33 x 24¼" (124.5 x 83.8 x 61.6 cm)
Signed, inscribed, and dated on top of base, next to boy's left foot: Chas. Grafly/Philadelphia 1897–8
Foundry mark on top of base at back: BUREAU BROS./PHILA.
Gift of Dr. Charles H. Drummond, 1987.1.2

THIS GROUP, along with *Symbol of Life* (q.v.), was modeled shortly after Charles Grafly returned to the United States from Paris. The theme of the sculpture

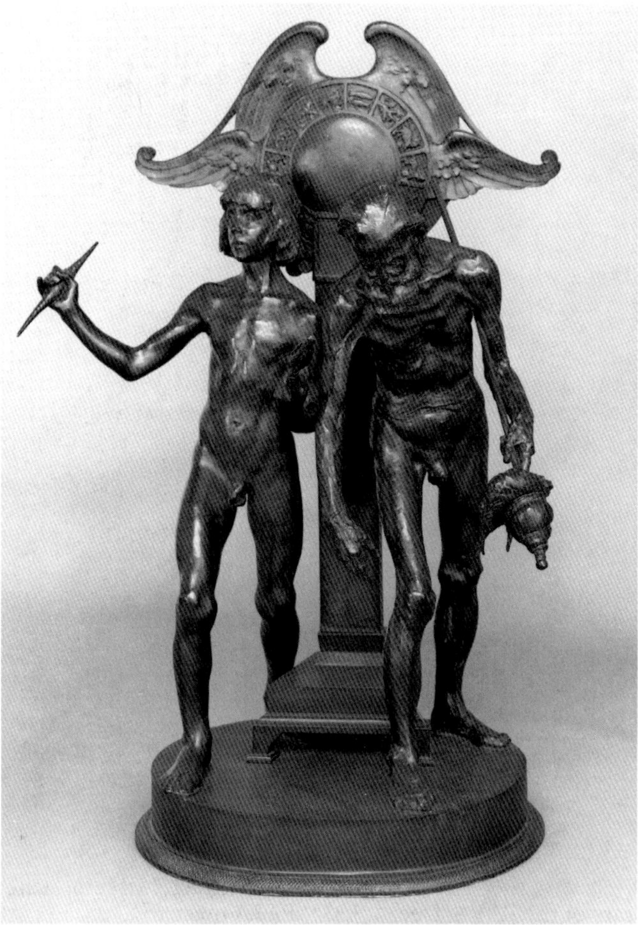

Grafly, *From Generation to Generation*

is the continuity of life. A youth and an old man stand before a winged dial marked with the signs of the zodiac. The old man carries a distaff with coarse wool from which thread will be spun onto the spool held by the youth. In their textured surface, the figures display more of the modeling style that Grafly learned in Paris than do those in *Symbol of Life* and his later works. The modeling of *From Generation to Generation* is less idealized and without the emphasis on outline that Grafly used later. The old man's sunken chest, loose skin, and the protruding veins of his upper arms are the closely observed features of a particular model.

No other versions of this work are extant, as the plaster was broken by 1908 and probably discarded.[1]

Note

1. Charles Grafly to J.T. Coolidge, Sr., Museum of Fine Arts, Boston, Feb. 20, 1908, Ablah Library, Wichita State University.

References

1899 Lorado Taft, "Charles Grafly Sculptor," *Brush and Pencil* 3 (March), p. 348 (ill.). **1901** Vittoria C. Dallin, "Charles Grafly's Work," *New England Magazine* 25 (Oct.), pp. 230–32. **1908** Leila Mechlin, "The National Sculpture Society's Exhibition at Baltimore—II; Imaginative Work," *International Studio* 25 (August), pp. 42–44 (ill.). **1974** Pamela H. Simpson, "The Sculpture of Charles Grafly," Ph.D. diss., University of Delaware, Newark, pp. 37–38, cat. no. 69 (ill.).

Exhibited

1899* cat. no. 801 (ill.). **1900** Paris, *Exposition Universelle,* cat. no. 25. **1901** Saint Botolph Club, Boston, *Exhibition of Sculpture by Mr. Chas. Grafly of Philadelphia,* checklist no. 3. **1901** Buffalo, *Pan-American Exposition,* cat. no. 1587, p. 68. **1901–2** Charleston, *South Carolina Inter-State and West Indian Exposition.* **1904** Saint Louis, *Louisiana Purchase Universal Exposition,* cat. no. 2119. **1906** Art Association of Indianapolis, John Herron Art Institute, *Inaugural Exhibition,* cat. no. 304. **1908** Museum of Fine Arts, Boston, *Renaissance and Modern Bronzes,* cat. no. 214. **1908** Fifth Regiment Armory, Baltimore, *Exhibition of the National Sculpture Society Under the Auspices of the Municipal Art Gallery of Baltimore,* cat. no. 146. **1909** Art Museum, Eden Park (Cincinnati Art Museum), *Sixteenth Annual Exhibition of American Art,* cat. no. 170. **1909–10** Buffalo Fine Arts Academy, Albright Art Gallery, *A Collection of Small Bronzes Lent by the National Sculpture Society,* cat. no. 58 (traveled to the Art Institute of Chicago; the City Art Museum, Saint Louis; and Worcester Art Museum in Massachusetts). **1926** Philadelphia, *Sesquicentennial International Exposition,* cat. no. 1128. **1930** PAFA, *Memorial Exhibition of Work by Charles Grafly,* cat. no. 43, as *Generation to Generation.* **1936** Temple University Art Galleries, Philadelphia, *Exhibition of Sculpture by Charles Grafly,* cat. no. 2. **1984–85** PAFA, *A Growing American Treasure: Recent Acquisitions and Highlights from the Permanent Collection.* **1986–87** PAFA, *Sculpture at the Pennsylvania Academy of the Fine Arts.*

Ex Collections

The artist, about 1899–1929; his family, 1929–87 (lent to the PAFA by Dorothy Grafly, 1941–80; by Dr. Charles H. Drummond, 1980–87).

Hugh Henry Breckenridge

1898
Bronze with green patina; cast in 1938
15¾ x 7¾ x 10¼" (40 x 19.7 x 26 cm)
Signed on back of neck: to my [friend] Breckenridg[e]/ Chas. Grafly
Sand cast by Bureau Brothers, Philadelphia
Pennsylvania Academy purchase, 1938.12

ALTHOUGH Charles Grafly enjoyed producing symbolic works, he gradually turned to portraiture. He had a talent for capturing not only likeness but also personality, and much of his reputation was based on this skill. Several writers considered him equal to JEAN ANTOINE HOUDON as a portraitist.[1]

From 1896 to 1929, Grafly created a series of portrait busts of artist friends. He referred to it as his "collection of the best in the profession, the real 'immortals.' "[2] This bust of Hugh Breckenridge (1870–1937) is commonly thought to be the first of the series. Two years earlier, however, in Paris in 1896, Grafly had made a bust of the painter Henry Ossawa Tanner.[3] Grafly and Breckenridge portrayed each other in 1898. Breckenridge's painting of Grafly (location unknown) was exhibited in the 1898 annual exhibition of the Pennsylvania Academy of the Fine Arts, and the plaster of this bust was shown the following year. The two artists had studied together at the Pennsylvania Academy and at the Académie Julian. Breckenridge also taught at the Academy, from 1894 to 1937, was Curator of Schools in 1907–8 and was active in the Academy Fellowship.

The plaster version of the bust was exhibited in the Pennsylvania Academy's 1930 memorial exhibition for Grafly. A year later, Breckenridge lent it to the Academy so that a bronze cast could be made.[4] In 1938 the bust was cast by Bureau Brothers, and the plaster was returned to Breckenridge's widow.[5] The bust was patinated a dappled green, probably at the request of the Academy. Because no casts were made of this bust in the sculptor's lifetime, it is not known what color he would have chosen. He did use green patinas in the busts of Emily Clayton Bishop and Henry Lorenz Viereck (qq.v.), but he more commonly specified tones of brown. A wooden box was supplied as the base for the Breckenridge bust. Grafly usually preferred stone bases, which, along with the manner in which he terminated the neck or shoulders, would indicate the size and mass of the rest of the sitter's body. Typically, Grafly supplied a sketch of the design for the base, specifying the dimensions and the type of stone, to the foundry at the time of casting. His special interest in stone dated from his years at Struthers Stoneyard, when he put together a small collection of stones of different types and colors.[6] The color of the stone base was matched with the personality of the sitter.

Grafly outlined his formula for modeling portrait busts in an article written with his daughter for the *Encyclopedia Britannica* in 1928.[7] He paid primary attention to the masses of the head by establishing its vertical and horizontal planes and then adding the details—facial features, hair, and neck. Light hair was indicated by subtle fluffy forms, whereas dark hair was given more definite shape and crisp shadows. He didn't show the sitter's clothing because he felt it would dissipate the focus and also date the portrait.

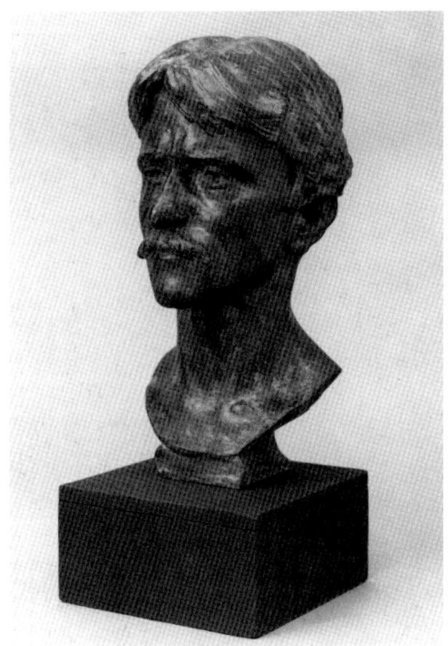

Grafly, *Hugh Henry Breckenridge*

Notes

1. Perhaps the first one to draw the comparison was Helen W. Henderson, *The Pennsylvania Academy of the Fine Arts and Other Collections of Philadelphia* (Boston, 1911), p. 206.

2. Charles Grafly to C. Powell Minnigerode, director, Corcoran Gallery of Art, Sept. 18, 1916, Ablah Library, Wichita State University.

3. Now in the Metropolitan Museum of Art, New York, gift of Jesse Tanner, 1948.

4. Hugh H. Breckenridge to John Andrew Myers, secretary of the PAFA, Dec. 4, 1931, PAFA object file.

5. There is no foundry mark on the Academy's bronze; but there is a bill, dated June 1, 1938, for "One bust cast in bronze and colored Green," PAFA object file. As of 1974, the plaster was in the collection of the sitter's widow.

6. Dorothy Grafly, *Sculptor's Clay*, typescript of biography of Charles Grafly, 1929, p. 171.

7. *Encyclopedia Britannica*, 14th ed., s.v. "portrait sculpture"; see also Charles and Dorothy Grafly to Warren E. Cox, Oct. 29, 1928, Ablah Library.

References

1899 Lorado Taft, "Charles Grafly Sculptor," *Brush and Pencil* 3 (March), p. 343 (ill.). **1938** "Gets Bronze Bust of Philadelphia," *Philadelphia Public Ledger*, July 18 (ill.), PAFA object file. **1938** "Grafly's Breckenridge," *Art Digest* 12 (August 1), p. 10 (ill.). **1974** Pamela H. Simpson, "The Sculpture of Charles Grafly," Ph.D. diss., University of Delaware, Newark, cat. no. 72 (ill.). **1984** Wayne Craven, *Sculpture in America*, Newark: University of Delaware, pp. 441, fig. 12.13, 462.

Exhibited

1948 Woodmere Art Gallery, Philadelphia, *American Art 1860–1914*. **1965** Newman Galleries, Philadelphia, *Daniel Garber Paintings; Charles Grafly Sculpture*. **1975–76** Whitney Museum of American Art, New York, *A Portrait of Young America*. **1976** PAFA, *In This Academy*, cat. no. 67. **1979** Governor's Residence, Harrisburg. **1984–85** PAFA, *A Growing American Treasure: Recent Acquisitions and Highlights from the Permanent Collection*.

James McManes

1900
Bronze with brown patina; sand cast
15½ x 8 x 9½" (39.4 x 20.3 x 24 cm)
Inscribed and dated beneath neck at back: PORTRAIT OF JAMES M^cMANES MADE BY CHARLES GRAFLY PHILADELPHIA 1900
Foundry mark at end of above inscription: CAST BY BUREAU BRO'S
Gift of Mrs. North Winship, 1964.10

CHARLES GRAFLY was apparently asked by the McManes family to model this posthumous bust.[1] A death mask, probably taken by the artist himself, was used as a reference.[2] Photographs of James McManes (1822–1899) were relied upon, as well.[3]

"I never liked my grandfather's hair all touseled [*sic*] up," complained McManes's granddaughter. "I never in my life saw him that way. He was always so particular about his appearance—and that hair does not go with a silk hat which he always wore—The rest of the bust is exactly like him."[4] Relatives of the subject were also disturbed by Grafly's decision to exclude a suggestion of clothing at the neck of the bust. The artist explained to them his desire to convey "timeless simplicity" in his portraits.[5]

Grafly, *James McManes*

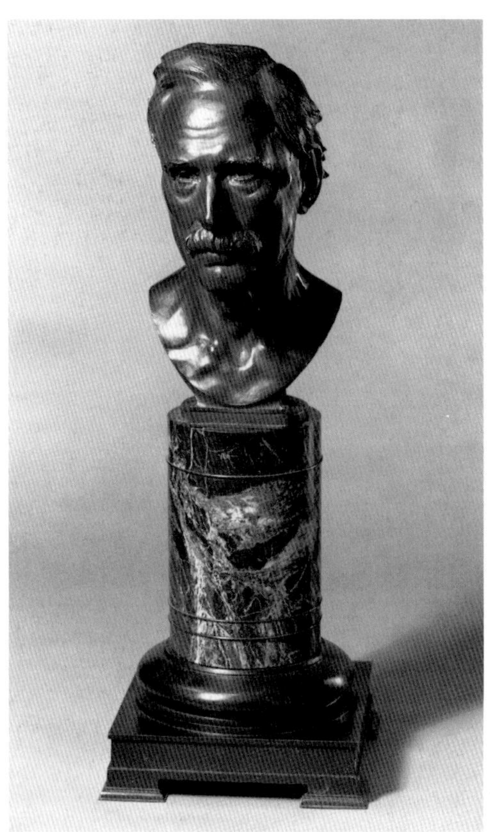

A photograph of this bust in clay or plaster was used as an illustration for an article on portrait sculpture by Charles Grafly and his daughter, Dorothy, in the *Encyclopedia Britannica.* It showed Grafly's method of modeling dark hair that had turned gray; the masses of the hair are heavy with a solid effect and shadows as if the hair was still dark.[6]

James McManes was an Irish-born politician who lived most of his life in Philadelphia and in his later years served as a Fairmount Park commissioner. In 1956 his granddaughter offered the bust to the Pennsylvania Academy of the Fine Arts. The gift was accepted, and in 1964 the sculpture was received by the Academy.[7]

The plaster version of the bust has no inscriptions and is at the Edwin A. Ulrich Museum of Art, Wichita State University. The Academy's bust, the only known bronze, is mounted on a green marble column with metal bands, atop a bronze footed base. It is similar to several other bases that Grafly chose for his portrait busts, such as the one for *Edward Hornor Coates* (q.v.).

Notes

1. Simpson 1974, p. 249.
2. John E.D. Trask to Charles Grafly, July 1, 1909, PAFA Archives.
3. Dorothy Grafly, *Sculptor's Clay,* typescript of unpublished biography of Charles Grafly, 1929, p. 154.
4. Catherine C. Winship to Louise Wallman, museum registrar of the PAFA, June 1, 1964, PAFA object file.
5. D. Grafly 1929, p. 112.
6. *Encyclopedia Britannica,* 14th ed., s.v. "portrait sculpture," pl. 15, no. 4.
7. C. Winship to Joseph T. Fraser, Jr., director of the PAFA, Oct. 7, 1956, and March 30, 1964, PAFA object file.

Reference

1974 Pamela H. Simpson, "The Sculpture of Charles Grafly," Ph.D. diss., University of Delaware, Newark, cat. no. 91, pp. 249, 250 (ill.).

Exhibited

1903* cat. no. 1109. **1904** *Louisiana Purchase Universal Exposition,* Saint Louis, cat. no. 2124. **1911** Saint Botolph Club, Boston, *Sculpture by Charles Grafly and Paintings by Daniel Garber,* checklist no. 14. **1965** Newman Galleries, Philadelphia, *Daniel Garber Paintings; Charles Grafly Sculpture.*

Ex Collection

The sitter's family, 1900–64.

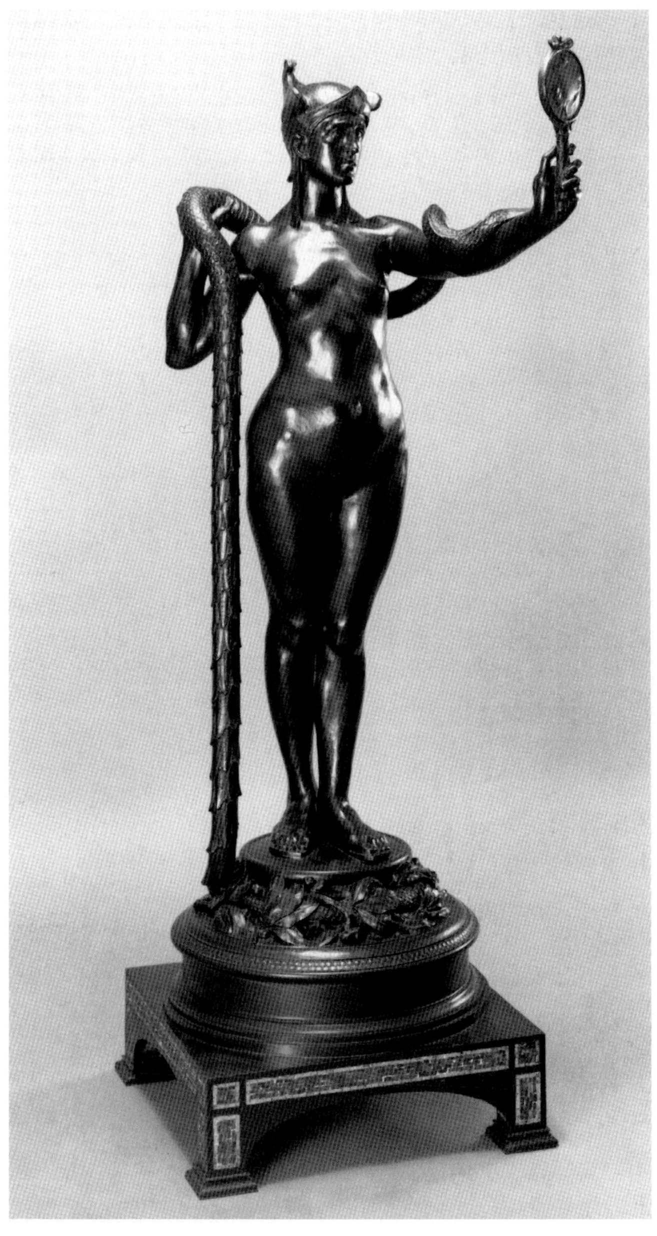

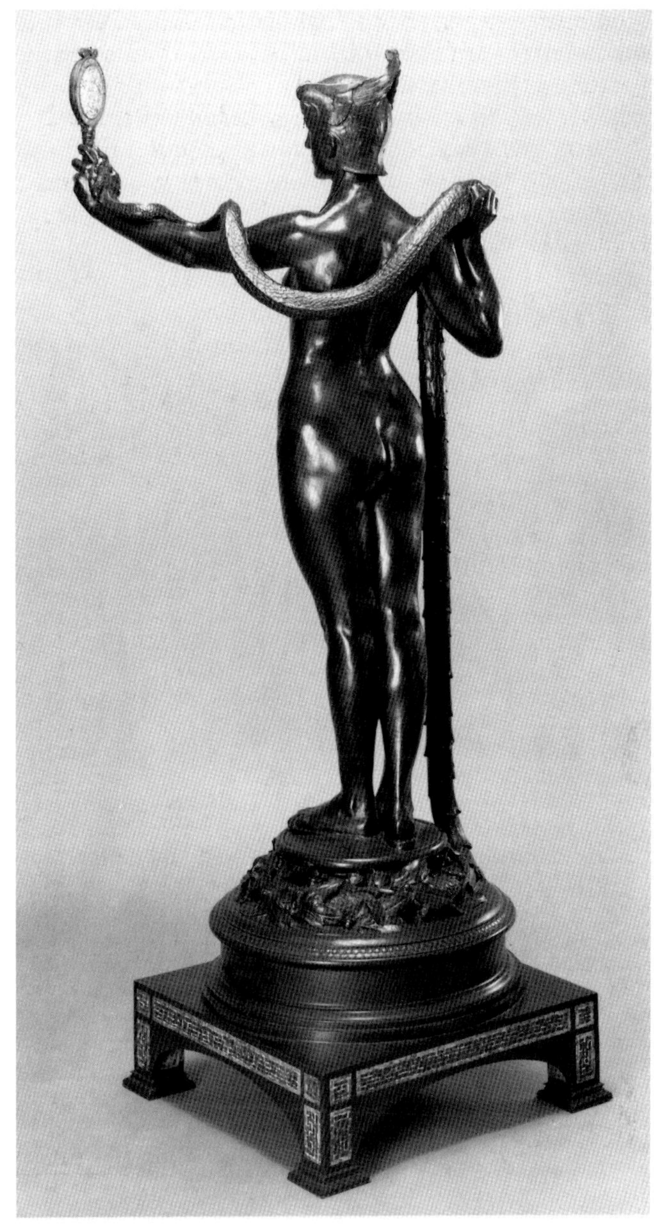

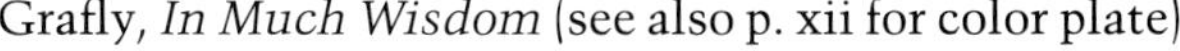

Grafly, *In Much Wisdom* (see also p. xii for color plate)

In Much Wisdom

1902
Bronze with black patina; sand cast in 1902–3; mosaic inlay of stone and gilded glass
63½ x 27¼ x 27¼" (161.3 x 69.2 x 69.2 cm)
Signed and dated on top of base next to figure's left foot: Charles Grafly/Philadelphia –1902 –
Foundry mark on top of base next to figure's right foot: Bureau Bro's/Bronze Founders
Henry D. Gilpin Fund, 1912.2

THIS IS the last of Charles Grafly's uncommissioned symbolic images. The Goddess of Wisdom is shown with her symbols, a mirror and a snake. The snake is wrapped around her and merges with the base on which she stands. The sculptor may have been influenced in the subject matter by William Rush's carved wooden figure of Wisdom that was for many years at the Fairmount Waterworks (Fairmount Park Commission, on loan since 1956 to the Museum of American Art of the Pennsylvania Academy of the Fine Arts). *In Much Wisdom* is unusual for Grafly in its ornament: the winged helmet decorated with gilded glass, and the base and mirror with gilded glass and turquoise mosaic.

In 1910 the statue was awarded a Gold Medal of

Honor for Sculpture at an exposition that traveled to Buenos Aires and Santiago. The whereabouts of the plaster version is unknown; but, like his earlier symbolic groups, it was probably broken and discarded.

Margaret Anderson, later West, a popular model at the Pennsylvania Academy, posed for this sculpture, as well as *Mermaid Fountain* by Grafly's student DANIEL C. MÜLLER.

References
1903 Helen W. Henderson, "Charles Grafly, Sculptor: An Apostle of Symbolism," *Booklovers Magazine* (Nov.), p. 500 (ill.). **1910** John E.D. Trask, "Charles Grafly, Sculptor: An Appreciative Note," *Art and Progress* 1 (Feb.), pp. 86–87 (ill.). **1939** "Forever Young and Fair: Model, Now 67, Recaptures Youth Looking at Academy Statues for Which She Posed as Girl," *Philadelphia Bulletin*, July 19, p. 10 (ill.). **1974** Pamela H. Simpson, "The Sculpture of Charles Grafly," Ph.D. diss., University of Delaware, Newark, cat. no. 97 (ill.), fig. 6, pp. 43–45.

Exhibited
1903* cat. no. 1110 (ill.). **1904** *Louisiana Purchase Universal Exposition*, Saint Louis, cat. no. 2120. **1908** Fifth Regiment Armory, Baltimore, *Exhibition of the National Sculpture Society Under the Auspices of the Municipal Art Gallery of Baltimore*, cat. no. 147. **1909** Art Museum, Eden Park (Cincinnati Art Museum), *Sixteenth Annual Exhibition of American Art*, cat. no. 171. **1910** *Exposicion Internacional de Arte del Centenario*, Buenos Aires, cat. no. 135 (traveled to Santiago). **1930** PAFA, *Memorial Exhibition of Work by Charles Grafly*, cat. no. 48 (ill.). **1974** Philadelphia National Bank, exhibition of works from the PAFA. **1974** PAFA, Peale House, *Selected Works from the Academy's 20th-Century Collection of Paintings and Sculpture*. **1976** Whitney Museum of American Art, New York, *200 Years of American Sculpture*, fig. 113, p. 71. **1978–79** PAFA, *350 Masterpieces of American Art: 1720–1978*. **1979** Brooklyn Museum, *The American Renaissance, 1876–1917*, cat. no. 245 (traveled to Washington, D.C., San Francisco, and Denver). **1984–85** PAFA, *A Growing American Treasure: Recent Acquisitions and Highlights from the Permanent Collection*. **1986–87** PAFA, *Sculpture at the Pennsylvania Academy of the Fine Arts*. **1994–96** PAFA, *Two Centuries of Collecting at the Museum of American Art*.

Ex Collection
The artist, about 1903–12.

Edward Hornor Coates

1903
Bronze with black patina; sand cast by 1905
18½ x 9¾ x 10" (47 x 24.8 x 25.4 cm)
Signed and dated on back of neck: Charles Grafly May 1903–
Inscribed on back beneath neck: EDWARD HORNOR COATES
Foundry mark beneath right side of neck: BUREAU BROS./ PHILA.
Gift of Mrs. E.H. Coates for Edward H. Coates memorial exhibition, 1923.9.13

THIS BUST was commissioned by Edward H. Coates (1846–1921) for his private collection.[1] He was the president of the Pennsylvania Academy of the Fine Arts for five terms, from 1890 to 1906. He served on the board of directors from 1877 to 1890, as treasurer, and on the committees on finance and instruction. Charles Grafly would have known Coates from both his student and teaching days and undoubtedly modeled him from life. Coates is portrayed without the mutton chops of Robert W. Vonnoh's 1893 portrait in oils (Museum of American Art of the Pennsylvania Academy of the Fine Arts).

In 1923 this bust, along with twenty-nine other American and European paintings and sculptures, was given to the Pennsylvania Academy by Mrs. Coates and shown in a memorial exhibition for her husband.[2] The bust is mounted on a pink marble column, atop a bronze footed base. The plaster version is at the Edwin A. Ulrich Museum of Art at Wichita State University.

Grafly, *Edward Hornor Coates*

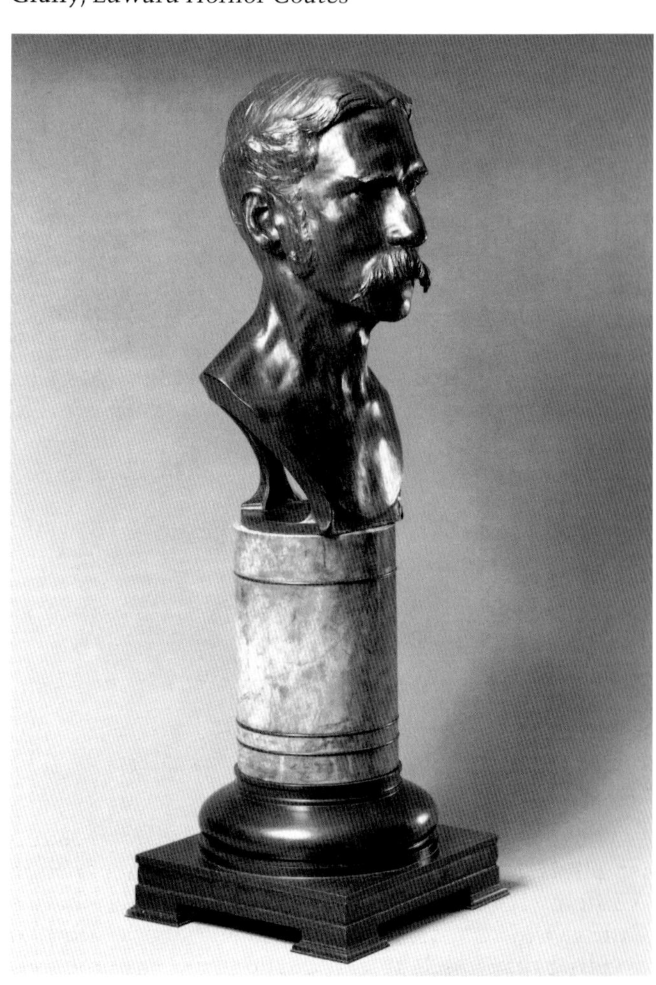

Notes

1. Simpson 1974, p. 274.

2. Minutes, meeting of the committee on collections and exhibitions, Nov. 5, 1923, PAFA Archives.

References

1905 "One Hundredth Anniversary Exhibition of the Academy of the Fine Arts Opens Its Doors," *Philadelphia Inquirer*, Jan. 22, p. 13 (ill.), clipping file, PAFA Archives. **1905** Helen W. Henderson, "Centenary Exhibition of the Pennsylvania Academy of the Fine Arts," *Brush and Pencil* 15 (March), pp. 155, 164 (ill.). **1910** John E.D. Trask, "Charles Grafly, Sculptor: An Appreciative Note," *Art and Progress* 1 (Feb.), p. 84 (ill.). **1911** Helen W. Henderson, *The Pennsylvania Academy of the Fine Arts and Other Collections of Philadelphia*, Boston, pp. 206, 207 (ill.). **1939** "Forever Young and Fair; Model, Now 67, Recaptures Youth Looking at Academy Statues for Which She Posed as Girl," *Philadelphia Bulletin*, July 19, p. 10 (ill.). **1974** Pamela H. Simpson, "The Sculpture of Charles Grafly," Ph.D. diss., University of Delaware, Newark, cat. no. 104 (ill.).

Exhibited

1905* cat. no. 970 (ill.). **1906** Art Association of Indianapolis, John Herron Art Institute, *Inaugural Exhibition*, cat. no. 302. **1908** Fifth Regiment Armory, Baltimore, *Exhibition of the National Sculpture Society Under the Auspices of the Municipal Art Gallery of Baltimore*, cat. no. 151. **1911** Saint Botolph Club, Boston, *Sculpture by Charles Grafly and Paintings by Daniel Garber*, checklist no. 10. **1922*** cat. frontispiece. **1923–24** PAFA, *The Edward H. Coates Memorial Collection*, cat. no. 30 (ill.). **1930** PAFA, *Memorial Exhibition of Work by Charles Grafly*, cat. no. 86 (ill.). **1948** Woodmere Art Gallery, Philadelphia, *American Art 1860–1914*. **1965** Newman Galleries, Philadelphia, *Daniel Garber Paintings; Charles Grafly Sculpture*. **1976** PAFA, *In This Academy*, cat. no. 16. **1980** PAFA, Peale House, *The Pennsylvania Academy Schools, 1876–1900*. **1996** Amon Carter Museum, Fort Worth, Texas, *Thomas Eakins and the Swimming Picture*, traveling exhib.

Ex Collections

Edward H. Coates, about 1905–21; his wife, 1921–23.

Walter Elmer Schofield

1905
Bronze with brown patina; sand cast in 1905–6
23 x 10½ x 10" (58.4 x 26.7 x 25.4 cm)
Signed, inscribed, and dated beneath right shoulder:
Charles Grafly/Philadelphia/DEC. 1905
Inscribed in relief on back: WALTER ELMER SCHOFIELD.
Foundry mark on back of base: BUREAU BROS./PHILA.
Gift of Dr. Charles H. Drummond, 1987.1.4

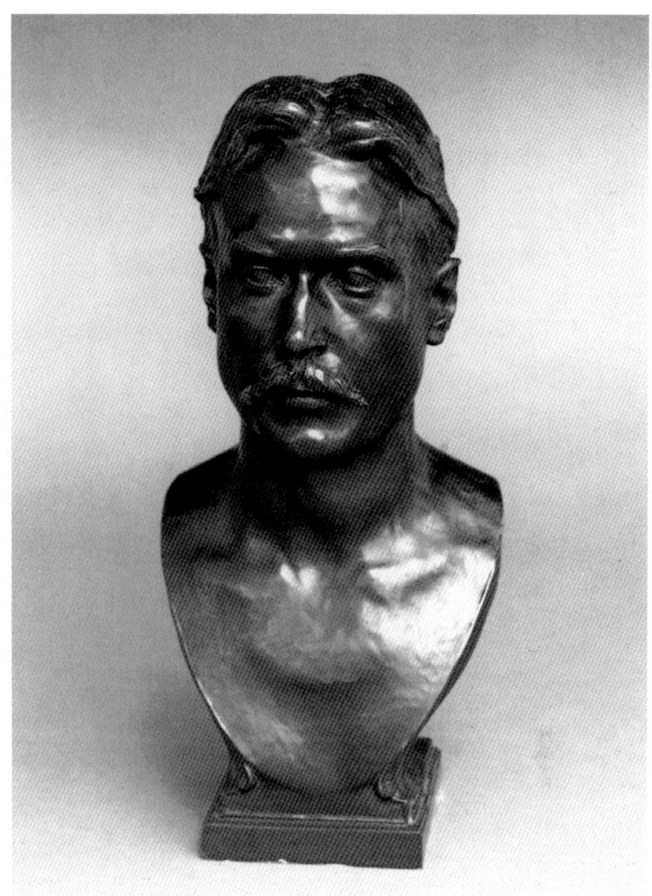

Grafly, *Walter Elmer Schofield*

WALTER E. SCHOFIELD (1867–1944), an impressionist landscape painter, studied at the Pennsylvania Academy of the Fine Arts at the same time as Charles Grafly. In 1901, after his marriage, Schofield began dividing his time between England and the environs of his native city, Philadelphia. This bust must have been modeled during one of his annual trips to the United States.

After this bust was modeled, two bronzes were cast. One was for the sitter, and the other was deposited at the Pennsylvania Academy in 1907. The former (now unlocated) was shown as belonging to Schofield in the 1911 exhibition at the Saint Botolph Club in Boston and in the 1930 Grafly memorial exhibition at the Pennsylvania Academy. It was probably the one included in the Panama-Pacific International Exposition. A plaster of this bust was Grafly's diploma portrait following his election as an academician by the National Academy of Design in 1905. Another plaster is in the Edwin A. Ulrich Museum of Art, Wichita State University.

An article by Anna Seaton-Schmidt shows a bronze bust of Schofield, perhaps the one formerly owned by the sitter, on a square bronze base.[1] The Pennsylvania Academy's bronze does not have a separate base.

Note

1. Anna Seaton-Schmidt 1918, p. 57.

References
1908 Leila Mechlin, "The National Sculpture Society's Exhibition at Baltimore—I; Monumental Work and Portraiture," *International Studio* 35 (July), p. 13 (ill.). **1918** Anna Seaton-Schmidt, "Charles Grafly in His Summer Home," *American Magazine of Art* 10 (Dec.), p. 57 (ill.). **1974** Pamela H. Simpson, "The Sculpture of Charles Grafly," Ph.D. diss., University of Delaware, Newark, cat. no. 124 (ill.).

Exhibited
1906* cat. no. 925. **1908** Fifth Regiment Armory, Baltimore, *Exhibition of the National Sculpture Society Under the Auspices of the Municipal Art Gallery of Baltimore*, cat. no. 149, listed incorrectly as lent by the sitter. **1915** San Francisco, *Panama-Pacific International Exposition*, cat. no. 3864. **1926** Corcoran Gallery of Art, Washington, D.C., *Special Exhibition of Portrait Busts of Noted American Painters and Sculptors by Charles Grafly*, cat. no. 11. **1926** Philadelphia, *Sesquicentennial International Exposition*, cat. no. 1132. **1929** Philadelphia Art Alliance, *Portraits of Prominent Philadelphians by Distinguished Artists*. **1929–30** Corcoran Gallery of Art, Washington, D.C., *Memorial Exhibition of Portrait Busts of Noted American Painters and Sculptors by Charles Grafly*, cat. no. 10. **1931** Museum of Fine Arts, Boston, *Memorial Exhibition of Sculpture by Charles Grafly*. **1965** Newman Galleries, Philadelphia, *Daniel Garber Paintings; Charles Grafly Sculpture*. **1987** Port of History Museum, Philadelphia, *The National Sculpture Society Celebrates the Figure*, cat. p. 69 (ill.). **1994–96** PAFA, *Two Centuries of Collecting at the Museum of American Art*.

Ex Collections
The artist, about 1906–29 (loaned to PAFA by Charles Grafly, 1907–29); the Grafly family, 1929–87 (loaned to PAFA by Grafly estate, 1929–87).

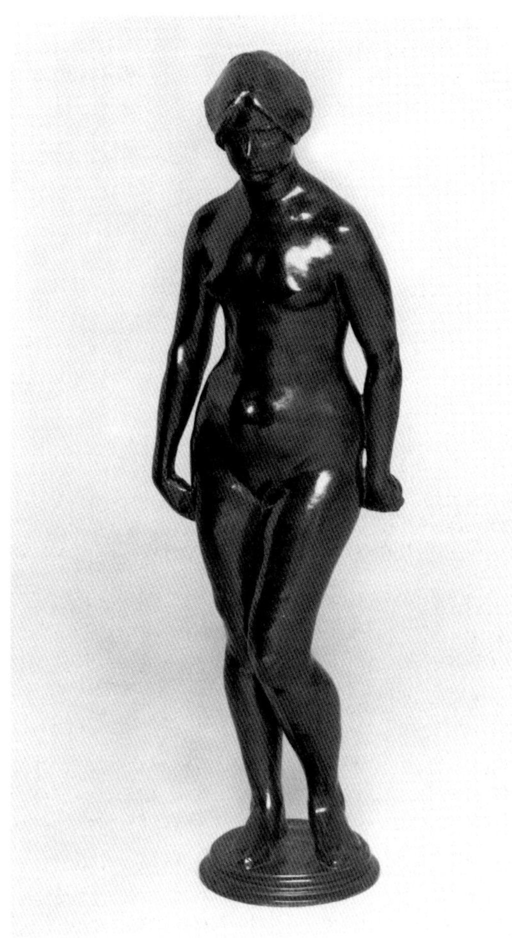

Grafly, *Maidenhood*

Maidenhood

1906
Bronze with red-brown patina; lost-wax cast by 1908
22¾ x 7 x 5" (57.8 x 17.8 x 12.7 cm)
Signed on top of base next to figure's right foot: CHARLES GRAFLY; dated between feet of figure: MCM/VI
Foundry mark on base beneath figure's left foot: ROMAN BRONZE WORKS N.Y.
Gift of Dorothy Grafly, 1957.22.1

In 1906 Charles Grafly made a series of nude female figures, but *Maidenhood* was the only one cast in bronze. It was probably a demonstration piece for one of the classes he taught. The illustration in the 1908 annual exhibition catalogue of the Pennsylvania Academy of the Fine Arts shows the figure on a large square stone base. Now, however, it has a separate small round wooden base, painted black. No other casts of this work are known, although several other studies of women done in 1906 are at the Edwin A. Ulrich Museum of Art, Wichita State University.

References
1908 "103rd Annual Exhibition At the Academy of Fine Arts," *Philadelphia Press*, Jan. 21 (ill.), clipping file, PAFA Archives. **1965** Ben Wolf, "Studio Letter: A Table Turned," *Jewish Exponent*, Feb. 12, p. 15 (ill.). **1972** Moissaye Marans, "Charles Grafly as Teacher," *National Sculpture Review* 21 (Fall), p. 20 (ill.). **1974** Pamela H. Simpson, "The Sculpture of Charles Grafly," Ph.D. diss., University of Delaware, Newark, cat. no. 140 (ill.).

Exhibited
1908* cat. no. 801 (ill.). **1909** Art Museum, Eden Park (Cincinnati Art Museum), *Sixteenth Annual Exhibition of American Art*, cat. no. 172. **1911** Saint Botolph Club, Boston, *Sculpture by Charles Grafly and Paintings by Daniel Garber*, checklist no. 1. **1915** San Francisco, *Panama-Pacific International Exposition*, cat. no. 2509. **1916** Buffalo Fine Arts Academy, Albright Art Gallery, *Exhibition of Contemporary American Sculpture*, held under the auspices of the National Sculpture Society, cat. no. 281. **1930** PAFA, *Memorial Exhibition of Work by Charles Grafly*, cat. no. 26. **1936** Temple University Art Galleries, Philadelphia, *Exhibition of Sculpture by Charles Grafly*, cat. no. 5. **1965** Newman Galleries, Philadelphia, *Daniel Garber Paintings; Charles Grafly Sculpture*. **1972** Cosmopolitan Club, Philadelphia, PAFA exhibition. **1980** PAFA,

Peale House, *The Pennsylvania Academy Schools, 1876–1900.* **1986–87** PAFA, *Sculpture at the Pennsylvania Academy of the Fine Arts.*

Ex Collections
The artist, about 1908–29; his family, 1929–57 (lent to PAFA by Dorothy Grafly, 1941–57).

Joseph Price

1906
Bronze with brown patina
24½ x 12¼ x 10½" (62.2 x 31.1 x 26.7 cm)
Signed and dated on back: Charles Grafly/JAN. 1906.
Inscribed in relief at front of base: JOSEPH PRICE. [and in smaller raised letters] SURGEON
Sand cast, probably by Bureau Brothers, Philadelphia
Gift of Mrs. Joseph H. Price, 1914.14

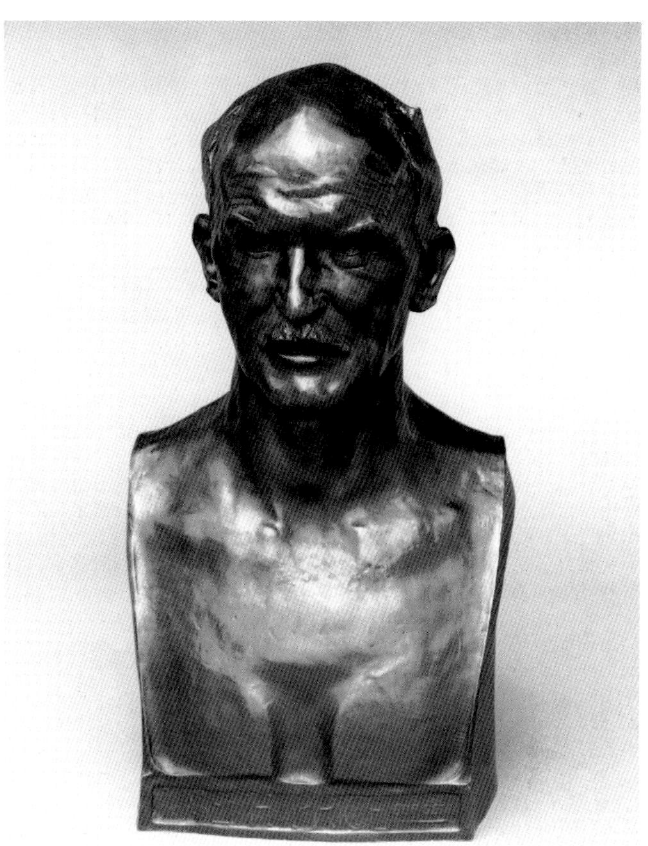

Grafly, *Joseph Price*

DR. JOSEPH PRICE (1853–1911) was born in Virginia and earned a medical degree from the University of Pennsylvania in 1877. He is well known in Philadelphia for his work in gynecological surgery. He helped found a hospital, later called the Joseph Price Memorial Hospital, that is no longer in existence. Mrs. Charles Grafly was one of his patients, and it was through her that the sculptor met the doctor and was commissioned to produce this bust.[1]

A rough preliminary sketch in plaster of the head and neck is in the Edwin A. Ulrich Museum of Art, Wichita State University. Grafly was able to suggest the strong personality by the stern gaze and mouth opened as if speaking, and the size of the man by the treatment of the shoulders and massive bare chest.[2] When the bust was shown at the 102nd annual exhibition of the Pennsylvania Academy of the Fine Arts, a critic considered it to be the best portrait that Grafly had produced thus far.[3]

The Pennsylvania Academy's bronze has no foundry mark; but, because it was sand cast, it was probably done by Bureau Brothers in Philadelphia. Sometime after 1906, Grafly switched from Bureau Brothers, a sand-casting foundry, to the Roman Bronze Works in New York, a predominantly lost-wax-casting foundry. For a time, the bust was on loan to the medical school of the University of Pennsylvania, where it was shown at the foot of the stairs in the library. It was presented to the Pennsylvania Academy by the sitter's widow in 1914. When exhibited in 1915 at the Panama-Pacific Exposition, it had a low rectangular marble base, now missing.

Three plasters of the completed bust were cast. One, painted buff, is in the collection of the College of Physicians of Philadelphia. It was originally owned by Frederick Newlin Price and was purchased by the college at auction in 1981.[4] It was shown in 1909 at the Cincinnati Art Museum's *Sixteenth Annual Exhibition of American Art.* A second plaster is in the Edwin A. Ulrich Museum of Art, Wichita State University. A third was owned by the Joseph Price Hospital; in 1920 Price's nephew Dr. J.W. Kennedy wrote to Grafly about replacing it with a bronze.[5] Grafly said that, to insure a better result for the bronze casting, he preferred to use the original plaster model, which he owned.[6] The hospital's plaster may have been damaged, or perhaps it was a later cast. By September of 1920, the bronze had been cast and was ready for shipment by the Roman Bronze Works.[7] Grafly chose a green patina for the bust as he thought it "most adaptable to its surroundings."[8] The present location of the plaster and the bronze are not known.

Notes

1. Simpson 1974, p. 327.
2. This bust was illustrated in clay or plaster in the *Encyclopedia Britannica,* 14th ed., s.v. "portrait sculpture," (pl. 15, no. 2), as an example of the way to indicate the massive size of a sitter.
3. "Fine Sculpture at the Academy of the Fine Arts," *Philadelphia Inquirer,* Feb. 3, 1907, p. 7, clipping file, PAFA Archives.

4. Julie S. Berkowitz, *The College of Physicians of Philadelphia Portrait Catalogue* (Philadelphia: College of Physicians of Philadelphia, 1984), pp. 173, 174 (ill.).

5. J.W. Kennedy to Charles Grafly, Jan. 26, 1920, Ablah Library, Wichita State University.

6. C. Grafly to J.W. Kennedy, Feb. 18, 1920, Ablah Library.

7. C. Grafly to J.W. Kennedy, Sept. 16, 1920; C. Grafly to Roman Bronze Works, Sept. 20, 1920; and Roman Bronze Works bill to C. Grafly, Sept. 23, 1920; all in Ablah Library.

8. C. Grafly to J.W. Kennedy, Sept. 28, 1920, Ablah Library.

References

1907 "Fine Sculpture at the Academy of the Fine Arts," *Philadelphia Inquirer,* Feb. 3, p. 7 (ill., plaster), clipping file, PAFA Archives. **1908** Leila Mechlin, "The National Sculpture Society's Exhibition at Baltimore—I; Monumental Work and Portraiture," *International Studio* 35 (July), p. 13 (ill., plaster). **1974** Pamela H. Simpson, "The Sculpture of Charles Grafly," Ph.D. diss., University of Delaware, Newark, cat. no. 138 (ill.).

Exhibited

1906 Art Institute of Chicago, *19th Exhibition of Oil Paintings and Sculpture by American Artists,* cat. no. 356. **1907*** cat. no. 613 (ill., plaster). **1911** Saint Botolph Club, Boston, *Sculpture by Charles Grafly and Paintings by Daniel Garber,* checklist no. 5. **1907** National Academy of Design, 82nd annual exhibition, cat. no. 424. **1908** Fifth Regiment Armory, Baltimore, *Exhibition of the National Sculpture Society Under the Auspices of the Municipal Art Gallery of Baltimore,* cat. no. 148 (ill.). **1915** San Francisco, *Panama-Pacific International Exposition,* cat. no. 3867, as *The Surgeon* (ill.). **1916** Buffalo Fine Arts Academy, Albright Art Gallery, *Exhibition of Contemporary American Sculpture,* held under the auspices of the National Sculpture Society, cat. no. 275, as *The Surgeon.* **1930** PAFA, *Memorial Exhibition of Work by Charles Grafly,* cat. no. 15. **1930** Brooklyn Museum, *Exhibition of Sculpture: Recent Work by Distinguished Sculptors,* cat. no. 140. **1955** PAFA, *150th Anniversary Exhibition,* cat. no. 193. **1965** Newman Galleries, Philadelphia, *Daniel Garber Paintings; Charles Grafly Sculpture.*

Ex Collections

The sitter, 1906–11; his wife, 1911–14.

Emily Clayton Bishop

1907
Bronze with green patina; lost-wax cast about 1912
15¾ x 8 x 11¼" (40 x 20.3 x 28.6 cm)
Signed on back at left: GRAFLY; dated at right: 1907
Inscribed on back beneath neck: SKETCH OF MISS BISHOP
Foundry mark on back of base: ROMAN BRONZE WORK[S]/N–Y–
Gift of friends of Miss Bishop, 1920.1.6

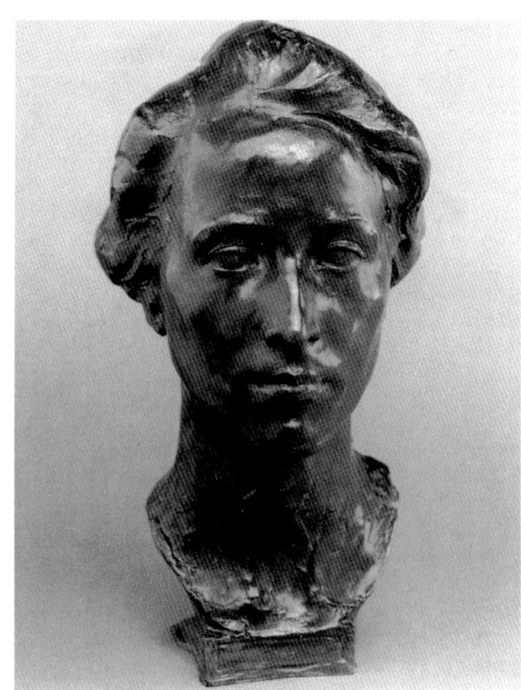

Grafly, *Emily Clayton Bishop*

AFTER she had been graduated by the Maryland Institute of Art and Design in Baltimore, EMILY CLAYTON BISHOP (1883–1912) attended the Pennsylvania Academy of the Fine Arts, where she was a very promising student of Charles Grafly from 1904 to 1910.

This portrait bust was modeled to honor Bishop for winning the composition prize in Grafly's class. She was given a plaster version, probably the only one that was cast at the time. Bishop may have included this bust with the plasters of her own work given to BEATRICE FENTON and Marjorie D. Martinet.[1] Following Bishop's untimely death, a bronze cast of the bust was ordered by her friends Fenton, Martinet, and probably Elizabeth Sparhawk-Jones and Anne West Strawbridge.[2] It was presented to the Pennsylvania Academy in 1920 with four reliefs and a portrait by Bishop for a memorial display at the school entrance.[3] A plaster that remained in Fenton's studio at her death in 1983 is now in the collection of her former student Joan S. Martin. Another plaster is owned by descendents of the sitter. It was once thought that there was a plaster of the bust at Wichita State University.[4] It is now believed that the bust in Wichita is not of Bishop but may be of Grafly's wife, Frances.[5]

The bust of Emily Bishop does not have a separate stone base, which is unusual for Grafly's portraiture. At the front, it has the standard rectangular block that he used as a transition; but the back of the bust is not hollowed out, and there is no provision for hardware to secure it to a separate base.

Notes

1. Beatrice Fenton to Joseph T. Fraser, Jr., director of the PAFA, Jan. 14, 1969, PAFA object file for Emily Clayton Bishop's six bronzes.

2. Exhibition card listing sculpture installation committee, ibid.

3. Minutes, meeting of the board of directors, Jan. 5, 1920, and minutes, meeting of committee on exhibition, Oct. 4, 1920, PAFA Archives.

4. Simpson 1974, pp. 332–33.

5. The author's examination revealed the features and structure of the head to be unlike those of Bishop but similar to other portraits of Mrs. Grafly.

Reference

1974 Pamela H. Simpson, "The Sculpture of Charles Grafly", Ph.D. diss., University of Delaware, Newark, cat. no. 141 (ill.).

Exhibited

1965 Newman Galleries, Philadelphia, *Daniel Garber Paintings; Charles Grafly Sculpture.* **1984–85** PAFA, *A Growing American Treasure: Recent Acquisitions and Highlights from the Permanent Collection.* **1986–87** PAFA, *Sculpture at the Pennsylvania Academy of the Fine Arts.*

Ex Collection

Beatrice Fenton and Marjorie D. Martinet, about 1912–20.

Henry Lorenz Viereck

1909
Bronze with green and brown patina; lost-wax cast in 1909–10
14½ x 8 x 9¼" (36.8 x 20.3 x 23.5 cm)
Inscribed, signed and dated on back beneath neck: HENRY LORENZ VIERECK ENTOMOLOGIST BY CHARLES GRAFLY 1909
Foundry mark on back of support for base: ROMAN BRONZE WORKS N.Y.
General Fund, 1926.3

A WELL-KNOWN NATURALIST, Henry Lorenz Viereck (1881–1931) grew up in Philadelphia and spent his early career there. Later he became a government entomologist and traveled widely. At the time this bust was modeled, he was working in Washington, D.C. Viereck was a close friend of Charles Grafly and often visited him and his family at their summer home in Massachusetts. The portrait was done from life on one of those visits.[1] It bears a close resemblance to the 1917 photograph of Viereck by John Howard Paine, especially in the shape of the head and such prominent features as the nose and ears.[2] Helen W. Henderson considered it to be one of Grafly's most successful portrait busts "in the delicacy of the surface modeling; the unity of its forms, both structural and superficial; while the character of the sitter is given with sympathy and appreciation."[3]

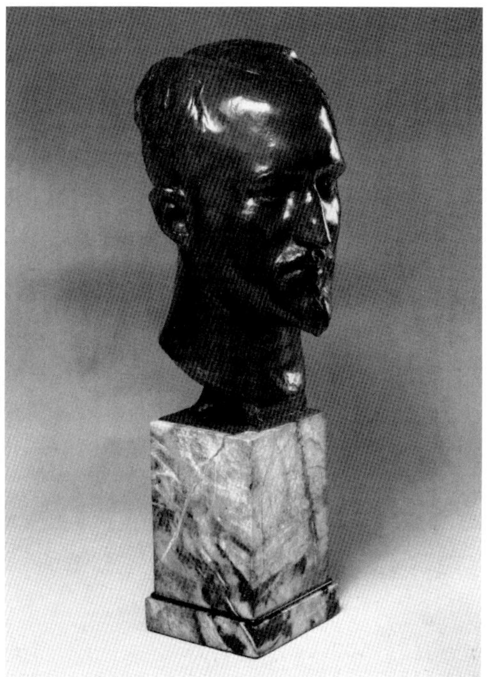

Grafly, *Henry Lorenz Viereck*

This portrait bust was apparently commissioned by Viereck, who paid the cost of the bronze casting.[4] Grafly worked with the foundry on the application of the patina by making "slight alterations."[5] In 1926 Viereck returned to Philadelphia and offered the bust to the Pennsylvania Academy of the Fine Arts at a modest price. He considered it his "most treasured possession which I regret I must part with in this way."[6] The Academy's bust is the only bronze that was cast. It is mounted on a rectangular base of green stone with a bronze band. Originally it was thought that this cast had been owned by Grafly and that the one owned by Viereck was unlocated.[7] When first exhibited at the Academy in 1910, the bust was titled *Henry Lorenz Viereck,* but for most of the subsequent exhibitions to which the sitter lent it, the title was either *The Entomologist* or *The Entomologist Viereck.* The plaster model that was illustrated in a 1910 article is in the Edwin A. Ulrich Museum of Art, Wichita State University.[8]

Notes

1. Dorothy Grafly, *Sculptor's Clay,* typescript of biography of Charles Grafly, 1929, pp. 154–55.

2. Rehn 1932, pl. 6, p. 140.

3. Henderson 1912, p. 384.

4. Simpson 1974, p. 339; Henry L. Viereck to Charles Grafly, Nov. 17, 1909, and May 16, 1910, Ablah Library, Wichita State University.

5. C. Grafly to Edward R. Smith, Columbia University, Dec. 30, 1910, Ablah Library.

6. H. Viereck to the PAFA, dated before Oct. 5, 1926,

on the back of a letter from John Andrew Myers to H. Viereck, Sept. 29, 1926, PAFA object file.

7. Simpson 1974, p. 339.

8. John E.D. Trask, "Charles Grafly, Sculptor: An Appreciative Note," *Art and Progress* 1 (Feb. 1910), p. 84 (ill.), pp. 86, 88 (ill.). "Forever Young and Fair: Model, Now 67, Recaptures Youth Looking at Academy Statues for Which She Posed as Girl," *Philadelphia Bulletin*, July 19, 1939, p. 10.

References

1912 Helen W. Henderson, *The Art Treasures of Washington*, Boston: L.C. Page and Company, pp. 383–84 (ill.). **1932** James A.G. Rehn, "Henry Lorenz Viereck, 1881–1931," *Entomological News* 43 (June), p. 146. **1974** Pamela H. Simpson, "The Sculpture of Charles Grafly," Ph.D. diss., University of Delaware, Newark, cat. no. 145 (ill.).

Exhibited

1910* cat. no. 815. **1910** Art Institute of Chicago, *23rd Annual Exhibition of Oil Paintings and Sculpture by American Artists*, cat. no. 98. **1910–11** National Academy of Design, *Winter Exhibition*, cat. no. 131. **1911** Saint Botolph Club, Boston, *Sculpture by Charles Grafly and Paintings by Daniel Garber*, checklist no. 13. **1915** San Francisco, *Panama-Pacific International Exposition*, cat. no. 2561. **1916** Buffalo Fine Arts Academy, Albright Art Gallery, *Exhibition of Contemporary American Sculpture*, held under the auspices of the National Sculpture Society, cat. no. 279. **1929** Philadelphia Art Alliance, *Portraits of Prominent Philadelphians by Distinguished Artists*. **1930** PAFA, *Memorial Exhibition of Work by Charles Grafly*, cat. no. 49. **1930** Brooklyn Museum, *Exhibition of Sculpture: Recent Work by Distinguished Sculptors*, cat. no. 144. **1931** Museum of Fine Arts, Boston, *Memorial Exhibition of Sculpture by Charles Grafly*. **1965** Newman Galleries, Philadelphia, *Daniel Garber Paintings; Charles Grafly Sculpture*.

Ex Collection

The sitter, about 1910–26.

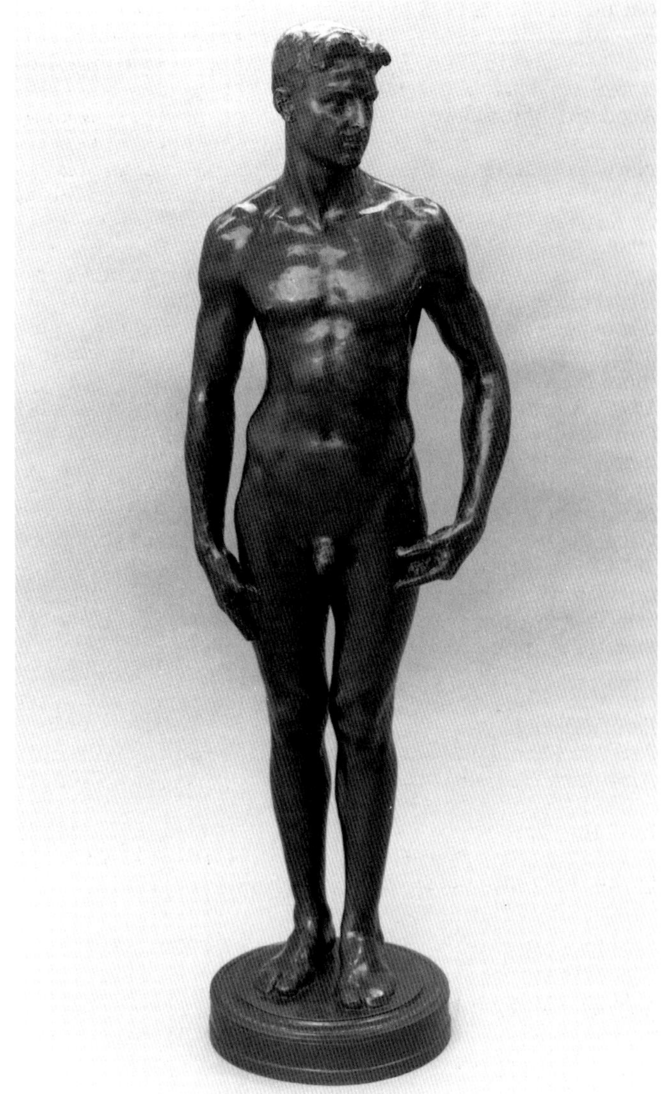

Grafly, *The Oarsman*

The Oarsman

1910
Bronze with red-brown patina; lost-wax cast
38¼ x 12 x 9½" (97.2 x 30.5 x 24.1 cm)
Signed and dated on top of base at front between feet: GRAFLY/–1910–
Foundry mark on back of base: ROMAN BRONZE WORKS N–Y–
Gift of Dorothy Grafly, 1969.22

THIS FIGURE of a rower was modeled in the summer of 1910 as a demonstration for the students in a class that Charles Grafly offered at his studio in Lanesville, Massachusetts.[1] Rowing subjects had been popular in the 1870s with Grafly's teacher THOMAS EAKINS. Because of their well-developed musculature, oarsmen would have been excellent models. Although this sculpture, like *Maidenhood* (q.v.), appears to be an anatomical study, it was cast in bronze and widely exhibited. It stands on a square base of red marble. A plaster with a metallic green surface is in the Edwin A. Ulrich Museum of Art, Wichita State University.

Note

1. Simpson 1974, p. 349.

Reference

1974 Pamela H. Simpson, "The Sculpture of Charles Grafly," Ph.D. diss., University of Delaware, Newark, cat. no. 152 (ill.).

Exhibited

1910–11 National Academy of Design, *Winter Exhibition*, cat. no. 92. **1911** Saint Botolph Club, Boston, *Sculpture by Charles Grafly and Paintings by Daniel Garber*, checklist no. 22. **1911** Art Institute of Chicago, *24th Annual Exhibition of American Oil Paintings and Sculpture,* cat. no. 149. **1915** San Francisco, *Panama-Pacific International Exposition,* cat. no. 3099. **1916** Buffalo Fine Arts Academy, Albright Art Gallery, *Exhibition of Contemporary American Sculpture,* held under the auspices of the National Sculpture Society, cat. no. 285. **1928** PAFA, annual Fellowship exhibition, cat. no. 126. **1928** Atlantic City Art Association, N.J., exhibition of American art. **1930** PAFA, *Memorial Exhibition of Work by Charles Grafly,* cat. no. 67. **1936** Temple University Art Galleries, Philadelphia, *Exhibition of Sculpture by Charles Grafly,* cat. no. 3. **1939–40** Art Institute of Chicago, *Half a Century of American Art,* cat. no. 194. **1948** Woodmere Art Gallery, Philadelphia, *American Art 1860–1914.* **1948** Walnut Street Art Association, Philadelphia, window display during the political conventions. **1955** Philadelphia Museum of Art, in cooperation with Artists Equity Association, *First Philadelphia Arts Festival Regional Exhibition,* cat. no. 269. **1965** Newman Galleries, Philadelphia, *Daniel Garber Paintings; Charles Grafly Sculpture.* **1974** Philadelphia National Bank, exhibition of works from the PAFA. **1974** PAFA, Peale House, *Selected Works from the Academy's 20th-Century Collection of Paintings and Sculpture.* **1976** PAFA, *In This Academy,* cat. no. 234. **1978–79** PAFA, *350 Masterpieces of American Art: 1720–1978.* **1986–87** PAFA, *Sculpture at the Pennsylvania Academy of the Fine Arts.* **1990** National Art Museum of Sport, Indianapolis, *Sport in Art from American Museums,* traveling exhib. cat., cat. no. 31 (ill.).

Ex Collections
The artist, 1910–29; his family, 1929–69 (lent to PAFA by Dorothy Grafly, 1941–69).

Thomas Anshutz

1912
Bronze with brown patina; lost-wax cast in 1912–13
17¾ x 13¼ x 10¾" (45.1 x 33.7 x 27.3 cm)
Signed on back at left: Grafly
Foundry mark on back of base: CAST BY ROMAN BRONZE WORKS N–Y
Gift of friends and admirers of Thomas Pollock Anshutz, 1913.12

THOMAS POLLOCK ANSHUTZ (1851–1912), the Kentucky-born painter, studied with THOMAS EAKINS at the Pennsylvania Academy of the Fine Arts in the 1870s and 1880s. When Eakins was asked to resign, Anshutz took over as instructor of painting and drawing from 1882 to 1912. Charles Grafly knew Anshutz well, first as his student and later as his colleague on the faculty. He referred to him fondly as "Tommy."[1] At an unknown date, Anshutz painted a portrait of Grafly modeling (Edwin A. Ulrich Museum of Art, Wichita State University).

In December 1911, when Anshutz was in failing health, a group of former students and friends met to discuss a possible tribute to him—a "testimonial fund [the goal of which] is to purchase one of Mr. Anshutz's representative works for the P.A.F.A. Permanent Collection, and also a bronze bust modeled by an eminent sculptor at a nominal price."[2] Grafly suggested *The Tanagra* as the painting to be presented because Anshutz thought it one of his best and the Pennsylvania Academy already owned one of his pastel drawings.[3] The painting was given to the Academy before Anshutz's death. Grafly was chosen to sculpt a portrait bust, and Anshutz's obituaries proclaimed the choice.[4] Grafly made a death mask and had the Tognarelli and Voigt Company in Philadelphia make five plaster casts: three were sent to his Philadelphia studio and the other two to his studio in Gloucester, Massachusetts.[5] Shortly after, one cast was received by the Pennsylvania Academy,[6] although none became part of the Academy's collection. In August 1912, Grafly received from the Philadelphia photographer William Shewell Ellis some photographs of Anshutz that Grafly felt would be of "great value to me in making the bust."[7] However,

Grafly, *Thomas Anshutz*

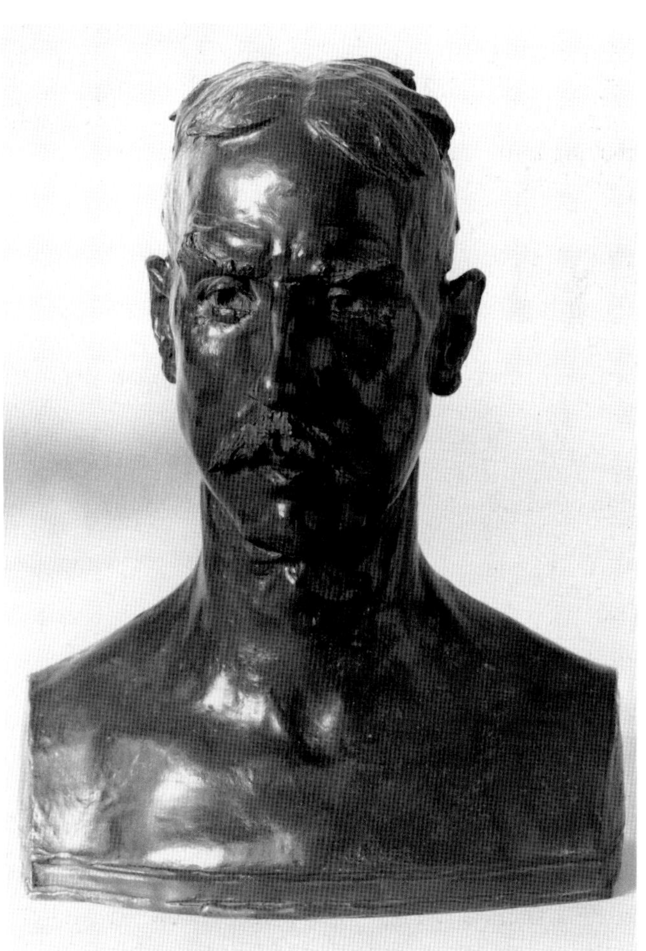

his attempts at modeling a portrait using the masks and photographs were unsuccessful. In an unusual move, Grafly gave up using the aids and proceeded to model a bust from memory in six hours.[8] At the Panama-Pacific International Exposition, the author and lecturer Helen Keller, who was blind and deaf, knew after touching all of Grafly's portrait busts that this one of Anshutz was different and said, "This is not the work of the same man. There is not the same feeling for construction, the same texture."[9]

The plaster bust was sent to the foundry in December 1912, and a bronze cast with a patina of "rich brown with very little green" was ready by the middle of January 1913.[10] Grafly received payment of five hundred dollars from F. Cresson Schell, the chairman of the Anshutz Memorial Committee in January.[11] The bust was shown in the Pennsylvania Academy's 1913 annual exhibition, in which it became the first winner of the George D. Widener Memorial Medal (then awarded as a monetary prize) and was accepted for the permanent collection. The friends and admirers of Anshutz who presented the bust were Helen W. Henderson, Charles E. Dana, Henry Thouron, Edward W. Redfield, Charles Grafly, F. Cresson Schell and Morris Hall Pancoast.[12]

The Sketch Club in Philadelphia, of which Anshutz had been president, wanted a bronze of Grafly's bust in 1913 but thought the funds would be too difficult to raise and requested instead a plaster cast to display in a "composition of the bust, Tommy's palette & brushes" in the assembly room.[13] There is no evidence that the Sketch Club ever received Grafly's bust. It does own a painted plaster death cast of Anshutz's head and neck that Grafly donated in 1921 and a bronze relief by ADAM PIETZ. The plaster original of the bust is painted beige and is in the Edwin A. Ulrich Museum of Art, Wichita State University.

The Pennsylvania Academy's bust was shown in early photographs with a rectangular marble base, but the base is no longer extant.

Notes

1. Dorothy Grafly, *Sculptor's Clay,* typescript of biography of Charles Grafly, 1929, p. 173.
2. Handwritten, undated note in an unknown hand, Ablah Library, Wichita State University.
3. Charles Grafly to F. Cresson Schell, Dec. 6, 1911, Ablah Library.
4. Obituaries, *Philadelphia Evening Bulletin* and *Philadelphia Public Ledger,* June 17, 1912; *Philadelphia Item,* June 23, 1912, PAFA Archives.
5. Tognarelli and Voigt Company bill to C. Grafly, July 6, 1912, Ablah Library.
6. John E.D. Trask to C. Grafly, July 12, 1912, Ablah Library.
7. William Shewell Ellis to C. Grafly, August 20, 1912, and C. Grafly to W.S. Ellis, August 27, 1912, Ablah Library.
8. According to Grafly's assistant George Demetrios (1896–1974); Simpson 1974, pp. 71, 72, 360.
9. D. Grafly 1929, p. 174.
10. C. Grafly to Roman Bronze Works, Dec. 30, 1912, and Roman Bronze Works bill to Grafly, Jan. 17, 1913, Ablah Library.
11. F.C. Schell to C. Grafly, Jan. 28, 1913, and Grafly receipt to Schell, Feb. 10, 1913, Ablah Library.
12. Minutes, meeting of board of directors, April 7, 1913, PAFA Archives.
13. F.C. Schell to C. Grafly, Jan. 31, 1913, Ablah Library.

References

1914 *American Art Annual* 11, before p. 317 (ill.). **1918** Anna Seaton-Schmidt, "Charles Grafly in His Summer Home," *American Magazine of Art* 10 (Dec.), p. 57 (ill.). **1921** Lorado Taft, *Modern Tendencies in Sculpture,* Chicago, p. 15 (ill.). **1970** Louis E. Marrits, *Modeled Portrait Sculpture,* South Brunswick and New York: A.S. Barnes and Company, p. 164 (ill.). **1972** Moissaye Marans, "Charles Grafly as Teacher," *National Sculpture Review* 21 (Fall), p. 20 (ill.). **1974** Pamela H. Simpson, "The Sculpture of Charles Grafly," Ph.D. diss., University of Delaware, Newark, pp. 71, 72, cat. no. 157 (ill.).

Exhibited

1913* cat. no. 721 (ill.). **1915** San Francisco, *Panama-Pacific International Exposition,* cat. no. 2562. **1916** Buffalo Fine Arts Academy, Albright Art Gallery, *Exhibition of Contemporary American Sculpture,* held under the auspices of the National Sculpture Society, cat. no. 277. **1926** Corcoran Gallery of Art, Washington, D.C., *Special Exhibition of Portrait Busts of Noted American Painters and Sculptors by Charles Grafly,* cat. no. 1. **1926** Philadelphia, *Sesquicentennial International Exposition,* cat. no. 1131. **1929–30** Corcoran Gallery of Art, Washington, D.C., *Memorial Exhibition of Portrait Busts of Noted American Painters and Sculptors by Charles Grafly,* cat. no. 1. **1930** PAFA, *Memorial Exhibition of Works by Charles Grafly,* cat. no. 17 (ill.). **1930** Brooklyn Museum, *Exhibition of Sculpture: Recent Works by Distinguished Sculptors,* cat. no. 141. **1931** Museum of Fine Arts, Boston, *Memorial Exhibition of Sculpture by Charles Grafly.* **1942** Philadelphia Art Alliance, *Memorial Exhibition of the work of Thomas Anshutz,* checklist [no. 15]. **1948** Woodmere Art Gallery, Philadelphia, *American Art, 1860 to 1914.* **1955** PAFA, *150th Anniversary Exhibition,* cat. no. 187 (ill.). **1975** William Penn Memorial Museum, Harrisburg, exhibition of works of art from the PAFA. **1975–76** Whitney Museum of American Art, New York, *A Portrait of Young America.* **1976** PAFA, *In This Academy,* cat. no. 17 (ill.). **1978–79** PAFA, *350 Masterpieces of American Art: 1720–1978.* **1980** PAFA, Peale House, *The Pennsylvania Academy Schools, 1876–1900.* **1984–85** PAFA, *A Growing American Treasure: Recent Acquisitions and Highlights from the Permanent Collection.* **1986–87** PAFA, *Sculpture at the Pennsylvania Academy of the Fine Arts.*

"E Pluribus Unum," Preliminary Sketch for the General George Gordon Meade Memorial

1916
Bronze with brown and green patina; lost-wax cast by 1929
18 x 11¼ x 13½" (45.7 x 28.6 x 34.3 cm)
Signed beneath back of slab at figure's right: CHARLES GRAFLY.
Foundry mark on back of base: ROMAN BRONZE WORKS N.Y.
Gift of Dorothy Grafly, 1957.22.2

A FIGURE representing General George Gordon Meade (1815–1872), a Civil War hero from Pennsylvania, is shown pulling together two slabs symbolizing the divided country. This rough sketch is one of Charles Grafly's first designs for his important commission for the Meade Memorial for the Capitol Mall in Washington, D.C. The project occupied much of the sculptor's time from 1915 to 1925. The unveiling took place in 1927.[1]

In June 1916, Grafly asked his studio assistant to pack and send to Washington, D.C., "the two (2) allegorical groups—the ones . . . holding together the rocks also the seated figure of Meade" so that he could show them to the committee sponsoring the memorial.[2] Of the two allegorical groups, one would have been the version later cast in bronze and given to the Pennsylvania Academy of the Fine Arts; the other had additional ornaments, including a sketchy horse's head crowning the composition.[3] At the meeting, the allegorical works and the seated figure were rejected, and a portrait of the general that could be viewed in the round was requested instead. Not long after, the Commission of Fine Arts set forth its requirements for the artwork and commented as follows on the allegorical group: "It is unnecessary in an expression of the character and abilities of General Meade to introduce any element that shall call attention to those differences which brought about the civil strife which gave to him opportunity for showing those abilities."[4] Ironically, this sketch was Grafly's favorite choice for the memorial. Only this one bronze was cast.

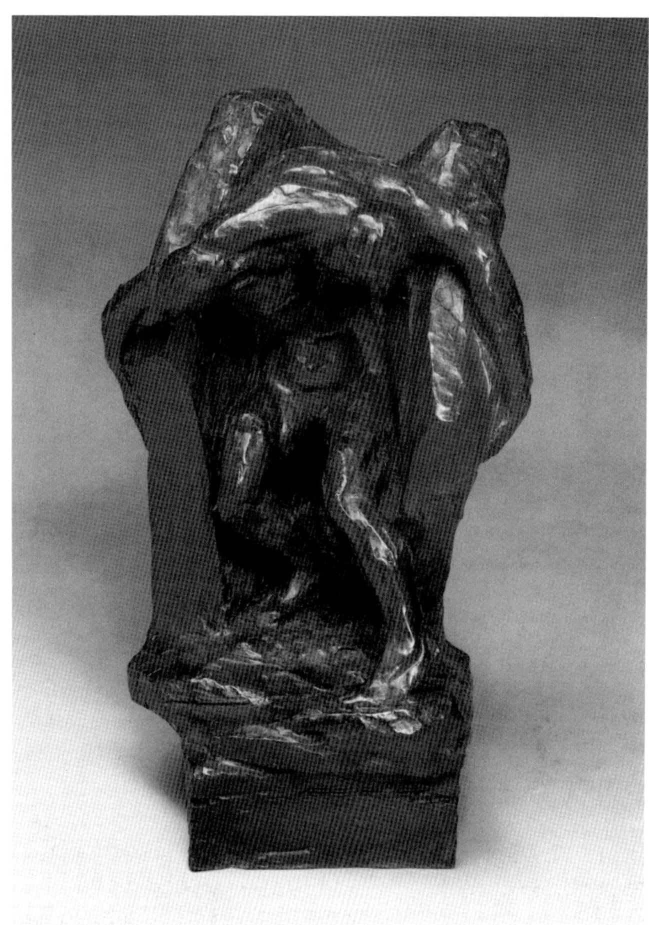

Grafly, *"E Pluribus Unum"*

Notes

1. The Meade Memorial is now in front of the U.S. District Court Building on Constitution Avenue between Third and Fourth streets NW, Washington, D.C.

2. Charles Grafly to Clyde Bathurst, stamped with the date June 12, 1916, Ablah Library, Wichita State University.

3. One example of the former plaster and two of the latter are at the Edwin A. Ulrich Museum of Art, Wichita State University.

4. Colonel Hart, U.S. Army, Secretary and Executive Officer of the Commission of Fine Arts, to Governor Martin G. Brumbaugh, Chairman, Meade Memorial Commission of the State of Pennsylvania, July 24, 1916, Ablah Library.

Reference

1974 Pamela H. Simpson, "The Sculpture of Charles Grafly," Ph.D. diss., University of Delaware, Newark, pp. 88, 89, cat. no. 193.

Exhibited

1929* cat. no. 440 (ill.). **1930** PAFA, *Memorial Exhibition of Work by Charles Grafly,* cat. no. 21. **1936** Temple University Art Galleries, Philadelphia, *Exhibition of Sculpture by Charles Grafly,* cat. no. 6. **1945** John Wanamaker department store, Philadelphia, *Portraits of Warriors.* **1955** PAFA, *150th Anniversary Exhibition,* cat. no. 192. **1965** Newman Galleries, Philadelphia, *Daniel Garber Paintings; Charles Grafly Sculpture.* **1986–87** PAFA, *Sculpture at the Pennsylvania Academy of the Fine Arts.*

Ex Collection

The artist's family, about 1929–57 (lent to the PAFA by Dorothy Grafly, 1941–57).

The Evangelist Felix

1919
Bronze with brown patina; lost-wax cast in 1919–20
23 x 11 x 10½" (58.4 x 27.9 x 26.7 cm)
Dated and signed on back: 1919 Grafly
Inscribed on back above signature: FELIX
Foundry mark on base at back: ROMAN BRONZE WORKS N[Y]
Gift of Dr. Charles H. Drummond, 1987.1.1

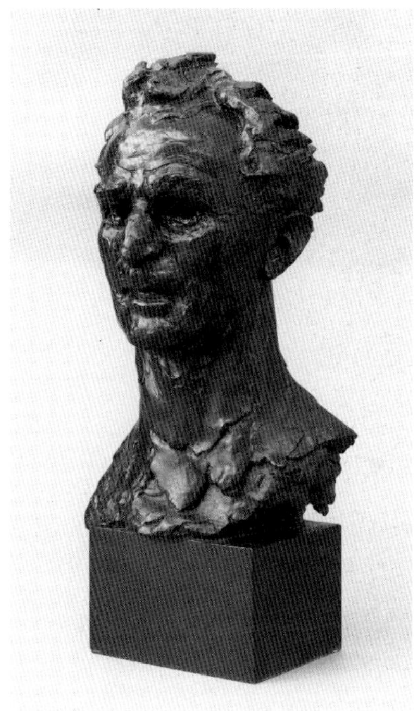

Grafly, *The Evangelist Felix*

FELIX POWELL was an evangelist whom Charles Grafly's daughter, Dorothy, met in Massachusetts in the summer of 1919 and introduced to her father. He had Felix pose for this "very sketchy head."[1] The rough modeling animates the features. It also shows Grafly's technique: he would leave the neck and shoulders until last and then smooth them, creating a suitable termination. Here he probably felt that the roughness of the neck was more appropriate to the treatment of the rest of the bust. As a base, he cast an integral square bronze box. An illustration of *The Evangelist Felix* in clay or plaster was published in the *Encyclopedia Britannica* to show the effect that a smile has on the other features of the face.[2] A plaster, painted white, is in the Edwin A. Ulrich Museum of Art, Wichita State University.

When shown at the annual exhibition of the Pennsylvania Academy of the Fine Arts in 1920, the bust attracted the attention of the painter and former Pennsylvania Academy student Yarnall Abbott, who saw "real strength and character" in it. To another critic, it was a "revealing study" that had "character and likeness and that misused word, soul."[3]

Notes

1. Charles Grafly to Elizabeth Wentworth Roberts, Concord Art Association, stamped with date Feb. 25, 1924, Ablah Library, Wichita State University.
2. *Encyclopedia Britannica,* 14th ed., s.v. "portrait sculpture," pl. 15, no. 1.
3. Yarnall Abbott, "Winners in Academy of Fine Arts Annual Exhibition; Comments on Art and Artists," *Philadelphia Press,* Feb. 15, 1920, and Harvey M. Watts, "Academy Opens Its 115th Annual," *Philadelphia Public Ledger,* Feb. 8, 1920, scrapbook, PAFA Archives.

References

1920 Yarnall Abbott, "Striking Canvases and Work of Sculptors at Academy's Annual Show; Comments on Art and Artists," *Philadelphia Press,* Feb. 8 (ill.), scrapbook, PAFA Archives. **1974** Pamela H. Simpson, "The Sculpture of Charles Grafly," Ph.D. diss., University of Delaware, Newark, cat. no. 190 (ill.).

Exhibited

1920* cat. no. 361 (ill.). **1924** Concord Art Association, Mass., *Eighth Annual Exhibition,* cat. no. 55. **1926** Philadelphia, *Sesquicentennial International Exposition,* cat. no. 1130. **1929** Library Hall, Wichita, under the direction of the Wichita Art Association, *Special Exhibition of Portrait Sculpture by Charles Grafly,* checklist no. 14. **1930** PAFA, *Memorial Exhibition of Work by Charles Grafly,* cat. no. 52. **1936** Temple University Art Galleries, Philadelphia, *Exhibition of Sculpture by Charles Grafly,* cat. no. 14. **1955** PAFA, *150th Anniversary Exhibition,* cat. no. 190.

Ex Collections

The artist, about 1920–29; his family, 1929–87 (lent to the PAFA by Dorothy Grafly, 1941–80; by Dr. Charles H. Drummond, 1980–87).

John E.D. Trask

About 1926
Bronze with brown patina; lost-wax cast by 1929
23¾ x 13½ x 12" (60.3 x 34.3 x 30.5 cm)
Signed on back: CHARLES GRAFLY
Foundry mark on back at bottom: ROMAN BRONZE WORK[S] N.Y.
Gift of Dr. Charles H. Drummond, 1987.1.3

JOHN ELLINGWOOD DONNELL TRASK (1871–1926) was active in the administration of the Pennsylvania Academy of the Fine Arts from 1897 to 1912. During much of that time, he was managing director; and he organized most of the exhibitions and wrote articles about American art. Trask served as U.S. commissioner for the International Fine Arts Exposition in Buenos Aires in 1910. He resigned from the Pennsylvania Academy in 1912 to become Director of Fine

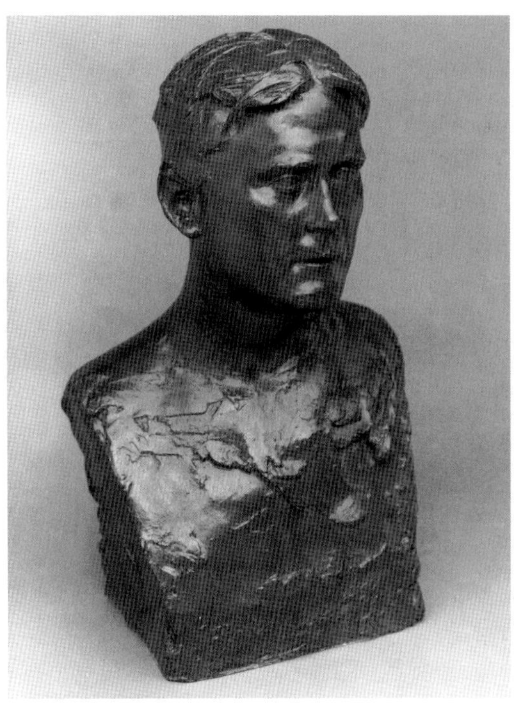

Grafly, *John E.D. Trask*

Arts at the Panama-Pacific International Exposition, in San Francisco. Trask had been a close friend of Charles Grafly for years. In fact, he served as Grafly's business manager from 1905 to 1912;[1] and, when he accepted the post at the exposition, Trask was able to help Grafly still further by securing for him the commission for the *Pioneer Mother Memorial.* In the 1920s, Trask opened a gallery of paintings and bronzes in New York. At his death, he was the art director of the upcoming Sesquicentennial International Exposition in Philadelphia.[2] It is not known when this bust was modeled, but Grafly may have been working on it at the time of Trask's death and never completed it. Both the plaster in the Edwin A. Ulrich Museum of Art, Wichita State University, and this bronze have mold lines at the sides, an unusual feature in Grafly's work. The sketchy representation of the sitter's chest forms a classical herm base such as was used on Grafly's early busts—for example, that of Joseph Price (q.v.)—and his 1925 portrait of Morris Gray.[3] The Trask bust also has a separate rectangular base of yellow marble with beveled edges.

Notes

1. Simpson 1974, p. 469.
2. "Pneumonia Victim, J.E.D. Trask Dies, Victim of his Zeal to Push Sesqui Art," *Philadelphia Public Ledger,* April 17, 1926, scrapbook, PAFA Archives.
3. For information on *Morris Gray,* see Kathryn Greenthal et al., *American Figurative Sculpture in the Museum of Fine Arts, Boston,* Boston: Museum of Finc Arts, pp. 290–92.

Reference

1974 Pamela H. Simpson, "The Sculpture of Charles Grafly," Ph.D. diss., University of Delaware, Newark, cat. no. 236 (ill.).

Exhibited

1929* cat. no. 604 (ill.). **1930** PAFA, *Memorial Exhibition of Work by Charles Grafly,* cat. no. 69. **1930** Brooklyn Museum, *Exhibition of Sculpture: Recent Work by Distinguished Sculptors,* cat. no. 155. **1936** Temple University Art Galleries, Philadelphia, *Exhibition of Sculpture by Charles Grafly,* cat. no. 17. **1965** Newman Galleries, Philadelphia, *Daniel Garber, Paintings; Charles Grafly Sculpture.*

Ex Collection

The artist's family, about 1929–87 (lent to the PAFA by Dorothy Grafly 1941–80; by Dr. Charles H. Drummond, 1980–87).

Charles R. Harley

1864–1930

Born in Philadelphia, Charles Richard Harley received his early training at the Spring Garden Institute and the Pennsylvania Academy of the Fine Arts. He attended the Pennsylvania Academy from 1888 to 1890 and again, supported by a scholarship, from 1892 to 1894.[1] His instructors included Thomas P. Anshutz, James P. Kelly, and CHARLES GRAFLY.

It is recorded that Harley received some instruction in New York from AUGUSTUS SAINT-GAUDENS and his studio assistant Philip Martiny (1858–1927).[2] This probably occurred after Harley's studies at the Pennsylvania Academy, sometime between 1895 and 1899. Most likely, this was also the period during which Harley went to Paris. He studied at the Ecole des Arts Décoratifs, the Académie Julian under Henri Michel Chapu (1833–1891), and the Ecole des Beaux-Arts under Jean Alexandre Joseph Falguière (1831–1900) and Jean Dampt (1853–1946).

By 1899 Harley was residing in Belmont, Massachusetts. That year, twelve of his sculptures provided the highlight of a fall exhibition at the Saint Botolph Club in Boston.[3] The critics reviewed his work favorably; and one wrote, "Mr. Harley manifests a capital vein of inventiveness and fancy."[4] Harley hoped that the exhibition would be installed at the Pennsylvania Academy, but scheduling precluded it.[5] Instead, two sculptures—*Our Mother of Sorrows* and *Pierrot at the Tribunal*—appeared in the Academy's annual exhibition in 1900. The two won him a bronze medal at the Pan-American Exposition, in Buffalo, the following year.[6] Harley also exhibited at the Pennsylvania Academy in 1894, 1901, 1912, and from 1916 to 1918. In addition to sculpture, he exhibited a few drawings and watercolors.

Between 1901 and 1917, Harley resided in New York.[7] In 1916 he and his artist sister, Jane Harley, began visiting the artist's colony in New Hope, Pennsylvania;[8] and two years later, Charles Harley settled there permanently.[9] In 1926, at the age of sixty-four, he married the photographer Agnes Williams Palmer.[10] She was a member of the Lenape Camera Club, an avant-garde women's photography club active in Bucks County about the turn of the century.

Notes

1. School registration card, PAFA Archives.
2. Mantle Fielding, *Dictionary of American Painters, Sculptors and Engravers* (New York: James F. Carr, 1965), p. 157.
3. Saint Botolph Club, Boston, *Exhibition of Sculptures by Charles R. Harley, and of Pictures by Several Boston Artists*, 1899, exhib. checklist, PAFA Archives.
4. "Mr. Harley's Sculptures at the St. Botolph Club," unknown Boston newspaper, Nov. 22, 1899, ibid.
5. Charles Harley to Harrison S. Morris, managing director of the PAFA, Dec. [4], 1899, and Morris to Harley, Dec. 7, 1899, ibid.
6. Lorado Taft, *The History of American Sculpture* (New York: Macmillan Company, 1903), p. 448.
7. Addresses listed in the PAFA's annual exhibition catalogues of 1901, 1912, 1916, and 1917.
8. Obituary, *Doylestown [Pa.] Daily Intelligencer*, Jan. 27, 1930, p. 1.
9. Address in the PAFA's annual exhibition catalogue, 1918.
10. Obituary, *Doylestown Daily Intelligencer.*

Memorial to James Philip Kelly

1894
Bronze with brown patina; sand cast
36½ x 24¾ x 3½" (93 x 63 x 9 cm)
Signed and dated at lower right: C.R. Harley '94
Inscribed at center top in arc: IN MEMORIAM; at upper left: ANNO/DNI MDCCCLIV·; at upper right: MDCCCXCIII·; on banner held by figure: JAMES PHILIP KELLY; at center left: BORN IN PHILADELPHIA PENN/SYLVANIA—DIED AT LVZE/RNE SWITZERLAND—/INSTRVCTOR AT THE PENN/SYLVANIA ACADEMY of THE/FINE ARTS FROM MDCCCLX/XXVI TO MDCCCXCIII—; at center right, a poem (see below); across bottom: THIS TABLET ERECTED BY HIS PVPILS AND FRIENDS/TO COMMEMORATE A HELPFVL LIFE·
Foundry mark stamped twice in arc at lower left edge: BUREAU BRO/P[H]ILA.
Gift of the pupils and friends of James Philip Kelly, 1895.3

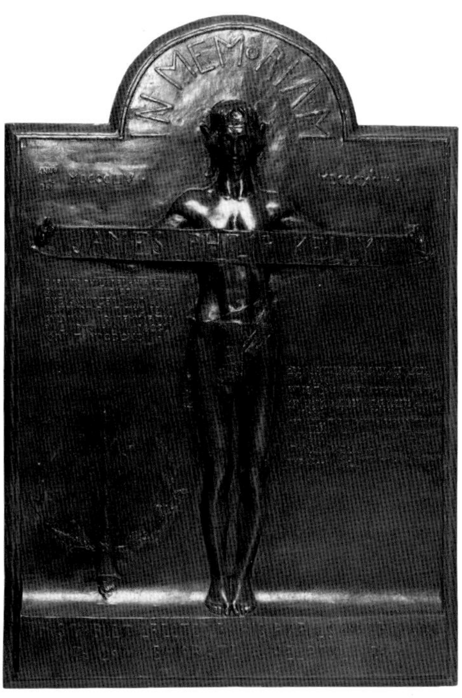

Harley, *Memorial to James Philip Kelly*

ON FEBRUARY 6, 1894, Charles R. Harley and two other students at the Pennsylvania Academy of the Fine Arts wrote to the managing director, Harrison S. Morris, on behalf of a group of students who wished to place on one of the walls of the school a memorial tablet honoring the late instructor James P. Kelly (1854–1893).[1]

A Philadelphia-born artist, Kelly had taught at the Pennsylvania Academy from 1886 to 1892; but his association with the Academy began much earlier, during the 1870s. Having been THOMAS EAKINS's student at the Philadelphia Sketch Club from 1874 to 1876, Kelly enrolled at the Pennsylvania Academy under Eakins in 1876 and took classes from 1879 to 1882.[2] In 1880, when Eakins was promoted to the position of professor of painting and drawing following the death of Christian Schussele, Kelly took over Eakins's role as chief demonstrator of dissection.[3] He later became one of the opponents of Eakins's dogmatic teaching methods and was among those who supported the complaints of some of the women students that Eakins lacked decorum in the life class.[4] After Eakins resigned in 1886, Kelly was engaged as instructor in painting and drawing. Modeling was added to his duties the following year, and he continued teaching these three subjects until 1892. Then he and Thomas P. Anshutz resigned their teaching posts at the Pennsylvania Academy in order to study in Paris.[5] Anshutz returned a year later to teach at the Academy; but Kelly died of rheumatic fever in Lucerne, Switzerland, in May of 1893.[6]

The idea for a memorial tablet honoring Kelly was well received by the Academy and the proceeds from an Academy auction of student caricatures of well-known American paintings was used for the purpose.[7] A competition among the students was then held for its design, and a jury composed of Wilson Eyre, John Stewardson, Henry Thouron, and CHARLES GRAFLY, selected Charles Harley's entry as the winner. His composition displays a standing male figure whose outstretched arms hold a banner inscribed with Kelly's full name. A poem, written in late Victorian style and most likely by Harley or another student, appears to the right of the figure:

> He had a sounding, swelling, prelude played
> Then broad'ning life sat smiling at the Helm,
> But death—as mothers bid their bairns from Play
> Her soothing finger on the harper laid;
> Calling him hence—so closed the helpful Day;
> Yet still the lingering echoes with us Bide
> As sweet vibrating bells their rhythm Hold
> Though o'er the hill, with silver Streaked sky
> The bellman's hand is on his lowly Gate.

Harley's design was cast in bronze and shown in the Pennsylvania Academy's annual exhibition in 1894–95. Following the exhibition, it was installed in one of the rooms in which life classes were held.

Notes

1. Charles Harley et al. to Harrison S. Morris, Feb. 6, 1894 (incorrectly dated 1893), PAFA Archives.
2. Student registration card, ibid.
3. Report of Dr. William W. Keen, May 10, 1879, ibid.
4. Lloyd Goodrich, *Thomas Eakins* (Cambridge: Harvard University Press, 1982), vol. 1, p. 285; also James Philip Kelly et al. to Pennsylvania Academy's board of directors, May 12, 1886, PAFA Archives.
5. Miscellaneous newspaper clippings in scrapbook, 1877–92, ibid.
6. Obituary, *Philadelphia Record,* May 24, 1893, p. 5.
7. "Students' Caricature Exhibition," *Philadelphia Ledger,* March 8, 1894, Thomas Hovenden Papers, microfilm, roll no. P13, frame no. 246, Archives of American Art, Smithsonian Institution, Washington, D.C. Curator Sylvia Yount brought this to our attention.

Exhibited

1894–95* cat. no. 250. **1994–95** PAFA, *Two Centuries of Collecting at the Museum of American Art.*

EDMUND STEWARDSON

1865–1892

Edmund Austin Stewardson was born in Philadelphia in 1865 into a socially prominent Quaker family. His father, Thomas Stewardson II, an attorney, and his mother, Margaret Haines Stewardson, inspired their children to artistic pursuits through their own fondness for art. Two sons, John and Emlyn, became renowned Philadelphia architects; and Edmund set out to be an artist in 1882, when he entered the Pennsylvania Academy of the Fine Arts to study under THOMAS EAKINS. He continued at the Academy until the spring of 1885.[1]

Following in the footsteps of Eakins, who had studied in Paris some twenty-one years earlier, Stewardson went there in 1887. Upon arriving, he immediately began studies under Henri Michel Chapu (1833–1891) at the Académie Julian. Among his fellow students, Stewardson quickly gained a reputation for knowledge of anatomy and dexterity in rendering musculature in clay.[2] Undoubtedly, this expertise was traceable to Eakins's tutelage at the Pennsylvania Academy. It helped Stewardson place first among seventy-two competitors for admission to the Ecole des Beaux-Arts.

Even after entering the Ecole, Stewardson continued to attend evening classes at the Académie Julian. During this time, he executed a grave stele that was selected by a jury comprised of Adolphe Bouguereau, Tony Robert-Fleury, Jules Joseph Lefebvre, and Gustave Boulanger to be preserved in the Académie Julian. Impressed by Stewardson's progress, Chapu asked him to become his assistant. It was in Chapu's private studio that Stewardson probably developed his skill in marble carving. He assisted Chapu on two major tombs, the Monument of Gustave Flaubert in Paris and the Monument of Cardinal de Bonnechose in Rouen. For the Universelle Exposition of 1889, Stewardson and his fellow Philadelphian CHARLES GRAFLY helped Chapu sculpt *Steam* (presumably destroyed), a large group of figures in plaster. At the Paris Salon of 1890, Stewardson received an honorable mention for *The Bather* (q.v.). When it was shown in the annual exhibition of the Society of American Artists in New York the following year, this sculpture earned him membership in the society.

Stewardson returned to Philadelphia in 1890 and set up a studio at 204 South Juniper Street, where he worked on a number of medallions and busts. By 1892 he had achieved sufficient recognition to be awarded desirable teaching positions at the University of Pennsylvania and the Pennsylvania Academy of the Fine Arts. Unfortunately, he died before he was able to begin either assignment.[3] The front page of the *Philadelphia Inquirer* of July 5, 1892, reported the tragic death of Stewardson and his friend W. Wharton Smith in a sailing accident off Newport, Rhode Island. Thomas Stewardson endowed a sculpture prize at the Pennsylvania Academy in memory of his son. The prize, like many that were given by

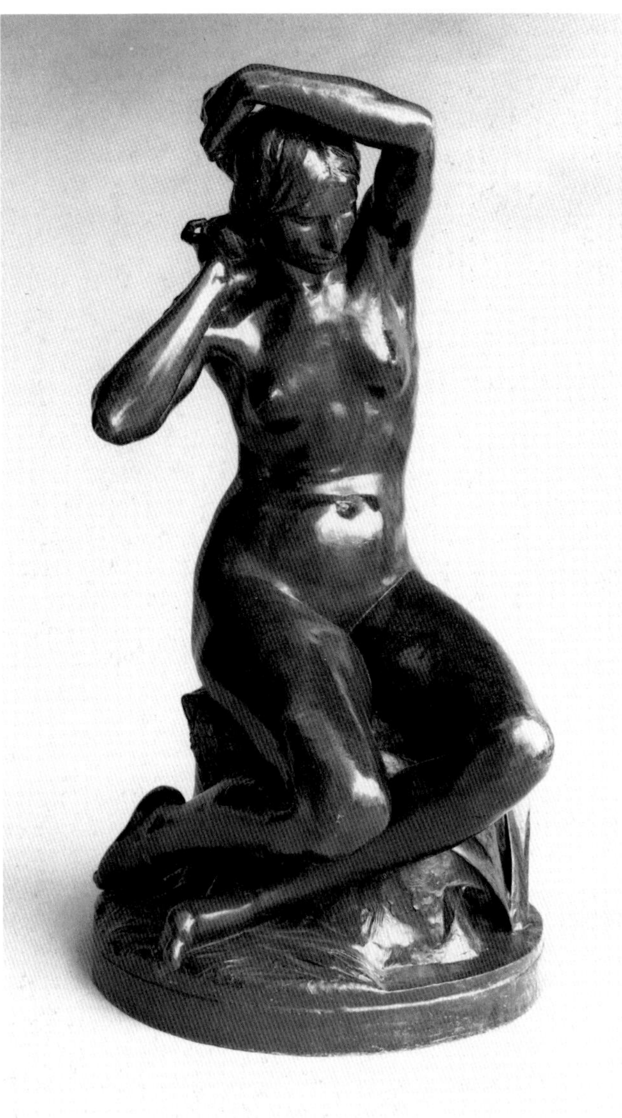

Stewardson, *The Bather*

the Ecole des Beaux-Arts, was originally awarded for the best full-length figure in relief or in the round, taken from life or the antique, and made within eighteen hours. It is still awarded annually by the Academy, although in 1922 the rules were changed and now specify that the work must be in the round and done from life.

Notes

1. Student Card and Student List, 1884–94, PAFA Archives.
2. *Stewardson* 1893, p. 24.
3. After considering available replacements for Stewardson, including JOHN JOSEPH BOYLE and Albert E. Harnisch (1843-after 1886), the board of directors of the Pennsylvania Academy appointed Charles Grafly to fill the vacancy.

References

1893 *Edmund Stewardson,* Philadelphia: privately printed, a memorial volume published by the artist's father.
1976 Libby W. Seaberg, "Edmund Stewardson," in *200 Years of American Sculpture,* exhib. cat., New York: David R. Godine in association with the Whitney Museum of American Art, pp. 312–13.

The Bather

1889–90
Bronze with brown patina; cast in 1895
48 x 25 x 25" (122 x 63.5 x 63.5 cm)
Signed and dated on back of base: Stewardson 1890; and signed faintly on front of base: EDMUND STEWARDSON
Sand cast by Motz, Paris
Gift of Thomas Stewardson, 1895.6

THOUGH TRAINED at the Ecole des Beaux-Arts in Paris, Edmund Stewardson never fully assimilated its lively modeling style. The few finished sculptures that he produced in his abbreviated lifetime are more akin to sculpture of the mid-nineteenth century. Stewardson wrote to his father on October 14, 1889, that he did not care for the "violent action suddenly frozen stiff" that he found in French works and preferred the "concentrated quiet" of Donatello.[1]

"Concentrated quiet" appropriately describes *The Bather.* Modeled in 1889 and 1890, it was the last sculpture that he executed under the eye of Henri Michel Chapu (1833–1891). The simple but charming depiction of a seated nude twisting her wet hair into a bun is free of symbolism. Stewardson received an honorable mention for the plaster model at the Paris Salon of 1890. In 1891, while *The Bather* was in the sixty-first annual exhibition of the Pennsylvania Academy of the Fine Arts, Edward H. Coates, the president of the Academy, wrote to Stewardson of the institution's desire to purchase it. Stewardson declined to sell because he hoped to translate the piece into marble, as Chapu had advised.[2]

In 1893, after Stewardson's death, his father gave the Pennsylvania Academy a plaster cast of *The Bather* (now lost). He retained the original plaster model in order to have it replicated in a more permanent material. Controversy raged among prominent artists over the suitability of bronze over marble, with THOMAS EAKINS advocating bronze for its fidelity to the original and AUGUSTUS SAINT-GAUDENS advising marble as closer to the artist's conception and ultimate intention. Thomas Stewardson finally sent the plaster to Paris in 1894, probably consigned to the care of the American sculptor Frederick MacMonnies (1863–1937), to have it cut in marble by Agathon Leonard (1841–1923), a sculptor of merit who had achieved recognition in the Paris Salons.[3] Following the completion of the marble, which had been accepted by the Metropolitan Museum of Art, in New York (where it remains today), Thomas Stewardson asked Edward Coates whether the Pennsylvania Academy wanted a bronze version. After receiving an affirmative reply, he had this bronze cast made in Paris by a Mr. Motz.[4]

Notes

1. *Edmund Stewardson* (Philadelphia: privately printed, 1893), pp. 45–46.
2. Edmund Stewardson to Edward H. Coates, undated [1891], PAFA Archives.
3. *Stewardson* 1893, pp. 8, 11, 15.
4. Thomas Stewardson to E.H. Coates, Feb. 25, 1895, PAFA Archives.

Reference

1977 Maurice Rheims, *19th Century Sculpture,* New York: Harry N. Abrams, p. [179], ill., cited erroneously on p. 168 as the marble version in the Metropolitan Museum of Art.

Exhibited

1904 *Louisiana Purchase Universal Exposition,* Saint Louis, cat. no. 2260. **1953** Philadelphia Art Alliance, *19th Century Philadelphia Architecture.* **1975** William Penn Memorial Museum, Harrisburg, exhibition of works of art from the PAFA. **1976** Whitney Museum of American Art, New York, *200 Years of American Sculpture,* cat. p. 73, fig. 118. **1978–79** PAFA, *350 Masterpieces of American Art.* **1986–87** PAFA, *Sculpture at the Pennsylvania Academy of the Fine Arts.* **1988** PAFA, *Sea and Shore.* **1994–96** PAFA, *Two Centuries of Collecting at the Museum of American Art.*

ATTRIBUTED TO EDMUND STEWARDSON

Study for "The Bather"

About 1889
Plaster, painted beige
16 x 8½ x 8¾" (40.6 x 21.6 x 22.2 cm)
Charles Bregler's Thomas Eakins Collection, purchased with the partial support of the Pew Memorial Trust, 1985.68.1.18

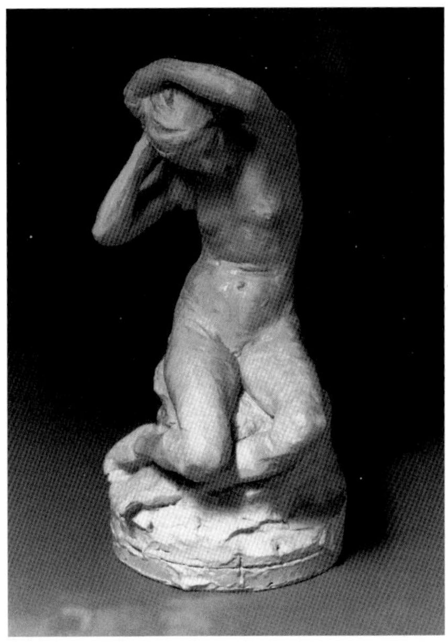

Attributed to Stewardson, *Study for "The Bather"*

THIS STUDY came to the Pennsylvania Academy of the Fine Arts in the collection of CHARLES BREGLER, an Academy student and loyal follower of THOMAS EAKINS. At first, it was thought to be a student work by Bregler, who would have had ample opportunity to copy Edmund Stewardson's plaster model, which for many years stood amid the Pennsylvania Academy's antique-cast collection. Now, however, the study is believed to be the original maquette for *The Bather* and possibly one of the "sketches" to which Stewardson referred in a letter to his father on July 16, 1889. Of two sketches that he liked best, one was a figure "sitting on the ground, brushing or doing something or other with her hair, the arms well up."[1] In this study, it is impossible to determine what the model is doing with her hair; but, in the final version, she is clearly twisting it into a bun. Here the model's hair hangs in front of her right shoulder rather than behind the shoulder, as it does in the final version. This suggests that the piece is a working model by Stewardson rather than a copy by Bregler after Stewardson's finished piece.

Bregler probably acquired this sculpture shortly after Stewardson's death. A photograph of about 1895 of Charles Bregler in his studio shows the maquette on the mantlepiece.[2] Although there is no evidence that Bregler and Stewardson were friends, they both studied under Eakins; and Bregler probably admired Stewardson's work, which was highly regarded by Eakins.

Notes

1. *Edmund Stewardson* (Philadelphia: privately printed, 1893), p. 45.
2. Photograph, PAFA Archives.

Reference

1997 Kathleen A. Foster, *Thomas Eakins Rediscovered,* New Haven, Conn.: Yale University Press.

Exhibited

1986–87 PAFA, *Sculpture at the Pennsylvania Academy of the Fine Arts.*

Ex Collections
Charles Bregler, Philadelphia, about 1892–1958; his second wife, Mary Picozzi Bregler, 1958–85.

Caroline Sidney Sinkler

1891
Bronze with black patina; cast about 1893
23 x 11¾ x 9½" (58.5 x 29.8 x 24.2 cm)
Signed around a vertical edge of integral base: EDMUND AUSTIN STEWARDSON [MD]CCCXCI
Sand cast, probably by Bureau Brothers, Philadelphia
Gift of Thomas Stewardson, 1893.4

FOR MANY YEARS, this bust was simply called *Portrait of a Lady.* In 1985, the identity of the sitter was discovered when a plaster version came to light in a private collection. The sitter, Caroline Sidney Sinkler (1860–1949), was thirty-one-years old in 1891, when Edmund Stewardson modeled her portrait. She was a woman of high society, the daughter of Charles Sinkler, and a descendant of a long line of prominent South Carolinians. The Sinkler family had settled in Philadelphia before the turn of the century.[1]

Stewardson's sculpture captures Caroline Sinkler in a graceful pose with her face tilted slightly upward and her hair in a French twist with tendrils escaping at the forehead and at the nape of the neck. Her air of sophistication is enhanced by the elegant neckline of her dress.

It was probably after this bust was modeled that Caroline Sinkler became engaged to John Stewardson.[2] John was Edmund's older brother and a partner in the Philadelphia architectural firm of Cope and Stewardson, which was noted for introducing the Collegiate Gothic style of architecture.[3] The couple never married; in 1896 John Stewardson, like Edmund four years earlier, drowned in a tragic accident. He fell through the ice while skating on the Schuylkill River.[4]

In her mature years, Caroline Sinkler became a great patron of the arts. She was awarded a gold medal by the Historical Society of Pennsylvania for the restoration of the Highlands, her Georgian manor in Montgomery County.[5]

Notes

1. Obituary, *Philadelphia Evening Bulletin,* May 6, 1949, clipping file, Department of Social Science and History, Free Library of Philadelphia.
2. Newspaper clipping, scrapbook, private collection.
3. Jean Barth Toll and Michael J. Schwager, eds., *Montgomery County: The Second Hundred Years* (Norristown, Pa.: Montgomery County Federation of Historical Societies, 1983), vol. 2, p. 1442.
4. "A Skater Drowned," *Philadelphia Inquirer,* Jan. 7, 1896, p. 1.
5. Toll and Schwager 1983, vol. 1, p. 804.

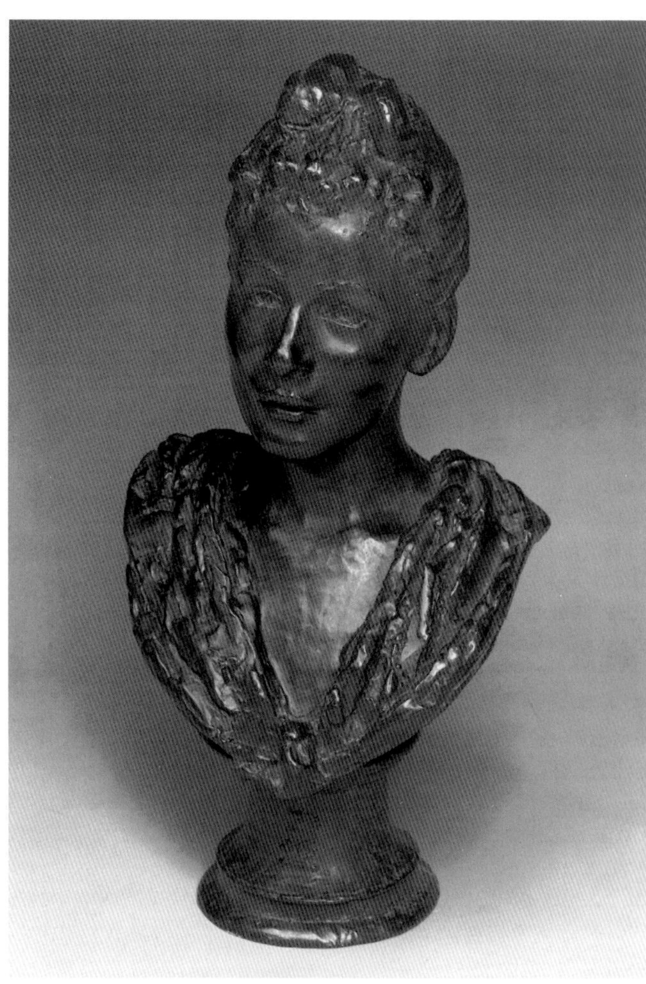

Stewardson, *Caroline Sidney Sinkler*

Exhibited
1915 San Francisco, *Panama-Pacific International Exposition,* cat. no. 2837, as *Portrait of a Lady.* **1953** Philadelphia Art Alliance, *19th Century Philadelphia Architecture.* **1962** PAFA, *Forgotten Favorites, Selections from the Permanent Collection,* as *Unknown Lady.* **1975** William Penn Memorial Museum, Harrisburg, exhibition of works of art from the PAFA. **1986–87** PAFA, *Sculpture at the Pennsylvania Academy of the Fine Arts.*

Charles Bregler

1865–1958

Charles Bregler was born into a German immigrant family in Philadelphia. His father, Wilhelm, a Civil War veteran, died when Charles was three. Forced to go to work at the age of twelve after the death of his mother, he learned to make fancy leather goods. He won a scholarship to the Franklin Institute, where he took evening drawing classes for a short time. Then, in 1883, Bregler enrolled at the Pennsylvania Academy of the Fine Arts and quickly advanced from the study of antique casts to life classes. He signed the futile student petition of 1886 that urged the directors of the Academy to ask THOMAS EAKINS to withdraw his resignation. Bregler followed Eakins to the Art Students' League of Philadelphia and continued to study with him.

In 1894, shortly after the demise of the league, Bregler returned to the Pennsylvania Academy, where he remained through the fall of 1895. He exhibited there in 1892, 1896–97, 1898, 1903, and 1934. He also exhibited in the World's Columbian Exposition, in Chicago in 1893. Interested primarily in landscape painting, he claimed in 1931 to have hundreds of pastel studies of the evening sky, some of which were shown in exhibitions of the Art Club of Philadelphia and in New York galleries. Bregler also painted portraits and made a few sculptures.

In a letter of 1931, he wrote, "To me the ultimate function of art is the bringing of joy and happiness into the lives of others."[1] To him "modern art," by which he meant abstract art, was "terrible stuff" that would pass into oblivion.[2]

Bregler is primarily remembered as the unofficial curator of the paintings that Thomas Eakins left to his wife, Susan. Although untrained as a restorer, Bregler was a careful craftsman who even succeeded in separating paintings on both sides of single wooden panels.[3] Devoted to the memory of Eakins, he published a two-part article, "Thomas Eakins as a Teacher," in *Arts* magazine.[4] It was based on notes that Bregler had taken during his formal training with the master. During Bregler's last years, he was writing a book on Eakins; but it was never published, and the manuscript today is unlocated.[5]

Notes

1. Charles Bregler to Samuel Murray, postmarked (month illegible) 24, 1931, Eakins-Murray letter file, Hirshhorn Museum and Sculpture Garden, Smithsonian Institution, Washington, D.C.
2. Quoted in "Samuel Murray Dies," *Art Digest* 16 (Jan. 1, 1942), p. 12.
3. Lloyd Goodrich, *Thomas Eakins* (Cambridge, Mass.: Harvard University Press for the National Gallery of Art, 1982), vol. 2, p. 283.
4. *Arts* 17 (March 1931), pp. 378–86; and 18 (Oct. 1931), pp. 28–42.
5. George Barker to Charles Bregler, July 30, 1944, PAFA Archives: "With all good wishes and congratulations on you[r] efforts to write a better book on Eakins."

References
1989 Kathleen A. Foster and Cheryl Leibold, *Writing about Eakins: A Guide to the Manuscripts in Charles Bregler's Thomas Eakins Collection,* Philadelphia: University of Pennsylvania Press, pp. 317–24, 337. **1997** Kathleen A. Foster, *Thomas Eakins Rediscovered,* New Haven, Conn.: Yale University Press.

Life Cast of Grandma's Face

1890
Plaster
8½ x 6 x 4½" (21.6 x 15.2 x 11.4 cm)
Inscribed on back: 6/29/90; and faintly: 6/29/8
Charles Bregler's Thomas Eakins Collection, purchased with the partial support of the Pew Memorial Trust, 1985.68.1.16

THE LIFE MASK is probably of Charles Bregler's paternal grandmother. It was made in conjunction with a painted portrait that Thomas Eakins saw and praised.[1]

The making of life casts was fairly common among portraitists working in a realistic mode at the turn of the century, especially among the sculptors and painters in Eakins's circle. Using casts as models

Bregler, *Life Cast of Grandma's Face*

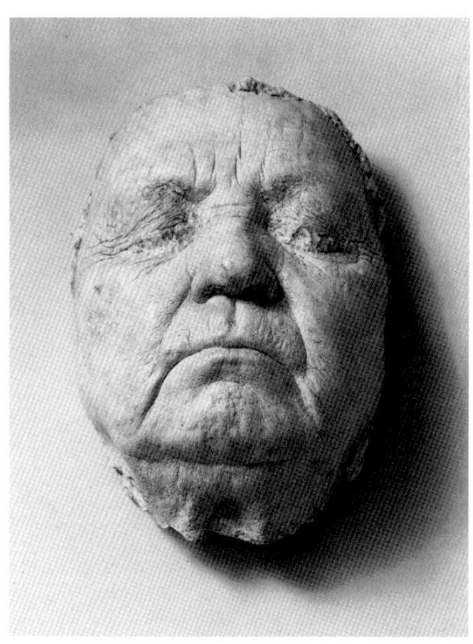

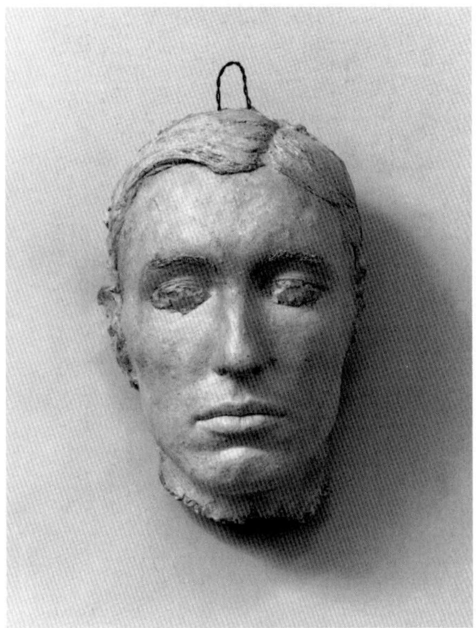

Bregler, *Life Cast of Young Man's Head*

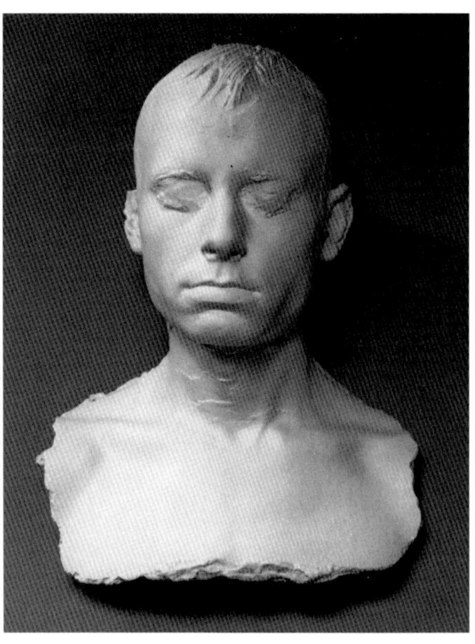

Bregler, *Life Cast of Young Man's Head and Torso*

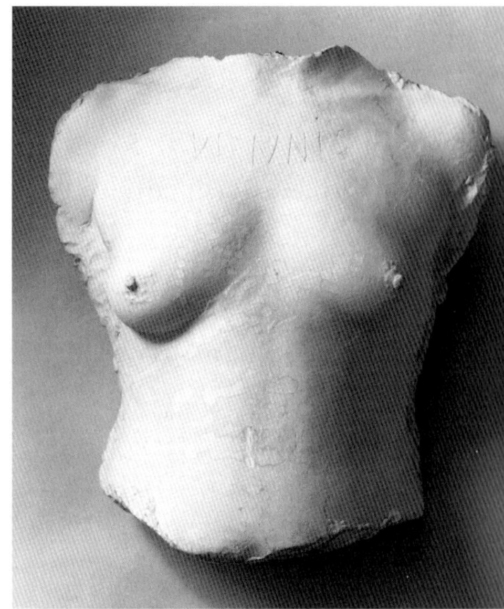

Bregler, *Life Cast of Young Woman's Torso*

greatly reduced the number of long, tiring sittings required of the subject. Photographs were also employed, but casts had the advantage of capturing the likeness in relief and full size.

Note

1. "Charles Bregler," *Arts* 17 (March 1931), p. 377, records Eakins's comments. The painting is in the Museum of American Art of the Pennsylvania Academy of the Fine Arts. It was lent to the World's Columbian Exposition, in Chicago in 1893, by Mrs. William Bregler, who presumably was the sitter.

Ex Collections

The artist, Philadelphia, 1890–1958; his second wife, Mary Picozzi Bregler, 1958–85.

Life Cast of Young Man's Head

1890
Plaster
10 x 6¾ x 5¼" (25.4 x 17.1 x 13.3 cm)
Inscribed on back: JULY 13TH/1890
Charles Bregler's Thomas Eakins Collection, purchased with the partial support of the Pew Memorial Trust, 1985.68.1.19

Ex Collections

The artist, Philadelphia, 1890–1958; his second wife, Mary Picozzi Bregler, 1958–85.

Life Cast of Young Man's Head and Torso

1890
Plaster, painted beige
16 x 12 x 6¾" (40.6 x 30.5 x 17.1 cm)
Inscribed on back: JULY 19TH/1890
Charles Bregler's Thomas Eakins Collection, purchased with the partial support of the Pew Memorial Trust, 1985.68.1.20

Ex Collections

The artist, Philadelphia, 1890–1958; his second wife, Mary Picozzi Bregler, 1958–85.

Life Cast of Young Woman's Torso

About 1890
Plaster, painted pink
16½ x 14¼ x 6¾" (41.9 x 36.2 x 17.1 cm)
Inscribed over sternum: DENNIS
Charles Bregler's Thomas Eakins Collection, purchased with the partial support of the Pew Memorial Trust, 1985.68.1.17

THIS LIFE CAST may date from about 1890, when Charles Bregler was attending the Art Students' League of Philadelphia and was known to be casting from life. The purpose of the cast is unknown, as is significance of the name inscribed over the breastbone.

Ex Collections
The artist, Philadelphia, about 1890–1958; his second wife, Mary Picozzi Bregler, 1958–85.

Elizabeth

About 1935
Plaster
7 x 5⅜ x 4″ (17.8 x 13.7 x 10.2 cm)
Signed on back of plinth: Bregler
Inscribed on front of plinth: ELIZABETH
Charles Bregler's Thomas Eakins Collection, purchased with the partial support of the Pew Memorial Trust, 1985.68.1.13

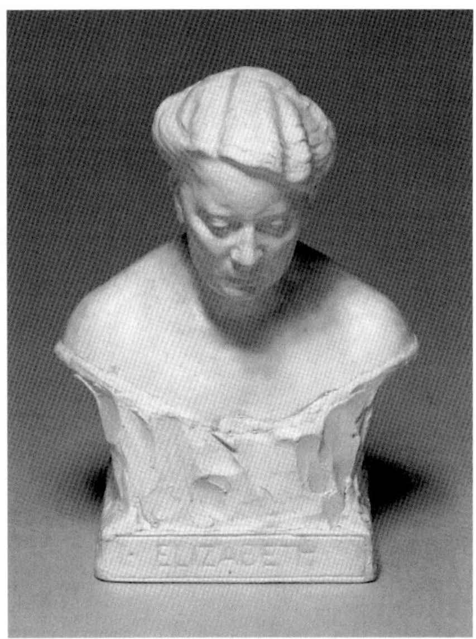

Bregler, *Elizabeth*

THIS BUST of Charles Bregler's first wife, Lizzie Yohn (1871–1944), demonstrates the artist's ability not only to capture a likeness but also to evoke personality. The slightly bowed head and downcast eyes betray the unenthusiastic attitude of a model who apparently did not enjoy posing. Unfortunately, the rough base detracts from the detail and fine finish of the portrait. There are three other plaster casts of this sculpture: two at the Museum of American Art of the Pennsylvania Academy of the Fine Arts and one in a private collection in Sellersville, Pennsylvania.

Charles Bregler and Elizabeth Yohn married in 1899. She was in ill health for her last twenty years. The bust may have been done posthumously as a memorial. He also portrayed her in pastels (location unknown) and in three oils (Museum of American Art of the Pennsylvania Academy of the Fine Arts).

Ex Collections
The artist, Philadelphia, about 1935–58; his second wife, Mary Picozzi Bregler, 1958–85.

Life Cast of Mary Bregler's Right Hand

1951
Plaster
9½ x 6½ x 2½″ (24.1 x 16.5 x 6.4 cm)
Inscribed and dated on back: HAND/of/MARY.L/JULY 23/1951
Charles Bregler's Thomas Eakins Collection, purchased with the partial support of the Pew Memorial Trust, 1985.68.1.15

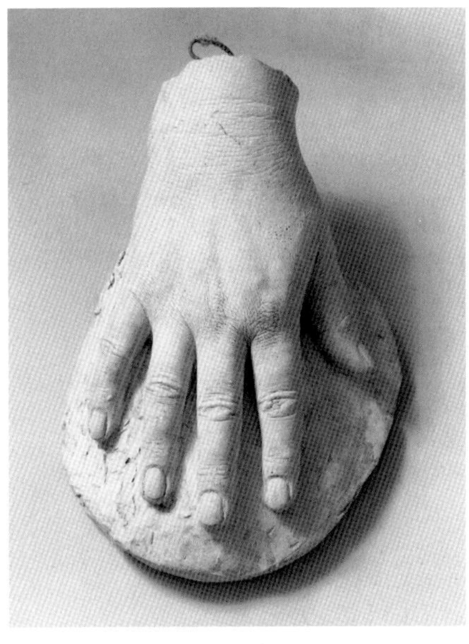

Bregler, *Life Cast of Mary Bregler's Right Hand*

PERHAPS Charles Bregler made this plaster cast at the same time that he photographed his second wife (1914–1987) and painted her portrait (Museum of American Art of the Pennsylvania Academy of the Fine Arts). The method of casting was first to grease the hand or dust it with some substance that would allow easy separation of the plaster from the skin. Then wet plaster was poured over the hand. When dry, the plaster mold was cut in half and removed. Often the inner surface was pigmented. The mold was reassembled with a wire armature inside, and plaster was poured into the mold so that it covered the armature and filled the mold. Once this was dry, the mold was chipped away. When the pigmented layer was reached, the sculptor knew that he must proceed slowly to avoid damaging the cast. Because plaster dries through crystallization, there is no shrinkage. Thus the life cast is an accurate reproduction.

Ex Collections
The artist, Philadelphia, 1951–58; his second wife, Mary Picozzi Bregler, 1958–85.

Walt Whitman

1953
Plaster, painted white
11¾ x 8½ x 6" (29.8 x 21.6 x 15.2 cm)
Dated and signed on back: Copyright/1953/by/ Chas Bregler
Inscribed on front: WALT WHITMAN
Charles Bregler's Thomas Eakins Collection, purchased with the partial support of the Pew Memorial Trust, 1985.68.1.14

CHARLES BREGLER'S reason for making a bust of Walt Whitman (1819–1892) sixty-one years after the poet's death, copyrighting it, and producing multiple plaster casts is unknown.[1] Perhaps he was inspired by another piece in his collection: the bust of Whitman (q.v.) by SAMUEL MURRAY.

There are certain parallels between the two sculptures—the roughly modeled beard, the indistinct eyelids and pupils, and the subject's name carved on an integral pedestal—but Bregler's portrait falls short as a realistic likeness and character study. Although some sense of the intellect of the "good gray poet" is conveyed by the prominent forehead and kindly eyes, the beard appears to be a solid mass plastered to the chest. Furthermore, the torso is not well formed and terminates crudely in the broad base. Other casts of this bust that Bregler painted in green or brown may have been intended to simulate bronze.[2]

Bregler, *Walt Whitman*

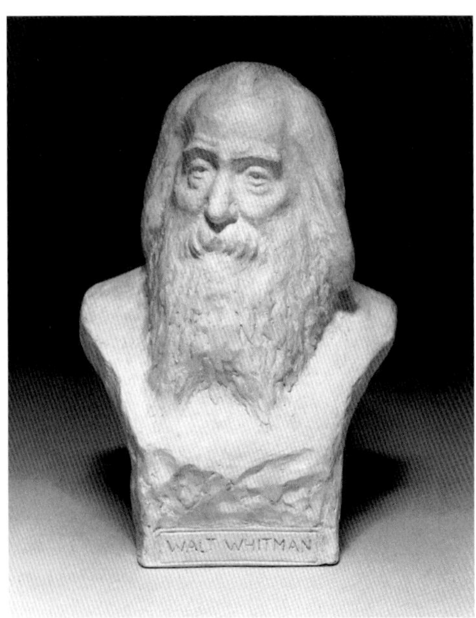

Notes

1. Copyright license GU 21204, dated April 9, 1953, is on file in the Copyright Office, Library of Congress, Washington, D.C.
2. Three other plaster casts are at the Museum of American Art of the Pennsylvania Academy of the Fine Arts.

Ex Collections
The artist, Philadelphia, 1953–58; his second wife, Mary Picozzi Bregler, 1958–85.

PAUL WAYLAND BARTLETT

1865–1925

As a young man, Paul Wayland Bartlett produced some truly modern-looking sculpture even though he eventually became a vociferous opponent of abstraction in art.[1] His experiments during the early 1890s in bronze casting by the lost-wax method and in the use of chemical patinas were quite revolutionary. In fact, his interest in every stage of the creation of a bronze anticipated the modernist emphasis on the artist's intimate interaction with his work from start to finish.

Born in New Haven, Connecticut, Paul was the son of the sculptor and critic Truman Howe Bartlett (1835–1923). When, in his mid-thirties, the elder Bartlett decided to pursue a career in sculpture, he moved his family to Paris. Thus Paul's early years were oriented around the Parisian art world, and he remained in Paris for most of his life. In his later years, however, he traveled frequently to the United States to complete commissions.

At the age of twelve, Bartlett modeled a bust of his grandmother that was exhibited at the Paris Salon in 1880. He studied at the Petite Ecole of the Ecole des Beaux-Arts under Pierre Jules Cavelier (1814–1894). It was not Cavelier, however, but Emmanuel Frémiet (1824–1910) who had a lasting influence on Bartlett and whom Bartlett called his teacher.[2] As a teenager, Bartlett attended Frémiet's animal modeling classes at the Jardins des Plantes and quickly became so proficient that he was hired as an assistant by the animal sculptor Joseph Antoine Gardet (1861–1891).[3]

At the Salon of 1887, Bartlett was awarded an honorable mention for his newly completed plaster *Bohemian Bear Tamer.* A bronze version of this piece is now in the Metropolitan Museum of Art, in New York. At the World's Columbian Exposition, in Chicago in 1893, Bartlett again exhibited *Bohemian Bear Tamer* along with a plaster of a native American titled *Ghost Dancer. Ghost Dancer* was exhibited the same year at the sixty-third annual exhibition of the Pennsylvania Academy of the Fine Arts.[4] Such themes were gaining popularity in the 1890s, and Bartlett may have been drawn to them for their distinctively American flavor. Bartlett's work had been previously shown twice at the Pennsylvania Academy: a small group of animal sculptures in 1882 and a bronze reduction of *Bohemian Bear Tamer* a decade later. He continued to participate in the Academy's annual exhibitions from 1896 to 1899 and in 1905, 1909, and 1913. Furthermore, he was a member of the jury of selection for sculpture for the annual exhibitions of 1900, 1906, 1913, 1916, and 1917.

Bartlett built a small foundry in his studio and was casting his own small works by 1892. He kept systematic notes on his techniques for lost-wax casting and his experiments with chemical patinas.[5] In the decorative-arts section of the 1895 Paris Salon, he exhibited a group of small bronzes depicting animals, fish, beetles, and crustaceans that he had cast and patinated himself. The group attracted a great deal of attention, especially from other artists who marveled at the array of colors in his patinas.

In 1898 Bartlett won a commission for two of the sixteen heroic bronze figures that adorn the upper story of the Rotunda in the Library of Congress. His figures of Christopher Columbus and Michelangelo established him as one of the foremost American sculptors of his day and provided the path to even grander commissions. His next major commission, an equestrian figure of the marquis de Lafayette, was a gift to France in return for the Statue of Liberty and was paid for by donations from American school children. It was installed in the courtyard of the Musée du Louvre, in Paris, in 1908. Two other major projects occupied Bartlett's attention during the years prior to World War I. The first, in 1908, was a commission by the United States Congress to sculpt an Apotheosis of Democracy for the pediment of the House of Representatives wing of the Capitol.[6] The second project, completed in 1915, was a group of six heroic figures for the attic of the main entrance of the New York Public Library.

Bartlett received many honors during his career. The French government elected him a chevalier of the Legion of Honor in 1895, an officer in 1908, and a commander in 1924. He also held an associate membership in the Académie des Beaux-Arts in both France and Belgium. In his native country, he was elected an academician of the National Academy of Design and served as president of the National Sculpture Society, both in New York.

Notes

1. Paul W. Bartlett, "What American Sculptors Owe to French Art," *New York Times,* Feb. 9, 1913, magazine sec., p. 13, gives his late views on modern tendencies in art.
2. The 1884 Salon catalogue described Bartlett as an "elève de Frémiet," and he described himself the same way in a letter to Harrison S. Morris, managing director of the PAFA, Nov. 3, 1895, PAFA Archives.
3. Shapiro 1985, p. 122.
4. After its exhibition in the sixty-third annual, *Ghost Dancer* remained at the Pennsylvania Academy. Bartlett had the molds for the piece and therefore felt no urgency in arranging for the plaster to be returned to him. The sculpture, now lost, was for many years located in the Academy's branch school in Chester Springs.
5. Shapiro 1985, p. 125.
6. For more on the pediment see: Thomas P. Somma, *The Apotheosis of Democracy, 1908–1916: The Pediment for the House Wing of the United States Capitol* (Newark: University of Delaware Press, 1995).

References

1905 Ellen Strong Bartlett, "Paul Bartlett: An American Sculptor," *New England Magazine* 33 (Dec.), pp. 369–82. **1925** Obituary, *New York Times,* Sept. 21, p. 1. **1925** Charles V. Wheeler, "Bartlett (1865–1925)," *American Magazine of Art* 16 (Nov.), pp. 573–85. **1984** Wayne Craven, *Sculpture in America,* Newark: University of Delaware Press, pp. 428–34. **1985** Michael Shapiro, *Bronze Casting and American Sculpture,* Newark: University of Delaware Press, pp. 121–32.

Crouching Statuette of Adam

1896
Plaster
9 x 7½ x 9½" (22.9 x 19.1 x 24.1 cm)
Signed and dated on top of base at figure's proper left side:
Paul W/Bartlett/'96
Gift of the artist, 1897.5.1

AFTER Paul Wayland Bartlett exhibited a group of small bronzes in the 1895 Paris Salon, Harrison S. Morris, the managing director of the Pennsylvania Academy of the Fine Arts, asked him to show them the next year in the Academy's sixty-sixth annual exhibition. Bartlett declined with the explanation that he could not reassemble enough of the group because some pieces had already been sent to the Avery Galleries in New York. Furthermore, he was concerned that they might give the false impression that he was mainly interested in diminutive bronzes, when actually he had executed the small pieces primarily to experiment with casting and patination.[1] Yet, there was so much interest that his reluctance to show small sculptures did not last long. In place of the earlier bronzes, however, Bartlett sent the Pennsylvania Academy two newly completed plaster statuettes, this figure and a standing Adam.

Bartlett called them *statuettes* rather than *studies*, implying that he considered them to be finished works.[2] Yet he did not bother to remove the ridges caused by the piece mold. Bartlett made no attempt to conceal his method of production and, like Auguste Rodin (1840–1917), often left these ridges on his small casts. Bartlett worked in Rodin's studio for a time during the early to mid 1890s, and the older artist's influence is readily apparent in this crouching Adam.[3] The huddled pose with head bowed to the knees is typical of personifications of Grief and is related to Rodin's *Femme Accroupie*, 1880–82 (terracotta, Musée Rodin, Paris; bronze, Rodin Museum, Philadelphia). The large hands and feet may also derive from Rodin. During the late nineteenth and early twentieth centuries, sculpted figures with large extremities were so closely associated with Rodin's influence that one American critic wrote, "We have seen in our land many a Bertha Broadfoot and many a Helen of the Large Hand created by those who had not Rodin's excuse for this avoidance of conventional proportion: they were not revealing the scarce-finished new beings of Paradise, or the muscular striding bulk of a John the Baptist in the Wilderness."[4]

Bartlett cast both the crouching and standing statuettes of Adam in bronze. They were included in his group of small bronzes that received a gold medal at the Pan-American Exposition in Buffalo in 1901 and the grand prize at the Saint Louis Exposition in 1904. This collection, which Morris had tried to obtain for exhibition in 1895, was finally shown at the Pennsylvania Academy in 1905. Bartlett had donated the plaster casts of both statuettes of Adam to the Academy in 1897, when they were in the sixty-sixth annual exhibition. The standing Adam was discovered to be irreparably damaged in 1970 and was destroyed.

Four bronzes of *Crouching Statuette of Adam* are known: *Study in Bronze* (Brookgreen Gardens, Murrells Inlet, South Carolina); *L'Homme Accroupi* (Musée d'Orsay, Paris); *Sorrow* (Washington County Museum of Fine Arts, Hagerstown, Maryland); and *Seated Male Nude* (Westmoreland County Museum of Art, Greensburg, Pennsylvania). The last two versions are known to be posthumous casts.

Bartlett, *Crouching Statuette of Adam*

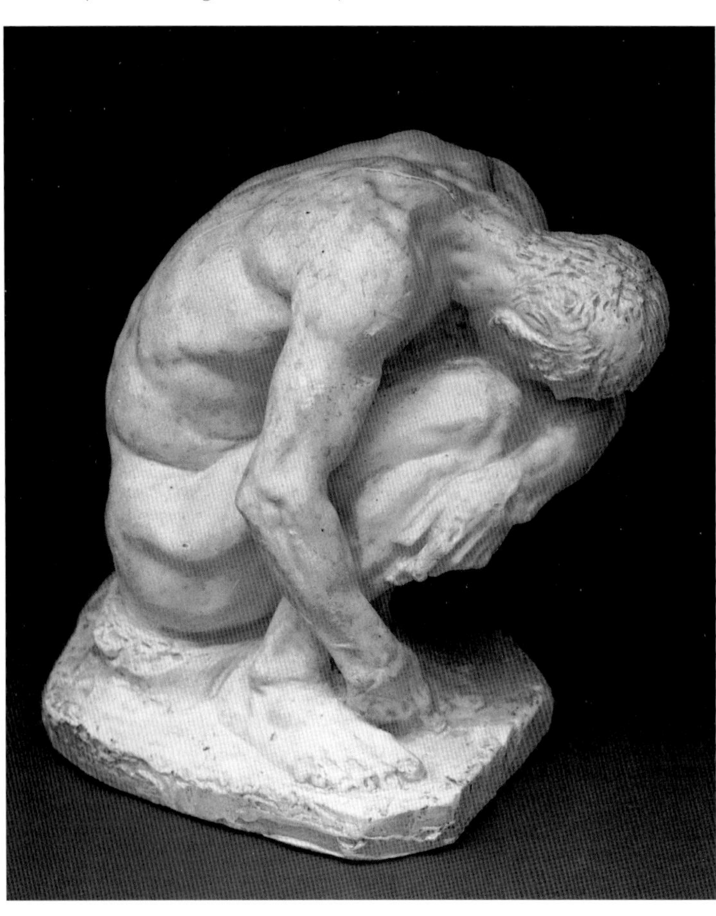

Notes

1. Paul Wayland Bartlett to Harrison S. Morris, Oct. 25, 1896, and Nov. 7, 1897, PAFA Archives.
2. Bartlett to Morris, Oct. 25, 1896, ibid.
3. I owe thanks to Thomas P. Somma for alerting me to the fact that Bartlett had worked in Rodin's studio.
4. Adeline Adams, *The Spirit of American Sculpture* (New York: National Sculpture Society, 1923), p. 224.

Exhibited

1896–97* cat. no. 659. **1986–87** PAFA, *Sculpture at the Pennsylvania Academy of the Fine Arts.*

R. Tait McKenzie

1867–1938

Born and reared near Ottawa, Canada, Robert Tait McKenzie was nine years old when his father, a Scottish Presbyterian minister, died. His family was left in financial hardship. As a youth, Robert drew, painted in watercolors, and pursued outdoor sports, such as ice skating, canoeing, and bow-and-arrow hunting. While at the Lisgar Collegiate Institute in Ottawa, he took night classes in charcoal drawing from casts and from life but was not satisfied with his work.[1] He financed his subsequent education at McGill University in Montreal by doing odd jobs, such as surveyor, steamship company clerk, and lumberman. McKenzie competed at the university in swimming, gymnastics, and track-and-field events, and fenced and played football. He earned a bachelor's degree in art in 1889 and a degree in medicine in 1892 and continued at McGill as an anatomy teacher and the medical director for physical training. In the summer of 1896, he toured Europe and kept a sketchbook journal of his trip.[2]

To illustrate a lecture that he gave in 1900 on the progress of fatigue in athletes, McKenzie modeled his first sculptures—masks titled *Effort, Breathlessness, Fatigue,* and *Exhaustion.*[3] These were so well-liked that he decided to continue sculpting. His next projects were to sculpt a sprinter and an ideal male athlete based upon the averages of the measurements of seventy-four sprinters and four hundred Harvard University athletes, respectively. *The Sprinter* was praised when shown at the Society of American Artists in New York in 1902, the Royal Academy in London in 1903, and the Paris Salon in 1904. A cast was purchased by the Fitzwilliam Museum in Cambridge, England. Commissioned by the Society of Directors of Physical Education in Colleges, *The Ideal College Athlete* is similar to classical Greek sculpture. It was bought by the Ashmolean Museum, Oxford. Both figures were in the seventy-third annual exhibition at the Pennsylvania Academy of the Fine Arts, in 1904. McKenzie began modeling athletes from life. Lacking any formal training in sculpture, he relied upon his intimate knowledge of human anatomy.

Dr. McKenzie traveled to England and France in the summer of 1904 and visited PAUL WAYLAND BARTLETT, who helped him find a Paris studio. In the fall, he came to the University of Pennsylvania in Philadelphia to be professor of physical therapy in the medical school and director of the Department of Physical Education. He also wrote textbooks, such as *Exercise in Education and Medicine* (1909). In 1907, he married Ethel O'Neil, a poet and musician. They formed an artistic circle centered upon private showings of Dr. McKenzie's latest sculpture. Solo public exhibitions were mounted by Doll and Richards gallery, Boston, in 1906, 1925–26, and 1936; the Herron Art Institute, Indianapolis, in 1908; McClees Galleries, Philadelphia, in 1913; the Art Club of Philadelphia in 1919; the Fine Arts Society, London, in 1920 and 1930; Ferargil Galleries, New York, in 1921; Galerie George Petit, Paris, in 1924; Grand Central Galleries, New York, in 1924, 1927, and 1934; the Art Gallery of Toronto in 1928; and the Philadelphia Art Alliance in 1931. His works were also shown in the annual exhibitions of 1904–11, 1918, 1920, and 1931 at the Pennsylvania Academy of the Fine Arts. Several sculptures adorn the campus of the University of Pennsylvania, including his first commemorative work, *Young Franklin,* for the tenth reunion of the class of 1904,[4] a portrait of the charismatic eighteenth-century preacher Reverend George Whitefield, and one of Provost Edgar Fahs Smith. A medallion of three hurdlers titled *The Joy of Effort* won a silver medal at the 1912 Olympic Games in Stockholm, where it is installed in a stadium.

During World War I, McKenzie volunteered to serve in the Canadian army. He was sent to England in 1915 where he developed innovative methods of physical training for recruits and wounded soldiers and designed masks to replace facial features mutilated in war. In 1918 he published a book based on his experiences, *Reclaiming the Maimed: A Handbook of Physical Therapy.* After the war, he resumed his teaching position at the University of Pennsylvania. He also received commissions for war memorials and portrait medallions. The Philadelphia Sketch Club, the Franklin Institute, and other organizations devoted to art, science, or athletics asked him to design medals. The Christine Wetherill Stevenson Memorial, a cast-stone relief combining a portrait and two ideal figures, was commissioned in 1928 by the Philadelphia Art Alliance in which McKenzie was active.

In 1931 the University of Pennsylvania awarded him the J. William White Research Professorship, which supported his work as a lecturer and sculptor, including the casting in bronze of many of his works. McKenzie returned to Almonte, Ontario, his boyhood town, and purchased a grist mill that he named Mill of Kintail after an ancestor's Scottish title. It was converted into a summer home and studio that is now the R. Tait McKenzie Memorial Museum.

The Lloyd P. Jones Gallery in the University of Pennsylvania's Gimbel Gymnasium has Dr. McKenzie's sculpture on permanent display.[5] His papers are in the university's archives. McKenzie's sculpture is in such collections as the Mutter Museum of the College of Physicians in Philadelphia, the Philadelphia Museum of Art, the University of Tennessee, Knoxville, the Metropolitan Museum of Art, the Yale University Art Gallery, and the National Gallery of Art, Ottawa.

Notes

1. Hussey 1930, pp. 3, 9. An addendum to this book, by the same name, was compiled in 1985 by Judy Millar under the auspices of the Ministry of Education, Nepean, Ontario. A copy is in Box #1, R. Tait McKenzie Papers, University of Pennsylvania Archives.

2. The journal with photographs inserted is in Box #2, ibid.

3. Casts of his *Four Studies of the Progress of Fatigue in Athletes* are in the College of Physicians of Philadelphia; the Lloyd P. Jones Gallery, University of Pennsylvania; the Museum of the School of Anatomy, Cambridge University; and the R. Tait McKenzie Memorial Museum.

4. The head was based on the bust by JEAN ANTOINE HOUDON, rendered youthful. The figure was sculpted from a live model. A bronze reduction is in Brookgreen Gardens, Murrells Inlet, S.C.

5. Most of the McKenzie sculptures on display in the gymnasium were given by the artist or purchased through the J. William White Fund. A checklist, published in 1987, lists about ninety sculptures by McKenzie, several of which are on loan. The sculptures of JOSEPH BROWN, who assisted McKenzie for seven years in the 1930s, are in an adjacent gallery.

References

R. Tait McKenzie Papers, University of Pennsylvania Archives, Philadelphia. **1910** Harrison S. Morris, "R. Tait McKenzie, Sculptor and Anatomist," *International Studio* 41 (July), pp. 11–14. **1918** Harold Donaldson Eberlein, "R. Tait McKenzie—Physician and Sculptor," *Century Magazine* 97 (Dec.), pp. 249–57. **1930** Christopher Hussey, *Tait McKenzie: A Sculptor of Youth,* Philadelphia: J.B. Lippincott Company (first published in London, England: Country Life, 1929). **1938** "McKenzie Dies," *Art Digest* 12 (May 15), p. 20. **1975** Andrew J. Kozar, *R. Tait McKenzie: The Sculptor of Athletes,* Knoxville: University of Tennessee Press. **1976** Philadelphia Museum of Art, *Philadelphia: Three Centuries of American Art,* Philadelphia, 1976, pp. 490–91.

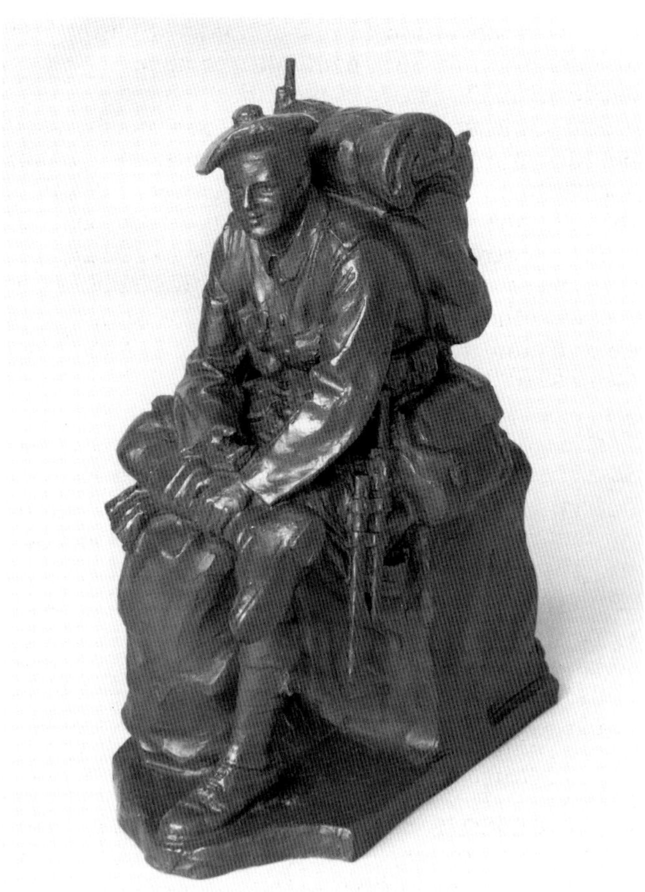

McKenzie, *Blighty*

Blighty

1915–17
Bronze with brown patina; lost-wax cast in 1917
16 x 7¼ x 11½" (40.6 x 18.4 x 29.2 cm)
Signed and dated on plinth at figure's left side:
©·R·Tait McKenzie·1917
Foundry mark on plinth at figure's right side:
ROMAN BRONZE WORKS N—Y—
Gift of the Estate of Emeline Maddock, 1949.13

Blighty (*Back to Blighty from the Ends of the Earth*[1] or *Six Days' Leave*[2]) was the only sculpture that R. Tait McKenzie produced while in England during the war.[3] It was begun in 1915 when he was medical officer at Heaton Park, Manchester. He was inspired by a young Scottish soldier on leave from France, dressed in the tam-o'-shanter and kilt of the Seaforth Highlanders, a fighting unit that wore the McKenzie tartan. The soldier wears the full service uniform with his kit, an overcoat, and a blanket roll topped by a trophy of war—a German helmet. He also has a rifle, an entrenching tool, and a cartridge belt. The sculpture's long title refers to the soldier's return home to England (or Great Britain).[4] *Blighty* is a slang term derived in the 1880s from a Hindi word.

McKenzie must have brought a plaster model of *Blighty* with him on his leave to Philadelphia in the winter of 1916–17. This cast, made in April 1917, was probably one of the first two made by the Roman Bronze Works, in New York.[5] It was displayed in November in the *British Allied Bazaar* at the Philadelphia Art Alliance, where it was purchased by Emeline Maddock. She offered the statue to the Pennsylvania Academy of the Fine Arts several months later for the same amount that she had paid.[6] The offer apparently was declined. The sculpture was donated to the Academy thirty-one years later by her estate.

At least ten other casts were produced by the Roman Bronze Works between 1917 and McKenzie's death in 1938. Perhaps others were made by the Gorham Company in New York, as a plaster model was moved to their office in Providence, Rhode Island, in 1934 to await further orders. *Blighty* was particularly popular in Great Britain; at least five casts were purchased there. Casts are known to be owned by Balmoral Castle, Scotland, and Major and Mrs. James Leys in Canada. One dated 1916 is on loan to the University of Pennsylvania by Professor and Mrs. Philip Rieff. Dates inscribed on the casts vary: 1916, 1917, and 1915–19.[7] These may indicate the dates the casts were made or McKenzie's changes to his original composition. One cast was shown in 1919 at an exhibition on the theme of war at the National Academy of Design, in New York.

After the war, McKenzie was commissioned to produce war memorials for Great Britain, Canada, and the United States. They often include a lone seated figure like *Blighty,* although it was never enlarged. When McKenzie's heart was buried at Saint Cuthbert's church in Edinburgh, his widow expressed "the intense admiration of his soul for the chivalry and the courage of the young Scot in the Great War."[8]

Notes

1. This title appears within a photograph published in the University of Pennsylvania's *Pennsylvania Gazette,* Oct. 15, 1920, p. 64, which shows the sculpture on display in the chapel at the R. Tait McKenzie Memorial Museum, Almonte, Ontario.

2. Rev. O.S. Duffield, "A Message from Art in War Time," *New York Christian Advocate,* Feb. 28, 1918, Scrapbook 1917–18, Box #8, R. Tait McKenzie Papers, University of Pennsylvania Archives, Philadelphia.

3. An unidentified publication, dated perhaps 1922, includes a photograph of the sculptor modeling *Blighty* in clay, clipping file, PAFA Library.

4. "What the McKenzie System Meant for the Soldier," *Philadelphia Public Ledger,* Oct. 1, 1916, Scrapbook 1914–17, Box #8, R. Tait McKenzie Papers, University of Pennsylvania Archives, reports a sentiment prevalent among the soldiers: "You are lucky if you're shot and killed, but d—n lucky if you're shot and wounded and get back to old 'Blighty'."

5. Roman Bronze Works to R. Tait McKenzie, April 6, 1917, and bill, April 30, 1917, Bronze foundry letters file, Box #2, ibid. One cast "for the [British Allied Bazaar]" was made at a reduced rate "to aid such a worthy cause." Fragments of a label originally on the sculpture, now in the object file, refer to the November exhibition at the Philadelphia Art Alliance.

6. Emeline Maddock to the [Director of the Pennsylvania] Academy of the Fine Arts, March 7, 1918, PAFA object file.

7. William J. Drake, Gorham Company, to R. Tait McKenzie, March 22, 1934, with a list of models, Bronze foundry letters file, Box #2, R. Tait McKenzie Papers, University of Pennsylvania Archives. At that time, *Blighty*'s base was broken and a piece was missing.

8. "Edinburgh Honors Canadian Sculptor," unidentified Scottish newspaper, Sept. [1938], Box #1, ibid.

References

1930 Christopher Hussey, *Tait McKenzie: A Sculptor of Youth,* Philadelphia: J.B. Lippincott Company, p. 56.
1975 Andrew J. Kozar, *R. Tait McKenzie: The Sculptor of Athletes,* Knoxville: University of Tennessee Press, p. 16.

Exhibited

1917 Philadelphia Art Alliance, *British Allied Bazaar.*

Ex Collections

Emeline Maddock, 1917–48; her nephew, 1948–49.

Duke Paoa Kahanomokee

1937–38
Plaster, painted red-brown
13 x 2½ x 4" (33 x 6.4 x 10.2 cm)
Signed and dated on base behind right foot: Tait McKenzie 19[3]7
Deposited by Mrs. R. Tait McKenzie, 1.1951

THIS unfinished figure is the last sculpture produced by R. Tait McKenzie. He was working on it the morning of his fatal heart attack.[1] It is a portrait of Duke Paoa Kahanomokee, the Hawaiian Olympic swimming champion, who was an inspiration to Hawaiian youth. The work was commissioned for Honolulu. This is one of at least two plasters made from McKenzie's unfinished model. Another, on a tall inscribed base, is in the J. William White Collection at the University of Pennsylvania, Philadelphia.[2] Joseph Brown was apparently asked to complete it; and in 1969, on a visit to Brown's studio, Andrew J. Kozar saw that he was working on a statue very similar to McKenzie's.[3] It is not known if it was completed.[4]

The sculpture was deposited at the Pennsylvania Academy of the Fine Arts in 1951 by the artist's wife, but she died the next year without making it a formal gift.

Notes

1. Jean McGill, *The Joy of Effort: A Biography of R. Tait McKenzie* (Bewdley, Ontario: Clay Publishing Company, 1980), p. 196.

2. Andrew J. Kozar, *R. Tait McKenzie: The Sculptor of Athletes* (Knoxville: University of Tennessee Press, 1975), p. 106 (ill.).

McKenzie, *Duke Paoa Kahanomokee*

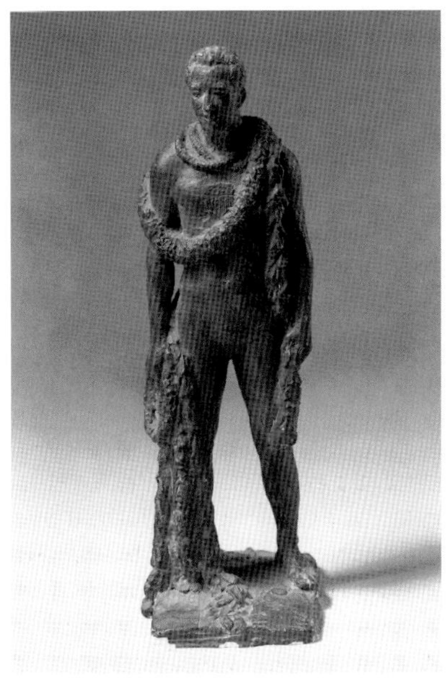

3. Kozar 1975, p. 36, n. 91.

4. McGill 1980, p. 224, mentions that the portrait was being completed in 1980 at the time of publication. It is not known if this is a reference to Joseph Brown's work.

Ex Collection
The artist's wife, 1938–51.

Philadelphia Sketch Club Medal of Honor, 1921: See Appendix.

Samuel Murray

1869–1941

Samuel Aloysius Murray was born in Philadelphia to William Murray, an Irish immigrant stonemason, and Margaretta Mary Hannigan Murray, the daughter of a linen merchant.[1] The eleventh of twelve children, Samuel was reared in a Roman Catholic family and educated in public and private schools in Philadelphia. He developed his first serious interest in art at the age of fifteen. In 1886 he enrolled at the Art Students' League of Philadelphia, where he met THOMAS EAKINS and began a warm friendship that lasted until Eakins died in 1916. The two men shared a studio from 1892 until about 1900, collaborated on several projects, and portrayed many of the same people, typically members of their families and close friends.

In 1890 Murray began a fifty-year teaching career at the Philadelphia School of Design for Women (now Moore College of Art and Design), where he taught clay modeling and anatomy. He exhibited regularly at the Pennsylvania Academy of the Fine Arts from 1892 until 1933. In March 1896, under the auspices of the Fairmount Park Art Association, the Pennsylvania Academy mounted the only one-man exhibition of Murray's work to be held in his lifetime. Murray showed his sculpture at the National Academy of Design, in New York, in 1892 and 1893; the World's Columbian Exposition, in Chicago in 1893; the Art Club of Philadelphia in 1894 (where he won a gold medal); the National Sculpture Society, in New York, in 1898 and 1908; the Exposition Universelle of 1900 in Paris; the Pan-American Exposition, in Buffalo in 1901 (where he was awarded an honorable mention); and the Louisiana Purchase Exposition, in Saint Louis in 1904 (where he won a silver medal).

Murray's monumental sculptures include the eight Prophets, 1896–98, for the Witherspoon Building in Philadelphia (only three survive—two in Alaska and one in a cemetery in Frazer, Pennsylvania); *Commodore Barry,* 1907, behind Independence Hall; Winged Victory and the pedimental reliefs on the Pennsylvania State Monument, 1909–10, and *Father William Corby,* 1909, both on the Gettysburg battlefield; the *Deshong Memorial,* 1910, in the Chester Rural Cemetery; the *Bishop Shanahan Memorial,* 1918, in Saint Peter's Church, Harrisburg; *Admiral George W. Melville,* 1923, in the Philadelphia Navy Yard; and *Senator Boies Penrose,* 1930, on the lawn of the state capitol in Harrisburg. In addition, Murray modeled nearly two hundred small portraits. Typically, they are miniature and lifesize busts and full-length statuettes twelve to eighteen inches high. He also executed several relief plaques. The Catholic clergy of Philadelphia, local businessmen, scientists, musicians, and artists comprised most of his subjects. Murray's best portraits are of the people he knew well, the close circle of family and friends that surrounded him and his mentor, Thomas Eakins. The largest collection of sculpture by Murray is in the Hirshhorn Museum and Sculpture Garden, in Washington, D.C.

Note

1. Five scrapbooks compiled by Murray and his wife, Jane (Jennie) Dean Kershaw Murray, are the richest and most comprehensive resources for study of the sculptor's life and work. They are in the Hirshhorn Museum and Sculpture Garden, Smithsonian Institution, Washington, D.C.

References

1979 Mariah Chamberlin-Hellman, "Samuel Murray, Thomas Eakins, and the Witherspoon Prophets," *Arts* 53 (May), pp. 134–39. **1979** Phyllis Rosenzweig, "Problems and Resources in Thomas Eakins Research: The Hirshhorn Museum's Samuel Murray Collection," *Arts* 53 (May), pp. 118–20. **1982** Lloyd Goodrich, *Thomas Eakins,* Cambridge, Mass.: Harvard University Press for the National Gallery of Art, 2 vols. **1982** Michael W. Panhorst, "Samuel Murray, Sculptor," master's thesis, University of Delaware. **1982** *Samuel Murray, the Hirshhorn Museum and Sculpture Garden Collection, Smithsonian Institution,* Washington, D.C.: Smithsonian Institution Press. **1997** Kathleen A. Foster, *Thomas Eakins Rediscovered,* New Haven, Conn.: Yale University Press.

Walt Whitman

1892
Plaster
13¾ x 7½ x 5½" (35 x 19 x 14 cm)
Signed and dated on back of base: COPYRIGHT/ MURRAY 1892
Inscribed in relief on front of base: Walt/Whitman
Charles Bregler's Thomas Eakins Collection, purchased

with the partial support of the Pew Memorial Trust, 1985.68.1.9

THIS IS a small but powerful portrait. The prominent forehead suggests the poet's intellect; the searching eyes, his strong but compassionate nature. Walt Whitman (1819–1892) was an abolitionist and served as a nurse in the Civil War. The shallow pupils of the eyes and the softly rounded edges of the eyelids contribute to the impression of a dreamer and seer. Deft modeling captures the fluffy, tangled look of Whitman's enormous beard.

On March 27, 1892, the day after Whitman died, Samuel Murray and Thomas Eakins, using waste molds, made casts of Whitman's face, shoulders, and right hand. As Murray explained, "Someday there might be a statue and the mask in this case would be invaluable."[1] Neither Murray nor Eakins ever received such a commission, however, and in 1897 they sold the casts to H. Buxton Forman of London along with a cast of Whitman's left hand and a reproduction of his head.[2] By that time, using the mask, the two casts of the shoulders, and probably photographs that he had taken earlier, Murray had already made this portrait.[3]

Although one of the first sculptures that Murray is known to have modeled, it was immediately recognized as a competent portrait. In anticipation of its popularity, Murray followed a practice common among sculptors at the time: he copyrighted the design.[4] A bronze cast was selected for exhibition at the World's Columbian Exposition, in 1893, and was shown in a preview exhibition that year at the Pennsylvania Academy of the Fine Arts. Several plaster replicas were sold or given away by the artist.

In addition to this plaster cast, which Murray apparently bequeathed to Charles Bregler, one bronze and one other plaster cast (both, Hirshhorn Museum and Sculpture Garden) were in Murray's studio at his death. He produced at least one more cast, probably in plaster, which he gave to Harrison S. Morris, the director of the Pennsylvania Academy (now unlocated).[5]

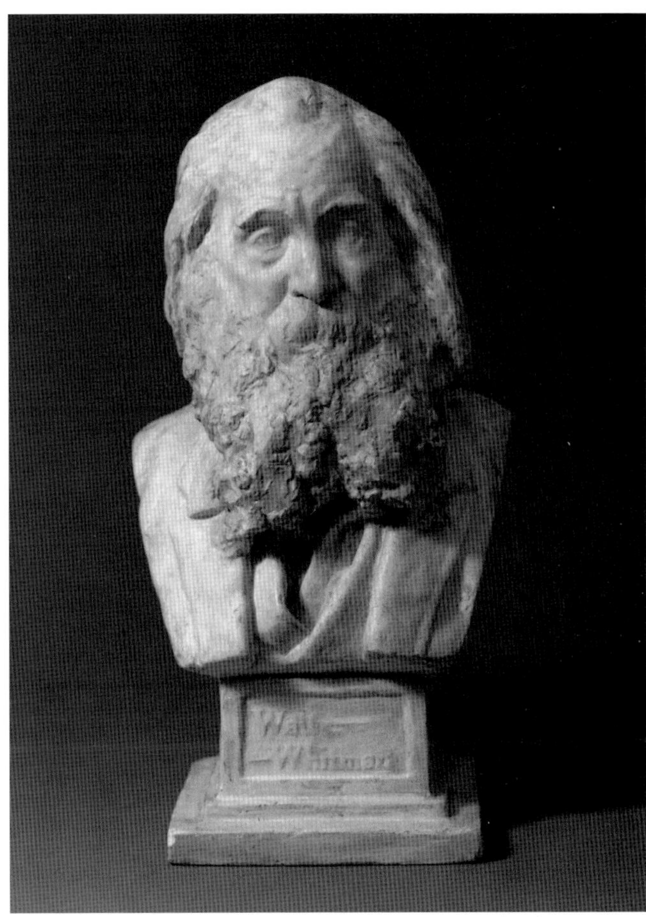

Murray, *Walt Whitman*

Notes

1. Samuel Murray to a Mr. Vanuxim, Oct. 19, 1898, Eakins-Murray Scrapbook 3, p. 8, Hirshhorn Museum and Sculpture Garden. A typescript signed by Eakins and Murray, dated June 1897, documents the making of the casts and states, "There were no other masks or molds taken from Walt after his death," ibid., p. 7. The mask and a cast of it, gifts of H. Buxton Forman, are in the collection of the Houghton Library, Harvard University, Cambridge; ill. in Gordon Hendricks, *The Life and Work of Thomas Eakins* (New York: Grossman Publishers, 1974), color pl. 36. Photo caption says mask was "essentially Murray's work, done with Eakins' advice."
2. Typescript, dated 1897, cited in n. 1.
3. William I. Homer, "Who Took Eakins's Photographs?" *Art News* 82 (May 1983), pp. 112–19, documents as the work of Murray a photograph of Whitman previously attributed to Eakins.
4. Copyright certificate 46142 for this bust is dated Nov. 12, 1892.
5. Hendricks 1974, p. 220.

Reference

1986 Kathleen A. Foster, "An Important Eakins Collection," *Antiques* 130 (Dec.), fig. 4, p. 1233.

Exhibited

1986–87 PAFA, *Sculpture at the Pennsylvania Academy of the Fine Arts.*

Ex Collections

The artist, Philadelphia, 1892–about 1941; Charles Bregler, Philadelphia, about 1941–58; his second wife, Mary Picozzi Bregler, 1958–85.

Benjamin Eakins

1894
Bronze with black patina; lost-wax cast in 1904
23 x 12¾ x 10" (58.4 x 32.4 x 25.4 cm)
Inscribed, signed, and dated on back: TO MY DEAR/ FRIEND/BENJAMIN·EAKINS/SAMUEL·MURRAY/1894
Inscribed in relief on front of plinth: –EAKINS–
Foundry mark on back: Roman Bronze Works N.Y. 1904.
Gift of Mrs. Samuel Murray, 1945.9

THOMAS EAKINS'S FATHER, Benjamin (1818–1899), was a writing master and a teacher of calligraphy. During the 1890s when Thomas and Susan Eakins lived with his father at 1729 Mount Vernon Street, Samuel Murray was a frequent dinner guest. Benjamin Eakins also accompanied the younger men to prizefights and on bicycle trips into the country.

Murray's familiarity with Benjamin Eakins undoubtedly contributed to the success of this portrait. The sculptor captured not only Eakins's appearance but also his personality. The slightly bowed head, straight lips, and intense gaze, which is emphasized by the deeply cut pupils, reveal Eakins as the gentle, pensive but strict man that he was. It may be that he posed at the same time for the painting by his son now in the Philadelphia Museum of Art.

The bust is among the earliest works that Murray modeled and exhibited.[1] He had studied art with Thomas Eakins for six years when he made the original plaster version of this sculpture. It won a gold medal in the 1894 exhibition of the Philadelphia Art Club. Murray also exhibited a version of this bust in the Exposition Universelle of 1900 in Paris—his only work to be exhibited outside the United States—and he showed a bust of Benjamin Eakins in the Louisiana Purchase Exposition, in Saint Louis in 1904. In 1902 Sadakichi Hartmann illustrated the plaster bust and four of Murray's other sculptures in *Modern American Sculpture* (New York: Paul Wenzel Publisher).

Note

1. This bronze cast is one of two made from the plaster model, 1894 (Hirshhorn Museum and Sculpture Garden). The other bronze is in the collection of the Philadelphia Museum of Art (see *Philadelphia: Three Centuries of American Art* [Philadelphia, 1976], cat. no. 378 [ill.]).

Reference

1974 Pamela Simpson, "The Sculpture of Charles Grafly," Ph.D. diss., University of Delaware, pp. 61, 63 (ill.).

Ex Collections

The artist, Philadelphia, 1904–41; his wife, Jane, 1941–45.

Murray, *Benjamin Eakins*

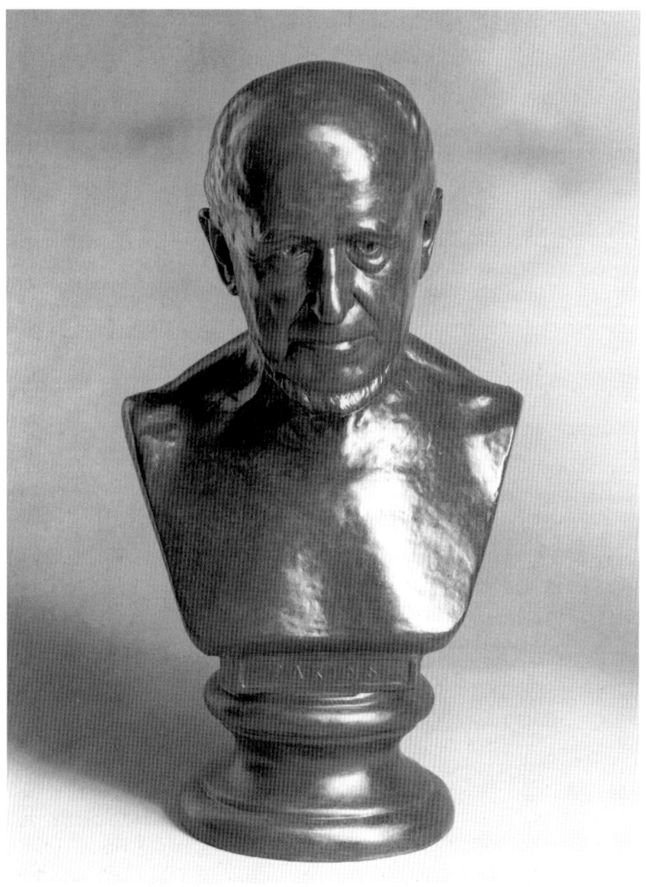

Susan Macdowell Eakins

1894
Plaster
24½ x 8½ x 9¾" (62.2 x 21.6 x 24.7 cm)
Signed and dated on top of base: MURRAY/94.
Charles Bregler's Thomas Eakins Collection, purchased with the partial support of the Pew Memorial Trust, 1985.68.1.10

SUSAN HANNAH MACDOWELL (1851–1938) was born in Philadelphia to William H. Macdowell, a distinguished engraver, and Hannah Trimble Gardner Macdowell.[1] The fifth of eight children reared in a progressive household, Susan showed an early interest in art. She saw Thomas Eakins for the first time in 1876 in Philadelphia, when Haseltine's Gallery exhibited his painting *The Gross Clinic,* 1875 (Jefferson Medical College, Philadelphia). Soon thereafter, she enrolled at the Pennsylvania Academy of the Fine Arts, where she studied until 1882 under Christian Schussele and Eakins. She married Eakins on January 19, 1884, and largely abandoned her own career to encourage his. Only after Eakins died thirty-two years later did she resume painting in earnest.

In this statuette, Samuel Murray combined com-

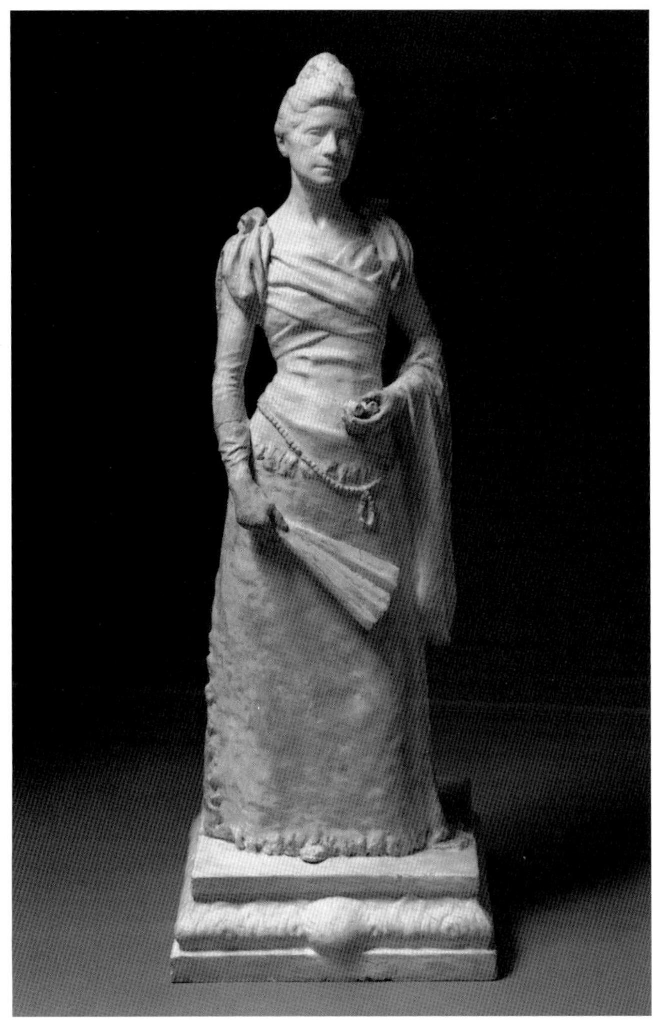

Murray, *Susan Macdowell Eakins*, plaster

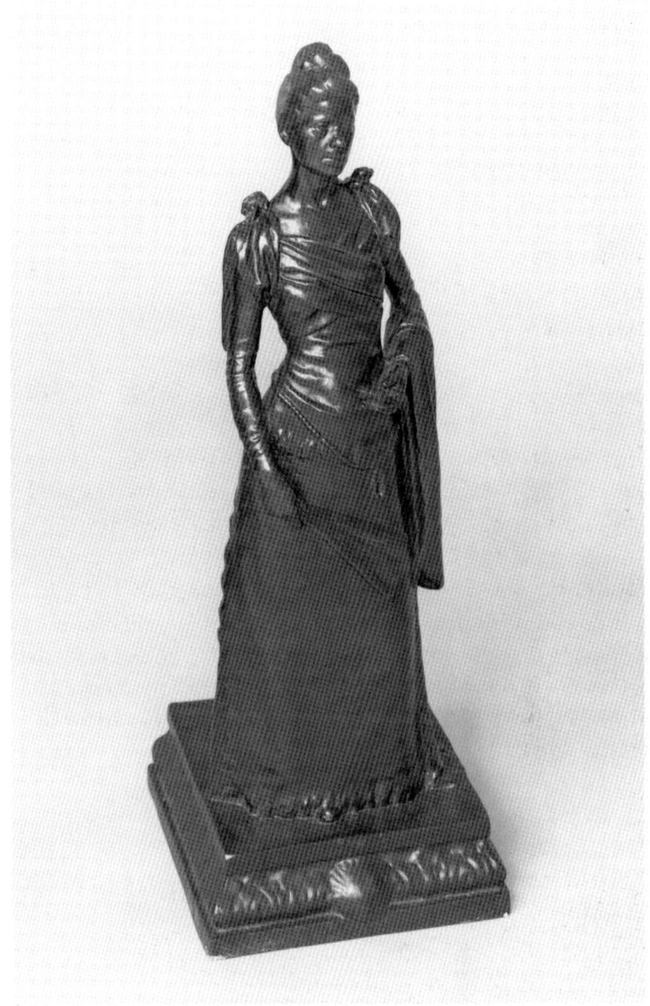

Murray, *Susan Macdowell Eakins*, bronze

prehensive knowledge of human anatomy with deep feeling for the subject. He depicted Mrs. Eakins dressed for an evening at the theater or the opera, as he must have seen her many times. The curves of the arms frame the upper torso and focus attention on the head and the characteristically stoical expression on the face. In profile, the curved spine and projecting head give the figure a lithe grace. The softly modulated surface of the floor-length skirt contrasts with the broad folds of the close-fitting bodice; and the vertical drapery at the shoulders accentuates her relaxed, contrapposto stance. Accessories, such as the opera glasses, fan, and beaded belt, are carefully organized to enhance the overall composition.

Murray made at least three casts of this portrait. The position of the left hand of this plaster figure and the shape and size of the opera glasses are slightly different from those of the bronze (q.v.), indicating that this detail was remodeled before the later cast was made. Unfortunately, the left hand of the only other known cast in this edition, the plaster figure in the collection of the Hirshhorn Museum and Sculpture Garden, was already missing when the statue was acquired by the museum. Therefore, a chronology of the three casts cannot be established without additional evidence.

In 1932 when Susan Macdowell Eakins painted *The Lewis Sisters* (private collection, Wilmington, Delaware), she included Murray's bronze statuette of herself. It stands on the piano in the portrait.[2]

Notes

1. For more information, see Susan P. Casteras, *Susan Macdowell Eakins, 1851–1938* (Philadelphia: PAFA, 1973); David Sellin, *Thomas Eakins, Susan Macdowell Eakins, Elizabeth Macdowell Kenton* (Roanoke, Va.: North Cross School, 1977); Kathleen A. Foster and Cheryl Leibold, *Writing about Eakins: A Guide to the Manuscripts in Charles Bregler's Thomas Eakins Collection* (Philadelphia: University of Pennsylvania Press, 1989), pp. 259–63, 309–

11; and Jeanette Toohey, "Susan Macdowell Eakins," unpublished manuscript, about 1993.

2. Casteras 1973, cat. no. 43 (ill.), p. 32.

Ex Collections

The artist, Philadelphia, 1894-about 1939; Charles Bregler, Philadelphia, about 1939–58; his second wife, Mary Picozzi Bregler, 1958–85.

Susan Macdowell Eakins

1894
Bronze with brown patina; sand cast before 1899
23¾ x 8½ x 9½" (60.3 x 21.6 x 24.1 cm)
Signed and dated on top of base: MURRAY/94.
Foundry mark on base: BUREAU BROS./PHILA.
Gift of Mrs. Samuel Murray, 1942.14

THIS IS PROBABLY the "portrait of Mrs. Eakins in bronze" that Samuel Murray mentioned in 1899 in a letter to Harrison S. Morris, the director of the Pennsylvania Academy of the Fine Arts. Murray wrote that he wished to enter it in that year's annual exhibition.[1] The catalogue listed the statue as *Portrait of a Lady,* lent by Thomas Eakins. The cast is probably also the sculpture about which Murray and CHARLES BREGLER corresponded after Mrs. Eakins's death. Bregler claimed that Mrs. Eakins had given it to him without Murray's knowledge. Murray argued that Mr. and Mrs. Eakins, who had given many of Murray's sculptures to friends, never gave away any without his prior approval.[2] From correspondence in Bregler's Eakins collection, it appears that Murray finally regained the figure.

The year after Murray's death, his widow donated this cast to the Pennsylvania Academy. It is the only known bronze cast of the figure. The plaster version (q.v.) that was in Bregler's collection at his death may have been given to him in consolation for the loss of the bronze.[3]

Notes

1. Samuel Murray to Harrison S. Morris, Jan. 5, 1899, PAFA Archives.

2. Samuel Murray to Charles Bregler, June 28, 1939, ibid. Murray also offered to exchange another statue for the bronze.

3. See n. 2.

References

1979 Mariah Chamberlin-Hellman, "Samuel Murray, Thomas Eakins, and the Witherspoon Prophets," *Arts* 53 (May), pp. 137, 138 (ill.). **1982** Lloyd Goodrich, *Thomas Eakins,* Cambridge: Harvard University Press, vol. 2, pp. 102–3, fig. 190.

Exhibited

1899* cat. no. 869. **1901** *Pan-American Exposition,* Buffalo, cat. no. 1624. **1948** Walnut Street Association, Philadelphia, window display during political convention. **1953** Philadelphia Art Alliance, *Philadelphia Architecture in the Nineteenth Century.* **1962** Philadelphia Museum of Art, *Eakins in Perspective: Works by Eakins and His Contemporaries,* cat. no. 93, adjunct to traveling exhibition *Thomas Eakins: A Retrospective Exhibition.* **1970–71** Worcester Art Museum, Mass., *Thomas Eakins: His Photographic Works.* **1975–76** Whitney Museum of American Art, New York, *A Portrait of Young America.* **1976** PAFA, *In This Academy,* cat. no. 239. **1978–79** PAFA, *350 Masterpieces of American Art: 1720–1978.* **1986–87** PAFA, *Sculpture at the Pennsylvania Academy of the Fine Arts.*

Ex Collections

Thomas Eakins, Philadelphia, by 1899–1916; his wife, Susan, 1916–39; Charles Bregler, Philadelphia, 1939; Samuel Murray, Philadelphia, 1939–41; his wife, Jane, 1941–42.

Thomas Eakins

1894
Bronze with brown patina; lost-wax cast about 1904
22¾ x 9¼ x 6¾" (57.8 x 23.5 x 17.1 cm)
Inscribed, signed, and dated on top of base: TO MY/DEAR MASTER/SAMUEL MURRAY/1894
Foundry mark on back of base: ROMAN BRONZE WORKS. N.Y.
Gift of the artist, 1941.10

IN JULY OF 1894, Thomas Eakins (1844–1916) wrote to the anthropologist Frank Hamilton Cushing, "I wish you were here now. Murray is just starting a statuette of me to go with that of my wife. He is modeling my naked figure before putting on the clothes and I wish you were modeling alongside of him."[1] The practice of modeling the nude figure and then adding clothes was common among realist sculptors at the turn of the century—when subjects could be persuaded to pose nude. In this portrait of Eakins, each fold of fabric tells of the underlying form. Small details like the sagging cloth at the ankles add to the realism of Murray's portrayal, for Eakins was known to be so casual about his painting attire that his sitters were sometimes perturbed.

Eakins felt that old clothes told something of the person who wore them. Therefore, he often asked his subjects to wear their most comfortable shoes or an old coat that had stretched to the shape and characteristic activities of its owner. Having shared a studio with Eakins for over a year before this portrait was made, Murray surely was aware of Eakins's preference for honest, even if unflattering, portraiture.

After eight years of seeing Eakins daily as a friend and colleague, Murray possessed an understanding and appreciation of his "dear master" unmatched by anyone except Eakins's wife. Murray met Eakins im-

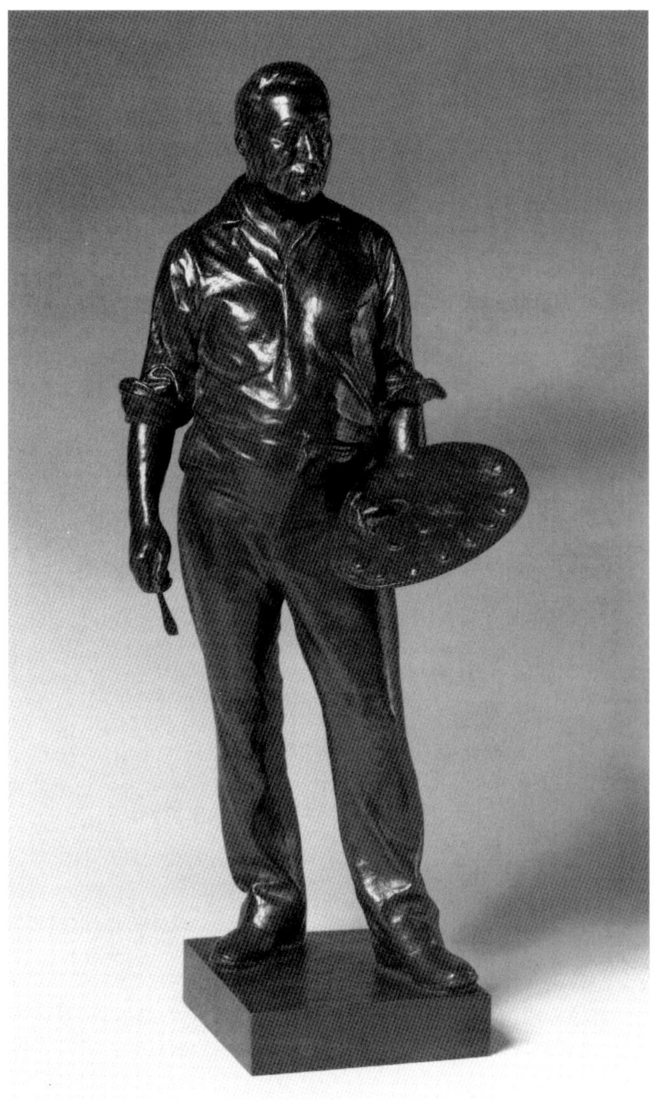

Murray, *Thomas Eakins,* 1894

mediately after the latter was forced to resign the post of director of the school and professor of painting at the Pennsylvania Academy of the Fine Arts. Their friendship endured throughout the trying final three decades of the painter's life. Murray knew Eakins's determination as an artist and the disappointment he felt over the public's failure to recognize his accomplishments. This *portrait d'apparat* of the painter about to lift his brush not only captures Eakins's characteristic appearance at work in the studio but also serves as a small-scale memorial to Murray's mentor. It was shown in plaster at the Pennsylvania Academy's 1895–96 annual exhibition and illustrated in the catalogue. Having seen a bronze cast of this portrait at the Louisiana Purchase Universal Exposition in Saint Louis in 1904, Thomas P. Anshutz wrote to Murray, "It is certainly a fine piece of work and great in character."[2]

Murray kept this statuette in his studio for over thirty-five years and then gave it to the Pennsylvania Academy.

Notes

1. Quoted in Goodrich 1982, vol. 2, p. 103. Gordon Hendricks, *The Life and Work of Thomas Eakins* (New York: Grossman Publishers, 1974), p. 228, erroneously dates letter 1895.

2. Undated letter on stationery of Louisiana Purchase Universal Exposition, Eakins-Murray Scrapbook 5, p. 59, Hirshhorn Museum and Sculpture Garden. The bronze shown in Saint Louis could be this cast or the one in the collection of the Hirshhorn Museum and Sculpture Garden. They are the only known casts of this portrait.

References

1982 Lloyd Goodrich, *Thomas Eakins,* Cambridge: Harvard University Press, vol. 2, pp. 103, 104, fig. 191. **1982** Linda Bantel, "Sculpture at the Pennsylvania Academy," *Antiques* 121 (March), p. 711, fig. 8.

Exhibited

1948 Woodmere Art Gallery, Philadelphia, *American Art, 1860–1914.* **1948** Walnut Street Association, Philadelphia, window display during political convention. **1953** Philadelphia Art Alliance, *Philadelphia Architecture in the Nineteenth Century.* **1962** Philadelphia Museum of Art, *Eakins in Perspective: Works by Eakins and His Contemporaries,* cat. no. 75, adjunct to traveling exhibition *Thomas Eakins: A Retrospective Exhibition.* **1969** Corcoran Gallery of Art, Washington, D.C., *The Sculpture of Thomas Eakins,* cat. no. 24 (ill.). **1970–71** Worcester Art Museum, Mass., *Thomas Eakins: His Photographic Works.* **1975–76** Whitney Museum of American Art, New York, *A Portrait of Young America.* **1976** PAFA, *In This Academy,* cat. no. 240 (ill.). **1978–79** PAFA, *350 Masterpieces of American Art: 1720–1978.* **1984–85** PAFA, *A Growing American Treasure: Recent Acquisitions and Highlights from the Permanent Collection.* **1986–87** PAFA, *Sculpture at the Pennsylvania Academy of the Fine Arts.*

Gertrude Murray

1894
Plaster, painted beige
10 x 7¾ x 5" (25.4 x 19.7 x 12.7 cm)
Signed and dated on back: MURRAY/94
Inscribed on bottom: MURRAY'S/SISTER; in pencil: Sister/of
Charles Bregler's Thomas Eakins Collection, purchased with the partial support of the Pew Memorial Trust, 1985.68.1.7

PAUL WAYLAND BARTLETT, a well-known sculptor active at the turn of the century, admired this bust of a "young girl with a melancholy expression" and wrote, "the man who can impart that expression to clay . . . has great genius and will be heard from in

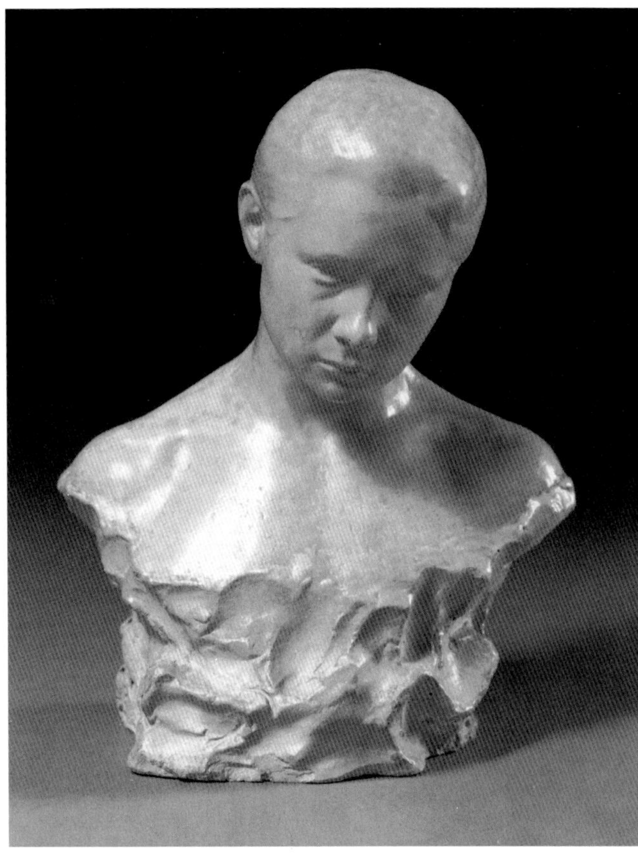

Murray, *Gertrude Murray*

the future."[1] Bartlett also noticed the family resemblance between Samuel Murray's sister Gertrude (before 1869–after 1944), as portrayed here, and the artist himself.

The bust is fully finished at the head and shoulders, yet the base is rough and seems hastily executed, as are a number of Murray's informal portraits.[2] The tilt of the head and pensive expression captured in *Gertrude Murray* evoke a sadness that is typical of four related sculptures: an unlocated bust entitled *Gerty,* shown in Eakins-Murray scrapbook 5 (p. 25); two small, full-length, ideal figures—one nude, the other draped—entitled *Grief* (Hirshhorn Museum and Sculpture Garden), which are both contemporaneous with *Gertrude Murray;* and a much later, lifesize, wax figure, also called *Grief* and based on the statuettes. It was unfinished when Murray died in 1941. The wax soon dried and cracked, and the sculpture was destroyed. All these works were modeled in the realistic style that the sculptor practiced throughout his career.

Thomas Eakins painted a portrait of Gertrude Murray[3] (unlocated) that was perhaps begun in 1894 at the same time she sat for her brother.

Notes

1. Untitled and undated newspaper clipping, Eakins-Murray Scrapbook 4, p. 29, Hirshhorn Museum and Sculpture Garden.

2. A photograph of this work in progress, titled *Study* by Murray and labeled unfinished, is in the PAFA object file.

3. Lloyd Goodrich, *Thomas Eakins: His Life and Work* (New York: Whitney Museum of American Art, 1933), p. 186, dates the portrait 1895.

Reference

1982 Michael W. Panhorst, "Samuel Murray, Sculptor," master's thesis, University of Delaware, p. 49, fig. 27.

Exhibited

1895* May have been shown as cat. no. 746, *Study of a Head.*

Ex Collections

The artist, Philadelphia, 1894–1941; Charles Bregler, Philadelphia, about 1941–58; his second wife, Mary Picozzi Bregler, 1958–85.

Life Cast of the Right Hand of Thomas Eakins

About 1894
Plaster, painted white
9 x 7½ x 2½" (22.9 x 19.1 x 6.4 cm)
Inscribed (by Charles Bregler) in cutoff at wrist: HAND OF/THOMAS/EAKINS
Charles Bregler's Thomas Eakins Collection, purchased with the partial support of the Pew Memorial Trust, 1985.68.1.12

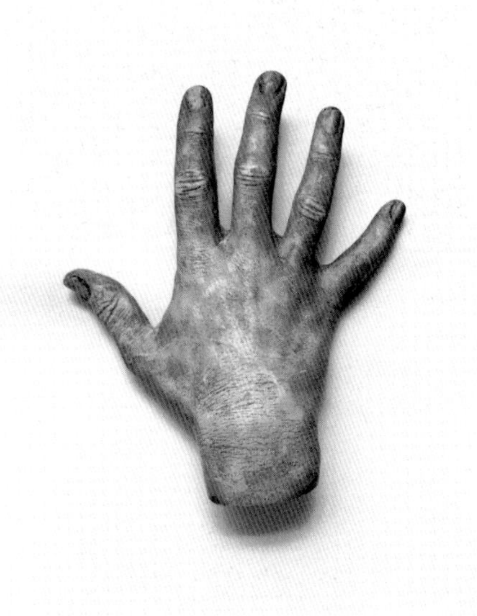

Murray, *Life Cast of the Right Hand of Thomas Eakins*

THIS HAND was cast from life, probably around 1894 when Murray was at work on two portraits of Thomas Eakins: a full-length statuette (q.v.) and a lifesize bust. It was common practice at the time for sculptors to make casts directly from the bodies of their subjects to ensure realistic portraits. Because Eakins taught that there was as much character in the hands as in the head, it is understandable that his protegé would want to make a cast of Eakins's right hand and that the painter would consent.

The Philadelphia Museum of Art owns a bronze cast of the hand and of the bust. The Hirshhorn Museum and Sculpture Garden owns a plaster cast of each.

Ex Collections
The artist, Philadelphia, about 1894–1941; Charles Bregler, Philadelphia, about 1941–58; his second wife, Mary Picozzi Bregler, 1958–85.

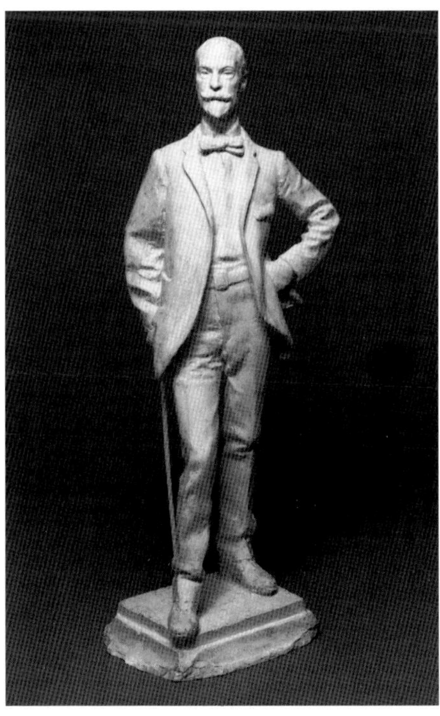

Murray, *David Wilson Jordan*

David Wilson Jordan

About 1895
Plaster and wood
13½ x 4½ x 3⅝" (34.3 x 11.4 x 9.2 cm)
Gift of Helen W. Henderson, 1951.26

THE PAINTER David Wilson Jordan (1859–1935) was born in Harrisburg and died in New York. He studied under Thomas Eakins at the Pennsylvania Academy of the Fine Arts about 1880 and became Eakins's close friend and staunch supporter. Both Jordan and his sister, Letitia Wilson Jordan Bacon, sat for Eakins. Jordan traveled widely and painted many landscapes. He was a dilettante and, until his marriage at the age of forty-eight, a gallant bachelor and much sought-after dancer.

In her obituary of Jordan, whom she had known, Helen Henderson remarked that this portrait was "immensely true of [Jordan] in his every day aspect." She added that the sculpture brings out Samuel Murray's "whimsical contention that knees in trousers give character to the figure."[1]

Thomas Anshutz wrote to Murray in 1903 or 1904, "I have not forgotten that I owe you a sketch for the little Jordan. But you will never get as good a one as it. We don't look on it as a sketch."[2] Indeed, the small figure is carefully detailed and fully finished down to the wrinkles in the coat sleeves and trouser legs. In 1979 the wooden walking stick was reconstructed.

Murray modeled another statuette of Jordan in 1920. It shows the frail and elderly painter mixing pigments on a palette. A heavy overcoat thrown over the shoulders suggests that he is working outdoors. Casts of this sculpture are in the Hirshhorn Museum (plaster, arms missing) and the New Britain Museum (bronze) in Connecticut.

Notes

1. Helen W. Henderson, "David Jordan Passes," *Philadelphia Inquirer*, Feb. 17, 1935, p. 14, society pages.
2. Thomas Anshutz to Samuel Murray, on Saint Louis World's Fair stationery, Eakins-Murray Scrapbook 5, p. 59, Hirshhorn Museum and Sculpture Garden. In addition to the statuette at the Museum of American Art of the Pennsylvania Academy, two plaster casts are known: one in a private collection and the other in the Hirshhorn Museum. The provenance of the work in private hands suggests that it may be the sculpture originally owned by Anshutz.

Reference
1973 Ruth Bowman, "The Artist as Model: A Portrait of David Wilson Jordan by Thomas Anshutz," *Register of the Museum of Art*, University of Kansas, Lawrence, 4 (Fall), p. 5, fig. 8.

Exhibited
1986–87 PAFA, *Sculpture at the Pennsylvania Academy of the Fine Arts.* **1991–92** PAFA, *Thomas Eakins Rediscovered: At Home, At School, At Work.*

Ex Collections
The sitter, Philadelphia, about 1895-about 1900; Helen W. Henderson, Philadelphia, about 1900–51.

William H. Macdowell

1897
Plaster
13½ x 7½ x 5½" (34.3 x 19.1 x 14 cm)
Inscribed, signed, and dated on back: To My/Friend/MRS. EAKINS/SAML. MURRAY/1897; dated on left side: APRI[L] 97
Charles Bregler's Thomas Eakins Collection, purchased with the partial support of the Pew Memorial Trust, 1985.68.1.8

WILLIAM H. MACDOWELL (about 1823–1906), a distinguished Philadelphia engraver, was painted and photographed many times by his daughter Susan Macdowell Eakins and her husband, Thomas Eakins. A number of their portraits depict him leaning to one side and cocking his head in the characteristic attitude captured by Samuel Murray in this sculpture.[1]

The old man's gaunt features emphasize the underlying structure of the forehead and cheekbones. The delineation of the disheveled hair and thin beard animates the portrait, which is further enlivened by the uneven shoulders and the lines of the coat lapels and vest. Rare in Murray's work, but effective in this instance, is the rough transitional passage that ties the tall, twisting form to its plinth.

Murray modeled two different busts of Macdowell, but only casts of this bust of 1897 are known today.[2] An earlier one, probably made in 1891, was shown the following years in the annual exhibition of the Pennsylvania Academy of the Fine Arts.[3] Lifesize and more formally balanced than the later one, it terminated cleanly at the middle of the chest and sat on a simple round pedestal. A plaster bust of Macdowell was shown in the third exhibition of the National Sculpture Society at the American Fine Arts Society, New York, in 1898.

Macdowell was known to be a pessimist with a propensity for predicting trouble, and this personality trait made Murray and Eakins choose him as the model for the prophet Jeremiah (no longer extant), one of ten colossal terracotta statues commissioned for the Witherspoon Building in Philadelphia in 1896 and later removed.[4]

Murray, *William H. Macdowell*

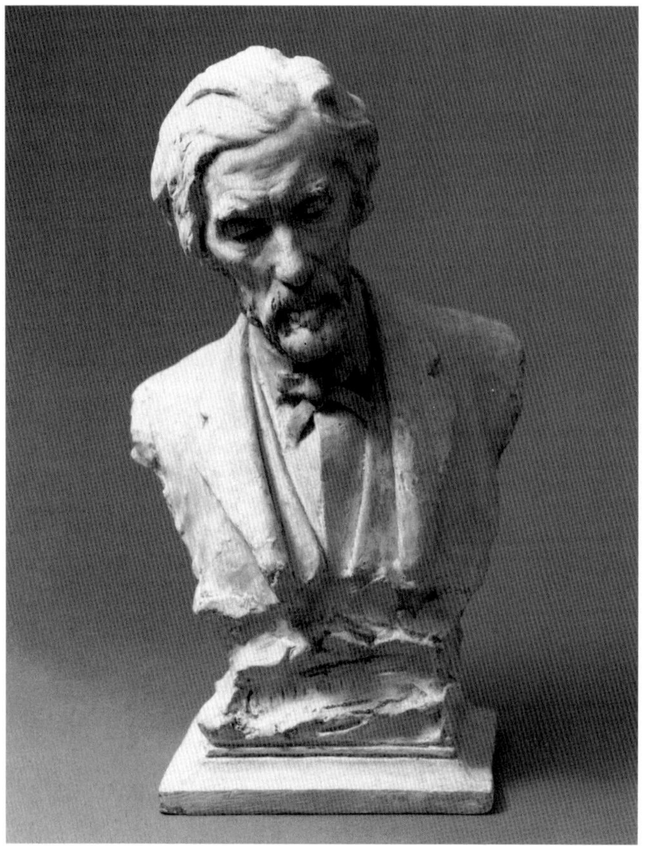

Notes

1. See examples in Susan Danly and Cheryl Leibold, *Eakins and the Photograph* (Washington, D.C. and London: Smithsonian Institution Press), 1994, cat. nos. 76–77, plate 15.
2. A bronze cast is in a private collection in Roanoke, Va.; and plaster casts are in three other private collections and in the Hirshhorn Museum and Sculpture Garden, Washington, D.C.
3. A photograph in Eakins-Murray Scrapbook 3, p. 21, Hirshhorn Museum and Sculpture Garden, shows Murray with the earlier bust of Macdowell (Gordon Hendricks, *The Life and Work of Thomas Eakins* [New York: Grossman Publishers, 1974], fig. 168, p. 120).
4. Mariah Chamberlin-Hellman, "Samuel Murray, Thomas Eakins and the Witherspoon Prophets," *Arts* 53 (May 1979), pp. 135–36, 138–39, fig. 9.

Exhibited
1986–87 PAFA, *Sculpture at the Pennsylvania Academy of the Fine Arts.*

Ex Collections
Susan Macdowell Eakins, Philadelphia, 1897-about 1939; Charles Bregler, Philadelphia, about 1939–58; his second wife, Mary Picozzi Bregler, 1958–85.

Frank Jay St. John

1900
Bronze with brown patina; lost-wax cast
13¼ x 9¼ x 5" (33.6 x 23.5 x 12.7 cm)
Inscribed, signed, and dated on back: TO MY FRIEND/ F. JAY. ST. JOHNS/S. MURRAY/1900
Foundry mark on back: ROMAN BRONZE WKS. N.Y.
Gift of Mr. and Mrs. Charles Nesbitt, 1977.23

FRANK JAY ST. JOHN (d. 1900), a businessman and

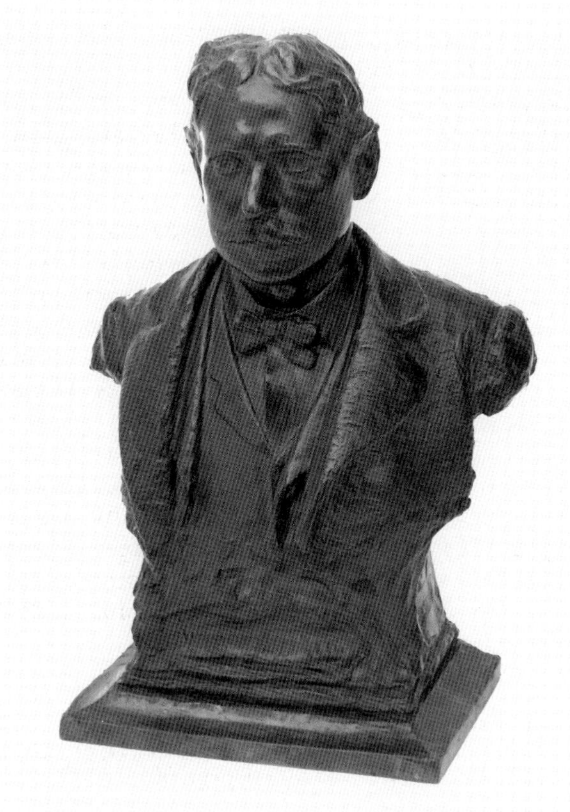

Murray, *Frank Jay St. John*

inventor, was one of at least forty people portrayedby both Samuel Murray and Thomas Eakins. Each artist made a portrait of him in 1900. Eakins's painting (private collection, New York) has St. John seated in profile, wearing his overcoat, and holding his hat in his lap. When he posed for Murray, St. John stood with his right hand in his pants pocket so that his jacket and overcoat were held open, as shown in a photograph probably taken by Eakins.[1] Although Murray's bust terminates near the middle of the chest, it is apparent from the way the lapels are pulled to one side that this sculpture is the result of the studio session recorded in the photograph.

Photographic documentation of such detailed correspondence between Murray's subjects and his portrait sculptures illustrates the naturalistic style that he practiced throughout his career. Yet nuances such as the open jacket and the mere suggestion of the pince-nez perched on the bridge of St. John's nose reveal the artistry of the sculptor.

Note

1. Reproduced in Gordon Hendricks, *Thomas Eakins: His Photographic Works* (Philadelphia: PAFA, 1969), fig. 50, and *The Photographs of Thomas Eakins* (New York: Grossman Publishers, 1972), fig. 234. The photograph also shows Murray's tiny bust of St. John's three-year-old daughter, Arcadia Willoughby St. John, modeled in 1899 (a plaster cast is in the Hirshhorn Museum and Sculpture Garden).

Exhibited

1978 PAFA, *The Last 3 Years—A Selection of Recent Acquisitions,* checklist p. 30. **1986–87** PAFA, *Sculpture at the Pennsylvania Academy of the Fine Arts.*

Ex Collections

The sitter, Philadelphia, 1900; his wife; their daughter, Mrs. Benjamin F. Chappelle, Reno, Nevada; her daughter, Caroline Chappelle, Oklahoma City, ?-about 1972; Mr. and Mrs. Charles Nesbitt, Oklahoma City, about 1972–77.

Mary Hallock (Mrs. Frank L. Greenewalt)

About 1903
Plaster, painted beige
24¾ x 17⅛ x 10½" (62.8 x 43.5 x 26.7 cm)
Inscribed in relief on front of pedestal: MARY HALLOCK
Charles Bregler's Thomas Eakins Collection, purchased with the partial support of the Pew Memorial Trust, 1985.68.1.11

MARY ELIZABETH HALLOCK (1871–1950), was born in Beirut and came to the United States in 1882. She

Murray, *Mary Hallock*

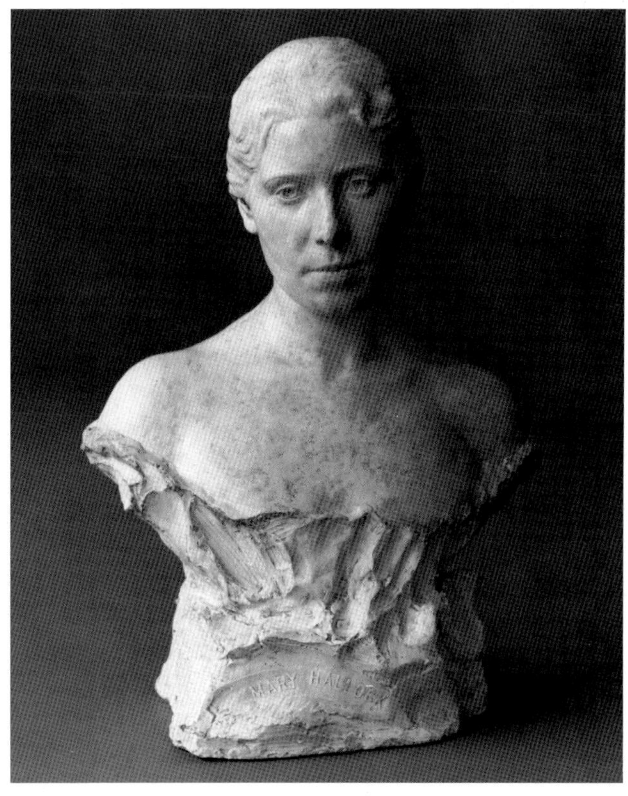

received a gold medal for piano performance from the Philadelphia Academy of Music from which she was graduated in 1893. By 1905 she married Dr. Frank Lindsey Greenewalt, a friend of Thomas Eakins, who painted each of them in 1903.[1]

During the 1910s, Mary Hallock Greenewalt appeared as a piano soloist with the Pittsburgh and Philadelphia symphony orchestras, went on a concert tour of North America, and recorded several works of Chopin for Columbia Records. She was a pioneer in the use of light to enhance the emotional impact of music; and in 1915 in the Egyptian Hall in Philadelphia, she introduced lighting effects into her piano recitals. She was awarded a gold medal in 1926 at the Philadelphia Sesquicentennial Exposition for her research on the synesthetic relationship of light and music. She invented and patented several machines for the projection of colored light keyed to music and in 1946 published *Nourathar: The Fine Art of Light Color Playing,* an early book on the integration of music and light effects.

This bust shows her to be confident and attractive. The eyes are contemplative. The compressed lips suggest determination. An art reviewer in 1905 described the bust as "graceful, sensitive, beautifully modeled and full of charm and temperament."[2] A bronze cast (now unlocated), used as an illustration in her book, was probably owned by Mrs. Greenewalt.

Notes

1. The 1903 portrait of Dr. Greenewalt is unlocated; the one of Mary Hallock is in the Wichita Art Museum. In 1905 Eakins modeled her profile in relief (unlocated). Both Murray and Eakins inscribed her portraits with her maiden name, although when Murray's bust was exhibited in November 1905, her married name was used in "Art and Artists," *Philadelphia Press,* Nov. 19, 1905 (ill.), scrapbook, microfilm, roll no. 54, frame no. 65, PAFA Archives.

2. Ibid.

Exhibited

1904–5 Art Club of Philadelphia, *Seventeenth Annual Exhibition of Oils and Sculpture.* **1908*** cat. no. 843. **1908** Fifth Regiment Armory, Baltimore, *Exhibition of the National Sculpture Society under the Auspices of the Municipal Art Gallery of Baltimore,* cat. no. 301. **1933*** cat. no. 530.

Ex Collections

Thomas Eakins, Philadelphia, about 1903–16; his wife, Susan, 1916–about 1939; Charles Bregler, Philadelphia, about 1939–58; his second wife, Mary Picozzi Bregler, 1958–85.

Thomas Eakins

1907
Plaster with lead palette, painted gold-green
9 x 9½ x 8⅝" (22.9 x 24.1 x 21.9 cm)
Inscribed and signed on top of base: TO MY DEAR FRIEND/ DR. F.H. MILLIKEN/SAMUEL MURRAY
Gift of Malcolm Sausser, 1928.12

THIS PORTRAIT OF THOMAS EAKINS is small in size but monumental in treatment and spirit. Large, simple sculptural masses punctuated by realistic details capture the stalwart presence of the aged painter. All the contours, as well as the painter's concentrated

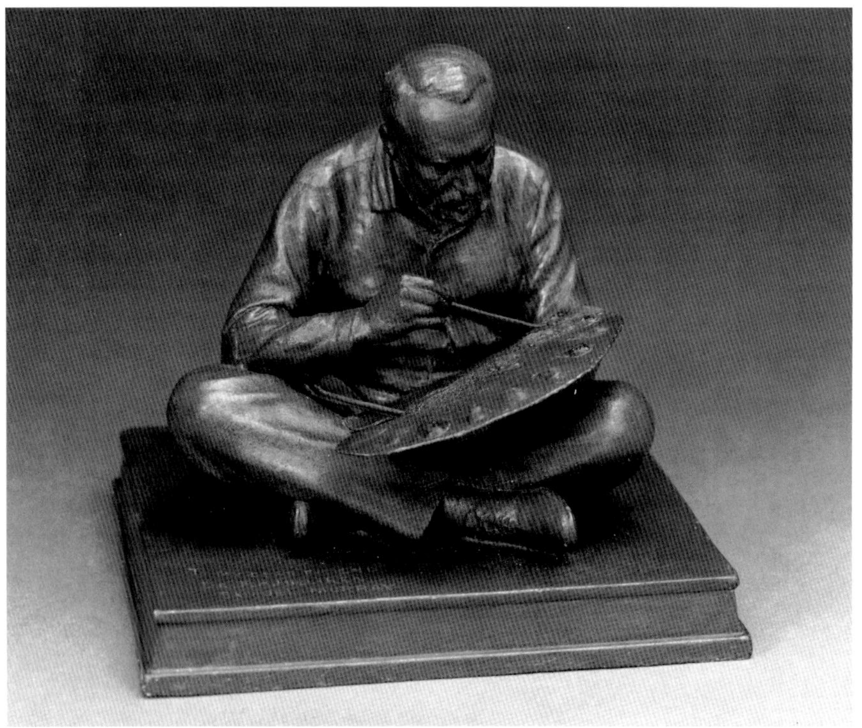

Murray, *Thomas Eakins,* 1907

gaze, direct attention to the right hand and brush at the center of the composition.

For this memorial to his mentor and friend, Samuel Murray portrayed Eakins in the herculean task of creating his largest picture. In 1889 Eakins painted much of *The Agnew Clinic* (University of Pennsylvania, Philadelphia) while seated cross-legged on the floor in front of the enormous canvas.[1] This commission was a rush job; and Eakins worked long hours, broken by occasional cat naps beside the picture.

Murray made at least eight other casts of this portrait—the largest edition that he ever produced.[2] All are inscribed 1907, but this inscription appears to have been cut into the original plaster.[3] The bronze in the Hirshhorn Museum collection was cast after Eakins died (it is inscribed with his birth and death dates), and the other casts may also postdate 1907. Murray kept three casts in his studio until his death and gave away or sold four others, which may have belonged to him or Eakins.[4] One bronze was bought by the Metropolitan Museum of Art, New York, in 1923; and a cast of unknown material was bought by Moore Institute of the Arts, Sciences, and Industry (now Moore College of Art and Design), Philadelphia, in 1940 or 1941.[5]

This plaster cast was given by Murray to his friend Dr. Frank Milliken, who posed for him at an unknown date. A second plaster without a dedication came to the Museum of American Art of the Pennsylvania Academy of the Fine Arts through Charles Bregler's Thomas Eakins collection.

Notes

1. Lloyd Goodrich, *Thomas Eakins* (Cambridge: Harvard University Press, 1982), vol. 2, p. 45. Goodrich, vol. 2, p. 99, states that Murray assisted Eakins in working out the perspective and laying in broad areas of *The Agnew Clinic.*

2. A bronze and two plasters are in the Hirshhorn Museum and Sculpture Garden, Washington, D.C.; a bronze in the Metropolitan Museum of Art; a plaster in the Detroit Institute of Arts; and a bronze and a plaster in a private collection in Larchmont, N.Y.

3. A tag attached to one of the plasters in the Hirshhorn Museum and Sculpture Garden (acc. no. 66.3719) indicates that it is the original plaster used to make the mold for a bronze cast of Eakins, but this tag may have been attached by the Roman Bronze Works in 1929 or 1930 when they made a bronze for Murray. This plaster may not be the original for the other casts.

4. In about 1984 a dealer, Robert Bahssin, in Larchmont, N.Y. issued an edition of about six bronzes cast by Excalibur Bronze in Brooklyn from a plaster that Murray inscribed to his friend and professional colleague, Charles Tefft.

5. The latter sale is recorded in a newspaper clipping, "Murray Honored by Institute," *Philadelphia Public Ledger,* Jan. 6, 1918, in Eakins-Murray Scrapbook 4, p. 14, Hirshhorn Museum and Sculpture Garden.

Exhibited

1953 Philadelphia Art Alliance, *Philadelphia Architecture in the Nineteenth Century.* **1986–87** PAFA, *Sculpture at the Pennsylvania Academy of the Fine Arts.* **1994–96** PAFA, *Two Centuries of Collecting at the Museum of American Art.*

Ex Collections

Dr. F.H. Milliken, Philadelphia, about 1907–?; Malcolm Sausser, Haverford, Pa., ?–1928.

Sergeant Kendall

1869–1938

William Sergeant Kendall was born in the small Harlem River village of Spuyten Duyvil, today part of the Bronx, New York.[1] He was educated at the Yonkers Military School and Brooklyn Polytechnic Institute, where he received his highest marks in drawing.[2] At the age of fourteen, he enrolled at the Students' Art Guild of the Brooklyn Art Association.[3] There, he first came under the tutelage of THOMAS EAKINS, then recognized as one of the country's leading art teachers.[4] It was surely Eakins who encouraged Kendall to model in clay, because Eakins believed modeling helped painters achieve a sense of depth. Although Kendall is primarily remembered as a painter of children, he enjoyed both modeling and carving and continued to sculpt throughout his career.[5] When Eakins quit teaching at the Students' Art Guild, Kendall followed him to the Pennsylvania Academy of the Fine Arts, in Philadelphia. There from November 1885 to February 1886, he attended the daytime life class.[6] He probably returned to New York shortly thereafter, for in November 1886, he began to study at the Art Students League of New York with Harry Siddons Mowbray and J. Carroll Beckwith.[7]

In 1888 Kendall went to Paris with his friend and fellow painter John Lambert. They both joined the atelier of the history painter Luc Olivier Merson; but, when Merson temporarily closed his atelier in 1889, Kendall enrolled at the Académie Julian, which was very popular with American students.[8] Merson sponsored Kendall in the semiannual entrance examination of the state-run Ecole des Beaux-Arts on March 6, 1889.[9] Kendall passed the examination, which entailed life drawing, modeling from antique casts, and elementary architectural design. Matriculation at the Ecole des Beaux-Arts did not require enrollment in the Ecole's ateliers, so Kendall continued to take most of his instruction at the Académie Julian. Among his teachers in Paris were Jules Joseph Lefebvre, Henri Lucien Doucet, and Benjamin Constant.[10]

While abroad, Kendall spent many summers in the art colonies at Concarneau and Le Pouldu in Brittany. He enjoyed painting Breton peasants, especially the women in their distinctive costumes. Breton genre scenes were very popular in the Paris Salon at this time, and Kendall's *Saint Yves, Pray For Us* (location unknown) was awarded an honorable mention in 1891. The same painting won the Walter Lippincott prize for figure painting at the sixty-third annual exhibition of the Pennsylvania Academy of the Fine Arts, in 1893–94. During the summer of 1891, Kendall traveled to Madrid to see and copy the work of Diego Velázquez.

Back in New York, he taught a women's painting class at Cooper Union from 1892 to 1895. He exhibited widely and showed regularly at the Pennsylvania Academy's annual exhibitions from 1894 to 1918 and occasionally thereafter. Early in 1896, Kendall married Margaret Weston Stickney, one of his painting students. In 1900, he painted *The End of the Day* (location unknown), a picture of his wife reading a bedtime story to their first child, Elisabeth. It was his earliest portrayal of motherhood—the theme of some of his best-known paintings, including *Beatrice,* 1906 (Museum of American Art, Pennsylvania Academy of the Fine Arts). For the next twenty-five years, his wife and three daughters were his primary models. He did not look upon the paintings as portraits, however, and he preferred to de-emphasize the fact that they depicted his family.[11] Kendall also painted landscapes and commissioned portraits.

He won many prizes for his paintings and sculpture, including medals at the World's Columbian Exposition of 1893, in Chicago; the Paris Exposition of 1900; the Pan-American Exposition of 1901, in Buffalo; the Louisiana Purchase Exposition of 1904, in Saint Louis; and the Panama-Pacific Exposition of 1915, in San Francisco. Kendall was awarded the Shaw prize by the Society of American Artists in 1901. That same year, he was elected an associate of the National Academy of Design, in New York; and, five years later, he was made an academician.

From 1906 to 1908, Kendall was an instructor in painting and drawing at the Pennsylvania Academy of the Fine Arts; and, from 1908 to 1910, he taught at the Carnegie Institute, in Pittsburgh.[12] In 1913 he succeeded John Ferguson Weir as dean of the Yale University School of Fine Arts. In the spring of 1922, following his divorce, he resigned from Yale. That summer, he married Christine Herter, a longtime friend and student and a member of a prominent New York family. They moved to Hot Springs, Virginia, where they built a house and stables and raised Arabian horses. Kendall continued to paint, but the female nudes of this period were not as popular as the earlier paintings of his children.

Notes

1. Robert Austin, "William Sergeant Kendall, Painter of Children," *Antiques* 124 (Nov. 1983), p. 1024, states that, as a boy, Kendall dropped his first name, William, in favor of his mother's maiden name, Sergeant.

2. Kendall's report cards from the Brooklyn Polytechnic Institute are preserved at the New-York Historical Society.

3. Austin 1983, p. 1024.

4. Lloyd Goodrich, *Thomas Eakins* (Cambridge: Harvard University Press, 1982), vol. 1, p. 188, notes that, at this time, Eakins was the director of the school of the PAFA, but he traveled to Brooklyn to teach at the art guild on Tuesdays and Thursdays.

5. The Museum of Fine Arts, Boston, owns a bronze bust by Kendall that depicts his eldest daughter, Elisabeth, and was cast in 1900.

6. Student List, 1884–95, PAFA Archives.

7. According to the records of the Art Students League, Kendall enrolled in the antique class in November 1886.

8. Austin 1983, p. 1024.

9. H. Barbara Weinberg, "Nineteenth-Century American Painters at the Ecole des Beaux-Arts," *American Art Journal* 13 (Autumn 1981), p. 74.

10. *Salon de 1891: Explication des Ouvrages de Peinture, Sculpture, Architecture, Gravure et Lithographie* (Paris: Paul Dupont, 1891), p. 78.

11. Sergeant Kendall to Harrison S. Morris, managing director of the PAFA, Oct. 25, 1897, PAFA Archives.

12. "Paintings by Kendall to be Displayed at Art Exhibition," *Columbus Enquirer,* March 10, 192[7], loose leaf, William Sergeant Kendall Scrapbook, New-York Historical Society.

References

William Sergeant Kendall Scrapbook, New-York Historical Society. **1905** Charles H. Caffin, "The Art of Sargeant [*sic*] Kendall," *Harper's Monthly Magazine* 117 (Sept.), pp. 568–77. **1915** Montrose J. Moses, "William Sergeant Kendall: Philosopher of Form and Color," *Hearst's Magazine* (Nov. 9), William Sergeant Kendall Papers, New-York Historical Society.

Quest

1910
Wood, polychromed; wood pedestal
34 x 14½ x 17" (86.5 x 36.8 x 43.2 cm)
Pedestal: 38⅝ x 17⅛ x 17⅛" (98.1 x 43.5 x 43.5 cm)
Gift of Mrs. William Sergeant Kendall, 1956.8

During the years when he was an art student in Paris, Sergeant Kendall spent many summer months on the coast in Brittany. The hardworking Breton peasants provided the subject matter for many of his early paintings and at least two sculptures—*Head of a Breton Girl,* a bronze of 1892, and *Quest.*[1] Kendall was fascinated by the deep religious conviction of the Bretons. In *Quest,* the intense gaze of the figure bespeaks a deep spirituality and unyielding faith. She seems to have paused for a moment of reflection during her chores, which typically would have included canning sardines and shucking oysters. The sculptor has emphasized her strong, capable hands.

Kendall began to carve *Quest* in January 1910.[2] He worked on it intermittently for many months. The model was Kendall's first cousin Anne Saunders Kendall, who was adopted by Kendall's parents and reared as his sister. A photograph of Anne posing for *Quest* shows her lying on her back on a couch.[3] The strange crook in the figure's neck undoubtedly stems from the model's reclining posture. The wood was probably in a horizontal position during the carving. On May 27, 1910, Kendall wrote in his journal, "I worked all morning on the wooden figure. I am much interested as I am getting hold of the right way to manage the carving. . . . Also I think I have solved the problem of the color of the jersey & [rushes]."

Painted wood carvings were not popular when Kendall executed *Quest.* Even in 1917, when direct carving had come into vogue, a critic for *Scribner's Magazine* wrote that *Quest* seemed like an anachronism.[4] Indeed, its closest antecedents were the cigar-store figures and ships' figureheads of the early nineteenth century. Nevertheless, *Quest* caused a sensation whenever it was exhibited and captured more attention than any of Kendall's other works. When it was shown at the Saint Botolph Club in Boston in 1913, one reviewer wrote, "Quest . . . quite leaves the rest of the collection in the shade."[5] At the Panama-Pacific Exposition, in 1915 in San Francisco, it won a silver medal.[6]

Shortly after *Quest* was completed, a crack appeared on the proper left side of the head; and Kendall had to split open the piece and add several slices of cherry wood in order to consolidate it.[7] Although the sculpture is carved from a single piece of wood, the pedestal (not shown in the photograph) is constructed of many pieces. Kendall adopted the style of French provincial cabinetry for the design of the pedestal.

After Sergeant Kendall's memorial exhibition closed at the Pennsylvania Academy in May 1939, *Quest* remained on indefinite loan to the Academy by Christine Herter Kendall, the artist's second wife. In 1956 she gave the piece to the Academy.

Notes

1. Charles H. Caffin, "The Art of Sargeant [*sic*] Kendall," *Harper's Monthly Magazine* 117 (Sept. 1905), p. 570, relates that *Head of Breton Girl* was refused admission to the Paris Salon because it was believed to have been cast from life.

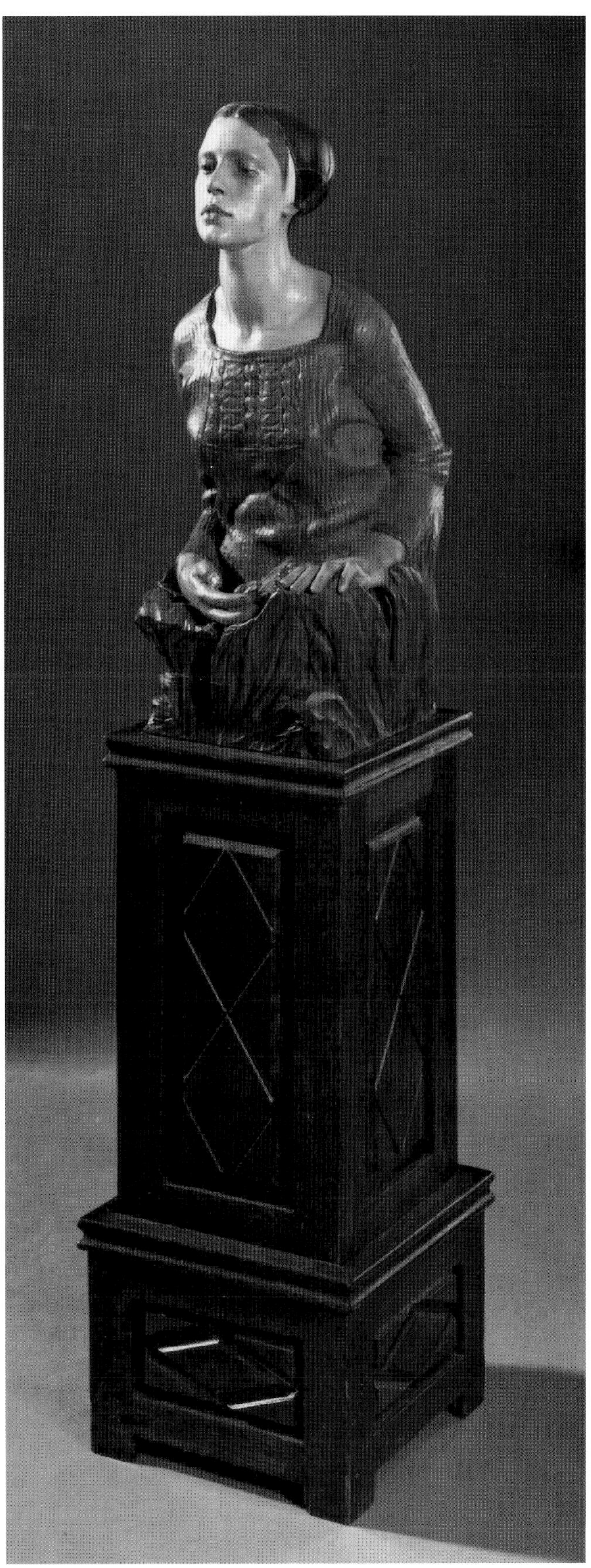

Kendall, *Quest* (see also frontispiece)

2. Kendall's journal, entry for Jan. 24, 1910, New-York Historical Society.

3. Copy photograph in PAFA object file.

4. Dana H. Carroll, "Polychrome Wood Carving," *Scribner's Magazine* 61 (May 1917), p. 643.

5. Unidentified newspaper clipping, William Sergeant Kendall Scrapbook, p. 49, New-York Historical Society.

6. Gy Blas, "Fine Kendall Paintings on Exhibition at Yale," *New Haven Register*, Jan. 15, 1939, scrapbook, PAFA Archives.

7. Virginia Norton Naudé, conservation report, Jan. 22, 1980, PAFA object file.

References

1913 *Providence Sunday Journal*, Dec. 28 (ill.), William Sergeant Kendall Scrapbook, New-York Historical Society. **1917** Dana H. Carroll, "Polychrome Wood Carving," *Scribner's Magazine* 61 (May), pp. 643–44 (frontispiece). **1922** Frank Jewett Mather, Jr., "Sergeant Kendall and His Art," *Yale Alumni Weekly* 31 (July 7), p. 1193 (ill.). **1982** Linda Bantel, "Sculpture at the Pennsylvania Academy," *Antiques* 121 (March), p. 711 (ill.). **1986** *Sculpture Review* 35 (Summer), p. 8 (ill.). **1986** Edward J. Sozanski, "A Sculptural Dialogue Links Past and Present," *Philadelphia Inquirer* (Nov. 9), p. 18-J (ill.).

Exhibited

1913 Yale University, School of the Fine Arts, New Haven, *Exhibition of Paintings, Drawings, Sculptures by William Sergeant Kendall, M.A., N.A.*, cat. no. 71. **1913** Saint Botolph Club, Boston, *Paintings by Sergeant Kendall*, checklist no. 64. **1913–14** Rhode Island School of Design, Providence, *Exhibition of the Work of Sergeant Kendall, M.A., N.A.*, cat. no. 72. **1915** Panama-Pacific Exposition, San Francisco, cat. no. 2465. **1916** National Academy of Design, New York, ninety-first annual exhibition, cat. no. 481. **1939** Yale University, Gallery of Fine Arts, *Memorial Exhibition of the Paintings, Drawings and Sculpture of William Sergeant Kendall*, cat. no. 46. **1939** PAFA, *Memorial Exhibition of the Work of Sergeant Kendall*, cat. no. 42. **1972** PAFA, *Acres of Art*, checklist no. 52. **1973** PAFA, *Held in Trust*, cat. no. 103. **1975–76** Whitney Museum of American Art, New York, *A Portrait of Young America*. **1976** PAFA, *In This Academy*, cat. no. 236 (ill.). **1978–79** PAFA, *350 Masterpieces of American Art, 1720–1978*. **1984–85** PAFA, *A Growing American Treasure: Highlights from the Permanent Collection*. **1986–87** PAFA, *Sculpture at the Pennsylvania Academy of the Fine Arts*. **1992–93** PAFA, *Masterworks of American Art: 1750–1950*. **1994–96** PAFA, *Two Centuries of Collecting at the Museum of American Art*.

A. Stirling Calder

1870–1945

Alexander Stirling Calder was the son of the Scottish-born sculptor Alexander Milne Calder (1846–1923) and Margaret Stirling Calder. The father's chief legacy is the elaborate sculptural decoration of Philadelphia's City Hall in which he was assisted by his young son.

Born in Philadelphia, A. Stirling Calder attended local public schools and harbored an early love for the theater.[1] He followed in his father's footsteps by enrolling at the Pennsylvania Academy of the Fine Arts. He was sixteen when he entered the Academy in the fall of 1885.[2] At that time, THOMAS EAKINS was the director of the school; and his curriculum emphasized the use of live models and the study of anatomy. When Eakins was forced to resign in February 1886, Calder signed the petition calling for his reinstatement.[3] Calder did not follow Eakins into the newly formed Art Students' League, however, but chose instead to continue his studies at the Academy under Thomas P. Anshutz and James P. Kelly (1854–1893). A prodigious talent, young Calder had two portrait heads accepted for the fifty-seventh annual exhibition of the Pennsylvania Academy in 1887. Throughout his career, Calder continued to exhibit at the Academy; he participated in another twenty-five annuals before his death in 1945.

Calder first traveled abroad in 1889 with classmates from the Pennsylvania Academy. In Paris they joined another contingent of Academy students, including CHARLES GRAFLY and Robert Henri. Calder returned to the Pennsylvania Academy as demonstrator of anatomy for the 1889–90 school year.[4] In this capacity, he assisted students in the dissecting room and gave demonstrations that complemented the anatomy lectures of Dr. William W. Keen. But Paris beckoned again, and Calder set sail in the fall of 1890 in the company of his friend Charles Grafly. Calder enrolled at the Académie Julian, where he studied under Grafly's former teacher Henri Michel Chapu (1833–1891). The following year, Calder was accepted into the atelier of Jean Alexandre Joseph Falguière (1831–1900) at the Ecole des Beaux-Arts.

Back in Philadelphia in 1892, Calder plunged into his career as a professional artist. His first major commission, won in competition, was a bronze statue of the Philadelphia surgeon Dr. Samuel Gross for Washington, D.C. In 1897 he began work on twelve large cast-stone statues depicting renowned Presbyterians for the facade of the Witherspoon Building in Philadelphia.[5] From 1900 to 1905, Calder was an instructor of modeling at the School of Industrial Art of the Pennsylvania Museum.[6] He received his first widespread acclaim at the Saint Louis Exposition, in 1904. He served on the advisory panel for sculpture and won a silver medal for his decorative statues, the most important of which was the French explorer Philippe François Renault.[7] Calder exhibited five sculptures at the hundredth anniversary exhibition of the Pennsylvania Academy in 1905. Among these were the marble sundial that he made for Philadelphia's Fairmount Park and the Celtic Cross Memorial to General William Joyce Sewell. The latter won him the Walter Lippincott prize at the anniversary exhibition.

In 1906 Calder contracted tuberculosis and was forced to move to a milder climate to convalesce. With financial assistance from the painter John Lambert, the Calders settled first in Arizona and then in California. In Pasadena, Calder modeled figures for the portico of the Throop Polytechnic Institute (now California Institute of Technology). With his health restored, he moved his family back east and in 1910 settled in Croton-on-Hudson, New York. That year, he taught sculpture in the evenings at the National Academy of Design in New York. During the 1911–12 school year he taught modeling there with Hermon Atkins MacNeil (1866–1947). In 1912 he was appointed acting chief of the Department of Sculpture under Karl Bitter (1867–1915) for the Panama-Pacific International Exposition to be held in San Francisco in 1915. Calder took a studio in the famed Tenth Street Studio Building in New York and, with several assistants, began to create the models for the exposition sculptures. After Bitter's death in 1915, Calder was responsible for the successful completion of the work in San Francisco. He was awarded the designer's medal for his figurative groups *The Nations of the East, The Nations of the West,* and *The Fountain of Energy.* Calder's next major work, the Depew Memorial Fountain (1915–17) in Indianapolis, was another of Bitter's unfinished projects. Calder retained the general scheme of his predecessor's sketch but created an entirely original work. The central figure is a daughter of Pan, clashing cymbals; and eight small children dance around her. *The Island,* another major work from the late 1910s, was a collaborative effort with the architect Paul Chalfin for the James Deering estate in Miami.

From 1918 to 1922, Calder taught modeling at the Art Students League in New York. About this time, the first manifestations of modernism became apparent in his work. His relief of Washington flanked by Wisdom and Justice for the War Memorial Arch in Washington Square in New York displays a new stylization and a tendency toward abstraction. By 1920 these aspects had become readily apparent. They can be seen in Calder's three reclining river personifications for the Swann Memorial Fountain in Philadelphia's Logan Circle. The Shakespeare Memorial, Calder's last major monument, was installed on Logan Circle in 1932. The model for the memorial was shown that year at the 127th annual exhibition of the Pennsylvania Academy and was awarded the James E. McClees prize. Calder also received the gold medal of the Architectural League of New York in 1932 for his statue of Leif Ericsson. It was given by the United States Government to the people of Iceland and installed at Reykjavik.

Notes

1. A. Stirling Calder, letter recounting experiences while studying at the Pennsylvania Academy, 1939, PAFA Archives. Calder erred in stating that he entered PAFA in the fall of 1886.
2. Student card, PAFA Archives.
3. Student petition to the board of directors of the Pennsylvania Academy, Feb. 15, 1886, ibid.
4. *Circular of the Committee on Instruction, 1889–1890* (school catalogue), ibid. Catalogue of the following year incorrectly listed him as demonstrator of anatomy.
5. Because of deterioration, the statues were removed in 1967. Six of them have been preserved at the present building of the Presbyterian Historical Society, 425 Lombard Street, Philadelphia.
6. Calder recalled that he had been invited back to Philadelphia in 1892 to become the assistant instructor of modeling at the Pennsylvania Academy (N. Calder 1947, p. 5). It is possible that his friend Charles Grafly recommended him for this position; however, there is no record that Calder ever taught modeling at the Academy.
7. Hayes 1977, p. 122.

References

1919 Henry Rankin Poore, "Stirling Calder, Sculptor," *International Studio* 67 (April), pp. 37–50. **1947** Nanette Calder, ed., *Thoughts of A. Stirling Calder on Art and Life,* New York: privately printed. **1977** Margaret Calder Hayes, *Three Alexander Calders,* Middlebury, Vt.: Paul S. Eriksson.

Man Cub

1901–2
Bronze with black patina; sand cast in 1905–6
48¾ x 15¼ x 13¾" (123.8 x 38.7 x 34.9 cm)
Signed on base near figure's left heel: *Calder*
Foundry mark stamped on top of base behind right foot: BUREAU BROS./PHILA.
Cast by the Pennsylvania Academy from the plaster purchased by subscription, 1905.9

MODELED FROM LIFE, *Man Cub* depicts the sculptor's son Alexander ("Sandy," 1898–1976, the originator of the mobile) at the age of three. A. Stirling Calder's thorough understanding of human anatomy is revealed in the child's pudgy figure. He appears ready to take a step forward. The position of his legs and the slightly outstretched left hand reinforce the suggestion of movement, while the ball in his right hand and his happy expression convey the playfulness of the moment. The sculpture has the freshness of a sketch. Quickly drawn, incised lines denote the eyebrows; and oblong voids represent the eyes.

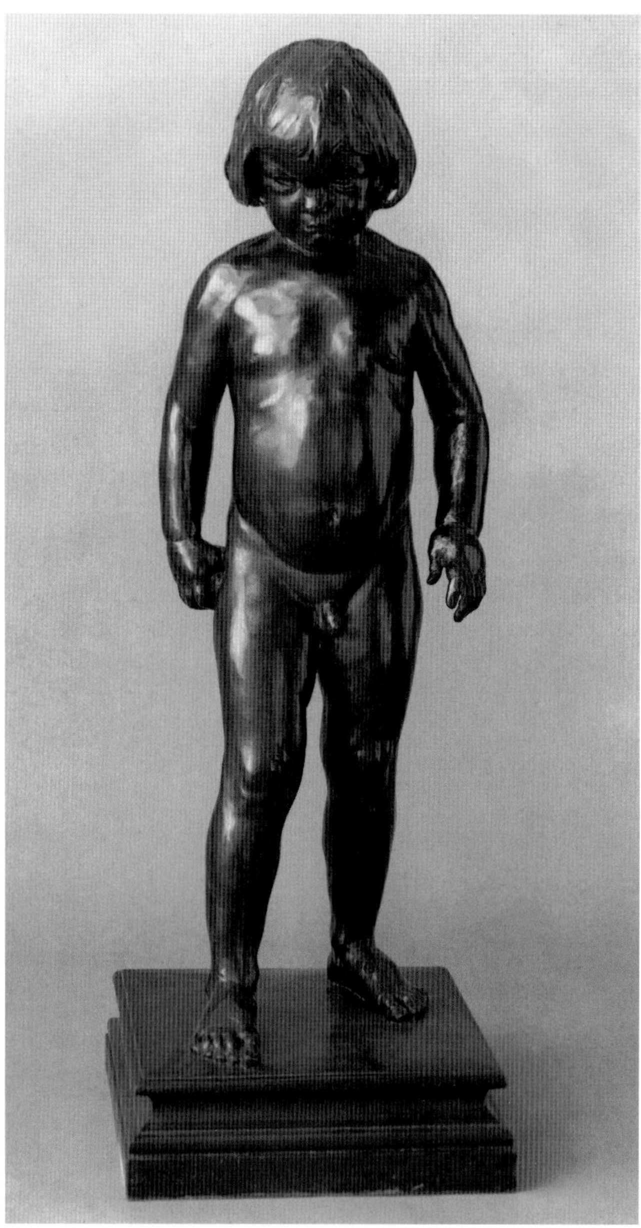

Calder, *Man Cub*

A. Stirling Calder completed a plaster cast of this piece in time to show it in the seventy-first annual exhibition of the Pennsylvania Academy of the Fine Arts, which opened on January 20, 1902. The plaster was shown again at the Louisiana Purchase Exposition, in Saint Louis in 1904. At the end of October 1905, the Pennsylvania Academy bought the plaster model. By then, Calder was seriously ill and in straitened financial circumstances. The purchase price of one thousand dollars was garnered through a quiet subscription campaign. John E.D. Trask, managing director of the Pennsylvania Academy, tried to avoid the appearance of a direct attempt to ease Calder's burden; but helping the sculptor was obviously the motivation of many of the donors.[1]

From the plaster, the Bureau Brothers foundry cast this bronze for the Pennsylvania Academy for $230.[2] It was finished by January 11, 1906, and placed in the 101st annual exhibition. According to the registrar's object files, the foundry returned the plaster to the Academy and it was stored in the basement. When an inventory of the collection was made in 1941, however, the plaster was not found. It may have deteriorated beyond repair or perhaps, during the intervening years, the Academy returned it to Calder. In 1918 Calder showed a plaster version in an exhibition of American sculpture at the Metropolitan Museum of Art, in New York. Following this exhibition, the Metropolitan's Committee on Purchases asked Calder for a bronze cast of *Man Cub*.[3] It was made by the Roman Bronze Works in 1922 and remains today in the Metropolitan Museum of Art.

Notes

1. John E.D. Trask to Albert Kelsey, Oct. 30, 1905, PAFA Archives.
2. Receipt from Bureau Brothers Bronze Statuary and Founders, Jan. 11, 1906, PAFA object file.
3. H.W. Kent to A. Stirling Calder, Jan. 18, 1922, Archives, Metropolitan Museum of Art.

References

1919 Henry Rankin Poore, "Stirling Calder, Sculptor," *International Studio* 67 (April), p. 48 (ill.). **1962** Bennard B. Perlman, *The Immortal Eight: American Painting from Eakins to the Armory Show, 1870–1913*, New York: Exposition Press, published as *Painters of the Ashcan School: The Immortal Eight*, New York: Dover Publications, 1988, p. 36 (ill.).

Exhibited

1906* cat. no. 903. **1912** Toledo Museum of Art, Ohio, *Exhibition of American Sculpture* (sponsored by the National Sculpture Society, New York), cat. no. 9. **1916** Pennsylvania Museum of Art, Memorial Hall, Philadelphia, *Americanization through Art*, cat. no. 261 (ill.). **1919** Luxembourg Museum, Paris, American art exhibition. **1926** Philadelphia, *Sesquicentennial Exposition*. **1953** Philadelphia Art Alliance, *Philadelphia Architecture in the Nineteenth Century*. **1960** Dallas Museum of Fine Arts, *Famous Families in American Art*, cat. no. 66 (ill.). **1961** Wilmington Society of the Fine Arts, Delaware Art Center, *Calder: Alexander Milne, Alexander Stirling and Alexander*, cat. no. 7 (ill.). **1974** Provident National Bank, Philadelphia, exhibition of Pennsylvania Academy works. **1975–76** Whitney Museum of American Art, New York, *A Portrait of Young America*. **1976–77** Whitney Museum of American Art, *Calder's Universe*, traveled to High Museum of Art, Atlanta; Walker Art Center, Minneapolis; Dallas Museum of Fine Arts. **1978–79** PAFA, *350 Masterpieces of American Art: 1720–1978*. **1981** Governor's Residence, Harrisburg, Pa., *Three Generations of the Calder Family*. **1982–83** Philadelphia College of Art, *Affects and Effects, Part I: Past Faculty of the Philadelphia College of Art*, p. 53, p. 14 (ill.). **1986–87** *Sculpture at the Pennsylvania Academy of the Fine Arts*.

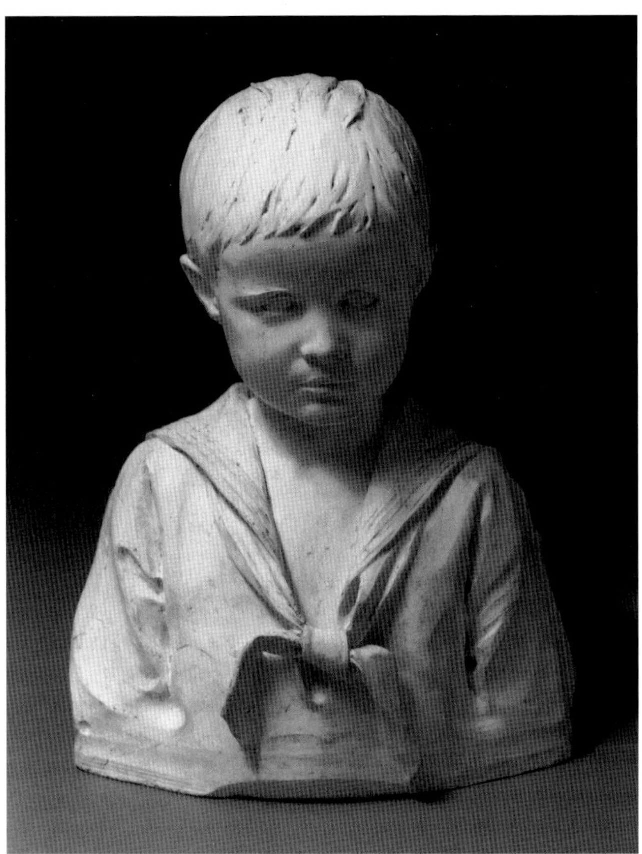

Calder, *Martin Philip Grey II*

Martin Philip Grey II

1902
Plaster
19 x 14 x 8" (48.2 x 35.5 x 20.3 cm)
Gift of Louise Grey Mitchell, Lucy Grey Stimson, and Norma Grey Kemball, in memory of their parents, Norman and Louise Booth Sinnickson Grey, 1954.8

IN THE YEARS immediately following his return from Paris, A. Stirling Calder's work consisted largely of portraiture. He modeled this bust of Martin Philip Grey II (1897–1902) just before the child's death in February 1902. Probably done from life, the bust displays Calder's simple and direct early style. Forms are reduced to their essentials so that a feeling of spontaneity pervades the portrait.

It is not clear whether the child's parents, who commissioned the bust, intended to have it translated into a more permanent medium. The bust remained in the Grey family for fifty-two years and was given to the Pennsylvania Academy in 1954 by the sitter's three sisters. During conservation in 1985, the removal of several unoriginal layers of white paint, revealed crisper forms and greater detail.

Exhibited
1903* cat. no. 1102, as *Portrait Bust of a Boy.* **1986–87** PAFA, *Sculpture at the Pennsylvania Academy of the Fine Arts.*

Naiad with Tragic Mask

About 1920
Plaster, painted green and white with evidence of gold leaf
16¼ x 9¾ x 11¼" (41.3 x 24.8 x 28.6 cm)
Funds provided by the Collectors' Circle, 1993.6

Naiad with Tragic Mask was produced a few years after Calder's 1917 commissions for the Swann Memorial Fountain and Shakespeare Memorial, both in Philadelphia's Logan Circle. The depiction of a mythological being—a water nymph—holding a Tragedy mask reveals the artist's continuing fascination with the theater and his growing interest in stylized abstraction. In fact, this sculpture is one of at least five known versions of the subject, produced in both plaster and bronze.[1] The greater naturalism of this piece

Calder, *Naiad with Tragic Mask*

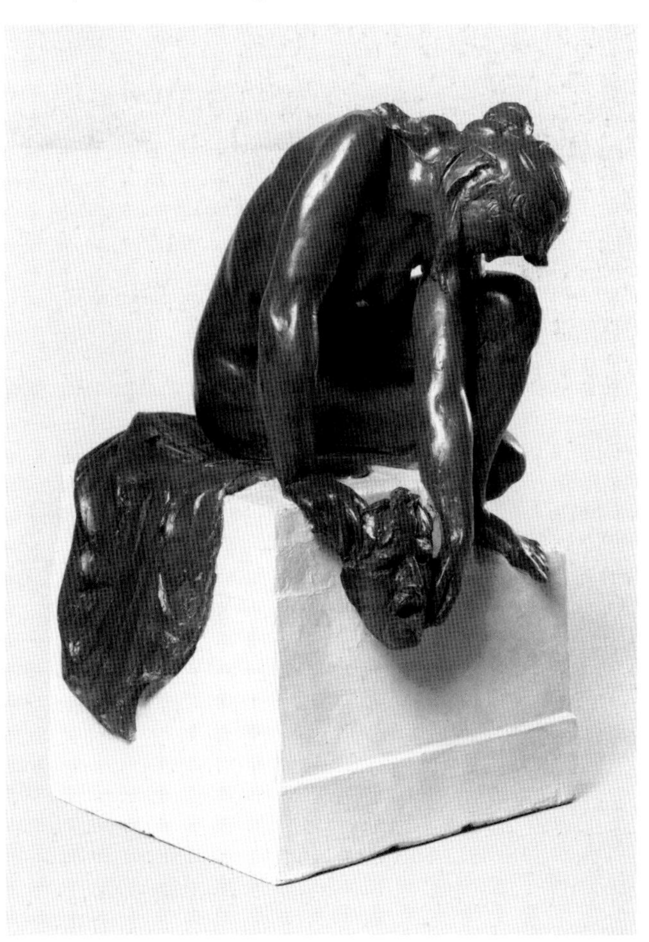

suggests that it may have been the working model. It is not known whether the work was ever realized as a public or private fountain.

Note

1. A larger plaster version is in the collection of the Montclair Art Museum, Montclair, N.J.; this version was exhibited in the Pennsylvania Academy's annual exhibition of 1921. A mid-size bronze version is owned by the Reading Public Museum, Reading, Pa. For a listing of other versions, see the Inventory of American Sculpture, National Museum of American Art, Smithsonian Institution.

Exhibited

1993–94 PAFA, *Masterworks of American Art: 1750–1950.* **1994–96** PAFA, *Two Centuries of Collecting at the Museum of American Art.*

Ex Collections

The artist, about 1920–45; Calder family; Janet DeTomassi, 1960s; Mr. and Mrs. Noel Glen; Hirschl and Adler Galleries, New York, 1993.

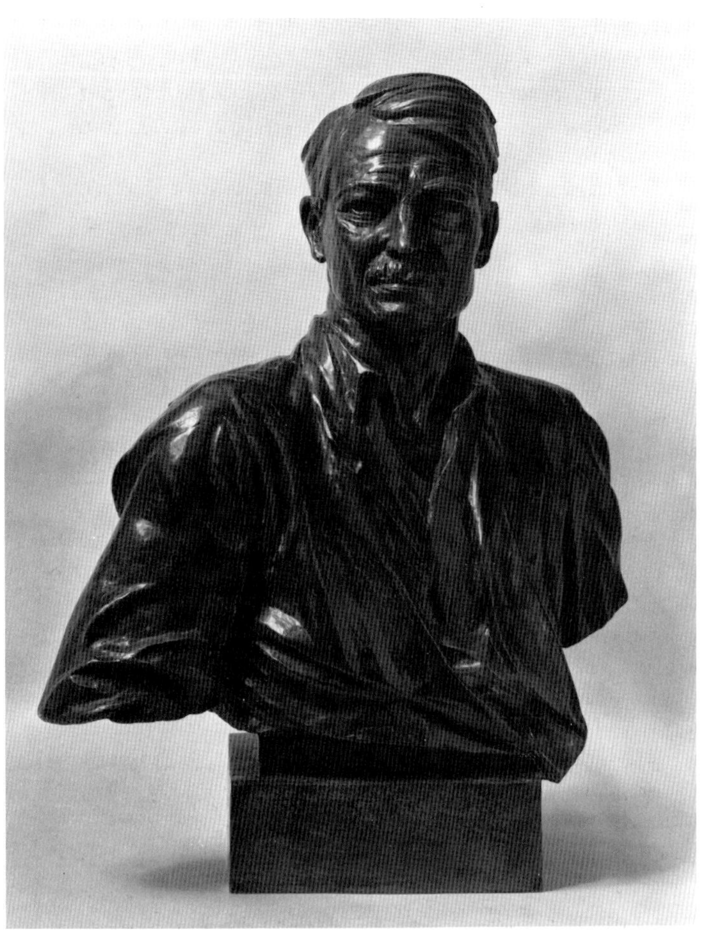

Calder, *Robert Henri*

Robert Henri, the painter-teacher with the gift of friendship

1934
Bronze with black patina; cast in 1947
32 x 25 x 18" (81.3 x 63.5 x 45.7 cm)
Signed on base under proper left shoulder: *Calder*
Lost-wax cast by E. Gargani and Sons, New York
Gift of Mrs. A. Stirling Calder, 1947.14

POSSESSED of a strong will and magnetic personality, Robert Henri (1865–1929) was the natural leader of the Ashcan school.[1] Concentrating on urban scenes, these artists advocated free artistic expression and individualism. As a much beloved teacher, Henri passed this vision on to a younger generation of artists.

A. Stirling Calder and Robert Henri probably met in 1886 when both were first-year students at the Pennsylvania Academy of the Fine Arts. They remained lifelong friends. Calder modeled this posthumous portrait of Henri in 1934. He showed it that year in plaster in *A Mile of Art,* the first municipal art exhibition held at the RCA Building, in Rockefeller Center, New York. The art critic Henry McBride included the bust among his "hints for purchase," a list of works that he singled out for their quality and beauty.[2] The plaster was not shown again until 1943, when it appeared in the Pennsylvania Academy's 138th annual exhibition. Calder specifically requested that the title in the Academy's catalogue read *Robert Henri, the painter-teacher with the gift of friendship.*[3] While the plaster was on view at the Academy, an attempt was made to secure funds for its purchase; but, in the turmoil of World War II, the appeal was unsuccessful. In 1947, two years after Calder's death, his wife had this bronze cast by E. Gargani and Sons. She presented it to the Pennsylvania Academy "to remind the Philadelphians of two men who began their art life in the Academy School."[4]

Notes

1. For biographical information on Henri, see *Robert Henri: Painter* (Wilmington, Del.: Delaware Art Museum, 1984), exhib. cat. for traveling show; and Bennard B. Perlman, *Robert Henri: His Life and Art* (New York: Dover Publications, 1991).
2. Henry McBride, "Municipal Art Exhibition Vast but Entertaining Show," *New York Sun,* March 3, 1934.
3. A. Stirling Calder to Joseph T. Fraser, Jr., undated, probably early Jan. 1943, PAFA object file.
4. Nanette Calder to J.T. Fraser, Feb. 20, 1947, PAFA Archives.

Reference

1982 Linda Bantel, "Sculpture at the Pennsylvania Academy," *Antiques* 121 (March), p. 712 (ill.).

Exhibited

1948 Woodmere Art Gallery, Philadelphia, *American Art, 1860–1914.* **1955** PAFA, *150th Anniversary Exhibition,* cat. no. 140 (ill.). **1961** Wilmington Society of the Fine Arts, Delaware Art Center, *Calder: Alexander Milne, Alexander Stirling and Alexander,* cat. no. 11. **1970** University of Nebraska Art Galleries, Sheldon Memorial Art Gallery, Lincoln, *American Sculpture,* cat. no. 37 (ill.). **1973** PAFA, *Held in Trust,* checklist no. 29. **1974** Provident National Bank, Philadelphia, exhibition of Pennsylvania Academy works. **1975–76** Whitney Museum of American Art, New York, *A Portrait of Young America.* **1976** PAFA, *In This Academy,* cat no. 247. **1980** PAFA, Peale House, *The Pennsylvania Academy Schools, 1876–1900.* **1986–87** PAFA, *Sculpture at the Pennsylvania Academy of the Fine Arts.* **1994–96** PAFA, *Two Centuries of Collecting at the Museum of American Art.*

Bessie Potter Vonnoh

1872–1955

Bessie Potter Vonnoh is primarily remembered for her diminutive sculptures portraying fashionable female figures in everyday activities.[1] During the 1920s and 1930s, however, she executed a number of large fountain and garden pieces. Both these facets of her oeuvre reflect the growing taste for bronze sculpture to adorn private homes in early twentieth-century America.[2] The ideals of motherhood and family embodied in many of Vonnoh's works were aptly suited to domestic environments.

Born in Saint Louis, Bessie Onahotema Potter was only two years old when her father was killed in a railroad accident. Shortly thereafter, she was stricken with a mysterious and painful illness, which her doctors were unable to diagnose but attempted to treat, at times confining her to an upright position by straps hung from the ceiling. This acute attack lasted for about a year.[3] In 1876 the Potters moved to Chicago. When Bessie's health had improved enough to allow her to attend school regularly, her favorite activity was clay modeling. Her work seemed so promising that her mother took her to see the sculptor Lorado Taft (1860–1936) for advice; and, as a result of his encouragement, she enrolled in 1889 for three years of study under Taft at the Art Institute of Chicago. He had studied in Paris at the Ecole des Beaux-Arts and was a staunch advocate of the naturalism and active modeling of the French school. He imparted this tradition to many of his students, especially Potter. When Taft was appointed supervisor for the enlargement of the sculptural decoration for the 1893 World's Columbian Exposition, in Chicago, he hired Potter and several other female students to assist him. Potter also executed an original statue, the personification of Art, for the Illinois State Building at the exposition.

According to Lorado Taft, Potter's early statuettes were inspired by the small bronze sculptures that Prince Paul Troubetzkoy (1866–1938) exhibited in the Italian section of the World's Columbian Exposition.[4] Certainly, the small scale and impressionistic style of the statuettes and portraits that Potter began to execute in 1894 are reminiscent of Troubetzkoy's work; but the subjects are far removed from the native Americans and horses that Troubetzkoy showed at the exposition.[5] Potter's first full-length statuettes portrayed friends attired in the long-skirted, balloon-sleeved dresses of the day.[6] Almost immediately, she gained attention for these works. In 1894 she had five sculptures accepted for the sixty-fourth annual exhibition at the Pennsylvania Academy of the Fine Arts. She showed works in the next two Pennsylvania Academy annuals and participated in another fifteen from 1899 to 1931.

In 1895 Potter traveled to Paris accompanied by her mother, Lorado Taft, and his sister, the sculptor Zulime Taft (1870-after 1940). During this three-month sojourn, Potter visited Auguste Rodin (1840–1917) in his studio. Back in Chicago, she continued to produce statuettes and portraits of fashionable women. With other Chicago artists, Potter formed "The Little Room," a club that met at her studio.[7] In 1898, following an eight-month visit to Italy, Potter began work on two major projects: a bust of Major General S.W. Crawford for the Smith Memorial in Philadelphia's Fairmount Park and a lifesize statue of the actress Maude Adams as *The American Girl.* The latter was to be cast in gold and placed in the Colorado State Exhibition at the Exposition Universelle in Paris in 1900; but, because of a controversy concerning its casting and payment, the piece was not part of the Colorado exhibit. Sadly, it was installed instead in a poor location next to a telescope in the Palais de l'Optique.[8]

Potter married the American impressionist painter Robert Vonnoh in 1899 and honeymooned in Paris. There, at the exposition of 1900, she was awarded a bronze medal for the bronze statuettes *Dancing Girl* and *Young Mother.* The Vonnohs remained in France for about a year before establishing a home in Rockland Lake, New York, in 1901.[9] In 1903 they moved to New York and began spending summers in Lyme, Connecticut. During the next two decades, Bessie Potter Vonnoh exhibited widely and won numerous awards. *Young Mother* and *Midsummer* were shown at the 1901 Pan-American Exposition, in Buffalo. At the 1904 Universal Exposition, in Saint Louis, she was awarded a gold medal for her ten entries. In 1906 she was elected an associate of the National Academy of Design, in New York. She won the Shaw prize at the National Academy in 1909 for *Enthroned,* a small group depicting a mother and her children. In 1913 a one-woman show of her small bronzes was mounted at the Brooklyn Museum, and her *Dancing Figure* appeared in the Armory Show. Vonnoh was a member of the National Sculpture Society and participated in many of its exhibitions. She was awarded the society's Watrous gold medal in 1921 for *Allegresse,* a group of three dancing girls.[10] That same year, she was elected an academician of the National Academy of Design.

Although she had no children of her own, Vonnoh often portrayed young children, especially in her fountains. The fountain at Ormond Beach Park, Florida, which she executed between 1913 and 1925, depicts a solitary child with hand outstretched for a bird to alight. Vonnoh used a similar theme in a bird bath, 1925–27, for the Roosevelt Bird Sanctuary, Oyster Bay, New York, and for her memorial to Frances Hodgson Burnett, 1937, in Central Park in New York. During the 1940s and 1950s, Vonnoh produced little; but she did some teaching at the Wayman Adams Old Mill Art School in Elizabethtown, New York.[11] In 1948, about fifteen years after Robert Vonnoh's death, she married the urologist Dr. Edward Keyes; but he died later that year. The sculptor died in 1955.

Notes

1. Most of the statuettes were intended to be cast in bronze; however, Vonnoh exhibited and sold numerous plaster casts, some of which were subtly polychromed. She also worked in terracotta. Five small terracottas were shown in the 1911 annual exhibition of the Pennsylvania Academy.

2. Small bronzes became more affordable in the late nineteenth century when the lost-wax casting method was brought from Europe. It replaced the more costly sand-casting technique.

3. Bessie Potter Vonnoh, "Tears and Laughter Caught in Bronze," *Delineator* 107 (Oct. 1925), p. 8. The health problem plagued her sporadically throughout her life. On Dec. 3, 1911, she wrote to John E.D. Trask, managing director of the PAFA: "My attack of [neuritis] has put me back in everything," PAFA Archives.

4. Lorado Taft, *The History of American Sculpture* (New York: Macmillan Company, 1903), p. 449.

5. See Kathryn Greenthal, *American Figurative Sculpture in the Museum of Fine Arts, Boston* (Boston: Museum of Fine Arts, 1986), p. 341.

6. Much later, when she was using classical garb for many of her figures, Vonnoh commented that she abhored the "balloon sleeves, wide skirts . . . [and] funny hats" of the turn of the century (*Delineator* 1925, p. 9).

7. Ibid., lists members of the club.

8. Greenthal 1986, p. 341.

9. May Brawley Hill, *Grez Days: Robert Vonnoh in France* (New York: Berry-Hill Galleries, 1987), p. 35, notes that the sculptor found the long stay in Paris uncomfortable, especially because she had not yet learned to speak French well. She made frequent trips to New York.

10. Sixteen of Vonnoh's sculptures, including a cast of *Allegresse,* are in the Corcoran Gallery of Art, Washington, D.C.

11. "Sculptress, 80, is Honored," *Philadelphia Inquirer,* August 17, 1952, p. 11, society pages.

References

1903 "A Sculptor of Statuettes," *Current Literature* 34 (June), pp. 699–702. **1909** "Some Sculpture by Mrs. Vonnoh," *International Studio* 38 (August), pp. 121–24. **1992** Julie A. Aronson, "Bessie Potter Vonnoh and Small Bronze Sculpture in America," Ph.D. diss., University of Delaware.

Young Mother

1896
Bronze with green-and-brown patina; lost-wax cast in 1913
14 x 13 x 15½" (35.6 x 33 x 39.4 cm)
Signed and dated on integral base at back: Bessie O Potter/ 1896/ Copyright/no XIX.
Foundry mark on back of integral base: ROMAN BRONZE WORKS N–Y–
Gift of Mrs. Edward H. Coates in memory of Edward H. Coates, 1923.9.8

MODELED IN 1896, *Young Mother* is believed to be Bessie Potter Vonnoh's first sculpture to portray the theme of motherhood.[1] Perhaps she was inspired by the representations of mothers and children by the French sculptor Jules Dalou (1838–1902) or the expatriate painter Mary Cassatt, which Vonnoh could have seen during her 1895 trip to Paris. In any event, motherhoood became one of her favorite themes.

This cast was owned by Edward H. Coates, a member of the board of directors of the Pennsylvania Academy of the Fine Arts from 1877 to 1890 and its president from 1890 to 1906. When Coates acquired this work is not known.

Young Mother was shown in plaster at the sixty-sixth annual exhibition of the Pennsylvania Academy in December 1896 to February 1897. The plaster was sold from the exhibition for thirty-five dollars. A second buyer ordered another plaster cast, which Vonnoh sold for twenty dollars.[2] *Young Mother* proved to be one of the sculptor's most popular pieces; according to her, thirty casts were made.[3] It seems likely, however, that Vonnoh did not include plasters in this count. The foundry ledgers of the Roman Bronze Works record the casting of sixteen bronze versions of the piece between December 1907 and December 1915.[4] They were cast in two sizes. The Pennsylvania Academy's cast, numbered nineteen, is in the larger size and was cast December 9, 1913.

Vonnoh showed *Young Mother* in numerous exhibitions. At the Exposition Universelle in Paris in 1900, it won a bronze medal. She also showed versions of it at the Pan-American Exposition, in Buffalo in 1901, and at the Louisiana Purchase Universal Exposition, in Saint Louis in 1904. It was shown in a 1909 exhibition of small bronzes that was organized by the National Sculpture Society, in New York, and toured various cities throughout the country. In 1915 a bronze version was shown at the Panama-Pacific International Exhibition, in San Francisco (erroneously catalogued as *Motherhood*). It was displayed on a classically inspired base, undoubtedly selected by Vonnoh and similar in design to the carved and gilded wood base that belongs to the bronze at the Museum of American Art of the Pennsylvania Academy.[5]

Notes

1. *Young Mother* has often been erroneously titled *Motherhood.* It has also been called *A Young Mother* or *The Young Mother,* sometimes by Vonnoh herself, who nonetheless usually called it *Young Mother.* See Bessie Potter to Harrison S. Morris, managing director of the PAFA, Dec. 31, 1896, about Feb. 2, 1897, and about March 12, 1897, PAFA Archives.

2. Bessie Potter Vonnoh to Harrison S. Morris, undated, received Feb. 9, 1897, PAFA Archives.

3. Albert TenEyck Gardner, *American Sculpture: A Catalogue of the Collection of the Metropolitan Museum of Art* (New York: Metropolitan Museum of Art, 1965), p. 112. Other bronze versions cast by Roman Bronze Works are at the Metropolitan Museum of Art and the National Academy of Design, both in New York. The Montclair Art Museum, N.J., owns a bronze dated 1899 with the foundry mark of the Henry Bonnard Bronze Company. A plaster version is owned by the Portland Museum of Art in Maine.

4. Roman Bronze Works, Ledger no. 2, p. 105, typed copy, PAFA research file. Ledger no. 2 begins with cast number eleven.

5. The base was conserved and regilded in 1986.

Reference

1989 Janis Conner and Joel Rosenkranz, *Rediscoveries in American Sculpture: Studio Works, 1893–1939,* Austin: University of Texas Press, p. 162 (ill.).

Exhibited

1924 PAFA, *The Edward H. Coates Memorial Collection,* cat. no. 29, erroneously as *Motherhood.* **1962** PAFA, *Forgotten Favorites: Selections from the Permanent Collection,* erroneously as *Motherhood.* **1974** PAFA, Peale House, *The Pennsylvania Academy and Its Women: 1850 to 1920,* cat. no. 38. **1975–76** Whitney Museum of American Art, New York, *A Portrait of Young America.* **1986–87** PAFA, *Sculpture at the Pennsylvania Academy of the Fine Arts.* **1987** Port of History Museum, Philadelphia, *National Sculpture Society Celebrates the Figure; Fifty-Fourth Annual Exhibition.* **1992–93** PAFA, *Masterworks of American Art: 1750–1950* **1994–96** PAFA, *Two Centuries of Collecting at the Museum of American Art.*

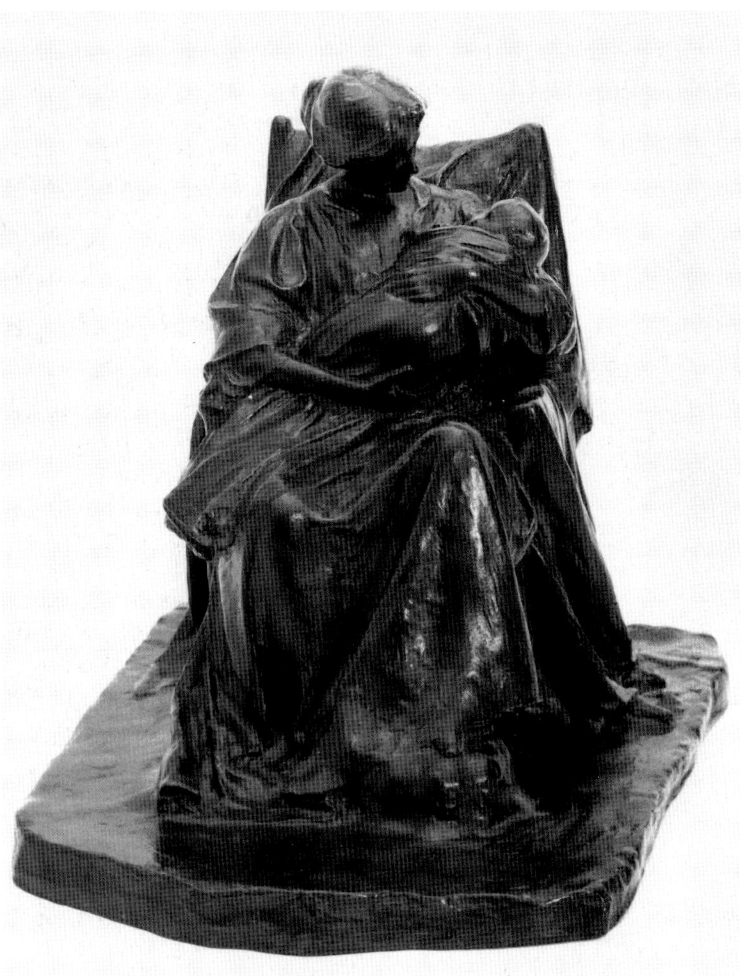

Vonnoh, *Young Mother*

Ex Collections

Edward H. Coates, about 1913–21; his wife, 1921–23.

Motherhood

1903
Bronze with brown patina; lost-wax cast in 1915
16½ x 6¼ x 8¼" (42 x 15.8 x 21 cm)
Signed and dated on integral base at back: Bessie Potter Vonnoh/Copyright 1903 no. xv
Foundry mark on side of integral base: ROMAN BRONZE WORKS N–Y–
General Fund Purchase, 1920.2

THE MODELS for *Motherhood,* Helena Franz Walter and three of her children—Helen, Josephine, and the baby, Charles—were residents of Rockland Lake,

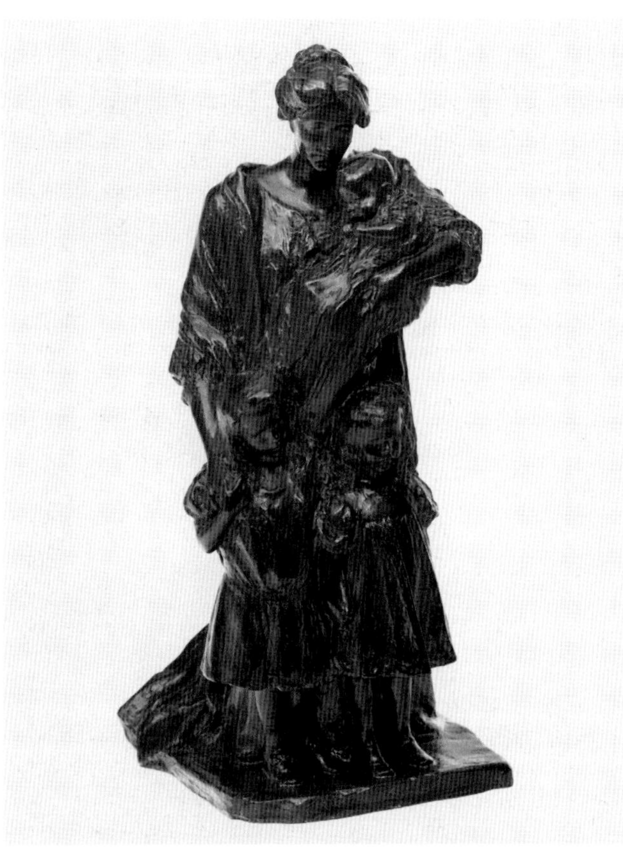

Vonnoh, *Motherhood*

New York, where Bessie Potter Vonnoh had her studio. According to Walter family tradition, Vonnoh stopped Helena Franz Walter on the street, told her that she was the most beautiful woman Vonnoh had ever seen, and asked her to pose with her children.[1] At least two sculptures resulted: *Enthroned,* 1902, and *Motherhood.* Although Vonnoh used photographs of the Walter family in her work, *Motherhood* is not a group portrait.[2] The figures are idealized. Vonnoh's impressionistic technique is marked by extremely subtle surface modulations. She merely hints at the facial features. The eyes, for instance, are indicated by shallow depressions.

In 1904 *Motherhood* was awarded the Shaw Memorial Prize at the exhibition of the Society of American Artists, in New York. Among the other exhibitions in which *Motherhood* (not this version) was shown are the hundredth annual exhibition of the Pennsylvania Academy of the Fine Arts, in 1905; the Louisiana Purchase Universal Exposition, Saint Louis, in 1904; a Montross Gallery exhibition, New York, in 1913; and an exhibition of contemporary American sculpture at the Albright Art Gallery, Buffalo, New York, in 1916.

Motherhood proved to be quite popular. The foundry ledgers of the Roman Bronze Works record the casting of seven bronzes between January 1908 and January 1916. According to the ledger, the Pennsylvania Academy's bronze, numbered fifteen, was cast in December 1915.[3] In 1919, at the Pennsylvania Academy's request, Bessie Potter Vonnoh sent two differently patinated bronze versions of *Motherhood* to the Academy.[4] This cast was selected for the permanent collection, and the other was returned to the sculptor.

Notes

1. Mary Walter Yin to Susan James-Gadzinski, June 30, 1985, PAFA object file.
2. Interview by Susan James-Gadzinski, Mary Mullen Cunningham, and Theresa Z. Esperdy of Josephine Walter Hudson and Helen Walter Draudt, Nov. 20, 1985, ibid.
3. Roman Bronze Works, Ledger no. 4, pp. 98–99, typed copy, PAFA research file. Ledger no. 4 begins with cast number nine.
4. Bessie Potter Vonnoh to John Andrew Myers, secretary of the PAFA, Feb. 15, 1920, PAFA Archives.

Reference

1982 Linda Bantel, "Sculpture at The Pennsylvania Academy," *Antiques* 121 (March), p. 710 (ill.).

Exhibited

1962 PAFA, *Forgotten Favorites: Selections from the Permanent Collection.* **1974** PAFA, *The Pennsylvania Academy and Its Women: 1850 to 1920,* cat. no. 39, fig. 14. **1986–87** PAFA, *Sculpture at the Pennsylvania Academy of the Fine Arts.*

Vonnoh, *The Dance*

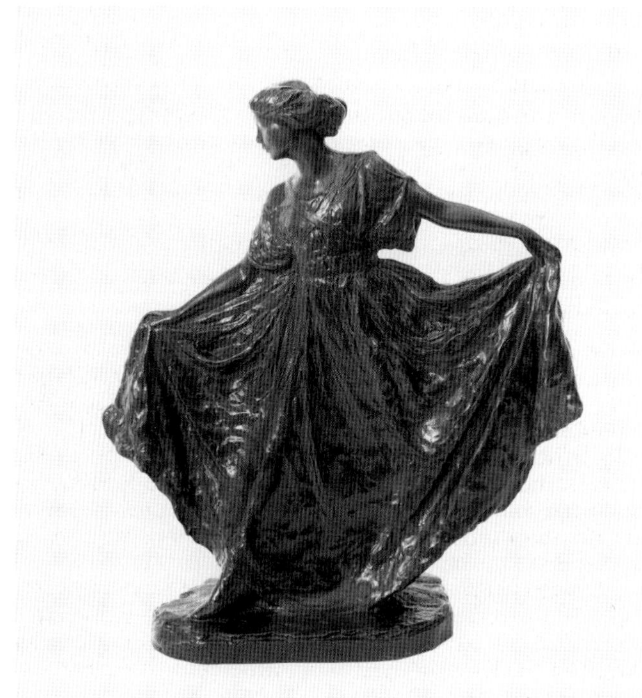

The Dance

1910
Bronze with brown-and-green patina; lost-wax cast possibly in 1913
12 x 10⅝ x 4¾" (30.5 x 27 x 12.1 cm)
Signed on integral base at back: Bessie Potter Vonnoh
Foundry mark on integral base at back: ROMAN BRONZE WORKS N Y A7
Henry D. Gilpin Fund, 1973.24

INFLUENCED by the English-born Aesthetic Movement, many artists of the American Renaissance looked to classical antiquity and the Renaissance for inspiration. This is manifest in the classical themes, motifs, and costumes that appear in American painting and sculpture between 1876 and 1917. Bessie Potter Vonnoh was increasingly drawn to classical attire after the turn of the century. The figure in *The Dance* wears a modified classical costume. *The Dance,* however, like many of Vonnoh's small works, also displays affinities with the art nouveau style. Female figures in elegant poses are the hallmark of this style, which reached its apogee in Paris at the Exposition Universelle of 1900.

The Dance is closely related to the sculptor's popular *Dancing Girl* of 1897 (versions in the Metropolitan Museum of Art, New York, and the Corcoran Gallery of Art, Washington, D.C.). In both pieces, the dancer steps to her right with an elegant pointed toe. Between February 1910, when Roman Bronze Works first cast this piece, and January 1916, twenty-one bronzes were made.[1] The statue in the Pennsylvania Academy of the Fine Arts, which is marked A7, may have been cast in 1913.[2] A different version in bronze had been shown in the Pennsylvania Academy's 106th annual exhibition, in 1911. That piece sold from the annual for $150.[3] Casts were shown in many exhibitions, among them the 1910 annual exhibition of the National Academy of Design, in New York; Vonnoh's 1913 exhibition at the Institute of Arts and Sciences in Brooklyn, New York; and the 1915 Panama-Pacific International Exhibition, in San Francisco.

Notes

1. May Brawley Hill, *The Woman Sculptor: Malvina Hoffman and Her Contemporaries* (New York: Berry-Hill Galleries, 1984), p. 22, states that Vonnoh ordered bronze casts of her works as needed and only rarely set an edition limit. Although she attempted to destroy the plaster models in her collection before her death, many remained at the Roman Bronze Works and posthumous bronze casts were made.
2. Roman Bronze Works, Ledger no. 4, pp. 104–5, typed copy, PAFA research file. Although the seventh version seems to have been cast in February 1913, there is no indication on the ledger that it was marked A7.
3. Sales Book, 1900–1959, PAFA Archives.

Exhibited

1972 Salem Fine Arts Center, Winston Salem, N.C.; North Carolina Museum of Art, Raleigh, *Women,* cat. no. 33 (ill.). **1974** PAFA, *The Pennsylvania Academy and Its Women: 1850 to 1920,* cat. no. 40. **1975–76** Whitney Museum of American Art, New York, *A Portrait of Young America.* **1979** Governor's Residence, Harrisburg, Exhibition of works from the collection of the Pennsylvania Academy. **1986–87** PAFA, *Sculpture at the Pennsylvania Academy of the Fine Arts.*

Ex Collections

Raydon Gallery, New York, by 1972; Berry-Hill Galleries, New York, 1972–73.

DANIEL C. MÜLLER

1872–1952

Born in Germany in 1872, Daniel Carl Müller was brought to the United States when he was nine years old. At first, his father, Johann Heinrich Müller, settled the family near Coney Island, in Brooklyn, New York. Then, in 1888, possibly at the behest of his fellow countryman, the Philadelphia carousel builder Gustav A. Dentzel, Johann Müller moved his family to Montgomery County, Pennsylvania.[1] Before his death two years later, Müller produced the Dentzel Company's first animal-shaped carousel figures.[2] Dentzel employed both of Müller's sons: Daniel and his younger brother, Alfred. Daniel excelled at the work and soon made his reputation as Dentzel's most skilled and creative carver.[3]

During the early 1890s, Daniel Müller attended the evening art classes of William Arnold Porter at the Spring Garden Institute in Philadelphia. In the 1893–94 school year, Müller took first prize in the evening modeling class.[4] By January 1893, he had begun to attend evening antique and life classes at the Pennsylvania Academy of the Fine Arts.[5] In May 1899, he ranked first in the modeling class conducted by CHARLES GRAFLY.[6] The following fall, the Pennsylvania Academy's Committee on Instruction approved Grafly's recommendation that Müller receive free admission to the modeling class.[7] Grafly modeled a bust of Müller in 1906 and showed it in the Pennsylvania Academy's 101st annual exhibition.[8] In 1912 Daniel Müller won the school's Edmund Stewardson Prize for the best full-length figure done within eighteen hours. He continued to attend classes until 1913. During his twenty years at the Academy, Müller studied almost exclusively at night

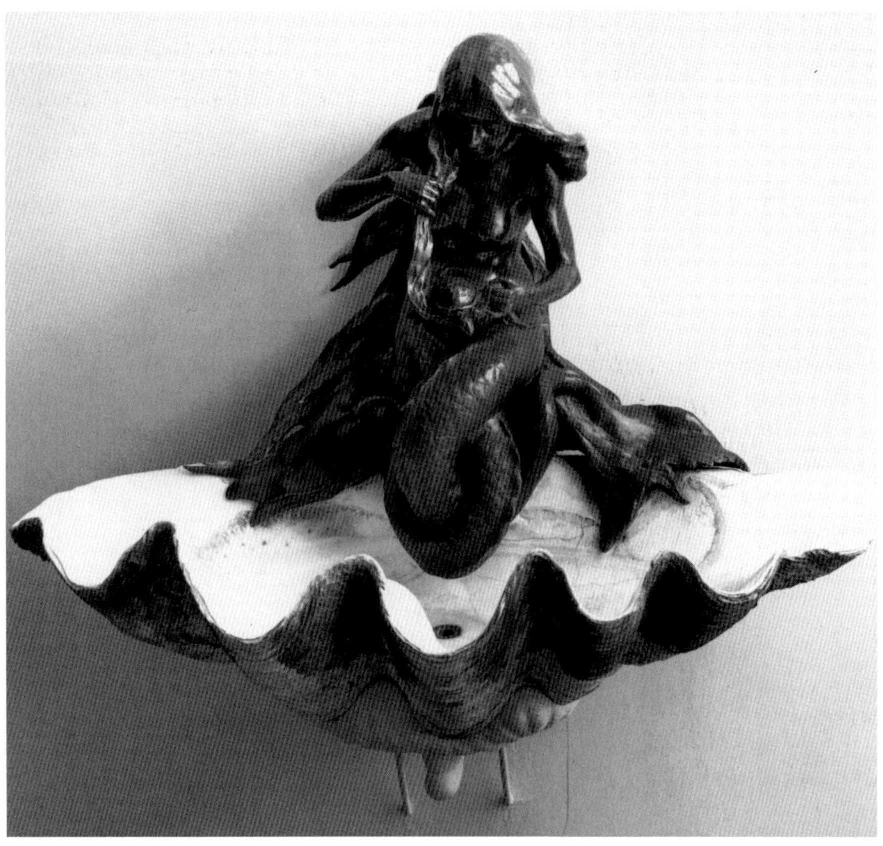

Müller, *Mermaid Fountain*

because, during the day, he was busy pursuing his career as a carousel maker.

In 1902 Daniel and Alfred Müller left Gustav Dentzel's employ to open their own carousel manufacturing company at 3560–62 North Marshall Street in Philadelphia. During the next few years, under Daniel Müller's direction, D.C. Müller and Brother made some of the most realistic and finely detailed wooden carousel horses ever produced. Daniel Müller's horses reveal his fine-art training. He paid close attention to anatomical detail and on occasion executed clay maquettes before carving.[9] He enjoyed creating historically accurate trappings for his horses and often turned to the Civil War for inspiration.[10]

One of D.C. Müller and Brother's major clients was T.M. Harton of Pittsburgh, who ordered many carousel animals and several complete carousels. He installed Müller-built carousels in such distant places as Cedar Point, Ohio; Binghamton, New York; and Montreal, Canada. Besides supplying individual clients, the Müllers designed and carved for other carousel manufacturers, including the Philadelphia Toboggan Company and the Dentzel Company.

With the outbreak of World War I, raw materials became scarce and business slowed considerably. On April 10, 1917, Daniel and Alfred Müller closed the doors of their shop for good, and both took jobs with William Dentzel, who had taken over the factory after the death of his father, Gustav, in 1909.[11] Daniel Müller continued to work for the Dentzel Company until William's death in 1928, when the factory closed after sixty years of production.

Notes

1. Fried 1978, p. 3.
2. Frederick Fried, *A Pictorial History of the Carousel* (Vestal, N.Y.: Vestal Press, 1964), p. 54.
3. Geoff Weedon and Richard Ward, *Fairground Art: The Art Forms of Travelling Fairs, Carousels and Carnival Midways* (New York: Abbeville Press, 1981), p. 88.
4. Annual report, Spring Garden Institute, for the year ended June 30, 1894.
5. Student Register, 1884–94, PAFA Archives.
6. Minutes, faculty meeting, May 20, 1899, ibid.
7. Minutes, meeting of Committee on Instruction, Oct. 31, 1900, ibid.
8. Now owned by Müller's daughter, Evelyn Müller Johnson.
9. Weedon and Ward 1981, p. 71.
10. Tobin Fraley, *The Carousel Animal* (Berkeley, Calif.: Zephyr Press, 1985), p. 11; Fried 1978, p. 5.
11. Ibid.

References

1978 Frederick Fried, "Daniel Carl Muller (1872–1952): Artist, Sculptor and Carousel Carver," *Merry-Go-Roundup*

5 (July), pp. 3–13. **1994** Tobin Fraley, *The Great American Carousel: A Century of Master Craftsmanship,* San Francisco: Chronicle Books, pp. 76–83.

Mermaid Fountain

1898
Bronze with red-brown patina; cast in 1905; and oyster shell
17 x 20 x 14" (43.2 x 50.8 x 35.6 cm)
Signed below figure's right thigh: D.C.Muller
Sand cast by Bureau Brothers, Philadelphia (repatinated in 1986 by Johnson Atelier, Mercerville, N.J.)
Pennsylvania Academy purchase, 1898.4

In February 1898, Daniel C. Müller's entry won a student competition for a drinking fountain to be placed in the Pennsylvania Academy of the Fine Arts. The entries were probably clay maquettes because, after winning, Müller was directed to carry out his design with several alterations recommended no doubt by the teachers CHARLES GRAFLY and Henry Thouron, who judged the competition.[1] It is not known if Müller's original scheme included the large oyster shell as the basin for the fountain or if the idea was suggested to him by Grafly or Thouron, both of whom might have known of the shell's existence in the Pennsylvania Academy's collection. The shell had been given to the Peale Museum in 1796 by Thomas Twining, a member of the family of English tea merchants. After the Peale Museum closed, the shell was aquired by the Pennsylvania Academy.[2]

Müller's fountain was not sent to the Bureau Brothers foundry for casting until 1905.[3] The delay was probably due to the Pennsylvania Academy's desire to cast it in conjunction with other pieces in order to get a better price. The fountain was eventually cast late in the summer of 1905 along with four busts from the Academy's collection. It was probably installed shortly thereafter on the ground floor opposite the grand staircase, where it remained until about 1925. In the fall of 1986, Müller's fountain was reinstalled in the Pennsylvania Academy, in the museum shop.

Notes

1. Minutes, meeting of Committee on Instruction, Feb. 23, 1898, PAFA Archives. Müller engaged a model occasionally hired by Grafly; see "Forever Young and Fair: Model, Now 67, Recaptures Youth Looking at Academy Statues for Which She Posed as Girl," *Philadelphia Bulletin,* July 19, 1939, p. 10.
2. Robert C. Alberts, *The Golden Voyage: The Life and Times of William Bingham, 1752–1804* (Boston: Houghton Mifflin Company, 1969), pp. 312, 314.
3. Bureau Brothers to Edward H. Coates, president of the PAFA, August 28, 1905, PAFA Archives.

References

1978 Frederick Fried, "Daniel Carl Muller (1872–1952): Artist, Sculptor and Carousel Carver," *Merry-Go-Roundup* 5 (July), p. 3 (ill. of artist with *Mermaid Fountain*). **1984** Charlotte Dinger, *Art of the Carousel,* Green Village, N.J.: Carousel Art, p. 115 (ill. of artist with *Mermaid Fountain*).

ADAM PIETZ

1873–1961

Born in Offenbach, Germany, where he first studied the art of die-engraving, Adam Pietz came to the United States in 1889. Shortly after his arrival, he began attending the Spring Garden Institute, where he received a gold medal for life-class work. He continued his studies at the Art Institute of Chicago and Drexel Institute before enrolling at the Pennsylvania Academy of the Fine Arts, where he was taught by Thomas Anshutz and CHARLES GRAFLY.[1]

In 1927 Pietz was appointed assistant engraver at the United States Mint in Philadelphia. When he retired in 1946, he was world famous for his die engravings and sculptures. During his years at the mint, Pietz engraved the dies for many U.S. coins and medals, commemorative coins for France and Belgium, and coinage for the first Republic of China. He also engraved the first five-cent airmail die for stamped envelopes and the special gold medal awarded by Congress for the first flight over the North Pole.[2]

Pietz specialized in portraiture and heraldic designs. He made busts, plaques, and bas-reliefs of many artists, musicians, and actors of his era and was a prolific medalist, as well. His work is represented in museums in this country and in London and Paris. Pietz participated in many annual exhibitions at the Pennsylvania Academy from 1901 to 1944 and in several annual watercolor exhibitions from 1909 to 1936. In 1931 he exhibited at the Philadelphia Sketch Club along with the engraver John Sinnock. Pietz was a member of the Fellowship of the Pennsylvania Academy of the Fine Arts, the Philadelphia Sketch Club, the American Numismatic Society, and the New York Numismatic Society.

Notes

1. Records in the PAFA Archives state that Pietz studied there in 1905–6. Pietz, however, recollected the dates as 1899–1903; see clipping file, PAFA Library.
2. Adam Pietz clipping file, Philadelphia Sketch Club Archives.

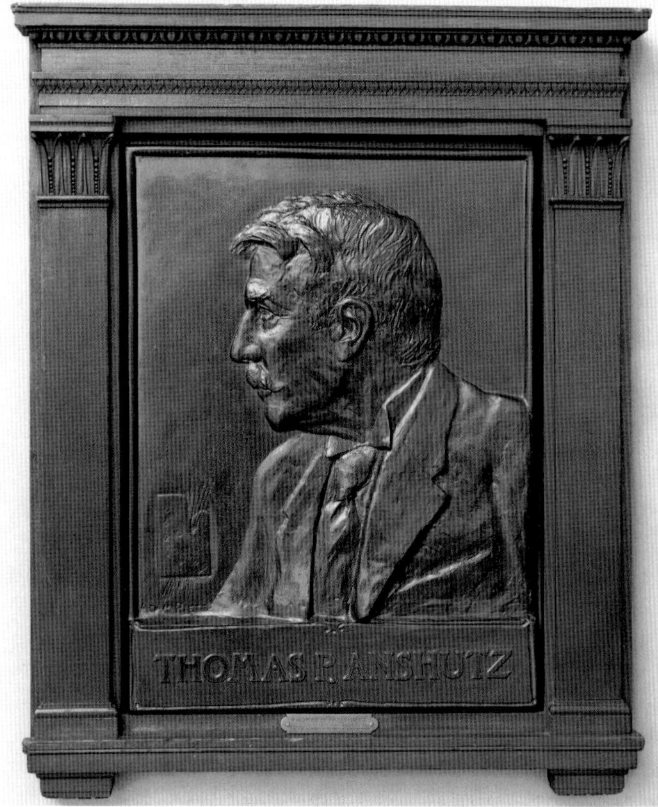

Pietz, *Thomas P. Anshutz*

Thomas P. Anshutz

1912–16
Bronze with brown patina
22 x 16½ x 1" (56 x 42 x 2.5 cm)
Signed at lower left: ADAM PIETZ
Inscribed at bottom: THOMAS P. ANSHUTZ
Sand cast, probably by Bureau Brothers, Philadelphia
Gift of the artist, 1938.6

ADAM PIETZ modeled this portrait of Thomas Anshutz (1851–1912), from life and later had it cast in bronze.[1] The date of the casting is not known. A portrait relief of Anshutz by Pietz in the collection of the Philadelphia Sketch Club is dated 1916, however, and Pietz may have had both portraits cast at the same time as a memorial to his former teacher. The Sketch Club portrait was cast at Bureau Brothers Foundry in Philadelphia. The relief in the Pennsylvania Academy was probably cast there, as well.

Pietz considered it easy to model a portrait from life and was pleased with his ability to "make the Bronze speak."[2] The textural interest in the entire figure, set against a smooth background, creates a feeling of spontaneity and liveliness. The painter's palette and brushes are depicted in the lower left corner of the relief, above the sculptor's name. The name of the sitter, in large raised letters, is across the bottom. The plaque is mounted in a classically inspired wooden frame.

Notes

1. For biographical information on Thomas Anshutz, see entry on portrait bust by CHARLES GRAFLY.
2. Adam Pietz clipping file, Philadelphia Sketch Club Archives.

Exhibited

1956 PAFA, *Living Philadelphia Artists Represented in the Permanent Collection of the Academy,* cat. no. 107. **1975** William Penn Memorial Museum, Harrisburg, exhibition of works of art from the PAFA. **1978–79** PAFA, *350 Masterpieces of American Art: 1720–1978.* **1986–87** PAFA, *Sculpture at the Pennsylvania Academy of the Fine Arts.* **1994–96** PAFA, *Two Centuries of Collecting at the Museum of American Art.*

Ex Collection

The artist, about 1916–38.

Parke C. Dougherty

1920
Bronze with yellow-ochre patina
14½ x 14½ x ¾" (36.8 x 36.8 x 1.9 cm)
Signed and dated at center right: ADAM PIETZ/SC./1920
Inscribed at center left: PARKE C./DOUGHERTY
Sand cast, probably by Bureau Brothers, Philadelphia
Gift of the artist, 1957.9

THE Philadelphia painter Parke Custus Dougherty (1867–1926) studied at the Pennsylvania Academy of the Fine Arts from 1885 to 1889. He participated regularly in the annual exhibitions from 1885 to 1921

Pietz, *Parke C. Dougherty*

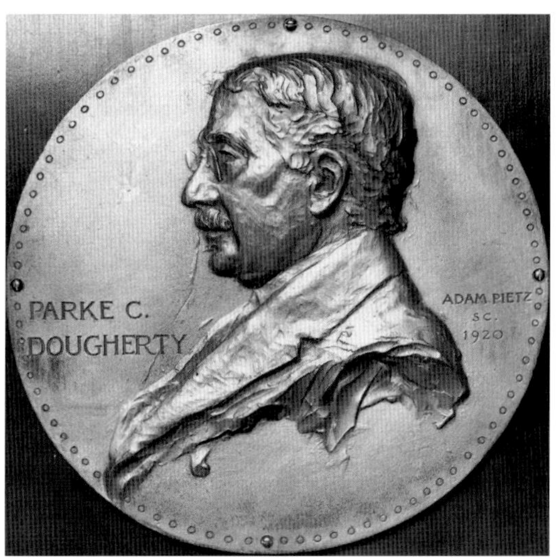

and, like Adam Pietz, belonged to the Fellowship of the Pennsylvania Academy. Dougherty was a member of the Philadelphia Sketch Club from 1899 until his death in 1926.

Adam Pietz modeled this portrait relief from life in 1920 and had it cast in bronze the same year. Dougherty was fifty-three at the time and is shown wearing pince-nez. His hair and mustache provide textural interest in the piece and contrast with the smooth facial planes and suit lapel. The edge of the relief is ornamented with incised circles.

Exhibited
1921 Salon de Paris. **1931*** cat. no. 430. **1956** PAFA, *Living Philadelphia Artists Represented in the Permanent Collection of the Academy,* cat. no. 106.

Ex Collection
The artist, 1920–57.

Locust Club Medal, 1923: See Appendix.

Henry Clews, Jr.

1876–1937

Henry Clews, Jr., was born in New York and reared there and in Newport, Rhode Island. His father was an English immigrant who became a Wall Street banker. His mother was Lucy Madison Worthington Clews, from Kentucky, a descendant of President James Madison. His grandfather James Clews was a potter in Staffordshire, England. Henry, Jr., was educated at the Groton School and by tutors. He then attended Amherst College in Massachusetts, Columbia University in New York, and two European universities. Clews worked briefly in his father's business before turning to art. A studio was set up in his family's house; and, without training, he began to paint portraits of the servants. While in Newport about 1900, he associated with the Paris-trained painters Howard Gardiner Cushing and Robert Winthrop Chanler, who must have encouraged his aspiration to become an artist. Shortly thereafter, Clews married his first wife, Louise, and moved to Paris. The marriage was short-lived, however, because of Clews's devotion to his art.

His early paintings were similar to those of James McNeill Whistler in their use of black and gray. His dandified lifestyle was also modeled after Whistler's. Clews soon adopted an impressionistic painting style with a brighter palette. By 1909, however, he had become dissatisfied with painting and set up a sculpture studio. There he modeled portrait heads in a style similar to that of Auguste Rodin (1840–1917), whose studio he often visited. Clews's lifelong rebelliousness and interest in human nature were revealed in his caricatures of members of high society and his series of imaginary grotesque deities. His subject matter drew criticism at exhibitions of his sculpture held between 1909 and 1914 in New York. He married Marie Elsie Whelen in 1914, and they remained permanently in France. At first, they lived in Paris in the former home of the sculptor Frederic Auguste Bartholdi (1834–1904). In 1918 they bought an eleventh-century monastery near Cannes, which they named the Château de la Napoule. They spent more than a decade rebuilding and decorating it. The sculptor designed imaginary, symbolic, and satirical architectural sculpture in a medieval vein to ornament his villa and brought a dozen Italian stone carvers to carry out the work. A critic called it "as fantastic as anything in 'Alice-in-Wonderland' but with a sharper bite."[1]

Clews's writings include the play *Mumbo Jumbo* (published in 1922) and "Dinkelspieliana" (an unpublished manuscript from the early 1930s). Both of them are criticisms of American society, including the art world with which he maintained close ties despite being an expatriate. In the 1930s Clews returned to modeling portraits to be cast in bronze and created such realistic depictions as *The Mayor of Mandelieu* (Metropolitan Museum of Art, New York).

Posthumous exhibitions of Clews's work were held at the Metropolitan Museum (1939), at the Pennsylvania Academy of the Fine Arts (1948) and in France at the Musée Massena, Nice (1948), and the Musée Jacquemart-André, Paris (1959). His widow created the La Napoule Art Foundation, Henry Clews Memorial. It was incorporated by the State University of New York in 1950 to promote the arts, the work of Henry Clews, and cultural exchange between the United States and France.

Note
1. Dorothy Grafly, "Henry Clews Memorial Show," *Boston Christian Science Monitor,* May 15, 1948, scrapbook, microfilm, roll no. 58, frame no. 555, PAFA Archives.

References
1940s *Henry Clews Sculptures,* La Napoule, France: Clews Museum, Château de la Napoule. **1940s** Marie Elsie Whelen Clews, "Myth-Mirth-Mystery," unpublished manuscript at La Napoule Art Foundation, La Napoule, France. **1984** Beatrice Gilman Proske, *Henry Clews, Jr., Sculptor,* Murrells Inlet, S.C.: Brookgreen Gardens (first printing 1953 in French).

Marie Elsie Whelen Clews

1917
Alabaster
19¼ x 19 x 12" (48.9 x 48.3 x 30.5 cm)
Signed and inscribed at back: HC/MMM [monogram]
Inscribed in red paint at center back: S.L. 3095.[1]9
Gift of Mrs. David J. Colton, 1986.18

ELSIE WHELEN (1879/80–1959) was the daughter of Henry Whelen, Jr., of Philadelphia, who served the Pennsylvania Academy of the Fine Arts for twenty years—as a member of the board of directors, as treasurer, and briefly as president. Elsie met Henry Clews in Newport in the summer of 1912. They were married in December 1914, after her divorce from Robert Goelet. She then took *Marie* as her first name perhaps to distinguish herself from her husband's sister, Elsie Clews Parsons, an anthropologist.

In 1915 Clews modeled his first portrait of his wife, *The Virgin of the Mancha,* and had it cast into bronze (La Napoule Art Foundation). She is shown as an idealized figure reminiscent of a Renaissance virgin. Describing a similar Renaissance sculpture in his play *Mumbo Jumbo,* Clews remarked on the small head "poised on a liliaceous neck" and the "tender, sensitive, compassionate smile and the wistful naïve purity and ethereal sweetness of her expression."[1] Clews thought of himself as the latter-day Cervantes character, Don Quixote de la Mancha, pointing out the foibles of society and trying to live in a land of myth, mirth, and mystery. He and his wife named their Paris home La Mancha; their son, "Little Mancha"; and their resident caretaker, Sancho.

The Pennsylvania Academy's bust of Marie Clews was carved in 1917. It is the sculptor's second and more realistic portrait of his wife, although she is still shown wearing a tiara of flowers. The translucent alabaster enhances the beauty of this tender portrait. Alabaster is an easily worked stone that has been used as a sculptural medium since Egyptian times. Polishing brings out the translucency. Clews began about 1908 to carve figures in alabaster. *Marie Elsie Whelen Clews* was singled out as his best portrait. It was also his own favorite.[2] The format of the bust, i.e., the truncation of the bust below the shoulders, and the use of costume are typical of the Renaissance Revival. The style originated in France in the 1860s and was popular in the United States between 1875 and 1910 with sculptors such as Herbert Adams (1858–1945).

The monogram on the back of the right shoulder includes three *M*'s that refer to myth, mirth, and mystery—the three values Clews tried to inspire in his life and work. Three casts of this bust were produced in bronze: one is at La Napoule, and two are in private collections in Philadelphia and New York. A bronze was shown in 1948 at the Pennsylvania Academy's Clews exhibition.

Clews, *Marie Elsie Whelen Clews*

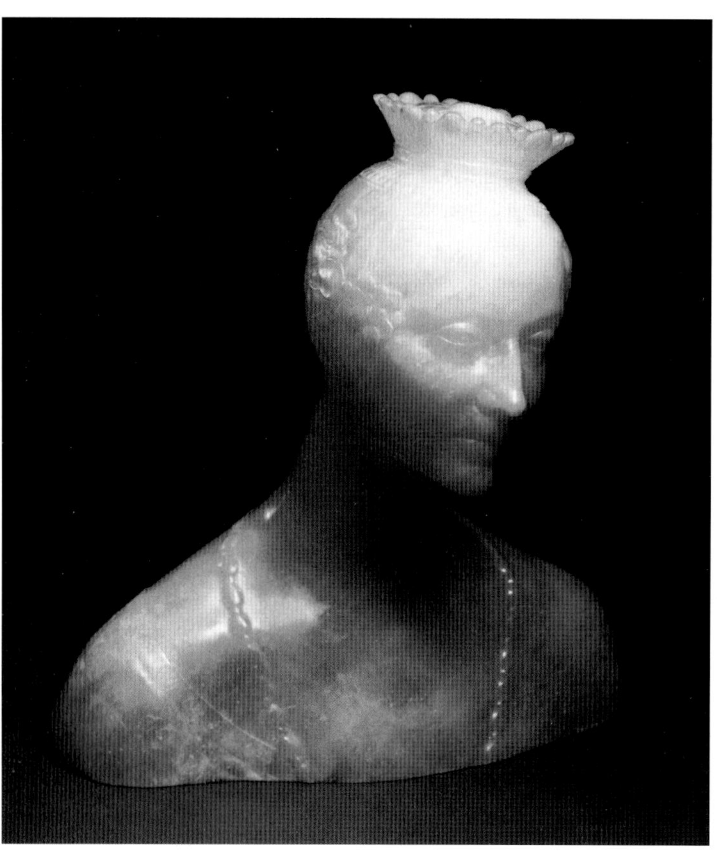

Notes

1. Quoted in Proske 1984, p. 9.
2. Pierre Borel, "L'oeuvre de Henry Clews," in *Henry Clews Sculptures,* 1940s.

References

1940s *Henry Clews Sculptures,* unpaginated essay, and p. 26 (ill.), as *Marie the Sculptor's Wife.* **1962** Lewis H. Van Dusen III, "Henry Clews, Jr.: The Life and Works of the Sculptor," Princeton University senior thesis, pl. 23, pp. 78–79, 131. **1984** Beatrice Gilman Proske, *Henry Clews, Jr., Sculptor,* Murrells Inlet, S.C.: Brookgreen Gardens, p. 7, fig. 3, p. 9.

Exhibited

1939 Metropolitan Museum of Art, *Exhibition of Sculpture by Henry Clews, Jr.,* cat. no. 9 (ill.). **1986–87** PAFA, *Sculpture at the Pennsylvania Academy of the Fine Arts.* **1993** PAFA, *Carved in Wood and Stone: Twentieth-Century Sculpture.*

Ex Collections

The artist, La Napoule, France, 1917–37; his second wife, Marie Elsie Whelen Clews, La Napoule, 1937-about 1959; her son, Peter Goelet, New York, about 1959-after 1962; La Napoule Art Foundation; Mr. and Mrs. David J. Colton; Mrs. David J. Colton, Sarasota, Florida, ?-1986.

Anna Hyatt Huntington

1876–1973

Anna Vaughn Hyatt was born in Cambridge, Massachusetts, into a socially prominent family. Her mother, Audella Beebe Hyatt, an academic painter, and her father, Alpheus Hyatt, a professor of paleontology and zoology, encouraged their daughter's early love for animals. Her interest in sculpture was kindled by her elder sister, Harriet (1868–1960). They both studied sculpture in Boston with Henry Hudson Kitson (1865–1947) and briefly shared a studio at home where they collaborated on projects in which Harriet modeled the human figures and Anna the animals. Anna's models were pets, farm animals, and wild animals from a local animal show. In 1902 she had her first solo exhibition, at the Boston Art Club. She soon moved to New York where she studied briefly at the Art Students League with sculptor Hermon Atkins MacNeil (1866–1947), learned horse modeling from Gutzon Borglum (1867–1941), and sketched animals at the Bronx Zoo. She shared a studio with the sculptor Abastenia St. Leger Eberle (1878–1942) with whom she collaborated on several figural groups, including *Men and Bull,* which won a bronze medal at the Louisiana Purchase Universal Exposition, in Saint Louis in 1904. In 1907 Hyatt traveled to France where she remained for several years while working on commissions for a lion mascot and an equestrian figure of Joan of Arc. In 1915 the monument to Joan of Arc, which had won an honorable mention at the 1910 Paris salon, was installed in New York, overlooking Riverside Park. Hyatt won a silver medal for ten sculptures displayed at the Panama-Pacific International Exposition, in San Francisco, in 1915. These accomplishments brought her wide recognition. In the early 1920s, she modeled two figures of Diana, the Roman goddess of the hunt. The actress Betty Davis is thought to have been the model for one of them, *Young Diana,* about 1923.[1]

In 1923 Hyatt married Archer Huntington, a philanthropist and scholar in Hispanic culture and literature. Together they did much to advance sculpture in the United States. For example, they donated one hundred thousand dollars in 1929 for an exhibition of fifteen hundred sculptures in San Francisco. In 1931 they founded Brookgreen Gardens in Murrells Inlet, South Carolina, a sculpture garden that grew to have an important collection of over four hundred works. The sculptor had gone there to recover from tuberculosis, which kept her from working for about seven years. When she began to work again, her output was extraordinary. It prompted a large retrospective exhibition at the American Academy of Arts and Letters in New York in 1936–37. A smaller show that included many lightweight aluminum casts traveled to about two dozen museums between 1937 and 1939; the Pennsylvania Academy of the Fine Arts hosted it in April 1939. In 1939 the Huntingtons donated their Fifth Avenue mansion to the National Academy of Design. They continued to live in South Carolina and at their country estate in Connecticut. The artist worked until she was well into her nineties, producing naturalistic sculptures of animals, often as commissions for large-scale equestrian groups.

Huntington's works are in about two hundred public collections; many are at Brookgreen Gardens, the Hispanic Society in New York, and the National Museum of American Art in Washington, D.C.

Note

1. "Statue found spot fitting for star," *Easton [Pa.] Express,* June 1983, p. A-2. There are casts of both Dianas in Brookgreen Gardens and elsewhere. The Museum of Fine Arts, Boston, owns one of the casts of *Young Diana.*

References

1968 Beatrice Gilman Proske, *Brookgreen Gardens Sculpture,* Murrells Inlet, S.C.: Brookgreen Gardens, pp. 168–80. **1976** Doris E. Cook, *Woman Sculptor: Anna Hyatt Huntington (1876–1973),* Hartford, Conn.: D.E. Cook. **1986** *American Figurative Sculpture in the Museum of the Fine Arts,* Boston: Museum of Fine Arts, pp. 352–59. **1989** Janis Conner and Joel Rosenkranz, *Rediscoveries in American Sculpture: Studio Works, 1893–1939,* Austin: University of Texas Press, pp. 71–78, 187.

Greyhounds Playing

1936
Bronze with brown patina; cast in 1937
39½ x 42¾ x 19¼" (100.3 x 108.7 x 48.9 cm)
Signed and dated on top of base behind taller dog: Anna Hyatt Huntington 1936
Foundry mark on side of base next to taller dog: ROMAN BRONZE WORKS.N.Y.
Lost-wax cast (figures); sand cast (base)
Gift of the artist, 1938.1

In the mid-1930s, when Anna Hyatt Huntington recovered from tuberculosis, she modeled several sculptures of greyhounds, including this one and the portraits *Speedy* and *Echo.* Dogs were among her favorite subjects for she had grown up with them and she and her husband raised them. Echo, for example, appears in at least five compositions in various poses.

Throughout her career, she chose to portray animals in action, often in pairs. They may be fighting or playing, as in this and a similar composition, *Fawns Playing,* 1936 (Corcoran Gallery of Art, Washington,

D.C.). Because the taller, more aggressive dog in *Greyhounds Playing* is a male and the other one is a female, the sculptor probably portrays a courtship display. Emphasis is placed on the rippling muscles and prominent ribs of the slender dogs and on their movement and heightened emotion.

An aluminum cast of this work (Art Gallery of Ontario) was awarded the George D. Widener Memorial Gold Medal in 1937 when it was displayed in the annual exhibition of the Pennsylvania Academy of the Fine Arts. There are at least two other aluminum casts, three other bronze casts, and one smaller, polychromed version in a latex ceramic compound.

The bronze in the Museum of American Art of the Pennsylvania Academy was cast in three parts. Each dog was cast by the lost-wax method, and the base was sand cast. The dogs are held together by a pin at their right forelegs and their feet are welded to the base. The surface was originally toned with a pigmented wax that had to be removed in 1985 because of embedded grime. The next year the sculpture was chemically patinated to simulate the brown of another bronze cast by the Roman Bronze Works of the same subject (Corcoran Gallery of Art, Washington, D.C.).

Reference

1939 "Noted Sculptress Exhibits Work at Academy," *Philadelphia Evening Bulletin,* April 8 (ill.), clipping file, PAFA Library.

Exhibited

1939 PAFA, *Exhibition of Sculpture by Anna Hyatt Huntington,* cat. no. 10 (ill. on cover). **1974** PAFA, *The Pennsylvania Academy and Its Women, 1850 to 1920,* cat. no. 44. **1986–87** PAFA, *Sculpture at the Pennsylvania Academy of the Fine Arts.* **1989** PAFA, *"The Birds and the Beasts Will Teach Us."*

Albert Laessle

1877–1954

Albert Laessle was born in Philadelphia to a German wood-carver and his wife, who had come to the United States in the 1850s. Albert developed an early fascination with art. His brother, Henry, whose interest in art had been discouraged by his parents, consulted CHARLES GRAFLY about possible schools for Albert.[1] On Grafly's advice, Laessle studied evenings at the Spring Garden Institute in Philadelphia from about 1893, when he won a second prize in freehand drawing, until his graduation in 1896. He then attended classes at Drexel Institute (now Drexel University) for about a year. In the fall of 1898, he was awarded free tuition to the Pennsylvania Academy of the Fine Arts, where he studied modeling with Grafly for six years. In 1901 Laessle received an honorable

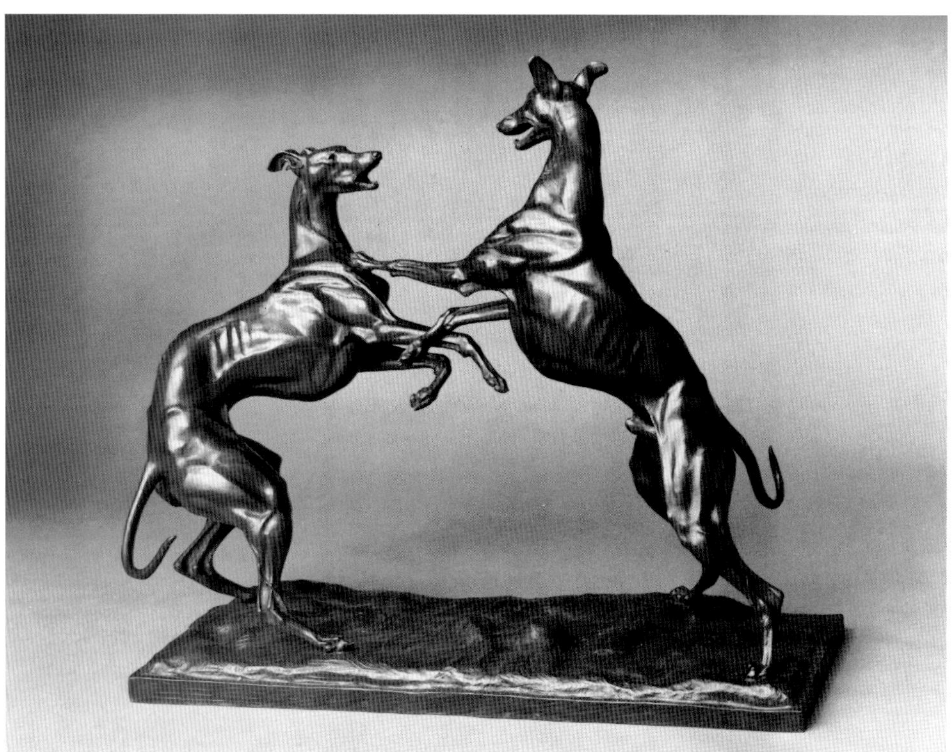

Huntington, *Greyhounds Playing*

mention in the competition for the Edmund Stewardson prize, which he won the following year. In 1904 he was awarded a William Emlen Cresson traveling scholarship for study in Paris. He received two extensions to the scholarship, which enabled him to remain in Paris for three years altogether. While there, he sculpted animals and exhibited in the 1907 Paris Salon. He received criticism from the sculptor Michel Léonard Béguine (1855–1929). Laessle also traveled in Italy and Switzerland. Before returning home, he married Mary Prudden Middleton, a fellow Pennsylvania Academy student.

Back in Philadelphia, Laessle became a prominent *animalier.* He shared a studio with Grafly for several years before establishing his own, near the Philadelphia Zoo. From 1901 to 1941, he participated regularly in the Pennsylvania Academy's annual exhibitions. He was included posthumously in a 1958 show of works owned by Philadelphia collectors. Laessle was awarded the Pennsylvania Academy's Fellowship Prize in 1915 for *Billy*[2] and in 1923 for *Drake Fountain,* 1921 (Cleveland Museum of Natural History). He won the George D. Widener Memorial Gold Medal in 1918 for *Penguins*[3] and the James E. McClees Prize in 1928 for *Duck and Turtle Fountain.*[4] The McClees Prize was a monetary award for the best sculptural group of at least two human figures or animals or a combination thereof, not less than one-third life size. Laessle also won a gold medal for a group of twenty sculptures in the Panama-Pacific International Exposition, in 1915 in San Francisco, and the first prize in sculpture in the exhibition *Americanization through Art,* in 1916 in Philadelphia. In 1926 thirty-six of his animal sculptures were awarded a gold medal at the Sesquicentennial International Exposition, in Philadelphia.

Laessle was hired by the Pennsylvania Academy in 1921 to teach animal sculpture at its country school, in Chester Springs. Farm and wild animals were plentiful to serve as subjects. Like Grafly, Laessle stressed anatomy and form; and a loyal following of students quickly formed. In 1920 he was one of the seven original sculptor members of the Society of Animal Painters and Sculptors founded by Henry Rankin Poore, who taught composition at the Pennsylvania Academy. From the 1920s to the 1940s, Laessle was active in the Fellowship of the Pennsylvania Academy. When Grafly was unable to complete a commission for a memorial to General Galusha Pennypacker, 1934 (Logan Square, Philadelphia), Laessle finished it according to Grafly's design. Four of Laessle's sculptures (*Pan, Billy, Dancing Goat,* and *Duck and Turtle Fountain*) were installed sometime after 1928 around a pool in Johnson Square in front of the Cooper Free Library in Camden, New Jersey. The park is now part of the campus of Rutgers University, and the library building is the university's Walt Whitman Poetry Center. Laessle was largely responsible for organizing the Pennsylvania Academy's 1930 memorial exhibition of the work of Charles Grafly.[5] In 1932 Laessle was elected an academician by the National Academy of Design and the National Institute of Arts and Letters, in New York. Ill health forced him to retire from teaching at the Pennsylvania Academy in 1939; and several years later, after his wife's death, he moved to Florida. From then on, he produced few sculptures.

Most of his sculpture is of animals. He did, however, model portrait busts of his friends and family, including one of Grafly, 1928 (National Institute of Arts and Letters, New York). A large collection of Laessle's work is in the National Museum of American Art, Smithsonian Institution, Washington, D.C.

Notes

1. "An Artist of Our Time: Albert Laessle, 1877-," *Philadelphia Public Ledger,* contemporary artists series, no. 32, undated clipping (after 1923), PAFA "Blue-Eyed Lizard" object file.
2. A cast of *Billy,* 1914, was a gift to Philadelphia from Eli Kirk Price II through the Fairmount Park Art Association and is installed in Rittenhouse Square. Other casts are owned by Rutgers University and the National Museum of American Art.
3. There are four bronze casts of *Penguins,* 1917. The Fairmount Park Art Association purchased one in 1918; it is installed outdoors at the entrance to the Bird House in the Philadelphia zoo. The other casts are in the California Palace of the Legion of Honor, San Francisco; Brookgreen Gardens, Murrells Inlet, S.C.; and the collection of the R.K. Mellon family in Pittsburgh.
4. Three bronzes of *Duck and Turtle Fountain,* 1926, were cast. They are in Brookgreen Gardens, the Cleveland Museum of Natural History, and Rutgers University.
5. Charles Grafly's wife, Frances, to Albert Laessle, Feb. 6, 1930, Albert Laessle Papers, Archives of American Art, Smithsonian Institution, Washington, D.C.

References

1924 D. Roy Miller, "A Sculptor of Animal Life," *International Studio* 80 (Oct.), pp. 23–27. **1976** Robert McCracken Peck, "Albert Laessle, American 'Animalier,' " *American Art Review* 3 (Jan.-Feb.), pp. 68–84. **1976** *Philadelphia: Three Centuries of American Art,* Philadelphia: Philadelphia Museum of Art, pp. 496–98. **1984** Wayne Craven, *Sculpture in America,* Newark: University of Delaware Press, pp. 544–45.

Embracing Figures

1899
Plaster, painted brown
11 x 4¾ x 4⅛" (27.9 x 12.1 x 10.8 cm)
Signed (incised in clay model) on rock beneath man's left

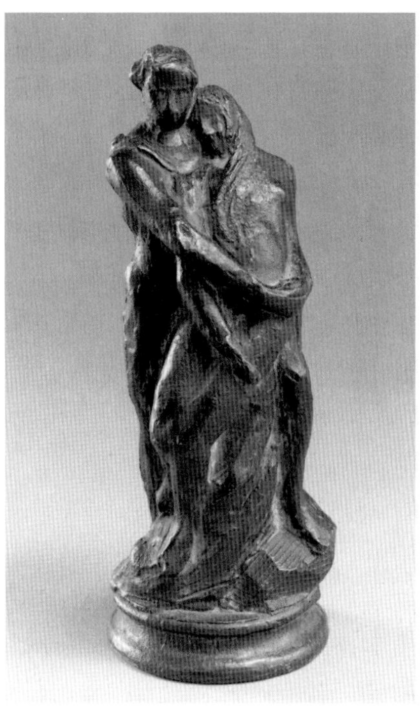

Laessle, *Embracing Figures*

foot: A. Laes; signed (incised into painted plaster) and dated in bottom: A. LAESSLE/1899
Gift of Janis Conner and Joel Rosenkranz, 1994.5

Embracing Figures was executed during Laessle's first year of study at the Pennsylvania Academy, while serving as a studio assistant to Charles Grafly. Significantly, the Rodinesque quality of the expressively modeled figures suggests Grafly's own production at this time. As an example of the early working methods of Laessle and his interest in process, the maquette is particularly revealing.

Ex Collections
Christie's, 1988; Conner-Rosenkranz Gallery, New York, 1988–94.

Turtle and Lizards

1902–3

a.
Plaster; cast in 1903–4
17 11/16 x 13½ x 20" (44.9 x 34.3 x 50.8 cm)
Signed, dated, and inscribed beneath turtle's right rear foot: ALBERT-LAESSLE. 1902–3./PHILADELPHIA.
Henry D. Gilpin Fund, 1904.4.2

b.
Bronze with brown patina; lost-wax cast in 1903–4
17½ x 13¼ x 19½" (44.5 x 33.7 x 49.5 cm)
Signed, dated, and inscribed beneath turtle's right rear foot: ALBERT-LAESSLE. 1902–3./PHILADELPHIA.
Foundry mark on base beneath turtle's left rear foot: Roman Bronze Works N.Y.
Henry D. Gilpin Fund, 1904.4.1

TURTLES were among Albert Laessle's favorite subjects. One of his earliest animal compositions was *Turtle and Crab,* about 1901 (plaster, destroyed), showing the two animals fighting over a dead crow.[1] A student had given a ten-pound snapping turtle to Charles Grafly for his dinner, and Laessle was offered the opportunity to use it as a model. When the resulting sculpture, *Turtle and Crab,* was exhibited in 1901 at the Philadelphia Art Club, it was denied a gold medal because the modeling was so realistic that it was thought to be cast from life.[2] For several months in 1901 and 1902, local newspapers, including the *Philadelphia Item,* carried news of the controversy; but neither Laessle nor Grafly would comment.

Laessle tried to put an end to the matter the following year by modeling *Turtle and Lizards* in wax and showing it at the seventy-second annual exhibition of the Pennsylvania Academy of the Fine Arts. The wax model was purchased by the Academy and cast in plaster and in bronze. In 1904 the bronze was exhibited at both the Pennsylvania Academy and at the Louisiana Purchase Universal Exposition, Saint Louis, where it was well received.[3]

The sculpture shows a turtle perched on a rock with two lizards peeking out of crevices. A snail is at the turtle's right side. A comparison of the plaster and the bronze reveals that, even with the precision of lost-wax casting, some of the fine details of the turtle's shell and wrinkled skin were lost. There are two other plasters of this group, but their present whereabouts is unknown.[4] Parts of the plaster cast in the Museum of American Art of the Pennsylvania Academy, especially portions of the tail, had broken and were reconstructed in 1985–86 by the Museum's sculpture conservator.

When Laessle was in Paris from 1904 to 1907, he continued to model compositions of turtles, including *Turning Turtle,* 1905 (Metropolitan Museum of Art, New York; Brookgreen Gardens, Murrells Inlet, S.C.; and three private collections). The animals were imported from Algiers to control insects in Parisian basements. When *Turning Turtle* was exhibited in the Paris Salon of 1907, it, too, was attacked as a life cast.

Notes

1. Robert McCracken Peck, "Albert Laessle, American 'Animalier,' " *American Art Review* 3 (Jan.-Feb. 1976), appendix, p. 83.
2. Miller 1924, p. 24.

3. Craven 1984, p. 544.
4. Peck 1976, appendix, p. 83.

References
1911 Helen W. Henderson, *The Pennsylvania Academy of the Fine Arts and Other Collections of Philadelphia,* Boston: L.C. Page and Company, p. 208. **1916** "Americanization Shown by Artists; Painters and Sculptors of Foreign Birth or Parentage Make Splendid Display," *Philadelphia Press,* Jan. 17, p. 8. **1924** D. Roy Miller, "A Sculptor of Animal Life," *International Studio* 80 (Oct.), pp. 24, 25 (ill.). **1976** *Philadelphia: Three Centuries of American Art,* Philadelphia: Philadelphia Museum of Art, p. 497. **1984** Wayne Craven, *Sculpture in America,* Newark: University of Delaware Press, pp. 544, 553, fig. 14.13.

Exhibited (plaster)
1986–87 PAFA *Sculpture at the Pennsylvania Academy of the Fine Arts.*

Exhibited (bronze)
1904* cat. no. 846. **1904** *Louisiana Purchase Universal Exposition,* Saint Louis, cat. no. 2162. **1912** Saint Botolph Club, Boston, *Paintings by Mr. Joseph T. Pearson, Jr.; Sculpture by Mr. Albert Laessle,* cat. no. 8. **1916** Pennsylvania Museum of Art, Memorial Hall, Philadelphia, *Americanization through Art,* cat. no. 258. **1922** Unknown institution, Baltimore, one-man exhibition. **1970** Free Library of Philadelphia, *Animal Sculpture for Children,* bookmobile. **1986–87** PAFA, *Sculpture at the Pennsylvania Academy of the Fine Arts.* **1987** Port of History Museum, Philadelphia, *National Sculpture Society Celebrates the Figure: Fifty-Fourth Annual Exhibition,* p. 72 (ill.). **1989** PAFA, *"The Birds and the Beasts Will Teach Us."* **1992–93** PAFA, *Masterworks of American Art, 1780–1950.*

The Blue-Eyed Lizard

1908
Bronze with brown patina; lost-wax cast by 1911
3⅜ x 9⅞ x 4¾" (8.5 x 24.8 x 12.1 cm)
Signed in front of lizard at left: ALBERT-LAESSLE; inscribed and dated at right: PHILA. 1908.
Foundry mark beneath lizard's left front leg: ROMAN BRONZE WORKS N.Y.
Gift of Mrs. Joseph Drexel, 1911.1

IN THIS sculpture, Albert Laessle captures a portion of the woodland floor. A realistic lizard is surrounded on his rocky perch by a larva and maple seedpods. The artist, who is known for choosing elegant stone bases, selected this green-and-orange marble, mounted on a brass plate. Two other bronze casts were made.[1] One is in the Cleveland Museum of Natural History; the other is now unlocated.

Note
1. Robert McCracken Peck, "Albert Laessle, American

Laessle, *Turtle and Lizards,* plaster

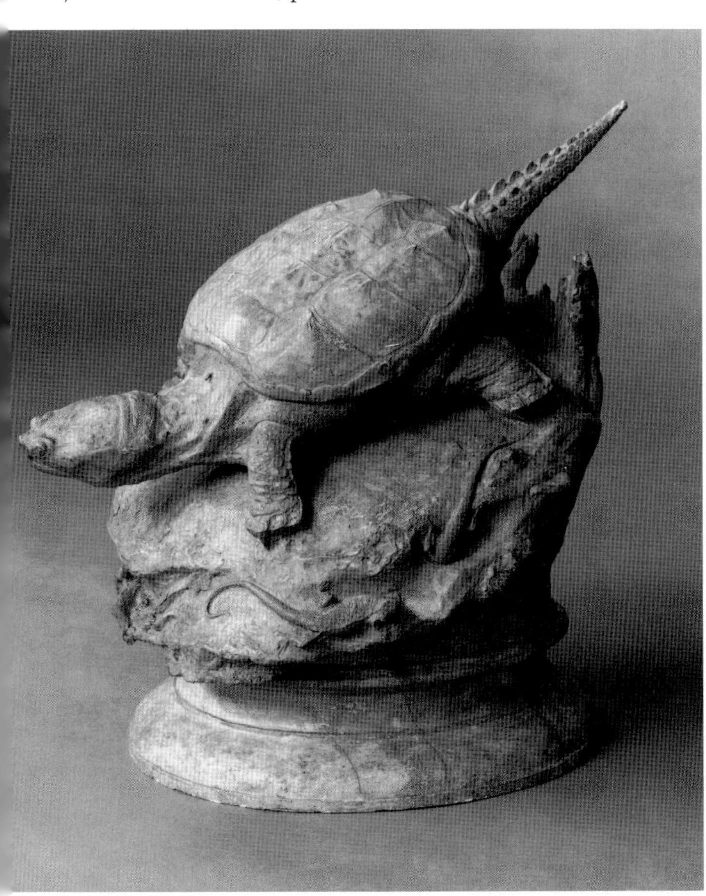

Laessle, *Turtle and Lizards,* bronze

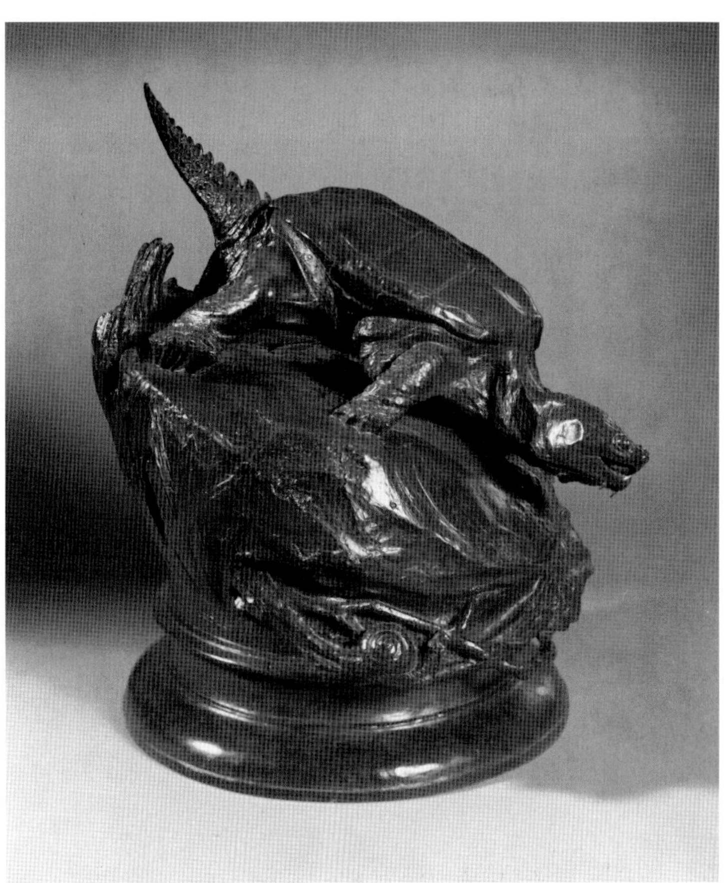

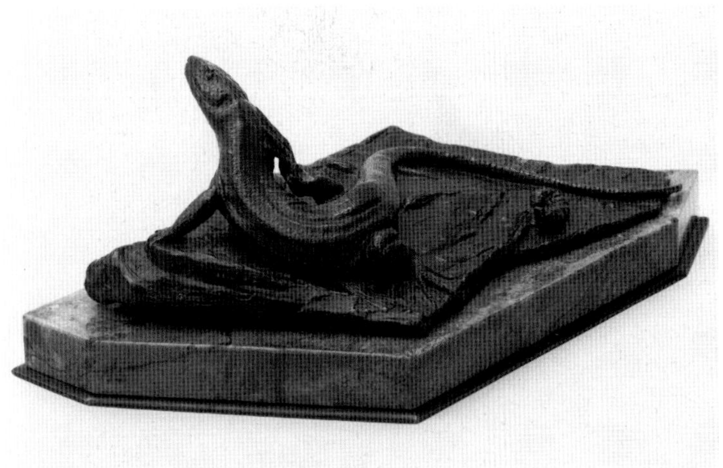

Laessle, *The Blue-Eyed Lizard*

'Animalier,' " *American Art Review* 3 (Jan.-Feb., 1976), appendix, p. 83.

References
1911 Helen W. Henderson, *The Pennsylvania Academy of the Fine Arts and Other Collections of Philadelphia,* Boston: L.C. Page and Company, pp. 208–9. **1924** D. Roy Miller, "A Sculptor of Animal Life," *International Studio* 80 (Oct.), pp. 25 (ill.), 27.

Exhibited
1911* cat. no. 838. **1912** Saint Botolph Club, Boston, *Paintings by Mr. Joseph T. Pearson Jr.; Sculpture by Mr. Albert Laessle,* cat. no. 7. **1915** *Panama-Pacific International Exposition,* San Francisco, cat. no. 3215. **1916** Pennsylvania Museum of Art, Memorial Hall, Philadelphia, *Americanization through Art,* cat. no. 306. **1916** Buffalo Fine Arts Academy, Albright Art Gallery, *Exhibition of Contemporary American Sculpture* (held under the auspices of the National Sculpture Society), cat. no. 436. **1972** Cosmopolitan Club, Philadelphia, exhibition of PAFA works. **1986–87** PAFA, *Sculpture at the Pennsylvania Academy of the Fine Arts.*

Heron and Fish

1910
Bronze with green-brown patina; lost-wax cast by 1912
16½ x 7 x 5¼" (42 x 17.8 x 13.3 cm)
Foundry mark behind heron's right leg: ROMAN BRONZE WORKS N.Y.
Gift of the heirs of Albert Laessle, 1973.29

BIRDS fascinated Albert Laessle. The details of the heron's anatomy and feathers, the two fish, and the shells and stones in relief on top of the plinth attest to the many hours of observation that Laessle must have devoted to the subject. He designed the beveled orange marble base.

Two other bronze casts were made (now unlocated).[1]

Note
1. Robert McCracken Peck, "Albert Laessle, American 'Animalier,' " *American Art Review* 3 (Jan.-Feb., 1976), appendix, p. 84.

Exhibited
1912* cat. no. 824. **1915** *Panama-Pacific International Exposition,* San Francisco, cat. no. 3225. **1916** Buffalo Fine Arts Academy, Albright Art Gallery, *Exhibition of Contemporary American Sculpture* (held under the auspices of the National Sculpture Society), cat. no. 446. **1986–87** PAFA, *Sculpture at the Pennsylvania Academy of the Fine Arts.* **1988** PAFA, *Sea and Shore.* **1994–96** PAFA, *Two Centuries of Collecting at the Museum of American Art.*

Ex Collections
The artist, until 1954; Mrs. Albert Laessle, Dr. Albert M. Laessle, and Paul Laessle, 1954–73.

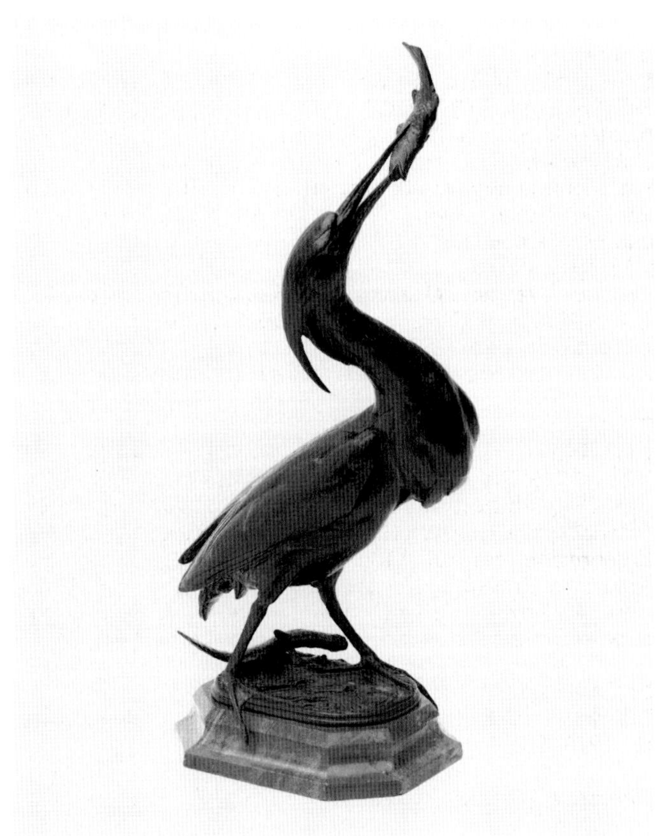

Laessle, *Heron and Fish*

Chanticleer

1912
Bronze with brown and red-brown patina; lost-wax cast in 1913
16 x 5¾ x 9½" (40.7 x 14.6 x 24.2 cm)
Signed, dated, and inscribed on top of base: ALBERT-LAESSLE 1912 PHILA.
Foundry mark at right of bird's right foot: ROMAN BRONZE WORKS N–Y–
Gift of the Fellowship of the Pennsylvania Academy of the Fine Arts, 1923.2

THIS crowing barnyard rooster developed from one that Albert Laessle modeled for Charles Grafly's 1904 marble figure *France* for the exterior of the New York Customs House. The orange stone base was designed by Laessle. Five other bronze casts were made of this work (now unlocated).[1] The painter and teacher Daniel Garber purchased a cast in 1913 from the 108th annual exhibition of the Pennsylvania Academy of the Fine Arts.

Note

1. Peck 1976, appendix, p. 84.

References

1913 "From Current Exhibitions," *Philadelphia Press*, Feb. 16, p. 12 (ill.). **1924** D. Roy Miller, "A Sculptor of Animal Life," *International Studio* 80 (Oct.), pp. 26, 27. **1925** Edward Longstreth, *The Art Guide to Philadelphia*, Philadelphia: Edward Longstreth, p. 131 (ill.). **1976** Robert McCracken Peck, "Albert Laessle, American 'Animalier,' " *American Art Review* 3 (Jan.-Feb.), pp. 76, 78, 79 (ill.), appendix, p. 84. **1984** Wayne Craven, *Sculpture in America*, Newark: University of Delaware Press, pp. 544–45. **1989** Janis Conner and Joel Rosenkranz, *Rediscoveries in American Sculpture: Studio Works, 1893–1939*, Austin: University of Texas Press, p. 107 (ill.).

Exhibited

1913 PAFA, Fellowship traveling exhibition, checklist no. 708. **1919** PAFA, Philadelphia Art Alliance, Fellowship annual exhibition, checklist no. 112. **1982** Woodmere Art Gallery, Chestnut Hill, Pa., *Pennsylvania Artistry: A Celebration*, cat. no. 113. **1984–85** PAFA, *A Growing American Treasure: Recent Acquisitions and Highlights from the Permanent Collection.* **1986–87** PAFA, *Sculpture at the Pennsylvania Academy of the Fine Arts.*

Ex Collection

Fellowship of the Pennsylvania Academy, purchase, probably 1913–23.

George D. Widener Memorial Gold Medal, 1916: See Appendix.

Sesquicentennial Medal of Award, 1926: See Appendix.

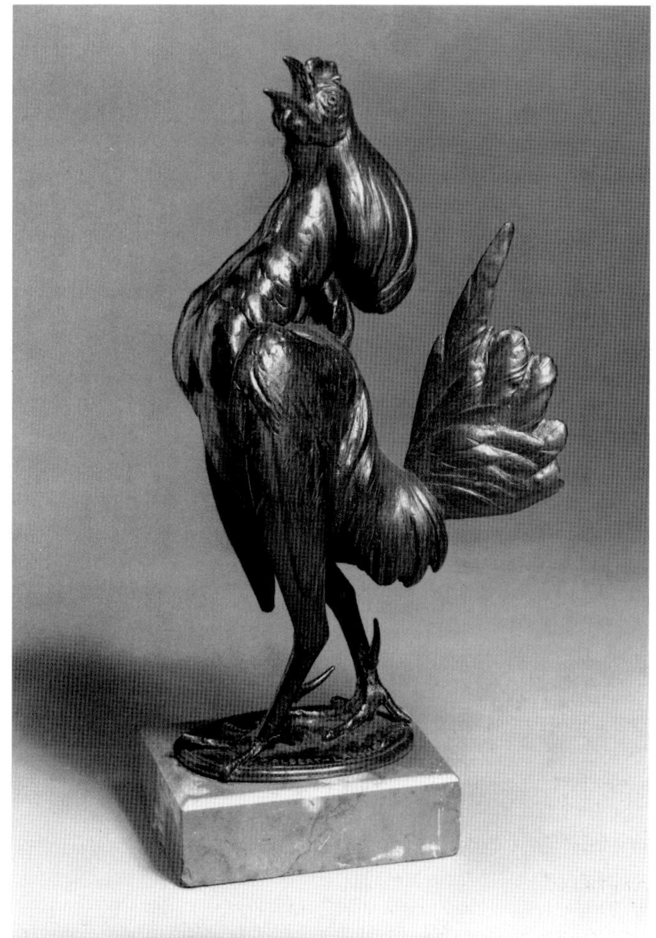

Laessle, *Chanticleer*

MAHONRI YOUNG

1877–1957

Mahonri Mackintosh Young is most often remembered as a sculptor, but he was also a successful painter and printmaker. In all media, Young was a realist. His subjects ranged from the cowboys, Indians, and animals of the American West to construction workers and city dwellers of Paris and New York. In sculpture, he was particularly skilled at capturing figures in motion. Bronze boxers and straining laborers are among his best-known works. They often prompt comparison to similar themes in the realist paintings of contemporary, Ashcan school artists like George Luks and George Bellows.

Mahonri Young was born in Salt Lake City in 1877, the year that his grandfather, the Mormon leader Brigham Young, died. As a child, Mahonri liked to draw and make objects from adobe. When he was still a boy, his father died and the family fell into dire financial straits. Young dropped out of high school to work as an artist for the Salt Lake Tribune.[1] To hone his skills, he took drawing lessons from the local artist James T. Harwood. Young's childhood interest in modeling was reawakened in 1897, when he had the opportunity to watch Cyrus E. Dallin (1864–1944) execute a statue of Brigham Young.

In 1899 determination to be an artist led Mahonri Young to New York and the Art Students League, where he studied with the impressionist painter Childe Hassam. Two years later, Young left for Paris. During the next four years, he attended several of the popular private art schools in Paris, including the académies Julian, Colarossi, and Delécluse. He made his first statuettes of workingmen during these years. His sculpture of an Alsatian boatman, entitled *Bovet Arthur—A Laborer,* 1904 (Newark Museum, New Jersey), captures the strong but weary body of an aging laborer. In 1911 it won the Helen Foster Barnett Prize at the annual exhibition of the National Academy of Design, in New York.

From Paris, Young returned to Salt Lake City in 1905, but his hometown lacked the large artistic community and opportunities to which he had become accustomed, and in 1909 he went east for good. Yet Young executed some of his most important commissions for Salt Lake City. The first of these was an architectural frieze of athletes, made in 1911 for the Deseret Gymnasium. The following year, he created the Sea Gull Monument for Temple Square. It commemorates the sea gulls that saved the crops of Mormon farmers from a plague of crickets and grasshoppers in 1848. Two of the relief panels for the Sea Gull Monument were exhibited in New York at the 1913 Armory Show, which Young helped to organize. His last major work for Salt Lake City, The Pioneer Monument (also called This Is the Place Monument), was completed in 1947. It depicts Brigham Young and two other Mormon leaders arriving in the Salt Lake valley.

In 1912, during the first of several trips to the Southwest, Young became fascinated with the native tribes and made drawings, paintings, etchings, and bas-reliefs of their daily life. The knowledge that he acquired earned him a commission from the American Museum of Natural History, in New York, for plaster groups of Apache, Navaho, and Hopi.

For the 1915 Panama-Pacific Exposition, in San Francisco, Young modeled architectural decorations for the portal of the Liberal Arts Palace. They included a relief panel, *The Useful Arts,* flanked by two niche figures, *Woman with the Distaff* and *Man with the Sledge Hammer.* He also exhibited sculptures and etchings at the exposition and was awarded a silver medal for sculpture.

In 1916 Young returned to the Art Students League in New York to teach. His tenure at the school lasted until 1943, with year-long absences in 1918–19 and 1939–40 and a lengthy leave between 1922 and 1934.[2] In the mid-1920s, he went back to Paris for two and a half years. During this time, he made many of his popular sculptures of boxers. *The Knockdown,* 1927 (Museum of Art, Brigham Young University, Provo) won him a gold medal at the 1932 Olympic Games in Los Angeles.

Throughout his career, Young modeled portraits. Many depict artist friends like Alfred Maurer, John Twachtman, and Emil Carlsen. His portrait of Carlsen was awarded the Maynard Prize at the National Academy of Design in 1932. Young's last major work was a statue of Brigham Young for Statuary Hall in the United States Capitol.

Notes

1. *Mahonri M. Young from the Brigham Young University Art Collection,* 1969, p. 2.
2. Archives of the Art Students League, New York.

References

1912 J. Lester Lewine, "The Bronzes of Mahonri Young," *International Studio* 47 (Oct.), pp. 55–59. **1918** Mahonri Young, "Life as Mahonri Young Sees It," *Touchstone* 4 (Oct.), pp. 8–18. **1969** *Mahonri M. Young from the Brigham Young University Art Collection,* New York: Brigham Young University and M. Knoedler and Company, catalogue for traveling exhibition. **1992** Roberta K. Tarbell, "Mahonri Young's Sculptures of Laboring Men, Walt Whitman, and Jean François Millet," *Walt Whitman and the Visual Arts,* New Brunswick, N.J.: Rutgers University Press, pp. 142–65.

Man with a Pick

1915
Bronze with black patina; lost-wax cast in 1918
28¼ x 8 x 10" (71.7 x 20.3 x 25.4 cm)
Signed on integral base between feet: YOUNG
Foundry mark incised on back of integral base: ROMAN BRONZE WORKS, INC N–Y
Gift of Mrs. John Wintersteen, 1982.11

MODELED IN 1915, *Man with a Pick* is one of Mahonri Young's many sculptures depicting workingmen.[1] He began to explore the theme of the worker about 1903, while he was studying in Paris. The paintings of toiling peasants by François Millet and the sculptures of downtrodden laborers by Constantin Meunier (1831–1905) inspired him. Unlike these French artists, however, Young insisted that his interest in workers was not intended as social commentary.[2] Aesthetic considerations were paramount in his choice of subjects, and he delighted in the balance and poise of working people and in the rhythmic nature of their tasks.[3] Nevertheless, during the early decades of the twentieth century, Young found little market in the United States for sculptures of laborers. For the most part, American art patrons were not interested in the subject, and they were uncomfortable with art that might be interpreted as social criticism. During the mid-1920s, when Young turned his attention to boxers (who shared many of the qualities that he found exciting in workers), he had more buyers for his work.

While studying in Paris, Young assimilated the Beaux-Arts style, which is characterized by actively worked surfaces. The result can be seen in the profusion of broken planes that reflect light and create a sense of movement in *Man with a Pick.* This sculpture is closely related to an earlier work, *The Heavy Sledge,* 1911 (plaster at Museum of Art, Brigham Young University, Provo). The poses are similar. Both figures hold tools over their heads and have slightly bent knees. According to the sculptor, only two casts of *Man with a Pick* were made.[4] The other one belongs to the Metropolitan Museum of Art, in New York.

Notes

1. This date was given to me by Daniel Hodgson who is working on a monograph on Young.
2. *Mahonri M. Young from the Brigham Young University Art Collection* (New York: Brigham Young University and M. Knoedler and Company, 1969), traveling exhib. cat., p. 3.
3. Mahonri Young, "Life as Mahonri Young Sees It," *Touchstone* 4 (Oct. 1918), p. 10.
4. Albert TenEyck Gardner, *American Sculpture: A Catalogue of the Collection of the Metropolitan Museum of Art* (New York: Metropolitan Museum of Art, 1965), p. 132.

Exhibited

1958 PAFA, *Twentieth Century American Painting and Sculpture from Philadelphia Private Collections,* cat. no. 46, as *Miner.* **1984–85** PAFA, *A Growing American Treasure: Acquisitions Since 1978,* cat. no. 218 (ill.). **1986–87** PAFA, *Sculpture at the Pennsylvania Academy of the Fine Arts.* **1987** PAFA, *Gifts of a Collector: Bernice McIlhenny Wintersteen (1900–1986),* checklist p. 6 (ill.). **1994–96** PAFA, *Two Centuries of Collecting at the Museum of American Art.*

Ex Collections

John D. McIlhenny, purchase from the sculptor, about 1915–25; his daughter Bernice McIlhenny Wintersteen (Mrs. John Wintersteen), 1925–82.

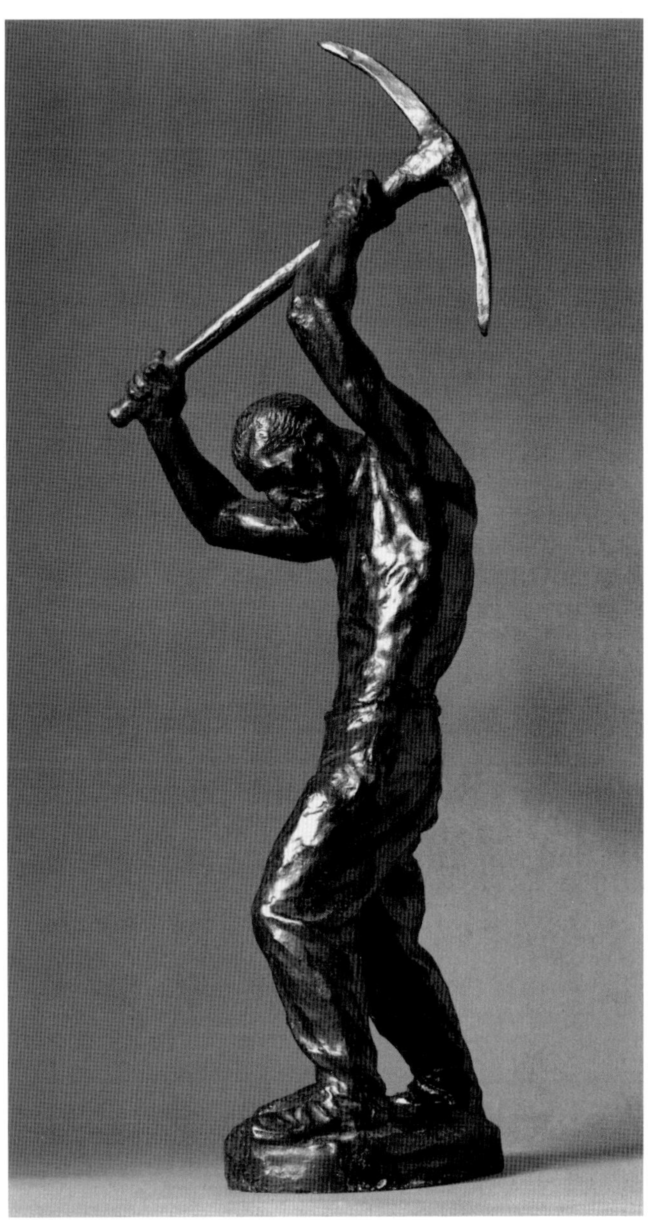

Young, *Man with a Pick*

Salvatore F. Bilotti

1879–1953

Salvatore Bilotti was born in Cosenza, Italy. When he came to the United States is not known. Presumably he had art training prior to entering the Pennsylvania Academy of the Fine Arts in 1904, because he did not take beginning classes. He studied life modeling with CHARLES GRAFLY at the Academy for three years and was awarded free tuition for his first two years. Bilotti won a summer Cresson traveling scholarship to Europe in 1906 and a two-year scholarship from 1907 to 1909. He was in Paris in 1907 at the same time as the fellow sculpture students ALBIN POLÁŠEK and John M. Bateman (b. 1887). Bilotti was in Rome in 1910 and in Paris until 1912. His work was shown regularly at the Pennsylvania Academy's annual exhibitions from 1905 to 1943, including the time that he was in Europe.

By 1914 Bilotti was living in New York, in Greenwich Village, among such sculptors as Polášek, Daniel Chester French (1850–1931), Henry Hudson Kitson (1865–1947), James Earle Fraser (1876–1953), Laura Gardin Fraser (1889–1966), and Victor D. Salvatore (1885–1965) and a stonecutter named Merli.[1] That year Bilotti won a collaborative prize from the Architectural League of New York. In 1917 his work was included in a New York benefit exhibit, *The Allies of Sculpture.* The following year he was listed as a member of the newly organized Whitney Studio Club, which was begun by the sculptor and patron Gertrude Vanderbilt Whitney (1875–1942) and was the predecessor of the Whitney Museum of American Art. Bilotti exhibited regularly in the Club's annual and sculpture exhibitions beginning in 1918, and was given a show there in 1921 with Gerome Brush and Harold Erskine (1879–1951). Bilotti was predominantly a stone carver of female figures. He also modeled portrait busts that were cast in bronze. He assisted Mrs. Whitney with stone carving,[2] and she purchased his bronze portrait of Lawrence Fellows, 1918 (Whitney Museum of American Art, New York).

By 1923 Salvatore Bilotti had produced a marble statue for the Chapel of the Little Sisters of the Poor in Our Lady of Lourdes, New York. Nine works including garden sculptures and a Classical Greek-type torso fragment in painted plaster were in the National Sculpture Society's 1923 *Exhibition of American Sculpture.* He was included in their 1929 *Contemporary American Sculpture* exhibition in San Francisco. His work was among those chosen to represent New York state in the *American Art Today* exhibition at the 1939 New York World's Fair. He exhibited in the 1940 and 1949 Sculpture International Exhibitions held at the Philadelphia Museum of Art and organized by the Fairmount Park Art Association.

His work is in the Whitney Museum of American Art and the Saint Louis Art Museum.

Notes

1. Ruth Sherwood, *Carving His Destiny, The Story of Albin Polášek* (Chicago: Ralph Fletcher Seymour, 1954), p. 239.

2. Roberta K. Tarbell, "Gertrude Vanderbilt Whitney as Patron," in *The Figurative Tradition and the Whitney Museum of American Art: Paintings and Sculpture from the Permanent Collection* (New York: Whitney Museum of American Art in association with Newark: University of Delaware Press and London and Toronto: Associated University Presses, 1980), p. 15.

Albert Rosenthal

1909
Bronze with green patina
16 x 7¼ x 10½" (40.6 x 18.4 x 26.7 cm)
Signed and dated on back at edge of neck: SF Bilotti 09
Lost-wax cast, possibly in Rome, Italy
Bequest of Albert Rosenthal, 1940.12.1

THE SITTER, Albert Rosenthal (1863–1939), was a portrait painter, etcher, and authority on American history and art. He studied at the Pennsylvania Academy of the Fine Arts in the 1880s, at the Ecole des Beaux-Arts in Paris with Jean Léon Gérôme, and in Munich. He is known for his portraits of Philadelphia's first ten mayors, in the city hall, and many of the Chief Justices of the Pennsylvania Supreme Court, in Harrisburg.

Salvatore F. Bilotti's training with Charles Grafly is evident in the strong modeling and the naturalistic yet simplified treatment of the features, including the hollow pupils that his teacher sometimes used. The bust was probably commissioned by Rosenthal,

Bilotti, *Albert Rosenthal*

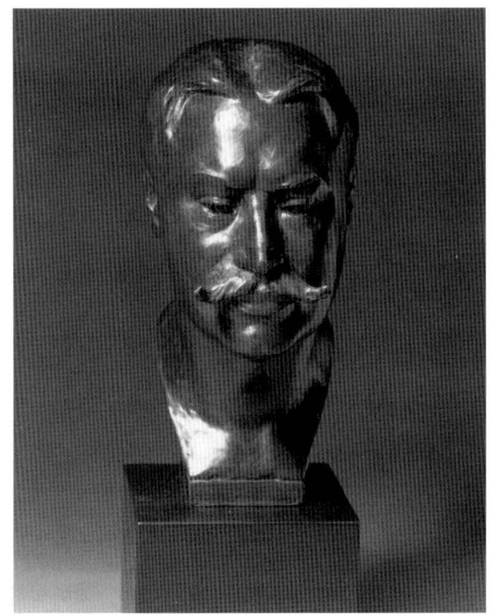

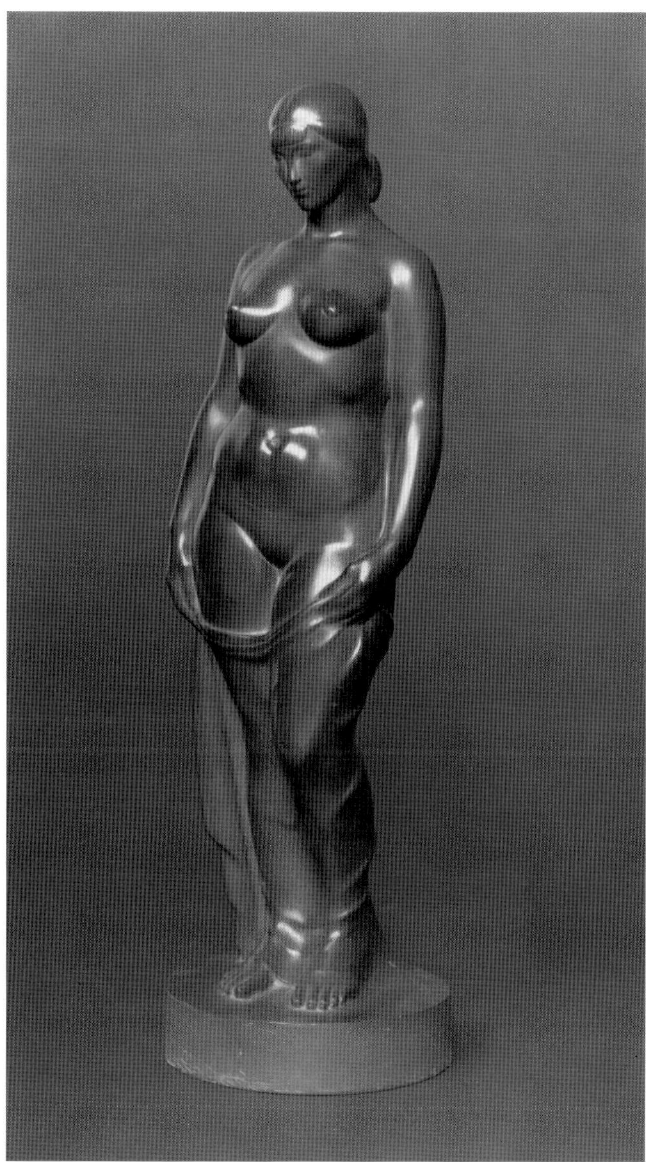

Bilotti, *Suzanne*

who may have posed in Rome. It was submitted for exhibition at the Pennsylvania Academy in 1910. The sitter bequeathed it to the Academy with his 1923 self-portrait and an 1899 portrait of his father, Max Rosenthal, an important engraver and lithographer. The present black wood base was made in 1987 to replace the original.

Exhibited
1910* cat. no. 810.

Suzanne

1938
Pyrophyllite
20¾ x 6½ x 5¾" (52.7 x 16.5 x 14.6 cm)
Signed and dated on top of base next to left foot:
S. BILOTTI/38
Henry D. Gilpin Fund, 1940.2

Suzanne is typical of one of Salvatore F. Bilotti's favorite subjects: the nude female figure partially clothed in diaphanous drapery that also serves as a support. The demure figure may refer to the story in the Old Testament Apocrypha of Susanna and the Elders in which Daniel saves the wrongly accused woman from death. This subject was especially popular in Renaissance art.

The sculpture is carved in a soft mineral resembling talc that the artist referred to as African Wonderstone. It was used by other artists of the period, including NATHANIEL CHOATE. Bilotti worked the surface until it was smooth and highly polished. *Suzanne* was illustrated in 1947 with other types of stone carvings in *The Materials and Methods of Sculpture* by Jack C. Rich. In 1949 it was chosen to represent Bilotti's work in the memorial exhibition for Juliana Force, a colleague of Gloria Vanderbilt Whitney at the Whitney Museum of American Art, New York.

Exhibited
1939 New York World's Fair, *American Art Today*, cat. no. 569 (ill.). **1940*** cat. no. 34. **1942** Metropolitan Museum of Art, New York, *Artists for Victory*, p. 22. **1949** Whitney Museum of American Art, New York, memorial exhibition for Juliana Force, cat. no. 147. **1986–87** PAFA, *Sculpture at the Pennsylvania Academy of the Fine Arts.*

ALBIN POLÁŠEK

1879–1965

Albin Polášek was born in Moravia in the Carpathian Mountains, which later became part of Czechoslovakia. Having shown an early talent for drawing and whittling, he was apprenticed at the age of sixteen to a furniture maker in Vienna. About 1898 he immigrated to the United States to join his brothers, who were ministers in Minnesota. Polášek carved wooden altar figures in factories there and in Iowa.

Upon seeing CHARLES GRAFLY's allegorical figures and portrait busts at the 1904 Louisiana Purchase

Universal Exposition, in Saint Louis, he decided to study with him at the Pennsylvania Academy of the Fine Arts. Polášek enrolled the following year and took many honors that Grafly wrote in 1907, "He gives promise of being one of the strongest students the Academy ever had."[1] He won an Edmund Austin Stewardson competition and one of the Charles Grafly prizes (probably in composition) in 1906. He also won William Emlen Cresson traveling scholarships in 1907, 1908, and in 1909 for summer travel. In 1907 he visited England, Belgium, Switzerland, Italy, France, and his birthplace, which was then part of Austria. He was especially impressed by Roman architecture, equestrian statues, and the anatomical sketches of Michelangelo.[2] In 1909 Polášek traveled in Greece. He won the 1910 Prix de Rome in Sculpture and received a three-year scholarship for study at the American Academy in Rome. In his final year, he was required to model a heroic figure. Accordingly, he executed *The Sower* (Art Institute of Chicago), which was awarded an honorable mention at the 1913 Paris Salon. In 1915 he was awarded the cash equivalent of the Pennsylvania Academy's George D. Widener Memorial Gold Medal for *Aspiration* (Samuel S. Fleisher Memorial and Detroit Institute of Arts), which depicts a woman kissing an angel.[3] The same year, at the Panama-Pacific International Exposition, in San Francisco, he received a silver medal for a group of ten portraits and figures. Polášek lived and worked in New York from 1913 to 1916. Then he accepted a teaching position at the Art Institute of Chicago, where he remained until 1943 except for a leave of absence to be a visiting professor at the American Academy in Rome in 1930 and 1931. In 1926 he was awarded a silver medal at the Sesquicentennial Exposition in Philadelphia. The National Academy of Design, in New York, elected him an associate in 1926 and an academician in 1933.

After World War II, Polášek spent summers in his native village and completed various commissions for the government of Czechoslovakia. Perhaps his most well-known composition is *Man Carving His Own Destiny*, which occupied his attention for over fifty years, beginning with his student days at the Pennsylvania Academy. It was modeled in several versions in different sizes. An early version, from 1920, is at the Samuel S. Fleisher Art Memorial in Philadelphia. The final version, carved in limestone by Robert A. Baillie (1880–1961) and Arthur E. Lorenzani (1886-after 1982) in 1961, is in Brookgreen Gardens, Murrells Inlet, South Carolina. Polášek's 1954 biography, written by his first wife, the sculptor and teacher Ruth Sherwood (1889–1953), derives its title from this sculpture.

In about 1951 Polášek suffered a stroke that left him paralyzed on one side; but, through sheer determination, he was still able to model in clay and paint. He died in 1965 in Winter Park, Florida. His home and two hundred of his sculptures and paintings now comprise the Albin Polasek Foundation. In 1989 a documentary about Polášek was filmed for Czech television. It included photographs of the Academy's sculpture, as well as works in Winter Park, Brookgreen Gardens, and the Art Institute of Chicago.

Notes

1. Charles Grafly to John E.D. Trask, secretary and managing director of PAFA, undated (stamped with date of receipt, Sept. 11, 1907), PAFA Archives.

2. Two undated letters from Albin Polášek to John E.D. Trask, 1907, are in the Cresson records, PAFA Archives.

3. In 1958 in gratitude for the Pennsylvania Academy's early support, he donated a sum equal to the funds he had been given for European travel. He also paid to have a Widener gold medal cast for himself. See Albin Polášek to Joseph T. Fraser, Jr., director of the PAFA, May 19, May 31, and Sept. 7, 1958, PAFA "Self-Portrait" object file.

References

1954 Ruth Sherwood, *Carving His Own Destiny: The Story of Albin Polášek*, Chicago: Ralph Fletcher Seymour. **1965** Obituary, *New York Times*, May 20, p. 43. **1968** Beatrice Gilman Proske, *Brookgreen Gardens Sculpture*, Murrells Inlet: Brookgreen Gardens, rev. ed., pp. 227–31. **1970** Emily Polasek, *Albin Polasek: Man Carving His Own Destiny*, Winter Park: Albin Polasek Foundation (contains inaccuracies). **1982** Regina Soria, "Albin Polášek," *Dictionary of Nineteenth-Century American Artists in Italy, 1760–1914*, Rutherford, N.J.: Fairleigh Dickinson University Press, pp. 251–52.

Francis Davis Millet

1912
Bronze with brown patina; lost-wax cast
16 x 9¾ x 9" (40.8 x 24.9 x 23 cm)
Signed at back behind neck: Albin Polašek
Inscribed and dated above signature at back edge of neck:
Roma Villa Amelia Jen. [*sic*] 1912.
Foundry mark on back of plinth: Fond. Nelli-Roma
Henry D. Gilpin Fund, 1913.9

FRANK MILLET (1846–1912) was a prominent mural painter and a founder of the American Academy in Rome, where Albin Polášek was studying when he modeled this bust. Impressed by a bust of Frederic Crowninshield, the director of the American Academy, which the sculptor had done in December 1911, Millet agreed to pose. "Let's have this fun," he exclaimed.[1] Never before had Millet consented to having his portrait modeled. The sittings, which were marked by animated discussions, occurred over a two-week period in January 1912. When the bust was

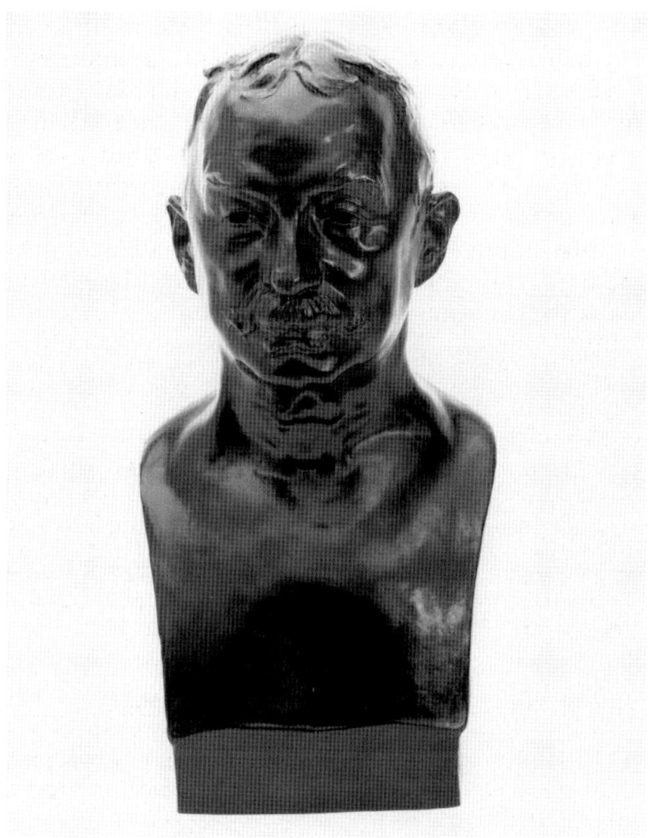

Polášek, *Francis David Millet*

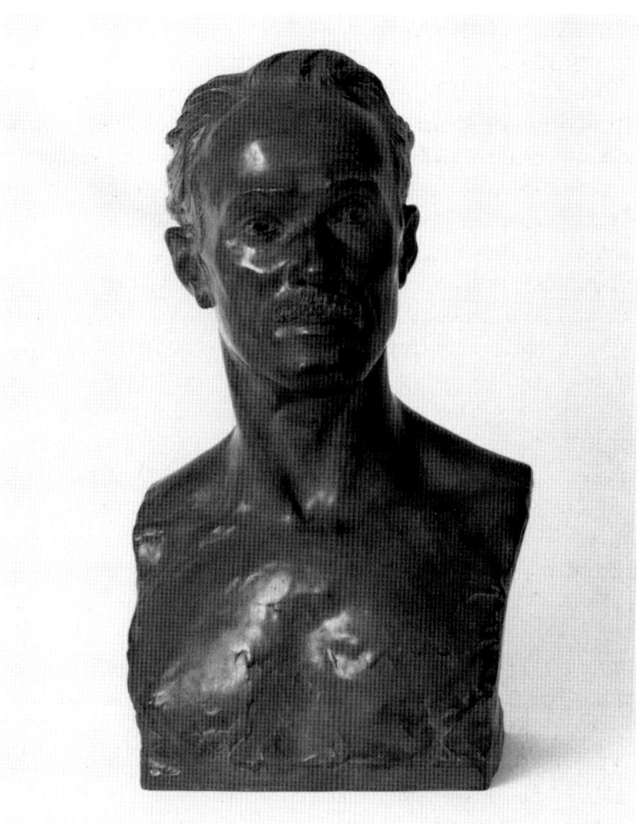

Polášek, *Self-Portrait*

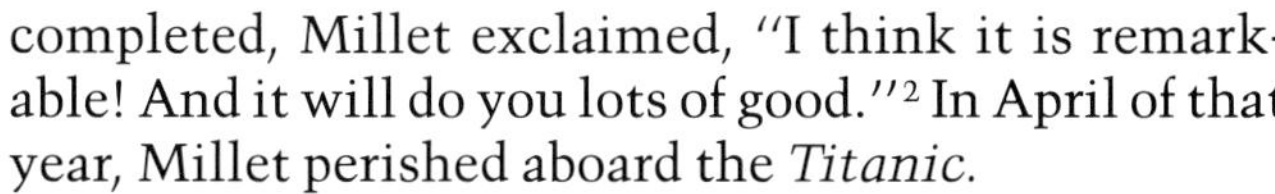

completed, Millet exclaimed, "I think it is remarkable! And it will do you lots of good."[2] In April of that year, Millet perished aboard the *Titanic.*

The solid structure of the head and the strong modeling are typical of portrait busts by Polášek's teacher Charles Grafly. The deep-set eyes impart a sense of vitality and convey the sense of humor of the sitter. The inscription should probably read either "Gen.", *January* in Italian, or "Jan." for the English abbreviation. This bust was admired by Grafly and John E.D. Trask at the Pennsylvania Academy, who had it cast in Rome at the Academy's expense in time to be shown in the 1913 annual exhibition.[3] Altogether nine bronzes were cast. One was shown at the Sesquicentennial Exposition, in Philadelphia. In 1934 four of Polášek's busts—Millet, Grafly and the painters Elihu Vedder and Charles W. Hawthorne—were installed in the Hall of American Artists at New York University.

Notes

1. Sherwood 1954, p. 231.
2. Ibid., p. 232.
3. John E.D. Trask to Albin Polášek, June 17, 1912, PAFA object file.

References

1954 Ruth Sherwood, *Carving His Own Destiny: The Story of Albin Polášek,* Chicago: Ralph Fletcher Seymour, pp. 123 (ill.), 231–32. **1970** Emily Polasek, *Albin Polasek: Man Carving His Own Destiny,* Winter Park: Albin Polasek Foundation (contains inaccuracies), pp. 16 (ill.), 17.

Exhibited

1913* cat. no. 717 (ill.). **1915** *Panama-Pacific International Exposition,* San Francisco, cat. no. 2865. **1917** Art Institute of Chicago, solo exhibition. **1986–87** PAFA, *Sculpture at the Pennsylvania Academy of the Fine Arts.*

Self-Portrait

1933
Bronze with green patina; lost-wax cast by 1935
21½ x 12¼ x 8" (54.7 x 31.2 x 20.5 cm)
Signed and dated on proper left at bottom: *Albin Polášek*/1933
Foundry mark on back at proper left: ROMAN BRONZE WORKS.N.Y.
Henry D. Gilpin Fund, 1935.5

THIS BUST shows Albin Polášek as the serious, determined artist who overcame many obstacles and became a success at his chosen profession. At the edges of the chest, the original clay was left rough, an allusion either to the process of creation or to his livelihood. Polášek may have modeled this self-portrait after his election as an academician of the National Academy of Design, in New York, although its collection does not contain a cast of this bust but only his 1915 bust of William Merritt Chase.

A cast of this self-portrait is in the Albin Polasek Foundation in Winter Park, Florida, where there is also a painted self-portrait of him modeling a portrait bust.

References

1937 *Brookgreen Gardens: Sculpture by Albin Polášek,* Murrells Inlet, S.C.: Brookgreen Gardens, ill. of clay original incorrectly attributed to PAFA. **1954** Ruth Sherwood, *Carving His Own Destiny: The Story of Albin Polášek,* Chicago: Ralph Fletcher Seymour, p. 81 (ill. of clay original incorrectly attributed to PAFA).

Exhibited

1935* cat. no. 403, as *Portrait Bust* (ill.). **1962** Woodmere Art Gallery, Philadelphia, *An Invited Exhibition by Pennsylvania Members of the National Academy of Design,* cat. no. 40. **1984–85** PAFA, *A Growing American Treasure: Recent Acquisitions and Highlights from the Permanent Collection.*

Edward McCartan

1879–1947

Edward Francis McCartan was born and reared in Albany, New York. His father, Michael McCartan, was born in Ireland, and his mother, Anna Hyland McCartan, was of Irish descent. After spending two years at Albany High School, Edward attended Pratt Institute in Brooklyn, where for six months he studied sculpture with Herbert Adams (1858–1945), then renowned for his decorative portrait busts of women. Between 1900 and 1903, McCartan attended the Art Students League in New York. He studied painting with George DeForest Brush, drawing with Kenyon Cox and Bryson Burroughs, and sculpture with George Grey Barnard (1863–1938).[1] McCartan gained some practical experience in the sculpture studios of Hermon Atkins MacNeil (1866–1947) and Karl Bitter (1867–1915). Under Bitter's direction, he worked on some of the large-scale sculpture decorations for the 1901 Pan-American Exposition, in Buffalo.

In 1907 McCartan sailed for Europe. During the next three years, he studied sporadically at the Ecole des Beaux-Arts in Paris with the sculptor Jean Antoine Injalbert (1845–1933). He spent a good deal of time at the Musée du Louvre, where he developed an enthusiasm for French eighteenth-century sculpture, particularly the elegant works of Clodion (1738–1814) and JEAN ANTOINE HOUDON. It was almost impossible for a young sculptor working in Paris during the early years of the twentieth century to escape the influence of Auguste Rodin (1840–1917), and McCartan was no exception. *The Kiss* (Albright-Knox Art Gallery, Buffalo, N.Y.), a composition of a mother and child that he began in Paris in 1908, shows the influence of Rodin.

Not long after his return to New York from Paris, McCartan began to be recognized for his ornamental and garden sculpture. In 1912 his design for a fountain won the Helen Foster Barnett Prize at the National Academy of Design. His sculpture *Pan,* about 1913, was exhibited at the 1915 Panama-Pacific Exposition, in San Francisco. The following year, *The Spirit of the Woods,* about 1914, was awarded the George D. Widener Memorial Gold Medal at the Pennsylvania Academy of the Fine Arts. Made for Welwyn, the estate of Mr. and Mrs. Harold Pratt, Glen Cove, New York, it depicts a dancing nymph with a baby faun in her arms. McCartan was especially attracted to mythological themes. One of his favorites was Diana, the goddess of the hunt. In his best-known sculpture of Diana, 1922–23, the goddess restrains a leaping greyhound (versions at the Metropolitan Museum of Art, New York; Fogg Art Museum, Cambridge, Mass.; and Brookgreen Gardens, Murrells Inlet, S.C.). His *Boy and Panther,* 1923 (Century Association, New York), depicting Dionysus, the god of wine, was awarded the James E. McClees Prize at the Pennsylvania Academy in 1931.

The sculptor won several important commissions for public sculpture. In 1922 he completed a memorial to Eugene Field, the author of children's books, to be placed in Lincoln Park in Chicago. It depicts a fairy watching over two sleeping children. Among his other major works are the stone allegorical figures of Industry and Transportation, 1928, that support the clock on the facade of the Helmsley Building (originally called the New York Central Building), in New York, and a pediment, completed about 1937, of the Department of Labor and Commerce Building, in Washington, D.C.

McCartan was very active as a teacher. In 1914 he joined the sculpture department of the School of Beaux-Arts Architects, in New York (renamed the Beaux-Arts Institute of Design and now called the National Institute for Architectural Education), and later became the department's director. From 1926 to 1929, he also taught modeling at the Art Students

League. He was appointed head of the Rinehart School of Sculpture at the Maryland Institute, in Baltimore, in 1943.

He became a fellow of the National Sculpture Society. In 1925 he was elected an academician of the National Academy of Design for which he served as vice president from 1940 to 1942. He was awarded a gold medal of honor by the Allied Artists of America in 1933. In 1944 he was elected to the American Academy of Arts and Letters.

Note

1. Student records, Archives of the Art Students League, New York.

References

1937 *Brookgreen Gardens: Sculpture by Edward McCartan,* Murrells Inlet, S.C.: Brookgreen Gardens. **1947** Obituary, *New York Herald Tribune,* Sept. 22, clipping file, PAFA Library. **1967** Loring Holmes Dodd, *Golden Moments in American Sculpture,* Cambridge, Mass.: Dresser, Chapman and Grimes, pp. 76–79. **1968** Beatrice Gilman Proske, "Edward McCartan," in *Brookgreen Gardens Sculpture,* Murrells Inlet: Brookgreen Gardens, rev. ed., pp. 221–23. **1989** Janis Conner and Joel Rosenkranz, *Rediscoveries in American Sculpture: Studio Works, 1893–1939,* Austin: University of Texas Press, pp. 113–22.

The Bather

1935
Bronze, gilded and coated with pigmented varnish; cast in 1938
26 x 9⅝ x 8½" (66.1 x 24.5 x 21.6 cm)
Signed on back of integral base: E. MCCARTAN/1935
Lost-wax cast by the Roman Bronze Works, New York
Henry D. Gilpin Fund, 1938.4

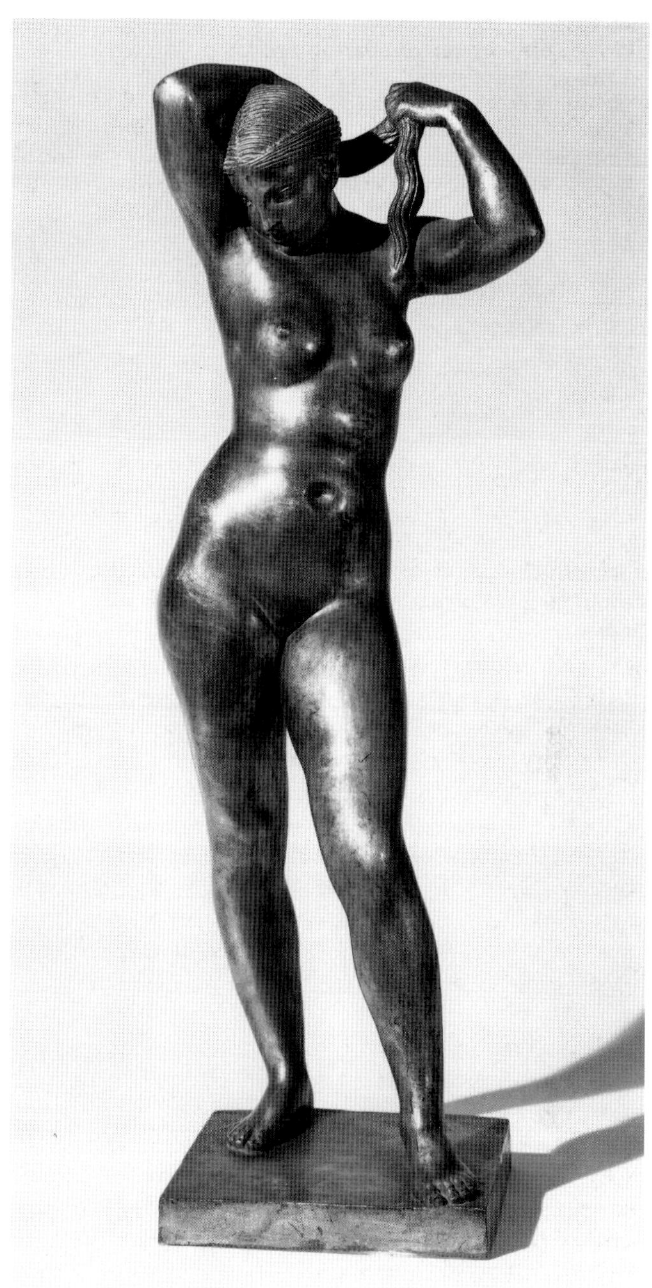

McCartan, *The Bather*

The Bather is typical of the decorative sculpture favored by the American public during the 1920s and 1930s. Edward McCartan simplified the figure's anatomy into solid rounded forms and emphasized outline to achieve a graceful rhythm. The exaggerated contrapposto and the formalized treatment of the hair call to mind the Archaic Greek-inspired sculpture of Paul Manship (1885–1966), the most popular American sculptor of the era.

Although it was completed in 1935, McCartan did not exhibit *The Bather* in plaster until 1938 at the 133rd annual exhibition of the Pennsylvania Academy of the Fine Arts. When John A. Myers, the secretary of the Academy, wrote to McCartan of the institution's wish to purchase a bronze cast for its permanent collection, he added that WALKER HANCOCK, one of the sculpture instructors, thought the piece would look "glorious" in gold leaf.[1] Although McCartan had envisioned it with a dark "Renaissance" patina, he was willing to accede to the Academy's wishes.[2] The sculpture was cast by the Roman Bronze Works, in New York, and McCartan oversaw the application of gold leaf and a protective coating of pigmented varnish.

Notes

1. John A. Myers to Edward McCartan, Feb. 16, 1938, PAFA Archives.
2. McCartan to Myers, Feb. 19, 1938, ibid.

Reference
1989 Janis Conner and Joel Rosenkranz, *Rediscoveries in American Sculpture: Studio Works, 1893–1939,* Austin: University of Texas Press, p. 121 (ill. and cover ill. in color).

Exhibited
1945* cat. no. 88. **1986–87** PAFA, *Sculpture at the Pennsylvania Academy of the Fine Arts.*

Frederick W. Härer

1879–1948

Frederick W. Härer was born in Blossburg, Pennsylvania, to a furnituremaker, who taught him to work in wood at an early age. About 1901 he briefly studied cast and life drawing at the Pennsylvania Academy of the Fine Arts with Thomas Anshutz and William Merritt Chase, respectively. He was awarded free tuition for two school years of further study, from 1908 to 1910. He also studied at the Pennsylvania Museum School of Industrial Art (now the University of the Arts). His early work appears to have been mostly in watercolor, for he exhibited regularly in the Pennsylvania Academy's annual watercolor exhibitions from 1911 to 1931. Many of the subjects appear to have been drawn from his travels to Spain and the West Indies.[1]

These travels probably influenced the designs for some of the picture frames that he carved and sold from the 1910s into the 1930s. Härer's frames are known for being completely hand-carved, for the use of sgraffito and punched decoration, and for burnished gilding. He came to be the "New Hope School" framemaker, producing simple but elegant frames, often enhanced with silver or gold leaf that nicely complemented their respective paintings.[2] Härer once said, "All my designs are based on fundamental truths that I hope will survive this period and all others, as the primitives have done."[3] The Pennsylvania Academy has a number of his signed frames on paintings by such American impressionists as Edward W. Redfield, Charles Morris Young, Adolphe Borie, Richard Blossom Farley, and especially Daniel Garber, who studied at the Academy when Härer first did and was a teacher when Härer returned. Traditional "Härer-type" Arts and Crafts style frames were later made by Härer's student Bernard Badura (1896–1986) and other Bucks County framemakers.

Probably in the late 1930s, Härer turned from framemaking to sculpture.[4] He carved animals in stone or wood, often gilded with metal leaf. From 1939 to his death in 1948, he showed his sculpture in the Pennsylvania Academy's annual exhibitions. His *Chinese Gander,* 1943 (Philadelphia Museum of Art) in wood with silver leaf, won the gold medal in 1944 at the annual exhibition of the Fellowship of the Pennsylvania Academy. It also won the Speyer Memorial Prize at the National Academy of Design, in New York, in 1945. Kraushaar Galleries probably began to represent him in the mid-1940s. In 1948 the Pennsylvania Academy bought *Hawk* (q.v.), and the Woodmere Art Museum bought *Catfish,* a wood sculpture with silver leaf made about 1939.

Because of his reputation in carving and gilding, Härer was asked in 1946 to repair and regild a broken nineteenth-century carved eagle (q.v.) that was then thought to be the work of WILLIAM RUSH. Härer also designed and made furniture and architectural details on commission for architects.[5]

Notes

1. Evidence of Härer's early travels appears in his oil painting *Borinquena,* about 1916 (Museum of American Art of the Pennsylvania Academy of the Fine Arts). It depicts a woman in the tropics and is reminiscent of the work of Paul Gauguin.
2. Suzanne Smeaton, *"The Art of The Frame": American Frames of the Arts and Crafts Period,* exhib. cat. (New York: Eli Wilner and Company, 1988), p. 24. A Härer frame was featured on both covers of the catalogue. See also Smeaton, "American Picture Frames of the Arts and Crafts Period, 1870–1920," *Antiques* 136 (Nov. 1989), pp. 1133–34.
3. Smeaton 1988, p. 22.
4. By 1939 the artist was referring to himself as "painter-sculptor-craftsman," artist's resumé, Sept. 29, 1939, PAFA object file for *Borinquena.*
5. Ibid.

References
1933 Peter Keenan, "Art and Artists," *New Hope Magazine* 1 (Sept.), pp. 6–7. **1948** Obituary, *New York Times,* April 28, p. 27.

Hawk

1947
Lead
10½ x 8⅜ x 13⅛" (26.6 x 21.3 x 33.3 cm)
Signed and dated (in 1948) on back of log: HARER/47/NO 1
Henry D. Gilpin Fund, 1948.5

Hawk, an image of a bird often seen in rural Pennsylvania, was modeled in clay, cast in plaster, and then cast in lead, probably by the artist.[1] Perhaps this was done in the studio of his student Bernard Badura, who was a stained-glass maker, as well as a painter, carver, and framemaker. Other examples of lead sculptures

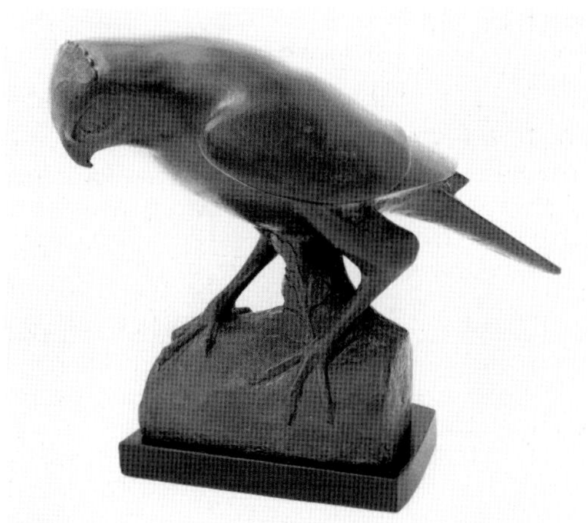

Härer, *Hawk*

by Frederick W. Härer are not known, although when he dated this piece retroactively in 1948,[2] Härer also incised "NO 1" to suggest that this was the first in a series. Whether other sculptures were actually produced is not known.

The hawk is shown sitting on a tree branch as if gazing intently at his prey. A smaller vertical branch with a leaf serves to support the bird. The sculpture is an overall matte gray, the color of the natural metal, with some areas of new metal visible over slight casting imperfections.[3] Lead is soft, so tool marks were easily made by the artist after casting. They emphasize the veining of the leaves and provide texture on the bird's chest and the log. The head, back, and wings appear smooth and streamlined with no attempt to delineate feathers.

Hawk was purchased from the 1948 annual exhibition of the Pennsylvania Academy of the Fine Arts. It is mounted on a wood base that is painted black.

Notes

1. "Hawk Sculptored By Harer In Pa. Exhibit," *Milford [N.J.] News*, Jan. 30, 1948, microfilm, roll no. 58, frame no. 526, PAFA Archives.

2. Joseph T. Fraser, Jr., director of the PAFA, to Frederick Härer, March 10, 1948, and Härer to Fraser, March 12, 1948, both in PAFA object file.

3. Virginia Norton Naudé, conservation report, Jan. 8, 1986, p. 1, ibid.

Exhibited

1947 National Academy of Design, New York, *First Half of 121st Annual Exhibition*, cat. no. 7. **1948*** cat. no. 180. **1958** Quaker City Federal Savings and Loan Association, Philadelphia, window display promoting the PAFA's 153rd annual exhibition. **1970** Free Library of Philadelphia, *Animal Sculpture for Children*, bookmobile. **1986–87** PAFA, *Sculpture at the Pennsylvania Academy of the Fine Arts*. **1989** PAFA, *"The Birds and the Beasts Will Teach Us."*

Giuseppe Donato

1881–1965

Giuseppe Donato was born in Maida, Calabria, Italy, and came to the United States about 1890. He learned cabinet making and wood carving from his father, Antonio. Because of his early artistic abilities, he was permitted to take classes for two years at the Philadelphia School of Industrial Art (now the University of the Arts) with the painter, photographer, and school director J. Liberty Tadd.[1] When he was graduated from high school in 1897, Donato won a city scholarship to attend the Pennsylvania Academy of the Fine Arts free of charge for three years (thereafter, the Academy paid his tuition in exchange for his assistance with casting). He studied sculpture with CHARLES GRAFLY and drawing with the painters William Merritt Chase, Thomas Anshutz, and Hugh Breckenridge. Donato won the school's first Edmund Stewardson competition in 1900 and was awarded the 1903 long-term William Emlen Cresson Traveling Scholarship for sculpture.

From 1903 to 1905 Giuseppe Donato traveled in Italy and France on the scholarship. He spent most of his time in Paris, where he attended classes at the Académies Colarossi and Julian. PAUL WAYLAND BARTLETT lent one of his studios to Donato. Bartlett also gave him periodic criticisms and may have introduced him to Auguste Rodin (1840–1917), whose pervasive influence on Donato's compositions and subject matter is evident. Rodin was said to have praised the work of the "young Italian."[2] Donato wrote to the Pennsylvania Academy from abroad and sent photographs of work in progress. They show that he was modeling portrait busts of several Americans and figural groups of mythological and biblical subjects. Photographs were later sent for display in the 1905 school competition.[3] In July 1905 before returning to Philadelphia and the Academy, he went back to Italy "where *Art* really lives in its highest form," especially to see the sculpture of Cellini, Michelangelo, and Donatello.[4]

Donato entered *The Age of Eternal Inspiration* (location unknown), also titled *That Burning Desire Within Me, Which Gives Me No Rest*, in the Pennsylvania Academy's 1906 annual exhibition. It was shown the same year in the Paris Salon, where it was apparently well received. Two years later, however, the nude male figure was rejected for exhibition by the Municipal Art Society of Baltimore when it was hosting the National Sculpture Society show.[5] This refusal to exhibit a nude figure caused some notoriety and was ironic inasmuch as Charles Grafly's *Symbol of Life* and *From Generation to Generation* (qq.v.), which incorporate male and female nudity, were both accepted into the show. In 1914 eleven of Donato's works were exhibited at the Pennsylvania Academy. They included *The Dance of Eternal Spring* (Italian Lake Park, Harrisburg),[6] and *Faun: Voice of the Forest* (location unknown), which were also shown the following year at the Panama-Pacific International Exposition, in San Francisco. In 1930 *Winged Thoughts, in Memory of Charles Grafly* (location unknown) was exhibited at the Pennsylvania Academy.

Like his teacher Grafly, Donato modeled portrait busts of many important people of his day, such as the Italian liberator Giuseppe Garibaldi, Benito Mussolini, the actor Robert B. Mantell, Mark Twain, and local figures, such as Dr. Russell Conwell, a clergyman and the founder of Temple University. In 1930 Donato produced a nine-foot-high bronze figure of Columbus on a ten-foot-high stone pedestal for Riverside Park, along the Delaware River, in Easton, Pennsylvania. The monument was the focus of a daylong celebration that featured a parade, speeches by political and religious leaders from Philadelphia and New York, a banquet, and a concert by the Apollo Grand Opera Company of Philadelphia.[7]

Giuseppe Donato took over Charles Grafly's seat on the Municipal Art Jury (later the Philadelphia Art Commission) in 1929 and served for at least thirty years. Donato's Philadelphia commissions include the west pediment of the Municipal Court Building, Nineteenth and Vine streets, which he executed in 1940, and a figure of Thomas Fitzsimmons, a signer of the Constitution, that was installed at Logan Circle in 1946. Other works are said to be in City Hall's Conversation Hall, and Saint John's Roman Catholic Church. Probably in the 1930s or 1940s, he served as the director of the art department at Lincoln College Preparatory School.[8] In addition, Donato was an inventor who successfully sued the Parker Pen Company for unauthorized use of his ideas. He also designed a mechanical pencil with changeable lead colors.

Notes

1. "Quakeress Statue is Italians' Pride," *Philadelphia Bulletin*, Oct. 3, 1908, microfilm, roll no. 55, frame no. 95, PAFA Archives.
2. "Sculptor Won Bride Within Five Days," *Philadelphia Inquirer*, March 20, 1906, microfilm, roll no. 54, frame no. 291, PAFA Archives.
3. Donato's letters are in the PAFA Archives; the photographs are in his clipping file in the PAFA Library.
4. Giuseppe Donato to Harrison S. Morris, managing director of the PAFA, July 14, 1905, PAFA Archives.
5. "Baltimore Won't Have Nude in Art," *Philadelphia North American*, April 19, 1908, microfilm, roll no. 55, frame no. 19, ibid.
6. In 1915 Donato won a court settlement of almost $24,000 from Milton S. Hershey for this bronze fountain of three nude female figures and a baby, representing the seasons. It had been commissioned for Hershey Park without a formal contract; and, after the size was doubled at Hershey's request, he refused to pay more for the larger version. "Remarkable Art Verdict," an unidentified New York newspaper clipping, Dec. 4, 1915 (ill.), Charles Henry Hart Scrapbooks, vol. 2, PAFA Archives.
7. "Columbus Statue Presented To City At Impressive Exercises," *Easton [Pa.] Express*, Dec. 15, 1930, pp. 1, 13. A model for this memorial was shown at the Pennsylvania Academy in 1930.
8. "Birthday Greetings to—Giuseppe Donato," unidentified newspaper, clipping file, PAFA Library.

References

1913 "Giuseppe Donato, Local Sculptor, Disciple of Nature," *Philadelphia Olney Times*, Jan. 27, microfilm, roll no. 55, frame no. 776, PAFA Archives. **1914** "Local Sculptor is Puzzle to Artists," *New York World Telegraph*, March 16, microfilm, roll no. 59, frame no. 202, PAFA Archives. **1965** "Giuseppe Donato Dies at 84, Sculptor, Art Commissioner," *Philadelphia Inquirer*, April 11, clipping file, PAFA Library.

John H. Converse

1912–13
Bronze with brown patina; lost-wax cast in 1913
20¾ x 9 x 9½" (52.7 x 22.9 x 24.2 cm)
Signed and dated beneath right side of neck:
©/G. Donato/1912–13/Phila.
Inscribed in relief at front of base: JOHN H. CONVERSE
Foundry mark on back: ROMAN BRONZE WORKS N–Y–
Deposited by John W. Converse, 1.1913

JOHN W. CONVERSE commissioned this posthumous portrait of his father, John Heman Converse (1840–1910), who had been president of the Baldwin Locomotive Works. He served on the board of directors of the Pennsylvania Academy of the Fine Arts from 1886 to 1910 and established the Academy's Gold Medal of Honor, designed by Daniel Dupuis (1849–1899), see Appendix. Using photographs and a death mask as guides, Giuseppe Donato depicted Converse as a younger man. The bust was in the process of being modeled by July 1913 and was completed by October.[1] Apparently, it had been redone sixteen times before the sculptor was satisfied. According to a 1914 newspaper article, only one bronze cast was made.[2]

Charles Grafly asked to see his former student's bust before its possible exhibition at the Pennsylvania Academy, and he reported favorably on the work.[3] The Academy recorded it as a loan by the subject's son. A newspaper at the time erroneously cited the

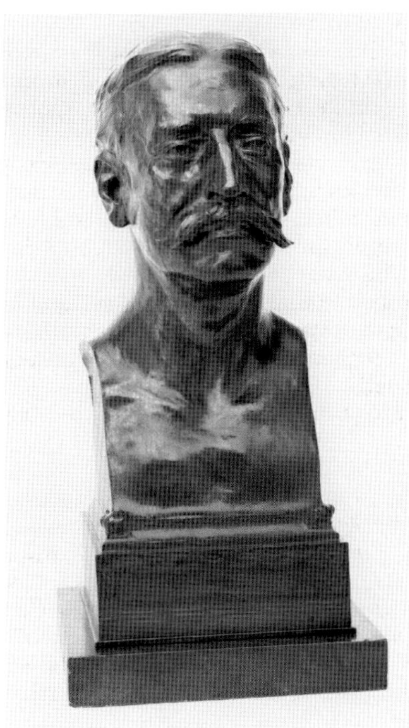

Donato, *John H. Converse*

work as given to the Pennsylvania Academy by the artist[4]; this confusion may have resulted from the fact that Donato delivered the bust to the Academy, and he thought at the time that it was intended as a gift.[5] The board of directors apparently assumed the work to be Academy property when, on November 3, 1913, they approved its loan to Donato for display in Chicago.

Upon seeing this bust at the Pennsylvania Academy in 1914, a critic wrote that it was "sufficiently in the academic style to show that [Donato] can do it, yet it contains notes of individuality and strength that relieve it of pedantry."[6] The portrait embodies many of the conventions that Donato's master, Charles Grafly, used in his works. Converse is shown bare-chested to avoid the distraction of clothing. The focus of attention is the structure of the head and the animation of the features. Such animation is difficult to achieve in a posthumous portrait. The bust is mounted on a red-brown marble base.

Notes

1. John F. Lewis, president of the PAFA, to Charles Grafly, July 31, 1913, and Oct. 7, 1913, both in Charles Grafly papers, Ablah Library Special Collections Archives, Wichita State University, Kansas.

2. "Bust of J.H. Converse Reproduced in Bronze," *Philadelphia North American,* Jan. 15, 1914 (ill.), microfilm, roll no. 56, frame no. 168, PAFA Archives.

3. Charles Grafly to John F. Lewis, draft, August 2, 1913, and note dated Oct. 10, 1913, at bottom of Lewis to Grafly, Oct. 7, 1913, ibid.

4. "Academy Gets Converse Bust; Likeness of Locomotive Builder is Work of Giuseppe Donato," *Philadelphia Bulletin,* Nov. 28, 1913, microfilm, roll no. 56, frame no. 144, PAFA Archives.

5. John F. Lewis to Giuseppe Donato, Jan. 14, 1914, and Donato to Lewis, Jan. 28, 1914, PAFA object file.

6. "Local Sculptor is Puzzle to Artists," *New York World Telegraph,* March 16, 1914, microfilm, roll no. 59, frame no. 202, PAFA Archives.

Exhibited

1913 Art Institute of Chicago, *26th Annual Exhibition of American Paintings and Sculpture,* cat. no. 400. **1914*** cat. no. 778. **1916** Pennsylvania Museum of Art, Memorial Hall, Philadelphia, *Americanization through Art,* cat. no. 287. **1923** Audubon Terrace, New York, *1923 Exhibition of National Sculpture of New York,* cat. no. 56. **1956** PAFA, *Living Philadelphia Artists Represented in the Permanent Collection of the Academy,* cat. no. 166. **1984–85** PAFA, *A Growing American Treasure: Recent Acquisitions and Highlights from the Permanent Collection.*

Gaston Lachaise

1882–1935

Born in Paris, Gaston Lachaise was the son of a prominent wood-carver and cabinetmaker, who taught his young son to carve. By school age, Gaston had already made a holy-water font.[1] At thirteen, he was studying with the sculptor Alphonse Moncel (b. 1866) at the Ecole Bernard Palissy, a training school for arts and crafts. After learning technical skills there for three years, Lachaise entered the atelier of the sculptor Gabriel Jules Thomas (1824–1905) at the Académie Nationale des Beaux-Arts. In 1899 the minimum-age rule was waived so that the sixteen-year-old Lachaise could exhibit in the Paris Salon. About 1902 a chance meeting with an American visitor, Isabel Dutaud Nagle, at the Musée de Cluny changed his life.[2] He decided to follow her to Boston; and, as a result, he gave up a school scholarship, a growing reputation in French academic circles, and the promise of a Prix de Rome. To earn enough money for the transatlantic passage, he went to work for the art nouveau designer René Lalique. Lachaise emigrated in 1906. He never returned to Europe because he felt that the United States was "the most favorable ground for the continuity of art."[3] He helped Henry Hudson Kitson (1865–1947) complete his commissions for Civil War monuments until 1912. In his spare time, Lachaise modeled rough statuettes of Isabel Nagle, one of which was exhibited in the 1913 Armory Show, in New York.[4]

In 1912 Lachaise left Boston for New York and soon became an assistant to Paul Manship (1885–1966), with whom he remained for about ten years. During that time, Lachaise married Isabel Nagle and became a United States citizen. He began his well-known, elegant, nude *Standing Woman,* which was shown in plaster at the Stephan Bourgeois Gallery in New York in 1918 as the focus of his first solo exhibition.[5] According to the critic Henry McBride, an early admirer of Lachaise's work, the sculptor was criticized for violating the classical tradition of the female nude.[6] Lachaise chose instead to portray the archetypal woman, reminiscent of prehistoric images of fertility goddesses.[7] Also in the 1918 exhibition were his popular, decorative, animal sculptures inspired by Manship's work.

Lachaise left Manship's employ in 1921 to accept a commission for a frieze of singing and dancing boys for the lobby of the old American Telephone and Telegraph Building, New York.[8] From 1922 to 1926, Lachaise was represented by the C.W. Kraushaar Galleries, which oversaw the casting in bronze of some of his works. In the 1920s, the sculptor became known for his insightful portraits of such people as e.e. cummings and Henry McBride.[9] They were associated with the *Dial,* a magazine that often used Lachaise's work as illustrations (he was the only sculptor to be featured thus). In 1927 he had a solo exhibition at Alfred Stieglitz's Intimate Gallery. At about that time, he made portraits of Stieglitz and the gallery associates Georgia O'Keeffe and John Marin. Lachaise may have turned to portraiture because of his admiration of the French portrait sculptor JEAN ANTOINE HOUDON and also because of his own experience assisting Manship with portraits such as that of John D. Rockefeller.

In 1935 the Museum of Modern Art in New York gave Lachaise a retrospective exhibition for which he chose the works. None of his early animal sculpture was included. When he died in the fall of that year, probably from an infection, he was working on a model for the group *Welcoming the Peoples* for the Ellen Phillips Samuel Memorial in Fairmount Park, Philadelphia. It was to consist of nude figures of a man and a woman, flanking a column with reliefs of people from different historic periods and cultures.[10]

Notes

1. Gerald Nordland, "Lachaise's 20th-Century Woman," *Arts in Virginia,* Virginia Museum of Fine Arts Bulletin (Spring 1980), p. 15.

2. Marsden Hartley, "Thinking of Gaston Lachaise," *Twice a Year,* nos. 3–4 (1939–40), reprinted in Hilton Kramer et al., *The Sculpture of Gaston Lachaise* (New York: Eakins Press, 1967), p. 27.

3. Gaston Lachaise, "A Comment on My Sculpture," *Creative Art* 3 (August 1928), p. 28, reprinted in *Massachusetts Review* 1 (August 1960), p. 696.

4. *Nude with Coat,* about 1912, plaster, 10¾" (27.3 cm) high, illustrated in Hilton Kramer et al. 1967, fig. 4; also exhibited in bronze as *Woman* in *Gaston Lachaise: Twenty Sculptures* at the Robert Schoelkopf Gallery, New York, in 1982.

5. Twelve bronzes of *Standing Woman* have been cast; four were produced in Lachaise's lifetime, beginning in 1927. Examples are at the Whitney Museum of American Art, in New York, and the Philadelphia Museum of Art.

6. Henry McBride, "Here's to Lachaise," in *Lachaise* (New York: Brummer Gallery, 1928), exhib. cat., unpaginated.

7. Nordland 1980, p. 17.

8. Beatrice Gilman Proske, *Brookgreen Gardens Sculpture* (Murrells Inlet, S.C.: Brookgreen Gardens, rev. ed., 1968), p. 419.

9. More than sixty portraits were shown in *Gaston Lachaise: Portrait Sculpture* in 1985 at the National Portrait Gallery, Smithsonian Institution, Washington, D.C.

10. "The Last Work of Gaston Lachaise," *American Magazine of Art* 29 (August 1936), pp. 518–19.

References

1931 Gilbert Seldes, "Profiles: Hewer of Stone," *New Yorker* 7 (April 4), pp. 28–31. **1991** Barbara Rose, *Gaston Lachaise Sculpture,* New York: Salander-O'Reilly Galleries. **1993** Sam Hunter, *Lachaise,* New York: Cross River Press.

Peacocks

1918
Bronze with gilding; lost-wax cast in 1922
22¼ x 55¾ x 9" (56.5 x 141.5 x 22.9 cm)
Signed and dated on top of base at right front:
G. LACHAISE/© 1922
Foundry mark on back at right: ROMAN BRONZE WORKS N–Y–
Gift of Mr. and Mrs. Lawrence Katz, 1985.8

GASTON LACHAISE wanted his animal sculptures, of sea gulls, sea lions, dolphins, penquins, and peacocks to "translate spiritual forces."[1] This decorative sculpture was modeled five years after he began working for Paul Manship and reflects Manship's influence in the frontal orientation with an emphasis on silhouette, the simplification of the forms, and the use of gilding. Fourteen casts of an unnumbered edition of twenty were produced in the 1920s, while the artist was represented by the C.W. Kraushaar Galleries in New York.[2] This cast originally had a dark patina with gold leaf that was applied by the artist probably with Riccardo Bertelli, the patina expert who founded the Roman Bronze Works in New York. Because weathering and cleaning had destroyed much of the patina, the sculpture was repatinated

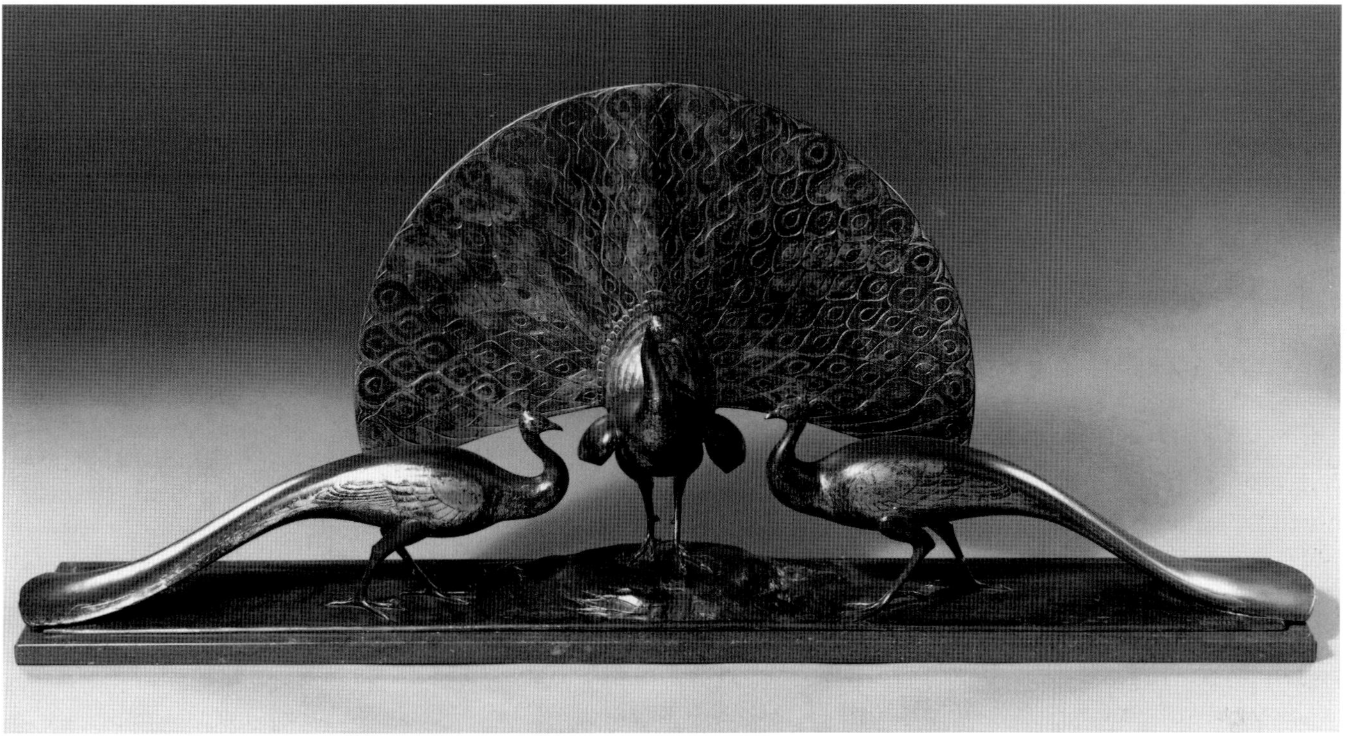

Lachaise, *Peacocks*

and gilded in 1986.[3] The original gilding on bronze casts belonging to the Metropolitan Museum of Art, in New York, and the Phillips Collection, in Washington, D.C., was used as a guide in recreating the surface intended by the artist. Lachaise probably knew of the ancient Roman tradition of gilding images of peacocks. In 1920 he produced marble garden sculptures of two peacocks perched on globes for the Deering Estate in Miami; and, later, he used the peacock in a design for a bronze fountain for a Long Island collector.[4]

The sculpture is displayed on a black marble base.

Notes

1. Gaston Lachaise, "A Comment on my Sculpture," *Creative Art* 3 (August 1928), p. 25, reprinted in *Massachusetts Review* 1 (August 1960), p. 694.

2. Eleven bronze casts of *Peacocks* have been located. In addition to the one in the Museum of American Art of the Pennsylvania Academy, four are in public collections: the Newark Museum, the Metropolitan Museum of Art, the Phillips Collection, and the Detroit Institute of Arts; the rest are in private collections (one cast is intended for the Philadelphia Museum of Art). Donald B. Goodall's unpublished manuscript "Gaston Lachaise: Sculptor," about 1966, lists the locations of the casts. The plaster model for *Peacocks* is unlocated.

3. According to a memorandum, dated Sept. 6, 1985, in the PAFA object file, this cast of *Peacocks* was installed outdoors probably in the 1940s and later cleaned by the owners.

4. The peacocks are illustrated in A.E. Gallatin, "Gaston Lachaise," *Arts* 3 (June 1923), p. 398. See also Donald B. Goodall, unpublished manuscript "Gaston Lachaise: Sculptor," about 1966, no. G13.71 and, for the fountain, which included two squirrels, no. G13.72.

Exhibited

1986–87 PAFA, *Sculpture at the Pennsylvania Academy of the Fine Arts.* **1994–96** PAFA, *Two Centuries of Collecting at the Museum of American Art.*

Ex Collections

Unknown Canadian collector, about 1922–about 1940; Mr. and Mrs. Lawrence Katz, Philadelphia, about 1940–85.

Emily Clayton Bishop

1883–1912

Emily Clayton Bishop had a short but productive career. At the time of her death, most art critics lauded her achievements and bemoaned the loss to the art world. One called her "the prototype of the moderns" and felt that her influence was very far-reaching.[1]

Born in Smithburg, Maryland, in 1883, Bishop was one of six artistically inclined sisters. In 1901 she enrolled at the Maryland Institute of Art, in Baltimore. She won a medal for best student work in 1902. She was graduated with highest honors in 1904 and received the Gold Medal of Honor. While at the institute, Bishop attended Johns Hopkins University for courses in art interpretation and criticism, which resulted in the granting of a teacher's certificate in 1903. She then won a scholarship to the Pennsylvania Academy of the Fine Arts.

At the Academy, she studied sculpture with CHARLES GRAFLY, who was already recognized as one of the most influential sculpture teachers in the country. One critic credited Grafly with exerting a "wholesome influence" upon the younger generation of American sculptors."[2] Grafly "ruled the destinies of young sculptors," wrote sculptor and author Lorado Taft (1860–1936), who praised him as one of America's best teachers.[3] Bishop also attended William Merritt Chase's life drawing classes. Chase reportedly asserted that Bishop drew better than any other student he ever had. It is said that he carried her drawings with him to New York to show to his classes at the Arts Students League.[4] Bishop eventually turned away from drawing and concentrated her studies exclusively on modeling.

Her student work, executed mostly for class assignments, ranges from portraiture and sculptural groups to public monuments and decorative sculpture. In these and even the most routine studies, Bishop enlivened her work with remarkable vitality, wit, and a keen self-awareness. She won many prizes, beginning with the Packard Prize (second place) in 1905 for drawing from live animals. She was twice awarded the McClellan Anatomy prize: first place and twenty-five dollars in 1906, and second place and ten dollars in 1907. Bishop won the Composition Prize for Sculpture in 1907. It included a portrait bust (q.v.) of the winner sculpted by Charles Grafly. The highest award was the William Emlen Cresson Traveling Scholarship of five hundred dollars, which Bishop won in 1907 and 1908. According to her friend BEATRICE FENTON, Bishop was only the second woman in the sculpture department to receive a Cresson traveling scholarship.[5] The summers of 1907, 1908, and 1909 found Bishop in Europe; but it is unclear how she financed the trip in 1909. Over the course of these three summers, she traveled extensively through Europe, pausing long enough in Paris to rent a studio in 1908.[6] She received honorable mention in the competition for the Edmund Stewardson Prize for sculpture in 1907, 1909, and 1910. In 1910 she was awarded a special prize of fifty dollars given by the president of the Pennsylvania Academy.

During her short lifetime, Emily Bishop participated in the annual exhibitions of the Pennsylvania Academy in 1907, 1910, 1911, and 1912. Her works were included in local and national exhibitions, as well. The National Sculpture Society sponsored a show in Baltimore in 1908 that featured two of her portrait busts. *The Bacchic Dancer* was shown in *Small Bronzes by American Sculptors* at the Art Institute of Chicago in 1910. After Bishop completed her studies at the Academy in 1910, she shared a studio with Beatrice Fenton.

The breadth of Bishop's commissions—portraits, decorative sculpture, fountains, stained glass-designs—shows her willingness to undertake any work that would aid her career. The fact that she received so many commissions while still a student underscores both her determination and her ability. She accepted portrait commissions for heads and busts in the round and in relief. John E.D. Trask, the secretary and manager of the Pennsylvania Academy, and Dr. Joseph Sailer, of Philadelphia, were early patrons. A portrait of a different sort was commissioned in 1908 for Saint Thomas's churchyard in Whitemarsh, Pennsylvania. The *Grave Slab of Elizabeth Walsh,* of cast concrete, is a full-length, nearly lifesize relief of the deceased young woman, wearing a long cloak and a bonnet. Bishop also executed a number of small genre figures in terracotta and painted plaster, no doubt in reaction to the growing market for small table-top figures. She fulfilled many decorative commissions for private homes, hotels, and other public buildings in Philadelphia and New Jersey. In 1909 she completed decorations for the clock tower of the Mask and Wig Dormitory, part of the Cope and Stewardson quadrangle at the University of Pennsylvania. The Philadelphia Cricket Club, one of the oldest and most exclusive clubs in the city, commissioned Bishop in 1910 to decorate the fireplace of the main ballroom. She designed a plaster lunette for the overmantle with a series of terracotta tiles surrounding the fireplace itself.

Emily Bishop died on March 1, 1912, just before her twenty-ninth birthday. Only weeks earlier, she had attained a professional triumph in the unveiling at the Academy of Music in Philadelphia of one of her most impressive commissions. The *Michael Hurly Cross Memorial Tablet,* commissioned by the Orpheus Club in 1911, received rave reviews in the Philadelphia and Baltimore papers. Bishop died quite suddenly at her home in Smithburg, where she had gone to rest. The cause of death is uncertain. A *New York Times* obituary cited heart disease; but other reports mentioned lung disease, both congenital and due to breathing plaster dust.[7] An article that appeared in the *Philadelphia Press* a year later attributed her death to "a nervous breakdown from overwork and tax on her energies, which caused her literally to starve to death."[8] Whatever the actual cause, the tragic nature of her death nearly overwhelms the obituaries and memorial articles that appeared at the time. The *New York Times* called her "one of the most promising of America's young sculptors."[9] "In her death," another writer lamented, "the American Art world lost a genius of the first order."[10]

Bishop had asked her friends and fellow students Beatrice Fenton and Marjorie Martinet to take charge of her work in the event of her death. Accordingly, they organized a memorial exhibition at the Pennsylvania Academy in conjunction with the 1913 annual exhibition. Nineteen works in bronze, plaster, and terracotta were shown, accompanied by a laurel wreath tied with a purple ribbon and a specially prepared pamphlet eulogizing Bishop. Fenton and Martinet had Bishop's works cast into bronze at their own expense in the expectation that the Academy would buy the lot, but the Academy declined on the basis of insufficient funds. Beatrice Fenton was responsible for maintaining the bulk of Bishop's work: in addition to the posthumous bronze casting, she preserved many plaster and clay models, as well as the drawings. Until her death in 1983, Fenton attempted to place Bishop's work in major collections. It can be seen in the Philadelphia Museum of Art and the National Museum of American Art, in Washington, D.C.

In the years immediately after Bishop's death, her work appeared in numerous shows, probably through the efforts of Beatrice Fenton. One of the most important was the 1915 Panama-Pacific International Exposition, in San Francisco, in which sixteen of her works were shown. Her sculpture was exhibited at the Philadelphia Plastic Club in 1914 and 1916; at the Peabody Institute, in Baltimore in 1915; and at the Kansas City Fine Arts Institute and the Buffalo Palace of the Fine Arts in 1916. In 1920 five of Bishop's sculptures along with the portrait bust of her that Charles Grafly had modeled, were installed in the lobby of the Pennsylvania Academy; soon after they became part of the collection.

Notes

1. J. Oldmixon Lambdin, *Baltimore Evening Sun,* May 2, 1917, clipping file, PAFA Library.

2. John E.D. Trask, *Catalogue Deluxe of the Department of Fine Arts, Panama-Pacific International Exposition* (San Francisco: Paul Elder and Company, 1915), p. 57.

3. Lorado Taft, *The History of American Sculpture,* 2nd ed. (1903: reprint, New York: Macmillan Company, 1924), p. 579.

4. Margie H. Luckett, *Maryland Women* (Baltimore: King Brothers, 1931), p. 33.

5. Beatrice Fenton to Joseph T. Fraser, Jr., director of the PAFA, Jan. 14, 1969, PAFA Archives.

6. Luckett 1931, p. 32.

7. "Emily Bishop, Young Sculptor Dead," *New York Times,* March 3, 1912, p. 15, and PAFA research file.

8. "Fame for Girl Sculptor Year after Death," *Philadelphia Press,* March 15, 1913, microfilm, roll no. 56, frame no. 49, PAFA Archives.

9. "Emily Bishop, Young Sculptor, Dead," 1912, p. 15.

10. Luckett 1931, p. 32.

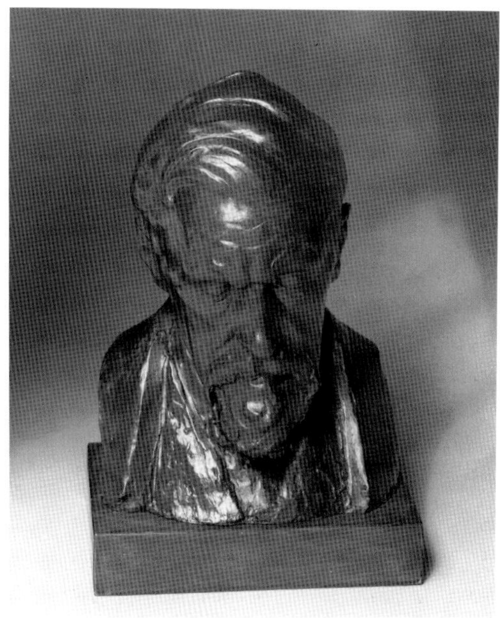

Bishop, *Portrait of Mr. Fenn*

Portrait of Mr. Fenn

1906
Bronze with brown patina; lost-wax cast after 1912
14 x 10 x 9¼" (35.6 x 25.4 x 23.6 cm)
Signed and dated on back of shoulders: Emily Clayton Bishop –1906–
Foundry mark at bottom back right side: ROMAN BRONZE WORKS INC. N.Y.
Gift of Marjorie D. Martinet and Beatrice Fenton, 1969.10.5

WHEN Emily Bishop first studied with Charles Grafly at the Pennsylvania Academy of the Fine Arts in 1904, he had already gained wide recognition as a sculptor and teacher. This portrait bust of Mr. Fenn in the style of her teacher is one of the earliest known examples of Bishop's work. Grafly reportedly remarked when he saw it that he would like to own it.

Mr. Fenn, a friend of Bishop's family, was a college science professor blinded in a scientific experiment.[1] The bust indicates his blindness by closed eyes, as do two small relief medallions of the same subject.[2] This work was probably the portrait bust exhibited in plaster in the Pennsylvania Academy's 1907 annual exhibition. It may be one of two plaster busts that Bishop entered in the National Sculpture Society's show in Baltimore in 1908.[3]

Notes

1. Interview with Suzanne Smith, Oct. 12, 1990, notes in PAFA research file.

2. One is in the Suzanne and Marvin Smith collection, Keedysville, Maryland; the other is in the collection of the Smithsburg Historical Society. A plaster cast of the bust is in the National Museum of American Art, Washington, D.C.

3. Beatrice Fenton states in her "List of Sculpture by Emily Clayton Bishop" that it was 1906; however, it may have been the 1908 show, p. 1, Suzanne and Marvin Smith collection.

An American Totem Pole

1907
Bronze with brown and green patina; cast after 1912
32⅝ x 4½ x 5⅛" (82.9 x 11.4 x 13 cm)
Signed and dated at back of base: Emily C. Bishop 1907
Sand cast, probably by Roman Bronze Works, New York
Gift of Marjorie D. Martinet and Beatrice Fenton, 1969.10.1

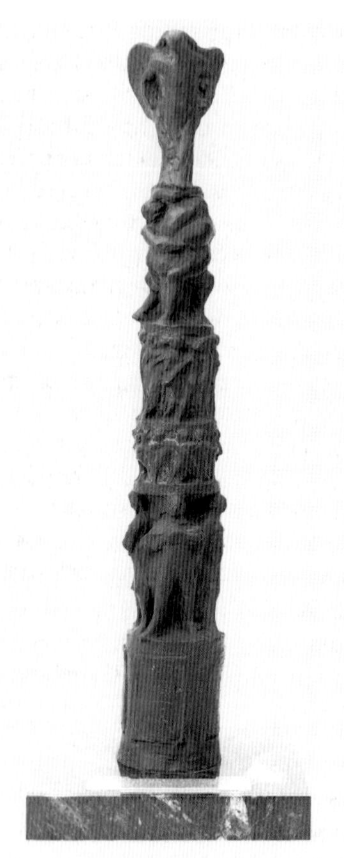

Bishop, *An American Totem Pole*

A REGULAR PART of the course work in Charles Grafly's sculpture class was the design of public monuments. These works were finished to scale and included a base and a likely architectural setting. Bishop executed a number of these works. *An American Totem Pole* is one of the best extant examples. Five groups of figures surmount one another to form the tall column. In the original clay model, the base of the pole was placed in the center of a broad square platform with stairs sweeping up on all sides. Bishop worked out a complete allegorical program, representing the history of the United States in five stages. Beatrice Fenton describes the allegory as follows:

> The four figures at the base represent respectively: Discover, Religious, Conqueror, Settler, the last a woman. Next above these, 13 figures of children, the 13 original states; above these, group of figures representing the country growing and developing; then two massive figures locked in gigantic struggle, the North and South of the Civil War, and surmounting them and crowning the column a figure, half man and half eagle, ready for the future, for whatever the coming event in the nation's life is to be.[1]

The only figures in "accurate" costume are the Conqueror, who wears the Spanish armor of the conquistador, and the Settler, who wears the simple dress of a pioneer woman. The Settler foreshadows Grafly's *Pioneer Mother Memorial,* 1913, which was dedicated to the women who crossed the Plains. Grafly and other contemporaries also borrowed the image of the winged figure that surmounts Bishop's *Totem Pole.*

This piece was awarded a special composition prize in the sculpture department at the Pennsylvania Academy in 1908. It is installed on a green marble base. A painted plaster version of this sculpture is in the collection of Suzanne and Marvin Smith, Keedysville, Maryland.

Note

1. Beatrice Fenton, "List of Sculpture by Emily Clayton Bishop," p. 6.

Classicism and the Renaissance

1907
Bronze with blue-green patina; lost-wax cast about 1913
14 x 5¾ x 4⅜" (35.5 x 14.5 x 11.2 cm)
Signed and dated on back just above plinth: Emily Clayton Bishop/1907

Foundry mark on back of plinth at left side: ROMAN BRONZE WORKS INC. N.Y.
Gift of Marjorie D. Martinet and Beatrice Fenton, 1969.10.2

FOLLOWING the award of her first Cresson traveling scholarship in 1907, Emily Clayton Bishop thanked the Pennsylvania Academy of the Fine Arts and stated her hope "to materialize in my work during the coming session some of the information gathered from those wonderful examples of the past and to show in the same form my appreciation of the advantages of the present."[1] She attempts this synthesis in *Classicism and the Renaissance.* Classicism is represented as a woman; Renaissance, as a man. This small two-figure piece was probably intended as an investigation in figural relationships. Having absorbed Grafly's interest in the symbolic character of sculpture, however, Bishop has imbued it with further meaning. According to Beatrice Fenton, Bishop's only comment on the piece was the rather cryptic "he loves her better than she does him."[2] A contemporary reviewer commented "For [Miss Bishop] there was a true parallel here with the eager seeking of the earlier art by the new in the great period of Italy's creative epoch." The same critic wrote that "sincerity, straight-forward seeing and thinking inform the group."[3] Too much nudity at the Pennsylvania Academy's 1913 annual exhibition caused complaints, with *Classicism and the Renaissance* being specifically mentioned as an example.[4]

This bronze is mounted on a green marble base. A painted plaster cast is in the Suzanne and Marvin Smith collection, Keedysville, Maryland; another is at the Smithsburg Historical Society.

Notes

1. Emily C. Bishop to the committee on instruction, Nov. 9, 1907, PAFA Archives.
2. Beatrice Fenton, "List of Sculpture by Emily Clayton Bishop," p. 4.
3. "Miss Bishop's Classicism and the Renaissance," *New York Sun,* Feb. 13, 1913, clipping file, PAFA Library.
4. "Too Much Nude at Academy Salon Prompts Protest," *New York World Telegraph,* Feb. 10, 1913, microfilm, roll no. 56, frame no. 29, PAFA Archives.

Exhibited

1913* cat. no. 750. **1914** Plastic Club, Philadelphia, *Exhibition of Sculpture and Paintings by Emily Clayton Bishop, Beatrice Fenton, Ada C. Williamson, Marjorie D. Martinet, Alice Kent Stoddard, Anne W. Strawbridge,* cat. no. 1. **1915** San Francisco, *Panama-Pacific International Exposition,* cat. no. 3347. **1916** Fine Arts Institute, Kansas City.

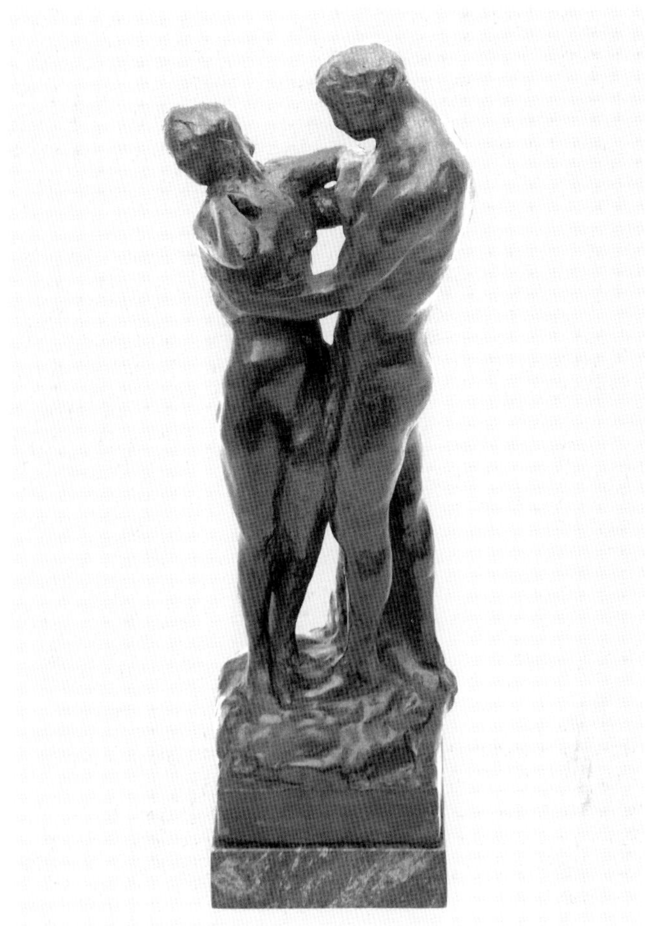

Bishop, *Classicism and the Renaissance*

Comedy

1907
Bronze with brown patina; lost-wax cast about 1913
11⅞ x 5½ x 5½" (30.2 x 14 x 14 cm)
Signed and dated on bronze base, starting at center back: Emily Clayton Bishop–1907–
Inscribed in a continuous line around bronze band affixed to base: QUIPS·AND·CRANKS·AND·WANTON·WILES· NODS·AND·BECKS·AND·WREATHED·SMILES
Foundry mark on lowest rim of base at back: ROMAN BRONZE WORKS N–Y–
Gift of Marjorie D. Martinet and Beatrice Fenton, 1969.10.3

Comedy was a school project designed for the entrance to a theatre. Words from Milton's *L'Allegro* are inscribed in relief around the base. The grinning personification of Comedy holds a comedy mask in her right hand. She is perched on a pedestal surrounded by three smiling children carved in relief.

The base is comprised of bronze and green marble.

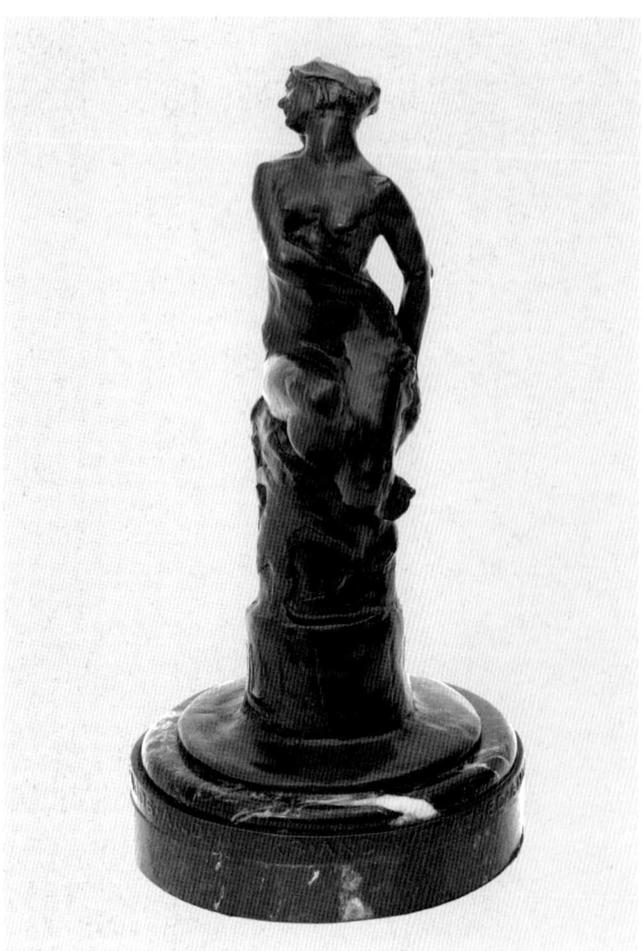

Bishop, *Comedy*

A plaster cast of the sculpture is in the National Museum of American Art, Washington, D.C., and another is in the Suzanne and Marvin Smith collection, Keedysville, Maryland.

Exhibited
1913* cat. no. 752. **1914** Plastic Club, Philadelphia, *Exhibition of Sculpture and Paintings by Emily Clayton Bishop, Beatrice Fenton, Ada C. Williamson, Marjorie D. Martinet, Alice Kent Stoddard, Anne W. Strawbridge,* cat. no. 6. **1915** San Francisco, *Panama-Pacific International Exposition,* cat. no. 3345. **1916** Fine Arts Institute, Kansas City.

Greed

1907
Bronze with brown patina; lost-wax cast about 1913
14⅛ x 9 x 9" (35.9 x 22.9 x 22.9 cm)
Signed and dated on back of second plinth, from top:
Emily Clayton Bishop/1907
Foundry mark on left side on lowest plinth: ROMAN BRONZE WORKS N.Y.
Gift of the Three Arts Club, 1913.3

EMILY CLAYTON BISHOP probably made this small figure group for one of Charles Grafly's composition classes at the Pennsylvania Academy of the Fine Arts. It could have fulfilled the requirements for an exercise in the "Aesthetic Significance of Form," dealing with light and shade, line, rhythm, and grace. In this assignment, students were asked to "develop the opportunities of Effect to their utmost; to select a subject involving shadows; to let it be original, having its positive side and its mysterious suggestive side."[1] The supposition that *Greed* was intended for this purpose is supported by Beatrice Fenton's comments that the piece was designed to show especially the "quality of color, light and shade," and that it was "remarkable for the way it composes as a group when viewed from any side."[2]

The composition consists of three figures—a man, a woman, and a large feline—intertwined or wrestling on a set of stairs. The dense tangle of limbs

Bishop, *Greed*

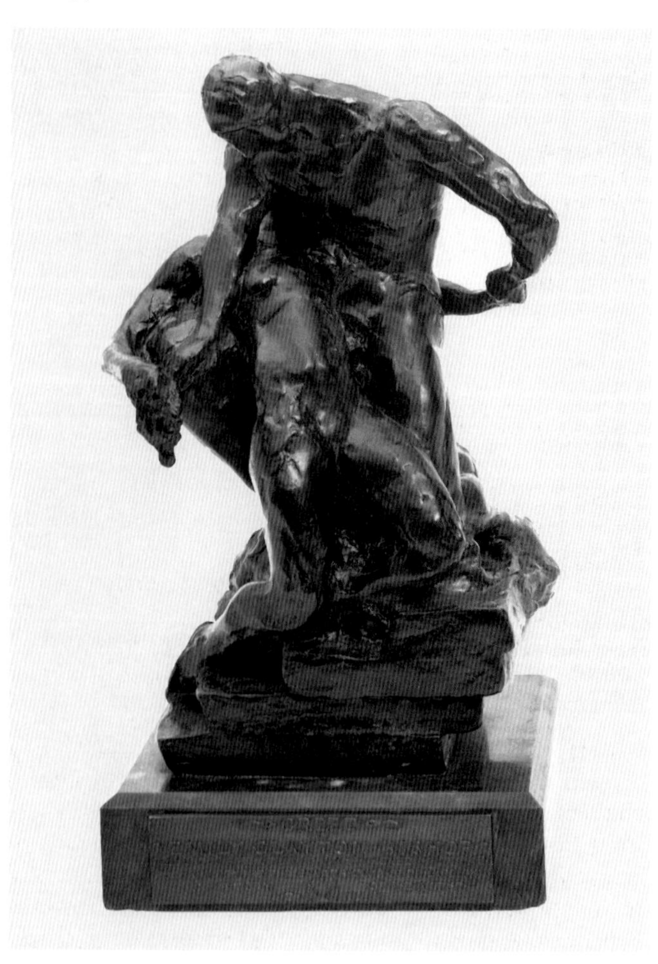

conveys emotional and physical endurance pushed to their limits. The female figure holds the skin of an animal's face in her right hand. The male figure is reminiscent of Rodin's *The Thinker*, 1879–89. Paul Manship, who was in the same composition class, also modeled wrestling figures during 1907–8. It is possible that Grafly suggested wrestling as a means of dealing with the assignment. Other sculptures by Bishop at that time depicted emotions—there were several entitled *Grief*, 1909–10, and one entitled *Joy*, 1909, which was destroyed.

Greed was presented to the Pennsylvania Academy in memory of Emily Bishop by the Three Arts Club, a group composed of women students of art, music, and drama, founded in 1906. Bishop, Fenton, and Marjorie Martinet were all members of the club.

In an article in the *Philadelphia Inquirer* in 1913, *Greed* is praised as "strong and beautifully modelled."[3] It is mounted on a maroon stone base. A clay model is in the Smithsburg Historical Society, in Maryland.

Notes

1. PAFA, *Syllabus for Composition Class, 1909–1910* (Philadelphia, 1909), p. 3.
2. Beatrice Fenton, "List of Sculpture by Emily Clayton Bishop," p. 10.
3. "Important Art Sales Recorded," *Philadelphia Inquirer*, Feb. 16, 1913, microfilm, roll no. 56, frame no. 31, PAFA Archives.

Exhibited

1913* cat. no. 767. **1915** San Francisco, *Panama-Pacific International Exposition*, cat. no. 3346. **1962** PAFA, *Forgotten Favorites: Selections from the Permanent Collection.* **1994–96** PAFA, *Two Centuries of Collecting at the Museum of American Art.*

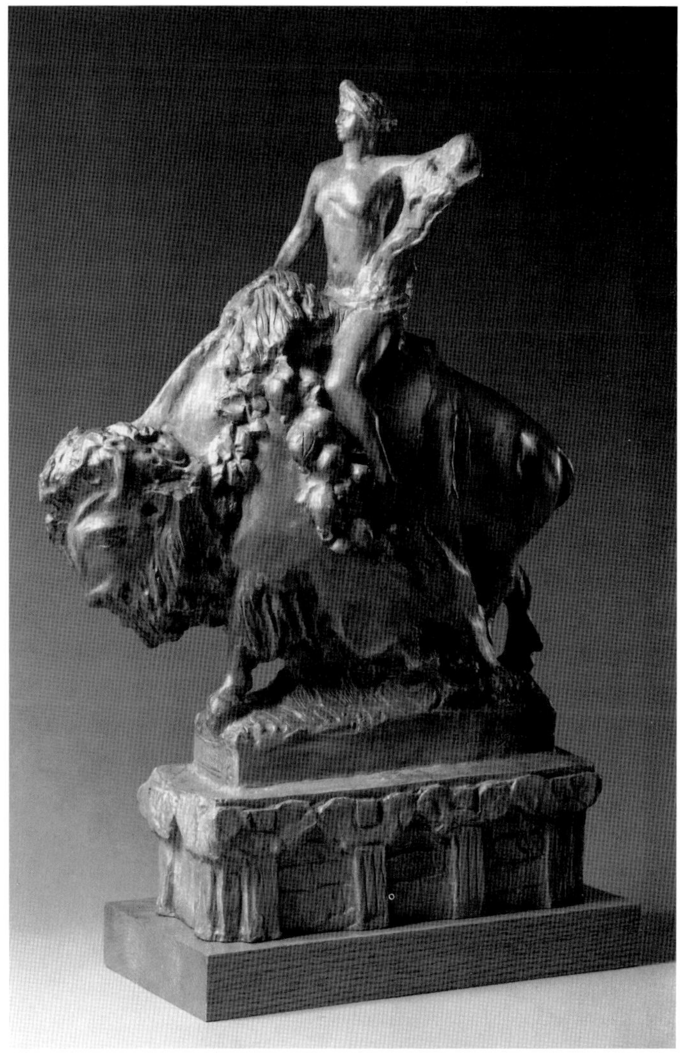

Bishop, *Conquest of the Great Northwest through Agriculture*

Conquest of the Great Northwest through Agriculture

1908
Bronze with green patina; cast about 1913
25½ x 8½ x 18" (64.8 x 21.6 x 45.7 cm)
Signed and dated on left side of base below buffalo's left rear foot: EMILY BISHOP 08
Sand cast, probably by Roman Bronze Works, New York
Gift of Marjorie D. Martinet and Beatrice Fenton, 1969.10.4

MONTHLY TOPICS suggested by Charles Grafly's students for the composition class were published in the Pennsylvania Academy of the Fine Arts' catalogue for 1908–9. Emily Clayton Bishop created *Conquest of the Great Northwest through Agriculture* in response to her own suggestion for the month of February. A triumphant and athletic female personification of Agriculture sits astride a monumental buffalo. Garlands and flowing drapery form her saddle. She holds in her arm a bountiful cornucopia. Her hair is piled high like a crown. Though buffalo were not a familiar sight in Philadelphia, art students on occasion had the opportunity to model from such exotic beasts. A 1904 photograph in the Pennsylvania Academy Archives shows sculpture students modeling from a water buffalo.

Conquest of the Great Northwest through Agriculture can be seen in a sculpture-exhibition photograph in the 1909–10 Pennsylvania Academy catalogue. It is mounted on a wood base. A painted plaster cast is in the Suzanne and Marvin Smith collection, Keedysville, Maryland; another is in the Washington County Museum of Fine Arts in Hagerstown, Maryland.

Reference
1982 Linda Bantel, "Sculpture at the Pennsylvania Academy," *Antiques* 121 (March), p. 713, fig. 13.

Exhibited
1913* cat. no. 756. **1914** Plastic Club, Philadelphia, *Exhibition of Sculpture and Paintings by Emily Clayton Bishop, Beatrice Fenton, Ada C. Williamson, Marjorie D. Martinet, Alice Kent Stoddard, Anne W. Strawbridge,* cat. no. 5. **1973** PAFA, *Held in Trust,* cat. no. 18. **1986–87** PAFA, *Sculpture at the Pennsylvania Academy of the Fine Arts.*

The Passing of the Seasons: Winter into Spring

1908
Bronze with green patina; lost-wax cast about 1913
12 x 24⅜ x 13¼" (30.5 x 62 x 33.6 cm)
Signed and dated behind woman's right shoulder:
Emily Clayton Bishop/–1908–
Foundry mark on bronze base below mother's left arm:
ROMAN BRONZE WORKS N–Y–
Gift of Marjorie D. Martinet and Beatrice Fenton,
1969.10.6

In *The Passing of the Seasons: Winter into Spring,* an allegory of the changing seasons is transformed by Emily Clayton Bishop's treatment into an uncompromising depiction of childbirth. There is a sharp contrast between the listless reclining woman who represents Winter and the defiantly upright boy who represents Spring. Winter is not old, as one might expect, but exhausted with barely enough energy to prop herself up. The agony of labor and childbirth is abundantly clear. The child, having absorbed the spirit from his mother's body, turns away from her. Bishop allegedly said that the child is "the wild mustard, the first thing to flower in the spring."[1] A critic of the time wrote that the sculptor "touched the world of imagination" in this piece.[2] She expected to carry out the design in a larger size in marble.[3] The woman's figure echoes Michelangelo's figure of Dawn on the Tomb of Lorenzo de' Medici, 1521, in the Medici Chapel, in Florence, which Bishop probably visited during her summer abroad in 1907.

The opportunity to buy this piece was offered to the Pennsylvania Academy in 1913 by Beatrice Fenton and other friends of Bishop. The offer was declined for lack of funds. The sculpture was eventually given to the Academy by Fenton and Marjorie Martinet in 1969. It is mounted on a stone base. A painted plaster version is in the Suzanne and Marvin Smith collection, Keedysville, Maryland.

Notes
1. Beatrice Fenton, "List of Sculpture by Emily Clayton Bishop," p. 5.
2. *New York Sun,* Feb. 13, 1913, clipping file, PAFA Library.
3. Beatrice Fenton, "List of Sculpture by Emily Clayton Bishop," p. 5.

Exhibited
1913* cat. no. 753. **1914** Plastic Club, Philadelphia, *Exhibition of Sculpture and Paintings by Emily Clayton Bishop, Beatrice Fenton, Ada C. Williamson, Marjorie D. Martinet, Alice Kent Stoddard, Anne W. Strawbridge,* cat. no. 3. **1915** San Francisco, *Panama-Pacific International Exposition,* cat. no. 3048. **1986–87** PAFA, *Sculpture at the Pennsylvania Academy of the Fine Arts.*

Bishop, *The Passing of the Seasons: Winter into Spring*

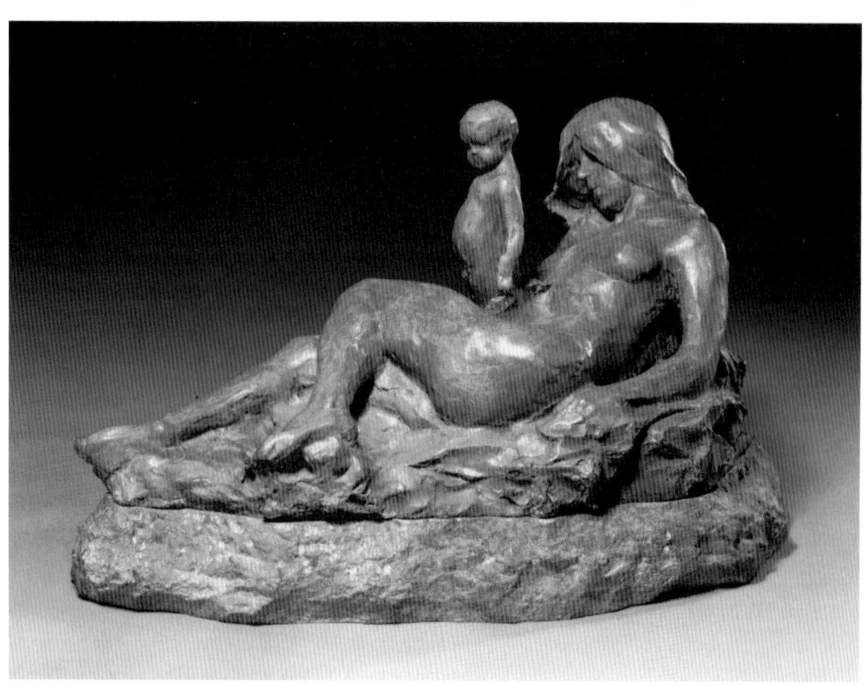

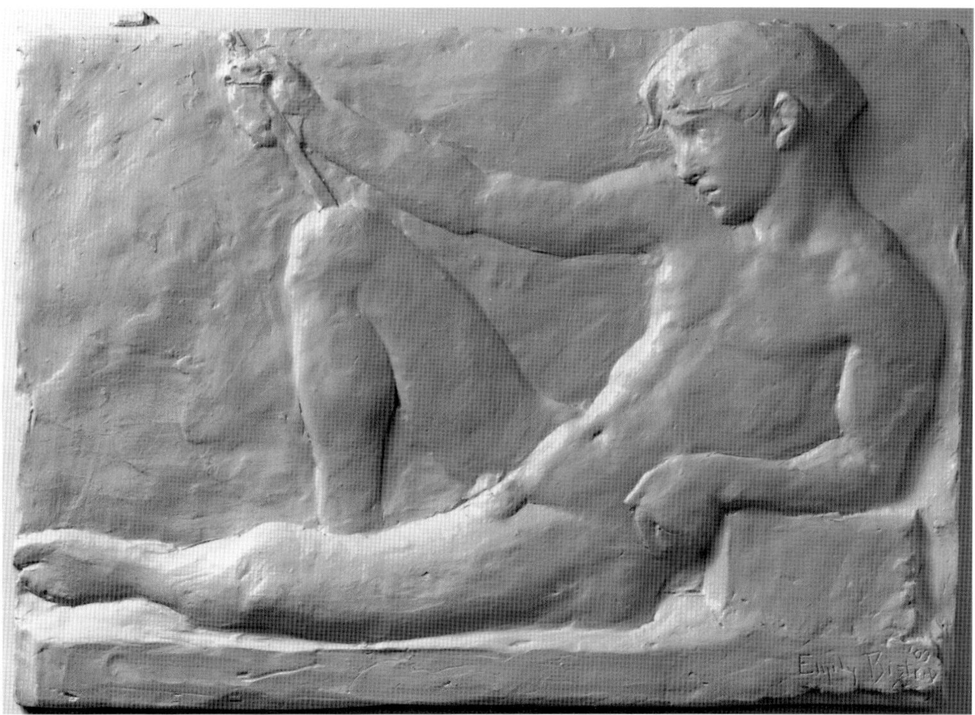

Bishop, *Academy Study of a Man*

Academy Study of a Man

1909
Plaster relief, painted white
17¾ x 24¾ x ¼ to 1¼″ (varies) (45.2 x 63 x .7 to 3.4 cm)
Signed and dated at lower right: Emily Bishop/'09
Gift of Beatrice Fenton, 1977.15

THE Pennsylvania Academy of the Fine Arts catalogue for 1909–10 states that relief work "from both the full-length figure and the head only" would be undertaken in the school year.[1] Emily Clayton Bishop completed numerous relief studies of female and male nudes. This reclining figure, holding a staff, was probably based on a model in the school. It is boldly placed, extending from one edge to the other. The inexpert depiction of the genitals contrasts with the authentic treatment of the rest of the body. This underscores the fact that women students were not permitted to work from a fully nude male model.

Note

1. PAFA, *School Circular, 1909–10,* p. 19.

Exhibited

1986–87 PAFA, *Sculpture at the Pennsylvania Academy of the Fine Arts.* **1990** PAFA, *Figure Studies: The Academic Tradition.*

The Bacchic Dancer

1909
Bronze with green-brown patina; cast about 1913
9½ x 7 x ½″ (24.1 x 17.8 x 1.3 cm)
Signed and dated at lower left: Emily C. Bishop—09
Inscribed at lower right: F/M/2
Sand cast, probably by Roman Bronze Works, New York
Gift of friends of the artist, 1920.1.2

EMILY CLAYTON BISHOP executed a number of relief studies for her composition classes at the Pennsylvania Academy of the Fine Arts in 1909 and 1910. *The Bacchic Dancer* and *The Greek Maiden's Dance of Joy* (q.v.) are examples. The school catalogue for 1909–10 specifically mentions dance as a subject. Students were instructed to produce designs that were "typical of freedom, abandon, joy, active life."[1] This rhythmic figure in low relief is characteristic of Bishop's work for it exemplifies "the spirit which prompted all her endeavor; that remarkable appreciation of the beauty of motion, that feeling for the joy of living that made itself felt in her sculpture."[2]

A bronze of this piece (location unknown) was cast in Bishop's lifetime, and was shown in several exhibitions of small bronzes throughout the country in 1909 and 1910.[3] A plaster cast is in the Suzanne and Marvin Smith collection, Keedysville, Maryland;

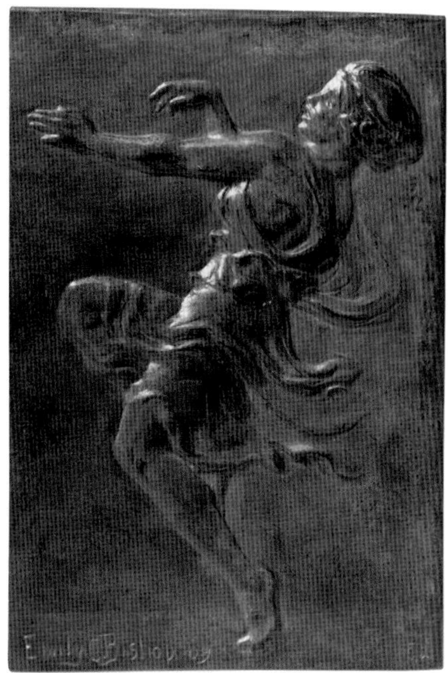

Bishop, *The Bacchic Dancer*

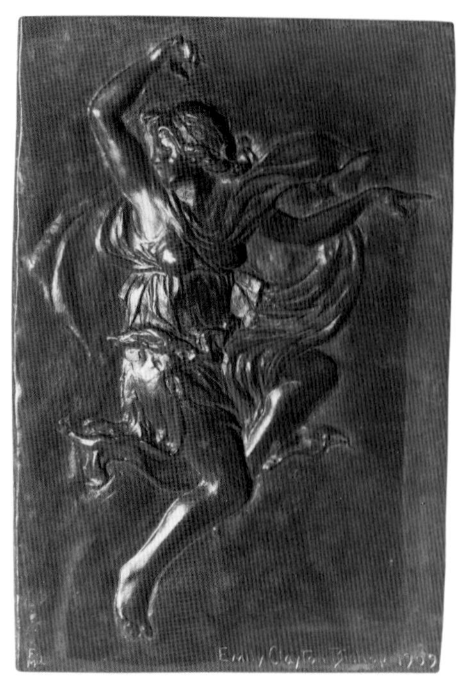

Bishop, *The Greek Maiden's Dance of Joy*

and a similar piece is in the National Museum of American Art, Washington, D.C. The inscription F/M/2 on this bronze cast is thought to mean it was the second cast supervised by Fenton and Martinet.

Notes

1. *School Circular, 1909–10,* p. 4.
2. John O. Lambdin, *Baltimore Evening Sun,* Dec. 17, 1914, quoted in First Annual Bulletin of the Maryland Institute Alumni Association, 1914–15.
3. Albright-Knox Art Gallery, Buffalo, 1909–10; The Art Institute of Chicago, 1910; Worcester Art Museum, Mass., 1910.

Exhibited

1913* cat. no. 764. **1915** Peabody Institute, Baltimore, *Exhibition of Sculpture and Paintings by Emily C. Bishop, Beatrice Fenton, Ada C. Williamson, Elizabeth Sparhawk-Jones, Anne W. Strawbridge, Alice Kent Stoddard, Marjorie D. Martinet,* cat. no. 5. **1915** San Francisco, *Panama-Pacific International Exposition,* cat. no. 1419. **1920** PAFA, *The Group of Sculpture by Emily Bishop.* **1986–87** PAFA, *Sculpture at the Pennsylvania Academy of the Fine Arts.*

The Greek Maiden's Dance of Joy

1909
Bronze with green-brown patina; cast about 1913
10⅜ x 7 x ⅝" (26.4 x 17.8 x 1.6 cm)
Signed and dated at lower right: Emily Clayton Bishop 1909
Inscribed at lower left: F/M/2
Sand cast, probably by Roman Bronze Works, New York
Gift of friends of the artist, 1920.1.3

In the first decades of the twentieth century, modern dance was a source of inspiration for many artists, and Emily Clayton Bishop was no exception. She executed a number of reliefs inspired by the dances of Isadora Duncan.[1] They all display the same sense of liberation and bacchic emotion that can be found in the work of Bishop's contemporaries. The dancers, be they wood nymphs or fauns, are lithe and athletic. They convey the emancipated energy that was so characteristic of Duncan, Pavlova, Nijinsky, and others. According to Beatrice Fenton, these reliefs illustrate maidens of Chalkis, dancing for joy at the sight of Greek ships in the distance.[2]

Both *The Bacchic Dancer* (q.v.) and *The Greek Maiden's Dance of Joy* were enthusiastically reviewed by contemporary art critics. One wrote that the Greek dancers portray a "sense of pagan joy" with a "marked individuality of their own."[3] In these pieces, as in most of her sculptures, Bishop took the spirit and the art of the past and made it her own. Two plaster casts are in the Suzanne and Marvin Smith collection, Keedysville, Maryland.

Notes

1. Beatrice Fenton, "List of Sculpture by Emily Clayton Bishop," p. 11.
2. Ibid.

3. John O. Lambdin, *The Baltimore Evening Sun,* March 17, 1915, clipping file, PAFA Library.

Reference
1914–15 *1st Annual Bulletin of the Maryland Institute Alumni Association,* Baltimore (ill.).

Exhibited
1913* cat. no. 765. **1915** Peabody Institute, Baltimore, *Exhibition of Sculpture and Paintings by Emily C. Bishop, Beatrice Fenton, Ada C. Williamson, Elizabeth Sparhawk-Jones, Anne W. Strawbridge, Alice Kent Stoddard, Marjorie D. Martinet,* cat. no. 3. **1915** San Francisco, *Panama-Pacific International Exposition,* cat. no. 1422. **1920** PAFA, *The Group of Sculpture by Emily Bishop.* **1986–87** PAFA, *Sculpture at the Pennsylvania Academy of the Fine Arts.*

Seated Nude

1909
Bronze with green-brown patina; cast by 1920
7¾ x 5¼ x ¾" (19.7 x 13.3 x 1.9 cm)
Signed and dated at lower right: Emily C. Bishop/'09
Sand cast, probably by Roman Bronze Works, New York
Gift of friends of the artist, 1920.14

THE MANY extant examples of Emily Clayton Bishop's relief studies of female and male nudes, including this one, *Standing Nude,* and *Academy Study of a Man* (qq.v.), show her to have been a proficient modeler. There are numerous related nude studies in various poses. The National Museum of American Art, Washington, D.C., owns several. Additional studies can be found in the Suzanne and Marvin Smith collection, Keedysville, Maryland, along with a plaster cast of the Academy's piece; a second plaster cast is in another private collection.

Bishop, *Seated Nude*

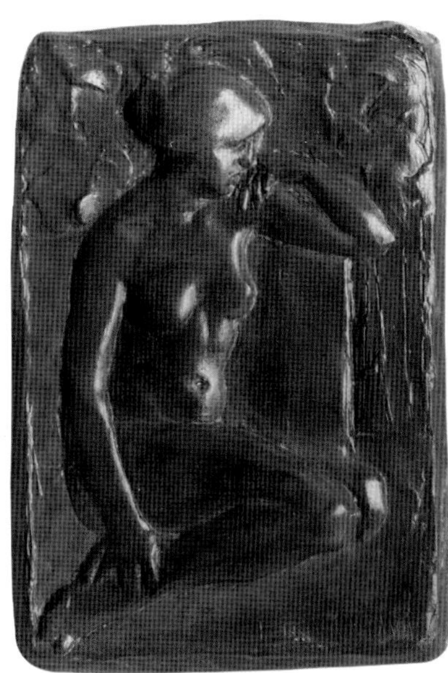

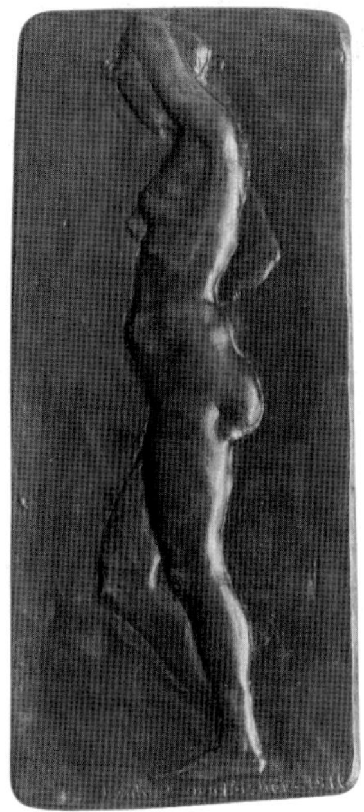

Bishop, *Standing Nude*

Exhibited
1920 PAFA, *The Group of Sculpture by Emily Bishop.* **1986–87** PAFA, *Sculpture at the Pennsylvania Academy of the Fine Arts.*

Standing Nude

1910
Bronze with green-brown patina; cast by 1920
8¾ x 3¾ x ¼" (22.3 x 9.5 x .6 cm)
Signed and dated at lower right: Emily Clayton Bishop—1910
Sand cast, probably by Roman Bronze Works, New York
Gift of friends of the artist, 1920.1.5

BETWEEN 1909 and 1911, Emily Clayton Bishop made many studies of the nude figure, all modeled simply and directly. Several, such as *Standing Nude,* exhibit extraordinary proficiency and clarity in the depiction of the human form.

The National Museum of American Art, in Washington, D.C., owns related sculptures. A painted plaster cast of the Academy's piece is in the Suzanne and Marvin Smith collection, Keedysville, Maryland, along with numerous related works.

Exhibited
1920 PAFA, *The Group of Sculpture by Emily Bishop.*

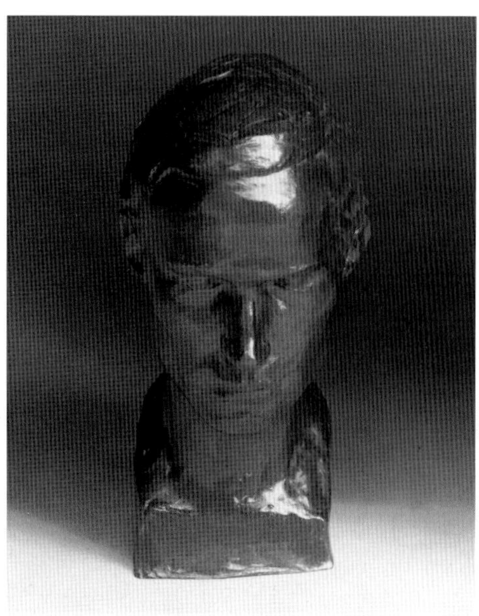

Bishop, *Portrait Head of a Young Painter*

Portrait Head of a Young Painter

1909
Bronze with green patina; lost-wax cast about 1913
15 x 7¼ x 10" (38.1 x 18.4 x 25.4 cm)
Signed and dated on right side near bottom: Emily Clayton Bishop—1909
Foundry mark on back at left side: ROMAN BRONZE WORKS N-Y-
Gift of friends of the artist, 1920.1.1

THE IDENTITY of the subject of this portrait is unknown. He is one of many students at the Pennsylvania Academy of the Fine Arts who served as models for their colleagues in Charles Grafly's Head Classes.[1] In this way, Emily Clayton Bishop executed numerous portraits of classmates and friends. Most of these sculptures are now unlocated. *Portrait Head of a Young Painter* was modeled in about five hours in the Pennsylvania Academy studios.[2] Also extant is the *Portrait of Painter Annie Strawbridge.*[3]

Portrait Head of a Young Painter is one of five pieces of Bishop's sculpture given to the Pennsylvania Academy by friends of the artist. It was included in a memorial group of her work placed at the entrance to the school in 1920. A newspaper article at the time cited the portrait bust as "an astonishingly forceful piece of work . . . and remarkably strong in its seizure and portrayal of character."[4]

Notes

1. A photograph in the PAFA Archives shows one such class. The model, seated at the center, is partly obscured. Beatrice Fenton is at the far left, and Emily Bishop is working in the center with her back to viewer.
2. Beatrice Fenton, "List of Sculpture by Emily Clayton Bishop," p. 2, Suzanne and Marvin Smith collection, Keedysville, Maryland.
3. The plaster bust of Strawbridge is in the Suzanne and Marvin Smith collection, along with three busts of unidentified men. A plaster cast of the Academy's piece is at the Washington County Museum of Fine Arts, Hagerstown, Maryland.
4. Unidentified newspaper article, Oct. 31, 1920, microfilm, roll no. 56, frame no. 700, PAFA Archives.

Exhibited
1913* cat. no. 749, 759, or 760. **1915** San Francisco, *Panama-Pacific International Exposition,* cat. no. 2866. **1920** PAFA, *The Group of Sculpture by Emily Bishop.*

JO DAVIDSON

1883–1952

Jo Davidson was born to Russian-Jewish parents on the Lower East Side, in New York. He showed an early interest in drawing and took classes at the New York Educational Alliance. When he was sixteen, he received a one-year scholarship to study at the Art Students League. He earned some money making burnt-wood drawings. Despite this early inclination toward art, Davidson became interested in medicine and began a course of study at Yale Medical School. Drawing classes at the Yale School of Art attracted him, however; and, after his first experience modeling clay there, he dropped medicine for a career in art. He returned to the Art Students League of New York to study modeling. From about 1901 to 1904, he worked in the studio of Hermon Atkins MacNeil (1866–1947) on MacNeil's *Fountain of Liberty* for the 1904 Louisiana Purchase Universal Exposition, in Saint Louis.

With the financial backing of a patron, Davidson went to Paris to complete his art education and studied briefly at the Ecole des Beaux-Arts. He became acquainted with the American painters and sculptors then in Paris and did their portraits. One example is the bust of John Marin, 1908 (National Portrait Gallery, Washington, D.C.). Davidson met Gertrude Vanderbilt Whitney (1877–1942), a sculptor and patron of the arts, who bought and commissioned works from him and assisted him later in New York. In 1909 he exhibited at the Salon d'Automne and had a show at the Baillie Gallery in London. The following year, he had a one-person show at the New York Cooperative Society. He submitted three works to the 1909 annual exhibition of the Pennsylvania

Academy of the Fine Arts, and continued to participate sporadically from 1934 to 1951. Seven of Davidson's sculptures and ten drawings were in the celebrated 1913 modernist show in the Armory in New York.

Over the years, he modeled portraits of the military leaders of World Wars I and II, presidents, industrialists, actors, artists, and writers. *Gertrude Stein,* about 1923 (Whitney Museum of American Art, New York), portrays her entire figure. Sometimes, probably to reduce the number of sittings, he would make terracotta life masks of his subjects, as he did in the case of *Mrs. Whitney,* 1910 (private collection); *Andrew W. Mellon,* 1927 (National Portrait Gallery, Washington, D.C.); *A New Englander,* about 1935 (collection of the sitter's family; bronze cast, Museum of Fine Arts, Boston).

In the 1920s, Davidson bought a home near Tours, France, and kept studios there and in Paris. In the 1940s, he lived briefly in Bucks County, Pennsylvania, before returning to France, where he died. A retrospective of about two hundred of his works was held at the American Academy of Arts and Letters, in New York, in 1947. In 1951 *Between Sittings,* an informal autobiography, was published.

A collection of his portraiture is installed permanently in the Jo Davidson room of the National Portrait Gallery, in Washington, D.C. His work is also in many other collections. A posthumous exhibition was held in New York in 1983 at the Hammer Galleries.

References
1978 *Jo Davidson: Portrait Sculpture,* Washington, D.C.: National Portrait Gallery, exhib. cat. **1984** Wayne Craven, *Sculpture in America,* Newark: University of Delaware Press, pp. 557–60. **1986** Kathryn Greenthal, Paula M. Kozol, and Jan Seidler Ramirez, *American Figurative Sculpture in the Museum of Fine Arts, Boston,* Boston: Museum of Fine Arts, pp. 394–98. **1989** Janis Conner and Joel Rosenkranz, *Rediscoveries in American Sculpture: Studio Works, 1893–1939,* Austin: University of Texas Press, pp. 10–18.

Samuel M. Vauclain

1924
Limestone, carved about 1926
24¼ x 28 x 14" (61.6 x 71.7 x 35.6 cm)
Signed (incised) on the back at right side: JO DAVIDSON
Deposited by Samuel M. Vauclain, 1.1927

SAMUEL M. VAUCLAIN (1856–1940) was the chairman of the Baldwin Locomotive Works of Philadelphia for more than two decades. He rose from a fifty-cents-a-day laborer to a business leader and a 1920 presidential candidate. He became an international hero during World War I when his plants produced locomotives and weaponry worth $250 million. He received the Distinguished Service Medal from the United States and awards from France, Italy, and Poland. After the war, he traveled to Europe, Russia, and South America to secure further contracts. In 1922 he became widely known for shipping twenty locomotives to the Southern Pacific Company in Los Angeles on a train dubbed the "Prosperity Special."

Vauclain's prominence and magnanimous personality made him an ideal subject for Davidson. The format of the bust, including massive shoulders and part of the chest, evoke the presence of the man who was described in a lengthy obituary in the *Philadelphia Inquirer,* February 5, 1940, as "tall and powerful" and "powerful-voiced, great-chested." Davidson liked to converse with his subjects while they posed in order to evince natural, relaxed expressions. Vauclain was captured in an animated moment with mouth slightly open and eyes focused on his companion. Details, such as the jowls and wrinkles of the seventy-year-old sitter, are honestly portrayed. A 1924 article compared this work to JEAN ANTOINE HOUDON's bust of Benjamin Franklin in its "patriarchal and whimsical simplicity."[1] The article was illustrated by photographs of Davidson's clay busts of Vauclain and John D. Rockefeller (bronze cast of 1925, National Portrait Gallery, Washington, D.C.). The bust of Vauclain was formerly inscribed in pencil

Davidson, *Samuel M. Vauclain*

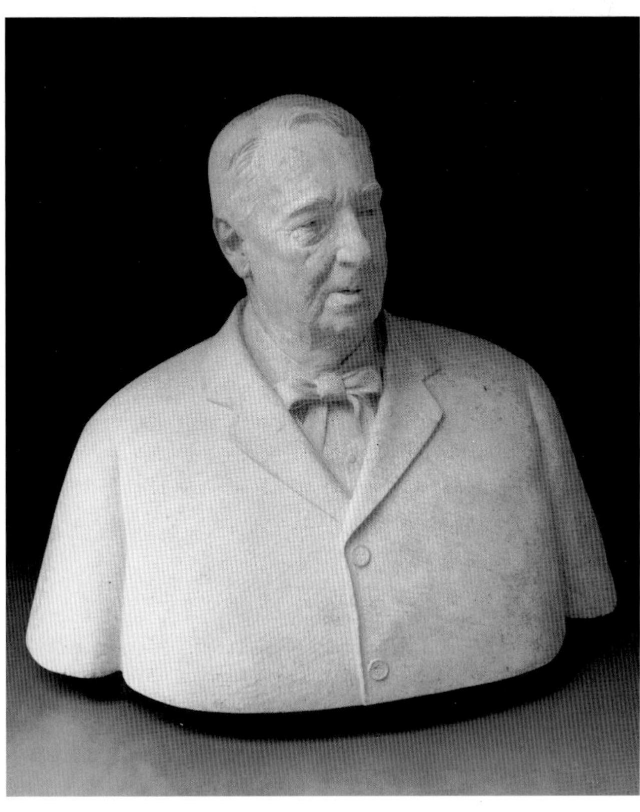

by an unidentified hand "NY 1924 PARIS 1926—NY 1927." The inscription was recorded and removed during conservation. The bust was apparently modeled in New York in 1924. The work may have continued in Paris in 1926,[2] or the bust may have been carved in stone at that time. The meaning of the reference to New York, 1927, is not known. Perhaps the sculptor refined further details in the carving at that time, or incised his signature.

The stone bust was shown at the Sequicentennial Exposition in Philadelphia in the latter half of 1926. It was apparently returned to the Baldwin Locomotive Works and then offered for loan to the Pennsylvania Academy of the Fine Arts in March 1927. The heavy weight of the piece may have made it unsuitable for display in a home. What happened to this plaster after it was translated into burgundy limestone is not known. This stone bust is now thought to be the only extant version.

Notes

1. Karl Freund, "Five Busts by Davidson," *International Studio* (Sept. 1924), pp. 427 (ill.), 428, 432.

2. Arthur L. Church, secretary and assistant treasurer, Baldwin Locomotive Works, to John A. Myers, managing director of the PAFA, March 26, 1927, PAFA object file.

Exhibited

1926 Philadelphia, *Sesquicentennial International Exposition*, cat. no. 1183. **1976** PAFA, *In This Academy*, cat. no. 278. **1993** PAFA, *Carved in Wood and Stone: Twentieth-Century Sculpture.*

Louis G. Milione, Sr.

1884–1955

Born in Padua, Louis Milione was a son of the portrait painter Carmen Milione, who brought his family to the United States in 1895. Louis studied art with William Arnold Porter at the Spring Garden Institute (now Spring Garden College), in Philadelphia, and sculpture with A. STIRLING CALDER at the Philadelphia Museum School of Industrial Art (now the University of the Arts). Under the name Louis Million, he studied sculpture with CHARLES GRAFLY at the Pennsylvania Academy of the Fine Arts from 1903 to 1910. In 1904 he won the Edmund Stewardson Prize in a competition requiring a full-length figure in the round to be created from a live model in eighteen hours. In 1908 the award of a William Emlen Cresson Traveling Scholarship enabled him to go to Italy, where he spent most of his time, and to Switzerland, France, and England.[1]

Milione's work, mostly portrait busts, was shown regularly in the annual exhibitions of the Pennsylvania Academy from 1909 to 1951. He also exhibited sculpture at the National Academy of Design, in New York in the 1910s; the 1916 *Americanization through Art* show by artists of foreign birth or parentage at Memorial Hall in Fairmount Park, where he won an honorable mention; the Sesquicentennial Exposition in 1926; and at the Sculpture International exhibitions of 1933 and 1940, sponsored by the Fairmount Park Art Association and held at the Philadelphia Museum of Art.

From 1922 to 1930, Milione taught sculpture at the Philadelphia Museum School of Industrial Art. A solo exhibition of his work was held in the school's gallery in 1922. He produced commissions for marble portrait busts and reliefs, fountains, memorials, and architectural ornamentation mostly in Philadelphia but also in New Jersey, Delaware, Ohio, Mississippi, and Wyoming. Among his commissions were a statue of Alfred du Pont and a model of Versailles Gardens for the du Pont estate in Wilmington, Delaware, and a statue of General Casimir Pulaski for Pulaski Park in Camden, New Jersey. In 1937 Milione was hired by the Pennsylvania Academy to examine the Greek sculpture *Ceres* that had been on the facade of its building at Broad and Cherry streets since 1876. He found the sculpture to be sadly deteriorated and deemed it a danger to passersby. It was removed, and pieces of the Pentelic marble were given to several sculptors, including CHARLES RUDY. Whether Milione received any is not known.

Milione carved thirteen shields between 1934 and 1940 for the Ninth Street facade of the Federal Courthouse and Post Office in Philadelphia. Each represented a state in the circuit of the federal district court. In 1940 he produced sculpture for the west pediment of the Municipal Court Building (now Family Court) at 1801 Vine Street. At the time of his death, in 1955, he was working on six large-scale sculptures of historic figures for the Lutheran Church of Wittenberg College in Ohio.

Note

1. Louis Million to the PAFA president, faculty, and board of directors, Oct. 5, 1908, Traveling scholarships and Cresson records, PAFA Archives.

References

1922 Dorothy Grafly, "Features of Sculpture Shown at the Academy; At the School of Industrial Art," *Philadelphia North American*, Feb. 12, scrapbook, PAFA Archives. **1955** "Louis G. Milione, Sculptor, Was 71," *New York Times*, March 29, p. 29. **1985** *Who Was Who in American Art*, Madison, Conn.: Sound View Press.

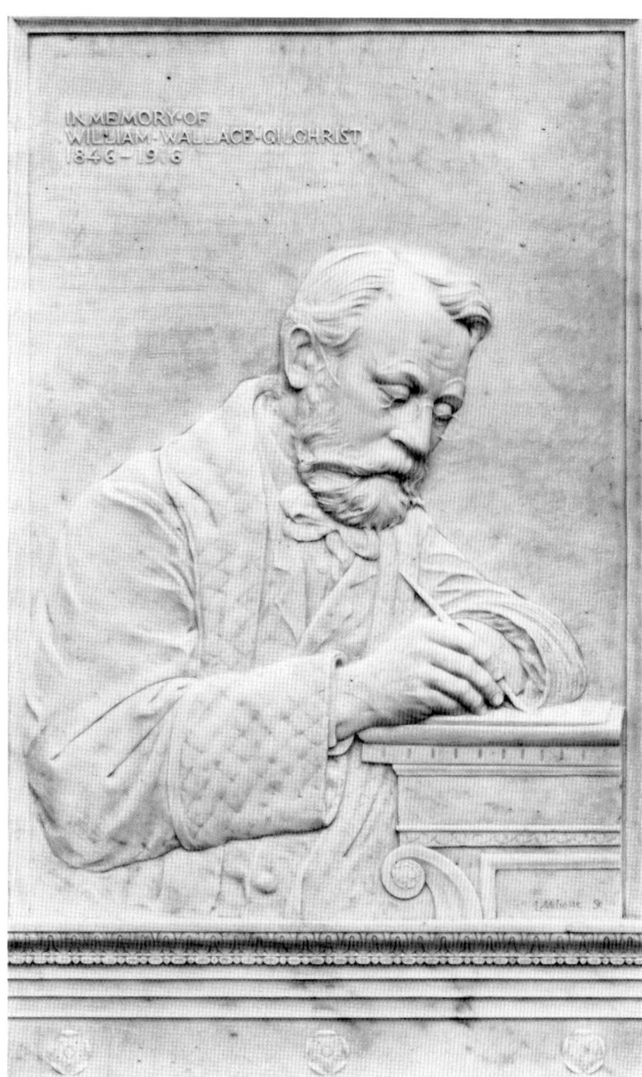

Milione, *Memorial to William Wallace Gilchrist*

Memorial to William Wallace Gilchrist

About 1921
Marble
47⅝ x 29 x 3" (121 x 73.7 x 7.6 cm)
Signed at lower right: L Milione Sc
Inscribed in relief at upper left: IN MEMORY·OF/WILLIAM·WALLACE·GILCHRIST/1846–1916
Gift of Mr. and Mrs. William L. Grala, 1986.33

THIS RELIEF was commissioned by the William Wallace Gilchrist Memorial Committee of the Academy of Music to honor the prominent Philadelphia composer, conductor, and organist. Gilchrist (1846–1916) studied at the University of Pennsylvania, taught at the Philadelphia Musical Academy (now Zeckwer-Hahn Philadelphia Musical Academy), and founded the Philadelphia Symphony Society and the Philadelphia Mendelssohn Club.

The memorial shows a three-quarter view of Gilchrist absorbed in writing music. Milione was probably given a photograph of the subject from which to work. The carving is sensitive, from the low relief of the eyeglass frames that merge with the background to the high relief of the nose. The marble relief was unveiled on April 29, 1921, after a memorial concert by the Philadelphia Orchestra conducted by Leopold Stokowski, which included Gilchrist's composition "A Symphonic Poem in G Major." The relief was installed for more than thirty years in the corridor serving the lobby of the Academy of Music on South Broad Street. It was removed in 1957 during the second stage of building renovations and given to one of the sculptor's sons, Louis G. Milione, Jr. The relief was donated to the museum at the Pennsylvania Academy of the Fine Arts in 1986 by a member of the board of trustees, William L. Grala, and his wife, Babette. The model for the memorial (location unknown) was displayed in 1922 at Milione's exhibition at the Philadelphia Museum School of Industrial Art.

Exhibited
1986–87 PAFA, *Sculpture at the Pennsylvania Academy of the Fine Arts.* **1994–96** PAFA, *Two Centuries of Collecting at the Museum of American Art.*

Ex Collections
Academy of Music, Philadelphia, 1921–57; Louis G. Milione, Jr., 1957–86.

José de Creeft

1884–1982

José de Creeft was born in Guadalajara, Spain, and reared in Barcelona. After the death of his father, the family became impoverished. At the age of eleven, José modeled religious figures to sell at a festival.[1] Two years later, he was apprenticed to a carver of religious figures and shortly thereafter to a bronze founder. In 1900 his family moved to Madrid, and he studied sculpture with Ignacio Zuloaga (1870–1945) and drawing with Rafael Hidalgo de Caviedes.[2] De Creeft soon entered into an apprenticeship with the official sculptor and medalist of Spain, Augustín Querol (1863–1909). By 1902 de Creeft had opened his own studio and was exhibiting portraits of children. He saw Eskimos carving ivory at an exposition and was impressed by the simplicity and power of their work.[3] He later recalled that moment as the beginning of his interest in direct carving. At the age of twenty-one, de Creeft moved to Paris. Urged by Zuloaga and Auguste Rodin (1840–1917) to undertake further study, he enrolled at the Académie Julian. After a year studying anatomy, perspective, and drawing, he won first prize in a student competition. Because of his reluctance to let other craftsmen transfer his plaster and clay maquettes into stone, de Creeft set out to learn how to use a pointing machine so that he could do the work himself. Therefore, between 1911 and 1914, he was employed by the Maison Gréber, which specialized in making replicas, enlargements, and reductions. He showed great skill in carving stone.

To free himself from the restrictions imposed by replicating already modeled forms, de Creeft began to carve directly into wood and stone in 1915–16. He was to become one of the earliest sculptors in the twentieth century to return to this ancient technique. The change in method became a turning point in his career, for he destroyed all of his previous work. This symbolically separated him from his academic training. During World War I, de Creeft worked sporadically as a caricaturist and a house painter.[4] In 1918 he received a commission from the French government to carve a granite war memorial for the town of Saugues.

De Creeft was one of the first artists to use found materials. He created a sensation when *Le Picador,* 1925 (location unknown), his innovative assemblage of scrap metal and rubber tubing, was shown in 1926 in Paris. From 1927 to 1929, de Creeft produced over two hundred architectural sculptures for a fortress on the island of Majorca. He was assisted in this commission by the American sculptor Alice Robertson Carr (b. 1899), who had studied with him in Paris. They married in 1929 and came to the United States to visit her relatives in Seattle. De Creeft exhibited his sculpture there and, shortly after moving to New York, at the Feragil Galleries. His work immediately gained wide recognition.

From about 1932 to 1939 and 1944 to 1970, de Creeft taught direct carving in wood and stone and also hammering in metals at the New School for Social Research, in New York. The Philadelphia Art Alliance gave him a joint exhibition with Alphonse Legros (1837–1911) in 1932 and a solo show the next year. Museums were soon acquiring his work: in New York, the Brooklyn Museum purchased his hammered lead *Semitic Head* in 1938; the Museum of Modern Art bought the lead portrait *Saturnia* in 1940; and, in the early 1940s, the Whitney Museum of American Art purchased *Cloud,* a stone female nude, and *Himalaya,* a hammered lead portrait. In 1942 de Creeft's 1923 granite portrait *Maternity* won first prize in the important Metropolitan Museum of Art exhibition *Artists for Victory;* and it became part of the museum's collection. *Rachmaninoff* (q.v.) was awarded the George D. Widener Memorial Gold Medal in 1945 at the 140th annual exhibition of the Pennsylvania Academy of the Fine Arts. The sculpture was purchased for the Academy's collection six years later. De Creeft exhibited regularly at the Pennsylvania Academy from 1943 to 1966.

In 1944, after his first marriage ended in divorce, de Creeft married another former sculpture student, Lorrie Goulet (b. 1925). From then until 1948 and from 1957 to 1979, he taught direct carving at the Art Students League in New York and offered a class at his studio. In 1948 he was elected an associate of the National Academy of Design, and in 1964 he became an academician. His first major American commission was *Poet,* 1956, a granite figure 8½ feet high for the Ellen Phillips Samuel Memorial in Philadelphia's Fairmount Park. Occasionally, departing from direct carving, de Creeft modeled works in clay to be cast into bronze. In 1959, for example, he completed a sixteen-foot-high bronze scene from *Alice in Wonderland,* a commission for New York's Central Park.

From 1960 to 1962, a retrospective exhibition sponsored jointly by the American Federation of the Arts and the Ford Foundation traveled from the Whitney Museum to thirteen other institutions. De Creeft was one of three American sculptors whose works were selected in 1973 for the permanent collection of contemporary art in the Vatican Museums. A retrospective exhibition was held at the Art Center of the New School for Social Research in 1974. Although known as a sculptor, de Creeft also produced many drawings, watercolors, and oil paintings during his long career.

Notes

1. Adelyn D. Breeskin and Virginia M. Mecklenburg, *José de Creeft: Sculpture and Drawings* (Washington, D.C.: Smithsonian Institution Press, 1983), National Museum of American Art exhib. cat., p. 8.
2. Ibid., chronology, p. 34.
3. José de Creeft, "Statement on Sculpture," a 1954 reprint in Jules Campos, *The Sculpture of José de Creeft* (New York: Kennedy Graphics and De Capo Press, 1972), p. 12.
4. Breeskin and Mecklenburg 1983, p. 10.

References

José de Creeft Papers, Archives of American Art, Smithsonian Institution, Washington, D.C. **1944** Eudora Welty, "José de Creeft," *Magazine of Art* 37 (Feb.), pp. 42–47.

Rachmaninoff

1943
Hammered lead
36½ x 27 x 22½" (92.8 x 68.6 x 57.1 cm)
Signed on scroll at left side of neck: Josè [*sic*] de CREEFT; on scroll at bottom edge of neck: de CREEFT
Lewis S. Ware Fund, 1951.20

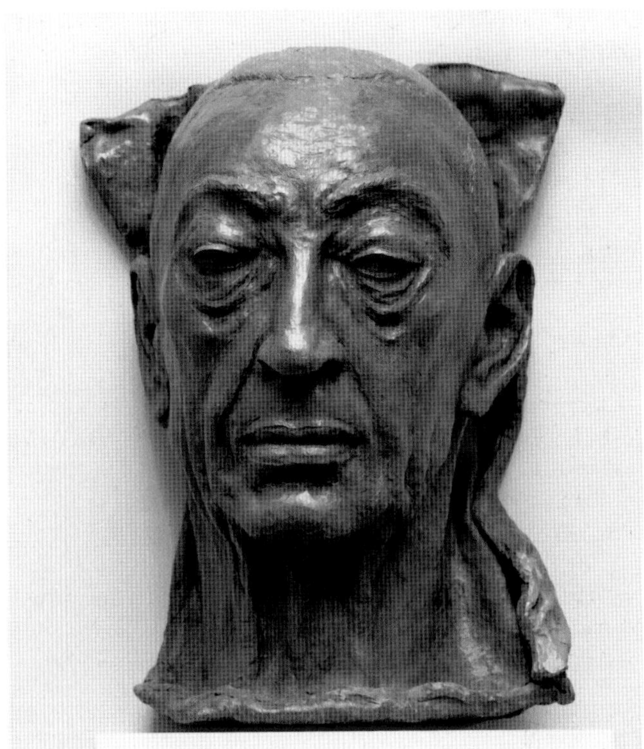

de Creeft, *Rachmaninoff*

IT TOOK six months to complete this monumental portrait of the great Russian composer, pianist, and conductor, Sergei Rachmaninoff (1873–1943). The work not only is a remarkable likeness of the man but also conveys the brooding power of his music. José de Creeft considered this work to be one of his best pieces of sculpture.[1] De Creeft had begun to shape metal by hammering. He eschewed copper (which SAUL BAIZERMAN used) in favor of lead because "lead is more serious in color, more lively, and more plastic. It has greater force."[2] He had been interested in lead since about 1918, when he produced clay figures with a cubist influence, had them cast in lead, and then chiseled the surface details. He referred to his hammered pieces as "beaten lead." They were made by securely clamping a sheet of lead in place, sketching rough guidelines with chalk directly on the sheet, and hammering it on both sides with a ball-peen hammer. The sheet used for *Rachmaninoff*, 49 by 52 by ½ inches, produced one of his largest portraits.[3]

De Creeft set out to produce a memorial portrait shortly after Rachmaninoff died in March 1943. For inspiration he listened to recordings of Rachmaninoff's music, conjured up memories of the concerts he had attended, and studied photographs. The result, according to the catalogue of the 1960 retrospective exhibition, was one of the best of de Creeft's beaten-lead portrait busts.[4] Upon completion, it was shown at the Passedoit Gallery in New York and was praised by critics. Malcolm Vaughan in his foreword to the catalogue called it a "spiritual portrait" and said, "Monumental, tender, articulate, austere, it well commemorates the heroic measure of the musician's genius."[5] *New York Herald Tribune* commented, "The 'Rachmaninoff' is more than an item, it is almost a show in itself. . . . [It] comes impressively to life."[6] The portrait won the George D. Widener Memorial Gold Medal when it was shown at the 140th annual exhibition of the Pennsylvania Academy of the Fine Arts, in 1945. The press unanimously praised the choice. The critic Peyton Boswell described *Rachmaninoff*, displayed in the rotunda, as "breathtakingly powerful and without doubt one of the great portraits of our time."[7] Later that year, it was chosen by New York critics to be included in a special exhibition at the art and antiques show in New York. In 1950 the bust was offered to the Pennsylvania Academy for purchase.[8] Negotiations with the artist were made through R. Sturgis Ingersoll, who had recently dealt with him in connection with the Fairmount Park commission for *Poet*.[9]

Because lead is such a malleable material, the portrait is supported on the inside by steel braces reinforced with concrete. Circular hammer marks can be seen on the forehead and the hair; the face has a more subtle faceted appearance. There are some small cracks around the eyes, nostrils, and lips, which were produced in the course of hammering. A wavy scroll that frames the composition on three sides is the remains of the edges of the original metal sheet. The color of the surface varies from rust red to shades of gray. Some of the dark gray areas were probably colored with pigments by the sculptor.

Notes

1. José de Creeft to Joseph T. Fraser, Jr., director of the PAFA, March 6, 1951, p. 2, PAFA object file.
2. Dorothy Grafly, "José de Creeft," *American Artist* 11 (March 1947), p. 31.
3. "Art: The Great Lead Face," *Newsweek* 22 (Dec. 6, 1943), p. 110.
4. Devree 1960, p. 14.
5. Malcolm Vaughan, typescript, enclosed in Edith Bry to J. T. Fraser, August 28, 1950, PAFA object file.
6. Quoted in "Art: The Great Lead Face," 1943.

7. Peyton Boswell, Jr., "Progressive Trend Distinguishes Pennsylvania Academy Annual," *Art Digest* (Feb. 1, 1945), p. 5.

8. Edith Bry to Joseph T. Fraser, Jr., August 28 and Sept. 13, 1950, PAFA object file.

9. R. Sturgis Ingersoll to José de Creeft, Feb. 5, 1951, PAFA object file.

References
1943 Maude Riley, "De Creeft Portrays Rachmaninoff in Lead," *Art Digest* 18 (Dec. 1), p. 16 (ill.). **1943** "The Passing Shows," *Art News* 42 (Dec. 1), p. 30 (ill.). **1945** Dorothy Grafly, "Art in Revolt," *Art Outlook* (Feb. 1) (ill.). **1945** Edward Alden Jewell, "Show Puts Critics on Spot," *New York Times,* Sept. 23, p. 2 (ill.). **1945** "The Armory 1945: The Contemporary and Antique Chosen by Critics and Dealers," *Art News* 44 (Oct. 1), p. 12 (ill.). **1945** Jules Campos, *José de Creeft,* New York: Erich S. Herrmann, p. 14, pl. 93. **1948** C. Ludwig Brummé, *Contemporary American Sculpture,* New York: Crown Publishers, pl. 25. **1950** John Cunningham, ed., *José de Creeft,* Athens, Georgia: University of Georgia Press, published with the National Sculpture Society, New York, p. 35 (ill.). **1954** Ruth Seltzer, "The Philadelphia Scene," *Philadelphia Sunday Bulletin,* Oct. 24, p. 21 (ill.). **1960** Charlotte Devree, *José de Creeft,* New York: American Federation of Arts, traveling exhib., pp. 11 (ill.), 14. **1972** Jules Campos, *The Sculpture of José de Creeft,* New York: Kennedy Graphics and Da Capo Press, pl. 195.

Exhibitions
1943 Passedoit Gallery, New York, *Jose de Creeft Recent Sculptures,* cat. no. 1, as *Sergei Rachmaninoff.* **1945*** cat. no. 85 (ill.). **1945** 17th Regiment Armory, New York, *Art and Antiques Show: Critics Choice.* **1948–49** New School for Social Research, New York. **1950** Cranbrook Academy of Art, Bloomfield Hills, Mich., *Modern Sculpture,* cat. no. 6. **1951** John Herron Art Institute, Indianapolis, *Sculpture of the 20th Century,* cat. no longer extant. **1970** University of Nebraska, Sheldon Memorial Art Gallery, Lincoln, *American Sculpture,* cat. no. 48 (ill.). **1986–87** PAFA, *Sculpture at the Pennsylvania Academy of the Fine Arts.*

Ex Collection
The artist, 1943–51.

Alfeo Faggi

1885–1966

Born in Florence, Alfeo Faggi received his first art lessons from his father, a fresco painter. His official training began at the age of thirteen when he entered the Academie delle Belle Arti in his native city. He followed a traditional academic course, which included drawing and modeling from casts and live models. After completing four years there, he augmented his education with several years of anatomical study in a local hospital. The rich artistic heritage of Italy exerted its force on the young sculptor, who particularly admired the work of Benvenuto Cellini (1500–1571).[1] Faggi, however, sought to break free of the pervasive influence of the Renaissance, as well as contemporary academic and neoclassical art with its attention to detail.[2] As early as 1910, Faggi's work showed a marked subordination of detail: the statuette *Reading Girl* (location unknown), for example, seems semiarticulated and impressionistic.[3]

Although Faggi was developing a personal style and exhibiting his work, he felt the need to escape Italy's influences, so in 1913 he immigrated to the United States. Shortly after settling in Chicago, he married Beatrice Butler, an accomplished musician whom he had met in Italy. His 1915 statuette of her (location unknown) is reminiscent of the earlier *Reading Girl.* During the three years after his arrival in Chicago, Faggi had important one-man shows: in 1914 at the Henry Reinhardt Galleries, in 1915 at the Art Institute of Chicago, and in 1916 at the Roullier Galleries. During these years, he created a number of sculptures depicting motherhood. He also executed religious works like the well-known standing *Saint Francis,* 1915 (Albright-Knox Art Gallery, Buffalo). Most of his sculptures from this period are elongated and columnar. Away from his native country, Faggi was better able to appreciate and profit from its art. He awakened to a new interest in late medieval and early Renaissance Italian art, particularly the work of the Pisani, Giotto, and Donatello.[4] Faggi was greatly attracted to the emotive content of the work of these artists, as he sought to instill strong feelings in his own works. This he did admirably in his 1916 *Pietà,* commmissioned by Mrs. Frank Lillie for the Church of Saint Thomas the Apostle in Chicago. In this sculpture, the dead Christ slumps in the lap of the seated Virgin so as to echo her form and almost melt into it.

With the outbreak of World War I, Faggi was called back to Italy to serve in the army. He returned to Chicago in 1919 and became an American citizen eight years later. An exhibition of his work at the Chicago Arts Club in 1919 caught the attention of a New York gallery owner, Stephen Bourgeois, who gave the sculptor his first one-man show in New York in 1921. Among the works that Faggi exhibited at the Bourgeois Gallery were his portrait heads of the poets Yone Noguchi, 1919 (Art Institute of Chicago) and Rabindranath Tagore, 1921 (location unknown). Many critics, including Stella Rubinstein and the poet Marianne Moore, responded to his work with glowing praise.[5]

In 1923 Faggi and his family moved to Woodstock, New York, a small artists' colony located in the tranquil Catskill Mountains. During the following three years, Faggi worked primarily on fourteen reliefs depicting the Stations of the Cross, which, like the earlier *Pietà,* were commissioned by Mrs. Lillie for the Church of Saint Thomas the Apostle. During the early 1930s, the sculptor opened his own school in Woodstock. He offered classes in sculpture, drawing, and composition from June to October. Woodstock remained his home, and Faggi became a founding member of the Woodstock Artists Association and served as one of its directors.

During the mid-1930s, Faggi began a series of nudes in the round and in relief. He exhibited widely throughout the 1930s and 1940s. In 1941 he was given a retrospective at the Albright Art Gallery (now the Albright-Knox Art Gallery). In 1942, at the Art Institute of Chicago's fifty-third annual exhibition of American paintings and sculpture, Faggi was awarded the Mr. and Mrs. Frank G. Logan Art Institute Medal for his bronze *From the Cross* (Columbus Museum of Art, Ohio). During the 1950s, Faggi frequently exhibited sculpture as well as line drawings at the Weyhe Gallery in New York.

Notes

1. Stella Rubinstein, "Alfeo Faggi," *Art in America* 9 (August 1921), p. 195.
2. "Faggi Fled from Ghosts of the 'Dead Great,'" *Art Digest* 6 (Sept. 1, 1932), p. 17.
3. See *Sculpture and Drawings by Alfeo Faggi* (Buffalo: Buffalo Fine Arts Academy, Albright Art Gallery, 1941).
4. Rubinstein 1921, p. 195; and Richard Offner, "An Approach," preface to *Exhibition of Sculpture by Alfeo Faggi* (New York: Bourgeois Gallery, 1921).
5. See Rubinstein 1921, pp. 192–202; and Marianne Moore, "Is the Real the Actual?" *Dial* 73 (Dec. 1922), pp. 620–22.

References

1941 "Albright Gallery Honors the Sensitive Sculpture of Alfeo Faggi," *Art Digest* 15 (March 1), p. 7. **1965** "Alfeo Faggi: Master in the Florence Tradition," *Woodstock Week,* July 9, Woodstock Artists Association Archives. **1976** "Alfeo Faggi," in *200 Years of American Sculpture,* New York: David R. Godine in association with the Whitney Museum of American Art, pp. 270–71.

The Holy Family

1949
Bronze with green patina; cast in 1952–53
32¼ x 33 x 1" (81.9 x 83.8 x 2.5 cm)
Signed and dated at lower right: A. FAGGI/1949; and faintly in relief at lower right: A. FAGGI/1949
Sand cast, probably by Modern Art Foundry, New York
Anonymous gift, 1953.2

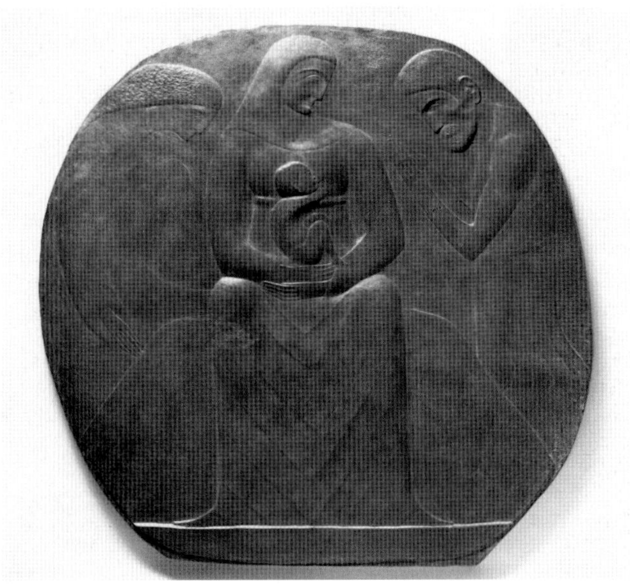

Faggi, *The Holy Family*

ALFEO FAGGI created a large number of religious sculptures, many of which are in low relief like this tondo entitled *The Holy Family.* Faggi's late reliefs display extremely subtle variations in the depth of surface and seem to occupy a place somewhere between sculpture and drawing. Because the modeling is limited, the forms are essentially rendered through calligraphic outline and texture.

Faggi admired Italian art of the late thirteenth and early fourteenth centuries, and its influence can be detected in his work. Here, both imagery and style bring to mind early Italian painting. Although Faggi's iconography is somewhat unusual, the central grouping of Mary and the infant Jesus recalls many enthroned Madonnas of the late thirteenth and early fourteenth centuries. There is also an austere mystical quality in the relief that is not unlike the paintings of Duccio and Cimabue. Stylistically, the geometric folds of Mary's garment could just as easily derive from Egyptian sculpture, which Faggi also admired.[1] His predilection for reducing complex forms to simple, rhythmic shapes is found in the art of both thirteenth-century Italy and ancient Egypt.

When Joseph T. Fraser, Jr., the director of the Pennsylvania Academy of the Fine Arts, visited New York's Weyhe Gallery in October 1952, he learned that friends of the sculptor were interested in presenting one of Faggi's pieces to the Academy if the institution would pay for its casting in bronze.[2] The Academy's board of directors accepted this proposal and chose *The Holy Family.* The Weyhe Gallery handled the casting.[3]

Notes

1. "Albright Gallery Honors the Sensitive Sculpture of Alfeo Faggi," *Art Digest* 15 (March 1, 1941), p. 7.

2. Minutes, meeting of the board of directors, Oct. 14, 1952, PAFA Archives.

3. Weyhe Gallery to Joseph T. Fraser, Jr., Feb. 10, 1953, PAFA object file.

Reference

1954 Annual report, Pennsylvania Academy of the Fine Arts (cover ill.).

Exhibited

1957 Atlantic City Art Center, N.J., *Alfeo Faggi's Sculpture and Drawings.* **1959** National Institute of Arts and Letters, New York, *Candidates for Grants Exhibition.* **1986–87** PAFA, *Sculpture at the Pennsylvania Academy of the Fine Arts.*

Alexander Portnoff

1887–1949

Alexander Portnoff was born in Odessa, Russia. He drew as a child and was urged to study architecture at the Odessa School of Fine Arts from which he received a Bachelor of Arts in 1906. He fondly remembered the training because "it steeped him in classicism."[1] He was imprisoned for his political views but was released by a sympathetic guard who appreciated his artistic talent.[2] Portnoff emigrated in 1908. He settled first in Canada and then came to Philadelphia. He worked during the day as a photographer and attended evening courses at the Philadelphia Museum School of Industrial Art (now the University of the Arts). From 1910 to 1915, he studied at the Pennsylvania Academy of the Fine Arts, where he took his first classes in clay modeling with CHARLES GRAFLY. In 1911 Portnoff was awarded a William L. Elkins Memorial Scholarship that paid his tuition. In 1912 he won the Packard Zoological Sketch First Prize for animal drawings done at the Philadelphia zoo. He won two William Emlen Cresson Traveling Scholarships—in 1912 he traveled to nine countries, including his native Russia, and in 1913 he spent most of his time in Paris, where he met Auguste Rodin (1840–1917).[3]

In 1915 Portnoff became a United States citizen and earned an honorable mention at the Panama-Pacific Exposition, in San Francisco. A group of his watercolors and sculptures were shown in the 1916 *Americanization through Art* exhibition of works by Pennsylvania artists of foreign birth, at Memorial Hall in Philadelphia. During World War I he produced cartoons in lithography on the theme of war. Later, he produced war memorials in Pennsylvania and New Jersey. Most of his commissions were for portrait busts of such people as the poet Carl Sandburg, 1926 (American Swedish Historical Museum and Foundation, Philadelphia); John Dewey, by 1933 (University of Chicago); Dr. Charles La Wall, 1921 (Philadelphia College of Pharmacy and Science); and Dr. Joseph Brinton, 1926 (Philadelphia Museum of Art). He also modeled busts of Ludwig von Beethoven, Leo Tolstoy, Abraham Lincoln, Walt Whitman, Karl Marx, and Sholom Aleichem (all unlocated).

Throughout his life, he traveled often to Russia, the Mediterranean countries, North Africa, Spain, and France. On these occasions, he made sketches in watercolor and lithographic crayon. He was a founder and director of the American-Russian Institute in Philadelphia, a society for the exchange of culture between the two nations. Solo exhibitions of his work were held in 1931 at the Montclair Art Museum in New Jersey, in 1933 at the Modern Gallery in New York, at an unknown date at the Milch Galleries in New York,[4] and in 1950 at a memorial exhibition of 145 works at the Pennsylvania Academy. In 1950 Mrs. Portnoff gave a group of his watercolors to Temple University Hospital in Philadelphia and a bust to the Pennsylvania Academy. For several years in the 1950s, she gave a cash prize in memory of her husband for the best head modeled by an Academy sculpture student. Portnoff's 1917 *Drawing #26* of four figures was given to the Pennsylvania Academy in 1955 by Mrs. Thomas Drake.

Notes

1. Robert Emmet Higginbotham, "Men of the Arts in Philadelphia," *Art Alliance Bulletin,* about 1933, p. 13, clipping file, PAFA Library.

2. Biography in *Memorial Exhibition of the Work of Alexander Portnoff,* exhib. cat. (Philadelphia: PAFA, 1950), unpaginated.

3. Alexander Portnoff to committee on instruction, PAFA, Jan. 25, and Nov. 30, 1913, 1912 and 1913 Cresson records, PAFA Archives.

4. *Alexander Portnoff: Portrait Busts and Drawings,* Milch Galleries, New York, Feb. 25–March 11 (n.d.), exhib. cat., essay by Christian Brinton, microfilm, roll no. NM2, frame nos. 69–71, Archives of American Art, Smithsonian Institution.

References

1949 Obituary, *Philadelphia Inquirer,* Dec. 21, p. 14. **1950** Dorothy Grafly, "In Memory of Alexander Portnoff," in *Memorial Exhibition of the Work of Alexander Portnoff,* exhib. cat., Philadelphia: PAFA, unpaginated. **1950** C.H. Bonte, "Academy Has Exhibition of Alex. Portnoff Work," *Philadelphia Inquirer,* April.

Richard T. Dooner

1929
Bronze with brown patina; lost-wax cast by 1931
23¾ x 9 x 11¾" (60.3 x 22.9 x 29.8 cm)
Signed and dated on top of base at back below neck:
A. Portnoff/1929
Foundry mark on edge of base at back: GORHAM CO. FOUNDERS/QGXS
Gift of Mrs. Alexander Portnoff, 1950.14

RICHARD T. DOONER (1878–1954) was a well-known Philadelphia portrait photographer. He probably met Alexander Portnoff while he also was working as a photographer shortly after arriving from Russia. An early supporter, Dooner was instrumental in bringing Portnoff to the Pennsylvania Academy of the Fine Arts.[1] Dooner may have studied at the Academy inasmuch as he served on the board of directors of the Fellowship of the Pennsylvania Academy from 1917 to 1927.[2] In the 1920s, he was an originator of Philadelphia's Art Week in which artists opened their studios to the public. When Dooner retired in 1945 after fifty years as a photographer, he had photographed sixty thousand people.

Portnoff liked to talk with his sitters and get to know them. He worked from live models who could participate in the sculptural process and influence the final product.[3] He has captured Dooner in an animated pose reminiscent of the strongly modeled works of his former teacher Charles Grafly. The bust also has the lively surface texture typical of works by Auguste Rodin, whom Portnoff admired. "I think it a splendid example of Portnoff's work," Dooner wrote, "and shows a fine knowledge of his craftsmanship."[4] The bust is mounted on a black marble base.

Notes

1. Richard T. Dooner to Joseph T. Fraser, Jr., director of the PAFA, [May] 1950, PAFA object file.
2. Dooner's student card in the PAFA Archives does not list any dates of admittance or classes attended.
3. Louise Lee Outlaw, "An Artist Tells How It's Done," *Philadelphia Record,* June 23, 1940, metropolitan section, p. 5.
4. Dooner to Fraser, [May] 1950, PAFA object file.

Exhibited

1931* cat. no. 369 (ill.). **1931** Montclair Art Museum, N.J., *Alexander Portnoff Sculpture,* cat. no. 11. **1932** Columbia University, New York, Philosophy Hall, *Portrait Busts by Alexander Portnoff,* cat. no. 7. **1933** Modern Art Gallery, New York, solo exhibition. **1933** Philadelphia Art Alliance. **1950** PAFA, *Memorial Exhibition of the Work of Alexander Portnoff,* cat. no. 4 (ill.). **1950** Long Beach Island Foundation for the Arts and Sciences, Loveladies, N.J., *Memorial Exhibition of Alexander Portnoff.* **1967** Samuel S. Fleisher Art Memorial, Philadelphia, *Exhibition of Works by Faculty Members, Present and Former.* **1986–87** PAFA, *Sculpture at the Pennsylvania Academy of the Fine Arts.*

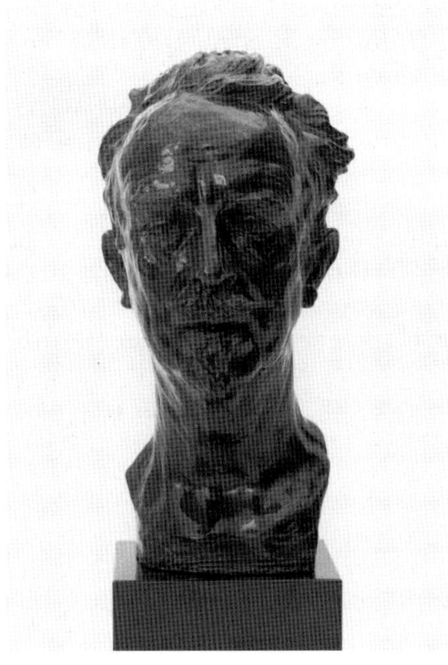

Portnoff, *Richard T. Dooner*

Ex Collections

The artist, about 1929–49; his wife, Marie, 1949–50.

BEATRICE FENTON

1887–1983

Beatrice Fenton was the daughter of Dr. Thomas Hanover Fenton, a prominent ophthalmologist, art patron, and president of the Art Club of Philadelphia. She was the granddaughter of Gustavus Remak, a Fairmount Park commissioner from 1867 until 1886. Beatrice was educated at home by governesses until the age of sixteen. Then she decided to become an animal painter like the French artist Rosa Bonheur. Her father showed THOMAS EAKINS her sketches of animals from the Philadelphia zoo. Eakins found the drawings too flat. "Get some clay and mold it," he advised, "learn a sense of form."[1] Accordingly, Fenton enrolled in a modeling class in 1903–4 taught by A. STIRLING CALDER at the Pennsylvania Museum School of Industrial Art (now the University of the Arts). In the summer of 1904, she made sculpture studies of her father's horses. That November, she began to study life modeling with CHARLES GRAFLY at the Pennsylvania Academy of the Fine Arts. Fenton remained Grafly's student until 1912. She studied cast drawing with Thomas Anshutz in 1905–6 and in the following two terms took William Merritt Chase's drawing classes.

Beatrice Fenton was awarded the George McClellan Anatomy Prize in 1907 and the Edmund Stewardson Prize in 1908. She won her first William Emlen Cresson Traveling Scholarship in 1909. It enabled her to spend a summer visiting Belgium, Germany, Austria, Italy, Greece, France, and England. She was particularly impressed by the works of Michelangelo and by the Parthenon, the friezes of which she knew from casts at the Pennsylvania Academy.[2] In 1910 a second Cresson scholarship enabled her to go to France for several months with her friend Marjorie D. Martinet, a painting student.[3] In May 1911 Fenton received a commendation and free tuition for the next year from the faculty and board of directors of the Pennsylvania Academy, who praised her "diligence and marked ability" and called her "a great stimulus to other students in Sculpture."[4]

For almost fifty years, beginning in 1911, Beatrice Fenton participated regularly in the annual and regional exhibitions of the Pennsylvania Academy of the Fine Arts and the exhibitions of its Fellowship. Her *Seaweed Fountain*, 1920, of a young girl draped in seaweed and poised on the back of a turtle, won two prizes in 1922: the George D. Widener Memorial Gold Medal and the Fellowship's annual prize, awarded by vote of the members. The fountain was installed the same year in Fairmount Park in a pond at the foot of Lemon Hill.[5] Fenton won the Percy M. Owens Memorial Prize for a distinguished Pennsylvania artist at the Fellowship's annual exhibition in 1967. She showed three portrait busts at the 1915 Panama-Pacific International Exposition, in San Francisco, and won an honorable mention for her bust of the painter Peter Moran (collection of the Art Club of Philadelphia). She was made an associate of the National Sculpture Society, New York, in 1927 and a Fellow about 1945. In 1931 she executed a commission for four limestone figures of children for the gateposts of Philadelphia's Children's Hospital, then located at Seventeenth and Bainbridge streets. The building was torn down in the mid-1970s and the figures presumably destroyed. One of nine Pennsylvania sculptors chosen to participate in the show *American Art Today* at the 1939 New York World's Fair, Fenton exhibited *Torso*, a bronze sculpture of a female figure.

In October 1942, she replaced SAMUEL MURRAY as instructor of sculpture at the Moore Institute and School of Design for Women (now Moore College of Art and Design). She taught life modeling there for the next twelve years and, on her retirement, was awarded an honorary doctorate of fine arts. She later taught life modeling of heads, figures, and low reliefs at her Germantown studio.

Fenton's memorial to Evelyn Taylor Price, a bronze sundial composed of two children holding a sunflower, was installed in Rittenhouse Square in 1947. She received a commission in 1950 to design the congressional medal that was awarded to Vice President Alben W. Barkley. In 1952 a major exhibition of her work was held at the Woodmere Art Gallery (now the Woodmere Art Museum) in Philadelphia. The gallery awarded her honorable mention in 1957 for her striding *Leopard* in stone. She also won the gallery's Violet Oakley Memorial Prize in 1962. Fenton was recognized for outstanding achievement by the award of the National Sculpture Society's Herbert Adams Memorial Medal in 1980.

Notes

1. George R. Dowdell, "Recognized Sculptress; Great Painter Discouraged Sculptress into Medium," *Germantown Courier*, April 12, 1962, clipping file, Woodmere Art Museum.

2. Beatrice Fenton to John Trask, secretary and managing director, August 11, 1909, student file, PAFA Archives.

3. Ethel Ramsey to Charles Ramsey, curator, Sept. 7, 1910, PAFA Archives.

4. Minutes, meeting of the board of directors, May 25, 1911, [p. 3], PAFA Archives.

5. *Seaweed Fountain* was moved to Fairmount Park's Horticultural Center in 1983. Two bronze casts are in private collections and one is in Brookgreen Gardens, Murrells Inlet, S.C. The composition was awarded a bronze medal at the Sesquicentennial Exposition in Philadelphia in 1926. For an article on the model, see Nessa Forman, "Found: Mary Wilson," *Philadelphia Evening Bulletin*, March 21, 1977, p. 1-B.

References

Beatrice Fenton Papers, Archives of American Art, Smithsonian Institution, Washington, D.C. **1976** *Philadelphia: Three Centuries of American Art*, Philadelphia: Philadelphia Museum of Art, pp. 521–22. **1983** Obituary, *Chestnut Hill Local*, Feb. 24, clipping file, Woodmere Art Museum.

Bacchanale

1934
Plaster, painted green
78 x 49½ x 22½" (198.1 x 125.7 x 57.2 cm)
Signed and dated on top of base next to satyr's left foot:
Beatrice Fenton Sc. 1934–
Gift of Joan S. Martin, 1987.19

BEATRICE FENTON's best-known body of work is a series of fanciful fountains and garden figures that began with *Seaweed Fountain* (Fairmount Park) in 1920 and continued through the 1940s.[1] Her garden sculptures were commissioned for estates in Chest-

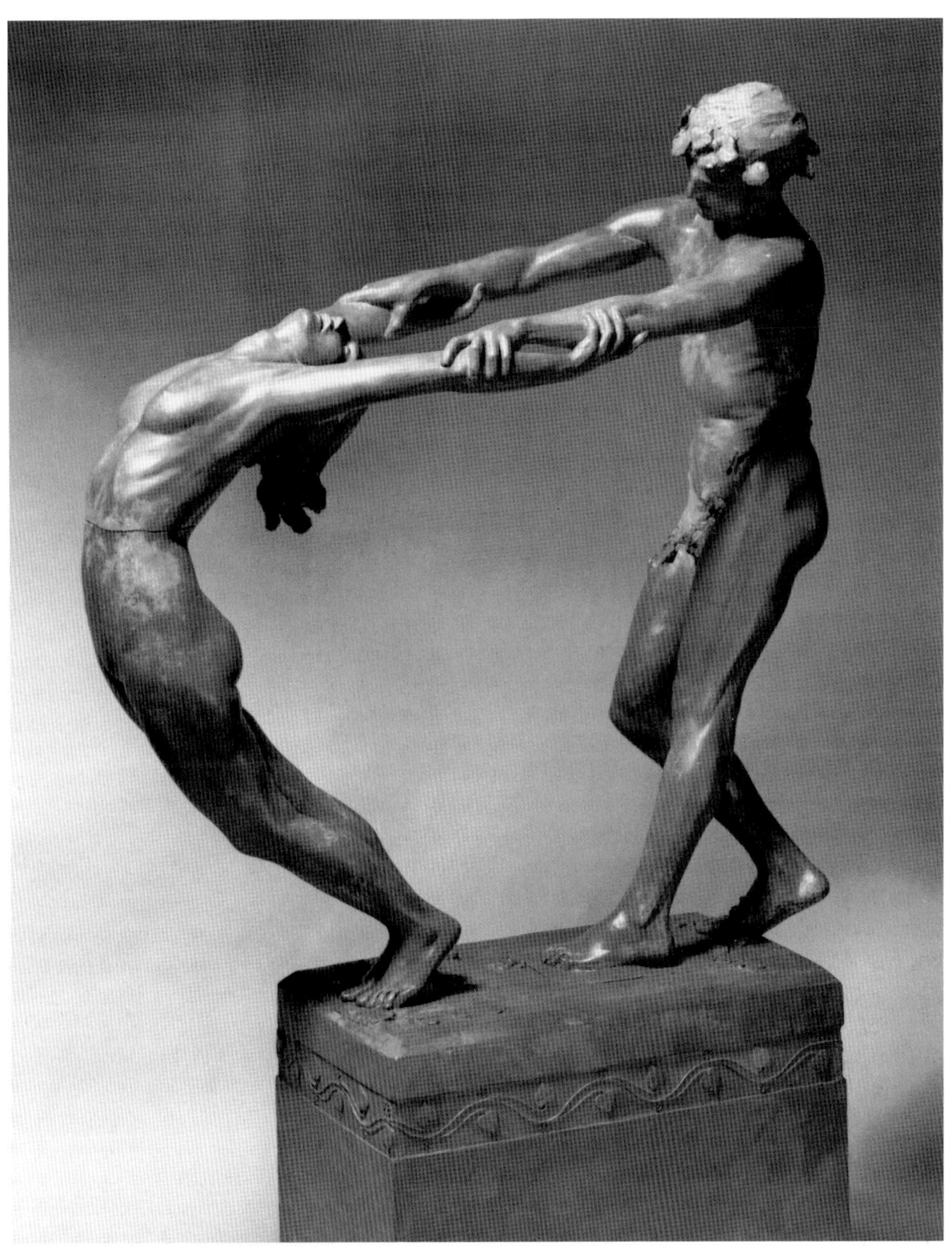

Fenton, *Bacchanale*

nut Hill and Main Line Philadelphia, as well as Rhode Island, Delaware, Maryland, South Carolina, Ohio, Arizona, and California.[2] Usually the gardens were already completed, and a niche or pedestal designed by a landscape architect was in place. Fenton would then design a grouping to conform in mood and shape to the surroundings.[3] Most of her fountains consist of a young child modeled from life coupled with one or more aquatic creatures, such as dolphins, a tortoise, a frog, a seahorse, a starfish, or angelfish.[4] She produced at least three adult groups that she considered appropriate for a garden setting: *Nereid Fountain,* 1928 (private collection, Huntington Valley, Pa.), of a female figure dancing on the backs of dolphins; *Daphne and Apollo* (date and location unknown)[5]; and *Bacchanale.*

In *Bacchanale,* a satyr, adorned with grape leaves, grasps the arms of a nymph and pulls her toward him in a graceful arc. They may have been inspired by the "Autumn Bacchanale" in Alexander Constantinovich Glazunov's ballet *Seasons,* that was performed in the 1910s by the renowned Russian ballerina Anna Pavlova and her partner Mikhail Mordkin.[6] The theme had apparently intrigued Fenton from at least 1926, when she requested a bid from the Bureau Brothers foundry in Philadelphia for a bronze cast of a *Bacchanale* consisting of figures 6 feet high on a base about 2½ feet high.[7] Her sketch was not completed, however, until 1930. That year, she received two bids from Bureau Brothers for casting a model of 38-inch figures with and without a base 16 inches in diameter and 20 inches high.[8] As models, Fenton hired a brother and sister gymnastic team.[9] Her concern for accurately portraying anatomy reflects her academic training at the Pennsylvania Academy of the Fine Arts. The carefully modulated bodies are in sharp contrast to the sketchy facial features.

This plaster group, the only known cast, was completed in 1934, published in a pamphlet in 1937, and exhibited in 1939. It is made up of four parts fitted together with roman joins, which suggest that the complicated composition was intended to be cast in sections into bronze and welded together.[10] The reason this was never realized may have been the expense involved in casting such a large piece into bronze. Or it may have been the erotic subject matter that caused the sculpture to remain in the artist's studio for almost fifty years. Sometime prior to 1952, a patron expressed interest in having the work cast for display in a park. The base was therefore raised to accommodate lettering, but the commission never materialized.[11] Perhaps it was still in negotiation in 1952 at the time of Fenton's exhibition at the Woodmere Art Gallery (now the Woodmere Art Museum). This may account for the sculpture's being left out of the exhibition. It is one of the few garden works not even included as a photograph.

Bacchanale was painted to simulate the modulated light-green patina that was popular in the period. Fenton used three or four different greens at one time to capture the variegated patina that would develop on differently textured surfaces of a bronze figure. Joan S. Martin, Fenton's student and the inheritor of her studio and its contents, commented that the sculptor would have painted the whole world green if she had had the chance.[12] It was one of the colors that Fenton chose for the patination of the casts that she had made of the sculptures of EMILY CLAYTON BISHOP.

In the course of forty years, areas of *Bacchanale* were repainted to hide abrasions, chips, and dirt. The new paint was toned to match the adjacent original paint that by then had darkened. When the sculpture was cleaned in 1989, the areas of inpainting by Joan S. Martin were removed; but all paint believed to be Beatrice Fenton's was retained.[13] A few patches of dark paint that greatly detracted from a reading of the sculptural forms were toned down with an easily removable paint. There was some patchiness in the original paint at the junction of the base's extension and it resulted from the application of paint to unprimed plaster. Because the effect had been acceptable to the artist, it was retained.

Notes

1. Two other garden sculptures from Fenton's studio went to public collections in 1987: *Boy and Starfish Fountain,* 1930, Historical Society of Pennsylvania, Philadelphia; and *Young Dryad,* 1940, Woodmere Art Museum.

2. "Art Alliance Sculpture Members," *Art Alliance Bulletin* (Jan. 1940), clipping file, PAFA Library.

3. Karin Dale, "Garden Counterpoint," unidentified Philadelphia area magazine, about 1939–40, p. 12, clipping file, PAFA Library.

4. Six such groups are illustrated in an undated pamphlet, *Garden Sculpture by Beatrice Fenton,* clipping file, PAFA Library. Fenton apparently advertised in newspapers for child models. Nels Nelson, "She Wanted Me to Pose in the Nude, But I Wouldn't Take Off My Shorts," *Philadelphia Daily News,* Feb. 23, 1971, p. 4, relates that, when he was a seven-year-old model, the sculptor assured him that she merely wanted "something living" and that the figure was "not a portrait."

5. Dale, "Garden Counterpoint," p. 13.

6. *The American Way in Sculpture, 1890–1930* (Cleveland: Cleveland Museum of Art, 1986), cat. no. 46, shows *Bacchanale Russe,* a 1917 sculpture by Malvina Hoffman (1887–1966).

7. Bureau Brothers, June 25, 1926, estimate of $2,100, card file, Beatrice Fenton Papers, Archives of American Art, Smithsonian Institution, Washington, D.C.

8. Bureau Brothers, March 31, 1930, estimates of $600 and $750, ibid.

9. Interview with Joan S. Martin by Mary Mullen Cunningham, July 1, 1987, notes in PAFA research file. Martin stated that no sketches are extant and that, if the sketch of 1930 was for the Pennsylvania Academy's piece, a more precise dating for the composition would be 1930–34.

10. Virginia Norton Naudé, conservation report, August 19, 1989, PAFA object file. Also, the hyphen after the composition date on the inscription may suggest that Fenton intended later to inscribe a cast date on the bronze.

11. Telephone interview with Joan S. Martin by Michelle E. Barger, Jan. 30, 1989, quoted ibid.

12. Ibid.

13. Naudé 1989.

Reference

1937 *Sculpture by Beatrice Fenton,* Murrells Inlet, S.C.: Brookgreen Gardens, ill. showing sculpture with its original base.

Exhibited

1939 Art Club Gallery, Philadelphia, *The Fellowship of the Pennsylvania Academy of the Fine Arts Annual Exhibition,* cat. no. 86. **1994–96** PAFA, *Two Centuries of Collecting at the Museum of American Art.*

Ex Collections

The artist, 1934–83; Joan S. Martin, 1983–87.

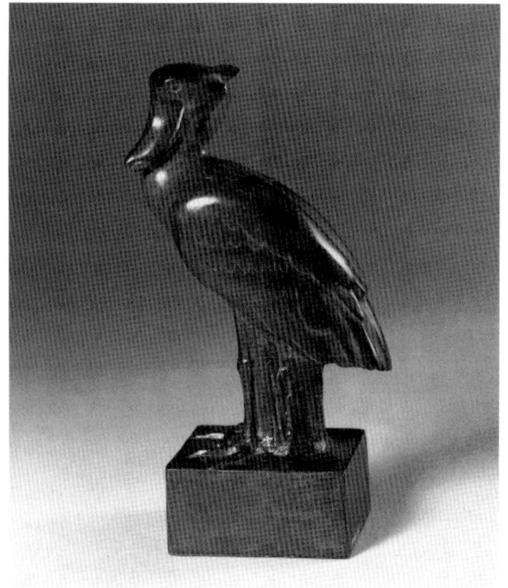

Fenton, *Shoe-bill Stork*

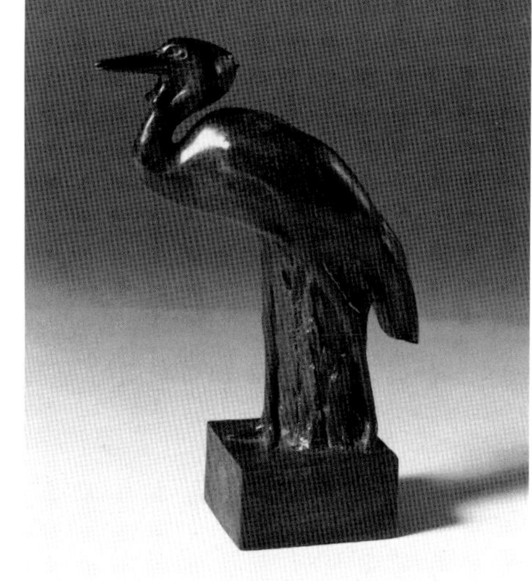

Fenton, *Wattled Crane*

Shoe-bill Stork

1942
Bronze with brown patina; cast in 1943
9½ x 3$\frac{1}{16}$ x 4¾" (24.1 x 7.8 x 12.1 cm)
Signed and dated on top of base: B. Fenton '42
Sand cast, probably by the Anton Basky Foundry, New York
Gift of the Fellowship of the Pennsylvania Academy of the Fine Arts, 1943.13.1

BEATRICE FENTON grew up around horses and spent time at the zoo sketching other animals. She probably received some training in modeling animals from Charles Grafly at the Pennsylvania Academy of the Fine Arts, but classes in the subject were not introduced until 1921. She continued to work at the zoo through at least the 1950s. Sculpting with plasteline from live animals "teaches you to be quick," she noted, "an antelope or penguin won't stand still while you model him."[1] Fenton had her models either copied in stone or cast in bronze with a patina imitating stone, as exemplified by this stork and the *Wattled Crane* (q.v.).

Shoe-bill Stork is simplified in form but realistic. The bird's broad bill rests on its chest, and its legs are poised as if wading through the reeds of its native African habitat. The vegetation supports the bird's thin legs, as in *Wattled Crane.* Several rows of incised vertical and wavy lines indicate the feathers on the bird's sides and back. Beatrice Fenton has portrayed a specific animal with a personality of its own. She probably modeled it at the Philadelphia zoo, which had one such stork, named Pete, from 1928 to 1948. From then until 1974, the zoo had several other shoe-bill storks. They are now rare.

Note

1. Quoted in Libby McCall, "Courier Portraits," *Germantown [Pa.] Courier,* April 10, 1952, clipping file, PAFA Library.

Exhibited

1944* cat. no. 180. **1956** PAFA, *Living Philadelphia Artists Represented in the Permanent Collection of the Academy,* cat. no. 133A. **1970** Free Library of Philadelphia, *Animal Sculpture for Children,* bookmobile. **1972** Cosmopolitan Club, Philadelphia, exhibition of art from the Pennsylvania Academy of the Fine Arts. **1986–87** PAFA, *Sculpture at the Pennsylvania Academy of the Fine Arts.* **1988** PAFA, *Sea and Shore.* **1989** PAFA, *"The Birds and the Beasts Will Teach Us."*

Wattled Crane

1943
Bronze with brown patina
10⅛ x 3$\frac{1}{16}$ x 6¾" (25.7 x 7.8 x 17.1 cm)
Signed and dated on top of base: B. Fenton '43
Sand cast, probably by the Anton Basky Foundry, New York
Gift of the Fellowship of the Pennsylvania Academy of the Fine Arts, 1943.13.2

PRODUCED some months after *Shoe-bill Stork* (q.v.), *Wattled Crane* was modeled on the same small scale and with the same format of integral base and vegetative support. The striding crane has a strong, sinuous outline. Its feathers are more subtly defined than those of the stork without the patterns of incised lines. The two fleshy pendants below the beak are wattles, hence the bird's name. The Philadelphia zoo had such a bird from 1941 to 1974, and it probably served as the model for this sculpture. Wattled cranes, although native to Africa, are fairly common in zoos in the United States. Beatrice Fenton created other images of cranes: a fountain shown in the 1941 annual exhibition of the Fellowship of the Pennsylvania Academy of the Fine Arts and *Demoiselle Crane* of about 1962, included that year in the members' exhibition of the Woodmere Art Gallery (now the Woodmere Art Museum), Philadelphia.

Beatrice Fenton often made small studies of animals to be enlarged later in stone, and that may have been her original intention for *Shoe-bill Stork* and *Wattled Crane.* It is not known if larger versions were produced. The plaster sculptures were shown at the 1943 annual exhibition of the Fellowship and were purchased by the Fellowship for presentation to the Academy. Between April and June of that year, they were cast in bronze, probably at the Anton Basky Foundry, which Fenton often used. She specified the color of the patinas. When the bronzes were completed, the plaster models were returned to her. Another bronze of the stork may have been cast, for one was offered for sale in 1952 at the Woodmere Art Gallery.

Exhibited
1956 PAFA, *Living Philadelphia Artists Represented in the Permanent Collection of the Academy,* cat. no. 133B. **1970** Free Library of Philadelphia, *Animal Sculpture for Children,* bookmobile. **1972** Cosmopolitan Club, Philadelphia, exhibition of art from the PAFA. **1986–87** PAFA, *Sculpture at the Pennsylvania Academy of the Fine Arts.* **1987** Port of History Museum, Philadelphia, *National Sculpture Society Fifty-Fourth Annual Exhibition,* p. 67 (ill.). **1988** PAFA, *Sea and Shore.* **1989** PAFA, *"The Birds and The Beasts Will Teach Us."*

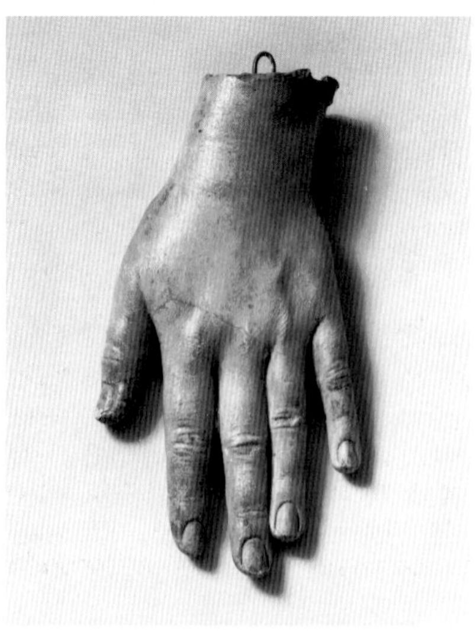

Attributed to Fenton, *Life Cast of Emily Clayton Bishop's Left Hand*

ATTRIBUTED TO BEATRICE FENTON

Life Cast of Emily Clayton Bishop's Left Hand

About 1907
Plaster, painted white
8⅜ x 4⅜ x 1⅞" (21.3 x 11.1 x 4.8 cm)
Inscribed on bottom: Emily Bishop's/hand/Cast from life
Gift of Powel Fenton, 1984.43

Ex Collections
The artist, about 1907–83; her brother, Powel Fenton, 1983–84.

See also EMILY CLAYTON BISHOP.

WHARTON ESHERICK

1887–1970

The Philadelphia-born artist, Wharton Harris Esherick showed an early interest in drawing. At the age of twenty, he studied painting briefly at Philadelphia School of Industrial Art (now the University of the Arts). In November 1908, he enrolled at the Pennsylvania Academy of the Fine Arts, where he studied drawing and painting with William Merritt Chase and Cecilia Beaux and later with Thomas P. Anshutz. After a brief stint as a newspaper illustrator, Esherick moved with his wife to a farmhouse in Paoli, Pennsylvania, in 1912 to pursue painting.

In 1919, while teaching drawing at an artists' colony in Fairhope, Alabama, Esherick purchased carving tools to make frames for his paintings. The next year, back in Pennsylvania, he produced his first sculpture, *The Race,* which featured game pieces of horses and riders in painted wood. By the mid-1920s, he had given up painting altogether and was working in wood—making woodcuts for book illustrations and carving furniture and sculpture.[1] Esherick particularly liked to carve oak. He used wood from trees near his home and studio. To accommodate this change from painting to carving, he needed a larger studio; and in 1926 he designed and built a new one (now the Wharton Esherick Museum). During the 1930s, he received commissions for interior designs and furniture. One of his commissions for a private home, his interior for a Pennsylvania Hill House with the Museum's prominent sculptural oak spiral staircase was on display at the 1939–40 New York World's Fair.

Esherick never studied sculpture. He considered his works to be "three-dimensional drawings."[2] This approach is borne out by his two methods of preparation: preliminary drawings on paper, used for *Darling,* and sketching on wood with chalk to bring out the natural form of a log, as in *Twin Twist* (qq.v.). He regularly exhibited his sculpture at the Pennsylvania Academy in the 1950s and 1960s. In 1951 he won the Academy's prize for sculpture in *A Regional Exhibition of Oil Painting and Sculpture, Philadelphia and Vicinity* for *Sad Sack,* 1949 (location unknown), a cubist interpretation in ebony of a World War II cartoon character.[3] The Architectural League of New York awarded Esherick its gold medal of honor in 1954 for pioneering in "the use of modern concepts of form in furniture, sculpture, and structural design."[4] The organic forms employed in Esherick's work have influenced many young furnituremakers.[5] His first major exhibition was held in 1958–59 at the Museum of Contemporary Crafts (now the American Craft Museum) in New York. In 1968 the Pennsylvania Academy mounted a retrospective exhibition of his sculpture, furniture, paintings, and prints at its Peale House galleries. The American Institute of Architects, New York, awarded him a posthumous craftsmanship medal in 1971. The following year, the Wharton Esherick Museum, in Paoli, was dedicated and opened to the public. In 1993 the site was designated a National Historic Landmark.

Notes

1. Mansfield Bascom, *Prints by Wharton Esherick* (Philadelphia: Woodmere Art Museum, 1984), pp. ii, iii.
2. Quoted in Gene Rochberg, *Drawings by Wharton Esherick* (New York: Van Nostrand Reinhold Company, 1978), [p. 1].
3. Listed incorrectly in exhibition catalogue as *Sad Sap.*
4. Artist's resumé, about 1968, p. 1, clipping file, PAFA Library.
5. Elizabeth Bidwell Bates and Jonathan L. Fairbanks, *American Furniture: 1620 to the Present* (New York: Richard Marek Publishers, 1981), p. 514.

References

1976 *Philadelphia: Three Centuries of American Art,* Philadelphia: Philadelphia Museum of Art, pp. 538–39.
1977 *The Wharton Esherick Museum: Studio and Collection,* Paoli: privately published.

Darling

1940
White oak
87¼ x 26¼ x 57½" (221.6 x 66.7 x 146.1 cm)
Signed with initials and dated on rear leg: W/E/MCM/XXXX
Henry D. Gilpin Fund, 1951.21

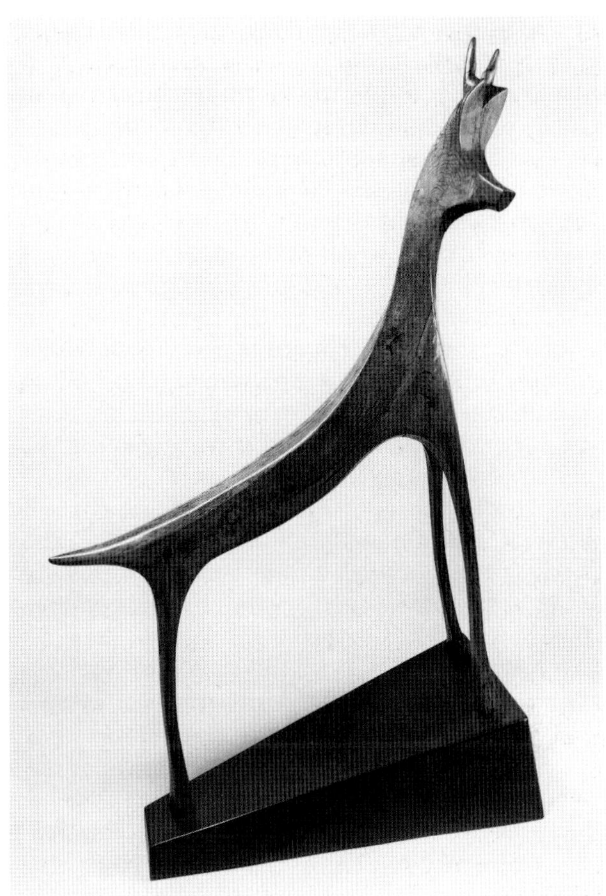

Esherick, *Darling*

ANIMALS were among Wharton Esherick's favorite subjects, especially in the 1930s, when he carved several horses. In 1939 he made pencil sketches entitled *Deer on the Lawn* (Wharton Esherick Museum, Paoli) in which he was probably working out the ideas for this sculpture.[1] *Darling* is carved from one large tree trunk. Its sinuous outline is reminiscent of the spare, flowing lines of Esherick's drawings. He was interested in warped surfaces and the fluid forms of nature without the intrusion of symmetry and sharp edges. Soon after the sculpture was completed, it was exhibited outdoors for about a year at the Hedgerow Theatre in Rose Valley. The head of *Darling* can be seen in the foreground of his small, undated woodcut *Hedgerow Snow* (private collection), showing the exterior of the theatre. Then, perhaps for as long as ten years, the sculpture stood in the woods outside Esherick's studio. It was periodically varnished to protect the surface from exposure to weather. Nonetheless, repairs had to be made in several areas (pieces were joined together with dowels)—most prominently where the deer's nose had weathered. Esherick called this a "nose job."[2] The original base—a *T*-shaped construction consisting of a long wooden plank set into a higher pyramidal piece—was designed for installation outdoors, where it would be "partly covered and surrounded by brush and vegetation."[3] *Darling* was exhibited in 1951 with this base at the 146th annual exhibition of the Pennsylvania Academy of the Fine Arts. After the Academy bought the sculpture, Esherick replaced the base with its current walnut box for installation indoors. He apparently hated parting with *Darling,* which had become a fixture outside his studio.[4]

When *Darling* was exhibited at the Argent Galleries in New York in 1944, a critic wrote "The silhouette is harsh and ungraceful; the scooped and wobbly legs of shiny oak look like bad furniture."[5] In contrast, a reviewer in 1951 "marveled at the curve of the head, the sauciness of the ears, and tail, the way the light caught the sculptured edges."[6] The artist particularly enjoyed the comment of a young viewer: "Your deer may have three legs, but I can't stop looking at it."[7] Esherick's horse sculpture *Cheeter,* 1934 (Wharton Esherick Museum), also has three legs, and *Jeeter (Hedgerow Horse),* 1934 (unlocated), has two.

Notes

1. For pencil sketches, see Rochberg 1978, [p. 1], figs. 12–14.

2. Conversation between Mansfield Bascom, Ruth Esherick Bascom, and Susan James-Gadzinski, Dec. 1, 1987.

3. Wharton Esherick to Joseph T. Fraser, Jr., director of the PAFA, April 14, 1951, PAFA object file.

4. Gertrude Benson, "Wood Sculpture Functions in Home and Landscape," *Philadelphia Inquirer,* July 15, 1951, TV/Radio section, p. 7.

5. Breuning 1944, p. 12.

6. Benson 1951 (July 15).

7. Gertrude Benson, "Leading American Artists Express Optimism on Eve of the New Year," *Philadelphia Inquirer,* Dec. 30, 1951, p. 8.

References

1944 Margaret Breuning, "Three Sculptors," *Art Digest* 18 (March 15), p. 12. **1950** Dorothy Grafly, "Wharton Esherick," *Magazine of Art* 43 (Jan.), p. 11, as *Deer.* **1976** *Philadelphia: Three Centuries of American Art,* Philadelphia: Philadelphia Museum of Art, p. 546. **1977** *The Wharton Esherick Museum: Studio and Collection,* Paoli: privately published, introduction, cat. no. 54. **1978** Gene Rochberg, *Drawings by Wharton Esherick,* New York: Van Nostrand Reinhold Company, [p. 19] (ill.).

Exhibited

1940–41 Hedgerow Theatre, Rose Valley, Pa., in garden. **1941–51** Outside the artist's studio, Paoli. **1944** Argent Galleries, New York, *Esherick, Faggi, Zadkine: Drawings and Sculpture,* checklist no. 5. **1950** Long Beach Island Foundation of the Arts and Sciences, Loveladies, N.J., exhibition of works by contemporary American artists. **1951*** cat. no. 336, incorrectly as *Reindeer.* **1956** PAFA, *Living Philadelphia Artists Represented in the Permanent Collection of the Academy,* cat. no. 150. **1958** Philadelphia Museum School of Art. **1958–59** Museum of Contemporary Crafts, New York, *The Furniture and Sculpture of Wharton Esherick,* cat. no. 78. **1972** PAFA, *Acres of Art,* checklist no. 32. **1974–88** Wharton Esherick Museum, Paoli, on loan. **1989** PAFA, *"The Birds and the Beasts Will Teach Us."* **1994–96** PAFA, *Two Centuries of Collecting at the Museum of American Art.*

Ex Collection

The artist, 1940–51.

Twin Twist

1940
White oak
183½ x 31¼ x 44" (466.1 x 79.4 x 111.8 cm)
Signed and dated at bottom: • • • W • E • /MCMXL
Harrison Earl Fund and gift of the Pennsylvania Academy Women's Committee, 1968.21

ACCORDING to its inscription, *Twin Twist* was carved in 1940, although it has been commonly dated 1944.[1] The log was found in Valley Forge by the lumberman Ed Ray, who supplied much of the wood for Wharton Esherick's sculpture.[2] Years later, Esherick remembered the phone call from his friend: "I have a crazy old twisted log. Shall I take it to the sawmill?" Esherick went to see the log and decided that it "would be ruined at a sawmill." Although he had no idea what to do with it, he was not "going to let a sawmill hack at it."[3]

The sculpture was carved outside his studio in Paoli. First, he sketched directly on the wood with chalk attached to a long stick. Then, chopping with an ax, he emphasized the natural twist that was present in the log. Esherick did not claim the entire credit for *Twin Twist.* "Somebody else was there first," he wrote, "fooling with that piece of wood."[4] The sculpture was left on display outdoors probably for as long as eighteen years.

In 1958 *Twin Twist* was brought indoors in preparation for Esherick's retrospective exhibition at the Museum of Contemporary Crafts (now the American Craft Museum) in New York.[5] A six-sided wooden base was constructed by the artist and painted black. In 1962 at the 163rd annual exhibition of the Pennsylvania Academy of the Fine Arts, the sculpture was displayed in the rotunda. It had never looked better, according to Esherick, and he hoped that someday it would be shown in that space again.[6] The Pennsylvania Academy purchased the work in 1968 from his retrospective exhibition at its Peale House galleries.

Twin Twist has been on loan to the Wharton Esherick Museum since 1975. Because of its height (over fifteen feet), it is installed in a sculpture well that the artist excavated in the ground floor of his studio in 1959 for the purpose of showing his larger sculptures. In 1986 and 1987, during an exhibition of the Pennsylvania Academy sculpture collection, *Twin Twist* was once again shown in the rotunda.

Notes

1. Grafly 1950, p. 11, and data sheet, 1968, PAFA object file.
2. Will Thompson, "The Stuff of Great Art Has Come from His Ax," *Philadelphia Inquirer*, Oct. 7, 1984, Art section, p. 1.
3. Wharton Esherick to Joseph T. Fraser, Jr., director of the PAFA, Jan. 11, 1969 (with a sketch of *Twin Twist*), PAFA object file.
4. Ibid.
5. Studio photograph, 1958, Archives, Wharton Esherick Museum.
6. Wharton Esherick to Joseph T. Fraser, Jr., Jan. 11, 1969, PAFA object file.

References

1950 Dorothy Grafly, "Wharton Esherick," *Magazine of Art* 43 (Jan.) pp. 9, 10, 11 (ill.). **1977** *The Wharton Esherick Museum: Studio and Collection*, Paoli, privately published, cat. no. 55.

Exhibited

1940–58 Outside the artist's studio, Paoli. **1958–59** Museum of Contemporary Crafts, New York, *The Furniture and Sculpture of Wharton Esherick*, cat. no. 67. **1960** Munson-Williams-Proctor Institute Museum of Art, Utica, N.Y., *Art Across America*. **1962*** cat. no. 142. **1963** Delaware Art Center, Wilmington, *Contemporary Crafts for Christmas Giving*, checklist no. 186. **1964** Philadelphia Art Alliance, *The Work of Wharton Esherick*. **1968** Philadelphia Civic Center Museum, *20th Anniversary Exhibition, Philadelphia Chapter Artists Equity Association*, cat. no. 42. **1968** PAFA, Peale House, *A Retrospective Exhibition of Sculpture, Furniture, Paintings, and Graphics by Wharton Esherick*, cat. no. 30. **1968–75** PAFA, Peale House. **1975–86** Wharton Esherick Museum, Paoli. **1986–87** PAFA, *Sculpture at the Pennsylvania Academy of the Fine Arts*. **1987-present** Wharton Esherick Museum, long-term loan.

Ex Collection

The artist, 1940–68.

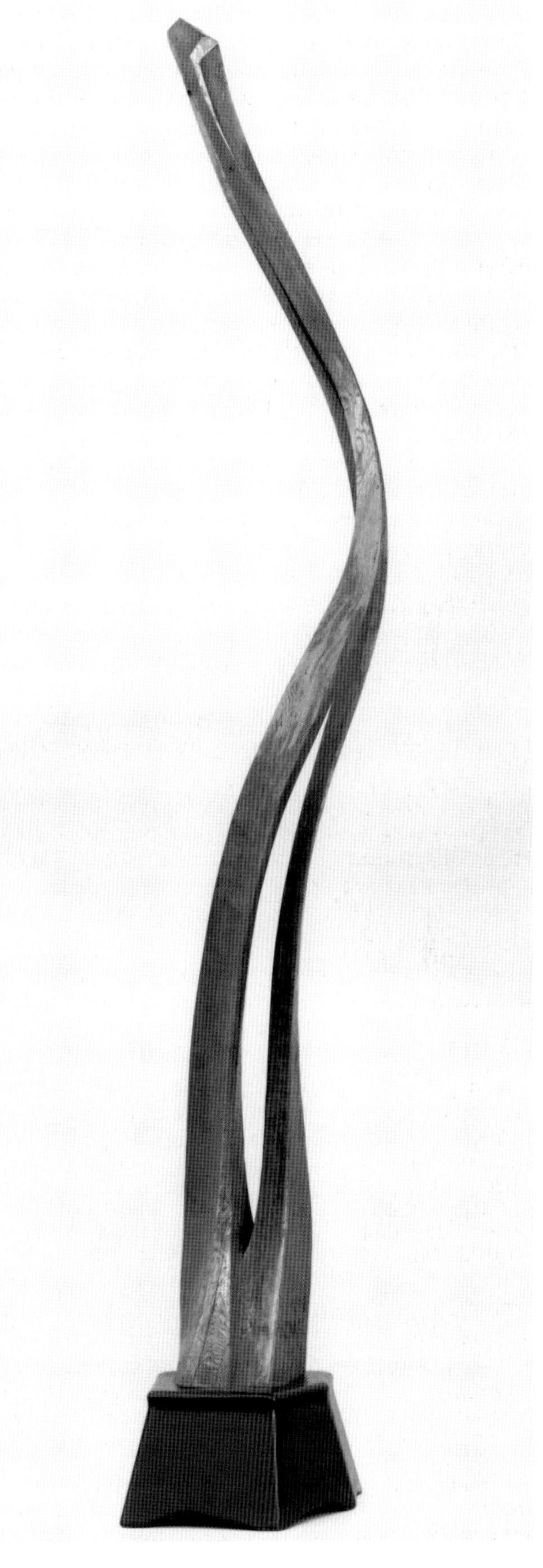

Esherick, *Twin Twist*

Waldemar Raemisch

1888–1955

Waldemar Raemisch was born in Berlin into a tailor's large family. At the age of fourteen, he was apprenticed to a metalsmith for four years. He then studied design at the Städtische Handwerkerschule, the municipal arts and crafts school. In 1911 he took classes in drawing and sculpture at the Staatliche Kunstgewerbe Museum. Raemisch was on an extensive tour that included Italy, Egypt, Israel, and Greece when World War I broke out. He joined the German Air Force, and, because of his sculptural ability, was assigned a job carving cemetery monuments for German soldiers.[1] He returned to Germany in 1918 and soon became head of metalwork, sculpture, and drawing at the Staatliche Kunstgewerbe Museum. Raemisch made decorative silver objects, such as candlesticks of human and animal figures, candelabras, coffee pots, and bronze vases. He produced commissions for German coinage, a wedding present for the Shah of Persia, bronze eagles for the Berlin Olympic stadium, and medals, trophies, and badges for the 1936 Olympic games in Berlin. He was removed from his post in 1937 by the Nazi regime.

In 1939 Raemisch accepted a position teaching industrial design and figure modeling at the Rhode Island School of Design, in Providence. He became head of the sculpture department in 1946 and remained there until his death in 1955. He had exhibitions in 1940 at Brown University, in 1941 at the Buchholz Gallery in New York, and in 1943 at the Providence Art Club. In 1944 he completed commissions for bronze portrait busts of Edward W. Forbes and Paul J. Sachs, former directors of the Fogg Art Museum at Harvard University, where Raemisch was a lecturer and Fellow. His *Pietà: 1944*, a granite figure of a mourning mother and her dead child, won the George D. Widener Memorial Gold Medal at the 1946 annual exhibition of the Pennsylvania Academy of the Fine Arts.[2]

In the early 1950s, he was awarded the commission for *The Preacher*, a ten-foot granite figure, one of a group of sculptures erected on the north terrace of the Ellen Phillips Samuel Memorial in Philadelphia's Fairmount Park. In 1954 he was commissioned to create two large-scale groups of sculpture, *The Great Mother* and *The Great Healer*, for the Youth Study Center designed by Carroll, Grisdale, and Van Alen on Benjamin Franklin Parkway. Raemisch died in Rome while supervising the bronze casting. The two sculptures were erected by his widow, Ruth Galland Raemisch, and his former student and assistant, the sculptor Gilbert Alfred Franklin (b. 1919). Memorial exhibitions were held in 1955 at the Rhode Island School of Design and in 1956 at the Philadelphia Art Alliance.

Raemisch's work is in the Fogg Art Museum of Harvard University, Cambridge; the Cranbrook Academy of Art, Bloomfield Hills, Michigan; and the National Museum of American Art, Washington, D.C. Wolfgang Behl (b. 1918), Raemisch's student in Berlin and Providence, owns a collection of his teacher's works including his landscape drawings.[3]

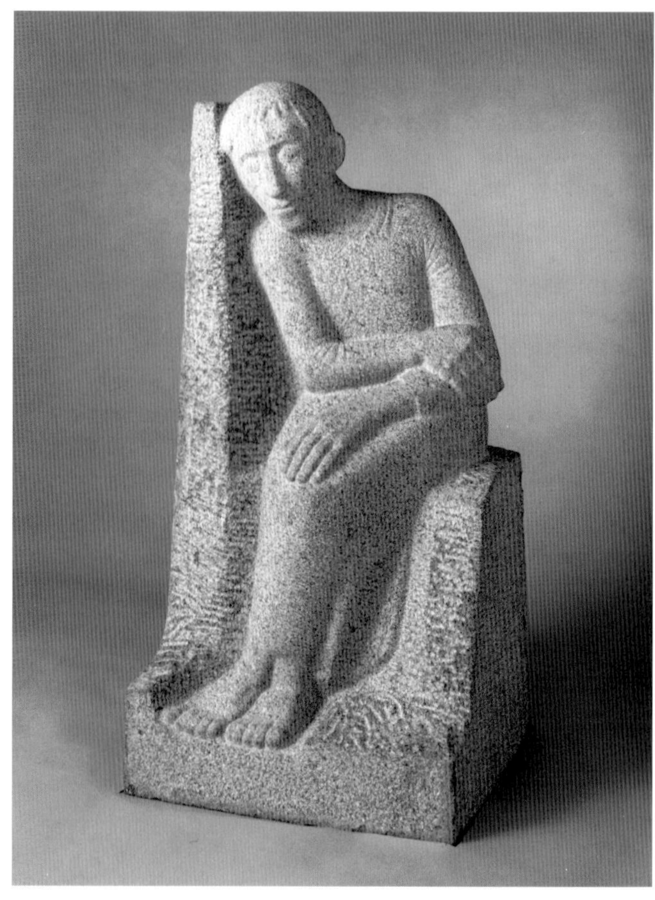

Raemisch, *Displaced Person*

Notes

1. Muriel Ciolkowska, "Raemisch—Metal Worker," *International Studio* 77 (June 1923), p. 235.
2. The sculpture was called *Terror from the Air* in the 1956 memorial exhibition at the Philadelphia Art Alliance.
3. Behl's *Prometheus*, 1962–63, is in the collection of the Museum of American Art of the Pennsylvania Academy of the Fine Arts.

References

1945 L.E.K., "Interview with an Artist," *Museum Notes*, Museum of Art, Rhode Island School of Design, 3 (March), unpaginated. **1955** Obituary, *New York Times*, April 16, clipping file, PAFA Library. **1956** "Memorial Exhibition of Raemisch Sculpture," *Art Alliance Bulletin* (Nov.), pp. 11–12.

Displaced Person

1942
Granite
37 x 18 x 17" (94.1 x 45.8 x 43.2 cm)
Collection Fund, 1956.19

Waldemar Raemisch's work of the 1940s consisted mainly of direct carvings in granite, his favorite medium; and it often dealt with themes of war. *Displaced Person* shows his empathy for others who, as a result of war, were alone in foreign surroundings and had to make do often with meagre resources. The statue is reminiscent of ancient Egyptian seated figures. The stubborn granite is ideal for Raemisch's simple formal style. The bench and head rest were given a texture that contrasts with the smoother surface of the figure.

The Pennsylvania Academy of the Fine Arts purchased this sculpture from the artist's widow while the work was on display at the memorial exhibition at the Philadelphia Art Alliance.

Exhibited

1945 Rhode Island School of Design, Providence, solo exhibition, as *The Tired Man.* **1955** Rhode Island School of Design, *Waldemar Raemisch Memorial Exhibition.* **1956** Philadelphia Art Alliance, *Waldemar Raemisch Memorial Exhibition,* cat. no. 17. **1993** PAFA, *Carved in Wood and Stone: Twentieth-Century Sculpture.*

Ex Collections

The artist, 1942–55; his wife, Ruth Galland Raemisch, 1955–56.

Saul Baizerman

1889–1957

The son of a Russian harnessmaker, Saul Baizerman showed an early interest in art. He served a brief apprenticeship to two painter-craftsmen and, at the age of thirteen, produced his first sculpture, a clay bust of his father. Saul attended the Imperial Art School in Odessa for one year while he worked as an artist's model. In 1905, after leaving school to work in a factory, he was sent to Siberia because of his political activities. He escaped from prison four years later.[1]

Baizerman then came to the United States, where he lived briefly with relatives in Boston before moving to New York. In the fall of 1910, he enrolled at the National Academy of Design to learn clay modeling. For nine years, beginning in 1911, he studied evenings at the Beaux-Arts Institute of Design (now the National Institute for Architectural Education) with the sculptor Solon Borglum (1868–1922) and the architect Lloyd Warren. In 1920 Baizerman won a competition for a Civil War monument but turned it down because he had become disillusioned with producing traditional academic sculpture. Instead, drawing upon his memories of the 1913 Armory Show, he began modeling a series of small stylized figures titled The City and the People. When the figures were cast in bronze, he was distressed to discover that the foundry workmen had smoothed the surface of the metal. Using a hammer to try to recover the lost texture, he discovered how responsive bronze is to hammering. He then tried hammering copper sheets—the medium of most of his subsequent work. At about this time, Baizerman married the painter Eugenie Silverman; and, during the next few years, they made several trips to Europe and one to Russia. In London in July 1924, the Dorien Leigh Galleries gave him his first solo exhibition (except for a 1921 show at his studio in New York). *Man with a Shovel* was shown in 1925 at the Salon des Indépendents in Paris.

The following year, the couple returned to New York. A fire in 1931 in his studio at Broadway and Sixty-fifth Street destroyed almost all of Baizerman's hammered copper sculpture. No photographs of the work had been taken. He did not sculpt for two years. Then, in 1933, he resumed work and exhibited small bronzes at the Eighth Street Gallery. His hammered copper sculpture was first exhibited in 1938 at the Artists' Gallery. From 1934 to 1940, he taught sculpture, drawing, and anatomy at the Baizerman Art School, which he and his wife operated in their Greenwich Village home/studio.

Eugenie, who had been a strong influence on her husband's life and work, died in 1949. That was the year in which Baizerman began to receive public recognition: the copper head *Silence,* 1936–37 (University of Minnesota Art Gallery, Minneapolis), won an honorable mention (a monetary award) at the 147th annual exhibition of the Pennsylvania Academy of the Fine Arts; *Slumber,* 1940–48, was purchased by the Whitney Museum of American Art, New York, which was the first institution to buy one of his hammered copper works; and the Philadelphia Art Alliance held a solo show of forty-three of his pieces. Baizerman had first exhibited at the Pennsylvania Academy in 1922, he participated regularly from 1934 to 1956, and a work was shown posthumously in 1958. Further recognition came in 1951 with a grant from the American Academy of Arts and Letters and in 1952 with the Pennsylvania Academy's purchase of *Ugesie* (q.v.) and the Guggenheim Foundation's award of a fellowship to assist in the completion of his large-scale groups of figures—the third and fourth Sculptural Symphonies. In 1953 a retrospective exhibition organized by the Walker Art Center, Minneapolis, traveled to Des Moines, San Francisco, and Ontario, Canada. At the time of his death, the

Institute of Contemporary Art, Boston, was organizing an exhibition of his sculpture. It was presented in his memory the following year.

Because Baizerman's work was independent of mainstream artistic movements, his contribution to American sculpture has become increasingly acclaimed with the passage of time.[2] He was an innovator in the technique of hammering copper into sculpture. Unfortunately, the toxic fumes from soldering the pieces together and the stress of constant noise may have hastened his death. Toward the end of his life, Baizerman said of his copper sculpture: "When [a piece] has taken away from me everything I have to give. When it has become stronger than myself. I become the empty one and it becomes the full one. When I am weak and it is strong the work is finished."[3]

Notes

1. Carl Goldstein, "The Sculpture of Saul Baizerman," *Arts* 51 (Sept. 1976), p. 122.
2. See, for example, reviews by Hilton Kramer: "Art," *Nation* (Feb. 9, 1963), pp. 127–28; "A Lost World," *New York Times,* Nov. 26, 1967, p. D-23; and "Show of Sculpture in the Heroic Style," *New York Times,* Jan. 22, 1972, p. 25.
3. Robert Goodnough, "Baizerman makes a sculpture," *Art News* 51 (March 1952), p. 67.

References

1952–57 Baizerman's journals, Special Collection, University of North Carolina, Greensboro. **1953** *Saul Baizerman,* exhib. cat., Minneapolis: Walker Art Center. **1975** Carl Goldstein, ed., "Saul Baizerman: The Journal, May 10, 1952," *Tracks* 1 (Spring), pp. 8–23. **1987** Melissa Dabakis, "The Sculpture of Saul Baizerman (1889–1957)," Ph.D. diss., Boston University. **1989** Melissa Dabakis, *Vision of Harmony: The Sculpture of Saul Baizerman,* Redding Ridge, Conn.: Black Swan Books.

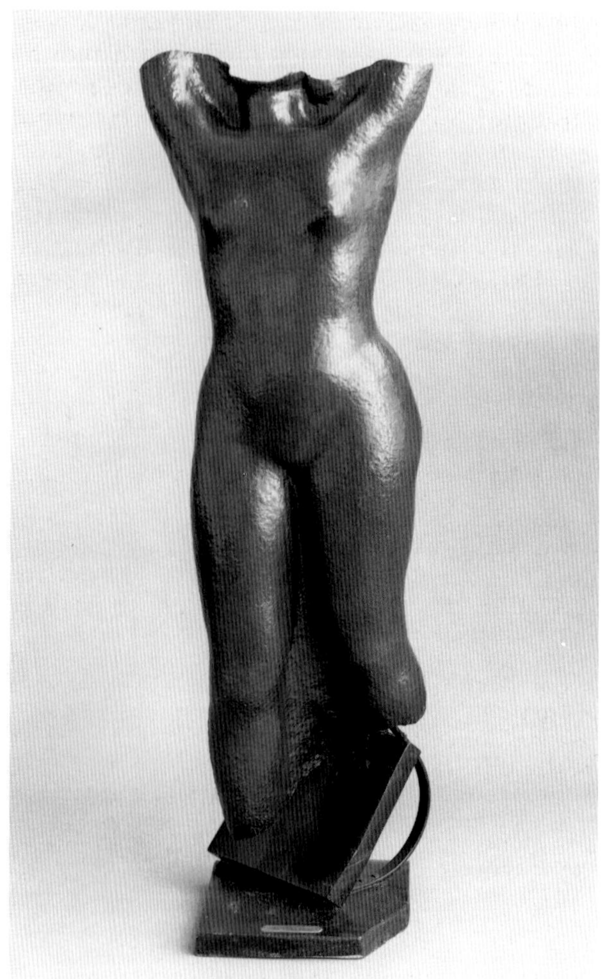

Baizerman, *Ugesie*

Ugesie

1939–40
Hammered copper
62 x 23 x 19¼" (157.5 x 58.4 x 48.9 cm)
Signed vertically at back: Baizerman
Henry D. Gilpin Fund, 1952.4

Ugesie, one of the sculptor's favorite works, depicts the torso of his teenage daughter, Ugesie (b. 1925/26), now known as Karen.[1] The forms of the hollow figure flow without emphasis on anatomical detail. The torso was hammered from a copper sheet.

Baizerman's method was to stabilize the copper sheet in a vertical position. He worked the metal according to a design in his mind without any preliminary drawings or sketches. Only details were modified later; the basic plan was never altered. The forms were established with the use of rubber and wooden mallets. Ear protectors were needed because of the loud noise. Gradually, the soft copper hardened under the stress of continuous hammer blows to both the front and the back of the sculpture. Baizerman did not anneal the copper as he worked, however, but learned to sense when the metal was near the breaking point. Occasionally splits did occur in *Ugesie,* especially near the edges of the back; and they were repaired with metal that was brazed to the copper. Natural patinas were then produced by the oxidation of the different metals. The surface that the sculptor tried to achieve in his hammered copper works can be compared to rippled seas or pitted stones.[2] Baizerman also designed the sculpture's two-part, black-painted wooden base with the attached curving steel straps.

Baizerman usually chose to sculpt the female figure, often a partial figure. His works straddle the boundary between sculpture in the round and relief.

Typically, he worked on several hammered copper works at one time. Each might take from two to seven years to complete. *Ugesie* was first exhibited in 1940 at the Whitney Museum of American Art, in New York. In a 1949 exhibition, the work was dated 1939–40.[3] The artist later mistakenly cited the date of execution as 1941.[4] When shown at the annual exhibition of the Pennsylvania Academy of the Fine Arts in 1952, *Ugesie* received the Alfred G.B. Steel Memorial Prize for the sculpture most deserving professional recognition for its distinction.

Notes

1. Saul Baizerman to Joseph T. Fraser, Jr., director of the PAFA, Jan. 30, 1952, PAFA object file.
2. *Saul Baizerman*, exhib. cat. (Minneapolis: Walker Art Center, 1953), p. 8.
3. *Fifth Summer Exhibition of Contemporary Art: Sculpture* (Iowa City: State University of Iowa, 1949), unpaginated.
4. Artist's response to PAFA questionnaire, May 2, 1952, PAFA object file.

References

1949 C. Ludwig Brummé, "Contemporary Sculpture: A Renaissance," *Magazine of Art* 42 (Oct.), p. 216 (ill.). **1950** Belle Krasne, "Art for Grants," *Art Digest* 25 (Dec. 15), p. 16 (ill.), as *Torso*. **1952** Dorothy Drummond, "Pennsylvania Academy Annual: Drastic Changes Due," *Art Digest* 26 (Feb. 1), pp. 8 (ill.), 27. **1953** Walker Art Center Calendar, Jan. (ill.). **1953** "Man with a Hammer," *Time* 61 (March 2), p. 62 (ill.).

Exhibited

1940 Whitney Museum of American Art, New York, *Annual Exhibition of Contemporary American Art*, cat. no. 114. **1948** Artists' Gallery, New York, *Baizerman: Paintings by Eugenie Baizerman and Sculpture by Saul Baizerman*, cat. no. 2. **1949** State University of Iowa, Iowa City, *Fifth Summer Exhibition of Contemporary Art: Sculpture*, cat. no. 5 (ill.). **1949** Philadelphia Art Alliance, *Saul Baizerman Sculpture*, cat. no. 15. **1950–51** American Academy of Arts and Letters, New York, *Exhibition of Works by Candidates for Grants in Art for the Year 1951*. **1951** Worcester Art Museum, Worcester, Mass., *Contemporary Art in the United States*, cat. no. 85. **1952*** cat. no. 231 (ill.). **1953** Walker Art Center, Minneapolis, *Saul Baizerman*, cat. no. 17. **1956** Artists' Gallery, New York, *Reunion on Lexington Avenue*. **1962** PAFA, *Forgotten Favorites: Selections from the Permanent Collection*. **1986–87** PAFA, *Sculpture at the Pennsylvania Academy of the Fine Arts*. **1994–96** PAFA, *Two Centuries of Collecting at the Museum of American Art*.

Ex Collection

The artist, 1940–52.

Carl Paul Jennewein

1890–1978

Carl Paul Jennewein was born in Stuttgart to Louis and Emilia Weber Jennewein. Louis was an engraver, who taught his trade to his son. At the age of thirteen, Carl left school for a three-year apprenticeship as a technician in a local museum. There he learned to model, cast in plaster, draw, and paint. He also attended classes in art history and architectural drawing at the University of Stuttgart.[1] Jennewein decided to go to New York after seeing images of buildings designed by McKim, Mead, and White. He arrived when he was sixteen and went to work for Buhler and Lauter, where his father had a friend. The firm made many of the sculptural decorations for buildings designed by McKim, Mead, and White. Meanwhile, Jennewein took drawing and painting classes at the Art Students League in the evenings. Soon he began to receive commissions for architectural ornament and mural decoration. For several years beginning in 1912, he traveled in France, Germany, Italy, and Egypt. In 1915 he became a United States citizen. The next year he was awarded a fellowship to study at the American Academy in Rome, where he remained until 1920. In Italy he met Gina Pirra, a painter and linguist, whom he married. Like Paul Manship (1885–1966), his predecessor at the American Academy, Jennewein was inspired by the classical sculpture of Italy and Greece. He determined to concentrate on sculpture from then on. His work combines simplified forms with elegant design and often includes portraits of his wife and children.

In 1920 he returned to New York and set up a studio. Shortly thereafter, he won commissions for the Darlington Memorial Fountain in Judiciary Square, Washington, D.C.; Pilgrim Memorial Fountain in Plymouth, Massachusetts; and the Barre War Memorial in Barre, Vermont. Within a few years, he received the most important commission of his career, for the west pediment and architectural ornament of the Philadelphia Museum of Art. He traveled in Greece with Charles Borie, one of the architects of the museum, to study surviving examples of polychromed architectural sculpture. Jennewein designed and executed a group of freestanding polychrome-glazed terracotta figures of Greek gods and goddesses. They represent Western Civilization and were installed in 1933. Leon V. Solon, an authority on ancient polychromy, advised on the use and placement of color in the composition. John Gregory (1879–1958) designed the east pediment, but it was never completed. A model is in the Philadelphia Museum of Art.

Jennewein's work was shown regularly at the annual exhibitions of the Pennsylvania Academy of the Fine Arts from 1924 to 1947. In 1926 *Nymph and Fawn* (Darlington Memorial Fountain) won the Academy's Fairmount Park Art Association Prize. *Indian and Eagle* was awarded the George D. Widener Memorial Gold Medal in 1932. It was later installed as the Tours War Memorial in Tours, France. In 1938 Jennewein exhibited the plaster for *The Spirit of Justice,* part of his commission for the interior and exterior decoration for the Department of Justice building in Washington, D.C.[2] At the next annual exhibition, Jennewein served as chairman of the jury of selection for sculpture and received the Pennsylvania Academy's medal of honor "in recognition of high achievement in his profession as a sculptor and for eminent services in the cause of art and the Academy."[3]

Jennewein was known for numerous collaborations with architects to produce sculpture in an architectural setting. His other commissions include eagles for the Arlington Memorial Bridge, in Washington, D.C.; The Soldiers and Sailors Memorial in Providence, Rhode Island; reliefs for the Education Building in Harrisburg; the Endecott Memorial in Boston; and reliefs over the entrances to the State Dining Room and the East Room of the White House. After his death in 1978, his estate of over two thousand drawings, paintings, plaster and bronze sculptures, and medals were given to the Tampa Museum, in Florida.

Jennewein, *Memory* (see also p. viii for color plate)

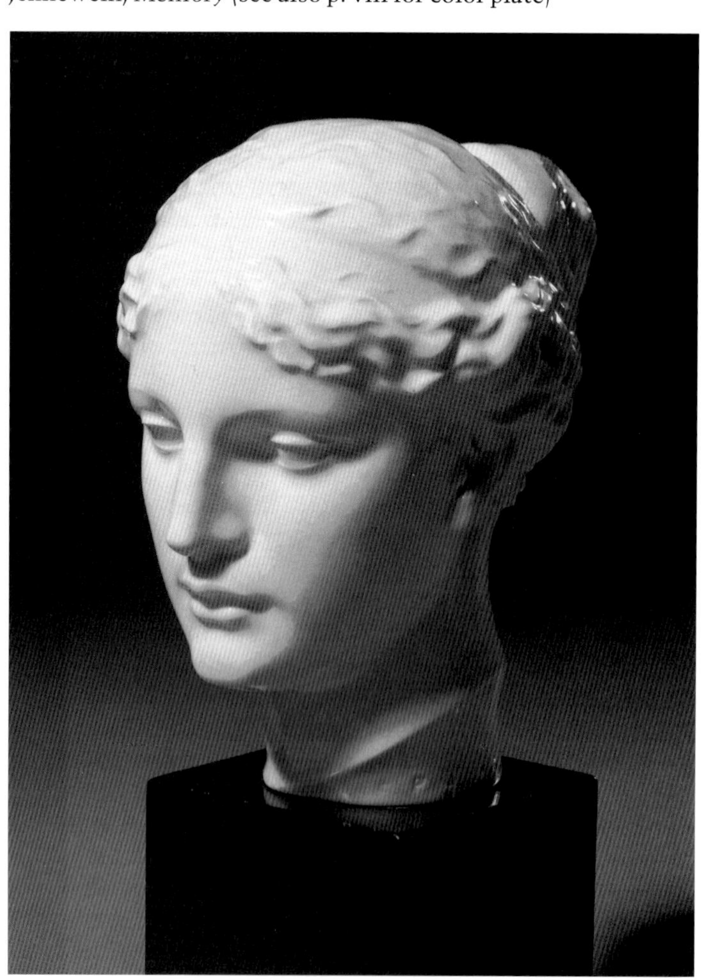

Notes

1. Conner and Rosenkranz 1989, p. 79.
2. The plaster (perhaps the full-size work, 12½ feet in height) was given to the Pennsylvania Academy at the close of the exhibition because the work had already been cast into its final form, in aluminum. The plaster was in use by drawing students until the summer of 1941, when it was destroyed. For details of the commission, see George Gurney, *Sculpture and the Federal Triangle* (Washington, D.C.: Smithsonian Institution Press, 1985), pp. 158–59, 163–96.
3. Minutes, meeting of the board of directors, Feb. 8, 1939, PAFA Archives.

References

Carl Paul Jennewein Papers, Archives of American Art, Smithsonian Institution, Washington, D.C. **1968** Beatrice Gilman Proske, *Brookgreen Gardens Sculpture,* Murrells Inlet, S.C.: Brookgreen Gardens, rev. ed., pp. 305–11. **1980** Shirley Reiff Howarth, *C. Paul Jennewein Sculptor,* Tampa: Tampa Museum. **1989** Janis Conner and Joel Rosenkranz, *Rediscoveries in American Sculpture: Studio Works, 1893–1939,* Austin: University of Texas Press. **1993** Robin R. Salmon, *Brookgreen Gardens Sculpture,* vol. 2, Murrells Inlet, S.C.: Brookgreen Gardens, pp. 56–64.

Memory

About 1928
Cream-white glazed porcelain; cast in 1935
10⅛ x 6⅞ x 9¼" (25.7 x 17.5 x 23.5 cm)
Signed and dated around left side and back of neck:
C.P. JENNEWEIN 1935
Cast by Somm Pottery in Tottenville, Staten Island, N.Y.
Joseph E. Temple Fund, 1936.11

Memory was probably modeled in either 1927 or 1929.[1] It was based on *Nymph and Fawn* (Darlington Memorial Fountain, Washington, D.C.), which was made in the early 1920s.[2] The head, similar to an idealized classical Greek sculpture, is elegant in form and simple in detail. The wistful facial expression implies reminiscence, a reference to the title. In the late 1920s and mid-1930s, Carl Paul Jennewein produced a series of such classical female heads. In about 1935, he began working with Walter Howat of the Somm Pottery in Tottenville, Staten Island, New York, to cast porcelain editions of the heads. The first two casts of *Memory,* of which this is one, were made between December 18, 1935, when the order was placed, and late January 1936, when they were to delivered.[3] The inscription was made by a signature die that the artist directed the craftsman to press into the wet clay. Five other porcelain casts were made in 1936. It may be that a total edition of ten were made.[4] Two casts were sold in 1947.[5] No other extant examples are known, and there may not be many because of their fragility. One was given by the artist to the American Academy and Institute of Arts and Letters, in New York, in 1938. It was later accidentally broken.

Another porcelain head, *Marietta,* is also a detail from an earlier full-length figure—the garden figure *Coral,* about 1928.[6] Jennewein was a proponent of porcelain casting into the 1940s. He helped found the Ceramic Center in New York.

In 1995 the head of *Memory* was installed on a cube of Nubian granite, similar to what the artist would have chosen, to replace a standard exhibition box of black painted wood.

Notes

1. Shirley Reiff Howarth, *C. Paul Jennewein Sculptor* (Tampa: Tampa Museum, 1980), p. 136, lists it in the chronology under 1927; whereas *C. Paul Jennewein* 1950, p. 21, gives the date as 1929. The inscription on the piece itself gives the date of casting.
2. Conner and Rosenkranz 1989, p. 86, n. 20.
3. Carl Paul Jennewein Papers, microfilm, roll no. 3323, frame nos. 126, 210.
4. Conner and Rosenkranz 1989, p. 86, n. 20.
5. Jennewein Papers, microfilm, roll no. 3324, frame no. 1270, has notations on a 1942 exhibition list.
6. Conner and Rosenkranz 1989, p. 86, n. 20.

References

1950 *C. Paul Jennewein,* Athens, Georgia: University of Georgia Press, published in collaboration with the National Sculpture Society as a part of The American Sculptors Series (p. 24 mistakenly cites *Greek Dance* as owned by the PAFA). **1989** Janis Conner and Joel Rosenkranz, *Rediscoveries in American Sculpture: Studio Works, 1893–1939,* Austin: University of Texas Press, pp. 83, 84 (ill.).

Exhibited

1936* cat. no. 349 (ill.). **1986–87** PAFA, *Sculpture at the Pennsylvania Academy of the Fine Arts.* **1995** Los Angeles County Museum of Art, *The Figure in American Sculpture: A Question of Modernity,* traveling exhib. cat., plate 54, p. 60.

The Hackney

1942
Bronze with black patina and gold leaf; cast in 1944
11½ x 11¼ x 3½" (29.2 x 28.6 x 8.9 cm)
Signed and dated on top of base in center: C.P. JENNEWEIN Sc./19©42

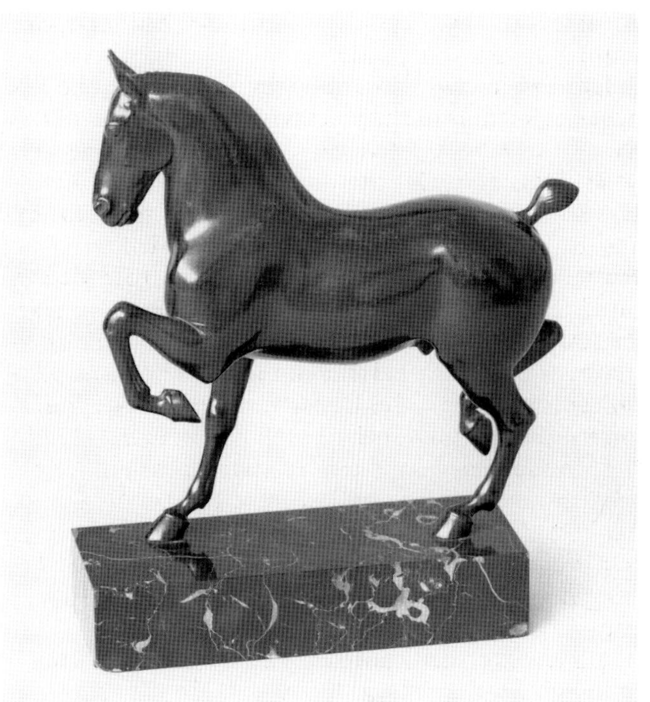

Jennewein, *The Hackney*

Lost-wax cast, probably by the Modern Art Foundry, New York
Henry D. Gilpin Fund, 1947.5

THIS HORSE is reminiscent of Renaissance statues in its regal appearance, as well as the elegant black patina with patches of red-brown and the gold leaf on the mane. Hackneys are large carriage horses. Their tails are clipped to keep them from getting caught in the vehicle. *The Hackney* captures the "high action" of the left front and right rear legs in trotting. The sculpture was the result of close observation of horses for several months and of helpful criticism offered by experts in judging horses. On June 24, 1942, Carl Paul Jennewein wrote to his friend the architect Charles Borie, "So, I am now making a horse, having only aesthetics in mind, which means, that I have to know as much as a taxidermist, but I must also leave out the non-essentials, in order to make it beautiful."[1] The cast owned by the Museum of American Art of the Pennsylvania Academy of the Fine Arts was probably the horse that Jennewein had cast in 1944 for fifty dollars at the Modern Art Foundry.[2] It was shown at the Century Association, in New York, in December 1946. Joseph T. Fraser, Jr., the director of the Pennsylvania Academy, and BRUCE MOORE saw it there and enthusiastically invited Jennewein to enter it in the upcoming Academy annual exhibition from which it was purchased.[3]

Pegasus, the winged horse, appears in many of Jennewein's classically inspired works, including an acroterion for the Philadelphia Museum of Art; the 1937 over-door relief, probably for the entrance to a residence, exhibited at the Pennsylvania Academy in 1939; the 1938–39 entrance pylons to the Brooklyn Public Library; and the announcement that he designed for his February 1936 exhibition at the Grand Central Art Galleries, in New York. These mythological horses are more idealized and less anatomically correct than *The Hackney.* A bronze *Pegasus* was apparently shown at the Philadelphia Art Alliance in 1946.[4] Jennewein retained his interest in horses, for in 1949 he designed the base for the trophy given to the winner of the Iroquois steeplechase in Nashville, Tennessee. He went there to see it awarded for the first time.[5]

Notes

1. Quoted in Howarth 1980, p. 53. Nearly two months earlier, Jennewein had been granted a copyright number: Copyright Office Remitter's Copy of Form, Receipt no. 27983, May 1, 1942, for "Horse 'Hackney'," Jennewein Papers, microfilm, roll no. 3324, frame no. 1346.

2. Jennewein Papers, microfilm, roll no. 3325, frame no. 1264.

3. Ibid., microfilm, roll no. 3326, frame no. 858.

4. Ibid., microfilm, roll no. 3325, frame no. 613.

5. "Sculptor Paul Jennewein To Attend Iroquois Here," *Nashville Morning Tennessean,* April 24, 1949, clipping file, PAFA Library.

References

1980 Shirley Reiff Howarth, *C. Paul Jennewein Sculptor,* Tampa: Tampa Museum, pp. 52–54, 137, 138, figs. 92, 110, 111. **1989** Janis Conner and Joel Rosenkranz, *Rediscoveries in American Sculpture: Studio Works, 1893–1939,* Austin: University of Texas Press, p. 84.

Exhibited

1945 National Academy of Design, N.Y., annual exhibition, cat. no. 16. **1946** Art Gallery, Century Association, N.Y. **1947*** cat. no. 217. **1970** Mississippi Art Association, exhibition in Old Capitol Museum, Jackson. **1970–71** PAFA, *200 Years of American Art* (traveling exhibition to seven southern museums). **1976** PAFA, *In This Academy,* cat. no. 286 (ill.). **1986–87** PAFA, *Sculpture at the Pennsylvania Academy of the Fine Arts.* **1989** PAFA, *"The Birds and the Beasts Will Teach Us."*

Robert Laurent

1890–1970

Robert Laurent was born in France, in the town of Concarneau, Brittany, an area rich in granite sculpture. His paternal grandfather was a weaver; his maternal grandfather, a fisherman. His father was a real estate agent. Robert was artistically inclined from an early age. When he was eleven years old, he met the American painter Hamilton Easter Field, who would radically change the boy's life.[1] Field had studied in Paris in the 1890s, developed a love of art history as well as modern art, and befriended many of the artists and writers of the day, including Gertrude and Leo Stein. In about 1901 when Field returned to the United States, the Laurent family accompanied him. They lived in Columbia Heights, New York, and spent summers in Ogunquit, Maine. Through Field's sponsorship, both areas would become artists' colonies. Laurent received some instruction in painting before he and his family returned to Brittany in 1904. Soon, through Field, he became an assistant to a Paris art dealer. While in Paris, Laurent became interested in sculpture after seeing the works of Aristide Maillol (1861–1944). Field decided to foster this interest by taking Laurent to Rome for several years. There Laurent took classes in drawing and perhaps in sculpture with the American painter, sculptor, and etcher Maurice Sterne (1878–1957), who was then living in Rome. Laurent learned to carve wood as an apprentice to the famous frame carver Giuseppe Doratori.

In 1910 Field and Laurent returned to the United States. Field began to promote the modern art emerging in Europe and established classes in New York and Maine. Laurent was enlisted as one of the teachers. He also made frames for the paintings of such artists as Childe Hassam, Robert Henri, and Leon Kroll. He decorated furniture in a low-relief style inspired by African sculpture and the work of Paul Gauguin. Field and Laurent often visited the renowned Armory Show in 1913 in New York. Among the works he saw there, Laurent was deeply moved by the sculptures of Wilhelm Lehmbruck (1881–1919), a German who was known for simplified female nudes. In 1915 Laurent's first major exhibition of wood carvings was held in New York. The critics, recognizing the uniqueness of his work, gave it favorable reviews. The Philadelphia collector and teacher Dr. Albert C. Barnes bought two reliefs from the show and ordered many frames. By 1917 Laurent had begun to carve wood in the round. In about 1919 he started carving in alabaster and other stones.

In 1917 Laurent became an American citizen. He enlisted in the Navy and was sent to Brittany to serve as an interpreter during World War I, and there he met his future wife. When Field died in 1922, Laurent became the sole heir to his property in New York and Maine. He helped establish the Hamilton Easter Field Foundation, which purchased works from many of the artists that Field had encouraged. (The collection is now in the Portland Museum of Art in Maine.)

Laurent chose early to concentrate on the female figure. He liked to work from live models and carve directly in wood or stone without preparing preliminary sketches. Translucent alabaster was one of his favorite materials. In the 1930s, he developed a technique of working in plaster that combined carving and modeling. It enabled him to work on a larger scale. One of his large plaster female nudes, *Reveil*, was soon purchased by the Whitney Museum of American Art, in New York. Laurent received commissions for public works, including the cast aluminum nude figure *The Goose Girl*, 1932, for Radio City Music Hall; *Spanning the Continent*, 1935, showing a man and a woman ploughing, for the Ellen Phillips Samuel Memorial in Philadelphia's Fairmount Park; a limestone relief, *Shipping*, 1938, for the Federal Trade Commission Building in Washington, D.C.; and two large-scale commissions, *The Hunt* and *Forester*, for the 1939 New York World's Fair. From 1934 to 1960, Laurent's work was shown regularly in the annual exhibitions of the Pennsylvania Academy of the Fine Arts.

For most of his career, the sculptor was also a teacher. He held classes in his studio in New York and in Ogunquit. For fifteen years at the Art Students League of New York, he taught one of the first classes in carving stone and wood. It was attended by CHAIM GROSS and CONCETTA SCARAVAGLIONE. In 1942, at the height of his career, Laurent accepted a position at Indiana University in Bloomington, originally a one-year appointment that was extended for eighteen years. His contract combined teaching and producing carvings for the school in Indiana limestone. Like alabaster and plaster, it could be carved with relative ease and it allowed him to work on a large scale. In the 1950s, he traveled to Paris and several times to Rome on sabbatical leaves. He was a sculptor-in-residence at the American Academy in Rome, and his sculpture *Birth of Venus* for the Showalter Fountain at Indiana University was cast there. Laurent retired in 1960. The following year, before he moved to Maine, a retrospective exhibition was held at Indiana University. In 1970 Laurent was elected a member of the National Institute of Arts and Letters, New York. The Robert Laurent catalogue raisonné project is underway at Rutgers University, in Camden, New Jersey, under the direction of Roberta K. Tarbell.

Note

1. For more information on Field and Laurent, see Doreen Bolger, "Hamilton Easter Field and His Contribution to American Modernism," *American Art Journal* 20, no. 2 (1988), pp. 79–107.

References

1961 *Laurent: Fifty Years of Sculpture*, Bloomington: Indiana University. **1972** *Robert Laurent Memorial Exhibition*, New York: Kraushaar Galleries. **1972** *The Robert Laurent Memorial Exhibition*, Durham: University of New Hampshire, exhibition traveled to University of North Carolina at Greensboro, Delaware Art Museum, and Indianapolis Museum of Art. **1984** Wayne Craven, *Sculpture in America*, Newark, Del.: University of Delaware Press, pp. 573–76.

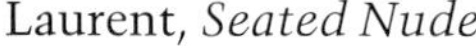
Laurent, *Seated Nude*

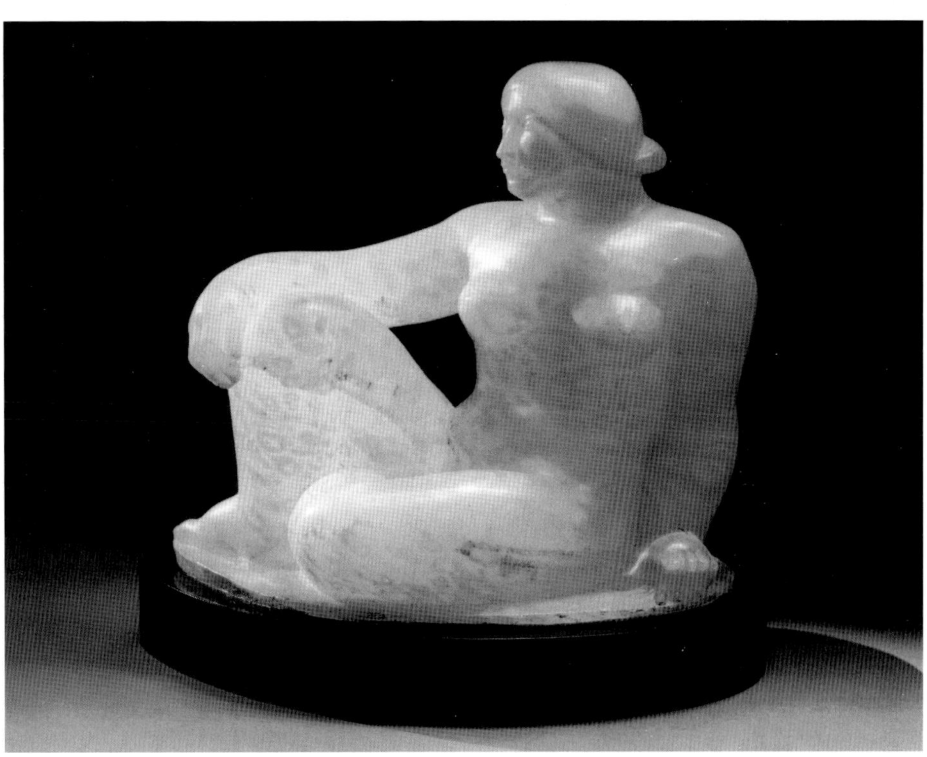

Seated Nude

1940
Alabaster
14¼ x 14½ x 9" (36.1 x 36.9 x 22.9 cm)
Signed on self-base at back: LAURENT
Henry D. Gilpin Fund, 1947.6

ROBERT LAURENT, like HENRY CLEWS, JR. and Edward Fenno Hoffman III (1916–1991), enjoyed working in alabaster. He liked its translucency when carved and polished. Between 1920 and 1970, Laurent made about fifty alabaster sculptures, more than any other American sculptor.[1] Many were figures of women, or mothers and children. They were carved in solid voluminous forms as in *Seated Nude.* Unlike his earlier alabaster carvings, this one has a hollow beneath the figure's right arm that allows more interplay of light and form. This work has the pronounced eyelids that Laurent used on most of his figures, probably based on the Etruscan sculptures that he must have seen in Rome. The sculpture is mounted on a black marble base.

Note

1. *Vanguard American Sculpture, 1913–1939* (New Brunswick, N.J.: Rutgers University Art Gallery, 1979), p. 48.

Reference

1984 Wayne Craven, *Sculpture in America,* Newark, Del: University of Delaware Press, pp. 575–76, 607, fig. 15.12.

Exhibited

1941 Valentine Gallery, New York, one-man show. **1944** John Herron Art Museum, Indiana University, Bloomington, *Sculpture by Robert Laurent and Others.* **1947*** cat. no. 144. **1974** Provident National Bank, Philadelphia, exhibition of PAFA works. **1974** PAFA, Peale House, *Selected Works from the Academy's 20th-Century Collection of Paintings and Sculpture.* **1976** PAFA, *In This Academy,* cat. no. 289, pp. 227–28, 309–10. **1986–87** PAFA, *Sculpture at the Pennsylvania Academy of the Fine Arts.* **1990** Hofstra Museum, Hofstra University, Hempstead, N.Y., *The Coming of Age of American Sculpture: The First Decades of the Sculptors Guild, 1930s–1950s.* **1992** Council for Creative Projects, Davis, Calif., *The Coming of Age . . . , traveling exhibition.* **1994–96** PAFA, *Two Centuries of Collecting at the Museum of American Art.*

JACQUES LIPCHITZ

1891–1973

Chaim Jacob Lipchitz was born in Druskieniki, Lithuania, and began carving figures in bread and clay at the age of thirteen. His mother encouraged his artistic pursuits; but his father, a building contractor, wanted him to become an architect or engineer. In 1909 he went to Paris, where he studied sculpture and drawing at the Ecole des Beaux-Arts and the Académie Julian. Upon his arrival in Paris, Lipchitz was given the name *Jacques* when he was issued an identification card. Soon he was introduced to avant-garde art by artists such as Diego Rivera, Amedeo Modigliani, Pablo Picasso, and Juan Gris. Rebelling against his own academic training, Lipchitz began to make cubist-inspired sculpture.

In 1920 he modeled a series of portraits, including one of Jean Cocteau (private collection) and perhaps two of Gertrude Stein (one is in the Baltimore Museum of Art). He was also given his first solo exhibition in Paris. Two years later, he met Dr. Albert C. Barnes, who encouraged him, bought several important sculptures, and commissioned five reliefs for his home (now the Barnes Foundation, Merion, Pennsylvania). Lipchitz became a French citizen in 1924 and was married soon after. He commissioned a house from his friend the architect Le Corbusier. Lipchitz began producing open-form sculptures that he called "transparents." They were cast in bronze by the lost-wax method. Some large-scale compositions were commissioned. Usually figurative, the works were often based on biblical or classical themes. Lipchitz's first retrospective exhibition was held in Paris in 1930. American critics saw his work in a solo show at the Brummer Gallery in New York in 1935 and recognized his original contribution to modern sculpture. At the 1937 Paris World's Fair, his large-scale commission *Prometheus* was prominently displayed.

During World War II, Lipchitz and his wife were forced to flee Paris, and in 1941 they settled in New York. With the help of friends and the American Rescue Committee, he was soon able to set up a studio and produce works for a successful show at the Buchholz Gallery in 1942. His sculptural themes drew upon the world political situation and emotional events in his life. After the war, the couple returned briefly to Paris, where he had an exhibition and was made a chevalier of the Legion of Honor.

At the 1952 annual exhibition of the Pennsylvania Academy of the Fine Arts, Lipchitz was awarded the George D. Widener Memorial Gold Medal for *Pro-*

metheus Strangling the Vulture.[1] This recasting of the Greek myth, reversing the role of victim, had been depicted by Lipchitz several times since 1931. A few days after the sculpture was shipped to the Academy, a fire destroyed his Manhattan studio and the early models for his 1950 commission for the Ellen Phillips Samuel Memorial in Fairmount Park. (It was eventually completed as *The Spirit of Enterprise* and installed in 1960.) While his new studio was being built at his home in Hastings-on-Hudson, New York, he used a studio at the Modern Art Foundry in Astoria, Long Island, where he experimented with the casting of small, spontaneously modeled sculptures in bronze. A traveling retrospective exhibition originated at the Museum of Modern Art, in New York, in 1954; another major exhibition toured Europe in 1958. His *Mother and Child,* about 1949 (unlocated), received the Alfred G.B. Steel Memorial Prize at the Pennsylvania Academy's 1956 annual exhibition. Lipchitz became an American citizen in 1958.

In the 1960s, Lipchitz spent his summers in Pietrasanta, Italy, casting his work in bronze at the Tommasi Foundry. Two major retrospective exhibitions traveled in 1963–64; one of 150 sculptures and drawings was seen on the east coast at the Philadelphia Museum of Art. In 1972 the Metropolitan Museum of Art held a major show, *My Life in Sculpture.* It was only a year before his death, but Lipchitz was busy with large-scale commissions: *Government for the People* (installed in 1976) for the plaza of the Municipal Services Building in Philadelphia, *Bellerophon Taming Pegasus* (installed in 1977) for Columbia University Law School, and *Our Tree of Life* (installed in 1978) for Hadassah University Hospital at Mount Scopus in Jerusalem.

In 1990 and 1991, *Jacques Lipchitz: A Life in Sculpture,* organized by Alan G. Wilkinson of the Art Gallery of Ontario in Toronto, traveled in Canada and the United States.

Note

1. The 1943–44 plaster sculpture was purchased by the Philadelphia Museum of Art, cast into bronze at the Modern Art Foundry, and installed at the east entrance of the museum. For a discussion of this and Lipchitz's other Prometheus sculptures, see John Tancock, "Prometheus Strangling the Vulture and The Spirit of Enterprise," in *Sculpture of a City: Philadelphia's Treasures in Bronze and Stone* (New York: Walker Publishing Company, 1974), pp. 258–65. Another bronze cast is at the Walker Art Center in Minneapolis.

References

1984 Wayne Craven, *Sculpture in America,* Newark, Del.: University of Delaware Press, pp. 616–23. **1989** Alan G. Wilkinson, *Jacques Lipchitz: A Life in Sculpture,* Toronto: Art Gallery of Ontario.

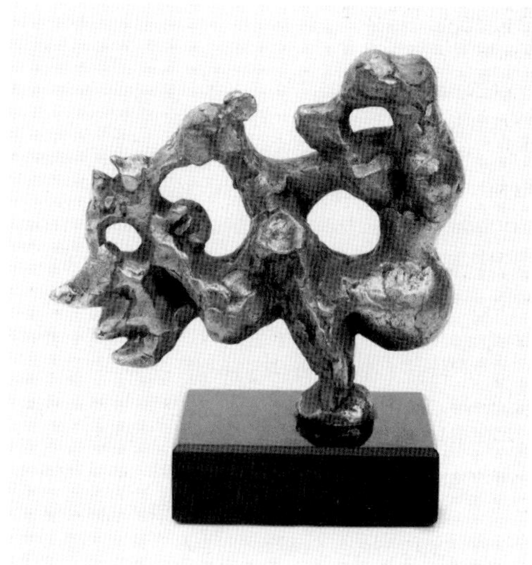

Lipchitz, *Untitled*

Untitled

Probably about 1945
Bronze with gilding
6 x 6¾ x 2½" (15.2 x 17.2 x 6.4 cm)
Signed on back: *J Lipchit[z]*
Lost-wax cast, probably by the Modern Art Foundry, New York
Gift of James P. and Ruth M. Magill, 1957.15.16

Jacques Lipchitz created small sculptures like this as a diversion while he was working on monumental commissions. This sketch came to the Museum of American Art of the Pennsylvania Academy of the Fine Arts with very little information, and efforts to identify the subject have been inconclusive.[1] The closest parallel is his *Mother and Child,* 1945 (unlocated) a 5¾-inch figure of similar silhouette.[2] The Museum's sculpture balances on a sphere as does *Prometheus Strangling the Vulture,* 1943–44 (Philadelphia Museum of Art). The extended arm could be grasping a baby as in a mother and child theme, or it might be holding a dagger that pierces either a head or a winged creature, such as a vulture.

In the 1940s and 1950s, Lipchitz often modeled spontaneously in wax and had the wax sculpture cast directly into bronze. Only a single work resulted from this method. When multiples were desired, Lipchitz would model in clay and have a craftsman cast the clay sculpture into plaster and the plaster into wax. The sculptor could then refine the surface by means of a hot spatula, and bits of wax could be added where needed. It is not known which method was used for this sculpture. Lipchitz's fingerprints can be seen everywhere, including the two wax "mushrooms," as he called them, that are adjacent to his signature.[3] His usual practice was to inscribe the edition number on a mushroom, but this piece does not have a number. He ordinarily cast in editions of seven, but this is said to be from an edition of five. No other examples are known to exist. This fact and the lack of an inscribed edition number may indeed mean that the sculpture is a unique cast. It is mounted on a black marble base.

One of the donors, James P. Magill, was a member of the board of directors of the Pennsylvania Academy from 1951 to 1962. He served on numerous committees, including the committee on collections and exhibitions. In 1957, when they donated this piece, he and his wife deeded their entire art collection to the Academy. Most of the paintings and sculpture remained in their possession until Mr. Magill's death in 1974.

Notes

1. James P. Magill and Ruth Marshall Magill Personal Property List, dated Dec. 13, 1957, p. 15, gives this description: "Bronze Sculpture, Jacques Lipchitz, 6", Free form golden bronze group, Edition of 5, Signed, Black enameled plinth," Magill Gift and Bequests file, PAFA Archives.

2. Jeanne L. Wasserman, Fogg Art Museum, Cambridge, to Susan James-Gadzinski, April 19, 1985, PAFA research file. *Mother and Child* is illustrated in H.H. Arnason, *Jacques Lipchitz: Sketches in Bronze* (New York: Frederick A. Praeger, 1969), fig. 132.

3. Eleanor C. Munro, "Sculptor in the Foundry: Lipchitz at Work," *Art News* 55 (March 1956), p. 30.

Exhibited

1958 PAFA, *Twentieth Century American Painting and Sculpture from Philadelphia Private Collections,* checklist no. 230, as *Golden Figure.*

Ex Collection

James P. and Ruth M. Magill, about 1945–74.

Isidore Binswanger

1891–1955

Isidore Binswanger was born in Cape May, New Jersey. He was educated in Philadelphia at the William Penn Charter School and at the Wharton School of the University of Pennsylvania, where he earned a business degree. At the death of his father in about 1914, he became president of the family business, the Thomas Porcelite Paint Company. In the 1920s, while recovering from surgery, he began to model in clay. Sculpture became his avocation. For several years about 1927, he took sculpture classes at the Graphic Sketch Club (now the Samuel S. Fleisher Art Memorial). Soon afterwards, he modeled busts of family members. In 1934 he studied at Temple University's Tyler School of Art with the painter Furman Joseph Finck, who had attended the Pennsylvania Academy of the Fine Arts in the 1920s. Several undated impressionistic landscapes by Binswanger in the collection of his descendants may date from this period. Later, he studied with the sculptor Boris Blai (1898–1985), who had founded the Tyler School of Art, and with ALEXANDER PORTNOFF.

Binswanger's commissioned portrait of the Philadelphia lawyer Robert B. Wolf was his first work to be cast in bronze.[1] It was shown in 1940 at the Fairmount Park Art Association's *Second Sculpture International,* held at the Philadelphia Museum of Art. His 1936 bust of Harry B. Hirsh, also commissioned, was shown in 1938 in the Pennsylvania Academy's 133rd annual exhibition, in 1939 in the exhibition *American Art Today* at the New York World's Fair, and 1940 in the *Second Sculpture International* in Philadelphia.[2]

While living in Longport, New Jersey, Binswanger kept a studio in Philadelphia in the former home of the conductor Leopold Stokowski.

Notes

1. The bronze is in the collection of the sitter, and the plaster is owned by Carole I. Binswanger, according to her 1985 chronological list of her father's work, PAFA research file.

2. The bronze was in a private collection in Palermo, Italy, in July 1954. Its present whereabouts is unknown according to Carole Binswanger's list, ibid.

Judge Theodore Rosen

1939
Plaster, painted green
16¼ x 10½ x 9¾" (41.3 x 26.7 x 24.7 cm)
Signed on back of base: BIN
Gift of Alfred Bendiner, 1962.1

ISIDORE BINSWANGER had apparently often asked his friend Theodore Rosen (1895–1940) to sit for a portrait.[1] Rosen was a prominent Philadelphia lawyer, who had been educated at the University of Pennsylvania. He served as an assistant district attorney, a judge in the Municipal Court, and, from 1938 until his death, a judge in the Court of Common Pleas. In World War I, he had been decorated for outstanding bravery after a mission that cost him an arm and an eye.

According to the Philadelphia artist Alfred Bendiner, who knew both men, Binswanger "caught the spirit of [Rosen] through a broken frame."[2] The bust

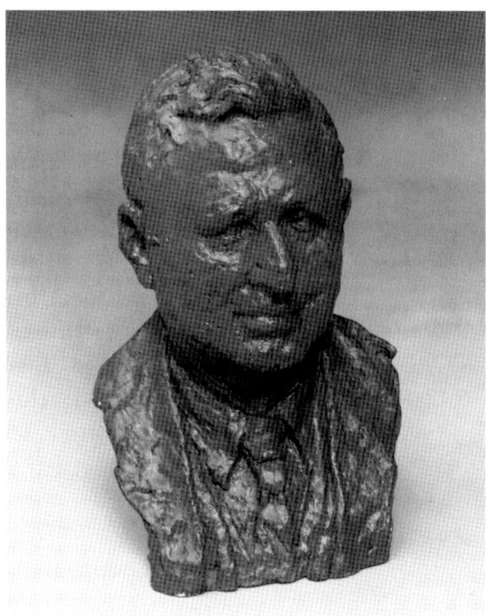

Binswanger, *Judge Theodore Rosen*

has the heavily textured surface that was characteristic of Binswanger's work and a thick overall coat of green paint, probably intended to simulate bronze. After Judge Rosen's death, his widow had the bust cast in bronze (location unknown). The bronze was exhibited in 1940 in the *Second Sculpture International* of the Fairmount Park Art Association. Of the two plasters that were made, this one was presented to Binswanger's friend Alfred Bendiner; the other was kept by the sculptor and is now owned by one of his daughters.

Notes

1. Esther K. Rosen to Joseph T. Fraser, Jr., director of the PAFA, Feb. 9, 1962, PAFA object file, gives biographical information.

2. Alfred Bendiner to Joseph T. Fraser, Jr., [Dec. 1961], PAFA object file, has an ink drawing of Bendiner offering the bust.

Reference

1962 "At the Academy," *Philadelphia Jewish Exponent*, May 18, p. 39 (ill.).

Ex Collection

Alfred Bendiner, gift from the artist, about 1940–61.

Oronzio Maldarelli

1892–1963

Born in Naples, Oronzio Maldarelli was the son of a goldsmith, Michael Maldarelli, and his wife, Louisa Rizzo Maldarelli. The family immigrated to New York in 1900. At the age of fourteen, Oronzio began attending evening art classes in drawing and painting at Cooper Union. After two years, he was admitted to the National Academy of Design, where he took classes in life drawing and studied sculpture with Hermon Atkins MacNeil (1866–1947). When he was seventeen, Maldarelli entered an apprenticeship with a jeweler, which enabled him to support his art training. In 1912 he began seven years of evening studies in sculpture at the Beaux-Arts Institute of Design (now the National Institute of Architectural Education) with Solon Borglum (1868–1922) and visiting artists, such as JO DAVIDSON, John Gregory (1879–1958), EDWARD MCCARTAN, and Elie Nadelman (1885–1964). Maldarelli became an American citizen in 1920.

Archaic and classical Greek sculpture inspired Maldarelli's early works. His first commission was for figures of Charity and Labor for a municipal building in Plainfield, New Jersey. In 1930 he won the Fairmount Park Art Association prize for "best decorative group for garden, park, or outdoor placement" for a realistic female figure, *Resignation* (location unknown) at the Sculpture-in-the-Open-Air exhibition in Rittenhouse Square in Philadelphia. A Guggenheim Fellowship enabled him to travel to Paris from 1931 to 1933. There, while associating with Heinz Warneke (1895–1983) and other American sculptors, he absorbed cubism and abstraction. A second Guggenheim Fellowship in 1943 would take him to Rome and Florence. The work done in Paris was shown in 1933 at his first one-man exhibition, at the Midtown Galleries in New York; another solo show was held there in 1948. Maldarelli soon combined abstraction with figuration to produce simplified, voluptuous images of nude females, often in pairs. His preference was for direct carving in stone or wood, although he also hammered in lead and modeled in clay, which was then either fired or cast into bronze. Sometimes, working from a live model, he produced drawings or small sketches in clay that he then enlarged and transformed from memory. A model might also be used at this stage, so that details could be clarified. Although he was not interested in capturing likenesses, Maldarelli usually used the proper names of female friends as the titles of his works.[1]

In 1935 he was awarded the commission for *Air-*

mail Pilot in a competition for twelve historical figures for the Postmaster General's reception room in the Department of the Post Office Building, Washington, D.C.[2] He also produced commissions for the Irish and French buildings at the New York World's Fair,[3] the New York City Housing Authority, the Towle Silver Company in Boston, the Public Library in Hartford, and a Madonna for Saint Patrick's Cathedral in New York. Maldarelli exhibited his work widely. It was shown at the New York World's Fair of 1939 and the Sculpture Internationals of 1940 and 1949 at the Philadelphia Museum of Art. It was also entered regularly in the annual exhibitions of the Pennsylvania Academy of the Fine Arts from 1927 to 1964. He was awarded the George D. Widener Memorial Gold Medal for *Bianca #2,* the most meritorious work in the 1951 annual exhibition.[4] In 1954 *Mountain Mother* won the Pennsylvania Academy's Garden Sculpture Prize for the "best work of sculpture suitable for a small garden" and in 1956 *Nahomi* won an honorable mention (both, location unknown). In 1959 and posthumously in 1963, solo exhibitions were held at the Paul Rosenberg and Company gallery in New York. Maldarelli was included in a 1966 show of works by former chairmen of juries for the annual exhibitions in the Pennsylvania Academy's Peale House galleries. His sculpture is in Brookgreen Gardens, Murrells Inlet, South Carolina; the Newark Museum; the Whitney Museum of American Art, New York; the Art Institute of Chicago; the Museum of Art, Ogunquit, Maine; and the Saint Louis Art Museum.

For about twenty-five years, Maldarelli taught sculpture at Columbia University and at Sarah Lawrence College, Bronxville, New York. His classes at Columbia were like a three-year apprenticeship in which the students learned by watching the master work and, as their skills developed, they assisted him. He made them begin by carving stone; only later could they proceed to modeling clay. He discouraged heavy reliance on the live model and urged his students to work from memory. Maldarelli retired from teaching in 1961. He continued to live and work in New York and Townshend, Vermont. He died of a heart attack while at work, carving marble.

Notes

1. "Woman on a Pedestal," *Time,* Nov. 15, 1948, p. 82.
2. For information, see George Gurney, *Sculpture and the Federal Triangle* (Washington, D.C.: Smithsonian Institution Press, 1985), pp. 296–322.
3. Ralph M. Pearson, *The Modern Renaissance in American Art Presenting the Work and Philosophy of Fifty-Four Distinguished Artists* (New York: Harper and Brothers, 1954), p. 261.
4. It was purchased by the Metropolitan Museum of Art, New York. Other known casts are in the Virginia Museum of Fine Arts, Richmond; and the National Museum of American Art, Washington, D.C. Several bronze casts were made of a nine-inch-high study for this work. One is in the Hirshhorn Museum and Sculpture Garden, Washington, D.C.

References

1940 Virginia Murphy, "An Interview with Oronzio Maldarelli Sculptor," *Art Education Today,* pp. 39–42. **1948** Ernest W. Watson, "Oronzio Maldarelli," *American Artist* 12 (March), pp. 35–39, 54. **About 1952** "Oronzio Maldarelli," *Amerika Illustrated,* no. 47, pp. 56–59 (in Russian, published by the U.S. Department of State). **1963** Henry Allen Moe, "A Letter to Oronzio Maldarelli," *National Sculpture Review,* 12 (Spring), pp. 14–15. **1968** Beatrice Gilman Proske, *Brookgreen Gardens Sculpture,* Murrells Inlet, S.C.: Brookgreen Gardens, rev. ed., pp. 428–31.

Gemini #2

1947–48
Marble
31½ x 23½ x 13" (80 x 59.7 x 33.1 cm)
Signed on front at lower right: O. MALDARELLI
Henry D. Gilpin Fund, 1949.8

WITH MARBLE, Oronzio Maldarelli said, "you can play a chisel as a musician plays an instrument."[1]

Maldarelli, *Gemini #2*

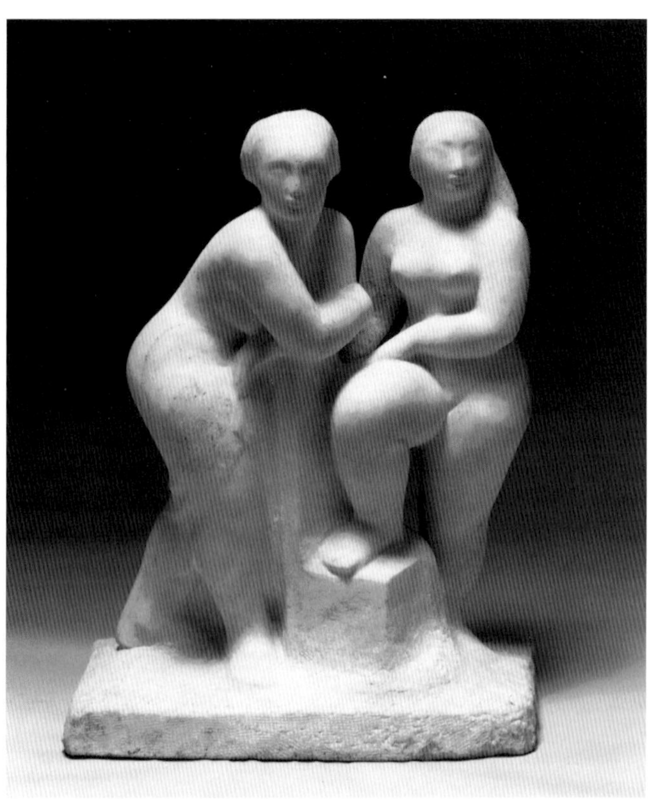

Gemini #2 was carved in his favorite kind of marble, which he called Milano, presumably because it was quarried in Italy, near Milan. This particular piece has prominent veins of iron pyrites, which create gray lines and patches that accentuate the form of the sculpture and create visual interest. The skin of the two figures was polished smooth, areas of the hair and drapery were given texture with a toothed chisel, and the base was left rough.

Maldarelli created a large-scale bronze group, *Gemini #1,* 1943 (location unknown).[2] A small study was made for each *Gemini:* the study for *Gemini #1* is bronze and 7″ high, and the one for *Gemini #2* is terracotta and 9½″ high (both, location unknown). It is likely that the sculpture at the Museum of American Art of the Pennsylvania Academy of the Fine Arts resembles its study very closely because a 1948 photograph shows the sculptor measuring with calipers while carving *Gemini #2*.[3] In this work, one can see that Maldarelli closely followed his maxim of trying "to create form, beautiful harmonies of shapes."[4] Details, such as facial features, hands, and feet, are subtly delineated.

The title *Gemini* refers to the constellation in the Northern Hemisphere that contains the twin stars Castor and Pollux, named after Zeus's twin sons in Greek mythology. Maldarelli made the twins female, for his interest was in the female figure.

Notes

1. "'The Only True Mission,' " *Time,* March 29, 1963, p. 68.
2. It was exhibited at the 1946 annual exhibition of the Pennsylvania Academy of the Fine Arts and at the *Third Sculpture International,* in 1949, held at the Philadelphia Museum of Art and sponsored by the Fairmount Park Art association, which purchased the work. On loan to the Philadelphia Museum of Art and displayed outdoors on the East Terrace, it was discovered missing in May 1972.
3. *American Artist* 12 (March 1948), p. 35.
4. "Woman on a Pedestal," *Time,* Nov. 15, 1948, p. 82.

Reference

1948 Ernest W. Watson, "Oronzio Maldarelli," *American Artist* 12 (March), p. 35 (ill., work in progress).

Exhibited

1948 Midtown Galleries, New York, *Oronzio Maldarelli.* **1949*** cat. no. 119. **1959** Paul Rosenberg and Company, New York, *An Exhibition of Sculpture (1948–1958) by Oronzio Maldarelli,* cat. no. 8 (ill.). **1993** PAFA, *Carved in Wood and Stone: Twentieth-Century Sculpture.*

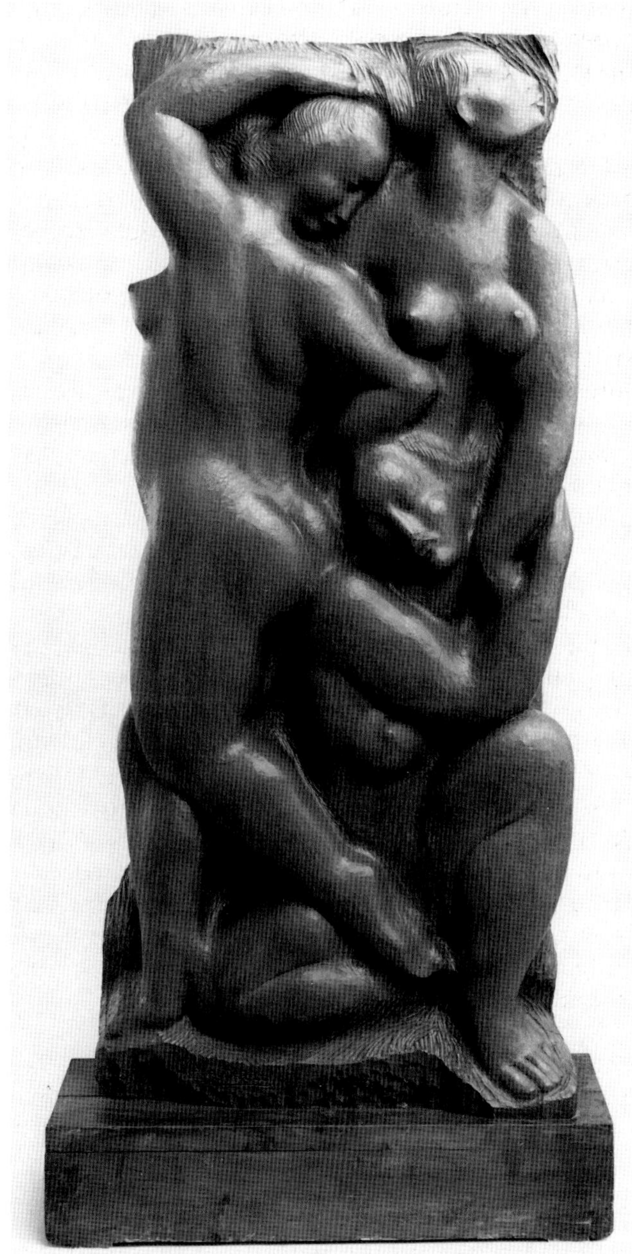

Maldarelli, *Triad*

Triad

1950
Mahogany
77½ x 36½ x 13¼″ (196.9 x 92.7 x 33.7 cm)
Signed on front at lower left: O. MALDARELLI
Gift of Abner Schreiber, Mae Martin, and Inez Bock in memory of Oronzio and Tillie Maldarelli, 1968.15

EARLY in his career, Oronzio Maldarelli became interested in African carvings. They probably influenced his later large-scale wood carvings like *Triad.*

It was carved from a single block of mahogany, a red-brown tropical hardwood, that came from Honduras. He once said, "Wood is a lot of fun. It is warm and friendly, fights less."[1] *Triad,* as its title implies, incorporates three women, two standing and one crouching, in a compact arrangement of limbs and forms. Like *Gemini #2* (q.v.), the facial features, hands, and feet in *Triad* are given only minor importance. Instead, figural form is emphasized by an overall faceting and texture is created by deeper gouges in the background and the hair. The base is a separate piece of wood, probably pine that has been stained.

Triad was shown in the controversial exhibition *American Sculpture 1951* at the Metropolitan Museum of Art, New York. One critic said that this sculpture was one of the few that gave her pleasure.[2] *Triad* won a medal at the Architectural League of New York in the mid-1950s. It was lent to the Pennsylvania Academy of the Fine Arts for four years and then donated to the Academy in 1968 in memory of the sculptor and his wife, Tillie, by their heirs. Another large relief by Maldarelli is *Dancers,* 1943 (Munson-Williams-Proctor Institute, Utica, N.Y.). It is carved of Slavic oak, stands 74¾ inches high, and incorporates two female figures.

Notes

1. Ernest W. Watson, "Oronzio Maldarelli," *American Artist* 12 (March 1948), p. 54.
2. Emily Genauer, "Art and Artists: Museum's Vast Scheme for Sculpture Show Ends in a Mediocre Display," *New York Herald Tribune,* Dec. 1951, microfilm, roll no. 1625, frame no. 289, Concetta Scaravaglione Papers, Archives of American Art, Smithsonian Institution, Washington, D.C.

Reference

1951 Howard Dupree, "Sculpture Again: The Metropolitan Permanent Collection as Background to the Current Show," *New York Times,* Dec. 16, sec. 2, p. 12 (ill.).

Exhibited

1951–52 Metropolitan Museum of Art, New York, *American Sculpture 1951,* pl. no. 20. **1953*** cat. no. 210. **1956** Village Art Center, New York, *Invitation Exhibition Honoring our Sculpture Jurors,* cat. no. 17. **1959** Paul Rosenberg and Company, New York, *An Exhibition of Sculpture (1948–1958) by Oronzio Maldarelli,* cat. no. 11. **1972** PAFA, *Acres of Art,* cat. no. 62. **1986–87** PAFA, *Sculpture at the Pennsylvania Academy of the Fine Arts.* **1993** PAFA, *Carved in Wood and Stone: Twentieth-Century Sculpture.*

Ex Collections

The artist, 1950–63; his heirs, 1963–68 (on loan to the Pennsylvania Academy, 1964–68).

Cornelia Chapin

1893–1972

Cornelia van Auken Chapin was born in Waterford, Connecticut, near her family's summer home in New London. Early in her studies at private schools in New York, she showed an interest in drawing and painting and was also encouraged to model in clay. The Egyptian collection at the Metropolitan Museum of Art particularly impressed her.[1] In the early 1920s, she studied sculpture with Gail Sherman Corbett (1871–1952), who had been a student of AUGUSTUS SAINT-GAUDENS. In 1934 Cornelia Chapin traveled to Paris and studied stone-carving with the renowned Spanish animal sculptor Mateo Hernández (1885–1949). She spent much of her time at the Vincennes Zoo, where she carved stones set on a pushcart. In 1936 *Tortoise* (Brooklyn Museum, New York), in volcanic rock, was exhibited at the Salon d'Automne, which elected her a member. In 1937 Chapin was awarded the Second Grand Prize in stone sculpture by a jury of forty-three nations at the Paris International Exposition of Art and Techniques. By 1938 she had returned to New York and was sculpting at the Bronx Zoo. She exhibited the same year in the first show of the Sculptors Guild. In addition, she was given an exhibition at the Fifteen Gallery in New York. Her mentor Mateo Hernández praised her in the catalogue as a woman "who has had the daring, the admirable energy and discipline to practice the technique of direct carving from life in blocks of hard stone and wood." He commented further that "her figures have each a distinct personality, the essential quality of each individual type. . . . Her work has warmth, humor, a classic simplicity and purity of impulse. She has made no false effort to compose but rather to choose, in all humility, that natural rhythm which best conveys the quality of life itself."[2]

Cornelia Chapin participated in the annual exhibitions of the Pennsylvania Academy of the Fine Arts in 1932, 1938, and from 1942 to 1951. During World War II, she served as sculpture chairman of the Artists for Victory, a relief agency formed by twenty-one New York art organizations. From 1951 to 1953, she was the sculpture member of the Art Commission of the City of New York. She lectured and demonstrated direct carving at museums and schools for many years. From the 1940s until her death, she shared a Manhattan studio with the sculptor MARION SANFORD.

Cornelia Chapin's *Giant Frog,* 1937–38, was installed in Rittenhouse Square in 1940 and can still be seen there. It is a four-foot granite carving on a base designed by Paul Cret, the well-known architect of Philadelphia's Rodin Museum. Her works in public and private collections include *Bear Cub* at the National Zoological Gardens, Washington, D.C.; *Christ the King* on the high altar of the Cathedral of Saint John the Divine, New York; and *Young Rhino* at Brookgreen Gardens, Murrells Inlet, South Carolina. In addition to sculpture in the round, she produced wood engravings and reliefs.

Notes

1. Proske 1968, p. 395.
2. Quoted in "Hernández Disciple," *Art Digest* 12 (April 15, 1938), p. 7.

References

Cornelia Chapin Papers, Archives of American Art, Smithsonian Institution, Washington, D.C. **1968** Beatrice Gilman Proske, *Brookgreen Gardens Sculpture,* Murrells Inlet, S.C.: Brookgreen Gardens, rev. ed., pp. 395–99. **1972** "Cornelia Chapin, Sculptor, Was 80," *New York Times,* Dec. 6, p. 50.

Black Beetle

1945
Cast stone, painted black
7 x 13⅛ x 24" (17.8 x 33.6 x 61 cm)
Signed and dated on top of base: CORNELIA CHAPIN/1945
Gift of George Biddle, 1951.1

Black Beetle is a hollow cast of cement and metallic particles. It was cast from a plasteline original that Cornelia Chapin modeled, according to Marion Sanford, from a beetle specimen that Chapin had received through the mail. There were no preliminary drawings or maquettes.[1] Known primarily for her animal sculpture, Chapin made only one other insect—a cast-stone grasshopper, *Mid-Summer Knight,* 1947 (location unknown), that was shown at the Pennsylvania Academy in 1950. Both sculptures are much larger than life. The forms are simplified, compact, and streamlined, and they are placed on what the artist called a "sustaining wall" or "support."[2]

In *Black Beetle,* the upraised arcs of the beetle's legs are only partly freed from the matrix in the manner of some ancient sculptures. This not only creates a feeling of solidity but also makes the figure easier to cast. The device, found in both her carved and her modeled pieces, was learned from Mateo Hernández, who borrowed the idea from Assyrian sculpture. The casting was done by John Rasmussen, an expert in cast stone who emigrated from Scandinavia and worked in New York from the 1930s to 1950s. The plasteline model was probably destroyed in the casting process. Only one cast was produced.[3]

Black Beetle was given to the Pennsylvania Academy of the Fine Arts in 1951 by the painter George Biddle, who had studied at the Academy from 1912 to 1914 and was married to HÉLÈNE SARDEAU.

Notes

1. Marion Sanford's response to questionnaire, July 31, 1984, PAFA Sanford research file and Sanford to Susan James-Gadzinski, May 29, [1985], PAFA Chapin research file.
2. Quoted in *An Exhibition by Seven Present-Day Women Artists* (Montclair, N.J.: Montclair Art Museum, 1951), p. 5.
3. Sanford to James-Gadzinski, May 29.

References

1946 Cornelia Van A. Chapin, N.A., "An Artist Looks at the Zoo," *Animal Kingdom* 49 (August 9), p. 151 (ill.). **1972–73** Charlotte Dunwiddie, "Even before Noah," *National Sculpture Review* 21 (Winter), p. 14 (ill.).

Exhibited

1946 Pen and Brush Galleries, New York, *Prize Award Exhibit—Cornelia Van A. Chapin: Small Sculpture,* checklist no. 8. **1946** New York Zoological Park, Bronx, Heads and Horns Museum Gallery, *Animals in Art: An Exhibi-*

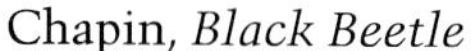
Chapin, *Black Beetle*

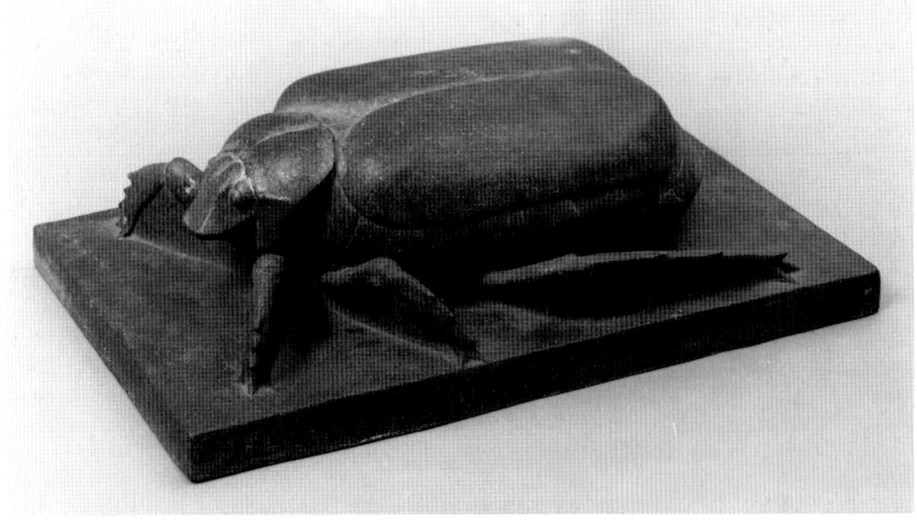

tion of Paintings, Sculpture, Carvings, Textiles, by Members of the New York Zoological Society, checklist no. 36. **1947*** cat. no. 91. **1947** Grand Central Art Galleries, New York, *Three Sculptors: Chapin, Duble, Sanford,* checklist no. 8. **1948** Lyman Allyn Museum, New London, Conn., *Exhibition of Small Sculpture by Cornelia Chapin.* **1949** National Academy of Design, New York, *123rd Annual Exhibition,* cat. no. 33, as *Garden Figure.* **1970** Free Library of Philadelphia, *Animal Sculpture for Children,* bookmobile. **1986–87** PAFA, *Sculpture at the Pennsylvania Academy of the Fine Arts.* **1989** PAFA, *"The Birds and the Beasts Will Teach Us."*

Ex Collection
George Biddle, Croton-on-Hudson, N.Y., about 1947–51.

Clara Bratt

1894–1972

Born in Kishineff, Romania, of a Russian father and an Austrian mother, Clara Bratt came to the United States alone in 1913 upon graduation from school. She settled in Milwaukee, where she worked as a milliner and studied drawing and painting in evening classes at the School of Fine and Applied Arts of the State Normal School.[1] By 1916 she had moved to Philadelphia and was working for a millinery company at Eighth and Arch streets. It was probably at this time that she studied drawing and modeling in the evenings at the Graphic Sketch Club (now the Samuel S. Fleisher Art Memorial). In February 1918, she was admitted to the Pennsylvania Academy of the Fine Arts for evening classes in life modeling. She remained there for the rest of the year and returned for the 1919–20 academic year.

In 1921 Clara Bratt spent six months in Paris, where she attended a modeling class, sketched nude models, studied outdoor monuments, and went to exhibitions.[2] From the 1920s until about 1934, she lived in Brooklyn, New York, and worked as a milliner. In 1934 at the age of forty, she returned to Philadelphia to study sculpture full-time with WALKER HANCOCK at the Pennsylvania Academy, where she remained for five years. Among the prizes she won were the Stewardson Prize in 1935 (second honorable mention) and 1937 and the Stimson Prize and the John F. Lewis, Jr., Prize in sculpture in 1936. She was awarded a William Emlen Cresson Traveling Scholarship in 1938 and spent four months touring France, Switzerland, Italy, Romania, and Yugoslavia. Clara Bratt served on the board of directors of the Pennsylvania Academy's Fellowship for the academic years 1942–43 and 1943–44 and took evening classes at the Academy in the spring of 1944. During the 1940s, she participated in annual and group exhibitions locally at the Woodmere Art Gallery (now the Woodmere Art Museum) and the Philadelphia Art Alliance and in New York at the National Academy of Design, Allied Artists of America, and National Association of Women Artists.

In September 1950, Bratt realized her dream of visiting Israel, where she had relatives.[3] She went back to Israel in 1955 for about a year and a half and finally, in 1959, settled permanently in Haifa. She had her first solo show in 1957 at the Chagall House in Haifa and a second one in 1959 at the Atran House in New York. During the 1960s, she exhibited with the Israel Painters and Sculptors Association in Haifa and Tel Aviv.

In 1967 a catalogue of her work was privately published in Hebrew and English with an appreciation by Ephraim Harris, who served for thirty-five years as the Haifa art critic for the *Jerusalem Post.* He credited her with a significant role in the emergence of an Israeli art.[4] Twenty-five of her sculptures are illustrated in the catalogue. Some are fountains and small groups of figures done in Philadelphia; others are realistic portrait busts of a range of Israeli citizens. Several of her works are in public and private collections in Israel, including the Museum of Modern Art in Haifa.

Notes

1. Clara Bratt to Eleanor Barker, Sept. 22, 1916, student file, PAFA Archives.
2. Bratt to Barker, Sept. 25, 1921, ibid.
3. Bratt to Mr. and Mrs. Joseph T. Fraser, Jr., August 28, 1950, student file, PAFA Archives.
4. Ephraim Harris, "An Appreciation of Clara Bratt," in *Sculpture: Clara Bratt* (Haifa: privately printed, 1967), [p. 2].

Sketch for Fountain

1936
Plaster, painted black
11 x 15½ x 10" (28 x 39.5 x 25.4 cm)
Signed on side of base below male figure: C. BRATT
Gift of the artist, 1944.13

THIS MODEL, executed in the fall of 1936, was Clara Bratt's contribution to the Twelfth Annual Collaborative Problem sponsored by the Association of the Alumni of the American Academy in Rome. The program was instituted at the Pennsylvania Academy of the Fine Arts by WALKER HANCOCK in 1933 soon after he began teaching there. The awarding of a collabora-

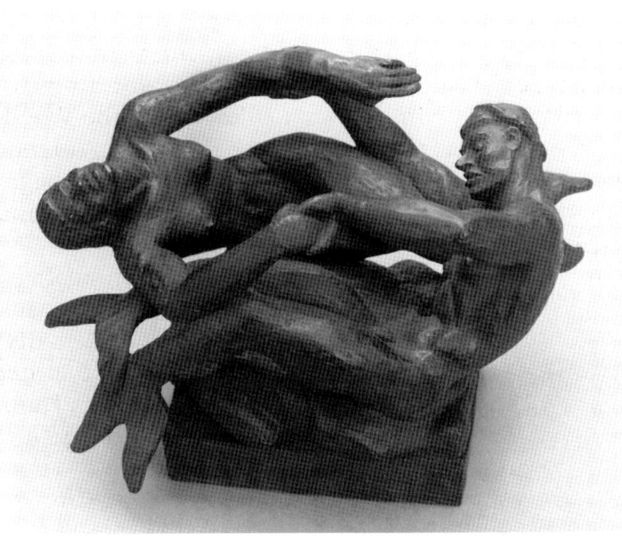

Bratt, *Sketch for Fountain*

tive scholarship for free tuition to the Pennsylvania Academy's own winners began in 1937. Each group of students consisted of a sculptor and a mural painter from the Academy and an architect and a landscape architect from the School of Fine Arts at the University of Pennsylvania. Although there is no information in the Academy's Archives on the assigned subject for 1936–37, it may have been to design an aquarium. Clara Bratt produced this sketch for a fountain. It is shown in situ in the proposed architectural drawing, a photograph of which is in the Academy's Archives. The fountain was to stand on a waterfront promenade in front of a mural designed by another Academy student, Fredrik Lund Ottesen.

The fountain is a circular composition of a merman and mermaid, holding each other's arms while balancing on a central crest of waves. The female figure looks skyward; and the male, wearing a wreath on his head, gazes at her. Their legs are covered with fish scales from the knees down, and each foot has a separate flipper. The plaster is painted black to simulate a bronze patina.

This work was probably the *Sketch for a Fountain* that was sold at the 1938 annual exhibition of the Fellowship of the Pennsylvania Academy.[1] It may have been purchased by the Fellowship, inasmuch as a 1942 list of "Items in Academy Belonging to Fellowship" includes "one black fountain by Clara Bratt."[2] Her 1967 catalogue mentions that one of her works is in the collection of the Fellowship of the Academy.[3] There is, however, no documentation that indicates how or when the fountain came into the Pennsylvania Academy's permanent sculpture collection.

According to her 1967 catalogue, she took a version of this fountain to Israel.[4] It may be the one, in either bronze or plaster, that was exhibited in 1959 and is illustrated by two views in the 1967 catalogue of her work. Clara Bratt's friend and supporter Carl Alpert remembers that she had always hoped to have a fountain, perhaps this one, installed in a public park in Israel.[5]

Notes

1. "Sales—Season 1937–38," *41st Annual Report of the Fellowship of the Pennsylvania Academy of the Fine Arts*, 1938, p. 7, PAFA Archives.
2. Mary Butler, compiler, "Items in Academy Belonging to Fellowship," June 22, 1942, PAFA Archives.
3. *Sculpture: Clara Bratt*, 1967, [p. 3].
4. Harris, "An Appreciation of Clara Bratt," ibid., [p. 1].
5. Carl Alpert to Susan James-Gadzinski, Feb. 5, 1986, PAFA object file.

Reference

Ephraim Harris, "An Appreciation of Clara Bratt," in *Sculpture: Clara Bratt*, Haifa: privately printed, 1967, [p. 1], 2 ills., [p. 18].

Exhibited

1938 PAFA, Fellowship annual exhibition, checklist no. 102, as *Sketch for Fountain.* **1942** PAFA, Fellowship annual exhibition, checklist no. 117, as *Garden Sculpture.* **1959** Atran House, New York, *Clara Bratt*, cat. no. 14.

Ex Collection

Fellowship of the Pennsylvania Academy of the Fine Arts, about 1938–44, purchased from the artist.

Philip Lagana

1896?–1963

Born in Italy, Filippo Lagana was known throughout his life as both Filippo and Philip.[1] He was the son of a sculptor, Domenico Lagana and may have studied art at the Academy in Rome before immigrating to the United States. Philip Lagana served in the U.S. Army during World War I. He worked as a cobbler for several years to support his studies at the Beaux-Arts Institute of Design in New York (now the National Institute for Architectural Education),[2] where he probably studied with the sculptor Solon Borglum (1868–1922). While there he won the second Paris Prize for sculpture and the Beaux-Arts medal for composition.

By 1928 Lagana was living and working in Darien, Connecticut, which remained his home for the rest of his life. He was a founding member of the Guild of the Seven Arts in Darien and a member of the Silvermine Guild, founded by Solon Borglum in New Canaan.[3] Lagana taught a popular clay modeling class in his studio and exhibited his sculpture at the Guild Hall in Darien. In 1928 he produced a memorial for the Veterans of Foreign Wars in Stamford, which commemorates the late Captain Ralph L. Taylor and the progress of aviation. It features an obelisk topped by a male figure grasping an airplane wing and standing within a mass of clouds.[4] One Connecticut newspaper referred to Lagana as "the well known cobbler-sculptor" when he exhibited a caricature statue, *Debutante,* that was painted and wore a cloth dress.[5] In 1929 Lagana was commissioned to model a trophy for the annual outboard-motor boat race of the Norwalk Country Club. It depicted a motor boat moving through waves and was produced in bronze and silver.[6]

From December 1929 to the summer of 1930, he took an advanced sculpture course in Rome.[7] When he returned to Darien, he set up his studio in the houseboat of the late, John Huffington, a painter of seascapes whose bust he modeled and had cast into bronze and whose 1930 posthumous exhibition he oversaw. The same exhibition featured what many considered to be Lagana's greatest sculpture, *Mother and Child.*[8] In 1931 his bust of the painter George Burroughs Torrey was displayed at the National Academy of Design, in New York, and drew praise from a French art critic.[9] In the early 1930s, Lagana exhibited three other busts at the National Academy of Design and two at the Pennsylvania Academy of the Fine Arts. On January 19, 1934, in a letter to Juliana Force at the Whitney Museum of American Art, in New York, Lagana asked for employment under the Public Works of Art Project and apparently was given short-term work related to a sculpture monument for a park in Norwalk, Connecticut.[10] In 1935 he was elected a member of the National Sculpture Society and remained a life-time member. In 1940 *Determination,* his plaster group of four boys, was shown at the Whitney Museum of American Art in an exhibition sponsored by the National Sculpture Society.

Notes

1. Because the bust owned by the Museum of American Art of the Pennsylvania Academy of the Fine Arts is signed "Ph." for *Philip,* that version of his name is used here.
2. Obituary, *Darien News Review,* Dec. 5, 1963, p. 2.
3. Scrapbooks of clippings dated about 1928–31, Guild of Seven Arts, Darien Historical Society, Darien.
4. "Lagana Designs Memorial Piece" and caption for photograph, *Darien News Review,* May 24, 1928, and June 14, 1928, respectively (ill.), ibid.
5. "Lagana's Statue Hit of Exhibition," *Norwalk Hour,* Jan. 23, 1929, ibid.
6. "Trophy Completed by Philip Lagana," *Norwalk Hour,* July 3, 1929 (ill.), ibid.
7. "Darien Sculptor Sails December 7 to Study in Italy," *Stamford Advocate,* Nov. 27, 1929, ibid.
8. "Lagana's 'Mother and Child' in First Showing at Exhibit," *South Norwalk Evening Sentinel,* August 21, 1930, ibid.
9. "Philip Lagana of Darien Praised for Bust of G.B. Torry," *Stamford Advocate,* April 23, 1931 (ill.), ibid.
10. Records of the Public Works of Art Project, Record Group 121, National Archives Correspondence of the Region 2 Office (New York area) with artists, 1933–34, F-N, Archives of American Art, microfilm, roll no. DC113, frame nos. 909–12.

References

1963 Obituary, *Darien News Review,* Dec. 5, p. 2. **1985** Peter Hastings Falk, ed., *Who Was Who in American Art,* Madison, Conn.: Sound View Press, p. 354 (mistakenly lists Philadelphia Museum of Art, rather than the Museum of American Art of the Pennsylvania Academy of the Fine Arts, as owning a work by him). **1984** Glenn B. Opitz, *Dictionary of American Sculptors,* Poughkeepsie, N.Y.: Apollo Book, p. 229 (mistakenly lists Pennsylvania Museum of Art as owning the portrait *Clarence Roe* [sic]).

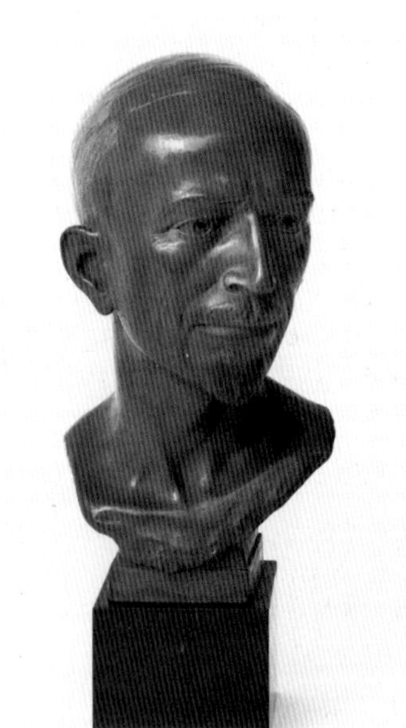

Lagana, *Clarence Herbert Rowe*

Clarence Herbert Rowe

1930
Bronze with green patina; lost-wax cast
15½ x 7⅝ x 8⅛" (39.4 x 19.4 x 20.6 cm)
Signed and dated beneath left shoulder: Ph. LAGANA 1930
Gift of the family of Clarence H. Rowe through the Fellowship of the Pennsylvania Academy of the Fine Arts, 1933.9

MUCH OF Philip Lagana's artistic production appears to have been portraiture in bronze or marble. He modeled busts of the former Supreme Court Chief Justice Charles Evans Hughes and the Italian poet Francesco Sofia Alessio, but his subjects were predominantly children and artists.

The artists he portrayed include painters: John Huffington, George Burroughs Torrey, George B. Wright, and this one of the etcher illustrator Clarence Herbert Rowe (1878–1930), who was born in Philadelphia and briefly attended the Pennsylvania Academy of the Fine Arts in the 1890s before traveling to Paris for further study. He displayed watercolors of French scenes at the 1900 and 1903 annual exhibitions of the Pennsylvania Academy. At the time of his unexpected death, in Cos Cob, Connecticut, Rowe seemed to be a "rising artist."[1] Lagana was chosen by his family to produce this posthumous portrait. It portrays a very severe-looking visage with an intent gaze and prominent veins at the temples. A bit of the iris of the eye was retained to give animation. The raw appearance of the edge of the cut-off of the composition at the chest level recalls that this bust was modeled in clay. It is not known where it was cast nor what foundries the sculptor used for his other busts. In fact, the whereabouts of all of his other works is unknown. This bust is mounted on a stone base.

The sitter's widow always intended that the bust be given to the Pennsylvania Academy as a memorial to her husband, but she died without having made arrangements. Family members offered the bust to the Fellowship of the Pennsylvania Academy which accepted it and then presented it to the Museum.[2]

Notes

1. Miss Leng Arrington to PAFA, Feb. 11, 1932, PAFA object file.
2. Arrington to PAFA, ibid.; Mary Butler, president of the Fellowship, to Arrington, Feb. 25, 1932; and Arrington to Butler, June 17, 1932, PAFA object file.

Ex Collections

The sitter's widow, New York, 1930–32; his descendants, 1932–33.

GLADYS EDGERLY BATES

b. 1896

Born in Hopewell, New Jersey, where her family had a summer home, Gladys Edgerly attended Gunston Hall, then a girls' boarding school, in Washington, D.C. In 1909–10 she took classes at the School of Industrial Arts in Trenton, New Jersey, with the painter Henry R. MacGinnis, who encouraged her and her younger sister, Beatrice, to attend the Corcoran School of Art in Washington, D.C. Although younger than usually allowed, they entered the Corcoran in 1910 at the ages of 13 and 11, respectively, and studied anatomy, drawing, and painting for about six years. In 1914 they went with their family to Italy where the girls sketched.

Six former Corcoran students, including the Edgerly sisters, came to Philadelphia in 1916 to study at the Pennsylvania Academy of the Fine Arts. In her first year, Gladys Edgerly took drawing and painting with Daniel Garber, Philip Hale, and Hugh Breckenridge. Because Garber advised his students to model at least one portrait bust, Edgerly enrolled in CHARLES GRAFLY's modeling class in the fall of 1917. She found him inspiring and decided to switch to the sculpture curriculum. In 1919 she won the Stimson Prize, served as a monitor in the women's life modeling class helping her fellow students between Grafly's Friday visits, and joined the Academy's Fellowship. Edgerly won a William Emlen Cresson Traveling Scholarship in 1920, as did her husband-to-be, the painting student Earl Kenneth Bates. The next year, Gladys traveled with her sister in England, France, and Italy for five months and was inspired by the stone carvings on medieval cathedrals and abbeys. After the trip, she returned for one year to the Pennsylvania Academy and studied with ALBERT LAESSLE at the Academy's summer school at Chester Springs. In 1923 she married Kenneth Bates and moved permanently to Mystic, Connecticut. They went camping on the western prairies in 1927, where Gladys Bates was greatly influenced by the forms of the landscape. The following year, the family traveled to France and Italy.

Bates entered sculpture in the Pennsylvania Academy's annual exhibitions of 1921, 1922, 1928 to 1936, 1939, and 1942 to 1951. At the 1931 annual exhibition, her mahogany figure *Eve,* was awarded the Fellowship Prize and the George D. Widener Memorial Gold Medal. It was later sold to a private collector. Her watercolors and pastels were shown in the Academy's annual watercolor exhibitions of 1926, 1927, 1934, and 1935.

In 1934, Bates had a joint exhibition at the New Jersey State Museum in Trenton with M. Elizabeth Price, who had studied painting at the Pennsylvania Academy from 1905 to 1907. Bates exhibited at the Art Club of Philadelphia in 1934 and at the Reading Museum in 1935, with a group of nine Philadelphia women painters. She was elected an associate of the National Sculpture Society, New York, in 1941 and became a fellow in 1945. Her first solo exhibition was held at the Pen and Brush Club in New York in 1945. She and her husband were included in a 1948 invitational exhibition of works by eight artist couples at the Woodmere Art Gallery (now the Woodmere Art Museum) in Philadelphia. Bates was one of twelve women sculptors, including Doris Caesar (1893–1971), Dorothea Greenbaum (1893–1986), and CLEO HARTWIG, in a 1950 exhibition at the Art Alliance of Philadelphia. In Connecticut in the 1950s and 1960s, she and her husband participated in several joint exhibitions. They were also active in the Mystic Art Association. In the late 1950s, she taught sculpture at the Madison Art Gallery and Studios in Madison, Connecticut, and at the Hartford Art School of the University of Hartford.

Morning, her 1935 plaster, is in the Metropolitan Museum of Art, New York; *Pan of the Laurentians,* a lead fountain of about 1930, is in the New Jersey State Museum, Trenton; *Venus with Shell,* a bronze fountain of about 1932, and *Noah's Wife,* 1934, a reclining figure in mahogany, are in the Madison Art Gallery. Other examples of her work in terracotta, cast stone, carved stone, and sculpmetal are in private collections.

Reference

1984 Interview with Gladys Bates by Linda Bantel and Susan James-Gadzinski (April 16), tapes in PAFA Archives.

Sleepy Girl

1938
Red-brown cast stone
14¾ x 27 x 14¼" (37.5 x 68.6 x 36.9 cm)
Joseph E. Temple Fund, 1939.1

Sleepy Girl shows a reclining woman who leans on her right elbow while braiding her hair. She wears a long cloth that falls in folds across her waist, hips, knees, and ankles. The sculpture is a reworking of *Morning,* 1935 (Metropolitan Museum of Art, New York), which won the Third Purchase Prize at the 1942 exhibition *Artists for Victory,* held by the Metropolitan Museum. Bates felt that the "hastily modeled" figure of 1935 had "a certain awkwardness" and hoped to achieve a "feeling of relaxation" in her next version.[1]

Sleepy Girl was produced by a mold that Bates made from her clay model. The work was cast by John Rasmussen of New York in a mixture of stone dust, cement, red pigment, and a special binding material.[2] An expert in this technique who worked for many artists, including CORNELIA CHAPIN, Rasmussen made eleven works in cast stone for Bates between 1934 and 1948.

Notes

1. Bates to Bantel, with artist's response to questionnaire, [May 18, 1984], PAFA object file.
2. Telephone conversation, Bates and Virginia Norton Naudé, Feb. 13, 1984, typed notes, ibid.

Reference

1968–69 *National Sculpture Review* 17 (Winter), back cover (ill.).

Exhibited

1938 Mystic Art Association, Conn., annual exhibition. **1939*** cat. no. 309 (ill.). **1986–87** PAFA, *Sculpture at the Pennsylvania Academy of the Fine Arts.*

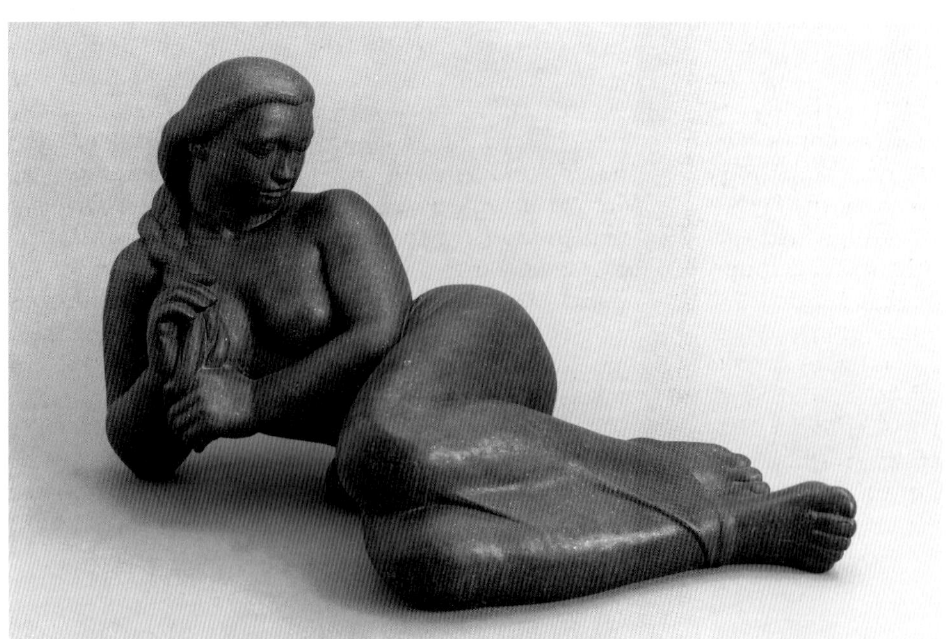

Bates, *Sleepy Girl*

Harry Rosin

1897–1973

Harry Baker Rosen was born in Philadelphia to Aaron Rosen, a Russian shoemaker who came to the United States in the 1880s, and Bertha Baker Rosen, who was from Alsace-Lorraine. By his early twenties, Harry had changed the spelling of his last name to Rosin.[1] Upon graduating from Central High School, he did wrought-iron work for three years with the master craftsman Samuel Yellin. Rosin later taught iron design at the School of Industrial Arts (now the University of the Arts) and operated his own workshop. Before and after serving in the United States Navy in 1918 he took night classes in modeling in the teacher's training course at the School of Industrial Arts. For two years in the early 1920s, he taught modeling and pottery at the Trenton Art School (now, Trenton State College) in New Jersey.

Harry Rosin came to the Pennsylvania Academy of the Fine Arts in the fall of 1921 to study modeling with CHARLES GRAFLY. He continued at the Academy in the summer of 1922 and full-time from 1923 to 1926. Then he was awarded a William Emlen Cresson Traveling Scholarship that enabled him to study and travel in France, Spain, Italy, Austria, Germany, and Hungary.[2] He returned to Philadelphia to study for several months of the 1926–27 academic year and in the evenings of the following year. He won the Edmund Stewardson Prize in the spring of 1928 for a full-length female nude modeled in competition. Much of his time until 1932 was spent working in Paris. While there in 1932, he exhibited in *Modern American Artists of Paris* and *Salon de L'Oeuvre Unique.*

He returned to the United States during the Depression and found little work available for a sculptor. A friend, the painter Saul Schary, who had studied at the Pennsylvania Academy in 1924–25, extolled the beauty of the island of Martinique and the relative economy of living there, so Rosin set off for the West Indies.[3] Through his Paris connections, he was soon commissioned to do work for the French government, including a twenty-foot-high figure of Christ for the façade of the Cathedral of Guadeloupe. Rosin went to Tahiti in 1933 and stayed until 1937 except for brief visits to Philadelphia. Nine of his sculptures, mostly untitled torsos and heads, were shown in the 1933 Sculpture International held at the Philadelphia Museum of Art and sponsored by the Fairmount Park Art Association. Rosin's first solo exhibition was held at the Gimbel Galleries in January 1936.[4]

In the late 1930s, the sculptor settled permanently in Bucks County, Pennsylvania, with his wife, Vilna Spitz, who was of Danish and Tahitian ancestry. He modeled portrait busts of the daughters of a local property owner, Tyson Nimick; and by 1940 Rosin had bartered the artwork for land on which to build a house, near the artists' colony of New Hope. The same year, he was selected from the sculptors exhibiting in the Second Sculpture International at the Philadelphia Museum of Art to produce full-length figures in limestone of a Puritan and a Quaker for the Ellen Phillips Samuel Memorial in Fairmount Park. He replaced ALBERT LAESSLE as an instructor in construction at the Pennsylvania Academy in the 1940–41 academic year and continued teaching figure construction and sculpture there until his death in 1973. During World War II, Rosin worked for a year at the General Motors Corporation in Trenton, where he made drawings and patterns for United States Navy bombers.[5]

Harry Rosin's work was shown regularly in the Pennsylvania Academy's annual exhibitions from 1934 to 1968. In 1939 he won the George D. Widener Memorial Gold Medal for his plaster *Hina Rapa* (q.v.). In 1941 he was awarded the Annual Fellowship Prize at the 136th annual exhibition for *Bather* (location unknown). The next year, he received the Fellowship Gold Medal of fifty dollars for one of his reclining female nudes. The Pennsylvania Academy gave Rosin one-person shows in 1945–46 in its Philadelphia Artists' Gallery and in 1965 and 1980 in its Peale House Galleries. In his spare time, the artist painted in oils, often Tahitian subjects.

The American Academy of Arts and Letters in New York awarded Harry Rosin a grant in 1946 "to further creative work by American artists and to honor them for achievement." The next year, a group of ten artists, including the Pennsylvania Academy instructor Franklin Watkins and the painter Morris Blackburn, who later taught there, purchased *Reclining Nude,* of pink-tinted cast stone, from Rosin and gave it to the Philadelphia Museum of Art. Rosin's *Mother and Child* was shown in *American Sculpture 1951: A National Competitive Exhibition* at the Metropolitan Museum of Art in New York and was singled out as "buoyant and beautifully posed."[6] A bronze cast of it was installed that year in Philadelphia in the lobby of the Children's Hospital (former location). The work is now on the hospital's Reath Terrace at Thirty-fourth Street and Civic Center Boulevard.

In 1956 Harry Rosin was commissioned to create a memorial to "Mr. Baseball," Connie Mack. The statue was moved from its original location near Connie Mack Stadium to the new Veteran's Stadium in 1972. Rosin's seated figure of John B. Kelly, the Olympic rowing champion, was installed in 1965 near Boat House Row on East River Drive (now called Kelly Drive after his son). The next year, the sculptor completed four large-scale panels of historic figures from four centuries for the newly built Chester County Courthouse in West Chester. Rosin was commissioned in 1972 to produce a series of medals depicting rare and endangered animals to commemorate the centennial of the Philadelphia zoo. A memorial exhibition to Harry Rosin was held in New Hope at the Baltic Galleries in 1973.

Notes

1. "Harry Rosin, 75, Renowned Sculptor," *Philadelphia Inquirer*, Sept. 29, 1973, p. 5-C.
2. Rosin 1941, p. 16.
3. Ibid.
4. Dorothy Grafly, "Rosin Finds South Seas Spell Glamour and Profits—Artists' Society Creates Rental Fee Issue," unidentified newspaper clipping, Jan. 5, 1936, faculty file, PAFA Archives.
5. "Exhibitor at International Sculpture Show: Honors and Fame Have Come to Former Trenton Teacher," *Trenton Sunday Times Advertiser*, August 7, 1949, p. 8.
6. Robert M. Coates, "The Art Galleries: Sculptures, Current, and Paintings, Past," *New Yorker* 27 (Dec. 15, 1951), p. 104.

References

1941 Harry Rosin, "A Sculptor's Story: Why and How Harry Rosin Came Here," *New Hope Towpath* 2 (April), pp. 16–17, 19. **1946** Dorothy Grafly, "Harry Rosin," *American Artist* 10 (Feb.), pp. 20–21, 39–40. **1973** *In Memoriam: Harry Rosin 1897–1973; Exhibition in honor of the sculptor by 10 New Hope artists with past and recent works by Harry Rosin*, New Hope: Baltic Studios. **1976** *Philadelphia: Three Centuries of American Art*, Philadelphia: Philadelphia Museum of Art, pp. 555–56.

Rosin, *Torso of Tehiva*

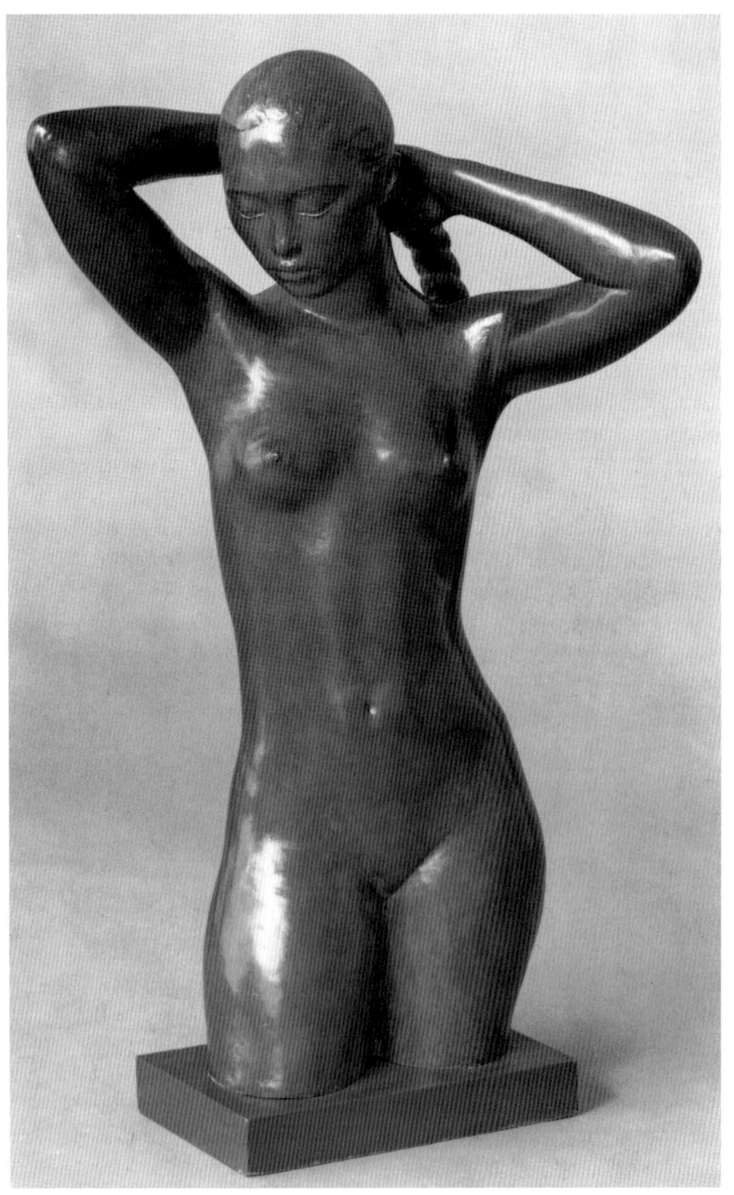

Torso of Tehiva

1933
Bronze with brown patina; cast in 1940s
30¾ x 17 x 13¾" (78.2 x 43.2 x 35 cm)
Signed on right thigh: H. ROSIN
Lost-wax cast, probably by Roman Bronze Works, New York
Bequest of Myer H. Goldman, 1971.18.1

THIS IS one of the works that Harry Rosin produced during his first year in Tahiti. The young Tahitian woman named Tehiva was apparently a favorite model.[1] Rosin claimed that "Tahitian women are the world's most perfect models."[2] He particularly liked their carriage and perfect proportions. Tehiva is shown with her arms raised, braiding her hair. She also posed for a portrait bust, *Head of Tehiva*, 1934, and *Tehiva Seated on Tiki*, about 1934 (both in private collections). A *tiki* is an ancestor or god from Polynesian mythology. Plasters of both these sculptures were shown in the 1980 Peale House solo exhibition. *Head of Tehiva* won the Thomas Bouregy Portrait Prize in 1956 from the Audubon Artists in New York. A cast of the head in plaster (present location unknown) was shown at the Pennsylvania Academy of the Fine Arts as part of the Ingersoll collection in 1956; another cast in an unknown medium, from a private collection, was shown at the Peale House in 1965.

The first version of *Torso of Tehiva*, in plaster, was shown in 1934 in the Pennsylvania Academy's 129th annual exhibition and in *A Century of Progress Exhibition of Paintings and Sculpture* at the Art Institute of Chicago (part of the Chicago World's Fair). It was also shown in the *Exhibition of Painting, Sculpture and Graphic Arts* at the Dallas Museum of Fine Arts (part of the Texas Centennial) in 1936. At the Pennsylvania Academy showing, the torso was praised for its "exquisite rosy texture [with] Oriental inflections."[3] Another critic commented, "From the standpoint of firm construction plus sensitive feeling 'Tehira' [*sic*] is perhaps the most satisfying single figure in the exhibition."[4] The plaster was in the artist's studio at his death and is now in a private collection. A cast in an unknown medium was purchased in the 1930s by the actor Frederic March on a visit to Tahiti.[5]

In the 1941 *Exhibition of American Sculpture* at the Carnegie Institute in Pittsburgh, Rosin showed a cast-stone version of *Torso of Tehiva* (Lyman Allyn Museum, New London, Connecticut). This may be the cast that was owned by the Russian-born illustrator and painter Boris Artzybasheff. Around 1940 Rosin was having works produced in pink-tinted cast stone.[6] One of these, *Reclining Nude,* about 1939, was given to the Philadelphia Museum of Art in 1947 and then cast in bronze in 1949.[7] Rosin may have followed the same progression with *Torso of Tehiva:* plaster to cast stone to bronze. Assuming this to be the case, the bronze in the Museum of American Art of the Pennsylvania Academy of the Fine Arts would have been cast after 1941, probably by the Roman Bronze Works in New York. They cast other pieces for Rosin; and the beautiful translucent light brown patina is probably the work of Riccardo Bertelli, the foundry's originator and a master at patination. The torso was then purchased by Myer H. Goldman, who bequeathed it and Rosin's *Reclining Nude* to the Pennsylvania Academy in 1971. *Torso of Tehiva* is mounted on a wood plinth painted brown.

Notes

1. A photograph of the model, Tehiva, and of the torso in plaster appear in "The Perfect Model is Discovered in the South Seas," *Philadelphia Inquirer,* Oct. 30, 1938, Picture Parade Section, p. 3.
2. Robert Matthews, "Men of the Arts in Philadelphia," *Philadelphia Arts,* Oct. 1939, p. 10, faculty file, PAFA Archives.
3. C.H. Bonte, "In Gallery and Studio: Sculpture in the Academy's annual exhibition," *Philadelphia Inquirer,* Feb. 4, 1934, p. 17-A.
4. Dorothy Grafly, "News of Art, Artists, and Current Exhibitions," *Philadelphia Public Ledger,* Jan. 28, 1934, section 3, p. 7.
5. Robert E. Baum, "Discovering Bucks County: Harry Rosin, Noted Sculptor, Is Building Home in New Hope for Himself and His Tahiti Bride; Lived on Martinique Island for Three Months," *Allentown [Pa.] Call,* July 14, 1940, clipping file, PAFA Library.
6. Ibid.
7. *Philadelphia: Three Centuries of American Art* (Philadelphia: Philadelphia Museum of Art, 1976), cat. no. 471, pp. 555–56.

Exhibited

1980 PAFA, Peale House, *Harry Rosin, Sculptor,* checklist no. 4. **1986–87** PAFA, *Sculpture at the Pennsylvania Academy of the Fine Arts.* **1993–96** James A. Michener Museum, Doylestown, Pa., *A Legacy of Bucks County Art.*

Ex Collection

Myer H. Goldman, 1940s-1971.

Hina Rapa

1935

a.
Plaster, painted brown
25 x 16 x 9" (63.5 x 38.8 x 23 cm)
Signed and dated within a rectangle at back: ROSIN/1935/TAHITI
Joseph E. Temple Fund, 1939.13.2

b.
Bronze with brown patina; lost-wax cast in 1939
24 x 16 x 9" (61.1 x 38.8 x 23 cm)
Signed and dated within a rectangle at back: ROSIN/1935/TAHITI
Foundry mark at back: ROMAN BRONZE WORKS N.Y.
Joseph E. Temple Fund, 1939.13.1

A TAHITIAN WOMAN named Hina Rapa, considered to be an exceptional beauty, was the model for this bust.[1] She is shown "emerging from an island pool into sparkling sunlight," hence the partly closed eyes and the backward tilt of the head, indicating the weight of her wet waist-length hair.[2] The torso is considered to be Rosin's masterpiece; it is the work for which he is best known. Like *Torso of Tehiva* (q.v.), it is smoothly and sensitively modeled. The hair has an overall texture. When shown at the Pennsylvania Academy of the Fine Arts in 1939, *Hina Rapa* was pronounced "outstanding in its sound handling of forms." The reviewer also noted that the sculpture "makes its impression by a notable simplicity of line, as well as by an absence of any affectation."[3]

At least two bronzes of *Hina Rapa* were cast before Rosin left Tahiti in 1937. Lewis Hirshon commissioned one, together with a bronze of the 1935 portrait bust of his wife, Eugenie.[4] Both pieces are now owned by his grandson Charles T. Hirshon in Santa Monica, California. The other bronze cast of *Hina Rapa* (present location unknown) was sold to Charles Nordhof, co-author of *Mutiny on the Bounty,* as a figurehead for his boat.[5]

The original, painted plaster of *Hina Rapa* was

awarded the George D. Widener Memorial Gold Medal in 1939 at the 134th annual exhibition of the Pennsylvania Academy. The Academy purchased it and had a bronze cast made at the Roman Bronze Works in New York between April 20 and May 6 of that year.[6] Its patination was to be as close as possible to the color of the paint on the plaster.[7]

Later, probably in 1971, Harry Rosin gave the Pennsylvania Academy permission to make another mold from the original plaster of *Hina Rapa* so that up to eleven plaster casts could be made for sale in the Academy's proposed store.[8] In February William Hanson, Rosin's former student, made a rubber mold at Peale House, one of the Academy's school buildings.[9] Five casts are known to have been made. The earliest were probably painted by the sculptor or by Hanson from Rosin's instructions, although Hanson later claimed he had not painted any of them.[10] After Rosin's death, the finishing was done by Paul Anthony Greenwood (1921–1985), the Academy's instructor of plaster casting from 1959 to 1960, and of sculpture from 1959 to 1985. The first cast was for Rosin's friend Henry Hotz, Jr., the administrator of the Pennsylvania Academy's school.[11] By the fall of 1971, one cast (perhaps cast number 2; present location unknown) had been purchased by William Micheel and installed in his office on a hexagonal wooden pedestal.[12]

Cast number 3 was sold to Bill Martone, who was then a painting instructor (present location unknown).[13] One of the final two casts was given to the Pennsylvania Academy for the school's cast collection in response to a request from Arthur De Costa, who taught cast drawing in the early 1970s and wanted a nonclassical example for his students.[14] Now painted beige, it continues to be a popular subject in the first-year class. This was probably the cast shown in the 1980 Peale House faculty-sponsored exhibition of Harry Rosin's work, rather than the plaster in the Museum. The painted surface of the latter was left unexhibitable by the preparations for the mold-making process. The last of the five casts, painted "chocolate brown" and somewhat shopworn, was sold in 1979 to Robert Stubbs, business manager in the 1970s.[15]

It may be that more than five of the proposed edition of eleven casts were produced. The Allentown Art Museum in Pennsylvania has a plaster painted reddish brown that was given in 1982 by Martin H. Ritter. He bought it directly from the artist, probably shortly before his death. It is unusual in having a dedicatory inscription: To SAM/ROSIN 1935. The identity of "Sam" and the reason for the dedication are unknown; Ritter thought that he was the first owner.[16] Another plaster, of unknown date, is in a private collection in Virginia. The artist must have kept a plaster for himself, as one was shown in the plaza of the Bucks County Playhouse in the summer of 1940 and in an exhibition in New York in June 1946 of works by recipients of grants from the American Academy of Arts and Letters.

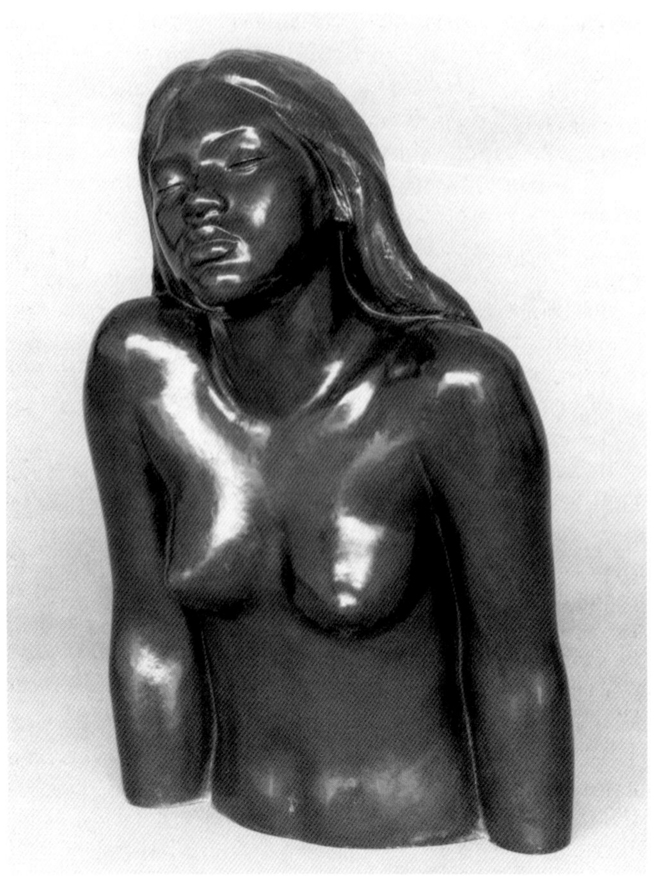

Rosin, *Hina Rapa*, bronze

Notes

1. "The Perfect Model is Discovered in the South Seas," *Philadelphia Inquirer*, Oct. 30, 1938, Picture Parade section, p. 2.

2. Pennsylvania Academy's Museum wall label for the bronze, in memoriam, Sept.-Oct. 1973, faculty file, PAFA Archives.

3. Dorothy Grafly, "Exhibits Fall Short of Staging," *Philadelphia Record*, Feb. 5, 1939, and C.H. Bonte, "Academy's Sculpture; Annual Contains Striking Works," a Philadelphia newspaper, Feb. 1939, both on microfilm, roll no. 57, frame no. 537, PAFA Archives.

4. Charles T. Hirshon to Susan James-Gadzinski, July 30, 1986, PAFA research file.

5. *Philadelphia: Three Centuries of American Art* (Philadelphia: Philadelphia Museum of Art, 1976), p. 556.

6. Riccardo Bertelli, Roman Bronze works, to Joseph T. Fraser, Jr., April 20, 1939, and receipt, May 6, 1939, PAFA object file.

7. Fraser to Roman Bronze Works, April 18, 1939, and

Bertelli to Fraser, April 20, 1939, PAFA object file.

8. Robert Stubbs, PAFA business manager, memorandum to file, April 30, 1975, PAFA object file.

9. Marilyn Fiegel to William G. Hanson, "Permission to cast Harry Rosin's 'Hina-Rippa [*sic*],' " n.d., and receipt, Feb. 2, 1971, PAFA object file.

10. Caption on reverse of photograph, Oct. 1971, "Cast in plaster and patina[t]ed by William Hansen [*sic*]. Purchased by William Micheel, and shown in his office," and James-Gadzinski, note to file, July 1, 1988, PAFA object file.

11. Stubbs memo., April 30, 1975, PAFA object file.

12. Photograph, Oct. 1971, PAFA object file.

13. Stubbs memo., April 30, 1975, PAFA object file.

14. Conversation with Arthur De Costa, July 20, 1988. (He taught drawing and painting at PAFA until 1988.)

15. Conversation with Fred Kelley, July 15, 1988.

16. Conversation with Patricia Delluva, Registrar, Allentown Art Museum, Pa., July 18, 1988.

References (plaster)
1939 "Academy Winners," *Art Digest* 13 (Feb. 1), p. 6 (ill.). **1939** "Sculpture Today," *Art Digest* 13 (June 1), p. 28 (ill.). **1939** Robert Matthews, "Men of the Arts in Philadelphia," *Philadelphia Arts* (Oct.), p. 10 (ill.), faculty file, PAFA Archives. **1941** Harry Rosin, "A Sculptor's Story: Why and How Harry Rosin Came Here," *New Hope Towpath* 2 (April), p. 17 (ill.), cited erroneously as *Nina Rapa.*

Reference (bronze)
1973 Henry Hotz, "The Teacher," catalogue essay in *In Memoriam: Harry Rosin 1897–1973,* New Hope: Baltic Studios, unpaginated (ill.).

Exhibited (plaster)
1939* cat. no. 314 (ill.). **1939** New York World's Fair, *American Art Today,* cat. no. 741 (ill.).

Exhibited (bronze)
1945–46 PAFA, *Harry Rosin, Portraits of Children and Other Recent Sculpture,* cat. no. 26. **1953** Fairmount Park Commission, Playhouse in the Park. **1956** PAFA, *Painting and Sculpture by Living Philadelphia Artists Represented in the Permanent Collection of the Academy,* cat. no. 131. **1960** PAFA, *Faculty Exhibition,* cat. no. 178. **1965** PAFA, Peale House, *Julian Levi; Harry Rosin,* checklist no. 24. **1973** PAFA, memorial tribute. **1974** Provident National Bank, Philadelphia, exhibition of PAFA works. **1975** William Penn Memorial Museum, Harrisburg, exhibition of works of art from the PAFA. **1986–87** PAFA, *Sculpture at the Pennsylvania Academy of the Fine Arts.*

Elizabeth W. Bendiner (also known as *Portrait of a Lady*)

1939
Plaster, painted brown and red
12 x 7 x 9½" (30.5 x 17.8 x 24.1 cm)
Signed and dated on back: 1939–ROSIN
Gift of Mrs. Alfred Bendiner, 1947.15

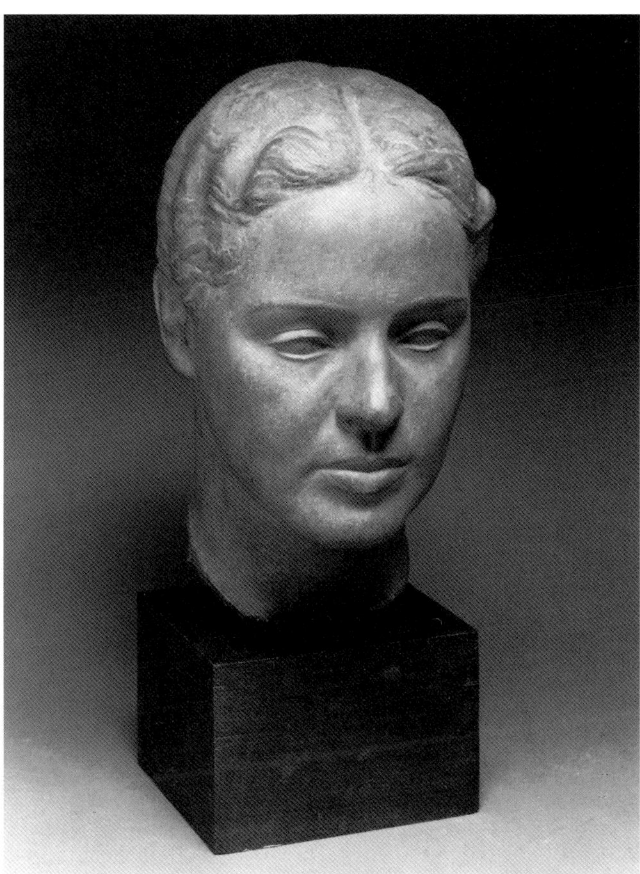

Rosin, *Elizabeth W. Bendiner*

THIS BUST of Betty Sutro Bendiner (1904–1991) was commissioned by her husband, Alfred, a painter, printmaker, and caricaturist and a friend of Harry Rosin. The couple first met in the 1920s while studying architecture at the University of Pennsylvania; they married in 1937. While Mrs. Bendiner was posing for her portrait at Rosin's studio at 201 South Tenth Street, a telegram arrived from the Pennsylvania Academy of the Fine Arts, announcing that he had won the George D. Widener Memorial Gold Medal.[1]

The portrait was modeled in clay, and two plasters and one bronze were cast. All three casts became the property of the sitter and her husband. One of the plasters, mounted on a wooden base, was given to the Pennsylvania Academy in 1947. It is painted brown with reddish highlights on the eyebrows, cheeks, lips, and hair, especially the chignon. The coloration is similar to that seen on Rosin's bronze *Head of Tory* (q.v.). The other plaster is painted an overall beige. The bronze, cast by the Roman Bronze Works in New York, has a dark brown patina. The bronze head has a more pronounced tilt than the plasters, probably a difference in mounting.

Mrs. Bendiner felt that the likeness was "too prissy" and often decorated the casts with a ribbon or a hat, which displeased the sculptor on one of his visits to her home.[2] When she donated the plaster to the Pennsylvania Academy in 1947, Mrs. Bendiner wished to remain anonymous, both as donor and sitter;[3] but, in 1987, she agreed to allow the portrait to be identified and the gift credited to her.

Notes

1. Conversation between Elizabeth W. Bendiner and Susan James-Gadzinski, Oct. 19, 1987. The announcement was probably made on Jan. 28, 1939, the day before the exhibition opening, as the notice appeared in the newspaper that day: "Philadelphians Honored at Academy Art Exhibit," *Philadelphia Evening Public Ledger*, p. 2.
2. Conversation with Mrs. Bendiner, March 7, 1985.
3. Minutes, board of directors, June 1947 annotation after May 12, 1947, p. 2, PAFA Archives.

Reference

1970 Louis E. Marrits, *Modeled Portrait Sculpture*, South Brunswick, N.J., and New York: A.S. Barnes and Company, p. 319 (ill.), as *Portrait of a Lady*.

Exhibited

1940* cat. no. 222, as *Portrait.* **1959** PAFA, *Paintings, Drawings, Prints, and Sculpture Collected and Owned by Fourteen Philadelphia Artists*, cat. no. 312, as *Head.* **1960** PAFA, *Faculty Exhibition*, cat. no. 180, as *Portrait of a Lady.* **1965** PAFA, *Memorial and Retrospective Exhibition of the Work of Alfred Bendiner 1899–1964.*

Ex Collection

Mr. and Mrs. Alfred Bendiner, 1939–47.

Reclining Nude

1940
Bronze with black patina; cast in 1940s
10½ x 18 x 9½" (26.6 x 45.8 x 24.2 cm)
Signed on back: HARRY/ROSIN
Lost-wax cast, possibly by Modern Art Foundry, New York
Bequest of Myer H. Goldman, 1971.18.2

Rosin, *Reclining Nude*

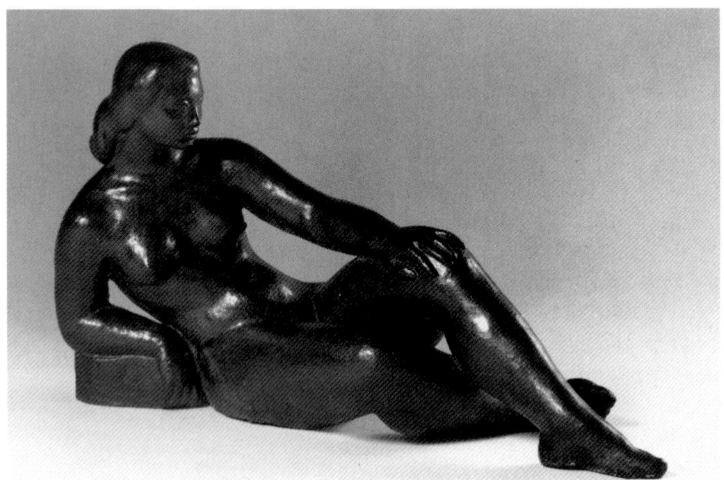

THIS IS one of the smallest works in a series of reclining female nudes that Harry Rosin produced in the late 1930s and early 1940s, several years after returning from Tahiti. The woman's face is less exotic than those in works done in Tahiti. A professional model posed for this piece.[1] Five reclining nudes were shown in 1945–46 at the one-man exhibition *Harry Rosin: Portraits of Children and Other Recent Sculpture* at the Pennsylvania Academy of the Fine Arts. Among them was the cast stone figure dated about 1939 that was given to the Philadelphia Museum of Art in 1947. It is forty-two inches long and shows the model in a somewhat more animated pose with her left arm raised. The four others were apparently a numbered edition titled *Reclining Nude.*[2] Number one, in plaster, was then owned by Mrs. John Wintersteen, and number two, in an unknown medium, was owned by Alfred G.B. Steel, both of Philadelphia. Numbers three and four were then part of the artist's collection; perhaps it was one of these that was later sold to Myer H. Goldman and presented to the Pennsylvania Academy in 1971.

It is not known if the example in the Museum of American Art of the Pennsylvania Academy of the Fine Arts was ever given a number in the edition or if there are other casts of it extant. There is no record of which foundry cast this piece. The black surface is not typical of the patinas seen on other works that Rosin had cast by the Roman Bronze Works. He also used the Modern Art Foundry, New York, in the 1940s; and this casting may have been made there. It won the Second Patrons Prize in 1965 at the Phillips Mill Art Exhibition.

Notes

1. Artist's response to questionnaire, about 1971, PAFA object file.
2. In 1949, Rosin related that until recently, he had called such works *nude* or *reclining nude* and assigned numbers to an edition of four. In 1948 he started assigning more specific titles to all his pieces. Reported in "Exhibited At International Sculpture Show; Honor and Fame Have Come To Former Trenton Teacher," *Trenton Sunday Times Advertiser*, August 7, 1949, p. 8.

Exhibited

1945–46 PAFA, *Harry Rosin: Portraits of Children and Other Recent Sculpture.* **1965** Phillips Mill Art Exhibition, New Hope, Pa., cat. no. 46. **1980** PAFA, Peale House, *Harry Rosin, Sculptor*, checklist no. 34.

Ex Collection

Myer H. Goldman, 1940s-71.

Head of Tory (Victoria Rosin, later Mrs. Carl Bieber)

1944
Bronze with brown, red, and gold patina; cast about 1945
7¾ x 5 x 6¾" (19.8 x 12.8 x 17.2 cm)
Inscribed at left side of neck: VICTORIA/[9] MOS.
Lost-wax cast, possibly by Modern Art Foundry, New York
Gift of the artist to honor Joseph T. Fraser, Jr., for his sympathetic help to the American artist, 1967.10

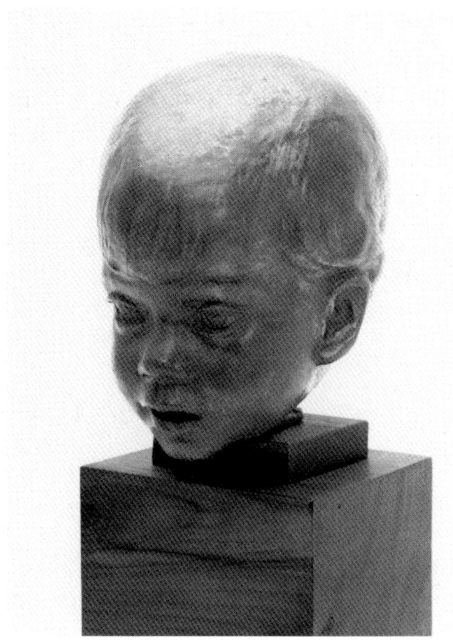

Rosin, *Head of Tory*

HARRY ROSIN'S DAUGHTER, Victoria (b. 1943), was one of his favorite subjects. In addition to this bust, modeled when she was nine months old, he made a painted portrait of her at about nineteen months for the family's 1944 Christmas card[1]; a pastel, *Tory at 3;* and a plaster, *Tory at 4.* The latter two were shown in Rosin's solo exhibition in 1980 at the Peale House galleries of the Pennsylvania Academy of the Fine Arts. By 1948 Rosin had done a pen-and-wash drawing of Tory that was included the same year in the Academy's 46th annual watercolor and print exhibition. In the summer of 1947 when Tory was four, she was painted in oils by Franklin Watkins. The painter Leon Karp did her portrait in December of that year. Her father also painted her at the ages fifteen and twenty-one (private collection).

Rosin started making portrait busts of children in about 1935 while he was in Tahiti. He was commissioned to model a portrait of two-year-old Miko, the daughter of Charles Nordhof, the co-author of *Mutiny on the Bounty.*

> That was my first lesson in how difficult it is to model a child. Whenever she was brought to my studio she began to cry. I finally found out that she thought it was a doctor's office. A great deal of the structural modeling of the head had to be done while Miko was asleep. That wasn't easy, but I persisted, and as a result became keenly aware of simple child forms that lend themselves naturally to the medium of sculpture. After that, I did several other Tahitian children. First I had to make friends with them by modeling little animals. Then, I'd concentrate on the head, look up to check with my model, and find it just wasn't there any more. That's why it takes longer to do children than older persons.[2]

Rosin preferred ten to twenty sittings with each model and found that the most time he could work with a child was an hour and a quarter or an hour and a half. Within that time he had only a ten-minute actual look at the child with most of the time spent working on the "structure of the forms." Fifteen of his portraits of children were exhibited at the Pennsylvania Academy in 1945–46 and were described by the critic Dorothy Grafly as "Alert, questioning, wistful—with more than a touch of tenderness—they suggest a baby world of fairy tale."[3]

To model this *Head of Tory,* Rosin put the baby in a crib and worked on the floor with clay for about fifteen to twenty minutes each day.[4] He had the finished bronze head patinated an overall light brown with reddish highlights throughout, especially on the lips and cheeks. There are also areas of shiny gold highlights. The inscription appears to have been made in the clay, and then just the name was retraced with an engraving tool in the bronze, as there is a distinct difference between the two lines in clarity and depth. The head, mounted on a wooden base, was presented to the Pennsylvania Academy of the Fine Arts by the sculptor to honor Joseph T. Fraser, Jr., who served as curator of schools from 1934 to 1942, secretary from 1938 to 1969 and director from 1946 to 1969.[5] The whereabouts of the original plaster is not known, and there is no record of other casts.

Notes

1. Harry Rosin to Alfred B. Steel and family, c/o Pennsylvania Academy, postmarked Dec. 23, 1944, Joseph T. Fraser, Jr. faculty file, PAFA Archives.
2. Dorothy Grafly, "Harry Rosin," *American Artist* 10 (Feb. 1946), p. 20.
3. Ibid.
4. Interview of Rosin by Jack Bookbinder, "Art and the Artist," WPTZ television series, 1955, film in PAFA Archives.
5. Rosin to Frank T. Howard, president of the PAFA, Sept. 6, 1967, PAFA object file.

Reference
1945 "Local Boy Makes Good—in Tahiti," *Philadelphia Record* (Dec. 8), p. 9 (ill.).

Exhibited
1945 PAFA, annual Fellowship exhibition, checklist no. 73, as *Victoria.* **1945–46** PAFA, *Harry Rosin: Portraits of Children and Other Recent Sculpture,* cat. no. 21 (ill.), as *Sculptor's Daughter.* **1960** PAFA, *Faculty Exhibition,* cat. no. 177. **1965** PAFA, Peale House, *Julian Levi, Harry Rosin,* checklist no. 36, as *Head of Victoria (Tory) 9 Months.* **1986–87** PAFA, *Sculpture at the Pennsylvania Academy of the Fine Arts.*

John Fulton Folinsbee

1945
Bronze with brown patina; lost-wax cast in 1946
11¼ x 6¼ x 8½" (28.5 x 15.9 x 21.6 cm)
Signed and dated at back: 1945–ROSIN
Foundry mark on bracket: ROMAN BRONZE CORP N.Y.
Gift of Harry Rosin, 1947.11

JOHN FULTON FOLINSBEE (1892–1972) was a portrait and landscape painter who was trained at the Art Students League of New York and at the Woodstock School of Art in Connecticut. Like Harry Rosin, he was a resident of New Hope, Pennsylvania, and probably met the sculptor there. A plaster cast of the bust was exchanged for Folinsbee's painting of Rosin's wife, Vilna (private collection). The plaster was included in Rosin's solo show at the Pennsylvania Academy of the Fine Arts in 1945–46, as owned by Mrs. John Folinsbee. In gratitude for the exhibition, Rosin invited the Academy to choose for its collection one of the works that had been shown.[1] The Academy already owned one of Rosin's figures, *Hina Rapa* (q.v.), and wanted a portrait. The Folinsbee bust was selected because his paintings were represented in the collection and he had been awarded a prize in an Academy annual.[2] Due to the war the bust was not cast until late in 1946. It was then shown at the National Academy of Design.

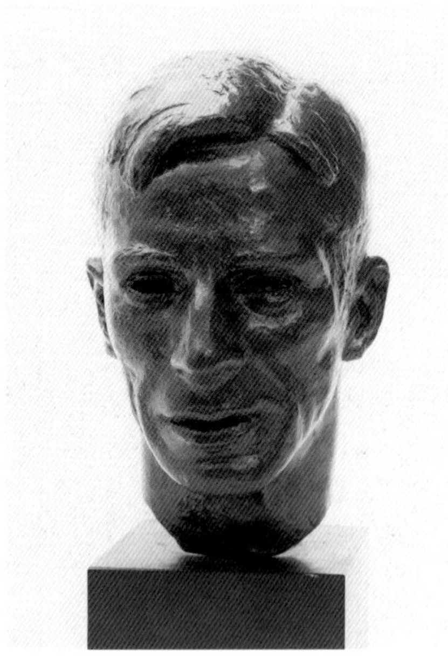

Rosin, *John Fulton Folinsbee*

The bust, mounted on a painted wooden base, has an overall texture that Rosin also used in the bust of Franklin Chenault Watkins (q.v.).

Notes
1. Rosin to Joseph T. Fraser, Jr., director of the PAFA, June 24, 1947, PAFA object file.
2. Note to file by unknown author, about 1947, PAFA object file. The award was the *Jennie Sesnan Medal* in 1931.

Exhibited
1947 National Academy of Design, New York, 1st half of 121st annual exhibition, cat. no. 52. **After 1952** Playhouse Galleries, New Hope, Pa., *John Folinsbee, N.A.,* ill. on cover of brochure. **1960** PAFA, *Faculty Exhibition,* cat. no. 174. **1980** PAFA, Peale House, *Harry Rosin, Sculptor,* checklist no. 38.

Franklin C. Watkins

1947
Bronze with brown patina; lost-wax cast
12¾ x 6½ x 10½" (32.4 x 16.5 x 26.7 cm)
Signed and dated at back: HARRY ROSIN 1947
Foundry mark at back: Modern Art Fdry. N.Y.
Henry D. Gilpin Fund, 1947.18

FRANKLIN CHENAULT WATKINS (1894–1972) studied painting and drawing at the Pennsylvania Academy of the Fine Arts in 1913 and from 1915 to 1920 and modeling in 1922–23. He received William Emlen Cresson Traveling Scholarships in 1917 and 1918. Watkins served at the Academy as an instructor of painting and a general critic from 1942 to 1971. He was a member of the board of trustees for twelve years and vice-president of the Fellowship for twenty-five years. Twenty of his still lifes, portraits, and religious paintings are in the permanent collection.

Harry Rosin and Watkins both taught at the Pennsylvania Academy in the 1940s. In the summer of 1947, Rosin went to Watkins's studio and summer home in Avalon, New Jersey, with his wife, Vilna, and daughter, Tory.[1] They spent two weeks there, while Rosin modeled the bust of Watkins. A plaster cast of that portrait was exchanged for Watkins's oil sketch of Tory (private collection).[2] The plaster was

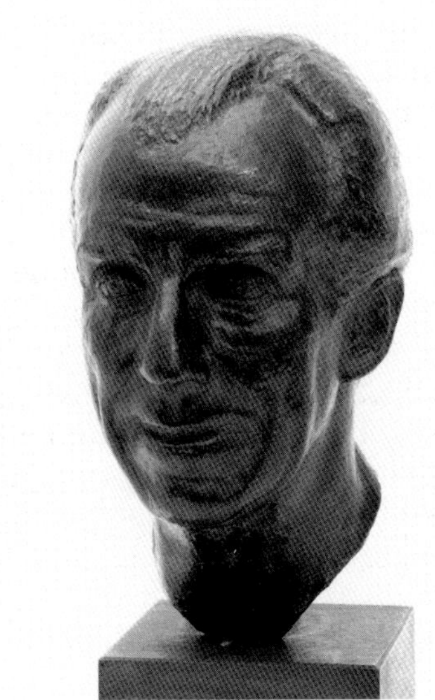

Rosin, *Franklin C. Watkins*

shown with the collection of the sitter in the 1959 Academy exhibition *Paintings, Drawings, Prints, and Sculpture Collected and Owned by Fourteen Philadelphia Artists.* An undated newspaper clipping shows the bust in Watkins's studio near a bronze cast of the head from the wooden figure *Allegory of the Schuylkill River* by WILLIAM RUSH.[3]

The bust of Watkins was cast in bronze in 1947, purchased the same year by the Pennsylvania Academy, and shown in the annual exhibition of 1948. The bust is modeled with an overall texture and captures an impression rather than a detailed likeness. It is mounted on a wooden base.

Notes

1. Rosin to Joseph T. Fraser, Jr., director of the PAFA, June 24, 1947, PAFA object file.
2. Artist's response to questionnaire, [1947], PAFA object file.
3. Clipping in faculty file, PAFA Archives.

References

1971/72–1973/74 PAFA, school catalogues.

Exhibited

1948* cat. no. 184. **1960** PAFA, *Faculty Exhibition,* cat. no. 193. **1965** PAFA, Peale House, *Julian Levi; Harry Rosin,* checklist no. 25. **1980** PAFA, Peale House, *Harry Rosin, Sculptor,* checklist no. 44.

Eleanor S. Gray (Mrs. J. Maurice Gray)

1967
Bronze with brown patina
21 x 19 x 10″ (53.3 x 48.3 x 25.4 cm)
Signed and dated at back: 1967—HARRY ROSIN
Lost-wax cast, probably by Modern Art Foundry, New York
Gift of J. Maurice Gray, 1968.9

A PATRON of the Philadelphia Orchestra, Eleanor Schramm Gray (1920–1967) had a strong interest in the visual arts, as well, and studied painting at the Pennsylvania Academy of the Fine Arts from 1960 to 1963. She and her husband, J. Maurice Gray, established a student prize for still-life painting in 1961 that evolved into the purchase prize named for her. A second fund was established in her name upon her death by her husband. It provides special prizes and awards to be made at the discretion of the faculty and administration, as well as tuition scholarships.

This bust was commissioned by J. Maurice Gray shortly after his wife's death.[1] Harry Rosin was given photographs as a guide, including, no doubt, the one that appears in several issues of the Academy's school catalogues in the 1970s and shows her, as here, with a pearl necklace and wearing her hair in a bun. By October 1967 bronzes were being cast, probably by the Modern Art Foundry, which Rosin often used.[2] One cast was given to the Pennsylvania Academy and the other, to the Philadelphia zoo. By 1970 the latter was installed in a niche in the Eleanor S. Gray hummingbird house, which became part of the tropical aviary of the Bird House in 1987.[3] The location of the plaster is unknown.

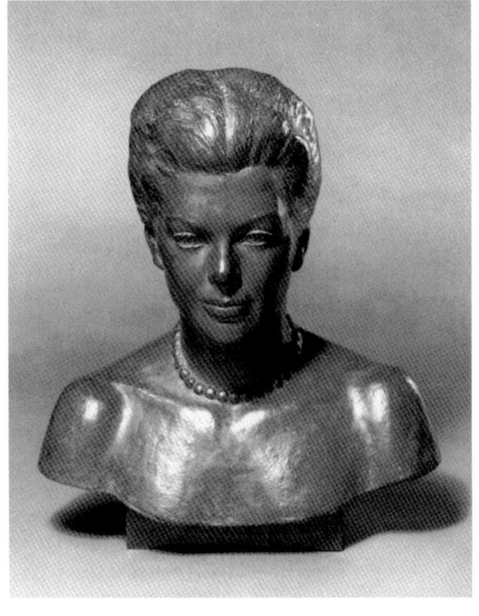

Rosin, *Eleanor S. Gray*

Notes

1. Rosin, note to file, [1968], PAFA object file.

2. Joseph T. Fraser, Jr. to J. Maurice Gray, Oct. 19, 1967, PAFA object file.

3. "Bird house at the Zoo is memorial," unidentified newspaper clipping, about 1968, faculty file, PAFA Archives.

Exhibited

1978–79 PAFA, *350 Masterpieces of American Art: 1720–1978.* **1980** PAFA, Peale House, *Harry Rosin, Sculptor,* checklist no. 40.

Aurelius Renzetti

1897–1975

Born in the Abruzzi region of Italy, Marcus Aurelius Renzetti was named after the second-century Roman emperor Marcus Aurelius Antoninus. As a child of four, Renzetti modeled figures from clay that he found near his village. In 1902 he and his mother came to the United States to join his father, who had set up a tailor shop in Philadelphia. At the age of about thirteen, Renzetti left school, apprenticed himself to a sculptor, and began studying at the Graphic Sketch Club (now the Samuel S. Fleisher Art Memorial). With the help of local art patrons, he was able to attend the Pennsylvania Academy of the Fine Arts from 1916 to 1923. He studied life modeling with CHARLES GRAFLY and won the Edmund Stewardson Prize in 1918. Renzetti went to Europe on William Emlen Cresson Traveling Scholarships in 1918 and 1921; won a cash prize for sculpture in 1920, donated by John F. Lewis, President of the board of trustees; and received Stimson Prize honorable mentions in 1920 and 1921. While a student at the Pennsylvania Academy, Renzetti spent more than a year repairing the terracotta Tanagra figurines in the Academy's collection.[1] He was also employed by the American Statuary and Decorating Company in Philadelphia to make religious statues.

After graduation, Renzetti worked briefly as a designer and carver for the Victor Talking Machine Company in Camden, New Jersey. Then in about 1922, he began teaching sculpture at the Graphic Sketch Club. In the late 1930s, he taught sculpture to the blind.

For thirty-six years, beginning in 1930, Renzetti taught sculpture at the Philadelphia Museum School of Industrial Art (now the University of the Arts). In 1961 he was awarded its first honorary degree in recognition of his outstanding teaching. He received the Alumni Association Award of Merit in 1965 and was given a one-man exhibition. When interviewed about the work in the show, he said, "Don't call it sculpture; that is too imposing. I call them things. Almost every piece shown here I did as a demonstration for the students at the school, and each one represents a challenge of another sort."[2] Even after his retirement in 1966, he continued to teach sculpture at the Young Men's Christian Association near his home in Arden, Delaware. In 1962 he received the annual award of the Da Vinci Art Alliance, Philadelphia, for his contribution to the art community. At about that time, he was blinded in one eye by a chip of marble and turned his attention from sculpture to photography and design.

Renzetti worked in a variety of materials, including clay, stone, cast stone, wood, bamboo, and metal. He participated in the Pennsylvania Academy's annual exhibitions from 1915 to 1918, 1920 to 1923, and in 1925 and 1938, as well as in several Fellowship annuals.

Notes

1. Martin Zipin, "Marcus Aurelius Renzetti: Abruzzi to Broad and Pine," *Jewish Exponent,* Nov. 5, 1965, clipping file, library, *Philadelphia Inquirer.*

2. Ibid.

References

1965 "Aurelius Renzetti describes his work as: Things I Like To Do," *Philadelphia Inquirer,* Dec. 12, magazine section, pp. 18–19. **1971** William P. Frank, "The Artist Renzetti, re-'discovered' in Arden, Del.," *Wilmington Morning News,* March 3, p. 29. **1975** William P. Frank, "Arden Sculptor Marcus Renzetti," *Wilmington Morning News,* June 30, p. 37.

Negresco

About 1938
Cast stone, painted purple-black
8½ x 5½ x 6½" (21.6 x 14 x 16.5 cm)
Gift of the Fellowship of the Pennsylvania Academy of the Fine Arts, 1940.10.1

THIS HEAD of a black man was probably influenced by African art. It is a hollow cast with streamlined contours that taper very slightly from the close-cropped hair to the thick neck. The eyes are indented beneath arching brows that create deep shadows. It is mounted on a high wooden base.

Negresco may have been made to show Aurelius Renzetti's students how to cast multiples from a stone original, using cement with stone dust and chips. The porous and textured surface of the sculpture suggests that it was cast from a carved stone work rather than a smoother, clay-modeled one. The

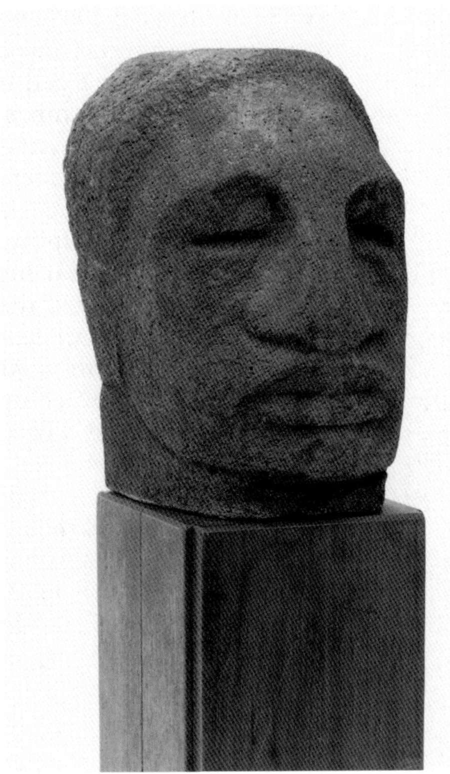

Renzetti, *Negresco*

broadly carved features and the sense of the artist's having worked within the confined space of a boulder reinforce the conjecture that the original was carved in stone. Cast stone was popular for producing inexpensive and durable multiples in the 1930s and 1940s.

Exhibited
1938 PAFA, Fellowship annual exhibition, cat. no. 109.

Reuben Nakian

1897–1986

A first generation Armenian-American, Reuben Nakian was born on Long Island and reared in New Jersey. He became interested in art at an early age and was encouraged by his parents to take drawing lessons at an academy in Jersey City when he was thirteen. He studied briefly at the Art Students League of New York in 1912. As a commercial artist, he produced lettering for mail-order houses and for *Century Magazine* from 1913 to 1915. In the evenings in 1915, he studied life drawing with Homer Boss and A.S. Baylinson at the Independent Art School, which was directed by Robert Henri, and clay modeling at the Beaux-Arts Institute of Design (now the National Institute for Architectural Education), in New York.

For three years, Nakian served as apprentice to Paul Manship (1885–1966) and his chief assistant, GASTON LACHAISE. Nakian learned to cast in bronze and made drawings and sculpture of animals. In 1919 he was awarded a Louis Comfort Tiffany Foundation Fellowship. He shared a studio with Lachaise in the early 1920s and then acquired a studio of his own through the award of a stipend and studio expenses by Gertrude Vanderbilt Whitney (1877–1942), who made him a member of the Whitney Studio Club. In 1926 his first solo exhibition was held at the Club galleries, and in 1930 he was included in a new-talent show at the Museum of Modern Art. He spent some time in France and Italy in 1931 on a Guggenheim Fellowship. While there he was impressed by ancient Roman portraiture and images from classical mythology.[1] In 1932–33 he modeled two series of realistic portrait busts: one was of artists, and the other depicted President Franklin D. Roosevelt and his cabinet.[2] The next year, Nakian gained recognition for an eight-foot-high plaster sculpture of the baseball hero Babe Ruth (location unknown).

In the late 1930s and early 1940s, Nakian turned from sculpture to drawing. By 1946, however, he was working in both media. From then until 1951, he taught at the Newark School of Fine and Industrial Arts, where he had access to a large kiln. He began a series of abstract terracotta reliefs, sculptures in the round, and drawings based on Greek mythology. He used these themes much the way that Pablo Picasso (1881–1973) did. They held interest for him throughout the rest of his life. His style became freer under the influence of abstract expressionism to which he was introduced by his friend Arshile Gorky, a painter who was also of Armenian descent. Nakian's subject matter became predominantly the female figure.

Beginning in the mid-1950s, Nakian made large-scale plaster sculptures. In the next two decades, he executed commissions of monumental sculptures for the facade of the Loeb Student Center at New York University and *Voyage in Crete* for the New York State Theater at Lincoln Center. They were cast in aluminum and in bronze, respectively. In 1961, fifty-eight of his works represented the United States in the São Paulo Biennal, in Brazil. In 1966 the Museum of Modern Art organized an important retrospective of Nakian's work. The Philadelphia College of Art (now the University of the Arts) awarded Nakian the Gold Medal for Excellence in 1967. The next year, ten of his monumental plaster works, including the series Judgment of Paris and Goddess with the Golden Thighs, represented the United States in the Thirty-fourth Venice Biennale. His work is owned by the Museum of Modern Art, the Whitney Museum of American Art, the Metropolitan Museum of Art, and Saint Vartan's Armenian Cathedral, in New York; the Hirshhorn Museum and Sculpture Garden and the National Museum of American Art, in Washington, D.C.; and the Art Institute of Chicago, among many others.

From 1948 until his death at the age of eighty-eight, Nakian lived in Stamford, Connecticut. In 1985, the year before his death, retrospective exhibitions were organized by the DiLaurenti Gallery in New York and the Milwaukee Art Museum, Wisconsin.

Notes

1. Wayne Craven, *Sculpture in America* (Newark: University of Delaware Press, 1984), p. 641.

2. Four busts from the FDR series were displayed in a 1983 exhibition concerning the New Deal period. It was mounted by the National Portrait Gallery, Washington, D.C., which owns the bust of Harry L. Hopkins, administrator of the Federal Emergency Relief Administration during the Depression, secretary of commerce, and special assistant to President Roosevelt in World War II.

References

1966 Frank O'Hara, *Nakian,* New York: Museum of Modern Art, exhib. cat. **1967** Anne G. Terhune, "The Sculpture of Reuben Nakian from 1920 to 1965," unpublished M.A. thesis, Institute of Fine Arts, New York University, New York, June. **1977** Hilton Kramer, "Nakian's Dazzling Artistry," *New York Times,* Sept. 25, sec. 2, pp. 1, 33. **1986** Grace Glueck, "Reuben Nakian, U. S. Sculptor, Dies," *New York Times,* Dec. 5, p. 20-D.

Saul Schary

1943
Bronze with black patina; lost-wax cast by 1980
12½ x 8⅝ x 9¾" (31.8 x 21.9 x 24.8 cm)
Inscribed at left side beneath neck: SCHARY
Foundry mark on back edge of bracket: Modern Art Fdry. N.Y.
Bequest of Mrs. Hope Skillman Schary, 1982.2

THIS PORTRAIT of the illustrator and painter Saul Schary (1904–1978) was modeled during Reuben Nakian's early explorations in abstract expressionism. The massive head has a forceful presence, indicative of the painter's personality. The surface is rough and broadly modeled with tool marks visible on the face and the artist's fingerprints on the back of the head and neck.

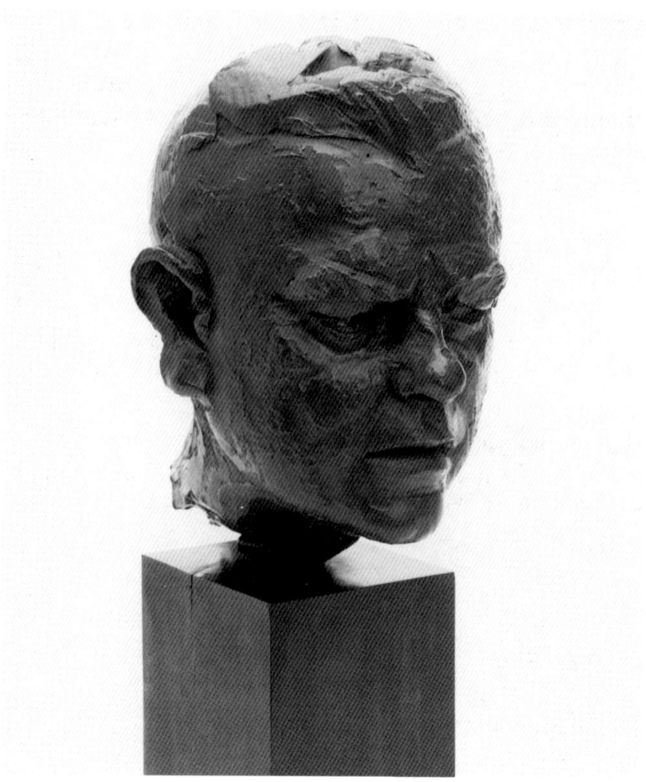

Nakian, *Saul Schary*

Schary posed for the portrait although he did not commission it. The plaster version (location unknown) became his property and was later cast into bronze at the Modern Art Foundry, Astoria, Long Island, without the knowledge of the sculptor.[1] It is therefore not known whether the color of the patina and surface appearance of the bronze would have pleased him. This bronze cast was bequeathed to the Pennsylvania Academy of the Fine Arts in 1982 by the sitter's widow. Schary had attended the Pennsylvania Academy in 1924–25, before studying in New York and Paris. His oil paintings and watercolors were shown in the Academy's annual exhibitions from 1932 to 1944. Arshile Gorky introduced Schary to Nakian, and they became friends.[2] This bust of Schary was displayed in a posthumous solo exhibition at the Pennsylvania Academy in 1980, which featured his portraits of Nakian and Gorky. It is mounted on a wooden base.

Nakian's first series of artists' portraits dated from 1932–33 and included busts of the painters Raphael Soyer and Peggy Bacon and the sculptor CONCETTA SCARAVAGLIONE. Ten portraits were shown in his 1933 solo exhibition at the Downtown Gallery in New York. They were all modeled with smooth surfaces. In 1943, however, when Nakian again turned to artists' portraits, he produced rough, energetic surfaces. In addition to this bust of Schary, he modeled art collector Dikran Kelekian (plaster, 1966, Egan Gallery, New York), and the painter Marcel Duchamp (bronze, about 1961, Hirshhorn Museum and Sculpture Garden, Washington, D.C.); the latter is considered one of his masterpieces.[3]

Notes

1. Artist's response to questionnaire, August 19, 1984, PAFA object file.
2. Ibid.
3. Grace Glueck, "Reuben Nakian, U.S. Sculptor, Dies," *New York Times,* Dec. 5, 1986, p. 20-D.

Exhibited

1980 PAFA, Peale House, *Saul Schary (1904–1978) Selected Works,* exhibition sponsored by PAFA faculty, listed in checklist as *Bronze Portrait Head of Schary.*

Sol Bauer

1898–1982

A native of Cleveland, Sol A. Bauer made watch fobs as a child by carving initials into soft beach stones from Lake Erie. His first figural composition was a stone image of the comic-book characters Mutt and Jeff. He continued to carve in high school and while earning a civil-engineering degree from the Case School of Applied Science (now Case Western Reserve University) in Cleveland. He was graduated in 1920 and, three years later, was licensed as a surveyor and civil engineer. He ran his own company, Bauer's Surveys, from 1926 to 1969. In 1927 he tried modeling a bust of Clarence Darrow from an image in *Vanity Fair* magazine but was unhappy with the clay version and carved it in wood. The following year, a local art dealer convinced Bauer to submit the wood portrait to the annual May show at the Cleveland Museum of Art, where it won first prize. Every year after that until 1956, he submitted his wood sculpture to the Cleveland Museum's exhibitions and often won awards.

While working as a surveyor, he took a few evening classes with the sculptor Walter A. Sinz (b. 1881) at the Cleveland School of Art (now the Cleveland Institute of Art), but Bauer considered himself to be basically self-taught.[1] He devoted about fifteen hours a week to carving pieces of wood that had been discarded at building sites. In sculpture Bauer preferred the discipline of the subtractive method of direct carving to the additive method of clay modeling. Each sculpture was begun with only a rough idea of what he wanted to do. The composition would often change depending upon the condition of the wood and its grain.

Between 1933 to 1958, Bauer participated in about a third of the annual exhibitions of the Pennsylvania Academy of the Fine Arts. Invited to enter work in *American Art Today* at the 1939 New York World's Fair, he showed a smoothly polished wood figure called *Slav Dancer.* Two of his sculptures were in the *Artists for Victory* exhibition at the Metropolitan Museum of Art in New York in 1942. In 1945 he received a commission from Saint Francis of Assisi Catholic Church in Gates Mills, Ohio for a wooden figure of Saint Joseph. Bauer's work is also represented in the Cleveland Museum of Art.

Note

1. Artist's response to questionnaire, Jan. 30, 1950, PAFA object file.

References

1941 Milton Widder, "Cleveland Artist Leader in Wood Carving Revival," *Cleveland Press,* August 23, *Cleveland Press* Collection, Cleveland State University Library. **1982** Alma Kaufman, "Sol A. Bauer, civil engineer, a talented sculptor in wood," *Cleveland Plain Dealer,* Jan. 20, library, *Plain Dealer.*

Processional

1948–49
Apple wood
29 x 17¼ x 16¾" (73.7 x 43.8 x 42.7 cm)
Signed and dated on top of base: SA BAUER/1949
Joseph E. Temple Fund, 1950.2

Processional is one of a series of dancers, carved singly or in groups of up to four figures. This work depicts three, full-length, stocky, female figures with their fists together and arms raised overhead. The artist saw in this work "a sad beauty, like the patient nobility I want to insinuate into their Oriental faces."[1] The figures were finished with a small gouge that created a uniform faceted surface. The hair and the base were worked with broader strokes. The sides of the base were left rough, and the top rim was beveled. A crack from the edge of the base to the center of the log developed in the process of carving and forced Bauer to compose the figures in a circle. In order to be self-supporting and less fragile, the dancers were left joined and given thick limbs. Unfortunately, after six months of work, an accident occurred during the carving. The sculpture was knocked off the workstand when the chisel hit a rotten area in the wood. Evidence of the artist's patching are visible on the lower back of the first figure in the procession and on the arms of the final figure.

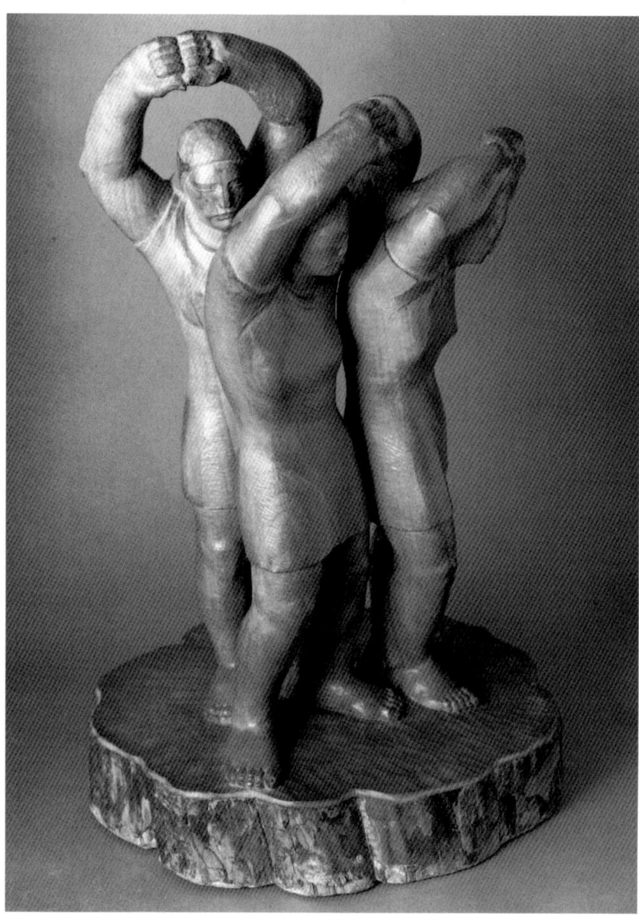

Bauer, *Processional*

Bauer won first prize in the wood-sculpture category at the annual exhibition of the Cleveland Museum of Art in 1949 for this work and *Kneeling Figure.* The next year, *Processional* was awarded an honorable mention in sculpture and a cash prize at the annual exhibition of the Pennsylvania Academy of the Fine Arts.

Note

1. "Art is Adventure for Wood Carver," *Cleveland Plain Dealer,* May 8, 1949, Cleveland State University Library.

References

1949 "Annual Exhibition," *Bulletin of the Cleveland Museum of Art* 36 (May), pp. 68, 74, 78 (ill.). **1950** Paul B. Metzler, "Shaker [Heights] Sculptor Wins Two Prizes with Oaken Work," *Cleveland Plain Dealer* (Jan. 23), Cleveland State University Library.

Exhibited

1949 The Cleveland Museum of Art, Cleveland, Ohio, *Thirty-First Annual Exhibition of Work by Cleveland Artists and Craftsmen.* **1950*** cat. no. 201 (ill.). **1971** Philadelphia Art Alliance, *Dance in Sculpture.* **1986–87** PAFA, *Sculpture at the Pennsylvania Academy of the Fine Arts.*

Hélène Sardeau

1899–1969

Born in Antwerp, Belgium, Hélène Sardeau came to the United States with her family about 1912. She briefly attended various art schools in New York, including the Art Students League, where she studied with MAHONRI YOUNG. Upon the death of her father about 1924, she and her sister Martine created a successful business making portrait dolls of famous people. Hélène modeled and painted the heads, and her sister made the costumes. The dolls were exhibited in Chicago and New York. With some of the profits, Hélène was able to live in Paris from 1926 to 1929, where she studied at the American School of Sculpture and had her work critiqued by the French sculptor Charles Despiau (1874–1946). In 1927 she designed and made masks for the Aeschylus festival in Delphi, Greece, and in 1928 she exhibited at the Salon d'Automne.

On her return to New York in 1929, she was given an exhibition at Ehrich Gallery. In 1929–30 she executed a commission for three figure groups in relief for the facade of the main Young Men's Hebrew Association in New York. She married the Philadelphia painter and sculptor George Biddle (1885–1973) in 1931, and they lived and worked in Italy for the next two years. Sardeau became an American Citizen in 1933. She was given a solo exhibition at the Mellon Galleries in Philadelphia and was commissioned to carve the limestone figure *Slave* for the Ellen Phillips Samuel Memorial in Fairmount Park. In 1934 her *Kneeling Figure* won the Avery Prize for sculpture at the Architectural League of New York. Sardeau exhibited her work in the first exhibition of the progressive group called the Sculptors Guild, in 1938 in New York. A solo exhibition of her sculpture and drawings was held in 1946 at the Robert Carlen Gallery, in Philadelphia.

In the 1940s Hélène Sardeau and her husband collaborated on two projects in which she executed reliefs and he painted murals: one at the National Library in Rio de Janeiro and the other at the Library of the Supreme Court in Mexico City. Her work is also in the Metropolitan Museum of Art and the Whitney Museum of American Art in New York and the Tel Aviv Museum in Israel. The Philadelphia Museum of Art owns the terracotta bust *Negro Lament,* 1941; the lifesize figure *Icarus,* 1951, which is displayed inside the east entrance to the museum; and a 1935 print.

References
1930 "New Sculptures by Hélène Sardeau," *Vanity Fair* 35, Dec., pp. 48–49. **1956** Frank Crotty, "Wife of Artist George Biddle is Famed Woman Sculptor; Spends Summers on Cape Cod," *Worcester [Mass.] Telegram,* April 29, clipping file, PAFA Library. **1969** Obituary, *New York Times,* March 25, p. 47.

Amazon

1932
Terracotta
14⅛ x 7⅛ x 8¼" (35.9 x 18.1 x 21 cm)
Signed and dated at base of neck at back: Hélène Sardeau./ 1932
Gift of George Biddle, 1950.16

HÉLÈNE SARDEAU'S SCULPTURES often depict themes from Greek myths. The Amazons were a race of female warriors who were said to have lived in Scythia, near the Black Sea. This head with serene half-closed eyes and a thick powerful neck represents such a woman. The treatment of the hair suggests the helmet worn by a warrior. The smooth slightly shiny surface of the hair and eyebrows was achieved by applying slip, or liquid clay, of a lighter color and then burnishing those areas.[1] The rustic appearance of the rest of the head and neck suggests antiquity and shows the marks of the sculptor at work. The dark stains at the bottom of the neck and the numerous fire cracks throughout indicate that the clay head was fired. The head is mounted on a white marble base.

Amazon was given to the Pennsylvania Academy of the Fine Arts in 1950 by the artist's husband, George Biddle, who responded to a letter sent to Academy stockholders and members soliciting donations of works by particular artists not yet represented in the permanent collection. Sometime probably in the 1940s, Sardeau produced another bust called *Amazon* that she carved in limestone and exhibited in New York in 1944 and in Philadelphia in 1946.

Note
1. Conservation report by Mitchell B. Merback and Virginia N. Naudé, August 12, 1986, PAFA object file.

Exhibited
1932 Galeria di Roma, Rome, joint exhibition with George Biddle. **About 1932** Ehrich Galleries, New York, solo exhibition. **About 1933** Julien Levy Gallery, New York, *Exhibition of Sculpture by Helene Sardeau,* cat. no. 12. **1933** Mellon Galleries, Philadelphia, *Sculpture by Hélène Sardeau,* cat. no. 10. **1986–87** PAFA, *Sculpture at the Pennsylvania Academy of the Fine Arts.*

Ex Collection
The artist, 1932–50.

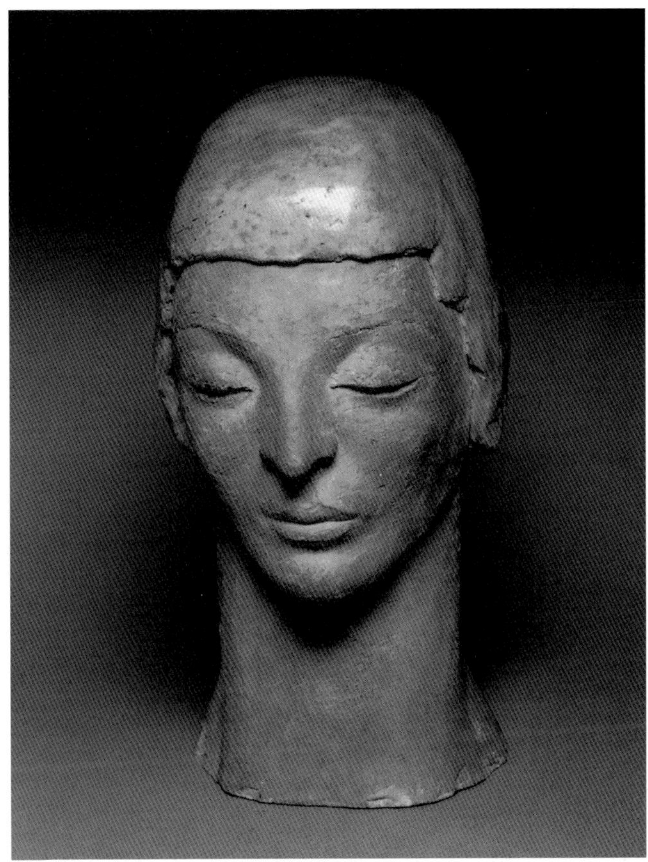

Sardeau, *Amazon*

Figure

1952
Bronze with brown patina; cast in 1952–53
28 x 15½ x 17" (71.2 x 39.5 x 43.2 cm)
Signed and dated on back near bottom edge: SARDEAU 1952
Sand cast in Rome, Italy
Henry D. Gilpin Fund, 1954.14

THIS attenuated figure of a woman is typical of Hélène Sardeau's work of the 1950s. (Another example *Kneeling Woman,* 1955 is in the Metropolitan Museum of Art.)

After *Figure* was exhibited in New York in 1954, it was sent, at the artist's request, to Modern Art Foundry in New York to serve as the model for another bronze cast. Sardeau thought the plaster model had probably been destroyed during the initial casting in Rome.[1] During conservation treatment in November 1984 a piece of a 1954 newspaper article was found inside the sculpture, which may indicate that the work in the Museum of American Art of the Pennsylvania Academy of the Fine Arts is actually

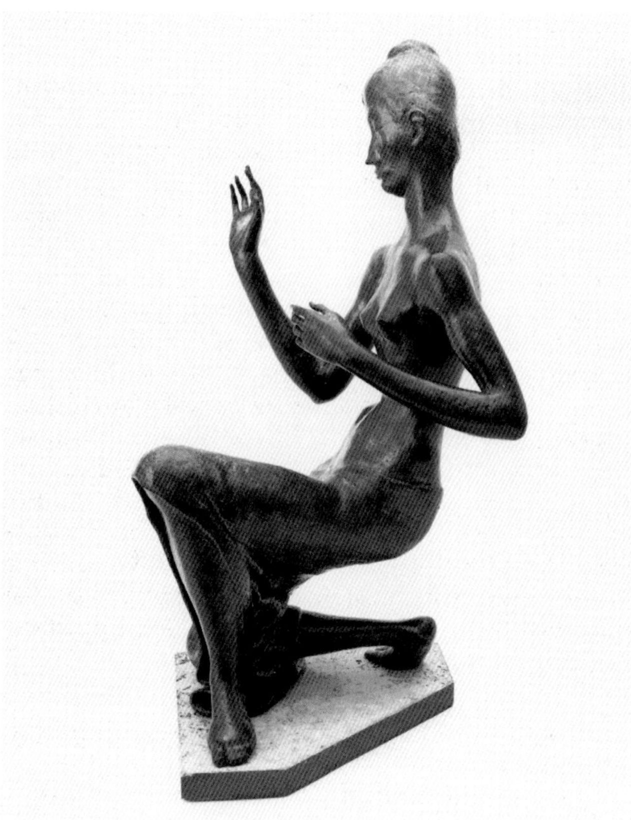

Sardeau, *Figure*

the second cast; the one made in New York. The whereabouts of the other cast is not known. This figure is mounted on a travertine base.

Note

1. Hélène Sardeau to Joseph T. Fraser, Jr., director of PAFA, Feb. 16, 1954, PAFA object file.

Exhibited

1953 Sculptors Guild, New York, cat. no. 138. **1954*** cat. no. 54 (ill.).

Nathaniel Choate

1899–1965

Nathaniel Choate was born in Southboro, Massachusetts. He was educated in Morristown, New Jersey, and at Harvard University, where he studied art history with Paul J. Sachs, Edward W. Forbes, and Denman Waldo Ross. Having been graduated in 1922, he studied painting in Paris at the Académies Colarossi and Delécluse,[1] and spent two summers doing mural decoration and portraiture in Italy. After a trip to Greece in 1924, he chose sculpture as his medium. For two years, he was art editor for the *Youth's Companion* magazine then published by the Atlantic Monthly Company in Boston. In the evenings, he took modeling classes with John Albert Wilson (b. 1878), who taught at Harvard's architectural school and at the Massachusetts Institute of Technology.

In 1927 Nathaniel Choate went back to Italy and worked near the marble quarries until about 1936. During that time, he made several trips to Africa and to the United States. His travels through Morocco and the Sudan in 1932 greatly affected his subsequent work, which often featured animals or people from different cultures. A group of bronze and stone works from his Moroccan trip were well received when shown at the Durand-Ruel Galleries in New York in November 1934. They were praised for "drawing beauty from the material" and for the way the "play of light" gave them "life."[2]

Choate returned to the United States in 1936 and settled near Phoenixville, Pennsylvania. His work was shown regularly at the annual exhibitions of the Pennsylvania Academy of the Fine Arts from 1935 to 1950. The Architectural League of New York awarded him its 1937 medal of honor in design and craftsmanship for excellence in stone carving and design. In 1938 he taught sculpture with CHARLES RUDY at the Pennsylvania Academy's Chester Springs summer school and had a second New York one-man show at the Arden Gallery. Choate designed reliefs for the entrance to the United States Pavilion at the New York World's Fair in 1939. In the late 1930s, he executed a relief, *The Four Winds*, for the Post Office in Pittman, New Jersey, for the Federal Works Agency. In 1940 and 1949, he participated in the *Sculpture International* juried exhibitions at the Philadelphia Museum of Art sponsored by the Fairmount Park Art Association. Choate managed his own ceramic firm, Aldham Kilns, from 1941 to 1947 when the factory burned down, destroying much of his life's work. His first one-man show in Philadelphia was held in 1948–49 at the Philadelphia Art Alliance. It included sculpture, paintings, and drawings, which were characterized by critics as "outstanding" and praised for "amazing versatility."[3]

Nathaniel Choate's work is in the Brookgreen Gardens, Murrells Inlet, South Carolina; the National Academy of Design, New York; and the Honolulu Academy of Arts. Among his commissions were emblems of the four Evangelists for the American Battle Monument at the military cemetery in Hamm, Luxembourg. Choate was elected an associate of the National Academy of Design in 1940 and an Academician in 1955. He was also a member of the National Sculpture Society for many years and served as first vice-president from 1953 to 1955.

Notes

1. Proske 1968, p. 380.
2. Mary Morsell, "Nathaniel Choate, Durand-Ruel Galleries," *Art News* 33 (Nov. 24, 1934), p. 9.
3. Dorothy Drummond, "Sculpture Show at Philadelphia Art Alliance," *Art Digest* 23 (Dec. 15, 1948), p. 30; and C.H. Bonte, "Choate at Alliance," *Philadelphia Inquirer,* Dec. 19, 1948, p. 15-SO.

References
1948–49 *Nat Choate: Sculpture, Paintings, and Drawings,* Philadelphia Art Alliance, exhib. brochure, [p. 4]. **1965** Obituary, *New York Times,* August 24, p. 31. **1968** Beatrice Gilman Proske, *Brookgreen Gardens Sculpture,* Murrells Inlet, S.C.: Brookgreen Gardens, pp. 380–82.

Moroccan Goat

By 1937
Pyrophyllite
7¼ x 9½ x 6¾" (18.4 x 24.1 x 17 cm)
Signed (incised) near animal's tail: NAT.CHOATE
Henry D. Gilpin Fund, 1943.7

One of Nathaniel Choate's favorite sculptural themes was exotic animals. *Moroccan Goat* may have been done from memories of his trip to Morocco in 1932 or from a drawing that he made there. The sculpture was probably carved directly in stone. Pyrophyllite is a soft mineral resembling talc. It was then commonly known as African Wonderstone but was sometimes confused with the much harder black Belgian marble. Choate used the same style for stone as for clay.[1] He refused to allow the properties of the material to interfere with his aesthetic. He was interested in creating sinuous forms to emphasize a striking silhouette.

Moroccan Goat shows an interplay of different textures. A regular pattern of deeply carved lines curves from the animal's head to his right shoulder. An overall pattern of shallow incised lines represents the hairs of the animal's coat. And a "fish scale" pattern differentiates the fur on the legs. Most of the carved lines are gray in contrast to the blackness of the smooth areas of the face, ears, and hooves. Other incised lines have been either toned or polished black to further emphasize the forms of the shoulders, the joints of the forelegs, and the curve of the hind legs.

This was one of three sculptures that won Choate the Architectural League of New York's medal of honor in 1937. *Moroccan Goat* was shown the following year in the annual exhibition of the Pennsylvania Academy of the Fine Arts. In 1943 when a bronze titled *Roan Antelope* was displayed at the Academy, it was purchased with the intention of exchanging it for *Moroccan Goat.*[2]

Notes

1. "Roundabout the Galleries," *Art News* 36 (May 7, 1938), p. 18.
2. Minutes, meeting of the board of directors, March 11, 1943, [p. 1].

Exhibited
1937 Architectural League of New York, annual exhibition. **1938*** cat. no. 338 (ill.). **1938** Arden Gallery, New York, *An Exhibition of Sculptures by Nathaniel Choate,* cat. no. 25 (medium mistakenly given as black Belgian marble). **1948–49** Philadelphia Art Alliance, *Nat Choate: Sculpture, Paintings, and Drawings,* cat. no. 1 (medium mistakenly given as Belgian marble). **1970** Free Library of Philadelphia, *Animal Sculpture for Children,* bookmobile. **1972** Cosmopolitan Club, Philadelphia, exhibition of PAFA works. **1974–85** Executive Mansion, Harrisburg, long-term loan. **1986–87** PAFA, *Sculpture at the Pennsylvania Academy of the Fine Arts.* **1989** PAFA, *"The Birds and the Beasts Will Teach Us."*

Choate, *Moroccan Goat*

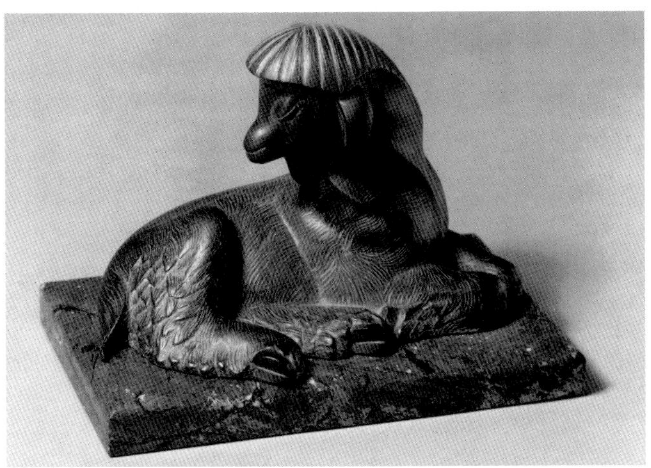

François Rubitschung

1899–about 1986

François H. Rubitschung was born to Swiss-German parents in Pforzheim in southern Germany. He developed an early interest in art, perhaps through his grand-uncle who was a well-known mural painter.[1] Rubitschung probably studied with Paul Baum, a famous painter and teacher. Although his interest was in sculpture, Rubitschung was encouraged by his father to pursue the jewelry trade, which seemed more lucrative. In the early 1920s, he went to Caracas to study goldsmithing and for several years operated two shops for custom-made jewelry. One of his patrons was the Venezuelan president. In 1924 at the urging of friends, Rubitschung visited the United States and, while in New York, lived among artists in Greenwich Village. After a trip to Germany, he returned to the United States and became a citizen in about 1930. He studied at various New York art schools, particularly the School of Sculpture at Columbia University. For four years he studied and taught there and came under the influence of ORONZIO MALDARELLI.

Rubitschung exhibited *Woman Figure,* a nude in marble, at the New York World's Fair of 1939–40. During World War II, he did defense work at the Sperry Gyroscope plant on Long Island. In 1945 at the twenty-ninth annual exhibition of the Brooklyn Society of Artists, held at the Brooklyn Museum, he won the first prize of a hundred dollar war bond for his marble *Sustenance.* At the *Third Sculpture International* exhibition, sponsored by Philadelphia's Fairmount Park Art Association in 1949, he exhibited an onyx figure called *Rima,* inspired by a character in the novel *Green Mansions.* The same year, he accepted a one-year teaching position at the University of Texas at Austin while the sculptor Charles Umlauf (b. 1911) was on a Guggenheim fellowship. Rubitschung lived in various Texas cities and taught classes in clay modeling, drawing, and carving to children and adults. For about twenty years, he was a caretaker at Heritage House in Austin, where he gave historic house tours and kept a studio. His commissions include a 260-foot-long mural on the life of the Texas cowboy for the Pearl Brewery in Austin and a large-scale glass sculpture of the explorer Hernando de Soto for a monument on the Mississippi River.[2] In 1962 Rubitschung was given an exhibition in Austin at Saint Edward's University Library. While he was primarily a direct carver in stone and wood, several examples in plaster, terracotta, and bronze were included in the show. One of his last works was a guest book for Lady Bird Johnson.[3]

Notes

1. Most of the biographical data in this entry comes from Mildred Shaw Nelson, "Sculpture Was His Aim," *Houston Chronicle,* magazine section, March 16, 1958, clipping file, PAFA Library.
2. Rick Smith, "An artist's drive helps sculptor past obstacles," *Austin American-Statesman,* Jan. 8, 1979, pp. 1 and 4-A, clipping file, Austin History Center, Austin Public Library.
3. Telephone conversation by Susan James-Gadzinski with Mrs. Allen Russell, May 27, 1994, notes in PAFA research file.

Octopus

1939
Marble
13 x 17½ x 7" (33.1 x 44.5 x 17.8 cm)
Henry D. Gilpin Fund, 1946.11

ANIMALS were among François Rubitschung's favorite subjects. *Octopus* was meant to be a timely representation of the Nazi movement in his native Germany. The sculpture shows the animal subduing its prey by wrapping it in its arms and injecting venom by biting. The sculptor used as his model a small octopus in the old New York Aquarium in Battery Park.[1] He visited there often to study the action of the animal's arms and their suckers, but the octopus spent most of its time hiding in a shell.

The design has been compacted to fit the size and shape of the boulder from which the figure was to be carved. Oronzio Maldarelli suggested this type of abstraction;[2] and much of Rubitschung's work from the late 1930s shows this influence in its increasingly abstract qualities. The focus of this composition is the off-center meeting of two curving arms with the suckers exposed. Balance is maintained by placing the animal's head to the left of center. Most of the contours of the stone are smooth and polished. Tool marks that appear as incised dots and lines help to define the forms by creating shadows. The artist called this stone "French black marble."[3]

Notes

1. Artist's response to questionnaire, [March 7, 1946], PAFA object file.
2. Margaret Taylor Dry, "Rubitschung's Sculpture Graces Many Austin Sites," *Austin American-Statesman,* May 6, 1973, p. 1, clipping file, Austin History Center, Austin Public Library.
3. Artist's response to questionnaire, [March 7, 1946].

Reference

1958 Mildred Shaw Nelson, "Sculpture Was His Aim," *Houston Chronicle,* magazine section, March 16 (ill.), clipping file, PAFA Library.

Exhibited

1941 A.C.A. Gallery, New York, *Exhibition of Paintings and Sculpture by Norman Barr, Earl Hoshall, Joseph Konzal, Sophia Korff, François H. Rubitschung, and Louis Tytell.* **1942–43** Metropolitan Museum of Art, *Artists for Victory,* cat. p. 30. **1946*** cat. no. 174. **1984–85** PAFA, *A Growing American Treasure: Recent Acquisitions and Highlights from the Permanent Collection.* **1986–87** PAFA, *Sculpture at the Pennsylvania Academy of the Fine Arts.* **1989** PAFA, *"The Birds and the Beasts Will Teach Us."* **1993** PAFA, *Carved in Wood and Stone: Twentieth-Century Sculpture.* **1994–96** PAFA, *Two Centuries of Collecting at the Museum of American Art.*

dancer Charlotte Crabtree for the esplanade along the Charles River in Boston and started working on several small sculptures of animals, including this one. She began the kangaroo by modeling in clay on December 12 at Boston's Franklin Park Zoo and reported two days later, "Had a good morning on my kangaroo."[1] The sculpture was completed in 1940 and cast in time to be shown in 1943 at the 138th annual exhibition of the Pennsylvania Academy of the Fine Arts, from which it was purchased. She was pleased by the honor for "there is no place where I would rather have it for I have, not only the greatest admiration for all the Academy stands for but also a personal interest in it for Mr. Charles Grafly was for many years my teacher and I owe much to his wise instruction."[2]

The figure of the kangaroo was modeled realistically from life, illustrating her intimate knowledge of her subject. She kept the forms simple and planar, avoiding too close an attention to details of the skin and features. Following Grafly's philosophy, she was interested in representing animals in their characteristic poses, often at rest.

The plaster model for *Kangaroo* remained in the sculptor's studio and has "an uneven copper-colored finish."[3] In October 1944 Lane had begun experimenting with applying color to the surfaces of her plasters and her *Kangaroo* was the first one she tried.[4]

Portraying kangaroos continued to be of interest to her. In the 1950s she produced several drawings of kangaroos reclining and bending.[5] They were probably drawn in the Central Park Zoo where she applied for a permit each year allowing her to draw. In 1963 she modeled another kangaroo running, in a smaller size, and had it cast in bronze and patinated a seafoam blue/green in 1970 at Roman Bronze Works in New York. It was shown at the National Academy of Design's 147th annual exhibition in 1973 where it won the Ellin P. Speyer Prize of $300 for the best depiction of an animal. The unique cast was purchased from the exhibition by David Labarre, a private collector.[6]

Notes

1. Ambler 1987, p. 61.
2. Katharine W. Lane to Joseph T. Fraser, Jr., director of the PAFA, Feb. 26, 1943, PAFA object file.
3. Louise Todd Ambler to Susan James-Gadzinski, August 5, 1986, PAFA object file.
4. Ambler 1987, p. 69.
5. Katharine Lane Weems Papers, Archives of American Art, Smithsonian Institution, Washington, D.C., sketchbook, microfilm, roll no. 724, frame nos. 811, 858, 860, 872.
6. Weems's reminiscences of the circumstances surrounding her second kangaroo sculpture have been confused in her memoir (pp. 113–14) with those of the earlier kangaroo. Ambler refers to information from Weems's diaries when discussing the Pennsylvania Academy's version. This kangaroo was offered for sale by Christie's in New York, Sept. 28, 1989, cat. no. 169 (ill.).

Reference

1987 Louise Todd Ambler, *Katharine Lane Weems: Sculpture and Drawings,* Boston: Boston Athenaeum, pp. 61, fig. 54, 67.

Exhibited

1943* cat. no. 91. **1986–87** PAFA, *Sculpture at the Pennsylvania Academy of the Fine Arts.* **1989** PAFA, *"The Birds and the Beasts Will Teach Us."*

Henry Kreis

1899–1963

Henry Godfrey Kreis was born in Essen, Germany, into a family of ten children. His father, an architect, often gave his children rolls of wallpaper and pencils to keep them busy drawing. Henry loved to draw and model small figures. Upon completing high school, he was apprenticed for four years to a stone carver named Goldkuhle; but Kreis had to spend more time selling tombstones and digging their foundations than actually carving stone. World War I intervened, and Kreis served in the army in Flanders. During quiet moments, he sketched horses and the landscape. He later completed his apprenticeship to Goldkuhle and thereby acquired a craft in which he could always find work while pursuing his desire to become a professional sculptor. He studied for three years with Joseph Wackerle (1880–1959) at the School of Applied Art in Munich. There Kreis carved mostly in wood within a workshop environment where students taught one another.

In 1923 the German postwar economy forced Kreis to leave school, and he decided to come to the United States. He became an American citizen in 1930. His first employment was as a maker of tombstones and monuments. Later he worked as a carver of building moldings and ornament while he studied evenings at the Beaux-Arts Institute of Design in New York. A successful commission to carve figures for a Florida residence led to a similar commission for a New York building and employment for five years as an assistant to the archaistic sculptors CARL PAUL JENNEWEIN and Paul Manship (1885–1966). Among other projects, Kreis worked with Jennewein on carvings for the Education Building in Harrisburg.[1] In 1930 he helped Jennewein with the pediment and acroteria for the new Greek Revival building of the Philadelphia Museum of Art.[2]

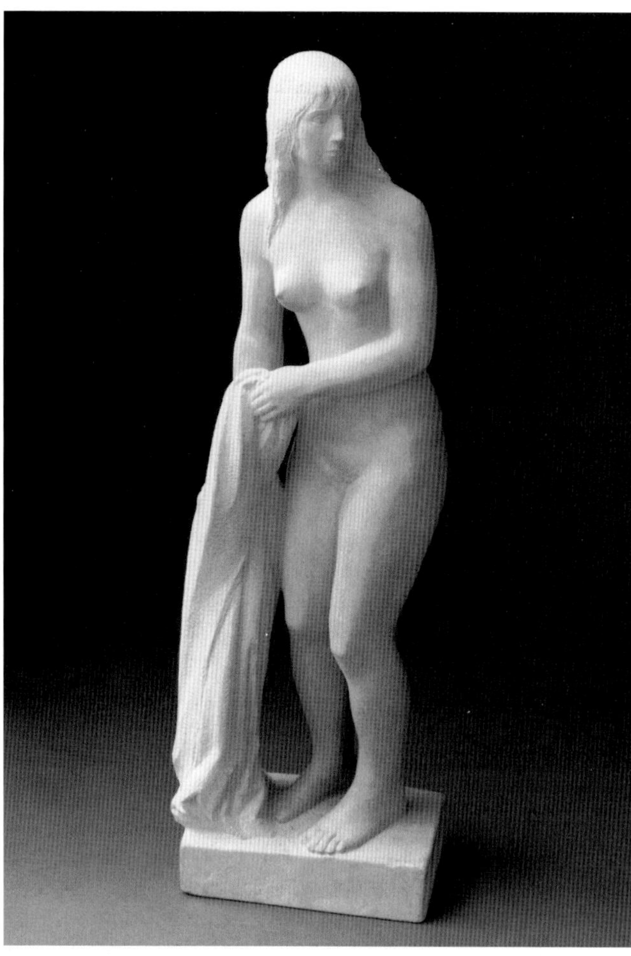

Kreis, *Bather*

In the early 1930s, Henry Kreis bought an old farm in Connecticut. Through the Treasury Department of the Works Progress Administration, he secured his first government commission, for a figure for the Bronx Post Office. From 1935 to 1954, he taught sculpture at the Hartford Art School in Connecticut. As a visiting artist in 1954, he provided criticism to the art students at Yale University's School of Design, in New Haven. He exhibited regularly at the National Sculpture Society, in New York and, from 1934 to 1962, in the annual exhibitions of the Pennsylvania Academy of the Fine Arts.

Kreis produced several medals, including the 1939 World's Fair medal and a 1940 special National Sculpture Society medal of honor for ANNA HYATT HUNTINGTON. As a result of a competition held in 1940 at the *Second Sculpture International* exhibition, sponsored by the Fairmount Park Art Association and held at the Philadelphia Museum of Art, he was awarded the commission for *The Birth of a Nation.* A ten-foot-high limestone relief, it stands on the south terrace of the Ellen Phillips Samuel Memorial in Fairmount Park, near the Philadelphia Museum of Art. The plaster scale model was awarded a George D. Widener Memorial Gold Medal for the most meritorious work in sculpture at the Pennsylvania Academy's 1943 annual exhibition. Kreis had won a third purchase prize of $2,500 the previous year for a seated female figure *Indian Summer,* 1937, in the *Artists for Victory* exhibition at the Metropolitan Museum of Art in New York.

Henry Kreis produced several historic monuments, religious commissions, and World War II memorials, including one at the Virginia Polytechnic Institute, in Blacksburg. While working on such major commissions, he often modeled small terracotta figures, mostly of women, for later use in large stone sculptures. He relied on impressions of everyday life and therefore rarely worked from live models, sometimes only for details. In its simplification, his work draws upon the tradition of gothic sculpture in German cathedrals and the work of the German sculptor Gerhard Marcks (1889–1981).

Kreis's first one-man show was held in 1948 at the Clay Club Sculpture Center in New York and consisted mostly of female figures. In 1951, because his work was considered among the most likely to gain a permanent place in American culture, he was elected a life member of the National Institute of Arts and Letters. The Wadsworth Athenaeum, in Hartford, gave him a joint show in 1955 with the painter Henry Schnakenberg. It included fifty-three of his sculptures—finished works in stone, studies in terracotta, and medals.

Henry Kreis's sculpture is in the Wadsworth Athenaeum, the Metropolitan Museum of Art, the Whitney Museum of American Art, and the National Academy of Design.

Notes

1. Shirley Reiff Howarth, *C. Paul Jennewein Sculptor* (Tampa: Tampa Museum, 1980), pp. 98–103.

2. Henry Kreis to Elizabeth Z. Swenson, Public Relations, PAFA, Dec. 17, 1948, clipping file, PAFA Library.

References

Henry Kreis Papers, Archives of American Art, Smithsonian Institution, Washington, D.C. **1938** Henry Kreis, "A Sculptor Speaks," *American Magazine of Art* 31 (Nov.), pp. 630–35, 673, reprinted in *Painters and Sculptors of Modern America,* New York: Thomas Y. Crowell Company, 1942, pp. 148–52. **1963** "Sculptor Henry Kreis, 63, Dies at His Home in Essex," *Middletown [Conn.] Press,* Jan. 22, clipping file, PAFA Library.

Bather

By 1942
Limestone
37¾ x 12 x 6⅝" (95.9 x 30.5 x 16.8 cm)
Signed on base at figure's left side: HENRY KREIS
Henry D. Gilpin Fund, 1942.5

IN THE *Bather,* a nude woman grasps her robe (a support for the figure) as if startled by an intruder. A variety of textures can be seen: the figure was carved with a smooth chisel and sanded; the hair and drapery were carved with a narrow-toothed chisel; and the base was carved with a wide-toothed chisel.[1] The eyes are blank as is common in Henry Kreis's monumental figures. The statue was carved in Alabama limestone, the same type of stone that the sculptor was then using for *The Birth of a Nation,* 1943.[2] He often worked in limestone, a common building stone that is softer than marble and more matte in finish.

Notes

1. Virginia Norton Naudé, Conservation report, April 17, 1986, p. 1, PAFA object file.
2. "These Works by Connecticut Artists May Win Part of the $6,000 Purse in Philadelphia," *Bridgeport Post,* Feb. 18, 1942, scrapbook, microfilm, roll no. 58, frame no. 80, PAFA Archives.

Exhibited
1942* cat. no. 87. **1942** Art Institute of Chicago, annual exhibition, cat. no. 257.

CONCETTA SCARAVAGLIONE

1900–1975

BORN on New York's Lower East Side to parents who had emigrated from Calabria, Italy, Concetta Scaravaglione was the youngest of nine children.[1] As a youth, she enjoyed making furniture and toys, especially a wagon for racing. In school she showed talent in drawing and received encouragement from her teacher, Cecilia Holman. Her family finally agreed to let her study sculpture with Frederick Roth (1872–1944) in a free class for women at the National Academy of Design. She was there from 1916 to 1920, when the class was canceled because of dwindling enrollment. She worked at perfume and lampshade factories to earn enough money to attend the Art Students League of New York in 1921. There she studied drawing with Boardman Robinson and earned scholarships that enabled her to attend until 1923. In 1924, when ROBERT LAURENT consented to teach her direct carving, she became one of his first students and one of an early group of American direct carvers.[2]

In 1925 Scaravaglione began her own long career of teaching—first at the Educational Alliance in New York; later at Sarah Lawrence College, in Bronxville; at Black Mountain College, near Asheville, North Carolina; and, from 1952–67, at Vassar College, in Poughkeepsie, New York. By 1925 she was exhibiting at the Whitney Studio Club, and in 1926 she was elected a member of the New York Society of Women Artists. She worked at the Louis Comfort Tiffany Foundation at Oyster Bay, Long Island in 1928. In 1931 she visited Italy and saw the birthplace of her parents. Her plaster *Standing Nude,* by 1933 (destroyed), was exhibited in the Fairmount Park Art Association's 1933 *International Exhibition of Sculpture,* in Philadelphia. The next year her *Mother and Child* in plaster (location unknown) won the George D. Widener Memorial Gold Medal as the most meritorious sculpture by an American citizen at the 129th annual exhibition of the Pennsylvania Academy of the Fine Arts. She exhibited regularly at the Academy until 1966. In 1934 she was singled out as "perhaps the most promising of the younger women sculptors . . . , whose work has largeness of scale and a feeling for full, round forms."[3]

In the 1930s, Concetta Scaravaglione worked on commissions for the Treasury Department's Section of Painting and Sculpture. They included the aluminum *Railway Mail Carrier of 1862,* 1935, for the Federal Post Office building, and a limestone relief, *Harvest,* 1937, for the Federal Trade Commission building, both in Washington, D.C. For the garden court of the Federal Building at the 1939 New York World's Fair, she produced a fourteen-foot-high group, *Woman with Mountain Sheep* (destroyed). She was active in the Sculptors Guild, and her *Girl with Gazelle,* 1936 (location unknown), a Federal Arts Project of the Works Progress Administration was praised at the Guild's first outdoor exhibition, in 1938.[4] A solo exhibition of her work was held at the Virginia Museum of Fine Arts, Richmond, in 1941. She was elected an associate member of the National Sculpture Society in 1944 and became a fellow in 1947. The Pennsylvania Academy purchased *Seated Girl* (q.v.) in 1946 and shortly after the American Academy of Arts and Letters and the National Institute of Arts and Letters gave her a thousand dollar award. In 1946 she learned welding from Theodore Roszak (1907–1981) and was working in the former studio of Frederick MacMonnies (1863–1937). The following year, she won the Prix de Rome, the first time that the competition was opened to women.

As a result, she was able to study at the American Academy in Rome until 1950.

In the 1960s and 1970s, Scaravaglione abandoned direct carving in favor of hammered and welded copper sheets. Her imagery continued to be simplified figures, predominantly women. A retrospective exhibition of her sculpture was held at the Vassar College Art Gallery upon her retirement in 1967. In 1974 she had her first exhibition at the Kraushaar Gallery in New York, and a posthumous show was held there in 1983. Her sculpture is in the Museum of Modern Art and the Whitney Museum of American Art, New York; the National Museum of American Art, Washington, D.C.; the Glasgow Museum, in Scotland; and Vassar College.

Notes

1. Concetta Scaravaglione, "My Enjoyment in Sculpture," *Magazine of Art* 32 (August 1939), p. 451. Most of the early biographical information in the entry comes from this source. It was reprinted in *The Sculpture of Concetta Scaravaglione*, exhib. cat., 1941 (Virginia Museum of Fine Arts), pp. 5–13, and in *Painters and Sculptors of Modern America* (New York: Thomas Y. Crowell Company, 1942), pp. 107–11.
2. Roberta Kupfrian Tarbell, *Catalogue Raisonné of William Zorach's Carved Sculpture*, Ph.D. diss., University of Delaware, p. 99.
3. Holger Cahill and Alfred H. Barr, Jr., eds., *Art in America* (New York: Reynal and Hitchcock, 1934), p. 59.
4. *Girl with Gazelle* was on the cover of *Art Digest* 12 (May 1, 1938).

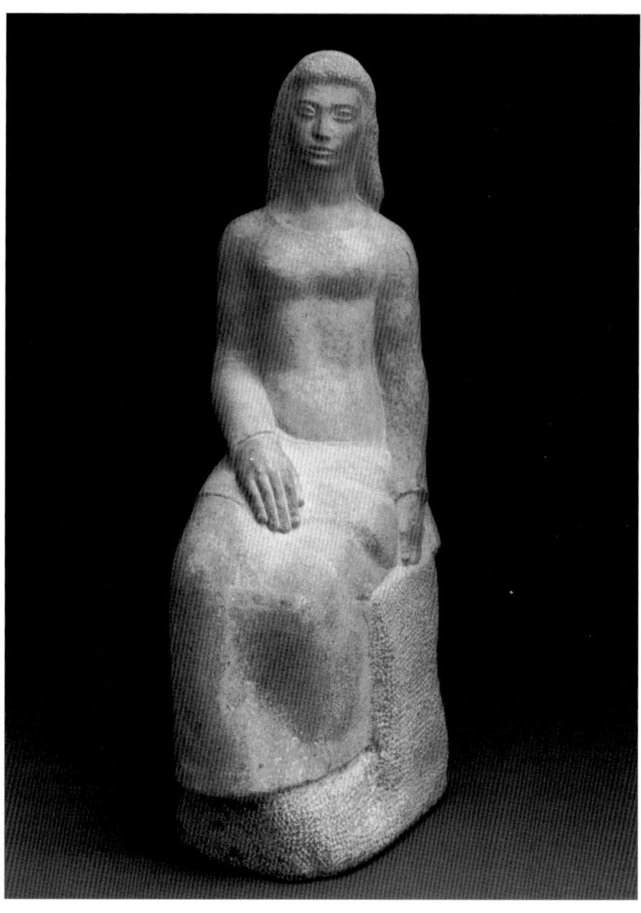

Scaravaglione, *Seated Girl*

Seated Girl

1939
Marble
32½ x 9 x 13" (82.6 x 22.9 x 33 cm)
Henry D. Gilpin Fund, 1946.12

CONCETTA SCARAVAGLIONE is known for her carved figures of women either alone like *Seated Girl* or with a child or an animal. *Seated Girl* is carved from what the artist called Napoleon Gray marble. The forms are bold and simplified; a rough texture defines the hair and base. This composition was apparently carved in marble in two sizes. A twenty-four-inch version called *Woman Waiting*, probably later than the piece in the Museum of American Art of the Pennsylvania Academy of the Fine Arts, was shown at the *Outdoor Sculpture Exhibition* of the Sculptors Guild in 1941 and illustrated in its catalogue.[1] According to the artist in 1946, *Seated Girl* had been shown only in the exhibition *Artists for Victory* in 1942 at the Metropolitan Museum of Art, New York.[2] That piece, however, was called *Woman Waiting*, as was the one for sale for $650 at the Art Institute of Chicago in 1941/42. *Seated Girl* had been shown at the Art Institute of Chicago in 1940/41 at a price of $750. It was shown at the 141st annual exhibition of the Pennsylvania Academy of the Fine Arts in 1946 and was purchased for the permanent collection.

Notes

1. *Outdoor Sculpture Exhibition* (New York: Sculptors Guild, 1941), cat. no. 44 (ill.), as *Woman Waiting*.
2. Artist's response to questionnaire, [1946], PAFA object file.

References

1939 *Art Digest* (April 15), p. 8 (ill. of work in progress). **1954** Ralph M. Pearson, *The Modern Renaissance in American Art*, New York: Harper and Brothers, fig. 175 (work in progress), p. 271.

Exhibited

1940 Whitney Museum of American Art, New York, *1940 Annual Exhibition of Painting, Sculpture, Watercolor, Drawing and Prints*, cat. no. 154. **1940** Fairmount Park Art Association, Philadelphia, *Sculpture International*, cat. no. 345. **1940–41** Art Institute of Chicago, *The Fifty-first Annual Exhibition of American Paintings and Sculpture*, cat. no. 312. **1946*** cat. no. 175. **1986–87** PAFA, *Sculpture at the Pennsylvania Academy of the Fine Arts*.

Ex Collection
The artist, 1939–46.

Walker Hancock

b. 1901

Walker Kirtland Hancock was born and reared in Saint Louis. His mother, Anna Spencer Hancock, had been a painter prior to her marriage, and she encouraged her son's interest in art.[1] At the age of nine, he made a cardboard model of the Parthenon with pedimental figures modeled in plasteline. In high school he was inspired by the art teacher Agnes Lodwick, who taught two-dimensional design and composition. As a result, he began attending Saturday classes at Washington University's School of Fine Arts. When Hancock was only fifteen, his design for a medal won second prize in a national competition held by the Saint Louis Art League. After graduation, he studied at Washington University from about 1918 to 1920. One of his teachers was the Danish-born sculptor Victor S. Holm (1876–1935), who had studied with the sculptor and author Lorado Taft (1860–1936) and had been a studio assistant to AUGUSTUS SAINT-GAUDENS. Hancock's other teacher was the painter and school administrator Edmund Henry Wuerpel. Hancock drew from antique casts, copied them full size in clay, drew and modeled from life, and made original compositions in plasteline.[2]

In the summer of 1920, Walker Hancock took intensive language classes in French and Italian at the University of Wisconsin. That fall he began studying at the Pennsylvania Academy of the Fine Arts with CHARLES GRAFLY, who was then considered the best teacher of sculpture in the country. Hancock excelled as Grafly's student. He won the Edmund Stewardson Prize in 1921 and William Emlen Cresson Traveling Scholarships in 1922 and 1923. His language training served him well on his two Cresson trips throughout Europe. Hancock sculpted in Grafly's studio in Gloucester, Massachusetts, in the summer of 1921; and he worked there alone in 1924 and 1925, after having finished his studies at the Pennsylvania Academy.

Toivo, the portrait of a Finnish boy, won the George D. Widener Memorial Gold Medal in 1925 at the Academy's 120th annual exhibition.[3] That year, against Grafly's advice, Hancock competed for and won the Prix de Rome, which enabled him to spend four years sculpting at the American Academy in Rome and traveling in Italy and elsewhere in Europe. Grafly's objection was based on his dislike of the archaistic style that Paul Manship (1885–1966) had adopted while studying at the American Academy in Rome. Its clear outlines and simplified forms were inspired by early Greek art. During his training at the American Academy, Hancock was assigned architectural problems to solve in collaboration with students of painting and architecture. He later instituted a similar program at the Pennsylvania Academy in which Academy students collaborated with architecture students and teachers at the University of Pennsylvania. It lasted from 1933 to 1959.

Walker Hancock had been asked by Charles Grafly in 1929 on his deathbed to succeed him as instructor of sculpture at the Pennsylvania Academy. Hancock accepted and taught there for thirty-eight years with interruptions for war service and for two years as sculptor-in-residence at the American Academy in Rome. He expanded the Pennsylvania Academy's curriculum to include work with the slow-motion camera, a class in stone carving taught by Philip Aliano (1877/78–1959) from 1938 to 1959, and a class in plaster casting.

For more than forty years, Hancock exhibited regularly at the Pennsylvania Academy. In 1932 his *Bird Charmer,* depicting a Zuni Indian, was awarded the Fellowship Prize at the 127th annual exhibition. A bronze cast was installed that year as a memorial fountain in the zoological gardens in Saint Louis.

In 1930 Walker Hancock bought property in Lanesville, Massachusetts, near Gloucester, and built a house and a studio. He drew models for his sculpture from the large Finnish community in the area. The athletic young men who swam in the pools in abandoned granite quarries on his property were particular favorites. He commuted from Gloucester to Philadelphia, as Grafly had done before him.

While teaching, Hancock worked on commissions for medals, such as the Eisenhower-Nixon inaugural medals, and for war memorials and portrait sculpture. Perhaps his most well-known commission is the Pennsylvania Railroad War Memorial—an angel lifting up a wounded soldier. Located in Philadelphia's Thirtieth Street Station, it was dedicated in 1952.[4] This work is Hancock's own favorite. In 1953 he received a Pennsylvania Academy medal of honor along with the painter and muralist George Harding "in view of their eminent position in the profession and in appreciation of their exemplary services to the Academy as members of its faculty."[5] Hancock's full-length figure of John Paul Jones was installed in 1957 as part of the memorial to General William M. Reilly on the west side of the Philadelphia Museum of Art. In the 1960s, Hancock supervised the completion of the colossal mountain carving Memorial to the Confederacy that the sculptor Gutzon Borglum (1867–1941) had begun about fifty years earlier at Stone Mountain, Georgia.

An exhibition of Hancock's small bronzes of basketball players was held in 1965 at the Pennsylvania Academy's Peale House Galleries.[6] In 1982 his male figure *Air* was installed at Philadelphia's Civic Center as part of the city's Century IV celebration. Since then he has sculpted busts of Chief Justice Warren E. Burger and President Gerald R. Ford, among others. In 1989 Hancock's fountain group depicting the Greek poet Arion on a dolphin was installed in a garden at Houston's Methodist Hospital.[7]

In 1991 Hancock was honored with the Dean's Award for Distinguished Service to the School of the Pennsylvania Academy of the Fine Arts. Also that year his bust of former President George Bush was unveiled in the United States Senate.

Notes

1. Much of the biographical information is from an interview, Dec. 3, 1984, with Walker Hancock by Linda Bantel and Susan James-Gadzinski. Tapes are in the PAFA Archives.
2. Walker Hancock to Zebulon Burke, Feb. 14, 1962, Walker Hancock Papers, microfilm, roll no. 1719, frame no. 542, Archives of American Art, Smithsonian Institution, Washington, D.C.
3. A bronze of *Toivo*, 1924 is in the Saint Louis Art Museum. Another is in a private collection, Cape Ann, Mass. The whereabouts of two others is unknown.
4. For more information, see Hancock, "The Pennsylvania Railroad Memorial," *American Artist* 16 (Oct. 1952), pp. 28–31, 69, 70. It was conserved in 1991, during the renovation of the train station.
5. PAFA, minutes of the board of directors, Feb. 16, 1953, PAFA Archives.
6. Forty small bronzes of basketball players are in the collection of the Cape Ann Historical Association. See *The Sculpture of Walker Hancock*, 1989, p. 53.
7. Ibid., p. 51 (ill.).

References

1924–78 Walker Hancock Papers, Archives of American Art, Smithsonian Institution, Washington, D.C. **1968** Beatrice Gilman Proske, *Brookgreen Gardens Sculpture*, Murrells Inlet, S.C.: Brookgreen Gardens, pp. 352–54. **1974** Adlai S. Hardin, "Walker Hancock: Distinguished Sculptor," John F. Harbeson, "Architectural Collaborator," and Joseph Thompson Fraser, Jr., "Gifted Teacher," *National Sculpture Review* 23 (Spring), pp. 8–11, 26, respectively. **1986** Kathryn Greenthal, *American Figurative Sculpture in the Museum of Fine Arts*, Boston: Museum of Fine Arts, pp. 465–68. **1989** *The Sculpture of Walker Hancock*, exhib. cat., Gloucester, Mass.: Cape Ann Historical Association.

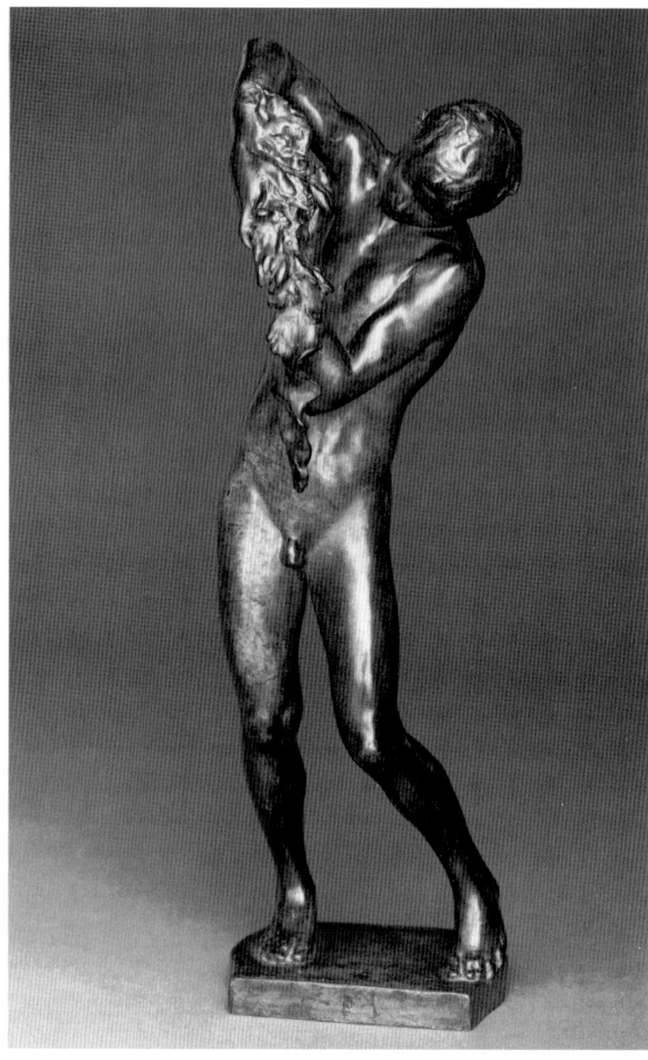

Hancock, *Kelp Water*

Kelp Water (also called *Seaweed Fountain*)

1921
Bronze with green patina; lost-wax cast in 1922
19½ x 6¼ x 6¼" (49.5 x 15.9 x 15.9 cm)
Signed on top of base: WALKER HANCOCK
Foundry mark on back of base: ROMAN BRONZE WORKS N–Y–
Gift of the Fellowship of the Pennsylvania Academy, 1924.3

Kelp Water was modeled in plastilene in the summer of 1921, when Walker Hancock was working in Charles Grafly's studio on the Massachusetts coast. The sculpture was inspired by the sight of children picking up the kelp that washed ashore near the cottage in which he was living. As a model, Hancock used Lauri Ronka, the young son of a Finnish missionary, serving the community around Lanesville. This sculpture was the first one that Hancock took really seriously. He worked on it during the day in Grafly's studio and during the evening in his cottage. Grafly's influence can be seen in the handling of forms, the strong sense of anatomy, and the impressionistic handling of the facial features.

According to Hancock, three other bronzes were probably cast at the Roman Bronze Works.[1] The green patination was chosen by the foundry. All three are in private collections. One was purchased by the grandmother of former president George Bush for her home in Maine. The plaster model was later destroyed by the artist. There is no evidence that the bronze in the Museum of American Art of the Pennsylvania Academy of the Fine Arts was intended to function as a fountain. All of the bronzes in private collections were piped for water. When one of them was shown in 1925, it was described as "piped for water to trickle from the sea-weed."[2] The Museum's bronze was the first one cast, in 1922, and was shown at the Academy's annual exhibition that year. *Kelp Water* was selected by a jury to be purchased from the Fellowship's 1924 annual exhibition and given to the Museum.

Notes

1. Taped interview with Walker Hancock by Linda Bantel and Susan James-Gadzinski, Dec. 3, 1984, tapes in PAFA Archives. *The Sculpture of Walker Hancock,* 1989, checklist, p. 60, lists four other bronzes, although no location is known for a fourth cast.

2. Grand Central Art Galleries, New York, exhibition of works by candidates for the Prix de Rome, May 1925, cat. no. 4, Walker Hancock clipping file, Saint Louis Art Museum.

Reference

1989 *The Sculpture of Walker Hancock,* Gloucester, Mass.: Cape Ann Historical Association, exhib. cat., checklist, p. 60.

Exhibited

1922* cat. no. 438 (ill.). **1923** National Sculpture Society, New York, *Exhibition of American Sculpture,* cat. p. 333. **1924** PAFA, annual Fellowship exhibition, held at the Art Club, Philadelphia, cat. no. 109. **1925** Grand Central Art Galleries, New York, exhibition of works by candidates for the Prix de Rome, cat. no. 4. **1986–87** PAFA, *Sculpture at the Pennsylvania Academy of the Fine Arts.*

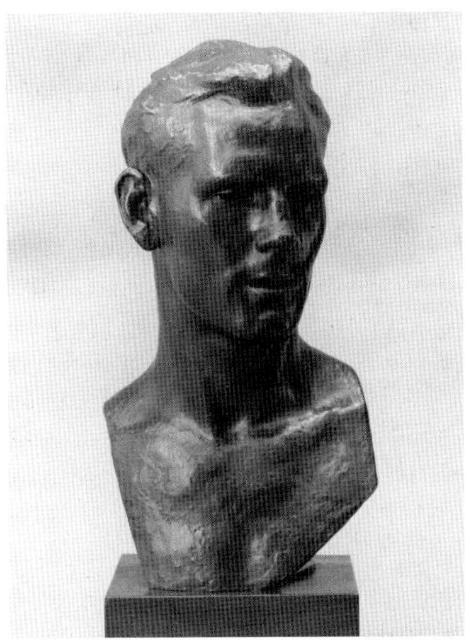

Hancock, *Young Lobsterman*

Young Lobsterman

1934
Bronze with brown patina; lost-wax cast by 1936
20 x 10½ x 10½" (50.8 x 26.6 x 26.6 cm)
Signed and dated on left shoulder: W. HANCOCK 1934
Foundry mark on back of support: CELLINI BRONZE WORKS N.Y.
Joseph E. Temple Fund, 1936.8

Young Lobsterman is a portrait of Eino Ahonen, a Finnish lobsterman from Lanesville, Massachusetts.[1] He appears to be strong and lean. A sense of animation is created by the use of an open mouth and the deep shadows of the hollow eyeballs. The bust terminates asymmetrically. The right side of the bare chest rests on the base, while the left side extends at a forty-five degree angle over the edge of the base, which is a separate wooden box. The bust was purchased from the 131st annual exhibition of the Pennsylvania Academy of the Fine Arts. Another bronze cast, with a walnut base, is in the National Academy of Design, New York. Unlike the cast in the Museum of American Art of the Pennsylvania Academy of the Fine Arts, that one is signed but not dated. It was given to the National Academy by Hancock in 1939 on his election as an academician and was specially cast for that purpose. The original plaster is in a private collection in Cape Ann, Massachusetts.[2]

Notes

1. Walker Hancock to Susan James-Gadzinski, postmarked Sept. 14, 1989, PAFA research file.

2. *The Sculpture of Walker Hancock,* 1989, checklist, p. 64.

References
1936–37 PAFA, *Winter School Circular*, p. 12 (ill.). **1965** Theodore B. White, *The Philadelphia Art Alliance: Fifty Years, 1915–1965*, Philadelphia: University of Pennsylvania Press, p. 59 (ill.).

Exhibited
1936* cat. no. 386 (ill.). **1936** National Academy of Design, New York, 111th annual exhibition, cat. no. 334. **1937** William Penn Charter School, Philadelphia. **1940** Mint Museum of Art, Charlotte, N.C., *Exhibition of Sculpture and Drawings by Walker Hancock and George Demetrios*, cat. no. 8. **1949** Woodmere Art Gallery, Philadelphia, Pa., *Contemporary Portraits*. **1952** Saint Botolph Club, Boston, *Sculpture and Photographs of Sculpture by Walker Hancock*. **1960** PAFA, *Faculty Exhibition*, cat. no. 140. **1989** Cape Ann Historical Association, Gloucester, *The Sculpture of Walker Hancock*, p. 27 (ill.).

Spiral

About 1935–39
Bronze with brown patina; lost-wax cast in 1939; repatinated in 1986
25¾ x 5 x 5½" (65.4 x 12.7 x 14 cm)
Dated and signed on top of base: ©/1939/W. HANCOCK
Foundry mark on side of base: ROMAN BRONZE WORKS. N.Y.
Joseph E. Temple Fund, 1940.8

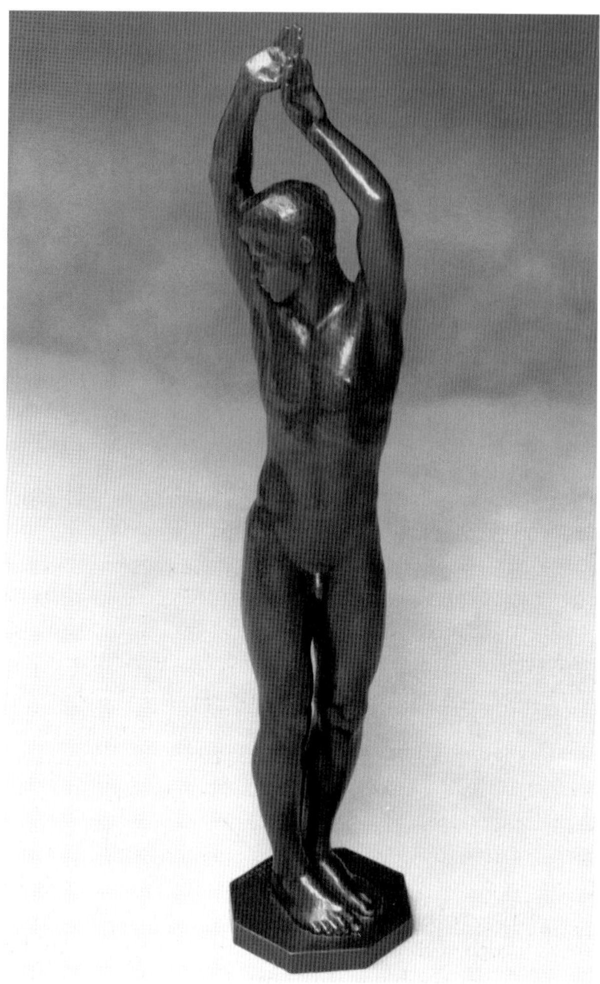
Hancock, *Spiral*

Spiral shows a young Finnish man poised as if to dive into a pool in the quarry on Walker Hancock's property in Lanesville, Massachusetts. Just before the dive, "somebody called him and he turned around, suddenly making this very interesting spiral pose."[1] Walker Hancock began modeling *Spiral* in about 1935. It was completed and cast in 1939. The original patina, applied by the master craftsman Riccardo Bertelli of Roman Bronze Works, consisted of gold leaf with a black coating, probably wax. This coating was damaged, most likely in the 1950s, when a hot gelatin mold material was used in a casting demonstration at the Pennsylvania Academy of the Fine Arts. Because Hancock felt the work to be unexhibitable in that condition, the decision was made to have it repatinated. In 1986 a brown patina, selected by the sculptor, was applied by the Johnson Atelier Technical Institute of Sculpture, near Princeton, New Jersey. The patina is similar to that on the cast of *Spiral* in the Museum of Fine Arts, Boston.

About six casts of *Spiral* exist. The first one produced was the one in the Museum of American Art of the Pennsylvania Academy of the Fine Arts. Two other casts were made soon after. One was sold from a 1946 exhibition at the Corcoran Gallery of Art (location unknown); the other is in a private collection in Mercer Island, Washington. A second version had been cast in Italy by 1968 and is in a private collection in Chadds Ford, Pennsylvania. In 1968 Hancock lengthened the diver's arms on his damaged plaster model while keeping the height of the figure the same. This third version was cast in bronze about 1970 by the Tallix Foundry in Beacon, New York (private collection, Cape Ann, Massachusetts). In about 1985 another was cast by the same foundry and given to the Museum of Fine Arts, Boston, by KATHARINE LANE WEEMS. It is inscribed with the dates 1930–1968. Hancock actually began working on the figure about 1935.[2]

Notes
1. Taped interview with Walker Hancock by Linda Bantel and Susan James-Gadzinski, Dec. 3, 1984, tapes in PAFA Archives.
2. Walker Hancock to Susan James-Gadzinski, [May 16, 1988], PAFA object file.

References
1940–41 PAFA, school catalogue, p. 9 (ill.). **1989** *The Sculpture of Walker Hancock*, exhib. cat., Gloucester: Cape Ann Historical Association, checklist, p. 65.

Exhibited
1940* cat. no. 112. **1952** Saint Botolph Club, Boston, *Sculpture and Photographs of Sculpture by Walker Hancock.* **1953** Cosmopolitan Club, Philadelphia. **1960** Wilkie-Buick Corporation, Philadelphia. **1960** PAFA, *Faculty Exhibition,* cat. no. 138. **1986–87** PAFA, *Sculpture at the Pennsylvania Academy of the Fine Arts.* **1992–93** PAFA, *Masterworks of American Art: 1750–1950.*

Head of a Finnish Boy

1939
Terracotta
15¾ x 8¼ x 8½" (40 x 21 x 21.6 cm)
Signed and dated on back: W. HANCOCK 1939
Gift of James P. and Ruth Marshall Magill (1959),
1957.15.11

THE SITTER for this sensitively modeled portrait was Alwin Jussila, who was from the Finnish community in Lanesville. The irises of the eyes, the knitted cap, and the sweater were subtlely tinted blue with egg tempera.[1] It is common to add color, often oil paint, to the surface of a terracotta sculpture after it has been fired.

Soon after *Head of a Finnish Boy* was modeled, Walker Hancock took lessons in modeling and casting terracotta at the Massachusetts Institute of Technology with Professor Frederick H. Norton. He tried two terracotta techniques. A mold was made of the clay head along with a plaster model. In one, clay was pressed into the sections of the mold, the pieces were attached and then fired. The cast in the Museum of American Art of the Pennsylvania Academy of the Fine Arts is the only pressed terracotta version. It has very thick walls and the surface appears to be dry in the areas of the eyes and nose. Two other casts of the head were made by the other technique: pouring white slip, or thinned clay made according to Norton's formula, into sections of the mold, piecing them together, and then firing. A poured terracotta sculpture has thinner walls than a pressed terracotta one, is lighter in weight, and will hardly shrink when fired. One of the poured casts was sold to provide money for Finnish relief at the time of the Finno-Russo War of 1939–40; the other cast was owned by the sitter's family[2] (both, location unknown).

The plaster model was originally owned by James P. and Ruth Marshall Magill, who preferred it to the terracotta. Hancock let them purchase it contrary to his usual policy of never releasing a unique plaster model.[3] The Magills deeded the bust to the Pennsylvania Academy in 1957 along with other sculpture, paintings, and works on paper. While the plaster head was on exhibit in the Academy's 1958 show *Twentieth Century American Painting and Sculpture from Philadelphia Private Collections,* it was accidentally broken. The pieces were returned to Hancock, who repaired the sculpture and kept it (now in the collection of the Cape Ann Historical Association, Gloucester, Massachusetts). As a replacement, he decided to give the Magills the terracotta that was in his studio. He tinted the hair and clothing in a similar manner to the plaster and used rasps and abrasive stones to give the terracotta the proper definition of form.[4] The replacement bust was sent to the Magills in May 1959. It came to the Pennsylvania Academy in 1974, soon after Mr. Magill's death. The bust at one time had its own wooden plinth, painted white, but it is no longer extant.[5] Hancock's *Kneeling Man* and *Resting Swimmer* (qq.v.) became part of the collection at the same time. While a student, Hancock lived near the Magills in Chestnut Hill, Pennsylvania, and came to know them well. James Magill served on the board of trustees of the Pennsylvania Academy from 1951 to 1962 and on the committee on instruction from 1958 to 1962, while Hancock was a faculty member.

Hancock, *Head of a Finnish Boy*

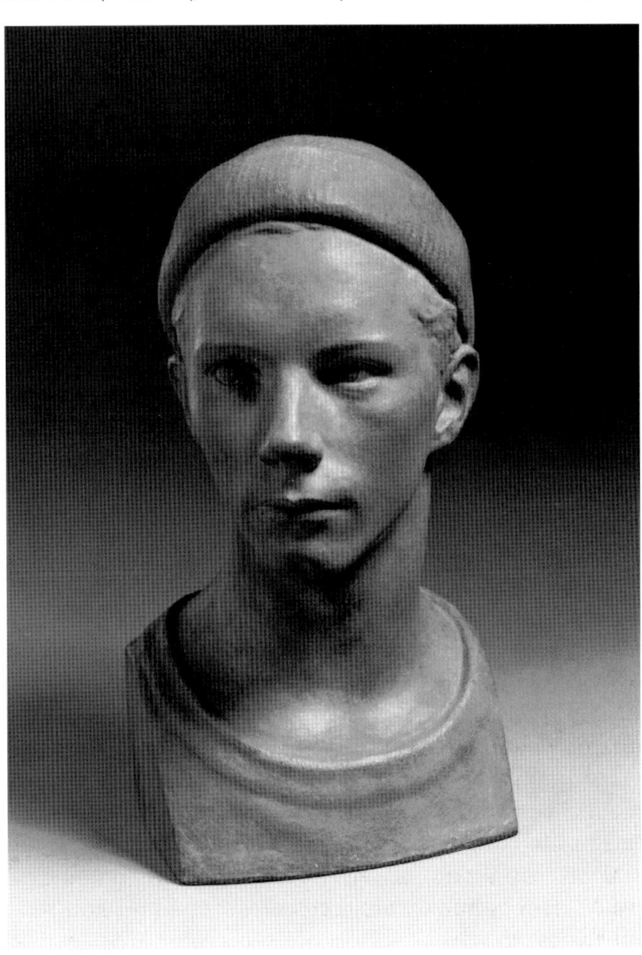

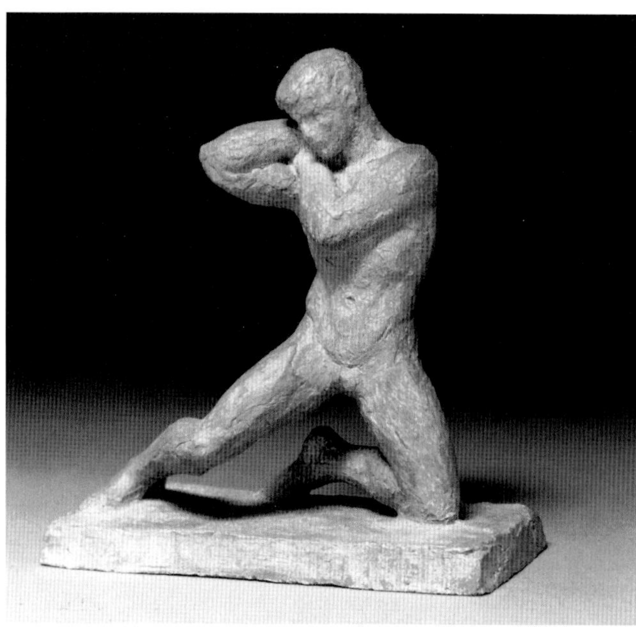

Hancock, *Kneeling Man*

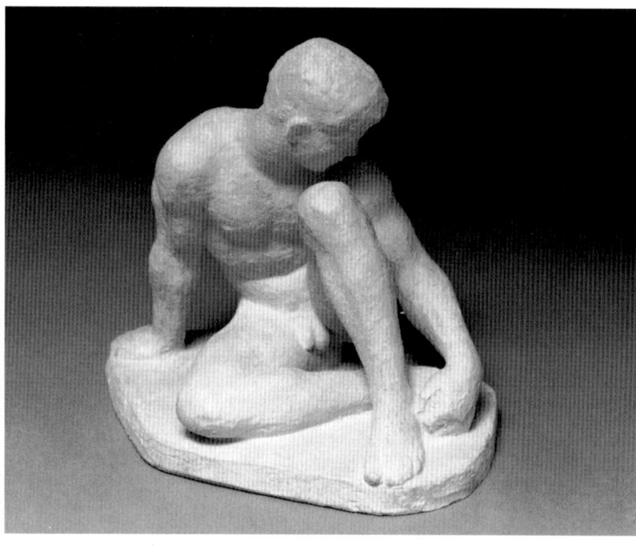

Hancock, *Resting Swimmer*

The plaster version of *Head of a Finnish Boy* was singled out as one of the best portrait busts in the Academy's 135th annual exhibition, in 1940.[6] It was used in an educational videotape on portraiture produced by the National Sculpture Society in the early 1980s. In 1987 a cast was made in polyester for a collector in Washington, D.C. This version will eventually go to the National Museum of American Art, in Washington, D.C.[7]

Notes

1. Walker Hancock to Joseph T. Fraser, Jr., director of the PAFA, May 29, 1959, PAFA Archives.
2. Taped interview with Walker Hancock by Linda Bantel and Susan James-Gadzinski, Dec. 3, 1984, tapes in PAFA Archives.
3. W. Hancock to J.T. Fraser, Jr., Nov. 28, 1958, PAFA Archives.
4. W. Hancock to J.T. Fraser, Jr., May 29, 1959, PAFA Archives.
5. "Personal Property Referred to in the Declaration of Trust of James P. Magill and Ruth Marshall Magill Dated December 13, 1957," p. 15, PAFA Archives.
6. Doris Brian, "Philadelphia Flavor in Its Annual: Prize-Winners and Others at the Pennsylvania Academy," *Art News* 38 (Feb. 10, 1940), pp. 8 (ill.), 17.
7. Artist's response to questionnaire, April 28, 1988, PAFA object file.

References

1989 Virgil Jones, "Walker Hancock. . . . an artist and his community," *Sculpture Review* 38 (Jan.–March), p. 15 (ill.). **1989** *The Sculpture of Walker Hancock*, exhib. cat., Gloucester, Mass.: Cape Ann Historical Association, checklist, p. 66 (medium incorrectly given as polyester).

Exhibited

1960 PAFA, *Faculty Exhibition*, cat. no. 133, as *Finnish Boy*. **1984–85** PAFA, *A Growing American Treasure: Recent Acquisitions and Highlights from the Permanent Collection*. **1986–87** PAFA, *Sculpture at the Pennsylvania Academy of the Fine Arts*.

Ex Collections

The artist, 1939–59; James P. and Ruth Marshall Magill, given as replacement for broken plaster, 1959–74.

Kneeling Man

Before 1949
Painted terracotta
6½ x 6 x 2½" (16.7 x 15.3 x 6.5 cm)
Gift of James P. and Ruth Marshall Magill, 1957.15.12

Kneeling Man is a study that was modeled in clay, fired, then painted red-brown. The pose is similar to the one that Walker Hancock used in his unfinished lifesize plaster *Revelation (Suddenly a Light)*, 1947 (private collection, Cape Ann, Mass.), which was shown in 1949 at the 144th annual exhibition of the Pennsylvania Academy of the Fine Arts. *Kneeling Man* was deeded to the Academy in 1957 and received in 1974.

Reference

1989 *The Sculpture of Walker Hancock*, exhib. cat., Gloucester, Mass.: Cape Ann Historical Association, checklist, p. 67.

Ex Collection

James P. and Ruth Marshall Magill, before 1949–74.

Resting Swimmer

1953
Terracotta
6½ x 7 x 5" (16.5 x 17.8 x 12.7 cm)
Signed and dated on bottom of base: Walker Hancock/1953
Inscribed above signature: For/Ruth/and/Jim
Gift of James P. and Ruth Marshall Magill, 1957.15.13

Ralph Humes

1901–1981

Born in Philadelphia, Ralph Hamilton Humes was reared in Pennsylvania and Virginia. As a teenager, he worked as a millwright while attending school. Later he studied photography. The outbreak of World War I disrupted his college plans. In the war, he served as an Army aerial photographer. While recovering from injuries to his eyes and hands suffered in an explosion, he was given modeling clay for physical therapy. He enjoyed sculpting and produced a portrait bust of a fellow patient that was shown to the sculptor Henry Kirke Bush-Brown (1857–1935), who recommended that Humes attend art school. Upon his discharge, he studied from 1922 to 1924 at the Rinehart School of Sculpture in Baltimore; the government paid his tuition the first year. Humes enrolled at the Pennsylvania Academy in 1925 for several years of study with CHARLES GRAFLY in Philadelphia and six years of study with ALBERT LAESSLE at the Academy's summer school in Chester Springs. At the 1926 Chester Springs exhibitions, Humes received a second prize for *Bantams* and a first prize for *Macaw and Sunflower.* The latter plaster sculpture was acquired by the Academy in 1930 and kept at Chester Springs (location unknown).[1] Humes served as monitor for the sculpture class in the summer of 1927. His duties included finding and posing models. In 1929 he was commissioned to do a portrait of a grand champion bull for the duPont family. He was awarded William Emlen Cresson Traveling Scholarships in 1929 and 1930. His 1929 winning submission consisted of a relief, a portrait bust, two full-length female figures, several figural groups, and several animals, including an elephant, birds, and a dog.[2] In two summers he traveled to England, France, Italy, Germany, and Belgium.

In 1932 when Ralph Humes was working on his own at Chester Springs, Laessle said that "his work is beginning to show a bigness that may put him in a class with the great sculptors."[3] That year Humes's *Wounded Crow* (Brookgreen Gardens, Murrells Inlet, South Carolina) won the Ellin P. Speyer Memorial Prize at the National Academy of Design, New York. Humes participated in the Pennsylvania Academy's annual exhibitions of 1929, 1933, 1935, and 1937. His *Walking Bear Cub* won the Fellowship Prize in 1937. Although he considered setting up a studio in Jenkintown, the Philadelphia suburb in which Laessle lived, Humes moved to Florida in 1934 with his wife Janet Chapman (1899–1983), a former Pennsylvania Academy of the Fine Arts sculpture student at Chester Springs.

In Florida Ralph Humes produced a fountain for the Coral Gables library and pursued his interests in animal and floral photography, raising orchids, and publishing sketches and articles on shells. For about eight years he lived in Arizona and produced a statue of Father Kino, the founder of the missions there. He was a fellow of the National Sculpture Society and a member of the Fellowship of the Pennsylvania Academy. Many of Humes's works are in private collections.

Notes

1. *Brookgreen Gardens: Sculpture by Ralph Hamilton Humes* (Murrells Inlet, S.C.: Brookgreen Gardens, 1937), clipping file, PAFA Library.
2. Photograph, PAFA school catalogue, 1929–30, p. 90.
3. Quoted in Laura Lee, "War Wounds Made Humes a Sculptor," *Philadelphia Evening Bulletin,* April 9, 1932, clipping file, Library of the *Philadelphia Inquirer.*

Reference

1968 Beatrice Gilman Proske, *Brookgreen Gardens Sculpture,* Murrells Inlet, S.C.: Brookgreen Gardens, pp. 488–90.

Whippet

About 1936
Bronze with brown patina; lost-wax cast
25⅛ x 25½ x 12½" (63.8 x 64.8 x 31.8 cm)
Signed on top of base: *Ralph Humes*
Foundry mark on edge of base between dog's hind feet: ROMAN BRONZE WORKS. N.Y.
Gift of the artist, 1968.12

RALPH HUMES claimed that he had chosen to pursue animal sculpture because he was "poor as the proverbial church-mouse and forced to find models that wouldn't charge a dollar an hour to pose."[1] Trained by Albert Laessle, whom he considered to be "one of the foremost teachers in the country," Humes excelled at modeling animals.[2]

Whippet is a lifelike standing figure of a racing dog.

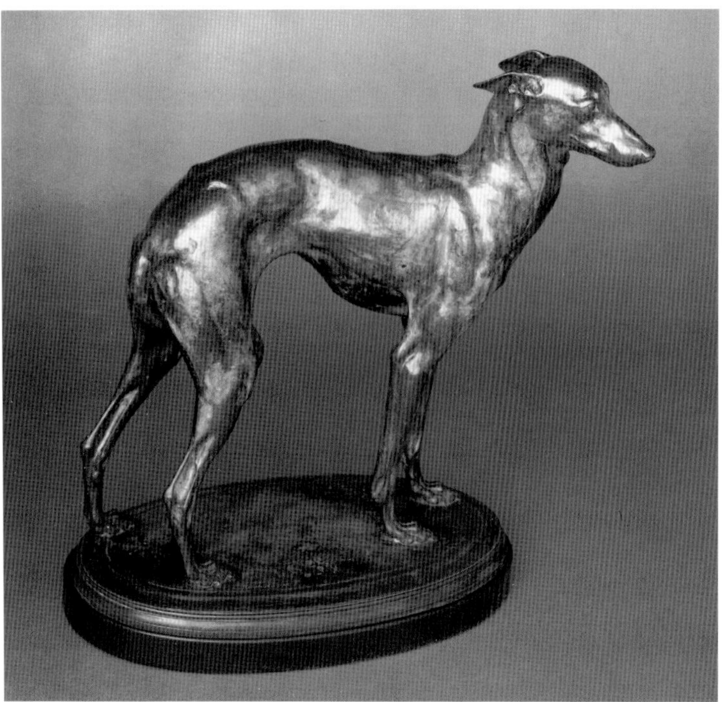

Humes, *Whippet*

References
1937 *Brookgreen Gardens: Sculpture by Ralph Hamilton Humes,* Murrells Inlet, S.C.: Brookgreen Gardens (ill.). **1937** "Sculpture 'Steals the Show' in Washington," *The Art Digest* 11 (Feb. 15), p. 10 (ill.). **1964** Everett DuPen, "Gardens and Fountains: It is essential that a garden should have a point of focus and that focus is provided by sculpture," *National Sculpture Review* 13 (Summer), p. 9 (ill.).

Exhibited
1936 New Haven Paint and Clay Club, Conn. **1937** Corcoran Gallery of Art, Washington, D.C., *46th Annual Exhibition of the Society of Washington Artists.* **1938** Florida Federation of Art, *46th Annual Exhibition of the Society of Washington Artists.* **1940** Whitney Museum of American Art, New York, *Sculpture Festival: Exhibition of Sculpture under the Auspices of the National Sculpture Society,* cat. no. 57 (ill.). **1940–41** Art Institute of Chicago, *51st Annual Exhibition of American Paintings and Sculpture,* cat. no. 284. **1941** Corcoran Gallery of Art, Washington, D.C., *50th Annual Exhibition of the Society of Washington Artists.* **1950** Fairchild Tropical Garden, Miami, painting and sculpture by E.C. Dean and Mr. and Mrs. R.H. Humes. **1975** William Penn Memorial Museum, Harrisburg, Pa., exhibition of works of art from the PAFA.

Ex Collection
The artist, about 1936–68.

The tendons, claws, and hair are carefully delineated. The curve of the tail imitates the arch of the underside of the belly. Humes was not totally satisfied with the patina of the bronze and wished that he could have had it repatinated before giving it to the Pennsylvania Academy of the Fine Arts.[3] Although the dappled browns do imitate the coloration of an animal's coat, the mottled effect obscures much of the modeling. Several paw prints appear on the top of the bronze base, which is mounted on a mahogany base.

Ralph Humes received numerous awards for *Whippet:* the Club Prize of the New Haven Paint and Clay Club in 1936, a gold medal from the Florida Federation of Art in 1938 (a one hundred dollar award for most meritorious work at the 1937 annual exhibition of the Society of Washington Artists), and a gold medal at its annual exhibition of 1941. He modeled several other sculptures of dogs, including a recumbent one that was in his winning submission to the 1929 competition for a Cresson traveling scholarship and a standing English setter in 1932.

Notes

1. Doris Reno, "Injury Led to Career for Sculptor Humes," *Miami [Fla.] Herald,* clipping file, PAFA Library.
2. Quoted in Laura Lee, "War Wounds Made Humes a Sculptor," *Philadelphia Evening Bulletin,* April 9, 1932, clipping file, Library of the *Philadelphia Inquirer.*
3. Ralph Humes to Joseph T. Fraser, Jr., director of the PAFA, April 9, 1968, PAFA object file.

Adlai S. Hardin

1901–1989

Adlai Stevenson Hardin was born in Minneapolis into a family of lawyers and ministers and was reared in Chicago. Adlai Stevenson, the Democratic presidential candidate in 1952 and 1956, was his first cousin. As a boy, Hardin was an accomplished whittler. After seeing an exhibition of wood sculpture at the Art Institute of Chicago with his father in 1916, he attended Saturday drawing classes there for about a year. Later, as a student at Princeton University, he took courses in art and architecture and produced drawings for the school's humor magazine. After his graduation in 1923, he visited Europe.

Until 1932 Hardin worked as a millwright for the Quaker Oats Company in Cedar Rapids, Iowa. Using the company's tools, he taught himself to carve figures in the evenings. He married in 1934, moved to Connecticut, and began taking evening life classes in Darien with the German-born sculptor Karl Lang (1892–1952). There Hardin had his first training in human anatomy and figure construction. Soon he was accepting commissions and having his work cast in bronze. In the 1930s he made sculpture for churches in Convent, New Jersey, and Harwichport, Massachusetts. He carved a crèche that won a competition held by the Arts and Crafts Guild in Philadelphia.

Adlai S. Hardin participated in the annual exhibitions of the Pennsylvania Academy of the Fine Arts in 1939–40, 1945, 1947–48, 1952, and 1954. The National Academy of Design, in New York, elected him an associate in 1951 and an academician in 1963. From 1957 to 1960, he served as president of the National Sculpture Society. During a twenty-seven-year career as a New York advertising executive, he sculpted in his spare time, and upon retirement in 1959 he was able to devote all his time to sculpture. In 1962 he was a sculptor-in-residence at the American Academy in Rome.

Hardin won many awards from the 1940s on, including the National Academy of Design Gold Medal for Sculpture in 1976. His late commissions include lifesize bronze figures of Saint Peter and Saint Paul installed in 1983 in Saint Patrick's Cathedral, New York, and four bronze figures produced in 1984 for Saint Joseph's Seminary, Yonkers, New York.[1]

Note

1. Artist's response to questionnaire, Sept. 2, 1984, PAFA object file.

References

1969 Walker Hancock, "Adlai S. Hardin," *National Sculpture Review* 18 (Spring), pp. 22, 26–27. **1993** Robin R. Salmon, *Brookgreen Gardens Sculpture*, Murrells Inlet, S.C.: Brookgreen Gardens, pp. 118–21, 223–24.

Amish Man

1938
Bronze with black patina; sand cast
28½ x 8 x 8" (72.4 x 20.3 x 20.3 cm)
Signed and dated on top of base: ADLAI S. HARDIN 38
Foundry mark on back of base: KUNST.F.DRY.N.Y.C.
Joseph E. Temple Fund, 1939.7

Amish Man was one of Adlai S. Hardin's first works to be sold.[1] The full-length, bearded figure represents a member of the religious community centered in rural Lancaster County, Pennsylvania. He wears traditional Amish garb—a flat-crowned hat and a long coat with a vest—and rests his hands on a cane. The choice of black as the patina for this figure is appropriate, for it is the prescribed color of most of the clothing worn by Amish men. Hardin produced this work from a newspaper photograph without preparing any preliminary drawings or maquettes.[2] His interest in the Amish may have been sparked by the national attention the group received during President Roosevelt's New Deal when they refused to accept subsidies to which they were entitled for not planting tobacco.

In the late 1930s and early 1940s, paintings and sculpture of the Amish by artists such as Vernon Kiehl Newswanger (1900–1980) and William W. Swallow (b. 1921) were common in the annual exhibitions of the Pennsylvania Academy of the Fine Arts. Hardin's *Amish Man* belongs to that genre. Artists working in the same tradition include H. RICHARD DUHME, JR., and MARION SANFORD.

Notes

1. Artist's response to questionnaire, Sept. 2, 1984, PAFA object file.
2. Ibid. The plaster model of *Amish Man* was kept by the artist.

References

1938 Edward Alden Jewell, "The Academy's 113th: What Happens When the Reviewer Gives All the Space Required by Prizes," *New York Times*, March 20, art sec., p. 9 (ill.). **1939** "News and Comment," *Magazine of Art* 32 (April), p. 240 (ill.). **1960** Frederic Whitaker, "The Sculpture of Adlai Hardin," *American Artist* 24 (Dec.), p. 55 (ill.). **1971–72** Robert A. Weinman, "Art . . . Evidence of the Spirit," *National Sculpture Review* 20 (Winter), p. 12 (ill.).

Exhibited

1938 National Academy of Design, New York, 113th annual exhibition, cat. no. 342, as *Amishman*. **1939*** cat. no. 370 (ill.). **1939** Connecticut Academy of Fine Arts, Hartford, 29th annual exhibition, held at the Wadsworth Athenaeum. **1975** William Penn Memorial Museum, Harrisburg, Pa., exhibition of works of art from the PAFA.

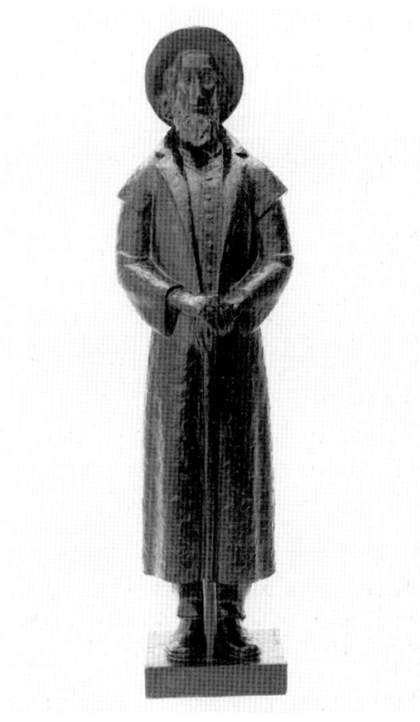

Hardin, *Amish Man*

Alice Decker

1901–1979

Born in Saint Louis, Alice Decker grew up in Montclair, New Jersey. In 1923 she was graduated from Smith College with a degree in psychology. After graduate studies in social work at Columbia University, she worked for the New York Neurological Institute. In 1928 while doing research in criminology for the Rockefeller Foundation, Decker took evening sculpture classes with ROBERT LAURENT at the Art Students League of New York. In 1929, she went to Paris and studied for three months with the sculptors Charles Despiau (1874–1946) and Emile Antoine Bourdelle (1861–1929).[1] She married the sculptor Duncan Ferguson (1901–1974), also a former student of Laurent. Decker, who occasionally returned to social work to support her sculpting, spoke of the career change as a natural one, from "pushing people around" to create social order to pushing clay around.[2]

In the 1930s, the Caproni Galleries of Boston offered for sale thirteen of her small animal sculptures in plaster. Some of the same works appeared in *The Sculptor's Way,* a book by Brenda Putnam (1890–1975), as suggested models from which to sculpt.[3] From the late 1930s into the 1940s, Decker's work was shown in group exhibitions at the Brooklyn Museum, the Whitney Museum of American Art, the Corcoran Gallery of Art, the Fairmount Park Art Association's *Third Sculpture International,* and the Sculptors Guild, New York, of which she was an early member.

Alice Decker remarried in 1938. The next year she executed a commission of three teak panels for the post office in Palmyra, Pennsylvania. She considered herself a self-taught carver.[4] In 1944, while her husband, Davidson Sommers, was in military service at Yellow Springs, Ohio, she had a solo exhibition of eight works in mahogany, teak, walnut, plaster, terracotta, and aluminum at Antioch College. She worked in a studio overlooking the Potomac River in Washington, D.C., from the mid-1940s to the mid-1950s, when illness forced her to stop sculpting. In 1949 her teak relief of five owls was installed in a public library in Saint Paul, Minnesota, as a memorial to a soldier killed in World War II. She participated in the annual exhibitions of the Pennsylvania Academy of the Fine Arts in 1950, 1951, and 1958. Aside from public commissions, her known works, primarily animals and portrait busts, are in private collections in Washington, D.C., and New York.

Notes

1. Undated form sent with letter from Alice Decker to Joseph T. Fraser, Jr., director of the PAFA, Jan. 29, [1950], PAFA object file.
2. Antioch College, Yellow Springs, Ohio, *Decker Sculpture Exhibit,* July 5–15, 1944, brochure, Elizabeth McCausland Papers, microfilm, roll no. D374, frame no. 215, Archives of American Art, Smithsonian Institution, Washington, D.C.
3. Brenda Putnam, *The Sculptor's Way: A Guide to Modelling and Sculpture* (New York: Farrar and Rinehart, 1939), pp. 19 (ill.), 20–21.
4. Undated form cited in n. 1.

Reference

1966 E. Benezit, *Dictionnaire de Peintres, Sculpteurs, Dessinateurs, et Graveurs,* Paris: Librarie Gründ, vol. 3, p. 98.

Whom Shall I Fear?

1940–48
Cherry wood
40⅛ x 15¼ x 16" (102 x 38.8 x 40.7 cm)
Joseph E. Temple Fund, 1950.5

Whom Shall I Fear? is one of Alice Decker's most important works. It is one of the largest; and, although she did not work on it continuously, it occupied her attention for many years. In 1940 she began carving the cherry log that came from a friend's orchard. Commenting later on her first glimpse of the log, she said, "the final form seemed very clear—I really take very little credit for releasing it." Before the sculpture could be completed, it had to be stored during the years that her husband served in World War II because the family had no permanent residence. After the war, she resumed work on it; but the wood had developed cracks from exposure to the elements. She felt that "there was something about the inner life of that log" that drove her to complete it in 1948.[1]

The sculpture is a full-length figure of a woman wearing a long robe and waist-length cloak. She pulls the cloak tightly about her with one hand and carries a bag in the other. The subtle diagonal folds of the drapery give a realistic sense of form to the figure. Its smooth, highly polished surface contrasts with the rough base. The sculpture is covered with checks and small cracks that are original. Many of them radiate from the core of the log at the back of the figure's neck. Davidson Sommers remembers that his wife planned to carve a child at the figure's left side where the bag is now, but that idea had to be changed when a knot or defect in the wood was discovered.[2] There are many breaks in the wood beneath the left hand,

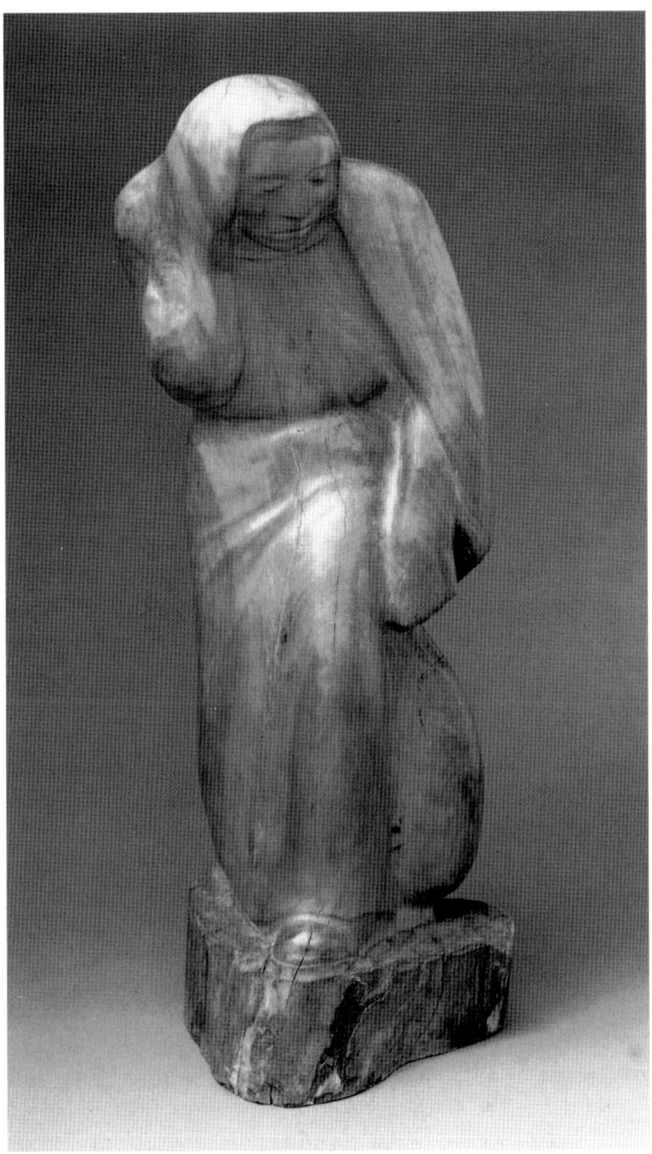

Decker, *Whom Shall I Fear?*

probably where the artist encountered difficulties in the wood.

Alice Decker's goal in sculpture was "to record a variety of moods and reactions to life; to communicate such emotion, by form that is simple, direct, and inevitable; to avoid cliches, heroics and sentimentality." She tried "to achieve economy of statement by avoiding large scale and irrelevant detail."[3] She never signed her work, because "Art should be anonymous."[4]

The title of this sculpture comes from the twenty-seventh Psalm: "The Lord *is* my light and my salvation; whom shall I fear?" Alice Decker was an avid reader of the Psalms, and this one had a special significance for her because she believed "it is certainly one for *all* artists to lean on."[5] Decker produced several other works based on Biblical subjects. *Flight,* about 1939 (private collection, Washington, D.C.) on a similar theme, was carved in cherry and cast in aluminum. It shows a draped, running female figure, sheltering in her arms a child wrapped in a bundle. In 1955 Decker carved an alabaster eagle with an eaglet (now in a private collection), based on a passage in the 103rd Psalm.[6]

Notes

1. Alice Decker to Joseph T. Fraser, Jr., director of the PAFA, Jan. 29, [1950], PAFA object file.
2. Davidson Sommers to Susan James-Gadzinski, April 20, 1985, PAFA research file.
3. Quoted in Antioch College, Yellow Springs, Ohio, *Decker Sculpture Exhibit,* 1944, brochure, Elizabeth McCausland Papers, microfilm, roll no. D374, frame no. 215, Archives of American Art, Smithsonian Institution, Washington, D.C.
4. Quoted in "Wood Carving Presented—Five Owls 'Roost' in Library," clipping from unidentified Saint Paul, Minnesota, newspaper, March 6, 1950, Alice Decker papers, private collection.
5. A. Decker to J.T. Fraser, Jr., Jan. 29, [1950], PAFA object file.
6. Harriet French, "Sculpture Is Her Forte: Artist Feels One Learns by Doing," *Washington Star,* Dec. 4, 1955, clipping file, Martin Luther King Memorial Library, District of Columbia Library, Washington, D.C.

Exhibited

1948 Corcoran Gallery of Art, Washington, D.C., *Sculptors of Maryland, Washington, Virginia,* cat. no. 5. **1949** Whitney Museum of American Art, New York, *1949 Annual Exhibition of Contemporary American Sculpture, Watercolors, Drawings,* cat. no. 13. **1950*** cat. no. 94. **1974** Provident National Bank, Philadelphia, exhibition of art works from the PAFA. **1986–87** PAFA, *Sculpture at the Pennsylvania Academy of the Fine Arts.* **1993** PAFA, *Carved in Wood and Stone: Twentieth-Century Sculpture.*

Richmond Barthé

1901–1989

Born in Bay Saint Louis, Missouri, Richmond Barthé was reared in New Orleans, where he received a grade school education. Because he was black, he was not allowed to enter art schools there so a priest suggested that he study at the Art Institute of Chicago. From about 1924 to 1927, Barthé was a student of the painter Charles Schroeder, who in 1927 encouraged him to try clay modeling to help develop a sense of depth in his paintings. His portrait busts of two friends were praised when exhibited that year at the Women's City Club in Chicago. Barthé then switched exclusively to sculpture. From about 1927 to 1928, he studied at the Art Institute with ALBIN POLÁŠEK, who had been a student of CHARLES GRAFLY at the Pennsylvania Academy of the Fine Arts.

About 1930, Barthé moved to New York. This was the time of the Harlem Renaissance. He attended the Art Students League for one year and met JO DAVIDSON, who praised his sculpture and suggested that he work on his own, away from instructors. In 1931 Barthé's sculpture was first exhibited at the Caz-Delbo Galleries in New York and received praise from the critics. In 1931 and 1932, he was awarded two Julius Rosenwald Fellowships. By 1934 the Whitney Museum of American Art had purchased his works: *Blackberry Woman*, 1932; *African Dancer*, 1933. He toured the museums of Europe in 1934, and received an honorary master of arts degree from Xavier University, in New Orleans. In 1937 he made reliefs for a Harlem River housing project. Chosen to participate in the *American Art Today* exhibition at the 1939 New York World's Fair, he showed *Mother and Son* (later destroyed), a pietà that was a comment on lynching. That year he began a series of portrait busts of actors, including John Gielgud and Lawrence Olivier. In 1941 and 1942, Barthé won Guggenheim Fellowships. His figure *Boxer* was shown in 1942 in the *Artists for Victory* exhibition at the Metropolitan Museum of Art, which purchased the sculpture.

Richmond Barthé submitted portraits and figures to the Pennsylvania Academy's annual exhibitions of 1938 and 1940–48. In 1946 he was commissioned to execute a bust of Booker T. Washington for the Hall of Fame, New York. The bust was shown the next year at the Pennsylvania Academy's 143rd annual exhibition. In 1949 he completed a monument to the eighteenth-century Haitian patriot Toussaint L'Ouverture for the government of Haiti. Barthé lived in Jamaica and then Europe for almost thirty years. His later years were spent in California.

References
1939 "The Story of Barthé," *Art Digest* 13 (March 1), p. 20. **1981** Lynn Moody Igoe and James Igoe, *250 Years of Afro-American Art: An Annotated Bibliography*, New York: R.R. Bowker Company, pp. 450–59. **1989** Grace Glueck, "Richmond Barthé, Sculptor, Dies," *New York Times*, March 16, p. 16-B.

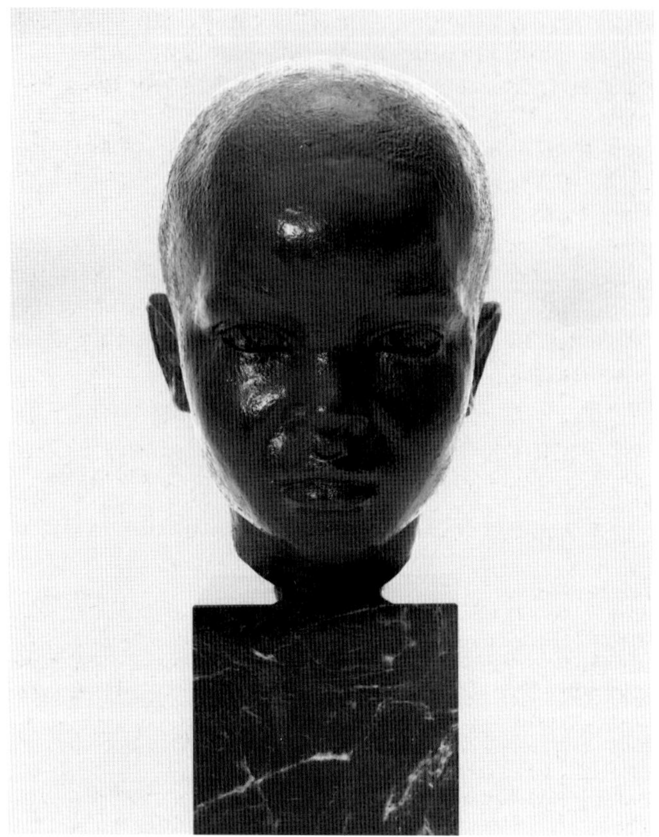

Barthé, *Julius*

Julius

About 1940
Bronze with black patina; cast in 1943
8¾ x 6¼ x 7¼" (22.2 x 15.9 x 18.4 cm)
Signed on bronze plate at left side of neck: BARTHÉ
Lost-wax cast by Modern Art Foundry, New York
Henry D. Gilpin Fund, 1943.2

RICHMOND BARTHÉ'S FRIEND Carl Van Vechten, well-known portrait photographer, music critic, and author of books on Harlem, commissioned this bust of his housekeeper's nephew. Julius posed for the bust when he was five years old and for a mask several years later.

Julius is a sensitive, realistic portrait of a young black boy with piercing deep-set eyes, the pupils of which are indicated in low relief. Barthé strove in his portraits for a "spiritual quality behind the eyes."[1] There is an overall surface pattern on the bust. The hair is suggested by intersecting pairs of incised parallel lines. At the foundry, some of the patina was rubbed off the nose, lips, cheeks, ears, and hair, creating red-brown highlights. The head is mounted on a green-black marble base.

Only two bronzes of this bust were cast by the

Modern Art Foundry. The Museum of American Art of the Pennsylvania Academy of the Fine Arts owns cast no. 2. Cast no. 1 (location unknown), was formerly in the Van Vechten collection.[2] It was exhibited at the Art Institute of Chicago in 1940–41; the International Print Society, in New York in 1945; and the Phillips Memorial Gallery, Washington, D.C. in 1946–47, with the mask of Julius and twenty-one other Barthé sculptures. Several bronzes of the mask of Julius were made: one is in the Santa Monica Art Museum in California; others were owned by movie stars of the 1940s.[3]

Notes

1. Artist's response to questionnaire (with annotated exhibition brochure), Sept. 18, 1984, PAFA research file.
2. Ibid.
3. Artist's response to questionnaire, cited in n. 1.

Exhibited

1943* cat. no. 210. **1955** Pyramid Club of Philadelphia, *Special Fall Exhibition.* **1963** Urban League of Philadelphia, Fine Arts Tea on the 100th Anniversary of the Emancipation Proclamation. **1970** Sheldon Memorial Art Gallery, University of Nebraska, Lincoln, *American Sculpture,* cat. no. 21 (ill.). **1974** University Museum, University of Pennsylvania, Philadelphia, *Second World Black and African Festival of Arts and Culture, Southeastern Region.* **1986–87** PAFA, *Sculpture at the Pennsylvania Academy of the Fine Arts.* **1990** Newark Museum, Newark, N.J., *Against the Odds: African-American Artists and the Harmon Foundation, 1923–1943,* traveling exhib. **1994–95** Reynolda House Museum of American Art, Winston-Salem, N.C.

Chaim Gross

1904–1991

Chaim Gross, the tenth child of Leah and Moses Gross, was born on March 17, 1904, in the Galician village of Wolowa, situated in the thickly wooded Carpathian Mountains of eastern Austria. When he was still a young child, his family moved a short distance to Slobodka Lesnia, where his father, a lumber merchant, took a job as controller of a large sawmill. Subsequently, the family relocated to the city of Kolomyja, which was invaded by Russian troops in 1914. As the ten-year-old boy watched in horror, soldiers cruelly attacked his parents. For the remaining years of World War I, Gross was repeatedly imprisoned and suffered many other hardships before being reunited with family members. Prior to attending a Budapest art academy for six months in 1919, Gross wandered from Kolomyja to Stryj, Silesia and Vienna. At the end of the war, he returned to Kolomyja only to be incarcerated again when hostilities erupted between Poland and Russia.

Gross escaped from his imprisonment and fled to Vienna, where he studied art for a year at the Kunstgewerbe Schule. In 1921 he was able to join his brother Naftoli Gross, a Yiddish-language poet, in New York. The seventeen-year old immigrant enrolled at the Educational Alliance Art School. In his first year in the United States he formed lifetime friendships with the artists SAUL BAIZERMAN, Peter Blume, Phillip Evergood, Adolph Gottlieb, Barnett Newman, CONCETTA SCARAVAGLIONE, Ben Shahn, and Moses and Isaac Soyer. Gross went on to study sculpture with Elie Nadelman (1882–1946) at the Beaux-Arts Institute of Design.

His 1926 decision to focus his creative life on the direct carving of wood was triggered by a course at the Art Students League with the direct carver ROBERT LAURENT. The choice was also shaped by pleasant childhood experiences associated with wood, such as exploring his father's lumber stocks and seeing relatives whittle and carve.

Gross lived a life of extreme privation in the late twenties and early thirties. Nonetheless, he remained committed to his art and carved figures in a variety of exotic woods. In 1932 the 144 Gallery in Greenwich Village gave him his first one-man exhibition. The same year, he married Renee Nechin. Gross was awarded a Louis Comfort Tiffany Foundation Fellowship in 1933. His second solo show was held in 1935 at the Boyer Gallery, Philadelphia. One of the first artists selected to participate in the New Deal arts projects initiated by President Franklin Delano Roosevelt, Gross received several important sculpture commissions for federal buildings in the 1930s. A popular instructor, he taught at the New School for Social Research and at the Educational Alliance. One of his first students was Louise Nevelson (1899–1988).

Holger Cahill, curator at the Museum of Modern Art, in New York, described Gross in 1935 as "one of the gifted young artists who is revitalizing contemporary American sculpture."[1] This attests to the early recognition that Gross received for his direct wood carvings. In a 1938 autobiographical statement, Gross noted, "I am essentially a carver and the harder the wood the more pleasure I get from chipping away and exposing the forms I want."[2] His career spanned seven decades, marked by multiple national and international exhibitions of his sculpture and drawings. A lignum vitae wood sculpture entitled *I Love My Baby,* 1948 (Collection of Vera and Albert A. List, New York) was shown in the 149th annual exhibition of the Pennsylvania Academy of the Fine Arts, where it was awarded honorable mention. In the late fifties, Gross expanded his techniques to modeling for bronze casting in order to fulfill several international outdoor commissions.

He died in New York at the age of eighty-seven in 1991. The Chaim Gross Studio Museum in New York opened to the public in 1995. A catalogue raisonné is forthcoming.

Notes

1. Cahill 1935.
2. Gross 1938, p. 696.

References

1935 Holger Cahill, "Chaim Gross," in *Sculpture by Chaim Gross,* exhib. brochure, Boyer Galleries, Philadelphia, clipping file, PAFA Library. **1938** Chaim Gross, "A Sculptor's Progress," *Magazine of Art* 31 (Dec.), pp. 694–98. **1957** Chaim Gross, *The Technique of Wood Sculpture,* New York: ARCO Publishing Company. **1974** National Collection of Fine Arts, Smithsonian Institution, *Chaim Gross: Sculpture and Drawings,* exhib. cat. **1977** Lowe Art Museum, University of Miami, *Chaim Gross: A Retrospective,* exhib. cat. **1991** John T. McQuiston, "Chaim Gross, 87, Wood Sculptor of Exuberant Human Forms, Dies," *New York Times,* May 7, p. 12-B.

Gross, *Balancing on a Unicycle*

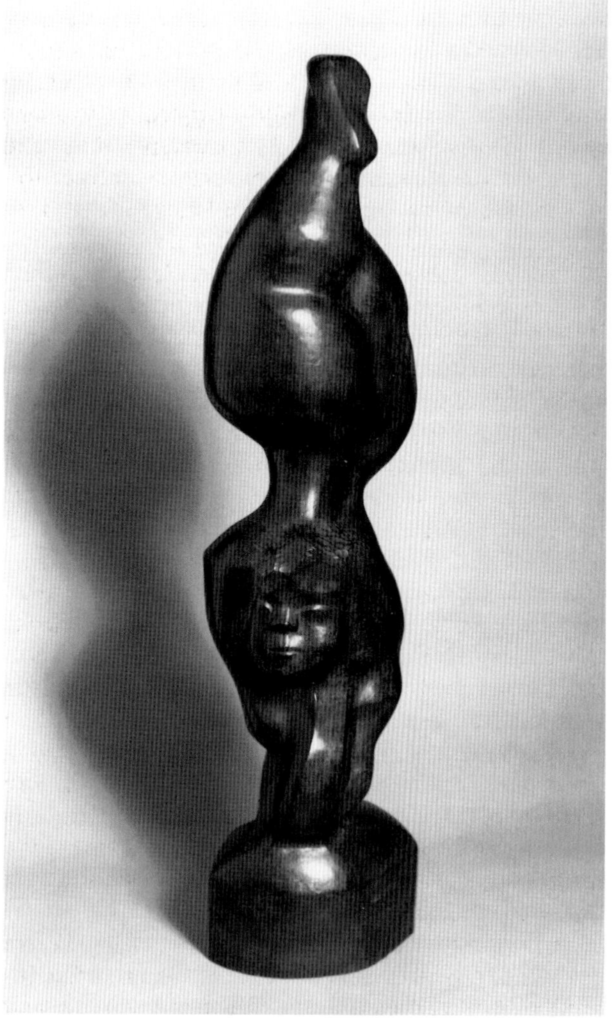

Balancing on a Unicycle

1940
Bronze with black patina; lost-wax cast in 1967 from ebony carving
41 x 11 x 7" (104.1 x 27.9 x 17.8 cm)
Signed on front of integral base above artist's cipher: CHAIM GROSS
Foundry mark on side of base: BEDI-MAKKY [N]YC
Gift of Mimi Gross, 1986.55

THROUGH HIS ART, Chaim Gross celebrated the human condition. He focused on female figures, the family, and circus performers. Subject matter was incidental to form:

> People have often asked me why I am interested in acrobatic figures. I am not interested in acrobats per se, but I use these subjects, because I find in them many possibilities of variations in forms and movement. . . . My acrobats allow me to combine and interlock forms and permit a flow of one form into another. In addition, this subject matter lends itself to spiraling which aids me in achieving a three-dimensional effect. This spiraling adds a lift to the figure, for the eye is carried upward and thus gives a monumental effect to even a small piece of sculpture.[1]

Two important instances of his abiding attention to images of acrobats are *Handlebar Riders,* acquired by New York's Museum of Modern Art in 1937, and *Girl on Wheel,* purchased by the Metropolitan Museum of Art in 1941. Gross's penchant for depicting female gymnasts is also seen to good advantage in *Balancing on a Unicycle,* the second of three bronze casts made in 1967 from a 1940 ebony carving.[2] This sculpture was a gift from the sculptor's daughter, the painter Mimi Gross.

The surface of the bronze cast of *Balancing on a Unicycle* closely imitates the polish and color of the original dark wood. The female acrobat's squarish face, enlivened by a slight smile, is characteristic of the sculptor's favored facial type. In a general way, it resembles his wife, Renee. Signs of the carved original are revealed in the cascade of hair framing the woman's face. Bold chisel marks on the crown and smaller strokes on the side delineate the locks of hair. With the exception of these choppy passages, the body of the plump, wasp-waisted performer is rendered in smooth, simplified volumes. By showing the acrobat balancing upside-down as she maneuvers a unicycle, Gross invites viewers to consider the human form as an upward spiral of interlocking forms.

Notes

1. Chaim Gross, "A Sculptor's Progress," *Magazine of Art* 31 (Dec. 1938), p. 697.

2. The ebony carving is listed in the sculptor's record book (collection of Chaim Gross Archives, the Renee and Chaim Gross Foundation, New York) as "Black figure on wheel."

Reference

Forthcoming April Paul, catalogue raisonné of the work of Chaim Gross, the Renee and Chaim Gross Foundation, New York.

Exhibited

1993 PAFA, *Carved in Wood and Stone: Twentieth-Century Sculpture.*

Charles Rudy

1904–1986

Charles Horace Rudy was born and reared in York, Pennsylvania. His father, J. Horace Rudy, was a stained-glass maker who had studied painting at the Pennsylvania Academy of the Fine Arts in 1892 and 1893 along with John Sloan, William Glackens, and Robert Henri. Charles's grandfather John Rudy was a painter of stagecoaches, carriages, and wagons.

Charles Rudy had made clay images of animals and developed a strong desire to work with his hands. From the age of about eight to eighteen he worked in his father's shop. He attended the Pennsylvania Academy from 1924 to 1928. After about six months of classes in drawing and painting with Daniel Garber at the Academy's summer school in Chester Springs, Rudy began to study head and life modeling with CHARLES GRAFLY. In the summer of 1925, he learned to model animals with ALBERT LAESSLE, at Chester Springs. A few months later, his *Goat and Toad* (location unknown) received a prize at the ninth annual exhibition at Chester Springs. Rudy was awarded William Emlen Cresson Traveling Scholarships in 1927 and 1928 that enabled him to go to Europe for five months each year. He was impressed by Madrid and Munich and was greatly influenced by the ancient art in Italy. In 1928 John F. Lewis, president of the Pennsylvania Academy's board of trustees, gave Rudy a cash prize for a mask he made. Rudy was considered by his Academy teachers to be an "unusually fine worker."[1] He made plaster casts for his fellow students of their sculpture and taught modeling at a local settlement house. For several years after graduation, he lived in York, where he set up a studio and completed his first commissions—memorials for the York public schools and the Masonic Temple. He also gave private lessons and assisted his father.

In 1931 Rudy married, moved to New York, and became the head of the sculpture department at the Cooper Union School of Art, where for ten years he taught stone and wood carving, modeling, and plaster casting. Having developed an interest in working in stone while helping his father install stained glass in the stone window frames of churches, Charles Rudy had taught himself to carve using tools that he bought from a local blacksmith and stone collected from New York demolition sites. In 1932 he produced his first stone carving, *Mother and Child* (private collection), a kneeling nude, supporting an infant on her back. In 1936 he won a national competition held by the United States Treasury Department's Section of Fine Arts for the design for a high-relief stone panel for the facade of the main post office in the Bronx, New York. Rudy designed a thirteen-foot marble sculpture called *Noah Receiving a Message from a Dove* that was carved in place by Louis Beretta. For its "idea and simplicity," it was awarded a Second Honorable Mention in 1937 at the fifty-first annual exhibition of the Architectural League of New York by a jury that included A. STIRLING CALDER. Rudy's bronze *Bather,* 1935 was shown in the *American Art Today* exhibition at the 1939 New York World's Fair; and he was one of six sculptors chosen to produce works for the fair's Federal Building. His contribution was a sculpture group entitled *Indian with Bear Cubs.*

Starting in 1938, when he shared the teaching of a summer session with NATHANIEL CHOATE, Rudy taught sporadically at Chester Springs until 1951. The Rudys had purchased a house in rural Bucks County in the 1930s, and in 1941 they took up permanent residence there. *Reclining Girl* (q.v.) was purchased that year by the Pennsylvania Academy from its 136th annual exhibition. In November of the following year, Rudy's first one-man show—sixteen works mostly based on rural themes—was held at the Philadelphia Art Alliance. He was awarded a Guggenheim Foundation Fellowship in 1942, the same year he assisted the war effort as an airplane welder in Willow Grove, Pennsylvania. From the scrap metal that he saved, he made small sculptures, which were featured in *Life* magazine.[2] In 1944 he received the American Academy of Arts and Letters Award. In the spring of 1946, Rudy was an artist-in-residence at Michigan State College (now Michigan

State University) in East Lansing, where he produced terracotta panels to decorate a dormitory dining room and had a one-man show of his work. From about 1948 to 1952, he created figures symbolizing Duty, Loyalty, and Service for the War Memorial at Virginia Polytechnic Institute, at Blacksburg with Donald De Lue (b. 1900) and HENRY KREIS, who Rudy credited along with WALKER HANCOCK as a major influence in his career.[3] For twenty-seven years beginning in 1949, Rudy served as a member of the Pennsylvania Arts Commission.

In the fall of 1949, Rudy taught sculpture at the Pennsylvania Academy while Walker Hancock, the head of the department, was on leave. Rudy replaced HARRY ROSIN in 1952/53 and then returned in the spring of 1955 to teach stone and wood carving. He was a regular participant in the Pennsylvania Academy's annual exhibitions from 1928 to 1962 and in the Fellowship annual exhibitions until 1974. In 1935 he won the Annual Fellowship Prize for *Joy Ride* (Brookgreen Gardens, Murrells Inlet, South Carolina), which depicts a boy and a pig. In 1949 he won the Annual Fellowship Alumni Association Prize for *Frustration* (private collection), a figure of a monkey. In 1947 *The Letter* (private collection), a 1945 portrait of his wife, Lorraine, won the Pennsylvania Academy's George D. Widener Memorial Gold Medal First Honorable Mention and a prize in memory of Dr. Herbert M. Howe, a member of the board of directors of the Pennsylvania Academy from 1898 to 1916.[4] The Academy gave Rudy a solo show of twenty-eight works in 1948 in the Philadelphia Artists' Gallery (a forerunner of the current Morris Gallery).

The National Academy of Design, in New York, elected Rudy an associate in 1952 and an academician in 1967. He designed five seven-foot-high bronze figures symbolizing the *Unity of Man and of Mutual Tolerance* for the Memorial Flag Pole of the University of Pennsylvania, dedicated in 1952. In the summer of 1954, he taught carving in stone and modeling in terracotta at the Skowhegan School of Painting and Sculpture in Maine, and the next year he completed a nine-foot-high figure for a memorial commissioned by the Sun Oil Company in Marcus Hook, Delaware, in memory of seamen killed in World War II. Rudy received a commission in 1955 for bronze tablets with relief portraits of Benjamin Franklin for a bridge that crosses the Delaware River and connects Philadelphia with Camden, New Jersey.

Exhibitions of Charles Rudy's work were held in Pennsylvania at the Dickinson College Art Gallery, Carlisle, in 1953, Lehigh University Art Galleries, Bethlehem, in 1955, and the Historical Society of York County in 1960. For the fifty-seventh issue of the Society of Medalists in 1958, he produced a medal symbolizing a Robert Browning poem. In 1962 Rudy was commissioned to sculpt ten figures of prominent Pennsylvanians, a group entitled *Penn's Treaty with the Indians,* and images of state seals and coats of arms for the facade and gates of the Pennsylvania State Historical Museum, in Harrisburg. In 1964 he completed an eighteen-foot-long granite relief for the exterior of the Lehigh County Courthouse, in Allentown. In the late 1960s, Rudy worked for four years under Walker Hancock on the Confederate memorial at Stone Mountain, Georgia, which had been designed by Gutzon Borglum (1867–1941) in 1917 and abandoned in the 1920s. As a consultant, Rudy supervised the work of thirty sculptors.

In 1971 he received the Percy M. Owens Memorial Prize for a distinguished Pennsylvania artist from the Fellowship of the Pennsylvania Academy. In 1976 the Academy presented an Outstanding Artist Award to him; and York, Pennsylvania, held a "Charles Rudy Day." He received a citation for excellence in the arts from Governor Richard Thornburgh in 1980 and an honorary degree from York College of Pennsylvania in 1981.

Notes

1. Charles Connick, "My Friend, J. Horace Rudy," *Stained Glass* 35 (Spring 1940), p. 5.
2. "Scrap Sculpture: An artist-welder in a war plant makes these from leftover steel," *Life* 15 (Dec. 20, 1943), pp. 81, 82, 84.
3. Interview with Mr. and Mrs. Charles Rudy, by Linda Bantel and Susan James-Gadzinski, May 1, 1984, tapes in PAFA Archives.
4. Three other bronze casts of *The Letter* were produced. One was awarded the first Charles K. Smith Prize at the eighth annual exhibition of the Woodmere Art Gallery, in Philadelphia in 1948. A cast was shown in the exhibition *American Sculpture 1951,* at the Metropolitan Museum of Art, New York, in 1951/52 and was acquired by the Metropolitan in 1966. Another cast received a gold medal at the fortieth annual exhibition of the National Sculpture Society, New York, in 1973 and was included in the 1976 Philadelphia Museum of Art exhibition and catalogue *Philadelphia: Three Centuries of American Art.* In 1980 the bust was in an exhibition of contemporary American art at the British Museum. A cast was given to the Philadelphia Museum of Art by Benjamin Bernstein in 1986. A cast is in a private collection in the Philadelphia area.

References

1940 Charles Rudy, "The Challenge of Form," *Magazine of Art* 33 (April), pp. 204–9, published in *Painters and Sculptors of Modern America,* New York: Thomas Y. Crowell Company, 1942, pp. 102–5. **1948** Dorothy Grafly, "Charles Rudy: An Interview by Dorothy Grafly," *American Artist* 12 (April), pp. 38–40, 62. **1975** James C.G. Conniff, "The Man Who Sculpts Monuments," *Philadelphia Inquirer,* magazine section, May 11, pp. 28–30, 32, 33. **1976** *Philadelphia: Three Centuries of American Art,* Philadelphia: Philadelphia Museum of Art, pp. 565–67.

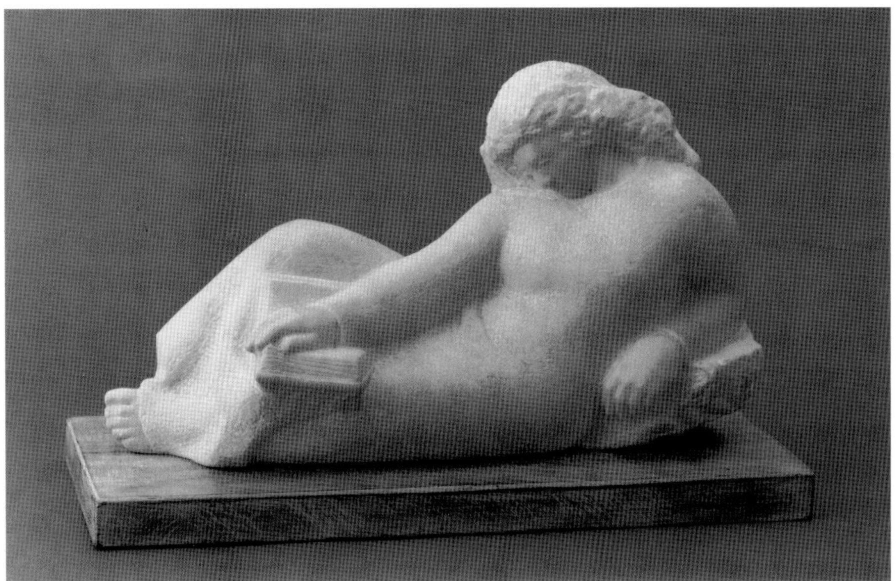

Rudy, *Reclining Girl*

Reclining Girl

1940
Vermont marble
10½ x 17¼ x 5½" (26.7 x 43.8 x 14 cm)
Signed and dated on back: C RUDY 1940; signed on back: CR [monogram]
Henry D. Gilpin Fund, 1941.11

Reclining Girl was carved from one of the leftover marble fragments from the panel *Noah Receiving a Message from a Dove,* 1937 (Post Office, Bronx, New York).[1] In handling the fragment, Charles Rudy tried to see how successfully he "might carry the forms around to the flat face of the stone rather than reduce the scale of the figure."[2] The back of the head and the dress from the waist downward are in the same plane, while the torso is carved in the round. The smooth surface of the open book and of the figure's face, neck, hands, and toes contrasts with the roughness of her hair, the support, and the overall pattern on the floor-length dress and the incised parallel lines at its neck and cuffs.

An image of *Reclining Girl* was used by the American Artists Group in New York for its 1941 Christmas card.[3] Mrs. Carey Etnier—whose son Stephen was a student at the Pennsylvania Academy of the Fine Arts and a friend of Charles Rudy—wished to commission a tomb monument in 1950 for her late husband and remembered the Academy's *Reclining Girl.* With the permission of the Academy, she had Rudy carve in marble a similar composition, enlarged beyond lifesize. This figure was, however, completely carved in the round and not bound by the severe restrictions on design that the fragment had imposed. Mrs. Etnier called the tomb monument *Book of Life* from a passage in Revelations. Rudy obtained her permission to make a mold of the marble; and in his studio with outside assistance, he produced a cast-stone replica made of cement with marble chips and dust that he had saved from the carving of the original monument. The cast-stone version will someday be erected in a Bucks County cemetery in memory of the sculptor and his wife.

Notes

1. *Bear Cub,* about 1942, and *The Mother,* 1942 (both in private collections), were also carved from marble fragments saved from the *Noah* panel.
2. Artist's statement, March 1942, PAFA object file.
3. Samuel Golden to Charles Rudy, Jan. 13, 1941, Charles Rudy Papers, private collection.

References

1948 Dorothy Grafly, "Charles Rudy: An Interview by Dorothy Grafly," *American Artist* 12 (April), p. 38 (ill.). **1948** "Former Yorker among America's Top Sculptors: Charles Rudy Got First Art Training in Father's Stained Glass Workshop," *York [Pa.] Gazette and Daily,* May 24, p. 14 (ill.). **1948** Jacques F. Schneir, *Sculpture in Modern America,* Berkeley: University of California Press, p. 33 (ill.). **1952** Orville Prescott, "Of This Year's Books, These Have Impressed Me Most," *New York Times Book Review,* June 8, p. 6 (ill.).

Exhibited

1941* cat. no. 222 (ill.). **1942** Guggenheim Foundation, New York, exhibition of works by candidates for fellowships. **1942** Philadelphia Art Alliance, *Sculpture by Charles Rudy.* **1944** American Academy of Arts and Letters, New York, exhibition of award-winners. **1946** Michigan State College Art Gallery, East Lansing, *Sculpture by*

Charles Rudy. **1948** PAFA, Philadelphia Artists' Gallery, *Exhibition of Sculpture by Charles Rudy,* checklist no. 8. **1955** Lehigh University Art Gallery, Bethlehem, Pa., *Sculpture of Charles Rudy and Ceramics of Victor Riu.* **1975** William Penn Memorial Museum, Harrisburg, Pa., exhibition of works of art from the PAFA. **1986–87** PAFA, *Sculpture at the Pennsylvania Academy of the Fine Arts.*

Pekin Drake

1941
Pentelic marble
10⅛ x 7 x 12¼" (25.7 x 17.8 x 31.1 cm)
Signed on plinth at duck's left side: C. RUDY
Joseph E. Temple Fund, 1942.9

IN AUGUST 1937 the Pennsylvania Academy of the Fine Arts took down a badly deteriorated, unrestorable Greek statue of Ceres from a stone pedestal at the second-floor level of the facade of its building at 118 North Broad Street and gave the fragments to several sculptors, including Charles Rudy.[1] From the four pieces that he received, Rudy carved *Pekin Drake, Two Hearts that Beat as One* (q.v.), *Waterbird,* dated between 1948 and 1956 (location unknown),[2] and *Medusa,* 1958 (private collection).[3]

Ducks and other birds were among Rudy's favorite subjects, and he often drew them. He remembered as a child being interested in the ducks he saw at farm markets. At their home in Ottsville, Pennsylvania, he and his wife raised ducks, and Mrs. Rudy remembers his placing a mirror in front of the drake that was the subject of this piece in order to entice it into remaining quiet on the sculpture stand.[4] The final form of *Pekin Drake* was influenced by the original shape of the stone. The base on which the duck is perched still shows the marks of the drill used to remove the original statue of Ceres from the Pennsylvania Academy facade.[5] The webbed feet of the duck were carved in low relief, and the stone between the legs and the upturned tail was left uncut to act as a support. The surface of the duck is smooth; and the forms, especially the breast and sides, are subtly delineated. A minimum of carved lines are used to indicate the duck's eyes, bill, nostrils, and tail feathers. The work is simple in form yet realistic—two characteristics that Rudy strived for. *Pekin Drake* was one of six sculptures chosen for commendation by the sculptors' jury at the 137th annual exhibition of the Pennsylvania Academy in 1942.

Rudy, *Pekin Drake*

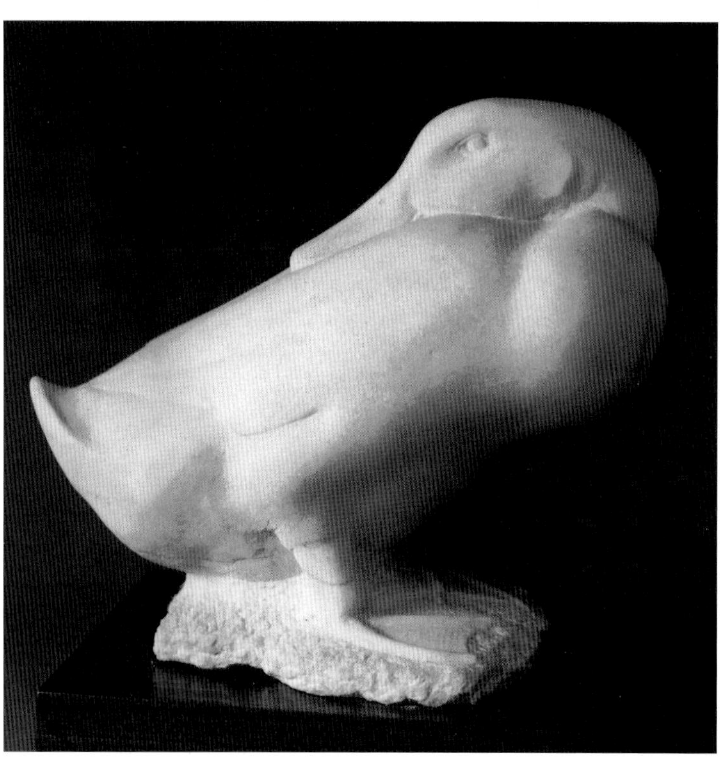

Notes

1. Statement by Charles J. Marsh, assistant to the secretary of the PAFA, July 27, 1937, and "Ceres Endures City's Climate 109 Years—but at Last Collapses, Marble Goddess is Removed from Academy Pedestal, Greek Statue 2300 Years Old Crumbles to Dust in Strange Land," *Philadelphia Record,* August 13, 1937, PAFA Archives.
2. Dorothy Grafly, "Charles Rudy: An Interview by Dorothy Grafly," *American Artist* 12 (April 1948), p. 40.
3. "Pentelic marble" was written in pencil in the artist's hand on the back of a photograph of *Medusa,* Charles Rudy Papers, private collection.
4. Conversation with Mrs. Charles Rudy, Linda Bantel, Cheryl Leibold, and Susan James-Gadzinski, Feb. 27, 1987.
5. Artist's statement, March 1942, PAFA object file.

References

1941 Eleanor Jewett, "November Full of Interesting Art Exhibits," *Chicago Sunday Tribune,* Nov. 9, p. 5 (ill.). **1945** Mary H. Spruance, "A Pennsylvania Sculptor—Charles Rudy," *Pennsylvania Clubwoman* 33 (Nov.), p. 9 (ill.). **1948** "Former Yorker among America's Top Sculptors: Charles Rudy Got First Art Training in Father's Stained Glass Workshop," *York [Pa.] Gazette and Daily,* May 24, p. 14 (ill.).

Exhibited

1941–42 Art Institute of Chicago, *The Fifty-second Annual Exhibition of American Paintings and Sculpture,* cat. no. 259. **1942*** cat. no. 302. **1942** Guggenheim Foundation, New York, exhibition of works by winners of fellowships. **1942** Philadelphia Art Alliance, *Sculpture by Charles Rudy.* **1943** National Academy of Design, New York, *117th Annual Exhibition,* cat. no. 35, sculpture section. **1944** American Academy of Arts and Letters, New York, exhibition of award-winners. **1948** PAFA, Philadelphia Artists' Gallery, *Exhibition of Sculpture by Charles Rudy,* cat. no. 6. **1949** Bonwit Teller, Philadelphia, window display for publicity for the annual PAFA Fellowship exhibition. **1954** Downtown Gallery, New York, *Skowhegan School Exhibition,* special exhibition of work by faculty members from the previous nine years. **1956** PAFA, *Painting and Sculpture by Living Philadelphia Artists Represented in the Permanent Collection of the Academy,* cat. no. 148. **1958** Quaker City Federal Savings and Loan Association, Philadelphia, window display promoting PAFA's 153rd annual exhibition. **1986–87** PAFA, *Sculpture at the Pennsylvania Academy of the Fine Arts.* **1988** PAFA, *Sea and Shore.* **1989** PAFA, *"The Birds and the Beasts Will Teach Us."* **1992–93** PAFA, *Masterworks of American Art: 1750–1950.* **1994–96** PAFA, *Two Centuries of Collecting at the Museum of American Art.*

Two Hearts that Beat as One

1945
Pentelic marble
10 x 12 x 6¼" (25.4 x 30.5 x 15.9 cm)
Signed and dated at left rear: 4 RUDY 5
Gift of Mrs. Alfred Bendiner, 1985.60

Two Hearts that Beat as One was based on a rough pencil sketch about two inches square, which is now lost.[1] Like *Pekin Drake* (q.v.), it was carved from a fragment of a deteriorated Greek statue of Ceres. Except the textured hair, the forms of *Two Hearts that Beat as One* are bold and curved with a smooth, polished finish. The original composition had to be altered because the area that was to be the figure's right foot was too fragile to carve, due to the deterioration of the marble. Evidence of a repair made by the sculptor in 1960 can be seen at the figure's left wrist.[2]

Charles Rudy liked this composition so much that he later modeled another version in clay (private collection).

Notes

1. Grafly 1948, p. 40.
2. Charles Rudy to Joseph T. Fraser, Jr., director of the PAFA, July 9, 1960, PAFA Archives.

Reference

1948 Dorothy Grafly, "Charles Rudy: An Interview by Dorothy Grafly," *American Artist* 12 (April), p. 40.

Exhibited

1946 Whitney Museum of American Art, New York, *1946 Annual Exhibition of Contemporary American Sculpture, Watercolors, and Drawings,* cat. no. 36. **1948** PAFA, Philadelphia Artists' Gallery, *Exhibition of Sculpture by Charles Rudy,* checklist no. 24. **1955** Lehigh University Art Gallery, Bethlehem, Pa., *Sculpture of Charles Rudy and Ceramics by Victor Riu.* **1959** PAFA, *Paintings, Drawings, Prints, and Sculpture Collected and Owned by Fourteen Philadelphia Artists,* cat. no. 314. **1986–87** PAFA, *Sculpture at the Pennsylvania Academy of the Fine Arts.* **1993** PAFA, *Carved in Wood and Stone: Twentieth-Century Sculpture.*

Ex Collection

Mr. and Mrs. Alfred Bendiner, 1947–85.

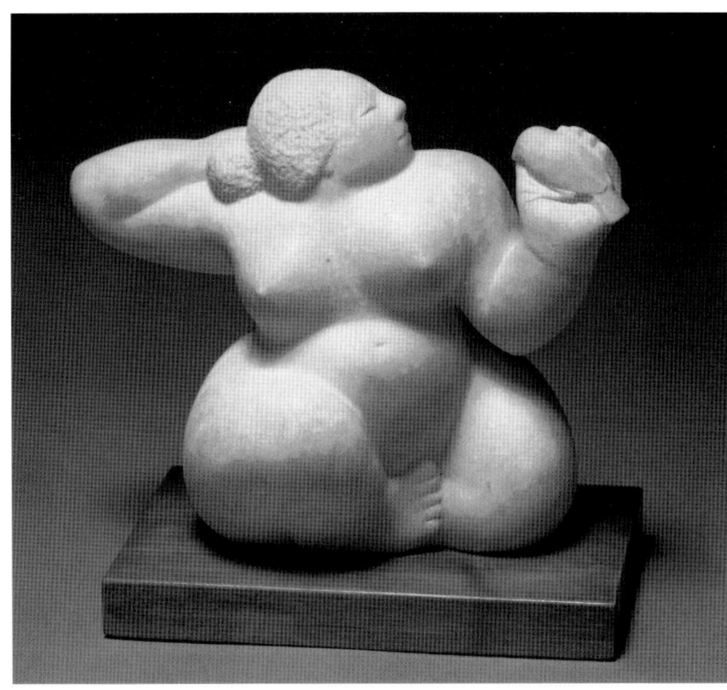

Rudy, *Two Hearts that Beat as One*

Marion Sanford

1904–1988

Born in Guelph, Ontario, of American parents, Marion Sanford spent most of her childhood in Warren, Pennsylvania, where her father farmed. After studying drawing and painting at the Pratt Institute in Brooklyn, New York, in the early 1920s, she returned to Warren and designed stage sets and costumes.[1] Later she studied sculpture briefly with Leo Lentelli (1879–1962) and ROBERT LAURENT at the Art Students League of New York. From about 1935 to 1941, she worked in the New York studio of Brenda Putnam (1890–1975), a former student of CHARLES GRAFLY in Boston. Marion Sanford did all the line drawings used to illustrate anatomy and sculpture techniques in Brenda Putnam's book *The Sculptor's Way.*[2] In 1939 Sanford modeled a relief *Weighing Cotton* for the post office in Winder, Georgia, as part of a Federal Art Project under the Works Progress Administration.[3] From 1941 to 1943, her work was supported by two grants from the Guggenheim Foundation. For about thirty years, she and the animal sculptor CORNELIA CHAPIN shared the former studio of Gutzon Borglum (1867–1941) in Manhattan. Chapin was the model for some of the figures in Marion Sanford's genre series Women at Work.

Sanford participated in the annual exhibitions of the Pennsylvania Academy of the Fine Arts from 1942 to 1951. In the 1950s, she executed several commissions for large-scale works: the altar for a church in Warren, a relief of the Epiphany for the reredos in Saint Mary's Chapel in Faribault, Minnesota, and a limestone figure of Hippocrates for the tower of a hospital in Warren. A large collection of her sculpture, in plaster and bronze, can be seen at the Warren County Historical Society. Her work is also in the Corcoran Gallery of Art, Washington, D.C., and Brookgreen Gardens, Murrells Inlet, South Carolina. From 1979 to her death in 1988, she lived in England, where she devoted much of her time to researching church sculpture and architecture.[4]

Notes

1. Beatrice Gilman Proske, *Brookgreen Gardens Sculpture* (Murrells Inlet, S.C.: Brookgreen Gardens, 1968), rev. ed., p. 463.

2. Brenda Putnam, *The Sculptor's Way: A Guide to Modelling and Sculpture* (New York: Farrar and Rinehart, 1939), p. 343.

3. The relief was moved in 1995 to the Barrow County Historical Society Museum in Winder. See Jim Kvicala, "Weighing Cotton: Museum Sculpture Ties Community with Its Past," *Winder [Ga.] News*, Sept. 27, 1995, pp. 1, 3-C.

4. Artist's response to questionnaire, July 31, 1984, PAFA object file.

Sanford, *Harvest*

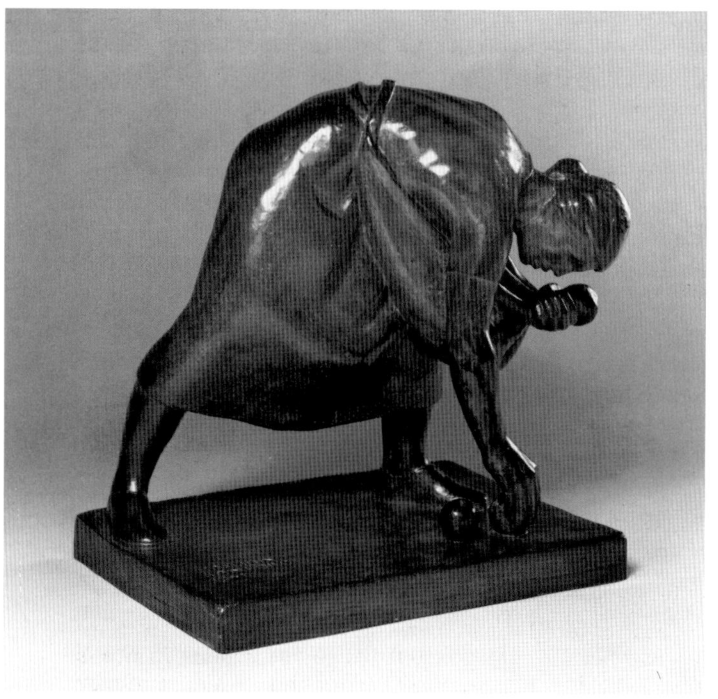

Harvest

1941
Bronze with gray-green patina; cast in 1942
14 x 13 x 9½" (35.6 x 33 x 24.1 cm)
Signed and dated on top of base: MARION/SANFORD/1941
Sand cast by Anton Basky Foundry, New York
Henry D. Gilpin Fund, 1942.10

Harvest is from the series Women at Work in which small female figures are shown performing such tasks as washing clothes, scrubbing floors, churning butter, and ploughing and planting fields. The sculptures, in plaster, bronze, and stone, date from 1939 through the 1940s. *Harvest* shows a muscular farmwoman bending to grasp a fallen apple with her right hand while her left hand clutches the gathered end of an apron already bulging with apples. The forms are boldly modeled with scant detail. Most of Marion Sanford's genre sculptures are based on memories of the farm scenes that she saw while growing up near Warren, in the northwestern corner of Pennsylvania. When interviewed in 1947 about her inspiration for the series, she said, "There's beauty in movements one makes while performing homely useful chores and there's unconscious grace in the succession of movements as the work proceeds."[1] In the 1940s, she was primarily interested in sculpting the human figure in action. Her work during that period is similar to the sculpture produced in the early decades of this century by MAHONRI YOUNG, who depicted laborers, and Abastenia St. Leger Eberle (1878–1972), who depicted children at play and women working.

Marion Sanford produced one preliminary drawing for *Harvest*, but its present whereabouts is unknown. The plaster cast of the clay original was purchased by the Pennsylvania Academy in 1942 from its 137th annual exhibition and was one of six sculptures chosen by the sculpture jury to receive special notice.[2] The Academy had it cast in bronze the same year and returned the plaster to the sculptor. Originally Sanford chose terracotta as the casting material for this piece, but Paul Manship (1885–1966), who also exhibited in the 1942 annual, convinced her that bronze would be more appropriate. She selected the "blue-green somewhat greyed" patina for the surface of the Academy's cast.[3] There are two other known bronzes, both with brown patinas. One is at the Warren County Historical Society, Warren, Pennsylvania; the other, at the National Academy of Design, in New York. It was probably the cast now at the National Academy that was awarded a gold medal at a 1945 exhibition of the Allied Artists of America.[4] Sanford gave the National Academy their version in 1963 as her diploma presentation. A plaster, painted to look like terracotta, is in a private collection.

Notes

1. Quoted in Sally MacDougall, "N.Y. Has Everything Marion Sanford Wants in Art," *New York World Telegram,* March 19, 1947, clipping file, Library of the *Philadelphia Inquirer.*

2. Marion Sanford to Joseph T. Fraser, Jr., director of the PAFA, March 11, 1942, PAFA object file.

3. M. Sanford to J. Fraser, April 28, 1942, ibid.

4. Beatrice Gilman Proske, *Brookgreen Gardens Sculpture* (Murrells Inlet, S.C.: Brookgreen Gardens, 1968), rev. ed., p. 464.

Exhibited

1943 Bonestell Gallery, New York, *Marion Sanford Sculpture,* checklist no. 11. **1947** Grand Central Art Galleries, New York, *Three Sculptors: Chapin, Duble, Sanford,* checklist no. 2. **1986–87** PAFA, *Sculpture at the Pennsylvania Academy of the Fine Arts.*

Bruce Moore

1905–1980

E. Bruce Moore was born in Bern, Kansas, to Elmer Bowdle Moore and Edna Browning Wooten Moore. The family moved to Wichita when Bruce was twelve. He soon began modeling in clay. In 1922 at the age of seventeen, he entered the Pennsylvania Academy of the Fine Arts and studied with CHARLES GRAFLY and ALBERT LAESSLE for four years. He took an animal sculpture class with Laessle at the Pennsylvania Academy's summer school in Chester Springs in 1923 and 1924. His facility at modeling animals helped him win William Emlen Cresson Traveling Scholarships in 1925 and 1926 for study in Europe, where he was impressed by the city of Florence and the works of Michelangelo.

In 1926 Moore returned to Wichita for three years. He taught at the Wichita Art Association and created designs using Western motifs for the exterior ornamentation of Wichita North High School. While there, he produced *Black Panther,* 1929 (Wichita Art Association), which won the prestigious George D. Widener Memorial Gold Medal in the Pennsylvania Academy's 1929 annual exhibition.[1] It is a stylized version of two sculptures (both, location unknown) that he made while a student at the Pennsylvania Academy.[2] Moore won Guggenheim Fellowships in 1929 and 1930 for study in Paris with the French sculptors Jean Dampt (1853–1946) and Louis Henri Bouchard (1875–1960). He also was given critiques of his work by the American expatriate sculptor Cecil Howard (1888–1956), who had trained in Antwerp with the French animalier Rembrandt Bugatti (1855–1916). In Paris Moore met Alice ("Aly") Hugli, a Swiss woman whom he married in 1932 in Switzerland.

In 1933 he briefly assisted Paul Manship (1885–1966) before working for four years on the commissions of the academic sculptor James Earle Fraser (1876–1953) in his studios in New York and Westport, Connecticut. During that time, Moore sketched animals in zoos and submitted work to the National Academy of Design, New York, where he won the Ellin P. Speyer Memorial Prize for *Pelican and Fish* and the Helen Foster Barnett Prize for *Saint Francis.*[3] From 1937 to 1939, he studied the human figure at the American Academy in Rome on an M.R. Cromwell traveling scholarship. In the 1940s, he lived in New York and commuted to Baltimore where he was the director and a teacher at the Rinehart School of Sculpture at the Maryland Institute. Moore's *Little Brother,* about 1941 (National Museum of American Art, Smithsonian Institution, Washington, D.C.), formerly *Brother and Sister,* was included in the 1942 *Artists for Victory* exhibition at the Metropolitan Museum of Art. His career was interrupted during World War II while he did war work in a New Jersey army hospital. Moore moved to Washington, D.C., in 1950 and, for about the next twenty years, worked on commissions, such as a heroic figure of General William Mitchell 1957 (Air and Space Museum, Smithsonian Institution); a thirty-foot figure of Columbia, 1960, for the National Memorial of the Pacific in Honolulu; two ten-foot-long tigers, about 1968, for Princeton University; doors, from the 1960s, for Grace Cathedral in San Francisco; and various medals. He continued to sketch animals in zoos and use animals and insects as subjects for linoleum-block prints, lithographs, and designs for Steuben Glass figures and engraved crystal vessels.

Moore's health began to fail in the early 1970s, and he stopped sculpting. In 1984 a retrospective exhibition was sponsored by the Wichita Art Museum and the Wichita Art Association, which had given him a one-man show in 1962.

Notes

1. A second cast is a promised gift to the National Museum of American Art, Smithsonian Institution, Washington, D.C., which, along with the Wichita Art Association, has a major collection of his work. *Striding Panther,* also modeled in 1929, is in the Whitney Museum of American Art, New York, and the collection of Wichita East High School. It was included in the Whitney's 1976 exhibition *200 Years of American Sculpture.*

2. PAFA, school catalogues, 1925–26, p. 45 (ill.), and 1926–27, p. 31 (ill.).

3. A cast of *Pelican and Fish* is in a park in Pratt, Kansas; another was installed at Brookgreen Gardens, Murrells Inlet, S.C., in 1936, with two other animal sculptures by

Moore. A cast of *Saint Francis* is in Brookgreen Gardens, and another is in the Wichita Art Museum.

References
1975 Howard Wilcox, *Bruce Moore: Notes Toward a Review of His Life and Art,* Washington: Estate Book Sales. **1984** Howard DaLee Spencer, *Bruce Moore: A Retrospective,* Wichita: Wichita Art Museum.

Fawn

1937
Bronze with brown patina; cast by 1941
13¼ x 13⅞ x 4½" (33.7 x 35.2 x 11.4 cm)
Signed and dated on back edge of plinth behind left foot:
BRUCE·MOORE [3]7
Lost-wax cast, probably in Rome
Henry D. Gilpin Fund, 1941.6

Fawn is a realistic depiction of a newborn deer feeding. It was modeled while Bruce Moore was working with James Earle Fraser in Westport. It is one of a series of fawns and young deer in poses such as suckling, sleeping, and alert. Moore probably had them cast into bronze while he was in Rome.[1] *Fawn* was purchased from the 1941 annual exhibition of the Pennsylvania Academy of the Fine Arts.

While a student at the Pennsylvania Academy in 1925, Moore had modeled a figure of a deer mortally wounded by an arrow.[2] Later, in 1948, he completed *Young Girl and Fawn (Girl with Deer),* a lifesize commission in bronze for the Wichita Art Association, which loaned the work to the Fairmount Park Art Association's *Third Sculpture International* at the Philadelphia Museum of Art the next year. Because of their elegant anatomy, deer and fawns have been popular subjects for sculptors, such as ANNA HYATT HUNTINGTON, Elie Nadelman (1882–1946), Paul Manship, and CARL PAUL JENNEWEIN.

Moore, *Fawn*

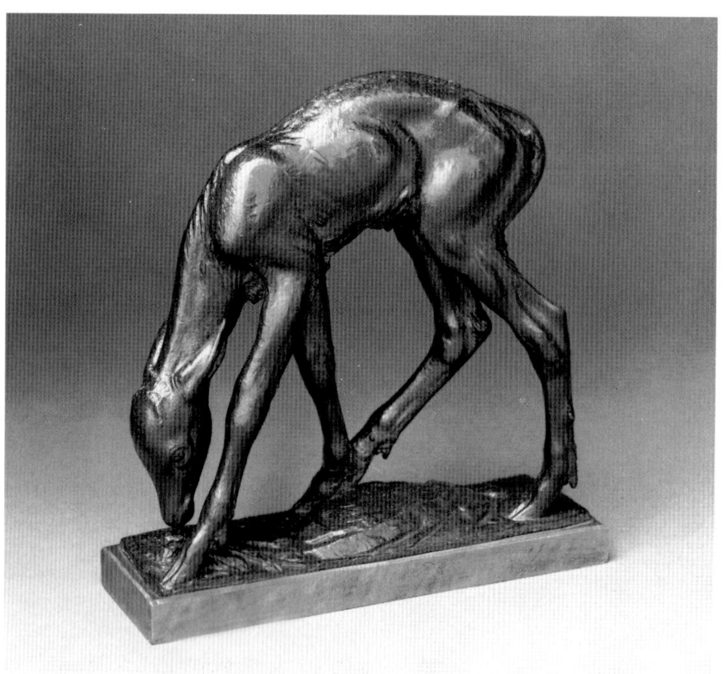

Notes
1. Hale P. Benton, American Academy in Rome, to Bruce Moore, Oct. 7, 1939, Bruce Moore Papers, Archives of American Art, Smithsonian Institution, Washington, D.C., lists three "young fawns" made of plaster in the described poses together with "One young Deer" in both plaster and bronze. The latter may be the Pennsylvania Academy's *Fawn.* The present whereabouts of the plaster is unknown, and it is not known whether other bronze casts were produced.
2. PAFA, school catalogue, 1925–26, p. 51 (ill.).

References
1942 "Sculpture and Drawings: Bruce Moore," *American Artist* 6 (June), p. 21 (ill.). **1972** Dorothy and Harold Wilcox, "Bruce Moore . . . his work," *National Sculpture Review* 21 (Summer), p. 20 (ill.). **1975** Howard Wilcox, *Bruce Moore: Notes Toward a Review of His Life and Art,* Washington: Estate Book Sales, pp. 20, 45, 66 (ill.).

Exhibited
1941* cat. no. 258 (ill.). **1949** Bonwit Teller, Philadelphia, window display for publicity for PAFA annual Fellowship exhibition. **1962** Wichita Art Association, *Bruce Moore: Animal Sculpture and Drawings,* cat. no. 22. **1979–85** Executive Mansion, Harrisburg, Pa., long-term loan. **1986–87** PAFA, *Sculpture at the Pennsylvania Academy of the Fine Arts.*

Anthony J. Lauck

b. 1908

Anthony Joseph Lauck was born and reared in Indianapolis and showed an early talent for drawing. After graduation from high school in 1926, he sold shoes, acted in amateur theatricals, played the banjo, and helped run his family's funeral home.[1] In 1932, with the encouragement of his parents, he entered the John Herron Art Institute (now the Herron School of Art of Indiana University). He studied drawing, design, oil painting, and clay modeling of the head and figure.[2] He developed a strong interest in sculpture, and in 1934 he studied at the Cranbrook Academy of Art in Bloomfield Hills, Michigan with the Swedish-born sculptor Carl Milles (1875–1955). Lauck was graduated from the Herron Art Institute in 1936.

During the final years of his art training, he felt

himself called to a spiritual life. In 1936 he entered the University of Notre Dame, Notre Dame, Indiana, to study for the priesthood. Ten years later, he was ordained into the Congregation of the Holy Cross. In 1946 and 1947, Lauck lived in Washington, D.C., and studied direct carving with the German-born sculptor Heinz Warneke (1895–1983) at the Corcoran School of Art, where he earned a certificate for advanced study in sculpture and painting. In the winter of 1948, he studied stone carving with ORONZIO MALDARELLI at Columbia University, in New York, and probably then studied sculpture with Hugo Robus (1885–1964) and painting with Julian Levi at the Art Students League of New York. In 1949 Lauck spent a year in Europe and, upon his return, studied sculpture with Ivan Meštrović (1883–1962) at Syracuse University.[3]

The Reverend Anthony J. Lauck, C.S.C., began teaching art at the University of Notre Dame in 1950. He went on to become chairman of the art department and director of the art collection, which became the Snite Museum of Art of which he is director emeritus. His sculptures were shown at the annual exhibitions of the Pennsylvania Academy of the Fine Arts in 1948–49, 1953–54, and 1966. In 1953 his limestone figure *Monk at Prayer,* 1948 (Butler Institute of American Art, Youngstown, Ohio), was awarded the Pennsylvania Academy's George D. Widener Memorial Gold Medal and was purchased by a Philadelphia collector. Many preliminary drawings, at least two small clay models, and 120 hours of carving were required to complete the composition.[4] In the 1950s, he created designs for stained-glass windows that were produced by the Conrad Schmitt Studios in Milwaukee for the Library and the Moreau Seminary at the University of Notre Dame.[5]

In 1967 Lauck began to make minimal slab sculptures, or "monoliths," of clay with incised decoration that were inspired by the ancient monument Stonehenge. They were exhibited with drawings and watercolors in a 1983 solo exhibition at the Vincent Visceglia Art Center, Caldwell College, in New Jersey. The University of Notre Dame Art Gallery held exhibitions of his work in 1968 and 1973, and a retrospective exhibition was held at the university's Snite Museum of Art upon his retirement from Notre Dame in 1980.

Notes

1. Larry Conner, "Wood, Clay, Stone," *Indianapolis Star Magazine,* April 19, 1953, p. 26, clipping file, PAFA Library.
2. Artist's response to questionnaire, March 15, 1985, PAFA object file.
3. Artist's response to questionnaire, April 19, 1953, PAFA object file, and Norman Kent, "Anthony Lauck, Priest and Artist," *American Artist* 25 (June 1961), pp. 27–28.
4. Conner 1953, p. 25.
5. Kent 1961, pp. 24–25, 95–98.

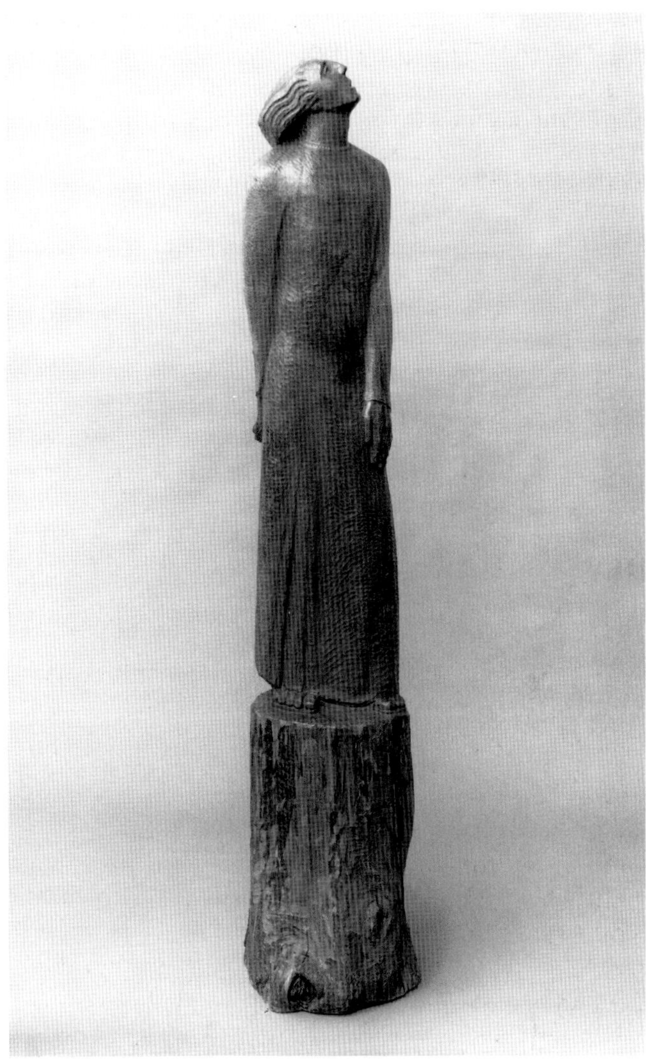

Lauck, *Saint John beside the Cross*

Saint John beside the Cross

1947
Black walnut
72½ x 11½ x 17" (184.2 x 29.2 x 43.2 cm)
Signed on top of base between the figure's feet: *A. Lauck*
Gift of the Fairmount Park Art Association, 1952.20

ANTHONY J. LAUCK considers this to be one of his best wood carvings.[1] It depicts Saint John the Evangelist, who was present at the Last Supper, the Crucifixion, and the Transfiguration. He stood beneath the cross for hours and heard some of Christ's last words. Lauck, who wanted to depict "the loneliness at the loss of the Lord, coupled with gaunt strength in the grace and courage He left behind," shows him gazing upward in rapt attention.[2]

The sculptor made several drawings (location unknown) and several plasteline maquettes (no longer extant) for this composition in 1946 and 1947. *Saint John beside the Cross* was carved from a log of Indiana black walnut, Lauck's favorite wood, with the natural shape of the log and the roots serving as the sculpture's base. The sculptor was trying to capture the form of the figure "through the sparkling hand-tooled look which only the gouge can produce."[3] The carving was done in Washington D.C., during his studies at the Corcoran School of Art. It required about six months of working six-hour days.[4]

Saint John beside the Cross was exhibited in 1949 at the Fairmount Park Art Association's *Third Sculpture International* and was one of seven sculptures purchased by the association. After being exhibited at the Philadelphia Museum of Art, where it had been temporarily housed, it was given to the Pennsylvania Academy in 1952. The next year, Father Lauck won the George D. Widener Memorial Gold Medal for *Monk at Prayer.*

Notes

1. Anthony Lauck to [William B. Stevens], director of the PAFA, March 31, 1980, PAFA object file.
2. Anthony Lauck, "The Third Sculpture International," *Right Angle,* July 1949, clipping file, PAFA Library.
3. Artist's response to questionnaire, March 15, 1985, PAFA object file.
4. Larry Conner, "Wood, Clay, Stone," *Indianapolis Star Magazine,* April 19, 1953, p. 26, clipping file, PAFA Library.

References

1949 Henri Marceau, "The Philadelphia story on sculpture," *Art News* 48 (May), p. 16 (ill.). **1949** "Indianapolis Priest's Sculpture Shown in East," *Indianapolis News,* May 12 (ill.), Anthony Lauck Papers, Archives of American Art, Smithsonian Institution, Washington, D.C. **1949** Emma Rivers Milner, "Notre Dame Priest Winning Fame as Religious Sculptor, Painter; Plans to Work with Mestrovic," *Indianapolis Times,* June 14 (ill.), ibid. **1949** Anthony Lauck, "The Third Sculpture International," *Right Angle* (July), Washington, D.C., clipping file, PAFA Library. **1949** "A C.S.C. Priest-Alumnus Wins Acclaim as Sculptor," *Notre Dame Alumnus* (July-August), p. 16. **1949** "Fairmount Park Art Unit Buys 7 Sculpture Works," *New York Times,* August 3, p. 16-L (ill.). **1949** Walter E. Baum, "New Sculpture Purchased for Park Includes Modern and Traditional; Fairmount Art Association Pays $20,000 for Seven Pieces at International Show," *Philadelphia Bulletin,* August 7, p. 7-M1 (ill.). **1949** Aline B. Louchheim, "Monuments in Parks; Sculpture Selected from the Philadelphia Show," *New York Times,* August 28, p. 6-X. **1961** Norman Kent, "Anthony Lauck Priest and Artist," *American Artist* 25 (June), p. 28 (ill.). **1964** Rev. Anthony Lauck, C.S.C., "The Touch of Marble . . . The Feel of Wood," *Today's Art* (Jan.), p. 7 (ill.). **n.d.** Anthony Lauck, "Modern Art Sacred Art? Rome Speaks," *Ava Maria,* p. 8 (ill.), clipping file, PAFA Library.

Exhibited

1948 Corcoran Gallery of Art, Washington, D.C., *Sculptors of Maryland, Washington, Virginia,* cat. no. 18. **1949** Auditorium Galleries, William H. Block Company, Indianapolis, *The 25th Annual Hoosier Salon,* cat. no. 82. **1949** Fairmount Park Art Association, Philadelphia, held at the Philadelphia Museum of Art, *Third Sculpture International,* cat. no. 153. **1976** Philadelphia Civic Center, *Exhibition of Liturgical Arts,* organized by the Forty-first International Eucharistic Congress, cat. no. 317 (ill.). **1980** Snite Museum of Art, University of Notre Dame, *Anthony J. Lauck, C.S.C.: Selected Works 1947 to 1980,* p. 4 (ill.). **1986–87** PAFA, *Sculpture at the Pennsylvania Academy of the Fine Arts.* **1993** PAFA, *Carved in Wood and Stone: Twentieth-Century Sculpture.*

Ex Collection

1949–52 Fairmount Park Art Association, Philadelphia (deposited at the Philadelphia Museum of Art near east entrance).

Joseph Brown

1909–1985

Joseph Brown, perhaps the best-known sculptor of sports figures in the United States, was also an educator and an athlete. Boxing was a favorite sport, as it was for most boys from his Devil's Pocket neighborhood in the Grays Ferry section of South Philadelphia. He dreamed of acquiring "a million bucks and a million friends" by following in the footsteps of his older brother, Harry "Kid" Brown, a professional prizefighter.[1] In 1927 Joseph won a football scholarship to Temple University. He played on the football team for two years and was captain of the boxing team. In his junior year, under an assumed name, he entered the professional ring as a light heavyweight. He fought and won nine bouts, four of which were knockouts. Still, he felt that there must be a better way to make a living, so he banked his prize money and continued his studies at Temple, where he was graduated in 1931 with a bachelor of science degree in Education.

Brown started sculpting quite by accident. In 1929, while still in college, he modeled for students in WALKER HANCOCK's sculpture class at the Pennsylvania Academy of the Fine Arts. Brown thought the figures that the students were making did not resemble him. Convinced that he could do better, he shaped the figure of a boxer in clay. Hancock, exclaimed "It looks like the best sculptor in the class is the model."[2] Thus encouraged, Brown decided to try sculpting on his own. Without any formal training, he executed and cast three figures that were later accepted in the 128th annual exhibition of the Pennsylvania Academy of the Fine Arts, in 1933.

From 1931 to 1938, Brown worked as an apprentice and studio assistant to R. TAIT MCKENZIE.[3] They first met while Brown was posing at the Pennsylvania Academy. McKenzie taught him to capture the rhythm and movement of sports figures and transfer the image to plaster and bronze.

In 1937 Brown became a part-time boxing coach at Princeton University. He commuted from Philadelphia until McKenzie's death in 1938. Then Brown moved permanently to Princeton to work full-time at the university. That same year he married Gwyneth King, a painter who studied briefly at the Pennsylvania Academy. During his first two years at Princeton, no one was aware of Brown's sculpting abilities. Finally, the academic dean noticed a small bronze done by him, and Brown was appointed Resident Fellow in Sculpture in 1939 under a new creative-arts program. He became a full professor of Art in 1962 and continued teaching sculpture until his retirement in 1977, when he was named professor emeritus. Joseph Brown was a member of the Philadelphia Art Commission from 1972 until 1984. He received an honorary degree from Western Maryland College in 1978, and Temple University awarded him an honorary doctorate in fine arts in 1980. The National Association of Sports and Physical Education inducted him into its Hall of Fame in 1980.

Brown produced more than four hundred major works throughout his long career. They are in museums, other institutions, and private collections worldwide. He had numerous one-man shows and exhibited in most of the major cities in the United States. His work appeared many times at the Pennsylvania Academy from 1933 to 1968. Brown created portrait busts of many well-known figures, such as Robert Frost, John Steinbeck, William Carlos Williams, Jimmy Durante, and Pope John Paul II. By far his most popular pieces, however, were naturalistic sculptures of athletes engaged in a wide variety of sports. *Gymnasts,* 1969, in front of McGonigal Hall, Temple University, is Brown's work, as is the massive bronze *Benjamin Franklin Craftsman,* commissioned by the Masonic Order of Pennsylvania in 1980 and erected on North Broad Street, opposite City Hall and the Masonic Temple. The major commission of his career was the design and execution of four heroic bronze statues of athletes installed in 1975 and 1976 at Veterans Stadium in Philadelphia. Brown saw them as "a monument to himself in his old hometown."[4] The same can be said about all of his sculptures in Philadelphia.

Notes

1. Joe Marshall, "Heroes with Feet of Clay," *Sports Illustrated,* Nov. 5, 1973, p. 44.
2. Tom Fox, "An old sculptor—then and now," *Philadelphia Inquirer,* Sept. 12, 1978, p. 1-B.
3. Telephone interview with Andrew J. Kozar, Ph.D. and Theresa Z. Esperdy, May 19, 1988, notes in PAFA research file. Kozar said that Brown told him that he had worked with McKenzie from 1931 to 1938.
4. Jan Schaffer, "Sculptor's Superstars Are Measured in Tons," *Philadelphia Inquirer,* Oct. 8, 1974, p. 3-C.

Counter-Punch No. 1

1935
Bronze with ochre and brown patina; lost-wax cast by 1936
8⅞ x 8¾ x 7⅛" (22.5 x 22.2 x 18.1 cm)
Signed and dated on top of base: Joe Brown/1935
Gift of J. Welles Henderson, 1971.21

"A STORY is best told," Joseph Brown wrote, "when it incites the viewer to imagine things that are actually not told in the story."[1] His sculpture invites the viewer to do this. In *Counter-Punch No. 1,* Brown depicts the boxing champion Mickey Walker "turning aside a left jab and beginning to counter with a left hook to the body."[2] The observer is left to draw

Brown, *Counter-Punch No. 1*

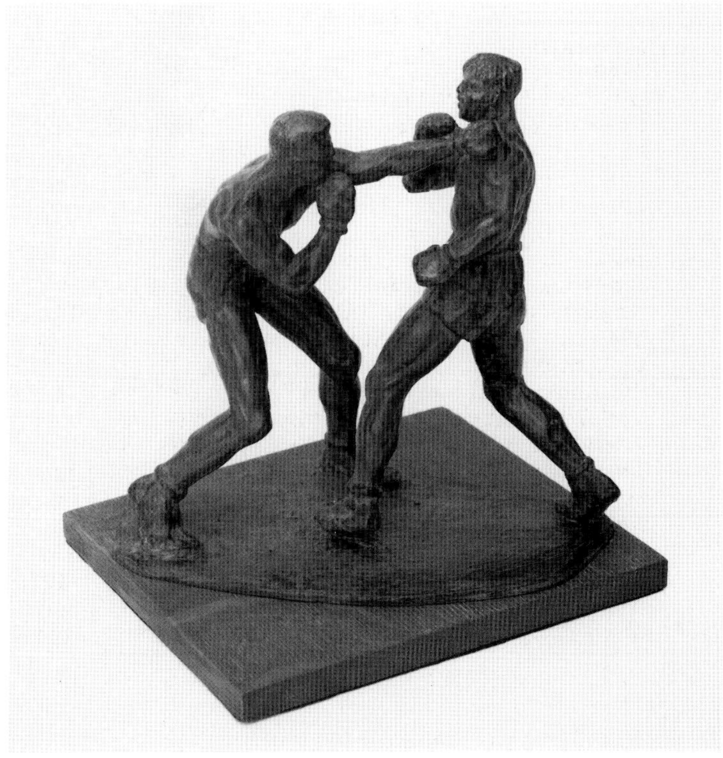

his own conclusion, however, as to the success of the counterpunch. According to Brown, "that's what gives the feeling of action—when you can't really tell."[3] A subtle distortion of proportions, evident in the arms and legs of both boxers, heightens the sculpture's sense of motion. The irregular surface of the piece and the various colors used in the patina further enhance the impression of spontaneity. Brown was an expert in modeling the human figure in action. The realistic handling of the swelling under Mickey Walker's left eye gives evidence of the considerable knowledge that Brown picked up from personal experience in the ring.

J. Welles Henderson, a member of the board of trustees of the Pennsylvania Academy of the Fine Arts from 1959 to 1968 and a member of the collections and exhibitions committee in the 1980s, purchased this bronze directly from the artist in 1968 and presented it to the Academy in 1971. Although approximately eight other casts have been made, their locations are unknown. The first cast is assumed to be the one in the Museum of American Art of the Pennsylvania Academy of the Fine Arts.[4] *Counter-Punch No. 1* is part of a series: *Counter-Punch No. 2* was modeled in 1936; *Counter-Punch No. 3,* in 1948.

Notes

1. Joe Brown, *"The Stadium Sculptures,"* pamphlet, about 1976.
2. Joe Brown, paper label affixed to bronze, Sept. 7, 1968, PAFA object file.
3. Quoted in Loni Stinnett, "Coffee Break with Professor Joe Brown," *Philadelphia Sunday Bulletin Magazine,* Oct. 21, 1962, p. 13.
4. J. Welles Henderson to R. Stubbs, business manager of the PAFA, Dec. 29, 1971, PAFA object file, refers to "the original piece."

References

1939 Joseph Brown, "The Manly Art of Sculpture," *Princeton Alumni Weekly* 40 (Nov. 17), pp. 189–91 (ill.). **1969** Joe Brown, Red Smith, Norman Thomas, *Joe Brown: Retrospective Catalogue 1932–1966,* privately printed, cat. no. 18 (ill.).

Exhibited

1936 Olympic Exhibition, Berlin. **1967** *Expo '67,* Montreal. **1968** Ibero American University, Mexico City, *Exhibition of the History and Art of the Olympic Games.* **1973** Mobile Art Gallery, Ala., *Where the Action Is (Sports in Art).* **1994** Union League of Philadelphia, *The Art of Sport.*

Ex Collections

The artist, 1935–68; J. Welles Henderson, 1968–71.

Brown, *Boxers*

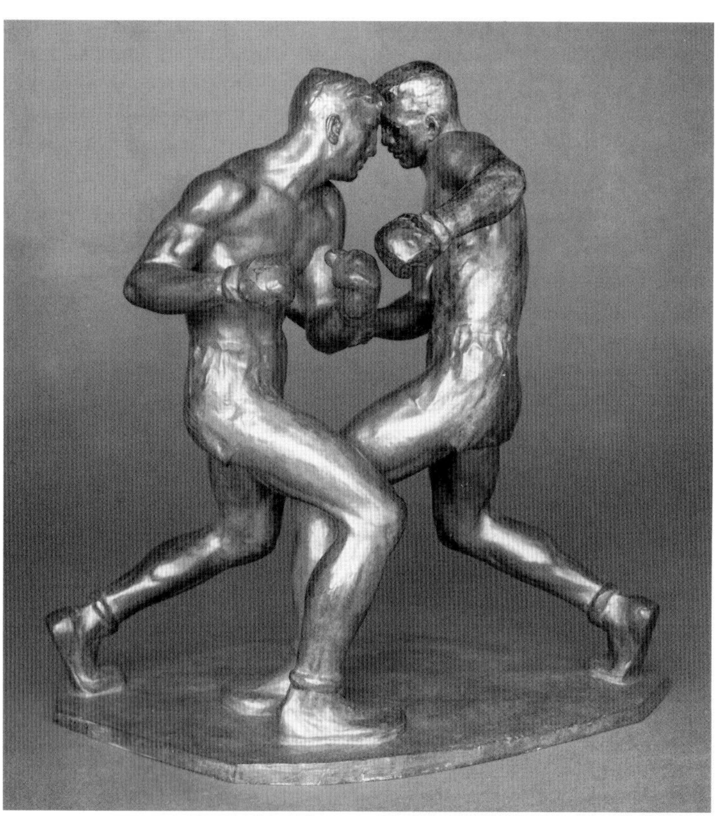

Boxers

1943
Bronze with green and brown patina; lost-wax cast by 1944
23 x 23¼ x 14¾" (58.4 x 59 x 37.3 cm)
Signed and dated on top of base: Joe Brown 1943
Purchased with funds from J. Brooks B. Parker, 1950.18

"FIGURATIVE SCULPTURE may be immobile, but that does not mean . . . that it therefore lacks movement."[1] *Boxers* is an excellent example of Joseph Brown's emphasis on motion. As in *Counter-Punch No. 1* (q.v.), the action is unresolved. It depicts an old trick used in the ring: the opponent's left arm is pushed in order to throw him off balance and into position for a left hook. This subject may have been suggested by watching Sugar Ray Robinson.

The two figures are realistically represented, the muscles modeled with the anatomical understanding of someone as familiar with boxing as Brown was. The piece was chased by the artist, and both figures are highly polished to a smooth surface. The boxers have been patinated with subtle differences, and the rich, variegated patination accentuates the muscles that are straining and taut.

In 1950 J. Brooks B. Parker donated the funds to purchase *Boxers.* Joe Brown was pleased to have this piece represent him in the Academy's collection because WALKER HANCOCK was directly responsible for his first "attempt at sculpture and the subject was a boxer."[2] Also, this was the first piece Brown did after losing the sight in his right eye and he was worried that his "sense of form and distance would have been so impaired" that he might have to give up sculpting.[3]

Boxers won the Helen Foster Barnett prize for sculpture at the National Academy of Design in 1944. This "original bronze" is assumed to be the one in the collection of the Museum of American Art of the Pennsylvania Academy of the Fine Arts.[4] About five other casts have been made but their locations are unknown. *Detail from Boxers*, 1943, whose face is more refined than most of Brown's pugilists, may have been a study for *Boxers*.

Notes

1. Joe Brown, "Movement and Figurative Sculpture," reprinted from *Quest*, Jan. 1975 in brochure, privately printed.
2. Joe Brown to Joseph T. Fraser, Jr., director of the PAFA, Oct. 16, 1950, PAFA object file.
3. Ibid.
4. Doris E. Brown, "Both Boxing and Sculpturing Taught by Princeton Professor," *New Brunswick [N.J.] Sunday Times*, April 26, 1953, clipping file, PAFA Library. The word "original" most likely means the first cast, which the Museum's bronze is assumed to be.

References

1952 "Two-Fisted Sculptor," *Pittsburgh Press*, April 27, (ill.). **1957** Bill Dougherty, "Professor of Sock-and Sculpture," *Newark, [N.J.] News*, Feb. 10, p. 21 (ill.). **1964** "He Sculpts What He Preaches," *Weirton, [W. Va.] Times*, June 26 (ill.). **1966** *Joe Brown: Retrospective Catalogue 1932–1966*, privately printed, cat. no. 13 (ill.). **1969** "Traveling Exhibit of National Sculpture Society," *National Sculpture Review* 18 (Summer), p. 20 (ill.). **1981–82** "Champions of American Sport, A Traveling Exhibition," *National Sculpture Review* 30 (Winter), p. 9 (ill.).

Exhibited

1944 National Academy of Design, New York, 118th annual exhibition, cat. no. 42A (ill.). **1945*** cat. no. 209. **1956** PAFA, *Living Philadelphia Artists Represented in the Permanent Collection of the Academy*, cat. no. 57. **1967** *Expo '67*, Montreal. **1968** Ibero Americana University, Mexico City, *Exhibition of the History and Art of the Olympic Games*. **1970** Fidelity Bank, Broad and Walnut Streets, Philadelphia, One-man traveling show: Fidelity Banks, Broad and Walnut Sts., and Rosemont, Pa.; Villanova University; Temple University. **1972–73** Provident National Bank, Philadelphia, *Exhibition of Sculpture by the Artist Joseph Brown*, cat. no. 29. **1974** PAFA, Peale House, *Selected Works from the Academy's 20th Century Collection of Paintings and Sculpture*. **1975** William Penn Memorial Museum, Harrisburg, Pa., exhibition of works of art from the PAFA. **1986–87** PAFA, *Sculpture at the Pennsylvania Academy of the Fine Arts*.

Ex Collection

The artist, 1943–50.

Cleo Hartwig

1911–1988

Born and reared in rural Webberville, Michigan, Cleo Hartwig developed a lifelong interest in birds and animals, that became subjects for her sculpture. At age thirteen she gained local notoriety for her snow and ice sculpture of a large dog.[1] During the summers of 1930 and 1931 Hartwig studied drawing at the Art Institute of Chicago. She received a bachelor's degree in art education in 1932 from Western Michigan University in Kalamazoo; she was later awarded two of their honorary degrees. After graduating she studied several summers at the International School of Art in the United States, including one spent in Europe.

In 1937 Hartwig went to New York to study stone carving with José de Creeft at the New School for Social Research. The next year she studied with him at his studio.[2] Hartwig particularly admired "the simplicity of forms and contours in his carvings."[3] She learned to carve directly in wood or stone from memory, without the use of maquettes, drawings, or live models. The subject emerged by the deliberate reduction of the material with bush hammers, chisels and rasps. While teaching at the Lenox School in New York in the late 1930s and early 1940s, Hartwig took evening classes in carving, modeling, and plaster casting at the Clay Club[4] (the Sculpture Center since 1951), which became the site of her first solo show in 1943. During the war she did technical illustrating for Bell Labs and Jordanoff Aviation Corporation. She received a commission in 1945 to ornament the facade of the Continental Casualties Building in New York and executed an eight-foot family group in aluminum. That year she began teaching sculpture and plastic design in the evenings at Cooper Union School of Art, in New York, and teaching modeling to children on the weekends at Montclair Art Museum in New Jersey. She taught various subjects at the latter institution until her retirement in 1971, when an exhibition of her sculpture was held. Her work regularly appeared in the Pennsylvania Academy annual exhibitions from 1945–62. A show of Hartwig's carvings, mostly of animals, traveled throughout Canada in 1949, in 1986 a solo exhibition was held at SUNY Plattsburgh, N.Y., and in 1987 one was held at Harmon-Meek Gallery in Naples, Florida.

In 1951 Cleo Hartwig married the Russian-born sculptor Vincent Glinsky (1895–1975), who won the Pennsylvania Academy's George D. Widener Memorial Gold Medal at the 131st annual exhibition, in

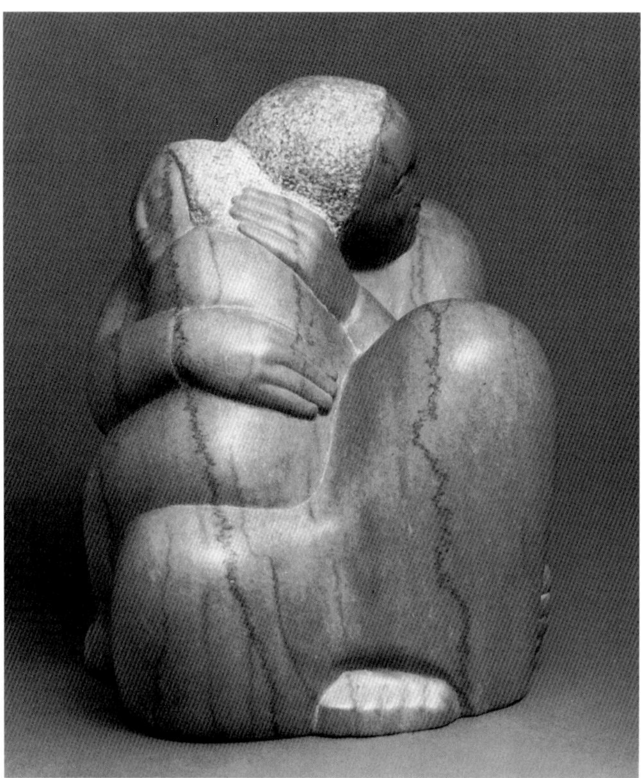

Hartwig, *Mother and Child*

1936, for a marble female figure *Awakening* (location unknown).[5] In 1972 a joint exhibition was held at the Sculpture Center in New York. The exhibition *Revealed Forms,* held in 1995 at the Erie Art Museum in Erie, Pennsylvania, included carvings by two sculptor-couples: Hartwig/Glinsky, and de Creeft/Lorrie Goulet.

Hartwig's work is represented in public and private collections, including Newark Museum, Detroit Institute of Arts, National Academy of Design, and Montclair Art Museum. *Homeward Spirit,* a five foot bronze figure of a woman holding a bird, of 1962, is in All Faiths' Memorial Tower in Paramus, New Jersey.

Notes

1. Enid Bell, "The Compatibles: Sculptors Hartwig & Glinsky," *American Artist* 32 (June 1968), p. 45.
2. Curriculum Vitae, Cleo Hartwig Papers, Archives of American Art, Smithsonian Institution, Washington, D.C.
3. Artist's response to questionnaire, April 10, 1985, PAFA object file.
4. For information on the Clay Club, see Catherine Sullivan, "Community of Sculptors: A Visit to the Clay Club Sculpture Center," *American Artist* 14 (April 1950), pp. 48–50, 71–73. Members Hartwig and de Creeft both have works illustrated.
5. A larger version of *Awakening,* that won the Pennsylvania Academy's Dr. Herbert M. Howe Memorial Prize at the 143rd annual exhibition in 1948, is in Brookgreen Gardens, Murrells Inlet, S.C.

References

1988 Constance L. Hays, "Cleo Hartwig, 80, Dies of Cancer; Her Sculpture Featured Animals," *New York Times,* June 20, p. 11-D. **1988** Albert Glinsky, Phyllis Mark, and Renata M. Schwebel, compilers, "A Tribute to Cleo Hartwig," *The Guild Reporter,* published by the Sculptors Guild, Inc., New York, 3 (Oct.), pp. 5–7.

Mother and Child

1940
Marble
13⅛ x 11½ x 12⅛" (33.4 x 29.2 x 30.9 cm)
Signed on back: C. HARTWIG
Henry D. Gilpin Fund, 1947.3

Mother and Child was carved from a fragment of a building block of what Cleo Hartwig called Tennessee marble.[1] It was made soon after she studied with José de Creeft. The simplicity of the forms of the intertwined figures is reminiscent of his work and of Eskimo sculpture. The sculpture is smooth and polished except for the texture of the hair which was created with a bush hammer.[2] The graining of the marble that runs through both figures, adds further color and visual interest. After Hartwig carved the block into an abstract composition, the subject of a mother and child suggested itself. Between 1937 and about 1945 she carved about five other groups of mothers and children.[3] One of them, *Young Mother* (whereabouts unknown), a nineteen-inch-high group in Vermont marble of a kneeling mother hugging her child, was shown at the Pennsylvania Academy's 140th annual exhibition in 1945. Hartwig also explored this theme in nature, with such animals as horses and pelicans as subjects.

The mother's left foot in *Mother and Child* was damaged during the installation of the Pennsylvania Academy's 142nd annual exhibition in 1947. After the show closed, Cleo Hartwig came to the Academy's stone room in the school on March 10, 1947 and recarved the toes.[4] The sculpture was then purchased for the museum's collection. It is mounted on a low wooden plinth with rounded corners.

Notes

1. Artist's response to questionnaire, [March 31, 1947], PAFA object file.
2. Ibid., April 10, 1985.
3. Curriculum Vitae, Cleo Hartwig Papers, Archives of American Art, Smithsonian Institution, Washington, D.C.
4. Hartwig to Joseph T. Fraser, Jr., director of the PAFA, March 17, 1947, PAFA object file.

Reference
1953 Cleo Hartwig, *The Work of the Sculptor Cleo Hartwig; A Collection of Photographs,* scrapbook, p. 27 (ill.), Central Research Library, New York Public Library.

Exhibited
1940 Clay Club Gallery, New York, *Sculpture in Stone,* checklist no. 20. **1942** National Academy of Design, New York, 116th annual exhibition, cat. no. 247. **1942** Art Institute of Chicago, *53rd Annual Exhibition of American Paintings and Sculpture,* cat. no. 250. **1943** Clay Club Gallery, New York, *Cleo Hartwig,* checklist no. 29. **1946** Nebraska Art Association, 56th annual exhibition, held at University of Nebraska, Lincoln, checklist no. 140. **1947*** cat. no. 224. **1986–87** PAFA, *Sculpture at the Pennsylvania Academy of the Fine Arts.*

Walter Rotan

b. 1912

Born in Baltimore, Walter W. Rotan was reared in rural Maryland and developed a lifelong interest in horses. At the age of ten, he began attending a modeling class for adults on Saturdays at the Maryland School of Fine and Practical Arts in Baltimore (now Maryland Institute, College of Art). He studied there in the evenings while in high school and graduated from the art school in 1929. Rotan made studies from the school's bronzes of animals in dramatic poses by the renowned French sculptor Antoine Louis Barye (1796–1875).[1] The sculptures are part of the George A. Lucas collection (now housed at the Baltimore Museum of Art).

Wishing to further improve his skill at modeling animals he came to the Pennsylvania Academy in the fall of 1930 to study with ALBERT LAESSLE at the Chester Springs country school. At that time the school was in operation year-round, and during the summer animals were used exclusively as models for sculpture students. Rotan exhibited a sculpture of a deer at the 15th student exhibition at Chester Springs in 1931 and in 1932 modeled a goat and a horse. In Laessle's class he also modeled portrait heads and compositions on particular themes. In 1933 he was awarded a William Emlen Cresson Traveling Scholarship enabling him to tour England, France, Italy and Germany, after which he traveled on his own in Egypt for several months. He returned to Chester Springs for study in the summer of 1934 and then studied privately with Laessle and modeled animals at the Philadelphia zoo. From 1935 to 1951 Rotan exhibited regularly at the Pennsylvania Academy, winning the Fellowship Prize for *Leonard,* a portrait of a black man (private collection). The bust was also exhibited in Philadelphia in 1949 at the *Third Sculpture International* of the Fairmount Park Art Association.

In the late 1930s he moved permanently to New York and began commuting to Taft School in Watertown, Connecticut, where he taught and was head of the Art Department until 1953. In about 1941 he married Kathleen Burnett Sullivan (b. 1911), who studied sculpture at the Academy with WALKER HANCOCK and Albert Laessle from 1930 to 1934. Rotan worked for his wife's business modeling portraits and figures from life for mannequins used in the fashion industry and at the Costume Institute of the Metropolitan Museum of Art. Two of his portrait busts and two of his animal sculptures received prizes at the National Academy of Design's annual exhibition between 1936 and 1945. In 1936 his bronze *Gazelle,* of 1935, was installed at Brookgreen Gardens in South Carolina and five years later his lifesize limestone group *Reclining Woman with Gazelle* came into their collection. Rotan was elected a member of the National Sculpture Society in 1939 and became a Fellow in 1959. In recent years he has modeled numerous horses from memory, drawing upon his childhood experiences in Maryland. The horses have been cast in plaster and are in the artist's collection.[2]

Notes
1. Conversation between Susan James-Gadzinski and Walter Rotan, March 22, 1988.
2. Ibid.

Reference
1968 Beatrice Gilman Proske, *Brookgreen Gardens Sculpture,* Murrells Inlet, S.C.: Brookgreen Gardens, pp. 490–92.

Herbert

1940
Bronze with black patina; cast in 1941
9½ x 6½ x 8" (24.2 x 16.5 x 20.3 cm)
Signed and dated on left side of neck: *W. Rotan/1940*
Lost-wax cast, probably by Modern Art Foundry, New York
Henry D. Gilpin Fund, 1941.12

IN THE early 1940s in the course of about three years, Walter Rotan modeled a series of portraits of black people. *Doris,* a portrait of a young girl in braids (private collection) and this bust of Herbert were modeled at about the same time using the children of housekeepers as sitters. For his portraits of adults Rotan hired non-professionals as models through an agency. These realistic portraits were done at about

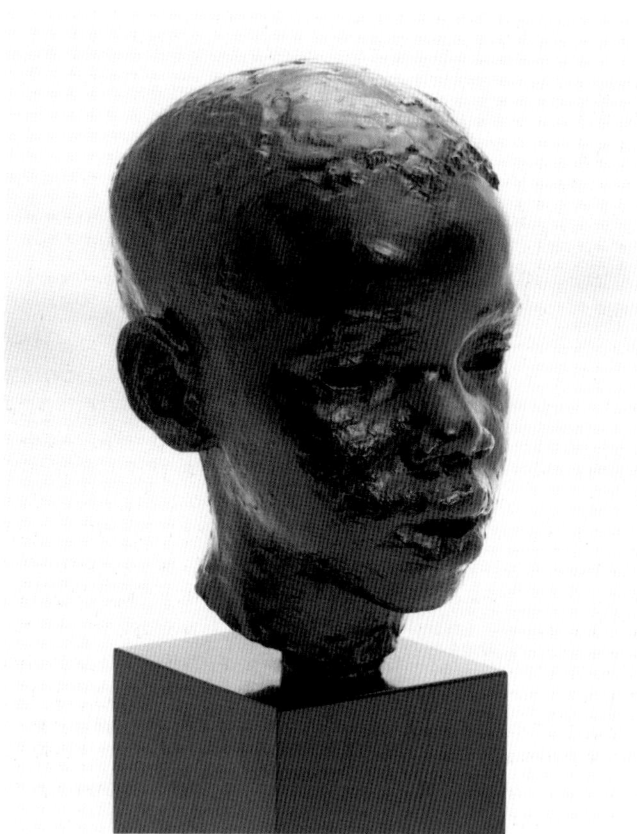

Rotan, *Herbert*

the same time that black artists were portraying subjects related to black life and history. The black sculptors Augusta Savage (1900–1962) and RICHMOND BARTHÉ produced similar portraits in bronze in the late 1930s and 1940s.

Herbert was modeled in a sketchy manner with an overall textured surface treatment. The eyes are hollow creating deep shadows. The bust was exhibited in plaster with a matte black patina (location unknown) at the Pennsylvania Academy's 136th annual exhibition in 1941. It was then purchased by the Academy for the purpose of having it cast in bronze. The artist did the overseeing of the casting in New York, probably at the Modern Art Foundry.[1] The bronze, mounted on a black marble base, was received at the Museum by April of 1941,[2] and the plaster remained for a time in the collection of the artist. Several years later Rotan had a second bronze of *Herbert* cast for himself.

Notes

1. Conversation by Walter Rotan and Susan James-Gadzinski, March 22, 1988.
2. Joseph T. Fraser, Jr., director of the PAFA, to Walter Rotan, April 25, 1941, PAFA object file.

Jane Wasey

b. 1912

Jane Wasey was born in Chicago and reared there and in Greenwich, Connecticut. At an early age she took classes at the Art Institute of Chicago. She went to Paris at age seventeen to further her education and to learn French.[1] Her first experience with clay modeling occurred while serving a three-year apprenticeship in the studio of the French academic sculptor Paul Landowski (1875–1961). She was an assistant on his large-scale *Christ of the Andes* for Rio de Janeiro and she learned to model from antique casts and from life.[2] Wasey returned to the United States in about 1931 and settled in New York. There she studied wood carving for two years with the Russian-born and German-trained sculptor Simon Moselsio (1890–1963), who is known for his carvings of animals and mothers and children.[3] In 1933 Wasey studied in New York with the direct carver John B. Flannagan (1895–1942), who taught her stone carving. She was to learn later that her maternal grandfather, Louis Gager, had been a stone mason. To support her sculpting, Wasey took on various odd jobs, such as doing design work for a glass company, packaging cosmetics, and making heads for dolls.[4]

In 1934 Jane Wasey's first exhibition was held in New York at Montross Gallery in conjunction with the mural paintings of her husband Domenico Mortellito. Included among Wasey's works was a human head carved in granite that is reminiscent of Flannagan's simplified, very minimal carving style.[5] Also shown were several groups of mothers and children. In the summer of 1939 Wasey studied stone carving in East Haddam, Connecticut, with German-born sculptor Heinz Warneke (1895–1983), who is known for his modeled and carved sculpture of animals.[6] She began exhibiting in the Pennsylvania Academy annual exhibitions the next year and her work was regularly submitted or invited until 1966. In 1948–49 Wasey taught carving, modeling, and plaster casting at Bennington College in Vermont, where her former teacher Moselsio had taught sculpture since 1933. She continued teaching privately from 1950–60, from her studio in New York. The works of this period are sleek abstract forms, either organic or geometric, of highly polished stone.

In the early 1970s she moved permanently to the coast of Maine, where she set up a studio. In 1976 Wasey began the work for which she is perhaps best known; her portrait of André the seal. He was a much-loved resident of the Boston Aquarium who used to migrate each year to Rockport, Maine. The sculptor presented Rockport with the two ton granite likeness that is installed outdoors at Marine Park Harbor. Wasey's first solo show since moving to Maine was held in 1986 at Kraushaar Galleries in New York and included works, mostly depictions of animals in stone and wood, spanning fifty years.[7] Works from the 1980s included several series of small human figures in bronze. In 1987 The William A. Farnsworth Library and Art Museum in Rockland, Maine presented a survey of her work from 1954 to 1987 in a joint exhibition with painter Howard Clifford. Jane Wasey's sculpture is in the Whitney Museum of American Art in New York, the Saint Louis Art Museum, and in various university and private collections.

Notes

1. Artist's response to questionnaire, May 23, 1988, PAFA object file.
2. Debby Smith, "Wasey Makes Her Own Animal Kingdom," *Camden [Maine] Herald,* Jan. 9, 1986, p. 8.
3. Artist's response to questionnaire, [March 4, 1948], PAFA object file; and Roberta Tarbell, "Direct Carving," *Vanguard American Sculpture, 1913–1939* (New Brunswick: Rutgers University Art Gallery, State University of New Jersey, 1979), p. 54.
4. Smith 1986, p. 8.
5. Jane Schwartz, "Jane Wasey, Domenico Mortellito, Montross Gallery," *Art News* 32 (March 3, 1934), p. 20 (ill.).
6. Heinz Warneke's granite *Cow Elephant and Calf,* 1962, is in the Philadelphia zoo. He is also known for his *Nittany Lion,* 1940, at Pennsylvania State University.
7. Kraushaar Galleries, New York, *Jane Wasey,* April 30-May 24, 1986, checklist.

Polar Bear

1947
Marble
9½ x 25¼ x 9½" (24.1 x 64.1 x 24.1 cm)
Signed (April 24, 1948) and dated on the bear's back:
J. WASEY/1947
Henry D. Gilpin Fund, 1948.18

IN THE SPRING of 1947, Jane Wasey made some sketches of zoo animals, as was often her practice. She was particularly captivated by the polar bears, at the Bronx Zoo and the New York Zoo, and decided to use them as a subject for sculpture.[1] Her wish was "to capture the ecstatic expression and pose of a bear swimming."[2] *Polar Bear* was carved that summer mostly from memory. The choice of white marble was appropriate to the subject and the overall coarse texture imitates the animal's fur. There is a subtle increase in the roughness of the stone's surface below a horizontal line symbolizing the water in which the bear is swimming. In contrast the bear's nose and nails are polished smooth and the eyes and mouth are indicated by incised lines. The swimming motion is shown by the bear's upraised left paw, a separate piece of marble that was probably joined by the sculptor in 1947 during the process of carving.

Polar Bear was shown in the Academy's 143rd annual exhibition in 1948, from which it was purchased. Critic Dorothy Grafly praised the "vitality and humor" of the show's sculpture section and mentioned in particular Wasey's "prone" bear.[3] Another

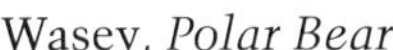
Wasey, *Polar Bear*

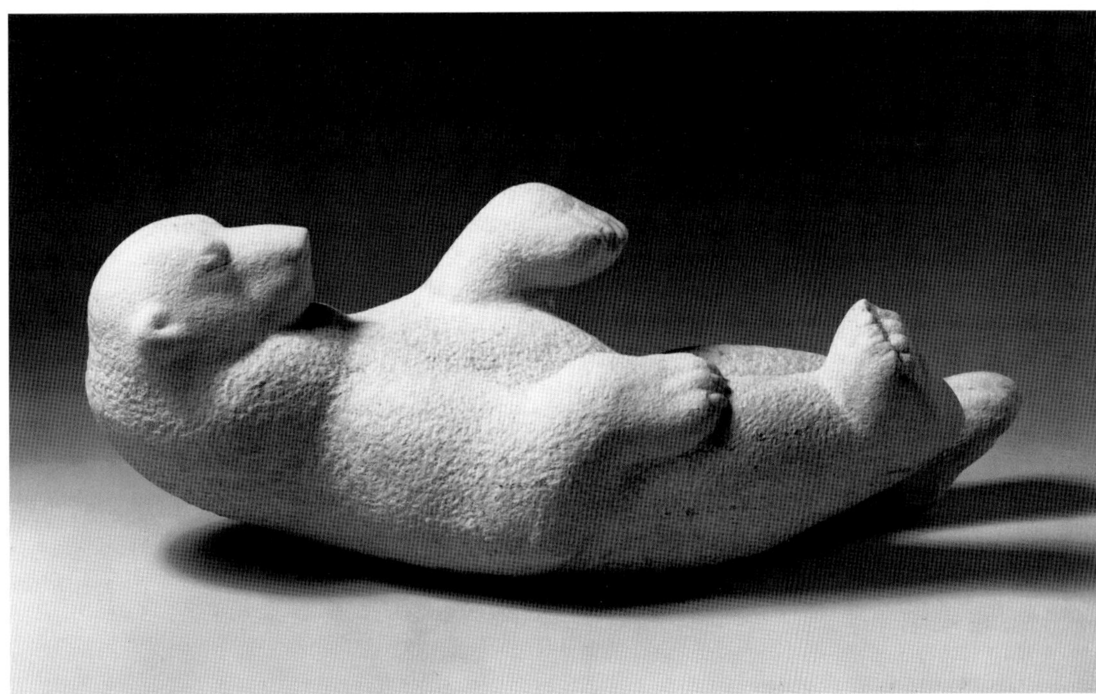

reviewer thought the "delightful" bear was "wonderfully captured."[4] In April 1948 the sculptor signed the piece at the request of director Joseph T. Fraser, Jr.[5] She usually doesn't sign her works "as I hate to change the surface."[6]

Notes

1. Wasey's sketches and sculptures of polar bears were all sold to private collectors according to her response to questionnaire, May 23, 1988, PAFA object file.
2. Artist's response to questionnaire, [March 4, 1948], ibid.
3. Dorothy Grafly, "Pennsylvania Academy's Annual Show: Trend to Creative Realism Is Discerned in Exhibition," *Boston Christian Science Monitor,* Jan. 24, 1948, p. 8.
4. Judith Kaye Reed, "Romanticism Displaces Abstractions at Pennsylvania Academy Show," *Art Digest* 22 (Feb. 1, 1948), p. 10.
5. Correspondence between Joseph T. Fraser, Jr. and Jane Wasey, March 10, April 18, 20, and 26, 1948, PAFA object file.
6. Artist's response to questionnaire, May 23, 1988, ibid.

Exhibited

1948* cat. no. 153. **1986–87** PAFA, *Sculpture at the Pennsylvania Academy of the Fine Arts.* **1989** PAFA, *"The Birds and the Beasts Will Teach Us."*

H. Richard Duhme, Jr.

b. 1914

Born and reared in Saint Louis, Herman Richard Duhme, Jr. showed an early interest in sculpture, modeling a puppy in clay at the age of nine and having it cast in plaster. While a student at John Burroughs School in Saint Louis, he took a modeling and composition course, and his relief was chosen for exhibition. During his senior year he met another Saint Louis native, WALKER HANCOCK, who was jurying a student exhibition at Burroughs. He convinced Duhme that he should study sculpture at the Pennsylvania Academy instead of studying architecture at Yale.[1]

In the fall of 1932, Duhme entered the Academy and in the course of his seven years there received recognition for his sculpture. He was awarded an honorable mention in John Harbeson's perspective class in 1933, and the next year was selected for an honorable mention in the Edmund Stewardson competition. In 1936 Duhme received an honorable mention in the Stimson competition, a Second Prize in the sculpture category in Henry R. Poore's composition class for a work on the subject *Discovery,* and a William Emlen Cresson Traveling Scholarship that enabled him to travel to England, Scotland and Italy that summer. He won collaborative scholarships as a member of the winning groups in the American Academy in Rome competitions of 1937 and 1938 held jointly with the University of Pennsylvania. Duhme was the first student to receive the newly created Ware Traveling Scholarship in 1938 that enabled him to travel the next year to Egypt, Israel, Syria, Switzerland, and spend over a month each in Greece and Italy.[2] He studied with Walker Hancock and served as his studio assistant during the summers of 1937 and 1938; in the latter year he worked on Hancock's fountains for the 1939 New York World's Fair. Duhme spent several summers at Chester Springs, including part of 1938 when he studied with CHARLES RUDY and NATHANIEL CHOATE, whose work he greatly admired and whose criticism he eagerly sought.[3]

Richard Duhme exhibited in the Academy annual exhibitions of 1938 to 1942 and in 1950. In 1941 and 1942 his work was shown in the annual exhibitions of the Fellowship, of which he had been a member since the late 1930s. His *Boy and Calf* won the Fellowship's 1941 May Audubon Post Prize. In about 1938 or 1940, Duhme was one of five current or former Academy sculpture students to form Sculptors Associated, a cooperative of Philadelphia artists willing to produce portrait busts, reliefs, garden sculpture, memorial sculpture, and portraits of pets on commission.[4] He returned to Saint Louis to teach sculpture at John Burroughs School in 1941–42, and taught there again in 1947 after four years of service in World War II. In the summer of 1946 he came back to Chester Springs to study under the G.I. Bill.

Richard Duhme began teaching at Washington University School of Fine Arts in Saint Louis in 1947, receiving a B.F.A. there in 1953, and retired in 1982 as Professor of Sculpture. He spent 1951 in Athens at the American School of Classical Studies. From the 1950s on he has taught sculpture at Chautauqua Institution Summer School in Chautauqua, New York. Duhme has produced numerous public and private commissions for Saint Louis and elsewhere, including a bronze *Lion Cub Fountain* in Mycenae, Greece.

Notes

1. H. Richard Duhme to Mrs. Joseph T. Fraser, Jr., Oct. 8, 1944, student file, PAFA Archives.
2. H.R. Duhme, Ware Scholarship Report, June 28, 1940, PAFA Archives.
3. Application for proctorship [at Chester Springs], [1940], student file, PAFA Archives.
4. *Sculptors Associated* [about 1938–40], brochure, ibid.

Reference
1982 Washington University, School of Fine Arts, Saint Louis, Mo., *Richard Duhme: Fifty Years of Sculpture*, exhib. brochure, with biographical data.

Model for Harvest Home

About 1938
Plaster, painted ochre
17 x 10½ x 19″ (43.2 x 26.7 x 48.3 cm)
Gift of the artist, 1985.61

THIS MODEL is composed of a group of figures of a man, a woman, and an ox in an agricultural scene. The muscular barefooted farm people are shown standing at the left side of the animal. They carry bundles of fruit and vegetables, and there are pumpkins, squash, and sheaves of corn arranged on a framework on the ox's back. Resting on the center of the plinth beneath the ox's stomach is a square support that is connected to and hidden by the legs of the man and woman. The plaster, cast in Philadelphia, was tinted to resemble terracotta.[1]

Harvest Home is a celebration of the harvest that is a time for feasting and thanksgiving. According to the artist the subject was chosen as the theme for a competition for ornamentation of the Agricultural Building at the Los Angeles County Fair in Pomona, California and the model was not completed in time to be submitted.[2] *Harvest Home* may have been the "sketch" Duhme was working on in July of 1938 in Gloucester, Massachusetts after he finished his job with Hancock.[3] He may have completed it later that summer while at Chester Springs where he would have had access to farm animals.

The Museum's permanent collection object card for *Harvest Home* has an early notation that the work was originally in the "School Collection (student work)." Although the sculpture was not officially given to the Museum until 1985, it was first accessioned in 1955 as a gift from the artist. It may have been part of the "material & equipment" Duhme had in storage at Chester Springs in 1946.[4] The sculpture may have remained there until the school closed in the 1950s, when the piece was turned over to the museum. A second plaster cast of this *Harvest Home* model is in the collection of the artist.

Notes

1. H. Richard Duhme to Linda Bantel, and artist's response to questionnaire, August 1, 1984, PAFA object file.
2. Ibid.
3. H.R. Duhme to Joseph T. Fraser, Jr., director of the PAFA, July 17, 1938, student file, PAFA Archives.
4. H.R. Duhme to J. Fraser, April [1946], ibid.

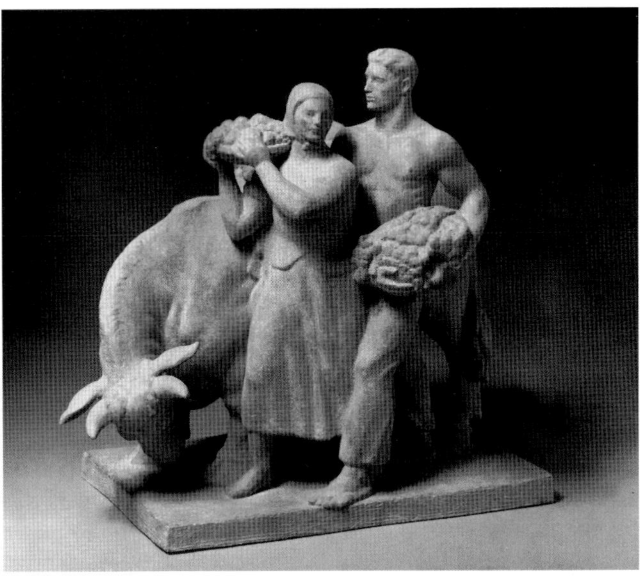

Duhme, *Model for Harvest Home*

Exhibited
1940* cat. no. 111.

Ex Collection
The artist, about 1938–85 (deposited in the Academy School about 1940–55; deposited in the Academy Museum 1955–85).

DEXTER JONES

1926–1986

Charles Dexter Weatherbee Jones III, was born in Ardmore, Pennsylvania, of Welsh descent. Because of a childhood accident, he was tutored at home in his early years. He was subsequently graduated from Radnor High School and took government courses at Saint Joseph's College in Philadelphia. During World War II, he worked in a metallurgy lab, and as an apprentice jeweler.

In 1947 he took sculpture classes at Chester Springs, the summer school of the Pennsylvania Academy of the Fine Arts. He studied sculpture in the regular classes of HARRY ROSIN and WALKER HANCOCK the following year. In 1948–49 he worked in New York as an assistant to JO DAVIDSON, Gwen Lux (b. 1908), and in the Ettl Studios, a foundry. Jones may also have worked as an assistant to Paul Manship (1885–1966) in New York the next year. He returned to the Pennsylvania Academy in 1951–53 to study with Hancock and CHARLES RUDY, with a full scholarship under the G.I. Bill, and in return was required to pose for the Portrait class. He won the school's Perspective Prize in 1952. Jones showed a portrait bust in each of the Pennsylvania Academy's 1950–52 annual exhibitions, and in several regional and fellowship exhibitions. He studied at the Accademia de Belle Arti in Florence in 1955–56, and visited European museums.

Like his teacher Jo Davidson, Dexter Jones specialized in making portraits, although he produced them in relief as well as in the round. Jones was commissioned to produce busts of such figures as Virginia Woolf, Eugene O'Neill, college presidents, doctors, and an army general. He also modeled portraits of friends such as the painter Jack Bookbinder (1981 relief, National Academy of Design) and trumpeter Dizzy Gillespie with whom he played music in his studio. His portrait busts and reliefs received awards from the National Sculpture Society in New York in 1959, 1961, 1973, and 1983.

Some of Jones's public commissions in Philadelphia include: the eleven-foot-high gilded bronze Great Seal of Philadelphia placed above the main entrance of the City's new Municipal Services Building in 1966, a dinosaur installed in 1971 in front of reptile house at the Philadelphia zoo, and photographic panels of his clown reliefs ornamenting the interiors of public transit vehicles of the Market-Frankford elevated since about 1980. His work is in the collections of the Woodmere Art Museum and the National Academy of Design. He was elected a Fellow of the National Sculpture Society in 1961, an Associate of the National Academy of Design in 1967, and an Academician in 1976.

References

1980 Wayne Robinson, "Dinosaurs, Clowns Get Dexterous Jones' Touch," *Philadelphia Bulletin* magazine, March 9, pp. 8–9. **1986** "Dexter Jones, sculptor; work won many prizes," *Philadelphia Inquirer,* June 30, p. 9-C.

Jo Davidson

1948
Brass
13⅝ x 10½ x 10¼" (34.5 x 26.6 x 26 cm)
Henry D. Gilpin Fund, 1952.13

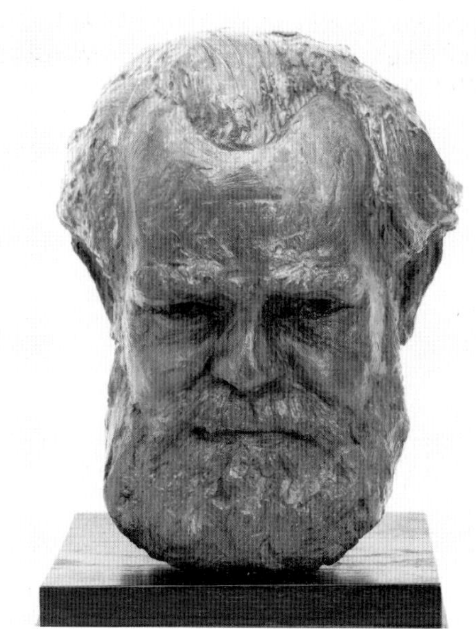

Jones, *Jo Davidson*

DEXTER JONES was working as an assistant in Jo Davidson's Fifty-eighth Street studio at the time this head was modeled.[1] He captured the imposing physical presence of his mentor, who was described as being "like a big friendly puppy . . . a black Newfoundland—with his bushy black hair, his bushy black beard, dancing brown eyes, and his sturdy, quick body, so altogether concerned with a rightful joy in life."[2] It is roughly finished and contains much of the same spirit as the self-portrait Davidson modeled in 1946 (bronze, National Portrait Gallery). Jones's bust was probably modeled in clay and cast in brass, using layers of varnish to tone the surface in gradations from bright brass to a deep matte brown.

This bust is installed on an oak base that is painted black, perhaps in memoriam since the bust was exhibited at the Pennsylvania Academy of the Fine Arts and purchased in the year of Davidson's death. Between 1910 and 1950, Davidson captured the likenesses of hundreds of the most influential people in the twentieth-century, and he was probably a strong factor in Jones's decision to pursue a similar path. It was a special honor to Jones that this bust was purchased while he was still a student at the Pennsylvania Academy.

It is not known how large an edition was produced, but in 1966 a bronze was for sale at a fundraiser for Florence artists sponsored by the Philadelphia chapter of the Artists Equity Association.

Notes

1. For a biography of Jo Davidson, see earlier catalogue entry.
2. Unidentified critic quoted in *Jo Davidson Portrait Sculpture,* exhib. cat., Washington, D.C.: National Portrait Gallery, Smithsonian Institution, 1978, unpaginated entry on Jo Davidson self-portrait.

Reference
1963 Albert d'Andrea, "On Portraiture . . . Something Old and Something New," *National Sculpture Review* (Spring), pp. 10–11 (ill.).

Exhibited
1950* cat. no. 160. **1951** National Academy of Design, New York, 126th annual exhibition, cat. no. 7. **1952** PAFA, fellowship annual exhibition. **1958–59** Philadelphia Art Alliance. **1962** Corning Glass Works, New York, National Sculpture Society exhibition. **1965** Philadelphia Art Alliance, exhibition of five sculptors. **1984–85** PAFA, *A Growing American Treasure: Recent Acquisitions and Highlights from the Permanent Collection.*

CHECKLIST OF SCULPTURE DATED 1951 TO 1995

Charles Bregler, 1865–1958

1. *Life Cast of Mary Bregler's Right Hand*
1951
See pages 149–50.

2. *Walt Whitman*
1953
See page 150.

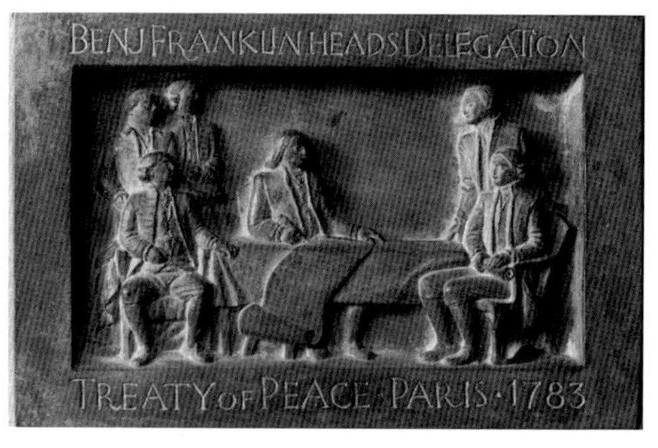

3

Paul Manship, 1885–1966

3. *Model for "Benjamin Franklin Heads Delegation, Treaty of Peace, Paris"*
About 1953
Bronze with green patina
6¾ x 10¼ x 1" (17.1 x 26 x 2.5 cm)
Inscribed at top: BENJ FRANKLIN HEADS DELEGATION; at bottom: TREATY OF PEACE PARIS 1783
Gift of Roy F. Nichols, 1968.17

Victor Riu, 1887–1974

4. *Resurgent Harmony*
1957
Granite
23 x 16⅛ x 13½" (58.4 x 41 x 34.3 cm)
Signed and dated underneath: VRiu/57
Henry D. Gilpin Fund, 1958.16

Doris Caesar, 1893–1971

5. *Standing Girl*
1951
Bronze with carbon-coated brown patina; lost-wax cast in 1951–52
72½ x 14¼ x 13¼" (184.2 x 36.2 x 33.7 cm)
Signed on top of base: Caesar
Foundry mark on back of base: MODERN ART FDRY NY
Gift of Mr. and Mrs. Mahlon Pitney, 1953.9

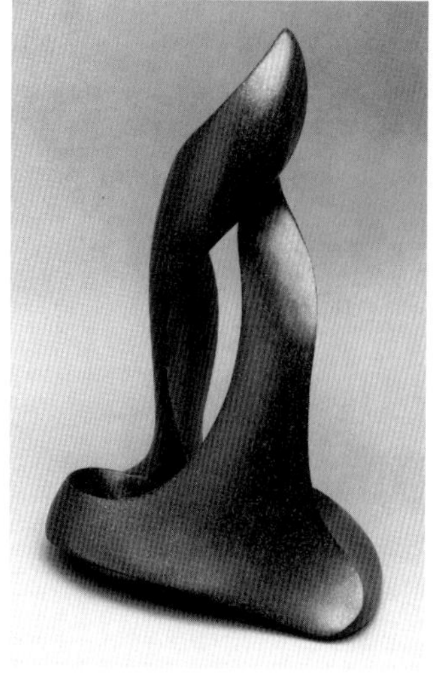
4

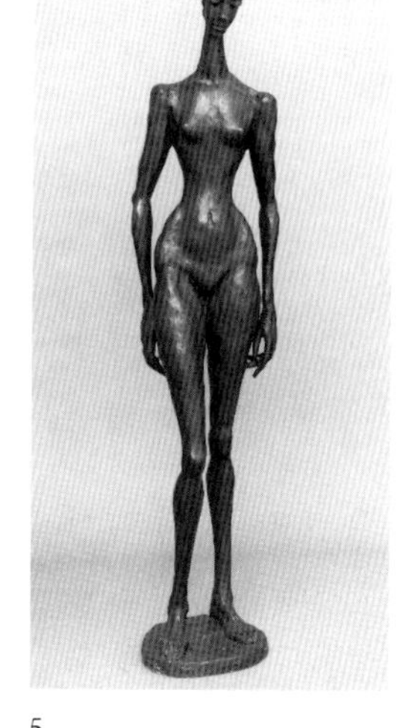
5

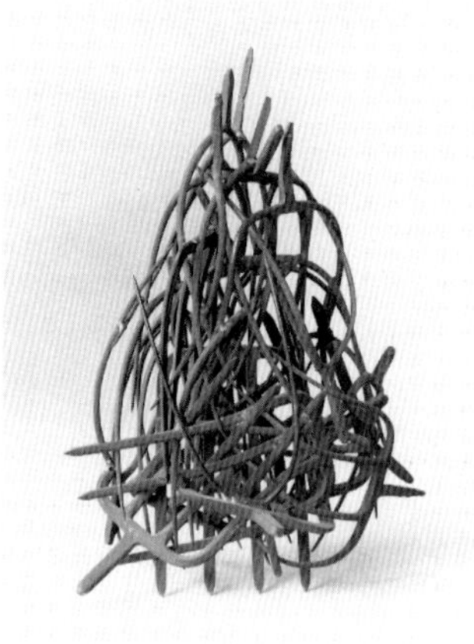
6

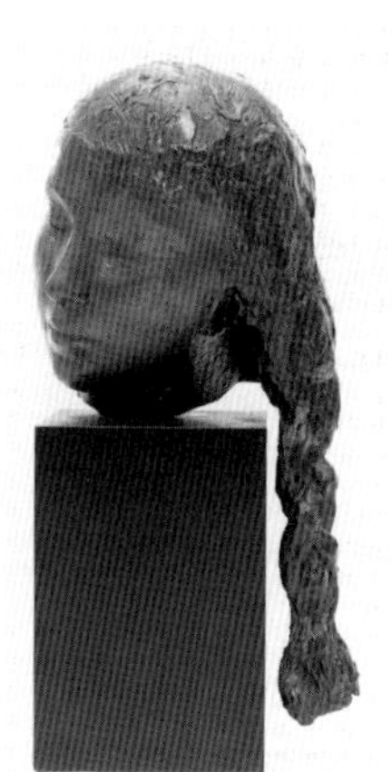
7

Lloyd R. Ney, 1893–1965

6. *Pitchforks*
1958
Welded steel
23½ x 16¼ x 16¾" (59.7 x 41.3 x 42.6 cm)
Gift of Bernard Davis, 1959.11

Dorothea Greenbaum, 1893–1986

7. *Braided Hair*
1962
Bronze with brown patina; lost-wax cast in 1963
17 x 8⅝ x 8" (43.2 x 21.9 x 20.3 cm)
Signed and dated on right side of neck: 62/Greenbaum
Foundry mark on left side of neck: MODERN ART/ [FOUNDRY]
Gift of the Ford Foundation, 1964.1.2

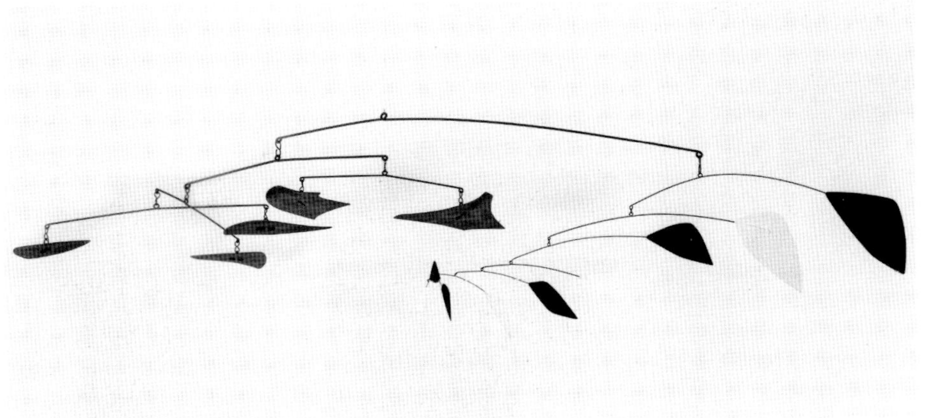
9

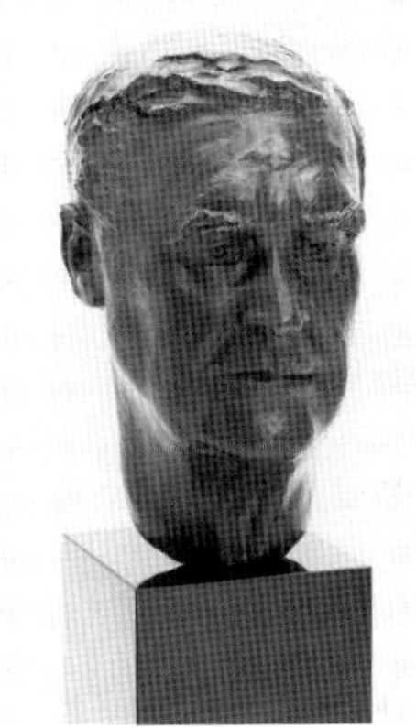
11

Harry Rosin, 1897–1973

8. *Eleanor S. Gray*
1967
See pages 263–64.

Alexander Calder, 1898–1976

9. *Route Barrée*
1962
Steel wire and sheet metal, painted red, white, and black
28 x 130 x 51″ (71.1 x 330.2 x 129.5 cm)
Signed and dated on reverse of largest blade: CA/62
Henry D. Gilpin Fund, 1962.16

Hélène Sardeau, 1899–1969

10. *Figure*
1952
See pages 269–70.

Margaret Wasserman Levy, b. 1899

11. *Henry S. Drinker,* 1880–1965
1954
Bronze with green patina
14 x 8⅛ x 9⅝″ (35.6 x 20.6 x 24.5 cm)
Lost-wax cast by Modern Art Foundry, New York
Gift of the artist, 1955.6

Louise Nevelson, 1899–1988

12. *Cascades Perpendiculars I*
1980–82
Wood, painted black
108½ x 34½ x 28″ (275.6 x 87.6 x 71.1 cm)
Gift of the friends of Bernice McIlhenny Wintersteen in honor of her 80th birthday, and the Ware Trust Fund, 1983.4

Walker Hancock, b. 1901

13. *Resting Swimmer*
1953
See pages 284–85.

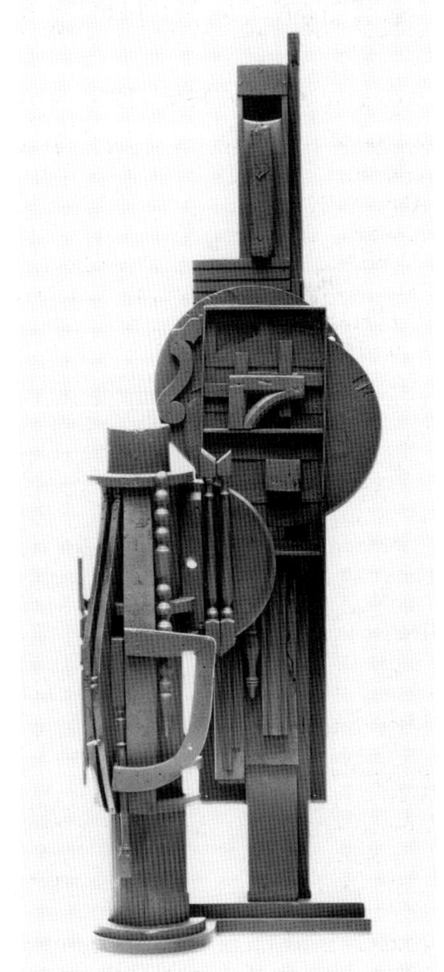
12

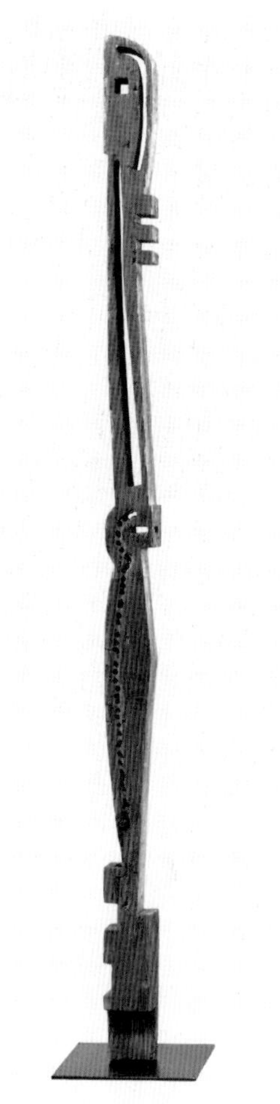

14

Arlie Sinaiko, 1902–1984

14. *Cadence*
1958
Driftwood
78 x 3⅞ x 3⅞" (198 x 9.8 x 9.8 cm)
Henry D. Gilpin Fund, 1960.12

Isamu Noguchi, 1904–1988

15. *Girl Torso*
1958
Marble
23 x 10 x 3" (58.5 x 25.4 x 7.5 cm)
Signed on bottom of figure: Noguchi
Henry D. Gilpin Fund, 1960.9

Bernard Frazier, 1906–1976

16. *Wounded Falcon*
1956
Ceramic
29 x 26 x 19¼" (73.7 x 66 x 48.9 cm)
Henry D. Gilpin Fund, 1958.11

David Smith, 1906–1965

17. *V.B. XXII*
1963
Welded steel
99⅝ x 14¼ x 13" (253 x 36.2 x 33 cm)
Signed and dated on back of base: David Smith 2–10–63
Inscribed on front of base: V-B XXII
Gift of Mr. and Mrs. David N. Pincus, 1980.28

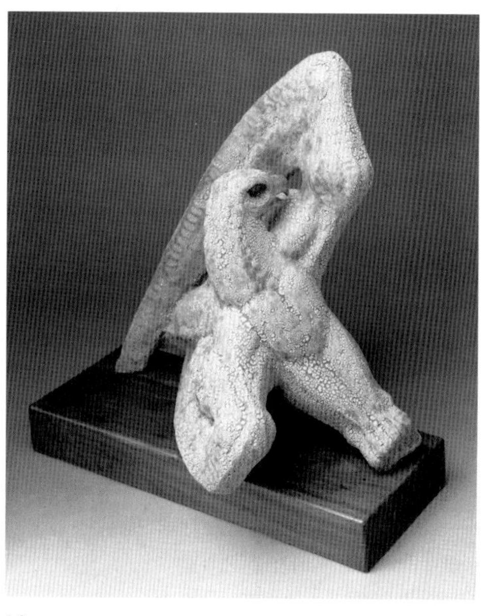

16

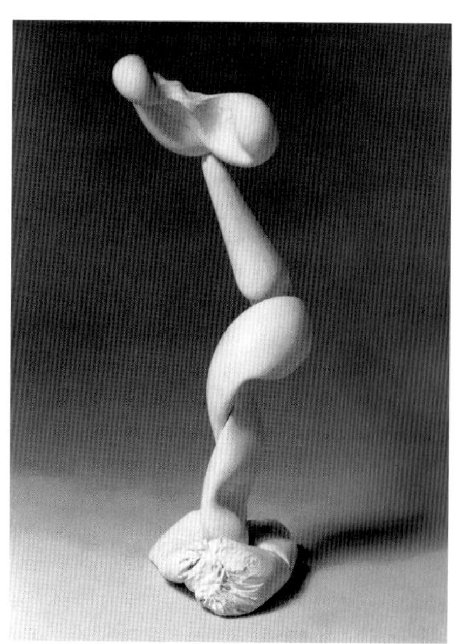

19

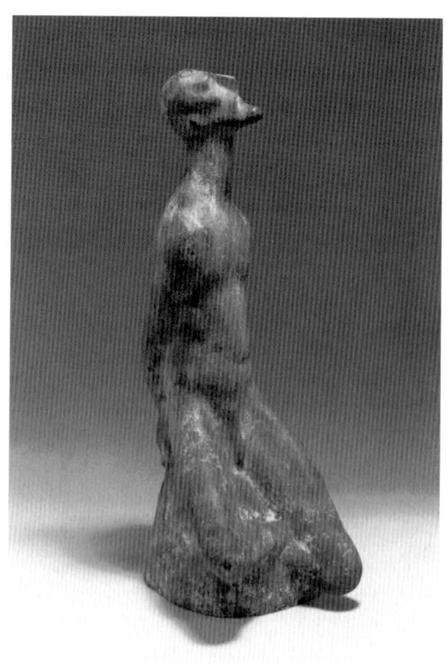

21

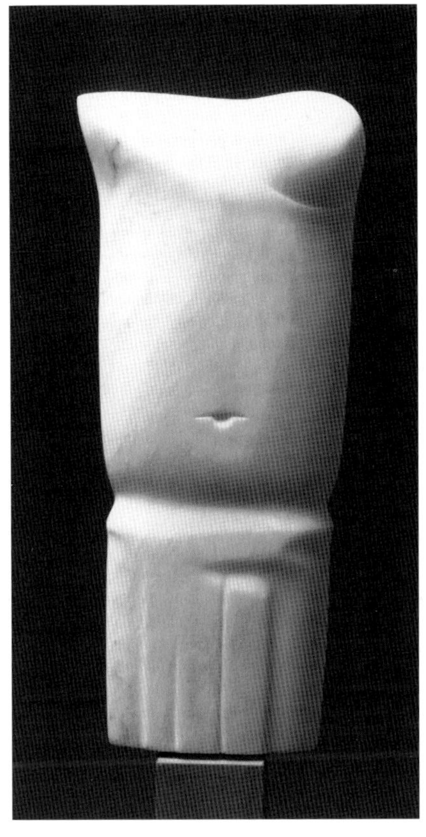

15

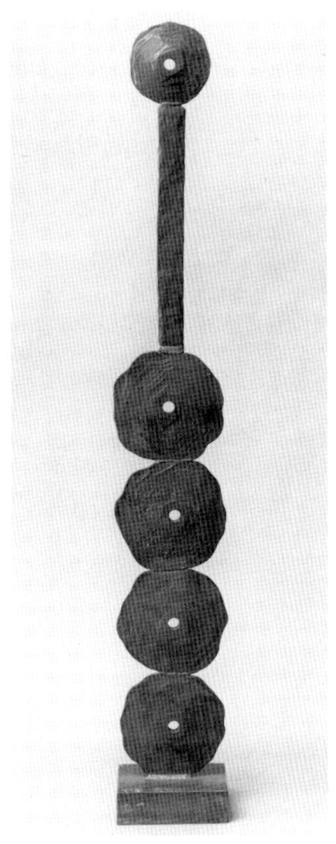

17

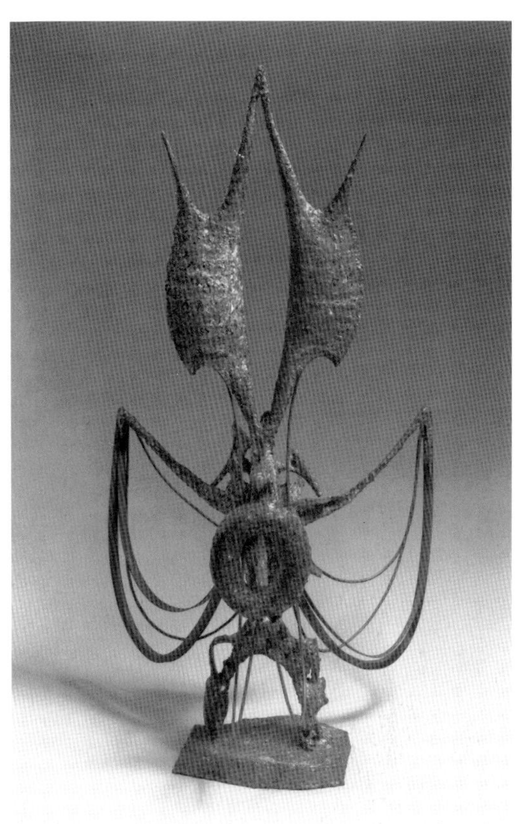

18

THEODORE ROSZAK, 1907–1981

18. *Ariadne*
1959–60
Nickel silver brazed onto steel
58¾ x 28½ x 28½" (149.2 x 72.4 x 72.4 cm)
Henry D. Gilpin Fund, 1968.10

PETER AGOSTINI, 1913–1993

19. *Butterfly*
1959
Plaster
25 x 10½ x 9¼" (63.5 x 26.7 x 23.5 cm)
Signed and dated on bottom section: AGOSTINI/59
Gift of Mr. and Mrs. Morris L. Weisberg, 1986.50.3

20. *Asian Head*
1971
Plaster
5 x 5½ x 7⅛" (12.7 x 14 x 18.1 cm)
Signed and dated on back: A 71
Gift of the artist in memory of Dorothy Weiss Bernstein, 1986.17

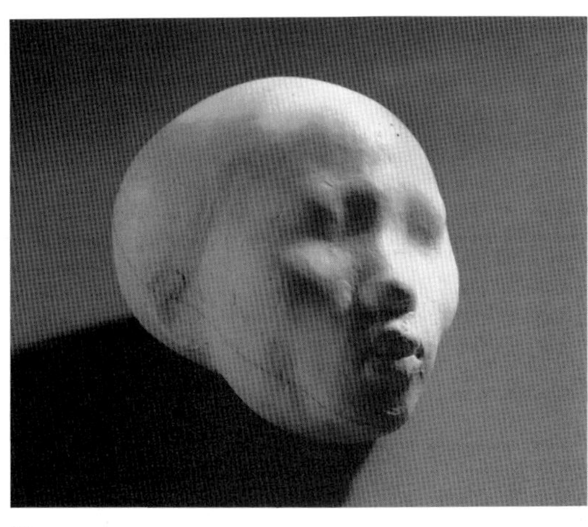

20

JOSEPH J. GREENBERG, 1915–1991

21. *Prisoner*
1952
Bronze with uneven patina; cast in 1953
48½ x 20 x 22" (123.2 x 50.8 x 55.9 cm)
Signed and dated on back below hands: GREENBERG/1952
Lost-wax cast by Fonderia M.A.F., Milan, Italy
Collection Fund, 1953.21

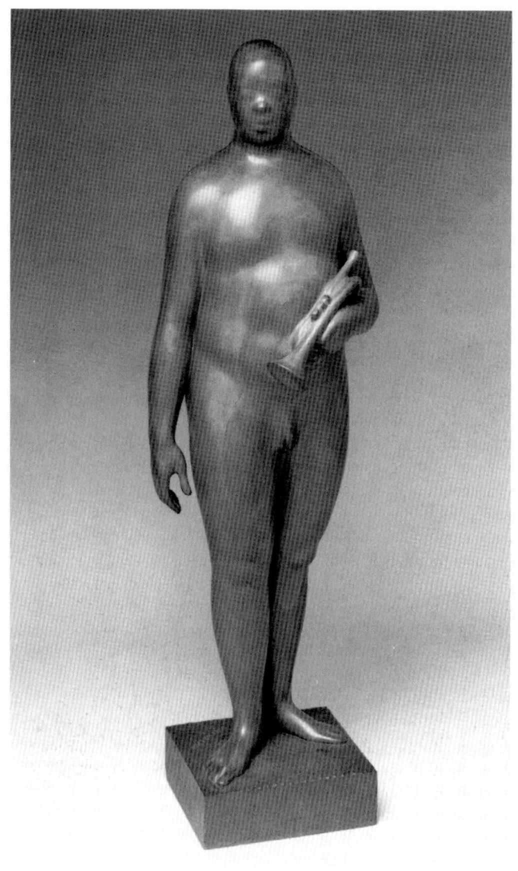

22

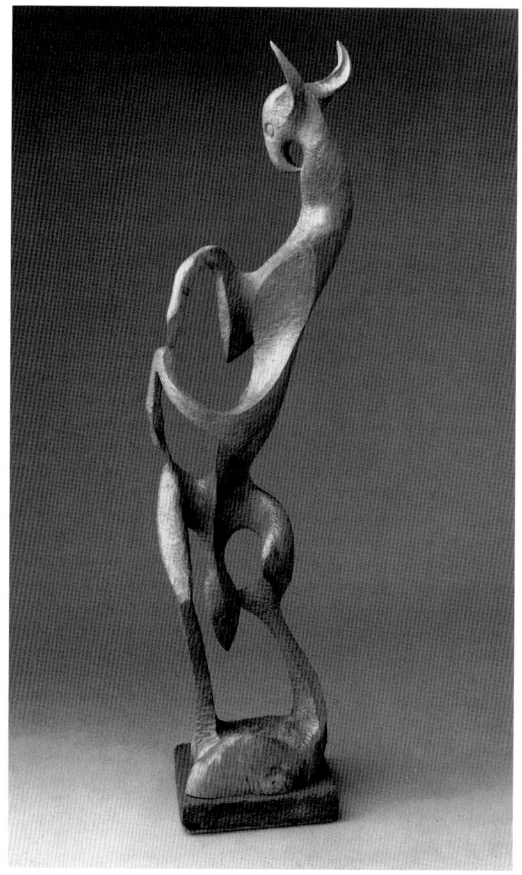

24

22. *The King* (Joe "King" Oliver, 1885–1938)
1955
Mahogany
50 x 15 x 11" (127 x 38.1 x 27.9 cm)
Signed and dated at top of base behind right foot:
J GREENBERG/1955
Gift of R. Sturgis Ingersoll, 1955.4

MARECHAL BROWN, 1915–1981

23. *Flight*
1953
Avodire and bubinga wood
Mobile of nine pieces (unassembled), 9" (22.9 cm) to 36⅞" (93.7 cm) in length
Henry D. Gilpin Fund, 1954.6

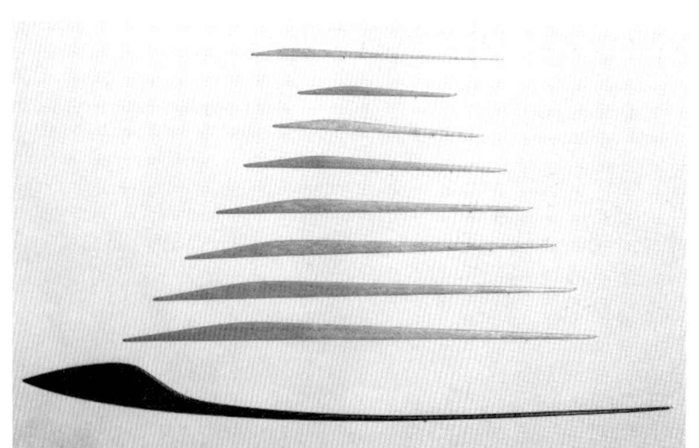

23

ADOLPH DIODA, 1915–1991

24. *Prancing Goat*
1955
Apple wood
58 x 19½ x 9½" (147.3 x 49.5 x 24.1 cm)
Gift of Carl Zigrosser, 1956.18.1

HARRY BERTOIA, 1915–1978

25. *Topiary Tree*
About 1966
Copper alloys and brass
27¼ x 14½ x 16" (69.2 x 36.8 x 40.6 cm)
Gift of Mr. and Mrs. Meyer P. Potamkin, 1977.1

26. *Tonal*
1967
Cupronickel and brass
72½ x 11⅞ x 11⅞" (184.2 x 30.2 x 30.2 cm)
Henry D. Gilpin Fund, 1968.4

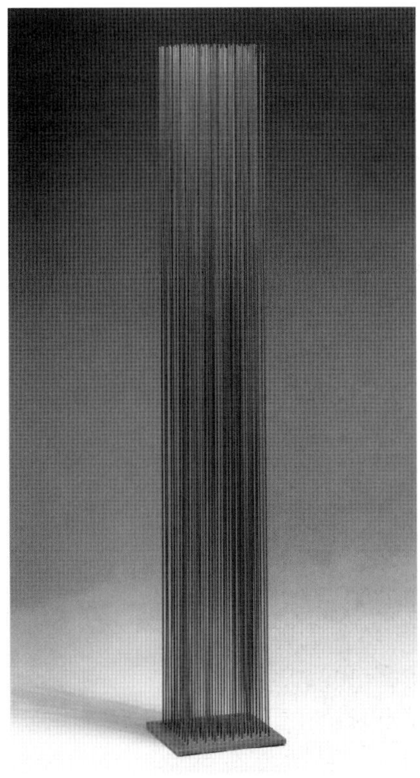

26

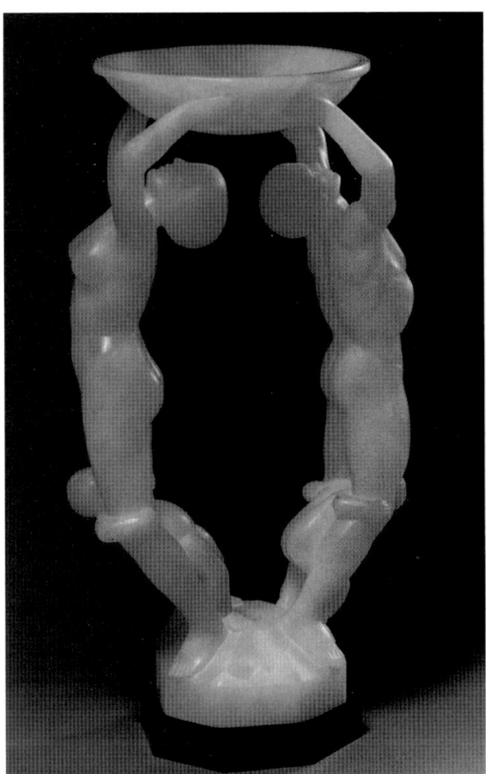

28

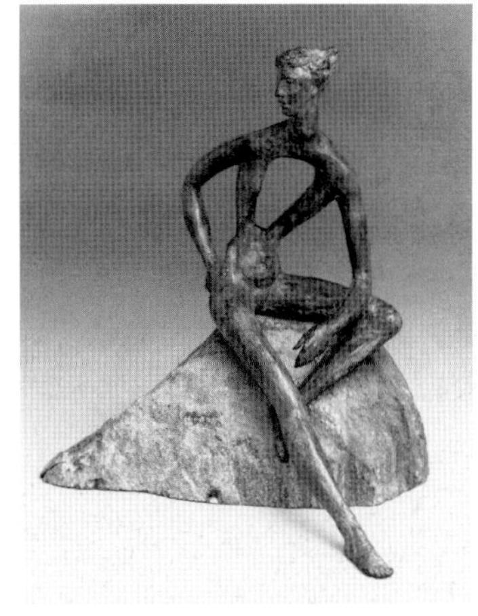

27

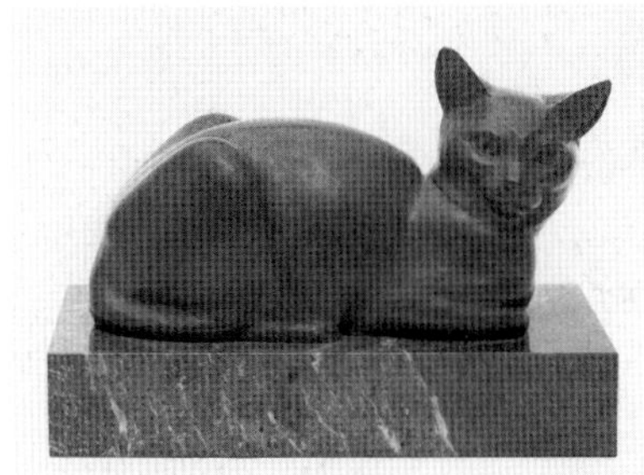

29

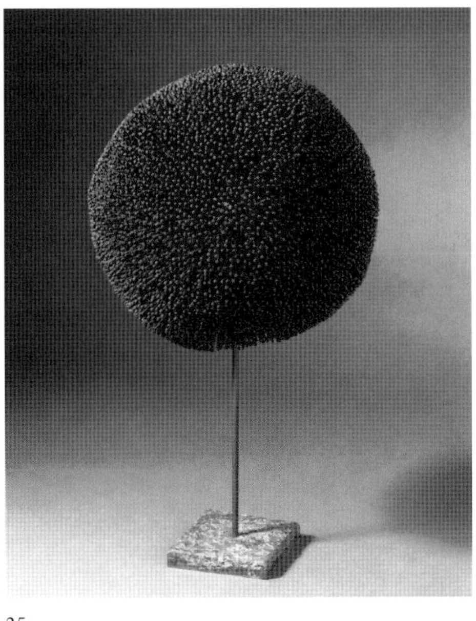

25

Henry Mitchell, 1915–1980

27. *Interlude*
1967
Bronze with green patina
22¾ x 20¾ x 19¼″ (57.8 x 52.7 x 48.9 cm)
Signed on inside of left foot: Mitchell
Lost-wax cast by Robert Barnes Foundry, Philadelphia
Funds provided by Mr. and Mrs. Clarence Morris in memory of Mrs. Morris Wenger, 1967.12

Edward Fenno Hoffman III, 1916–1991

28. *The Idealists*
1957
Alabaster
18 x 9¾ x 7⅜″ (45.7 x 24.8 x 18.7 cm)
Signed and dated on side of integral plinth: EDWARD/FENNO/HOFFMAN III/1957
Gift of Anna Hyatt Huntington, 1961.5

29. *Reclining Cat*
1969
Bronze with gray patina
6½ x 12 x 5½″ (16.5 x 30.5 x 14 cm)
Signed and dated at back: E.F. Hoffman III. 1969
Lost-wax cast by Modern Art Foundry, New York
Gift of the artist, 1974.29

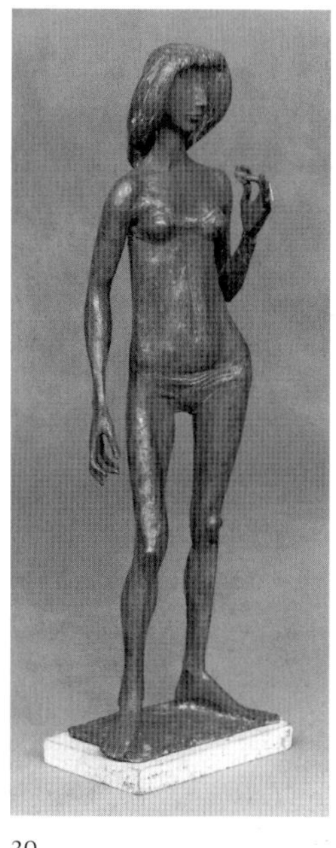

30

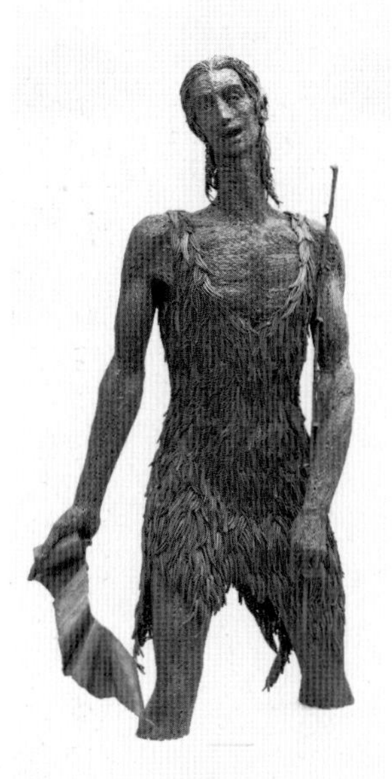

35

Milton Hebald, b. 1917

30. *Bikini*
1957
Bronze with areas of silver leaf; cast in 1957–58
31 x 10⅛ x 7½" (78.7 x 25.7 x 19.1 cm)
Signed and dated on top of base behind feet:
HEBALD Sc 195[8] #2
Lost-wax cast by Fonderia Nicci, Rome, Italy
Gift of the Ford Foundation, 1964.1.3

Wolfgang Behl, b. 1918

31. *Prometheus*
1962–63
Chestnut, driftwood, and other woods
69½ x 50 x 35" (176.5 x 127 x 88.9 cm)
Gift of the Ford Foundation, 1964.1.1

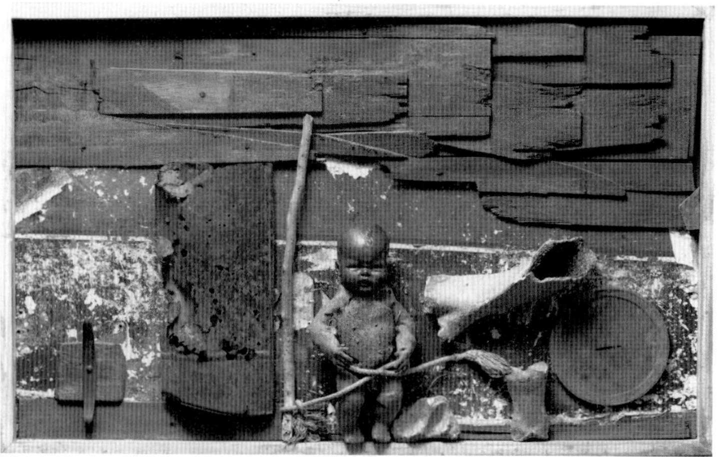

37

Robert H. Cook, b. 1921

32. *Reach*
1957
Olive wood
49 x 14½ x 13⅝" (124.5 x 36.8 x 34.6 cm)
Henry D. Gilpin Fund, 1958.7

Elena Kepalas, b. 1921

33. *Creation*
1964
Bronze with green patina
16⅞ x 12⅛ x 7" (42.9 x 30.8 x 17.8 cm)
Signed and dated at back: 64 EK
Lost-wax cast by Modern Art Foundry, New York
Joseph E. Temple Fund, 1968.8

Richard Stankiewicz, 1922–1983

34. *Dark Mother*
About 1955
Welded steel
50 x 31 x 26" (127 x 78.7 x 66 cm)
Contemporary Arts Purchase Fund, 1983.19

Kahlil Gibran, b. 1922

35. *Voice in the Wilderness*
1957
Welded iron
83½ x 36 x 22" (212.1 x 91.4 x 55.9 cm)
Signed on rectangle welded to back of scroll: K. GIBRAN
Gift of Mrs. Herbert C. Morris, 1961.3

Leonard Baskin, b. 1922

36. *Seated Woman*
1961
Oak
54 x 21 x 25½" (137.1 x 53.3 x 64.8 cm)
Henry D. Gilpin and Joseph E. Temple funds, 1966.2

Don Baum, b. 1922

37. *A Little Walk*
1964
Found objects
23¼ x 36¾ x 3⅞" (59 x 93.3 x 9.8 cm)
Gift of James Arthur Varchmin, 1986.49.2

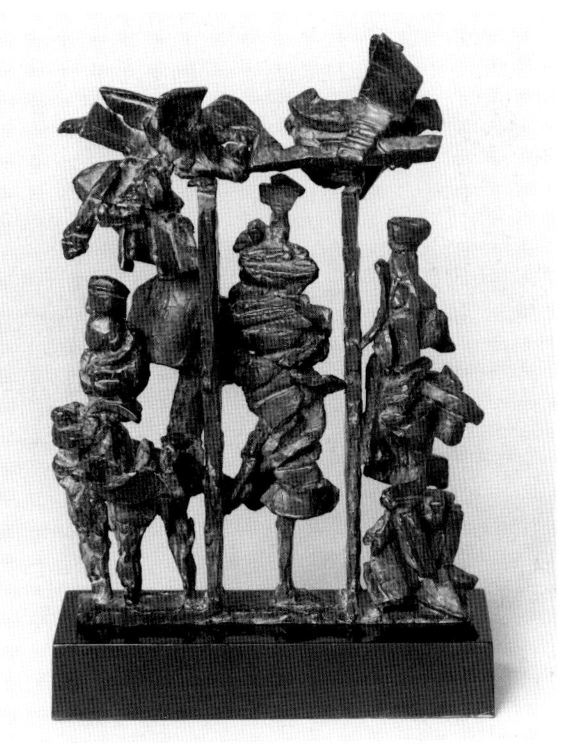

33

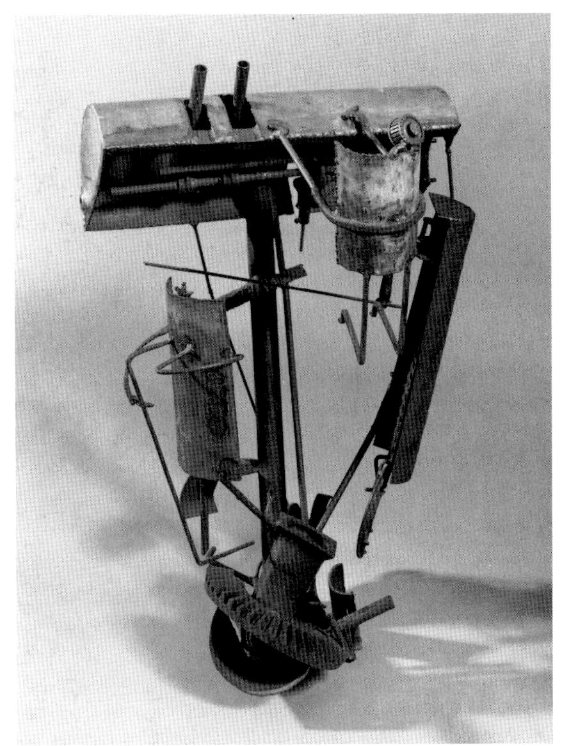

34

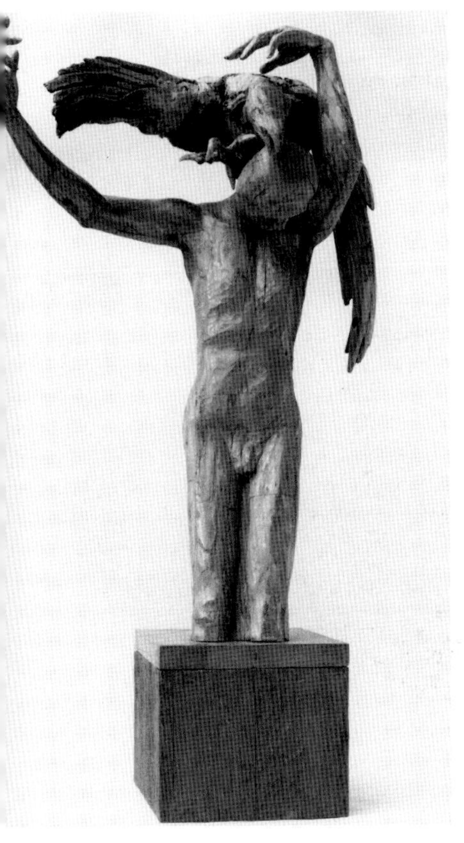

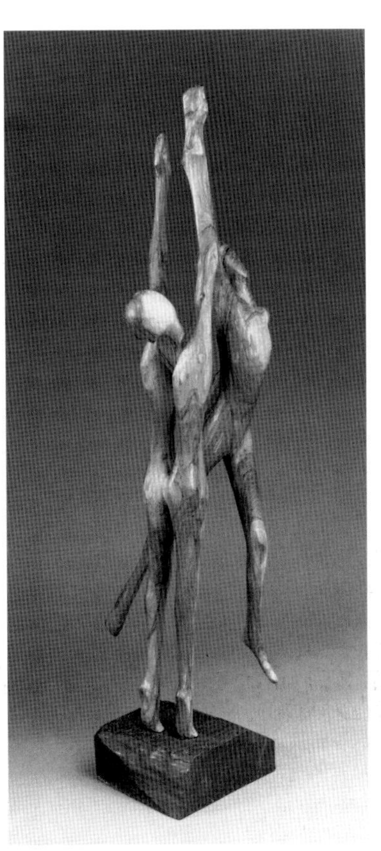

32

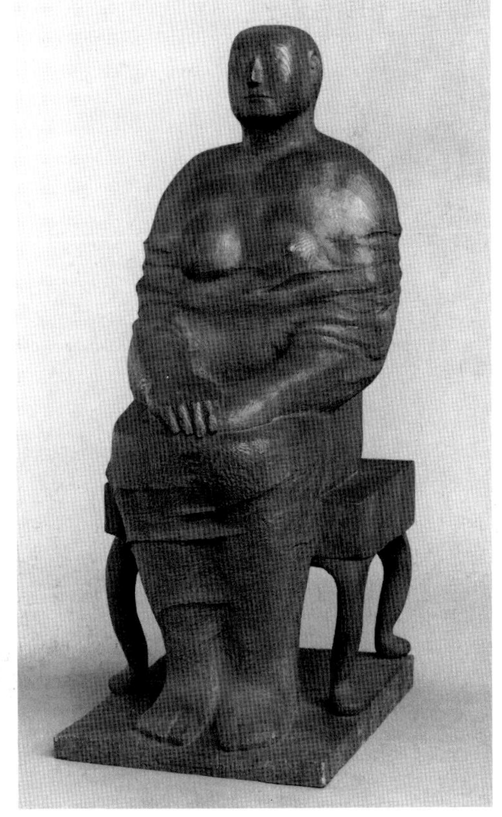

36

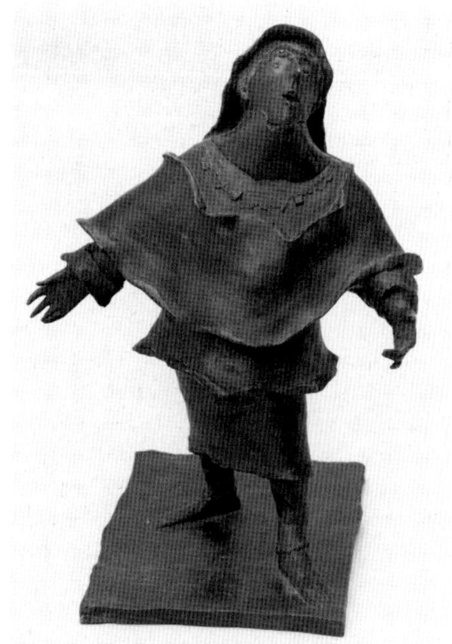

38

DAVID ARONSON, b. 1923

38. *The Singer*
1964
Bronze with brown patina; sand cast by 1967
14⅞ x 10⅞ x 9⅛" (37.8 x 27.6 x 23.2 cm)
Signed on top of base at right of right foot: Aronson
Foundry mark underneath base: BEDI-RASSY/ N.Y.C./SP/XII
Joseph E. Temple Fund, 1968.3

GEORGE SEGAL, b. 1924

39. *Girl against a Post*
1973
Plaster and cloth with wood
72¼ x 21 x 21½" (183.5 x 53.3 x 54.6 cm)
Funds provided by the National Endowment for the Arts, the Pennsylvania Academy's Women's Committee, and an anonymous donor, 1974.9.2

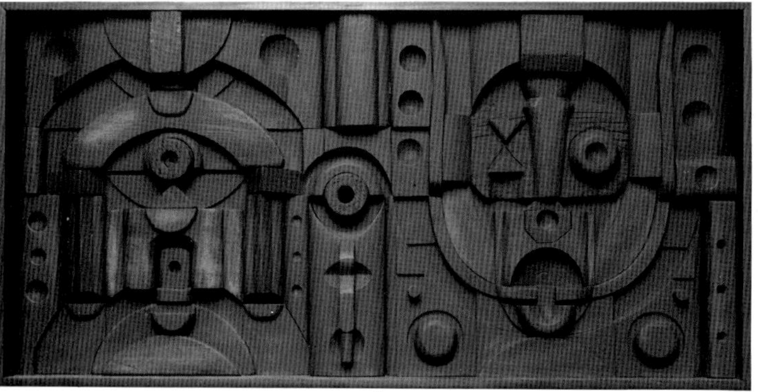

42

BRUNO LUCCHESI, b. 1926

40. *Wash Line*
1963
Bronze with green patina
51⅝ x 27 x 17" (131.1 x 68.6 x 43.2 cm)
Signed on left foot: B. LUCCHESI
Cast by Fonderia Tommasi, Pietrasanta, Italy
Joseph E. Temple Fund, 1964.4

FUMIO YOSHIMURA, b. 1926

41. *Blue Bird*
1967
Steel, painted blue, and blue fiberglass
84½ x 93 x 51" (214.6 x 236.2 x 129.5 cm)
Henry D. Gilpin Fund, 1970.2

DAN MILLER, b. 1928

42. *Hero and Leander*
1963–64
Wood, painted black
25⅜ x 49½ x 3⅝" (64.5 x 125.7 x 9.2 cm)
Signed and dated on back: 1964 ©/DAN MILLER
Inscribed on back: HERO AND LEANDER
Joseph E. Temple Fund, 1964.6

NORMAN CARLBERG, b. 1928

43. *Poto Negro*
1964
Epoxy, painted black, over a plaster core, and brass
14 x 16 x 15¼" (35.6 x 40.6 x 38.7 cm)
Henry D. Gilpin Fund, 1968.5

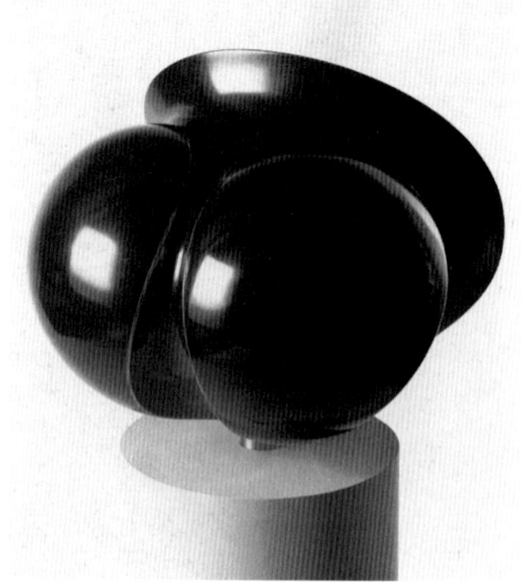

43

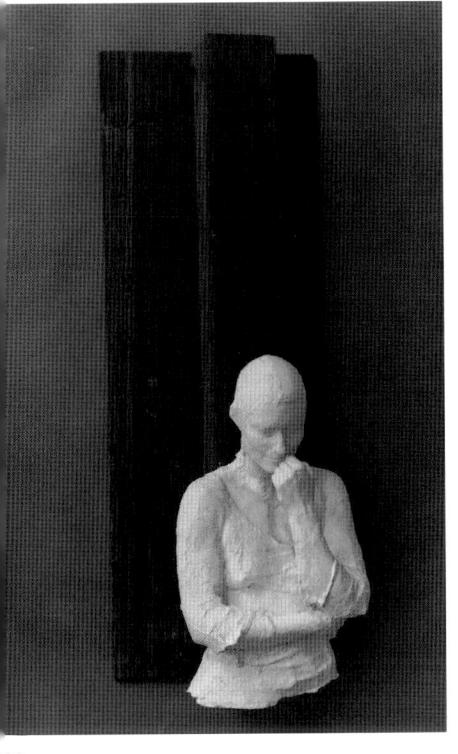

39

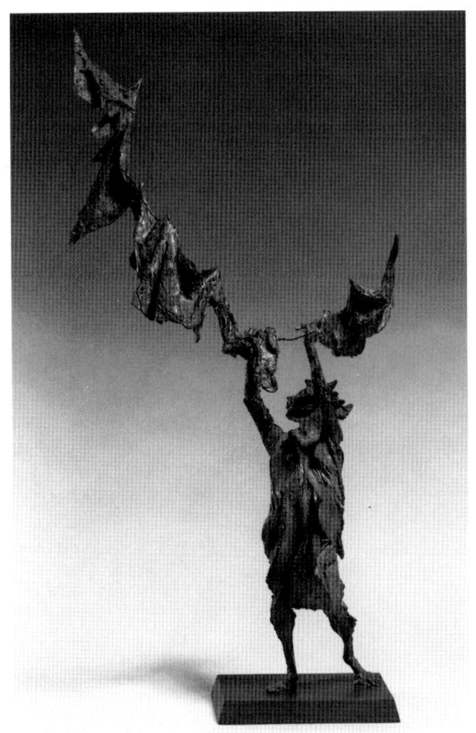

40

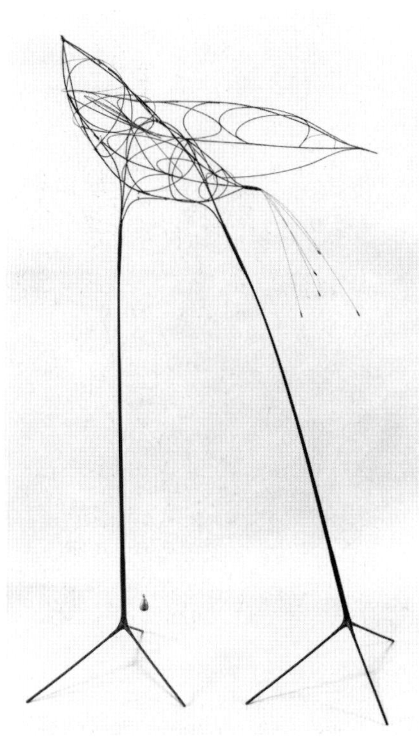

41

Jack Zajac, b. 1929

44. *Goat in Stakes, No. 1*
1957
Bronze with uneven patina
28⅞ x 17 x 12⅛" (73.3 x 43.2 x 30.8 cm)
Lost-wax cast probably in Rome, Italy
Gift of the Ford Foundation, 1962.5.3

45. *Small Skull and Horn, after Orvieto*
1976
Bronze with brown patina
15⅛ x 23⅛ x 10¾" (38.4 x 58.7 x 27.3 cm)
Lost-wax cast probably in Rome, Italy
Gift of Mr. and Mrs. Meyer P. Potamkin, 1991.2

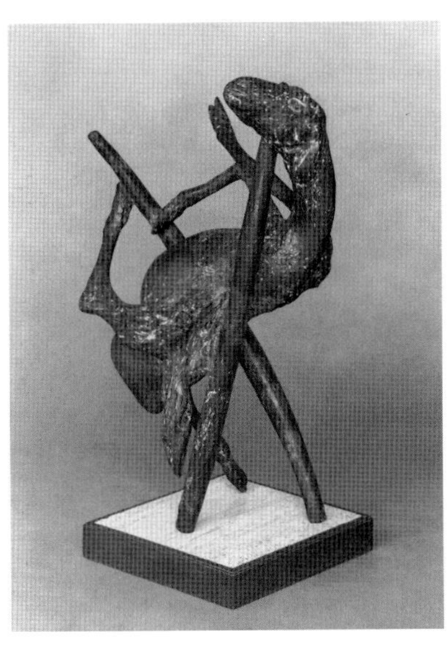

44

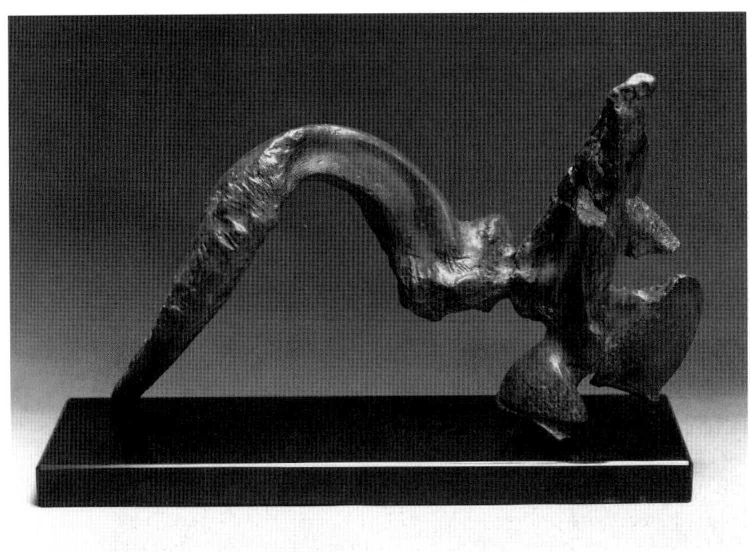

45

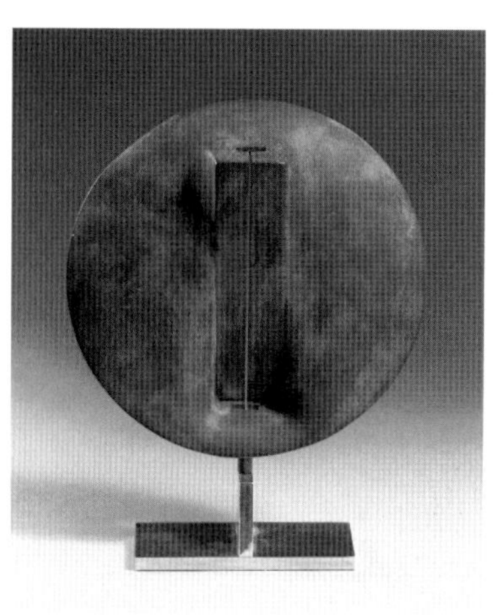
48

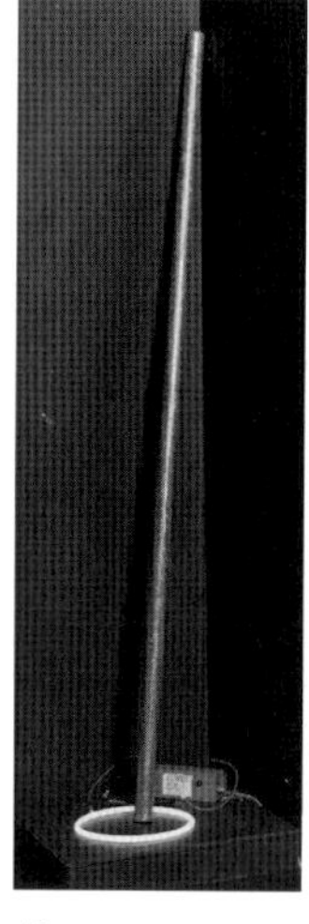
49

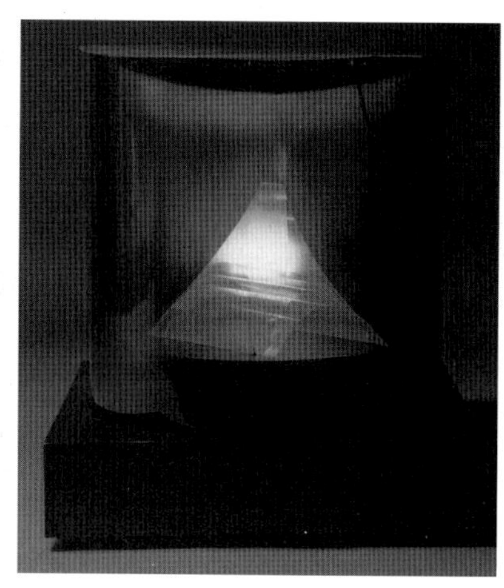
51

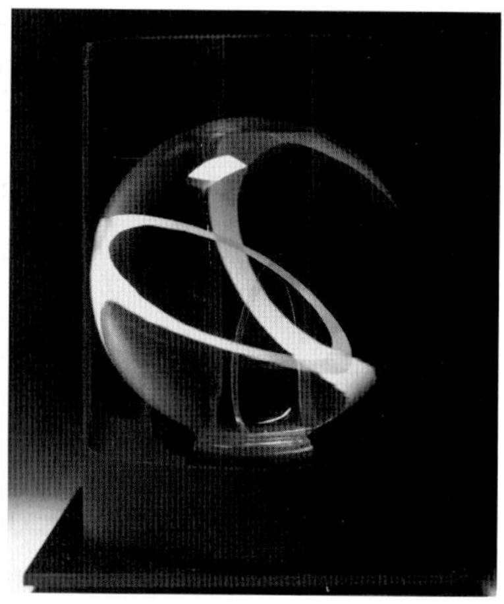
52

Bill Freeland, b. 1929

46. *Galway Rocker*
1982
Wood, canvas, stone, wire, and rope
14 x 10 x 16" (35.6 x 25.4 x 40.6 cm)
John Lambert Fund, 1985.13

Lee Bontecou, b. 1931

47. *Grounded Bird*
1957
Bronze with green patina; cast in 1958
17¼ x 62 x 15" (43.8 x 157.5 x 38.1 cm)
Signed and dated on outside of left foot: BONTECOU 58
Lost-wax cast probably by Giovanni Brothers, Rome, Italy
Joseph E. Temple Fund, 1960.2

James Wines, b. 1932

48. *Disc X*
By 1973
Bronze with gray-black patina
9¾ x 9¾ x 2¼" (24.8 x 24.8 x 5.7 cm)
Signed on back of disc at lower right edge: WINES
Inscribed on back of disc at lower left edge: 92–100
Gift of Dr. and Mrs. Paul Todd Makler, 1973.3

Rafael Ferrer, b. 1933

49. *Neon Corner*
1970
Galvanized steel pole, circular neon tubing, and transformer
Pole: 84 x 2 x 2" (213.4 x 5.1 x 5.1 cm); tubing: 12" diam. (30.5 cm); transformer: 3 x 4¼ x 9¼" (7.6 x 10.8 x 23.5 cm)
Signed and dated on paper label attached to transformer: FERRER/1970/35/50/Rafael Ferrer
Gift of Dr. and Mrs. Paul Todd Makler, 1972.6

Mary Frank, b. 1933

50. *Woman Lying Down*
1980
Stoneware (ten sections)
11¾ x 39 x 84" (29.8 x 99.1 x 213.4 cm)
Henry D. Gilpin Fund, 1981.14 a-j

Adam Peiperl, b. 1935

51. *Ice Palace*
1969–86
Glass, polystyrene, water, magnet, and polarized film with light
19¾ x 17¾ x 21¾" (50.2 x 45.1 x 55.2 cm)
Gift of the artist, 1969.30

52. *Astralite #138*
1970
Glass, plastic, and polarized film with light
22½ x 18 x 22" (57.2 x 45.7 x 55.9 cm)
Signed and dated on top of base: Astralite 138/A. Peiperl/April 1970
Signed and dated on glass plate that seals globe: Astralite 138/A Peiperl/March 1970
Gift of the artist, 1970.8

Italo Scanga, b. 1935

53. *Untitled (Pax with Dog)*
1986
Wood, polychromed
96 x 34 x 11½" (243.8 x 86.4 x 29.2 cm)
John Lambert Fund and by exchange with the artist, 1989.9

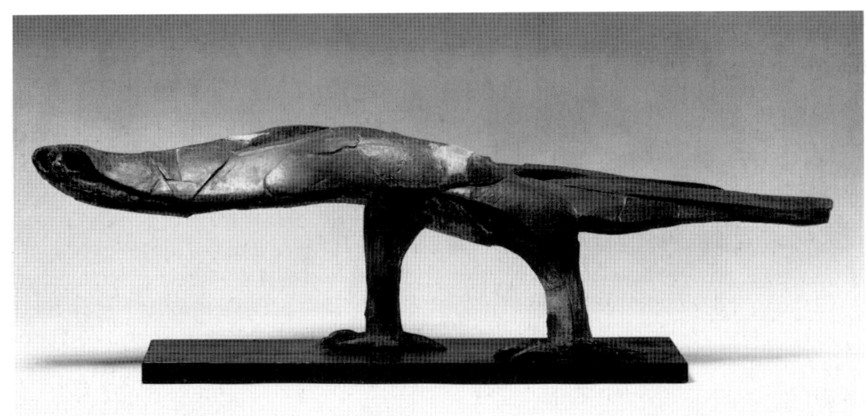

47

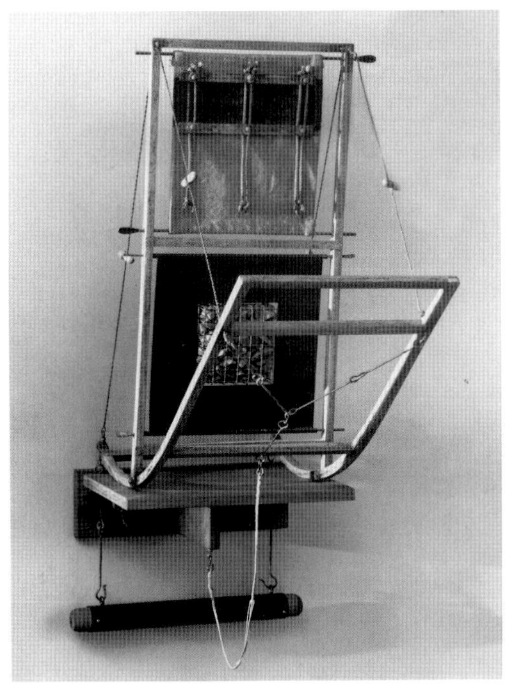

46

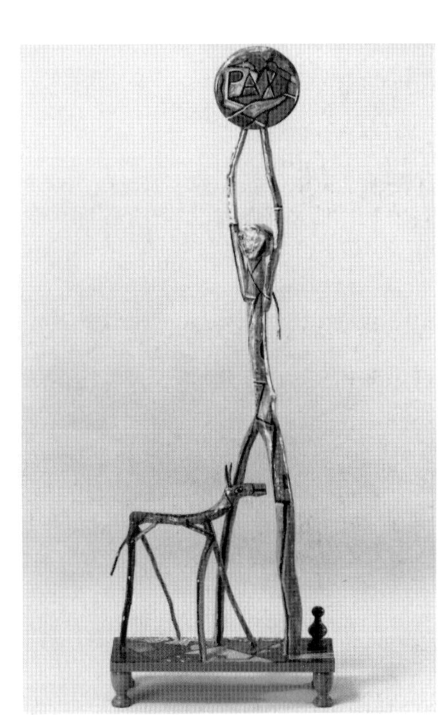

53

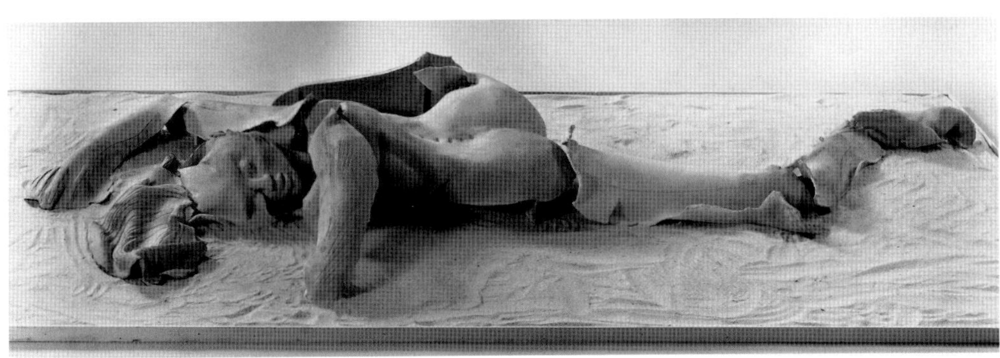

50

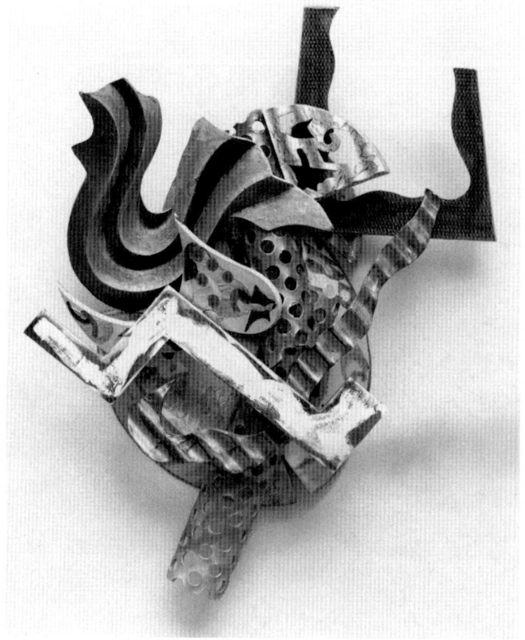
54

Frank Stella, b. 1936

54. *The Press Gang Sailor*
1986
Mixed media on anodized aluminum, light-colored alloy
62⅞ x 48¼ x 12⅞" (160.4 x 122.6 x 32.7 cm)
Pennsylvania Academy Purchase Fund, 1986.38

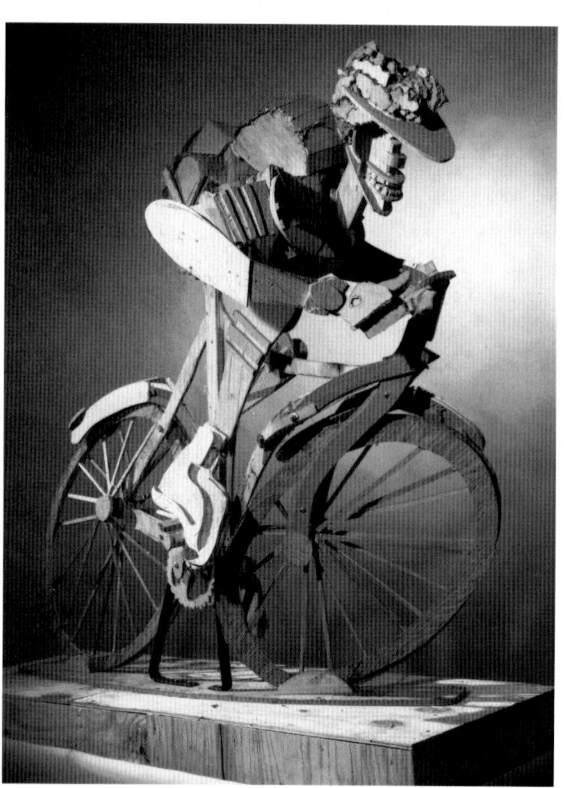
55

Red Grooms, b. 1937

55. *The Bicyclist*
1975–76
Working model for welded steel sculpture of cyclist on Brooklyn Bridge in *Ruckus Manhattan*, 1976
Assorted wood and corrugated cardboard
50½ x 65½ x 28¾" (128.3 x 166.4 x 73 cm)
Signed and dated in pencil on curved support: Red Grooms 1976
Gift of the artist in memory of Dorothy Weiss Bernstein, 1986.45

Dennis Oppenheim, b. 1938

56. *Roots in Cubism, Hearts in the Stars (Forest for Cézanne)*
1983–84
Model for project in Berlin, Germany
Wood, galvanized steel, stone, and ceramic
31 x 24½ x 21¾" (78.7 x 62.2 x 55.2 cm)
Contemporary Arts Purchase Fund, 1984.11

Patrick M. Kelly, b. 1939

57. *Pick Up Ten*
1963
Welded steel
19 x 17¾ x 20½" (48.3 x 45.1 x 52.1 cm)
Gift of the Ford Foundation, 1964.1.4

Charles Fahlen, b. 1939

58. *Speed King*
1974
Cardboard, rhoplex, wood, polyester resin, wire mesh, fiberglass, latex rubber, and paint
99 x 53 x 14½" (251.5 x 134.6 x 36.8 cm)
Signed and dated on back: SPEED KING/1974/C FAHLEN
Gift of subscribers to Marion Locks benefit, and Mr. and Mrs. Charles E. Mather III, 1975.17.2

59. *Model for "Turk's Head"*
1983
Plywood
13½ x 13 x 4" (34.3 x 33 x 10.2 cm)
Gift of the artist, 1986.32

60. *Turk's Head*
1983–84
Aluminum, painted blue, and steel
51 x 48½ x 15" (129.5 x 123.2 x 38.1 cm)
Gift of Frederick R. McBrien III, by exchange, and the John Lambert Fund, 1984.15

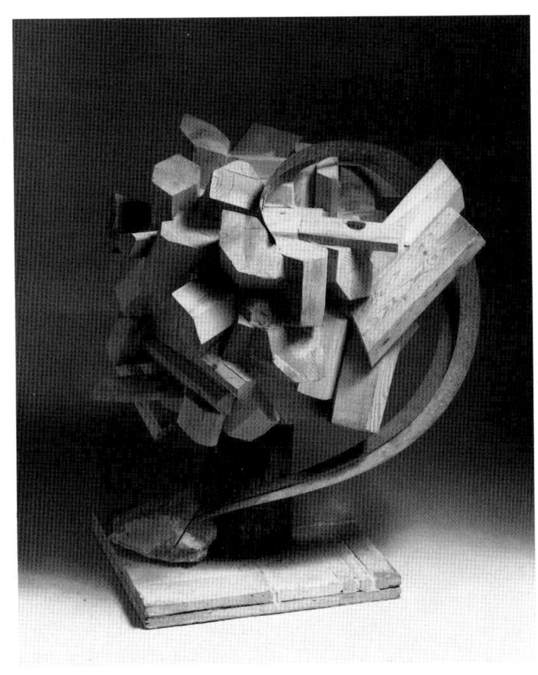

56

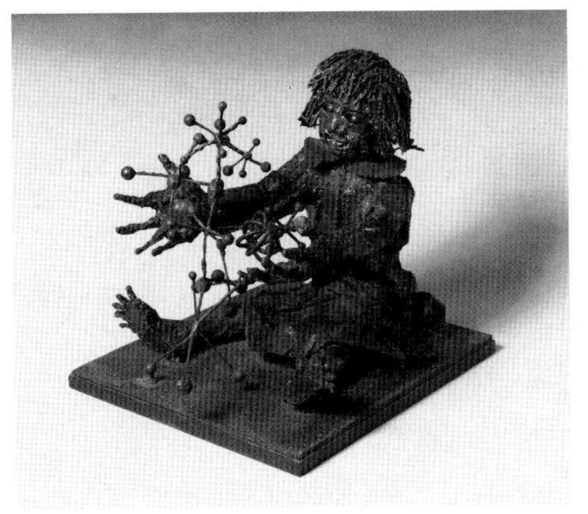

57

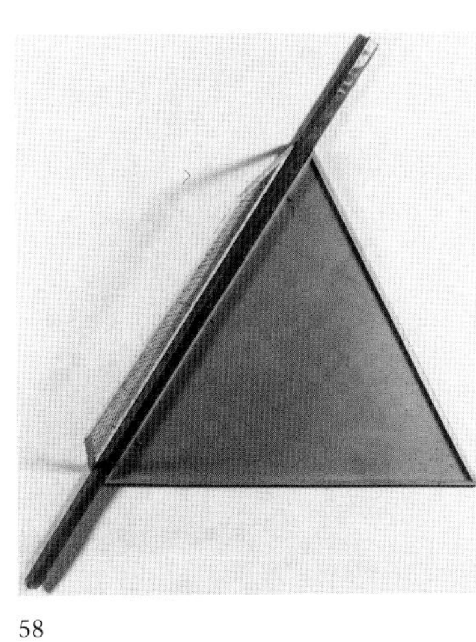

58

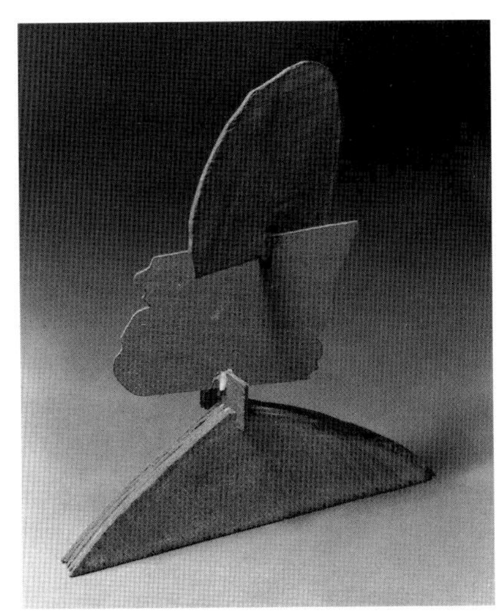

59

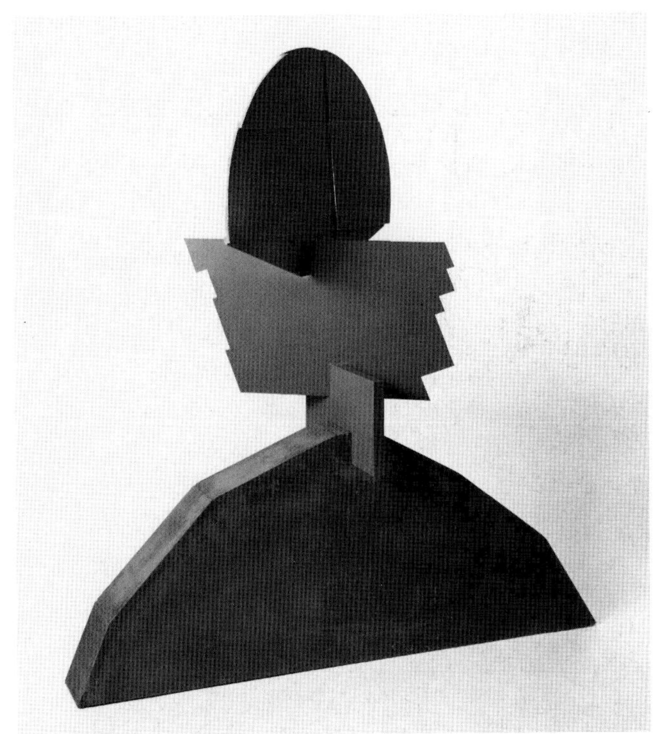

60

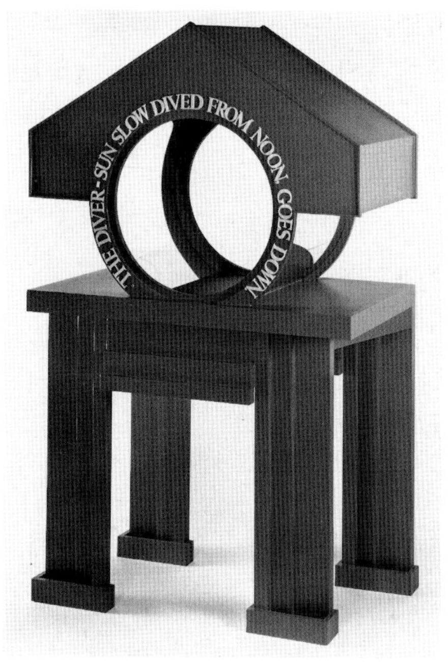

61

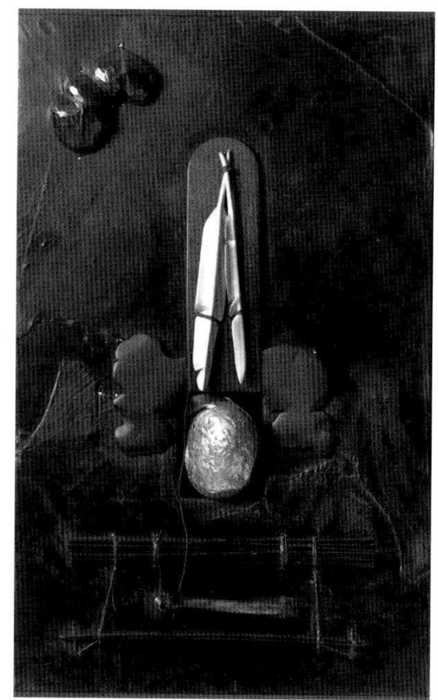
62

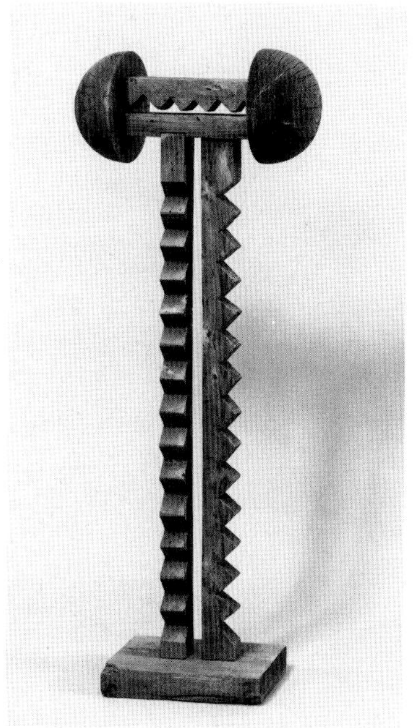
66

SIAH ARMAJANI, b. 1939

61. *Dictionary for Building: Fireplace Mantel with Mirror*
1982–83
Wood, painted green and yellow, and mirrored plastic
79¾ x 48¾ x 23½" (202.6 x 123.8 x 59.7 cm)
Inscribed with applied letters, painted yellow, encircling hollow cylinder in pediment: THE DIVER-SUN SLOW DIVED FROM NOON, GOES DOWN.
Gift of the Dietrich Foundation in memory of Henry S. McNeil, 1983.5

RALPH D. CAPARULO, b. 1939

62. *Kaga No Tori*
1989
Leather, brass, wood, metallic wax, and twine
32½ x 20½ x 9" (82.6 x 52.1 x 22.9 cm)
Signed on back in brown ink: RALPH D/CAPARULO/DEC 1984; on back in black ink: *Caparulo*
Other inscriptions on back
Pennsylvania Academy Purchase Prize from the 92nd Annual Fellowship Exhibition, Academy Art Purchase Fund, 1989.23

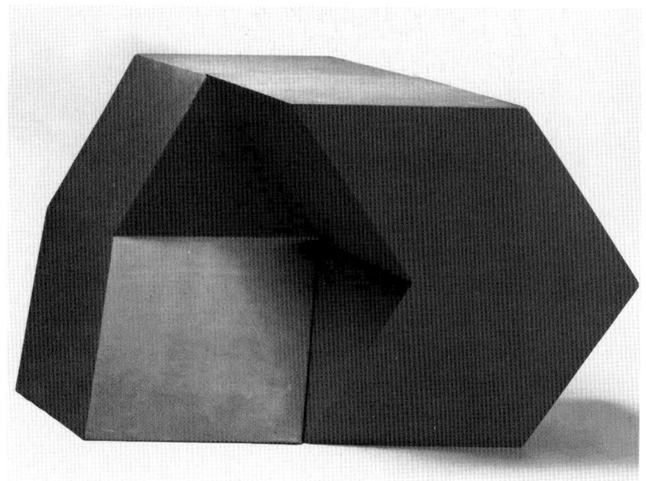
63

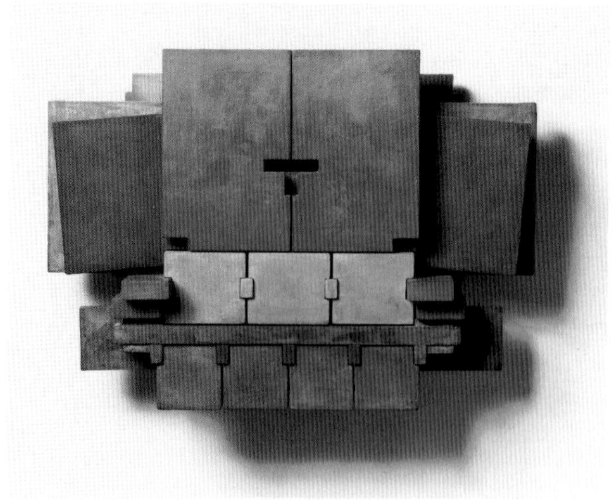
67

Robinson Fredenthal, b. 1940

63. *Untitled*
1973
Model for a sculpture
Plywood, painted rust red (two sections)
Each part: 27 x 47 x 27½″ (68.6 x 119.4 x 69.9 cm)
Pennsylvania Academy commission for Fredenthal exhibition, 1973.16

Herbert George, b. 1940

64. *Head #17 (Light and Shade, Self-Portrait)*
1985
Hydrocal, polychromed, and steel rods
30½ x 22 x 11″ (77.5 x 55.9 x 27.9 cm)
John Lambert Fund, 1987.17

Nancy Graves, b. 1940

65. *Hay Fervor*
1985
Bronze and steel with polychrome patina, baked enamel, and polyurethane paint
95¾ x 87 x 38¼″ (243.2 x 221 x 97.2 cm)
Signed and dated on edge of sickle bar: N.S. GRAVES IX85
Inscribed on edge of sickle bar at 54″ (137.2 cm), before signature: "HAY FERVOR"
Foundry mark on edge of sickle bar after date: T/X
Purchased with funds provided by Dr. Luther W. Brady, Mr. and Mrs. Daniel W. Dietrich II, Mrs. Robert English, Mr. and Mrs. Henry F. Harris, Mr. and Mrs. J. Welles Henderson, Mr. and Mrs. Leonard I. Korman, Mr. Harvey S. Shipley Miller, Mr. and Mrs. Allen J. Model, Mr. and Mrs. Stewart Resnick, Mr. and Mrs. George M. Ross, Mr. and Mrs. Stanley C. Tuttleman, and the Women's Committee, 1987.7

Stephen Porter, b. 1941

66. *Ladders #2*
1963
Weathered pine
63¼ x 25½ x 12¼″ (160.7 x 64.8 x 31.1 cm)
Gift of the Betty Parsons estate, 1985.43

Perry Gunther, b. 1941

67. *Tziquin*
1989
Wood with acrylic paint and marble dust
14 x 19 x 5⅝″ (35.6 x 48.3 x 14.3 cm)
Henry D. Gilpin Fund, 1989.18

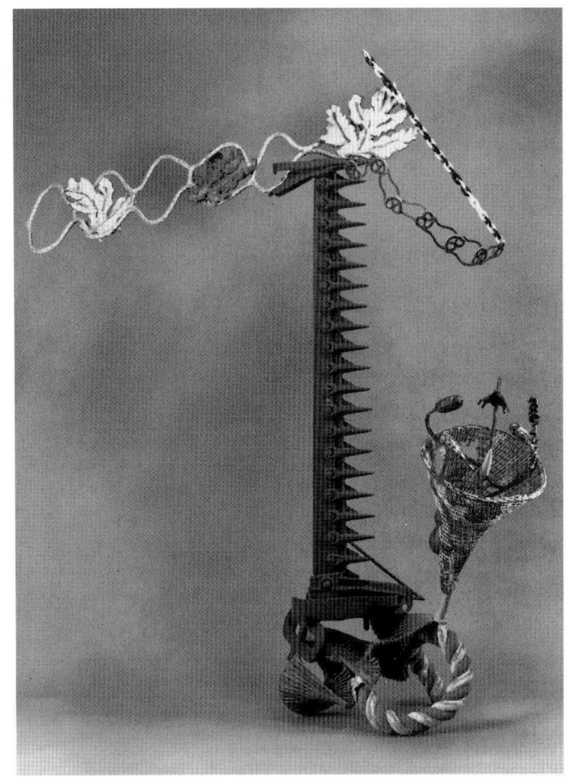

65

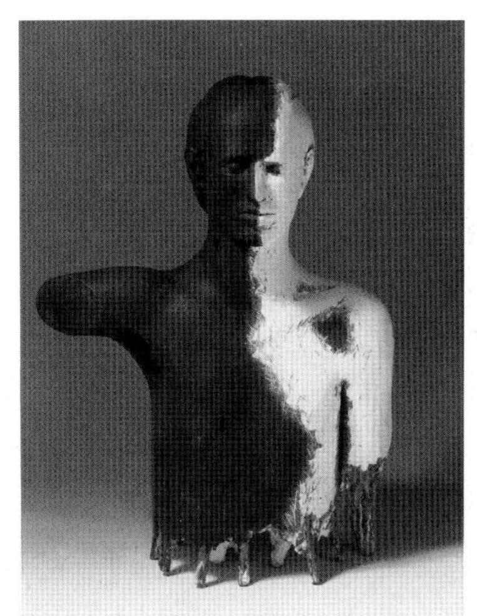

64

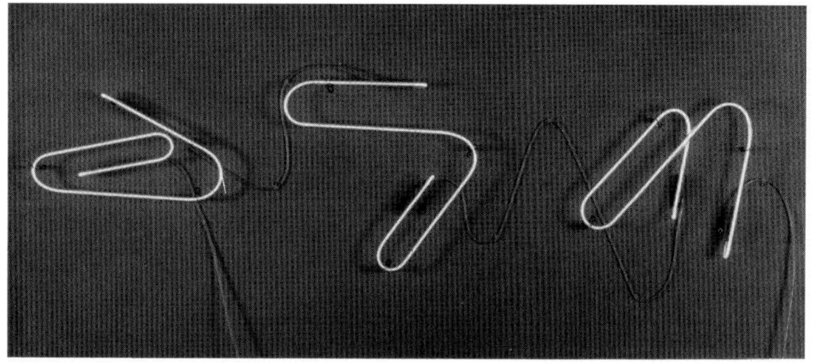

68

Annson Kenney, 1944–1981

68. *Variations on Three Bauhaus Bends*
1981
Argon in clear glass (three pieces), and transformer
18 x 65⅜ x 1¾" (45.7 x 166 x 4.4 cm)
John Lambert Fund, 1990.13 a-c

James Lloyd, b. 1944

69. *Portal Figure*
1985
Epoxy resin with graphite and iron oxide powder
29 x 15 x 13" (73.7 x 38.1 x 33 cm)
Pennsylvania Academy Purchase Prize from the 88th Annual Fellowship Exhibition, and Henry D. Gilpin Fund, 1985.64

Eric Parks, b. 1948

70. *Young Woman (Turning Point)*
1972
Bronze with brown patina; cast in 1972–73
26¼ x 6¾ x 6⅝" (66.7 x 17.1 x 16.8 cm)
Signed at back on edge of dress: ERIC PARKS
Cast by Parks family foundry, Hockessin, Del.
Gift of Mrs. Henry Dupont and anonymous donors, 1975.3

Barbara Schwartz, b. 1948

71. *Ariel*
1984
Bronze with polychrome patina and oil paint
23 x 17¾ x 2½" (58.4 x 45.1 x 6.4 cm)
Signed on back: BS
Cast by Johnson Atelier, Merchantville, N.J.
Gift of Aladar Marberger and Lawrence di Carlo, 1988.24

Eiko Fan, b. 1951

72. *Life Is a Cycle*
1993
Wood
89¼ x 52 x 56½" (226.7 x 132.1 x 143.5 cm)
Museum of American Art of the Pennsylvania Academy Purchase Prize from the 97th Annual Fellowship Exhibition, 1995.5

Tom Butter, b. 1952

73. *S.C.*
1985
Fiberglass and polyester resin
92 x 40 x 23" (233.7 x 101.6 x 58.4 cm)
Contemporary Arts Purchase Fund and Henry D. Gilpin Fund, 1985.63

Judy Moonelis, b. 1953

74. *Untitled*
1983
Glazed terracotta
28¼ x 24 x 16¼" (71.8 x 61 x 41.3 cm)
Signed and dated at back: JUDY MOONELIS 1983
Joseph E. Temple Fund, 1984.1

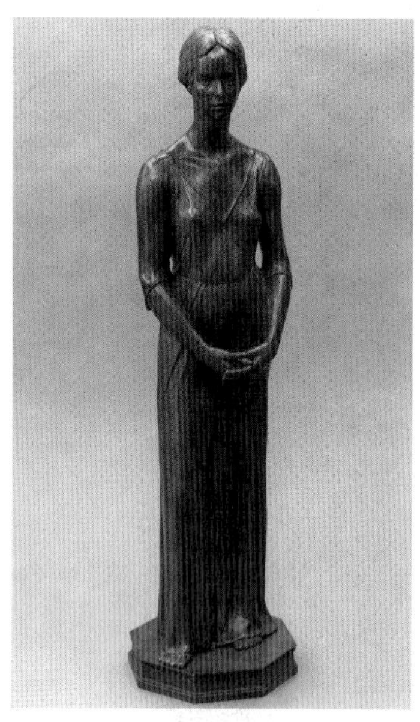

70

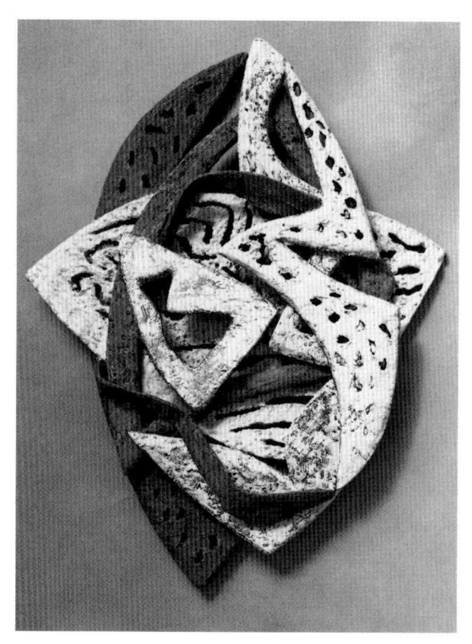

71

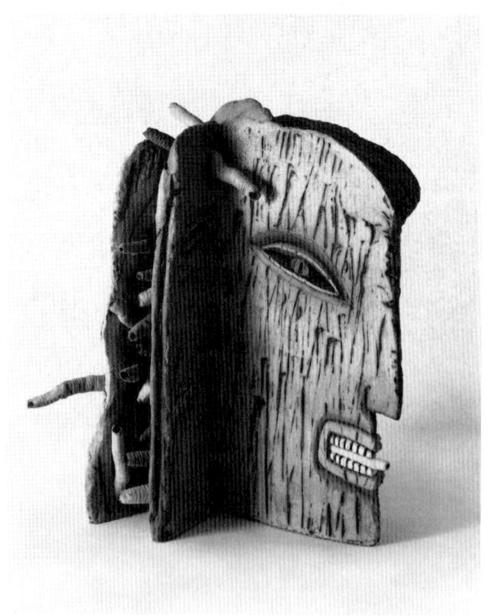

74

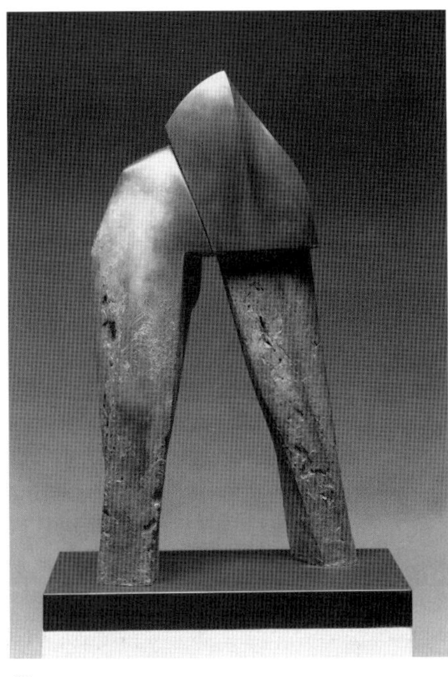

69

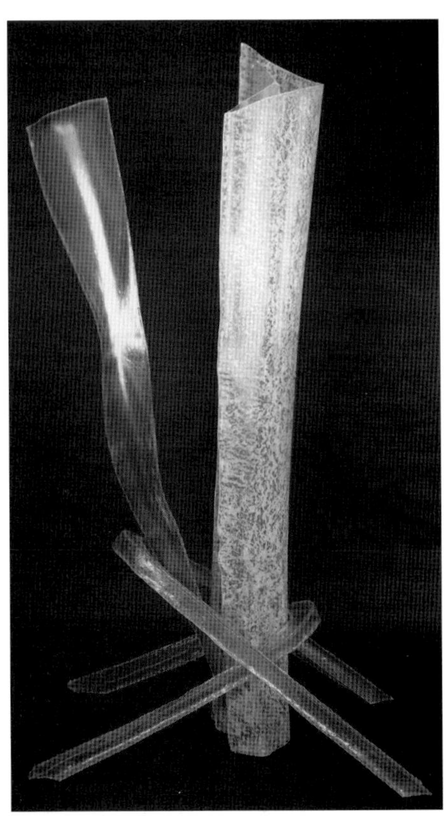

73

72

Phoebe Adams, b. 1953

75. *Half Laugh*
1985
Bronze with rust, black, white, and green patina
38¼ x 29¼ x 12″ (97.2 x 74.3 x 30.5 cm)
Cast by Johnson Atelier, Merchantville, N.J.
Henry D. Gilpin Fund, 1985.14

75

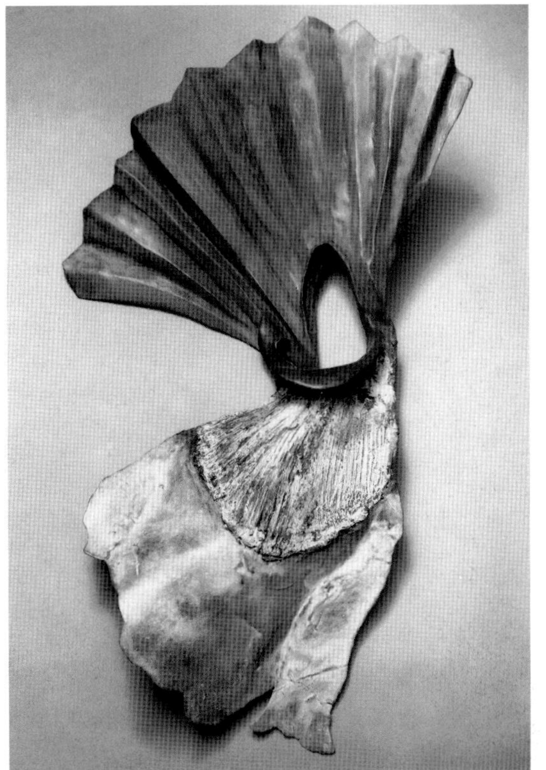

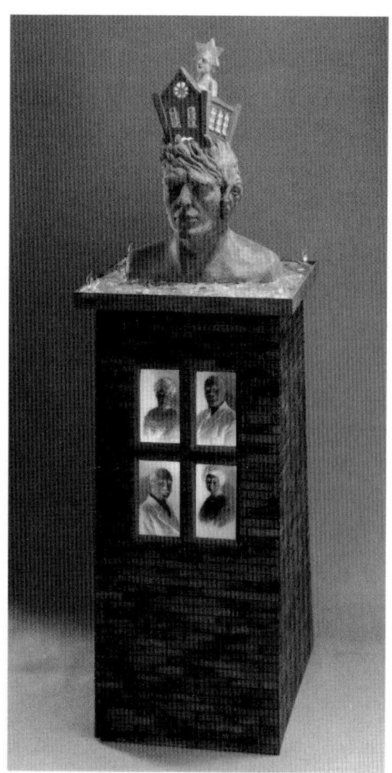

76

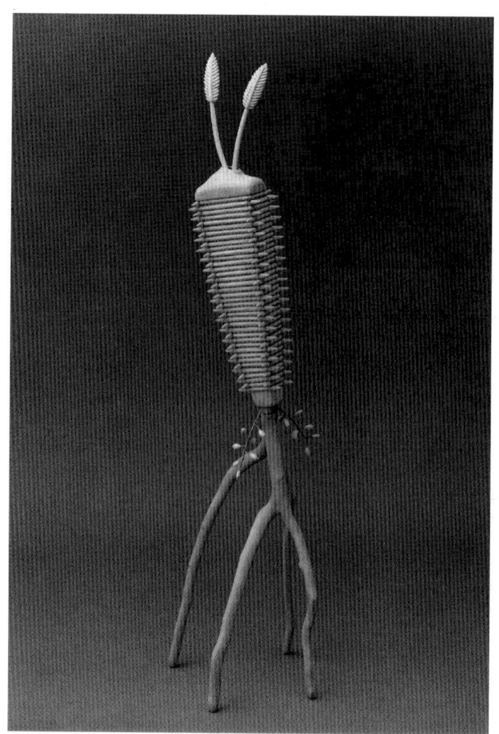

77

Jonathan Hertzel, b. 1953

76. *Kristallnacht: A Sleep of Reason*
1991
Mixed media
67 x 22 x 36″ (170.2 x 55.9 x 91.4 cm)
Pennsylvania Academy Purchase Prize from the 95th Annual Fellowship Exhibition, 1992.7

Brian Meunier, b. 1954

77. *Kernel*
1984
Wood, painted green and yellow, and copper wire
58 x 15 x 14″ (147.3 x 38.1 x 35.6 cm)
John Lambert Fund, 1984.29

APPENDIX: MEDALS AND CAMEOS CHECKLIST

MEDALS

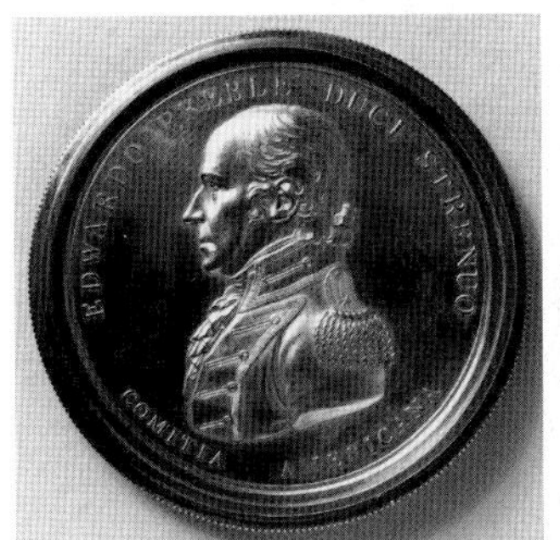
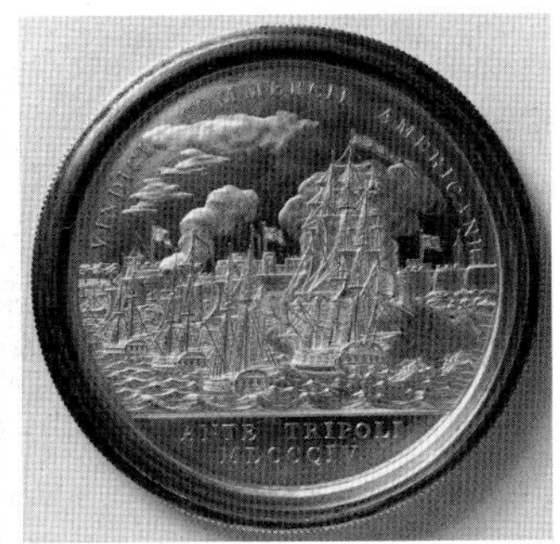
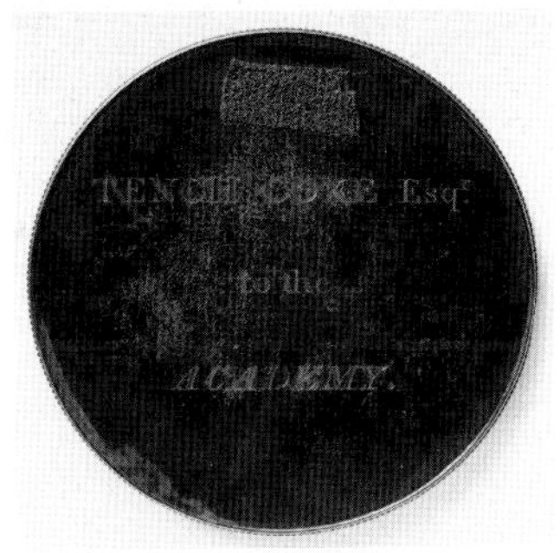

JOHN REICH, 1768–1833

Commodore Edward Preble Medal
1806
Gilded silver
2½″ diam. (6.4 cm)
Silver case (lid missing): 2¾″ diam. (7 cm)
Signed on obverse on truncation: R.
Inscribed on obverse (front) around upper edge: EDWARDO PREBLE DUCI STRENUO [Edward Preble, the valiant commander]; at lower edge: COMITIA AMERICANA [American Congress]
Inscribed on reverse (back) around upper edge: VINDICI COMMERCII AMERICANI [To the vindicator of American commerce]; in exergue: ANTE TRIPOLI/ MDCCCIV. [off Tripoli 1804]
Engraved on bottom of case: TENCH COXE Esqr./to the/ ACADEMY.
Gift of Tench Coxe, 1807.3

MORITZ FURST, 1782-after 1841

The Death of Turnus
1808
Obverse of medal
Bronze with black patina
2¹⁄₁₆″ diam. (5.2 cm)

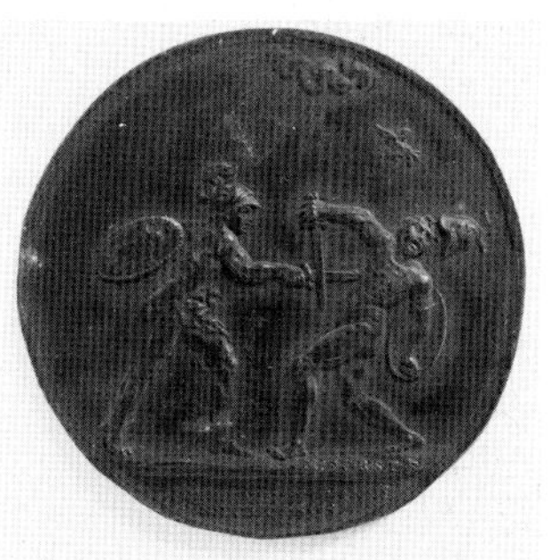

Signed above exergue at right: M:FURST-F; dated in exergue after inscription: 1808
Inscribed in exergue: THE DEATH OF TURNUS/N YORK
Source unknown, 1986.x.35

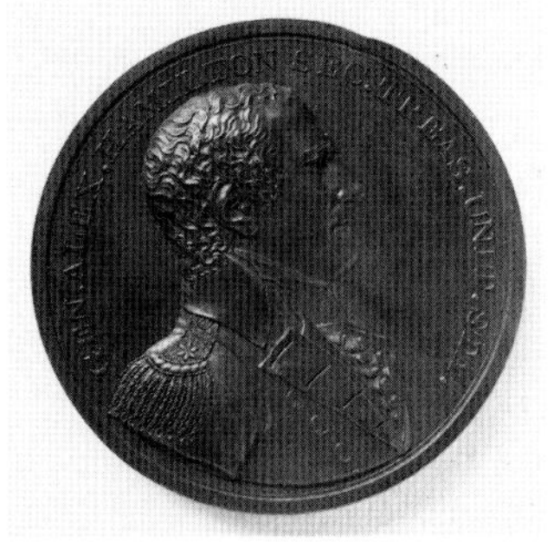
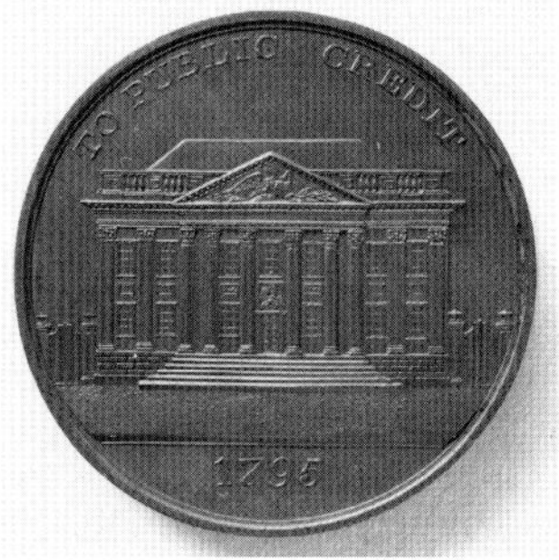

General Alexander Hamilton Medal
1808
Bronze with red-brown patina; cast about 1860
1¹⁵⁄₁₆″ diam. (4.9 cm)
Signed on obverse on truncation: F
Signed on reverse on line separating building from exergue at left: F
Inscribed on obverse around edge: GEN.ALEX.HAMILTON SEC.TREAS.UNIT.STA.
Inscribed on reverse around upper edge: TO PUBLIC CREDIT; in exergue: 1795
Cast by the Pennsylvania Academy from original dies in the collection, 1860.3

General Alexander Hamilton Medal
1808
Obverse of medal
Lead, cast about 1860
2″ diam. (5.1 cm)
Inscribed around edge: GEN.ALEX.HAMILTON SEC.TREAS.UNIT.STA.
Source unknown, 1986.x.37

General Alexander Hamilton Medal
1808
Reverse of medal
Lead, cast about 1860
1¹⁵⁄₁₆″ diam. (4.9 cm)
Inscribed around upper edge: TO PUBLIC CREDIT; in exergue: 1795
Source unknown, 1986.x.38

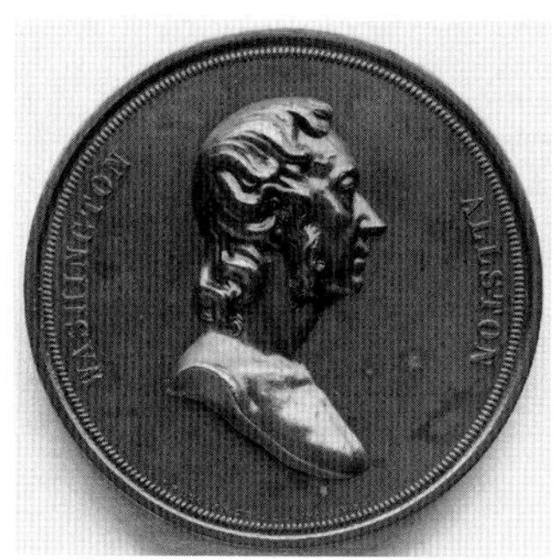
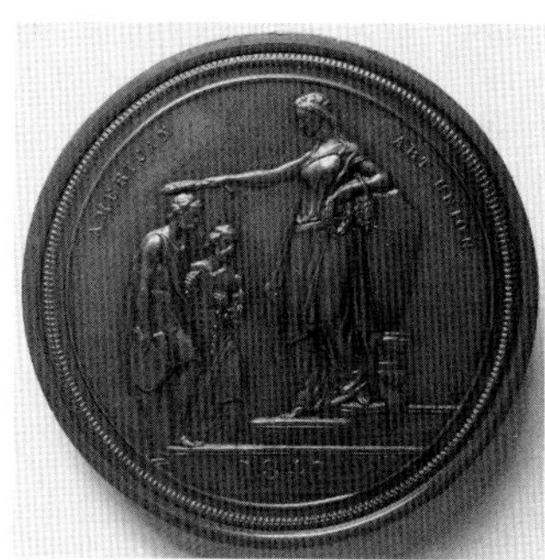

CHARLES CUSHING WRIGHT, 1796–1854
PAUL PETER DUGGAN, before 1810–1861

The Washington Allston Medal
1847
Bronze with red-brown patina
2½″ diam. (6.4 cm)
Signed on obverse around lower edge: P.P.DUGGAN DEL. C.C. WRIGHT SC.
Signed on reverse under steps: P.P.DUGGAN DEL./CC WRIGHT S^{c}; dated in exergue: 1847
Inscribed on obverse around edge: WASHINGTON ALLSTON
Inscribed on reverse around upper edge: AMERICAN ART-UNION
Source unknown, 1986.x.18

The Washington Allston Medal
1847
Bronze with brown patina
2½″ diam. (6.4 cm)
Signed on obverse around lower edge: P.P.DU[GGAN DEL. C.C. WRIGHT SC.]
Signed on reverse under steps: P.P.DUGGAN DEL./CC WRIGHT S^{c}; dated in exergue: 1847
Inscribed on obverse around edge: WASHINGTON ALLSTON
Inscribed on reverse around upper edge: AMERICAN ART-UNION
Source unknown, 1986.x.19

WILLIAM H. KEY, about 1828–1900

National School of Elocution and Oratory
J.A. Price Medal
About 1873
Bronze with brown patina

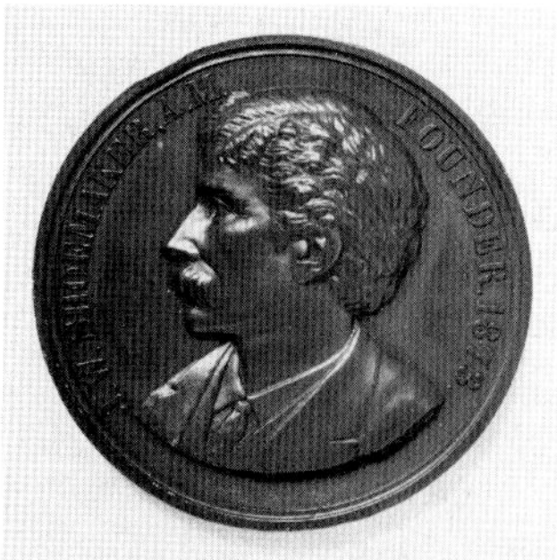
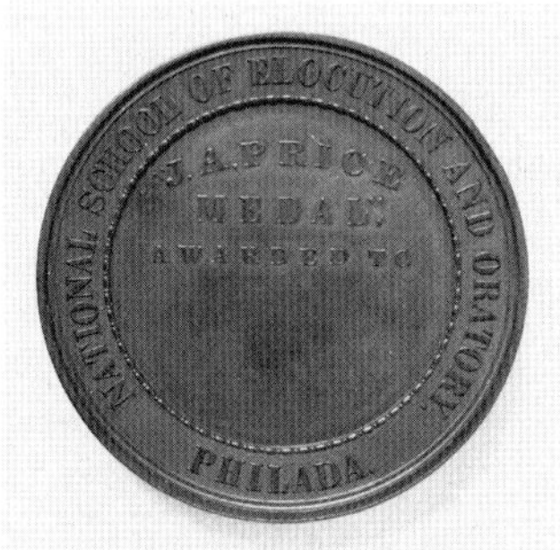

1⁹⁄₁₆″ diam. (4 cm)
Signed on obverse on truncation: KEY F.
Inscribed on obverse around left edge: J.W. SHOEMAKER, A.M.; around right edge: FOUNDER, 1873.
Inscribed on reverse around edge: NATIONAL SCHOOL OF ELOCUTION AND ORATORY.; at lower edge: PHILADA.; in upper center: "J.A. PRICE/MEDAL,"/AWARDED TO
Gift of Col. J.A. Price, 1881.7

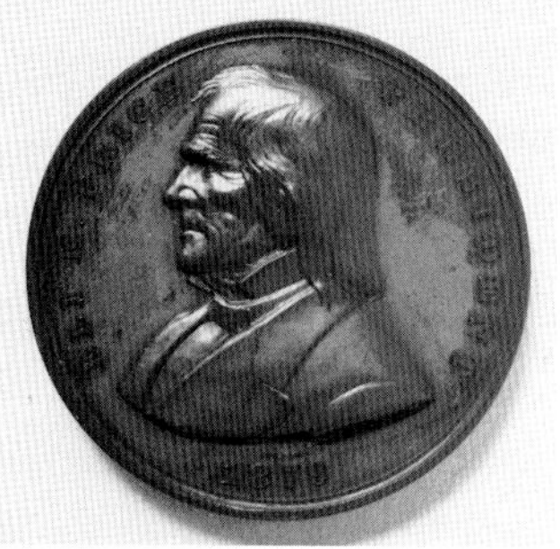
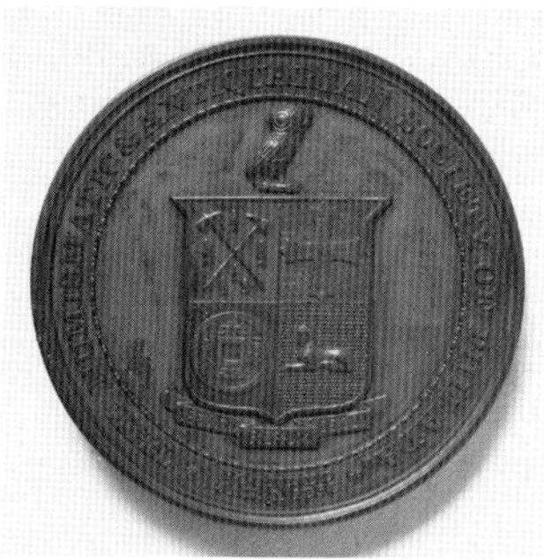

Eli Kirk Price Numismatic and Antiquarian Society Medal
1879
Bronze with red-brown patina
1⅝″ diam. (4.1 cm)
Signed on obverse on truncation: W.H. KEY F.
Inscribed on obverse around upper edge: ELI K. PRICE PRESIDENT; at lower edge: 1879
Inscribed on reverse around edge: THE NUMISMATIC & ANTIQUARIAN SOCIETY OF PHILADA.; at lower edge: FOUNDED/JAN.1.1858.; on ribbon below shield: VESTIGIA/RERUM/SEQUI [Follow the course of events]
Gift of Henry M. Phillips, 1879.11

HENRY MITCHELL, about 1835–1909

The Corcoran Gallery of Art Gold Medal
1884 and 1906
Gold
2¹⁄₁₆″ diam. (5.2 cm)
Signed on obverse at lower right: HENRY MITCHELL, SC.
Inscribed on obverse around edge: EXHIBITION • CONTEMPORARY • AMERICAN • OIL • PAINTINGS •

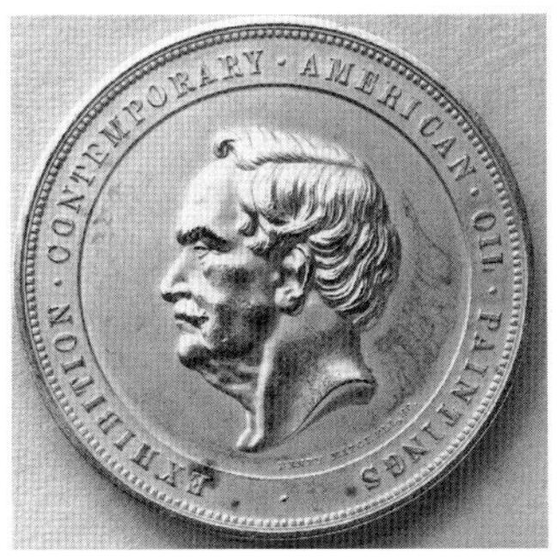

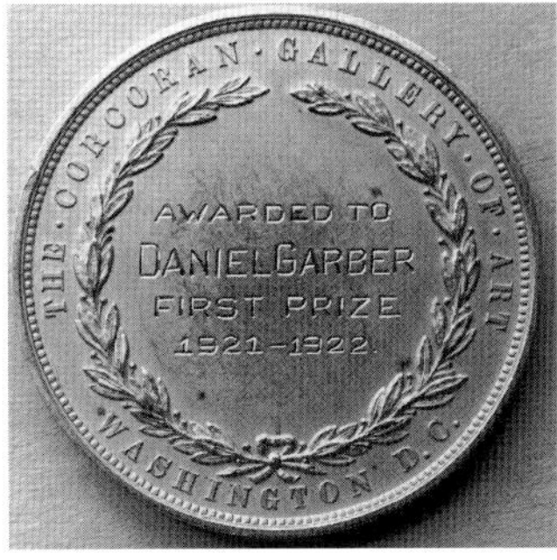

Inscribed on reverse around upper edge: THE · CORCORAN · GALLERY · OF · ART; at lower edge: WASHINGTON D.C.; engraved in center: AWARDED TO DANIEL GARBER/FIRST PRIZE/1921–22.
Gift of John Franklin Garber and Tanis Page, 1979.3.6

The Corcoran Gallery of Art Silver Medal
1884 and 1906
Silver
2¹⁄₁₆″ diam. (5.2 cm)
Signed on obverse at lower right: HENRY MITCHELL, SC.
Inscribed on obverse around edge: EXHIBITION · CONTEMPORARY · AMERICAN · OIL · PAINTINGS ·
Inscribed on reverse around upper edge: THE · CORCORAN · GALLERY · OF · ART; at lower edge: WASHINGTON D.C.; engraved in center: AWARDED/TO/DANIEL GARBER/SECOND/PRIZE/DECEMBER 1912
Gift of John Franklin Garber and Tanis Page, 1979.3.3

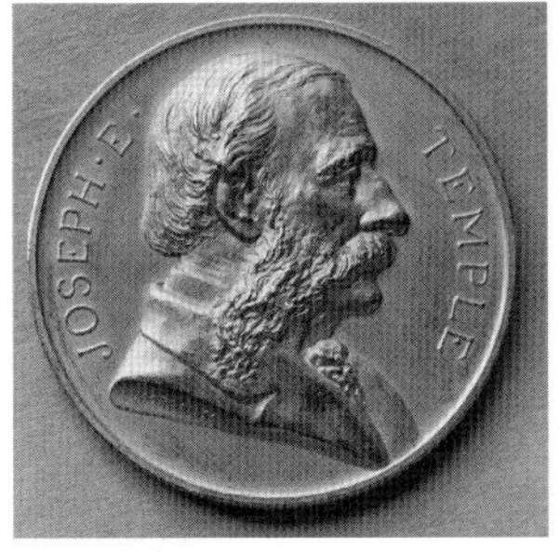

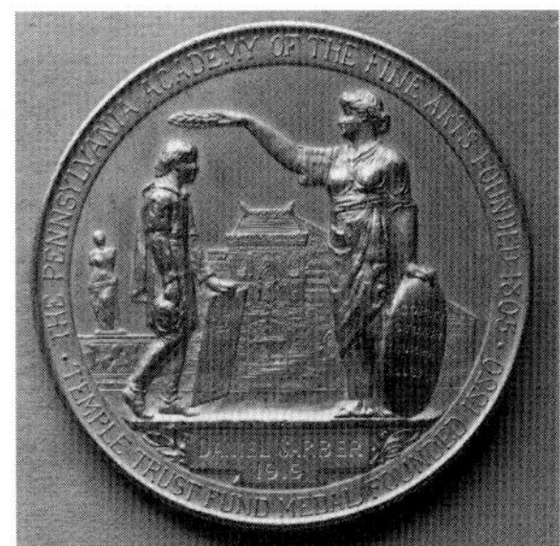

George T. Morgan, 1845–1925

Temple Trust Fund Medal
1883
Gold, struck about 1919
2⅛″ diam. (5.4 cm)
Signed on obverse on truncation of bust: MORGAN Sc.
Inscribed on obverse around edge: JOSEPH · E · TEMPLE
Inscribed on reverse around upper edge: THE PENNSYLVANIA ACADEMY OF THE FINE ARTS FOUNDED 1805; around lower edge: TEMPLE TRUST FUND MEDAL FOUNDED 1880; on shield: COPLEY/STUART/TRUMBULL/ALLSTON; engraved in exergue: DANIEL GARBER/1919
Gift of John Franklin Garber and Tanis Page, 1979.3.5

Temple Trust Fund Medal
1883
Zinc alloy
2⅛″ diam. (5.4 cm)
Inscribed as above, without engraving
Gift of the artist, 1885.5

Temple Trust Fund Medal
1883
Bronze with red-brown patina
2⅛″ diam. (5.4 cm)
Inscribed as above
Source unknown, 1986.x.20

Temple Trust Fund Medal
1883
Bronze with red-brown patina
2⅛″ diam. (5.4 cm)
Inscribed as above
Source unknown, 1986.x.21

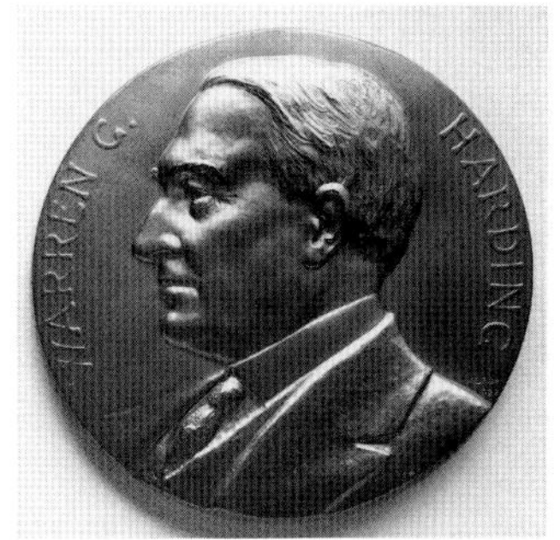

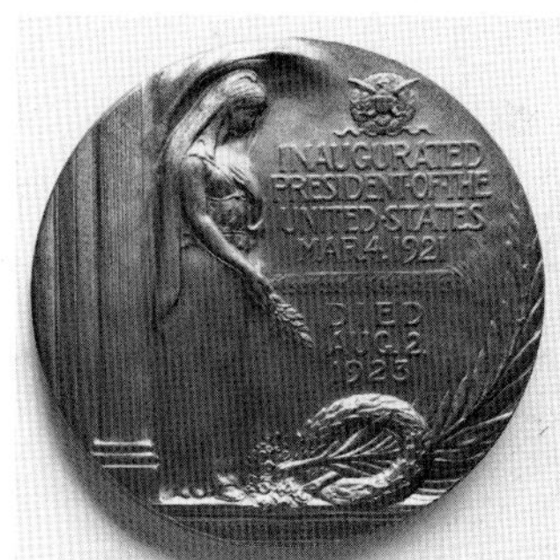

Warren G. Harding Presidential Medal
1922–23
Bronze with gold patina
3″ diam. (7.6 cm)
Signed and dated on obverse at lower right: MORGAN/1922
Signed on reverse at lower center: · · MORGAN · ·
Inscribed on obverse around edge: WARREN G. HARDING
Inscribed on reverse: INAUGURATED/PRESIDENT · OF · THE/UNITED · STATES/MAR.4.1921/DIED/AUG.2./1923
Source unknown, 1986.x.31

Attributed to Henry J. Ellicott, 1847–1901

Commemorative Medal of the 50th Anniversary of the Monument Cemetery
1888
Bronze with brown patina
2¼″ diam. (5.7 cm)
Inscribed on obverse around edge: JOHN SARTAIN PRESIDENT 1888
Inscribed on reverse: COMMEMORATIVE/OF THE 50TH/ANNIVERSARY OF THE/MONUMENT/CEMETERY; in the

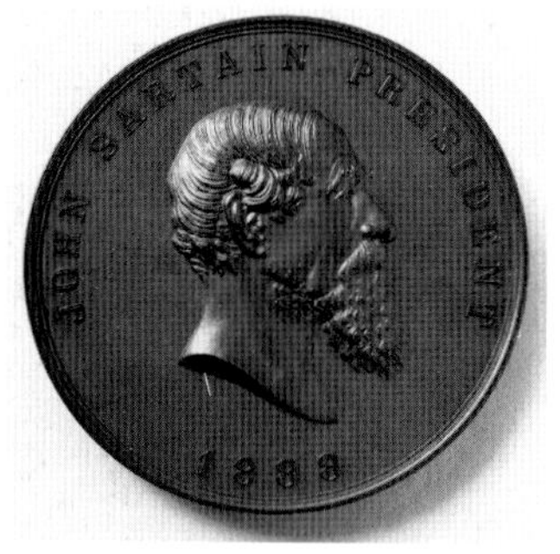

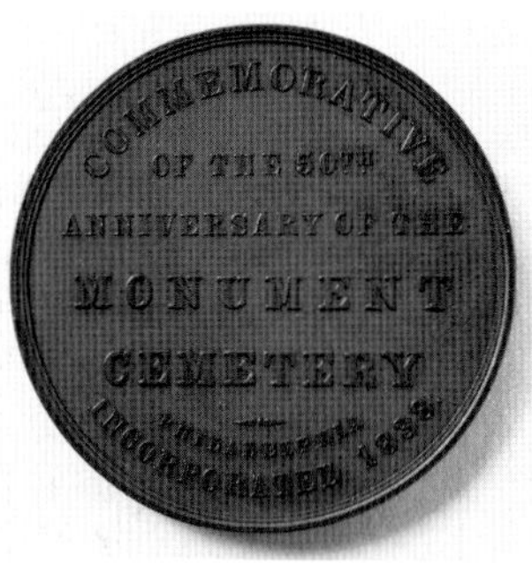

exergue: PHILADELPHIA/INCORPORATED 1838.
Gift of the artist, 1891.17

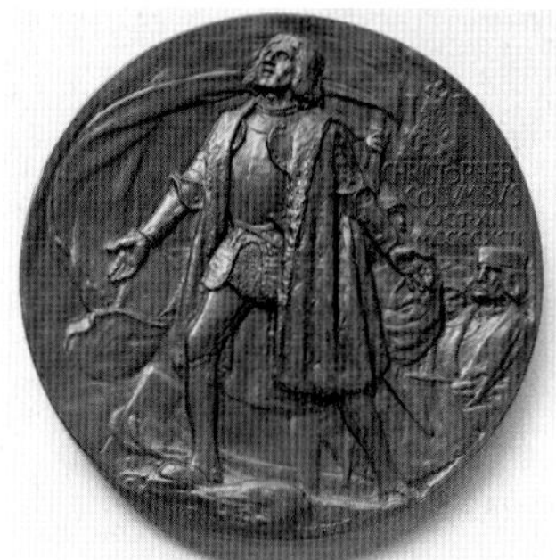

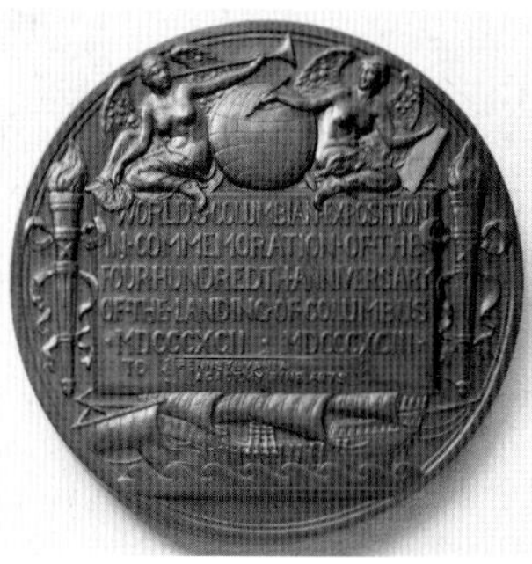

Augustus Saint-Gaudens, 1848–1907
Charles E. Barber, 1840–1917

World's Columbian Exposition Commemorative Presentation Medal
1892–94
Bronze
3″ diam. (7.6 cm)
Signed on obverse at bottom center: AVGVSTVS·SAINT·GAVDENS·FECIT
Signed (engraved) on reverse at bottom center: C.E. BARBER. FECIT
Inscribed on obverse at upper right: PLVS/VLTRA/CHRISTOPHER/COLVMBVS/OCT.XII/MCCCCXCII
Inscribed on reverse at center: WORLD'S·COLUMBIAN·EXPOSITION/IN·COMMEMORATION·OF·THE/FOUR·HUNDREDTH·ANNIVERSARY/OF·THE·LANDING·OF·COLUMBUS/·MDCCCXCII·MDCCCXCIII·/TO; on plate in relief: PENNSYLVANIA/ACADEMY FINE ARTS
Presented to the Pennsylvania Academy for its school exhibition at the World's Columbian Exposition, 1986.x.22

Daniel Dupuis, 1849–1899

Pennsylvania Academy Gold Medal of Honor
1893
Gold
2½″ diam. (6.4 cm)

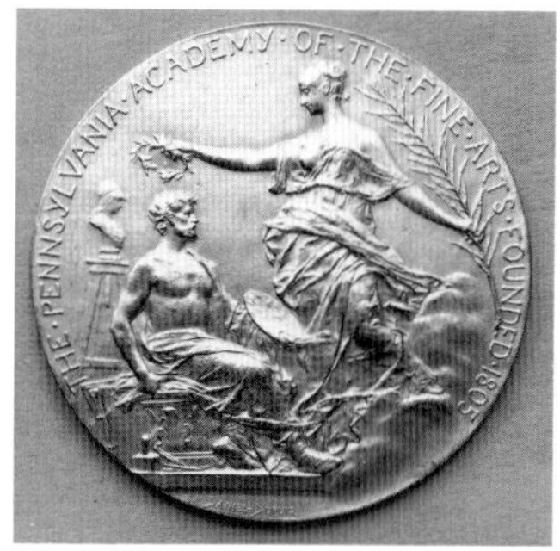

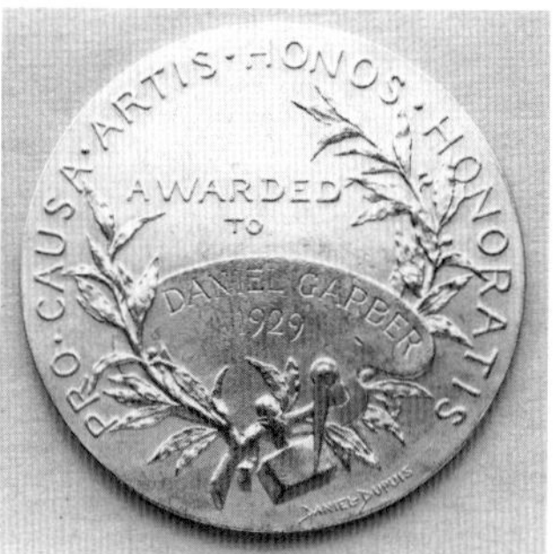

Signed on obverse and reverse at lower edge: DANIEL-DUPUIS
Inscribed on obverse around edge: THE·PENNSYLVANIA·ACADEMY·OF·THE·FINE·ARTS·FOUNDED·1805
Inscribed on reverse around edge: PRO·CAUSA·ARTIS·HONOS·HONORATIS; at center: AWARDED/TO; engraved: DANIEL GARBER/ 1929
Gift of John Franklin Garber and Tanis Page, 1979.3.9

John Joseph Boyle, 1851–1917

Art Club of Philadelphia Medal
About 1890
Gold
1¾″ diam. (4.4 cm)
Signed on reverse below left foot of figure: Boyle
Inscribed on obverse at left edge: ARS; at right edge: OPUS; within ribbon motif at left: PAINTING/SCULPTURE/ARCHITECTURE

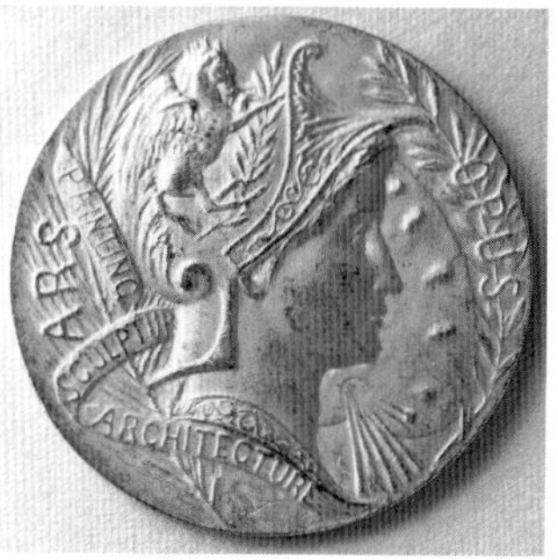

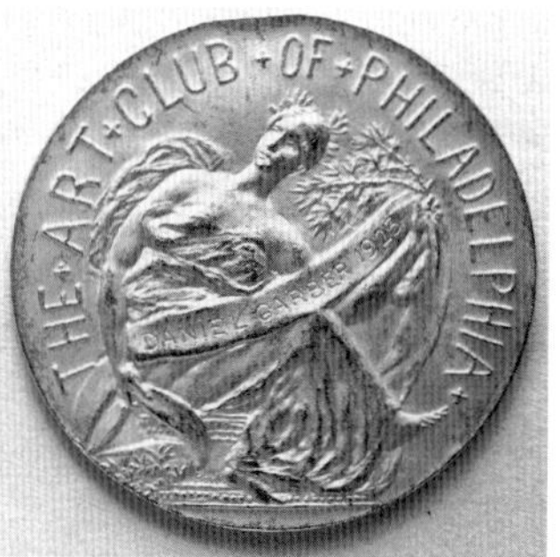

Inscribed on reverse around upper edge: THE + ART + CLUB + OF + PHILADELPHIA +; engraved around figure holding a banner: DANIEL GARBER 1923
Gift of John Franklin Garber and Tanis Page, 1979.3.8

Carol H. Beck Gold Medal
1909
Bronze with brown patina
2″ diam. (5.1 cm)
Signed and dated on obverse in exergue: ·MDCCCCIX·/J.J. Boyle

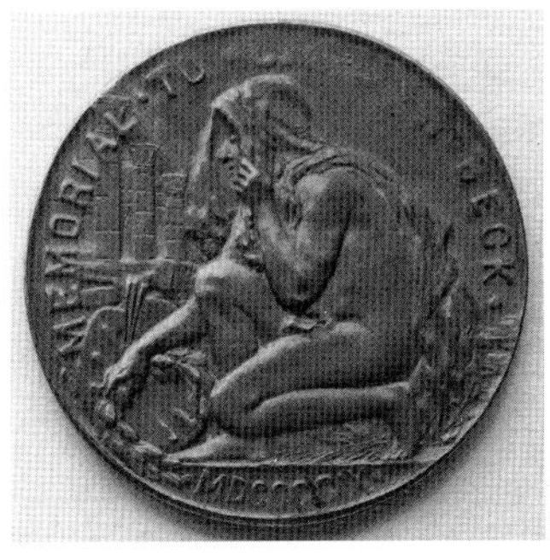

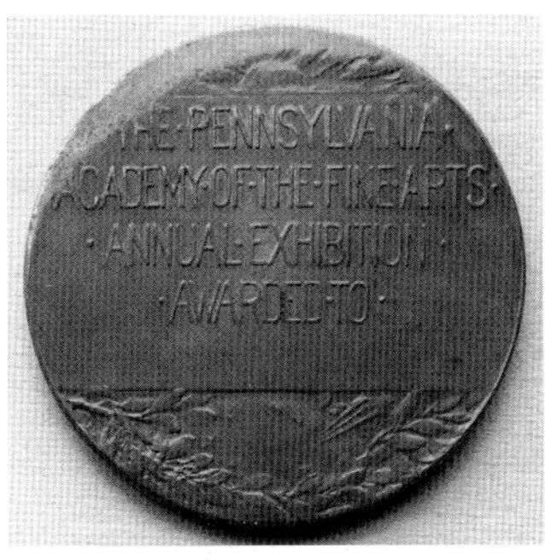

Inscribed on obverse in exergue: MEMORIAL·TO·BECK
Inscribed on reverse at center: THE·PENNSYLVANIA·/ ACADEMY·OF·THE·FINE·ARTS·/·ANNUAL· EXHIBITION·/·AWARDED·TO·
Source unknown, 1986.x.26

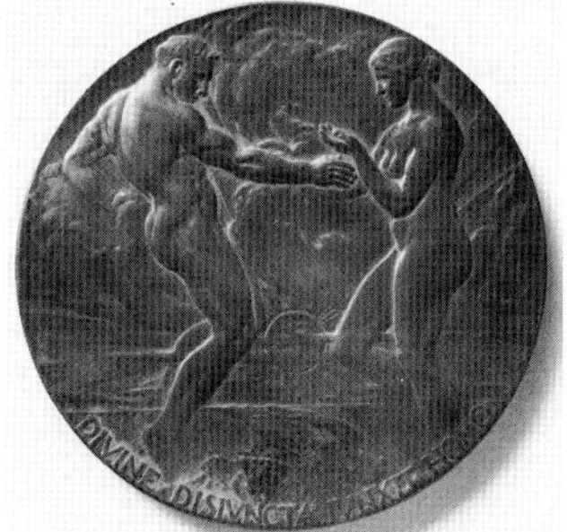
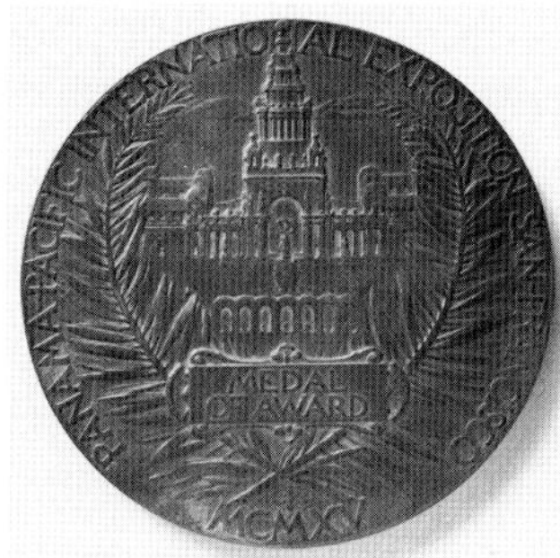

John Flanagan, 1865–1952

Panama-Pacific International Exposition Medal of Award
1915
Bronze with brown patina
2¾″ diam. (7 cm)
Signed on obverse within last O of inscription: JF
Inscribed on obverse around lower edge: DIVINE DISIVNCTA IVNXIT HOMO [Divinely separated, humanly joined]
Inscribed on reverse around edge: PANAMA-PACIFIC INTERNATIONAL EXPOSITION SAN-FRANCISCO/ MCMXV; in lower center: MEDAL/OF AWARD
Gift of John Franklin Garber and Tanis Page, 1979.3.4

Panama-Pacific International Exposition Medal of Award
1915
Bronze with brown patina
2¾″ diam. (7 cm)
Inscribed as above
Source unknown, 1986.x.27

The Joseph Pennell Memorial Medal
1928
Bronze with gold patina
2¾″ diam. (7 cm)

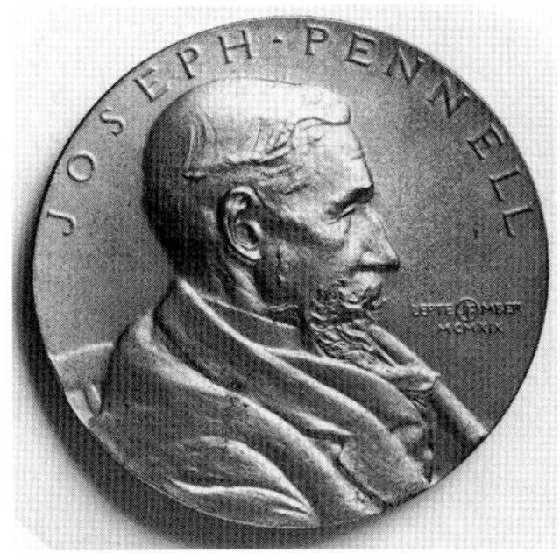

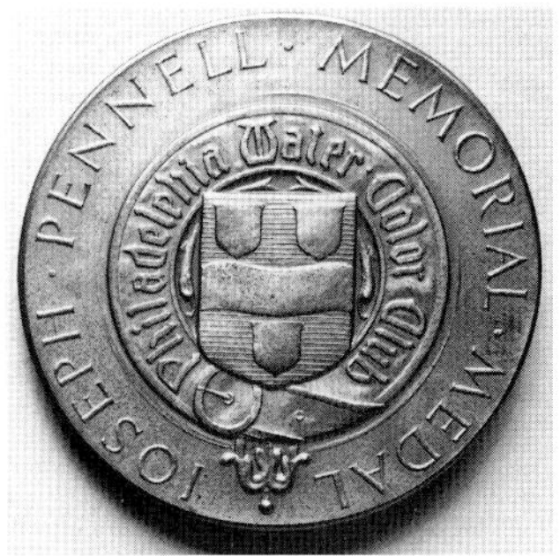

Signed and dated on obverse (artist's initials within a circle surrounded by name of month): SEPTEJFMBER/ MCMXIX [S is reversed]
Inscribed on obverse around upper edge: JOSEPH▲PENNELL
Inscribed on reverse around edge: IOSEPH·PENNELL· MEMORIAL·MEDAL; at center around shield: Philadelphia Water·Color·Club
Engraved on rim: DANIEL GARBER 1942
Gift of John Franklin Garber and Tanis Page, 1979.3.11

Hermon Atkins MacNeil, 1866–1947

Medal of Honor for Sculpture, Architectural League of New York
1909
Gold
2½″ diam. (6.4 cm)
Signed on obverse at lower right: H.A.MacNeil/FECIT
Signed on reverse at lower right: H.A.MAC
Inscribed on obverse across center field: STATVARIÆ ARTIS/PER IT ISSIMO

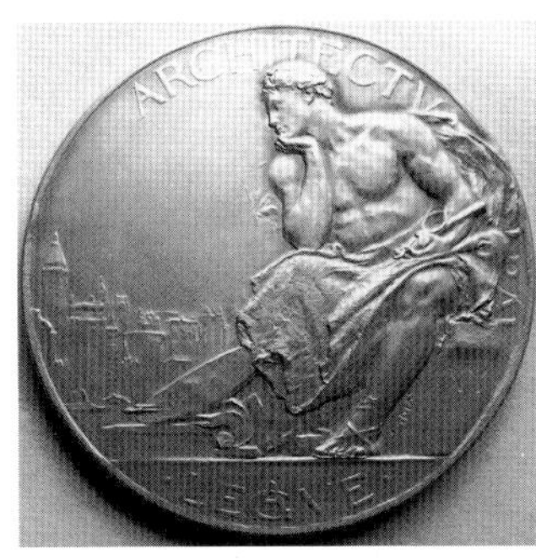
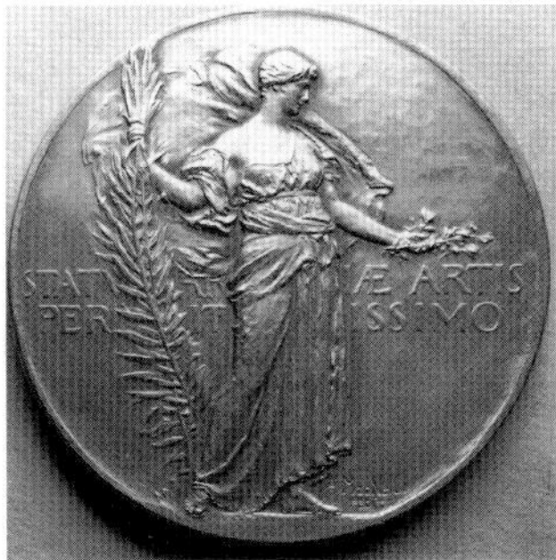

Inscribed on reverse around top edge: ARCHITECTVRAL; in exergue: ·LEAGVE· (A and G are intertwined); on throne at lower right: NY
Engraved on rim: A. STIRLING CALDER 1932
Gift of Margaret Calder Hayes, 1986.54

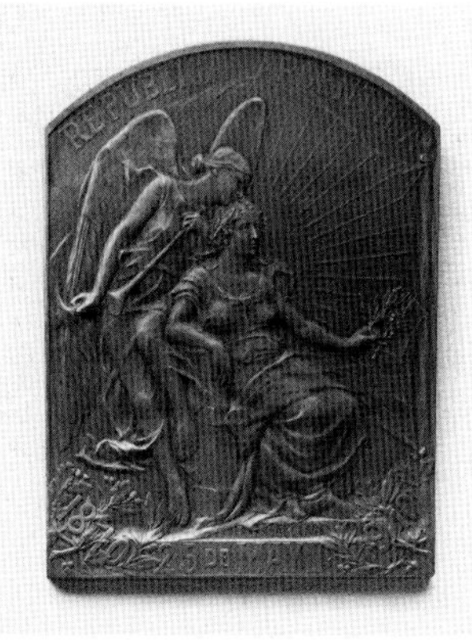
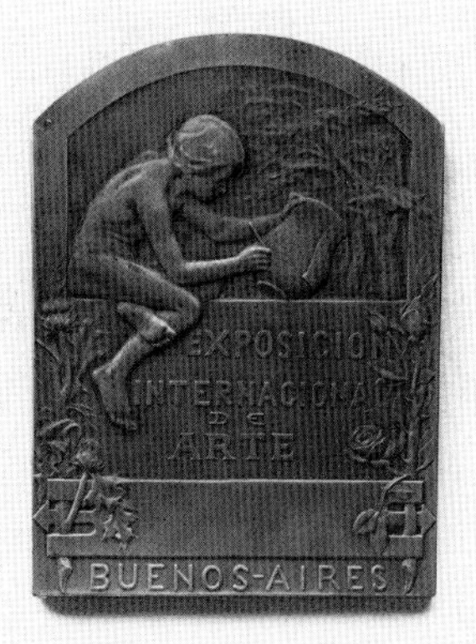

Ernesto De la Carcova, 1867–1927

Buenos-Aires Exposicion International de Arte Medal
1910
Bronze with brown patina
3½ x 2⅝" (8.9 x 6.7 cm)
Signed on obverse and reverse at lower right: E DELA CARCOVA
Inscribed on obverse at upper edge: REPUBLICA ARGENTINA at upper right: RA; at center of lower edge: 25 DE MAYO; at lower left: 1810; at lower right: 1910
Inscribed on reverse at center: EXPOSICION/ INTERNACIONAL/DE/ARTE; at lower edge: BUENOS-AIRES
Foundry mark on lower rim: ▲BRONZE
Gift of John Franklin Garber and Tanis Page, 1979.3.1

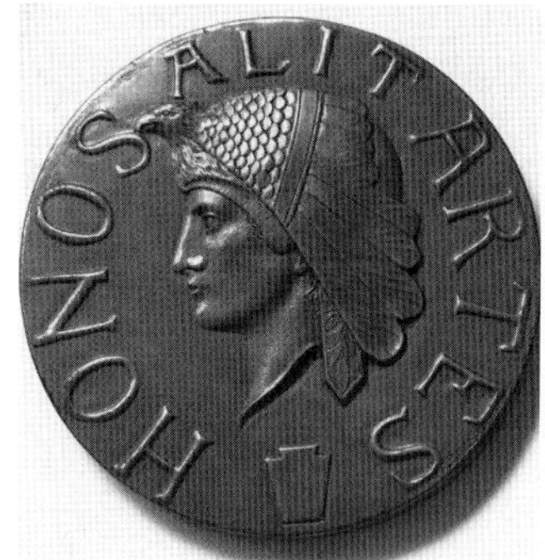
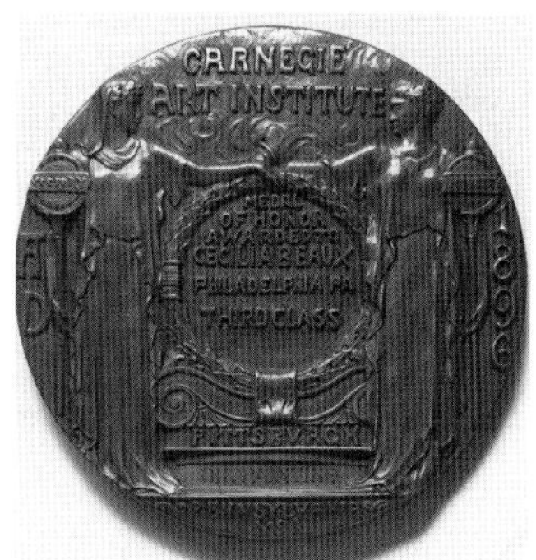

Kate Wilson, active about 1896–1931

Carnegie Art Institute Medal of Honor of the Third Class
1896
Bronze with brown patina
3 7/16" diam. (8.7 cm)
Signed on obverse: F.K. WILSON
Inscribed on obverse around edge: HONOS ALIT ARTES
Inscribed on reverse at top center: CARNEGIE/ART INSTITUTE; at left edge: VICTORY/A/D; at right edge: INDUSTRY/1/8/9/6; in center, on six lines: MEDAL/OF HONOR/AWARDED TO/CECILIA BEAUX/PHILADELPHIA PA/THIRD CLASS; beneath scroll: PITTSBVRGH; engraved: OIL PAINTING; inscribed in exergue: PENNSYLVANIA/VSA
Gift of Cecilia D. Saltonstall, 1988.17.2

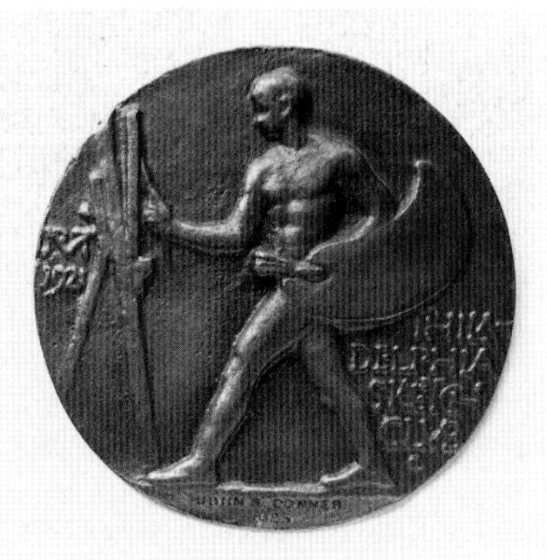

R. Tait McKenzie, 1867–1938

Philadelphia Sketch Club Medal of Honor
1921
Bronze with brown patina; cast in 1925
3¾" diam. (9.5 cm)
Signed and dated in monogram at left: RTM/1921
Inscribed at lower right: PHILA-/DELPHIA/SKETCH/CLVB; engraved at lower center: JOHN R. CONNER/1925
Source unknown, 1986.x.30

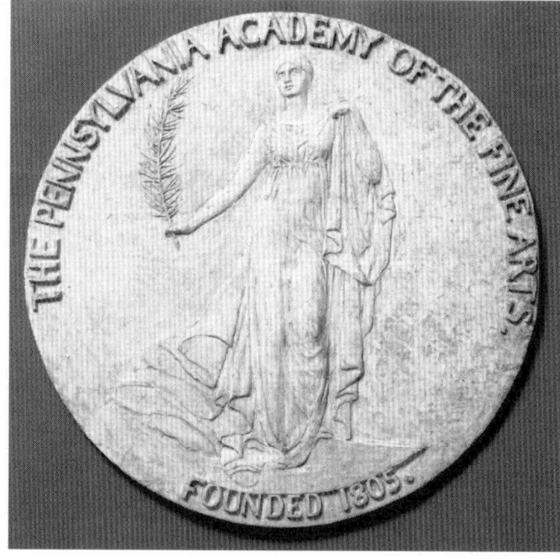

Mary P. Middleton
(Mrs. Albert Laessle, 1870–1944)

Sketch model for obverse of the Jennie Sesnan Prize
1902
Plaster
15" diam. (38.1 cm)
Signed on reverse: M.P. Middleton/1004 Chestnut St/ Phila
Inscribed in relief on obverse around upper edge: THE PENNSYLVANIA ACADEMY OF THE FINE ARTS.; in relief at lower center: FOUNDED 1805.
Source unknown, 1970.15

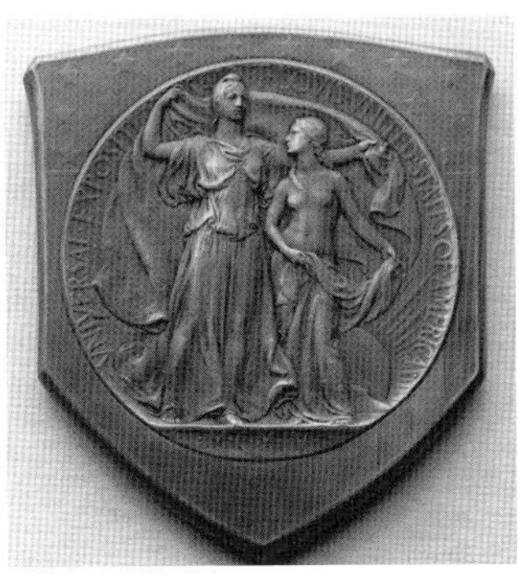

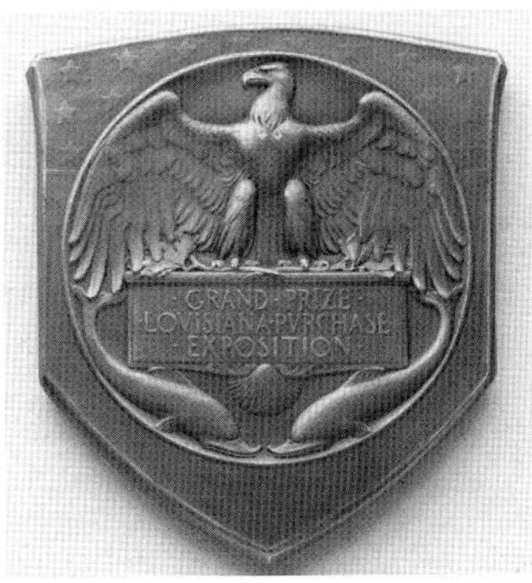

ADOLPH A. WEINMAN, 1870–1952

Louisiana Purchase Exposition Grand Prize Medal
1904
Bronze with brown patina
$2\frac{15}{16}$ x $2\frac{9}{16}$″ (7.5 x 6.5 cm)
Signed on obverse at lower right: A.A. WEINMAN/FECT.; dated in exergue: ▼M▼C▼M▼IV▼
Inscribed on obverse around edge of circle: VNIVERSAL▼ EXPOSITIO[N▼]SAINT▼LOVIS▼VNITED▼STATES▼OF▼ AMERICA▼
Inscribed on reverse in center: ▼GRAND▼PRIZE▼/ ▼LOVISIANA▼PVRCHASE▼/▼EXPOSITION▼
Source unknown, 1986.x.25

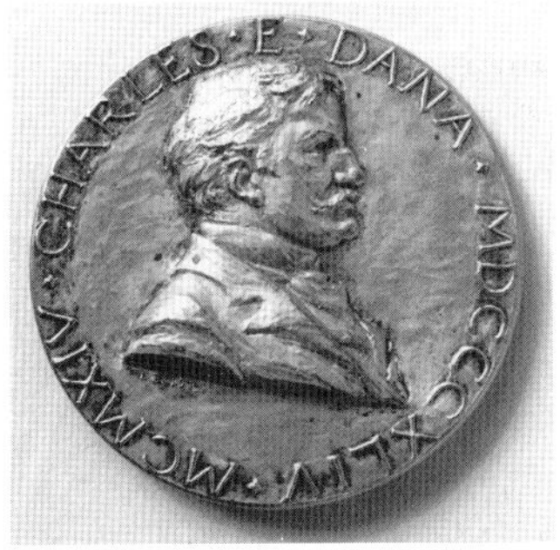

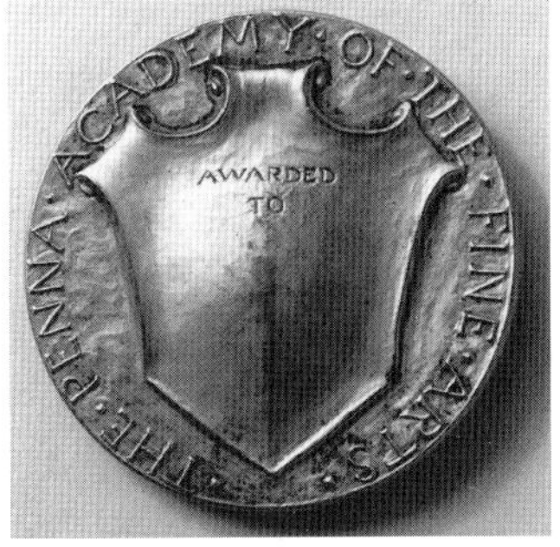

LOUISA EYRE, 1872–1952

Charles E. Dana Medal
1919
Bronze with brown patina; wood frame
$2\frac{1}{4}$″ diam. (5.7 cm), sight
Signed and dated below bust: L.E. 1919
Gift of Dr. Clark S. Marlor, 1990.11

ADAM PIETZ, 1873–1961

Locust Club Medal
1923
Gold
2″ diam. (5.1 cm)

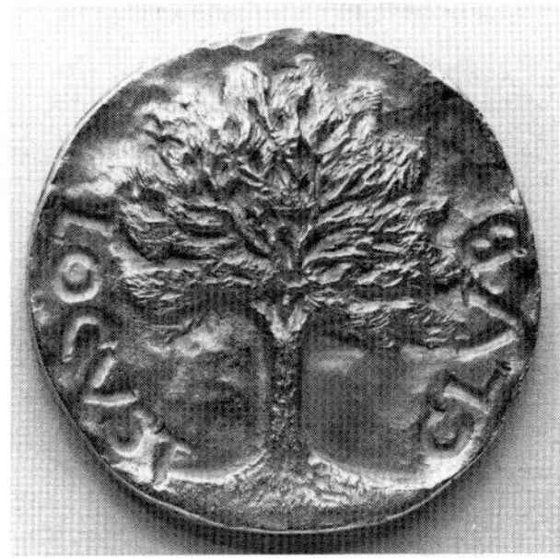

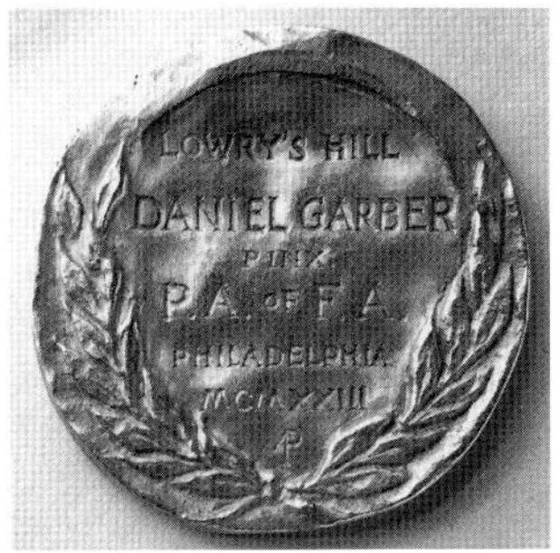

Signed (in monogram) on reverse at lower center: AP
Inscribed on obverse around edge: LOCVST CLVB
Engraved on reverse: LOWRY'S HILL/DANIEL GARBER/ PINX./P.A. OF F.A./PHILADELPHIA/MCMXXIII
Gift of John Franklin Garber and Tanis Page, 1979.3.7

HANS SCHULER, 1874–1951

The One Hundredth Anniversary Medal of the Maryland Institute
1925
Bronze with brown patina
2″ diam. (5.1 cm)
Signed (in monogram) on obverse at lower left: HS

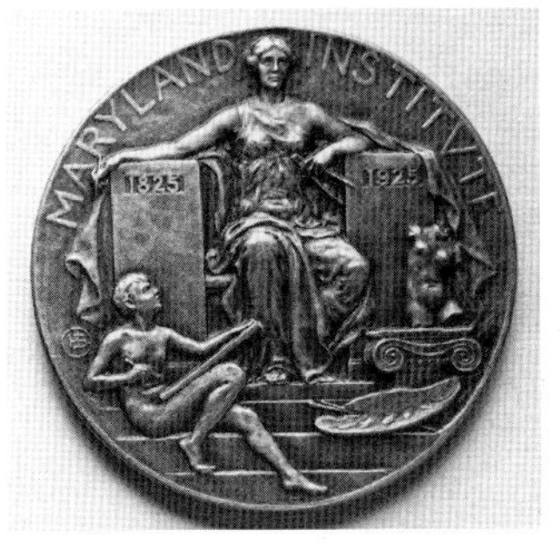

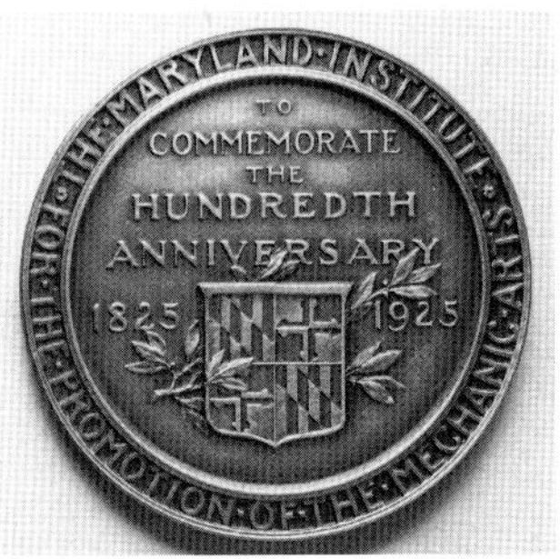

Inscribed on obverse around top edge: MARYLAND INSTITVTE; on throne: 1825–1925
Inscribed on reverse around upper edge: ⋆THE·MARYLAND ·INSTITUTE⋆; around lower edge: FOR·THE· PROMOTION·OF·THE·MECHANIC·ARTS; in center: TO/ COMMEMORATE/THE/HUNDREDTH/ANNIVERSARY/ 1825 1925
Foundry mark on rim: MEDALLIC ART CO. NY.
Gift of the Maryland Institute, 1925.17

The Baltimore and Ohio Railroad Centenary Medal
1927
Bronze with brown patina
$2\frac{3}{4}$″ diam. (7 cm)
Signed (in monogram within circle) on obverse at left edge: HS

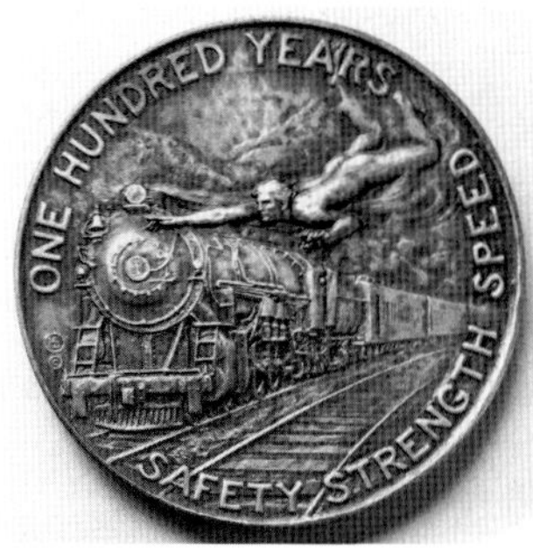

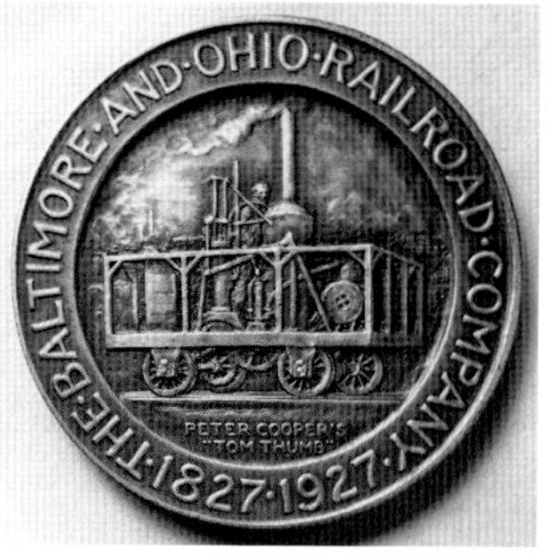

Inscribed on obverse around edge: ONE HUNDRED YEARS/ SAFETY STRENGTH SPEED; below monogram: ©
Inscribed on reverse around edge: THE · BALTIMORE · AND · OHIO · RAILROAD · COMPANY · /1827 · 1927 · ; in exergue: PETER COOPER'S/"TOM THUMB"
Foundry mark on rim: MEDALLIC ART CO. N.Y.
Gift of the Baltimore and Ohio Railroad Company, 1927.13

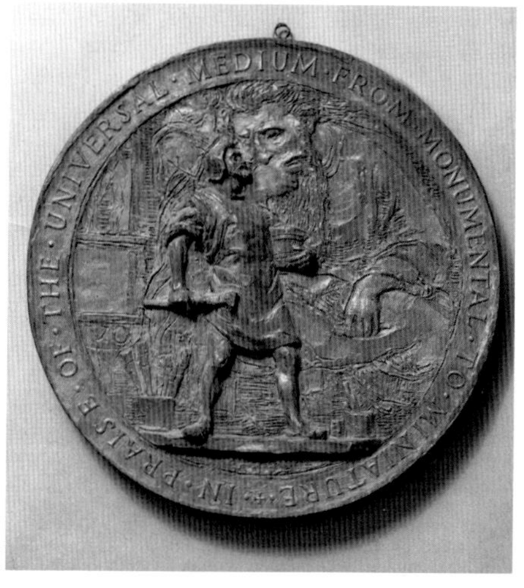

Violet Oakley, 1874–1961

Model for obverse of the Philadelphia Water Color Club Medal
1945
Plaster, painted blue, with gilding
13⅛" diam. (33.3 cm)
Signed at lower left: V.O.
Inscribed around edge: · IN · PRAISE · OF · THE · UNIVERSAL · MEDIUM · FROM · MONUMENTAL · TO · MINIATURE · +
Gift of the Philadelphia Water Color Club, 1945.25

The Philadelphia Water Color Club Medal
1945
Bronze with brown patina
3" diam. (7.6 cm)
Signed on obverse at left: V.O.

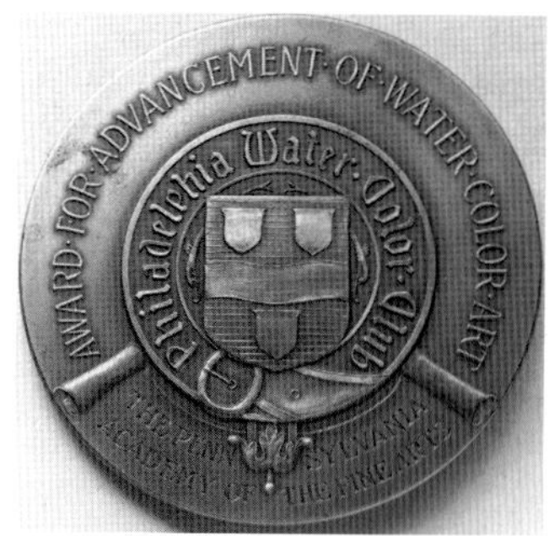

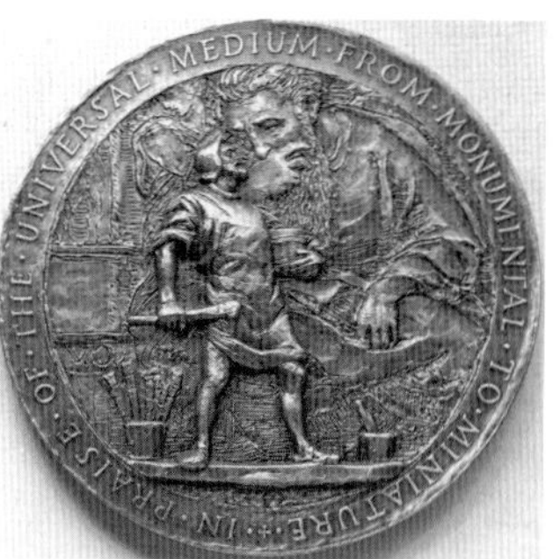

Inscribed on obverse around edge: · IN · PRAISE · OF · THE · UNIVERSAL · MEDIUM · FROM · MONUMENTAL · TO · MINIATURE · +
Inscribed on reverse around edge: AWARD · FOR · ADVANCEMENT · OF · WATER · COLOR · ART; around center shield: Philadelphia Water · Color · Club; engraved in exergue: THE PENNSYLVANIA/ACADEMY OF THE FINE ARTS
Foundry mark on rim: MEDALLIC ART CO. N.Y./BRONZE
Gift of the Philadelphia Water Color Club, 1945.19

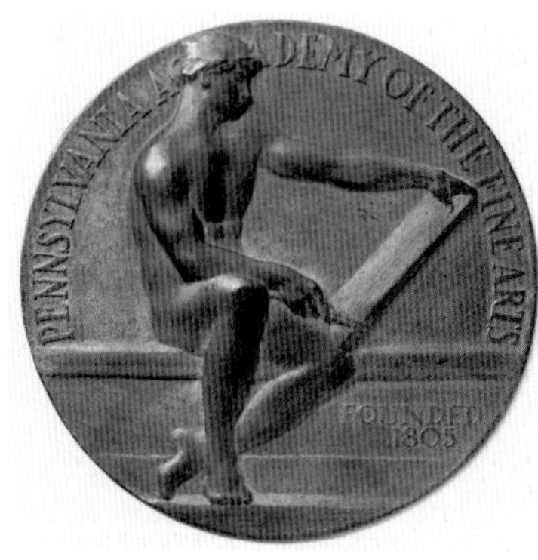

H. Lyman Saÿen, 1875–1918

Model for obverse of the Jennie Sesnan Prize
1902
Bronze with green patina
7⅛" diam. (18.1 cm)
Signed in exergue at lower right: H LYMAN SAYEN
Inscribed around upper edge: PENNSYLVANIA ACADEMY OF THE FINE ARTS; at lower right: FOUNDED/1805
Foundry mark on reverse: # 10.02
Gift of Ann Sayen, 1967.16

Model for obverse of the Jennie Sesnan Prize
1902
Bronze with brown patina
7" diam. (18 cm)
Signed in exergue at lower right: H LYMAN SAYEN
Inscribed around upper edge: PENNSYLVANIA ACADEMY OF THE FINE ARTS; at lower right: FOUNDED/1805
Source unknown, 1986.x.36

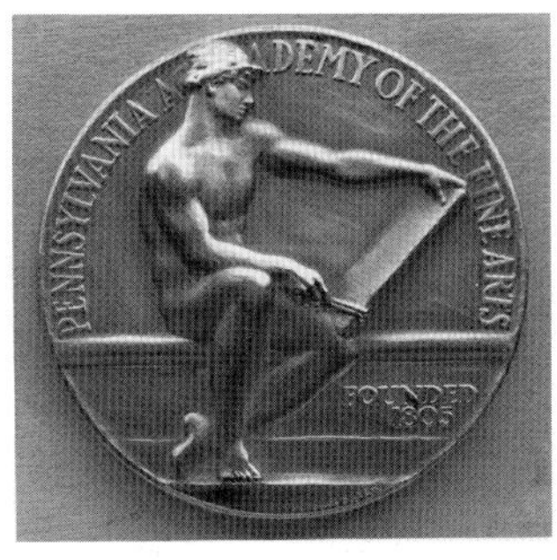

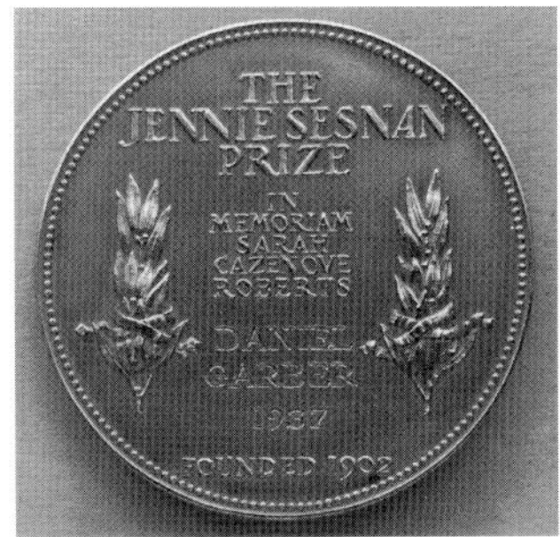

The Jennie Sesnan Prize
1902
Gold
1¾″ diam. (4.4 cm)
Signed on obverse in exergue at lower right: H LYMAN SAYEN
Inscribed on obverse around upper edge: PENNSYLVANIA ACADEMY OF THE FINE ARTS; at lower right: FOUNDED/1805
Inscribed on reverse on upper half: THE/JENNIE SESNAN/PRIZE/IN/MEMORIAM/SARAH/CAZENOVE/ROBERTS; engraved: DANIEL/GARBER/1937; at lower edge: FOUNDED 1902
Gift of John Franklin Garber and Tanis Page, 1979.3.10

The Jennie Sesnan Prize
1902
Bronze with brown patina
1¾″ diam. (4.4 cm)
Inscribed as above, without engraving
Source unknown, 1986.x.23

The Jennie Sesnan Prize
1902
Bronze with brown patina
1¾″ diam. (4.4 cm)
Inscribed as above
Source unknown, 1986.x.24

Joseph Maxwell Miller, 1877–1933

James Cardinal Gibbons Jubilee Medal
1911
Bronze with brown patina
2¾″ diam. (7 cm)
Signed on obverse at lower left: J M MILLER/-FECIT-
Inscribed on obverse around edge: JAMES CARDINAL GIBBONS
Inscribed on reverse around edge: SACERDOS [Ordination]· 30·JUN·1861 + EPISCOPUS [Bishop]·16·AUG·1868 ARCHIEPISCOPUS [Archbishop]·3·OCT·1877· CARDINALIS [Sacred College of Cardinals]· 30·JUN·1886; in exergue: 1861 1911/EMITTE/TUUM/SPIRITUM [Send forth thy spirit]
Foundry mark on rim: MEDALLIC ART CO. NY
Gift of Michael Jenkins, 1914.18

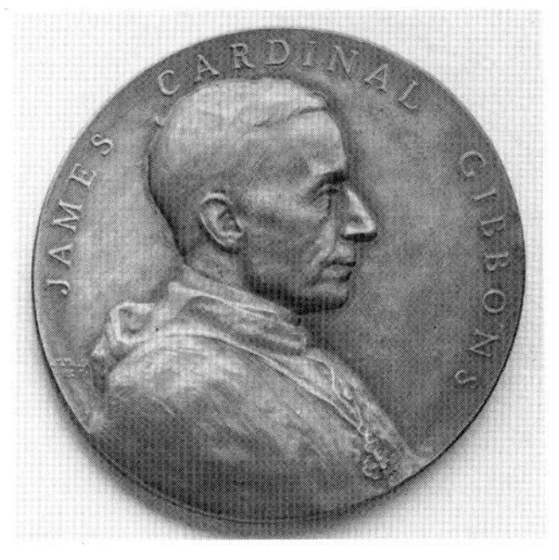

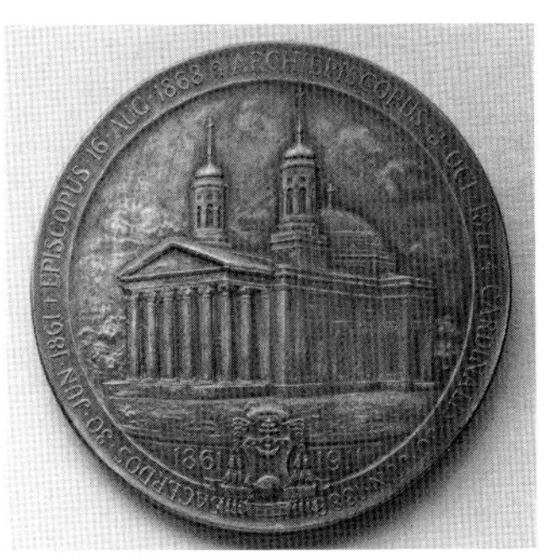

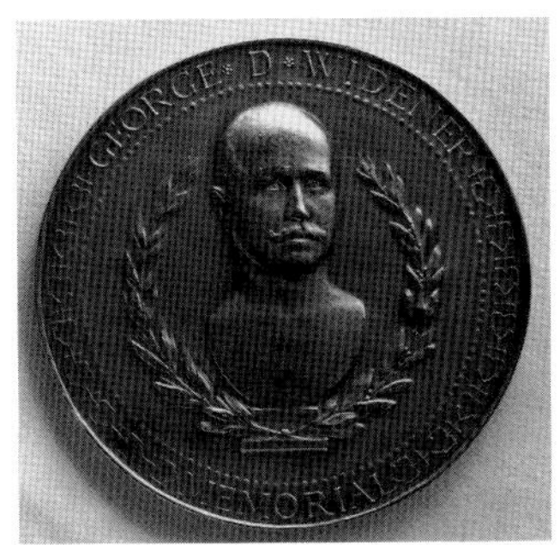

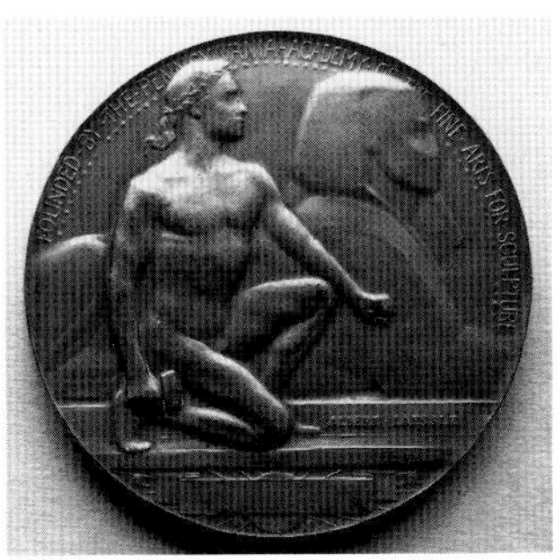

Albert Laessle, 1877–1954

George D. Widener Memorial Gold Medal
1916
Bronze with brown patina
2″ diam. (5.1 cm)
Signed on reverse at lower right: ALBERT·LAESSLE
Inscribed on obverse around edge: GEORGE*D*WIDENER/MEMORIAL
Inscribed on reverse around upper edge: FOUNDED-BY-THE-PENNSYLVANIA-ACADEMY-OF-THE-FINE-ARTS FOR SCULPTURE
Source unknown, 1986.x.28

Sesquicentennial Medal of Award
1926
Bronze with gold patina
3″ diam. (7.6 cm)
Signed on obverse at lower right: ALBERT LAESSLE
Inscribed on reverse around edge: ▲SESQUICENTENNIAL▲INTERNATIONAL▲EXPOSITION▲PHILADELPHIA▲/1776–1926; at center: MEDAL/OF AWARD
Foundry mark on rim: B.B.B. C^{O} PHILA
Source unknown, 1986.x.32

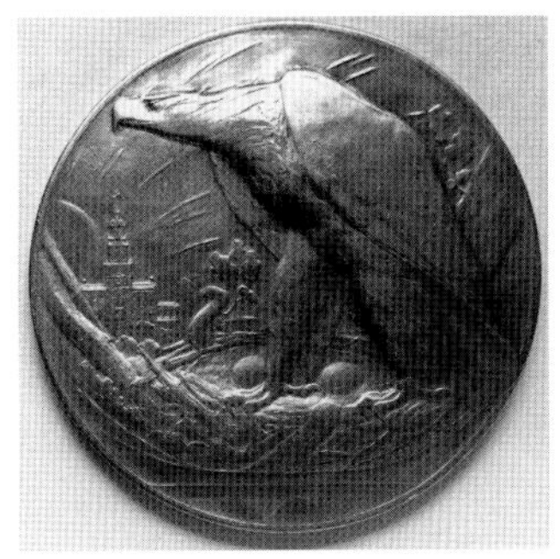

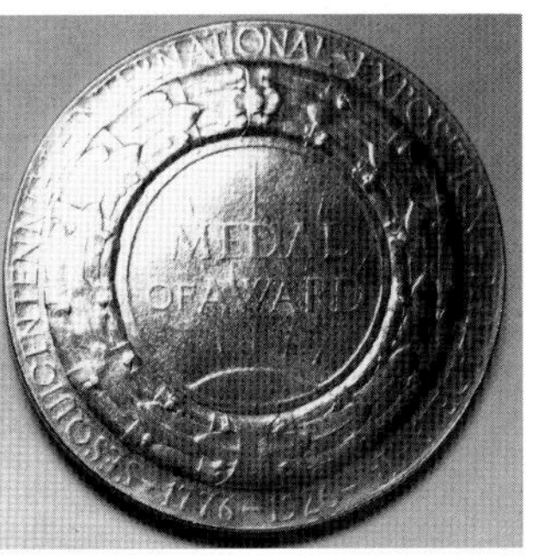

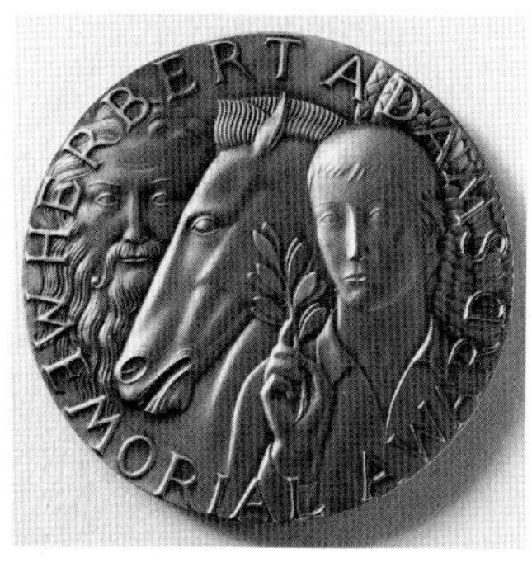

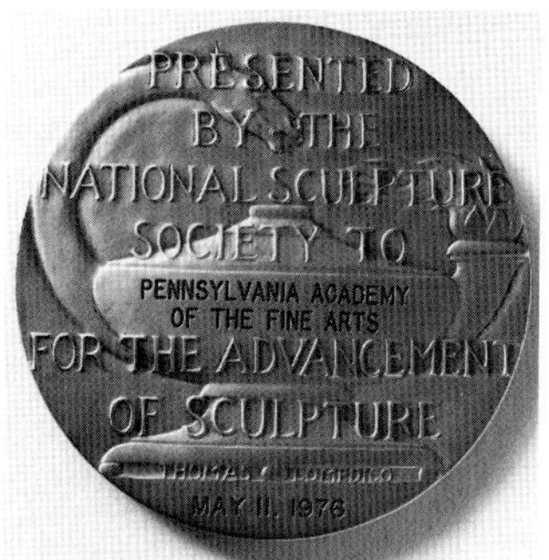

Thomas Lo Medico, 1904–1985

Herbert Adams Memorial Award
1946
Bronze with gold patina
2 11/16″ diam. (6.8 cm)
Signed on reverse above exergue: thomas lomedico
Inscribed on obverse around edge: herbert adams/memorial award
Inscribed on reverse: presented/by the/national sculpture/society to; engraved: pennsylvania academy/of the fine arts; inscribed: for the advancement/of sculpture; engraved in exergue below signature: may 11.1976
Foundry mark on rim: medallic art co. n.y./bronze
Gift of the National Sculpture Society, 1976.25

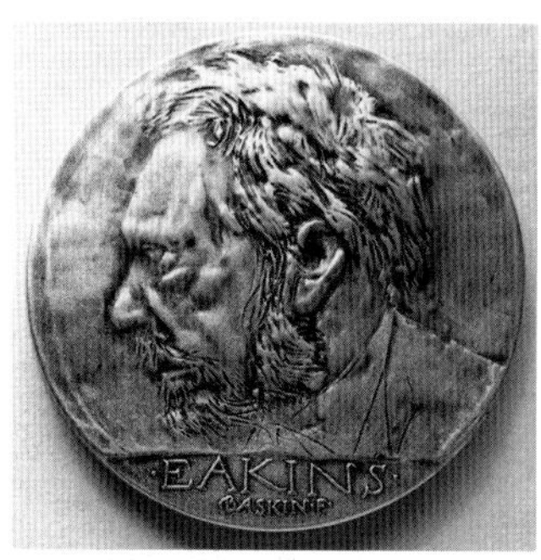

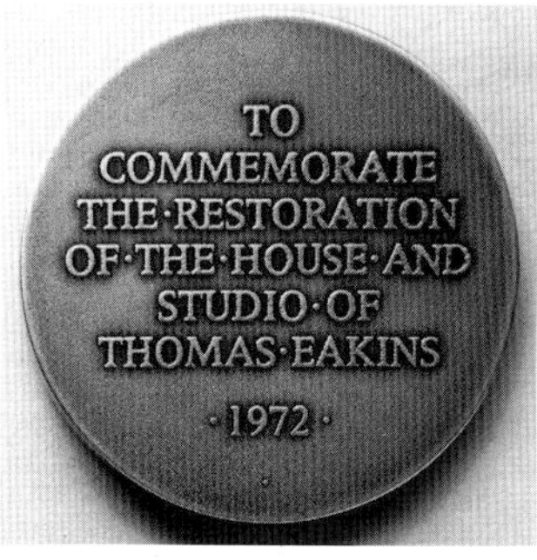

Leonard Baskin, b. 1922

Thomas Eakins Medal
1972
Silver
2 1/2″ diam. (6.4 cm)
Signed on obverse in exergue: baskin·f·
Inscribed on obverse above signature: ·eakins·
Inscribed on reverse: to/commemorate/the·restoration/of·the·house·and/studio·of/thomas·eakins/·1972·
Foundry mark on rim: sterling © F 72/0782
Gift of Seymour Adelman, 1973.5

Thomas Eakins Medal
1972
Silver
2 1/2″ diam. (6.4 cm)
Inscribed as above
Foundry mark on rim: sterling © F 72/0392
Source unknown, 1986.x.33

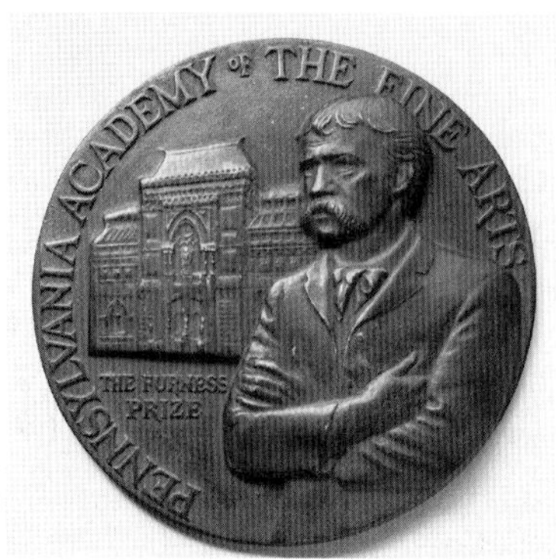

Alexander Hromych, b. 1940

Model for obverse of the Furness Prize
1976
Plaster, painted brown
7 5/16″ diam. (18.6 cm)
Signed (in monogram) at lower edge: AH
Inscribed around edge: pennsylvania academy of the fine arts; at lower left: the furness/prize
Source unknown, 1986.x.34

V. Conti, n.d.
After a design by Di Fausto, n.d.

Commemorative Medal of the Inauguration of the Fountain of the Sea Horses
1926
Bronze with brown patina
2 9/16″ diam. (6.5 cm)
Signed on obverse at lower left: di favsto·dis.; at lower right: d.conti·mod.
Inscribed on obverse around edge: to the american nation from the italian nation in the sesqvicentennial anniversary/of the declaration of independence-1776–1926

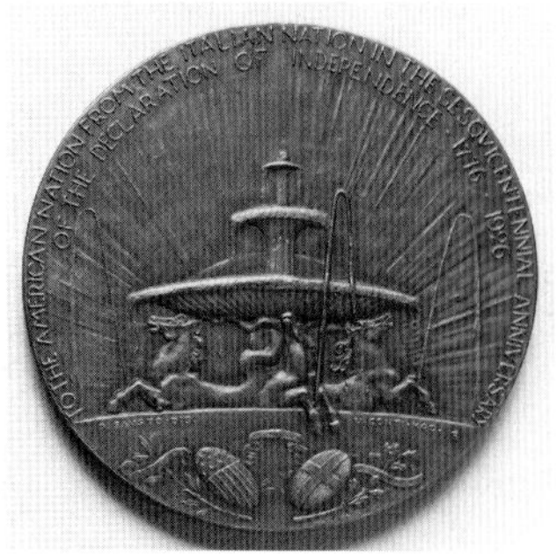

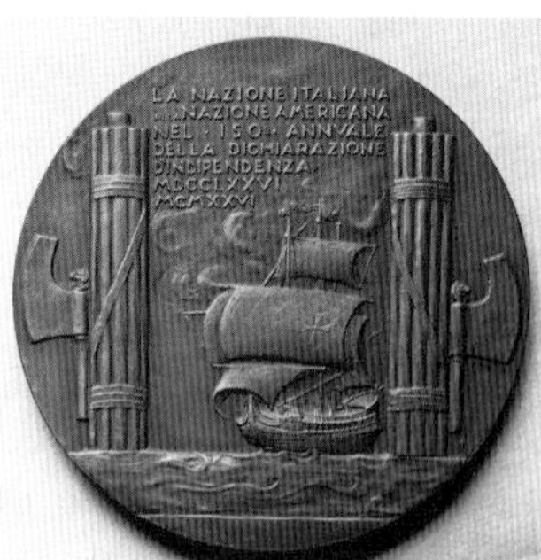

Inscribed on reverse: LA NAZIONE ITALIANA/ALLA NAZIONE AMERICANA/NEL·150º· ANNVALE/DELLA DICHIARAZIONE/D'INDIPENDENZA/MDCCLXXVI/ MCMXXVI
Foundry marks on obverse and reverse at lower right edge beneath a crown: Z
Gift of the Italian Government, 1928.19

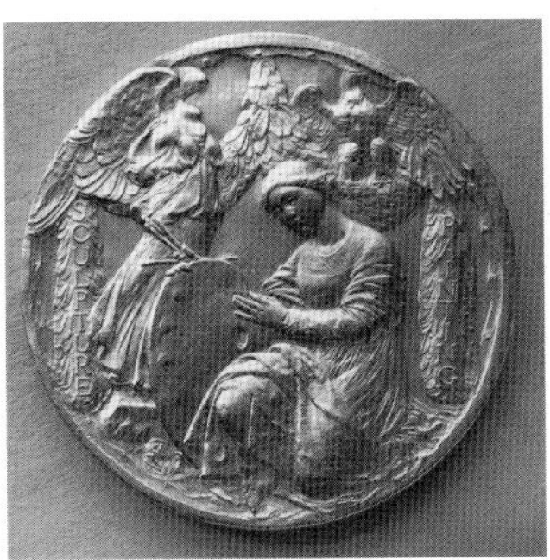

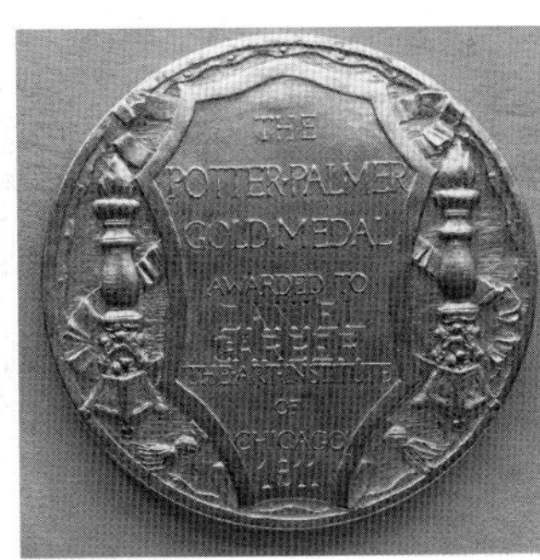

UNIDENTIFIED ARTIST

The Potter Palmer Gold Medal
1910
Gold
2″ diam. (5.1 cm)
Inscribed on obverse at left side: SCULPTURE; at right side: PAINTING
Inscribed on reverse: THE/POTTER·PALMER/GOLD MEDAL/AWARDED TO; engraved: DANIEL/GARBER; inscribed: THE·ART·INSTITUTE/OF/CHICAGO; engraved: 1911
Gift of John Franklin Garber and Tanis Page, 1979.3.2

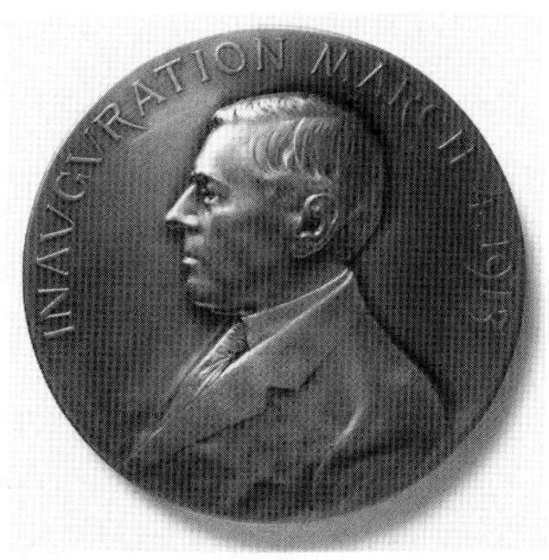

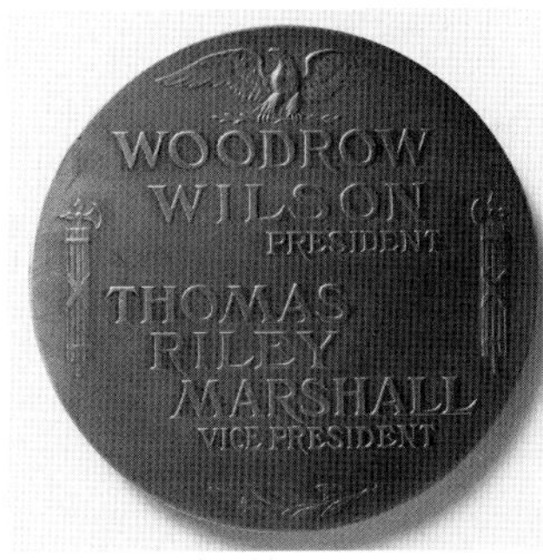

UNIDENTIFIED ARTIST

Woodrow Wilson Inaugural Medal
1913
Bronze with gold patina
2¾″ diam. (7 cm)
Inscribed on obverse around edge: INAVGVRATION MARCH 4, 1913
Inscribed on reverse: WOODROW/WILSON/PRESIDENT/ THOMAS/RILEY/MARSHALL/VICE PRESIDENT
Foundry mark on rim: WHITEHEAD-HOAG
Gift of William Corcoran Eustis, 1913.19

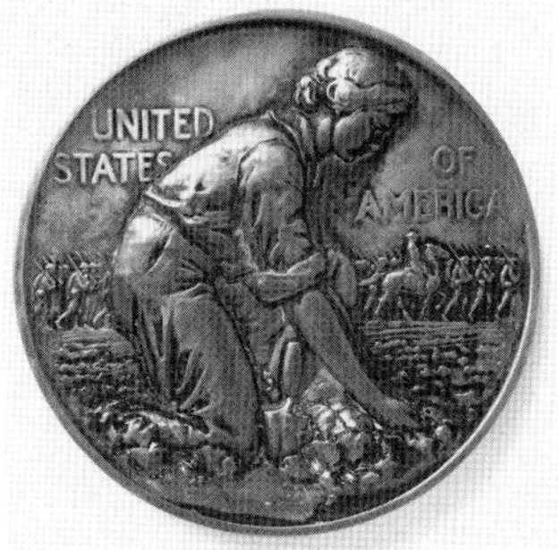

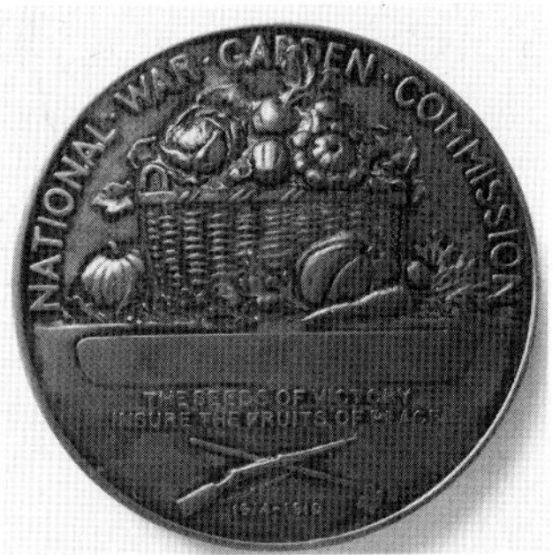

UNIDENTIFIED ARTIST

National War Garden Commemorative Medal
1919
Bronze with brown patina
3″ diam. (7.6 cm)
Inscribed on obverse at upper left: UNITED/STATES; at upper right: OF/AMERICA
Inscribed on reverse around upper edge: NATIONAL·WAR· GARDEN·COMMISSION; at lower center: THE SEEDS OF VICTORY/INSURE THE FRUITS OF PEACE; in exergue: 1914–1919; at lower right edge: TIFFANY & CO.
Foundry mark on rim: BRONZE/m
Source unknown, 1986.x.29

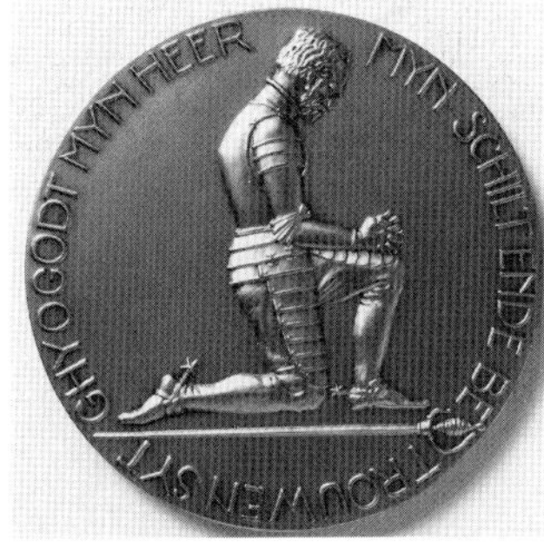

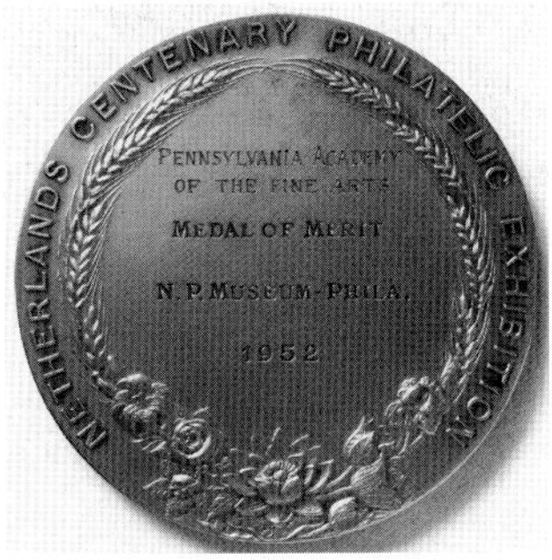

UNIDENTIFIED ARTIST

Netherlands Centenary Philatelic Exhibition Medal
1952
Bronze with gold patina
2⅜″ diam. (6.2 cm)
Inscribed on obverse around edge: GHYOGODT MYN HEER MYN SCHILT ENDE BE TROUWEN SYT
Inscribed on reverse around edge: NETHERLANDS CENTENARY PHILATELIC EXHIBITION; engraved in center: PENNSYLVANIA ACADEMY/OF THE FINE ARTS/ MEDAL OF MERIT/N.P. MUSEUM-PHILA./ 1952
Gift of the National Philatelic Society, 1952.25

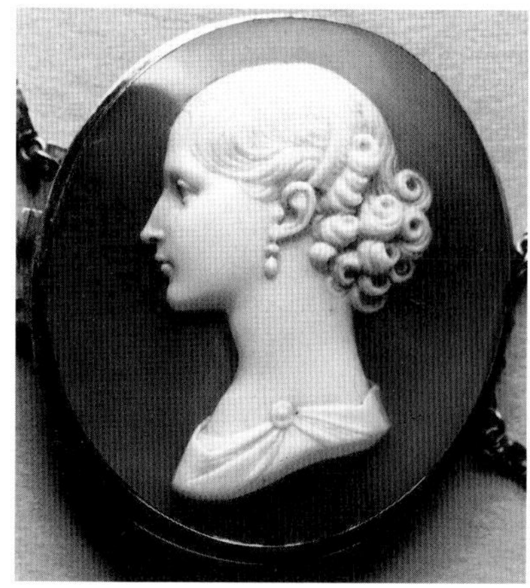

G. DIES (probably Italian, n.d.)

Anne McKean Hoffman Kerr (d. after 1854)
About 1835
Shell, silver
1¾ x 1½″ (4.4 x 3.8 cm)
Signed beneath the bust: G. Dies
Bequest of Fredericka Mary Kerr, 1942.12.4

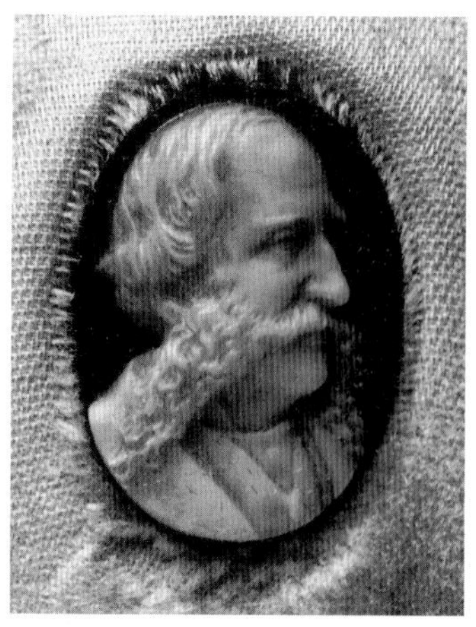

UNIDENTIFIED ARTIST

Joseph E. Temple, 1811–1886
By 1887
Glass
¾ x ½″ (1.9 x 1.3 cm)
Gift of the James E. Caldwell Co., 1887.6

Joseph E. Temple, 1811–1886
By 1887
Glass
¾ x ½″ (1.9 x 1.3 cm)
Anonymous gift, through Mrs. T. Hollingsworth Andrews, 1922.15

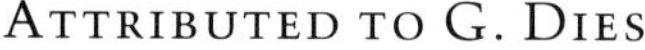

ATTRIBUTED TO G. DIES

David Hoffman, 1784–1854
About 1835
Shell
1¾ x 1½″ (4.4 x 3.8 cm)
Bequest of Fredericka Mary Kerr, 1942.12.2

Mary McKean Hoffman, 1797–1882
About 1835
Shell
1¾ x 1½″ (4.4 x 3.8 cm)
Bequest of Fredericka Mary Kerr, 1942.12.3

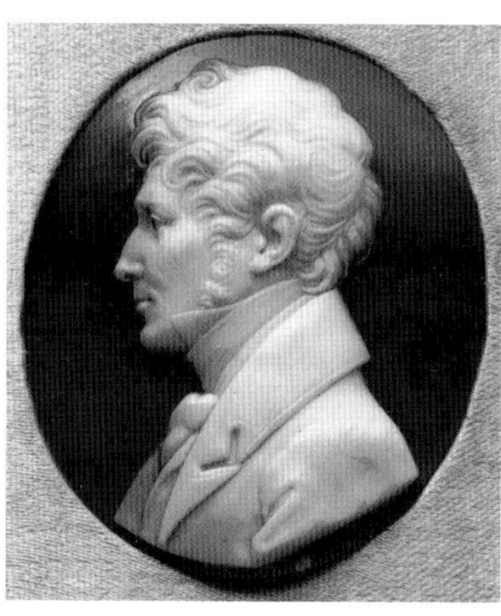

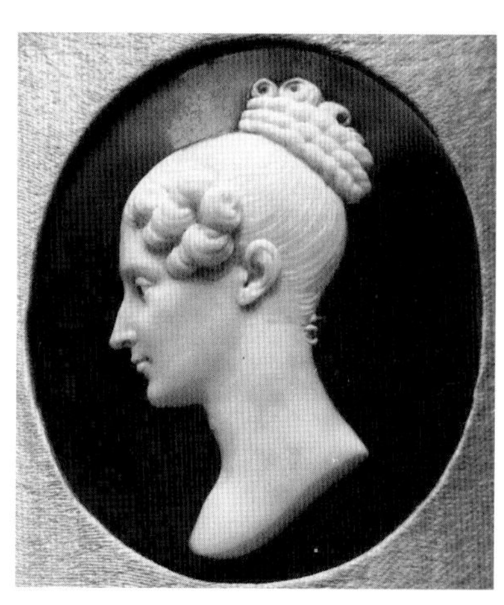

Selected Bibliography

Bach, Penny Balkin. *Public Art in Philadelphia.* Philadelphia: Temple University Press, 1992.

Bantel, Linda. "Sculpture at the Pennsylvania Academy of the Fine Arts." *Antiques* 121 (March 1982), pp. 706–13.

Clark, William J., Jr. *Great American Sculptures.* Philadelphia: Gebbie and Barrie, 1878.

Conner, Janis and Joel Rosenkranz. *Rediscoveries in American Sculpture: Studio Works, 1893–1939.* Austin: University of Texas Press, 1989.

Craven, Wayne. *Sculpture in America.* Newark: University of Delaware Press, 1984, new and rev. ed.

Gardner, Albert TenEyck. *American Sculpture: A Catalogue of the Collection of the Metropolitan Museum of Art.* New York: Metropolitan Museum of Art, 1965.

Gerdts, William H. *American Neo-Classic Sculpture: The Marble Resurrection.* New York: Viking Press, 1973.

Greenthal, Kathryn, Paula M. Kozol, and Jan Seidler Ramirez. *American Figurative Sculpture in the Museum of Fine Arts, Boston.* Boston: Museum of Fine Arts, 1986.

Gurney, George. *Sculpture and the Federal Triangle.* Washington, D.C.: Smithsonian Institution Press, 1985.

Inventory of American Sculpture. Washington, D.C.: National Museum of American Art, Smithsonian Institution, database since 1993.

Naudé, Virginia Norton, ed. *Sculptural Monuments In an Outdoor Environment.* Philadelphia: Pennsylvania Academy of the Fine Arts, 1985.

Opitz, Glenn B., ed. *Dictionary of American Sculptors.* Poughkeepsie, N.Y.: Apollo, 1984.

Philadelphia: Three Centuries of American Art. Philadelphia: Philadelphia Museum of Art, 1976.

Proske, Beatrice Gilman. *Brookgreen Gardens Sculpture.* Murrells Inlet, S.C.: Brookgreen Gardens, 1968, rev. ed.

Salmon, Robin R. *Brookgreen Gardens Sculpture.* Murrells Inlet, S.C.: Brookgreen Gardens, vol. 2, 1993.

Sellin, David. *The First Pose, 1876: Turning Point in American Art; Howard Roberts, Thomas Eakins and a Century of Philadelphia Nudes.* New York: W.W. Norton and Company, 1976.

Shapiro, Michael. *Bronze Casting and American Sculpture.* Newark: University of Delaware Press, 1985.

Taft, Lorado. *The History of American Sculpture.* New York: Macmillan Company, 1930, rev. ed.

———. *Modern Tendencies in Sculpture.* Chicago: University of Chicago Press, 1921.

200 Years of American Sculpture. New York: David R. Godine in association with the Whitney Museum of American Art, 1976.

Wainwright, Nicholas B., ed. *Sculpture of a City: Philadelphia's Treasures in Bronze and Stone.* New York: Walker Publishing Company, 1974.

Index

W

Y

Z

Authors' Index